Contents

II Key to map pages

IV Administrative and Postcode boundaries

VI Key to map symbols

1 Street maps

77 Central London

77 Key to map pages and key to symbols

78 Large-scale street maps

174 Index

290 List of numbered locations

310 Central London bus routes

312 London Underground

314 West End theatres and

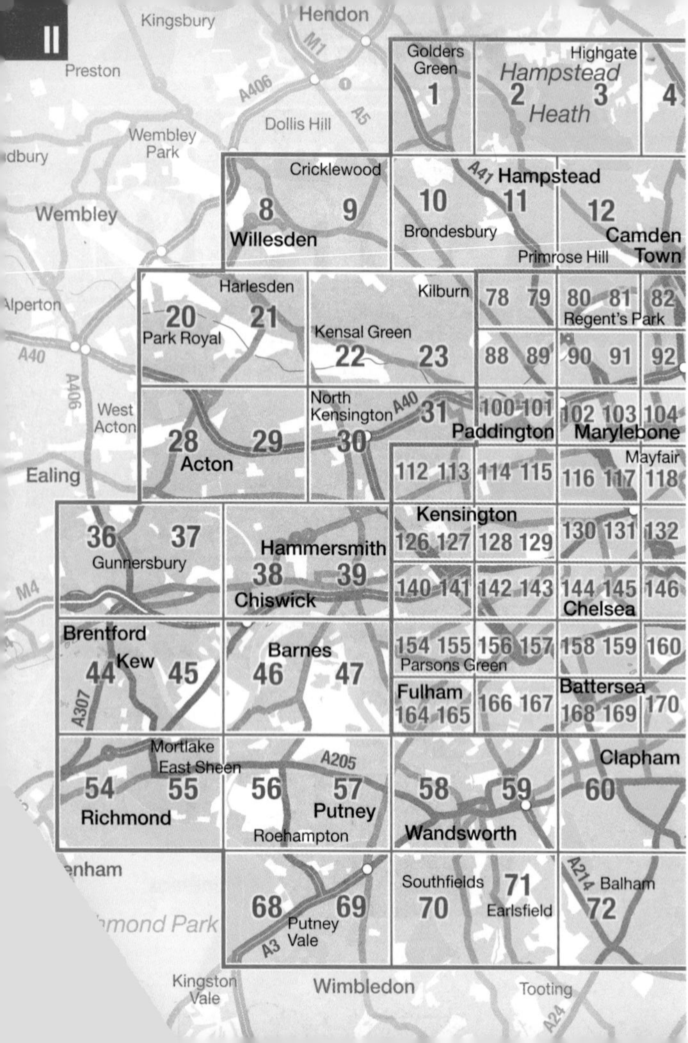

Kingsbury
Hendon
Preston
M1
A406
A5
Dollis Hill
Wembley Park
Golders Green 1
Highgate
Hampstead Heath 2 3
4
Wembley
Cricklewood
Willesden 8 9
10 Brondesbury
A41 Hampstead 11
12 Camden Town
Primrose Hill
Alperton
A40
A406
Harlesden
20 Park Royal 21
Kilburn
Kensal Green 22 23
78 79 80 81 82
Regent's Park
88 89 90 91 92
West Acton
28 Acton 29
North Kensington A40 31
30
100 101 Paddington
102 103 104 Marylebone
Ealing
112 113 114 115
Mayfair
116 117 118
Kensington
126 127 128 129
130 131 132
36 37 Gunnersbury
Hammersmith
38 39 Chiswick
M4
140 141 142 143 144 145 146
Chelsea
Brentford
44 Kew 45
A307
Barnes
46 47
154 155 156 157 158 159 160
Parsons Green
Fulham 164 165
166 167
Battersea 168 169 170
Mortlake
East Sheen
54 55 Richmond
A205
56 57 Putney
Roehampton
58 59 Wandsworth
Clapham 60
68 69 Putney Vale
A3
Southfields 70
71 Earlsfield
A214
Balham 72
Kingston Vale
Wimbledon
Tooting
A24

Key to map pages

Atlas pages at 3½ inches to 1 mile are shown in blue

Central London atlas pages at 7 inches to 1 mile are shown in red (See page 77)

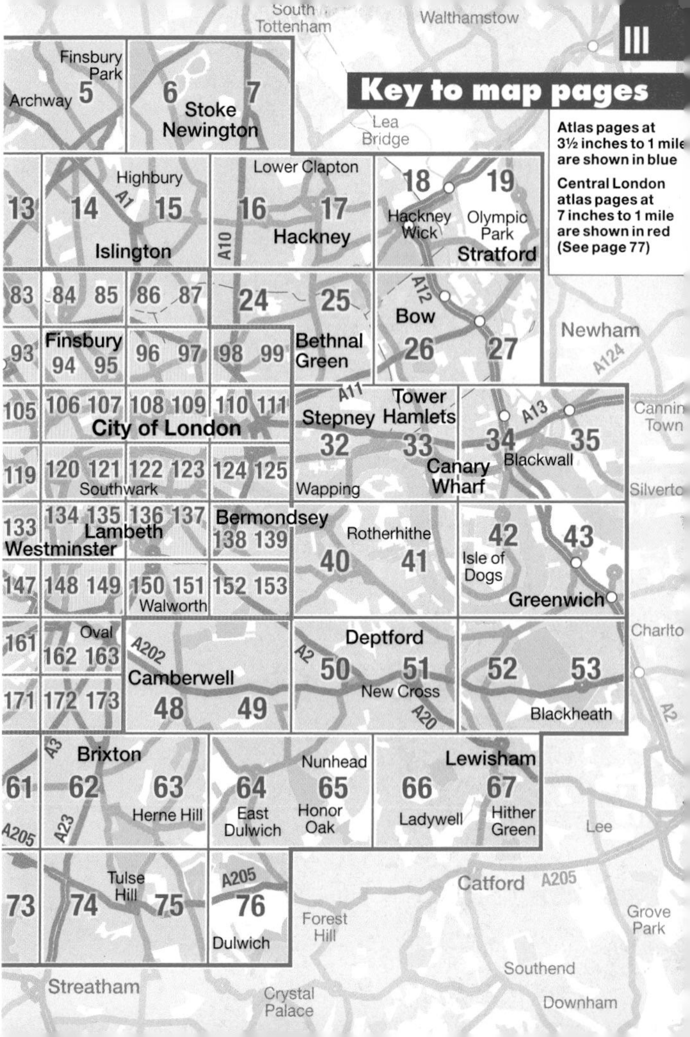

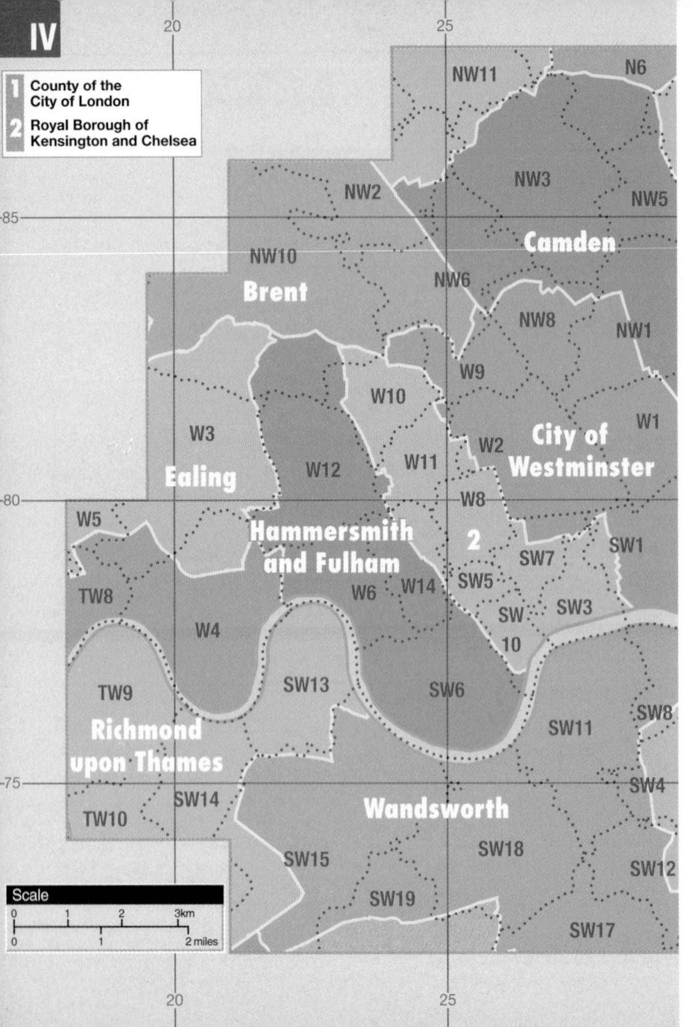
IV
1 County of the City of London
2 Royal Borough of Kensington and Chelsea
20
25
85
80
75
NW11
N6
NW3
NW5
NW2
Camden
NW10
Brent
NW6
NW8
NW1
W9
W10
W3
W1
City of Westminster
W2
Ealing
W12
W11
W8
W5
Hammersmith and Fulham
2
SW7
SW1
TW8
W6
W14
SW5
SW3
SW 10
W4
TW9
SW13
SW6
SW8
SW11
Richmond upon Thames
SW4
SW14
TW10
Wandsworth
SW18
SW15
SW12
SW19
SW17
Scale
0 1 2 3km
0 1 2 miles

Administrative and Postcode boundaries

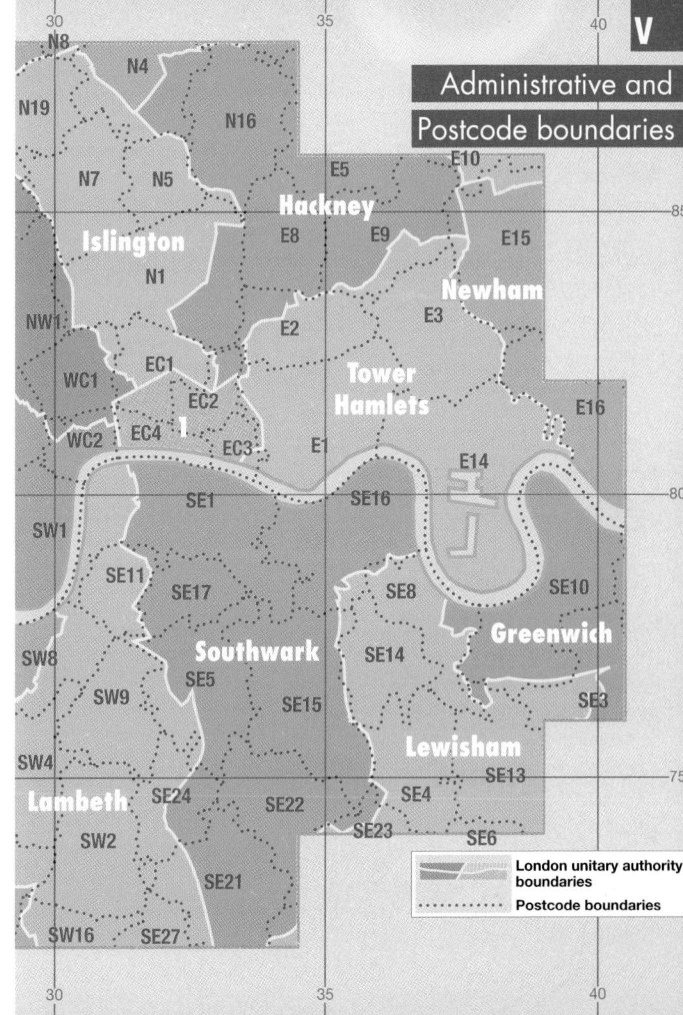

Key to map symbols

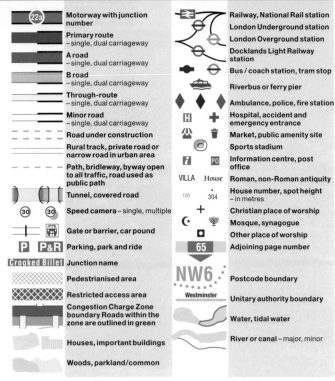

22a Motorway with junction number

Primary route – single, dual carriageway

A road – single, dual carriageway

B road – single, dual carriageway

Through-route – single, dual carriageway

Minor road – single, dual carriageway

Road under construction

Rural track, private road or narrow road in urban area

Path, bridleway, byway open to all traffic, road used as public path

Tunnel, covered road

30 30 Speed camera – single, multiple

Gate or barrier, car pound

P P&R Parking, park and ride

Crooked Billet Junction name

Pedestrianised area

Restricted access area

Congestion Charge Zone boundary Roads within the zone are outlined in green

Houses, important buildings

Woods, parkland/common

Railway, National Rail station

London Underground station

London Overground station

Docklands Light Railway station

Bus / coach station, tram stop

Riverbus or ferry pier

Ambulance, police, fire station

H Hospital, accident and emergency entrance

Market, public amenity site

Sports stadium

i PO Information centre, post office

VILLA House Roman, non-Roman antiquity

100 • 304 House number, spot height – in metres

Christian place of worship

Mosque, synagogue

Other place of worship

65 Adjoining page number

NW6 Postcode boundary

Westminster Unitary authority boundary

Water, tidal water

River or canal – major, minor

The map scale on the pages numbered in blue is 3½ inches to 1 mile
5.52 cm to 1 km • 1: 18 103

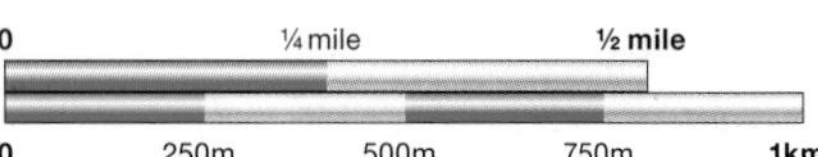

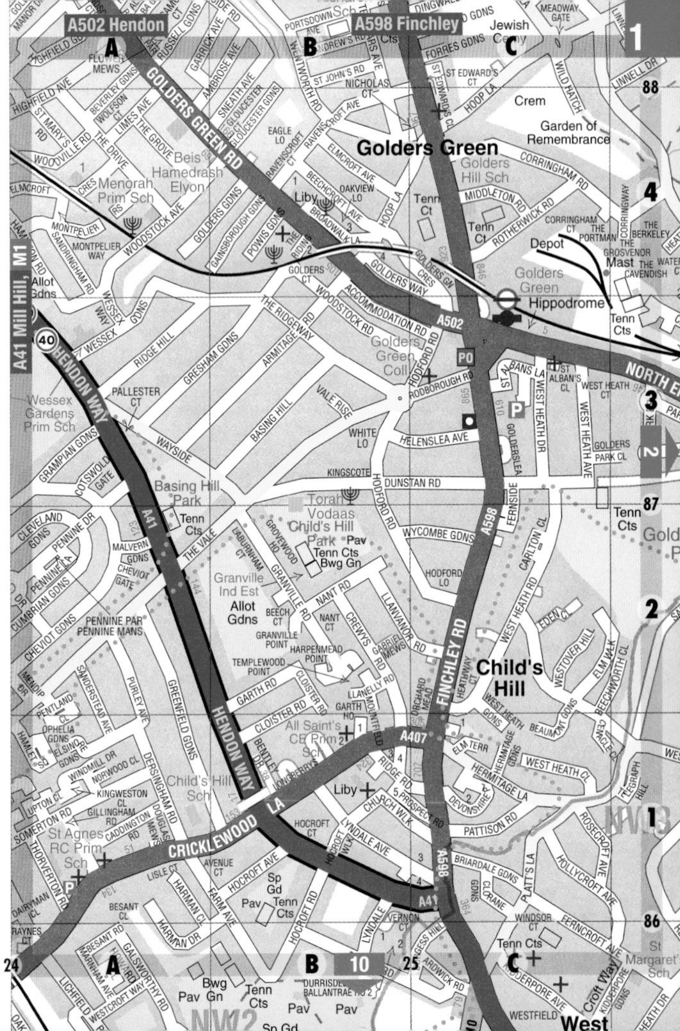

A502 Hendon
A598 Finchley
A
B
C
1
88
4
3
2
1
87
86
24
25
10
Golders Green
Child's Hill
NW11
NW2
Golders Green Rd
Hendon Way
Finchley Rd
Cricklewood La
North End
A41 Mill Hill, M1
A41
A502
A598
A407
40
Jewish Cemy
Crem
Garden of Remembrance
Golders Hill Sch
Menorah Prim Sch
Beis Hamedrash Elyon
Golders Green Hippodrome
Depot
Mast
Golders Green Coll
Wessex Gardens Prim Sch
Basing Hill Park
Torah Vodaas
Child's Hill Park
Granville Ind Est
Allot Gdns
All Saint's CE Prim Sch
Child's Hill Sch
St Agnes RC Prim Sch
St Margaret's Sch
Tenn Cts
Bwg Gn
Pav
Sp Gd
Liby
PO
Woodstock Ave
Wessex Gdns
Ridge Hill
Gresham Gdns
Armitage Rd
Basing Hill
Vale Rise
Wayside
The Vale
Dunstan Rd
Hodford Rd
Helenslea Ave
Rodborough Rd
Wycombe Gdns
Granville Rd
Nant Rd
Crewys Rd
Llanvanor Rd
Garth Rd
Cloister Rd
Ridge Rd
Prospect Rd
Church Wlk
Lyndale Ave
Hocroft Ave
Hocroft Rd
Farm Ave
Pattison Rd
Briardale Gdns
Platt's La
Hollycroft Ave
Rosecroft Ave
Ferncroft Ave
West Heath Rd
West Heath Dr
West Heath Ave
Westover Hill
Beechworth Cl
Corringham Rd
Rotherwick Rd
Middleton Rd
Hoop La
Accommodation Rd
Golders Way
The Ridgeway
Pennine Dr
Cleveland Gdns
Cotswold Gate
Grampian Gdns
Cheviot Gdns
Dersingham Rd
Greenfield Gdns
Purley Ave
Sanderstead Ave
Somerton Rd
Thorverton Rd
Besant Rd
Galsworthy Rd
Harman Dr
Kidderpore Ave
Ardwick Rd
Croft Way
West

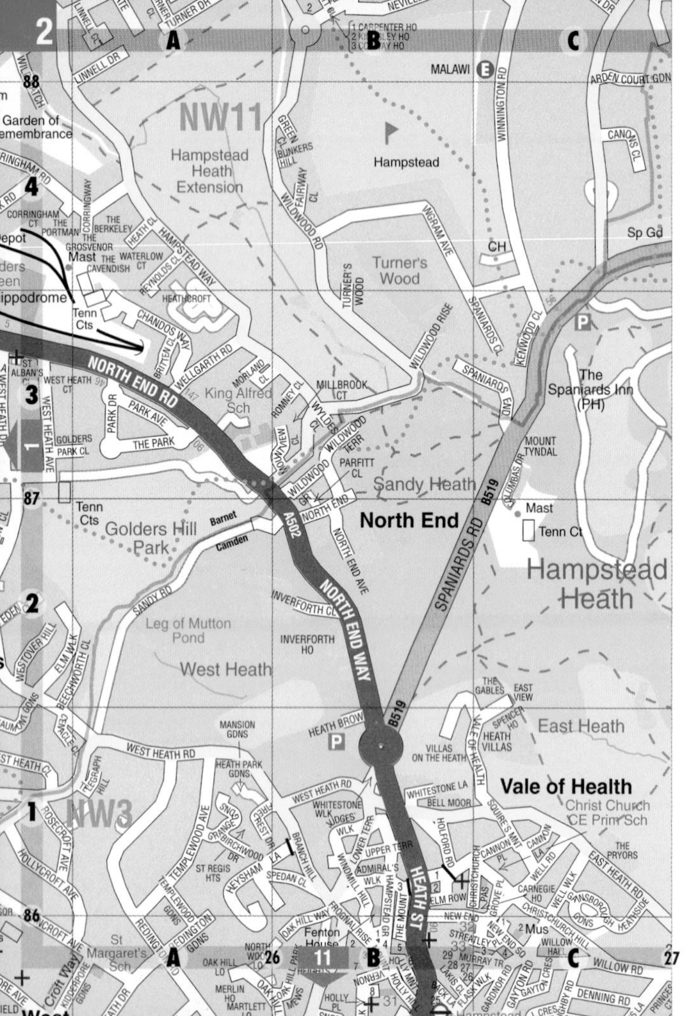

2
A
B
C
1 CARPENTER HO
TURNER DR
LINNELL CL
LINNELL DR
NEVILLE
MALAWI
WINNINGTON RD
ARDEN COURT GDNS
CANONS CL
88
Garden of Remembrance
NW11
Hampstead Heath Extension
GREEN CL
BUNKERS HILL
FAIRWAY CL
Hampstead
WILDWOOD RD
WIGRAM AVE
4
CORRINGHAM CT
THE PORTMAN
CORRINGWAY
THE BERKELEY
THE GROSVENOR
HEATH CL
HAMPSTEAD WAY
Depot
Mast
THE CAVENDISH
WATERLOW CT
REYNOLDS CL
HEATHCROFT
Hippodrome
Tenn Cts
CHANDOS WAY
Turner's Wood
TURNER'S WOOD
CH
SPANIARDS CL
KENWOOD CL
Sp Gd
WILDWOOD RISE
SPANIARDS END
The Spaniards Inn (PH)
ST ALBAN'S CL
WEST HEATH CT
NORTH END RD
BRITTEN CL
WELLGARTH RD
MORLAND CL
King Alfred Sch
MILLBROOK CT
ROMNEY CL
WYLDES CL
3
PARK DR
PARK AVE
WEST HEATH AVE
WEST HEATH DR
GOLDERS PARK CL
THE PARK
WOODVIEW CL
WILDWOOD TERR
WILDWOOD GR
PARFITT CL
Sandy Heath
MOUNT TYNDAL
COLUMBAS DR
B519
87
Tenn Cts
Golders Hill Park
Barnet
Camden
A502
NORTH END
North End
NORTH END AVE
SPANIARDS RD
Mast
Tenn Ct
Hampstead Heath
2
EDEN CL
WESTOVER HILL
ELM WLK
BEECHWORTH CL
SANDY RD
Leg of Mutton Pond
INVERFORTH CL
INVERFORTH HO
NORTH END WAY
West Heath
THE GABLES
EAST VIEW
SPENCER HO
HEATH VILLAS
East Heath
BEAUMONT GDNS
CEDAR CL
MANSION GDNS
HEATH BROW
VILLAS ON THE HEATH
VALE OF HEALTH
WEST HEATH RD
WEST HEATH CL
TELEGRAPH HILL
HEATH PARK GDNS
WEST HEATH RD
WHITESTONE WLK
JUDGES' WLK
WHITESTONE LA
BELL MOOR
Vale of Health
Christ Church CE Prim Sch
1
NW3
ROSECROFT AVE
HOLLYCROFT AVE
TEMPLEWOOD AVE
GRANGE GDNS
BIRCHWOOD DR
FIRECREST DR
BRANCH HILL
LOWER TERR
UPPER TERR
HOLFORD RD
SQUIRE'S MT
CANNON PL
CANNON LA
WELL RD
THE PRYORS
EAST HEATH RD
ST REGIS HTS
HEYSHAM LA
SPEDAN CL
WINDMILL HILL
ADMIRAL'S WLK
HAMPSTEAD GR
HEATH ST
ELM ROW
CHRISTCHURCH PAS
GROVE PL
CARNEGIE HO
WELL WLK
GANSBOROUGH GDNS
HEATHSIDE
CHRISTCHURCH HILL
86
TEMPLEWOOD GDNS
REDINGTON GDNS
REDINGTON RD
OAK HILL WAY
FROGNAL RISE
THE MOUNT
NEW END
STREATLEY PL
NEW END SQ
Mus
WILLOW HALL
St Margaret's Sch
Croft Way
KIDDERPORE GDNS
OAK HILL LO
NORTH WOOD LO
26
11
Fenton House
HOLLY MT
MURRAY TR
LAKIS CL
FLASK WLK
GAYTON RD
GAYTON CRES
WILLOUGHBY RD
WILLOW RD
DENNING RD
27
MERLIN HO
MARTLETT LO
OAK HILL PARK MEWS
HOLLY PL
VERNON
HOLLY HILL
BACK LA
Hampstead
West

A
B
C
3
Highgate
CH
Allot
Gdns
Highgate (Prim Sch)
NORTH HILL
SHELDON AVE
VIEW RD
DENEWOOD RD
COURTENAY AVE
COMPTON AVE
STORMONT RD
Tenn Cts
BROADLANDS RD
BISHOPSWOOD RD
Mallinson
Sp Ctr
Highgate
Sp Gd
St Michael's
CE Prim Sch
Highgate Pre-
Prep & Jun Sch
Pav
Haringey
Camden
HAMPSTEAD LA
B519
B550
PARK
FLATS
Kenwood
House
N6
MILLFIELD LA
FITZROY PK
HIGHFIELDS GR
THE HEXAGON
FITZROY CL
Allot
Gdns
Bwg
Gn
Open Air
Stage
Ken Wood
115
HIGHGATE HIGH ST
THE GROVE
HIGHGATE WEST HILL
SOUTH GR
BACON'S LA
1 POND SQ
2 BURLINGTON CT
3 CHESTERFIELD HO
WITANHURST
LA
Highgate
Cemy
Highgate
Sch
HOLLY TERR
HOLLY LODGE
GDNS
WESTHILL
PK
ROBIN
GR
ROBIN GR
OAKESHOTT AVE
HILLWAY
MAKEPEACE AVE
LANGBOURNE AVE
BROMWICH AVE
SWAIN'S LA
HOLLY LODGE
MANS
MAKEPEACE
MANS
LANGBOURNE
MANS
MERTON LA
Parliament
Hill
Highgate
Ponds
MILLFIELD PL
N6
HOLLY
VILLAGE
WEST HILL
CT
BROOKFIELD
ST ANN'S
CL
CHURCH
WLK
ST ALBAN'S RD
HYLDA
CT
COULTS
CRES
ST ALBAN'S
VILLAS
La Sainte
Union RC
Sec Sch
Tenn Cts
Bwg Gn
William
Ellis Sch
HIGHGATE RD
WOODSOME RD
Hampstead
Ponds
NW3
SOUTH HILL PK
GDNS
SOUTH HILL PK
Parliament Hill
Sch
Willow
Road
27
A
B
12
28
C
TANZA RD
NASSINGTON RD
Hampstead
Heath
Keats
Hampstead Hill
Pre Prep Sch
Athletics
Gd
Sw Pool
Gospel
Oak
Brookfield
Prim
Sch
88
87
86
4
2
1

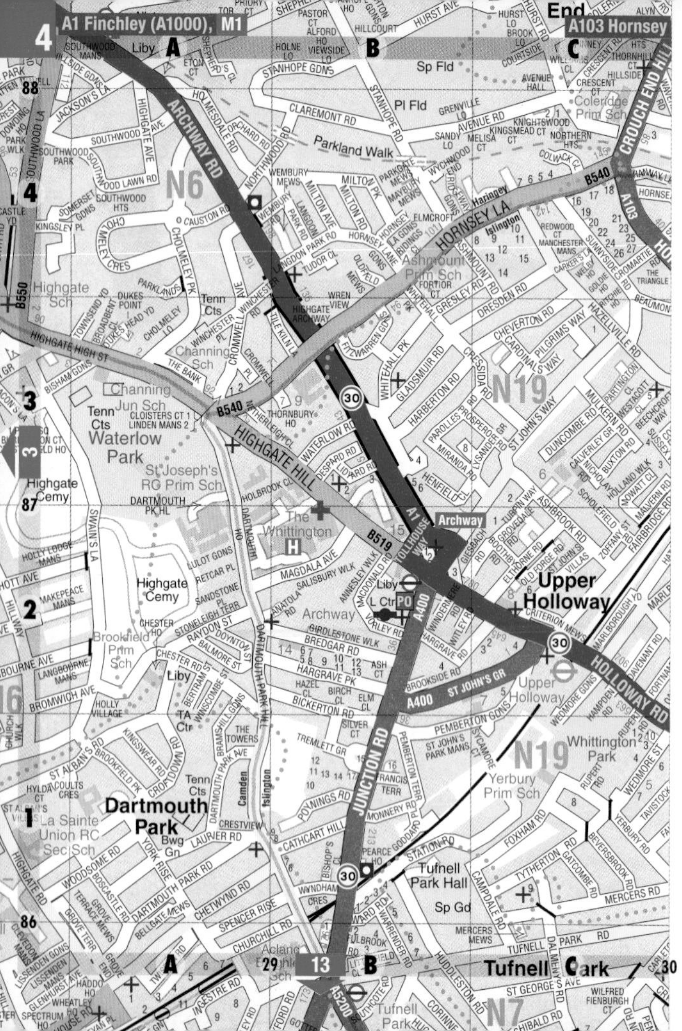
4
A1 Finchley (A1000), M1
End
A103 Hornsey
A
B
C
Liby
SOUTHWOOD MANS
ETON CT
PASTOR CT
ALFORD HO
HOLNE LO
VIEWSIDE LO
HILLCOURT
HURST AVE
HURST LO
BROOK LO
COURTSIDE
STANHOPE GDNS
Sp Fld
AVENUE HALL
CRESCENT CT
HILLSIDE
Coleridge Prim Sch
CROUCH END HILL
88
JACKSON'S LA
HIGHGATE AVE
HOLMESDALE RD
ARCHWAY RD
CLAREMONT RD
STANHOPE RD
Pl Fld
GRENVILLE LO
AVENUE RD
KNIGHTSWOOD
KINGSMEAD CT
NORTHERN HTS
SANDY LO
MELISA CT
SOUTHWOOD AVE
SOUTHWOOD LA
ORCHARD RD
NORTHWOOD RD
Parkland Walk
SOUTHWOOD PARK
SOUTHWOOD LAWN RD
N6
WEMBURY MEWS
MILTON AVE
MILTON PK
MILTON RD
PARKGATE MEWS
MAYBURY MEWS
WYCHWOOD END
COLWICK CL
B540
HORNSEY LA
CASTLE YD
SOMERSET GDNS
SOUTHWOOD HTS
CAUSTON RD
LANGDON PARK RD
HORNSEY LA GDNS
ELMCROFT
Haringey
Islington
REDWOOD CT
MANCHESTER MANS
SUNNYSIDE RD
A103
KINGSLEY PL
CHOLMELEY CRES
CHOLMELEY PK
TUDOR CL
OLDFIELD MEWS
Ashmount Prim Sch
ASHMOUNT RD
CARKER'S LA
WELBY HO
GOLDIE HO
CROMARTIE RD
THE TRIANGLE
NORTH RD
B550
Highgate Sch
PARKLANDS
DUKES POINT
Tenn Cts
CROMWELL AVE
WINCHESTER RD
WREN VIEW
FORTIOR CT
GRESLEY RD
DRESDEN RD
RITCHIE HO
BEAUMONT
TOWNSEND YD
BROADBENT CL
DUKES HEAD YD
CHOLMELEY LO
WINCHESTER PL
HIGHGATE ARCHWAY
TILE KILN LA
FITZWARREN GDNS
WHITEHALL PK
CHEVERTON RD
CARDINALS WAY
PILGRIMS WAY
HAZELLVILLE RD
HIGHGATE HIGH ST
Channing Sch
THE BANK
CROMWELL PL
GLADSMUIR RD
HARBERTON RD
CRESSIDA RD
N19
PARTINGTON CL
WESTACOTT CL
BISHAM GDNS
Channing Jun Sch
Tenn Cts
CLOISTERS CT
LINDEN MANS
THORNBURY HO
NETHERLEIGH CL
30
PAROLLES RD
PROSPERO RD
MIRANDA RD
LYSANDER GR
ST JOHN'S WAY
DUNCOMBE RD
MULKERN RD
BEECHCROFT WAY
3
Waterlow Park
St Joseph's RC Prim Sch
HIGHGATE HILL
WATERLOW RD
DESPARD RD
LIDYARD RD
HENFIELD CL
CALVERLEY GR
NICHOLAY RD
BUXTON RD
HOLLAND WLK
NOWAIT CL
MALVERN RD
SUSSEX WAY
Highgate Cemy
87
DARTMOUTH PK HL
HOLBROOK CL
DARTMOUTH HO
The Whittington
H
A1
Archway
TOLLHOUSE WAY
GIESBACH RD
TURPIN WAY
GROVEDALE RD
ASHBROOK RD
SCHOLEFIELD RD
ZOFFANY ST
FAIRBRIDGE RD
SWAIN'S LA
HOLLY LODGE MANS
B519
LULOT GDNS
RETCAR PL
MAGDALA AVE
SALISBURY WLK
ANNESLEY WLK
MACDONALD RD
BOOTHBY RD
ELTHORNE RD
OLD FORGE RD
ST JOHN'S VILLAS
SHOTT AVE
2
MAKEPEACE MANS
HILLWAY
Highgate Cemy
SANDSTONE PL
STONELEIGH TERR
ANATOLA RD
Liby
L Ctr
PO
A400
WINDERMERE RD
WITLEY RD
Upper Holloway
CRITERION MEWS
MARLBOROUGH YD
CHESTER HO
RAYDON ST
DOYNTON ST
Archway
GIRDLESTONE WLK
VORLEY RD
HARGRAVE RD
Brookfield Prim Sch
BALMORE ST
BREDGAR RD
ASH CT
HOLLOWAY RD
DAVENANT RD
LANGBOURNE AVE
LANGBOURNE MANS
CHESTER RD
Liby
HARGRAVE PK
BROOKSIDE RD
ST JOHN'S GR
Upper Holloway
BROMWICH AVE
BERTRAM ST
WINSCOMBE ST
HAZEL CL
BIRCH CL
ELM CL
BICKERTON RD
A400
PEMBERTON GDNS
WEDMORE GDNS
HAMPDEN RD
RUPERT RD
HOLLY VILLAGE
TA Ctr
BRAMSHILL GDNS
THE TOWERS
SILVER CT
ST JOHN'S PARK MANS
SYCAMORE CT
CHURCH WLK
KINGSWEAR RD
CROFTDOWN RD
DARTMOUTH PARK HILL
TREMLETT GR
PEMBERTON TERR
N19
Whittington Park
WEDMORE ST
ST ALBAN'S RD
BROOKFIELD PK
DARTMOUTH PARK AVE
FRANCIS TERR
JUNCTION RD
RUPERT RD
HYLDA CT
COULTS CRES
Tenn Cts
Camden
Islington
POYNINGS RD
MONNERY RD
Yerbury Prim Sch
TAVISTOCK
ST ALBAN'S VILLAS
1
La Sainte Union RC Sec Sch
Dartmouth Park
CRESTVIEW
CATHCART HILL
GODDARD PL
FOXHAM RD
YERBURY RD
Bwg Gn
LAURIER RD
STATION RD
BEVERSBROOK RD
HIGHGATE RD
WOODSOME RD
YORK RISE
PEARCE HO
Tufnell Park Hall
CAMPDALE RD
TYTHERTON RD
GATCOMBE RD
BOSCASTLE RD
DARTMOUTH PARK RD
BISHOP'S CL
30
TERRACE MEWS
GROVE TERR
CHETWYND RD
WYNDHAM CRES
WARD RD
WARRENDER RD
Sp Gd
MERCERS RD
86
GROVE TERR
BELLGATE MEWS
SPENCER RISE
MERCERS MEWS
CLEVEDON MANS
CHURCHILL RD
FULBROOK
TUFNELL PARK RD
LISSENDEN GDNS
Acland Burghley Sch
29
13
DALMENY RD
Tufnell Park
30
LISSENDEN MANS
GLENHURST AVE
HADDO HO
WHEATLEY HO
INGESTRE RD
A5200
SOUTHCOTE RD
HUDDLESTON RD
ST GEORGE'S AVE
WILFRED FIENBURGH CT
SPECTRUM HO
Tufnell Park
CORINNE RD
N7
ARCHIBALD RD

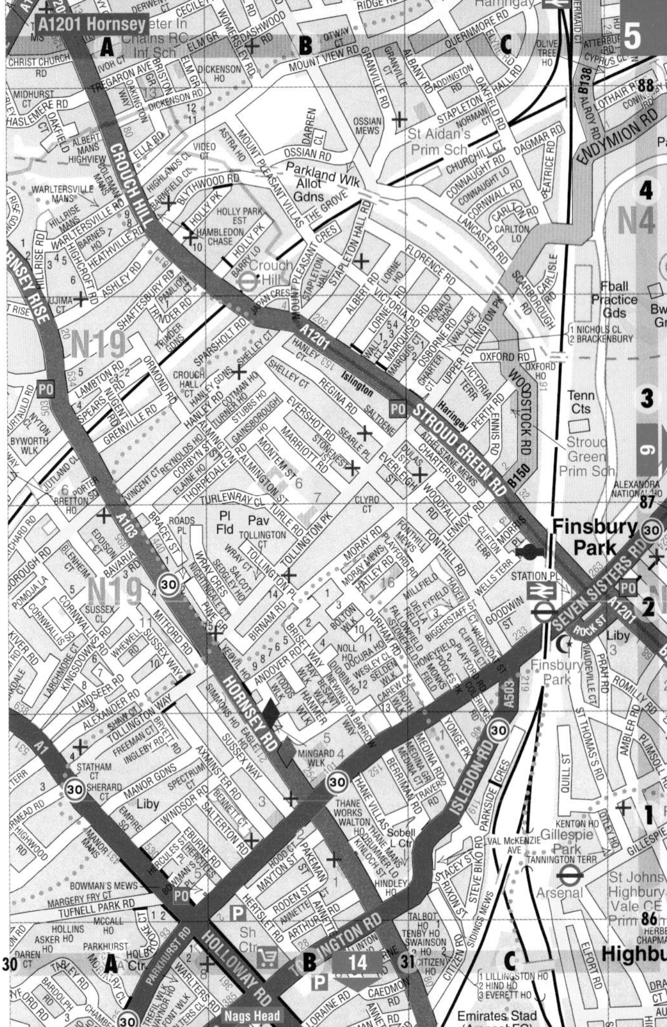

5
A1201 Hornsey
A
B
C
Harringay
St Peter In Chains RC Inf Sch
CHRIST CHURCH RD
TREGARON AVE
BRISTON GR
ELM GR
DICKENSON HO
DICKENSON RD
WOMERSLEY RD
DASHWOOD RD
OTWAY CT
MOUNT VIEW RD
GRANVILLE RD
GRANVILLE CT
ALBANY RD
QUERNMORE RD
OLIVE TREE HO
ATTERBURY RD
CYPRUS CL
B138
ALROY RD
LOTHAIR RD
88
ENDYMION RD
Pav
MIDHURST CT
HASLEMERE RD
OAKFIELD CT
ALBERT MANS
HIGHVIEW
CROUCH HILL
ELLA RD
VIDEO CT
ASTRA HO
MOUNT PLEASANT RD
DARREN CL
OSSIAN RD
OSSIAN MEWS
ADDINGTON RD
STAPLETON HALL RD
NORMAN CT
St Aidan's Prim Sch
CHURCHILL CT
DAGMAR RD
CONNAUGHT RD
CONNAUGHT LO
CORNWALL RD
BEATRICE RD
Parkland Wlk
Allot Gdns
WARLTERSVILLE MANS
HIGHLANDS CL
BARNFIELD CL
BLYTHWOOD RD
HOLLY PK
HOLLY PARK EST
HAMBLEDON CHASE
THE GROVE
MOUNT PLEASANT VILLAS
CARLTON RD
CARLTON LO
LANCASTER RD
4
N4
HILLRISE MANS
WARLTERSVILLE RD
BARNES HO
HEATHVILLE RD
HIGHCROFT RD
HILLRISE RD
HORNSEY RISE
ASHLEY RD
SHAFTESBURY RD
PAMLION CT
TRUNDER RD
BARRY LO
Crouch Hill
HOLLY LO
MOUNT PLEASANT CRES
STAPLETON HALL
ALBERT RD
LORNE HO
FLORENCE RD
SCARBOROUGH RD
CARLISLE RD
Fball Practice Gds
Bwg Gn
UJIMA CT
N19
TRINDER GDNS
SPARSHOLT RD
SHELLEY CT
JAPAN CRES
A1201
VICTORIA RD
LORNE RD
MARQUIS RD
MARQUIS CT
RONALD SHAY
OSBORNE RD
WALLACE LO
UPPER TOLLINGTON PK
1 NICHOLS CL
2 BRACKENBURY
OXFORD RD
OXFORD HO
LAMBTON RD
ORMOND RD
CROUCH HALL CT
HANLEY GDNS
COTMAN HO
SHELLEY CT
HANLEY CT
Islington
REGINA RD
SALTDENE
CHARTER CT
VICTORIA TERR
Haringey
PERTH RD
WOODSTOCK RD
Tenn Cts
3
PO
SPEARS RD
NUGENT RD
GRENVILLE RD
HANLEY RD
TURNER HO
STUBBS HO
GAINSBOROUGH HO
EVERSHOT RD
MARRIOTT RD
STONENEST ST
SEARLE PL
STROUD GREEN RD
ATHELSTANE MEWS
CHARTERIS RD
ENNIS RD
Stroud Green Prim Sch
9
BYWORTH WLK
JUTLAND CL
PORTER SQ
BRETTON HO
VINCENT CT
REYNOLDS HO
CORBYN ST
ELAINE HO
ALMINGTON ST
THORPEDALE RD
MONTEM ST
DULAS ST
EVERLEIGH ST
WOODFALL RD
LENNOX RD
B150
ALEXANDRA NATIONAL HO
87
TURLEWRAY CL
TURLE RD
CLYRO CT
Pl Fld
Pav
ROADS PL
TOLLINGTON CT
TOLLINGTON PK
FONTHILL MEWS
FONTHILL RD
CLIFTON TERR
MORRIS PL
Finsbury Park
BLENHEIM CT
EDDISON CT
BAVARIA RD
BRACEY ST
A103
WRAY CT
SALCOT
MORAY RD
MORAY MEWS
PLAYFORD RD
HATLEY RD
WELLS TERR
STATION PL
SEVEN SISTERS RD
PARK
POMOJA LA
CORNWALLIS SQ
CORNWALLIS RD
SUSSEX CL
MITFORD RD
WHEWELL RD
SUSSEX WAY
NIGHTINGALE CT
WRAY CRES
SEDGLEY HO
PINE GR
BIRNAM RD
TOLLINGTON PL
BOLTON WLK
DURHAM RD
MILLFIELD
DELLA PATH
FYFIELD
HADEN CT
BIGGERSTAFF ST
GOODWIN ST
ROCK ST
Liby
2
KINGSDOWN RD
LARCHMORE CT
YEOVIL HO
ANDOVER RD
BRISET WAY
NOLL HO
DOCURA HO
WESLEY CL
SELDEN WLK
FALLOWFIELD
STONEFIELD
HONEYFIELD
POOLES PK
MONKSFIELD
CLIFTON CT
WHADCOAT ST
PLAYFORD RD
A503
Finsbury Park
VAUDEVILLE CT
PRAH RD
ROMILLY RD
LANDSEER RD
ALEXANDER RD
TOLLINGTON WAY
SHAW CT
FREEMAN CT
BRYETT RD
INGLEBY RD
HORNSEY RD
SIMMONS HO
TODDS WLK
RAY WLK
BESANT WLK
HAMMER WLK
DIBDIN HO
NEWINGTON BARROW WAY
CAREW CL
YONGE PK
ISLEDON RD
ST THOMAS'S RD
AMBLER RD
PLIMSOLL RD
A1
STATHAM CT
SHERARD CT
MANOR GDNS
SPECTRUM CT
AXMINSTER RD
EAGLET CT
SUSSEX WAY
MINGARD WLK
MEDINA RD
MEDINA GR
MEDINA CT
BERRIMAN RD
TRAVERS RD
PARKSIDE CRES
QUILL ST
30
Liby
EMPIRE SQ
WINDSOR RD
BENNETT CT
SALTERTON RD
THANE WORKS
WALTON HO
THANE VILLAS
THANE MANS
DRUMMER LO
KINLOCH ST
Sobell L Ctr
VAL McKENZIE AVE
Gillespie Park
KENTON HO
OTLEY HO
GILLESPIE RD
TANNINGTON TERR
1
HIGHWOOD RD
MANOR MANS
HERCULES ST
HERCULES PL
EBURNE RD
HOOD CT
MAYTON ST
PAKEMAN ST
HINDLEY HO
STACEY ST
STEVE BIKO RD
RIXON ST
Arsenal
St Johns Highbury Vale CE Prim Sch
BOWMAN'S MEWS
MARGERY FRY CT
TUFNELL PARK RD
BOWMAN'S PL
RODEN ST
ANNETTE CT
ARTHUR RD
TOLLINGTON RD
TALBOT HO
TENBY HO
SWAINSON HO
SIDINGS MEWS
86
HERBERT CHAPMAN CT
HOLLINS HO
ASKER HO
MCCALL HO
PARKHURST CT
HOLBROOKE CT
Sh Ctr
HERTSLET RD
PARKHURST RD
HOLLOWAY RD
14
CITIZEN HO
CITIZEN RD
1 LILLINGSTON HO
2 HIND HO
3 EVERETT HO
ELFORT RD
Highbury
DAREN CT
TABLEY RD
BARDOLPH RD
WALTERS RD
TREFIL WLK
FONT WLK
Nags Head
LORAINE RD
CAEDMON RD
Emirates Stad (Arsenal FC)
DRAKELEY CT
AUBERT

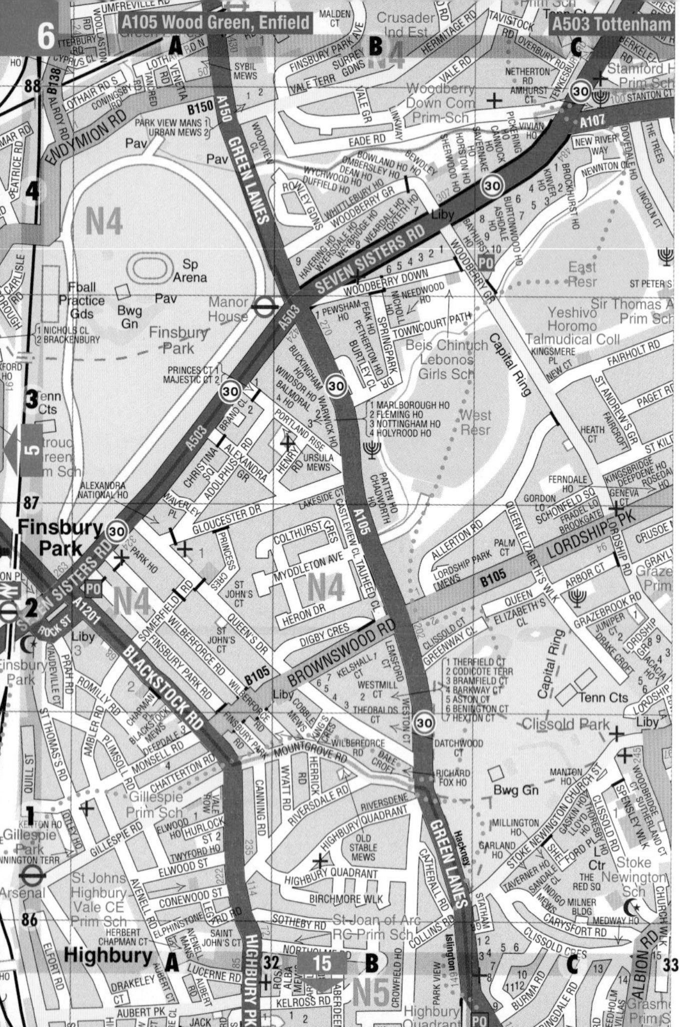
6
A105 Wood Green, Enfield
A503 Tottenham
A
B
C
N4
N4
N4
N4
N5
Finsbury Park
Manor House
Sp Arena
Fball Practice Gds
Bwg Gn
Pav
Pav
Pav
Woodberry Down Com Prim Sch
Crusader Ind Est
East Resr
West Resr
Beis Chinuch Lebonos Girls Sch
Yeshivo Horomo Talmudical Coll
Sir Thomas Abney Prim Sch
Capital Ring
Capital Ring
Clissold Park
Tenn Cts
Bwg Gn
Gillespie Prim Sch
Gillespie Park
St Johns Highbury Vale CE Prim Sch
St Joan of Arc RC Prim Sch
Stoke Newington Sch
Highbury Quadrant
Highbury
Arsenal
Hackney
Islington
Liby
PO
SEVEN SISTERS RD
GREEN LANES
A105
A150
A503
A107
A1201
B105
B150
B138
ENDYMION RD
BLACKSTOCK RD
HIGHBURY PK
BROWNSWOOD RD
LORDSHIP PK
WOODBERRY DOWN
WOODBERRY GR
EADE RD
MOUNTGROVE RD
RIVERSDALE RD
HIGHBURY QUADRANT
BIRCHMORE WLK
WILBERFORCE RD
FINSBURY PARK RD
SOMERFIELD RD
QUEEN'S DR
GLOUCESTER DR
MYDDLETON AVE
COLTHURST CRES
HERON DR
DIGBY CRES
GILLESPIE RD
ELWOOD ST
CONEWOOD ST
STOKE NEWINGTON CHURCH ST
CLISSOLD RD
CLISSOLD CRES
CARYSFORT RD
ALBION RD
ALLERTON RD
QUEEN ELIZABETH'S WLK
GRAZEBROOK RD
FAIRHOLT RD
ST ANDREW'S GR
TOWNCOURT PATH
SPRINGPARK DR
PORTLAND RISE
ALEXANDRA GR
CHRISTINA SQ
CANNING RD
WYATT RD
HERRICK RD
MONSELL RD
CHATTERTON RD
ROMILLY RD
AMBLER RD
PLIMSOLL RD
ST THOMAS'S RD
QUILL ST
AVENELL RD
SOTHEBY RD
NORTHOLME RD
KELROSS RD
AUBERT PK
DRAKELEY CT
ELFORT RD
LUCERNE RD
CROWFIELD HO
CATHERALL RD
BURMA RD
30
32
15
33
86
87
88
4
3
2
1
5

A10 Tottenham
A
B
C
88
87
86
4
3
2
1
33
34
16
AMHURST PK
Stamford Hill
Hackney
OLINDA RD
Springfield Com Prim Sch
Ravensdale Com Est
RAVENSDALE RD
WATERMINT QUAY
CLAYTON CT
Allot Gdns
Sp Gd
Tenn Cts
PRIESTLEY CL
ROOKWOOD RD
LEABOURNE RD
MOUNDFIELD RD
CASTLEWOOD RD
CRAVEN WLK
LINGWOOD RD
ASHTEAD RD
OVERLEA RD
SPRING HILL
BUCCLEUCH HO
EGERTON RD
ROCKWOOD CT
TOWER CT
CLAPTON COMM
Talmud Torah Machzikei Hadass Sch
A107
THE GARDENS
SUMMIT EST
Clapton Common
WEBB EST
Springfield
E5
YET LEV CT
FAWCETT EST
SPRINGFIELD CT
AMHURST PARK
CLOCK HO
HANOVER CT
STANARD CL
HAMBLYN CT
MAYFIELD HO
NORTHFIELD RD
RAV PINTER CL
LINTHORPE RD
COLBERG PL
Holmleigh Prim Sch
Liby
BROADWAY MEWS
LEWESTON PL
PORTLAND AVE
CROMDALE CT
BRAYDON RD
DUNSMURE RD
CLAYS CT
CARLTON MANS
HOLMLEIGH RD
ARRAN HO
CHEVIOT HO
COTSWOLD HO
BRECON HO
WICKLOW HO
MALVERN HO
SIDLAW HO
QUANTOCK HO
SULLIVAN CT
KILPATRICK CT
DARENTH RD
FIRSBY RD
CLARKE PATH
WALSHAM CL
FELDMAN CL
Tyssen Prim Sch
BROAD COMMON EST
OLDHILL ST
FORBURG RD
CHARDMORE RD
Upper Clapton
Jubilee JMI Sch
Capital Ring
GILDA CRES
HADLEY CT
GEDRA CT
SEYMOUR CT
FILEY AVE
A107 Hackney
UPPER CLAPTON RD
BERGHOLT CRES
DENVER RD
CRANWICH RD
DURLEY RD
PARK LEA CT
WEST BANK
EAST BANK
ALLANBRIDGE
BETHUNE RD
N16
GLASERTON RD
WILDERTON RD
FAIRHOLT CL
HEATHLAND RD
GRANGECOURT RD
ST ANDREW'S MEWS
SANDFORD CT
OXTED CT
LEATHERHEAD CL
DEAN HO
ERICSON HO
LOCKE HO
KIRKLEY HO
JONES HO
COLLETTE HO
Toldos Sch
ROYAL CL
REIZEL CL
LYNMOUTH RD
LAMPARD GR
Beis Malka Girls Sch
MARGARET RD
KYVERDALE RD
WINDUS WLK
OSBALDESTON RD
MANOR RD
COLLISON PL
MANOR PAR
WINDUS RD
STAMFORD HILL
ARK CT
CAZENOVE RD
LISTRIA LO
B105
BELFAST RD
Abney Park Cemy
MARTABAN RD
HUGH ST
GAITSKELL HO
Stoke Newington
Tawhid Boys Sch
ALKHAM RD
GEORGE DOWNING EST
RAINES CT
KEATES EST
FOUNTAYNE RD
EPPING HO
MORLEY HO
DURLSTON RD
HOGAN WAY
GELDESTON RD
FERNHILL HO
MELTON HO
WEALD SQ
WENSDALE HO
KNIGHTLAND HO
AVENUE HO
ROSSINGTON ST
ROSSENDALE ST
CHARNWOOD ST
B111
Liby
STOKE NEWINGTON
PEPPIE CL
MEROE CT
BOUVERIE RD
SAVANA
YOAKLEY RD
LISTER CT
BRETT CL
BOUVERIE MEWS
FLEETWOOD ST
SUMMERHOUSE RD
ABNEY PARK CT
GIBSON GDNS
A10
WILMER PL
Northwold Prim Sch
NORTHWOLD RD
STOKE NEWINGTON COMM
ALCONBURY RD
NARFORD RD
REIGHTON RD
ICKBURGH RD
STOKE NEWINGTON CHURCH ST
B104
PO
FLANDERS HO
KERSLEY RD
DEFOE RD
BEAVIS HO
BRODIA RD
BECK HO
LANCELL ST
DUMONT RD
AYRSOME RD
STOKE NEWINGTON HIGH ST
LAWRENCE CT
CLEVENDON CL
SMALLEY CL
SANFORD TERR
RECTORY RD
N16
NORCOTT RD
BROOKE RD
JENNER RD
BENTHAL RD
MAURY RD
EVERING RD
LAUNDRESS LA
BROOKE RD
NEWCOME HO
WALSINGHAM RD
Ickburgh Sch
HAWKSLEY RD
KYNASTON RD
CHESHOLM RD
LAVERS RD
SHANNON CT
DYNEVOR RD
MANLEY CT
LESWIN RD
TYSSEN RD
BAYSTON RD
DARVILLE RD
OAK PARK MEWS
Rectory Road
NILE CL
RENDLESHAM RD
KENNINGHALL RD
NAPOLEON RD
OLDFIELD RD
HARCOMBE RD
SANDBROOK RD
N16
YORKSHIRE CL
VICTORIAN GR
ORMSBY PL
HOLLAR RD
BATLEY RD
LESWIN PL
GLADING TERR
HEATHERLEY CT
Benthal Prim Sch
STELLMAN CL
OTTAWAY CT
OTTAWAY ST
MONTEAGLE WAY
MUIR RD
DELLA PATH
BRACKENFIELD
OLYMPUS SQ
BARBAULD RD
NEVILL RD
POPHAM CT
ORPEN WLK
VICTORIAN RD
A10 EVERING RD
MANSE RD
ALBION GR
ATHELSTAN HO
LONDESBOROUGH RD
GUN ST
STOR RD
Recn Gd
SYDNER MEWS
SYDNER RD
Shacklewell
THE BEECHERS
Nightingale Prim Sch
CLAPTON WAY
NOLAN WAY
GUDDEN DR
TIGER WAY
BEATTY RD
FOULDEN TERR
WALFORD RD
RECTORY RD
DOWNS RD
CLONBROCK RD
SHAKESPEARE WLK
ALLEN RD
BRIGHTON RD
FOULDEN RD
FARLEIGH PL
FARLEIGH RD
AMHURST TERR
MONRO WAY 1
SEATON POINT 2
WORSLEY GR 3
Downsview Sch

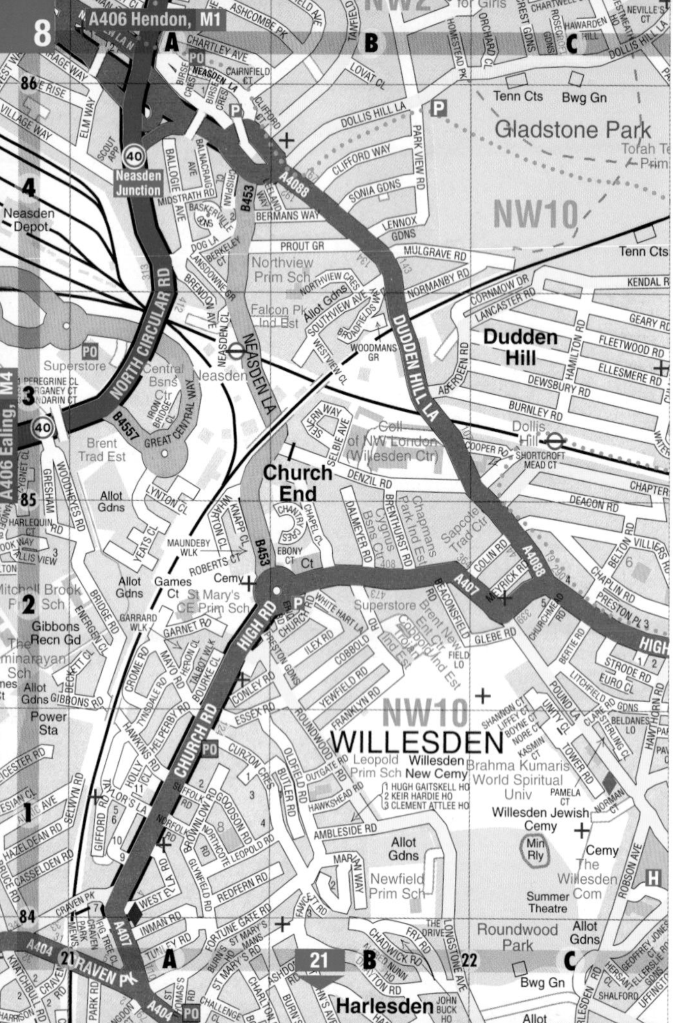

A406 Hendon, M1
A406 Ealing, M4
Neasden Junction
Neasden Depot
Gladstone Park
NW10
Dudden Hill
Neasden
Church End
WILLESDEN
Harlesden
NORTH CIRCULAR RD
DUDDEN HILL LA
NEASDEN LA
HIGH RD
CHURCH RD
CRAVEN PK
A4088
B453
A407
A404
B4557
Northview Prim Sch
Falcon Pk Ind Est
Central Bsns Ctr
Brent Trad Est
Coll of NW London (Willesden Ctr)
Chapmans Park Ind Est
Cygnus Bsns Ctr
Sapcote Trad Ctr
Superstore
St Mary's CE Prim Sch
Mitchell Brook Prim Sch
Gibbons Recn Gd
Power Sta
Leopold Prim Sch
Willesden New Cemy
Brahma Kumaris World Spiritual Univ
Willesden Jewish Cemy
The Willesden Com
Summer Theatre
Newfield Prim Sch
Roundwood Park
Dollis Hill
Tenn Cts
Bwg Gn
Allot Gdns
Games Ct
21
22

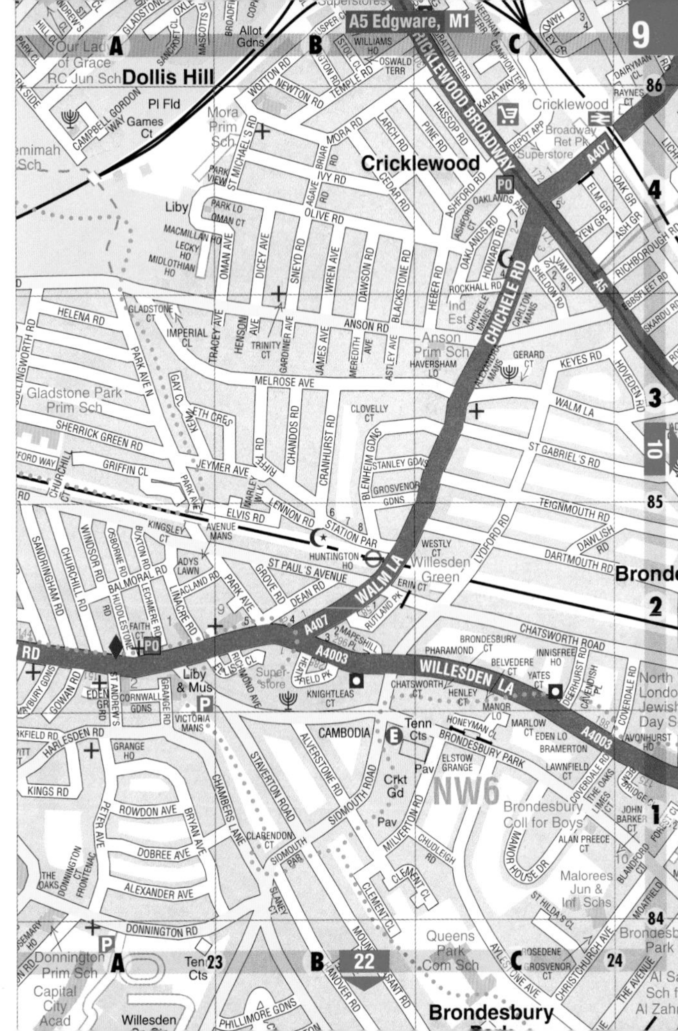

A5 Edgware, M1
Dollis Hill
Cricklewood
Willesden Green
NW6
Brondesbury
Cricklewood Broadway
Chichele Rd
Walm La
Willesden La
A407
A5
A4003
Our Lady of Grace RC Jun Sch
Mora Prim Sch
Anson Prim Sch
Gladstone Park Prim Sch
Brondesbury Coll for Boys
Malorees Jun & Inf Schs
North West London Jewish Day Sch
Queens Park Com Sch
Donnington Prim Sch
Capital City Acad
Liby
Liby & Mus
Superstore
Ind Est
Tenn Cts
Crkt Gd
Pav
Allot Gdns
Pl Fld
Games Ct
Helena Rd
Melrose Ave
Anson Rd
Olive Rd
Ivy Rd
Mora Rd
Sherrick Green Rd
Griffin Cl
Jeymer Ave
Elvis Rd
Lennon Rd
Station Par
St Paul's Avenue
Balmoral Rd
Dean Rd
Chatsworth Road
St Gabriel's Rd
Teignmouth Rd
Dartmouth Rd
Walm La
Keyes Rd
Harlesden Rd
Kings Rd
Rowdon Ave
Dobree Ave
Alexander Ave
Donnington Rd
Brondesbury Park
Sidmouth Road
Staverton Road
Chambers Lane
Alverstone Rd
Milverton Rd
Chudleigh Rd
Manor House Dr
Christchurch Ave
Aylestone Ave
Phillimore Gdns
A
B
C
4
3
2
1
86
85
84
10
22
23
24

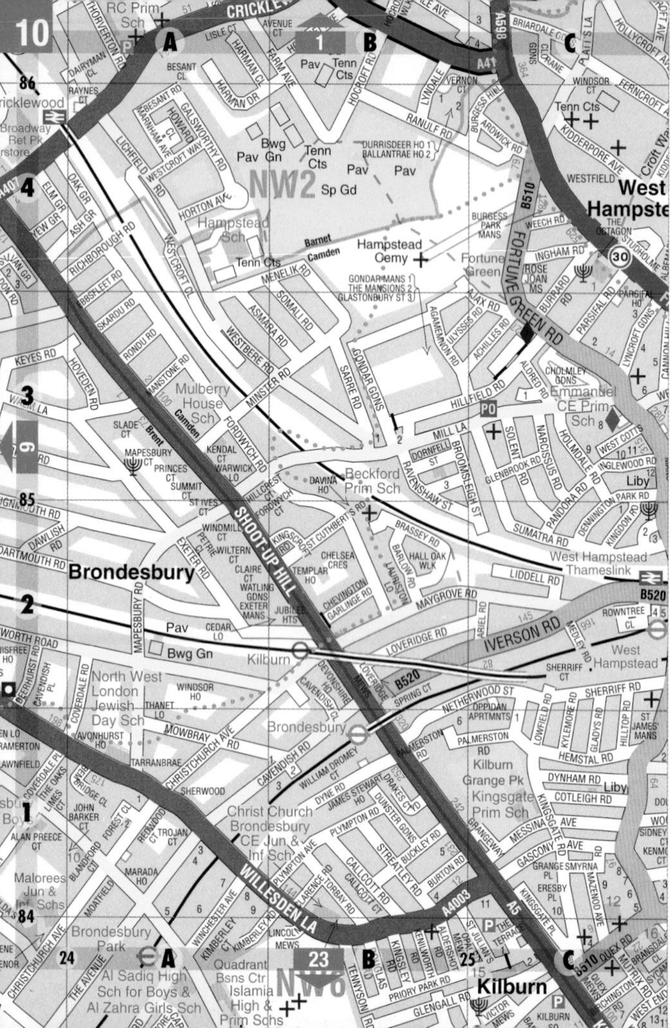
A
1
B
C
86
Cricklewood
Broadway Ret Pk
RC Prim Sch
HORVERTON RD
DAIRYMAN CL
RAYNES CT
BESANT CL
BESANT RD
LISLE CT
HARMAN CL
HARMAN DR
AVENUE CT
FARM AVE
Pav
Tenn Cts
HOCROFT RD
LYNDALE
VERNON CT
BRIARDALE GDNS
CLORANE GDNS
PLATT'S LA
HOLLYCROFT AVE
WINDSOR CT
FERNCROFT AVE
Tenn Cts
KIDDERPORE AVE
WESTFIELD
Croft Way
West Hampstead
THE OCTAGON
STUDHOLME
30
A598
A41
A407
B510
B520
A5
A4003
MARNHAM AVE
HOWARD CL
GALSWORTHY RD
WESTCROFT WAY
LICHFIELD RD
Bwg Gn
Pav
Tenn Cts
NW2
Sp Gd
DURRISDEER HO 1
BALLANTRAE HO 2
RANULF RD
BURGESS HILL
ARDWICK RD
4
ELM GR
OAK GR
YEW GR
ASH GR
RICHBOROUGH RD
HORTON AVE
Hampstead Sch
WESTCROFT CL
Barnet
Camden
Hampstead Cemy
BURGESS PARK MANS
WEECH RD
INGHAM RD
FORTUNE GREEN RD
Fortune Green
ROSE JOAN MS
BURRARD RD
PARSIFAL RD
PARSIFAL HO
LYNCROFT GDNS
SYLVAN GR
ELDON RD
EBBSFLEET RD
SKARDU RD
RONDU RD
Tenn Cts
MENELIK RD
SOMALI RD
ASMARA RD
WESTBERE RD
GONDAR MANS 1
THE MANSIONS 2
GLASTONBURY ST 3
AGAMEMNON RD
ULYSSES RD
AJAX RD
ACHILLES RD
ALDRED RD
CHOLMLEY GDNS
Emmanuel CE Prim Sch
KEYES RD
HOVEDEN RD
MANSTONE RD
Mulberry House Sch
MINSTER RD
SARRE RD
GONDAR GDNS
HILLFIELD RD
PO
3
WEST COTTS
INGLEWOOD RD
Liby
9
SLADE CT
Brent
Camden
FORDWYCH RD
MILL LA
DORNFELL ST
BROOMSLEIGH ST
SOLENT RD
NARCISSUS RD
HOLMDALE RD
GLENBROOK RD
MAPESBURY CT
KENDAL CT
WARWICK LO
PRINCES CT
SUMMIT CT
ST IVES CT
HILLCREST CT
FORDWYCH CT
DAVINA HO
Beckford Prim Sch
RAVENSHAW ST
PANDORA RD
DENNINGTON PARK RD
KINGDON RD
SUMATRA RD
85
TEIGNMOUTH RD
DAWLISH RD
DARTMOUTH RD
WINDMILL CT
PETRIE CL
EXETER RD
WILTERN CT
SHOOT-UP HILL
KINGSCROFT RD
ST CUTHBERT'S RD
BRASSEY RD
BARLOW RD
HALL OAK WLK
LAURISTON LO
CHELSEA CRES
TEMPLAR HO
CLAIRE CT
WATLING GDNS
EXETER MANS
JUBILEE HTS
CHEVINGTON
GARLINGE RD
MAYGROVE RD
West Hampstead Thameslink
LIDDELL RD
Brondesbury
2
MAPESBURY RD
Pav
CEDAR LO
Bwg Gn
Kilburn
LOVERIDGE RD
ARIEL RD
IVERSON RD
MEDLEY RD
ROWNTREE CL
West Hampstead
SHERRIFF CT
SHERRIFF RD
DEERHURST RD
CAVENDISH PL
COVERDALE RD
North West London Jewish Day Sch
WINDSOR HO
THANET LO
MOWBRAY RD
DEVONSHIRE HO
CAVENDISH CL
LOVERIDGE MEWS
SPRING CT
NETHERWOOD ST
OPPIDAN APRTMNTS
LOWFIELD RD
KYLEMORE RD
GLADYS RD
HILLTOP RD
ST JAMES' MANS
AVONHURST HO
CHRISTCHURCH AVE
Brondesbury
PALMERSTON RD
HEMSTAL RD
LAWNFIELD
TARRANBRAE
CAVENDISH RD
WILLIAM DROMEY CT
Kilburn Grange Pk
DYNHAM RD
COTLEIGH RD
1
COVERDALE PL
THE OAKS
LIMES CT
BRIDGE CL
JOHN BARKER CT
FOREST CL
SHERWOOD
REDWOOD CT
TROJAN CT
DYNE RD
JAMES STEWART HO
DRAKES CTYD
DUNSTER GDNS
Christ Church Brondesbury CE Jun & Inf Sch
Kingsgate Prim Sch
GRANGEWAY
MESSINA AVE
KINGSGATE RD
ALAN PREECE CT
BLANDFORD CT
MARADA HO
PLYMPTON RD
PLYMPTON AVE
STREATLEY RD
BUCKLEY RD
BURTON RD
GASCONY AVE
GRANGE PL
SMYRNA RD
MAZENOD AVE
ERESBY PL
Malorees Jun & Inf Schs
MOATFIELD
WILLESDEN LA
CLARENCE RD
TORBAY RD
CALLCOTT RD
CALLCOTT CT
84
WINCHESTER AVE
KIMBERLEY RD
KINGSGATE PL
Brondesbury Park
CHRISTCHURCH AVE
24
THE AVENUE
LINCOLN MEWS
23
KINGSLEY RD
KENILWORTH RD
ALDERSHOT RD
ST JULIAN'S RD
OPAL MEWS
THE TERRACE
25
QUEX RD
QUEX MEWS
MUTRIX RD
BRANSDALE CL
SYCAMORE CT
Al Sadiq High Sch for Boys & Al Zahra Girls Sch
Quadrant Bsns Ctr
Islamia High & Prim Schs
NW6
TENNYSON RD
DOUGLAS RD
PRIORY PARK RD
GLENGALL RD
Kilburn
VICTOR MEWS
KILBURN SQ
BIRCHINGTON RD
WEST END LA

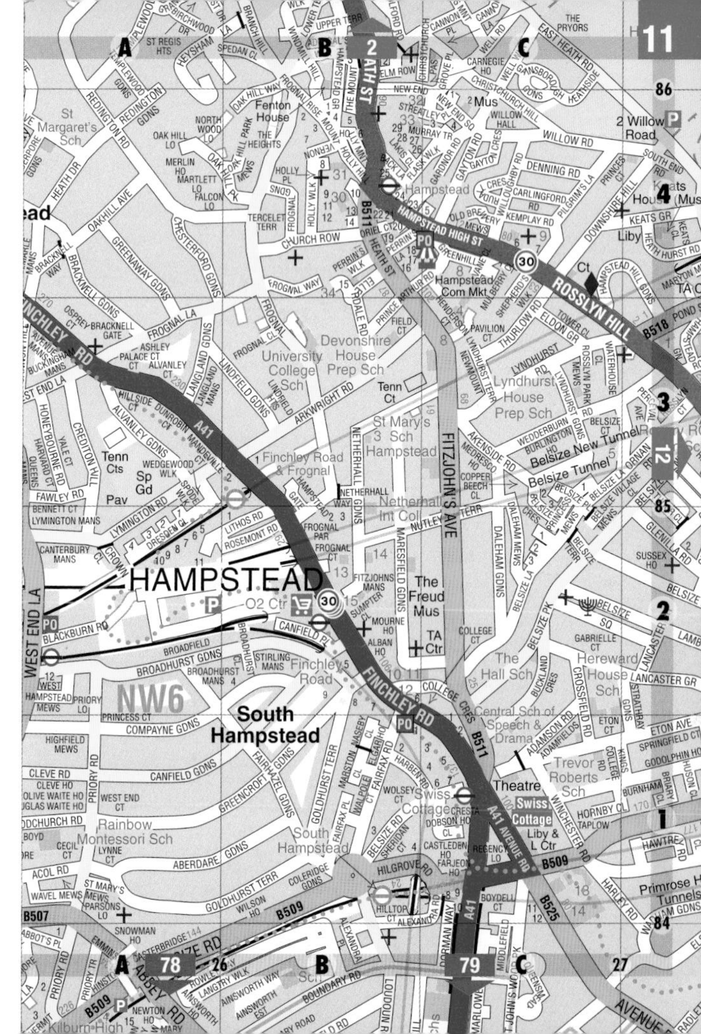
A
B
C
2
86
4
3
12
85
2
1
84
A
78
26
B
79
C
27
HAMPSTEAD
South Hampstead
NW6
Fenton House
2 Willow Road
Keats House (Mus)
Hampstead
Hampstead Com Mkt
University College Sch
Devonshire House Prep Sch
Lyndhurst House Prep Sch
St Mary's 3 Sch Hampstead
Netherhall Int Col
The Freud Mus
The Hall Sch
Hereward House Sch
Central Sch of Speech & Drama
Trevor Roberts Sch
Theatre
Swiss Cottage
Liby & L Ctr
Rainbow Montessori Sch
St Margaret's Sch
Finchley Road & Frognal
Finchley Road
Swiss Cottage
South Hampstead
O2 Ctr
Belsize New Tunnel
Belsize Tunnel
Primrose Hill Tunnels
HAMPSTEAD HIGH ST
ROSSLYN HILL
HEATH ST
FINCHLEY RD
FITZJOHN'S AVE
A41 AVENUE RD
WEST END LA
FROGNAL
FROGNAL LA
CHURCH ROW
ARKWRIGHT RD
WILLOW RD
EAST HEATH RD
DOWNSHIRE HILL
BELSIZE PK
BELSIZE LA
BOUNDARY RD
ABBEY RD
GOLDHURST TERR
ABERDARE GDNS
CANFIELD GDNS
COMPAYNE GDNS
BROADHURST GDNS
NETHERHALL GDNS
MARESFIELD GDNS
LYNDHURST GDNS
LANCASTER GR
ETON AVE
ADAMSON RD
WINCHESTER RD
COLLEGE CRES
HILGROVE RD
B509
B511
B518
B525
B507
A41

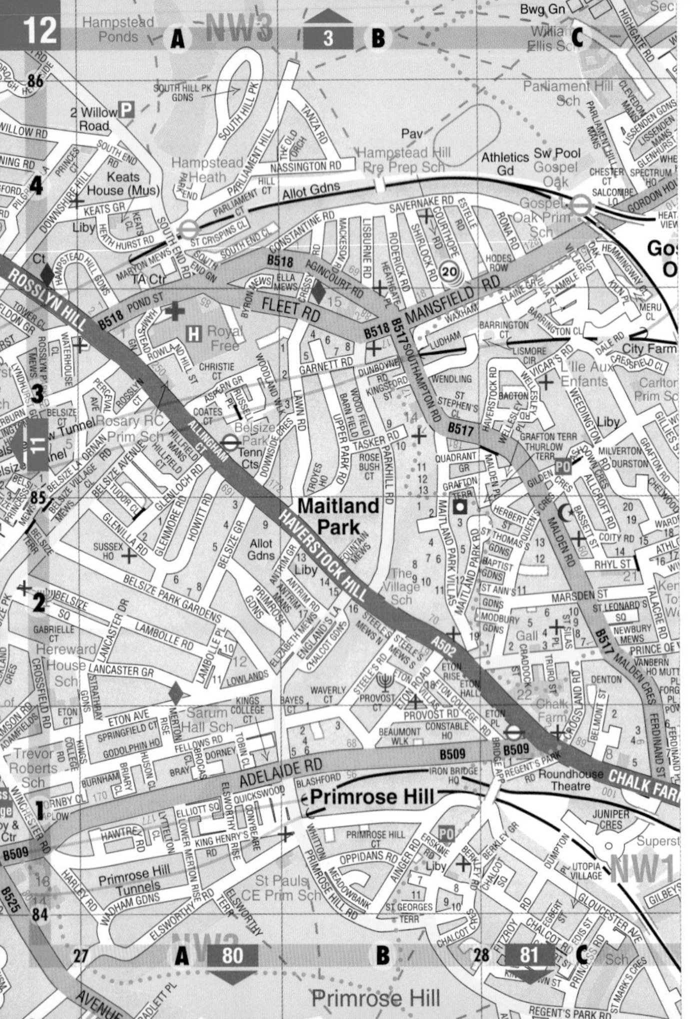
NW3
A
3
B
C
Hampstead Ponds
Bwg Gn
William Ellis Sch
HIGHGATE RD
SOUTH HILL PK GDNS
SOUTH HILL PK
2 Willow Road
WILLOW RD
TANZA RD
THE OLD ORCH
PARLIAMENT HILL
NASSINGTON RD
Hampstead Heath
Pav
Hampstead Hill Pre Prep Sch
Parliament Hill Sch
Athletics Gd
Sw Pool
Gospel Oak
Gospel Oak Prim Sch
Allot Gdns
Keats House (Mus)
KEATS GR
KEATS CL
DOWNSHIRE HILL
PRINCES CT
SOUTH END RD
HILL CT
PARLIAMENT CT
ST CRISPINS CL
SOUTH END CL
CONSTANTINE RD
SAVERNAKE RD
COURTHOPE RD
ESTELLE RD
RONA RD
MACKESON RD
LISBURNE RD
RODERICK RD
SHIRLOCK RD
HEATHGATE PL
Liby
HEATH HURST RD
HAMPSTEAD HILL GDNS
MARYON MEWS
TA Ctr
SOUTH END GN
B518
AGINCOURT RD
CRESSY RD
ELLA MEWS
BYRON MEWS
FLEET RD
POND ST
ROSSLYN HILL
MANSFIELD RD
B517
HODES ROW
ELAINE GR
JULIA ST
LAMBLE ST
OAK VILLAGE
HEMMINGWAY CL
KILN PL
MERU CL
BARRINGTON CT
BARRINGTON CL
WAXHAM
LUDHAM
DALE RD
City Farm
CRESSFIELD CL
LISMORE CIR
VICAR'S RD
L'Ile Aux Enfants
Carlton Prim Sch
Royal Free
H
ROWLAND HILL ST
CHRISTIE CT
WOODLAND WLK
GARNETT RD
DUNBOYNE RD
KINGSFORD ST
SOUTHAMPTON RD
WENDLING
ST STEPHEN'S CL
HAVERSTOCK RD
BACTON
WELLESLEY RD
WEEDINGTON RD
GILLIES ST
PERCEVAL AVE
ROSSLYN CT
ASPERN GR
RUSSELL PL
COATES CT
LAWN RD
BARN FIELD
WOOD FIELD
UPPER PARK RD
TASKER RD
PARKHILL RD
Belsize Park
Tenn Cts
Rosary RC Prim Sch
ALLINGHAM CT
HILLFIELD MANS
HILLFIELD CT
Tunnel
11
BELSIZE LA
ORNAN RD
BELSIZE AVENUE
BELSIZE VILLAGE
TUDOR CL
GLENLOCH RD
HOWITT RD
DOWNSIDE CRES
TROYES HO
ROSE BUSH CT
QUADRANT GR
GRAFTON TERR
THURLOW TERR
GILDEN CRES
GRAFTON TERR
PO
ASHDOWN CRES
ALLCROFT RD
MILVERTON
DURSTON
GRAFTON RD
CHELWOOD
Maitland Park
HAVERSTOCK HILL
MAITLAND PARK VILLAS
MAITLAND PARK RD
MALDEN PL
HERBERT ST
QUEEN'S CRES
MALDEN RD
BASSETT ST
COITY RD
RHYL ST
GLENILLA RD
GLENMORE RD
BELSIZE GR
Allot Gdns
SUSSEX HO
Liby
FOUNTAIN MEWS
ANTRIM GR
ANTRIM RD
ANTRIM MANS
The Village Sch
ST THOMAS'S GDNS
BAPTIST GDNS
ST ANN'S GDNS
MODBURY GDNS
MARSDEN ST
ST LEONARD'S SQ
NEWBURY MEWS
PRINCE OF WALES RD
TALACRE RD
BELSIZE PARK GARDENS
BELSIZE SQ
GABRIELLE CT
LAMBOLLE RD
LAMBOLLE PL
LANCASTER DR
PRIMROSE GDNS
ELIZABETH MEWS
ENGLAND'S LA
CHALCOT GDNS
STEELE'S MEWS N
STEELE'S MEWS S
A502
Gall
ST SILAS PL
CRADDOCK ST
TRURO ST
VANBERN HO
Hereward House Sch
LANCASTER GR
STRATHRAY GDNS
LOWLANDS
KINGS COLLEGE CT
BAYES CT
WAVERLY CT
STEELE'S RD
PROVOST CT
ETON ROAD
ETON VILLAS
ETON COLLEGE RD
ETON RISE
ETON HALL
ETON PL
DENTON
BELMONT ST
CROGSLAND RD
MALDEN CRES
FERDINAND ST
Chalk Farm
CROSSFIELD RD
ETON CT
ETON AVE
SPRINGFIELD CT
GODOLPHIN HO
MERTON RISE
Sarum Hall Sch
FELLOWS RD
BROCAS CL
DORNEY
TOBIN CL
PROVOST RD
CONSTABLE HO
BEAUMONT WLK
B509
BRIDGE APP
REGENT'S PARK RD
Roundhouse Theatre
CHALK FARM
Trevor Roberts Sch
KINGS COLLEGE RD
BRIARY CL
HUSON CL
BRAY
BURNHAM
ADELAIDE RD
BLASHFORD
IRON BRIDGE HQ
QUICKSWOOD
ELSWORTHY RISE
CONYBEARE
Primrose Hill
ELLIOTT SQ
LYTTELTON CL
JUNIPER CRES
Superst
WINCHESTER RD
HAWTREY RD
LOWER MERTON RISE
KING HENRY'S RD
WHITTON
PRIMROSE HILL CT
ERSKINE RD
AINGER RD
BERKLEY RD
BERKLEY GR
CHALCOT SQ
DUMPTON PL
UTOPIA VILLAGE
NW1
GILBEYS
B525
HARLEY RD
Primrose Hill Tunnels
WADHAM GDNS
ELSWORTHY RD
ELSWORTHY TERR
St Pauls CE Prim Sch
OPPIDANS RD
MEADOWBANK
PRIMROSE HILL RD
ST GEORGES TERR
CHALCOT CRES
FITZROY RD
CHALCOT RD
EGBERT ST
EDIS ST
GLOUCESTER AVE
PRINCESS RD
ST MARK'S CRES
Sch
27
A
80
B
28
81
C
ADLETT PL
AVENUE
Primrose Hill
REGENT'S PARK RD
KING ST

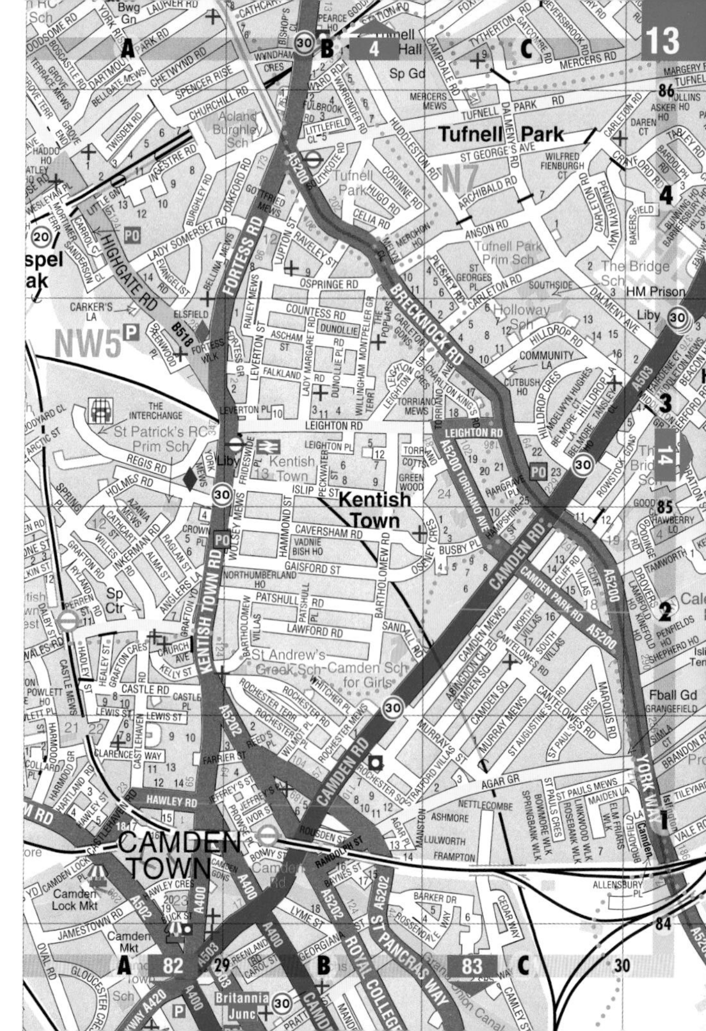
A
B
C
4
13
86
Tufnell Park
N7
NW5
Kentish Town
CAMDEN TOWN
Gospel Oak
LAURIER RD
YORK RISE
WOODSOME RD
BOSCASTLE RD
GROVE TERRACE MEWS
DARTMOUTH PARK RD
BELLGATE MEWS
CHETWYND RD
SPENCER RISE
CHURCHILL RD
TWISDEN RD
INGESTRE RD
Acland Burghley Sch
WYNDHAM CRES
BISHOP'S CL
PEARCE HO
GODWIN
STATION RD
Tufnell Hall
CAMPDALE RD
TYTHERTON RD
GATCOMBE RD
BEVERSBROOK RD
MERCERS RD
Sp Gd
MERCERS MEWS
DALMENY RD
TUFNELL PARK RD
HUDDLESTON RD
WARRENDER RD
FULBROOK
LITTLEFIELD CL
SOUTHCOTE RD
Tufnell Park
HUGO RD
CORINNE RD
ST GEORGE'S AVE
WILFRED FIENBURGH CT
ARCHIBALD RD
CARLETON RD
PENDERYN WAY
CRAYFORD RD
BARDOLPH RD
TABLEY RD
DAREN CT
ASKER HO
COLLINS
TUFNELL
MARGERY FRY
MORTIMER TERR
CARROL CL
SANDERSON CL
WESLEYAN PL
LITTLE GN ST
HIGHGATE RD
PO
LADY SOMERSET RD
BURGHLEY RD
OAKFORD RD
GOTTFRIED MEWS
FORTESS RD
LUPTON ST
RAVELEY ST
CELIA RD
MERCHON HO
MELYN CL
ANSON RD
Tufnell Park Prim Sch
BAKERS FIELD
The Bridge Sch
HM Prison
BELLINA MEWS
EVANGELIST RD
OSPRINGE RD
RAILEY MEWS
COUNTESS RD
DUNOLLIE
ASCHAM ST
LEVERTON ST
MONTPELIER GR
THE POPLARS
CARLETON GDNS
BRECKNOCK RD
PLESHEY RD
ST GEORGES PL
SOUTHSIDE
DALMENY AVE
Holloway Sch
HILLDROP RD
Liby
CARKER'S LA
ELSFIELD
B518
GREENWOOD PL
FORTESS WLK
FORTESS GR
FALKLAND RD
LADY MARGARET RD
DUNOLLIE PL
WILLINGHAM TERR
LEIGHTON CRES
LEIGHTON GR
CHARLTON KING'S RD
TORRIANO MEWS
TORRIANO AVE
COMMUNITY LA
CUTBUSH HO
HILLDROP CRES
MOELWYN HUGHES CT
BELMORE LA
HILLDROP LA
TANSLEY CL
A503
ROWSTOCK GDNS
THE INTERCHANGE
St Patrick's RC Prim Sch
WOODYARD CL
ARCTIC ST
LEVERTON PL
LEIGHTON RD
LEIGHTON PL
TORRIANO COTTS
GREENWOOD
A5200 TORRIANO AVE
HARGRAVE PL
REGIS RD
YORK MEWS
FRIDESWIDE PL
Kentish Town
PECKWATER ST
ISLIP ST
HOLMES RD
SPRING PL
AZANIA MEWS
CATHCART ST
INKERMAN RD
CROWN PL
WOLSEY MEWS
HAMMOND ST
CAVERSHAM RD
VADNIE BISH HO
BARTHOLOMEW RD
OSENEY CRES
BUSBY PL
HAMPSHIRE ST
CAMDEN RD
CLIFF RD
CLIFF VILLAS
A5200
GOODINGE RD
DROVERS
TAMWORTH
HAWBERRY LO
85
14
GRAFTON RD
RYLAND RD
WILLES RD
ALMA ST
RAGLAN ST
KENTISH TOWN RD
GAISFORD ST
NORTHUMBERLAND HO
ANGLERS LA
GRAFTON YD
Sp Ctr
PERREN ST
DALBY ST
PATSHULL RD
PATSHULL PL
BARTHOLOMEW VILLAS
LAWFORD RD
SANDALL RD
CAMDEN PARK RD
CAMDEN MEWS
NORTH VILLAS
SOUTH VILLAS
CANTELOWES RD
ABINGDON CL
CAMDEN SQ
PENFIELDS HO
SHEPHERD HO
WALES RD
HADLEY ST
HEALEY ST
GRAFTON CRES
CHURCH AVE
KELLY ST
St Andrew's Greek Sch
Camden Sch for Girls
CASTLE MEWS
POWLETT HO
CASTLE RD
CASTLE PL
LEWIS ST
ROCHESTER TERR
ROCHESTER RD
ROCHESTER PL
WHITCHER PL
ROCHESTER MEWS
MURRAY ST
MURRAY MEWS
ST AUGUSTINE'S RD
ST PAUL'S CRES
MARQUIS RD
Fball Gd
GRANGEFIELD
HARMOOD GR
CLARENCE WAY
CASTLEHAVEN RD
FARRIER ST
REED'S PL
WILMOT PL
CAMDEN RD
ROCHESTER SQ
STRATFORD VILLAS
AGAR GR
ST PAULS MEWS
MAIDEN LA
YORK WAY
BRANDON RD
COLLARD PL
HARTLAND RD
HAWLEY ST
HAWLEY RD
JEFFREY'S ST
JEFFREY'S PL
PROWSE PL
IVOR ST
NETTLECOMBE
ASHMORE
MANSTON
LULWORTH
FRAMPTON
SPRINGBANK WLK
BOWMORE WLK
ST PAULS CRES
ROSEBANK WLK
LINKWOOD WLK
ELM FRIARS WLK
BROADFIELD LA
TILEYARD RD
VALE ROYAL
CAMDEN
CAMDEN TOWN
CASTLEHAVEN RD
ROUSDEN ST
RANDOLPH ST
BONNY ST
CAMDEN GDNS
Camden Rd
AGAR PL
CAMDEN LOCK PL
Camden Lock Mkt
A502
HAWLEY CRES
BUCK ST
A400
BAYNES ST
A5202
ALLENSBURY PL
BARKER DR
ROSSENDALE WAY
CEDAR WAY
84
JAMESTOWN RD
Camden Mkt
LYME ST
GEORGIANA ST
ROYAL COLLEGE ST
ST PANCRAS WAY
OVAL RD
GLOUCESTER CRES
GREENLAND RD
CAROL ST
82
29
83
30
Britannia Junc
Grand Union Canal
CAMLEY ST
A420
P

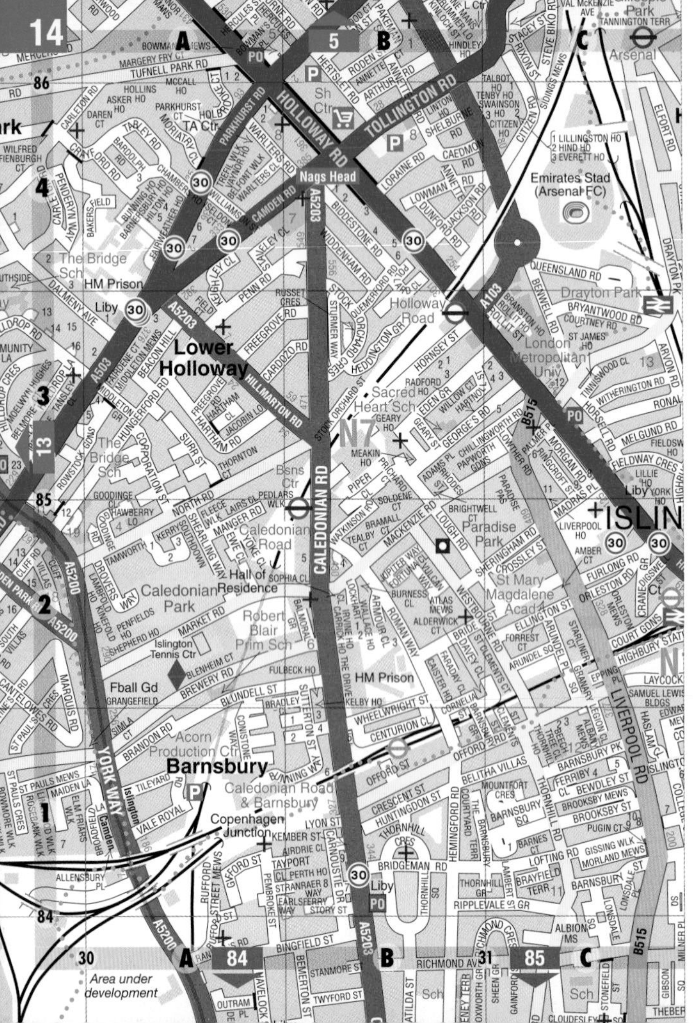

5
A
B
C
86
85
84
4
3
2
1
13
84
85
30
31
HOLLOWAY RD
TOLLINGTON RD
CAMDEN RD
CALEDONIAN RD
HILLMARTON RD
PARKHURST RD
TUFNELL PARK RD
MARGERY FRY CT
BOWMAN'S MEWS
Nags Head
Sh Ctr
A5203
A503
A103
A5200
B515
YORK WAY
LIVERPOOL RD
Emirates Stad (Arsenal FC)
Arsenal
Gillespie Park
Drayton Park
Holloway Road
London Metropolitan Univ
Lower Holloway
HM Prison
The Bridge Sch
Liby
TA Ctr
Caledonian Road
Caledonian Park
Hall of Residence
Robert Blair Prim Sch
Islington Tennis Ctr
Fball Gd
Acorn Production Ctr
Barnsbury
Caledonian Road & Barnsbury
Copenhagen Junction
Bsns Ctr
Sacred Heart Sch
N7
Paradise Park
St Mary Magdalene Acad
ISLIN
HM Prison
QUEENSLAND RD
BRYANTWOOD RD
MARKET RD
BREWERY RD
BRANDON RD
VALE ROYAL
COPENHAGEN
BRIDGEMAN RD
RICHMOND AV
BINGFIELD ST
OFFORD RD
CRESCENT ST
HUNTINGDON ST
THORNHILL RD
BARNSBURY RD
MACKENZIE RD
WESTBOURNE RD
ORLESTON RD
HOLLOWAY RD
Area under development

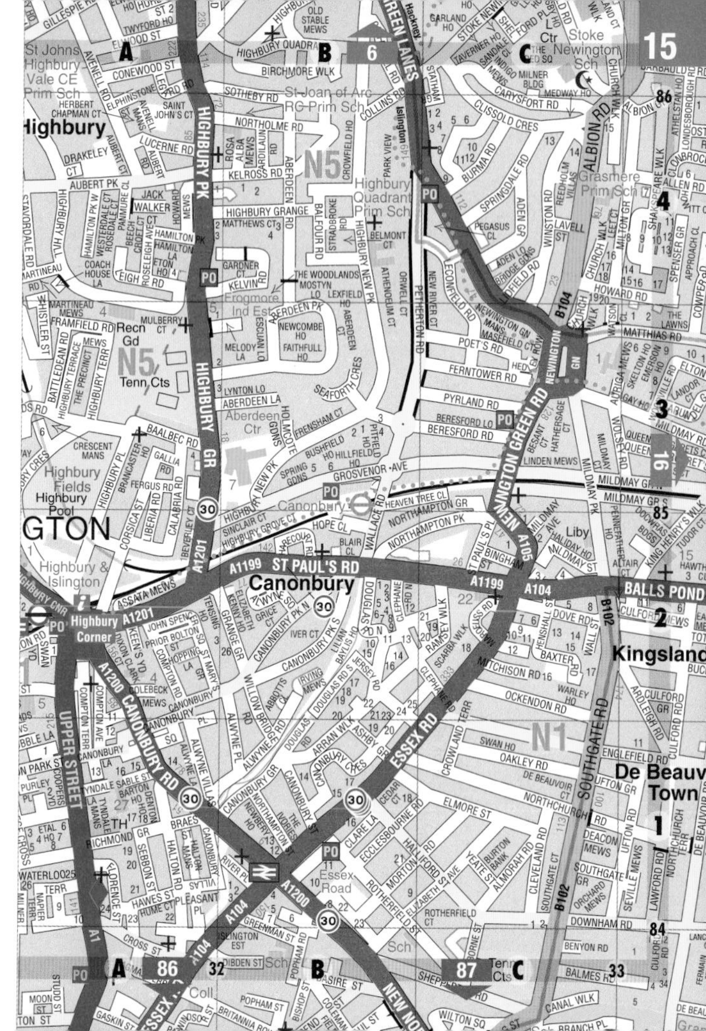
A
B
C
6
16
86
87
85
84
4
3
2
1
Highbury
Canonbury
Kingsland
De Beauv
Town
Stoke Newington Sch
N5
N1
GTON
HIGHBURY PK
HIGHBURY GR
GREEN LANES
HIGHBURY NEW PK
NEWINGTON GREEN RD
ALBION RD
ST PAUL'S RD
A1199
A1201
A1200
A104
A105
B104
B102
A1
BALLS POND
SOUTHGATE RD
UPPER STREET
CANONBURY RD
ESSEX RD
Highbury Corner
Highbury & Islington
Highbury Fields
Highbury Pool
Canonbury
Essex Road
Aberdeen Ctr
Frogmore Ind Est
Highbury Quadrant Prim Sch
St Joan of Arc RC Prim Sch
St Johns Highbury Vale CE Prim Sch
Grasmere Prim Sch
Recn Gd
Tenn Cts
Liby
HIGHBURY QUADRANT
BIRCHMORE WLK
SOTHEBY RD
NORTHOLME RD
KELROSS RD
HIGHBURY GRANGE
GROSVENOR AVE
NORTHAMPTON GR
NORTHAMPTON PK
CLISSOLD CRES
CARYSFORT RD
SPRINGDALE RD
POET'S RD
FERNTOWER RD
PYRLAND RD
BERESFORD RD
MILDMAY GR
MILDMAY PK
MATTHIAS RD
HOWARD RD
MITCHISON RD
OCKENDON RD
OAKLEY RD
NORTHCHURCH RD
ELMORE ST
DOWNHAM RD
CANONBURY PK N
CANONBURY PK S
CANONBURY GR
CANONBURY ST
CANONBURY CRES
DOUGLAS RD
ALWYNE RD
ALWYNE VILLAS
CONEWOOD ST
AUBERT PK
LUCERNE RD
DRAKELEY CT
BAALBEC RD
CORSICA ST
LIBERIA RD
CALABRIA RD
HIGHBURY PL
ROTHERFIELD ST
ECCLESBOURNE RD
ALMORAH RD
CLEVELAND RD
ENGLEFIELD RD
ESSEX RD
GREENMAN ST
POPHAM RD
POPHAM ST
CANAL WLK
BALMES RD
NEW NORTH RD

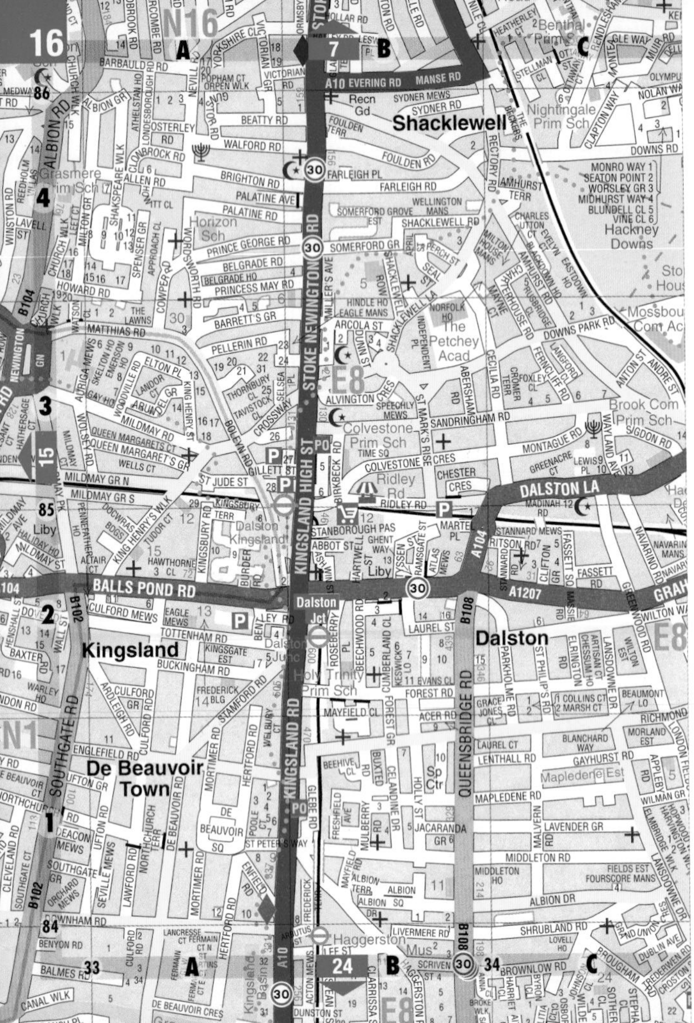

N16
A
B
C
7
Shacklewell
A10 EVERING RD
MANSE RD
SYDNER MEWS
SYDNER RD
Recn Gd
BARBAULD RD
YORKSHIRE CL
VICTORIAN GR
VICTORIAN RD
POPHAM CT
ORPEN WLK
ALBION GR
ALBION RD
CHURCH WLK
OSTERLEY RD
BEATTY RD
WALFORD RD
BROCK RD
FOULDEN TERR
FOULDEN RD
FARLEIGH PL
FARLEIGH RD
BRIGHTON RD
PALATINE AVE
PALATINE RD
ALLEN RD
Grasmere Prim Sch
Horizon Sch
SHAKSPEARE WLK
WORDSWORTH RD
PRINCE GEORGE RD
SOMERFORD GROVE EST
SOMERFORD GR
WELLINGTON MANS
SHACKLEWELL RD
BELGRADE RD
BELGRADE HO
PRINCESS MAY RD
HOWARD RD
MATTHIAS RD
THE LAWNS
BARRETT'S GR
PELLERIN RD
HINDLE HO
EAGLE MANS
ARCOLA ST
SHACKLEWELL LA
NORFOLK HO
The Petchey Acad
RECTORY RD
AMHURST TERR
AMHURST RD
DOWNS PARK RD
DOWNS RD
Nightingale Prim Sch
Hackney Downs
MONRO WAY 1
SEATON POINT 2
WORSLEY GR 3
MIDHURST WAY 4
BLUNDELL CL 5
VINE CL 6
Mossbou Com Ac
Benthal Prim
CLAPTON WAY
NOLAN WAY
STOKE NEWINGTON RD
ELTON PL
MILDMAY RD
QUEEN MARGARET'S GR
WELLS CT
MILDMAY GR N
MILDMAY GR S
ST JUDE ST
BOLEYN RD
CROSSWAY
E8
ALVINGTON CRES
SPEECHLY MEWS
Colvestone Prim Sch
COLVESTONE CRES
TIME SQ
Ridley Rd
RIDLEY RD
SANDRINGHAM RD
ST MARK'S RISE
CHESTER CRES
MONTAGUE RD
GREENACRE CT
Brook Com Prim Sch
SIGDON RD
WAYLAND AVE
DALSTON LA
MADINAH RD
15
85
Liby
KINGSBURY TERR
Dalston Kingsland
KINGSLAND HIGH ST
STANBOROUGH PAS
ABBOT ST
GHENT WAY
HARTWELL ST
Liby
MARTEL PL
STANNARD MEWS
RITSON RD
CLIFTON GR
FASSETT SQ
FASSETT RD
NAVARINO RD
NAVARINO MANS
HAWTHORNE CL
BALLS POND RD
A1207
A104
B102
B108
Dalston Jct
CULFORD MEWS
EAGLE MEWS
LEY RD
TOTTENHAM RD
Kingsland
KINGSGATE EST
Dalston Junc
BUCKINGHAM RD
Dalston
LAUREL ST
EVANS CL
FOREST RD
Holy Trinity Prim Sch
ROSEBERRY PL
BEECHWOOD RD
CUMBERLAND CL
KESWICK
PARKHOLME RD
ST PHILIP'S RD
ELRINGTON RD
LANSDOWNE DR
GREENWOOD RD
WILTON EST
BEAUMONT LO
RICHMOND RD
MORLAND EST
COLLINS CT
MARSH CT
GRACE JONES CL
FREDERICK BLG
STAMFORD RD
MAYFIELD CL
ACER RD
LAUREL CT
LENTHALL RD
GAYHURST RD
BLANCHARD WAY
Mapledene Est
QUEENSBRIDGE RD
SOUTHGATE RD
N1
ENGLEFIELD RD
De Beauvoir Town
UFTON GR
UFTON RD
MORTIMER RD
HERTFORD RD
KINGSLAND RD
BEEHIVE CL
BUXTED RD
CELANDINE DR
HOLLY ST
Sp Ctr
MAPLEDENE RD
LAVENDER GR
JACARANDA GR
DE BEAUVOIR SQ
DE BEAUVOIR RD
NORTHCHURCH TERR
DEACON MEWS
SOUTHGATE GR
SEVILLE MEWS
LAWFORD RD
ST PETER'S WAY
ENFIELD RD
FRESHFIELD AVE
MULBERRY RD
GLEBE RD
FREDERICK TERR
MAYFIELD RD
ALBION TERR
ALBION SQ
ALBION DR
MIDDLETON RD
MIDDLETON HO
FIELDS EST
FOURSCORE MANS
SHRUBLAND RD
LOVELL HO
GRAND UNION CRES
DUBLIN AVE
CLEVELAND RD
SOUTHGATE CT
ORCHARD MEWS
DOWNHAM RD
84
BENYON RD
BALMES RD
33
CANAL WLK
LANCRESSE CT
FERMAIN CT
DE BEAUVOIR CRES
Kingsland Basin
A10
ACTON MEWS
ARBUTUS ST
Haggerston
LEE ST
Mus
24
LIVERMERE RD
SCRIVEN ST
34
BROWNLOW RD
HAGGERSTON RD
CLARRISSA ST
DUNSTON ST
BROUGHAM RD

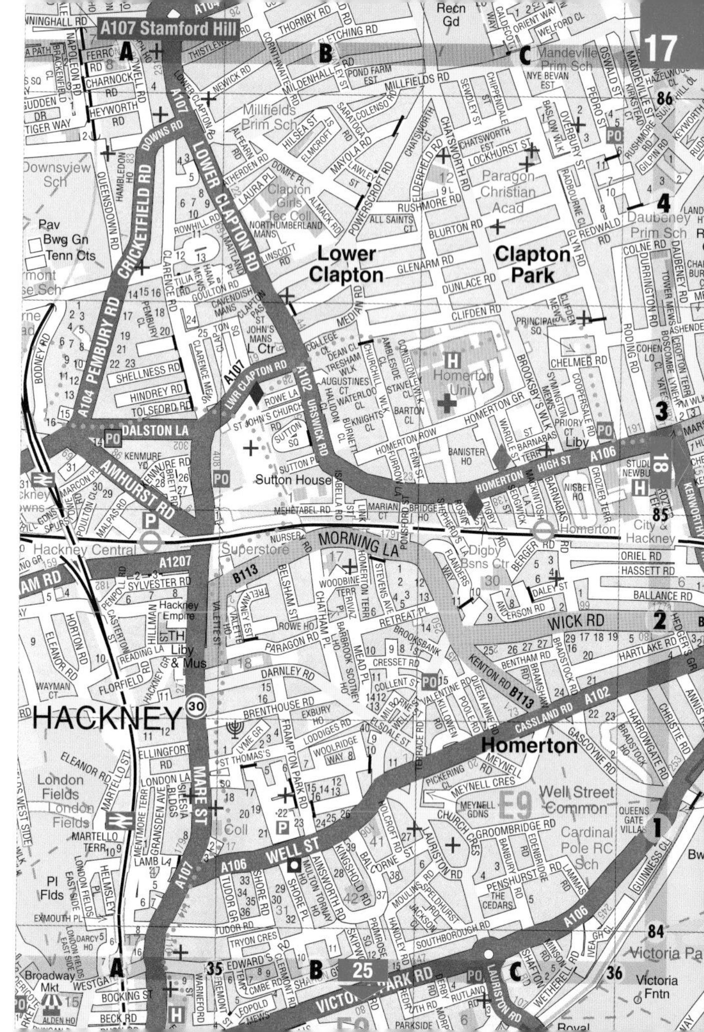
A107 Stamford Hill
A
B
C
86
Mandeville Prim Sch
NYE BEVAN EST
MILLFIELDS RD
Millfields Prim Sch
Downsview Sch
CRICKETFIELD RD
LOWER CLAPTON RD
DOWNS RD
Clapton Girls Tec Coll
CHATSWORTH RD
Paragon Christian Acad
Daubeney Prim Sch
Lower Clapton
Clapton Park
GLENARM RD
DUNLACE RD
CLIFDEN RD
A104 PEMBURY RD
SHELLNESS RD
HINDREY RD
TOLSFORD RD
DALSTON LA
AMHURST RD
LWR CLAPTON RD
A102 URSWICK RD
Homerton Univ
HOMERTON GR
HOMERTON ROW
HOMERTON HIGH ST
A106
18
85
Sutton House
Hackney Central
Homerton
City & Hackney
MORNING LA
Superstore
A1207
B113
SYLVESTER RD
Hackney Empire
Liby & Mus
WICK RD
HARTLAKE RD
Digby Bsns Ctr
KENTON RD
CASSLAND RD
A102
HACKNEY
30
Homerton
MARE ST
A107
Well Street Common
E9
London Fields
WELL ST
A106
Cardinal Pole RC Sch
QUEENS GATE VILLAS
PI Flds
Broadway Mkt
35
B
25
C
36
VICTORIA PARK RD
Victoria Park
Victoria Fntn
84
LAURISTON RD

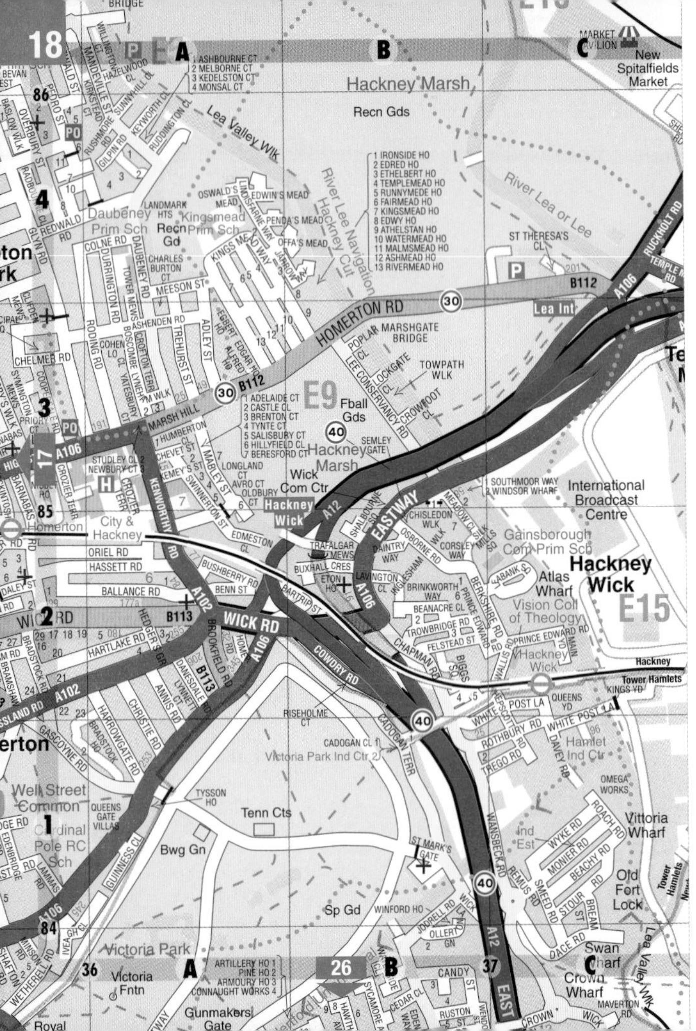

17
86
85
84
36
26
37

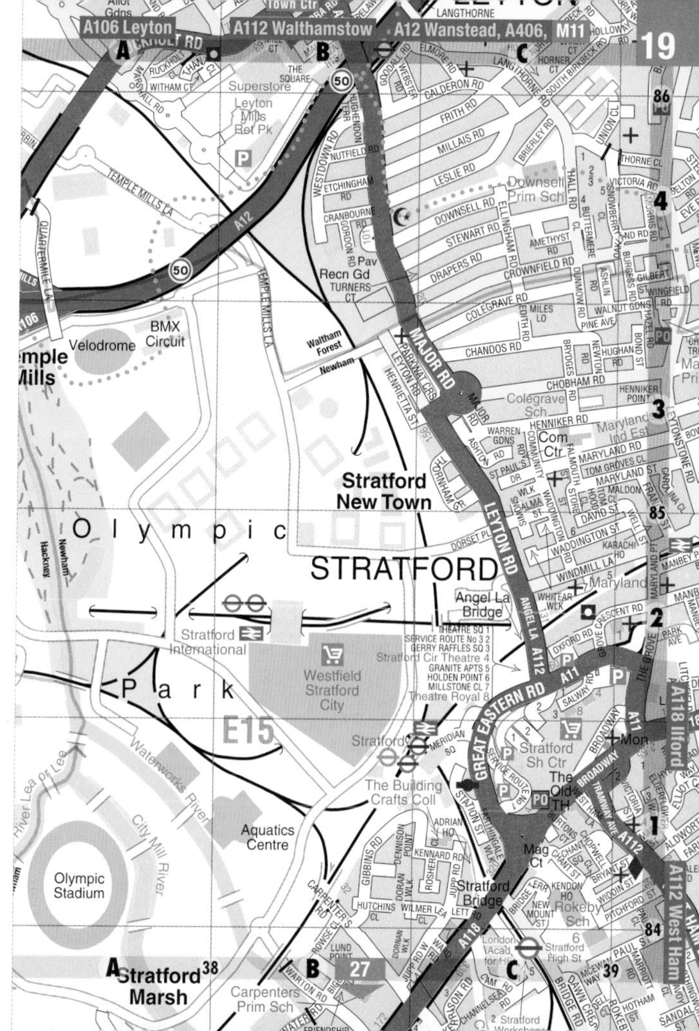
A106 Leyton
A112 Walthamstow
A12 Wanstead, A406, M11
LANGTHORNE
Superstore
Leyton Mills Ret Pk
TEMPLE MILLS LA
A12
QUARTERMILE LA
A106
Velodrome
BMX Circuit
Temple Mills
Recn Gd
Pav
Waltham Forest
Newham
MAJOR RD
LEYTON RD
Downsell Prim Sch
Colegrave Sch
Com Ctr
Maryland Ind Est
Maryland
Stratford New Town
STRATFORD
Olympic Park
Stratford International
Westfield Stratford City
E15
Angel La Bridge
THEATRE SQ 1
SERVICE ROUTE No 3 2
GERRY RAFFLES SQ 3
Stratford Cir Theatre 4
GRANITE APTS 5
HOLDEN POINT 6
MILLSTONE CL 7
Theatre Royal 8
Stratford
GREAT EASTERN RD
A11
Stratford Sh Ctr
The Old TH
BROADWAY
A118 Ilford
18
A112 West Ham
Waterworks River
City Mill River
River Lea or Lee
Olympic Stadium
Aquatics Centre
The Building Crafts Coll
Stratford Bridge
Rokeby Sch
Stratford High St
London Acad for HE
Stratford Marsh
38
27
39
84
85
86
Carpenters Prim Sch
A
B
C
1
2
3
4

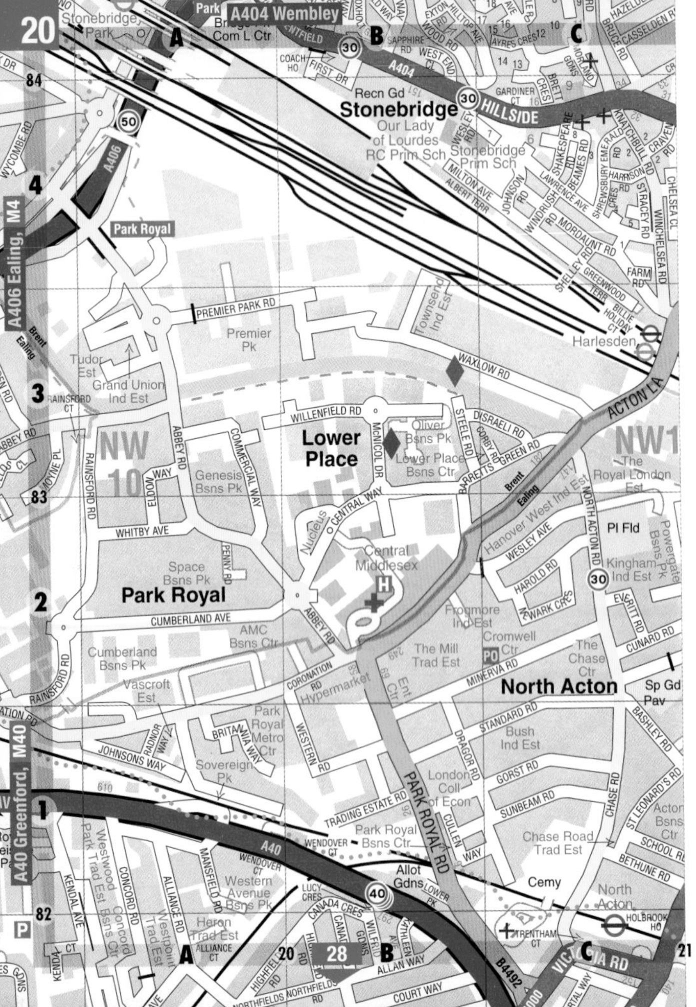
Stonebridge Park
A404 Wembley
A
B
C
84
Recn Gd
Stonebridge
HILLSIDE
Our Lady of Lourdes RC Prim Sch
Stonebridge Prim Sch
SAPPHIRE RD
WEST END CL
A404
FIRST DR
COACH HO
GARDINER CT
BRETT CRES
MORLAND GDNS
HAZELDEAN RD
CASSELDEN RD
BRUCE RD
WESLEY RD
SHAKESPEARE RD
BEAMES RD
EMERALD RD
KNATCHBULL RD
CRAVEN RD
HARRISON RD
STRACEY RD
CHELSEA CL
WINCHELSEA RD
MILTON AVE
ALBERT TERR
JOHNSON RD
WINDRUSH RD
LAWRENCE AVE
SHREWSBURY CRES
MORDAUNT RD
SHELLEY RD
GREENWOOD TERR
FARM RD
BILLIE HOLIDAY CT
Harlesden
WYCOMBE RD
A406
4
A406 Ealing, M4
Park Royal
PREMIER PARK RD
Premier Pk
Townsend Ind Est
WAXLOW RD
Tudor Est
Grand Union Ind Est
3
RAINSFORD CT
WILLENFIELD RD
Oliver Bsns Pk
Lower Place
Lower Place Bsns Ctr
McNICOL DR
STEELE RD
DISRAELI RD
CORBY RD
BARRETTS GREEN RD
ACTON LA
NW10
NW10
ABBEY RD
COMMERCIAL WAY
Genesis Bsns Pk
ELDON WAY
RAINSFORD RD
MOYNE PL
83
Brent
Ealing
Royal London Est
NORTH ACTON RD
Hanover West Ind Est
CENTRAL WAY
Nucleus
WHITBY AVE
Space Bsns Pk
PENNY RD
Central Middlesex
H
Park Royal
2
WESLEY AVE
HAROLD RD
NEWARK CRES
Pl Fld
Powergate Bsns Pk
Kingham Ind Est
30
EVERITT RD
CUNARD RD
CUMBERLAND AVE
ABBEY RD
AMC Bsns Ctr
Cumberland Bsns Pk
Frogmore Ind Est
Cromwell Ctr
The Mill Trad Est
The Chase Ctr
MINERVA RD
North Acton
Sp Gd Pav
RAINSFORD RD
Vascroft Est
CORONATION RD
Hypermarket
Ent Ctr
BASHLEY RD
STANDARD RD
Bush Ind Est
CORONATION RD
RADNOR WAY
BRITANNIA WAY
Park Royal Metro Ctr
WESTERN RD
DRAGOR RD
JOHNSONS WAY
Sovereign Pk
PARK ROYAL RD
GORST RD
London Coll of Econ
SUNBEAM RD
CHASE RD
ST LEONARD'S RD
Acton Bsns Ctr
A40 Greenford, M40
1
TRADING ESTATE RD
Park Royal Bsns Ctr
CULLEN WAY
Chase Road Trad Est
SCHOOL RD
BETHUNE RD
A40
WENDOVER CT
Westwood Park Trad Est
Concord Bsns Ctr
MANSFIELD RD
Western Avenue Bsns Pk
Allot Gdns
LOWER PK
Cemy
North Acton
HOLBROOK HO
82
KENDAL AVE
CONCORD RD
ALLIANCE RD
Westpoint Trad Est
Heron Trad Est
ALLIANCE CT
LUCY CRES
CANADA CRES
40
WILFRID GDNS
KATHLEEN AVE
TRENTHAM CT
P
KENDAL CT
A
20
28
B
ALLAN WAY
C
21
VICTORIA RD
B4492
HIGHFIELD RD
NORTHFIELDS RD
COURT WAY
PORTAL WAY
A4000

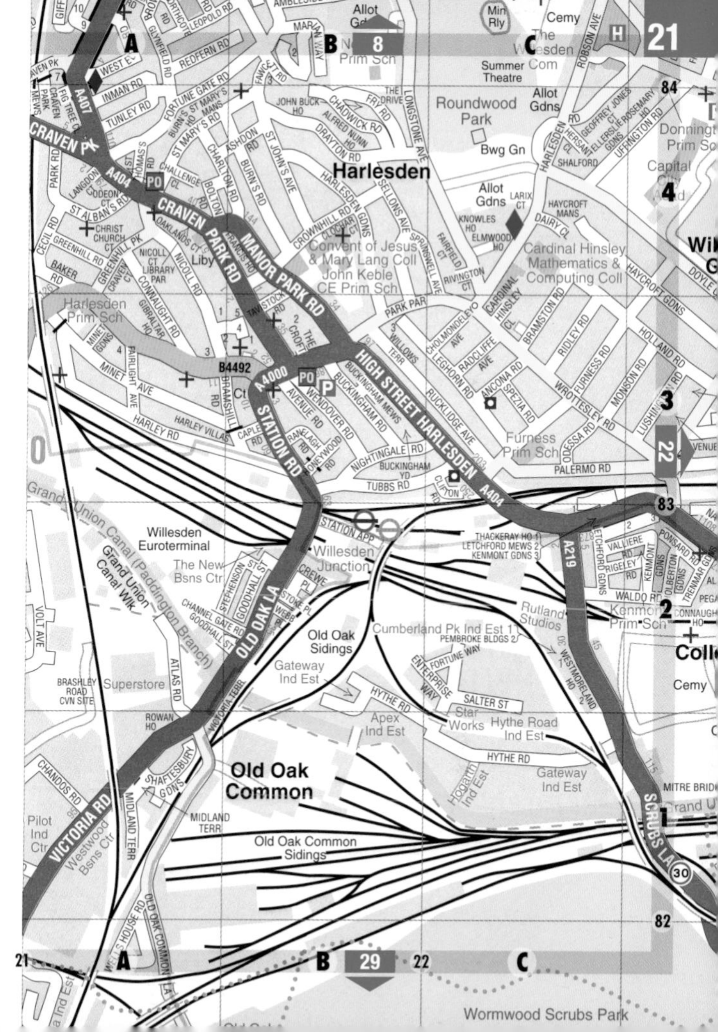

21
8
29
22
84
83
82
A
B
C
1
2
3
4
Harlesden
Old Oak Common
Roundwood Park
Bwg Gn
Allot Gdns
Cemy
Min Rly
Summer Theatre
The Willesden Com
Craven Pk
Craven Park Rd
Manor Park Rd
High Street Harlesden
Station Rd
Old Oak La
Victoria Rd
Scrubs La
A407
A404
A4000
A219
B4492
Harlesden Prim Sch
Convent of Jesus & Mary Lang Coll
John Keble CE Prim Sch
Cardinal Hinsley Mathematics & Computing Coll
Furness Prim Sch
Kenmont Prim Sch
Willesden Euroterminal
The New Bsns Ctr
Willesden Junction
Grand Union Canal (Paddington Branch)
Grand Union Canal Wlk
Old Oak Sidings
Gateway Ind Est
Cumberland Pk Ind Est
Rutland Studios
Apex Ind Est
Star Works
Hythe Road Ind Est
Old Oak Common Sidings
Superstore
Brashley Road Cvn Site
Pilot Ind Ctr
Westwood Bsns Ctr
Wormwood Scrubs Park
Liby
Capital City Acad
Donnington Prim Sch

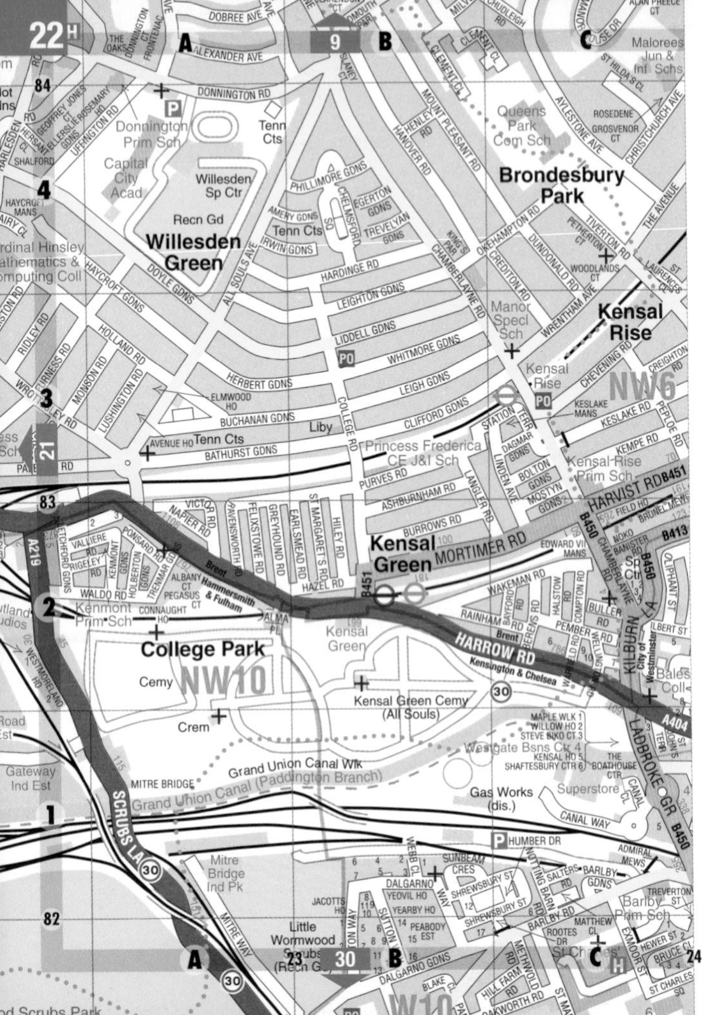

H
A
B
C
9
DOBREE AVE
CLARENDON CT
ALEXANDER AVE
THE OAKS
DONNINGTON CT
FRONTENAC
DONNINGTON RD
MILVERTON RD
CHUDLEIGH RD
CLEMENT CL
ALAN PREECE CT
MANOR HOUSE DR
Malorees Jun & Inf Schs
ST HILDA'S CL
84
GEOFFREY JONES CT
ELLERSLIE
ROSEMARY HO
UFFINGTON RD
HARLESDEN RD
HERSANT CL
SHALFORD
Donnington Prim Sch
Tenn Cts
Capital City Acad
Willesden Sp Ctr
Recn Gd
Willesden Green
MOUNT PLEASANT RD
HENLEY RD
HANOVER RD
Queens Park Com Sch
AYLESTONE AVE
ROSEDENE
GROSVENOR CT
CHRISTCHURCH AVE
Brondesbury Park
THE AVENUE
PHILLIMORE GDNS
CHELMSFORD SQ
EGERTON GDNS
AMERY GDNS
TREVELYAN GDNS
IRWIN GDNS
4
HAYCROFT MANS
AIRY CL
Cardinal Hinsley Mathematics & Computing Coll
HAYCROFT GDNS
DOYLE GDNS
ALL SOULS AVE
HARDINGE RD
LEIGHTON GDNS
KING'S PAR
CHAMBERLAYNE RD
OKEHAMPTON RD
CREDITON RD
DUNDONALD RD
PETHERTON CT
TIVERTON RD
WOODLANDS CT
ST LAURENCES CL
WRENTHAM AVE
Kensal Rise
Manor Specl Sch
LIDDELL GDNS
WHITMORE GDNS
PO
RIDLEY RD
FURNESS RD
HOLLAND RD
MONSON RD
LUSHINGTON RD
HERBERT GDNS
ELMWOOD HO
COLLEGE RD
LEIGH GDNS
CHEVENING RD
CREIGHTON RD
NW6
3
WROTTESLEY RD
BUCHANAN GDNS
Liby
CLIFFORD GDNS
STATION TERR
KESLAKE MANS
KESLAKE RD
PEPLOE RD
KEMPE RD
21
AVENUE HO
Tenn Cts
BATHURST GDNS
Princess Frederica CE J&I Sch
DAGMAR GDNS
LINDEN AVE
BOLTON GDNS
MOSTYN GDNS
Kensal Rise Prim Sch
HARVIST RD
B451
PURVES RD
ASHBURNHAM RD
LANGLER RD
FIELD HO
BRUNEL MEWS
83
VICTOR RD
NAPIER RD
PAVENSWORTH RD
FELIXSTOWE RD
GREYHOUND RD
EARLSMEAD RD
ST MARGARET'S RD
HILEY RD
BURROWS RD
B450
CHAMBERLAYNE RD
NOKO
BANISTER RD
B413
A219
VALLIERE RD
RIGELEY RD
ETCHFORD GDNS
KENMONT GDNS
HOLBERTON GDNS
PONSARD RD
TRENMAR GDNS
ALBANY CT
PEGASUS CT
Brent
Hammersmith & Fulham
HAZEL RD
Kensal Green
MORTIMER RD
EDWARD VII MANS
Sp Ctr
OLIPHANT ST
2
WALDO RD
Kenmont Prim Sch
CONNAUGHT HO
ALMA PL
WAKEMAN RD
RAINHAM RD
BAYFORD RD
BERENS RD
HALSTOW RD
COMPTON RD
BULLER RD
PEMBER RD
WELLINGTON RD
WARFIELD RD
KILBURN LA
City of Westminster
GILBERT ST
Bales Coll
Kensal Green
College Park
Cemy
NW10
HARROW RD
Brent
Kensington & Chelsea
WESTMORELAND HO
Crem
Kensal Green Cemy (All Souls)
30
A404
MAPLE WLK 1
WILLOW HO 2
STEVE BIKO CT 3
Westgate Bsns Ctr 4
KENSAL HO 5
SHAFTESBURY CTR 6
THE BOATHOUSE CTR
LADBROKE GR
ST JOHNS TERR
Gateway Ind Est
Grand Union Canal Wlk
Grand Union Canal (Paddington Branch)
MITRE BRIDGE
Gas Works (dis.)
Superstore
CANAL CL
CANAL WAY
B450
1
SCRUBS LA
HUMBER DR
ADMIRAL MEWS
NOTTING BARN RD
Mitre Bridge Ind Pk
WEBB CL
SUNBEAM CRES
DALGARNO WAY
YEOVIL HO
YEARBY HO
JACOTTS HO
SHREWSBURY ST
SALTERS RD
BARLBY GDNS
TREVERTON ST
Barlby Prim Sch
PEABODY EST
MATTHEW CL
BARLBY RD
ROOTES DR
EXMOOR ST
HEWER ST
MITRE WAY
82
Little Wormwood Scrubs (Recn Gd)
SUTTON WAY
METHWOLD RD
St Charles' H
BRUCE CL
24
23
30
DALGARNO GDNS
BLAKE CL
HILL FARM RD
OAKWORTH RD
ST CHARLES SQ
Wormwood Scrubs Park
W10

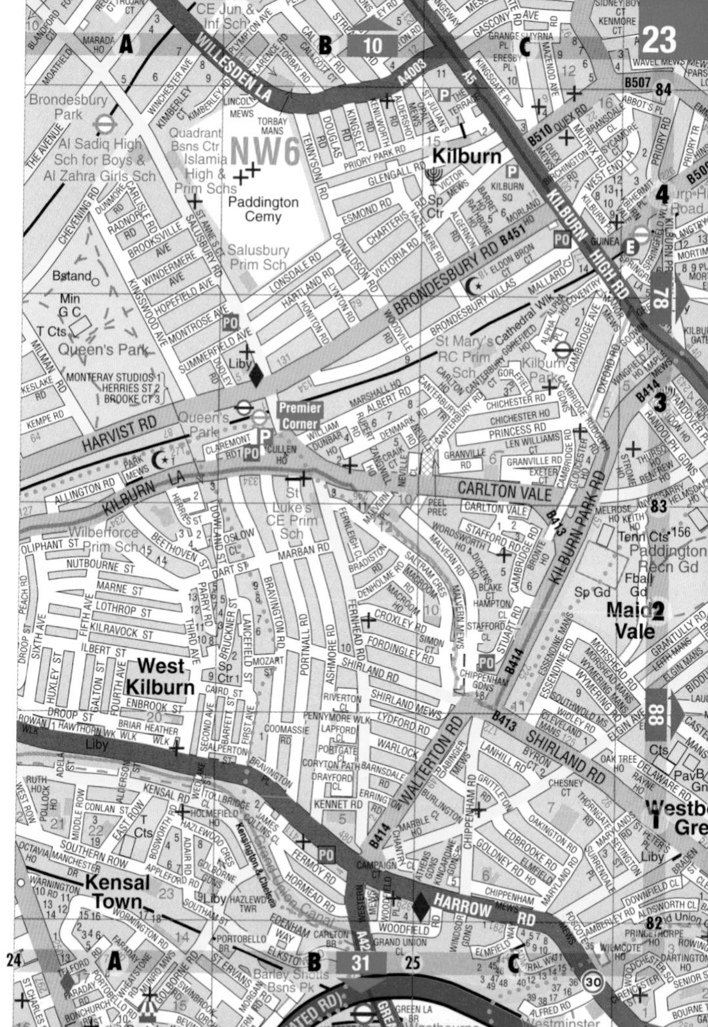

23
A
B
C
10
WILLESDEN LA
A4003
A5
B507
84
Brondesbury Park
Al Sadiq High Sch for Boys & Al Zahra Girls Sch
Quadrant Bsns Ctr
Islamia High & Prim Schs
NW6
Paddington Cemy
Salusbury Prim Sch
Kilburn
KILBURN HIGH RD
B510
QUEX RD
BRONDESBURY RD
B451
BRONDESBURY VILLAS
Queen's Park
Min G C
Bstand
T Cts
MONTERAY STUDIOS
HERRIES ST
BROOKE CT
HARVIST RD
Queen's Park
Premier Corner
Liby
KILBURN LA
St Luke's CE Prim Sch
St Mary's RC Prim Sch
Kilburn Park
CARLTON VALE
KILBURN PARK RD
B413
B414
78
4
3
83
2
Paddington Recn Gd
Tenn Cts
Fball Gd
Sp Gd
Maida Vale
Wilberforce Prim Sch
West Kilburn
SHIRLAND RD
WALTERTON RD
88
Westbourne Green
1
82
HARROW RD
Kensal Town
Grand Union Canal
Kensington & Chelsea
Barley Shotts Bsns Pk
24
31
25
30
A
B
C
Westminster

16
98
99
87
97
110
111
83
84
82
A
B
C
1
2
3
4
Haggerston
Hoxton
Britannia L Ctr
Haggerston Park
Fball Gd
Columbia Rd
Spitalfields
Broadgate
Old Spitalfields
Shoreditch High St
Brick Lane
Geffrye Mus
Art Gal
Govt Offices
TA Ctr
Bwg Gn
Allen Gdns
Osmani Prim Sch
Grand Union Canal
(Regent's Canal)
Kingsland Basin
St Leonard's
BETH
E8
E2
E1
EC2
KINGSLAND RD
SHOREDITCH HIGH ST
QUEENSBRIDGE RD
HACKNEY RD
COLUMBIA RD
GOSSET ST
BETHNAL GREEN RD
CHESHIRE ST
BRICK LA
GREAT EASTERN ST
CITY RD
EAST RD
PITFIELD ST
CURTAIN RD
COMMERCIAL
WARNER PL
VALLANCE RD
MIDDLETON RD
ALBION DR
SHRUBLAND RD
DOWNHAM RD
DE BEAUVOIR CRES
WHISTON RD
DUNSTON RD
LABURNUM ST
REGENT'S ROW
DOVE ROW
HOXTON ST
NUTTALL ST
WILMER GDNS
FALKIRK ST
CRONDALL ST
HABERDASHER ST
OLD ST
Haggerston
Hoxton
A10
A1208
A1202
A5201
A1209
B108
B101
B118
B134
B135
B122
B100

25
17
32
A
B
C
4
3
2
1
HACKNEY
South Hackney
Globe Town
Mile End
INAL GREEN
STEPNEY
E8
E9
E3
E2
E1
Victoria Park
Victoria Fntn
Royal Gate East
Royal Gate West
Crown Gate East
Crown Gate West
Gore Gate
Regent's Canal
Lauriston Prim Sch 6
London Chest
Morpeth Sec Sch
Meath Gardens
Allot Gdns
Mile End Park
Univ of London
Weavers Fields
Bethnal Green
Broadway Mkt
Cambridge Heath
Works
Super store
Mus
Liby
Cts
Anchor Ret Pk
Stepney Green
Swanlea Sch
Superstore
Crossrail Sta u/c
Pl Flds
Bnstand
Twig Folly Bridge
Grove Road Bridge
Skew Bridge
A106 WELL ST
VICTORIA PARK RD
LAURISTON RD
A1205
A107
CAMBRIDGE HEATH RD
A1208
B127 BISHOP'S WAY
SEWARDSTONE RD
OLD FORD RD
B118
BETHNAL GREEN RD
ROMAN RD
B119
GROVE RD
A1209
GLOBE RD
B120
B135
THREE COLTS LA
MILE END RD
A11
B121
STEPNEY GN
CHAPEL RD
MORPETH RD
GORE RD
MEATH CRES
HAVERFIELD RD
WESTFIELD WAY

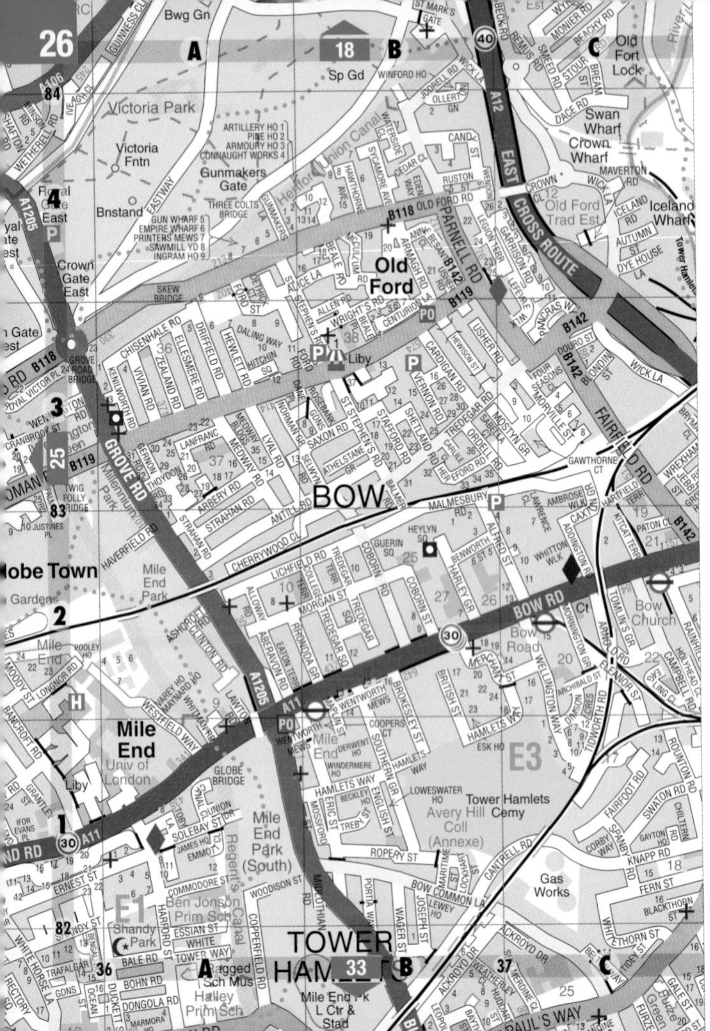

18
33
25
A
B
C
1
2
3
4
Bwg Gn
ST MARK'S GATE
GUINNESS CL
Sp Gd
WINFORD HO
Victoria Park
Victoria Fntn
Gunmakers Gate
Bnstand
EASTWAY
Royal Gate East
Crown Gate East
ARTILLERY HO 1
PINE HO 2
ARMOURY HO 3
CONNAUGHT WORKS 4
GUN WHARF 5
EMPIRE WHARF 6
PRINTERS MEWS 7
SAWMILL YD 8
INGRAM HO 9
THREE COLTS BRIDGE
SKEW BRIDGE
Hertford Union Canal
GUNMAKERS LA
WETHERELL RD
SHAFTON RD
IVE AGH CL
A106
A1205
A12
EAST CROSS ROUTE
OLD FORD RD
B118
B119
B142
PARNELL RD
Old Ford
Old Ford Trad Est
Old Fort Lock
Swan Wharf
Crown Wharf
Iceland Wharf
MAVERTON RD
WICK LA
ICELAND RD
AUTUMN ST
DYE HOUSE LA
DACE RD
STOUR RD
BREAM ST
SMEED RD
MONIER RD
BEACHY RD
REMUS RD
CROWN CL
CAND ST
RUSTON ST
WENDON ST
LEGION TERR
GARRISON RD
CEDAR CL
SYCAMORE AVE
HAWTHORNE AVE
WATERSIDE CL
JODRELL RD
OLLERTON GN
ANNIE BESANT CL
ARMAGH RD
USHER RD
McCULLUM RD
BEALE RD
ALICE LA
ALLEN RD
WRIGHT'S RD
CENTURION LA
ST STEPHEN'S RD
DALING WAY
HITCHIN SQ
FORD RD
CHISENHALE RD
VIVIAN RD
ZEALAND RD
ELLESMERE RD
DRIFFIELD RD
HEWLETT RD
KENILWORTH RD
GROVE RD
GROVE ROAD BRIDGE
Liby
PO
CARDIGAN RD
VERNON RD
HEWISON ST
PANCRAS WAY
DOURO ST
BLONDIN ST
FOUR SEASONS CL
MORVILLE ST
MOSTYN GR
TREDEGAR RD
SABELLA
ORDELL RD
FAIRFIELD RD
WICK LA
GAWTHORNE CT
HARTFIELD TERR
KITCAT TERR
PATON CL
WREXHAM RD
JEBB ST
BOW
MALMESBURY RD
LAWRENCE CL
AMBROSE WLK
CAXTON GR
ADDINGTON RD
WHITTON WLK
ALFRED ST
BENWORTH ST
HARLEY GR
HEYLYN SQ
GUERIN SQ
COBORN RD
COBORN ST
LICHFIELD RD
TREDEGAR TERR
COLLEGE TERR
MORGAN ST
TREDEGAR SQ
ALLOWAY RD
ABERAVON RD
EATON TERR
RHONDDA GR
BOW RD
Bow Road
Bow Church
MERCHANT ST
BRITISH ST
WELLINGTON WAY
MORNINGTON GR
TOMLIN'S GR
ARNOLD RD
ELEANOR ST
CAMPBELL RD
ARCHIBALD ST
TIDWORTH RD
HAMLETS WAY
ESK HO
E3
A11
WENTWORTH MEWS
Mile End
DERWENT HO
WINDERMERE HO
SOUTHERN GR
COOPERS CT
BROKESLEY ST
LOWESWATER HO
ENGLISH ST
BECKLEY HO
ERIC ST
MOSSFORD ST
TREBY ST
Tower Hamlets Cemy
Avery Hill Coll (Annexe)
ROPERY ST
MARITIME ST
LOCKHART ST
CANTRELL RD
BOW COMMON LA
LEWEY HO
JOSEPH ST
Gas Works
FAIRFOOT RD
SWATON RD
ROUNTON RD
CHILTERN RD
GAYTON HO
CORBY WAY
SPANBY RD
KNAPP RD
FERN ST
BLACKTHORN ST
WHITETHORN ST
TIDEY ST
ACKROYD DR
ST PAUL'S WAY
GALE ST
Furze Green
FURZE ST
TOWER HAMLETS
Mile End Pk L Ctr & Stad
WAGER ST
PORTIA WAY
MIDLOTHIAN RD
COPPERFIELD RD
WOODISON ST
Regent's Canal
Mile End Park (South)
Mile End Park
Millennium Park
Globe Town
Gardens
HAVERFIELD RD
CHERRYWOOD CL
STRAHAN RD
ARBERY RD
LANFRANC RD
THOYDON RD
GERNON RD
MEDWAY RD
LYAL RD
SELWYN RD
ATHELSTANE GR
SAXON RD
STAFFORD RD
SHETLAND RD
BALMER RD
ANTILL RD
TWIG FOLLY BRIDGE
JUSTINES PL
ASHCROFT RD
CLINTON RD
LONGNOR RD
MOODY ST
BANCROFT RD
ROOLEY HO
MAYNARD HO
HARVEY HO
WHITMAN RD
WESTFIELD WAY
LAWTON RD
Mile End
Univ of London
GLOBE BRIDGE
UNION CL
CANAL CL
TOBY LA
SOLEBAY ST
JAMES HO
EMMOTT CL
COMMODORE ST
Ben Jonson Prim Sch
ESSIAN ST
WHITE TOWER WAY
HARFORD ST
E1
Shandy Park
BALE RD
BOHN RD
DONGOLA RD
Ragged Sch Mus
Halley Prim Sch
ERNEST ST
SHANDY ST
BENGAL CT
TRAFALGAR GDNS
WHITE HORSE LA
OCEAN ST
DUCKETT ST
IFOR EVANS PL
GRANTLEY ST
Liby
H
ROYAL VICTOR PL
CRANBROOK ST
82
83
84
36
37
30
40

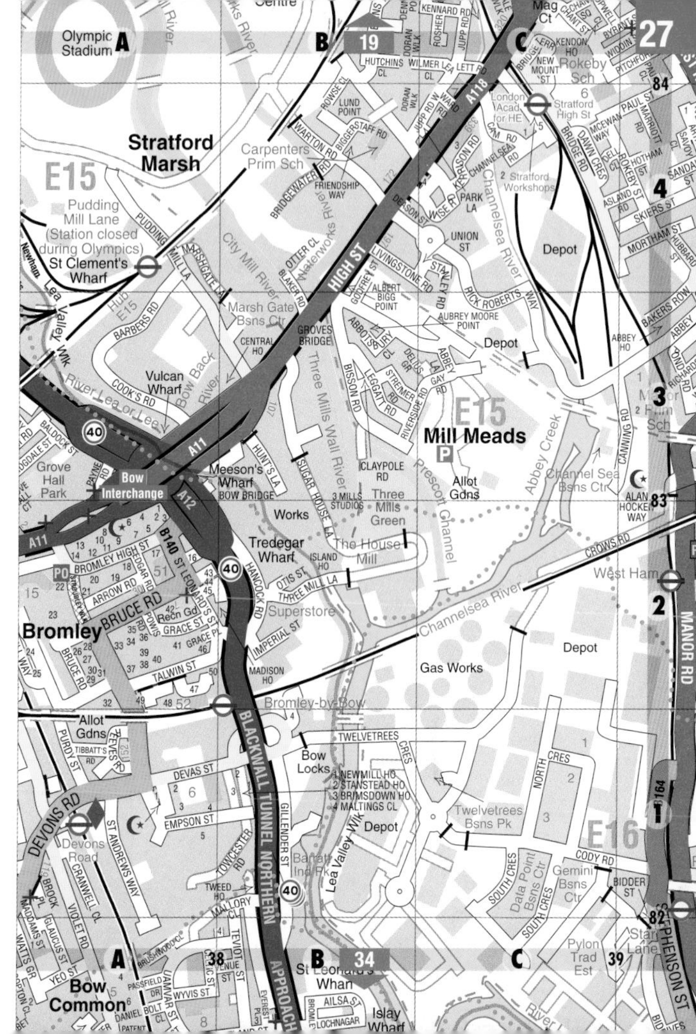

Olympic Stadium
A
B
19
C
Stratford Marsh
E15
Pudding Mill Lane
(Station closed during Olympics)
St Clement's Wharf
Carpenters Prim Sch
Rokeby Sch
London Acad for HE
Stratford High St
Stratford Workshops
Depot
HIGH ST
A118
City Mill River
Waterworks River
Marsh Gate Bsns Ctr
GROVES BRIDGE
CENTRAL HO
Three Mills Wall River
Channelsea River
Lea Valley Wlk
Hub E15
Vulcan Wharf
Bow Back River
River Lea or Lee
Grove Hall Park
Bow Interchange
A11
A12
B140
Meeson's Wharf
BOW BRIDGE
Works
Tredegar Wharf
3 MILLS STUDIOS
Three Mills Green
The House Mill
Mill Meads
Allot Gdns
Prescott Channel
Abbey Creek
Channel Sea Bsns Ctr
CROWS RD
West Ham
MANOR RD
Bromley
BROMLEY HIGH ST
BRUCE RD
Recn Gd
Superstore
Gas Works
Depot
Bromley-by-Bow
BLACKWALL TUNNEL NORTHERN APPROACH
TWELVETREES CRES
Bow Locks
1 NEWMILL HO
2 STANSTEAD HO
3 BRIMSDOWN HO
4 MALTINGS CL
Depot
Twelvetrees Bsns Pk
E16
Data Point Bsns Ctr
Gemini Bsns Ctr
CODY RD
Barratt Ind Pk
Devons Road
DEVONS RD
ST ANDREWS WAY
DEVAS ST
EMPSON ST
Pylon Trad Est
Star Lane
STEPHENSON ST
Bow Common
St Leonard's Wharf
Islay Wharf
34
38
39
82
83
84

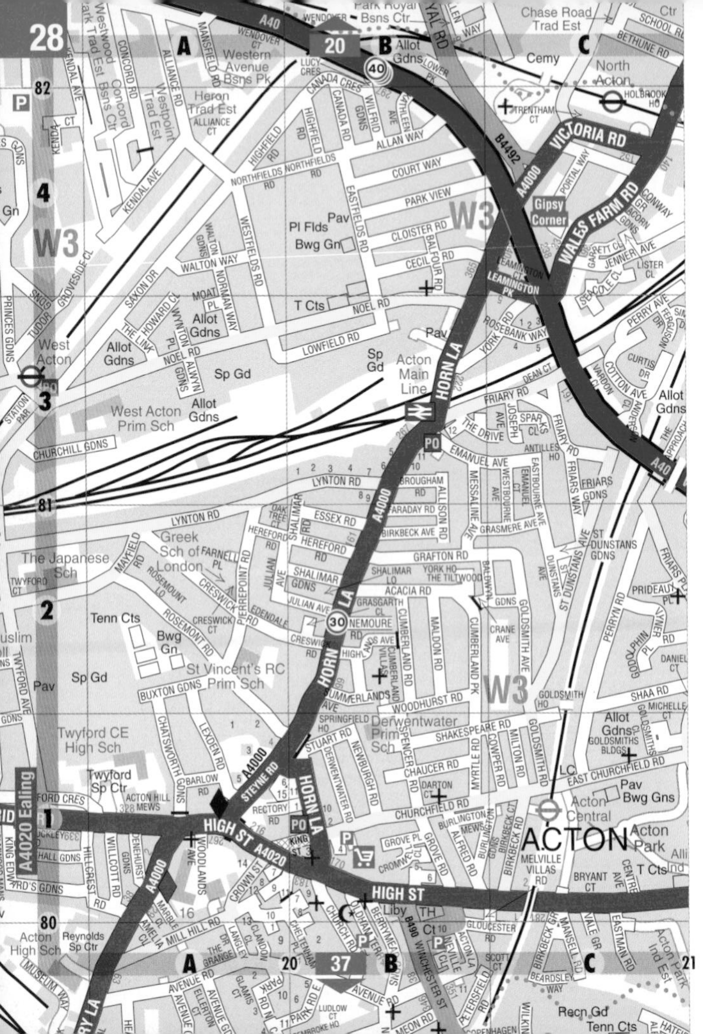
A40
20
40
B4492
A4000
VICTORIA RD
WALES FARM RD
Gipsy Corner
North Acton
W3
HORN LA
A4000
A4020 Ealing
HIGH ST A4020
HIGH ST
STEYNE RD
B490 WINCHESTER ST
West Acton
Acton Main Line
Acton Central
ACTON
Acton Park
The Japanese Sch
Greek Sch of London
St Vincent's RC Prim Sch
Twyford CE High Sch
West Acton Prim Sch
Derwentwater Prim Sch
Acton High Sch
Reynolds Sp Ctr
Twyford Sp Ctr
Western Avenue Bsns Pk
Heron Trad Est
Westpoint Trad Est
Chase Road Trad Est
Acton Park Ind Est
LYNTON RD
CHURCHILL GDNS
NOEL RD
LOWFIELD RD
NORTHFIELDS RD
EAST CHURCHFIELD RD
CHURCHFIELD RD
MELVILLE VILLAS RD
37
21
A
B
C
1
2
3
4
80
81
82

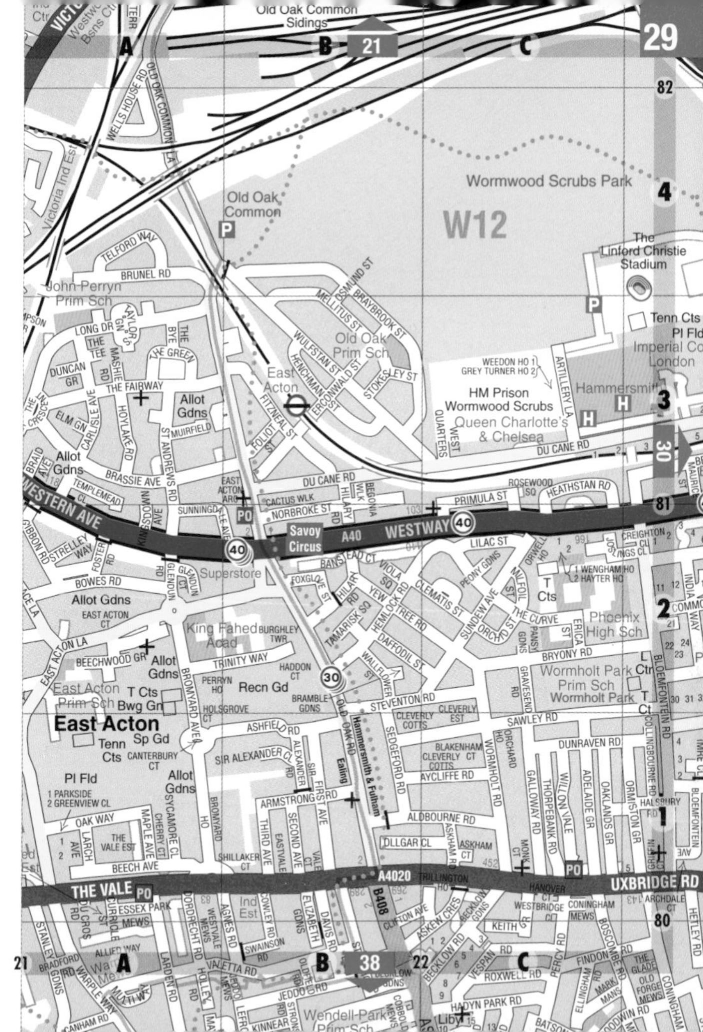

29
A
B
21
C
82
4
3
2
1
81
80
30
38
22
21
Old Oak Common Sidings
Westway Bsns Ctr
Victoria Ind Est
WELLS HOUSE RD
OLD OAK COMMON LA
Wormwood Scrubs Park
Old Oak Common
W12
The Linford Christie Stadium
Tenn Cts
Pl Fld
Imperial Coll London
Hammersmith
Queen Charlotte's & Chelsea
HM Prison Wormwood Scrubs
WEEDON HO
GREY TURNER HO
ARTILLERY LA
WEST QUARTERS
DU CANE RD
TELFORD WAY
BRUNEL RD
John Perryn Prim Sch
LONG DR
TAYLOR GN
THE TEE
MASHIE RD
THE BYE
THE GREEN
DUNCAN GR
THE FAIRWAY
Allot Gdns
ELM GN
CARLISLE AVE
HOYLAKE RD
ST ANDREWS RD
MUIRFIELD
BRASSIE AVE
TEMPLEMEAD CL
BRAID AVE
OSMUND ST
BRAYBROOK ST
MELLITUS ST
Old Oak Prim Sch
WULFSTAN ST
HENCHMAN ST
ERCONWALD ST
STOKESLEY ST
East Acton
FITZNEAL ST
FOLIOT ST
DU CANE RD
EAST ACTON ARC
CACTUS WLK
NORBROKE ST
HILARY RD
BEGONIA WLK
PRIMULA ST
ROSEWOOD SQ
HEATHSTAN RD
WESTERN AVE
SUNNINGDALE AVE
KINGSDOWN AVE
Savoy Circus
A40
WESTWAY
40
LILAC ST
CREIGHTON CL
JOSLINGS CL
1 WENGHAM HO
2 HAYTER HO
INDIA WAY
COMMONWEALTH
GIBBON RD
STRELLEY WAY
FOSTER RD
GLENDUN RD
GLENDUN CT
Superstore
BANSTEAD CT
FOXGLOVE ST
VIOLA SQ
CLEMATIS ST
PEONY GDNS
MILFOIL ST
ORWELL HO
BOWES RD
Allot Gdns
EAST ACTON CT
King Fahed Acad
BURGHLEY TWR
YEW TREE RD
HEMLOCK RD
TAMARISK SQ
DAFFODIL ST
SUNDEW AVE
ORCHID ST
THE CURVE
ERICA ST
PANSY GDNS
Phoenix High Sch
BRYONY RD
EAST ACTON LA
BEECHWOOD GR
TRINITY WAY
HADDON CT
WALLFLOWER ST
BLOEMFONTEIN RD
Wormholt Park Prim Sch
Wormholt Park
GRAVESEND RD
East Acton Prim Sch
T Cts
Bwg Gn
BROMYARD AVE
PERRYN HO
Recn Gd
BRAMBLE GDNS
30
STEVENTON RD
CLEVERLY COTTS
CLEVERLY EST
SAWLEY RD
HOLSGROVE CT
East Acton
ASHFIELD RD
Tenn Cts
Sp Gd
CANTERBURY CT
SIR ALEXANDER CL
ALEXANDER RD
Ealing
Hammersmith & Fulham
OLD OAK RD
SEDGEFORD RD
BLAKENHAM CT
CLEVERLY CT
CLEVERLY COTTS
AYCLIFFE RD
WORMHOLT RD
ORCHARD HO
DUNRAVEN RD
GALLOWAY RD
THORPEBANK RD
WILLOW VALE
ADELAIDE GR
OAKLANDS GR
ORMISTON GR
COLLINGBOURNE RD
IMRE CL
BLOEMFONTEIN AVE
HALSBURY RD
Pl Fld
1 PARKSIDE
2 GREENVIEW CL
OAK WAY
THE VALE EST
LARCH AVE
MAPLE AVE
CHERRY CT
SYCAMORE CL
BROMYARD HO
ARMSTRONG RD
SIR FIRST AVE
THIRD AVE
SECOND AVE
EASTVALE
VALE CT
ALDBOURNE RD
DILLGAR CL
ASKHAM RD
ASKHAM CT
MONK CT
PO
BEECH AVE
SHILLAKER CT
A4020
TRILLINGTON HO
HANOVER
UXBRIDGE RD
ARCHDALE CT
THE VALE
ESSEX PARK MEWS
DU CROS RD
CURRICLE ST
DORDRECHT RD
WESTVALE MEWS
AGNES RD
Ind Est
COWLEY RD
ELIZABETH GDNS
DAVIS RD
B408
CLIFTON AVE
ASKEW CRES
BECKLOW GDNS
KEITH GR
WESTBRIDGE CL
CONINGHAM MEWS
HETLEY RD
STANLEY GDNS
ALLIED WAY
Warple Mews
BRADFORD RD
WARPLE WAY
LARDEN RD
VALETTA RD
SWAINSON RD
HOLLEY RD
BECKLOW RD
VESPAN RD
ROXWELL RD
PERCY RD
FINDON RD
BOSCOMBE RD
ELLINGHAM RD
MARKHAM MANS
THE GLADE
OLD FORGE MEWS
CONINGHAM RD
JEDDO RD
OLDFIELD RD
STRONSA RD
Wendell Park Prim Sch
HADYN PARK RD
Liby
GOODWIN RD
BATSON ST
CANHAM RD
KINNEAR RD
LEFROY RD
COBBOLD MEWS

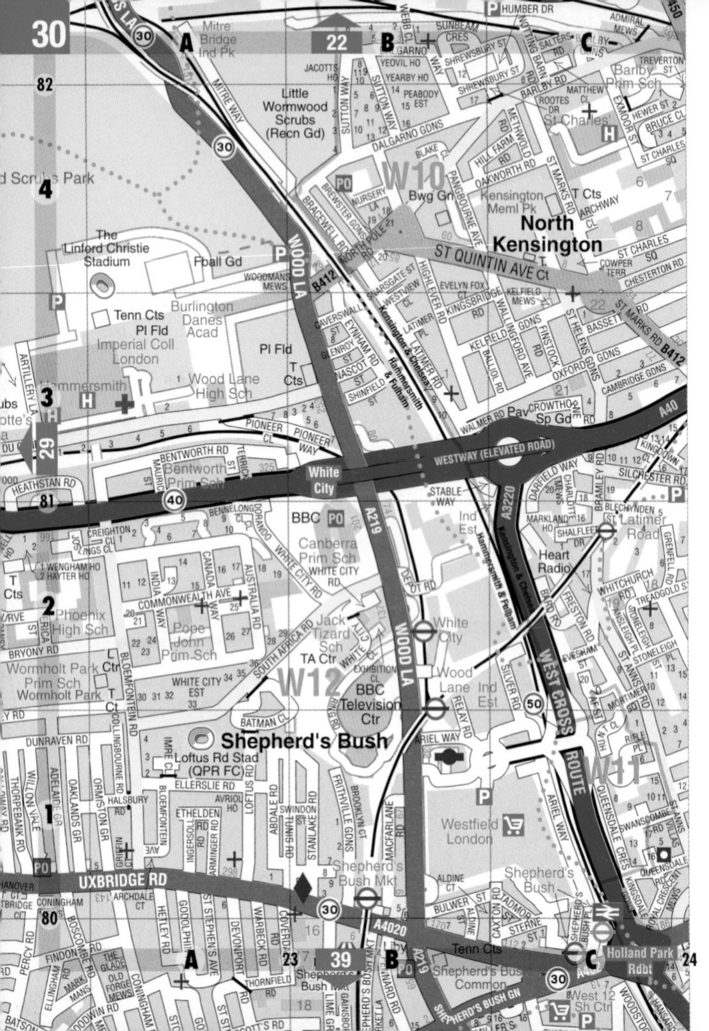

Mitre Bridge Ind Pk
22
Little Wormwood Scrubs (Recn Gd)
Wormwood Scrubs Park
The Linford Christie Stadium
Fball Gd
Tenn Cts
Pl Fld
Burlington Danes Acad
Imperial Coll London
Hammersmith
Wood Lane High Sch
WOOD LA
W10
North Kensington
ST QUINTIN AVE
Kensington Meml Pk
St Charles'
Barlby Prim Sch
WESTWAY (ELEVATED ROAD)
White City
Bentworth Prim Sch
BBC
Canberra Prim Sch
Phoenix High Sch
Pope John Prim Sch
Wormholt Park Prim Sch
Wormholt Park
W12
BBC Television Ctr
Shepherd's Bush
Loftus Rd Stad (QPR FC)
Latimer Road
Heart Radio
Wood Lane Ind Est
WEST CROSS ROUTE
W11
Westfield London
Shepherd's Bush
Shepherd's Bush Mkt
UXBRIDGE RD
Shepherd's Bush Common
Holland Park Rdbt
West 12 Sh Ctr
29
39
24

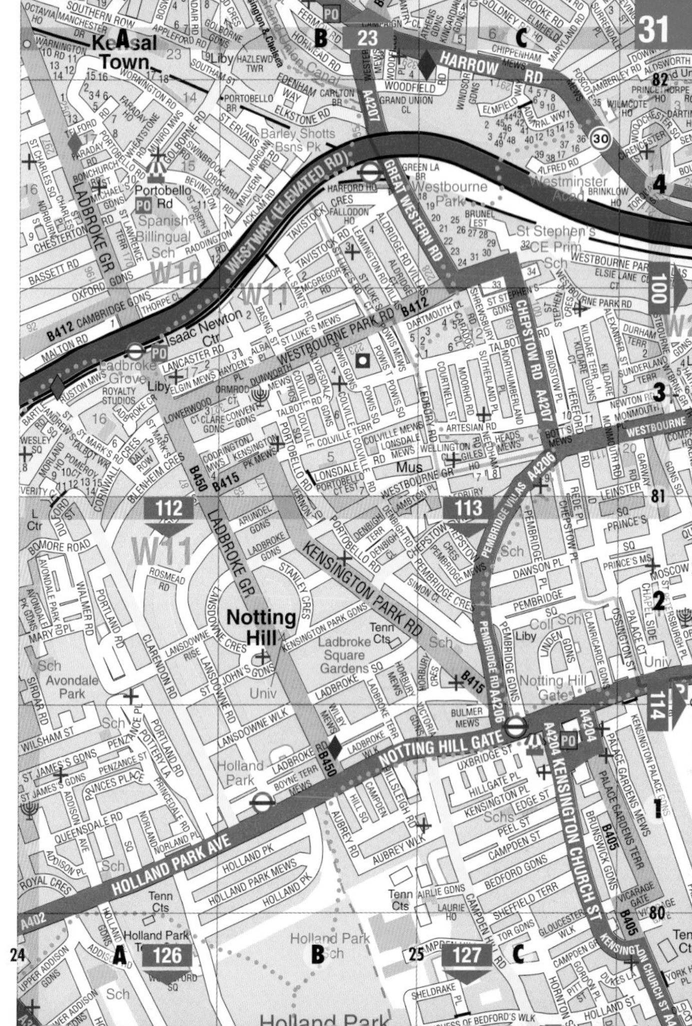

Kensal Town
Portobello Rd
Spanish Bilingual Sch
W10
W11
W2
WESTWAY (ELEVATED RD)
HARROW RD
GREAT WESTERN RD
Westbourne Park
Westminster Acad
St Stephen's CE Prim Sch
Barley Shotts Bsns Pk
Grand Union Canal
LADBROKE GR
Ladbroke Grove
Isaac Newton Ctr
WESTBOURNE PARK RD
CHEPSTOW RD
PEMBRIDGE VILLAS
LEDBURY RD
PORTOBELLO RD
KENSINGTON PARK RD
WESTBOURNE GR
Mus
Notting Hill
Ladbroke Square Gardens
Notting Hill Gate
NOTTING HILL GATE
HOLLAND PARK AVE
KENSINGTON CHURCH ST
Avondale Park
Holland Park
CAMPDEN HILL RD
PALACE GARDENS TERR
KENSINGTON PALACE GDNS
Tenn Cts
Univ
Coll Sch
112
113
114
100
23
126
127
A
B
C
1
2
3
4
24
25
80
81
82

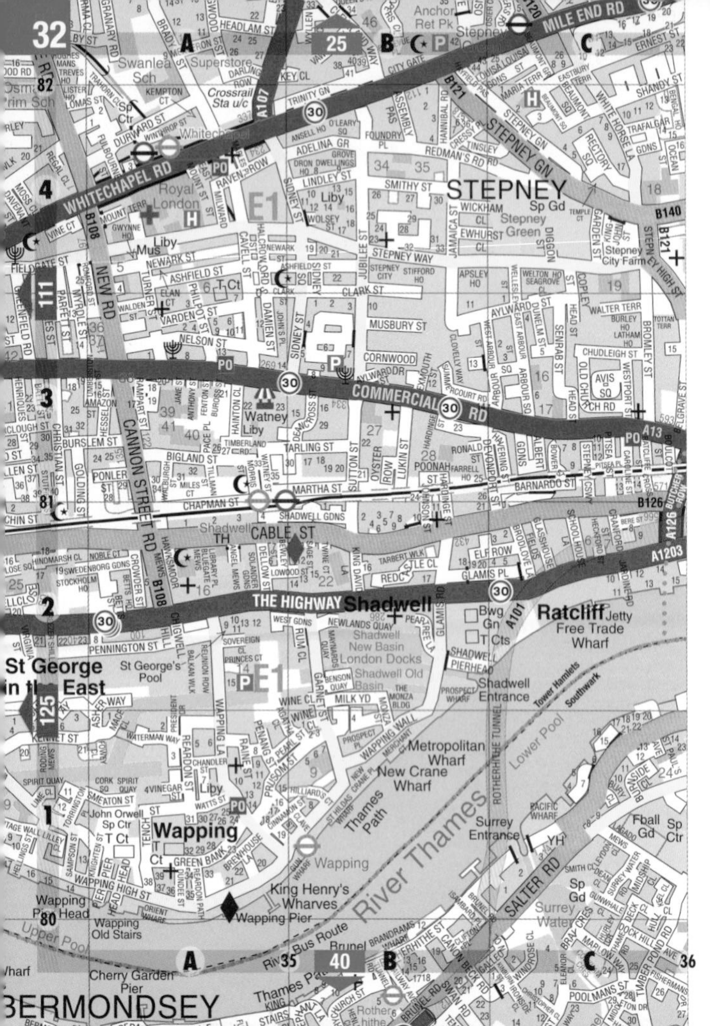

25
MILE END RD
WHITECHAPEL RD
Whitechapel
Royal London
Swanlea Sch
Superstore
Crossrail Sta u/c
A107
STEPNEY
Stepney Green
Sp Gd
STEPNEY GN
Stepney City Farm
STEPNEY HIGH ST
STEPNEY WAY
B140
B121
B108
E1
Watney Liby
COMMERCIAL RD
A13
111
NEW RD
CANNON STREET RD
CABLE ST
Shadwell
THE HIGHWAY
A1203
A126
B126
A101
Ratcliff
Free Trade Wharf
St George in the East
St George's Pool
125
Shadwell New Basin London Docks
Shadwell Old Basin
Shadwell Entrance
ROTHERHITHE TUNNEL
Metropolitan Wharf
New Crane Wharf
Thames Path
Wapping
King Henry's Wharves
Wapping Pier
Wapping Pier Head
Wapping Old Stairs
River Thames
Lower Pool
Upper Pool
Tower Hamlets
Southwark
Surrey Entrance
Surrey Water
SALTER RD
Fball Gd
Sp Ctr
Cherry Garden Pier
River Bus Route
40
BERMONDSEY
36
80
81
82

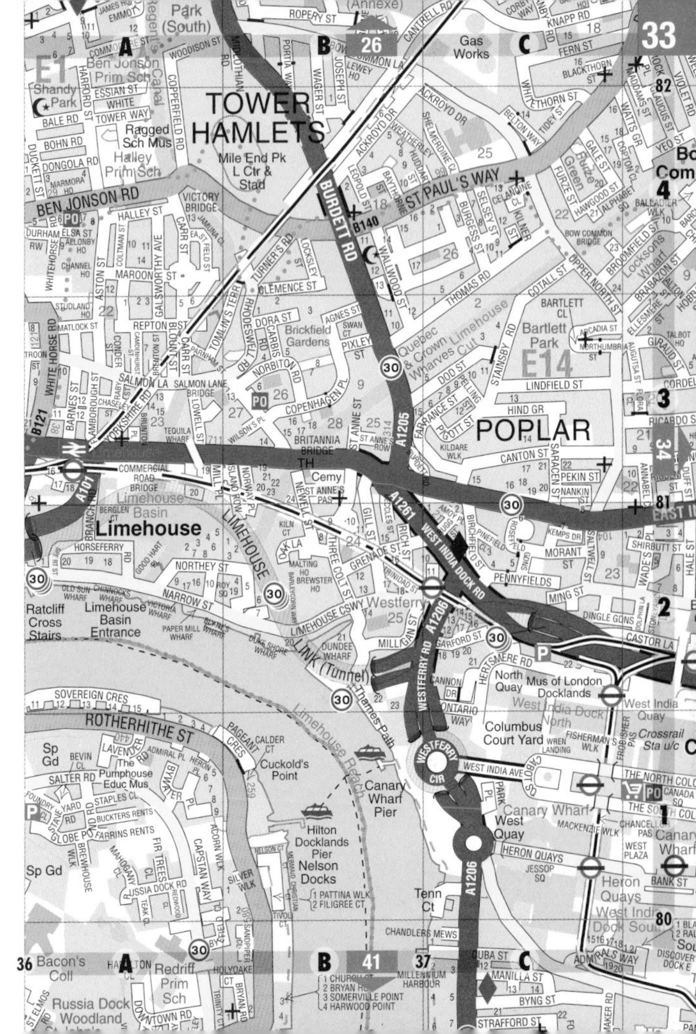

26
A
B
C
Park (South)
(Annexe)
ROPERY ST
CANTRELL RD
KNAPP RD
FERN ST
Gas Works
E1
Ben Jonson Prim Sch
Shandy Park
HARFORD ST
ESSIAN ST
WHITE
TOWER WAY
BALE RD
BOHN RD
DONGOLA RD
DUCKETT ST
MARMORA HO
Ragged Sch Mus
Halley Prim Sch
COPPERFIELD RD
WOODISON ST
TOWER HAMLETS
Mile End Pk L Ctr & Stad
MIDLOTHIAN RD
PORTIA WAY
WAGER ST
JOSEPH ST
LEWEY HO
ACKROYD DR
WEATHERLEY CL
SHELMERDINE CL
HUDDART ST
LEOPOLD ST
BAYTHORNE ST
WHITETHORN ST
BLACKTHORN ST
BELTON WAY
TIDEY ST
ST PAUL'S WAY
CELANDINE CL
SELSEY ST
BURGESS ST
KILNER ST
FURZE ST
Furze Green
GALE ST
HAWGOOD ST
ALPHABET SQ
NADDAMS ST
WATTS GR
COPTON CL
YEO ST
VIOLET RD
Bow Comm
BALLADIER WLK
BOW COMMON BRIDGE
BROOMFIELD ST
Locksons Wharf
BRABAZON ST
BEN JONSON RD
VICTORY BRIDGE
HALLEY ST
DURHAM RW
ELSA ST
WHITEHORSE RD
CHANNEL HO
COLTMAN ST
GALSWORTHY AVE
CARR ST
MAROON ST
ASTON ST
BURDETT RD
B140
WALLWOOD ST
THOMAS RD
COTALL ST
UPPER NORTH ST
TURNER'S RD
LOCKSLEY ST
CLEMENCE ST
STUDLAND HO
MATLOCK ST
REPTON ST
BLOUNT ST
TOMLIN'S TERR
RHODESWELL RD
DORA ST
CARBIS RD
AGNES ST
SWAN CT
PIXLEY ST
Brickfield Gardens
Quebec & Crown Wharves
Limehouse Cut
STAINSBY RD
BARTLETT CL
Bartlett Park
ARCADIA ST
NORTHUMBRIA ST
E14
ELLESMERE ST
GIRAUD ST
TALBOT HO
AUGUSTA ST
WHITE HORSE RD
CONDER ST
SALMON LA
SALMON LANE BRIDGE
LOWELL ST
NORBITON RD
COPENHAGEN PL
DOD ST
LINDFIELD ST
HIND GR
CORDELIA
BARNES ST
FLAMBOROUGH ST
CHASELEY ST
YORKSHIRE RD
TEQUILA WHARF
WILSON'S PL
BRITANNIA BRIDGE
ST ANNE ST
ST ANNE'S ROW
A1205
FARRANCE ST
PIGOTT ST
KILDARE WLK
POPLAR
CANTON ST
SARACEN ST
RICARDO ST
B121
Limehouse
A101
COMMERCIAL ROAD BRIDGE
MILL PL
ISLAND ROW
NORWAY PL
TH Cemy
NEWELL ST
ST ANNE'S PAS
PEKIN ST
NANKIN ST
ANNABEL CL
DUFF ST
34
EAST INDIA
Limehouse Basin
BERGLEN CT
BRANCH RD
HORSEFERRY RD
NORTHEY ST
KILN CT
OAK LA
GILL ST
RICH ST
A1261
WEST INDIA DOCK RD
BIRCHFIELD ST
PINEFIELD CL
KEMPS DR
MORANT ST
SALTWELL ST
SHIRBUTT ST
WADE'S PL
HALE ST
GRENADE ST
MALTING HO
BREWSTER HO
THREE COLT ST
TRINIDAD ST
PENNYFIELDS
MING ST
NARROW ST
Ratcliff Cross Stairs
Limehouse Basin Entrance
VICTORIA WHARF
PAPER MILL WHARF
DUKE SHORE WHARF
LIMEHOUSE CSWY
Westferry
A1206
DINGLE GDNS
CASTOR LA
DUNDEE WHARF
LINK (Tunnel)
MILLIGAN ST
GARFORD ST
HERTSMERE RD
North Quay
Mus of London Docklands
West India Quay
SOVEREIGN CRES
ROTHERHITHE ST
PAGEANT CRES
CALDER CT
Thames Path
Limehouse Reach
WESTFERRY RD
CANNON DR
ONTARIO WAY
West India Dock North
Columbus Court Yard
WREN LANDING
FISHERMAN'S WLK
FROBISHER PAS
Crossrail Sta u/c
Sp Gd
BEVIN CL
LAVENDER RD
ADMIRAL PL
HERON PL
The Pumphouse Educ Mus
Cuckold's Point
SALTER RD
BYWATER PL
STAPLES CL
FOUNDRY CL
STAVE YARD RD
BUCKTERS RENTS
GLOBE POND RD
FARRINS RENTS
Canary Wharf Pier
WESTFERRY CIR
WEST INDIA AVE
CABOT SQ
PARK PL
THE NORTH COLONNADE
CANADA SQ
THE SOUTH COLONNADE
Canary Wharf
West Quay
MACKENZIE WLK
CHANCELLOR PAS
BREWHOUSE WLK
MAHOGANY CL
FIR TREES CL
CAPSTAN WAY
ACORN WLK
RUSSIA DOCK RD
Hilton Docklands Pier
Nelson Docks
SILVER WLK
1 PATTINA WLK
2 FILIGREE CT
HERON QUAYS
JESSOP SQ
WEST PLAZA
BANK ST
Heron Quays
West India Dock South
Sp Gd
Tenn Ct
CHANDLERS MEWS
80
1 BLAKE
2 RALE
DISCOVERY DOCK E
36
Bacon's Coll
Redriff Prim Sch
HOLYOAKE CT
41
37
CUBA ST
ADMIRALS WAY
1 CHURCH
2 BRYAN
3 SOMERVILLE POINT
4 HARWOOD POINT
MILLENNIUM HARBOUR
MANILLA ST
BYNG ST
Russia Dock Woodland
DOWNTOWN RD
BRYAN RD
STRAFFORD ST

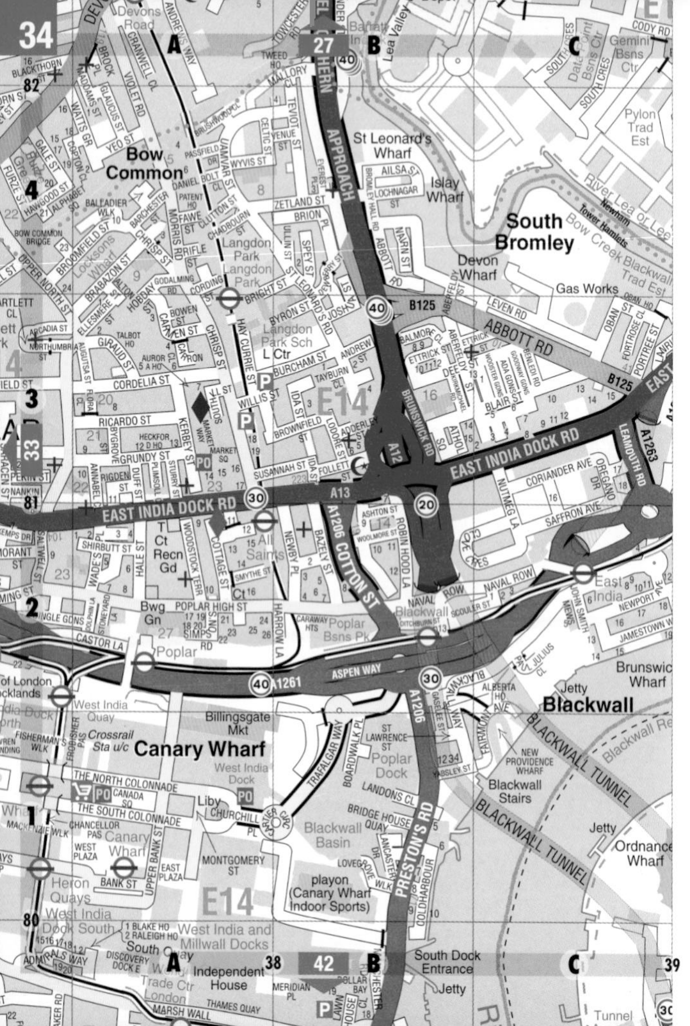

Bow Common
South Bromley
Blackwall
Canary Wharf
Poplar
St Leonard's Wharf
Islay Wharf
Devon Wharf
Gas Works
Bow Creek Blackwall Trad Est
River Lea or Lee
Newham
Tower Hamlets
Pylon Trad Est
Gemini Bsns Ctr
Langdon Park
Langdon Park Sch
L Ctr
E14
EAST INDIA DOCK RD
ABBOTT RD
B125
A12
A13
A1206
A1261
A1263
COTTON ST
ASPEN WAY
APPROACH
BRUNSWICK RD
LEAMOUTH RD
PRESTON'S RD
BLACKWALL TUNNEL
All Saints
East India
Poplar Bsns Pk
Billingsgate Mkt
West India Quay
Crossrail Sta u/c
West India Dock
Blackwall Basin
Poplar Dock
Brunswick Wharf
New Providence Wharf
Blackwall Stairs
Ordnance Wharf
Jetty
playon (Canary Wharf Indoor Sports)
Heron Quays
West India Dock South
West India and Millwall Docks
South Quay
Independent House
South Dock Entrance
THE NORTH COLONNADE
THE SOUTH COLONNADE
CHURCHILL PL
MARSH WALL
ADMIRALS WAY
Recn Gd
Bwg Gn
27
42
33

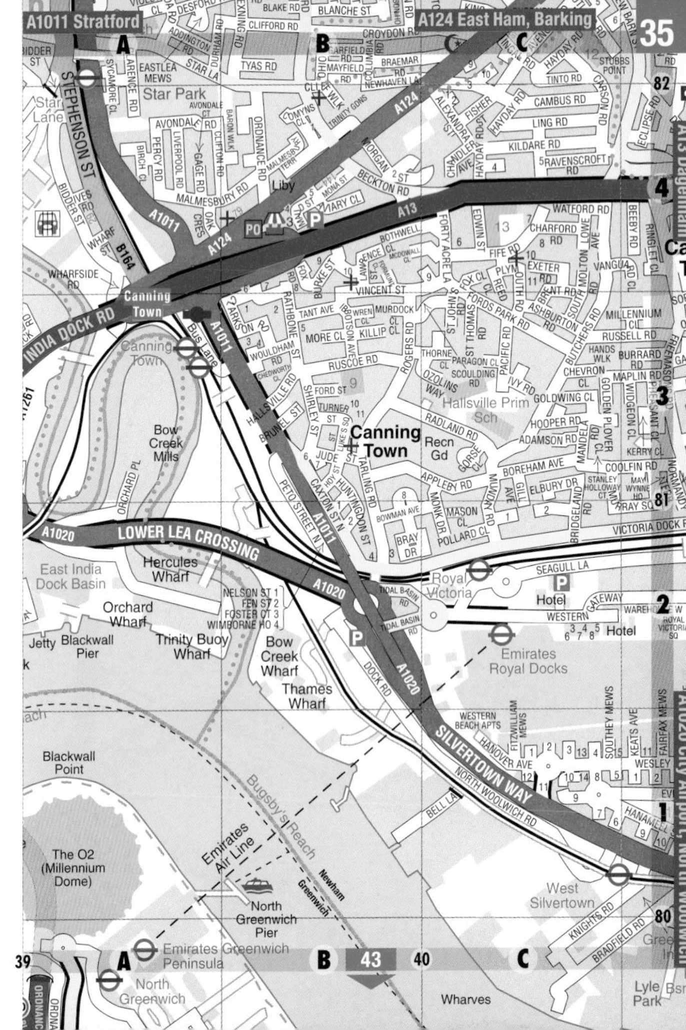

A1011 Stratford
A124 East Ham, Barking
A
B
C
82
A13 Dagenham
4
3
2
1
81
80
A1020 City Airport, North Woolwich
39
43
40
Star Park
Star Lane
STEPHENSON ST
BIDDER ST
EASTLEA MEWS
STAR LA
TYAS RD
CLIFFORD RD
BLAKE RD
BLANCHE ST
CROYDON RD
MAYFIELD RD
BRAEMAR RD
NEWHAVEN LA
AVONDALE RD
LIVERPOOL RD
GAGE RD
CLIFTON RD
ORDNANCE RD
PERCY RD
BIRCH CL
MALMESBURY RD
MORGAN ST
BECKTON RD
TINTO RD
CAMBUS RD
LING RD
KILDARE RD
RAVENSCROFT RD
HAYDAY RD
FISHER ST
CHANDLER AVE
ALEXANDRA ST
Liby
PO
A1011
A124
A13
B164
WHARFSIDE RD
WHARF ST
Canning Town
INDIA DOCK RD
Bus Lane
WATFORD RD
CHARFORD RD
FIFE RD
EXETER RD
BOTHWELL CL
VINCENT ST
FORTY ACRE LA
EDWIN ST
BEEBY RD
VANGUARD CL
MILLENNIUM CL
RUSSELL RD
BURRARD RD
MAPLIN RD
CHEVRON CL
GOLDWING CL
FORDS PARK RD
ASHBURTON RD
BUTCHERS RD
PACIFIC RD
ST THOMAS RD
ST JOHN'S RD
ROGERS RD
THORNE CL
PARAGON CL
SCOULDING RD
OZOLINS WAY
IVY RD
Hallsville Prim Sch
TANT AVE
MURDOCK CL
KILLIP CL
MORE CL
WOULDHAM RD
RUSCOE RD
RATHBONE ST
FORD ST
TURNER ST
SHIRLEY ST
HALLSVILLE RD
BRUNEL ST
Canning Town
JUDE ST
TARLING RD
RADLAND RD
Recn Gd
HOOPER RD
ADAMSON RD
BOREHAM AVE
COOLFIN RD
KERRY CL
GOLDEN PLOVER CL
WIDGEON CL
MANDELA RD
APPLEBY RD
ELBURY DR
BRIDGELAND RD
MONK DR
MASON CL
POLLARD CL
BOWMAN AVE
BRAY DR
MUNDAY RD
GILL AVE
VICTORIA DOCK RD
Bow Creek Mills
ORCHARD PL
PETO STREET N
CAXTON ST N
HUNTINGDON ST
A1020
LOWER LEA CROSSING
East India Dock Basin
Hercules Wharf
Orchard Wharf
Trinity Buoy Wharf
Jetty
Blackwall Pier
NELSON ST 1
FEN ST 2
FOSTER CT 3
WIMBORNE HO 4
Bow Creek Wharf
Thames Wharf
TIDAL BASIN RD
DOCK RD
Royal Victoria
SEAGULL LA
Hotel
WESTERN GATEWAY
Emirates Royal Docks
WESTERN BEACH APTS
HANOVER AVE
FITZWILLIAM MEWS
SOUTHEY MEWS
KEATS AVE
FAIRFAX MEWS
WESLEY
SILVERTOWN WAY
NORTH WOOLWICH RD
BELL LA
HANAMEL ST
Blackwall Point
Bugsby's Reach
Emirates Air Line
The O2 (Millennium Dome)
North Greenwich Pier
Newham
Greenwich
West Silvertown
KNIGHTS RD
BRADFIELD RD
Emirates Greenwich Peninsula
North Greenwich
Wharves
Lyle Park

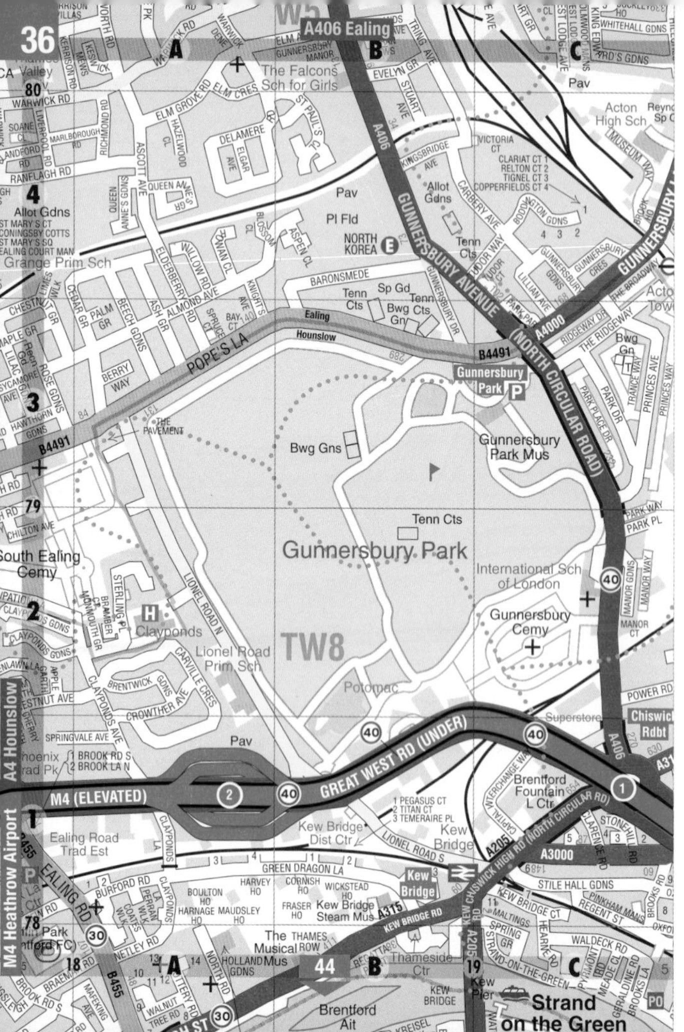

A406 Ealing
A
B
C
The Falcons Sch for Girls
ELM CRES
ELM GROVE RD
ST PAUL'S CL
DELAMERE RD
ELGAR AVE
HAZELWOOD CL
ASCOTT AVE
RICHMOND RD
WARWICK RD
SOANE CL
MARLBOROUGH RD
LIVERPOOL RD
RANELAGH RD
KERRISON RD
KESWICK MEWS
EVELYN GR
STUART AVE
TRING AVE
KINGSBRIDGE AVE
VICTORIA CT
CLARIAT CT 1
RELTON CT 2
TIGNEL CT 3
COPPERFIELDS CT 4
Acton High Sch
MUSEUM WAY
Pav
Allot Gdns
CARBERY AVE
BODDINGTON GDNS
Pl Fld
NORTH KOREA
Tenn Cts
GUNNERSBURY AVENUE
GUNNERSBURY GDNS
GUNNERSBURY CRES
THE BROADWAY
A4000
LILLIAN AVE
TUDOR WAY
ST MARY'S CT
CONINGSBY COTTS
ST MARY'S SQ
EALING COURT MAN
Grange Prim Sch
QUEEN ANNE'S GDNS
QUEEN ANNE'S GR
BLOSSOM CL
ASPEN CL
ROWAN CL
WILLOW RD
ELDERBERRY RD
ALMOND AVE
ASH GR
BEECH GDNS
PALM GR
CEDAR GR
CHESTNUT GR
LIMES WLK
MAPLE GR
LILAC GDNS
SYCAMORE AVE
HAWTHORN GDNS
ROSE GDNS
BERRY WAY
SPRUCE CT
BAY CT
KNIGHT'S AVE
BARONSMEDE
Sp Gd
Bwg Cts
Bwg Gn
GUNNERSBURY DR
Ealing
Hounslow
POPE'S LA
B4491
(NORTH CIRCULAR ROAD)
RIDGEWAY DR
THE RIDGEWAY
Acton Town
Gunnersbury Park
PARK PLACE DR
PARK DR
TRANCE WAY
PRINCES AVE
PRINCES WAY
THE PAVEMENT
Bwg Gns
Gunnersbury Park Mus
Tenn Cts
Gunnersbury Park
International Sch of London
PARK WAY
PARK PL
MANOR GDNS
MANOR WAY
MANOR CT
Gunnersbury Cemy
CHILTON AVE
South Ealing Cemy
CLAYPONDS GDNS
BRAMBER CT
MONMOUTH GR
STERLING PL
Clayponds
LIONEL ROAD N
Lionel Road Prim Sch
TW8
CARVILLE CRES
BRENTWICK GDNS
CROWTHER AVE
CLAYPONDS AVE
APPLE GARTH
CHESTNUT AVE
SPRINGVALE AVE
Potomac
POWER RD
Superstore
Chiswick Rdbt
A406
GREAT WEST RD (UNDER)
Pav
1 BROOK RD S
2 BROOK LA N
M4 (ELEVATED)
A4 Hounslow
M4 Heathrow Airport
Ealing Road Trad Est
1 PEGASUS CT
2 TITAN CT
3 TEMERAIRE PL
Kew Bridge Dist Ctr
Kew Bridge
LIONEL ROAD S
Brentford Fountain L Ctr
CAPITAL INTERCHANGE WAY
NORTH CIRCULAR RD
CLARENCE RD
STONEHILL RD
A205
A3000
GREEN DRAGON LA
CLAYPONDS LA
EALING RD
BURFORD RD
BOULTON HO
HARVEY HO
CORNISH HO
WICKSTEAD HO
HARNAGE HO
MAUDSLEY HO
FRASER HO
Kew Bridge Steam Mus
A315
KEW BRIDGE RD
KEW BRIDGE CT
STILE HALL GDNS
PINKHAM MANS
REGENT ST
MALTINGS
SPRING GR
STRAND-ON-THE-GREEN
HEARNE RD
WALDECK RD
PYRMONT RD
MEADE CL
GERALDINE RD
BROOKS LA
BROOKS RD
The Musical Mus
THAMES ROW
Thameside Ctr
KEW BRIDGE
Kew Pier
Strand on the Green
44
HOLLAND GDNS
NORTH RD
NETLEY RD
COATES WLK
PERRAN WLK
B455
BRAEMAR RD
BROOK RD S
MAFEKING AVE
WALNUT TREE RD
Brentford Ait
KREISEL
Park
Brentford FC

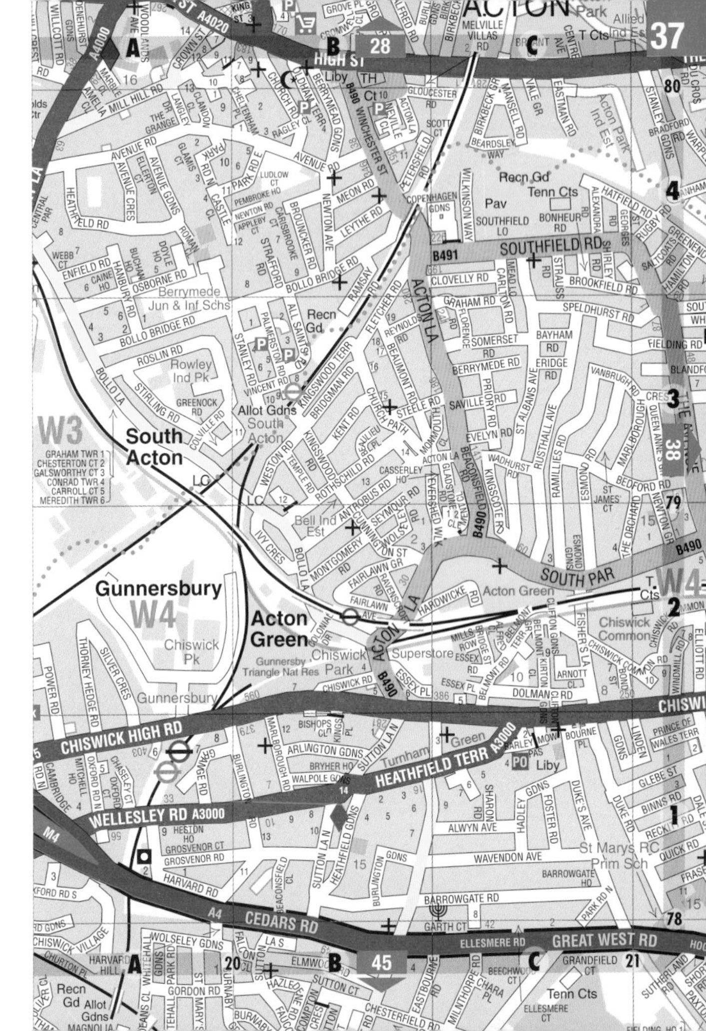

ACTON
South Acton
Gunnersbury
Acton Green
W3
W4
HIGH ST
CHISWICK HIGH RD
HEATHFIELD TERR A3000
WELLESLEY RD A3000
CEDARS RD
GREAT WEST RD
SOUTHFIELD RD
SOUTH PAR
ACTON LA
B490 WINCHESTER ST
BOLLO BRIDGE RD
AVENUE RD
Berrymede Jun & Inf Schs
Rowley Ind Pk
Bell Ind Est
Chiswick Pk
Chiswick Park
Gunnersby Triangle Nat Res
Chiswick Common
Acton Park Ind Est
Recn Gd
Tenn Cts
Allot Gdns
Superstore
Turnham Green
St Marys RC Prim Sch
GRAHAM TWR 1
CHESTERTON CT 2
GALSWORTHY CT 3
CONRAD TWR 4
CARROLL CT 5
MEREDITH TWR 6
28
38
45

29
46
37
THE VALE
A4020
B408
BEECH AVE
ESSEX PARK MEWS
ALLIED WAY
Warple Mews
Acton Park Ind Est
VALETTA RD
JEDDO RD
Wendell Park Prim Sch
COBBOLD RD
HADYN PARK RD
ASKEW RD
Liby
BATSON ST
Greenside Prim Sch
Southfield Prim Sch
The Good Shepherd RC Prim Sch
WENDELL PARK
BASSEIN PARK RD
ASHCHURCH TERR
B408
SOUTHFIELD RD
WHELLOCK RD
W12
Bedford Park
FIELDING RD
BLANDFORD RD
Tenn Cts
THE AVENUE
BLENHEIM RD
Ealing
Hounslow
Allot Gdns
FLANCHFORD RD
A402
SEVEN STARS CNR
B408 PADDENSWICK RD
John Betts Prim Sch
Bndstd
Bwg Gn
Ravenscourt Park
STAMFORD BROOK RD
B409
GOLDHAWK RD
BATH RD
B490
B409
FLANDERS RD
Turnham Green
W4
Stamford Brook
RAVENSCOURT GDNS
Tenn Cts
HAMLET GDNS
Ravenscourt Pk Prep Sch
KING ST
A315
A402
Chiswick Common
CHISWICK COMMON RD
TURNHAM GREEN TERR
B491
CHISWICK HIGH RD
A316
CHISWICK LA
T Cts
GREAT WEST RD
A4
CHISWICK
St Marys RC Prim Sch
Recn Gd
40
Thames Path
CHISWICK MALL
River
St Paul's Sch
Tenn Cts
GREAT WEST RD
HOGARTH
A4
Hogarth's House
Hogarth Bsns Pk
Roundabout
Fullers Brewery
Pl Fld
The Swedish Sch
LONSDALE RD
Flds
21
22
80
79
78
A
B
C
4
3
2
1

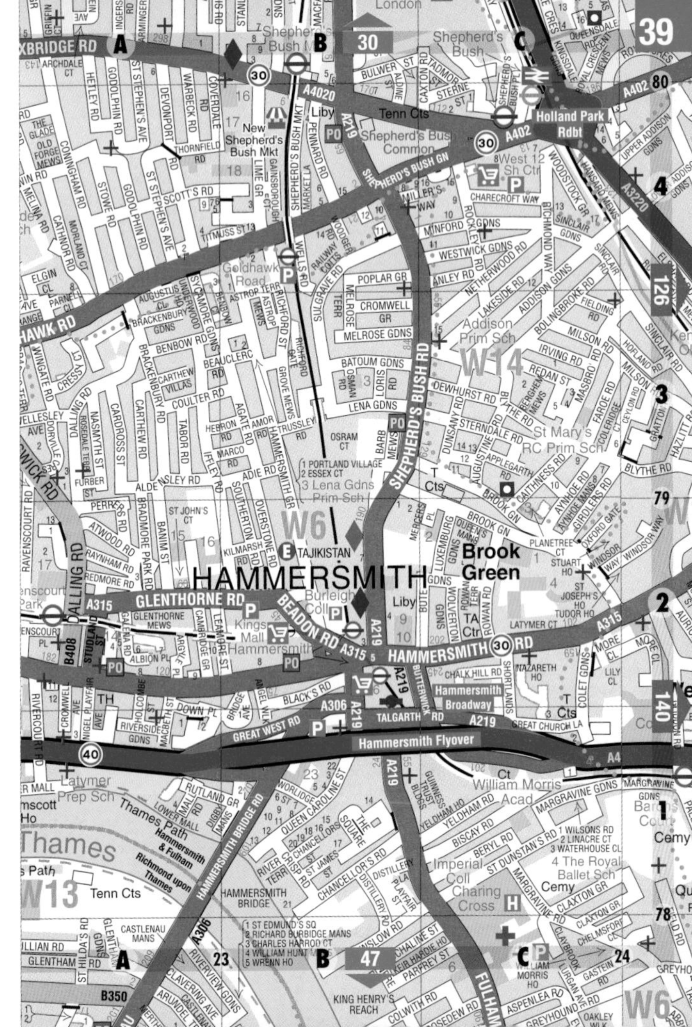

30
HAMMERSMITH
Brook Green
W6
W14
Shepherd's Bush
Holland Park Rdbt
Shepherd's Bush Common
New Shepherd's Bush Mkt
West 12 Sh Ctr
Goldhawk Road
Addison Prim Sch
St Mary's RC Prim Sch
3 Lena Gdns Prim Sch
TAJIKISTAN
Burleigh Coll
Kings Mall
Hammersmith Broadway
Hammersmith Flyover
Latymer Prep Sch
William Morris Acad
Imperial Coll
Charing Cross
Thames
Thames Path
Hammersmith & Fulham
Richmond upon Thames
HAMMERSMITH BRIDGE
KING HENRY'S REACH
UXBRIDGE RD
A4020
A219
A402
A3220
A315
A306
A4
B408
B350
SHEPHERD'S BUSH RD
SHEPHERD'S BUSH GN
GOLDHAWK RD
GLENTHORNE RD
BEADON RD
HAMMERSMITH RD
TALGARTH RD
GREAT WEST RD
DALLING RD
HAMMERSMITH BRIDGE RD
FULHAM
1 PORTLAND VILLAGE
2 ESSEX CT
1 WILSONS RD
2 LINACRE CT
3 WATERHOUSE CL
4 The Royal Ballet Sch
1 ST EDMUND'S SQ
2 RICHARD BURBIDGE MANS
3 CHARLES HARROD CT
4 WILLIAM HUNT M
5 WRENN HO
126
140
79
80
78
47
23
24

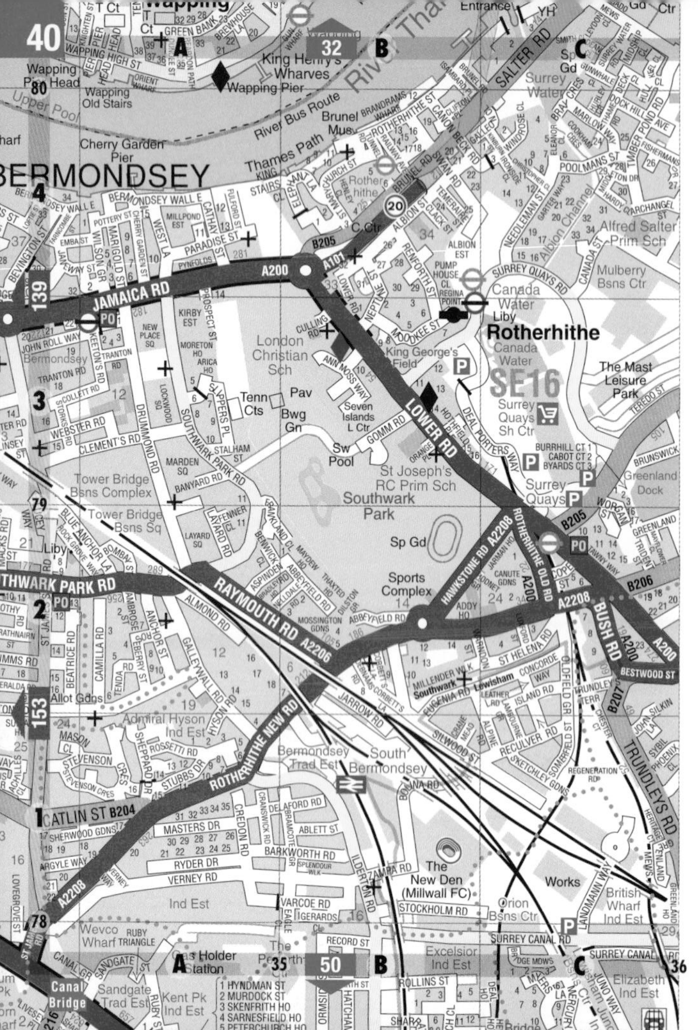

32
50
139
153
79
78
80
35
36
A
B
C
1
2
3
4
Wapping
Wapping High St
Wapping Pier Head
Wapping Old Stairs
King Henry's Wharves
Wapping Pier
Upper Pool
River Thames
River Bus Route
Cherry Garden Pier
BERMONDSEY
Brunel Mus
Thames Path
King Stairs Cl
Bermondsey Wall E
Rotherhithe St
Salter Rd
Surrey Water
Rotherhithe
Canada Water
Liby
SE16
Surrey Quays Sh Ctr
The Mast Leisure Park
Alfred Salter Prim Sch
Mulberry Bsns Ctr
Albion Channel
Jamaica Rd
A200
A101
B205
Lower Rd
London Christian Sch
King George's Field
Seven Islands L Ctr
Tenn Cts
Pav
Bwg Gn
Sw Pool
St Joseph's RC Prim Sch
Southwark Park
Southwark Park Rd
Sp Gd
Sports Complex
Tower Bridge Bsns Complex
Tower Bridge Bsns Sq
Raymouth Rd
A2206
Rotherhithe New Rd
Rotherhithe Old Rd
Hawkstone Rd
A2208
Bush Rd
B206
B207
Bestwood St
Greenland Dock
Surrey Quays
Trundleys Rd
Admiral Hyson Ind Est
Bermondsey Trad Est
South Bermondsey
Catlin St
B204
Masters Dr
Ryder Dr
Verney Rd
Ind Est
Ilderton Rd
The New Den (Millwall FC)
Stockholm Rd
Orion Bsns Ctr
Works
British Wharf Ind Est
Landmann Way
Surrey Canal Rd
Excelsior Ind Est
Wevco Wharf
Ruby Triangle
Gas Holder Station
Canal Bridge
Sandgate Trad Est
Kent Pk Ind Est
Elizabeth Ind Est
1 HYNDMAN ST
2 MURDOCK ST
3 SKENFRITH HO
4 SARNESFIELD HO
5 PETERCHURCH HO

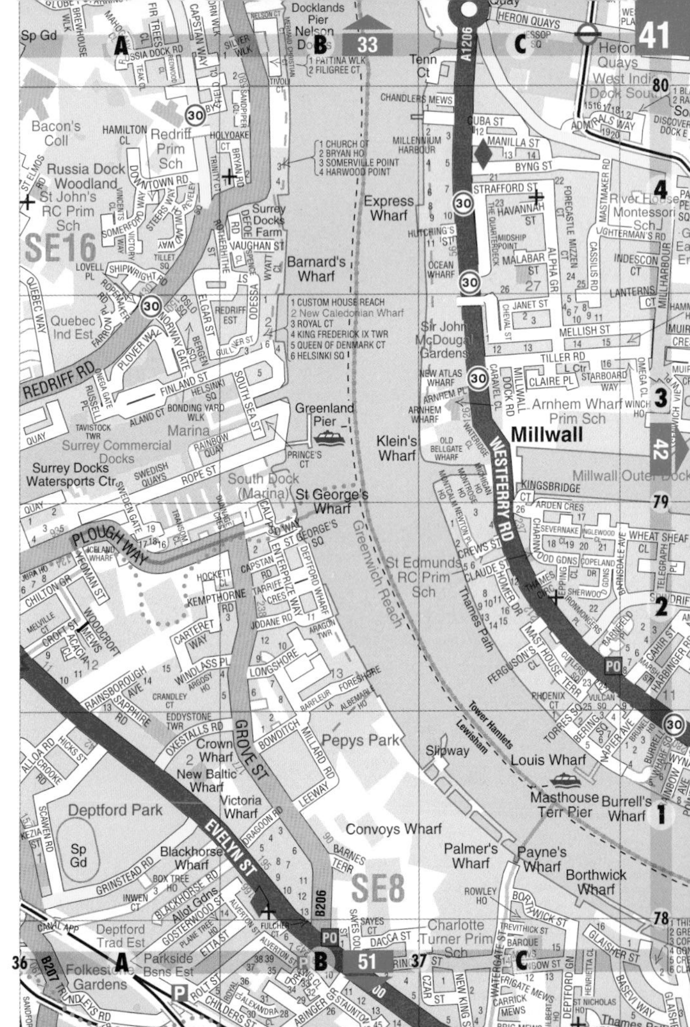
33
51
42
A
B
C
SE16
SE8
Millwall
Russia Dock Woodland
Redriff Prim Sch
Bacon's Coll
St John's RC Prim Sch
Surrey Docks Farm
Barnard's Wharf
Quebec Ind Est
Surrey Commercial Docks
Surrey Docks Watersports Ctr
Marina
Greenland Pier
South Dock (Marina)
St George's Wharf
Greenwich Reach
Express Wharf
Klein's Wharf
Sir John McDougal Gardens
St Edmunds RC Prim Sch
Thames Path
Arnhem Wharf Prim Sch
Millwall Outer Dock
River House Montessori Sch
Heron Quays
West India Dock South
Docklands Pier
Nelson Dock
Tenn Ct
Pepys Park
Crown Wharf
New Baltic Wharf
Victoria Wharf
Deptford Park
Blackhorse Wharf
Convoys Wharf
Palmer's Wharf
Payne's Wharf
Borthwick Wharf
Louis Wharf
Masthouse Terr Pier
Burrell's Wharf
Slipway
Tower Hamlets
Lewisham
Charlotte Turner Prim Sch
Deptford Trad Est
Parkside Bsns Est
Folkestone Gardens
Allot Gdns
REDRIFF RD
PLOUGH WAY
EVELYN ST
GROVE ST
WESTFERRY RD
A1206
B206
B207
ROPE ST
FINLAND ST
SOUTH SEA ST
HERON QUAYS
MANILLA ST
BYNG ST
STRAFFORD ST
MELLISH ST
TILLER RD
1 CHURCH CT
2 BRYAN HO
3 SOMERVILLE POINT
4 HARWOOD POINT
1 CUSTOM HOUSE REACH
2 New Caledonian Wharf
3 ROYAL CT
4 KING FREDERICK IX TWR
5 QUEEN OF DENMARK CT
6 HELSINKI SQ
1 PATTINA WLK
2 FILIGREE CT
1 THISTL
2 GREEN
3 CORBI
4 GONSO
5 CREEKS
6 CLARE
36
37
78
79
80

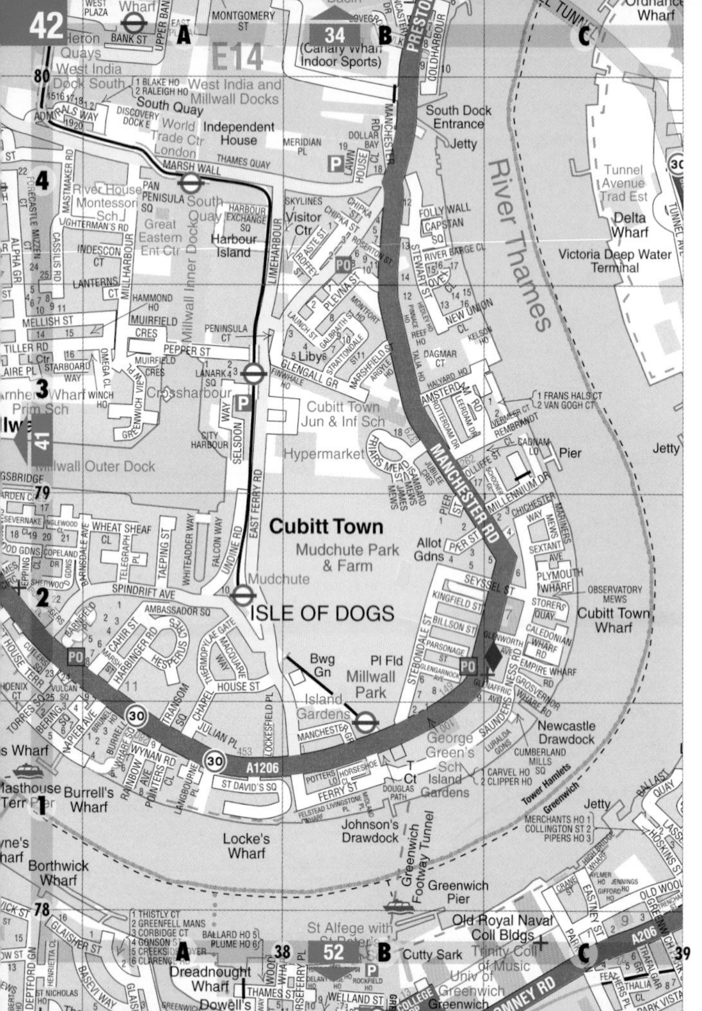

WEST PLAZA
MONTGOMERY ST
Basin
34
(Canary Wharf Indoor Sports)
PRESTON
Ordnance Wharf
Heron Quays
BANK ST
UPPER BANK
E14
West India Dock South
1 BLAKE HO
2 RALEIGH HO
West India and Millwall Docks
South Quay
ADMIRALS WAY
DISCOVERY DOCK E
World Trade Ctr London
Independent House
MERIDIAN PL
MANCHESTER RD
DOLLAR BAY
South Dock Entrance
Jetty
River Thames
Tunnel Avenue Trad Est
Delta Wharf
Victoria Deep Water Terminal
TUNNEL AVE
MARSH WALL
THAMES QUAY
LAWN HOUSE CL
PAN PENISULA SQ
South Quay
River House Montessori Sch
MASTMAKER RD
FORECASTLE CT
MIZZEN CT
LIGHTERMAN'S RD
Great Eastern Ent Ctr
HARBOUR EXCHANGE SQ
Harbour Island
Millwall Inner Dock
SKYLINES
Visitor Ctr
CHIPKA ST
ROSERTON ST
FOLLY WALL
CAPSTAN SQ
RIVER BARGE CL
STEWART ST
DOVEY CL
NEW UNION CL
INDESCON CT
ALPHA GR
CASSILIS RD
MILLHARBOUR
LIMEHARBOUR
ASTE ST
ROFFEY ST
PLEVINA ST
MONTFORT HO
LANTERNS CT
HAMMOND HO
MUIRFIELD CRES
MELLISH ST
PENINSULA CT
LAUNCH ST
GALBRAITH ST
STRATTONDALE ST
PINNACE HO
REEF HO
TALIA HO
DAGMAR CT
KELSON HO
TILLER RD
L Ctr
STARBOARD WAY
OMEGA CL
PEPPER ST
MUIRFIELD CRES
LANARK SQ
Liby
GLENGALL GR
MARSHFIELD ST
ARGYLE HO
HALYARD HO
AMSTERDAM RD
LEERDAM DR
ROTTERDAM DR
1 FRANS HALS CT
2 VAN GOGH CT
VERMEER CT
REMBRANDT CL
Wharf
WINCH HO
GREENWICH VIEW PL
Crossharbour
FINWHALE HO
Cubitt Town Jun & Inf Sch
Prim Sch
SELSDON WAY
CITY HARBOUR
41
Millwall Outer Dock
Hypermarket
FRIARS MEAD
ISAMBARD MEWS
ST JAMES MEWS
JUBILEE CRES
MANCHESTER RD
OLLIFFE ST
SCHOONER CL
CADNAM LO
Pier
Jetty
MILLENNIUM DR
79
WHEAT SHEAF CL
SEVERNAKE CL
INGLEWOOD CL
COPELAND DR
BARNSDALE AVE
TELEGRAPH PL
TAEPING ST
WHITEADDER WAY
FALCON WAY
UNDINE RD
EAST FERRY RD
Cubitt Town
Mudchute Park & Farm
PIER ST
Allot Gdns
CHICHESTER WAY
MARINERS MEWS
SEXTANT AVE
PLYMOUTH WHARF
SEYSSEL ST
OBSERVATORY MEWS
STORERS QUAY
Cubitt Town Wharf
KINGFIELD ST
BILLSON ST
CALEDONIAN WHARF RD
SPINDRIFT AVE
Mudchute
ISLE OF DOGS
AMBASSADOR SQ
BARNFIELD PL
CAHIR ST
HARBINGER RD
HESPERUS CRES
THERMOPYLAE GATE
MACQUARIE WAY
STEBONDALE ST
PARSONAGE ST
GLENGARNOCK AVE
GLENWORTH AVE
NESS RD
EMPIRE WHARF RD
GROSVENOR WHARF RD
PO
CUTLERS SQ
Bwg Gn
Pl Fld
Millwall Park
HOUSE ST
VULCAN SQ
TORRES SQ
BERING SQ
NAPIER AVE
BRUNEL HO
BURRELL WHARF SQ
TRANSOM SQ
CHAPEL HO
JULIAN PL
LOCKESFIELD PL
Island Gardens
MANCHESTER GR
GLENAFFRIC AVE
SAUNDERS NESS RD
Newcastle Drawdock
LURALDA GDNS
CUMBERLAND MILLS SQ
30
A1206
WYNAN RD
RAINBOW AVE
POINTERS CL
LANGBOURNE PL
ST DAVID'S SQ
POTTERS LO
HORSESHOE CL
FERRY ST
George Green's Sch
Island Gardens
T Ct
1 CARVEL HO
2 CLIPPER HO
Tower Hamlets
Greenwich
s Wharf
Masthouse Terr Pier
Burrell's Wharf
FELSTEAD WHARF
LIVINGSTONE PL
MIDLAND PL
DOUGLAS PATH
Johnson's Drawdock
Greenwich Footway Tunnel
Jetty
MERCHANTS HO 1
COLLINGTON ST 2
PIPERS HO 3
BALLAST QUAY
HOSKINS ST
HIGHBRIDGE WHARF
Locke's Wharf
Borthwick Wharf
AYLMER HO
JENNINGS HO
GIFFORD HO
CRANE ST
OLD WOOL
Greenwich Pier
78
1 THISTLY CT
2 GREENFELL MANS
3 CORBIDGE CT
4 GONSON ST
5 CREEKSIDE
6 CLARENCE
GLAISHER ST
BALLARD HO 5
PLUME HO 6
Old Royal Naval Coll Bldgs
EASTNEY ST
PARK ROW
GREENWICH PARK
St Alfege with St Peter's
Trinity Coll of Music
A206
TRAFALGAR GR
38
52
Cutty Sark
39
Dreadnought Wharf
THAMES ST
Dowell's Wharf
HORSEFERRY PL
DELANY HO
ROCKFIELD HO
WELLAND ST
COLLEGE APP
Univ of Greenwich
Greenwich
ROMNEY RD
FEATHERS PL
THALIA CL
PARK VISTA
HENRIETTA CL
DEPTFORD GN
ST NICHOLAS HO
BASEVI WAY
GREENWICH QUAY
Thames Path
A B C
1 2 3 4

The O2 (Millennium Dome)
A
B
35
C
Emirates Air Line
North Greenwich Pier
Emirates Greenwich Peninsula
North Greenwich
West Silvertown
KNIGHTS RD
BRADFIELD RD
80
Wharves
Bugsby's Reach
Jetty
4
3
2
1
79
78
ORDNANCE CRES
BLACKWALL TUNNEL APP
A102
EDMUND HALLEY WAY
EAST PARKSIDE
MILLENNIUM WAY
RIVER WAY
Busway
WEST PARKSIDE
The Millennium Prim Sch
JOHN HARRISON WAY
FARADAY LO
Gas Works
Bay Wharf
BOORD ST
DREADNOUGHT ST
Primrose Wharf
MORDEN WHARF RD
TUNNEL AVE
Morden Wharf
PETERBOAT CL
Refineries
Thames Path
Wharf
OSIER LA
BEQUEREL CT
CHILD LA
SCHOOL BANK RD
FARNSWORTH CT
KILBY CT
A2203
GREENWICH
SE10
WEST PARKSIDE
SOUTHERN WAY
BUGSBY'S WAY
COTTRELL CT
MOSELEY ROW
PEARTREE WAY
HORN LINK WAY
LOMBARD WALL
BROCKLEBANK RD
Brocklebank Road Ind Est
WILLOUGHBY WAY
SALUTATION RD
Works
TWYCROSS MS
Lawrence Trad Est
BLACKWALL LA
Piper's Wharf
MAURITIUS RD
AZOF ST
Peninsular Ret Pk
Angerstein Bsns Pk
Superstore
PENINSULAR PARK RD
FELLTRAM WAY
A206 Woolwich
HORN LA
ALDEBURGH PL
ALDEBURGH ST
FEARON ST
Badcocks Wharves
Lovell's Wharf
CHRISTCHURCH WAY
BELLOT ST
ARMITAGE RD
LENTHORP RD
HARRIOTT CL
MERCERS CL
WILLIAMSON CL
GLENFORTH ST
FINGAL ST
GLENISTER RD
COLLERSTON HO
CHILVER ST
DANDRIDGE CL
DENHAM ST
RAINTON RD
HARDMAN RD
DUPREE RD
FAIRTHORN RD
FARMDALE RD
GURDON RD
PELTON RD
BANNING ST
CARADOC ST
HADRIAN ST
A206
Liby
KEMSING RD
COMBEDALE RD
PO
Area u/c
PARK MEWS
CALVERT RD
CHEVENING RD
HALSTOW RD
East Greenwich Pleasaunce
ORMISTON RD
Westcombe Park
STATION CRES
TRAFALGAR RD
WOODLAND GR
EARLSWOOD ST
TYLER ST
COLOMB ST
WALNUT TREE RD
ANNANDALE RD
TUSKAR ST
WOODLANDS PARK RD
VANBRUGH HILL
DINSDALE RD
HUMBER RD
MYCENAE RD
WESTCOMBE
EASTCOMBE AVE
SANDTOFT
EVERSLEY
BERNARD
LEMMON
Maze Hill
RESTELL CL
39
A
B
53
40
C
KIRKSIDE RD
HARDY CT
RAMSHOT AVE

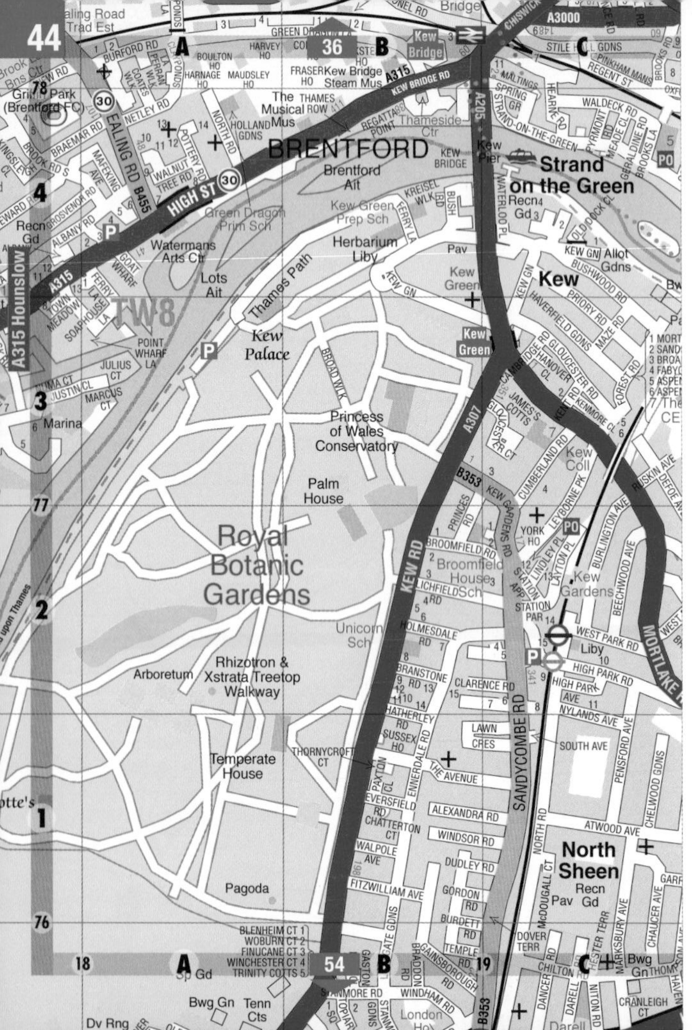

36
54
A
B
C
78
77
76
18
19
4
3
2
1
BRENTFORD
Strand on the Green
Kew
North Sheen
Royal Botanic Gardens
Kew Palace
Princess of Wales Conservatory
Palm House
Rhizotron & Xstrata Treetop Walkway
Temperate House
Arboretum
Pagoda
Kew Bridge
Kew Bridge Steam Mus
The Musical Mus
Brentford Ait
Lots Ait
Watermans Arts Ctr
Green Dragon Prim Sch
Kew Green Prep Sch
Herbarium Liby
Kew Green
Kew Pier
Kew Coll
Broomfield House Sch
Unicorn Sch
Kew Gardens
Thames Path
Thameside Ctr
Griffin Park (Brentford FC)
Marina
TW8
A315 Hounslow
A315
A3000
A205
A307
B353
B455
HIGH ST
KEW BRIDGE RD
EALING RD
KEW RD
MORTLAKE RD
SANDYCOMBE RD
KEW GARDENS RD
STATION APP
STATION PAR
WEST PARK RD
HIGH PARK RD
HIGH PARK AVE
NYLANDS AVE
SOUTH AVE
ATWOOD AVE
NORTH RD
CLARENCE RD
LAWN CRES
ALEXANDRA RD
WINDSOR RD
DUDLEY RD
GORDON RD
BURDETT RD
TEMPLE RD
GAINSBOROUGH RD
FITZWILLIAM AVE
WALPOLE AVE
CHATTERTON CT
EVERSFIELD RD
ENNERDALE RD
PAXTON CL
THE AVENUE
SUSSEX HO
HATHERLEY RD
BRANSTONE RD
HOLMESDALE RD
LICHFIELD RD
BROOMFIELD RD
PRINCES RD
CUMBERLAND RD
LEYBORNE PK
BURLINGTON AVE
BEECHWOOD AVE
RUSKIN AVE
KENT RD
GLOUCESTER RD
HAVERFIELD GDNS
PRIORY RD
BUSHWOOD RD
FOREST RD
KENMORE CL
CAMBRIDGE RD
HANOVER CL
JAMES'S COTTS
GLOUCESTER CT
LINDLEY PL
LAYTON PL
YORK HO
PENSFORD AVE
CHELWOOD GDNS
MARKSBURY AVE
CHAUCER AVE
McDOUGALL CT
DOVER TERR
CHILTON RD
DANCER RD
DARELL RD
NITON RD
HESTER TERR
CRANLEIGH CT
STANMORE RD
WINDHAM RD
BRADDON RD
GASTON GDNS
BLENHEIM CT 1
WOBURN CT 2
FINUCANE CT 3
WINCHESTER CT 4
TRINITY COTTS 5
THORNYCROFT CT
STRAND-ON-THE-GREEN
OLDDOCK CL
WATERLOO PL
KEW GN
FERRY LA
KREISEL WLK
BUSH RD
REGATTA POINT
THAMES ROW
HOLLAND GDNS
NORTH RD
POTTERY RD
WALNUT TREE RD
NETLEY RD
BRAEMAR RD
MAFEKING AVE
GROSVENOR RD
ALBANY RD
BROOK RD S
GOAT WHARF
FERRY LA
SOAPHOUSE LA
TOWN MEADOW
POINT WHARF LA
JULIUS CT
JUSTIN CL
MARCUS CT
BURFORD RD
BOULTON HO
HARNAGE HO
MAUDSLEY HO
HARVEY HO
FRASER HO
GREEN DRAGON LA
STILE HALL GDNS
PINKHAM MANS
REGENT ST
WALDECK RD
PYRMONT RD
MEADE CL
GERALDINE RD
BROOKS LA
HEARNE RD
SPRING GR
MALTINGS
CHISWICK
Recn Gd
Allot Gdns
Pav
Liby
Sp Gd
Bwg Gn
Tenn Cts
Dv Rng
Ealing Road Trad Est
Brook Bns Ctr
KINGSLEIGH CL

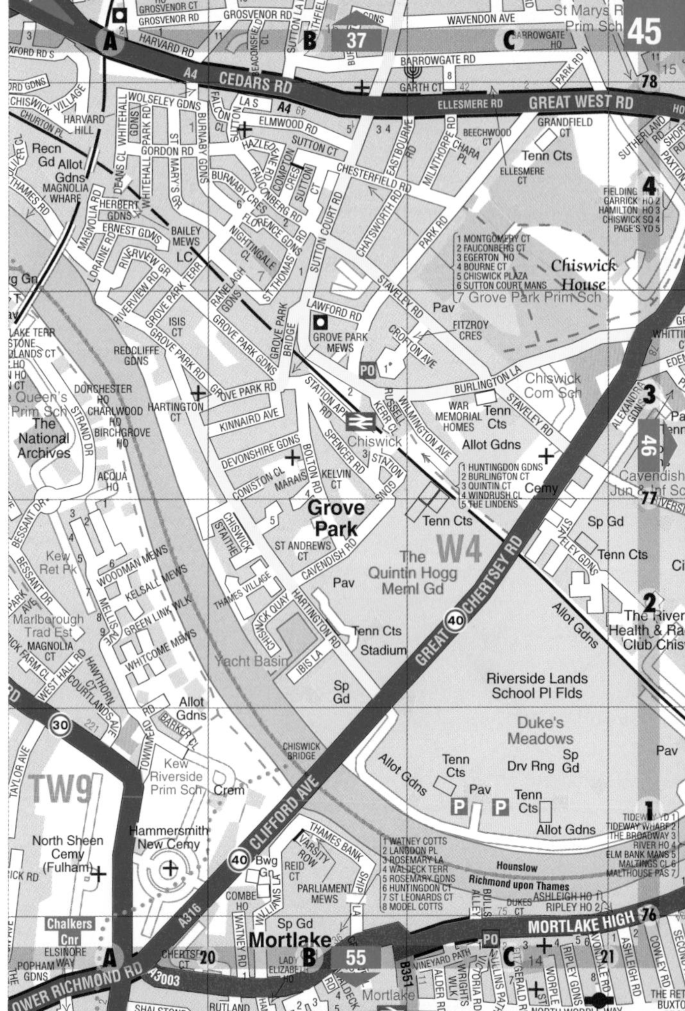
37
CEDARS RD
GREAT WEST RD
ELLESMERE RD
Chiswick House
Grove Park
W4
The Quintin Hogg Meml Gd
GREAT CHERTSEY RD
Riverside Lands School Pl Flds
Duke's Meadows
CLIFFORD AVE
Chiswick
The National Archives
Kew Ret Pk
Marlborough Trad Est
Yacht Basin
Kew Riverside Prim Sch
Crem
Hammersmith New Cemy
North Sheen Cemy (Fulham)
TW9
Mortlake
MORTLAKE HIGH
LOWER RICHMOND RD
Chalkers Cnr
NORTH WORPLE WAY
Hounslow
Richmond upon Thames
Cavendish Jun & Inf Sch
Chiswick Com Sch
7 Grove Park Prim Sch
1 MONTGOMERY CT
2 FAUCONBERG CT
3 EGERTON HO
4 BOURNE CT
5 CHISWICK PLAZA
6 SUTTON COURT MANS
1 HUNTINGDON GDNS
2 BURLINGTON CT
3 QUINTIN CT
4 WINDRUSH CL
5 THE LINDENS
1 WATNEY COTTS
2 LANGDON PL
3 ROSEMARY LA
4 WALDECK TERR
5 ROSEMARY GDNS
6 HUNTINGDON CT
7 ST LEONARDS CT
8 MODEL COTTS
TIDEWAY YD 1
TIDEWAY WHARF 2
THE BROADWAY 3
RIVER HO 4
ELM BANK MANS 5
MALTINGS CL 6
MALTHOUSE PAS 7
FIELDING HO 1
GARRICK HO 2
HAMILTON HO 3
CHISWICK SQ 4
PAGE'S YD 5
46
55

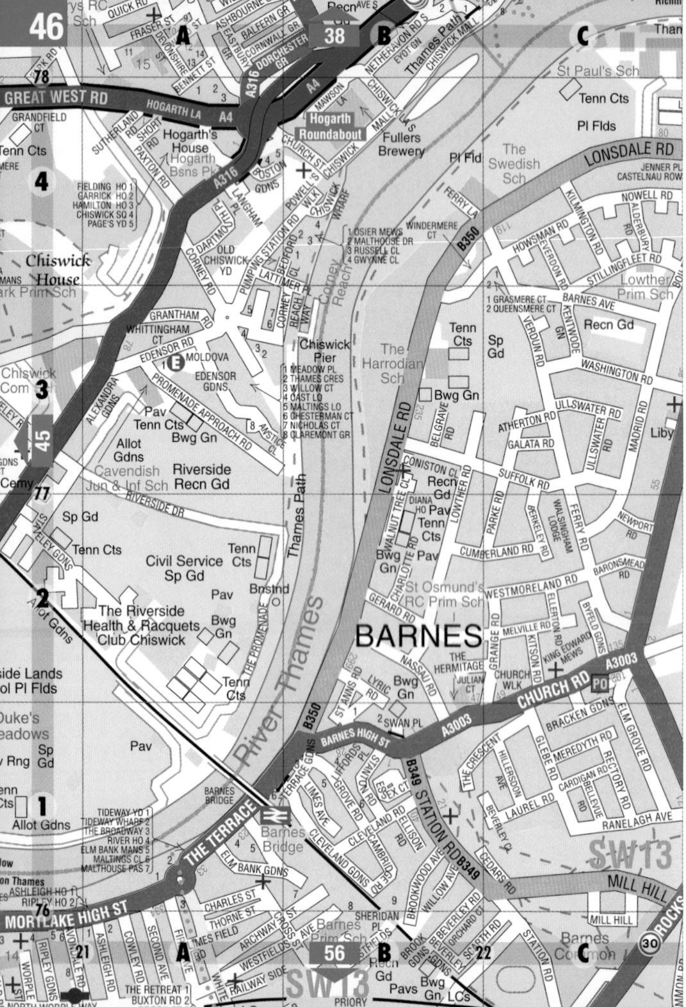
38
40
A
B
C
QUICK RD
FRASER ST
DEVONSHIRE ST
BENNETT ST
WILTON
ASHBOURNE GR
BALFERN GR
EASTBURY GR
CORNWALL GR
DORCHESTER GR
AIREDALE AVE S
Recn
NETHERAVON RD S
EYOT GN
Thames Path
CHISWICK MALL
St Paul's Sch
Tenn Cts
Pl Flds
78
GREAT WEST RD
HOGARTH LA
A4
A316
GRANDFIELD CT
Tenn Cts
SUTHERLAND RD
SHORT RD
PAXTON RD
Hogarth's House
Hogarth Bsns Pk
MAWSON LA
Hogarth Roundabout
CHISWICK LA S
Fullers Brewery
CHURCH ST
CHISWICK
BOSTON GDNS
Pl Fld
The Swedish Sch
LONSDALE RD
JENNER PL
CASTELNAU ROW
4
FIELDING HO 1
GARRICK HO 2
HAMILTON HO 3
CHISWICK SQ 4
PAGE'S YD 5
LANGHAM PL
POWELL'S WLK
CHISWICK WHARF
FERRY LA
WINDERMERE CT
NOWELL RD
KILMINGTON RD
ALDERBURY RD
HOWSMAN RD
EVERDON RD
DARTMOUTH PL
PUMPING STATION RD
BEDFORD CL
1 OSIER MEWS
2 MALTHOUSE DR
3 RUSSELL CL
4 GWYNNE CL
B350
STILLINGFLEET RD
Chiswick House
OLD CHISWICK YD
CORNEY RD
LATTIMER PL
CORNEY REACH WAY
Corney Reach
Lowther Prim Sch
1 GRASMERE CT
2 QUEENSMERE CT
BARNES AVE
VERDUN RD
KENTWODE GN
Recn Gd
GRANTHAM RD
WHITTINGHAM CT
EDENSOR RD
MOLDOVA
EDENSOR GDNS
Chiswick Pier
The Harrodian Sch
Tenn Cts
Sp Gd
WASHINGTON RD
Chiswick Com
3
1 MEADOW PL
2 THAMES CRES
3 WILLOW CT
4 OAST LO
5 MALTINGS LO
6 CHESTERMAN CT
7 NICHOLAS CT
8 CLAREMONT GR
Bwg Gn
ULLSWATER RD
ALEXANDRA GDNS
PROMENADE APPROACH RD
ANSTICE CL
Pav
Tenn Cts
Bwg Gn
45
Allot Gdns
LONSDALE RD
BELGRAVE RD
ATHERTON RD
GALATA RD
ULLSWATER RD
MADRID RD
Liby
Cavendish Jun & Inf Sch
Riverside Recn Gd
CONISTON CL
LOWTHER RD
SUFFOLK RD
Cemy
77
RIVERSIDE DR
Thames Path
WALNUT TREE CL
DIANA HO
Recn Gd
Pav
Tenn Cts
PARKE RD
BERKELEY RD
WALSINGHAM LODGE
FERRY RD
NEWPORT RD
Sp Gd
STAVELEY GDNS
Tenn Cts
Civil Service Sp Gd
Tenn Cts
Bwg Gn
Pav
CHARLOTTE RD
CUMBERLAND RD
BARONSMEAD RD
2
Allot Gdns
Pav
Bnstnd
The Riverside Health & Racquets Club Chiswick
Bwg Gn
River Thames
St Osmund's RC Prim Sch
GERARD RD
WESTMORELAND RD
ELLERTON RD
BYFIELD GDNS
BARNES
GRANGE RD
MELVILLE RD
KITSON RD
KING EDWARD MEWS
THE PROMENADE
Tenn Cts
NASSAU RD
THE HERMITAGE
JULIAN CT
CHURCH WLK
CHURCH RD
A3003
PO
ST ANNS RD
LYRIC RD
Bwg Gn
B350
BARNES HIGH ST
2 SWAN PL
A3003
BRACKEN GDNS
ELM GROVE RD
Pav
GLEBE RD
MEREDYTH RD
THE CRESCENT
HILLERSDON AVE
CARDIGAN RD
BELLEVUE RD
RECTORY RD
1
Allot Gdns
BARNES BRIDGE
TERRACE GDNS
LIMES AVE
GROVE RD
LIFFORDS PL
STANTON RD
ESSEX CT
B349
STATION RD
LAUREL RD
BEVERLEY CL
RANELAGH AVE
TIDEWAY YD 1
TIDEWAY WHARF 2
THE BROADWAY 3
RIVER HO 4
ELM BANK MANS 5
MALTINGS CL 6
MALTHOUSE PAS 7
THE TERRACE
Barnes Bridge
CLEVELAND GDNS
CLEVELAND RD
CAMBRIDGE RD
ELLISON RD
BROOKWOOD AVE
WILLOW AVE
CEDARS RD
SW13
MILL HILL
ELM BANK GDNS
ASHLEIGH HO 1
RIPLEY HO 2
CHARLES ST
THORNE ST
SHERIDAN PL
ROCKS
MILL HILL
76
MORTLAKE HIGH ST
ARCHWAY ST
CROSS ST
Barnes Prim Sch
Barnes Common
30
A
21
B
22
C
56
RIPLEY GDNS
ASHLEIGH RD
COWLEY RD
SECOND AVE
WESTFIELDS
RAILWAY SIDE
Recn Gd
Pavs
Bwg Gn
LCs
WORPLE ST
THE RETREAT 1
BUXTON RD 2
BROOK CT 3
NORTH WORPLE WAY
LC
PRIORY GDNS
SW13
STATION RD
MELINA CT 1

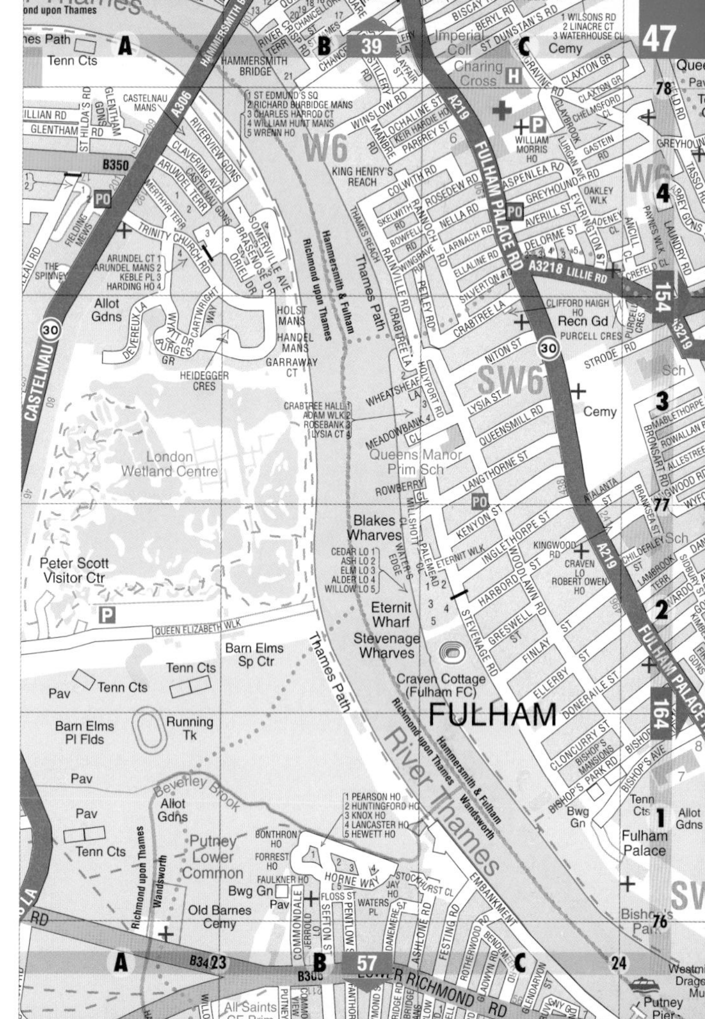

47
39
57
154
164
A
B
C
1
2
3
4
W6
SW6
FULHAM
River Thames
Thames Path
Hammersmith & Fulham
Richmond upon Thames
Wandsworth
HAMMERSMITH BRIDGE
London Wetland Centre
Peter Scott Visitor Ctr
Barn Elms Sp Ctr
Barn Elms Pl Flds
Putney Lower Common
Old Barnes Cemy
Craven Cottage (Fulham FC)
Fulham Palace
Bishop's Park
Charing Cross
Imperial Coll
Queens Manor Prim Sch
Blakes Wharves
Eternit Wharf
Stevenage Wharves
King Henry's Reach
Beverley Brook
CASTELNAU
FULHAM PALACE RD
LOWER RICHMOND RD
LILLIE RD
QUEEN ELIZABETH WLK
Putney Pier
All Saints CE Prim

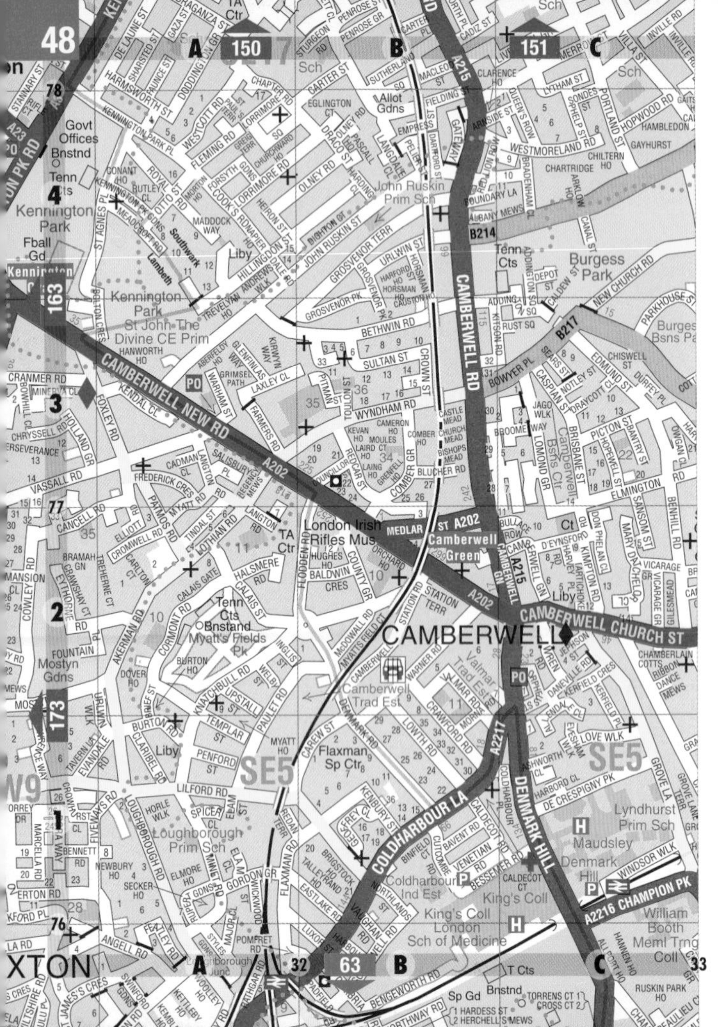

150
151
A
B
C
Govt Offices Bnstnd
Kennington Park
Fball Gd
Kennington Park
St John The Divine CE Prim
CAMBERWELL NEW RD
A202
CAMBERWELL RD
A215
B214
B217
Burgess Park
Burgess Bsns Park
John Ruskin Prim Sch
Allot Gdns
Southwark
Lambeth
163
173
London Irish Rifles Mus
TA Ctr
MEDLAR ST
Camberwell Green
CAMBERWELL
CAMBERWELL CHURCH ST
Camberwell Bsns Ctr
Myatt's Fields Pk
Mostyn Gdns
Camberwell Trad Est
Valmar Trad Est
Flaxman Sp Ctr
SE5
Loughborough Prim Sch
Coldharbour Ind Est
COLDHARBOUR LA
A2217
DENMARK HILL
King's Coll
King's Coll London Sch of Medicine
Maudsley
Denmark Hill
Lyndhurst Prim Sch
A2216 CHAMPION PK
William Booth Meml Trng Coll
Loughborough Junc
32
63
33
BRIXTON
WYNDHAM RD
VASSALL RD
LOTHIAN RD
WESTMORELAND RD
GROSVENOR TERR
JOHN RUSKIN ST
BETHWIN RD
LOVE WLK
DE CRESPIGNY PK
GROVE LA
FLAXMAN RD
LILFORD RD

49
A
152
B
153
C
OLD KENT RD
A2
A2208
TRAFALGAR AVE
B215
ALBANY RD
Burgess Park
SE15
SE1
Cobourg Prim Sch
LONCROFT RD
WAITE ST
GLENGALL TERR
GLENGALL RD
OSSORY RD
Superstore
Surrey Ret Pk
Cantium Ret Pk
Acorn Wharf
Nye's Wharf
Canal Bridge
Sandgate Trad Est
Wevco Wharf
RUBY TRIANGLE
SANDGATE ST
RUBY ST
CANAL GR
LIVESEY PL
BIANCA RD
LATONA RD
HAYMERLE RD
ST GEORGE'S WAY
DRAGON RD
WELLS WAY
LONGHOPE CL
NEWENT CL
Gloucester Prim Sch
DANIEL GDNS
LYNBROOK GR
PECKHAM GR
BLAKE'S RD
SAMUEL ST
CRONIN ST
GARNIES CL
EAST SURREY GR
CATOR ST
SUMNER RD
WILLOWBROOK RD
PECKHAM PARK RD
B216
PECKHAM HILL ST
COMMERCIAL WAY
SOUTHAMPTON WAY
PENTRIDGE ST
DIAMOND ST
STANSWOOD GDNS
SEDGMOOR PL
HAVIL ST
ST GILES RD
GABLES CL
DALWOOD ST
FLORIAN
WOODHOUSE AVE
MOODY RD
KELLY AVE
WATTS ST
GATONBY ST
HASLAM ST
STOPES ST
COMPTON CL
ASHMORE CL
GRENARD CL
LISFORD ST
PIONEER ST
JOCELYN ST
BONAR RD
BULLER CL
GOLDSMITH RD
MARMONT RD
FURLEY RD
STAFFORDSHIRE ST
BIRD IN BUSH RD
LYMPSTONE GDNS
FRIARY RD
LEDBURY ST
FENHAM RD
PENNETHORNE RD
BEWICK MEWS
MEETING HOUSE
SE15
50
77
78
4
3
2
1
PECKHAM RD
A202
Peckham
PECKHAM HIGH ST
30
Gall
MISTRAL
Liby
L Ctr
Aylesham Sh Ctr
Bellenden Rd Ret Pk
HANOVER PK
A2215
RYE LA
Tuke Sch
CONSORT RD
Harris Acad at Peckham
KINGFISHER HO
GANNET HO
HERON HO
OSPREY HO
GRUMMANT RD
TALFOURD PL
TALFOURD RD
LYNDHURST SQ
LYNDHURST WAY
BUSHEY HILL RD
Lucas Gdns
WILSON RD
DAGMAR RD
MAUDE RD
VESTRY RD
SHENLEY RD
CROFTON RD
GRACE'S RD
LINNELL RD
OSWYTH RD
GAIRLOCH RD
FEARNLEY HO
PEMBURY HO
LETTSOM ST
HARDEN HO
MCNEIL RD
CACTUS CL
AINSWORTH CL
HIGHSHORE RD
OLIVER MEWS
ELM GR
HOLLY GR
MONCRIEFF ST
CERISE RD
CICELY RD
CLAYTON RD
LYNDHURST GR
Recn Gd
Bellendon Rd Bsns Ctr
Peckham Rye
BLENHEIM GR
CHURCHILL CL
ALMOND CL
BOURNEMOUTH RD
BIRCH CL
HAZEL CL
COPELAND RD
BRAYARDS RD
SANDLINGS CL
GODMAN RD
GROVELANDS CL
CAMBERWELL GR
LINWOOD CL
Print Village Ind Est
CHADWICK RD
DRAYMANS MS
CHOUMERT RD
CHOUMERT MEWS
CHOUMERT GR
ALPHA ST
BELLENDEN RD
GROVE PK
THE BIRCHES
QUEENS CT
THE LIMES
CANNING CROSS
GROVE LA
Allot Gdns
A
B
64
C
33
34
76
JOHN HARRIS HO
REEDHAM ST
COSTA ST
MCDERMOTT RD
WAGHORN ST
ANSTEY RD
NIGEL RD
TROY TOWN FLATS
HUGUENOT SQ
PHILIP WLK
AUSTINS CT
SCYLLA RD
GALATEA SQ
IVANHOE RD
AVONDALE RISE
MALFORT RD
BROMAR RD
GROVE HILL RD
GLEBELANDS CL
MALDON CL
HOWDEN ST
WINGFIELD MEWS
MAXTED RD
SE15

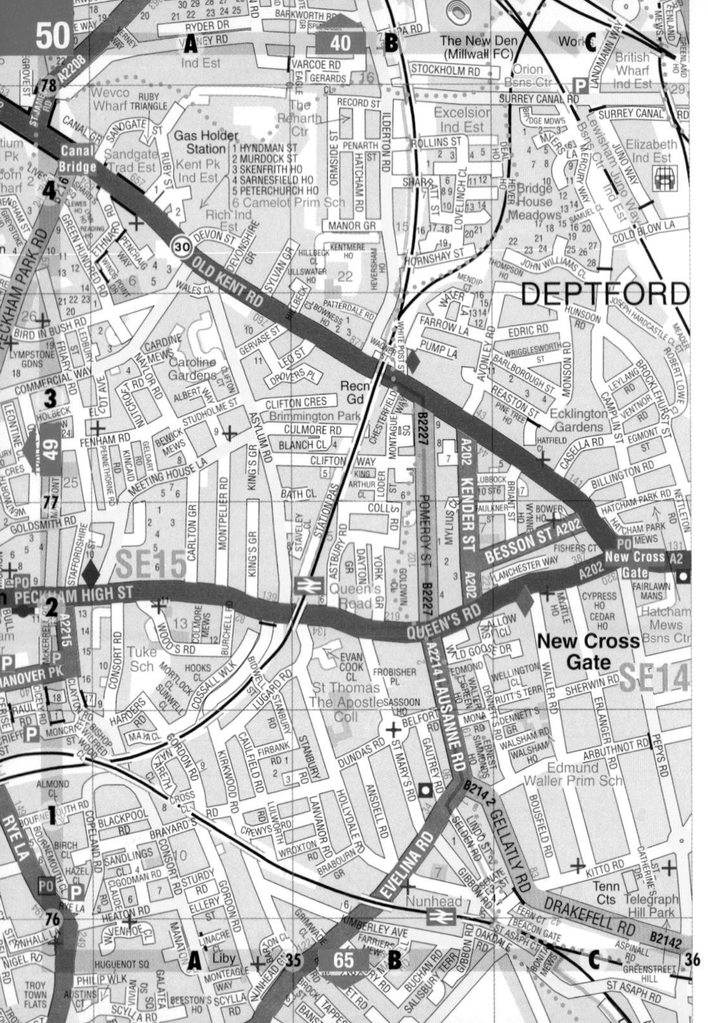

A
B
C
40
The New Den
(Millwall FC)
Works
British Wharf Ind Est
RYDER DR
VERNEY RD
Ind Est
BARKWORTH RD
VARCOE RD
GERARDS CL
STOCKHOLM RD
Orion Bsns Ctr
LANDMANN WAY
78
A2208
Wevco Wharf
RUBY TRIANGLE
RECORD ST
The Penarth Ctr
SURREY CANAL RD
Excelsior Ind Est
CANAL GR
SANDGATE ST
Gas Holder Station
1 HYNDMAN ST
2 MURDOCK ST
3 SKENFRITH HO
4 SARNESFIELD HO
5 PETERCHURCH HO
6 Camelot Prim Sch
ORMSIDE ST
PENARTH ST
HATCHAM RD
ILDERTON RD
ROLLINS ST
Elizabeth Ind Est
Lewisham Bsns Ctr
Juno Way Ind Est
JUNO WAY
MERCURY WAY
Canal Bridge
Sandgate Trad Est
Kent Pk Ind Est
RUBY ST
Rich Ind Est
SHARRATT ST
LOVELINCH CL
Bridge House Meadows
4
B216
MANOR GR
HORNSHAY ST
COLDBLOW LA
JOHN WILLIAMS CL
GREEN HUNDRED RD
ETHNARD RD
PENCRAIG WAY
DEVON ST
DEVONSHIRE GR
30
OLD KENT RD
SYLVAN GR
HILLBECK CL
KENTMERE HO
ULLSWATER HO
HEVERSHAM HO
22
THOMPSON HO
MENDIP CT
DEPTFORD
PECKHAM PARK RD
WINDSOR POINT
WALES CL
HILLBECK CL
BOWNESS CL
PATTERDALE RD
WATER LA
HUNSDON RD
JOSEPH HARDCASTLE CL
BIRD IN BUSH RD
LYMPSTONE GDNS
FRIARY RD
LEDBURY ST
CARDINE MEWS
NAYLOR RD
Caroline Gardens
GERVASE ST
LEO ST
DROVERS PL
WAGNER ST
WHITE POST ST
FARROW LA
PUMP LA
EDRIC RD
WRIGGLESWORTH ST
BARLBOROUGH ST
AVONLEY RD
MONSON RD
ROBERT LOWE CL
BROCKLEHURST ST
LEYLANG RD
COMMERCIAL WAY
3
HOLBECK ROW
TALBOT AVE
NUTCROFT RD
ALBERT WAY
CLIFTON CT
STUDHOLME ST
CLIFTON CRES
Brimmington Park
Recn Gd
CHESTERFIELD WAY
MONTAGUE SQ
B2227
REASTON ST
PINE TREE HO
Ecklington Gardens
CAMPLIN ST
VENTNOR RD
EGMONT ST
LEONTINE CL
49
FENHAM RD
PENNETHORNE RD
KINCAID RD
GELDART RD
BEWICK MEWS
ASYLUM RD
CULMORE RD
BLANCH CL
CLIFTON WAY
KING ARTHUR CL
LODER ST
A202
HATFIELD CL
CASELLA RD
BILLINGTON RD
MEETING HOUSE LA
KING'S GR
BATH CL
COLLS RD
POMEROY ST
KENDER ST
LUBBOCK ST
BRIANT ST
HATCHAM PARK RD
NETTLETON RD
WENTWORTH CRES
77
GOLDSMITH RD
STAFFORDSHIRE ST
CARLTON GR
MONTPELIER RD
STATION PAS
STAVELEY CL
ASTBURY RD
DAYTON GR
YORK GR
GOLDMIN CL
MYLIUS CL
FAULKNER ST
WYNNE HO
BOWER HO
HATCHAM PARK MEWS
SE15
BESSON ST
FISHERS CT
LANCHESTER WAY
PO
New Cross Gate
A2
FAIRLAWN MANS
PECKHAM HIGH ST
2
A2215
Queen's Road
QUEEN'S RD
MYRTLE HO
CYPRESS HO
CEDAR HO
Hatcham Mews Bsns Ctr
MCKERRELL RD
WOOD'S RD
COLMORE MEWS
BURCHELL RD
SALLOW CL
WILD GOOSE DR
New Cross Gate
SE14
HANOVER PK
CONSORT RD
Tuke Sch
HOOKS CL
MORTLOCK CL
SUNWELL CL
COSSALL WLK
BIDWELL ST
LUGARD RD
EVAN COOK CL
FROBISHER PL
A2214 LAUSANNE RD
EDMOND CT
WALTER GREEN HO
WELLINGTON CL
RUTT'S TERR
WALLER RD
SHERWIN RD
ERLANGER RD
CICELY RD
CLAYTON RD
BISHOP WILFRED WOOD CL
HARDERS RD
MAYA CL
St Thomas The Apostle Coll
SASSOON HO
BELFORT RD
MONA RD
SIMMONDS HO
DENNETT'S GR
DENNETT'S RD
WALSHAM RD
WALSHAM HO
ARBUTHNOT RD
PEPYS RD
MONCRIEFF ST
GORDON RD
NAZARETH CL
STANBURY RD
CAULFIELD RD
FIRBANK RD
KIRKWOOD RD
DUNDAS RD
ST MARY'S RD
GAUTREY RD
Edmund Waller Prim Sch
ALMOND CL
RYE LA
1
BOURNEMOUTH RD
BLACKPOOL RD
COPELAND RD
CROSS CL
BRAYARD'S RD
LULWORTH RD
CREWYS RD
LANVANOR RD
HOLLYDALE RD
ANSDELL RD
B214 2
GELLATLY RD
LINDO ST
SELDEN RD
BOUSFIELD RD
BIRCH CL
HAZEL CL
SANDLINGS CL
CONSORT RD
WROXTON RD
BRABOURN GR
EVELINA RD
GIBBON RD
SENATE ST
KITTO RD
ST CATHERINE'S DR
GODMAN RD
STURDY RD
CLAUDE RD
Nunhead
Tenn Cts
Telegraph Hill Park
PO
RYE LA
HEATON RD
ELLERY ST
GORDON RD
DRAKEFELL RD
B2142
76
FENHAM RD
MANATON CL
WIVENHOE CL
LINACRE CL
KIMBERLEY AVE
FARRIERS MEWS
FERN CT
BEACON GATE
ST ASAPH CT
NIGEL RD
HUGUENOT SQ
Liby
A
35
65
B
BUCHAN RD
SALISBURY TERR
GIBBON RD
OAKDALE RD
BONITA MEWS
C
ASPINALL RD
GREENSTREET HILL
36
TROY TOWN FLATS
PHILIP WLK
AUSTINS CT
VIVIAN SQ
GALATEA SQ
BEESTON'S HO
MONTEAGLE WAY
SCYLLA RD
NUNHEAD GR
ST ASAPH RD

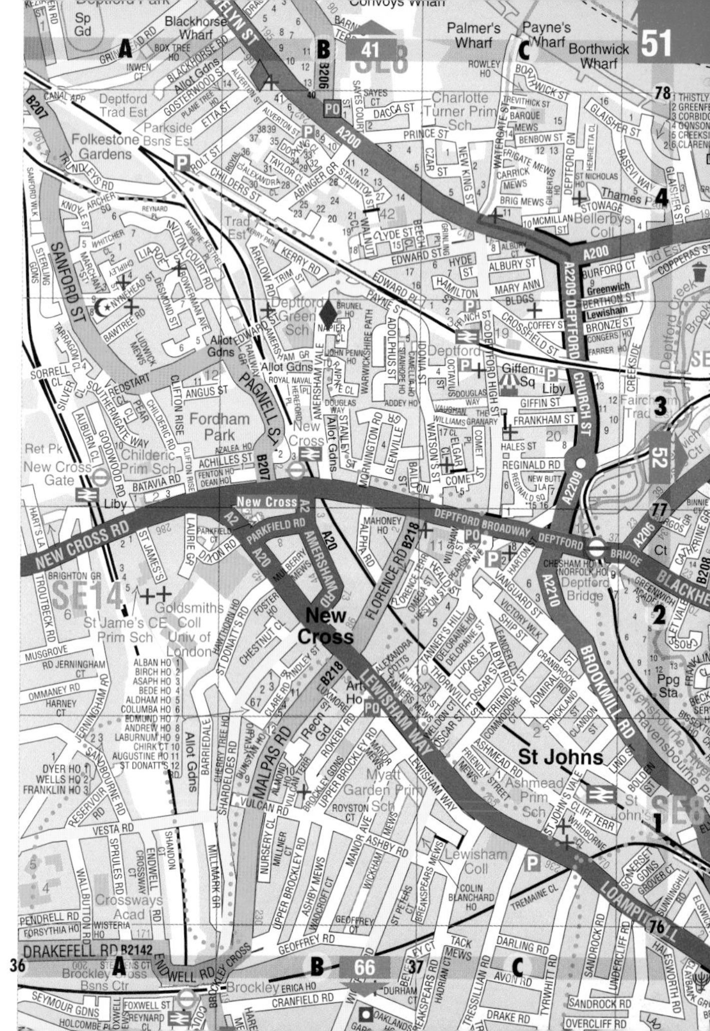

51
41
52
66
36
37
76
77
78
A
B
C
1
2
3
4
SE8
SE14
Convoys Wharf
Palmer's Wharf
Payne's Wharf
Borthwick Wharf
Blackhorse Wharf
Sp Gd
Deptford Park
EVELYN ST
GRINSTEAD RD
BOX TREE HO
BLACKHORSE RD
INWEN CT
Allot Gdns
GOSTERWOOD ST
PLANE TREE HO
ETTA ST
ALVERTON ST
B206
SAYES COURT
SAYES CT
DACCA ST
PO
A200
Charlotte Turner Prim Sch
PRINCE ST
ROWLEY HO
BORTHWICK ST
TREVITHICK ST
BARQUE MEWS
BENBOW ST
GLAISHER ST
HENRIETTA CL
DEPTFORD GN
WATERGATE ST
FRIGATE MEWS
CARRICK MEWS
BRIG MEWS
GILBERT HO
ST NICHOLAS HO
STOWAGE
Thames Pl
BASEVI WAY
MCMILLAN ST
Bellerbys Coll
1 THISTLY
2 GREENFE
3 CORBIDG
4 GONSON
5 CREEKSIL
6 CLARENC
B207
CANAL APP
Deptford Trad Est
Parkside Bsns Est
Folkestone Gardens
TRUNDLEYS RD
ROLT ST
CHILDERS ST
ROYAL
ALEXANDRA CL
TAYLOR CL
DORKING CL
ABINGER GR
STAUNTON ST
WALNUT
LYDE ST
BEECH
GRINLING PL
CZAR ST
NEW KING ST
SANFORD WLK
KNOYLE ST
ARCHER SQ
REYNARD PL
MILTON COURT RD
MAGPIE
KESTREL
Trad Est
KERRY PATH
KERRY RD
ARKLOW RD
TRIM ST
EDWARD ST
HYDE ST
ALBURY ST
A209 DEPTFORD CHURCH ST
BURFORD CT
Greenwich
BERTHON ST
Lewisham
BRONZE ST
CONGERS HO
FARRER HO
CREEKSIDE
COPPERAS ST
Ind Est
Deptford Creek
STERLING GDNS
SANFORD ST
WHITCHER CL
MARCHANT ST
CHIPLEY
LIARDET ST
NYNEHEAD ST
BAWTREE RD
DESMOND ST
BOWERMAN AVE
Deptford Green Sch
BRUNEL HO
NAPIER CL
EDWARD PL
HAMILTON ST
MARY ANN BLDGS
COFFEY ST
CROSSFIELD ST
FRENCH ST
Deptford
DEPTFORD HIGH ST
TARRAGON CL
LUDWICK MEWS
Allot Gdns
RAILWAY GR
JOHN PENN HO
WARWICKSHIRE PATH
ADOLPHUS ST
STANHOPE HO
CAMELLIA HO
IDONIA ST
OCTAVIUS ST
Giffen Sq
Liby
SORRELL CL
SILVER
SOUTHERNGATE WAY
REDSTART CL
PEAR CL
CHILDERIC RD
CLIFTON RISE
ANGUS ST
Fordham Park
PAGNELL ST
ROYAL NAVAL PL
HEREFORD
AMERSHAM VALE
DOUGLAS WAY
ADDEY HO
DOUGLAS WAY
VAUGHAN WILLIAMS
THE GRANARY
GIFFIN ST
FRANKHAM ST
HALES ST
Ret Pk
New Cross Gate
AUBURN CL
GOODWOOD RD
Childeric Prim Sch
AZALEA HO
ACHILLES ST
FENTON HO
DEAN HO
BATAVIA RD
New Cross
STANLEY ST
MORNINGTON RD
GLENVILLE GR
BAILDON ST
WATSON'S ST
ELGAR CL
COMET ST
COMET PL
REGINALD RD
REGINALD SQ
NEW BUTT LA
A2209
Fairchild Trad
HART'S LA
Liby
New Cross
A2
NEW CROSS RD
PARKFIELD RD
PARKFIELD CT
DIXON RD
LAURIE GR
ST JAMES'S
A20
MULBERRY MEWS
AMERSHAM RD
MAHONEY HO
ALPHA RD
FLORENCE RD
B218
DEPTFORD BROADWAY
WILSHAW ST
PEARSON'S AVE
HARTON ST
DEPTFORD BRIDGE
CHESHAM HO
NORFOLK HO
Deptford Bridge
A206
ARGOS
CATHERINE GR
B208
BLACKHEATH
GREENWICH ACADEMY
BINNIE CT
TROUTBECK RD
BRIGHTON GR
Goldsmiths Coll Univ of London
St James's CE Prim Sch
HAWTHORN HO
ST DONATT'S RD
FOSTER HO
CHESTNUT CL
New Cross
LEWISHAM WAY
FLORENCE TERR
OMEGA ST
HEALD ST
HESTON ST
VANGUARD ST
VICTORY WLK
SHIP ST
A2210
BROOKMILL RD
MUSGROVE RD
JERNINGHAM CT
JERNINGHAM RD
OMMANEY RD
HARNEY CT
ALBAN HO 1
BIRCH HO 2
ASAPH HO 3
BEDE HO 4
ALDHAM HO 5
COLUMBA HO 6
EDMUND HO 7
ANDREW HO 8
LABURNUM HO 9
CHIRK CT 10
AUGUSTINE HO 11
ST DONATT'S 12
Allot Gdns
BARRIEDALE
CHERRY TREE HO
FINDLEY ST
CLARE RD
LUXMORE ST
Art Ho
ALEXANDRA COTTS
TANNER'S HILL
TANNERS MEWS
NICHOLAS ST
DELORAINE HO
DELORAINE ST
THORNVILLE ST
LUCAS ST
OSCAR ST
ALBYN RD
LEANDER CT
FRIENDLY ST
CRANBROOK
ADMIRAL
STRICKLAND
CLANDON ST
COMMODORE CT
ASHMEAD RD
St Johns
LIND ST
BOLDEN ST
Ravensbourne River
Ravensbourne Pa
Ppg Sta
FRANKLIN
BECK
SERV
BISSEXTILE HO
DYER HO 1
WELLS HO 2
FRANKLIN HO 3
SANDBOURNE RD
RESERVOIR RD
SHARDELOES RD
DUNSTAN HO
MALPAS RD
Recn Gd
ROKEBY RD
ALMOND HO
VULCAN TERR
BROCKLEY GDNS
UPPER BROCKLEY RD
MANOR MEWS
Myatt Garden Prim Sch
LEWISHAM WAY
FRIENDLY STREET MEWS
Ashmead Prim Sch
ST JOHN'S VALE
CLIFF TERR
WHIDBORNE CL
St John's
VESTA RD
SPRULES RD
CROSSWAY CT
ENDWELL RD
SHANDON CT
MILLMARK GR
VULCAN RD
NURSERY CL
MILLNER CT
ROYSTON CT
MANOR AVE
ASHBY RD
WICKHAM MEWS
BREAKSPEARS MEWS
Lewisham Coll
COLIN BLANCHARD HO
TREMAINE CL
LOAMPIT VALE
SOMERSET GDNS
GROVER CT
SUNNINGHILL RD
ELSWICK RD
WALLBUTTON RD
Crossways Acad
PENDRELL RD
FORSYTHIA HO
WISTERIA RD
UPPER BROCKLEY RD
ASHBY MEWS
WOODCROFT CT
GEOFFREY CT
ST PETERS CT
BREAKSPEARS RD
HADRIAN CT
TACK MEWS
DARLING RD
AVON RD
TRESSILLIAN RD
TYRWHITT RD
SANDROCK RD
UNDERCLIFF RD
HALESWORTH RD
DRAKEFELL RD B2142
ENDWELL RD
BROCKLEY CROSS
GEOFFREY RD
BEVERLEY CT
Brockley Cross Bsns Ctr
Brockley
ERICA HO
CRANFIELD RD
DURHAM
OAKLANDS
SEYMOUR GDNS
FOXWELL ST
REYNARD CL
HOLCOMBE PL
DRAKE RD
SANDROCK RD
OVERCLIFF RD

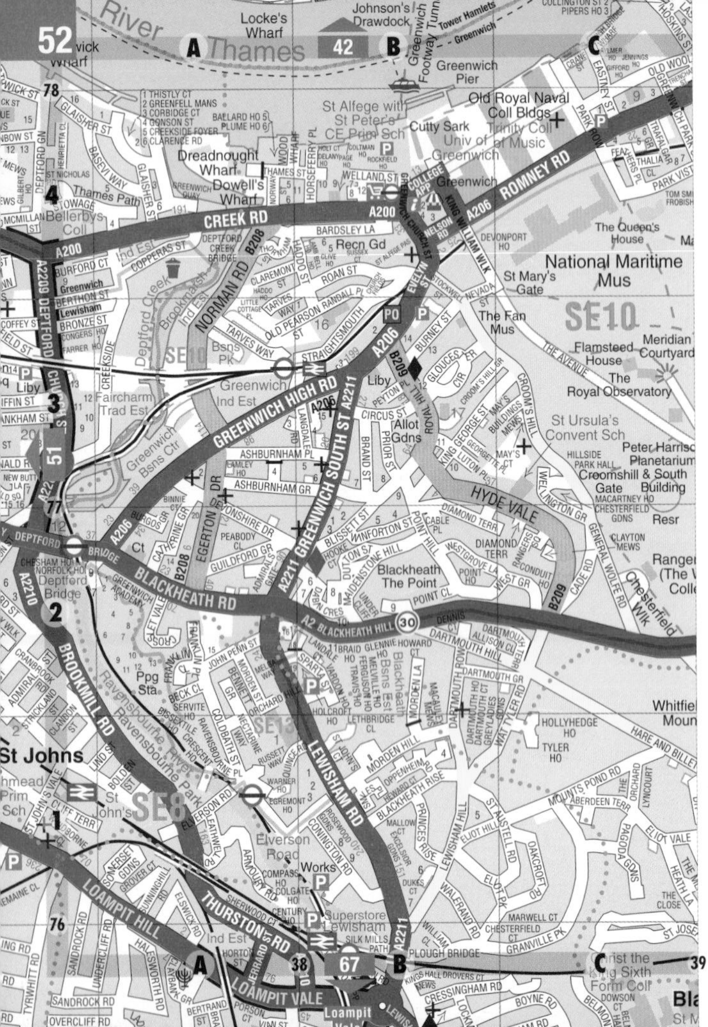
River Thames
Locke's Wharf
Johnson's Drawdock
Greenwich Footway Tunnel
Tower Hamlets
Greenwich
42
A
B
C
Greenwich Pier
Old Royal Naval Coll Bldgs
Trinity Coll of Music
Cutty Sark
Univ of Greenwich
St Alfege with St Peter's CE Prim Sch
Dreadnought Wharf
Dowell's Wharf
Thames Path
Bellerbys Coll
CREEK RD
A200
ROMNEY RD
A206
The Queen's House
National Maritime Mus
St Mary's Gate
The Fan Mus
SE10
Flamsteed House
Meridian Courtyard
The Royal Observatory
St Ursula's Convent Sch
Peter Harrison Planetarium
Croomshill & South Building
Resr
NORMAN RD
B208
Recn Gd
Deptford Creek
Brookmarsh Ind Est
Bsns Pk
Greenwich Ind Est
Faircharm Trad Est
Greenwich Bsns Ctr
GREENWICH HIGH RD
GREENWICH SOUTH ST
A2211
ROYAL HILL
B209
HYDE VALE
Allot Gdns
Liby
PO
DEPTFORD CHURCH ST
A209
51
4
3
2
1
DEPTFORD BRIDGE
Deptford Bridge
A2210
BROOKMILL RD
BLACKHEATH RD
A2 BLACKHEATH HILL
30
Blackheath The Point
Blackheath Bsns Est
DARTMOUTH ROW
Ppg Sta
Ravensbourne Park
Ravensbourne River
SE8
SE13
St Johns
LEWISHAM RD
LEWISHAM HILL
Elverson Road
Works
Superstore Lewisham
LOAMPIT HILL
LOAMPIT VALE
Loampit Vale
THURSTON RD
Ind Est
PLOUGH BRIDGE
67
38
39
76
77
78
Christ the King Sixth Form Coll

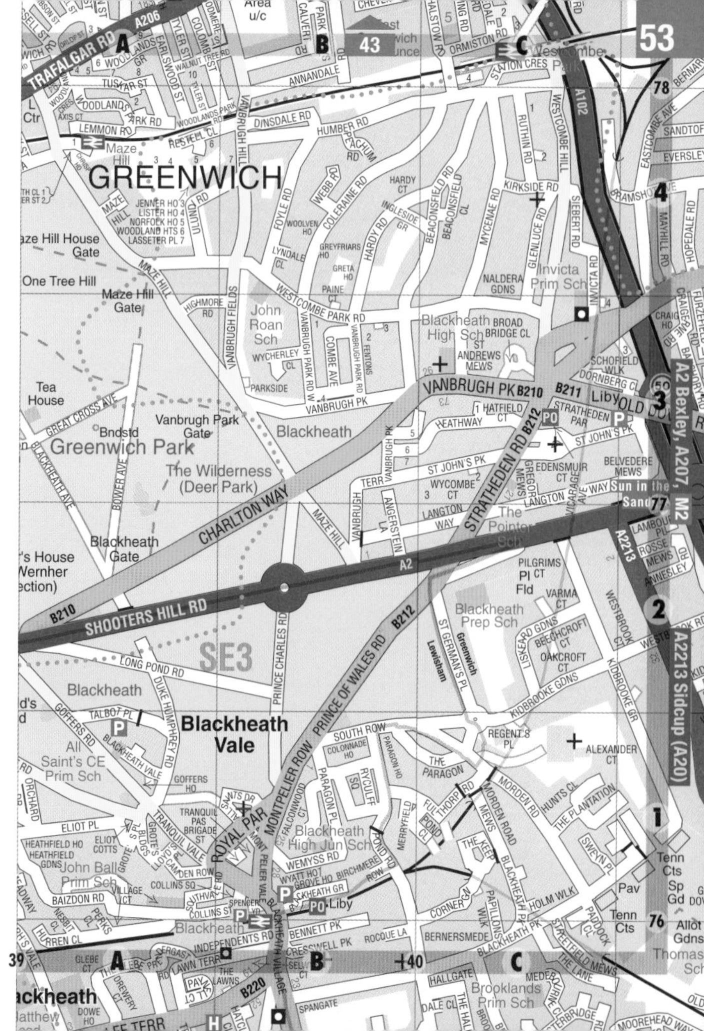

53
GREENWICH
Greenwich Park
Blackheath
Blackheath Vale
SE3
The Wilderness (Deer Park)
SHOOTERS HILL RD
CHARLTON WAY
VANBRUGH PK
STRATHEDEN RD
PRINCE OF WALES RD
PRINCE CHARLES RD
MAZE HILL
WESTCOMBE PARK RD
LONG POND RD
KIDBROOKE GDNS
A2 Bexley, A207, M2
A2213 Sidcup (A20)
John Roan Sch
Blackheath High Sch
Invicta Prim Sch
The Pointer Sch
Blackheath Prep Sch
All Saint's CE Prim Sch
Blackheath High Jun Sch
John Ball Prim Sch
Brooklands Prim Sch
Maze Hill
Westcombe Park
Tea House
Maze Hill Gate
Vanbrugh Park Gate
Blackheath Gate
One Tree Hill

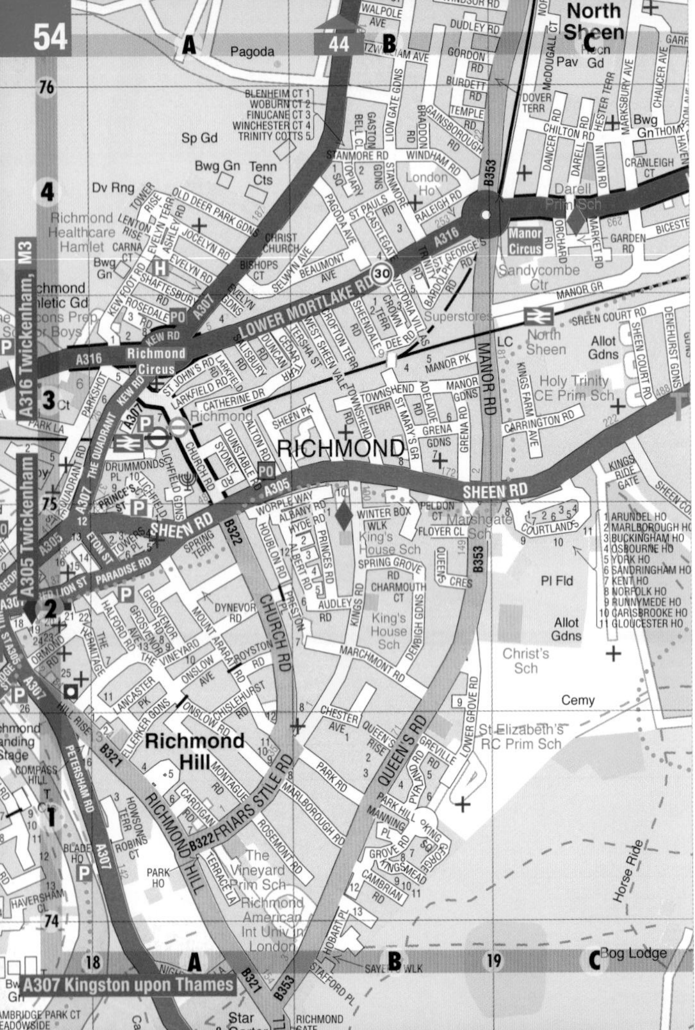

44
A
B
C
North Sheen
RICHMOND
Richmond Hill
Richmond Circus
Manor Circus
LOWER MORTLAKE RD
SHEEN RD
MANOR RD
QUEEN'S RD
CHURCH RD
RICHMOND HILL
FRIARS STILE RD
PETERSHAM RD
KEW RD
THE QUADRANT
PARADISE RD
RED LION ST
Pagoda
Sp Gd
Bwg Gn
Tenn Cts
Dv Rng
Richmond Healthcare Hamlet
CHRIST CHURCH
London Ho
Darell Prim Sch
Sandycombe Ctr
Superstores
North Sheen
Allot Gdns
Holy Trinity CE Prim Sch
King's House Sch
Marshgate Sch
Pl Fld
Christ's Sch
Cemy
St Elizabeth's RC Prim Sch
The Vineyard Prim Sch
Richmond American Int Univ in London
Horse Ride
Bog Lodge
1 ARUNDEL HO
2 MARLBOROUGH HO
3 BUCKINGHAM HO
4 OSBOURNE HO
5 YORK HO
6 SANDRINGHAM HO
7 KENT HO
8 NORFOLK HO
9 RUNNYMEDE HO
10 CARISBROOKE HO
11 GLOUCESTER HO
BLENHEIM CT 1
WOBURN CT 2
FINUCANE CT 3
WINCHESTER CT 4
TRINITY COTTS 5
A316 Twickenham, M3
A305 Twickenham
A307 Kingston upon Thames
76
75
74
18
19
4
3
2
1

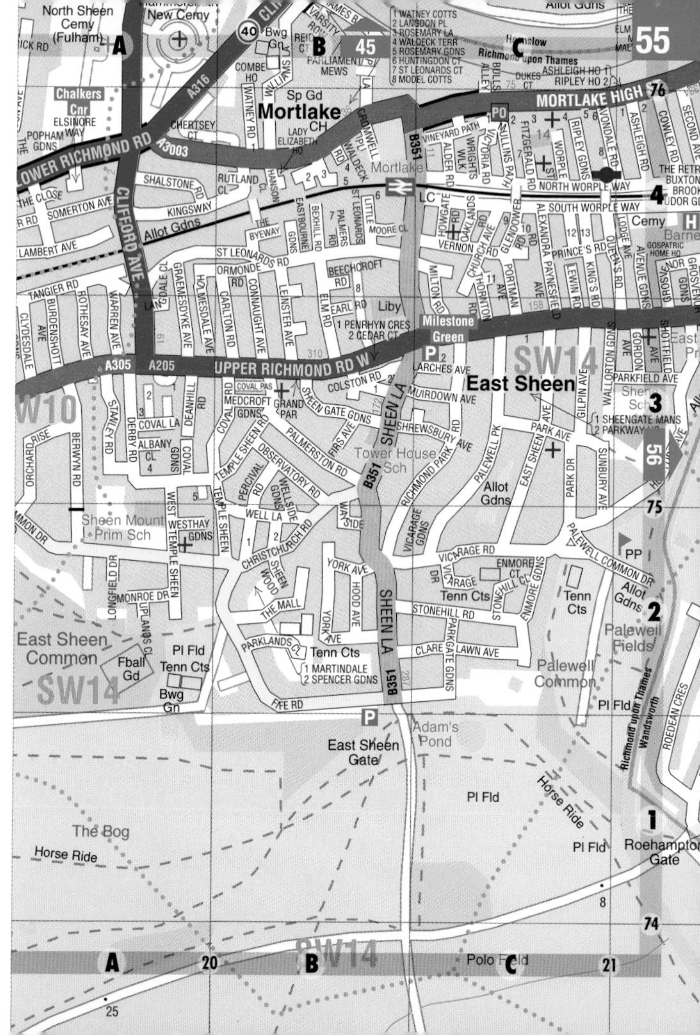

North Sheen Cemy (Fulham)
New Cemy
Mortlake
East Sheen
Milestone Green
UPPER RICHMOND RD W
MORTLAKE HIGH
LOWER RICHMOND RD
CLIFFORD AVE
SHEEN LA
East Sheen Common
East Sheen Gate
Adam's Pond
Roehampton Gate
Palewell Common
Palewell Fields
Tower House Sch
Sheen Mount Prim Sch
The Bog
Horse Ride
Polo Field
SW14
1 WATNEY COTTS
2 LANGDON PL
3 ROSEMARY LA
4 WALDECK TERR
5 ROSEMARY GDNS
6 HUNTINGDON CT
7 ST LEONARDS CT
8 MODEL COTTS
1 PENRHYN CRES
2 CEDAR CT
1 SHEENGATE MANS
2 PARKWAY
1 MARTINDALE
2 SPENCER GDNS
Richmond upon Thames
Wandsworth

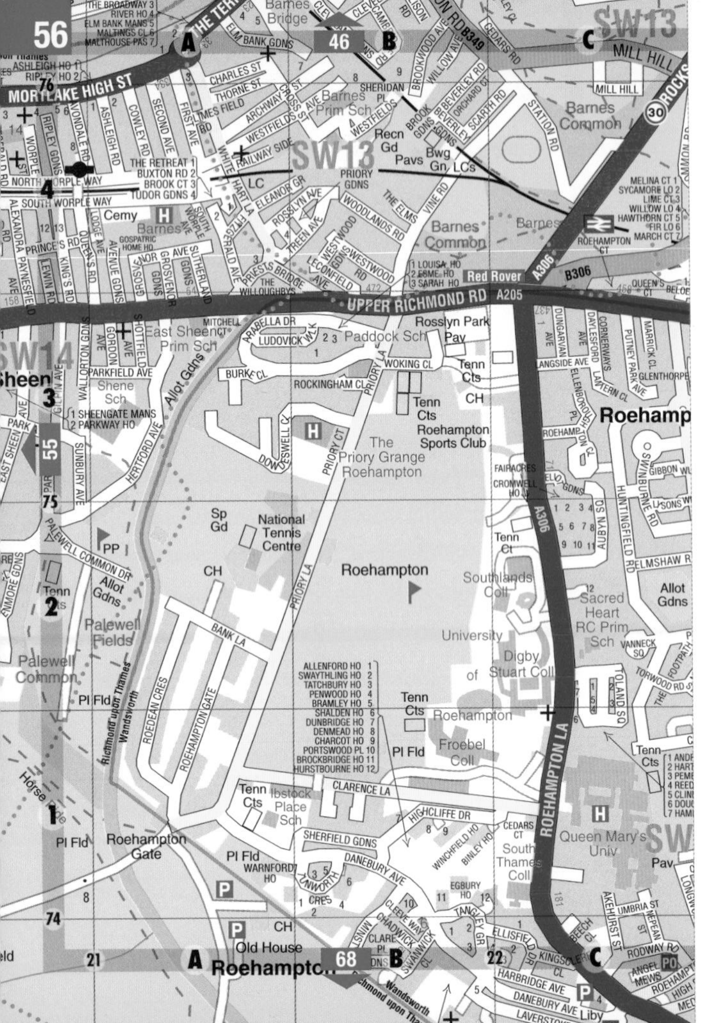
THE BROADWAY 3
RIVER HO 4
ELM BANK MANS 5
MALTINGS CL 6
MALTHOUSE PAS 7
THE TERR
Barnes Bridge
ELM BANK GDNS
46
A
B
C
SW13
MILL HILL
ASHLEIGH HO 1
RIPLEY HO 2
76
MORTLAKE HIGH ST
CHARLES ST
THORNE ST
ARCHWAY ST
CROSS ST
Barnes Prim Sch
SHERIDAN PL
WESTFIELDS
BROOKWOOD AVE
WILLOW AVE
BEVERLEY RD
ORCHARD CT
SCARTH RD
STATION RD
CEDARS RD
B349
Barnes Common
30
ROCKS
RIPLEY GDNS
AVONDALE RD
ASHLEIGH RD
COWLEY RD
SECOND AVE
FIRST AVE
LIMES FIELD RD
WESTFIELDS AVE
RAILWAY SIDE
Recn Gd
Pavs
Bwg Gn
LCs
BROOK GDNS
BEVERLEY GDNS
WORPLE ST
THE RETREAT 1
BUXTON RD 2
BROOK CT 3
TUDOR GDNS 4
NORTH WORPLE WAY
SOUTH WORPLE WAY
WHITE HART LA
LC
PRIORY GDNS
ELEANOR GR
ROSSLYN AVE
TREEN AVE
WOODLANDS RD
THE ELMS
VINE RD
MELINA CT 1
SYCAMORE LO 2
LIME CT 3
WILLOW LO 4
HAWTHORN CT 5
FIR LO 6
MARCH CT 7
Barnes
ROEHAMPTON CT
4
Cemy
H
Barnes
ALEXANDRA RD
PRINCE'S RD
QUEEN'S RD
LODGE AVE
GOSPATRIC HOME HO
SOUTH WORPLE AVE
FITZGERALD AVE
WESTWOOD GDNS
WESTWOOD RD
LECONFIELD AVE
1 LOUISA HO
2 ESME HO
3 SARAH HO
Red Rover
A306
B306
QUEEN'S CT
PAYNESFIELD AVE
LEWIN RD
KING'S RD
AVENUE GDNS
GROSVENOR AVE
GROSVENOR GDNS
SUTHERLAND GDNS
PRIESTS BRIDGE
THE WILLOUGHBYS
UPPER RICHMOND RD
A205
MITCHELL CT
ARABELLA DR
LUDOVICK WLK
Paddock Sch
Rosslyn Park
Pav
DUNGARVAN AVE
DAYLESFORD AVE
CORNERWAYS
PUTNEY PARK AVE
MARRICK CL
SW14
Sheen
WALLORTON GDNS
GORDON AVE
SHOTTFIELD AVE
East Sheen Prim Sch
PARKFIELD AVE
Shene Sch
BURKE CL
WOKING CL
Tenn Cts
LANGSIDE AVE
ELLENBOROUGH PL
LANTERN CL
GLENTHORPE
ROCKINGHAM CL
PRIORY LA
CH
Roehampton
3
GILPIN AVE
1 SHEENGATE MANS
2 PARKWAY HO
Allot Gdns
PARK
EAST SHEEN AVE
55
SUNBURY AVE
HERTFORD AVE
DOWNESWELL CL
H
PRIORY CT
The Priory Grange Roehampton
Roehampton Sports Club
ROEHAMPTON CL
FAIRACRES
CROMWELL HO
ELLOYD GDNS
SWINBURNE RD
GIBBON WK
HUNTINGFIELD RD
AUBYN SQ
75
PALEWELL PARK
Sp Gd
National Tennis Centre
Tenn Ct
A306
PALEWELL COMMON DR
PP
Roehampton
Southlands Coll
ELMSHAW RD
Allot Gdns
2
Tenn Cts
ENMORE GDNS
Palewell Fields
Palewell Common
BANK LA
University
of
Roehampton
Digby Stuart Coll
Sacred Heart RC Prim Sch
VANNECK SQ
TORWOOD RD
THE FOOTPATH
ALLENFORD HO 1
SWAYTHLING HO 2
TATCHBURY HO 3
PENWOOD HO 4
BRAMLEY HO 5
SHALDEN HO 6
DUNBRIDGE HO 7
DENMEAD HO 8
CHARCOT HO 9
PORTSWOOD PL 10
BROCKBRIDGE HO 11
HURSTBOURNE HO 12
Pl Fld
ROEDEAN CRES
ROEHAMPTON GATE
Richmond upon Thames
Wandsworth
Froebel Coll
TOLAND SQ
1 ANDR
2 HART
3 PEME
4 REED
5 CLIN
6 DOUG
7 HAMI
Horse Ride
1
Tenn Cts
Ibstock Place Sch
CLARENCE LA
HIGHCLIFFE DR
ROEHAMPTON LA
H
Pl Fld
Roehampton Gate
Pl Fld
SHERFIELD GDNS
WINCHFIELD HO
BINLEY HO
CEDARS CT
South Thames Coll
Queen Mary's Univ
Pav
WARNFORD HO
DANEBURY AVE
TUNWORTH CRES
EGBURY HO
P
74
CLEEVE WAY
CHADWICK
TANGLEY GR
ELLISFIELD DR
UMBRIA ST
NEPEAN ST
AKEHURST ST
BEECH CL
CH
Old House
P
CLARE PL
SWANWICK CL
KINGSCLERE CL
RODWAY RD
PO
ANGEL MEWS
21
A
Roehampton
68
B
22
C
HARBRIDGE AVE
DANEBURY AVE
LAVERSTOKE
Liby
Richmond upon Thames
Wandsworth

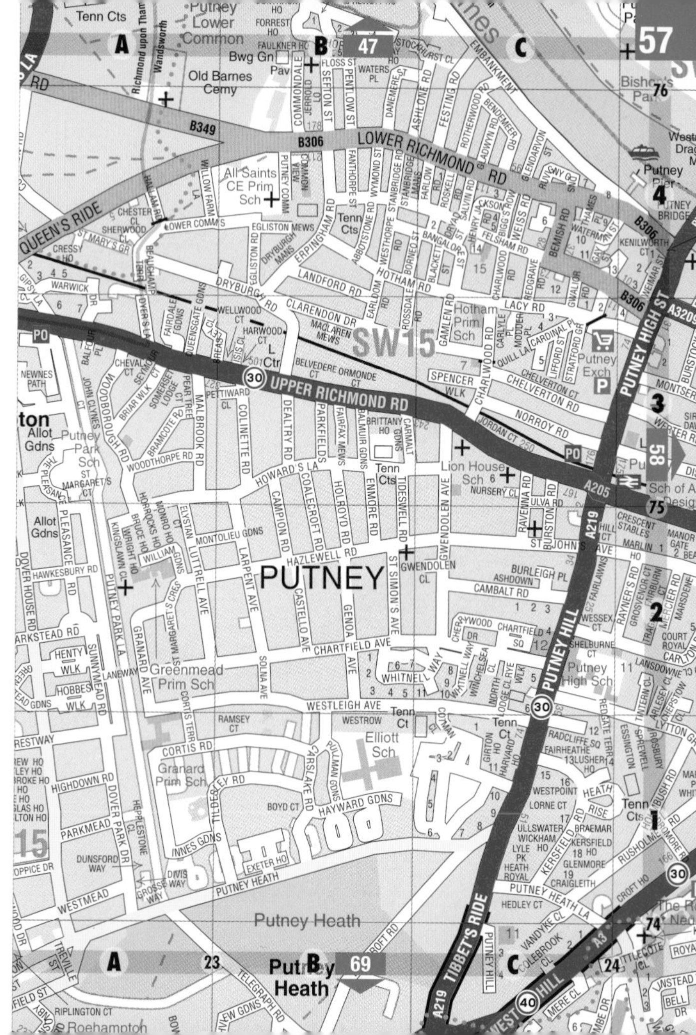

A
B
47
C
Tenn Cts
Putney Lower Common
Richmond upon Thames
Wandsworth
Old Barnes Cemy
Bwg Gn
Pav
FORREST HO
FAULKNER HO
COMMONDALE
JERROLD
FLOSS ST
SEFTON ST
PENTLOW ST
WATERS PL
DANEMERE ST
ASHLONE RD
STOCKHURST CL
FESTING RD
EMBANKMENT
Bishop's Park
76
B349
B306
LOWER RICHMOND RD
ROTHERWOOD RD
BENDEMEER RD
GLADWYN RD
GLENDARVON ST
Westminster Dragon Mu
Putney Pier
4
PUTNEY BRIDGE
QUEEN'S RIDE
HALLAM RD
WILLOW FARM LA
All Saints CE Prim Sch
PUTNEY COMM
COMMON VIEW
FANTHORPE ST
WYMOND ST
STANBRIDGE RD
STANBRIDGE MANS
FARLOW RD
ROSKELL RD
SALVIN RD
CHESTER CL
SHERWOOD CT
LOWER COMMS
EGLISTON MEWS
ERPINGHAM RD
Tenn Cts
ABBOTSTONE RD
WESTHORPE RD
BORNEO ST
BANGALORE ST
BLACKETT ST
DRYAD ST
HENRY JACKSON RD
BIGG'S ROW
WEISS RD
BEMISH RD
THAMES PL
WATERMAN ST
GAY ST
KENILWORTH CT
B306
ST MARY'S GR
CRESSY HO
BEAUCHAMP TERR
EGLISTON RD
DRYBURGH MANS
LANDFORD RD
HOTHAM RD
FELSHAM RD
CHARLWOOD RD
REDGRAVE RD
GWALIOR RD
WEIMAR ST
GIPSY LA
WARWICK DR
DRYBURGH RD
CLARENDON DR
EARLDOM RD
ROSSDALE RD
GAMLEN RD
Hotham Prim Sch
LACY RD
A3209
PUTNEY HIGH ST
PO
BALFOUR PL
FAIRDALE GDNS
QUEENSGATE GDNS
WELLWOOD CT
HARWOOD CT
MACLAREN MEWS
SW15
CARLYLE PL
MODDER PL
CARDINAL PL
LIFFORD ST
STRATFORD GR
Putney Exch
BURSTOCK RD
NEWNES PATH
CHEVAL CT
SEYMOUR
ISIS CL
L Ctr
BELVEDERE CT
ORMONDE CT
QUILL LA
SPENCER WLK
CHELVERTON CT
CHELVERTON RD
MONTSERRAT
3
ton
Allot Gdns
JOHN CLYNES CT
WOODBOROUGH RD
BRIAR WLK
SOMERSET LODGE
PEAR TREE CT
PETTIWARD CL
30
UPPER RICHMOND RD
NORROY RD
SIR ABRAHAM DAWES
WERTER RD
Putney Park Sch
BRAMCOTE RD
MALBROOK RD
COLINETTE RD
DEALTRY RD
PARKFIELDS
FAIRFAX MEWS
BALMUIR GDNS
BRITTANY HO
CARMALT GDNS
JORDAN CT
PO
58
THE PLEASANCE
ST MARGARET'S CT
WOODTHORPE RD
HOWARD'S LA
Tenn Cts
Lion House Sch
DISRAELI
Sch of Art Design
75
Allot Gdns
PLEASANCE RD
HORROCKS HO
MONRO HO
ELYSTAN CT
CAMPION RD
COALECROFT RD
HOLROYD RD
ENMORE RD
TIDESWELL RD
GWENDOLEN AVE
NURSERY CL
RAVENNA RD
BURSTON RD
ULVA RD
A205
A219
CRESCENT STABLES
MANOR GATE
DOVER HOUSE RD
HAWKESBURY RD
KINGSLAWN CL
WRIGHT HO
BRUCE HO
WILLIAM GDNS
MONTOLIEU GDNS
LUTTRELL AVE
LARPENT AVE
HAZLEWELL RD
ST SIMON'S AVE
GWENDOLEN CL
ST JOHN'S AVE
HILL CT
MARLIN HO
BEAUMONT
PUTNEY
BURLEIGH PL
ASHDOWN
CAMBALT RD
FAIRLAWNS
RAYNER'S RD
GROSVENOR CT
FAIRBURN CT
MERCIER RD
MARSDENE
2
ARKSTEAD RD
HENTY WLK
SUNNYMEAD RD
PUTNEY PARK LA
GRANARD AVE
ST MARGARET'S CRES
CASTELLO AVE
GENOA AVE
CHARTFIELD AVE
CHERRYWOOD DR
CHARTFIELD SQ
WESSEX CT
SHELBURNE CT
PUTNEY HILL
COURT ROYAL
CARLTON DR
LANSDOWNE CT
GREENMEAD GDNS
HOBBES WLK
LANEWAY
Greenmead Prim Sch
SOLNA AVE
WHITNELL WAY
WINCHELSEA CL
NORTH LODGE CL
RYE WLK
Putney High Sch
TINTERN CL
ARLESEY CL
CHEPSTOW CL
CORTIS TERR
WESTLEIGH AVE
Tenn Ct
RAMSEY CT
WESTROW
COTMAN CL
Tenn Ct
REDGATE TERR
ESSINGTON
SPREWELL
ROSBURY
LYTTON GR
RESTWAY
CORTIS RD
Elliott Sch
GIRTON HO
HARVARD HO
RADCLIFFE SQ
FAIRHEATHE
LUSHER HO
HIGHDOWN RD
DOVER PARK DR
Granard Prim Sch
TILDESLEY RD
PULLMAN GDNS
CARSLAKE RD
WESTPOINT
HEATH RISE
HOMEBUSH RD
MAPLE PINE WHITE
BOYD CT
HAYWARD GDNS
LORNE CT
Tenn Cts
1
PARKMEAD
HEPPLESTONE CL
ULLSWATER
WICKHAM HO
BRAEMAR
KERSFIELD RD
KERSFIELD HO
LYLE PK
HEATH ROYAL
GLENMORE
CRAIGLEITH
RUSHOLME RD
15
OPPICE DR
DUNSFORD WAY
INNES GDNS
EXETER HO
DIVIS WAY
GROSSE WAY
PUTNEY HEATH
PUTNEY HEATH LA
HEDLEY CT
CROFT HO
30
H
The Royal Neuro
WESTMEAD
Putney Heath
TIBBET'S RIDE
PUTNEY HILL
VANDYKE CL
COLEBROOK CL
A3
74
LITTLECOTE CL
ROYAL
TREVILLE ST
A
23
B
Putney Heath
69
C
24
TELEGRAPH RD
A219
40
WEST HILL
IMERE CL
MBE DR
UNSTEAD WAY
BELL DR
RIPLINGTON CT
Roehampton
FIELD ST
VIEW GDNS

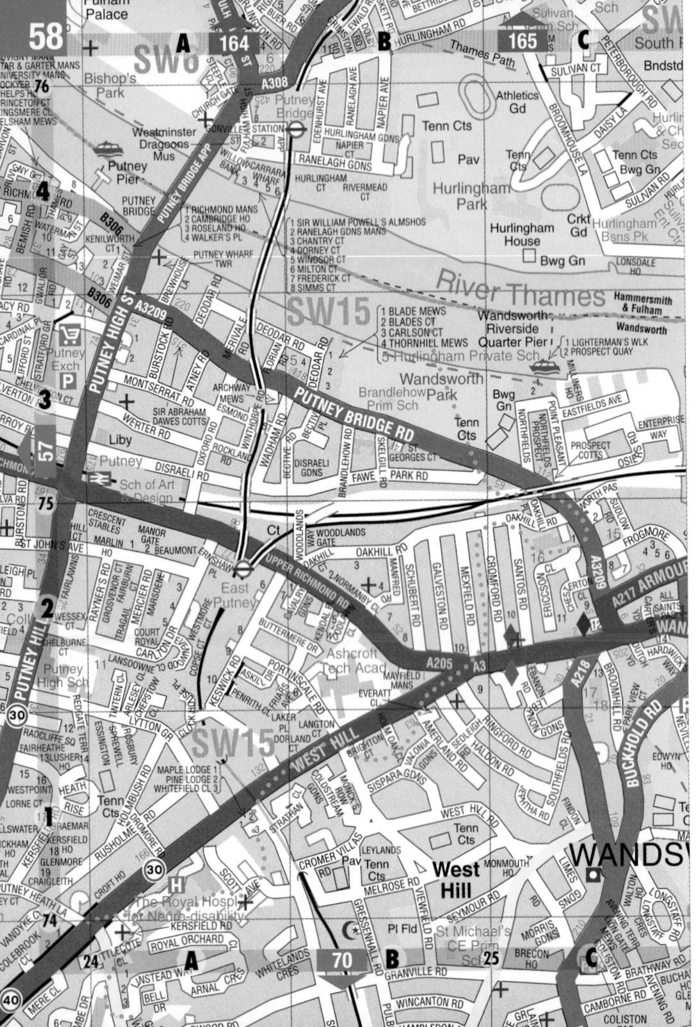

Fulham Palace
SW6
Bishop's Park
Westminster Dragoons Mus
Putney Pier
Putney Bridge
Hurlingham Park
Hurlingham House
River Thames
SW15
Wandsworth Riverside Quarter Pier
Wandsworth Park
Brandlehow Prim Sch
PUTNEY BRIDGE RD
PUTNEY HIGH ST
PUTNEY BRIDGE APP
UPPER RICHMOND RD
WEST HILL
PUTNEY HILL
East Putney
Putney Exch
Liby
Sch of Art & Design
Ashcroft Tech Acad
Putney High Sch
The Royal Hospl for Neuro-disability
St Michael's CE Prim Sch
West Hill
WANDSW
Hammersmith & Fulham
Wandsworth

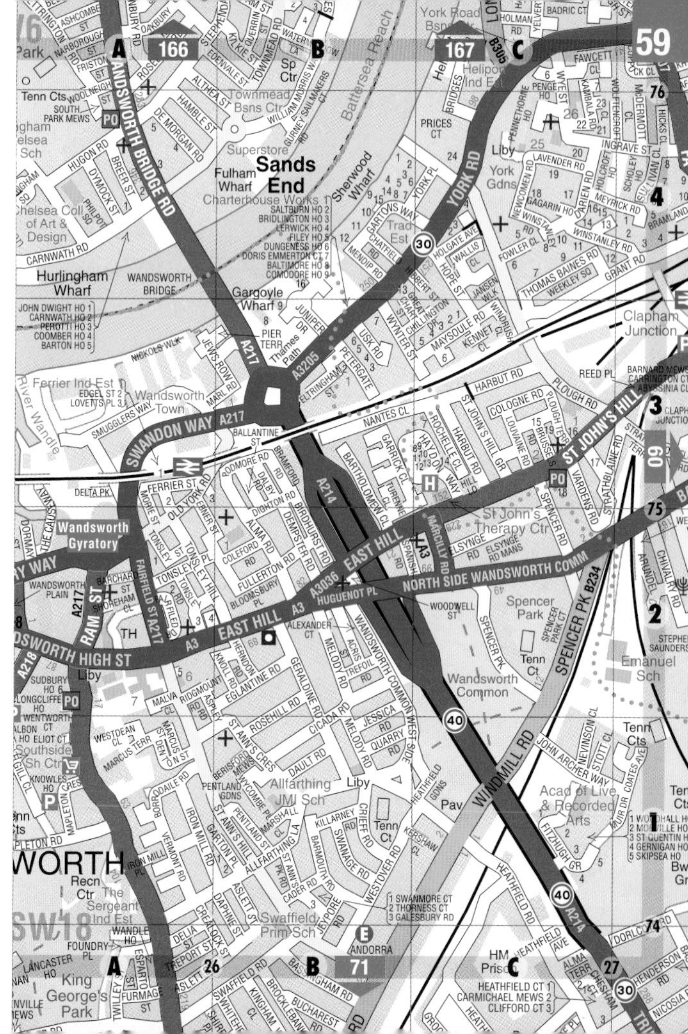
166
167
71
60
A
B
C
Sands End
Fulham Wharf
Charterhouse Works
Townmead Bsns Ctr
Superstore
Battersea Reach
Sherwood Wharf
York Road Bsns Ctr
Heliport Ind Est
Hurlingham Wharf
Chelsea Coll of Art & Design
Wandsworth Bridge
Gargoyle Wharf
Thames Path
Ferrier Ind Est
River Wandle
Wandsworth Town
Wandsworth Gyratory
Swandon Way
Wandsworth Bridge Rd
York Rd
East Hill
Wandsworth High St
North Side Wandsworth Comm
St John's Hill
Clapham Junction
St John's Therapy Ctr
Spencer Park
Wandsworth Common
Windmill Rd
Spencer Pk
Emanuel Sch
Acad of Live & Recorded Arts
Allfarthing JMI Sch
Swaffield Prim Sch
Southside Sh Ctr
The Sergeant Ind Est
King George's Park
HM Prison
SW18
A217
A3205
A214
A3036
A3
B305
B234
A218
Trad Est
Tenn Cts
Liby
PO
Recn Ctr
Pav
Bwg Gn
SALTBURN HO 2
BRIDLINGTON HO 3
LERWICK HO 4
FILEY HO 5
DUNGENESS HO 6
DORIS EMMERTON CT 7
BALTIMORE HO 8
COMODORE HO 9
JOHN DWIGHT HO 1
CARNWATH HO 2
PEROTTI HO 3
COOMBER HO 4
BARTON HO 5
EDGEL ST 2
LOVETTS PL 3
BARNARD MEWS 1
CARRINGTON CT 2
ABYSSINIA CL 3
1 WOODHALL HO
2 MORVILLE HO
3 ST QUENTIN HO
4 GERNIGAN HO
5 SKIPSEA HO
1 SWANMORE CT
2 THORNESS CT
3 GALESBURY RD
HEATHFIELD CT 1
CARMICHAEL MEWS 2
CLIFFORD CT 3
STEPHEN SAUNDERS CT

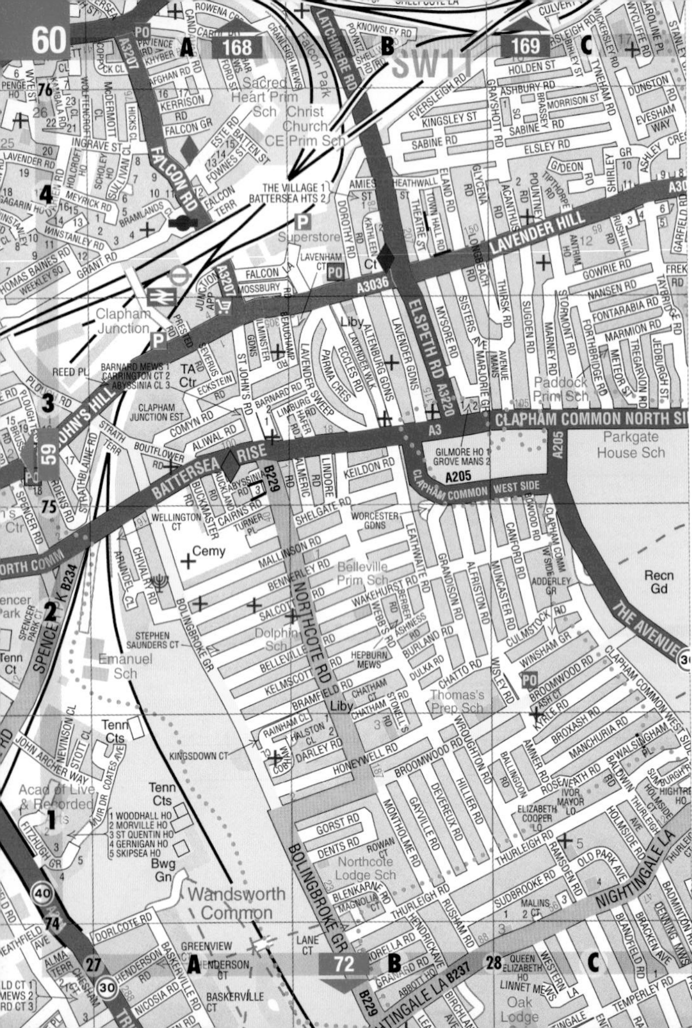
168
169
SW11
A
B
C
Falcon Park
Sacred Heart Prim Sch
Christ Church CE Prim Sch
LATCHMERE RD
FALCON RD
A3207
KNOWSLEY RD
HOLDEN ST
ASHBURY RD
MORRISON ST
EVERSLEIGH RD
KINGSLEY ST
SABINE RD
ELSLEY RD
DUNSTON RD
EVESHAM WAY
KERRISON RD
FALCON GR
INGRAVE ST
LAVENDER RD
MEYRICK RD
WINSTANLEY RD
GRANT RD
THOMAS BAINES RD
WEEKLEY SQ
THE VILLAGE 1
BATTERSEA HTS 2
Superstore
FALCON TERR
LAVENDER HILL
A3036
GIDEON RD
TIPTHORPE RD
ELAND RD
GLYCENA RD
ACANTHUS RD
POUNTNEY RD
RUSH HILL RD
GOWRIE RD
NANSEN RD
FONTARABIA RD
MARMION RD
TAYBRIDGE RD
JEDBURGH ST
METEOR ST
TREGARVON RD
FORTHBRIDGE RD
STORMONT RD
MARNEY RD
SUGDEN RD
THIRSK RD
MYSORE RD
SISTERS AVE
LONGBEACH RD
ELSPETH RD
A3220
LAVENDER GDNS
ALTENBURG GDNS
LAVENDER WLK
ECCLES RD
PARMA CRES
LAVENDER SWEEP
BEAUCHAMP RD
ILMINSTER GDNS
ST JOHN'S RD
Liby
Clapham Junction
FALCON LA
LAVENHAM CT
MOSSBURY RD
Paddock Prim Sch
CLAPHAM COMMON NORTH SIDE
A3
A205
Parkgate House Sch
GILMORE HO 1
GROVE MANS 2
CLAPHAM COMMON WEST SIDE
KEILDON RD
LINDORE RD
ALMERIC RD
BATTERSEA RISE
B229
ST JOHN'S HILL
BARNARD MEWS 1
CARRINGTON CT 2
ABYSSINIA CL 3
REED PL
TA Ctr
CLAPHAM JUNCTION EST
COMYN RD
ALIWAL RD
ECKSTEIN RD
BOUTFLOWER RD
STRATH TERR
STRATHBLAINE RD
PLOUGH RD
SPENCER RD
59
75
NORTH COMM
WELLINGTON CT
BUCKMASTER RD
CAIRNS RD
SHELGATE RD
WORCESTER GDNS
MALLINSON RD
Cemy
BENNERLEY RD
Belleville Prim Sch
WAKEHURST RD
SALCOTT RD
NORTHCOTE RD
Dolphin Sch
BELLEVILLE RD
KELMSCOTT RD
BRAMFIELD RD
HEPBURN MEWS
CHATHAM RD
STONELL'S RD
LEATHWAITE RD
GRANDISON RD
ALFRISTON RD
MUNCASTER RD
CANFORD RD
ADDERLEY GR
CULMSTOCK RD
WINSHAM GR
BROOMWOOD RD
Recn Gd
THE AVENUE
Thomas's Prep Sch
WISLEY RD
CHATTO RD
DULKA RD
BURLAND RD
WROUGHTON RD
HILLIER RD
DEVEREUX RD
GAYVILLE RD
MONTHOLME RD
HONEYWELL RD
DARLEY RD
KINGSDOWN CT
RAINHAM CL
HALSTON CL
BOLINGBROKE GR
CHIVALRY RD
ARUNDEL CL
STEPHEN SAUNDERS CT
Emanuel Sch
SPENCER PK
B234
Spencer Park
Tenn Ct
Tenn Cts
NEVINSON CL
STOTT CL
JOHN ARCHER WAY
COATES AVE
MUIR DR
Acad of Live & Recorded Arts
1 WOODHALL HO
2 MORVILLE HO
3 ST QUENTIN HO
4 GERNIGAN HO
5 SKIPSEA HO
FITZHUGH GR
Bwg Gn
Wandsworth Common
GORST RD
DENTS RD
ROWAN CT
Northcote Lodge Sch
BLENKARNE RD
MAGNOLIA CT
THURLEIGH RD
HENDRICK AVE
RUSHAM RD
BALLINGDON RD
AMNER RD
KYRLE RD
BROXASH RD
MANCHURIA RD
WALSINGHAM PL
BALDWIN RD
ROSENEATH RD
IVOR MAYOR LO
ELIZABETH COOPER LO
HOLMSIDE RD
THURLEIGH AVE
NIGHTINGALE LA
OLD PARK AVE
RAMSDEN RD
SUDBROOKE RD
MALINS CT
BLANDFIELD RD
BRACKEN AVE
DENNING MWS
BADMINTON RD
CLAPHAM COMMON WEST SIDE
DORLCOTE RD
HEATHFIELD AVE
ALMA TERR
CHESHAM
HENDERSON RD
BASKERVILLE RD
NICOSIA RD
GREENVIEW CT
HENDERSON CT
BASKERVILLE CT
LANE CT
72
GRANARD RD
ABBOTT HO
NIGHTINGALE LA B237
BIRCHLANDS AVE
QUEEN ELIZABETH HO
LINNET MEWS
WESTERN LA
TEMPERLEY RD
Oak Lodge
74
27
28
30
40

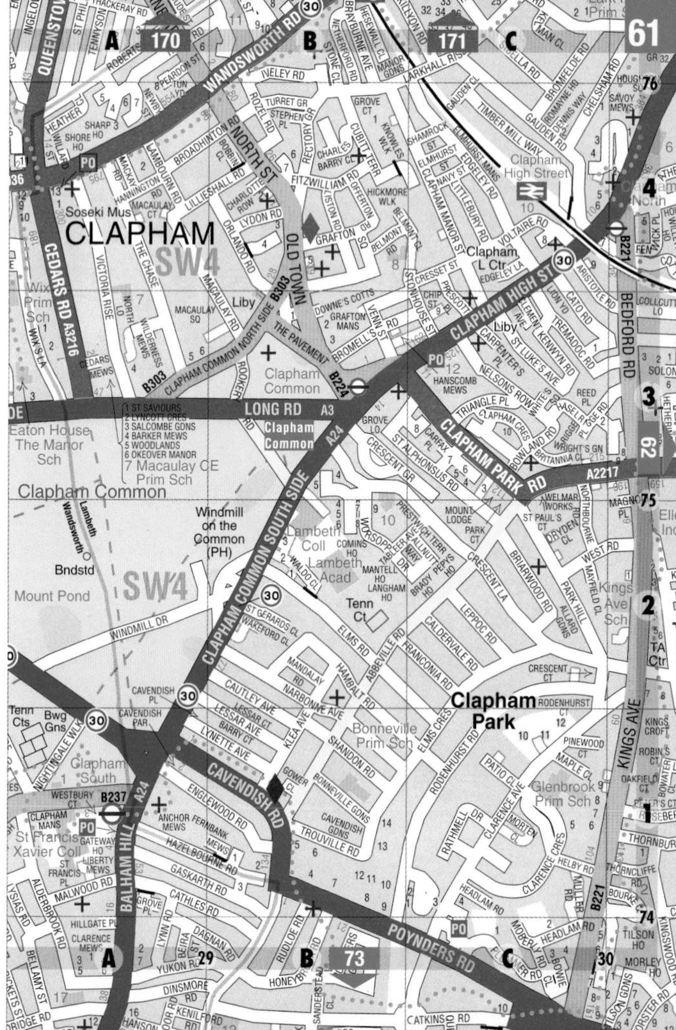

CLAPHAM
SW4
Clapham Common
Clapham Park
Clapham High Street
Clapham North
Clapham South
Clapham Common
WANDSWORTH RD
CLAPHAM HIGH ST
CLAPHAM PARK RD
CLAPHAM COMMON SOUTH SIDE
CLAPHAM COMMON NORTH SIDE
LONG RD
CEDARS RD
BEDFORD RD
KINGS AVE
CAVENDISH RD
POYNDERS RD
BALHAM HILL
OLD TOWN
NORTH ST
WINDMILL DR
Windmill on the Common (PH)
Lambeth Coll
Lambeth Acad
Bonneville Prim Sch
Glenbrook Prim Sch
St Francis Xavier Coll
Macaulay CE Prim Sch
Eaton House The Manor Sch
Soseki Mus
Mount Pond
1 ST SAVIOURS
2 LYNCOTT CRES
3 SALCOMBE GDNS
4 BARKER MEWS
5 WOODLANDS
6 OKEOVER MANOR
170
171
73
62

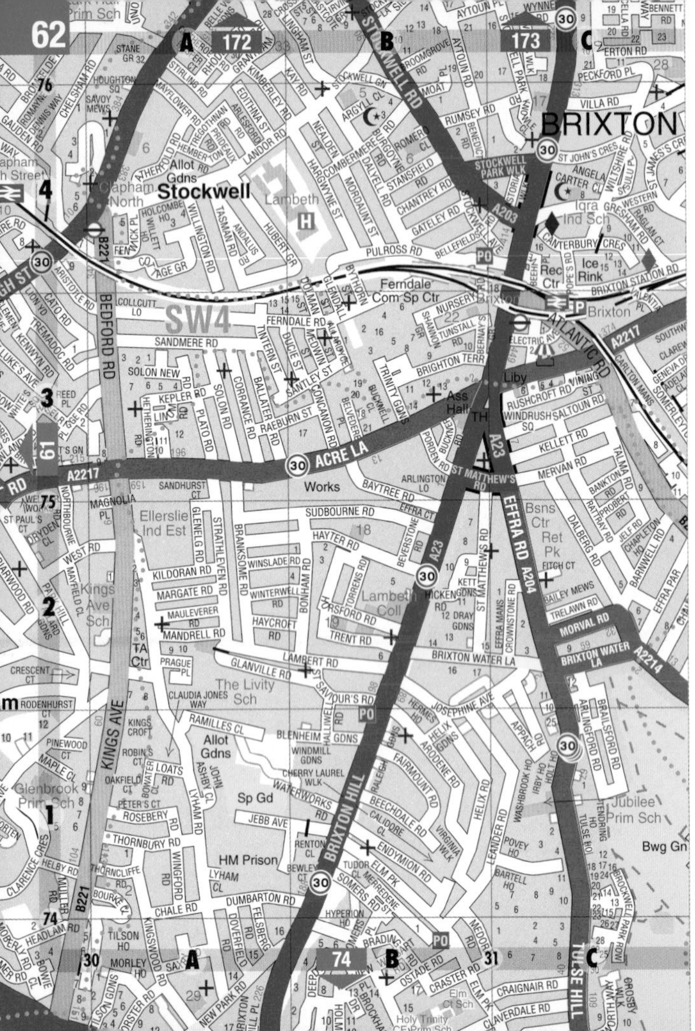

172
173
74
61
A
B
C
1
2
3
4
BRIXTON
Stockwell
SW4
Clapham North
Clapham High Street
Prim Sch
STANE GR
HOUGHTON SQ
SAVOY MEWS
CHELSHAM RD
BROMFELDE RD
ROMAYNE
DENNIS WAY
GAUDEN RD
STIRLING RD
MAYFLOWER RD
BELLEVUE
KIMBERLEY RD
GRANTHAM
LINGHAM ST
KAY RD
EDITHNA ST
ARLESFORD RD
REGOTHNAN
PRIDEAUX RD
HEMBERTON RD
LANDOR RD
ATHERFOLD RD
Allot Gdns
HOLCOMBE HO
WILLETT HO
WILLINGTON RD
TASMAN RD
ANDALUS RD
HUBERT GR
Lambeth
H
NEALDEN ST
HARGWYNE ST
COMBERMERE RD
MORDAUNT ST
DALYELL RD
BURGOYNE RD
ARGYLL CL
STOCKWELL GN
STOCKWELL RD
BROOMGROVE RD
AYTOUN RD
AYTOUN PL
MOAT PL
RUMSEY RD
BENEDICT RD
ROMERO CL
STANSFIELD RD
CHANTREY RD
GATELEY RD
BELLEFIELDS RD
PULROSS RD
STOCKWELL PARK WLK
STOCKWELL PARK RD
WYNNE RD
KNOWLE CL
VILLA RD
PECKFORD PL
ST JOHN'S CRES
WILTSHIRE RD
ST JAMES'S CRES
ANGELA CARTER CL
Iqra Ind Sch
WESTERN RD
GRESHAM RD
RAGLAN CT
CANTERBURY CRES
Rec Ctr
Ice Rink
POPE'S RD
BRIXTON STATION RD
A203
PO
ASTORIA WLK
STOCKWELL AVE
COTTAGE GR
FENWICK PL
ARISTOTLE RD
LION YD
CATO RD
TREMADOC RD
KENWYN RD
LUKE'S AVE
BEDFORD RD
B221
COLLCUTT LO
SANDMERE RD
SOLON NEW RD
KEPLER RD
LINOM RD
HETHERINGTON RD
SOLON RD
CORRANCE RD
BALLATER RD
TINTERN ST
DUCIE ST
MEDWIN ST
ALLARDYCE ST
SANTLEY ST
CONCANON RD
RAEBURN ST
FERNDALE RD
DOLMAN ST
GLENDALL ST
BYTHORN ST
Ferndale Com Sp Ctr
NURSERY RD
SHANNON GR
TUNSTALL RD
BERNAY'S GR
BRIGHTON TERR
TRINITY GDNS
BUCKNER CL
BELVEDERE PL
Ass Hall
TH
Liby
ELECTRIC AVE
Brixton
ATLANTIC RD
A2217
CARLTON MANS
SOMERLEYTON
GENEVA DR
VINING ST
RUSHCROFT RD
WINDRUSH SQ
SALTOUN RD
KELLETT RD
MERVAN RD
TALMA RD
BANKTON RD
RATTRAY RD
PROBERT RD
JELF RD
CHAPLETON HO
DALBERG RD
BARNWELL RD
EFFRA PAR
Bsns Ctr
Ret Pk
FITCH CT
BAILEY MEWS
TRELAWN RD
MORVAL RD
BRIXTON WATER LA
A2214
A23
A204
EFFRA RD
ST MATTHEW'S RD
ACRE LA
30
Works
BAYTREE RD
ARLINGTON LO
PORDEN RD
SUDBOURNE RD
EFFRA CT
HAYTER RD
BEVERSTONE RD
SANDHURST CT
MAGNOLIA PL
Ellerslie Ind Est
GLENELG RD
STRATHLEVEN RD
BRANKSOME RD
WINSLADE RD
BONHAM RD
WINTERWELL RD
HAYCROFT RD
TORRENS RD
HORSFORD RD
TRENT RD
Lambeth Coll
HICKEN RD
KETT GDNS
DRAY GDNS
EFFRA MANS
CROWNSTONE RD
KILDORAN RD
MARGATE RD
MAULEVERER RD
MANDRELL RD
NORTHBOURNE
WEST RD
MAYFIELD CL
PARK HILL
ST PAUL'S CT
DRYDEN CL
Kings Ave Sch
TA Ctr
PRAGUE PL
GLANVILLE RD
LAMBERT RD
ST SAVIOUR'S RD
The Livity Sch
CLAUDIA JONES WAY
RAMILLES CL
CRESCENT CT
RODENHURST CT
PINEWOOD CT
MAPLE CL
Glenbrook Prim Sch
KINGS AVE
KINGS CROFT
ROBIN'S CT
LOATS RD
OAKFIELD CT
BOWATER CL
PETER'S CT
ROSEBERY RD
THORNBURY RD
THORNCLIFFE RD
BOURKE CL
WINGFORD RD
LYHAM RD
LYHAM CL
JOHN ASHBY CL
Allot Gdns
Sp Gd
HM Prison
JEBB AVE
WATERWORKS RD
CHERRY LAUREL WLK
WINDMILL GDNS
BLENHEIM GDNS
HALLIWELL RD
BRIXTON HILL
RENTON CL
BEWLEY CT
TUDOR CL
ELM PK
SOMERS RD
MERREDENE ST
HERMES HO
HELIX GDNS
HELIX RD
ARODENE RD
JOSEPHINE AVE
FAIRMOUNT RD
BEECHDALE RD
CALIDORE CL
VIRGINIA WLK
ENDYMION RD
RALEIGH GDNS
LEANDER RD
WASHBROOK HO
IRBY HO
HOLT HO
APPACH RD
POVEY HO
BARTELL HO
ARLINGFORD RD
BRAILSFORD RD
Jubilee Prim Sch
TENDRING HO
TULSE HO
TULSE HILL
Bwg Gn
BROCKWELL PARK ROW
CROSBY WLK
WORTHY
HELBY RD
CLARENCE CRES
MULLER RD
HEADLAM RD
BOWIE CL
TILSON HO
MORLEY HO
CHALE RD
KINGSWOOD RD
DUMBARTON RD
DOVERFIELD RD
FELSBERG RD
NEW PARK RD
HYPERION HO
BRADING RD
OSTADE RD
CRASTER RD
ELM PK
MEDORA RD
CRAIGNAIR RD
CLAVERDALE RD
Elm Ct Sch
Holy Trinity CE Prim Sch
TILSON GDNS

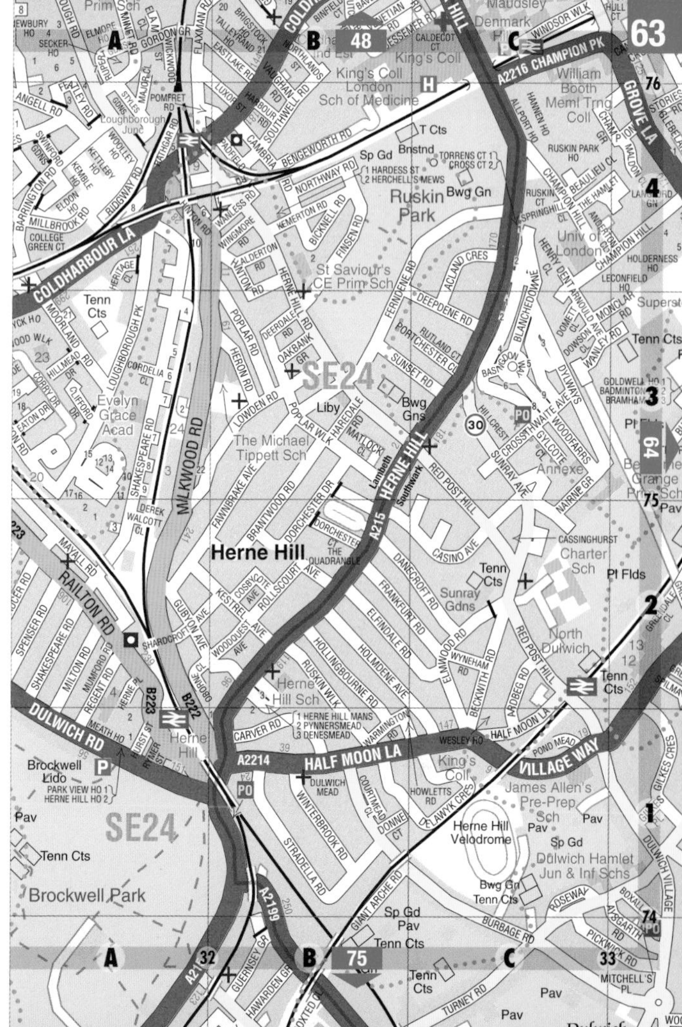

A
B
C
48
75
64
Herne Hill
SE24
Coldharbour La
Milkwood Rd
Herne Hill
A215
Half Moon La
A2214
Village Way
Dulwich Rd
Railton Rd
A2216 Champion Pk
Grove La
Denmark Hill
Ruskin Park
King's Coll
King's Coll London Sch of Medicine
William Booth Meml Trng Coll
Univ of London
St Saviour's CE Prim Sch
The Michael Tippett Sch
Evelyn Grace Acad
Loughborough Junc
Charter Sch
North Dulwich
James Allen's Pre-Prep Sch
Herne Hill Velodrome
Dulwich Hamlet Jun & Inf Schs
Herne Hill Sch
Brockwell Lido
Brockwell Park
Sunray Gdns
Liby
Bwg Gns
Tenn Cts
Pav
Sp Gd
Pl Flds
Lambeth
Southwark
Red Post Hill
Casino Ave
Ferndene Rd
Deepdene Rd
Dulwich Village
Giant Arche Rd
Burbage Rd
Stradella Rd
Winterbrook Rd
Turney Rd
A2199
B223
B222

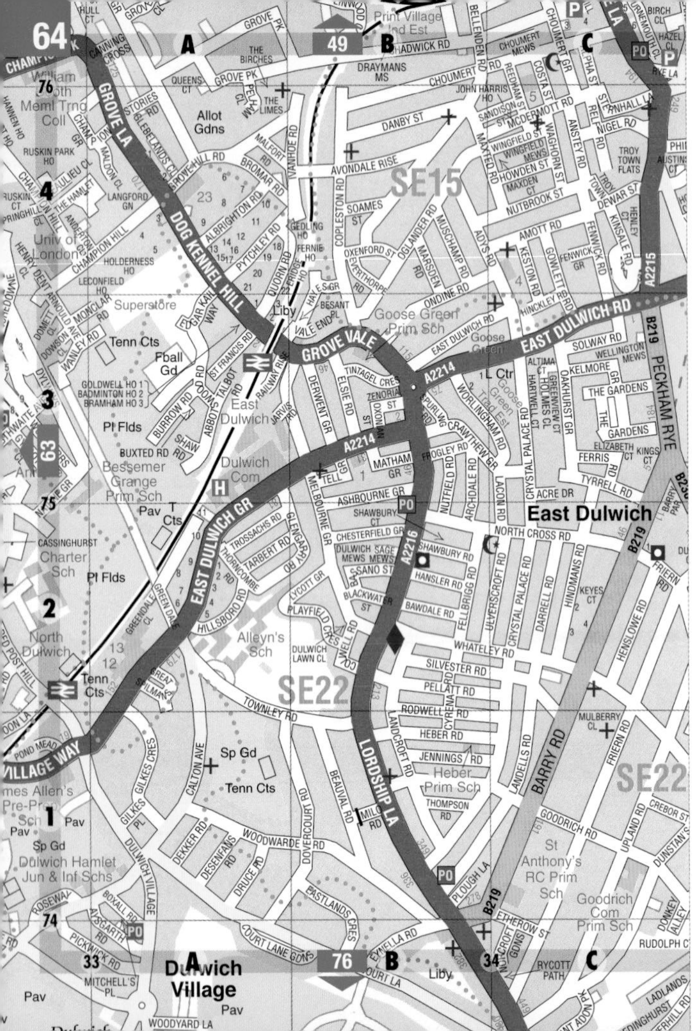

49
76
63
SE15
SE22
East Dulwich
Dulwich Village
North Dulwich
GROVE LA
DOG KENNEL HILL
GROVE VALE
EAST DULWICH RD
EAST DULWICH GR
LORDSHIP LA
PECKHAM RYE
BARRY RD
VILLAGE WAY
CHAMPION HILL
A2214
A2216
A2215
B219
Allot Gdns
Superstore
Tenn Cts
Fball Gd
Pl Flds
Bessemer Grange Prim Sch
Dulwich Com
Alleyn's Sch
Goose Green Prim Sch
Heber Prim Sch
St Anthony's RC Prim Sch
Goodrich Com Prim Sch
Dulwich Hamlet Jun & Inf Schs
Charter Sch
Univ of London
William Booth Meml Trng Coll
Print Village Ind Est
Liby
Sp Gd
Pav
L Ctr
Goose Green Trad Est

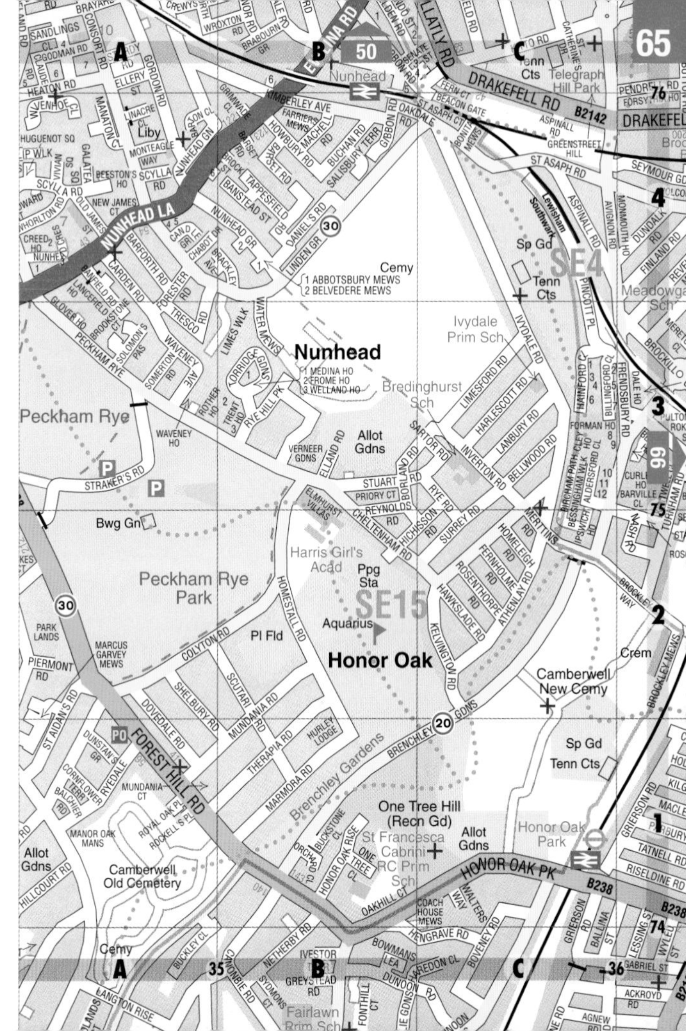

50
66
76
75
74
35
36

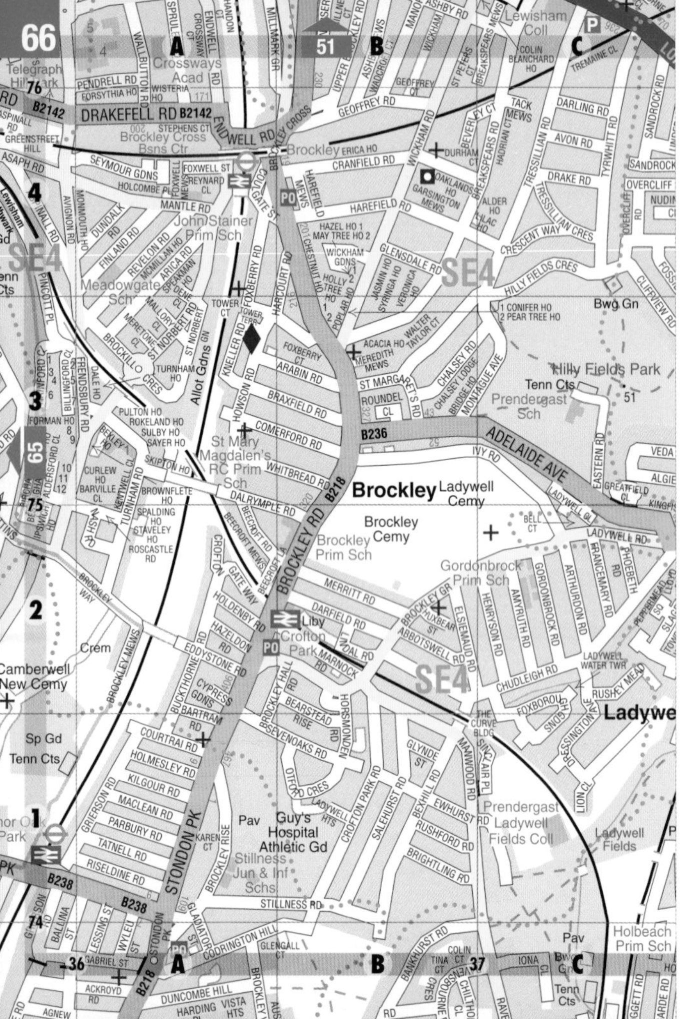

A
B
C
51
4
3
2
1
65
Telegraph Hill Park
Crossways Acad
DRAKEFELL RD B2142
Brockley Cross Bsns Ctr
ENDWELL RD
BROCKLEY CROSS
Brockley
Lewisham Coll
COLIN BLANCHARD HO
TREMAINE CL
GEOFFREY RD
CRANFIELD RD
HAREFIELD RD
SEYMOUR GDNS
FOXWELL ST
HOLCOMBE PL
MANTLE RD
John Stainer Prim Sch
SE4
Meadowgate Sch
DARLING RD
AVON RD
DRAKE RD
SANDROCK
OVERCLIFF
CRESCENT WAY
HILLY FIELDS CRES
Bwg Gn
Hilly Fields Park
Tenn Cts
Prendergast Sch
ADELAIDE AVE
B236
IVY RD
Brockley
Ladywell Cemy
Brockley Cemy
Brockley Prim Sch
St Mary Magdalen's RC Prim Sch
BROCKLEY RD
B218
WHITBREAD RD
COMERFORD RD
BRAXFIELD RD
ARABIN RD
FOXBERRY CT
Allot Gdns
Gordonbrock Prim Sch
LADYWELL RD
MERRITT RD
DARFIELD RD
Liby
Crofton Park
ABBOTSWELL RD
CHUDLEIGH RD
Ladywell
Crem
Camberwell New Cemy
Sp Gd
Tenn Cts
HOLDENBY RD
HAZELDON RD
EDDYSTONE RD
COURTRAI RD
HOLMESLEY RD
KILGOUR RD
MACLEAN RD
PARBURY RD
TATNELL RD
RISELDINE RD
STONDON PK
B238
Pav
Guy's Hospital Athletic Gd
Stillness Jun & Inf Schs
STILLNESS RD
Prendergast Ladywell Fields Coll
Ladywell Fields
Holbeach Prim Sch
CODRINGTON HILL
DUNCOMBE HILL
BROCKLEY RISE
SEVENOAKS RD
BEARSTEAD RISE
CROFTON PARK RD
SALEHURST RD
BEXHILL RD
EWHURST RD
RUSHFORD RD
BRIGHTLING RD
36
37
74
75
76

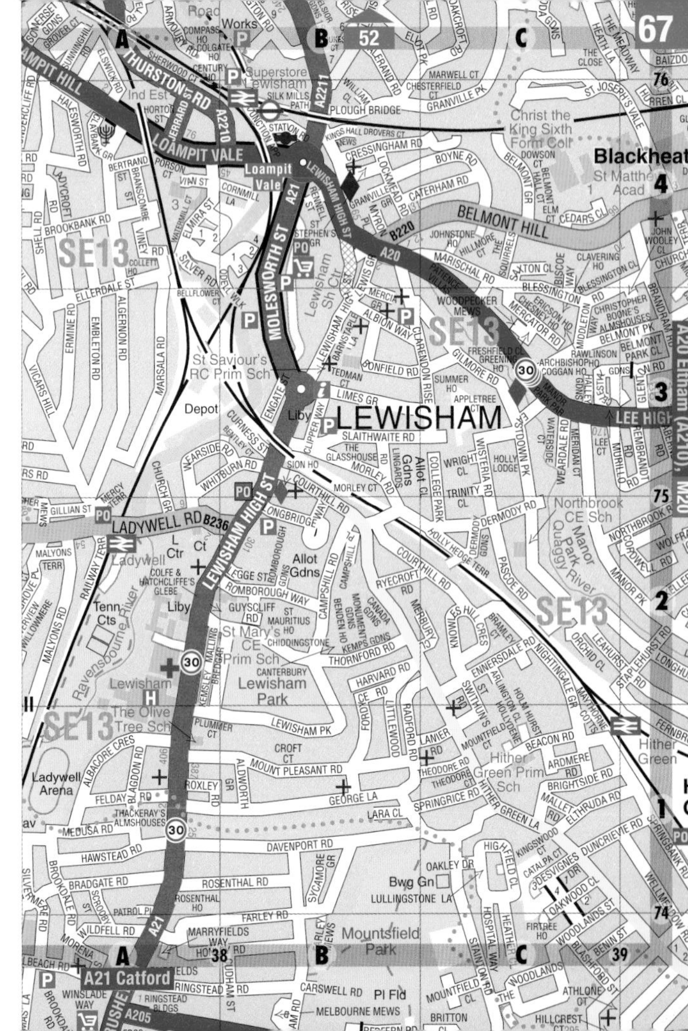

A
B
C
52
LOAMPIT HILL
THURSTON RD
LOAMPIT VALE
Loampit Vale
LEWISHAM HIGH ST
MOLESWORTH ST
A21
A20
B220
BELMONT HILL
Blackheath
SE13
LEWISHAM
Lewisham Sh Ctr
Superstore Lewisham
Christ the King Sixth Form Coll
St Matthew Acad
St Saviour's RC Prim Sch
Depot
Liby
LADYWELL RD
B236
Ladywell
Northbrook CE Sch
Manor Park
Quaggy River
Allot Gdns
St Mary's CE Prim Sch
Lewisham Park
Lewisham
The Olive Tree Sch
Ladywell Arena
Hither Green Prim Sch
Hither Green
Bwg Gn
Mountsfield Park
A21 Catford
A205
A20 Eltham (A210), M20
LEE HIGH
PLOUGH BRIDGE
CRESSINGHAM RD
BOYNE RD
CATERHAM RD
MARISCHAL RD
BLESSINGTON RD
GILMORE RD
LIMES GR
SLAITHWAITE RD
MORLEY RD
COURTHILL RD
LEWISHAM PK
MOUNT PLEASANT RD
GEORGE LA
DAVENPORT RD
ROSENTHAL RD
HITHER GREEN LA
SPRINGBANK RD
ELLERDALE ST
BROOKBANK RD
VICARS HILL
HAWSTEAD RD
MEDUSA RD
NIGHTINGALE GR
ENNERSDALE RD
MANOR PK
STAPLEHURST RD
DUNCRIEVIE RD
ELTHRUDA RD
BRIGHTSIDE RD
76
75
74
38
39
4
3
2
1

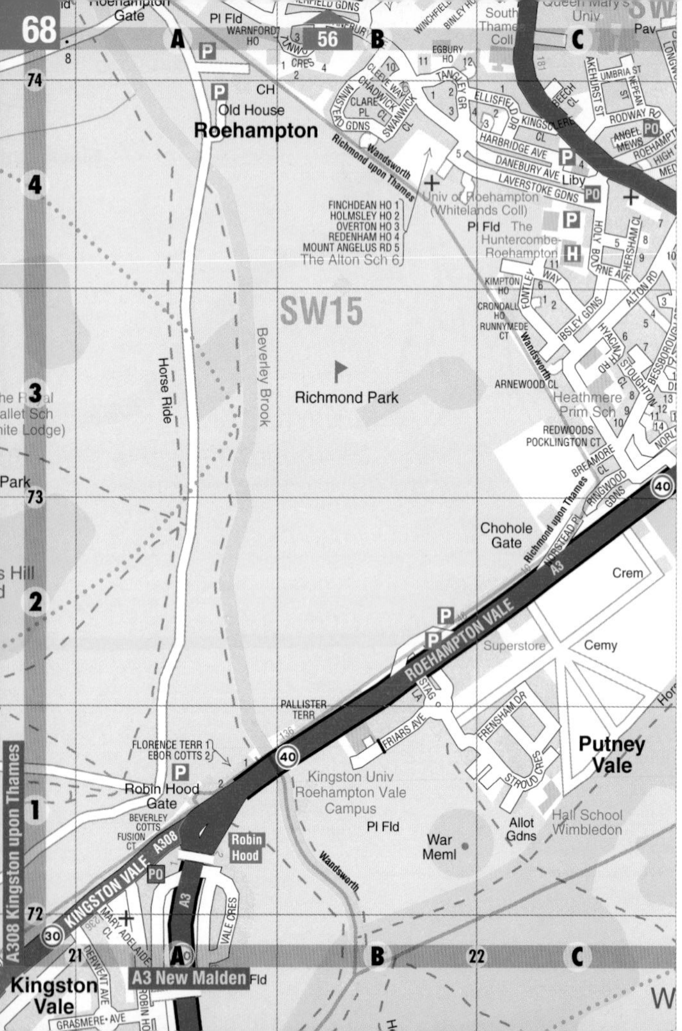

Roehampton Gate
Pl Fld
WARNFORD HO
56
Old House
CH
Roehampton
Richmond upon Thames
Wandsworth
FINCHDEAN HO 1
HOLMSLEY HO 2
OVERTON HO 3
REDENHAM HO 4
MOUNT ANGELUS RD 5
The Alton Sch 6
Univ of Roehampton (Whitelands Coll)
Pl Fld
The Huntercombe-Roehampton
South Thames Coll
Queen Mary's Univ
Pav
EGBURY HO
TANGLEY GR
ELLISFIELD DR
KINGSCLERE CL
HARBRIDGE AVE
DANEBURY AVE
LAVERSTOKE GDNS
Liby
PO
MINSTEAD GDNS
CLARE PL
CHADWICK CL
SWANWICK CL
CLEEVE WAY
UMBRIA ST
NEPEAN ST
AKEHURST ST
RODWAY RD
ANGEL MEWS
ROEHAMPTON HIGH ST
BEECH CL
HOLYBOURNE AVE
HERSHAM CL
KIMPTON HO
CRONDALL HO
RUNNYMEDE CT
FONTLEY WAY
IBSLEY GDNS
ALTON RD
HYACINTH RD
STOUGHTON CL
BESSBOROUGH
ARNEWOOD CL
Heathmere Prim Sch
REDWOODS
POCKLINGTON CT
BREAMORE CL
RINGWOOD GDNS
SW15
Richmond Park
Horse Ride
Beverley Brook
The Royal Ballet Sch (White Lodge)
Park
Chohole Gate
NORSTEAD PL
A3
Crem
ROEHAMPTON VALE
Superstore
Cemy
STAG LA
FRIARS AVE
FRENSHAM DR
STROUD CRES
PALLISTER TERR
Putney Vale
FLORENCE TERR 1
EBOR COTTS 2
Robin Hood Gate
BEVERLEY COTTS
FUSION CT
A308
KINGSTON VALE
Kingston Univ Roehampton Vale Campus
Pl Fld
War Meml
Allot Gdns
Hall School Wimbledon
Robin Hood
MARY ADELAIDE CL
VALE CRES
DERWENT AVE
ROBIN HOOD
GRASMERE AVE
Kingston Vale
A3 New Malden
A308 Kingston upon Thames
74
73
72
21
22
A
B
C

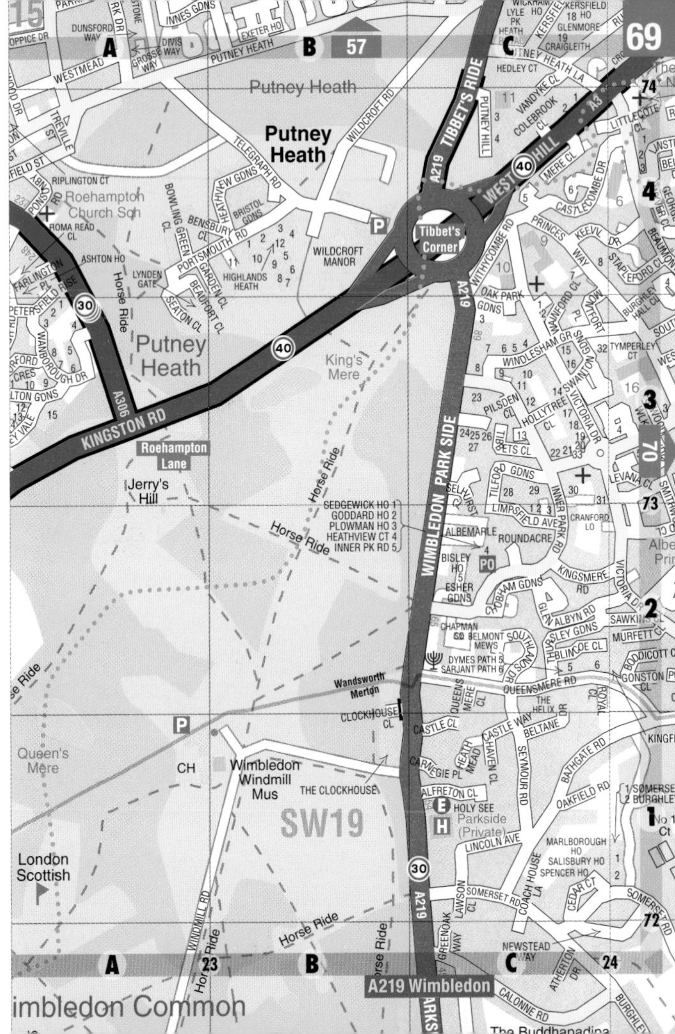

A
B
57
C
Putney Heath
Putney Heath
Tibbet's Corner
TIBBET'S RIDE
WEST HILL
A3
A219
PUTNEY HEATH
WESTMEAD
TELEGRAPH RD
WILDCROFT RD
WILDCROFT MANOR
PORTSMOUTH RD
HIGHLANDS HEATH
Roehampton Church Sch
Horse Ride
Putney Heath
KINGSTON RD
A306
Roehampton Lane
Jerry's Hill
King's Mere
WIMBLEDON PARK SIDE
SEDGEWICK HO 1
GODDARD HO 2
PLOWMAN HO 3
HEATHVIEW CT 4
INNER PK RD 5
Wandsworth
Merton
CLOCKHOUSE CL
Queen's Mere
CH
Wimbledon Windmill Mus
THE CLOCKHOUSE
SW19
London Scottish
WINDMILL RD
Horse Ride
A219 Wimbledon
Wimbledon Common
QUEENSMERE RD
ROUNDACRE
KINGSMERE RD
SOMERSET RD
CALONNE RD
Parkside (Private)
HOLY SEE
LINCOLN AVE
SEYMOUR RD
OAKFIELD RD
BATHGATE RD
70
73
72
74
23
24

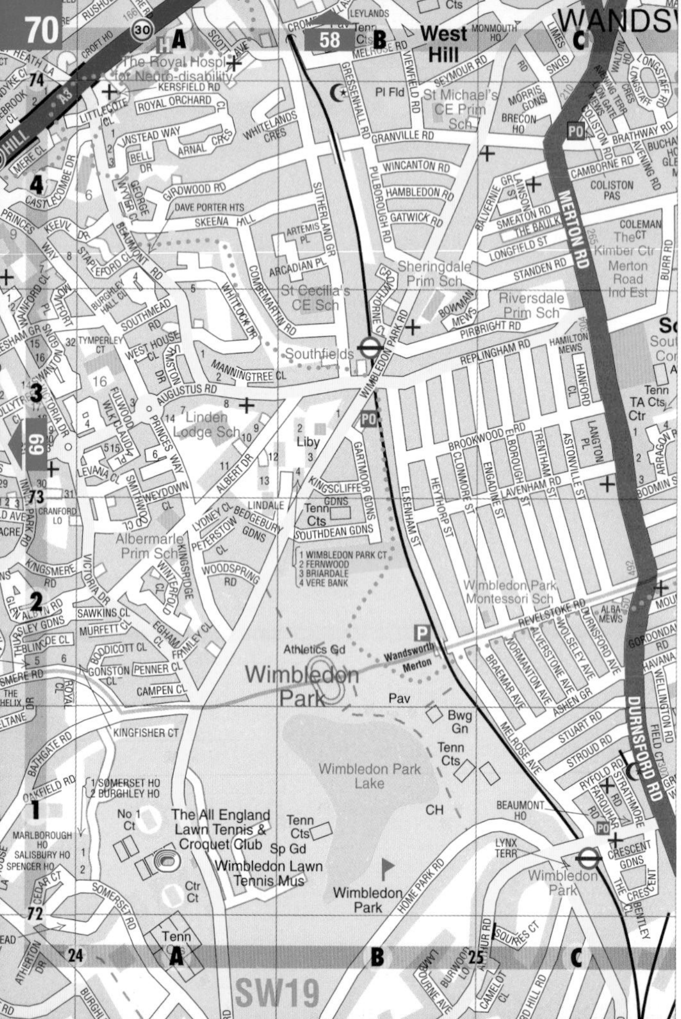

70
WANDSW
West Hill
58
69
SW19
The Royal Hospl for Neuro-disability
KERSFIELD RD
ROYAL ORCHARD
LITTLECOTE CL
WHITELANDS CRES
ARNAL CRES
BELL DR
GIRDWOOD RD
DAVE PORTER HTS
SKEENA HILL
CASTLECOMBE DR
PRINCES WAY
KEEVIL DR
STAPLEFORD CL
BEAUMONT RD
BURGHLEY HALL CL
SOUTHMEAD RD
WEST HOUSE CL
TYMPERLEY CT
AUGUSTUS RD
MANNINGTREE CL
WHITLOCK DR
COMBEMARTIN RD
ARCADIAN PL
ARTEMIS PL
SUTHERLAND GR
St Cecilia's CE Sch
Southfields
GRESSENHALL RD
GRANVILLE RD
WINCANTON RD
HAMBLEDON RD
GATWICK RD
PULBOROUGH RD
VIEWFIELD RD
SEYMOUR RD
MELROSE RD
LEYLANDS
Pl Fld
St Michael's CE Prim Sch
MORRIS GDNS
BRECON HO
MONMOUTH HO
LIMES GDNS
Sheringdale Prim Sch
Riversdale Prim Sch
BOWMAN MEWS
PIRBRIGHT RD
REPLINGHAM RD
HAMILTON MEWS
HANFORD CL
SMEATON RD
THE BAULK
LONGFIELD ST
STANDEN RD
MERTON RD
COLISTON PAS
CAMBORNE RD
BRATHWAY RD
The Kimber Ctr
Merton Road Ind Est
COLEMAN CT
BURR RD
WIMBLEDON PARK RD
Linden Lodge Sch
Liby
KINGSCLIFFE GDNS
GARTMOOR GDNS
SOUTHDEAN GDNS
Tenn Cts
LINDALE
1 WIMBLEDON PARK CT
2 FERNWOOD
3 BRIARDALE
4 VERE BANK
BROOKWOOD RD
CLONMORE ST
ENGADINE ST
ELBOROUGH ST
TRENTHAM ST
ASTONVILLE ST
LANGTON PL
LAVENHAM RD
ELSENHAM ST
HEYTHORP ST
Tenn TA Cts Ctr
Albermarle Prim Sch
ALBERT DR
LYDNEY CL
BEDGEBURY GDNS
PETERSTOW CL
WOODSPRING RD
KINGSRIDGE
WINTERFOLD CL
VICTORIA DR
KINGSMERE RD
SAWKINS CL
MURFETT CL
BODDICOTT CL
GONSTON CL
PENNER CL
CAMPEN CL
EGHAM CL
FRIMLEY CL
Wimbledon Park Montessori Sch
REVELSTOKE RD
ALBA MEWS
DURNSFORD AVE
WOLSELEY AVE
ALVERSTONE AVE
NORMANTON AVE
BRAEMAR AVE
ASHEN GR
MELROSE AVE
STUART RD
STROUD RD
Athletics Gd
Wandsworth
Merton
Wimbledon Park
Pav
Bwg Gn
Tenn Cts
Wimbledon Park Lake
CH
KINGFISHER CT
BATHGATE RD
OAKFIELD RD
1 SOMERSET HO
2 BURGHLEY HO
MARLBOROUGH HO
SALISBURY HO
SPENCER HO
CEDAR CT
SOMERSET RD
No 1 Ct
The All England Lawn Tennis & Croquet Club
Wimbledon Lawn Tennis Mus
Sp Gd
Ctr Ct
Wimbledon Park
HOME PARK RD
BEAUMONT HO
LYNX TERR
RYFOLD RD
FARQUHAR RD
STRATHMORE RD
CRESCENT GDNS
THE CRESCENT
DURNSFORD RD
WELLINGTON RD
HAVANA RD
GORDONDALE RD
SQUIRES CT
ARTHUR RD
BURWOOD LO
CAMELOT CL
AUGHTON DR

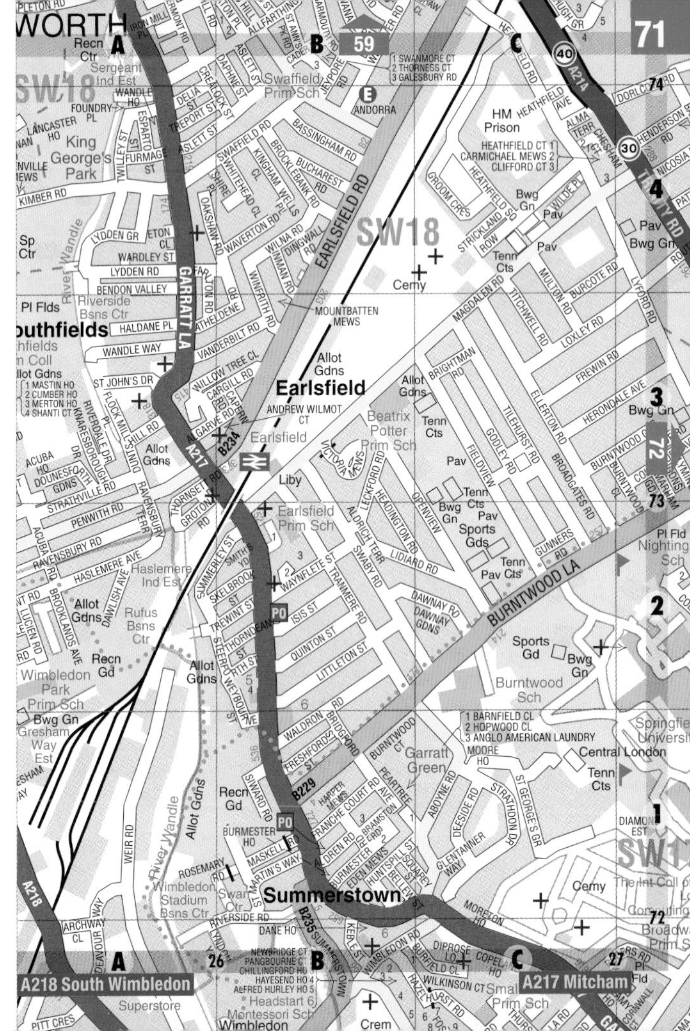

59
72
73
74
26
27
SW18
SW17
Earlsfield
Southfields
Summerstown
Garratt Green
King George's Park
HM Prison
GARRATT LA
EARLSFIELD RD
MAGDALEN RD
BURNTWOOD LA
TRINITY RD
A217
A218
B229
B234
B235
A214
1 SWANMORE CT
2 THORNESS CT
3 GALESBURY RD
HEATHFIELD CT 1
CARMICHAEL MEWS 2
CLIFFORD CT 3
1 MASTIN HO
2 CUMBER HO
3 MERTON HO
4 SHANTI CT
1 BARNFIELD CL
2 HOPWOOD CL
3 ANGLO AMERICAN LAUNDRY
NEWBRIDGE CT
PANGBOURNE CT
CHILLINGFORD HO
HAYESEND HO
ALFRED HURLEY HO
Earlsfield Prim Sch
Beatrix Potter Prim Sch
Burntwood Sch
Swaffield Prim Sch
Wimbledon Park Prim Sch
Haslemere Ind Est
Rufus Bsns Ctr
Riverside Bsns Ctr
Wimbledon Stadium Bsns Ctr
Gresham Way Est
Springfield University
Central London
Nightingale Sch
Headstart Montessori Sch
A218 South Wimbledon
A217 Mitcham

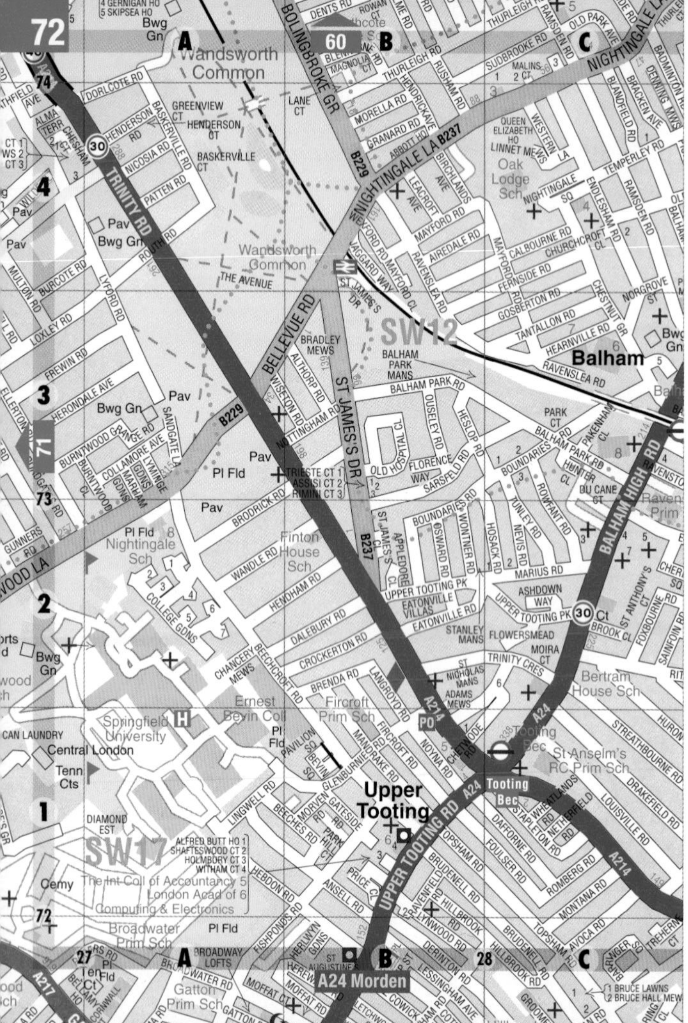
Wandsworth Common
TRINITY RD
BELLEVUE RD
ST JAMES'S DR
NIGHTINGALE LA
BALHAM HIGH RD
UPPER TOOTING RD
SW12
SW17
Balham
Upper Tooting
Tooting Bec
A24 Morden

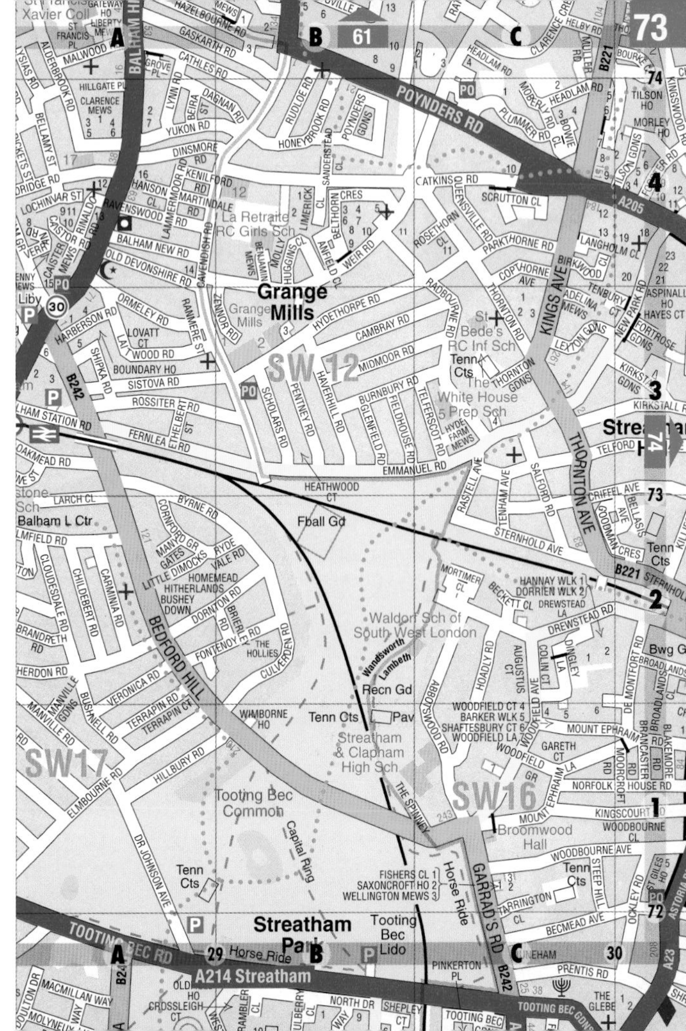

73
61
74
A
B
C
1
2
3
4
Xavier Coll
ST FRANCIS PL
GATEWAY HO
LIBERTY MEWS
BALHAM HILL
HAZELBOURNE RD
MEWS
GASKARTH RD
CATHLES RD
ALDERBROOK RD
MALWOOD RD
GROVE PL
HILLGATE PL
CLARENCE MEWS
LYNN RD
BEIRA ST
DAGNAN RD
YUKON RD
BELLAMY ST
DINSMORE RD
KENILFORD RD
HANSON CL
MARTINDALE RD
LOCHINVAR ST
RINALDO RD
RAVENSWOOD RD
LAMMERMOOR RD
CAVENDISH RD
CAISTER MEWS
BALHAM NEW RD
OLD DEVONSHIRE RD
La Retraite RC Girls Sch
BENJAMIN MEWS
MOLLY HUGGINS CL
LIMERICK CL
RUDLOE RD
HONEYBROOK RD
SANDERSTEAD CL
POYNDERS GDNS
POYNDERS RD
BELTHORN CRES
ANFIELD CL
WEIR RD
CATKINS RD
QUEENSVILLE RD
ROSETHORN CL
SCRUTTON CL
PARKTHORNE RD
COPTHORNE AVE
RADBOURNE RD
THORNTON RD
HEADLAM RD
MOBERLY RD
PLUMMER RD
BOWIE CL
CLARENCE CRES
HELBY RD
MULLER RD
B221
TILSON HO
MORLEY HO
KINGSWOOD RD
ILSON GDNS
A205
LANGHOLM CL
BIRKWOOD CL
ADELINA MEWS
TENBURY CT
NEW PARK RD
ASPINALL HO
HAYES CT
FORTROSE GDNS
LEXTON GDNS
KIRKSTALL GDNS
KIRKSTALL RD
TIERNEY RD
KINGS AVE
Liby
PO
P
30
Grange Mills
ZENNOR RD
RANMERE ST
ORMELEY RD
HARBERSON RD
LOVATT CT
LAITWOOD RD
SHIPKA RD
BOUNDARY HO
SISTOVA RD
ROSSITER RD
ETHELBERT ST
B242
HYDETHORPE RD
CAMBRAY RD
MIDMOOR RD
SW 12
SCHOLARS RD
PENTNEY RD
HAVERHILL RD
BURNBURY RD
GLENFIELD RD
FIELDHOUSE RD
TELFERSCOT RD
HYDE FARM MEWS
St Bede's RC Inf Sch
Tenn Cts
The White House Prep Sch
THORNTON GDNS
Streatham
TELFORD AVE
BALHAM STATION RD
FERNLEA RD
OAKMEAD RD
LARCH CL
Balham L Ctr
ELMFIELD RD
EMMANUEL RD
HEATHWOOD CT
Fball Gd
RASTELL AVE
TENHAM AVE
SALFORD RD
THORNTON AVE
CRIFFEL AVE
BELLASIS AVE
GOODMAN CRES
KILLIESER AVE
STERNHOLD AVE
B221 STERNHOLD AVE
Tenn Cts
BYRNE RD
CORNFORD GR
MANOR GATES
RYDE VALE RD
LITTLE DIMOCKS
HOMEMEAD
HITHERLANDS
BUSHEY DOWN
DORNTON RD
BRIERLEY RD
CLOUDESDALE RD
CHILDEBERT RD
CARMINIA RD
BRANDRETH RD
BEDFORD HILL
FONTENOY RD
THE HOLLIES
CULVERDEN RD
MORTIMER CL
BECKETT CL
HANNAY WLK
DORRIEN WLK
DREWSTEAD LA
DREWSTEAD RD
Waldon Sch of South West London
Wandsworth
Lambeth
Recn Gd
HOADLY RD
AUGUSTUS CT
COLIN CT
DINGLEY LA
Bwg Gn
BROADLANDS AVE
DE MONTFORT RD
VERONICA RD
MANVILLE GDNS
MANVILLE RD
BUSHNELL RD
TERRAPIN RD
TERRAPIN CT
WIMBORNE HO
Tenn Cts
Pav
Streatham & Clapham High Sch
ABBOTSWOOD RD
WOODFIELD CT
BARKER WLK
SHAFTESBURY CT
WOODFIELD LA
WOODFIELD AVE
MOUNT EPHRAIM RD
GARETH CT
WOODFIELD GR
MOUNT EPHRAIM LA
MOORCROFT RD
BRANCASTER RD
BROADLANDS CL
BLAKEMORE RD
NORFOLK HOUSE RD
SW17
HILLBURY RD
ELMBOURNE RD
Tooting Bec Common
Capital Ring
THE SPINNEY
SW16
KINGSCOURT RD
WOODBOURNE CL
WOODBOURNE AVE
Broomwood Hall
DR JOHNSON AVE
Tenn Cts
FISHERS CL
SAXONCROFT HO
WELLINGTON MEWS
Horse Ride
GARRAD'S RD
TARRINGTON CL
BECMEAD AVE
STEEP HILL
OCKLEY RD
ST GILES HO
ASTORIA PAR
Streatham Park
Tooting Bec Lido
TOOTING BEC RD
29
Horse Ride
A214 Streatham
PINKERTON PL
B242
PRENTIS RD
THE GLEBE
A23
MACMILLAN WAY
MOLYNEUX DR
OLD HO
CROSSLEIGH CT
NORTH DR
SHEPLEY CT
TOOTING BEC GDNS

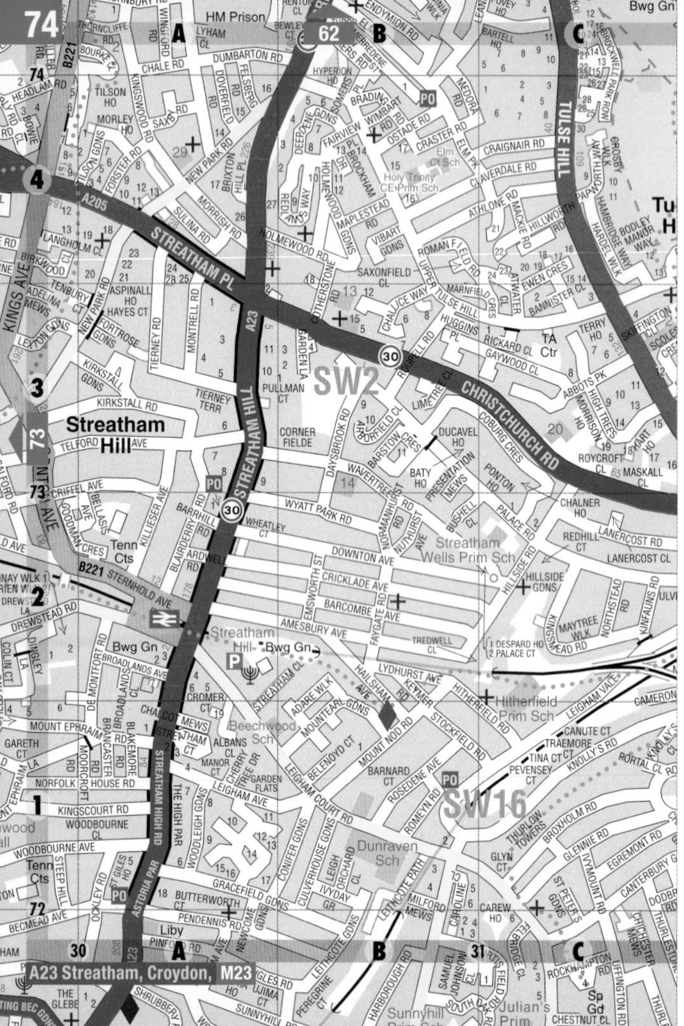

HM Prison
Thorncliffe Rd
Wingford Rd
Lyham Cl
Dumbarton Rd
Chale Rd
Kingswood Rd
Hyperion Ho
Endymion Rd
Merredene St
Somers Pl
Bradinc
Wimbart Rd
Ostade Rd
Medora Rd
Craster Rd
Elm Pk
Elm Ct Sch
Craignair Rd
Claverdale Rd
Holy Trinity CE Prim Sch
Bartell Ho
Povey Ho
Tulse Hill
Brockwell Park Row
Crosby Wlk
Papworth Way
Hambridge Way
Hardel Wlk
Bodley Manor Way
Bourke Cl
Headlam Rd
Tilson Ho
Morley Ho
Bowie Cl
Tilson Gdns
Forster Rd
New Park Rd
Saxby Rd
Doverfield Rd
Felsberg Rd
Brixton Hill Pl
Deepdene Gdns
Fairview Pl
Brockham Dr
Holmewood Rd
Holmewood Gdns
Redlands Way
Maplestead Rd
Vibart Gdns
Athlone Rd
Mackie Rd
Hillworth Rd
Sulina Rd
Morrish Rd
A205
Streatham Pl
Langholm Cl
Birkwood Cl
Tenbury Ct
Adelina Mews
Kings Ave
Aspinall Ho
Hayes Ct
Fortrose Gdns
Lexton Gdns
Tierney Rd
Montrell Rd
Cotherstone Rd
Saxonfield Cl
Chalice Way
Upper Tulse Hill
Roman Rise
Romanfield Rd
Marnfield Cres
Atwater Cl
Ewen Cres
Bannister Cl
Huggins Pl
Rickard Cl
Gaywood Cl
TA Ctr
Terry Ho
Skiffington Cl
Scoles Cres
A23
Garden La
SW2
Roupell Rd
Christchurch Rd
Kirkstall Gdns
Kirkstall Rd
Tierney Terr
Pullman Ct
Streatham Hill
Limetree Cl
Abbots Pk
High Trees
Morrison Ho
Hart Ho
Streatham Hill
Telford Ave
Corner Fielde
Daysbrook Rd
Horsfield Cl
Barstow Cres
Ducavel Ho
Coburg Cres
Roycroft Cl
Maskall Cl
Salford Rd
Criffel Ave
Bellasis Ave
Goodman Cres
Killieser Ave
Barrhill Rd
Wyatt Park Rd
Wheatley Ct
Wavertree Rd
Normanhurst Rd
Nuthurst Ave
Baty Ho
Presentation Mews
Ponton Ho
Bushell Cl
Palace Rd
Chalner Ho
Lanercost Rd
Redhill Ct
Lanercost Cl
Tenn Cts
Blairderry Rd
Ardwell Rd
Downton Ave
Cricklade Ave
Barcombe Ave
Emsworth St
Faygate Rd
Streatham Wells Prim Sch
Hillside Rd
Hillside Gdns
B221 Sternhold Ave
Drewstead Rd
Drewstead La
Colin Ct
Dingley La
Bwg Gn
Broadlands Ave
Broadlands Cl
De Montfort Rd
Amesbury Ave
Tredwell Cl
Streatham Hill Bwg Gn
Streatham Cl
1 Despard Ho
2 Palace Ct
Kingsmead Rd
Maytree Wlk
Northstead Rd
Kinfauns Rd
Lydhurst Ave
Hailsham Ave
Keymer Rd
Hitherfield Rd
Hitherfield Prim Sch
Leigham Vale
Cameron
Cromer Ct
Chalcot Mews
Adare Wlk
Mountearl Gdns
Mount Ephraim Rd
Brancaster Rd
Blakemore Rd
Streatham Ct
St Albans Cl
Beechwood Sch
Manor Ct
Cherry Tree Dr
Garden Flats
Belenoyd Ct
Mount Nod Rd
Stockfield Rd
Canute Ct
Traemore Ct
Tina Ct
Pevensey Ct
Knolly's Rd
Portal Cl
Gareth Ct
Mount Ephraim La
Moorcroft Rd
Norfolk House Rd
Streatham High Rd
The High Par
Leigham Ave
Leigham Court Rd
Barnard Ct
Rosedene Ave
Romeyn Rd
SW16
Thurlow Towers
Broxholm Rd
Glennie Rd
Egremont Rd
Ivymount Rd
Canterbury Gr
Kingscourt Rd
Woodbourne Cl
Woodbourne Ave
Woodleigh Gdns
Conifer Gdns
Culverhouse Gdns
Leigh Orchard Cl
Dunraven Sch
Glyn Ct
Steep Hill
Ockley Rd
St Giles Ho
Astoria Par
Gracefield Gdns
Ivyday Gr
Leithcote Path
Milford Mews
Caroline Ct
Carew Ho
St Peter's Gdns
Chichester Mews
Thurlestone Rd
Becmead Ave
Butterworth Ct
Pendennis Rd
Newcome Gdns
Leithcote Gdns
Felbridge Cl
Liby
Pinfold Rd
A23 Streatham, Croydon, M23
The Glebe
Shrubbery Rd
Peregrine Ct
Harborough Rd
Samuel Johnson Cl
Curtis Field Rd
South Oak Rd
Sunnyhill Rd
Sunnyhill Prim Sch
St Julian's Prim
Rockhampton Rd
Uffington Rd
Sp Gd
Chestnut Cl
Tooting Bec Gdns

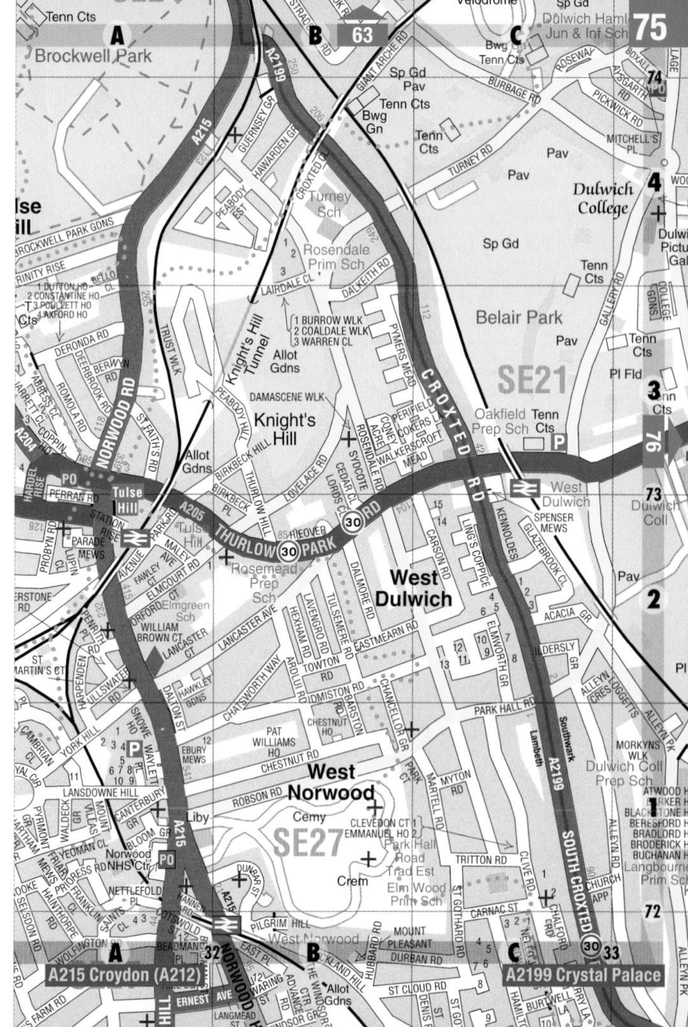
A
B
C
63
Brockwell Park
Tenn Cts
Dulwich Hamlet Jun & Inf Sch
Sp Gd
Bwg Gn
Tenn Cts
Sp Gd
Pav
A2199
A215
GIANT ARCHE RD
GUERNSEY GR
HAWARDEN GR
CROXTED CL
PEABODY EST
Turney Sch
Rosendale Prim Sch
ROSEWAY
BURBAGE RD
PICKWICK RD
AYSGARTH RD
MITCHELL'S PL
TURNEY RD
Pav
Dulwich College
Sp Gd
Tenn Cts
Dulwich Picture Gall
GALLERY RD
COLLEGE GDNS
Belair Park
Pav
Tenn Cts
Pl Fld
SE21
Tulse Hill
BROCKWELL PARK GDNS
TRINITY RISE
1 DUTTON HO
2 CONSTANTINE HO
3 POULLETT HO
4 AXFORD HO
BELLO CL
DERONDA RD
DEERBROOK RD
BERWYN RD
ROMOLA RD
ABBESS CL
JARRETT CL
COPPIN HO
A204
NORWOOD RD
TRUST WLK
ST FAITH'S RD
LAIRDALE CL
DALKEITH RD
1 BURROW WLK
2 COALDALE WLK
3 WARREN CL
Knight's Hill Tunnel
Allot Gdns
PYMERS MEAD
CROXTED RD
DAMASCENE WLK
Knight's Hill
PEABODY HILL
BIRKBECK HILL
THURLOW HILL
LOVELACE RD
SYDCOTE
ROSENDALE RD
CONEY ACRE
PERIFIELD
COKERS LA
WALKERSCROFT MEAD
Oakfield Prep Sch
Tenn Cts
P
76
HARDEL RISE
PO
PERRAN RD
Tulse Hill
STATION RISE
A205
BIRKBECK PL
CEDAR CL
LORDS CL
30
THURLOW PARK RD
HIEOVER
West Dulwich
SPENSER MEWS
KENNOLDES
GLAZEBROOK CL
LING'S COPPICE
CARSON RD
73
Dulwich Coll
PROBYN RD
PARADE MEWS
LUPIN CL
PARK RD
MALEY AVE
FAWLEY CT
ELMCOURT RD
AVENUE PARK RD
Rosemead Prep Sch
West Dulwich
Pav
DALMORE RD
ORFORD CT
Elmgreen Sch
WILLIAM BROWN CT
LANCASTER CT
LANCASTER AVE
HEXHAM RD
LAVENGRO RD
TULSEMERE RD
EASTMEARN RD
ELMWORTH GR
ACACIA GR
GILDERSLY GR
2
PENRITH PL
ST MARTIN'S CT
HARPENDEN RD
ULLSWATER RD
CHATSWORTH WAY
ARDLUI RD
TOWTON RD
IDMISTON RD
BARSTON RD
CHANCELLOR GR
ALLEYN CRES
LOGGETTS
ALLEYN PK
PARK HALL RD
HAWKLEY GDNS
DALTON ST
SNOWE HO
CHESTNUT HO
PAT WILLIAMS HO
Lambeth
Southwark
MORKYNS WLK
Dulwich Coll Prep Sch
CAMBRIAN CL
YORK HILL
WAYLETT PL
EBURY MEWS
CHESTNUT RD
West Norwood
PARK CT
MYTON RD
MARTELL RD
ATWOOD HO
BARKER HO
BLACKSTONE HO
BERESFORD HO
BRADLORD HO
BRODERICK HO
BUCHANAN HO
1
LANSDOWNE HILL
CANTERBURY GR
ROBSON RD
Liby
Cemy
SE27
CLEVEDON CT 1
EMMANUEL HO 2
Park Hall Road Trad Est
Crem
Elm Wood Prim Sch
TRITTON RD
CLIVE RD
SOUTH CROXTED RD
ALLEYN RD
Langbourne Prim Sch
PYRMONT GR
WALDECK GR
VILLAS
MOUNT
YEOMAN CL
BLOOM GR
Norwood NHS Ctr
PO
A215
DUNBAR ST
MEWS
FRIAR
PROGRESS RD
FRANKLIN
SAINTS CL
HAINTHORPE RD
SELSDON RD
NETTLEFOLD PL
HANNEN RD
COTSWOLD ST
PILGRIM HILL
West Norwood
MOUNT PLEASANT
HUBBARD RD
ST GOTHARD RD
CARNAC ST
CHALFORD RD
CHURCH APP
72
DURBAN RD
WOLFINGTON RD
BEADMAN PL
32
NORWOOD HIGH ST
EAST PL
KNOLLAND HILL
33
A215 Croydon (A212)
A2199 Crystal Palace
ERNEST AVE
WARING ST
ADVANCE RD
CTR
THE WINDSORS
Allot Gdns
ST CLOUD RD
DENIS
BURTWELL LA
HAMILTON RD
LANGMEAD ST
WINDSOR GR
ALLEYN PK

Hamlet Schs
A
B
C
64
DULWICH VILLAGE
DEKKER
DESENFANS RD
DRUCE RD
DOVE
EASTLANDS CRES
PO
PLOUGH LA
B219
St Anthony's RC Prim Sch
Goodrich Com Prim Sch
DUNSTANS
DONKEY ALLEY
RUDOLPH CT
ROSEWAY
74
BOXALL RD
AYSGARTH RD
PO
PICKWICK RD
COURT LANE GDNS
EYNELLA RD
COURT LA
Liby
ETHEROW ST
NORCROFT GDNS
RYCOTT PATH
Dulwich Village
MITCHELL'S PL
Pav
LADLANDS
BREDINGHURST
OVERHILL RD
MOUNT ADON PK
4
Dulwich College
WOODYARD LA
EDWARD ALLEYN HO
Tenn Cts
Dulwich Park
Pav
A2216
BELVOIR CL
BELVOIR RD
NORMAN CT
Dulwich Picture Gall
Tenn Cts
FRANK DIXON CL
Tenn Cts
SUNDERLAND CT
MELFORD CT
MELFORD
BEW CT
CAMPBELL CT
GALLERY RD
COLLEGE GDNS
MAXWELL CT
Park
Pav
Tenn Cts
FRANK DIXON WAY
Bwg Gn
Sp Gd
Pav
A205
The Grove
A205 Catford
SE21
3
Pl Fld
ALLISON GR
RYECOTES MEAD
Tenn Cts
Allot Gdns
Tenn Cts
30
DULWICH COMM
Sp Gd
Tenn Cts
BYRON CT 1
GLENNIE CT 2
McLEOD CT 3
DUKES CT 4
GLOUCESTER CT 5
T Cts
Pav
HIGH CL
ASHDOWN CT
75
HAMBLEDON PL
Tenn Cts
Liby
POND COTTS
Pav
Pav
SE21
Allot Gdn
73
West Dulwich
SPENSER MEWS
Dulwich Coll
GLAZEBROOK CL
Tenn Cts
Dulwich & Sydenham
COLLEGE RD
Pl Fld
Pav
2
ACACIA GR
GRANGE LA
CH
ILDERSLY GR
Sp Gd
Pl Fld
HUNTS SLIP RD
Pav
TOLLGATE DR
Toll
Allot Gdns
Allot Gdns
SE26
ALLEYN CRES
LOGGETTS
Pl Fld
GAINSBOROUGH CT
Tenn Cts
Bwg Gn
Pav
FERRINGS
ALLEYN PK
Games Ct
Dulwich
Dulwich Wood
Sydenham Wood (Nat Res)
WOODHALL DR
WOODHALL AVE
PECKARMANS WOOD
Southwark
Lambeth
MORKYNS WLK
CONSTABLE WLK
STONEHILLS CT
Dulwich Coll Prep Sch
A2199
8 DASHWOOD HO
9 DOWELL HO
10 GARRAWAY HO
11 BREAKSPEARE
CRESCENT WOOD RD
THE DULWICH OAKS
COUNTISBURY HO
1
ATWOOD HO 1
BARKER HO 2
BLACKSTONE HO 3
BERESFORD HO 4
BRADLORD HO 5
BRODERICK HO 6
BUCHANAN HO 7
SOUTH CROYDON RD
ALLEYN RD
Tenn Cts
LOW CROSS WOOD LA
CROUCHMANS CL
SYDENHAM HILL
DROITWICH CL
Langbourne Prim Sch
Sydenham Hill
CANBURY MEWS
CHURCH APP
Kingsdale Sch
BOWEN DR
GREAT BROWNINGS
WOODSYRE
72
CHALFORD RD
LYALL AVE
KINSEY HO
JULIAN HO
ST CLEMENT'S HEIGHTS
WELLS PARK CT 1
BRADFORD CL 2
PETER'S PATH 3
CHURCHLEY VILLAS 4
HOLLOW COMBE 5
Sydenham High 6 Sch Jun Dept
WELLS
33
A
Liby
PO
B
34
C
ALLEYN PK
ROUSE GDNS
SEELEY DR
HITHERWOOD CT
COLLEGE
ROCK HILL
DOME HILL PK
TALISMAN SQ
VIGILANT CL
Sydenham Wells Park
Tenn Cts
BURTWELL LA
BERRY LA
CHESTNUT PL

Key to central London map pages

78 79 St John's Wood | Primrose Hill 80 81 Regent's | 82 83 Somers | Islington 84 85 King's Cross | 86 87 | A10

Maida Vale 88 89 Westbourne Green | Park 90 91 Lisson | Town 92 93 | St Pancras 94 95 | Finsbury Shoreditch 96 97 | 98 99 Bethnal Green

Bloomsbury

Paddington 100 101 | Grove 102 103 Marylebone | Fitzrovia 104 105 | Holborn 106 107 St Giles | 108 109 City | Spitalfields 110 111 Whitechapel | A40 | A11 | A13

Notting Hill 112 113 | Bayswater 114 115 Kensington | 116 117 Hyde Park | Mayfair 118 119 St James | Strand 120 121 South Bank | 122 123 Southwark | 124 125 St George in the East | A3220

Kensington Gardens | Holland Pk 126 127 West | 128 129 | Knightsbridge 130 131 Brompton | Green Park 132 133 | Waterloo 134 135 | The Borough 136 137 | 138 139 Bermondsey

Westminster

Kensington 140 141 Earl's Ct | South Kensington 142 143 | 144 145 Belgravia | Victoria 146 147 Pimlico | Lambeth 148 149 Vauxhall | Newington 150 151 Kennington | 152 153 Walworth | A4

West Brompton 154 155 Parsons Green | Chelsea 156 157 Walham Green | 158 159 Battersea Park | 160 161 Nine Elms | 162 163 | A2 | A202

Fulham 164 165 | 166 167 | Battersea 168 169 | 170 171 | South Lambeth 172 173 Stockwell

Congestion Charge Zone

Additional symbols on enlarged maps

All other symbols may be found on page VI

- **Primary route** – single, dual carriageway
- **A road** – single, dual carriageway
- **B road**
- **Through route**
- **Minor road**
- **One way street**
- **No access in direction shown**
- **Congestion Charge Zone boundary Streets within the zone are outlined in green** – for further information call 0845 900 1234
- **Public building**
- **Railway or bus station building**
- **Place of interest**
- **Embassy, museum, theatre**

The map scale on the pages numbered in red is 7 inches to 1 mile
11.04 cm to 1 km • 1:9051

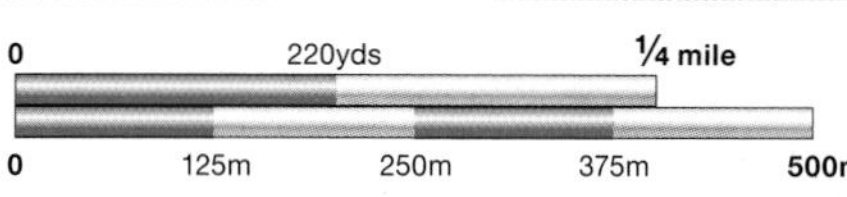

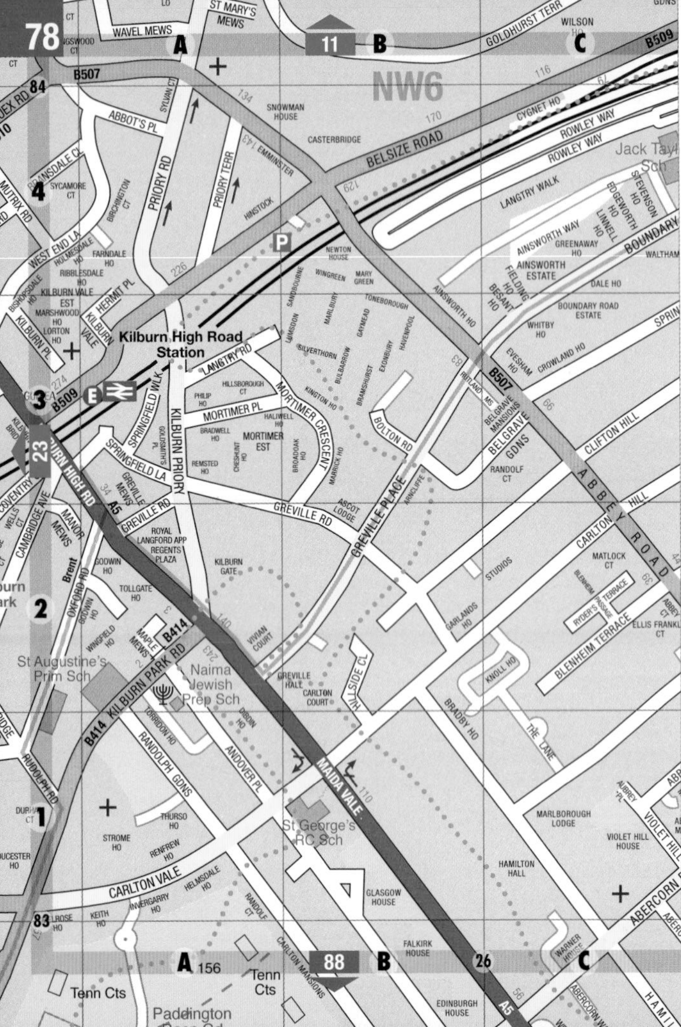

78
WAVEL MEWS
ST MARY'S MEWS
11
A
B
C
GOLDHURST TERR
WILSON HO
B509
B507
84
NW6
SNOWMAN HOUSE
CASTERBRIDGE
BELSIZE ROAD
CYGNET HO
ROWLEY WAY
Jack Tayl Sch
ABBOT'S PL
SYLVAN CT
PRIORY RD
PRIORY TERR
EMMINSTER
HINSTOCK
BRANSDALE CL
SYCAMORE CT
MUTRIX RD
4
BIRCHINGTON CT
WEST END LA
HOLMESDALE HO
FARNDALE HO
RIBBLESDALE HO
KILBURN VALE EST
MARSHWOOD HO
LORTON HO
KILBURN PL
HERMIT PL
KILBURN VALE
LANGTRY WALK
EDGEWORTH HO
STEVENSON HO
LINNELL HO
AINSWORTH WAY
GREENAWAY HO
AINSWORTH ESTATE
BOUNDARY
WALTHAM
NEWTON HOUSE
WINGREEN
MARY GREEN
SANDBOURNE
FIELDING HO
BESANT HO
DALE HO
TONEBOROUGH
AINSWORTH HO
BOUNDARY ROAD ESTATE
WHITBY HO
LUMSDON
MARLBURY
GAYMEAD
HAVENPOOL
Kilburn High Road Station
LANGTRY RD
SILVERTHORN
BULBARROW
EXONBURY
EVESHAM HO
CROWLAND HO
B507
RUTLAND MS
BRAMSHURST
KINGTON HO
HILLSBOROUGH CT
PHILIP HO
MORTIMER PL
MORTIMER CRESCENT
B509
3
SPRINGFIELD WLK
HALIWELL HO
BRADWELL HO
MORTIMER EST
BOLTON RD
BELGRAVE MANSIONS
BELGRAVE GDNS
CLIFTON HILL
23
KILBURN HIGH RD
SPRINGFIELD LA
KILBURN PRIORY
GOLDSMITH'S PL
CHESHUNT HO
REMSTED HO
BROADOAK HO
MARRICK HO
RANDOLF CT
GREVILLE PLACE
ARNCLIFFE
COVENTRY
WELLS CT
CAMBRIDGE AVE
MANOR MEWS
GREVILLE MEWS
A5
GREVILLE RD
ASCOT LODGE
ABBEY ROAD
CARLTON HILL
ROYAL LANGFORD APP
REGENTS PLAZA
GODWIN HO
KILBURN GATE
MATLOCK CT
STUDIOS
Brent
OXFORD RD
TOLLGATE HO
BLENHEIM PASSAGE
RYDER'S TERRACE
2
GODWIN HO
WINGFIELD HO
MAPLE MEWS
B414
VIVIAN COURT
GARLANDS HO
ABBEY CT
ELLIS FRANKLIN CT
St Augustine's Prim Sch
KILBURN PARK RD
Naima Jewish Prep Sch
GREVILLE HALL
CARLTON COURT
HILLSIDE CL
KNOLL HO
BLENHEIM TERRACE
B414
TORRIDON HO
RANDOLPH GDNS
DIDDN HO
ANDOVER PL
BRADBY HO
THE LANE
RUDOLPH RD
MAIDA VALE
1
THURSO HO
St George's RC Sch
MARLBOROUGH LODGE
AUBREY PL
VIOLET HILL
VIOLET HILL HOUSE
STROME HO
RENFREW HO
GLOUCESTER HO
HAMILTON HALL
CARLTON VALE
HELMSDALE HO
INVERGARRY HO
GLASGOW HOUSE
ABERCORN PL
KEITH HO
RANDOLF CT
83
FALKIRK HOUSE
WARNER HOUSE
A
156
88
B
26
C
CARLTON MANSIONS
Tenn Cts
Tenn Cts
Paddington
EDINBURGH HOUSE
ABERCORN W
A5
HAMILTON

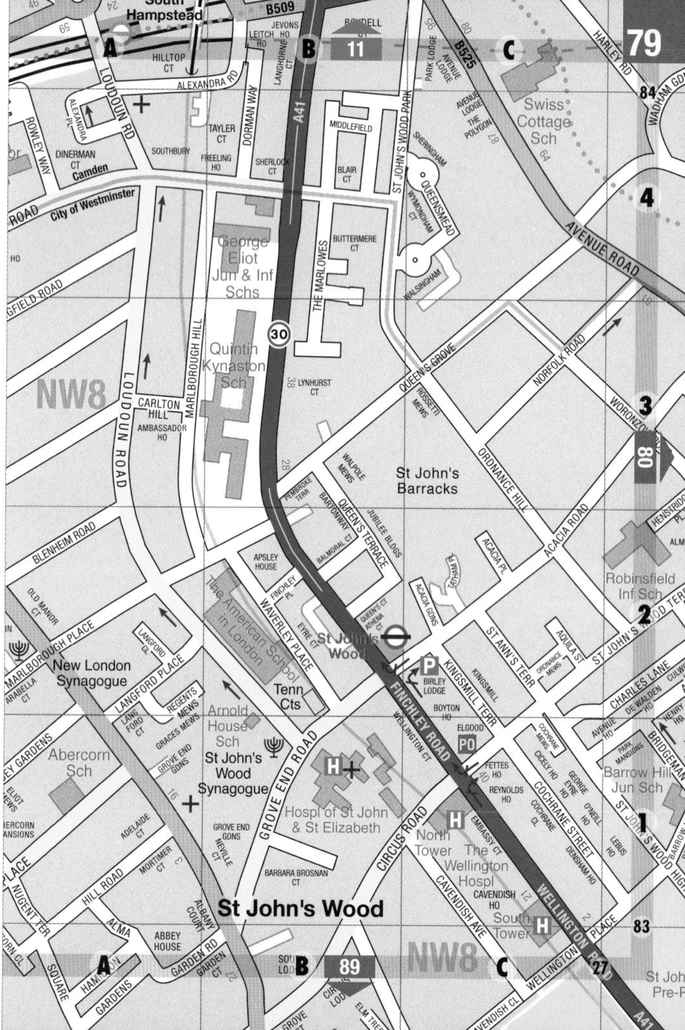

South Hampstead
B509
JEVONS HO
LEITCH HO
BOYDELL CT
11
HILLTOP CT
LANGHORNE CT
A
B
C
B525
PARK LODGE
AVENUE LODGE
HARLEY RD
WADHAM GDNS
84
ALEXANDRA RD
ALEXANDRA PL
LOUDOUN RD
ROWLEY WAY
TAYLER CT
DORMAN WAY
A41
MIDDLEFIELD
ST JOHN'S WOOD PARK
AVENUE LODGE
THE POLYGON
Swiss Cottage Sch
DINERMAN CT
Camden
SOUTHBURY
FREELING HO
SHERLOCK CT
BLAIR CT
SHERINGHAM
QUEENSMEAD
WYMONDHAM CT
City of Westminster
ROAD
4
AVENUE ROAD
BUTTERMERE CT
George Eliot Jun & Inf Schs
THE MARLOWES
WALSINGHAM
HO
GFIELD ROAD
30
Quintin Kynaston Sch
LYNHURST CT
QUEEN'S GROVE
NORFOLK ROAD
NW8
LOUDOUN ROAD
MARLBOROUGH HILL
CARLTON HILL
AMBASSADOR HO
ROSSETTI MEWS
WORONZOW RD
3
80
ORDNANCE HILL
St John's Barracks
WALPOLE MEWS
PEMBROKE TERR
BARTON WAY
QUEEN'S TERRACE
JUBILEE BLDGS
ACACIA ROAD
HENSTRIDGE PL
ALMSHO
BLENHEIM ROAD
APSLEY HOUSE
BALMORAL CT
ACACIA PL
TATHAM PL
Robinsfield Inf Sch
OLD MANOR CT
FINCHLEY PL
WAVERLEY PLACE
The American School in London
QUEEN'S CT
ATHENA CT
ACACIA GDNS
2
ST JOHN'S WOOD TERRACE
MARLBOROUGH PLACE
LANGFORD CL
EYRE CT
St John's Wood
P
BIRLEY LODGE
ST ANN'S TERR
AQUILA ST
ORDNANCE MEWS
CHARLES LANE
CULWORTH HO
New London Synagogue
LANGFORD PLACE
Tenn Cts
FINCHLEY ROAD
KINGSMILL TERR
KINGSMILL
DE WALDEN
ARABELLA CT
REGENTS MEWS
LANG FORD CT
GRACES MEWS
Arnold House Sch
BOYTON HO
WELLINGTON CT
ELGOOD
COCHRANE MEWS
AVENUE HO
HENRY HO
BRIDGEMAN ST
PO
PARK MANSIONS
GARDENS
Abercorn Sch
GROVE END GDNS
St John's Wood Synagogue
GROVE END ROAD
H
FETTES HO
CICELY HO
GEORGE EYRE HO
Barrow Hill Jun Sch
REYNOLDS HO
COCHRANE STREET
O'NEILL HO
ELIOT MEWS
16
Hospl of St John & St Elizabeth
CIRCUS ROAD
EMBASSY CT
COCHRANE CL
ST JOHN'S WOOD HIGH ST
1
ABERCORN MANSIONS
ADELAIDE CT
GROVE END GDNS
NEVILLE CT
North Tower
The Wellington Hospl
DENSHAM HO
LEBUS HO
BARROW HILL RD
PLACE
MORTIMER CT
HILL ROAD
BARBARA BROSNAN CT
CAVENDISH AVE
CAVENDISH HO
NUGENT TER
ALBANY COURT
St John's Wood
South Tower
WELLINGTON ROAD
WELLINGTON PLACE
83
ALMA
ABBEY HOUSE
GARDEN RD
89
NW8
SQUARE
GARDEN CT
WELLINGTON
27
St John's Pre-Prep
GARDENS
CAVENDISH CL
ELM TREE

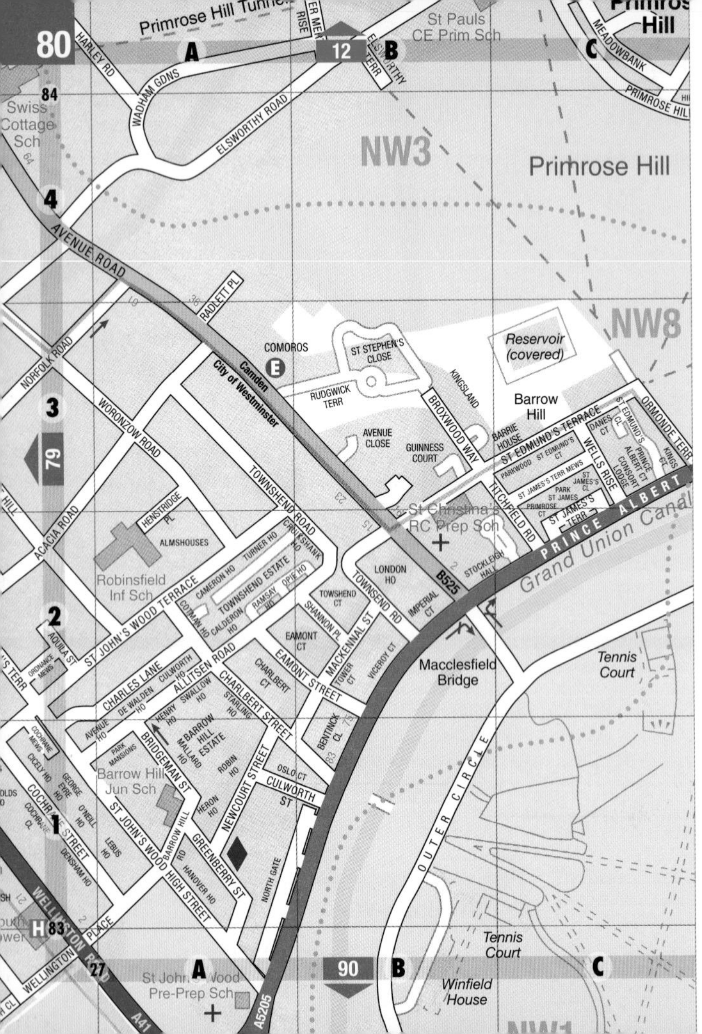

Primrose Hill Tunnel
A
12
B
C
Primrose Hill
St Pauls CE Prim Sch
HARLEY RD
WADHAM GDNS
ELSWORTHY ROAD
ELSWORTHY TERR
MEADOWBANK
PRIMROSE HILL
84
Swiss Cottage Sch
NW3
Primrose Hill
4
AVENUE ROAD
RADLETT PL
NORFOLK ROAD
NW8
Reservoir (covered)
COMOROS
ST STEPHEN'S CLOSE
Camden
City of Westminster
RUDGWICK TERR
KINGSLAND
Barrow Hill
3
79
WORONZOW ROAD
AVENUE CLOSE
GUINNESS COURT
BROXWOOD WAY
BARRIE HOUSE
ST EDMUND'S TERRACE
ST EDMUND'S CT
DANES CT
ST EDMUND'S CL
WELLS RISE
ORMONDE TERR
PRINCE ALBERT CT
CONSORT LODGE
KINGS CT
PARKWOOD
ST JAMES'S TERR MEWS
ST JAMES'S CL
PARK ST JAMES
PRIMROSE CT
ST JAMES'S TERR
TOWNSHEND ROAD
TITCHFIELD RD
PRINCE ALBERT
Grand Union Canal
HENSTRIDGE PL
ACACIA ROAD
ALMSHOUSES
St Christina's RC Prep Sch
CRUIKSHANK HO
TURNER HO
LONDON HO
STOCKLEIGH HALL
Robinsfield Inf Sch
CAMERON HO
TOWNSHEND ESTATE
OPIE HO
B525
2
ST JOHN'S WOOD TERRACE
COTMAN HO
CALDERON HO
RAMSAY HO
TOWSHEND CT
SHANNON PL
TOWNSEND RD
IMPERIAL CT
AQUILA ST
EAMONT CT
MACKENNAL ST
VICEROY CT
Macclesfield Bridge
Tennis Court
ORDNANCE MEWS
CHARLES LANE
CULWORTH HO
ALLITSEN ROAD
CHARLBERT CT
EAMONT STREET
TOWER CT
DE WALDEN HO
SWALLOW HO
CHARLBERT STREET
STARLING HO
AVENUE HO
HENRY HO
BARROW HILL ESTATE
BENTINCK CL
COCHRANE MEWS
PARK MANSIONS
BRIDGEMAN ST
MALLARD HO
ROBIN HO
OUTER CIRCLE
CICELY HO
GEORGE EYRE HO
Barrow Hill Jun Sch
OSLO CT
CULWORTH ST
NEWCOURT STREET
COCHRANE STREET
COCHRANE CL
O'NEILL HO
1
ST JOHN'S WOOD HIGH STREET
HERON HO
BARROW HILL RD
LEBUS HO
GREENBERRY ST
DENSHAM HO
HANOVER HO
NORTH GATE
WELLINGTON ROAD
WELLINGTON PLACE
H
83
Tennis Court
27
A
90
B
C
St John's Wood Pre-Prep Sch
Winfield House
A5205
A41

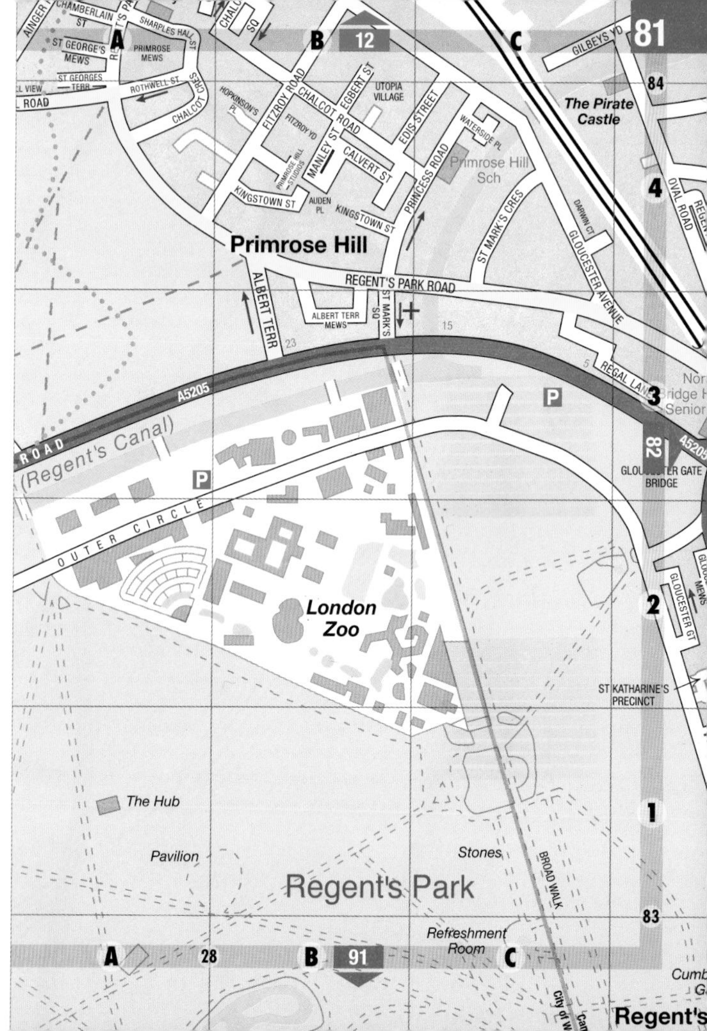

81
12
91
84
83
28
A
B
C
1
2
3
4
82
Primrose Hill
London Zoo
Regent's Park
The Pirate Castle
Primrose Hill Sch
The Hub
Pavilion
Stones
Refreshment Room
BROAD WALK
REGENT'S PARK ROAD
A5205
(Regent's Canal)
OUTER CIRCLE
ALBERT TERR
ALBERT TERR MEWS
ST MARK'S SQ
ST MARK'S CRES
GLOUCESTER AVENUE
REGAL LANE
DARWIN CT
PRINCESS ROAD
KINGSTOWN ST
AUDEN PL
CALVERT ST
MANLEY ST
PRIMROSE HILL STUDIOS
FITZROY YD
FITZROY ROAD
CHALCOT ROAD
EGBERT ST
UTOPIA VILLAGE
EDIS STREET
WATERSIDE PL
HOPKINSON'S PL
CHALCOT CRES
ROTHWELL ST
PRIMROSE MEWS
SHARPLES HALL ST
CHAMBERLAIN ST
ST GEORGE'S MEWS
ST GEORGES TERR
AINGER
GILBEYS YD
OVAL ROAD
GLOUCESTER GATE BRIDGE
GLOUCESTER GT
GLOUCESTER MEWS
ST KATHARINE'S PRECINCT
CHALCOT SQ

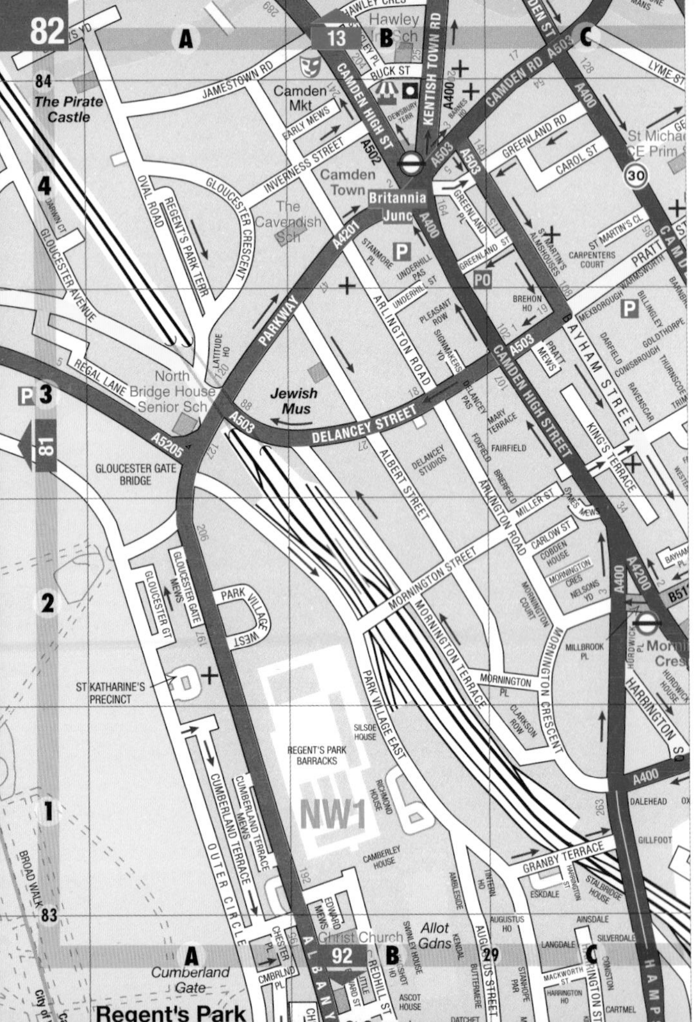

13
81
84
83
92
A
B
C
1
2
3
4
Camden High St
Kentish Town Rd
Camden Rd
Hawley Cres
Buck St
Jamestown Rd
The Pirate Castle
Camden Mkt
Early Mews
Inverness Street
Camden Town
Britannia Junc
Gloucester Crescent
Oval Road
Regent's Park Terr
The Cavendish Sch
Parkway
Greenland Rd
Carol St
St Martin's Cl
Carpenters Court
Pratt St
Bayham Street
Arlington Road
Albert Street
Delancey Street
Jewish Mus
North Bridge House Senior Sch
Regal Lane
Gloucester Avenue
Darwin Ct
Latitude Ho
Gloucester Gate Bridge
Mornington Street
Mornington Terrace
Mornington Crescent
Park Village East
Park Village West
Gloucester Gate Mews
Gloucester Gt
St Katharine's Precinct
Regent's Park Barracks
NW1
Cumberland Terrace
Cumberland Terrace Mews
Outer Circle
Broad Walk
Cumberland Gate
Regent's Park
Albany St
Granby Terrace
Augustus Street
Harrington Sq
Hampstead Rd
Allot Gdns
Christ Church
Miller St
Carlow St
King's Terrace
Millbrook Pl
Delancey Studios
Fairfield
Mary Terrace
Pleasant Row
Stanmore Pl
Underhill Pas
Greenland Pl
Greenland St
Mexborough
Billingley
Goldthorpe
Conisbrough
Ravenscar
Darfield
Cobden House
Mornington Cres
Nelsons Yd
Mornington Pl
Clarkson Row
Silsoe House
Richmond House
Camberley House
Eskdale
Ainsdale
Langdale
Silverdale
Dalehead
Gillfoot
Stalbridge House
Mackworth St
Harrington Ho
Cartmel
Redhill St
Edward Mews
Chester Pl
Cmbrlnd Pl
Ascot House
Swinley House
Kendal
Buttermere
Stanhope Par
Ambleside
Tintern Ho
Augustus Ho
Dewsbury Terr
A400
A503
A502
A4201
A5205
A4200
St George's

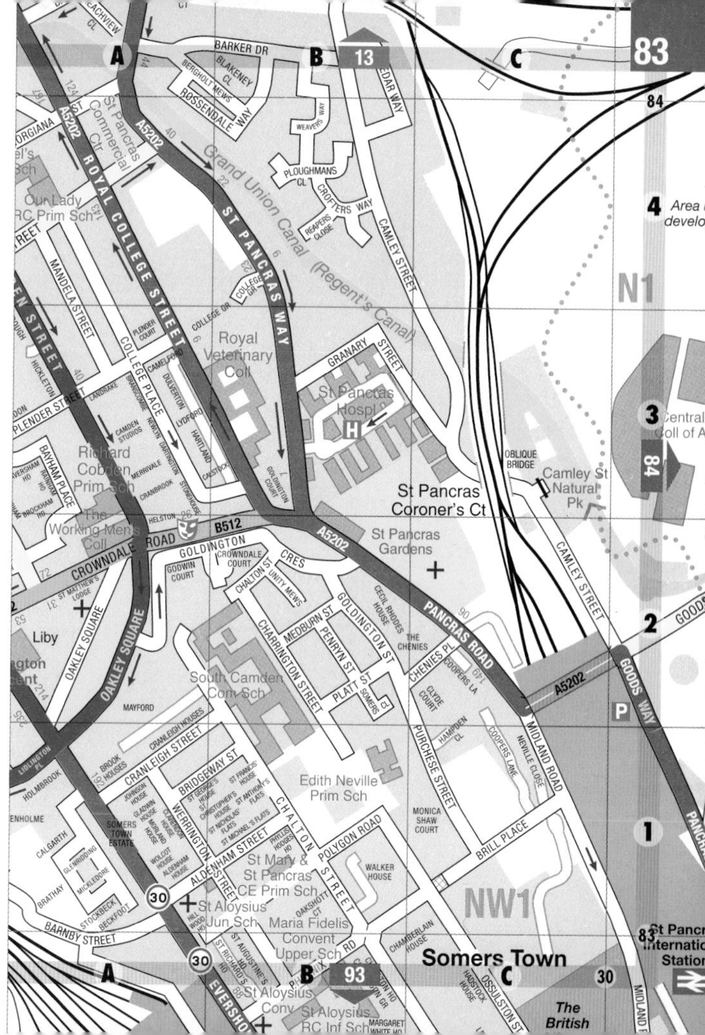

83
13
84
93
A
B
C
N1
NW1
Somers Town
Grand Union Canal (Regent's Canal)
BARKER DR
BLAKENEY CL
BERGHOLT MEWS
ROSSENDALE WAY
WEAVERS WAY
PLOUGHMANS CL
CROFTERS WAY
REAPERS CLOSE
CEDAR WAY
CAMLEY STREET
ROYAL COLLEGE STREET
St Pancras Commercial Ctr
ST PANCRAS WAY
A5202
Our Lady RC Prim Sch
MANDELA STREET
PLENDER COURT
COLLEGE GR
COLLEGE PLACE
Royal Veterinary Coll
GRANARY STREET
St Pancras Hospl
PLENDER STREET
BAYHAM PLACE
Richard Cobden Prim Sch
The Working Men's Coll
CROWNDALE ROAD
B512
GOLDINGTON CRES
CROWNDALE COURT
GODWIN COURT
St Pancras Coroner's Ct
St Pancras Gardens
OBLIQUE BRIDGE
Camley St Natural Pk
Central Coll of A
Area develo
PANCRAS ROAD
GOODS WAY
OAKLEY SQUARE
Liby
South Camden Com Sch
CHARRINGTON STREET
MEDBURN ST
PENRYN ST
GOLDINGTON ST
PLATT ST
CHENIES PL
THE CHENIES
CECIL RHODES HOUSE
MIDLAND ROAD
PURCHESE STREET
CLYDE COURT
COOPERS LANE
NEVILLE CLOSE
Edith Neville Prim Sch
CRANLEIGH STREET
BRIDGEWAY ST
WERRINGTON STREET
CHALTON STREET
POLYGON ROAD
MONICA SHAW COURT
BRILL PLACE
ALDENHAM STREET
St Mary & St Pancras CE Prim Sch
WALKER HOUSE
St Aloysius Jun Sch
Maria Fidelis Convent Upper Sch
BARNBY STREET
CHAMBERLAIN HOUSE
OSSULSTON ST
St Aloysius Conv
St Aloysius RC Inf Sch
The British
St Pancras International Station

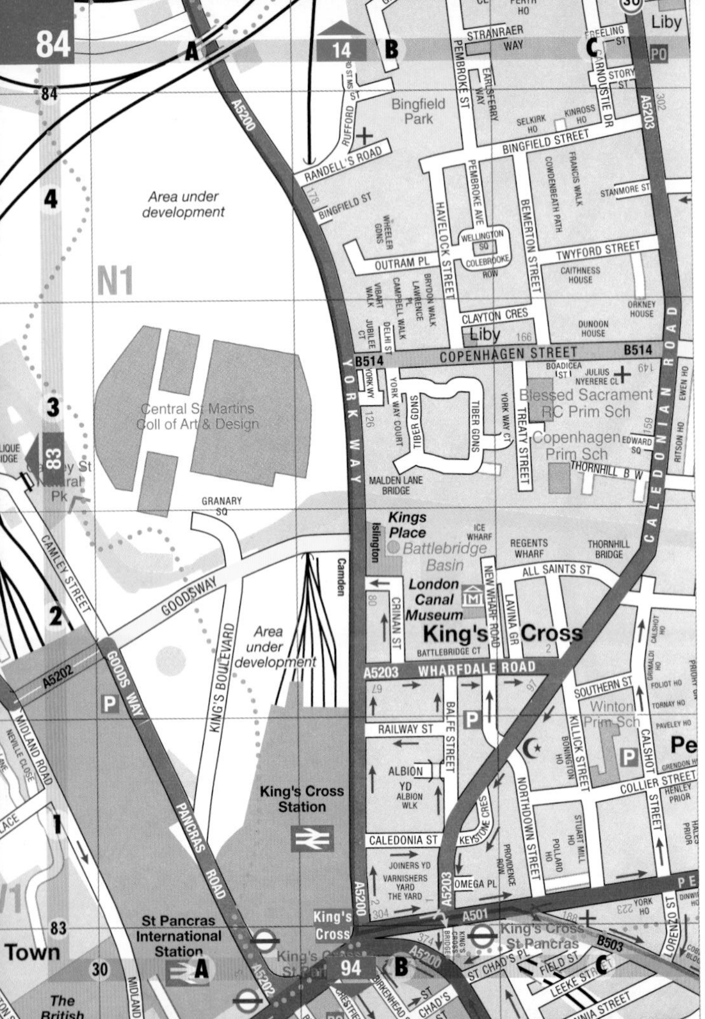

84
14
94
A
B
C
N1
Area under development
Bingfield Park
Central St Martins Coll of Art & Design
Kings Place
Battlebridge Basin
London Canal Museum
King's Cross
King's Cross Station
St Pancras International Station
Copenhagen Prim Sch
Blessed Sacrament RC Prim Sch
Winton Prim Sch
YORK WAY
CALEDONIAN ROAD
COPENHAGEN STREET
WHARFDALE ROAD
PANCRAS ROAD
GOODS WAY
GOODSWAY
KING'S BOULEVARD
CAMLEY STREET
MIDLAND ROAD
BINGFIELD STREET
RANDELL'S ROAD
TWYFORD STREET
HAVELOCK STREET
BEMERTON STREET
PEMBROKE ST
STRANRAER WAY
ALL SAINTS ST
NORTHDOWN STREET
CALSHOT STREET
COLLIER STREET
ST CHAD'S PL
LEEKE STREET
Town
The British

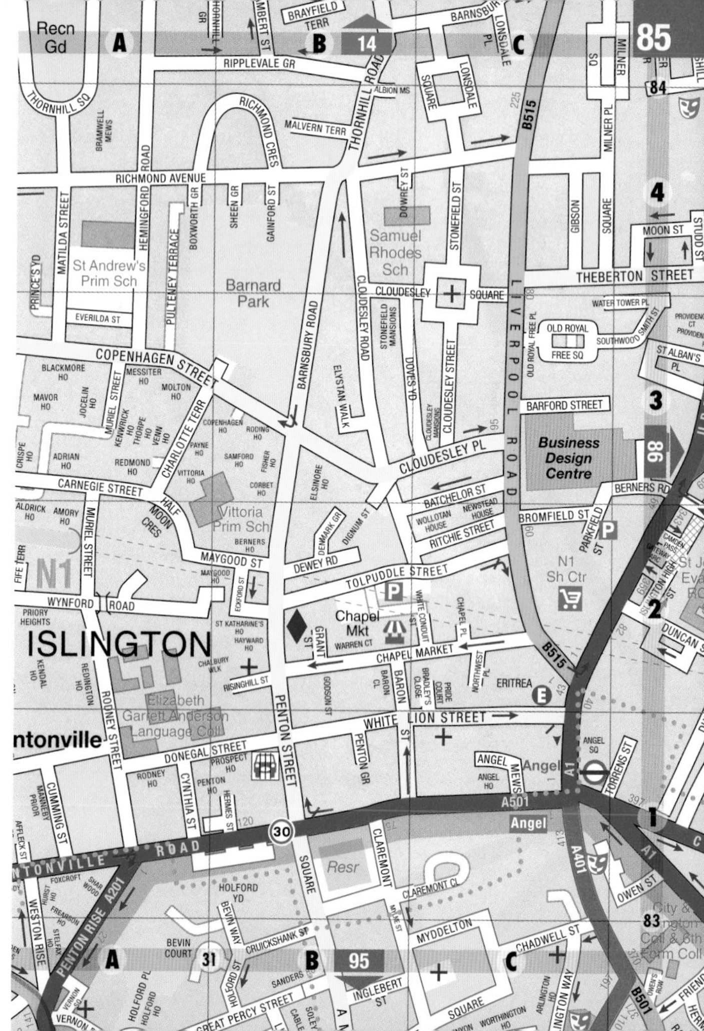

ISLINGTON
Barnard Park
Business Design Centre
N1 Sh Ctr
Chapel Mkt
Vittoria Prim Sch
St Andrew's Prim Sch
Samuel Rhodes Sch
Elizabeth Garrett Anderson Language Coll
Angel
LIVERPOOL ROAD
PENTON STREET
BARNSBURY ROAD
COPENHAGEN STREET
RICHMOND AVENUE
CALEDONIAN ROAD
PENTONVILLE ROAD
WHITE LION STREET
CHAPEL MARKET
TOLPUDDLE STREET
CLOUDESLEY SQUARE
THEBERTON STREET
MYDDELTON SQUARE

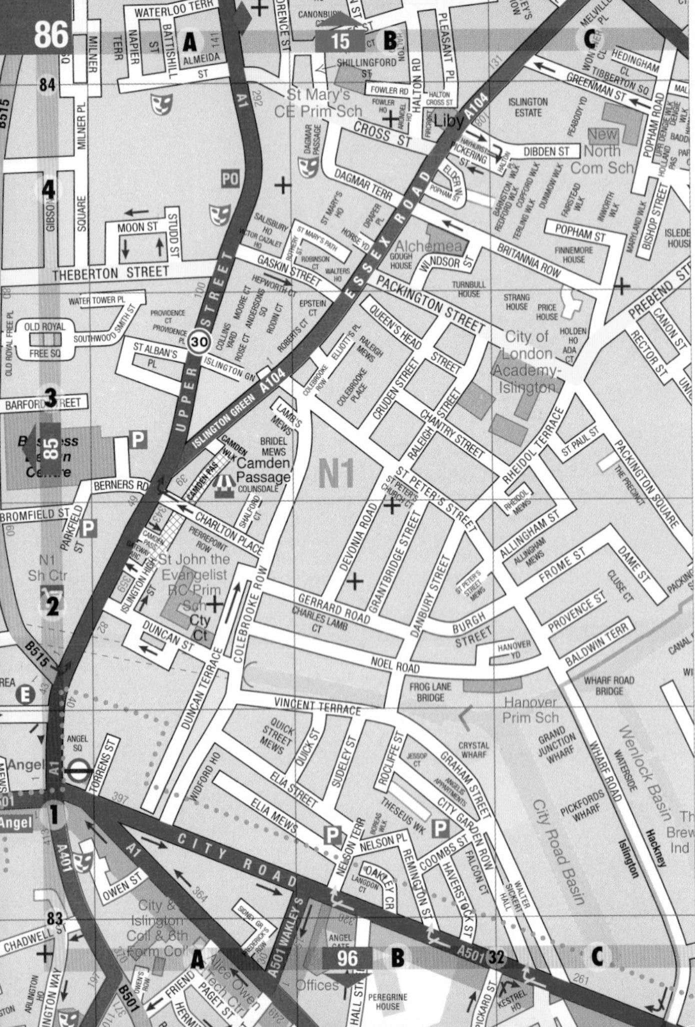

86
A
B
C
15
84
4
3
2
1
83
96
A
B
C
WATERLOO TERR
NAPIER TERR
BATTISHILL ST
ALMEIDA ST
MILNER SQ
MILNER PL
B515
GIBSON SQUARE
MOON ST
STUDD ST
THEBERTON STREET
WATER TOWER PL
OLD ROYAL FREE SQ
OLD ROYAL FREE PL
SOUTHWOOD SMITH ST
PROVIDENCE CT
PROVIDENCE PL
ST ALBAN'S PL
BARFORD STREET
Business Design Centre
85
BERNERS RD
BROMFIELD ST
PARKFIELD ST
N1 Sh Ctr
B515
E
Angel
ANGEL SQ
TORRENS ST
A1
A401
OWEN ST
City & Islington Coll & 6th Form Coll
CHADWELL ST
ARLINGTON WAY
FRIEND
PAGET ST
A501
B501
A1
PO
UPPER STREET
30
ISLINGTON GREEN
A104
ISLINGTON GN
COLLINS YARD
ROSE CT
MOORE CT
ANDERSONS SQ
RODIN CT
ROBERTS CT
SALISBURY HO
VICTOR CAZALET HO
GASKIN STREET
HEPWORTH CT
EPSTEIN CT
BOTHERY ST
ST MARY'S PATH
ROBINSON CT
WALTERS HO
ST MARY'S HO
DAGMAR PASSAGE
DAGMAR TERR
St Mary's CE Prim Sch
CANONBURY
SHILLINGFORD ST
FOWLER RD
FOWLER HO
HALTON RD
HALTON CROSS ST
PLEASANT PL
CROSS ST
Liby
ESSEX ROAD
A104
HORSE YD
DRAPER PL
Alchemea
GOUGH HOUSE
WINDSOR ST
PACKINGTON STREET
ELLIOTT'S PL
RALEIGH MEWS
COLEBROOKE ROW
COLEBROOKE PLACE
QUEEN'S HEAD STREET
CRUDEN STREET
CHANTRY STREET
RALEIGH STREET
LAMB'S MEWS
BRIDEL MEWS
CAMDEN WLK
CAMDEN PAS
Camden Passage
COLINSDALE
SHALFORD CT
N1
CHARLTON PLACE
PIERREPOINT ROW
St John the Evangelist RC Prim Sch
City Ct
ISLINGTON HIGH ST
DUNCAN ST
DUNCAN TERRACE
COLEBROOKE ROW
GERRARD ROAD
CHARLES LAMB CT
DEVONIA ROAD
GRANTBRIDGE STREET
ST PETER'S STREET
ST PETER'S CHURCH CT
DANBURY STREET
BURGH STREET
ST PETER'S STREET MEWS
NOEL ROAD
HANOVER YD
FROG LANE BRIDGE
VINCENT TERRACE
QUICK STREET MEWS
QUICK ST
SUDELEY ST
WIDFORD HO
ELIA STREET
ELIA MEWS
ROCLIFFE ST
JESSOP CT
THESEUS WK
GRAHAM STREET
ANGELIS APPARTMENTS
CITY GARDEN ROW
CRYSTAL WHARF
NELSON TERR
NELSON PL
REMINGTON ST
COOMBS ST
HAVERSTOCK ST
FALCON CT
OAKLEY CR
LANGDON CT
CITY ROAD
WAKLEY ST
SIDNEY GR
FREDERICK'S ROW
ANGEL GATE
Offices
HALL ST
PEREGRINE HOUSE
PICKARD ST
KESTREL HO
A501
32
WALTER SICKERT HALL
City Road Basin
Hanover Prim Sch
GRAND JUNCTION WHARF
PICKFORDS WHARF
WHARF ROAD
WATERSIDE
Wenlock Basin
Islington
Hackney
WHARF ROAD BRIDGE
BALDWIN TERR
PROVENCE ST
CLUSE CT
DAME ST
FROME ST
ALLINGHAM ST
ALLINGHAM MEWS
RHEIDOL MEWS
RHEIDOL TERRACE
ST PAUL ST
PACKINGTON SQUARE
THE PRECINCT
City of London Academy-Islington
HOLDEN HO
ADA CT
STRANG HOUSE
PRICE HOUSE
TURNBULL HOUSE
FINNEMORE HOUSE
POPHAM ST
BRITANNIA ROW
PREBEND ST
CANON ST
RECTOR ST
ISLINGTON ESTATE
PEABODY YD
DIBDEN ST
PICKERING ST
ELDER WK
POPHAM ST
BARNSTON WLK
REDFORD WLK
COPFORD WLK
TERLING WLK
DUNMOW WLK
FAIRSTEAD WLK
INWORTH WLK
MARYLAND WLK
BISHOP STREET
New North Com Sch
POPHAM ROAD
HEDINGHAM CL
TIBBERTON SQ
GREENMAN ST
MELVILLE PL
ISLEDEN HOUSE

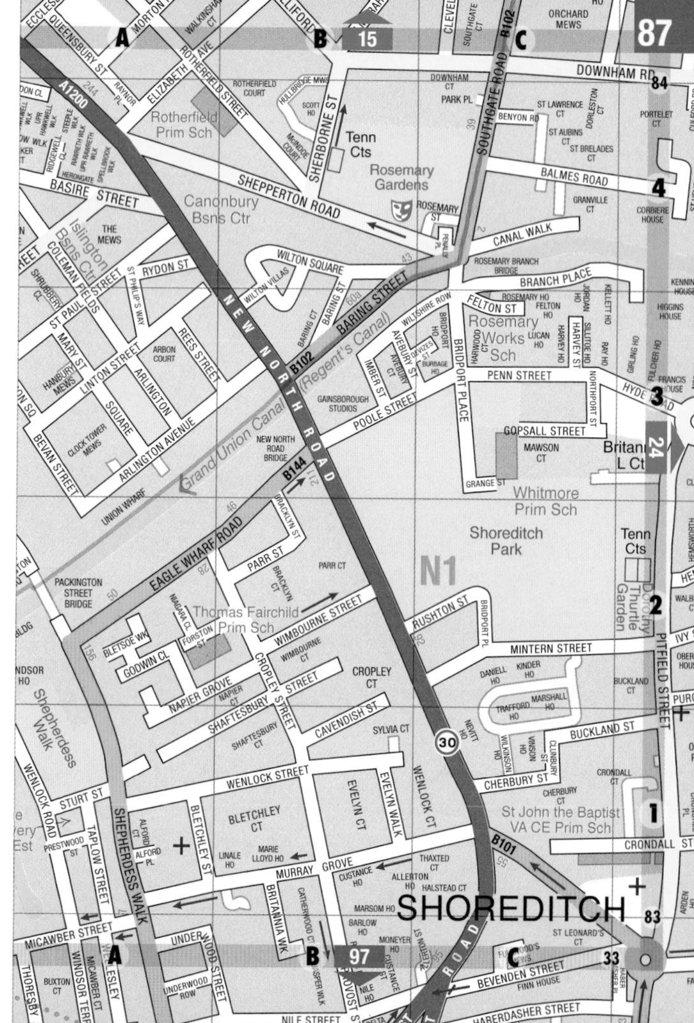

87
A
B
15
C
A
B
97
C
84
4
3
24
2
1
83
33
30
N1
SHOREDITCH
A1200
B102
B144
B101
NEW NORTH ROAD
SOUTHGATE ROAD
DOWNHAM RD
ORCHARD MEWS
QUEENSBURY ST
MORTON RD
WALKINSHAW CT
ROTHERFIELD STREET
ELIZABETH AVE
RAYNOR PL
ROTHERFIELD COURT
Rotherfield Prim Sch
SHERBORNE ST
SCOTT HO
MCINDOE COURT
Tenn Cts
Rosemary Gardens
DOWNHAM CT
PARK PL
BENYON RD
ST LAWRENCE CT
DORLESTON CT
ST AUBINS CT
ST BRELADES CT
PORTELET CT
CULFORD RD
BALMES ROAD
GRANVILLE CT
CORBIERE HOUSE
ST HELIER CT
BASIRE STREET
SHEPPERTON ROAD
Canonbury Bsns Ctr
Islington Bsns Ctr
THE MEWS
ROSEMARY ST
CANAL WALK
ROSEMARY BRANCH BRIDGE
BRANCH PLACE
WILTON SQUARE
WILTON VILLAS
BARING STREET
BARING ST
BARING CT
RYDON ST
ST PHILIP'S WAY
COLEMAN FIELDS
ST PAUL STREET
SHRUBBERY CL
MARY ST
HANBURY MEWS
LINTON STREET
ARBON COURT
REES STREET
ARLINGTON SQUARE
ARLINGTON AVENUE
CLOCK TOWER MEWS
BEVAN STREET
Grand Union Canal (Regent's Canal)
UNION WHARF
GAINSBOROUGH STUDIOS
NEW NORTH ROAD BRIDGE
POOLE STREET
WILTSHIRE ROW
AVEBURY ST
AVEBURY CT
IMBER ST
DEVIZES ST
BURBAGE HO
BRIDPORT HO
BRIDPORT PLACE
FELTON ST
ROSEMARY HO
FELTON HO
Rosemary Works Sch
LUCAN HO
HARWOOD CT
HARVEY HO
HARVEY ST
JORDAN HO
KELLETT HO
SILLITOE HO
RAY HO
GIRLING HO
FULCHER HO
NORRIS HO
KENNING HOUSE
HIGGINS HOUSE
FRANCIS HOUSE
HYDE ROAD
PENN STREET
NORTHPORT ST
GOPSALL STREET
MAWSON CT
Britannia L Ct
GRANGE ST
Whitmore Prim Sch
Shoreditch Park
Tenn Cts
Dorothy Thurtle Garden
EAGLE WHARF ROAD
BRACKLYN ST
BRACKLYN CT
PARR ST
PARR CT
PACKINGTON STREET BRIDGE
NIAGARA CL
FORSTON ST
Thomas Fairchild Prim Sch
WIMBOURNE STREET
WIMBOURNE CT
RUSHTON ST
BRIDPORT PL
MINTERN STREET
BLETSOE WK
GODWIN CL
NAPIER GROVE
NAPIER CT
CROPLEY STREET
CROPLEY CT
SHAFTESBURY STREET
SHAFTESBURY CT
CAVENDISH ST
SYLVIA CT
DANIELL HO
KINDER HO
TRAFFORD HO
MARSHALL HO
NEVITT HO
WILKINSON HO
VINSON HO
CLUNBURY ST
BUCKLAND ST
BUCKLAND CT
PITFIELD STREET
CHERBURY ST
CHERBURY CT
CRONDALL CT
St John the Baptist VA CE Prim Sch
CRONDALL STRE
Shepherdess Walk
WENLOCK ROAD
STURT ST
WENLOCK STREET
BLETCHLEY CT
EVELYN CT
EVELYN WALK
WENLOCK CT
PRESTWOOD ST
TAPLOW STREET
SHEPHERDESS WALK
ALFORD CT
ALFORD PL
BLETCHLEY ST
LINALE HO
MARIE LLOYD HO
MURRAY GROVE
CUSTANCE HO
THAXTED CT
ALLERTON HO
HALSTEAD CT
MARSOM HO
BARLOW HO
MONEYER HO
BRITANNIA WK
CATHERWOOD CT
MICAWBER STREET
WELLESLEY
UNDERWOOD STREET
UNDERWOOD ROW
THORESBY ST
BUXTON CT
WINDSOR TERR
MICAWBER CT
NILE STREET
NILE HO
CUSTANCE ST
PROVOST ST
ST LEONARD'S CT
BEVENDEN STREET
FINN HOUSE
HABERDASHER STREET

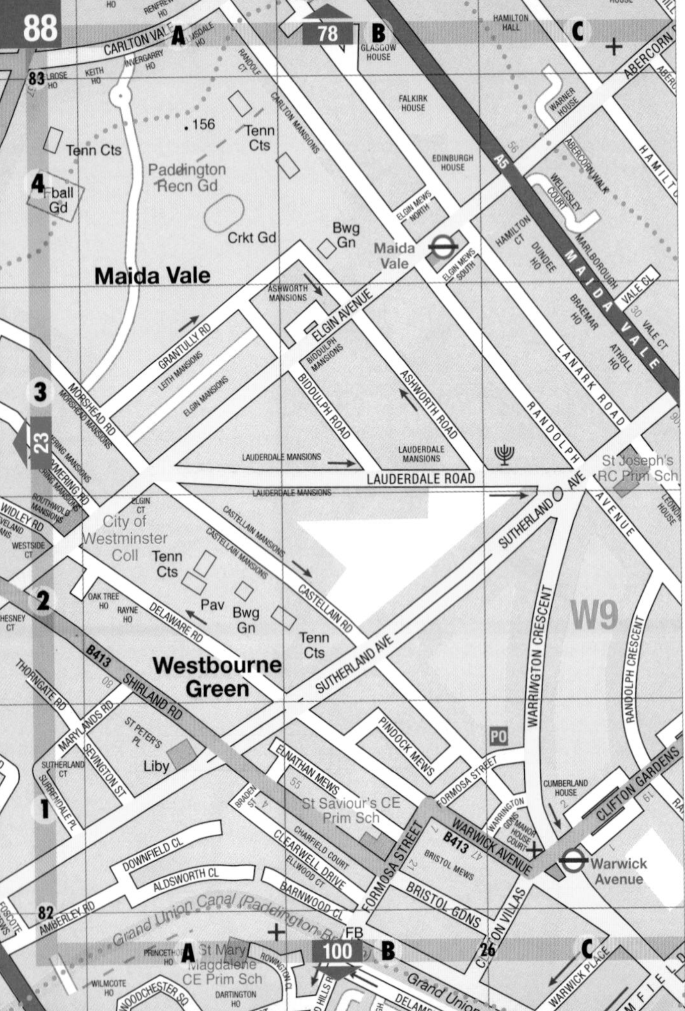

78
A
B
C
1
2
3
4
23
83
82
100
26
Maida Vale
Westbourne Green
W9
Paddington Recn Gd
Crkt Gd
Tenn Cts
Fball Gd
Bwg Gn
Pav
Maida Vale
Warwick Avenue
City of Westminster Coll
St Joseph's RC Prim Sch
St Saviour's CE Prim Sch
St Mary Magdalene CE Prim Sch
Liby
PO
FB
RC Sch
Grand Union Canal (Paddington Br)
CARLTON VALE
ABERCORN PL
MAIDA VALE
A5
ELGIN AVENUE
GRANTULLY RD
MORSHEAD RD
LAUDERDALE ROAD
ASHWORTH ROAD
BIDDULPH ROAD
RANDOLPH AVE
LANARK ROAD
SUTHERLAND AVE
CASTELLAIN RD
DELAWARE RD
SHIRLAND RD
B413
WARRINGTON CRESCENT
RANDOLPH CRESCENT
CLIFTON GARDENS
WARWICK AVENUE
FORMOSA STREET
PINDOCK MEWS
ELNATHAN MEWS
BRISTOL MEWS
BRISTOL GDNS
CLIFTON VILLAS
CLEARWELL DRIVE
CHARFIELD COURT
ELLWOOD CT
BARNWOOD CL
DOWNFIELD CL
ALDSWORTH CL
AMBERLEY RD
THORNGATE RD
MARYLANDS RD
SEVINGTON ST
ST PETER'S PL
SURRENDALE PL
SUTHERLAND CT
WIDLEY RD
WARWICK PLACE
WOODCHESTER SQ
DELAMERE T
ROWINGTON CL
BRADEN ST
HAMILTON HALL
GLASGOW HOUSE
FALKIRK HOUSE
EDINBURGH HOUSE
WARNER HOUSE
ABERCORN WALK
WELLESLEY COURT
MARLBOROUGH
HAMILTON CT
DUNDEE HO
BRAEMAR HO
ATHOLL HO
VALE CL
VALE CT
ELGIN MEWS NORTH
ELGIN MEWS SOUTH
RANDOLPH CT
CARLTON MANSIONS
ASHWORTH MANSIONS
BIDDULPH MANSIONS
LEITH MANSIONS
ELGIN MANSIONS
LAUDERDALE MANSIONS
MORSHEAD MANSIONS
CASTELLAIN MANSIONS
SOUTHWOLD MANSIONS
ELGIN CT
CLEVELAND MANS
WESTSIDE CT
CHESNEY CT
OAK TREE HO
RAYNE HO
CUMBERLAND HOUSE
WARRINGTON GDNS
MANOR HOUSE COURT
STROME HO
RENFREW HO
INVERGARRY HO
KEITH HO
ROSE HO
LEONORA HOUSE
PRINCETHORPE HO
WILMCOTE HO
DARTINGTON HO
FOSCOTE MEWS

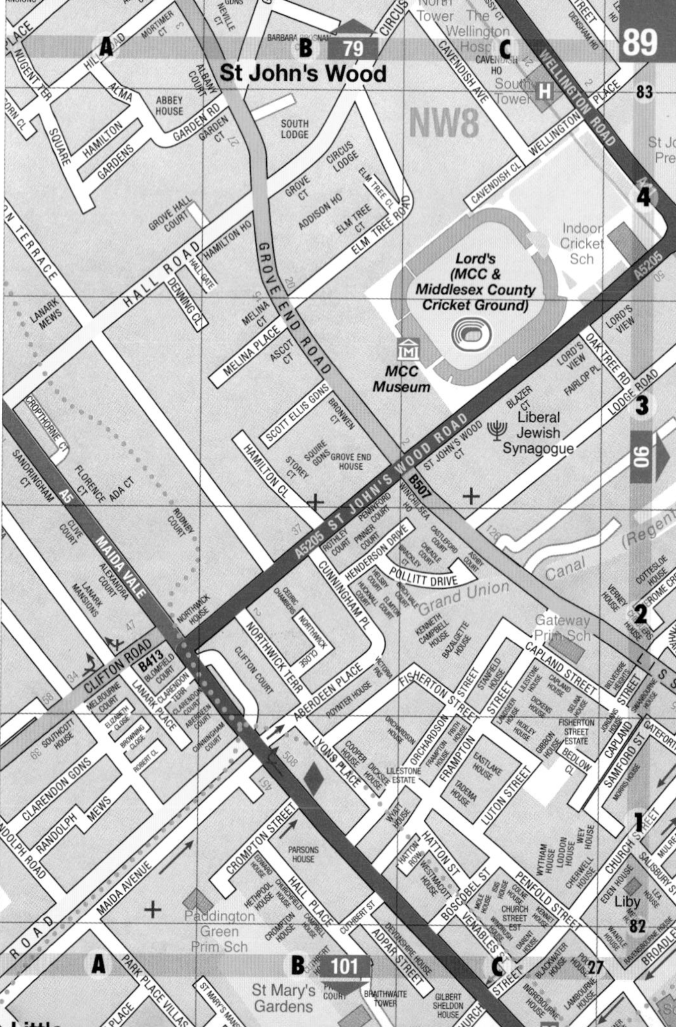
St John's Wood
NW8
79
A
B
C
83
4
3
2
1
82
90
101
Lord's
(MCC &
Middlesex County
Cricket Ground)
MCC
Museum
Liberal
Jewish
Synagogue
Indoor
Cricket
Sch
Gateway
Prim Sch
Paddington
Green
Prim Sch
St Mary's
Gardens
Wellington Hosp
South Tower
North Tower
Grand Union
Canal
(Regent's
WELLINGTON ROAD
GROVE END ROAD
HALL ROAD
A5205 ST JOHN'S WOOD ROAD
MAIDA VALE
CLIFTON ROAD
MAIDA AVENUE
ELM TREE ROAD
LODGE ROAD
CUNNINGHAM PL
ABERDEEN PLACE
FISHERTON STREET
NORTHWICK TERR
LYONS PLACE
CROMPTON STREET
HALL PLACE
LUTON STREET
PENFOLD STREET
HATTON ST
BOSCOBEL ST
CAPLAND STREET
CHURCH STREET
SALISBURY ST
BROADLEY ST
FRAMPTON
ORCHARDSON
POLLITT DRIVE
HENDERSON DRIVE
MELINA PLACE
HAMILTON CL
CLARENDON GDNS
RANDOLPH MEWS
PARK PLACE VILLAS
ADPAR STREET
CAVENDISH AVE
CAVENDISH CL
GARDEN RD
HAMILTON GARDENS
ABBEY HOUSE
SOUTH LODGE
CIRCUS LODGE
GROVE HALL COURT
LANARK MEWS
LANARK PLACE
Liby

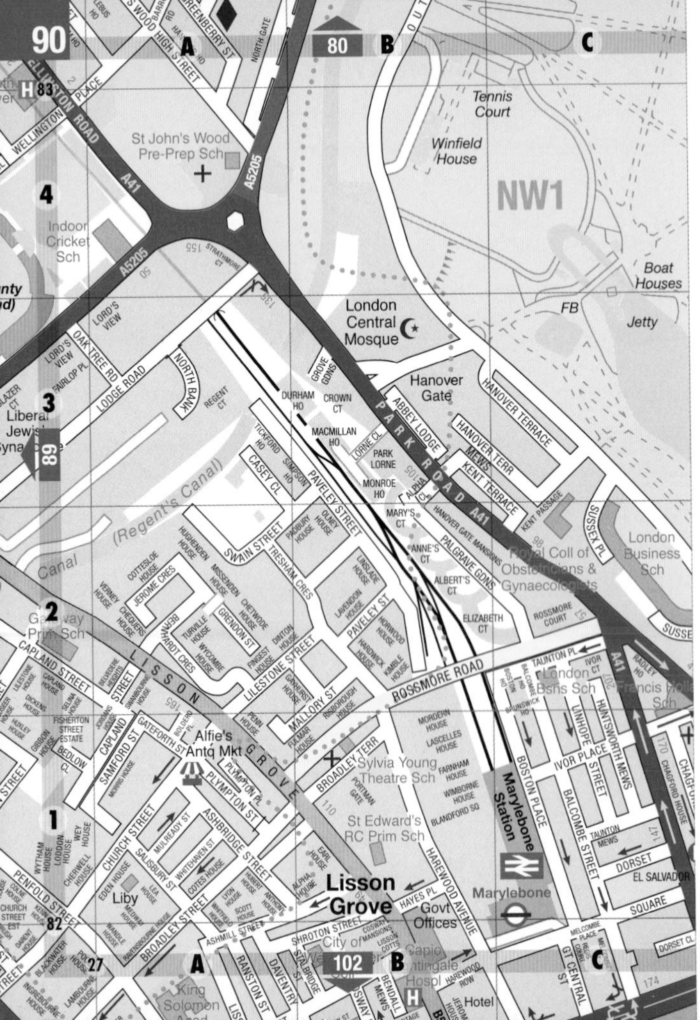

80
A
B
C
4
3
2
1
89
102
H 83
82
27
NW1
Tennis Court
Winfield House
Boat Houses
FB
Jetty
St John's Wood Pre-Prep Sch
Indoor Cricket Sch
Liberal Jewish Synagogue
London Central Mosque
Hanover Gate
Royal Coll of Obstetricians & Gynaecologists
London Business Sch
London Bsns Sch
Francis Holland Sch
Gateway Prim Sch
Alfie's Antq Mkt
Sylvia Young Theatre Sch
St Edward's RC Prim Sch
Lisson Grove
Liby
Govt Offices
Marylebone Station
Marylebone
City of Westminster Coll
Capio Nightingale Hospl
King Solomon Acad
Hotel
Regent's Canal
Canal
WELLINGTON ROAD
WELLINGTON PLACE
HIGH STREET
GREENBERRY ST
NORTH GATE
LEBUS HO
A41
A5205
STRATHMORE CT
LORD'S VIEW
OAK TREE RD
FAIRLOP PL
LODGE ROAD
NORTH BANK
REGENT CT
DURHAM HO
CROWN CT
GROVE GDNS
MACMILLAN HO
LORNE CL
PARK LORNE
MONROE HO
ALPHA CL
MARY'S CT
ANNE'S CT
ALBERT'S CT
ELIZABETH CT
PARK ROAD
ABBEY LODGE
HANOVER TERR MEWS
HANOVER TERRACE
KENT TERRACE
KENT PASSAGE
SUSSEX PL
HANOVER GATE MANSIONS
PALGRAVE GDNS
ROSSMORE COURT
ROSSMORE ROAD
TICKFORD HO
CASEY CL
SIMPSON HO
PAVELEY STREET
SWAIN STREET
TRESHAM CRES
LINSLADE HOUSE
LAVENDON HOUSE
PAVELEY ST
HORWOOD HOUSE
HARDWICK HOUSE
KIMBLE HOUSE
HUGHENDEN HOUSE
COTTESLOE HOUSE
JEROME CRES
MISSENDEN HOUSE
CHETWODE HOUSE
VERNEY HOUSE
CHEQUERS HOUSE
BERNHARDT CRES
TURVILLE HOUSE
GRENDON ST
WYCOMBE HOUSE
FINGEST HOUSE
DINTON HOUSE
LILESTONE STREET
GARNHURST HOUSE
MALLORY ST
RISBOROUGH HOUSE
PENN HOUSE
FULMAR HOUSE
LISSON GROVE
CAPLAND STREET
LILESTONE HOUSE
CAPLAND HOUSE
SELINA HOUSE
DICKENS HOUSE
FISHERTON STREET ESTATE
GIBBON HOUSE
BEDLOW CL
SAMFORD ST
GATEFORTH ST
BOLDERO PL
PLYMPTON PL
PLYMPTON ST
BROADLEY TERR
PORTMAN GATE
MORDERN HOUSE
LASCELLES HOUSE
FARNHAM HOUSE
WIMBORNE HOUSE
BLANDFORD SQ
TAUNTON PL
IVOR CT
BOSTON HO
BALCOMBE HO
BRUNSWICK HO
LINHOPE STREET
HUNTSWORTH MEWS
IVOR PLACE
BOSTON PLACE
BALCOMBE STREET
TAUNTON MEWS
DORSET SQUARE
EL SALVADOR
RADLEY HO
CHAGFORD HOUSE
MELCOMBE PLACE
DORSET CL
GT CENTRAL ST
CHURCH STREET
MULREADY ST
SALISBURY ST
WHITEHAVEN ST
COTES HOUSE
ASHBRIDGE STREET
EDEN HOUSE
LEA HOUSE
MEDWAY HOUSE
BROADLEY STREET
ASHMILL STREET
WYTHAM HOUSE
LODDON HOUSE
CHERWELL HOUSE
WEY HOUSE
PENFOLD STREET
CHURCH STREET EST
BLACKWATER HOUSE
LAMBOURNE HOUSE
INGREBOURNE HOUSE
ALPHA HOUSE
EARL HOUSE
HAYES PL
HAREWOOD AVENUE
HAREWOOD ROW
SHROTON STREET
COSWAY MANSIONS
LISSON COTTS
RANSTON ST
DAVENTRY ST
STALBRIDGE ST
BENDALL MEWS
JEROME HOUSE

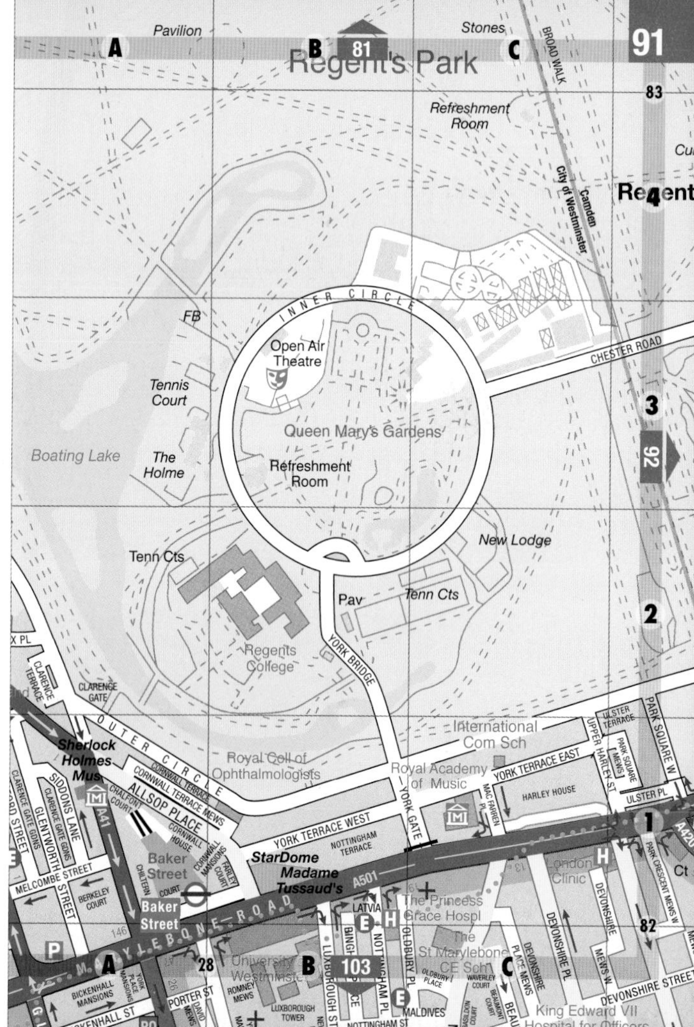

Regent's Park
Pavilion
Stones
BROAD WALK
Refreshment Room
City of Westminster
Camden
INNER CIRCLE
CHESTER ROAD
Open Air Theatre
Queen Mary's Gardens
Refreshment Room
FB
Tennis Court
Boating Lake
The Holme
Tenn Cts
New Lodge
Pav
Tenn Cts
Regents College
YORK BRIDGE
CLARENCE TERRACE
CLARENCE GATE
OUTER CIRCLE
International Com Sch
Royal Coll of Ophthalmologists
Royal Academy of Music
Sherlock Holmes Mus
YORK TERRACE EAST
UPPER HARLEY ST
ULSTER TERRACE
PARK SQUARE MEWS
PARK SQUARE W
HARLEY HOUSE
ULSTER PL
MAC FARREN PL
YORK GATE
YORK TERRACE WEST
NOTTINGHAM TERRACE
CORNWALL TERRACE
CORNWALL TERRACE MEWS
ALLSOP PLACE
CHALFONT COURT
CORNWALL HOUSE
CORNWALL MANSIONS
FARLEY COURT
Baker Street
CHILTERN COURT
StarDome
Madame Tussaud's
A501
MARYLEBONE ROAD
A4201
London Clinic
PARK CRESCENT MEWS W
DEVONSHIRE
DEVONSHIRE PL
DEVONSHIRE PLACE MEWS
DEVONSHIRE MEWS W
DEVONSHIRE STREET
SIDDONS LANE
CLARENCE GATE GDNS
GLENTWORTH STREET
MELCOMBE STREET
BERKELEY COURT
A41
LATVIA
The Princess Grace Hospl
The St Marylebone CE Sch
University of Westminster
LUXBOROUGH ST
NOTTINGHAM PL
OLDBURY PL
OLDBURY PLACE
WAVERLEY COURT
BEAUMONT COURT
BASILDON COURT
MALDIVES
NOTTINGHAM ST
LUXBOROUGH TOWER
ROMNEY MEWS
PORTER ST
DAVID MEWS
BICKENHALL MANSIONS
YORK PLACE MANSIONS
King Edward VII Hospital for Officers
X PL
Ct
Cur
Regent'
A
B
C
1
2
3
4
81
82
83
92
103
28
146

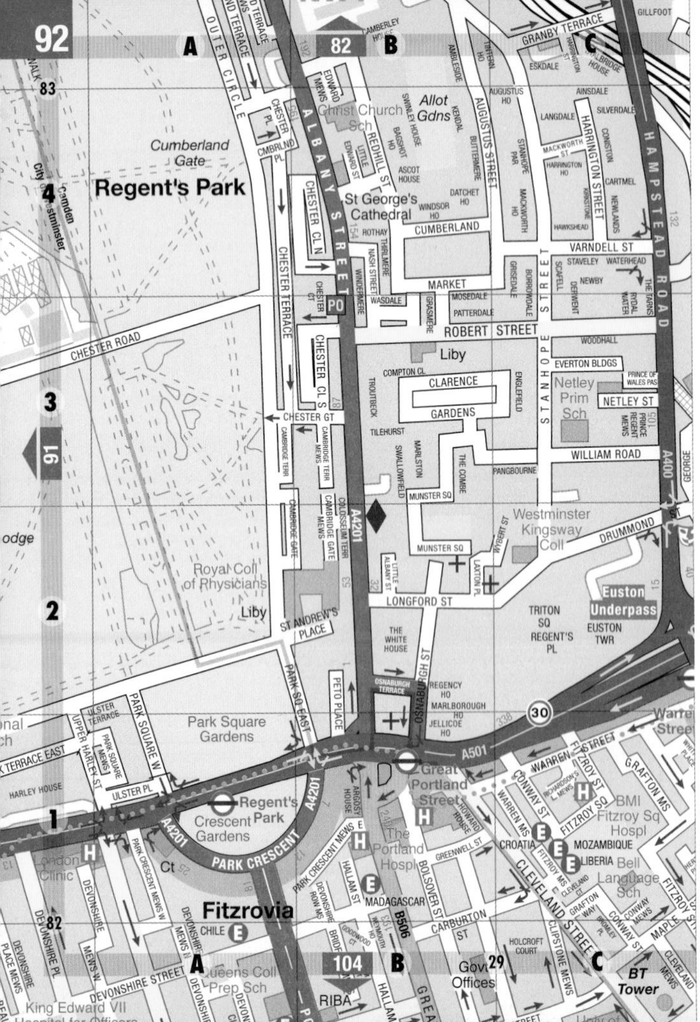

Regent's Park
Cumberland Gate
Chester Road
Outer Circle
Albany Street
Christ Church Sch
Allot Gdns
St George's Cathedral
Augustus Street
Hampstead Road
Granby Terrace
Harrington Street
Cumberland Market
Robert Street
Stanhope Street
Varndell St
Liby
Clarence Gardens
Netley Prim Sch
Netley St
William Road
Munster Sq
Westminster Kingsway Coll
Drummond St
Longford St
Euston Underpass
Triton Sq
Regent's Pl
Euston Twr
Royal Coll of Rhysicians
St Andrew's Place
Park Sq East
Chester Terrace
Chester Gt
Cambridge Gate
Osnaburgh St
Osnaburgh Terrace
Park Square Gardens
Park Square W
Ulster Terrace
Ulster Pl
Upper Harley St
Park Square Mews
Harley House
Regent's Park
Park Crescent
Crescent Gardens
Great Portland Street
London Clinic
Fitzrovia
Chile
Madagascar
Croatia
Mozambique
Liberia
Warren Street
Fitzroy Sq
BMI Fitzroy Sq Hospl
Bell Language Sch
The Portland Hospl
Conway St
Cleveland Street
Carburton St
Bolsover St
Hallam St
Devonshire Street
Devonshire Pl
King Edward VII Hospital for Officers
Queens Coll Prep Sch
RIBA
Govt Offices
Holcroft Court
Clipstone Mews
Grafton Way
BT Tower
A4201
A501
A400
B506

82
91
104

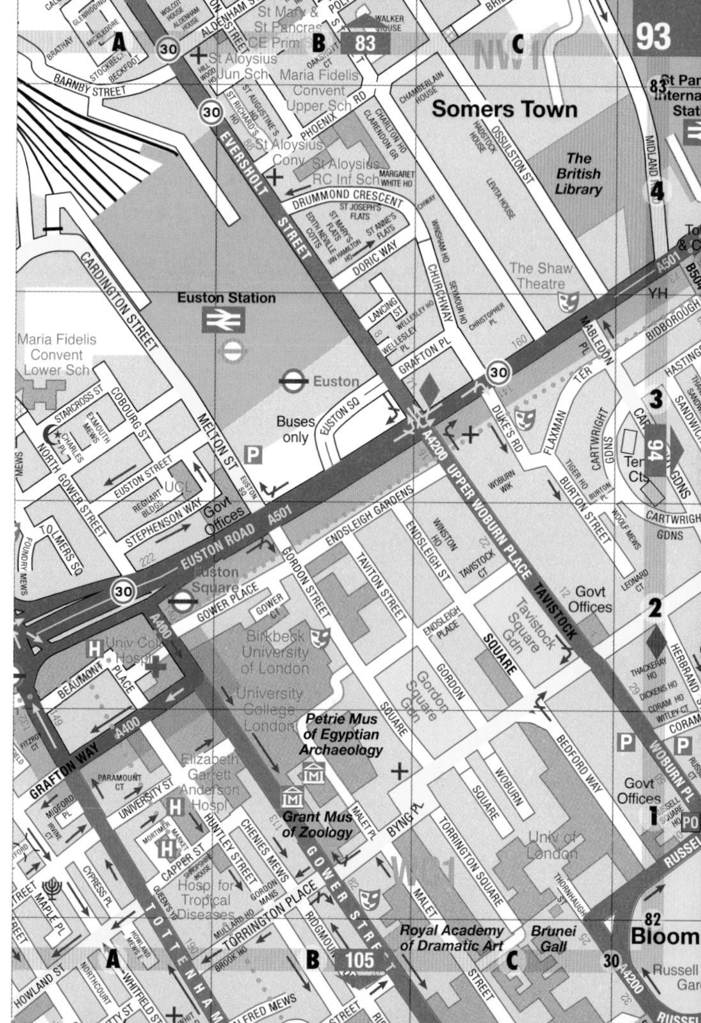

93
Somers Town
The British Library
Euston Station
Euston
Euston Square
Buses only
Govt Offices
The Shaw Theatre
Maria Fidelis Convent Lower Sch
Maria Fidelis Convent Upper Sch
St Aloysius Jun Sch
St Aloysius Conv
St Aloysius RC Inf Sch
St Mary & St Pancras CE Prim
Birkbeck University of London
University College London
Petrie Mus of Egyptian Archaeology
Grant Mus of Zoology
Elizabeth Garrett Anderson Hospl
Hospl for Tropical Diseases
Univ Coll Hospl
Royal Academy of Dramatic Art
Brunei Gall
Univ of London
Tavistock Square Gdn
Gordon Square Gdn
EUSTON ROAD
EVERSHOLT STREET
UPPER WOBURN PLACE
TAVISTOCK SQUARE
GOWER STREET
TOTTENHAM
GRAFTON WAY
CARDINGTON STREET
MELTON ST
NORTH GOWER STREET
GORDON STREET
ENDSLEIGH GARDENS
ENDSLEIGH ST
TAVITON STREET
BEDFORD WAY
WOBURN PL
TORRINGTON PLACE
HUNTLEY STREET
CHENIES MEWS
DRUMMOND CRESCENT
OSSULSTON ST
MIDLAND RD
CHURCHWAY
DUKE'S RD
BURTON STREET
FLAXMAN TER
CARTWRIGHT GDNS
BIDBOROUGH
HASTINGS
MABLEDON PL
GOWER PLACE
BEAUMONT PLACE
UNIVERSITY ST
CAPPER ST
MAPLE PL
HOWLAND ST
WHITFIELD ST
ALFRED MEWS
BYNG PL
MALET PL
TORRINGTON SQUARE
HERBRAND ST
CORAM
RUSSELL
Blooms
83
94
105
A
B
C
NW1
WC1
1
2
3
4

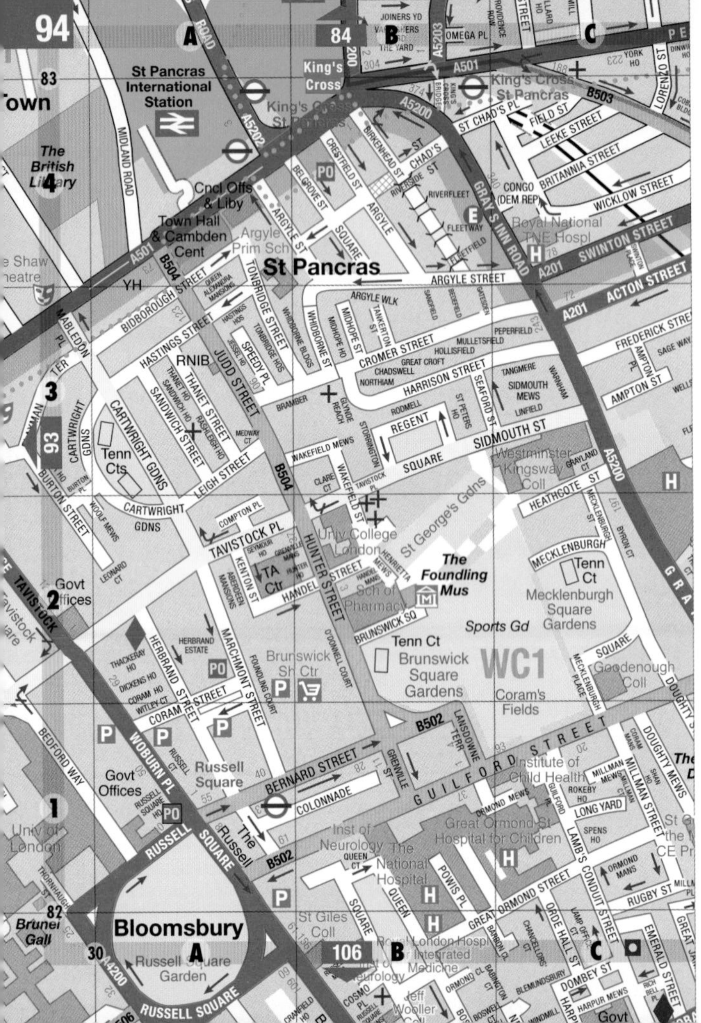

A
84
B
C
St Pancras International Station
King's Cross
King's Cross St Pancras
The British Library
Cncl Offs & Liby
Town Hall & Cambden Cent
Argyle Prim Sch
St Pancras
Royal National TNE Hospl
RNIB
Tenn Cts
Westminster Kingsway Coll
Univ College London
St George's Gdns
The Foundling Mus
Sch of Pharmacy
TA Ctr
Mecklenburgh Square Gardens
Sports Gd
Brunswick Sh Ctr
Brunswick Square Gardens
WC1
Coram's Fields
Goodenough Coll
Govt Offices
Russell Square
Institute of Child Health
Great Ormond St Hospital for Children
Inst of Neurology
The National Hospital
St Giles Coll
Royal London Hospl for Integrated Medicine
Univ of London
Brunei Gall
Bloomsbury
Russell Square Garden
106
93
GRAY'S INN ROAD
JUDD STREET
HUNTER STREET
GUILFORD STREET
BERNARD STREET
RUSSELL SQUARE
WOBURN PL
ARGYLE STREET
SWINTON STREET
ACTON STREET
CROMER STREET
HARRISON STREET
SIDMOUTH ST
REGENT SQUARE
TAVISTOCK PL
MARCHMONT STREET
HERBRAND STREET
CORAM STREET
GREAT ORMOND STREET
LAMB'S CONDUIT STREET
MIDLAND ROAD

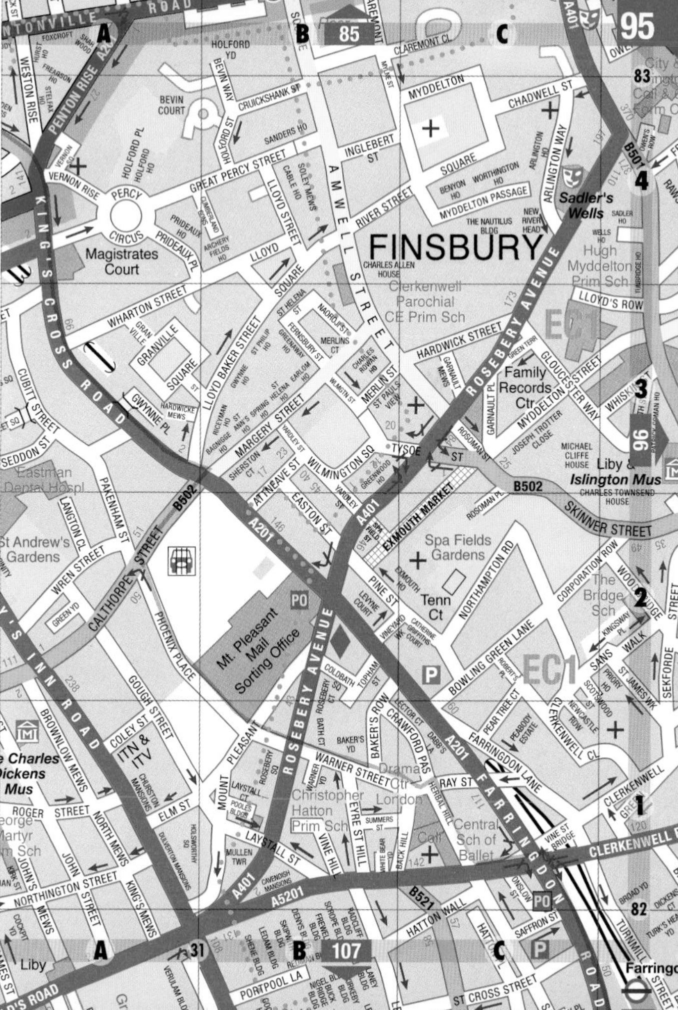

FINSBURY
Magistrates Court
Sadler's Wells
Hugh Myddelton Prim Sch
Clerkenwell Parochial CE Prim Sch
Family Records Ctr
Liby & Islington Mus
Spa Fields Gardens
Mt. Pleasant Mail Sorting Office
Eastman Dental Hospl
St Andrew's Gardens
The Bridge Sch
Christopher Hatton Prim Sch
Drama Ctr London
Central Sch of Ballet
ITN & ITV
Charles Dickens Mus
PENTONVILLE ROAD
KING'S CROSS ROAD
ROSEBERY AVENUE
AMWELL STREET
FARRINGDON ROAD
GRAY'S INN ROAD
CLERKENWELL ROAD
SKINNER STREET
EXMOUTH MARKET
FARRINGDON LANE

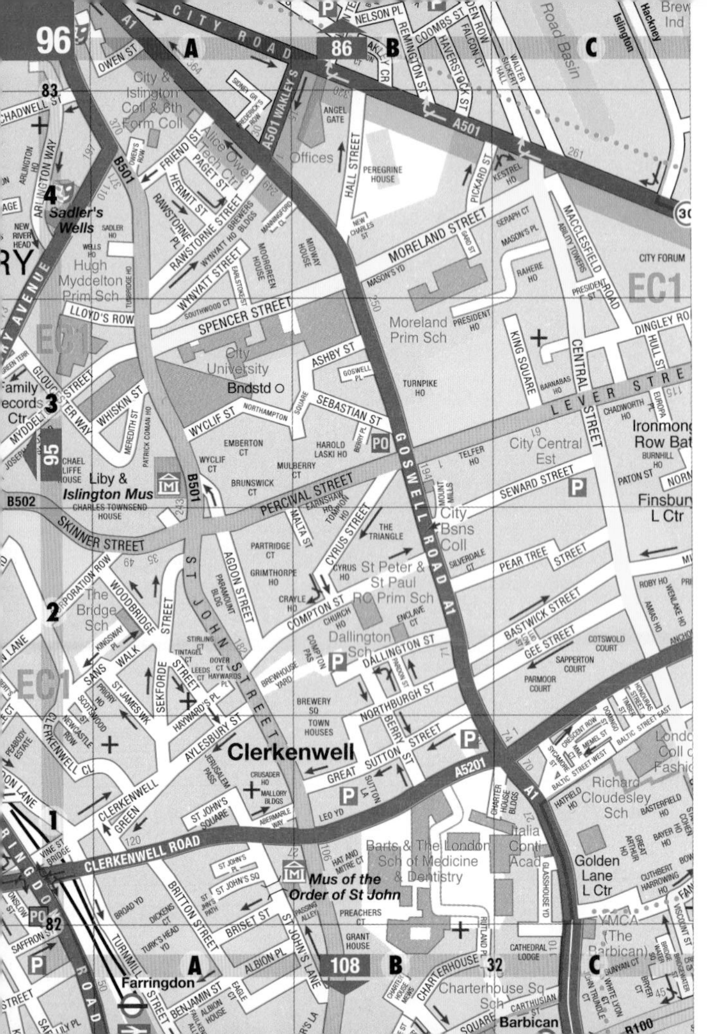

86
108
82
83
95
32
A
B
C
1
2
3
4
CITY ROAD
A1
A501
B501
B502
A5201
B100
EC1
Road Basin
Islington
Hackney
City & Islington Coll & 6th Form Coll
Alice Owen Tech Ctr
Offices
Sadler's Wells
Hugh Myddelton Prim Sch
City University
Bndstd
Moreland Prim Sch
City Central Est
Liby & Islington Mus
City Bsns Coll
St Peter & St Paul RC Prim Sch
The Bridge Sch
Dallington Sch
Clerkenwell
Mus of the Order of St John
Barts & The London Sch of Medicine & Dentistry
Italia Conti Acad
Richard Cloudesley Sch
Golden Lane L Ctr
YMCA (The Barbican)
Charterhouse Sq Sch
Farringdon
Barbican
Finsbury L Ctr
CITY FORUM
OWEN ST
NELSON PL
REMINGTON ST
COOMBS ST
HAVERSTOCK ST
FALCON CT
WALTER SICKERT HALL
WAKLEY ST
ANGEL GATE
HALL STREET
PEREGRINE HOUSE
PICKARD ST
KESTREL HO
MORELAND STREET
MACCLESFIELD ROAD
CHADWELL ST
ARLINGTON WAY
FRIEND ST
PAGET ST
HERMIT ST
RAWSTORNE ST
RAWSTORNE STREET
RAWSTORNE PL
WYNYATT STREET
SPENCER STREET
LLOYD'S ROW
MASON'S YD
SERAPH CT
MASON'S PL
RAHERE HO
PRESIDENT HO
KING SQUARE
CENTRAL STREET
DINGLEY ROAD
HULL ST
LEVER STREET
ASHBY ST
SEBASTIAN ST
NORTHAMPTON SQUARE
WYCLIF ST
GOSWELL ROAD
TURNPIKE HO
BARNABAS HO
CHADWORTH HO
Ironmonger Row Baths
PATON ST
SEWARD STREET
PERCIVAL STREET
SKINNER STREET
ST JOHN STREET
AGDON STREET
CYRUS STREET
MALTA ST
THE TRIANGLE
PEAR TREE STREET
BASTWICK STREET
GEE STREET
COMPTON ST
DALLINGTON ST
NORTHBURGH ST
BERRY ST
SUTTON LA
GREAT SUTTON STREET
WOODBRIDGE STREET
SANS WALK
SEKFORDE STREET
ST JAMES WK
HAYWARD'S PL
AYLESBURY ST
JERUSALEM PASS
CLERKENWELL GREEN
CLERKENWELL CL
CLERKENWELL ROAD
ST JOHN'S SQUARE
BRITTON STREET
BRISET ST
ST JOHN'S LANE
ALBION PL
TURNMILL STREET
FARRINGDON ROAD
BENJAMIN ST
CHARTERHOUSE ST
CARTHUSIAN ST
GLASSHOUSE YD
RUTLAND PL
CATHEDRAL LODGE
BALTIC STREET WEST
BALTIC STREET EAST
GOLDEN LANE

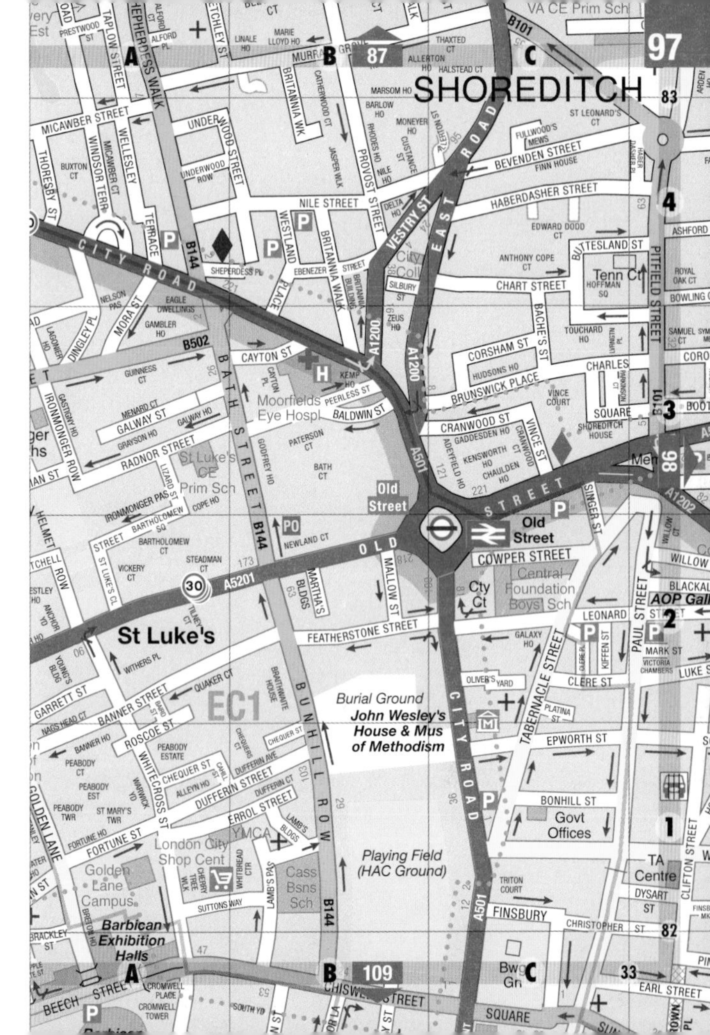

97
87
SHOREDITCH
83
CITY ROAD
EAST ROAD
VESTRY ST
NILE STREET
HABERDASHER STREET
BEVENDEN STREET
PITFIELD STREET
CHART STREET
CORSHAM ST
BRUNSWICK PLACE
CRANWOOD ST
CHARLES SQUARE
Moorfields Eye Hospl
St Luke's CE Prim Sch
Old Street
OLD STREET
COWPER STREET
Central Foundation Boys' Sch
St Luke's
EC1
BATH STREET
BUNHILL ROW
WHITECROSS ST
GOLDEN LANE
FEATHERSTONE STREET
LEONARD ST
PAUL STREET
TABERNACLE STREET
Burial Ground
John Wesley's House & Mus of Methodism
Playing Field (HAC Ground)
Govt Offices
TA Centre
London City Shop Cent
Golden Lane Campus
Cass Bsns Sch
Barbican Exhibition Halls
FINSBURY SQUARE
CHISWELL STREET
BEECH STREET
EARL STREET
109
98
82

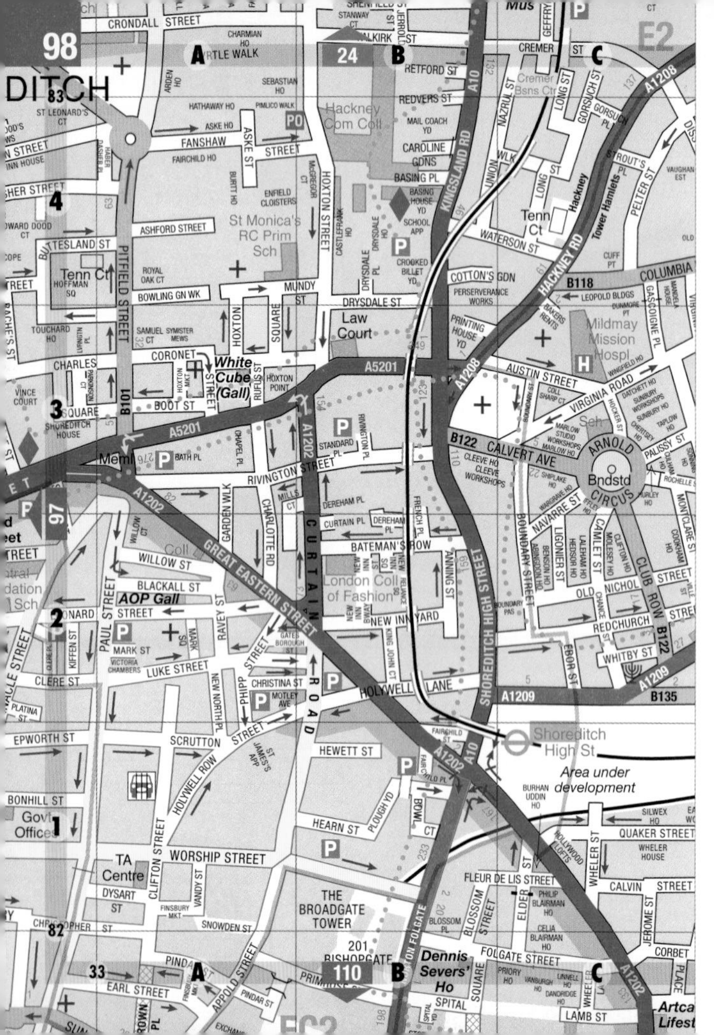
DITCH
A
B
C
24
E2
CRONDALL STREET
CHARMIAN HO
MYRTLE WALK
STANWAY CT
JERROLD ST
FALKIRK ST
CREMER ST
GEFFRYE
Mus
RETFORD ST
REDVERS ST
MAIL COACH YD
CAROLINE GDNS
BASING PL
BASING HOUSE YD
SCHOOL APP
Hackney Com Coll
ARDEN HO
SEBASTIAN HO
HATHAWAY HO
PIMLICO WALK
ASKE HO
ASKE ST
FANSHAW STREET
FAIRCHILD HO
BURTT HO
ENFIELD CLOISTERS
McGREGOR CT
HOXTON STREET
CASTLEFRANK HO
DRYSDALE HO
DRYSDALE PL
CROOKED BILLET YD
St Monica's RC Prim Sch
ST LEONARD'S CT
HABER DASHER PL
ASHFORD STREET
BUTTESLAND ST
ROYAL OAK CT
Tenn Ct
HOFFMAN SQ
BOWLING GN WK
MUNDY ST
DRYSDALE ST
Law Court
TOUCHARD HO
SAMUEL CT
SYMISTER MEWS
HOXTON
SQUARE
CHARLES SQUARE
CORONET ST
White Cube (Gall)
HOXTON MKT
RUFUS ST
HOXTON POINT
A5201
VINCE COURT
SHOREDITCH HOUSE
BOOT ST
B101
PITFIELD STREET
Meml
BATH PL
CHAPEL PL
RIVINGTON PL
STANDARD PL
RIVINGTON STREET
A1202
MILLS CT
DEREHAM PL
CURTAIN PL
DEREHAM PL
CHARLOTTE RD
GARDEN WALK
WILLOW CT
WILLOW ST
BLACKALL ST
AOP Gall
GREAT EASTERN STREET
CURTAIN ROAD
BATEMAN'S ROW
London Coll of Fashion
NEW INN YARD
FRENCH PL
ANNING ST
RAVEY ST
LEONARD STREET
PAUL STREET
MARK ST
MARK SQ
VICTORIA CHAMBERS
LUKE STREET
GATESBOROUGH ST
CHRISTINA ST
MOTLEY AVE
KING JOHN CT
HOLYWELL LANE
KIFFEN ST
CLERE PL
CLERE ST
TABERNACLE STREET
PLATINA ST
NEW NORTH PL
PHIPP ST
EPWORTH ST
SCRUTTON STREET
ST JAMES'S APP
HEWETT ST
FAIRCHILD ST
FAIRCHILD PL
BONHILL ST
HOLYWELL ROW
Govt Offices
PLOUGH YD
HEARN ST
BOWL CT
TA Centre
CLIFTON STREET
WORSHIP STREET
VANDY ST
DYSART ST
FINSBURY MKT
CHRISTOPHER ST
SNOWDEN ST
THE BROADGATE TOWER
201 BISHOPSGATE
PINDAR ST
APPOLD STREET
EARL STREET
PRIMROSE ST
110
NORTON FOLGATE
BLOSSOM PL
BLOSSOM STREET
Dennis Severs' Ho
SPITAL SQUARE
SPITAL YD
KINGSLAND RD
A10
NAZRUL ST
UNION WLK
Cremer Bsns Ctr
LONG ST
GOSSET ST
GORSUCH PL
A1208
HACKNEY RD
Hackney
Tower Hamlets
LONG ST
Tenn Ct
WATERSON ST
STROUT'S PL
PELTER ST
VAUGHAN EST
CUFF PT
COLUMBIA ROAD
B118
LEOPOLD BLDGS
DUNMORE PT
COTTON'S GDN
PERSERVERANCE WORKS
PRINTING HOUSE YD
BAKERS RENTS
MANDELA HOUSE
GASCOIGNE PL
Mildmay Mission Hospl
WINGFIELD HO
AUSTIN STREET
VIRGINIA ROAD
DATCHETT HO
SUNBURY HO
SUNBURY WORKSHOPS
TAPLOW HO
CHERTSEY HO
COLL SHARP CT
BOUNDARY ST
HOCKER ST
MARLOW STUDIO WORKSHOPS
MARLOW HO
Sch
B122
CALVERT AVE
CLEEVE HO
CLEEVE WORKSHOPS
ARNOLD CIRCUS
Bndstd
PALISSY ST
SHIPLAKE HO
WARGRAVE HO
NAVARRE ST
ROCHELLE ST
HURLEY HO
MONTCLARE ST
COOKHAM HO
LIGONIER ST
BENSON HO
HEDSOR HO
LALEHAM HO
CAMLET ST
MOLESEY HO
CLIFTON HO
CLUB ROW
BOUNDARY STREET
ABINGDON HO
OLD NICHOL STREET
CHANCE ST
REDCHURCH STREET
SHOREDITCH HIGH STREET
BOUNDARY PAS
EBOR ST
WHITBY ST
A1209
B135
Shoreditch High St
Area under development
BURHAN UDDIN HO
SILWEX HO
QUAKER STREET
WHELER ST
WHELER HOUSE
HOLLYWOOD LOFTS
CALVIN STREET
FLEUR DE LIS STREET
PHILIP BLAIRMAN HO
CELIA BLAIRMAN HO
ELDER ST
JEROME ST
CORBET PLACE
FOLGATE STREET
PRIORY HO
VANBURGH HO
LINNELL HO
DANDRIDGE HO
WHEELER PL
LAMB ST
Artcart Lifest
SPITAL ST
EC2
97
33
82
1
2
3
4

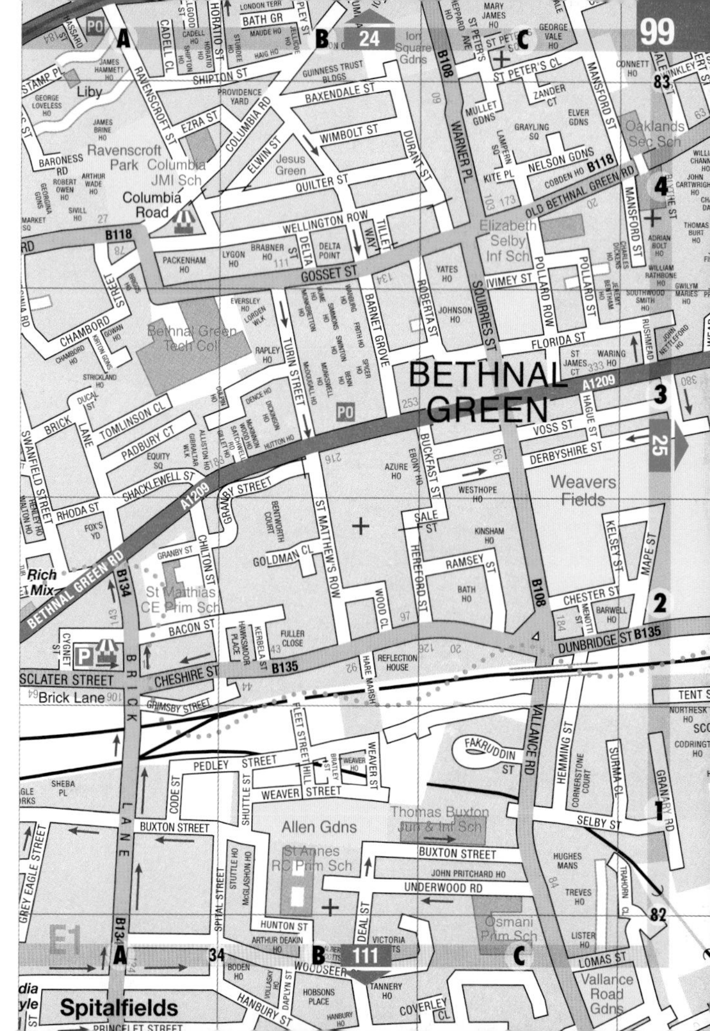
A
B
C
24
25
111
4
3
2
1
83
82
BETHNAL
GREEN
Spitalfields
E1
Brick Lane
Weavers
Fields
Ravenscroft
Park
Columbia
JMI Sch
Columbia
Road
Jesus
Green
Ion
Square
Gdns
Oaklands
Sec Sch
Elizabeth
Selby
Inf Sch
Bethnal Green
Tech Coll
St Matthias
CE Prim Sch
Allen Gdns
St Annes
RC Prim Sch
Thomas Buxton
Jun & Inf Sch
Osmani
Prim Sch
Vallance
Road
Gdns
Rich
Mix
Liby
PO
LONDON TERR
BATH GR
MAUDE HO
HAIG HO
JELLICOE HO
CADELL HO
HORATIO HO
SHIPTON HO
STURDEE HO
HORATIO ST
CADELL CL
PLEY ST
GUINNESS TRUST BLDGS
SHIPTON ST
BAXENDALE ST
PROVIDENCE YARD
RAVENSCROFT ST
EZRA ST
COLUMBIA RD
ELWIN ST
WIMBOLT ST
DURANT ST
QUILTER ST
WELLINGTON ROW
TILLETT WAY
DELTA ST
DELTA POINT
BRABNER HO
LYGON HO
PACKENHAM HO
GOSSET ST
B118
B108
B134
B135
A1209
MARY JAMES HO
ST PETER'S AVE
ST PETER'S CL
GEORGE VALE HO
MANSFORD ST
CONNETT HO
ZANDER CT
ELVER GDNS
GRAYLING SQ
MULLET GDNS
LAMPERN SQ
NELSON GDNS
COBDEN HO
KITE PL
OLD BETHNAL GREEN RD
WARNER PL
JOHN CARTWRIGHT HO
THOMAS BURT HO
ADRIAN BOLT HO
WILLIAM RATHBONE HO
GWILYM MARIES HO
SOUTHWOOD SMITH HO
RUSHMEAD
JOHN NETTLEFORD HO
CHARLES DICKENS HO
JEREMY BENTHAM HO
POLLARD ST
POLLARD ROW
IVIMEY ST
SQUIRRIES ST
YATES HO
JOHNSON HO
ROBERTA ST
BARNET GROVE
FLORIDA ST
ST JAMES CT
WARING HO
HAGUE ST
VOSS ST
DERBYSHIRE ST
WESTHOPE HO
KINSHAM HO
BUCKFAST ST
EBONY HO
AZURE HO
SALE ST
HEREFORD ST
RAMSEY ST
BATH HO
KELSEY ST
MAPE ST
CHESTER ST
MENOTTI ST
BARWELL HO
DUNBRIDGE ST
WOOD CL
ST MATTHEW'S ROW
BENTWORTH COURT
GOLDMAN CL
GRANBY STREET
GRANBY ST
CHILTON ST
BACON ST
FULLER CLOSE
KERBELA ST
HAWKSMOOR PLACE
CHESHIRE ST
REFLECTION HOUSE
HARE MARSH
GRIMSBY STREET
SCLATER STREET
CYGNET ST
BRICK LANE
BETHNAL GREEN RD
SHACKLEWELL ST
RHODA ST
FOX'S YD
SWANFIELD STREET
HENLEY HO
WALTON HO
EQUITY SQ
PADBURY CT
TOMLINSON CL
DUCAL ST
STRICKLAND HO
CHAMBORD ST
CHAMBORD HO
GOWAN HO
KIRTON GDNS
BRIGGS HO
TURIN STREET
RAPLEY HO
EVERSLEY HO
LORDEN WLK
DENCE HO
DICKINSON HO
HUTTON HO
GEORGE LOVELESS HO
JAMES HAMMETT HO
JAMES BRINE HO
STAMP PL
BARONESS RD
ARTHUR WADE HO
ROBERT OWEN HO
SIVILL HO
GEORGINA GDNS
MARKET SQ
VALLANCE RD
FAKRUDDIN ST
HEMMING ST
CORNERSTONE COURT
SURMA CL
GRANARY RD
TENT ST
NORTHESK HO
CODRINGTON HO
SELBY ST
HUGHES MANS
TREVES HO
LISTER HO
TRAHORN CL
LOMAS ST
BUXTON STREET
JOHN PRITCHARD HO
UNDERWOOD RD
DEAL ST
VICTORIA
TANNERY HO
COVERLEY CL
HUNTON ST
ARTHUR DEAKIN HO
STUTTLE HO
McGLASHON HO
SPITAL STREET
BODEN HO
VOLLASKY HO
DAPLYN ST
HOBSONS PLACE
HANBURY HO
HANBURY ST
WOODSEER ST
PRINCELET STREET
GREY EAGLE STREET
SHEBA PL
CODE ST
PEDLEY STREET
SHUTTLE ST
WEAVER STREET
FLEET STREET HILL
BRATLEY ST
WEAVER HO
WEAVER ST
BUXTON STREET

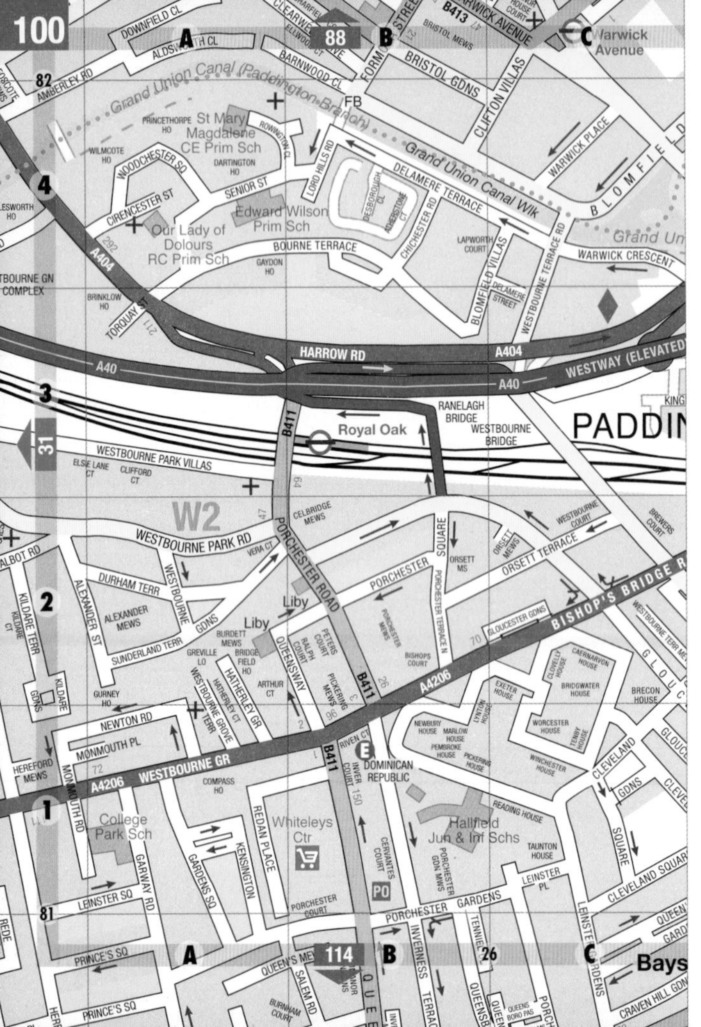

A
B
C
88
Warwick Avenue
DOWNFIELD CL
ALDSWORTH CL
AMBERLEY RD
82
Grand Union Canal (Paddington Branch)
BARNWOOD CL
BRISTOL MEWS
BRISTOL GDNS
WARWICK AVENUE
B413
CLIFTON VILLAS
WARWICK PLACE
BLOMFIELD
FB
PRINCETHORPE HO
St Mary Magdalene CE Prim Sch
DARTINGTON HO
WILMCOTE HO
WOODCHESTER SQ
ROWINGTON CL
LORD HILLS RD
DELAMERE TERRACE
Grand Union Canal Wlk
DESBOROUGH CL
ATHERSTONE CT
4
CIRENCESTER ST
SENIOR ST
Edward Wilson Prim Sch
Our Lady of Dolours RC Prim Sch
BOURNE TERRACE
GAYDON HO
CHICHESTER RD
LAPWORTH COURT
BLOMFIELD VILLAS
DELAMERE STREET
WESTBOURNE TERRACE RD
WARWICK CRESCENT
Grand Union
A404
BRINKLOW HO
TORQUAY ST
HARROW RD
A40
WESTWAY (ELEVATED)
3
B411
Royal Oak
RANELAGH BRIDGE
WESTBOURNE BRIDGE
PADDIN
31
WESTBOURNE PARK VILLAS
ELSIE LANE CT
CLIFFORD CT
W2
CELBRIDGE MEWS
WESTBOURNE PARK RD
VERA CT
PORCHESTER ROAD
PORCHESTER SQUARE
ORSETT MS
ORSETT MEWS
WESTBOURNE COURT
ORSETT TERRACE
BREWERS COURT
BISHOP'S BRIDGE RD
2
KILDARE TERR
ALEXANDER ST
DURHAM TERR
ALEXANDER MEWS
WESTBOURNE GDNS
SUNDERLAND TERR
Liby
BURDETT MEWS
BRIDGEFIELD HO
GREVILLE LO
QUEENSWAY
RALPH COURT
PETERS COURT
PORCHESTER MEWS
PORCHESTER TERRACE N
BISHOPS COURT
GLOUCESTER GDNS
A4206
ARTHUR CT
PICKERING MEWS
GURNEY HO
NEWTON RD
HATHERLEY GR
HATHERLEY CT
WESTBOURNE GROVE TERR
CLOVELLY HOUSE
CAERNARVON HOUSE
BRIDGWATER HOUSE
EXETER HOUSE
LYNTON HOUSE
BRECON HOUSE
WORCESTER HOUSE
TENBY HOUSE
NEWBURY HOUSE
MARLOW HOUSE
PEMBROKE HOUSE
PICKERING HOUSE
WINCHESTER HOUSE
RIVEN CT
DOMINICAN REPUBLIC
MONMOUTH PL
HEREFORD MEWS
WESTBOURNE GR
1
MONMOUTH RD
COMPASS HO
INVER COURT
CLEVELAND GDNS
College Park Sch
Whiteleys Ctr
REDAN PLACE
KENSINGTON GARDENS SQ
GARWAY RD
CERVANTES COURT
PO
Hallfield Jun & Inf Schs
READING HOUSE
TAUNTON HOUSE
PORCHESTER GDN MWS
LEINSTER PL
CLEVELAND SQUARE
LEINSTER SQ
81
PORCHESTER COURT
PORCHESTER GARDENS
INVERNESS TERRACE
LEINSTER GARDENS
PRINCE'S SQ
114
QUEEN'S MEWS
SALEM RD
BURNHAM COURT
QUEENSWAY
Bays
CRAVEN HILL GDNS

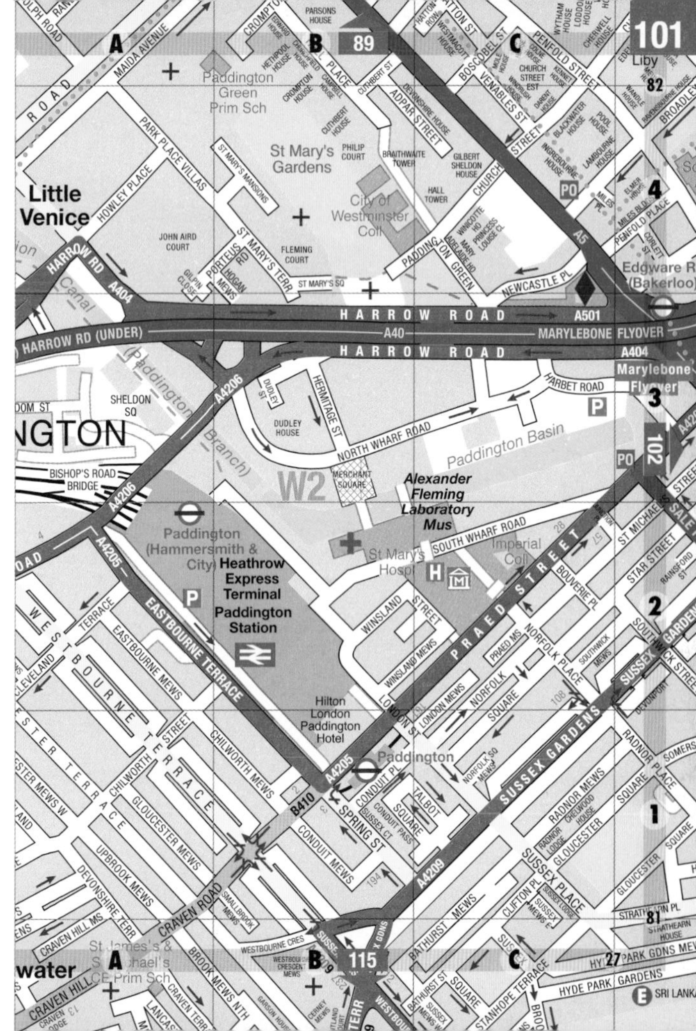

89
102
115
Little Venice
Paddington Green Prim Sch
St Mary's Gardens
City of Westminster Coll
HARROW ROAD
A501
HARROW RD (UNDER)
A40
MARYLEBONE FLYOVER
A404
Marylebone Flyover
Edgware Rd (Bakerloo)
Paddington Basin
W2
Alexander Fleming Laboratory Mus
St Mary's Hospl
Imperial Coll
Paddington (Hammersmith & City)
Heathrow Express Terminal
Paddington Station
Hilton London Paddington Hotel
Paddington
PRAED STREET
SUSSEX GARDENS
EASTBOURNE TERRACE
WESTBOURNE TERRACE
NORTH WHARF ROAD
SOUTH WHARF ROAD
SHELDON SQ
BISHOP'S ROAD BRIDGE
CRAVEN ROAD
HYDE PARK GARDENS
St James's & St Michael's CE Prim Sch
SRI LANKA

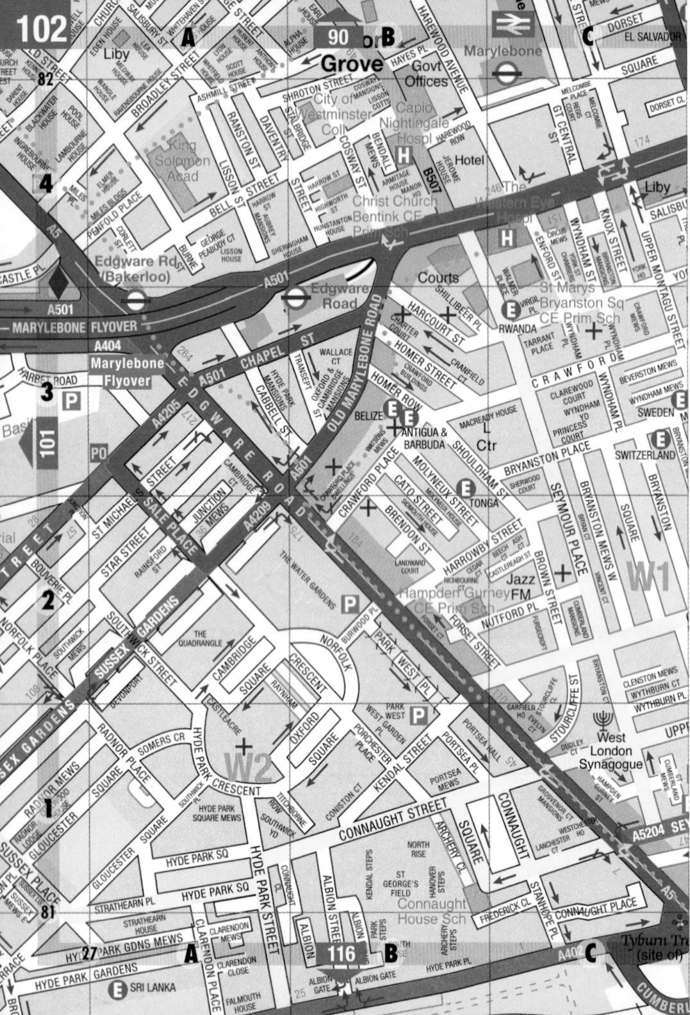

A
B
C
91
82
4
3
2
1
104
117
28
81
Baker Street
StarDome
Madame Tussaud
London Clinic
The Princess Grace Hospl
The St Marylebone CE Sch
University of Westminster
King Edward VII Hospital for Officers
BBC London Radio
The Heart Hospl
American Intercontinental Univ
St Vincent's RC Prim Sch
British Dental Association
Wallace Collection
Davies Laing & Dick Coll
Wigmore Hall
Western Marble Arch Synagogue
Cumberland Hotel
Marble Arch
Parklife Oxford St
West London Coll
West One Shop Cent
Bond Street
London Coll of Fashion
Albemarle College
MARYLEBONE ROAD
MELCOMBE STREET
BERKELEY COURT
CHILTERN COURT
CORNWALL MANSIONS
FARLEY COURT
YORK TERRACE
NOTTINGHAM TERRACE
BICKENHALL MANSIONS
YORK PLACE MANSIONS
BICKENHALL ST
PORTER ST
DAVID MEWS
ROMNEY MEWS
YORK MANSIONS
LUXBOROUGH TOWER
NEWCASTLE HOUSE
LUXBOROUGH HOUSE
LUXBOROUGH STREET
BINGHAM PLACE
NOTTINGHAM PL
OLDBURY PL
OLDBURY PLACE
WAVERLEY COURT
BEAUMONT COURT
BASILDON COURT
NOTTINGHAM ST
BRENDON HOUSE
TREBOROUGH HOUSE
DEVONSHIRE PLACE MEWS
DEVONSHIRE PL
DEVONSHIRE MEWS W
DEVONSHIRE STREET
DEVONSHIRE MEWS S
DEVONSHIRE
BEAUMONT ST
DUNSTABLE MEWS
UPPER WIMPOLE ST
CLARKES MEWS
BEAUMONT MEWS
MARYLEBONE HIGH STREET
PADDINGTON STREET
B524
GLOUCESTER PLACE
BAKER STREET
HONDURAS
MALDIVES
LATVIA
KYRGYZSTAN
LITHUANIA
ANGOLA
SHERLOCK MEWS
CHILTERN STREET
KENRICK PL
DURWESTON MEWS
SPRING MEWS
MONTAGU MANSIONS
MONTAGU ROW
CLAY ST
DURWESTON ST
ST ANDREW'S MANSIONS
GROTTO PAS
OSSINGTON BLDGS
ASHLAND PL
GARBUTT PLACE
MOXON ST
AYBROOK ST
CRAMER ST
MARYLEBONE ST
MAYBURY COURT
WESLEY ST
WESLEY CT
WHEATLEY ST
DE WALDEN ST
WESTMORLAND ST
WOODSTOCK MEWS
BROWNING MEWS
WIMPOLE MEWS
WEYMOUTH
DORSET STREET
WENDOVER HO
BROADSTONE PL
WENDOVER COURT
MANCHESTER STREET
MONTAGU MEWS N
BRYMON COURT
MONTAGU PLACE
MONTAGU COURT
RODMARTIN STREET
GLOUCESTER PLACE MEWS
ST VINCENT ST
CROSS KEYS CL
BULSTRODE PL
MARYLEBONE LA
BULSTRODE ST
MARYLEBONE MEWS
BLANDFORD STREET
ADMIRAL COURT
MANCHESTER MEWS
KENDALL PL
SPANISH PL
JACOB'S WELL MEWS
HERON PL
THAYER STREET
BENTINCK MS
BENTINCK ST
BENTINCK MANSIONS
WELBECK STREET
WELBECK WAY
WIMPOLE ST
MONTAGU SQUARE
MONTAGU MEWS W
CARLTON HOUSE
ROBERT ADAM ST
MANCHESTER SQUARE
HINDE ST
HINDE MS
MARYLEBONE LANE
EASLEY'S MEWS
GEORGE STREET
PORTMAN CLOSE
FITZHARDINGE HOUSE
BAKER'S MS
FITZHARDINGE ST
DUKE'S MS
MANDEVILLE PL
JASON CT
PORTMAN TOWERS
MONTAGU MEWS S
MONTAGU ST
PORTMAN SQUARE
ORCHARD COURT
SEYMOUR MEWS
WIGMORE STREET
B406
ST CHRISTOPHER'S PLACE
ALDBURGH MEWS
BRUNSWICK MEWS
GREAT CUMBERLAND PLACE
UPPER BERKELEY STREET
BERKELEY MEWS
NEW QUEBEC ST
QUEBEC MEWS
A41
A5204
GRAY'S YD
JAMES STREET
SARSDEN BLDGS
BOURNE MEWS
STRATFORD PL
EDWARDS MEWS
PICTON PLACE
TANZANIA
BOTSWANA
BARRETT ST
GEES CT
BILTON TOWERS
SEYMOUR STREET
OLD QUEBEC ST
PORTMAN MEWS STH
ORCHARD ST
BIRD ST
DUKE STREET
BRYANSTON STREET
GRANVILLE PL
PORTMAN ST
CUMBERLAND COURT
A40
MARBLE ARCH
TYBURN WAY
LUMLEY ST
BALDERTON FLATS
STALBRIDGE FLATS
DUKE ST MANSIONS
BALDERTON ST
CLARENDON FLATS
BROWN HART GARDENS
WEIGHHOUSE ST
GILBERT ST
BINNEY ST
DUKE'S YD
ST ANSELM PLACE
DAVIES STREET
ARGENTINE
NORTH ROW
NORTH AUDLEY ST
PROVIDENCE CT
GEORGE YD
A4202
DUNRAVEN
BRAZIL
GREEN STREET
LEES CT
LEES PL
ITALY
SOUTH MOLTON

PARK CRESCENT
Fitzrovia
92
Portland Hospl
MADAGASCAR
GREENWELL ST
CROATIA
MOZAMBIQUE
LIBERIA
Bell Language Sch
CLEVELAND STREET
A
B
C
82
DEVONSHIRE PL
DEVONSHIRE MEWS W
DEVONSHIRE MEWS N
CHILE
BOLSOVER ST
B506
CARBURTON ST
HOLCROFT COURT
CONWAY ST
MAPLE ST
FITZROY ST
DEVONSHIRE STREET
Queens Coll Prep Sch
DEVONSHIRE CL
BRIDFORD MEWS
HALLAM COURT
RIBA
Govt Offices
BT Tower
CLEVELAND MEWS
King Edward VII Hospl for Officers
4
UPPER WIMPOLE ST
DEVONSHIRE MEWS S
CHINA
POLAND
PORTLAND PLACE
HALLAM STREET
GREAT PORTLAND STREET
CLIPSTONE STREET
CLIPSTONE MEWS
Univ of Westminster
WEYMOUTH STREET
WEYMOUTH MEWS
KENYA
Portland Place Schs
CAVENDISH MEWS N
HANSON STREET
OGLE STREET
Blake Coll
WIMPOLE MEWS
HARLEY STREET
Royal Coll of Radiologists
NEW CAVENDISH STREET
GOSFIELD ST
GREAT TITCHFIELD ST
FOLEY STREET
WESTMORLAND ST
The Heart Hospl
BROWNING MEWS
DUCHESS MEWS
DUCHESS STREET
BBC Broadcasting Ho
GILDEA ST
RIDING HOUSE STREET
NASSAU ST
MANSFIELD MEWS
Royal Coll of Midwives
LANGHAM STREET
MIDDLETON PLACE
BOURLET CL
3
103
HARLEY PL
MANSFIELD ST
NAMIBIA
ALL SOULS PLACE
Univ of Westminster
British Dental Association Mus
Queen's Coll
CHANDOS ST
United International Coll
B506
LITTLE TITCHFIELD ST
BYWELL PL
QUEEN ANNE STREET
QUEEN ANNE MEWS
PORTLAND PL
LANGHAM PL
RIDING HO ST
BULSTRODE ST
Davies Laing & Dick Coll
W1
The Langham Hotel
Law Ct
ST ANDREWS CHAMBERS
LISTER HOUSE
WIGMORE PL
WIMPOLE STREET
DEAN'S MEWS
CAVENDISH PLACE
A5204
MORLEY HOUSE
LITTLE PORTLAND ST
BENTINCK MS
BENTINCK ST
WELBECK WAY
WELBECK STREET
BENTINCK MANSIONS
Wigmore Hall
CAVENDISH
Univ of Westminster
MARGARET STREET
MARGARET COURT
2
MARYLEBONE LANE
MARCOL HOUSE
MARKET
KENT HO
Cowdray Hall Royal College of Nursing
MARYLEBONE
LTC Coll
WIGMORE STREET
B406
SQUARE
JOHN PRINCE'S ST
GREAT CASTLE STREET
GT CASTLE ST
PLACE
ALDBURGH MEWS
HENRIETTA PLACE
HOLLES ST
London Coll of Fashion
OXFORD CIRCUS
JAMES STREET
BOURNE MEWS
CHAPEL PLACE
OLD CAVENDISH ST
A40
Radcliffe Coll
HILLS PL
RAMILLIES ST
ST CHRISTOPHER'S PLACE
STRATFORD PL
VERE ST
TANZANIA
BOTSWANA
OXFORD STREET
SWALLOW PL
ARGYLL STREET
HILLS PLACE
Oxford Circus
B524
Bond Street
B406
UNION YD
HAREWOOD PLACE
PRINCES ST
LITTLE ARGYLL STREET
1
DERING ST
HANOVER
JERVIS CT
A4201
GREAT MARLBOROUGH
SEDLEY PLACE
WOODSTOCK STREET
BLENHEIM STREET
TENTERDEN STREET
LITTLE MARLBOROUGH ST
West One Shop Cent
London Coll of Fashion
SOUTH MOLTON STREET
SOUTH MOLTON LANE
GLOBE YD
HAUNCH OF VENISON YD
Crossrail Sta u/c
SQUARE
HANOVER ST
POLLEN ST
REGENT STREET
Carnaby
KINGLY STREET
81
GILBERT ST
BINNEY ST
ST ANSELM'S PLACE
DAVIES MEWS
Shane Global Lang Cent
Handel House Mus
MEXICO
ST GEORGE STREET
MASON'S ARMS MEWS
29
MILL ST
B406
DAVIES STREET
DUKE'S YD
BROOK STREET
118
NEW BOND STREET
ARGENTINE
Claridge's Hotel
AVERY ROW
MADDOX
CONDUIT STREET
NEW BURLINGTON PL
Govt Offices
TENISON CT
BROOK'S MEWS
ITALY

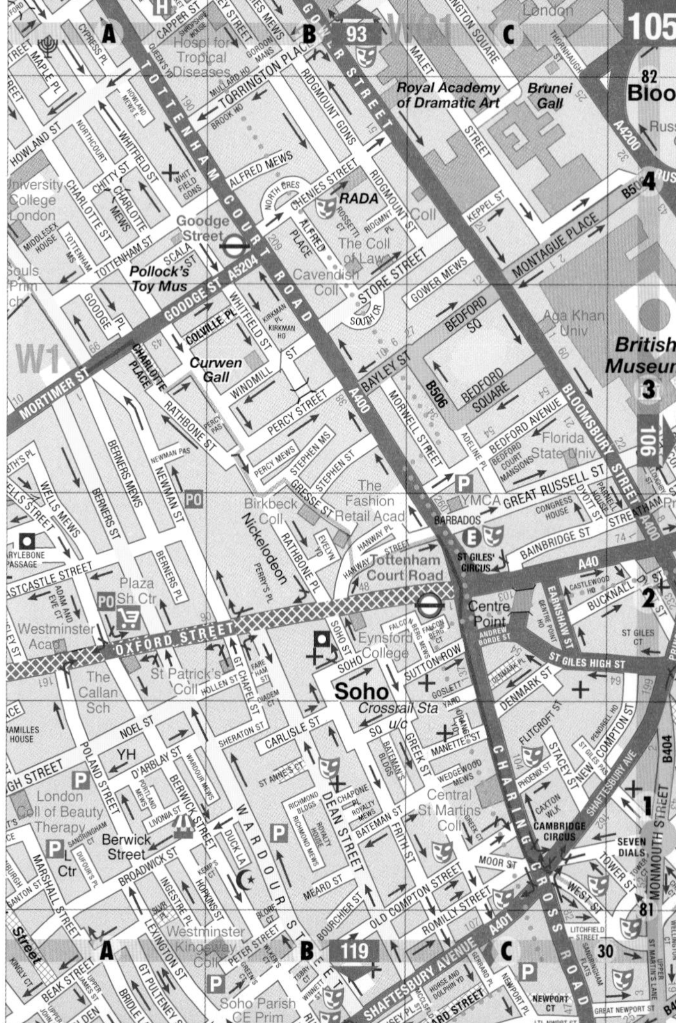

A
B
C
93
119
106
W1
WC1
Bloomsbury
British Museum
Royal Academy of Dramatic Art
Brunei Gall
RADA
Goodge Street
Pollock's Toy Mus
Curwen Gall
Birkbeck Coll
Nickelodeon
The Fashion Retail Acad
Tottenham Court Road
Centre Point
Soho
Crossrail Sta u/c
Eynsford College
St Patrick's Coll
The Callan Sch
Westminster Acad
Plaza Sh Ctr
London Coll of Beauty Therapy
Berwick Street
Westminster Kingsway Coll
Soho Parish CE Prim
Central St Martins Coll
Aga Khan Univ
Florida State Univ
The Coll of Law
Cavendish Coll
University College London
Hospl for Tropical Diseases
YMCA
TOTTENHAM COURT ROAD
GOWER STREET
BLOOMSBURY STREET
CHARING CROSS ROAD
OXFORD STREET
SHAFTESBURY AVENUE
GREAT RUSSELL ST
BEDFORD SQUARE
WARDOUR STREET
DEAN STREET
OLD COMPTON STREET
GOODGE ST
MORTIMER ST
TORRINGTON PLACE
MONTAGUE PLACE
ST GILES HIGH ST
MONMOUTH STREET
CAMBRIDGE CIRCUS
SEVEN DIALS

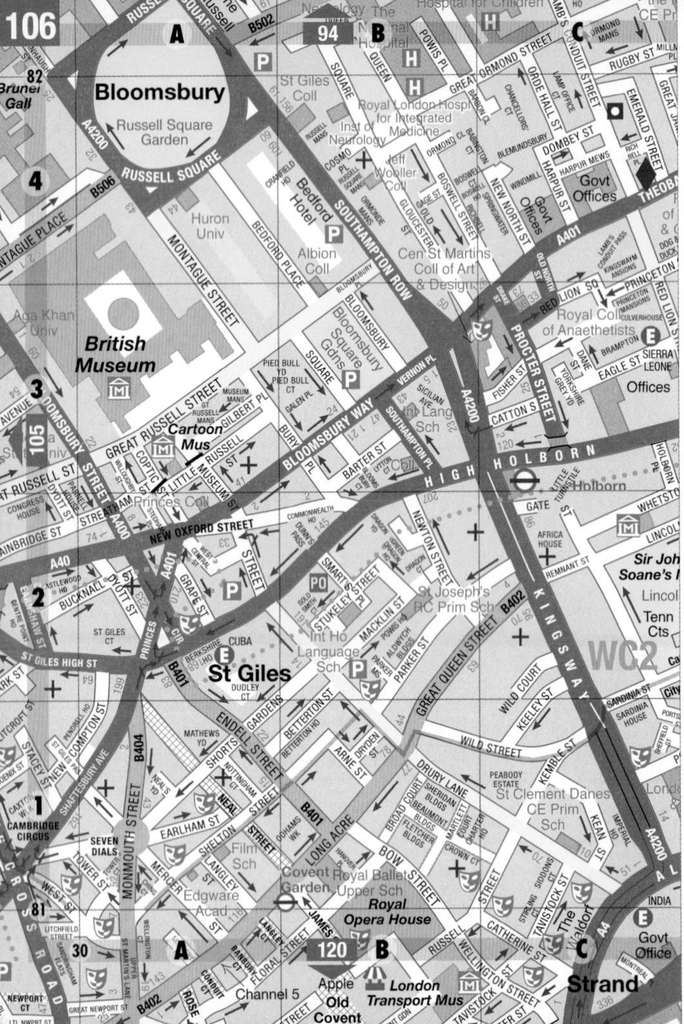

106
A
B
C
94
Bloomsbury
Russell Square Garden
RUSSELL SQUARE
A4200
B502
B506
MONTAGUE PLACE
Brunei Gall
Huron Univ
MONTAGUE STREET
BEDFORD PLACE
Bedford Hotel
Albion Coll
SOUTHAMPTON ROW
St Giles Coll
Inst of Neurology
Royal London Hospl for Integrated Medicine
Jeff Wooller Coll
GREAT ORMOND STREET
ORDE HALL ST
LAMB'S CONDUIT STREET
EMERALD STREET
RUGBY ST
DOMBEY ST
HARPUR MEWS
HARPUR ST
Govt Offices
THEOBALDS
NEW NORTH ST
BOSWELL STREET
GLOUCESTER ST
OLD GLOUCESTER ST
Cen St Martins Coll of Art & Design
A401
RED LION SQ
PRINCETON ST
Royal Coll of Anaethetists
PROCTER STREET
EAGLE ST
SIERRA LEONE
Offices
FISHER ST
CATTON ST
HIGH HOLBORN
Holborn
GATE ST
Aga Khan Univ
British Museum
BLOOMSBURY STREET
GREAT RUSSELL STREET
Cartoon Mus
BLOOMSBURY SQUARE
Bloomsbury Square Gdns
BLOOMSBURY WAY
VERNON PL
SOUTHAMPTON PL
Int Lang Sch
BARTER ST
BURY PL
LITTLE RUSSELL ST
MUSEUM ST
COPTIC ST
STREATHAM ST
Princes Coll
NEW OXFORD STREET
BAINBRIDGE ST
A40
A400
DYOTT ST
BUCKNALL ST
ST GILES HIGH ST
ST GILES CT
PRINCES CIR
SHAFTESBURY AVE
NEW COMPTON ST
STACEY ST
CAMBRIDGE CIRCUS
SEVEN DIALS
TOWER ST
WEST ST
CHARING CROSS ROAD
MONMOUTH STREET
B404
EARLHAM ST
NEAL STREET
SHORTS GARDENS
ENDELL STREET
B401
St Giles
CUBA
DUDLEY CT
MATHEWS YD
SHELTON ST
MERCER ST
LANGLEY ST
Film Sch
Edgware Acad
Covent Garden
Royal Ballet Upper Sch
Royal Opera House
BOW STREET
LONG ACRE
FLORAL STREET
JAMES ST
120
Apple
Old Covent
London Transport Mus
Channel 5
ROSE ST
B402
SMARTS PL
STUKELEY STREET
MACKLIN ST
PARKER ST
Int Ho Language Sch
St Joseph's RC Prim Sch
NEWTON STREET
GREAT QUEEN STREET
KINGSWAY
A4200
WC2
WILD COURT
KEELEY ST
WILD STREET
KEMBLE ST
DRURY LANE
PEABODY ESTATE
St Clement Danes CE Prim Sch
KEAN ST
AFRICA HOUSE
REMNANT ST
Sir John Soane's
LINCOLN
Tenn Cts
SARDINIA ST
SARDINIA HOUSE
RUSSELL ST
WELLINGTON STREET
CATHERINE ST
TAVISTOCK ST
The Waldorf
INDIA
Govt Office
Strand
A4
NEWPORT CT
GREAT NEWPORT ST
LITCHFIELD STREET
30
81
82
1
2
3
4
105

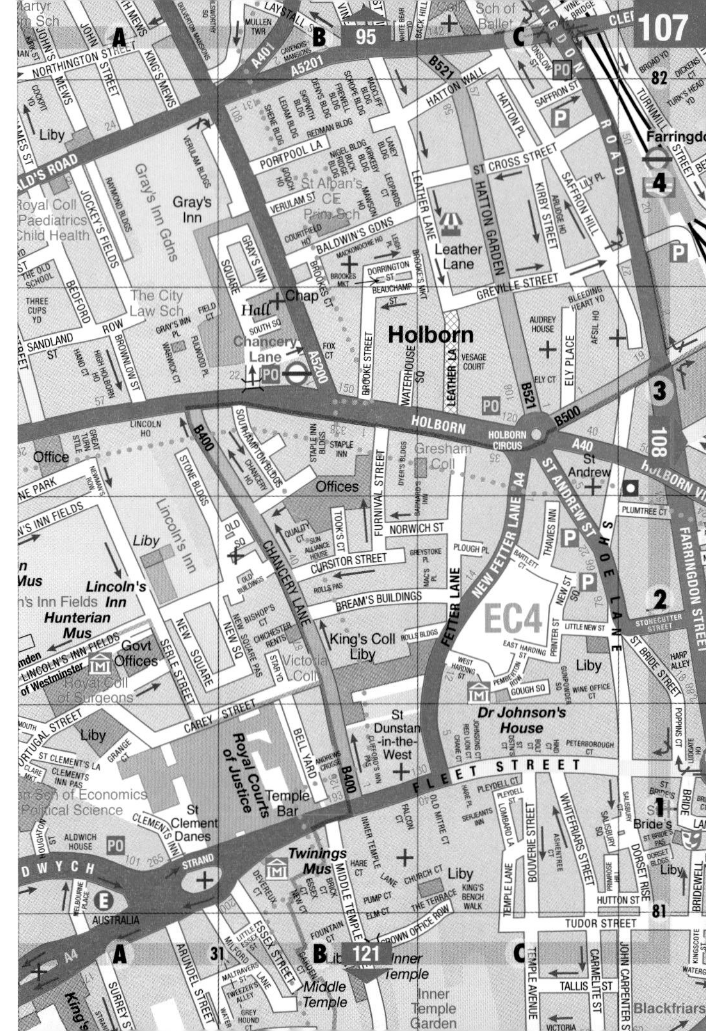

95
121
108
A
B
C
1
2
3
4
Holborn
EC4
Gray's Inn
Gray's Inn Gdns
The City Law Sch
Chancery Lane
Lincoln's Inn
Lincoln's Inn Fields
Hunterian Mus
Royal Coll of Surgeons
Govt Offices
Royal Courts of Justice
Temple Bar
St Clement Danes
St Dunstan-in-the-West
Dr Johnson's House
Twinings Mus
Inner Temple
Middle Temple
Inner Temple Garden
Leather Lane
Holborn Circus
St Andrew
Gresham Coll
Offices
King's Coll Liby
Victoria Coll
Royal Coll Paediatrics Child Health
St Bride's
Blackfriars
Farringdon
Sch of Ballet
Liby
Office
Chap
Hall
AUSTRALIA
ALDWICH HOUSE
HOLBORN
FLEET STREET
STRAND
ALDWYCH
THEOBALD'S ROAD
NORTHINGTON STREET
JOHN STREET
JOHN'S MEWS
KING'S MEWS
JOCKEY'S FIELDS
BEDFORD ROW
SANDLAND ST
BROWNLOW ST
HIGH HOLBORN
GRAY'S INN ROAD
PORTPOOL LA
VERULAM ST
BALDWIN'S GDNS
BROOKE'S CT
BROOKE STREET
LEATHER LANE
HATTON GARDEN
HATTON WALL
HATTON PL
ST CROSS STREET
KIRBY STREET
SAFFRON HILL
SAFFRON ST
GREVILLE STREET
ELY PLACE
ELY CT
FARRINGDON ROAD
FARRINGDON STREET
TURNMILL STREET
CLERKENWELL ROAD
HOLBORN VIADUCT
ST ANDREW ST
NEW FETTER LANE
FETTER LANE
SHOE LANE
CHANCERY LANE
SOUTHAMPTON BLDGS
FURNIVAL STREET
NORWICH ST
CURSITOR STREET
BREAM'S BUILDINGS
NEW SQUARE
SERLE STREET
CAREY STREET
PORTUGAL STREET
BELL YARD
ST BRIDE STREET
STONECUTTER STREET
BOUVERIE STREET
WHITEFRIARS STREET
TUDOR STREET
TEMPLE AVENUE
CARMELITE ST
JOHN CARPENTER ST
TALLIS ST
ESSEX STREET
ARUNDEL STREET
SURREY ST
MIDDLE TEMPLE LANE
INNER TEMPLE LANE
CROWN OFFICE ROW
KING'S BENCH WALK
THE TERRACE
CHURCH CT
BRIDEWELL PL
DORSET RISE
SALISBURY SQ
HUTTON ST
A401
A5201
A5200
B521
B400
B500
A40
A4

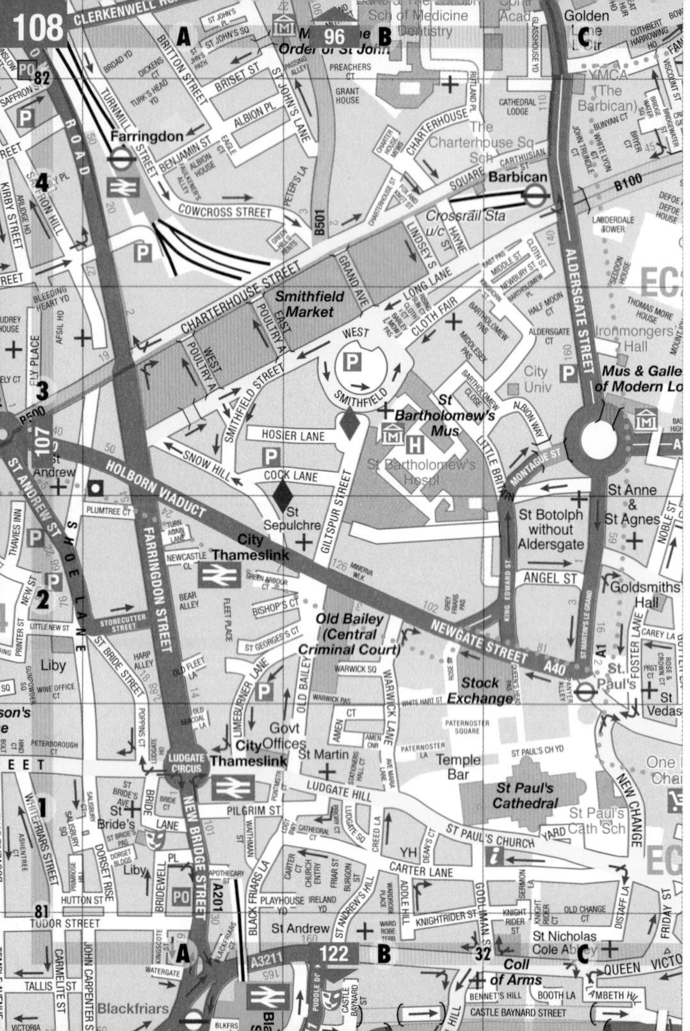

CLERKENWELL RD
96
122
107
82
81
A
B
C
1
2
3
4
Order of St John
Sch of Medicine
Dentistry
Golden Lane
Farringdon
Barbican
Crossrail Sta u/c
Charterhouse Sq Sch
The Barbican
YMCA
B100
B501
B500
A40
A1
A201
A3211
ROAD
TURNMILL STREET
BRITTON STREET
BRISET ST
ALBION PL
ST JOHN'S LANE
ST JOHN'S SQ
BROAD YD
DICKENS CT
TURK'S HEAD YD
BENJAMIN ST
EAGLE CT
COWCROSS STREET
PETER'S LA
PREACHERS CT
GRANT HOUSE
CHARTERHOUSE
CHARTERHOUSE STREET
CATHEDRAL LODGE
GLASSHOUSE YD
CARTHUSIAN ST
SQUARE
ALDERSGATE STREET
LAUDERDALE TOWER
SEDDON HOUSE
THOMAS MORE HOUSE
Ironmongers' Hall
Mus & Gallery of Modern London
Smithfield Market
GRAND AVE
LONG LANE
CLOTH FAIR
WEST POULTRY AVE
EAST POULTRY AVE
WEST SMITHFIELD
SMITHFIELD STREET
BARTHOLOMEW PAS
MIDDLESEX PAS
HALF MOON CT
ALDERSGATE CT
City Univ
St Bartholomew's Mus
St Bartholomew's Hospl
LITTLE BRITAIN
MONTAGUE ST
HOSIER LANE
COCK LANE
SNOW HILL
HOLBORN VIADUCT
GILTSPUR STREET
St Sepulchre
City Thameslink
FARRINGDON STREET
St Andrew
ST ANDREW ST
SHOE LANE
PLUMTREE CT
KIRBY STREET
SAFFRON HILL
ELY PLACE
BLEEDING HEART YD
St Botolph without Aldersgate
St Anne & St Agnes
NOBLE ST
ANGEL ST
Goldsmiths' Hall
KING EDWARD ST
NEWGATE STREET
Old Bailey (Central Criminal Court)
BISHOP'S CT
ST GEORGE'S CT
FLEET PLACE
BEAR ALLEY
NEWCASTLE CL
STONECUTTER STREET
ST BRIDE STREET
HARP ALLEY
OLD FLEET LA
LIMEBURNER LANE
OLD BAILEY
WARWICK SQ
WARWICK LANE
Stock Exchange
St Paul's
FOSTER LANE
CAREY LA
St Vedast
Liby
WINE OFFICE CT
PETERBOROUGH CT
LUDGATE CIRCUS
Govt Offices
City Thameslink
St Martin
AMEN CT
PATERNOSTER SQUARE
Temple Bar
ST PAUL'S CH YD
St Paul's Cathedral
LUDGATE HILL
PILGRIM ST
St Bride's
BRIDE LANE
NEW BRIDGE STREET
ST PAUL'S CHURCH YARD
St Paul's Cath Sch
NEW CHANGE
CARTER LANE
YH
CREED LA
DEAN'S CT
WHITEFRIARS STREET
DORSET RISE
SALISBURY SQ
HUTTON ST
TUDOR STREET
BRIDEWELL PL
PLAYHOUSE YD
IRELAND YD
BLACK FRIARS LA
St Andrew
ST ANDREW'S HILL
KNIGHTRIDER ST
GODLIMAN ST
OLD CHANGE CT
DISTAFF LA
FRIDAY ST
St Nicholas Cole Abbey
Coll of Arms
QUEEN VICTORIA
BENNET'S HILL
BOOTH LA
LAMBETH HILL
CASTLE BAYNARD STREET
CARMELITE ST
JOHN CARPENTER ST
TALLIS ST
Blackfriars
WATERGATE
VICTORIA

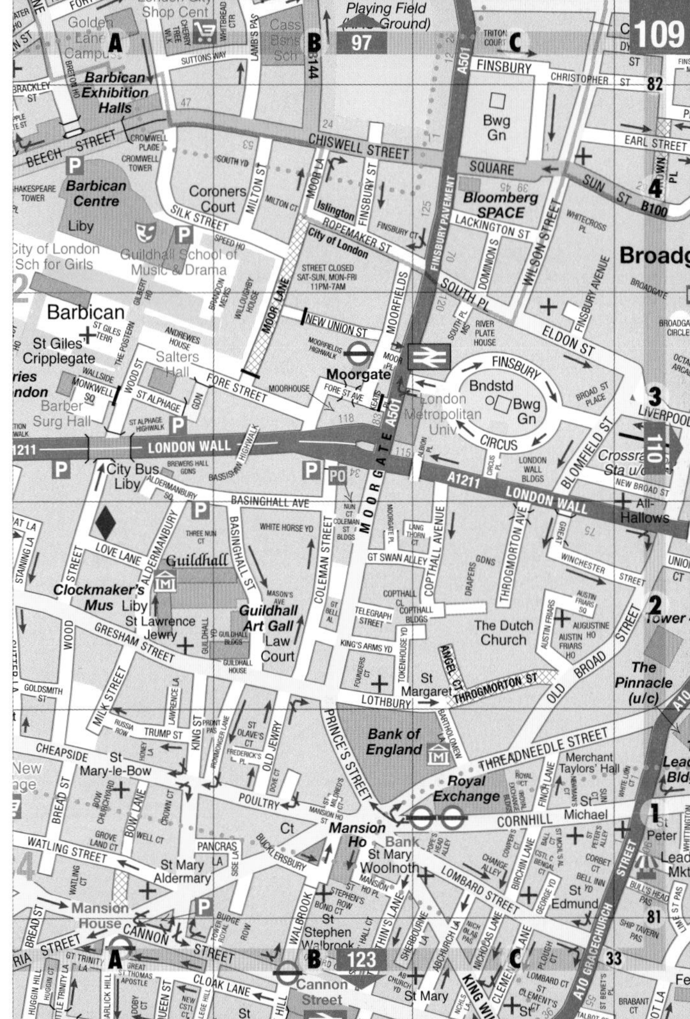
A
B
C
97
Playing Field
Golden Lane Campus
Shop Cent
CHERRY TREE WLK
WHITBREAD CTR
LAMB'S PAS
Cass Bsns Sch
B144
TRITON COURT
SUTTONS WAY
Barbican Exhibition Halls
BRETON HO
BRACKLEY ST
A501
FINSBURY
CHRISTOPHER ST
82
Bwg Gn
BEECH STREET
CROMWELL PLACE
CROMWELL TOWER
CHISWELL STREET
EARL STREET
SQUARE
SUN ST
B100
4
SHAKESPEARE TOWER
Barbican Centre
SOUTH YD
MILTON ST
MILTON CT
Coroners Court
MOOR LA
Islington
FINSBURY ST
FINSBURY CT
Bloomberg SPACE
LACKINGTON ST
WHITECROSS PL
WILSON STREET
Liby
SILK STREET
ROPEMAKER ST
City of London
FINSBURY PAVEMENT
City of London Sch for Girls
Guildhall School of Music & Drama
SPEED HO
STREET CLOSED SAT-SUN, MON-FRI 11PM-7AM
MOORFIELDS
DOMINION S
Broadgate
BROADGATE
FINSBURY AVENUE
SOUTH PL
Barbican
GILBERT HO
BRANDON MEWS
WILLOUGHBY HOUSE
MOOR LANE
NEW UNION ST
SOUTH PL MS
RIVER PLATE HOUSE
ELDON ST
BROADGATE CIRCLE
St Giles' Cripplegate
ST GILES TERR
THE POSTERN
ANDREWES HOUSE
MOORFIELDS HIGHWALK
MOOR PL
FINSBURY
OCTAGON ARCADE
Salters Hall
WOOD ST
WALLSIDE
Moorgate
Bndstd
Bwg Gn
MONKWELL SQ
FORE STREET
MOORHOUSE
FORE ST AVE
London Metropolitan Univ
BROAD ST PLACE
3
LIVERPOOL
ST ALPHAGE
GDN
Barber Surg Hall
ST ALPHAGE HIGHWALK
118
KEATS PL
CIRCUS
BLOMFIELD ST
110
A1211
LONDON WALL
A501
MOORGATE
ALBION PL
Crossrail Sta u/c
City Bus Liby
BREWERS HALL GDNS
BASSISHAW HIGHWALK
PO
CIRCUS PL
LONDON WALL BLDGS
NEW BROAD ST
ALDERMANBURY SQ
BASINGHALL AVE
NUN CT
COLEMAN ST BLDGS
All-Hallows
THREE NUN CT
WHITE HORSE YD
MOORGATE PL
LANG THORN CT
COPTHALL AVENUE
THROGMORTON AVE
GREAT WINCHESTER STREET
UNION CT
STAINING LA
LOVE LANE
ALDERMANBURY
Guildhall
BASINGHALL ST
COLEMAN STREET
GT SWAN ALLEY
DRAPERS GDNS
Clockmaker's Mus
Liby
MASON'S AVE
Guildhall Art Gall
COPTHALL CL
COPTHALL BLDGS
AUSTIN FRIARS SQ
2
Tower 42
St Lawrence Jewry
GT BELL AL
TELEGRAPH STREET
The Dutch Church
AUSTIN FRIARS
AUGUSTINE HO
AUSTIN FRIARS HO
WOOD
GRESHAM STREET
GUILDHALL YD
GUILDHALL BLDGS
Law Court
KING'S ARMS YD
OLD BROAD STREET
GUILDHALL HOUSE
TOKENHOUSE YD
FOUNDERS CT
ANGEL CT
St Margaret
THROGMORTON ST
The Pinnacle (u/c)
GOLDSMITH ST
MILK STREET
LAWRENCE LA
LOTHBURY
A10
RUSSIA ROW
TRUMP ST
KING ST
PRONT PAS
IRONMONGER LANE
ST OLAVE'S CT
OLD JEWRY
PRINCE'S STREET
Bank of England
BARTHOLOMEW LA
THREADNEEDLE STREET
Merchant Taylors' Hall
CHEAPSIDE
St Mary-le-Bow
FREDERICK'S PL
Royal Exchange
ROYAL EXCHANGE BLDGS
FINCH LANE
St Michael
The Leadenhall Bldg
BREAD ST
BOW CHURCHYARD
BOW LANE
CROWN CT
POULTRY
DOVE CT
ST MILDRED'S CT
MANSION HO ST
CORNHILL
1
St Peter
WHITTINGTON AVE
GROVE LAND CT
WELL CT
Ct
Mansion Ho
Bank
POPE'S HEAD ALLEY
COWPER'S CT
BALL CT
ST MICHAEL'S AL
ST PETER'S ALLEY
WATLING STREET
PANCRAS LA
BUCKLERSBURY
St Mary Woolnoth
CHANGE ALLEY
BIRCHIN LANE
CORBET CT
Leadenhall Mkt
St Mary Aldermary
SISE LA
MANSION HO PL
LOMBARD STREET
GEORGE YD
BELL INN YD
WATLING CT
St Edmund
STREET
BULL'S HEAD PAS
LIME ST PAS
Mansion House
BUDGE ROW
WALBROOK
ST STEPHEN'S ROW
BOND CT
St Stephen Walbrook
HALL CT
ST SWITHIN'S LANE
SHERBOURNE LA
ABCHURCH LA
NICHOLAS LANE
CLEMENT'S LANE
81
SHIP TAVERN PAS
BREAD ST
CANNON STREET
GRACECHURCH
A10
33
GT TRINITY LA
123
PLOUGH CT
LOMBARD CT
ST CLEMENT'S CT
GREAT ST THOMAS APOSTLE
CLOAK LANE
Cannon Street
AB CHURCH YD
St Mary
KING WILLIAM
ST BENET'S PL
BRABANT CT
POT LA
HUGGIN HILL
LITTLE TRINITY LA
GARLICK HILL
QUEEN ST
NEW CSTL CT
COLLEGE HILL
St Michael
St Clement
TALBOT CT
SKINNERS

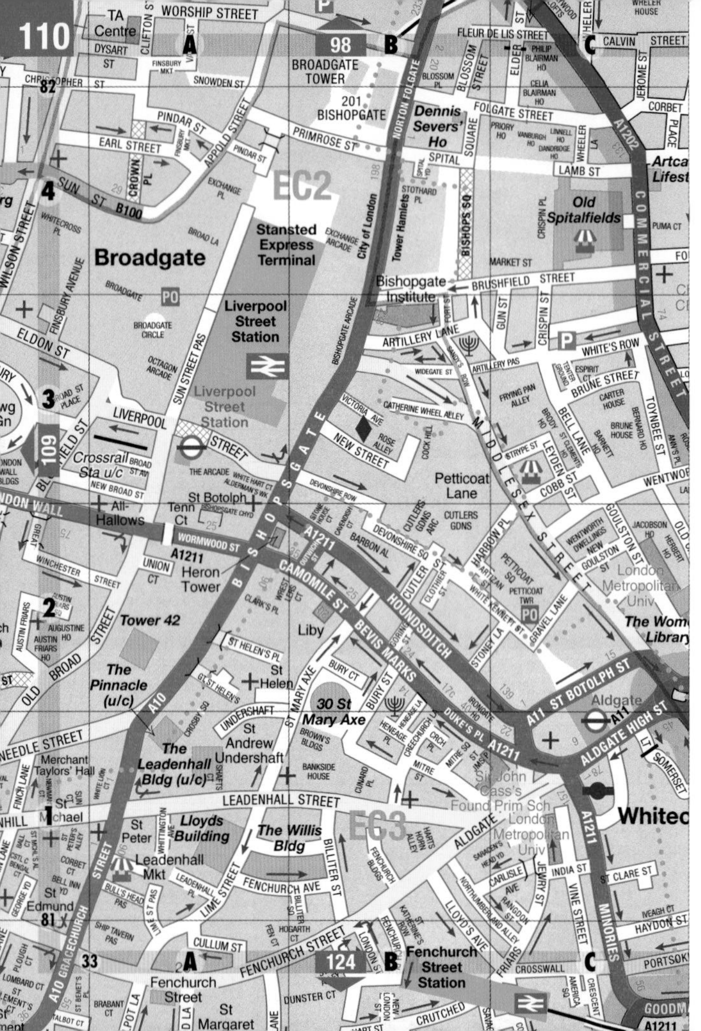

TA Centre
WORSHIP STREET
CLIFTON ST
DYSART ST
FINSBURY MKT
SNOWDEN ST
CHRISTOPHER ST
98
BROADGATE TOWER
201 BISHOPGATE
FLEUR DE LIS STREET
PHILIP BLAIRMAN HO
CELIA BLAIRMAN HO
CALVIN STREET
JEROME ST
CORBET PLACE
BLOSSOM PL
BLOSSOM STREET
ELDER ST
WHEELER HOUSE
FOLGATE STREET
Dennis Severs' Ho
NORTON FOLGATE
PRIORY HO
VANBURGH HO
LINNELL HO
DANDRIDGE HO
WHEELER LA
A1202
PINDAR ST
APPOLD STREET
EARL STREET
PRIMROSE ST
PINDAR ST
SPITAL SQUARE
LAMB ST
Artca Lifest
CROWN PL
EXCHANGE PL
EC2
SUN ST
B100
STOTHARD PL
BISHOPS SQ
Old Spitalfields
COMMERCIAL STREET
WHITECROSS PL
BROAD LA
Stansted Express Terminal
EXCHANGE ARCADE
City of London
Tower Hamlets
CRISPIN PL
PUMA CT
WILSON STREET
Broadgate
MARKET ST
FINSBURY AVENUE
BROADGATE
PO
Bishopgate Institute
BRUSHFIELD STREET
Liverpool Street Station
BROADGATE CIRCLE
BISHOPGATE ARCADE
GUN ST
CRISPIN ST
ELDON ST
ARTILLERY LANE
WHITE'S ROW
OCTAGON ARCADE
SUN STREET PAS
WIDEGATE ST
SANDY'S ROW
ARTILLERY PAS
ESPIRIT CT
BRUNE STREET
TENTER GROUND
Liverpool Street Station
FRYING PAN ALLEY
CARTER HOUSE
BROAD ST PLACE
LIVERPOOL STREET
VICTORIA AVE
CATHERINE WHEEL ALLEY
BRODY HO
BELL LANE
ST CLEMENTS HO
BARNETT HO
BERNARD HO
BRUNE HOUSE
TOYNBEE ST
109
BLOMFIELD ST
Crossrail Sta u/c
BROAD ST AV
ROSE ALLEY
NEW STREET
COCK HILL
MIDDLESEX STREET
STRYPE ST
LEYDEN ST
ANN'S PL
LONDON WALL BLDGS
THE ARCADE
WHITE HART CT
ALDERMAN'S WK
NEW BROAD ST
DEVONSHIRE ROW
Petticoat Lane
COBB ST
WENTWORTH
LONDON WALL
All-Hallows
St Botolph
Tenn Ct
BISHOPSGATE CHYD
STONE HOUSE CT
CAVENDISH CT
CUTLERS GDNS ARC
CUTLERS GDNS
WENTWORTH DWELLINGS
GOULSTON ST
JACOBSON HO
GREAT WINCHESTER ST
WORMWOOD ST
A1211
BISHOPSGATE
OUTWICH ST
A1211
BARBON AL
DEVONSHIRE SQ
HARROW PL
NEW GOULSTON ST
HERBERT HO
WINCHESTER STREET
UNION CT
Heron Tower
CAMOMILE ST
CUTLER ST
CLOTHIER ST
ARTIZAN ST
PETTICOAT SQ
WHITE KENNETT ST
PETTICOAT TWR
London Metropolitan Univ
AUSTIN FRIARS SQ
AUSTIN FRIARS
AUGUSTINE HO
AUSTIN FRIARS HO
OLD BROAD STREET
Tower 42
CLARK'S PL
WREST LEYS CT
HOUNDSDITCH
BEVIS MARKS
STONEY LA
GRAVEL LANE
PO
The Women's Library
Liby
ST HELEN'S PL
BURY CT
SPRING ST
The Pinnacle (u/c)
A10
GT ST HELEN'S
St Helen
ST MARY AXE
BURY ST
A11 ST BOTOLPH ST
Aldgate
A11
CROSBY SQ
UNDERSHAFT
30 St Mary Axe
HENEAGE LA
HENEAGE PL
CREECHURCH LA
CRCH PL
DUKE'S PL
IRONGATE HO
A1211
ALDGATE HIGH ST
NEEDLE STREET
The Leadenhall Bldg (u/c)
St Andrew Undershaft
BROWN'S BLDGS
BANKSIDE HOUSE
MITRE ST
MITRE SQ
ST JMS PL
Sir John Cass's Found Prim Sch
SOMERSET
Merchant Taylors' Hall
SHAFTS CT
CUNARD PL
FINCH LANE
WHITE LION CT
SUN CT
St Michael
LEADENHALL STREET
EC3
London Metropolitan Univ
Whitec
A1211
CORNHILL
WHITTINGTON AVE
St Peter
Lloyds Building
The Willis Bldg
HARTS HORN ALLEY
ALDGATE
SARACEN'S HEAD YD
BALL CT
ST MICHAEL'S AL
ST PETER'S ALLEY
CORBET CT
Leadenhall Mkt
BILLITER ST
FENCHURCH BLDGS
CARLISLE AVE
INDIA ST
ST CLARE ST
BELL INN YD
BULL'S HEAD PAS
LEADENHALL PL
LIME STREET
FENCHURCH AVE
JEWRY ST
VINE STREET
MINORIES
St Edmund
81
GEORGE YD
LIME ST PAS
BILLITER SQ
NORTHUMBERLAND ALLEY
RANGOON ST
IVEAGH CT
HAYDON ST
SHIP TAVERN PAS
HOGARTH CT
FEN CT
KATHERINE'S ROW
LLOYD'S AVE
GRACECHURCH STREET
PLOUGH CT
CULLUM ST
FENCHURCH STREET
LONDON ST
Fenchurch Street Station
FRIARS
CROSSWALL
PORTSOKEN
33
A
124
B
C
LOMBARD CT
ST CLEMENT'S CT
Fenchurch Street
St Margaret
DUNSTER CT
NEW LONDON ST
CRUTCHED
AMERICA SQ
CRESCENT
GOODMAN'S
A1211
BRABANT CT
ST BENET'S PL
TALBOT CT

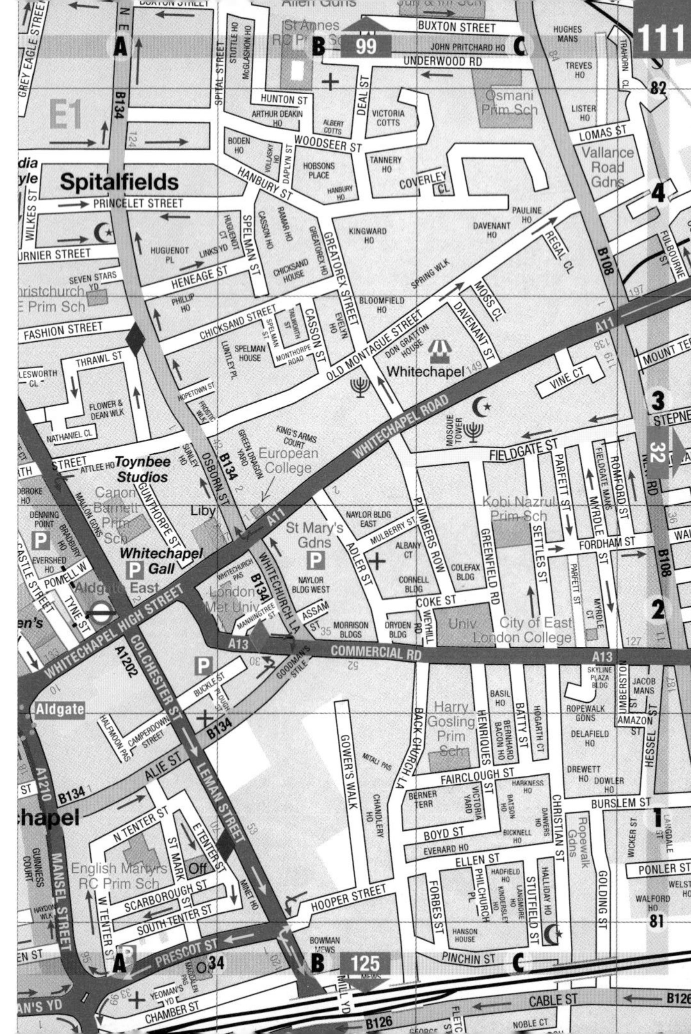

99
125
32
81
82
E1
Spitalfields
Whitechapel
Toynbee Studios
Whitechapel Gall
Aldgate East
Aldgate
BUXTON STREET
JOHN PRITCHARD HO
UNDERWOOD RD
HUNTON ST
ARTHUR DEAKIN HO
VICTORIA COTTS
WOODSEER ST
HOBSONS PLACE
TANNERY HO
COVERLEY CL
HANBURY ST
PRINCELET STREET
HUGUENOT PL
HENEAGE ST
SPELMAN ST
GREATOREX STREET
KINGWARD HO
DAVENANT HO
PAULINE HO
REGAL CL
SPRING WLK
BLOOMFIELD HO
MOSS CL
DAVENANT ST
CHICKSAND STREET
CHICKSAND HOUSE
CASSON ST
OLD MONTAGUE STREET
DON GRATTON HOUSE
FASHION STREET
THRAWL ST
FLOWER & DEAN WLK
NATHANIEL CL
SPELMAN HOUSE
LUNTLEY PL
WHITECHAPEL ROAD
VINE CT
MOUNT TERR
STEPNEY
FIELDGATE ST
PARFETT ST
MYRDLE ST
ROMFORD ST
FORDHAM ST
European College
Kobi Nazrul Prim Sch
Canon Barnett Prim Sch
GUNTHORPE ST
OSBORN ST
St Mary's Gdns
NAYLOR BLDG EAST
NAYLOR BLDG WEST
MULBERRY ST
ALBANY CT
PLUMBERS ROW
ADLER ST
COLEFAX BLDG
CORNELL BLDG
GREENFIELD RD
SETTLES ST
COKE ST
WHITECHURCH LA
London Met Univ
WHITECHAPEL HIGH STREET
COMMERCIAL RD
Univ
City of East London College
MORRISON BLDGS
DRYDEN BLDG
GOODMAN'S STILE
COLCHESTER ST
ALIE ST
LEMAN STREET
GOWER'S WALK
BACK CHURCH LA
Harry Gosling Prim Sch
HENRIQUES ST
BATTY ST
HOGARTH CT
SKYLINE PLAZA BLDG
JACOB MANS
ROPEWALK GDNS
AMAZON ST
DELAFIELD HO
DREWETT HO
DOWLER HO
HESSEL ST
FAIRCLOUGH ST
BURSLEM ST
BOYD ST
EVERARD HO
ELLEN ST
CHRISTIAN ST
Ropewalk Gdns
GOLDING ST
PONLER ST
WALFORD HO
N TENTER ST
English Martyrs RC Prim Sch
SCARBOROUGH ST
SOUTH TENTER ST
HOOPER STREET
FORBES ST
PHILCHURCH PL
STUTFIELD ST
HALLIDAY HO
HANSON HOUSE
MANSEL STREET
PRESCOT ST
BOWMAN MEWS
PINCHIN ST
CABLE ST
CHAMBER ST
MILL YD
NOBLE CT
A11
A13
B134
B108
B126
A1202
A1210

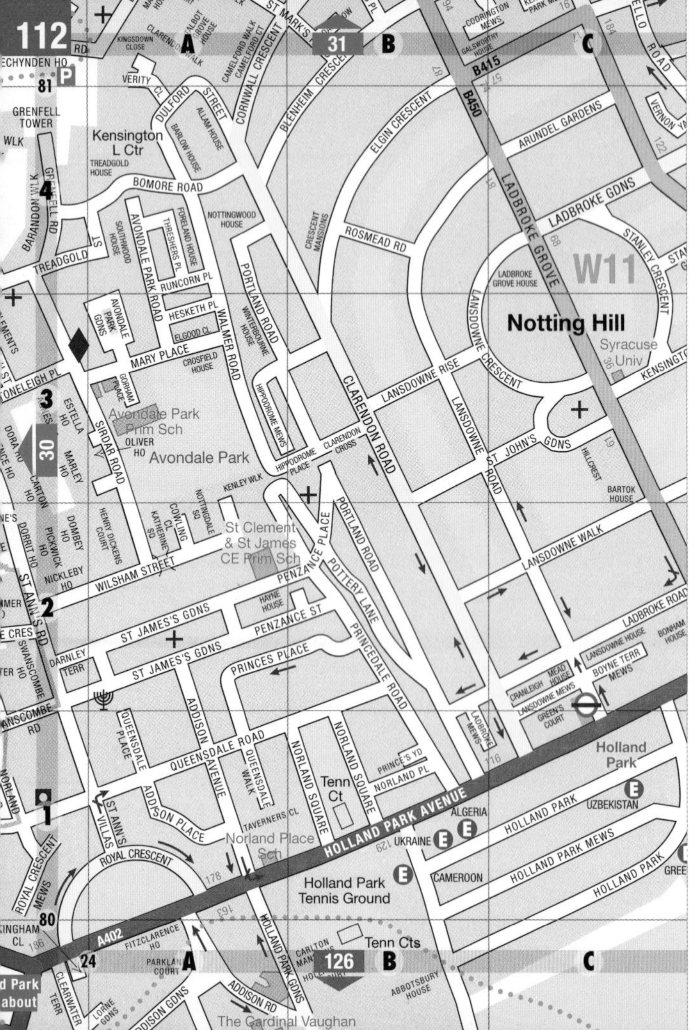

31
126
30
A
B
C
1
2
3
4
W11
Notting Hill
Holland Park
Kensington L Ctr
Avondale Park
Avondale Park Prim Sch
St Clement & St James CE Prim Sch
Norland Place Sch
Holland Park Tennis Ground
Tenn Ct
Tenn Cts
Syracuse Univ
The Cardinal Vaughan
GRENFELL TOWER
LADBROKE GROVE
CLARENDON ROAD
HOLLAND PARK AVENUE
PORTLAND ROAD
WALMER ROAD
LANSDOWNE CRESCENT
LANSDOWNE RISE
LANSDOWNE ROAD
LANSDOWNE WALK
ELGIN CRESCENT
ARUNDEL GARDENS
LADBROKE GDNS
STANLEY CRESCENT
ROSMEAD RD
ST JOHN'S GDNS
BLENHEIM CRESCENT
CORNWALL CRESCENT
DULFORD STREET
BOMORE ROAD
TREADGOLD ST
AVONDALE PARK ROAD
RUNCORN PL
HESKETH PL
ELGOOD CL
MARY PLACE
SIRDAR ROAD
WILSHAM STREET
PENZANCE PLACE
PENZANCE ST
POTTERY LANE
PRINCEDALE ROAD
ST JAMES'S GDNS
PRINCES PLACE
QUEENSDALE ROAD
ADDISON AVENUE
ADDISON PLACE
NORLAND SQUARE
NORLAND PL
ROYAL CRESCENT
ROYAL CRESCENT MEWS
ST ANN'S RD
ST ANN'S VILLAS
HOLLAND PARK
HOLLAND PARK MEWS
HOLLAND PARK GDNS
ADDISON RD
CLEARWATER TERR
LADBROKE ROAD
BOYNE TERR MEWS
HIPPODROME MEWS
HIPPODROME PLACE
CLARENDON CROSS
KENLEY WLK
ALGERIA
UKRAINE
UZBEKISTAN
CAMEROON
B415
B450
A402

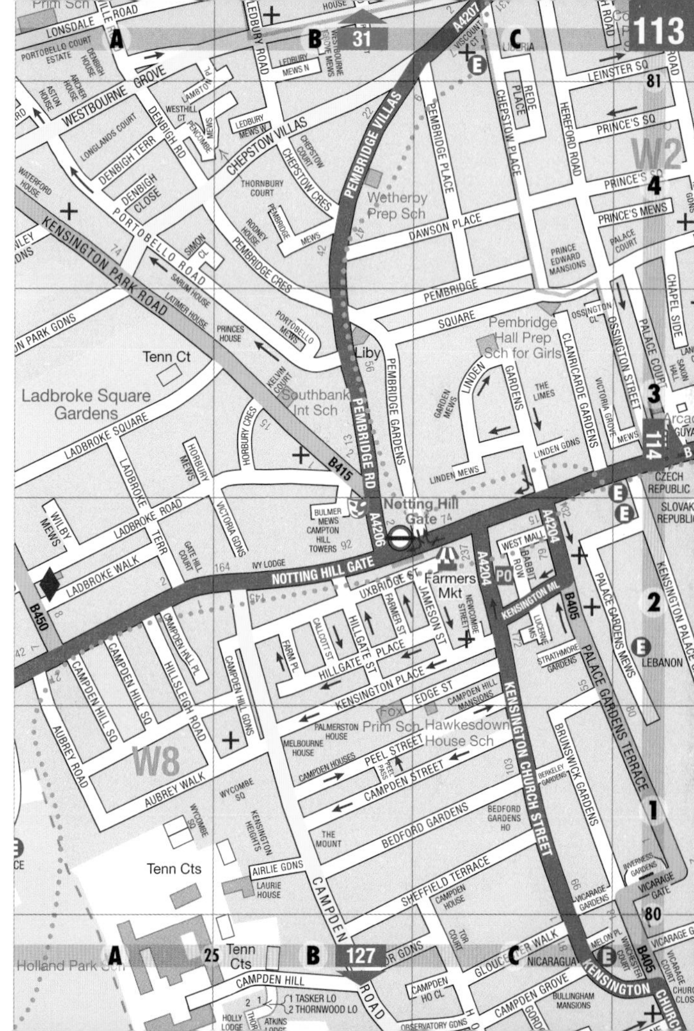

31
A4207
PEMBRIDGE VILLAS
PEMBRIDGE PLACE
CHEPSTOW PLACE
REDE PLACE
HEREFORD ROAD
LEINSTER SQ
PRINCE'S SQ
W2
PRINCE'S MEWS
PALACE COURT
PRINCE EDWARD MANSIONS
DAWSON PLACE
Wetherby Prep Sch
CHEPSTOW VILLAS
CHEPSTOW CRES
THORNBURY COURT
WESTBOURNE GROVE
LONSDALE ROAD
LEDBURY ROAD
LEDBURY MEWS N
LEDBURY MEWS W
PORTOBELLO COURT ESTATE
DENBIGH HOUSE
ARCHER HOUSE
ASTON HOUSE
LONGLANDS COURT
DENBIGH TERR
DENBIGH RD
DENBIGH CLOSE
WESTHILL CT
PENCOMBE MEWS
LAMBTON PL
WATERFORD HOUSE
KENSINGTON PARK ROAD
PORTOBELLO ROAD
SIMON CL
SARUM HOUSE
LATIMER HOUSE
PEMBRIDGE CRES
RODNEY HOUSE
PEMBRIDGE MEWS
PEMBRIDGE SQUARE
Pembridge Hall Prep Sch for Girls
OSSINGTON CL
OSSINGTON STREET
CHAPEL SIDE
PORTOBELLO MEWS
PRINCES HOUSE
Liby
Tenn Ct
Ladbroke Square Gardens
LADBROKE SQUARE
KELVIN COURT
Southbank Int Sch
PEMBRIDGE RD
PEMBRIDGE GARDENS
LINDEN GARDENS
GARDEN MEWS
THE LIMES
CLANRICARDE GARDENS
VICTORIA GROVE
MEWS
114
LINDEN GDNS
LINDEN MEWS
CZECH REPUBLIC
SLOVAK REPUBLIC
HORBURY CRES
HORBURY MEWS
B415
LADBROKE TERR
LADBROKE ROAD
WILBY MEWS
VICTORIA GDNS
BULMER MEWS
CAMPTON HILL TOWERS
Notting Hill Gate
A4206
A4204
WEST MALL
BABBIT ROW
PO
LADBROKE WALK
GATE HILL COURT
IVY LODGE
NOTTING HILL GATE
UXBRIDGE ST
FARMER ST
JAMESON ST
Farmers Mkt
NEWCOMBE STREET
KENSINGTON MALL
B405
PALACE GARDENS MEWS
KENSINGTON PALACE GARDENS
LEBANON
B450
CAMPDEN HILL SQ
CAMPDEN HILL PL
HILLSLEIGH ROAD
CAMPDEN HILL GDNS
FARM PL
CALLCOTT ST
HILLGATE ST
HILLGATE PLACE
KENSINGTON PLACE
EDGE ST
CAMPDEN HILL MANSIONS
LUCERNE MS
STRATHMORE GARDENS
PALACE GARDENS TERRACE
KENSINGTON CHURCH STREET
AUBREY ROAD
W8
AUBREY WALK
PALMERSTON HOUSE
MELBOURNE HOUSE
Fox Prim Sch
Hawkesdown House Sch
PEEL STREET
PEEL PASS
CAMPDEN HOUSES
CAMPDEN STREET
BERKELEY GARDENS
BRUNSWICK GARDENS
WYCOMBE SQ
KENSINGTON HEIGHTS
THE MOUNT
BEDFORD GARDENS
BEDFORD GARDENS HO
Tenn Cts
AIRLIE GDNS
LAURIE HOUSE
CAMPDEN
SHEFFIELD TERRACE
CAMPDEN HOUSE
TOR COURT
INVERNESS GARDENS
VICARAGE GATE
VICARAGE GARDENS
80
MELON PL
WINCHESTER COURT
VICARAGE COURT
VICARAGE GATE
CHURCH CLOSE
KENSINGTON CHURCH
Holland Park Sch
25
Tenn Cts
127
ROAD
CAMPDEN HILL
GLOUCESTER WALK
NICARAGUA
CAMPDEN HO CL
CAMPDEN GROVE
BULLINGHAM MANSIONS
1 TASKER LO
2 THORNWOOD LO
HOLLY LODGE
OBSERVATORY GDNS

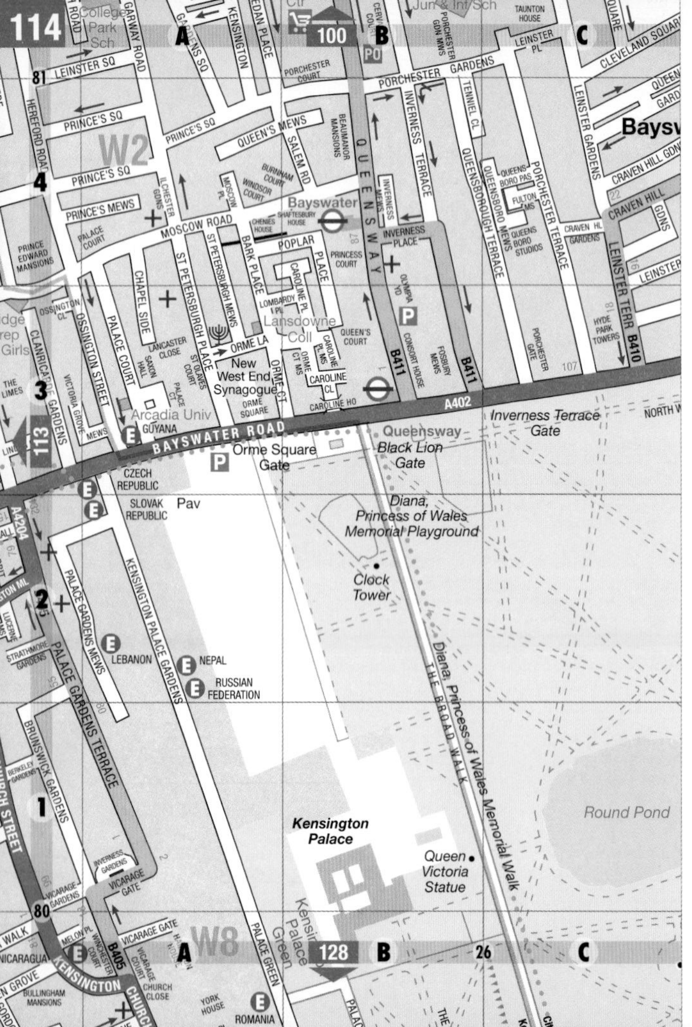

A
100
B
C
W2
Bayswater
LEINSTER SQ
PRINCE'S SQ
PRINCE'S MEWS
HEREFORD ROAD
GARWAY ROAD
KENSINGTON GARDENS SQ
PORCHESTER COURT
PORCHESTER GARDENS
QUEEN'S MEWS
SALEM RD
BEAUMANOR MANSIONS
QUEENSWAY
INVERNESS TERRACE
TENNIEL CL
QUEENSBOROUGH TERRACE
QUEENSBORO MEWS
PORCHESTER TERRACE
LEINSTER GARDENS
CLEVELAND SQUARE
CRAVEN HILL GDNS
CRAVEN HILL
LEINSTER TERR
TAUNTON HOUSE
MOSCOW ROAD
ILCHESTER GDNS
PALACE COURT
PRINCE EDWARD MANSIONS
CHAPEL SIDE
ST PETERSBURGH PLACE
ST PETERSBURGH MEWS
BARK PLACE
POPLAR PLACE
CAROLINE PL
LOMBARDY PL
Lansdowne Coll
ORME LA
ORME CT
ORME SQUARE
New West End Synagogue
CAROLINE CL
CAROLINE HO
PRINCESS COURT
QUEEN'S COURT
INVERNESS PLACE
OLYMPIA YD
CONSORT HOUSE
FOSBURY MEWS
PORCHESTER GATE
HYDE PARK TOWERS
B411
B410
A402
BAYSWATER ROAD
OSSINGTON STREET
CLANRICARDE GARDENS
VICTORIA GROVE MEWS
LANCASTER CLOSE
SAXON HALL
ST OLAVES COURT
Arcadia Univ
GUYANA
CZECH REPUBLIC
SLOVAK REPUBLIC
Pav
113
Orme Square Gate
Queensway
Black Lion Gate
Inverness Terrace Gate
Diana, Princess of Wales Memorial Playground
Clock Tower
Diana, Princess of Wales Memorial Walk
THE BROAD WALK
Round Pond
Kensington Palace
Queen Victoria Statue
A4204
PALACE GARDENS MEWS
PALACE GARDENS TERRACE
KENSINGTON PALACE GARDENS
STRATHMORE GARDENS
LEBANON
NEPAL
RUSSIAN FEDERATION
BRUNSWICK GARDENS
BERKELEY GARDENS
CHURCH STREET
INVERNESS GARDENS
VICARAGE GATE
VICARAGE GARDENS
MELON PL
WINCHESTER COURT
VICARAGE COURT
B405
KENSINGTON CHURCH
NICARAGUA
BULLINGHAM MANSIONS
CHURCH CLOSE
YORK HOUSE
ROMANIA
PALACE GREEN
Kensington Palace Green
W8
128
26
1
2
3
4

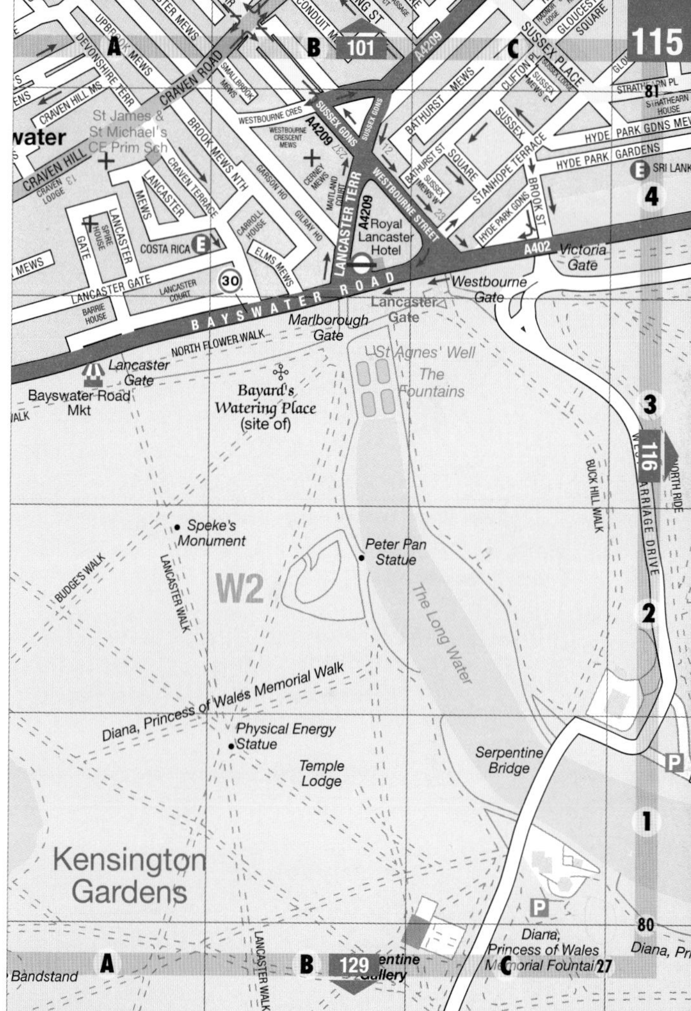

A
B
C
101
CRAVEN ROAD
UPBROOK MEWS
DEVONSHIRE TERR
CRAVEN HILL MS
CONDUIT MS
SMALLBROOK MEWS
WESTBOURNE CRES
WESTBOURNE CRESCENT MEWS
SUSSEX GDNS
A4209
BATHURST MEWS
CLIFTON PL
SUSSEX PLACE
GLOUCESTER SQUARE
STRATHEARN PL
STRATHEARN HOUSE
HYDE PARK GDNS MEWS
HYDE PARK GARDENS
SRI LANKA
St James &
St Michael's
CE Prim Sch
water
CRAVEN HILL
CRAVEN LODGE
LANCASTER MEWS
CRAVEN TERRACE
BROOK MEWS NTH
GARSON HO
CERNEY MEWS
MAITLAND COURT
LANCASTER TERR
WESTBOURNE STREET
BATHURST ST
SUSSEX SQUARE
SUSSEX MEWS W
STANHOPE TERRACE
HYDE PARK GDNS
BROOK ST
CARROLL HOUSE
GILRAY HO
ELMS MEWS
Royal
Lancaster
Hotel
SPIRE HOUSE
GATE
LANCASTER
COSTA RICA
MEWS
LANCASTER GATE
LANCASTER COURT
BARRIE HOUSE
30
BAYSWATER ROAD
A402
Victoria
Gate
Westbourne
Gate
Lancaster
Gate
Marlborough
Gate
NORTH FLOWER WALK
Lancaster
Gate
Bayswater Road
Mkt
WALK
Bayard's
Watering Place
(site of)
St Agnes' Well
The
Fountains
4
3
2
1
116
WEST CARRIAGE DRIVE
NORTH RIDE
BUCK HILL WALK
Speke's
Monument
Peter Pan
Statue
BUDGE'S WALK
LANCASTER WALK
W2
The Long Water
Diana, Princess of Wales Memorial Walk
Physical Energy
Statue
Temple
Lodge
Serpentine
Bridge
P
Kensington
Gardens
80
Diana,
Princess of Wales
Memorial Fountain
27
Diana, Pri
Bandstand
129
entine
Gallery

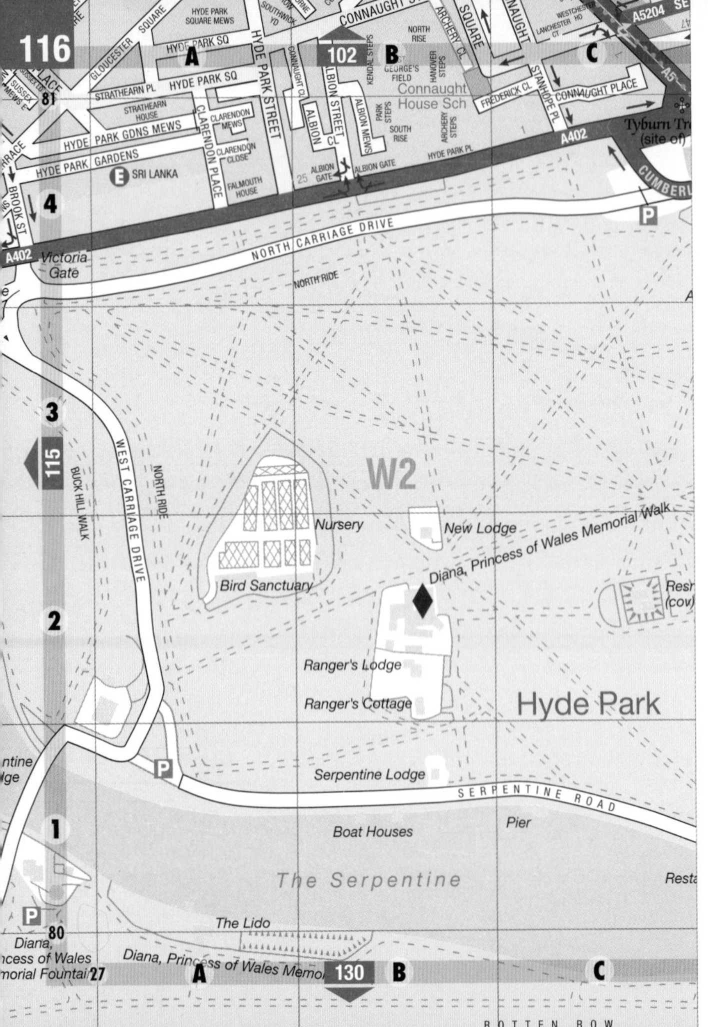

102
130
115
A
B
C
4
3
2
1
81
80
27
Hyde Park Square Mews
Hyde Park Sq
Gloucester Square
Strathearn Pl
Strathearn House
Hyde Park Gdns Mews
Hyde Park Gardens
Clarendon Place
Clarendon Mews
Clarendon Close
Falmouth House
Sri Lanka
Hyde Park Street
Connaught Cl
Albion Street
Albion Cl
Albion Mews
Albion Gate
Kendal Steps
St George's Field
Park Steps
South Rise
North Rise
Hanover Steps
Archery Steps
Archery Cl
Connaught House Sch
Hyde Park Pl
Connaught Sq
Frederick Cl
Stanhope Pl
Connaught Place
Westchester Ho
Lanchester Ct
A5204
A5
A402
Tyburn Tree (site of)
Cumberland
Brook St
Victoria Gate
North Carriage Drive
North Ride
West Carriage Drive
Buck Hill Walk
W2
Nursery
Bird Sanctuary
New Lodge
Diana, Princess of Wales Memorial Walk
Ranger's Lodge
Ranger's Cottage
Hyde Park
Serpentine Lodge
Serpentine Road
Pier
Boat Houses
The Serpentine
The Lido
Diana, Princess of Wales Memorial Fountain
Rotten Row

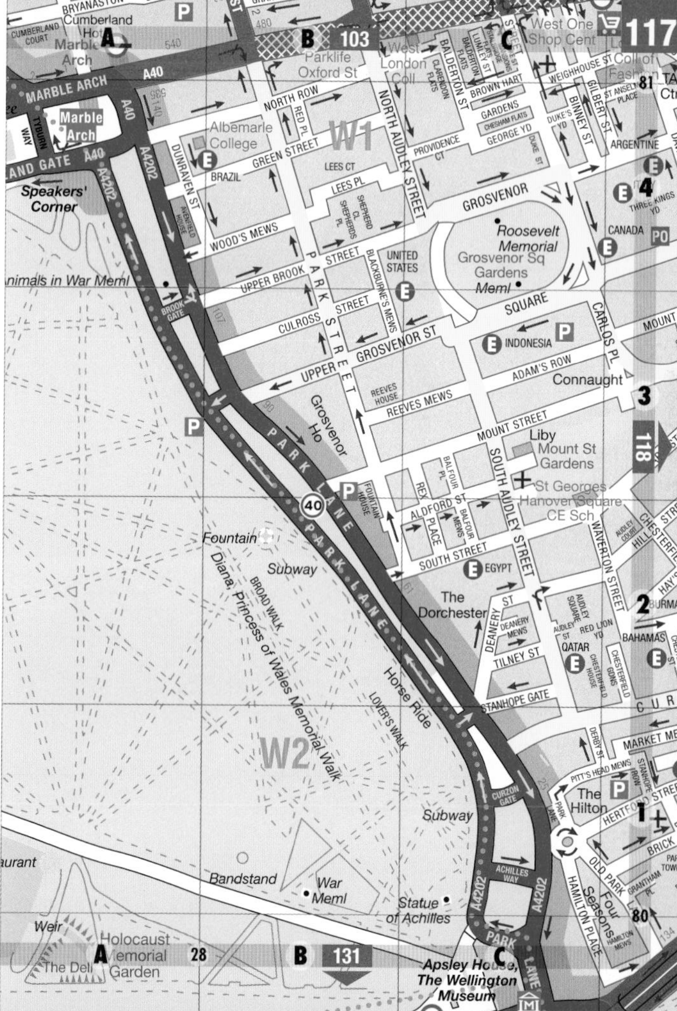
A
B
103
C
1
2
3
4
118
A
B
131
C
28
80
81
W1
W2
Bryanaston Street
Granville Pl
Cumberland Court
Cumberland Hotel
Marble Arch
Parklife Oxford St
West London Coll
West One Shop Cent
Coll of Fashion
TA Ctr
A40
Marble Arch
Tyburn Way
Land Gate
A4202
Speakers' Corner
North Row
Red Pl
Albemarle College
Green Street
Dunraven St
Brazil
Avenfield House
Wood's Mews
Lees Ct
Lees Pl
Shepherd Cl
Shepherds Pl
North Audley Street
Balderton St
Balderton Flats
Clarendon Flats
Lumley St
Lumley Flats
Brown Hart Gardens
Chesham Flats
George Yd
Duke St
Providence Ct
Weighhouse St
Duke's Yd
Binney St
Gilbert St
St Anselm's Place
Argentine
Davies Street
Three Kings Yd
Canada
PO
Grosvenor
Roosevelt Memorial
Grosvenor Sq Gardens
Meml
United States
Blackburne's Mews
Upper Brook Street
Park Street
Culross Street
Upper Grosvenor St
Square
Indonesia
Carlos Pl
Mount Row
Carpenter St
Adam's Row
Connaught
Animals in War Meml
Brook Gate
Reeves House
Reeves Mews
Mount Street
Liby
Mount St Gardens
St Georges Hanover Square CE Sch
Grosvenor Ho
Park Lane
40
Fountain House
Balfour Pl
Rex Place
Aldford St
Balfour Mews
South Audley Street
South Street
Egypt
Waverton Street
Audley Court
Hill Street
Chesterfield Hill
Hay's
Burma
Fountain
Subway
Broad Walk
Diana, Princess of Wales Memorial Walk
Horse Ride
Lover's Walk
The Dorchester
Deanery St
Deanery Mews
Tilney St
Stanhope Gate
Audley Square
Audley St
Red Lion Yd
Qatar
Chesterfield House
Chesterfield Gdns
Bahamas
Chesterfield St
Curzon
Derby St
Market Mews
Pitt's Head Mews
Stanhope Row
Hertford Street
The Hilton
Park Lane
Curzon Gate
Subway
Brick
Park Towers
Down Street
Old Park Lane
Grantham Pl
Hamilton Place
Four Seasons
Hamilton Mews
Achilles Way
Bandstand
War Meml
Statue of Achilles
Weir
Holocaust Memorial Garden
The Dell
Apsley House, The Wellington Museum

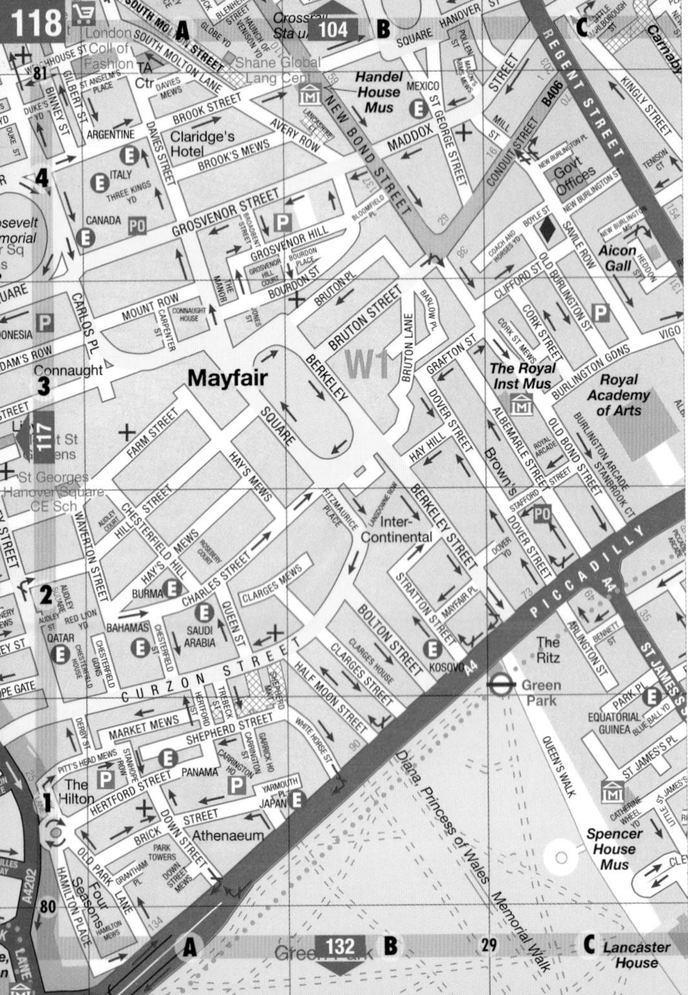
104
132
117
Mayfair
W1
Crossrail
London Coll of Fashion
Shane Global Lang Cent
Handel House Mus
Claridge's Hotel
Govt Offices
Aicon Gall
The Royal Inst Mus
Royal Academy of Arts
Brown's
Inter-Continental
The Ritz
Green Park
The Hilton
Athenaeum
Four Seasons
Spencer House Mus
Lancaster House
Diana, Princess of Wales Memorial Walk
Connaught
St Georges Hanover Square CE Sch
SOUTH MOLTON STREET
NEW BOND STREET
REGENT STREET
BROOK STREET
GROSVENOR STREET
GROSVENOR HILL
MOUNT ROW
BERKELEY SQUARE
BRUTON STREET
BRUTON LANE
DOVER STREET
ALBEMARLE STREET
OLD BOND STREET
BERKELEY STREET
PICCADILLY
CURZON STREET
CHARLES STREET
HALF MOON STREET
CLARGES STREET
BOLTON STREET
STRATTON STREET
QUEEN'S WALK
DOWN STREET
HERTFORD STREET
SHEPHERD STREET
WAVERTON STREET
FARM STREET
HILL STREET
CONDUIT STREET
SAVILE ROW
KINGLY STREET
MADDOX ST
DAVIES STREET
CARLOS PL
A4
B406

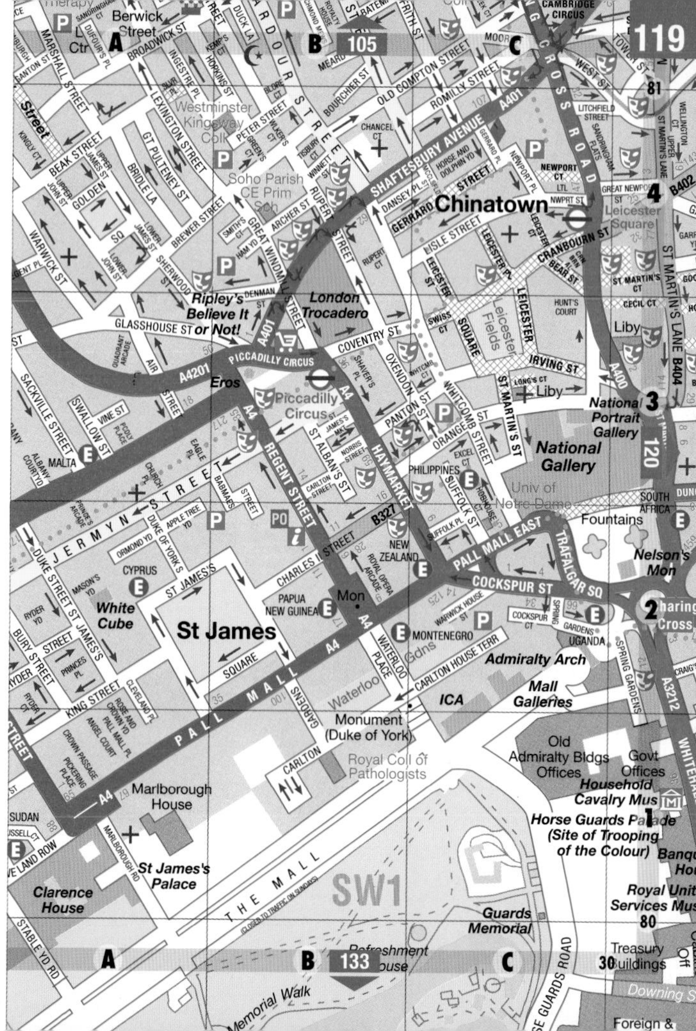
Chinatown
St James
London Trocadero
Ripley's Believe It or Not!
Piccadilly Circus
Eros
National Gallery
National Portrait Gallery
Nelson's Mon
Admiralty Arch
Mall Galleries
ICA
Marlborough House
St James's Palace
Clarence House
White Cube
Horse Guards Parade (Site of Trooping of the Colour)
Household Cavalry Mus
Banqueting House
Royal United Services Museum
Guards Memorial
Treasury Buildings
Old Admiralty Bldgs Offices
Govt Offices
Monument (Duke of York)
Royal Coll of Pathologists
SW1
THE MALL
PALL MALL
SHAFTESBURY AVENUE
CHARING CROSS ROAD
REGENT STREET
HAYMARKET
JERMYN STREET
WHITEHALL
COCKSPUR ST
TRAFALGAR SQ
PALL MALL EAST
COVENTRY ST
LEICESTER SQUARE
Leicester Square
Charing Cross
105
133
120

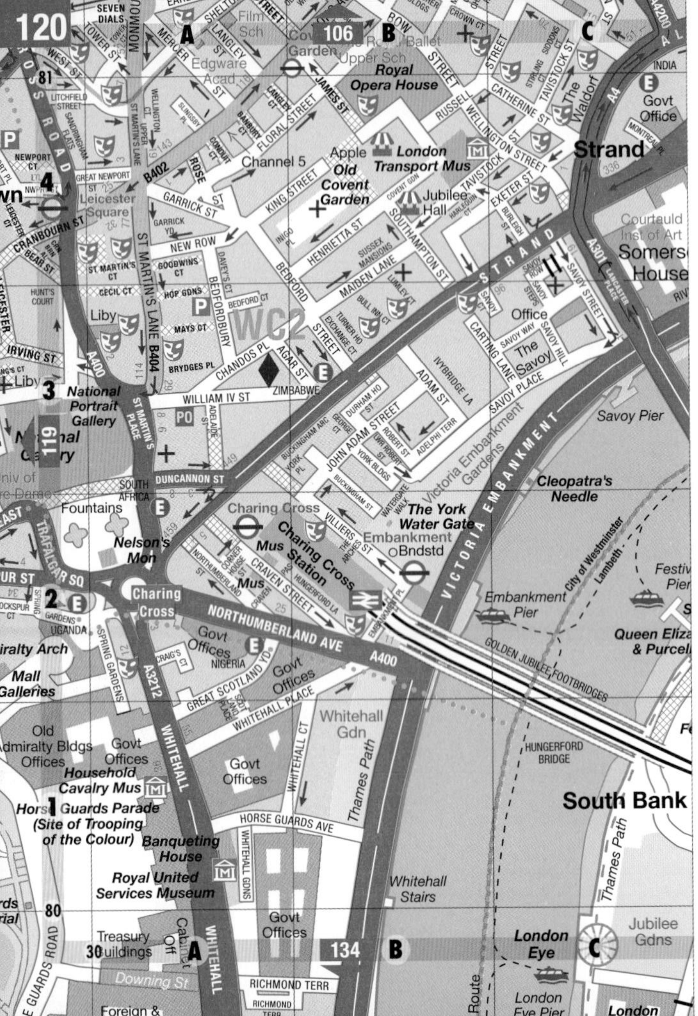

106
134
119
WC2
Royal Opera House
London Transport Mus
Old Covent Garden
Jubilee Hall
Strand
The Savoy
Savoy Pier
Somerset House
Courtauld Inst of Art
National Portrait Gallery
Charing Cross
Charing Cross Station
Embankment
Victoria Embankment Gardens
The York Water Gate
Cleopatra's Needle
Embankment Pier
Golden Jubilee Footbridges
Hungerford Bridge
South Bank
Nelson's Mon
Trafalgar Sq
Northumberland Ave
Whitehall
Whitehall Gdn
Horse Guards Ave
Household Cavalry Mus
Horse Guards Parade (Site of Trooping of the Colour)
Banqueting House
Royal United Services Museum
Treasury Buildings
Downing St
London Eye
Jubilee Gdns
London Eye Pier
Queen Elizabeth Hall & Purcell Room
Festival Pier
Leicester Square
Charing Cross Road
St Martin's Lane
Thames Path
Victoria Embankment
Govt Offices
Old Admiralty Bldgs
Mall Galleries
Admiralty Arch
Whitehall Stairs
Richmond Terr

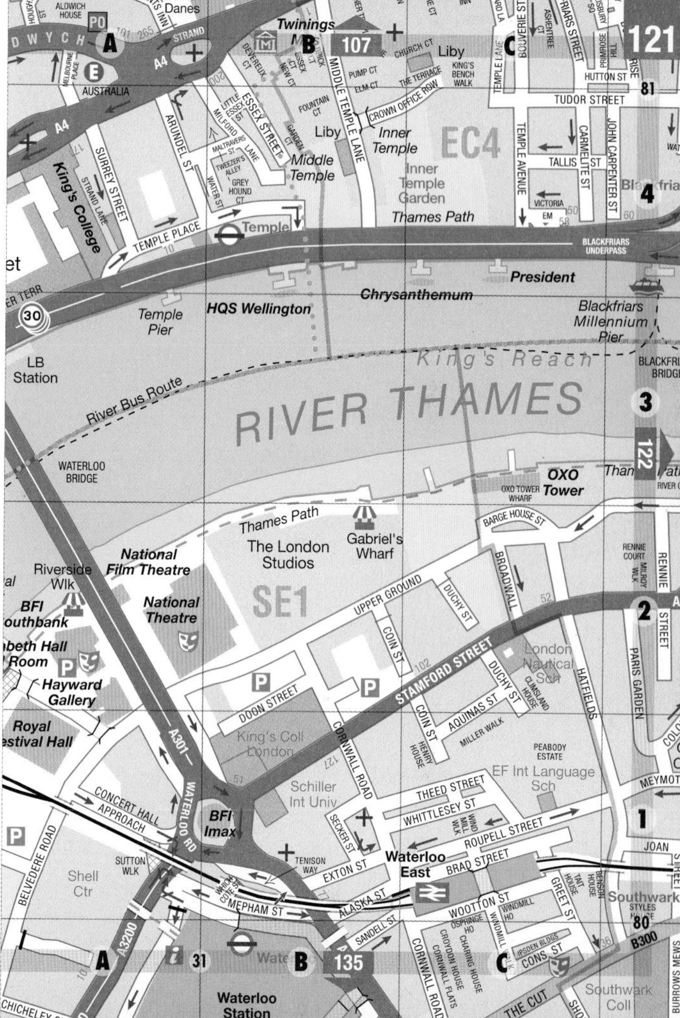

107
122
135
80
81
31
A
B
C
1
2
3
4
RIVER THAMES
King's Reach
River Bus Route
EC4
SE1
Twinings
Inner Temple
Middle Temple
Inner Temple Garden
Thames Path
King's College
Temple
Temple Pier
HQS Wellington
Chrysanthemum
President
Blackfriars Millennium Pier
BLACKFRIARS BRIDGE
BLACKFRIARS UNDERPASS
WATERLOO BRIDGE
LB Station
OXO Tower
OXO TOWER WHARF
Gabriel's Wharf
The London Studios
National Film Theatre
National Theatre
Riverside Wlk
BFI Southbank
Hayward Gallery
Royal Festival Hall
King's Coll London
Schiller Int Univ
BFI Imax
Waterloo East
Waterloo Station
Shell Ctr
London Nautical Sch
EF Int Language Sch
PEABODY ESTATE
Southwark
Southwark Coll
STRAND
ALDWICH HOUSE
AUSTRALIA
MELBOURNE PLACE
SURREY STREET
STRAND LANE
ARUNDEL ST
TEMPLE PLACE
ESSEX STREET
LITTLE ESSEX ST
MILFORD LANE
MALTRAVERS ST
TWEEZER'S ALLEY
GREYHOUND CT
WATER ST
DEVEREUX CT
NEW CT
FOUNTAIN CT
GARDEN CT
MIDDLE TEMPLE LANE
PUMP CT
ELM CT
CHURCH CT
THE TERRACE
KING'S BENCH WALK
CROWN OFFICE ROW
TEMPLE LANE
BOUVERIE STREET
ASHENTREE CT
WHITEFRIARS STREET
PRIMROSE HILL
HUTTON ST
TUDOR STREET
TEMPLE AVENUE
CARMELITE ST
JOHN CARPENTER ST
TALLIS ST
VICTORIA EM
KINGSCOTE ST
WATERGATE
BARGE HOUSE ST
UPPER GROUND
DUCHY ST
COIN ST
BROADWALL
STAMFORD STREET
HATFIELDS
CLIMSLAND HOUSE
AQUINAS ST
MILLER WALK
HENRY HOUSE
DOON STREET
CORNWALL ROAD
THEED STREET
WHITTLESEY ST
WINDMILL WLK
ROUPELL STREET
BRAD STREET
SECKER ST
EXTON ST
TENISON WAY
WATERLOO RD
CONCERT HALL APPROACH
SUTTON WLK
BELVEDERE ROAD
MEPHAM ST
ALASKA ST
SANDELL ST
WOOTTON ST
OSPRINGE HO
WINDMILL HO
CROYDON HOUSE
CORNWALL FLATS
CHARING HOUSE
IPSDEN BLDGS
CONS ST
THE CUT
GREET ST
TAIT HOUSE
BENSON HOUSE
JOAN STREET
STYLES HOUSE
B300
RENNIE COURT
MILROY WLK
RENNIE STREET
PARIS GARDEN
MEYMOTT ST
COLOMBO
RIVER COURT
BURROWS MEWS
CHICHELEY ST
A4
A301
A3200
A3200

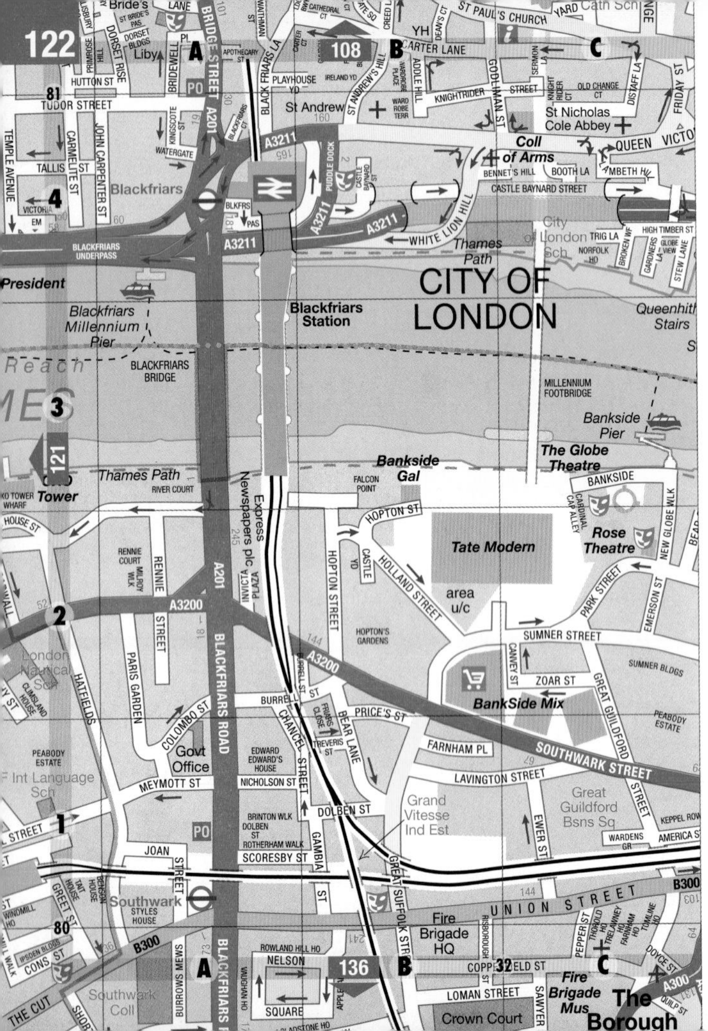

CITY OF LONDON
Blackfriars Station
Blackfriars Millennium Pier
BLACKFRIARS BRIDGE
MILLENNIUM FOOTBRIDGE
Bankside Pier
The Globe Theatre
Rose Theatre
Tate Modern
Bankside Gal
BankSide Mix
Thames Path
President
Queenhithe Stairs
City of London Sch
Coll of Arms
St Nicholas Cole Abbey
St Andrew
QUEEN VICTORIA
CARTER LANE
ST PAUL'S CHURCH YARD
BLACKFRIARS UNDERPASS
BLACKFRIARS ROAD
SOUTHWARK STREET
UNION STREET
HOPTON STREET
HOLLAND STREET
SUMNER STREET
GREAT GUILDFORD STREET
PARIS GARDEN
HATFIELDS
TUDOR STREET
TEMPLE AVENUE
CARMELITE ST
JOHN CARPENTER ST
BRIDGE STREET
WHITE LION HILL
CASTLE BAYNARD STREET
BANKSIDE
NEW GLOBE WLK
PARK STREET
Southwark
Fire Brigade HQ
Fire Brigade Mus
Crown Court
The Borough
Govt Office
Grand Vitesse Ind Est
Great Guildford Bsns Sq
Southwark Coll
London Nautical Sch
Int Language Sch
OXO Tower
108
121
136

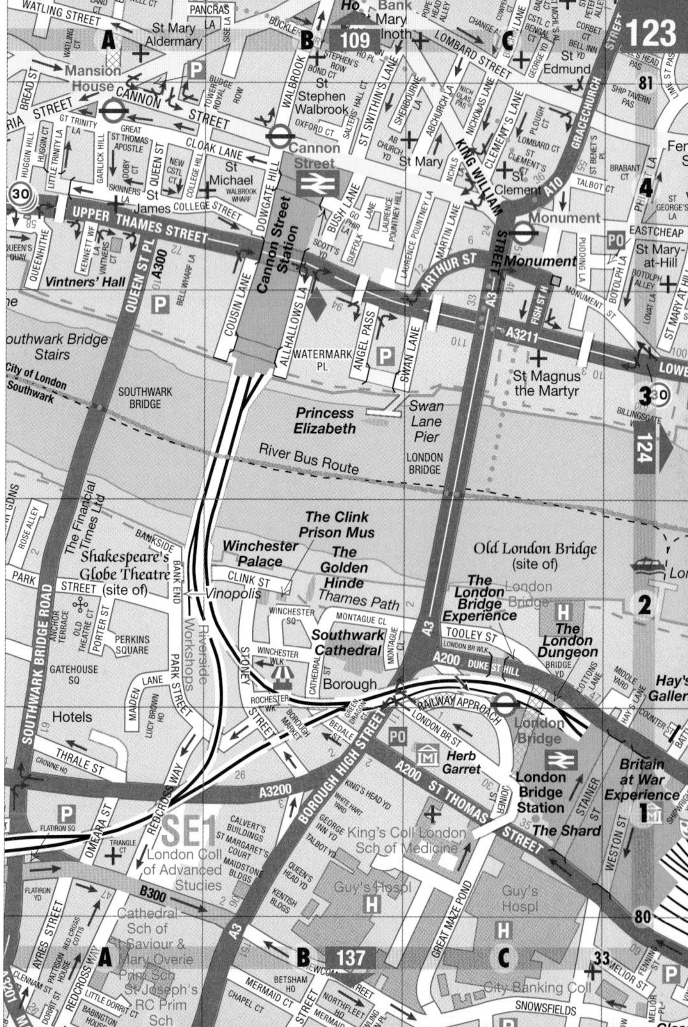
A
B
C
109
St Mary Aldermary
WATLING STREET
PANCRAS LA
Bank
St Mary Woolnoth
LOMBARD STREET
St Edmund
Mansion House
CANNON STREET
BREAD ST
BUDGE ROW
WALBROOK
St Stephen Walbrook
OXFORD CT
ST SWITHIN'S LANE
SHERBOURNE LA
ABCHURCH LA
NICHOLAS LANE
CLEMENT'S LANE
GRACECHURCH STREET
81
SHIP TAVERN PAS
LIME ST PAS
GT TRINITY LA
GREAT ST THOMAS APOSTLE
CLOAK LANE
Cannon Street
St Michael
St Mary
AB CHURCH YD
KING WILLIAM
LOMBARD CT
St Clement
TALBOT CT
BRABANT CT
ST BENET'S PL
Fenchurch St
4
HUGGIN HILL
HUGGIN CT
LITTLE TRINITY LA
GARLICK HILL
QUEEN ST
COLLEGE HILL
SKINNERS LA
St James
COLLEGE STREET
WALBROOK WHARF
DOWGATE HILL
BUSH LANE
LAURENCE POUNTNEY HILL
LAURENCE POUNTNEY LA
MARTIN LANE
A10
Monument
ST GEORGE'S LA
EASTCHEAP
30
UPPER THAMES STREET
QUEENHITHE
QUEEN'S QUAY
KENNETT WF LA
VINTNERS CT
QUEEN ST PL
A300
Cannon Street Station
SCOTT'S YD
SUFFOLK LA
ARTHUR ST
STREET
A3
Monument
PUDDING LA
BOTOLPH LA
St Mary-at-Hill
BOTOLPH ALLEY
ST MARY AT HILL
LOVAT LA
Vintners' Hall
BELL WHARF LA
COUSIN LANE
ALLHALLOWS LA
ANGEL PASS
SWAN LANE
FISH ST H
MONUMENT ST
A3211
Southwark Bridge Stairs
WATERMARK PL
St Magnus the Martyr
LOWER
City of London
Southwark
SOUTHWARK BRIDGE
Princess Elizabeth
Swan Lane Pier
3
BILLINGSGATE
124
River Bus Route
LONDON BRIDGE
ROSE ALLEY
The Financial Times Ltd
BANKSIDE
The Clink Prison Mus
Winchester Palace
The Golden Hinde
Old London Bridge (site of)
Shakespeare's Globe Theatre (site of)
PARK STREET
BANK END
CLINK ST
Vinopolis
Thames Path
The London Bridge Experience
London Bridge
2
WINCHESTER SQ
MONTAGUE CL
TOOLEY ST
LONDON BR WLK
The London Dungeon
ANCHOR TERRACE
OLD THEATRE CT
PORTER ST
PERKINS SQUARE
Riverside Workshops
WINCHESTER WLK
Southwark Cathedral
CATHEDRAL ST
A200
DUKE ST HILL
BRIDGE YD
COTTONS LANE
MIDDLE YARD
HAY'S LANE
Hay's Galleria
SOUTHWARK BRIDGE ROAD
GATEHOUSE SQ
MAIDEN LANE
LUCY BROWN HO
PARK STREET
STONEY STREET
ROCHESTER WK
Borough
RAILWAY APPROACH
GREEN DRAGON CT
LONDON BR ST
London Bridge
COUNTER ST
BATTLE BR
Hotels
BOROUGH MARKET
BEDALE ST
BOROUGH HIGH STREET
PO
Herb Garret
Britain at War Experience
THRALE ST
CROWNE HO
REDCROSS WAY
A3200
A200
ST THOMAS STREET
London Bridge Station
STAINER ST
1
KING'S HEAD YD
WHITE HART YARD
GEORGE INN YD
JOINER ST
SE1
CALVERT'S BUILDINGS
ST MARGARET'S COURT
King's Coll London Sch of Medicine
The Shard
WESTON ST
FLATIRON SQ
OMEARA ST
TRIANGLE CT
London Coll of Advanced Studies
TALBOT YD
MAIDSTONE BLDGS
QUEEN'S HEAD YD
FLATIRON YD
B300
Guy's Hospl
Guy's Hospl
KENTISH BLDGS
GREAT MAZE POND
80
Cathedral Sch of St Saviour & Mary Overie Prim Sch
AYRES STREET
RED CROSS COTTS
PATTISON HOUSE
REDCROSS WAY
A
B
137
C
33
MELIOR ST
FENNING ST
St Joseph's RC Prim Sch
LITTLE DORRIT CT
BABINGTON HOUSE
CLENNAM ST
DORRIT ST
MERMAID CT
BETSHAM HO
CHAPEL CT
NORTHFLEET HO
City Banking Coll
SNOWSFIELDS
A3201

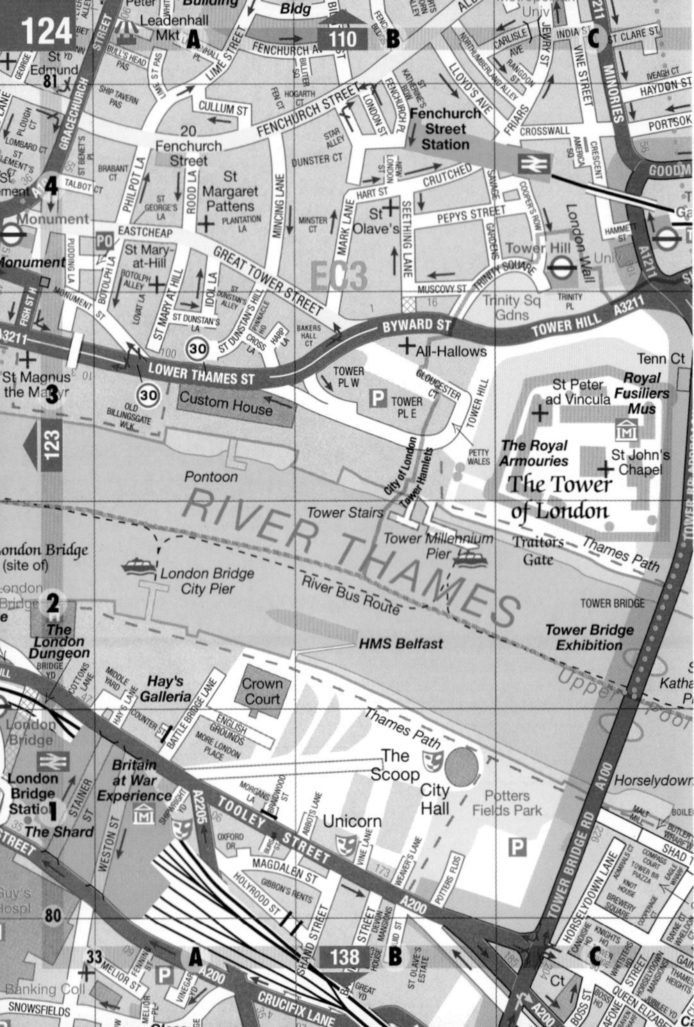

Leadenhall Mkt
Fenchurch Street Station
20 Fenchurch Street
St Margaret Pattens
St Olave's
Monument
St Mary-at-Hill
EC3
Tower Hill
Trinity Sq Gdns
All-Hallows
St Magnus the Martyr
Custom House
Tower Stairs
Tower Millennium Pier
St Peter ad Vincula
Royal Fusiliers Mus
The Royal Armouries
St John's Chapel
The Tower of London
Traitors Gate
Thames Path
RIVER THAMES
Pontoon
River Bus Route
London Bridge City Pier
HMS Belfast
Tower Bridge Exhibition
TOWER BRIDGE
The London Dungeon
Hay's Galleria
Crown Court
The Scoop
City Hall
Potters Fields Park
Britain at War Experience
London Bridge Station
The Shard
Unicorn
Horselydown
TOOLEY STREET
TOWER BRIDGE RD
LOWER THAMES ST
BYWARD ST
GREAT TOWER STREET
FENCHURCH STREET
MINORIES
CRUTCHED
PEPYS STREET
EASTCHEAP
MARK LANE
MINCING LANE
SEETHING LANE
GRACECHURCH STREET
CRUCIFIX LANE
MAGDALEN ST

110
123
138

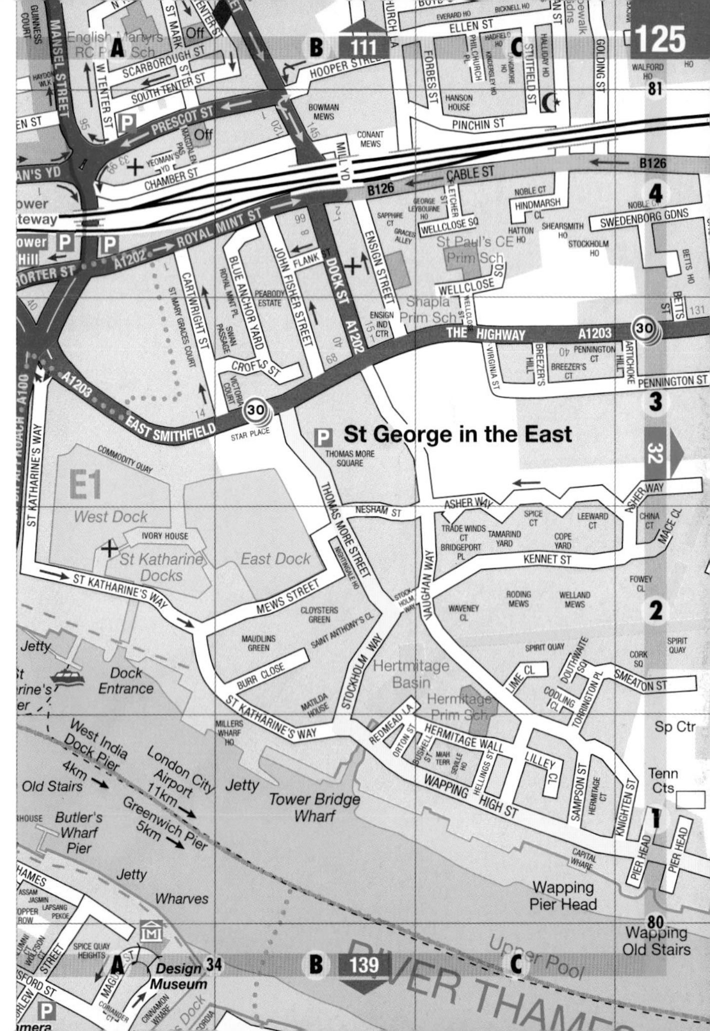

A
B
C
111
139
1
2
3
4
32
34
80
81
St George in the East
E1
West Dock
East Dock
St Katharine Docks
Dock Entrance
Hertmitage Basin
Hermitage Prim Sch
St Paul's CE Prim Sch
Shapla Prim Sch
English Martyrs RC Prim Sch
MANSEL STREET
GUINNESS COURT
W TENTER ST
SCARBOROUGH ST
SOUTH TENTER ST
PRESCOT ST
CHAMBER ST
YEOMAN'S YD
HOOPER STREET
BOWMAN MEWS
CONANT MEWS
MILL YD
ELLEN ST
EVERARD HO
BICKNELL HO
FORBES ST
HANSON HOUSE
PHILCHURCH PL
STUTFIELD ST
HALLIDAY HO
GOLDING ST
PINCHIN ST
WALFORD HO
B126
CABLE ST
NOBLE CT
HINDMARSH CL
HATTON HO
SHEARSMITH HO
STOCKHOLM HO
SWEDENBORG GDNS
BETTS HO
BETTS ST
WELLCLOSE SQ
SAPPHIRE CT
GRACES ALLEY
ROYAL MINT ST
A1202
A1203
A100
CARTWRIGHT ST
ST MARY GRACES COURT
BLUE ANCHOR YARD
JOHN FISHER STREET
FLANK ST
DOCK ST
ENSIGN STREET
ENSIGN IND CTR
PEABODY ESTATE
SWAN PASSAGE
ROYAL MINT PL
CROFTS ST
VICTORIA COURT
THE HIGHWAY
VIRGINIA ST
BREEZER'S HILL
PENNINGTON CT
BREEZER'S CT
ARTICHOKE HILL
PENNINGTON ST
EAST SMITHFIELD
STAR PLACE
THOMAS MORE SQUARE
THOMAS MORE STREET
COMMODITY QUAY
ST KATHARINE'S WAY
IVORY HOUSE
NESHAM ST
ASHER WAY
SPICE CT
LEEWARD CT
CHINA CT
MACE CL
TRADE WINDS CT
TAMARIND YARD
BRIDGEPORT PL
COPE YARD
KENNET ST
VAUGHAN WAY
FOWEY CL
RODING MEWS
WELLAND MEWS
WAVENEY CL
MEWS STREET
CLOYSTERS GREEN
SAINT ANTHONY'S CL
MAUDLINS GREEN
BURR CLOSE
STOCKHOLM WAY
MATILDA HOUSE
MILLERS WHARF HO
SPIRIT QUAY
CORK SQ
LIME CL
DOUTHWAITE SQ
CODLING CL
TORRINGTON PL
SMEATON ST
REDMEAD LA
HERMITAGE WALL
ORTON ST
BUSHELL ST
MIAH TERR
SEVILLE HO
HELLINGS ST
LILLEY CL
WAPPING HIGH ST
SAMPSON ST
HERMITAGE CT
KNIGHTEN ST
PIER HEAD
CAPITAL WHARF
Sp Ctr
Tenn Cts
Wapping Pier Head
Wapping Old Stairs
Upper Pool
RIVER THAMES
Jetty
West India Dock Pier 4km
London City Airport 11km
Greenwich Pier 5km
Old Stairs
Tower Bridge Wharf
Butler's Wharf Pier
Wharves
Design Museum
SPICE QUAY HEIGHTS
CINNAMON WHARF
CORIANDER CT
LAPSANG
ASSAM
JASMIN
PEKOE
Off

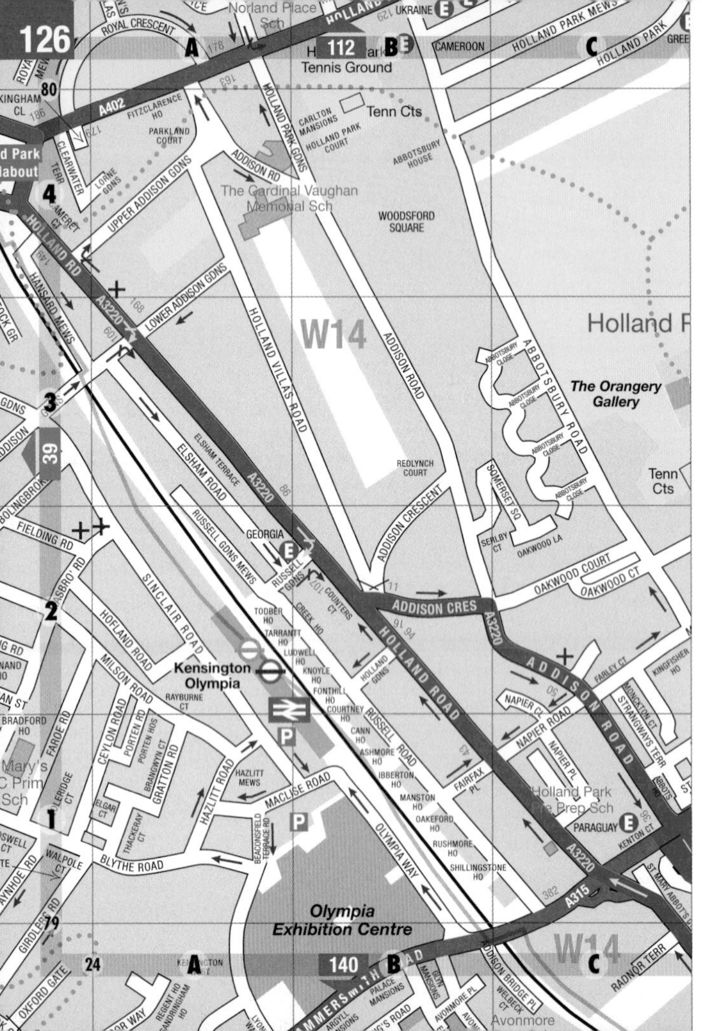

Norland Place Sch
ROYAL CRESCENT
UKRAINE
HOLLAND PARK MEWS
112
Holland Park Tennis Ground
CAMEROON
HOLLAND PARK
A
B
C
80
A402
FITZCLARENCE HO
PARKLAND COURT
HOLLAND PARK GDNS
CARLTON MANSIONS
HOLLAND PARK COURT
Tenn Cts
ABBOTSBURY HOUSE
CLEARWATER TERR
LORNE GDNS
UPPER ADDISON GDNS
ADDISON RD
The Cardinal Vaughan Memorial Sch
WOODSFORD SQUARE
4
HOLLAND RD
A3220
HANSARD MEWS
LOWER ADDISON GDNS
HOLLAND VILLAS ROAD
W14
ADDISON ROAD
Holland P
ABBOTSBURY CLOSE
ABBOTSBURY ROAD
The Orangery Gallery
3
39
ELSHAM TERRACE
ELSHAM ROAD
REDLYNCH COURT
Tenn Cts
ADDISON CRESCENT
SOMERSET SQ
FIELDING RD
RUSSELL GDNS MEWS
GEORGIA
RUSSELL GDNS
SERLBY CT
OAKWOOD LA
OAKWOOD COURT
OAKWOOD CT
SINCLAIR ROAD
COUNTERS CT
CREEK HO
ADDISON CRES
2
HOFLAND ROAD
TODBER HO
TARRANTT HO
LUDWELL HO
KNOYLE HO
FONTHILL HO
COURTNEY HO
HOLLAND GDNS
HOLLAND ROAD
ADDISON ROAD
FARLEY CT
KINGFISHER HO
MILSON ROAD
Kensington Olympia
RAYBURNE CT
NAPIER CL
NAPIER ROAD
NAPIER PL
MONCKTON CT
STRANGWAYS TERR
BRADFORD HO
FAROE RD
CEYLON ROAD
PORTEN RD
PORTEN HOS
BRANGWYN CT
GRATTON RD
RUSSELL ROAD
CANN HO
ASHMORE HO
IBBERTON HO
MANSTON HO
OAKEFORD HO
RUSHMORE HO
SHILLINGSTONE HO
FAIRFAX PL
HAZLITT ROAD
HAZLITT MEWS
MACLISE ROAD
Holland Park Pre Prep Sch
PARAGUAY
KENTON CT
1
ELGAR CT
THACKERAY CT
BEACONSFIELD TERRACE RD
OLYMPIA WAY
A3220
A315
WALPOLE CT
BLYTHE ROAD
ST MARY ABBOT'S PL
Olympia Exhibition Centre
79
GIRDLERS RD
24
140
HAMMERSMITH ROAD
PALACE MANSIONS
GLYN MANSIONS
ADDISON BRIDGE PL
WELBECK CT
AVONMORE PL
RADNOR TERR
OXFORD GATE
REGENT HO
SANDRINGHAM HO
ARGYLL MANSIONS
Avonmore

KENSINGTON
A
B
C
113
128
141
79
80
1
2
3
4
Tenn Cts
Holland Park Sch
Park
YH
Commonwealth Institute
Leighton House Mus
St Barnabas & St Philip CE Prim Sch
St Mary Abbots CE Prim Sch
TH
Liby
JORDAN
NICARAGUA
ARMENIA
SENEGAL
CAMPDEN HILL ROAD
CAMPDEN HILL
SHEFFIELD TERRACE
BEDFORD GDNS
AIRLIE GDNS
LAURIE HOUSE
THE MOUNT
TOR GDNS
TOR COURT
CAMPDEN HOUSE
CAMPDEN HO CL
GLOUCESTER WALK
CAMPDEN GROVE
BULLINGHAM MANSIONS
HORNTON STREET
GORDON PLACE
PITT ST
DUKES LANE
CARMEL CT
HOLLAND PL
HOLLAND STREET
GREGORY PL
DRAYSON MEWS
KENSINGTON CHURCH STREET
VICARAGE GARDENS
VICARAGE GATE
MELON PL
WINCHESTER COURT
B405
OBSERVATORY GDNS
CAMPDEN HILL COURT
1 TASKER LO
2 THORNWOOD LO
HOLLY LODGE
THORNWOOD GDNS
ATKINS LODGE
SHELDRAKE PLACE
DUCHESS OF BEDFORD HOUSE
ACADEMY GDNS
CAMPDEN HILL GATE
DUCHESS OF BEDFORD'S WALK
UPPER PHILLIMORE GARDENS
PHILLIMORE PLACE
PHILLIMORE GARDENS
ARGYLL ROAD
ESSEX VILLAS
STAFFORD TERRACE
PHILLIMORE WALK
PHILLIMORE COURT
STAFFORD CT
HORNTON PLACE
HORNTON COURT
HOLLAND WLK
ILCHESTER PLACE
PARK CLOSE
MELBURY ROAD
STAVORDALE LODGE
MELBURY COURT
PHILLIMORE GDNS CL
TROY CT
KENSINGTON HIGH STREET
A315
ALLEN HO
EDEN CL
ADAM AND EVE MEWS
IVERNA CT
IVERNA GARDENS
WRIGHT'S LANE
CHENISTON GARDENS
PHILLIMORE TERR
WYNNSTAY GDNS
ALLEN MANSIONS
ALLEN STREET
ABINGDON CT
ABINGDON VILLAS
ABINGDON GDNS
ABINGDON ROAD
VANTAGE PL
ILCHESTER MANSIONS
ABINGDON MANSIONS
WARWICK CHAMBERS
PATER ST
COPE PLACE
B316
PO
LEONARD CT
EDWARDES SQ
HOLLAND PARK ROAD
KENBROOK HO
MARY ABBOTS TERR
EARLS TERR
EDWARDES PL
ST MARY ABBOT'S PL
EDWARDES SQUARE
PEMBROKE PLACE
PEMBROKE MEWS
SOUTH EDWARDES SQ
EARLS WALK
PEMBROKE SQUARE
PEMBROKE SQ
PEMBROKE GARDENS CLOSE
PEMBROKE GDNS
PEMBROKE STUDIOS
PEMBROKE WLK
PEMBROKE VILLAS
SCARSDALE VILLAS
INKERMAN TERR
ALMA TERR
STRATFORD STUDIOS
BLITHFIELD ST
SHAFTESBURY MEWS
STRATFORD ROAD
RADLEY MEWS
LEXHAM MEWS
SUNNINGDALE GDNS
LEXHAM GARDENS
MARLOES ROAD
CEDAR HO
ZETLAND HO
RUTLAND
FALKLAND
SCARSDALE PLACE
A3220
WARWICK GARDENS
DURRELS HO
CHATSWORTH CT
HUNTINGDON HO
SHERBOURNE CT
EARLS

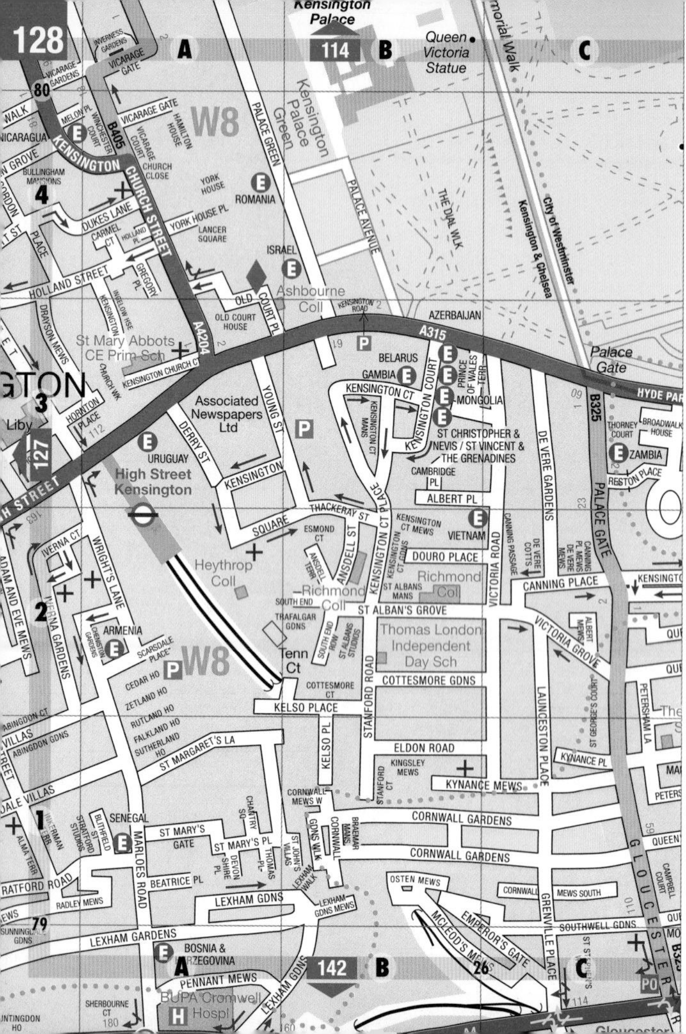
Kensington Palace
114
A
B
C
Queen Victoria Statue
Memorial Walk
W8
INVERNESS GARDENS
VICARAGE GATE
VICARAGE GARDENS
80
MELON PL
WINCHESTER COURT
B405
VICARAGE GATE
VICARAGE COURT
HAMILTON HOUSE
PALACE GREEN
Kensington Palace Green
NICARAGUA
KENSINGTON CHURCH STREET
CHURCH CLOSE
BULLINGHAM MANSIONS
YORK HOUSE
ROMANIA
PALACE AVENUE
THE DIAL WALK
Kensington & Chelsea
City of Westminster
4
DUKES LANE
YORK HOUSE PL
LANCER SQUARE
CARMEL CT
HOLLAND PL
ISRAEL
HOLLAND STREET
GREGORY PL
OLD COURT PL
Ashbourne Coll
KENSINGTON ROAD
INGELOW HSE
KENSINGTON
DRAYSON MEWS
OLD COURT HOUSE
AZERBAIJAN
A4204
A315
St Mary Abbots CE Prim Sch
BELARUS
PRINCE OF WALES TERR
Palace Gate
GAMBIA
KENSINGTON CT
KENSINGTON COURT
MONGOLIA
HYDE PARK
CHURCH WK
KENSINGTON CHURCH CT
YOUNG ST
Associated Newspapers Ltd
KENSINGTON CT MANS
B325
3
HORNTON PLACE
DERRY ST
ST CHRISTOPHER & NEVIS / ST VINCENT & THE GRENADINES
THORNEY COURT
BROADWALK HOUSE
Liby
127
URUGUAY
DE VERE GARDENS
ZAMBIA
CAMBRIDGE PL
High Street Kensington
KENSINGTON
RESTON PLACE
HIGH STREET
ALBERT PL
PALACE GATE
THACKERAY ST
KENSINGTON CT MEWS
SQUARE
ESMOND CT
VIETNAM
CANNING PASSAGE
IVERNA CT
WRIGHT'S LANE
ANSDELL ST
KENSINGTON CT PLACE
DOURO PLACE
DE VERE COTTS
DE VERE MEWS
CANNING PL MEWS
Heythrop Coll
ANSDELL TERR
KENSINGTON CT GDNS
Richmond Coll
VICTORIA ROAD
CANNING PLACE
KENSINGTON
ADAM AND EVE MEWS
ST ALBANS MANS
Richmond Coll
2
IVERNA GARDENS
SOUTH END
ST ALBAN'S GROVE
TRAFALGAR GDNS
VICTORIA GROVE
ALBERT MEWS
ARMENIA
CHENISTON GARDENS
SCARSDALE PLACE
SOUTH END ROW
ST ALBANS STUDIOS
Thomas London Independent Day Sch
Tenn Ct
W8
CEDAR HO
STANFORD ROAD
COTTESMORE GDNS
PETERSHAM LA
ZETLAND HO
COTTESMORE CT
ABINGDON CT
RUTLAND HO
KELSO PLACE
LAUNCESTON PLACE
ST GEORGE'S COURT
VILLAS
ABINGDON GDNS
FALKLAND HO
SUTHERLAND HO
ST MARGARET'S LA
KELSO PL
ELDON ROAD
KYNANCE PL
STREET
KINGSLEY MEWS
STANFORD CT
KYNANCE MEWS
PETERS
DALE VILLAS
CORNWALL MEWS W
CHANTRY SQ
1
CORNWALL GARDENS
INKERMAN TERR
STRATFORD STUDIOS
BLITHFIELD ST
SENEGAL
ST MARY'S GATE
CORNWALL GDNS WLK
BRAEMAR MANS
ALMA TERR
MARLOES ROAD
ST MARY'S PL
DEVONSHIRE PL
THOMAS PL
ST JOHN'S VILLAS
CORNWALL GARDENS
QUEEN'S
CAMPBELL COURT
RATFORD ROAD
BEATRICE PL
LEXHAM WALK
OSTEN MEWS
CORNWALL MEWS SOUTH
GRENVILLE PLACE
LEXHAM GDNS
LEXHAM GDNS MEWS
RADLEY MEWS
MCLEOD'S MEWS
EMPEROR'S GATE
GLOUCESTER
79
SUNNINGDALE GDNS
LEXHAM GARDENS
SOUTHWELL GDNS
BOSNIA & HERZEGOVINA
142
ST STEPHEN'S
A
B
26
C
PENNANT MEWS
LEXHAM GDNS
BUPA Cromwell Hospl
SHERBOURNE CT
HUNTINGDON HO
Gloucester

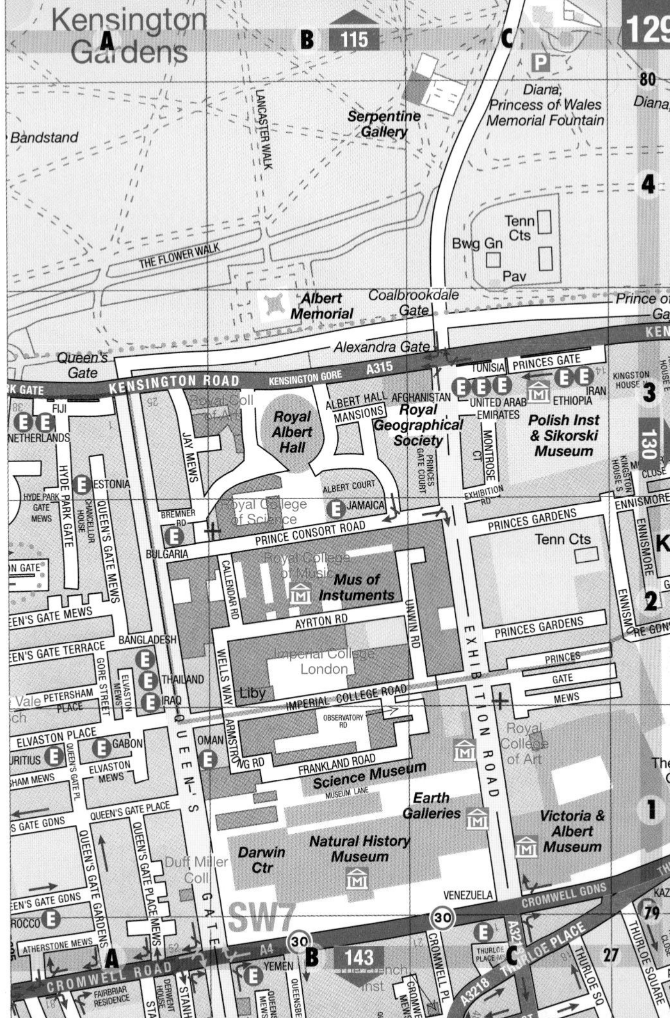
Kensington Gardens
A
B
115
C
Serpentine Gallery
Diana, Princess of Wales Memorial Fountain
Bandstand
LANCASTER WALK
THE FLOWER WALK
Tenn Cts
Bwg Gn
Pav
Albert Memorial
Coalbrookdale Gate
Prince of Wales Gate
Alexandra Gate
Queen's Gate
KENSINGTON ROAD
KENSINGTON GORE
A315
Royal Albert Hall
Royal Geographical Society
Polish Inst & Sikorski Museum
ALBERT HALL MANSIONS
JAY MEWS
PRINCES GATE
PRINCES GATE COURT
MONTROSE CT
EXHIBITION RD
ALBERT COURT
Royal College of Science
PRINCE CONSORT ROAD
PRINCES GARDENS
Tenn Cts
ENNISMORE GDNS
Royal College of Music
Mus of Instuments
CALLENDAR RD
AYRTON RD
UNWIN RD
WELLS WAY
Imperial College London
Liby
IMPERIAL COLLEGE ROAD
OBSERVATORY RD
EXHIBITION ROAD
PRINCES GATE MEWS
Royal College of Art
FRANKLAND ROAD
Science Museum
MUSEUM LANE
Earth Galleries
Natural History Museum
Darwin Ctr
Victoria & Albert Museum
QUEEN'S GATE
HYDE PARK GATE
QUEEN'S GATE MEWS
QUEEN'S GATE TERRACE
GORE STREET
ELVASTON MEWS
PETERSHAM PLACE
ELVASTON PLACE
QUEEN'S GATE PLACE
QUEEN'S GATE GDNS
QUEEN'S GATE GARDENS
QUEEN'S GATE PLACE MEWS
ATHERSTONE MEWS
Duff Miller Coll
SW7
CROMWELL ROAD
CROMWELL GDNS
CROMWELL PL
THURLOE PLACE
THURLOE SQ
THURLOE SQUARE
A3218
A4
30
143
FIJI
NETHERLANDS
ESTONIA
BULGARIA
BANGLADESH
THAILAND
IRAQ
GABON
OMAN
JAMAICA
TUNISIA
AFGHANISTAN
UNITED ARAB EMIRATES
ETHIOPIA
IRAN
VENEZUELA
YEMEN
KAZAKH
130
4
3
2
1
80
79
27

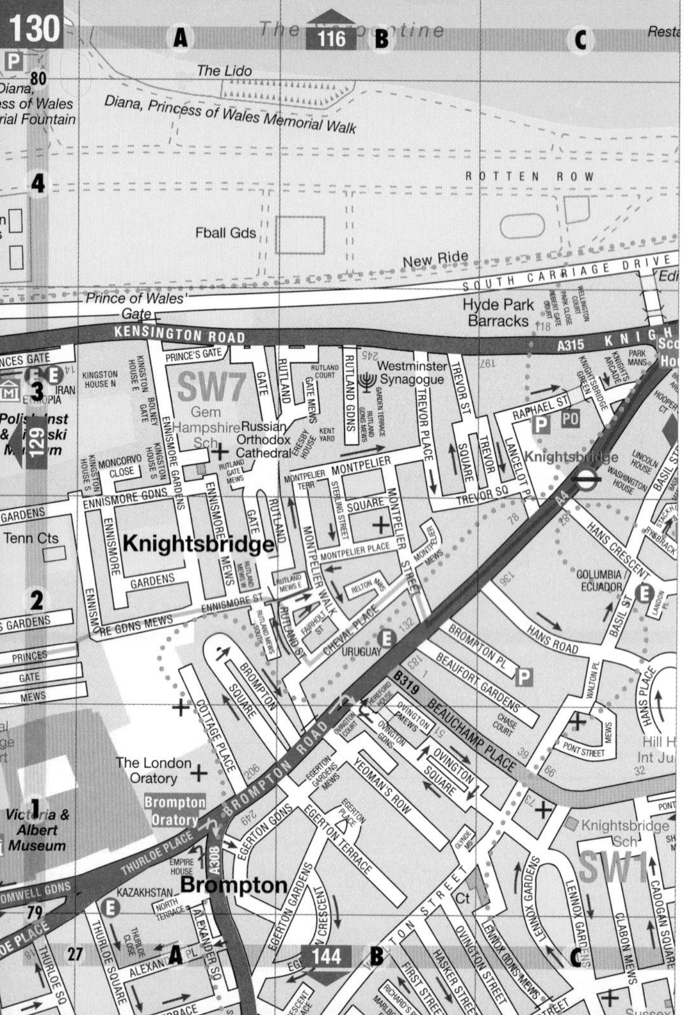

A
116
B
C
The Lido
Diana, Princess of Wales Memorial Walk
ROTTEN ROW
Fball Gds
New Ride
SOUTH CARRIAGE DRIVE
Prince of Wales' Gate
Hyde Park Barracks
KENSINGTON ROAD
A315
KNIGHTSBRIDGE
PRINCE'S GATE
SW7
Gem
Hampshire Sch
Russian Orthodox Cathedral
Westminster Synagogue
RUTLAND GATE
RUTLAND GDNS
TREVOR PLACE
TREVOR ST
TREVOR SQUARE
TREVOR SQ
RAPHAEL ST
KNIGHTSBRIDGE GREEN
LANCELOT PL
Knightsbridge
MONTPELIER SQUARE
MONTPELIER PLACE
MONTPELIER WALK
MONTPELIER STREET
ENNISMORE GARDENS
ENNISMORE GDNS
ENNISMORE ST
ENNISMORE GDNS MEWS
Knightsbridge
Tenn Cts
CHEVAL PLACE
URUGUAY
BROMPTON SQUARE
HANS CRESCENT
HANS ROAD
HANS PLACE
BASIL ST
COLUMBIA / ECUADOR
BROMPTON PL
BEAUFORT GARDENS
B319
BEAUCHAMP PLACE
PONT STREET
WALTON PL
COTTAGE PLACE
The London Oratory
BROMPTON ROAD
Brompton Oratory
THURLOE PLACE
A308
Brompton
EGERTON GDNS
EGERTON TERRACE
YEOMAN'S ROW
OVINGTON SQUARE
OVINGTON GDNS
WALTON STREET
LENNOX GARDENS
LENNOX GDNS MEWS
CLABON MEWS
CADOGAN SQUARE
Knightsbridge Sch
SW1
Victoria & Albert Museum
KAZAKHSTAN
THURLOE SQUARE
ALEXANDER SQ
ALEXANDER PL
EGERTON CRESCENT
OVINGTON STREET
HASKER STREET
FIRST STREET
144

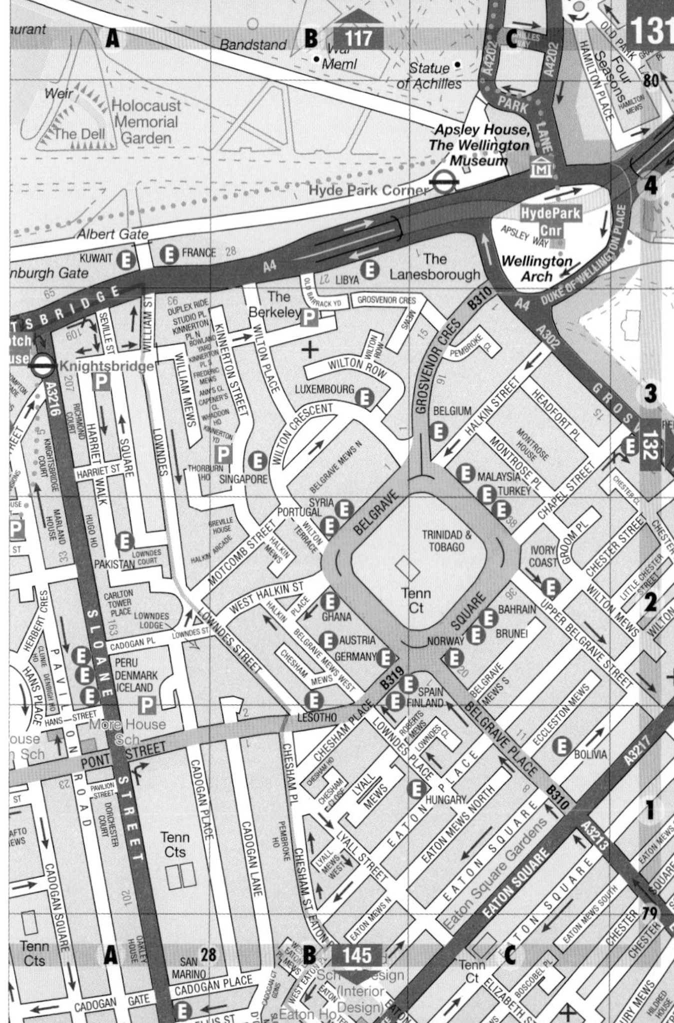

131
A
B
C
117
145
1
2
3
4
132
134
80
79
Bandstand
War Meml
Statue of Achilles
Weir
Holocaust Memorial Garden
The Dell
Apsley House, The Wellington Museum
Hyde Park Corner
HydePark Cnr
Apsley Way
Wellington Arch
Duke of Wellington Place
Park Lane
A4202
Old Park Lane
Hamilton Place
Hamilton Mews
Four Seasons
Albert Gate
Kuwait
France
Libya
The Lanesborough
The Berkeley
A4
A302
B310
Old Barrack Yd
Grosvenor Cres
Grosvenor Cres Mews
Pembroke Cl
Wilton Row
Wilton Place
Wilton Crescent
Luxembourg
Belgium
Halkin Street
Headfort Pl
Montrose House
Montrose Pl
Malaysia
Turkey
Chapel Street
Groom Pl
Chester Street
Chester Mews
Chester Cl
Little Chester Street
Wilton Mews
Wilton Street
Grosvenor Place
Knightsbridge
A3216
Seville St
William St
William Mews
Duplex Ride
Studio Pl
Kinnerton Pl N
Bowland Yard
Kinnerton Pl S
Frederic Mews
Ann's Cl
Capener's Cl
Whaddon Ho
Kinnerton Yd
Kinnerton Street
Thorburn Ho
Singapore
Belgrave Mews N
Syria
Portugal
Wilton Terrace
Halkin Mews
Motcomb Street
Greville House
Halkin Arcade
Belgrave Square
Trinidad & Tobago
Tenn Ct
Ivory Coast
Bahrain
Brunei
Norway
Upper Belgrave Street
West Halkin St
Halkin Place
Ghana
Austria
Germany
Belgrave Mews West
Chesham Mews
Lowndes Street
Lowndes Square
Lowndes Court
Lowndes Lodge
Lowndes St
Pakistan
Carlton Tower Place
Cadogan Pl
Peru
Denmark
Iceland
Harriet Walk
Harriet St
Hugo Ho
Richmond Court
Knightsbridge Court
Marland House
Sloane Street
Herbert Cres
Hans Place
Hans Street
Pavilion Road
Clunie Ho
Denbigh Ho
More House Sch
Pont Street
B319
Spain
Finland
Lesotho
Chesham Place
Lowndes Place
Roberts Mews
Lowndes Cl
Belgrave Mews S
Belgrave Place
Eccleston Mews
Bolivia
A3217
Chesham Ho
Chesham Close
Lyall Mews
Lyall Mews West
Lyall Street
Hungary
Eaton Place
Eaton Mews North
Eaton Square
Eaton Square Gardens
A3213
Eaton Mews South
Eaton Mews N
Chester Square
Chester Row
Pembroke Ho
Chesham St
Cadogan Place
Cadogan Lane
Cadogan Square
Cadogan Gate
Dorchester Court
Pavilion Street
Oakley House
San Marino
Tenn Cts
Elizabeth St
Boscobel Pl
Hildred House
Ellis St
Eaton Ho
Sch of Design (Interior Design)

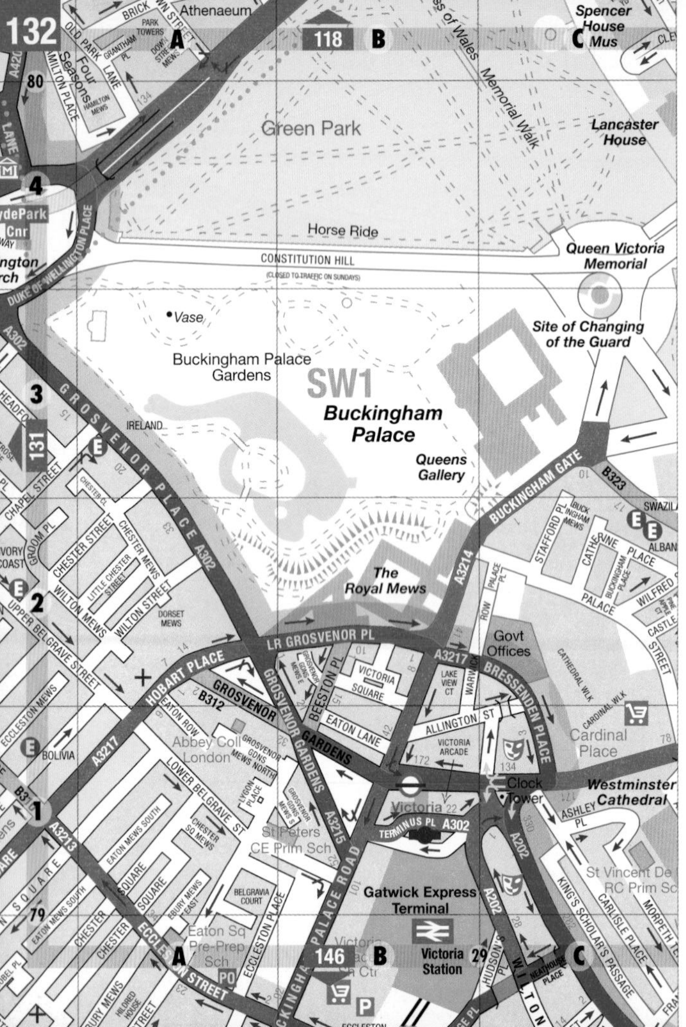
118
146
131
Green Park
Horse Ride
Constitution Hill
(Closed to traffic on Sundays)
Queen Victoria Memorial
Site of Changing of the Guard
Spencer House Mus
Lancaster House
Athenaeum
Four Seasons
Vase
Buckingham Palace Gardens
SW1
Buckingham Palace
Queens Gallery
The Royal Mews
Govt Offices
Cardinal Place
Westminster Cathedral
Clock Tower
Victoria
Gatwick Express Terminal
Victoria Station
Abbey Coll London
St Peters CE Prim Sch
Eaton Sq Pre-Prep Sch
St Vincent De RC Prim Sc
Grosvenor Place
Duke of Wellington Place
Buckingham Gate
Lr Grosvenor Pl
Hobart Place
Grosvenor Gardens
Bressenden Place
Buckingham Palace Road
Eccleston Street
Terminus Pl
Memorial Walk
Ireland
Bolivia
Ivory Coast
Chester Street
Wilton Street
Upper Belgrave Street
Lower Belgrave St
Eaton Lane
Victoria Square
Allington St
Victoria Arcade
Ashley Pl
Carlisle Place
King's Scholar's Passage
Neathouse Place
Wilton Road
Hudson's Pl
Eccleston Place
Belgravia Court
Stafford Pl
Catherine Place
Palace Street
Wilfred St
Castle
Dorset Mews
Chester Mews
Wilton Mews
Eaton Row
Eccleston Mews
Hamilton Place
Old Park Lane
Brick
Park Towers
Grantham Pl
Hamilton Mews
Chapel Street
Groom Pl
Little Chester Street
Chester Cl
Headfort
Lygon Place
Beeston Pl
Warwick Row
Palace Pl
Lake View Ct
Cathedral Wlk
Cardinal Wlk
Eaton Mews South
Chester Sq Mews
Ebury Mews East
Ebury Mews
Hildred House
A302
A3217
A3214
A3215
A3213
A202
B312
B323
A420
Hyde Park Cnr
Swaziland
Alban

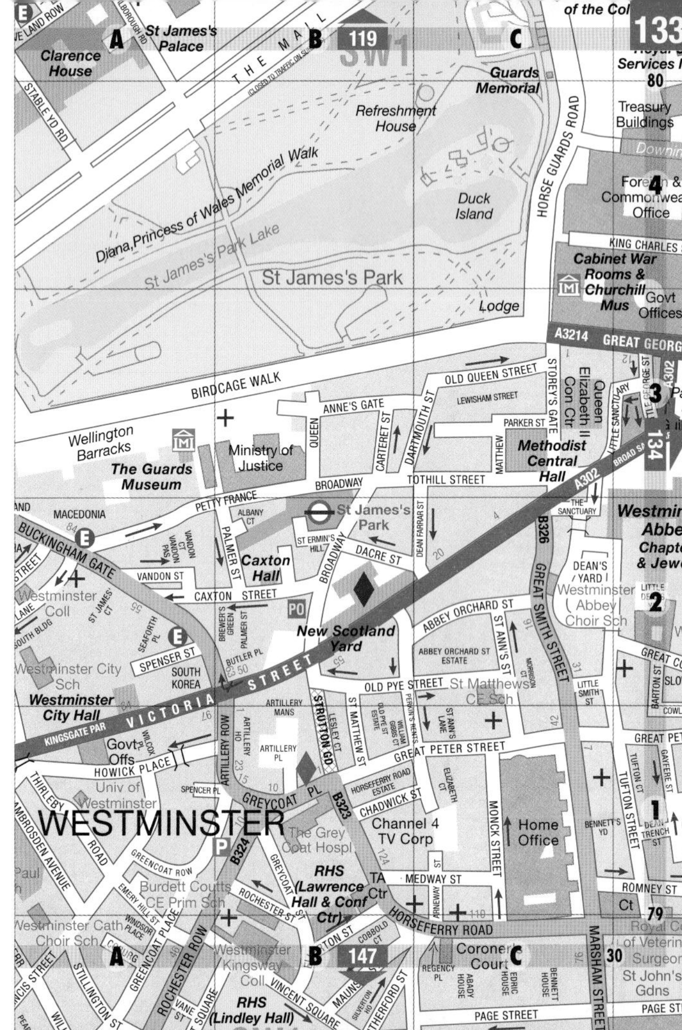
St James's Palace
Clarence House
THE MALL
119
SW1
Guards Memorial
Services Mu
80
Treasury Buildings
Refreshment House
HORSE GUARDS ROAD
Diana, Princess of Wales Memorial Walk
Duck Island
Foreign & Commonwealth Office
KING CHARLES ST
St James's Park Lake
St James's Park
Cabinet War Rooms & Churchill Mus
Govt Offices
Lodge
A3214 GREAT GEORGE ST
BIRDCAGE WALK
OLD QUEEN STREET
STOREY'S GATE
Queen Elizabeth II Con Ctr
LEWISHAM STREET
ANNE'S GATE
PARKER ST
Wellington Barracks
The Guards Museum
Ministry of Justice
QUEEN
CARTERET ST
DARTMOUTH ST
MATTHEW
Methodist Central Hall
LITTLE SANCTUARY
BROAD SANCTUARY
134
BROADWAY
TOTHILL STREET
A302
PETTY FRANCE
MACEDONIA
ALBANY CT
St James's Park
THE SANCTUARY
Westminster Abbey Chapter & Jewel
BUCKINGHAM GATE
VANDON CT
VANDON PAS
PALMER ST
Caxton Hall
ST ERMIN'S HILL
BROADWAY
DACRE ST
DEAN FARRAR ST
B326
DEAN'S YARD
VANDON ST
CAXTON STREET
Westminster Coll
ST JAMES' CT
SEAFORTH PL
BREWER'S GREEN
PALMER ST
PO
New Scotland Yard
ABBEY ORCHARD ST
GREAT SMITH STREET
Westminster Abbey Choir Sch
LITTLE DEAN'S
SPENSER ST
SOUTH KOREA
BUTLER PL
VICTORIA STREET
ABBEY ORCHARD ST ESTATE
ST ANN'S ST
MORRISON CT
GREAT COLLEGE
Westminster City Sch
OLD PYE STREET
St Matthews CE Sch
LITTLE SMITH ST
SLOVEN
BARTON ST
COWLEY
Westminster City Hall
ARTILLERY MANS
STRUTTON GD
ST MATTHEW ST
LESLEY CT
OLD PYE ST ESTATE
WILLIAM GIBBS CT
PERKIN'S RENTS
ST ANN'S LANE
GREAT PETER
KINGSGATE PAR
VICTORIA
WILCOX PL
Govt Offs
ARTILLERY ROW
ARTILLERY HO
ARTILLERY PL
GREAT PETER STREET
TUFTON CT
GAYFERE ST
LORD NORTH STREET
HOWICK PLACE
SPENCER PL
HORSEFERRY ROAD ESTATE
ELIZABETH CT
THIRLEBY ROAD
Univ of Westminster
GREYCOAT PL
B323
CHADWICK ST
TUFTON STREET
BENNETT'S YD
DEAN TRENCH ST
WESTMINSTER
AMBROSDEN AVENUE
The Grey Coat Hospl
Channel 4 TV Corp
MONCK STREET
Home Office
P
B324
GREENCOAT ROW
GREYCOAT ST
RHS (Lawrence Hall & Conf Ctr)
TA Ctr
MEDWAY ST
ARNEWAY ST
ROMNEY ST
Burdett Coutts CE Prim Sch
EMERY HILL ST
ROCHESTER ST
Ct
79
Royal Coll of Veterinary Surgeons
HORSEFERRY ROAD
Westminster Cath Choir Sch
WINDSOR PLACE
GREENCOAT PLACE
COBBOLD CT
MARSHAM STREET
147
Coroners Court
30
REGENCY PL
ABADY HOUSE
EDRIC HOUSE
BENNETT HOUSE
ROCHESTER ROW
Westminster Kingsway Coll
St John's Gdns
STILLINGTON ST
VINCENT SQUARE
SILVERTON HO
RHS (Lindley Hall)
PAGE STREET
PAGE STREET

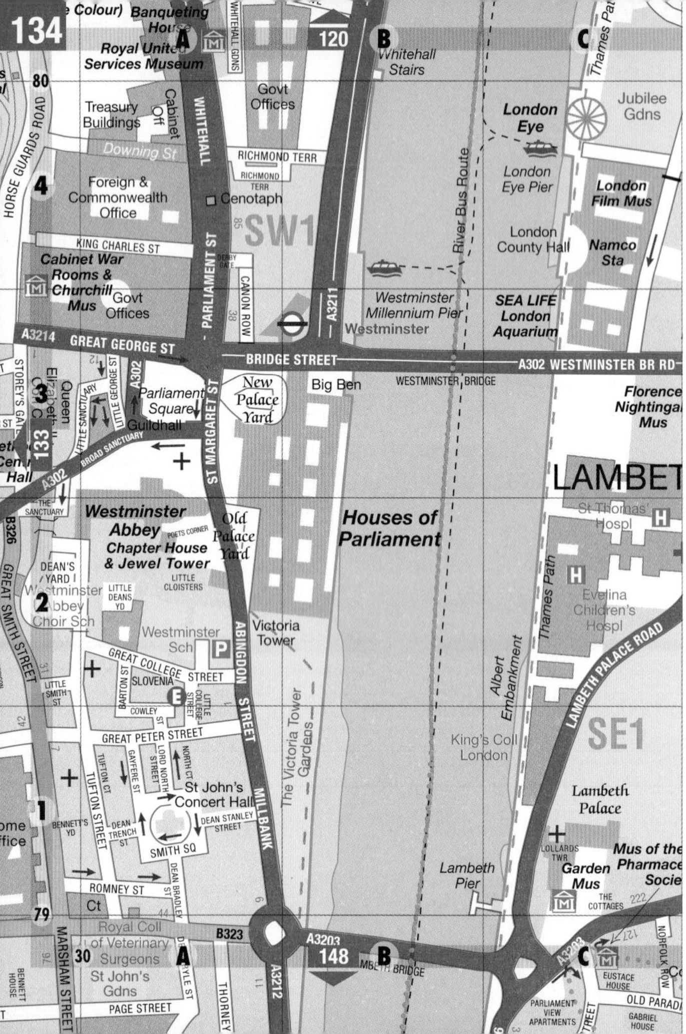

Banqueting House
Royal United Services Museum
120
Whitehall Stairs
Treasury Buildings
Cabinet Off
Govt Offices
WHITEHALL
HORSE GUARDS ROAD
Downing St
RICHMOND TERR
Cenotaph
SW1
Foreign & Commonwealth Office
KING CHARLES ST
Cabinet War Rooms & Churchill Mus
Govt Offices
PARLIAMENT ST
CANON ROW
A3211
London Eye
Jubilee Gdns
London Eye Pier
London Film Mus
London County Hall
Namco Sta
River Bus Route
Westminster Millennium Pier
Westminster
SEA LIFE London Aquarium
A3214 GREAT GEORGE ST
BRIDGE STREET
A302 WESTMINSTER BR RD
WESTMINSTER BRIDGE
Big Ben
New Palace Yard
Parliament Square
Guildhall
ST MARGARET ST
STOREY'S GATE
LITTLE GEORGE ST
BROAD SANCTUARY
LITTLE SANCTUARY
Queen Elizabeth II Conf Centre
133
Florence Nightingale Mus
LAMBETH
St Thomas' Hospl
THE SANCTUARY
Westminster Abbey
POETS CORNER
Old Palace Yard
Houses of Parliament
Chapter House & Jewel Tower
LITTLE CLOISTERS
DEAN'S YARD
Westminster Abbey Choir Sch
LITTLE DEANS YD
Westminster Sch
Victoria Tower
Thames Path
Evelina Children's Hospl
GREAT SMITH STREET
B326
GREAT COLLEGE STREET
SLOVENIA
BARTON ST
COWLEY ST
LITTLE COLLEGE STREET
ABINGDON STREET
Albert Embankment
LAMBETH PALACE ROAD
LITTLE SMITH ST
SE1
GREAT PETER STREET
TUFTON CT
GAYFERE ST
LORD NORTH STREET
NORTH CT
The Victoria Tower Gardens
King's Coll London
TUFTON STREET
St John's Concert Hall
MILLBANK
Lambeth Palace
BENNETT'S YD
DEAN TRENCH ST
DEAN STANLEY STREET
SMITH SQ
LOLLARDS TWR
Garden Mus
Mus of the Pharmaceutical Society
Lambeth Pier
ROMNEY ST
DEAN BRADLEY ST
THE COTTAGES
Royal Coll of Veterinary Surgeons
B323
A3203
148
LAMBETH BRIDGE
St John's Gdns
MARSHAM STREET
A3212
DERYLE ST
THORNEY
PAGE STREET
BENNETT HOUSE
EUSTACE HOUSE
PARLIAMENT VIEW APARTMENTS
OLD PARADISE
GABRIEL HOUSE
NORFOLK ROW

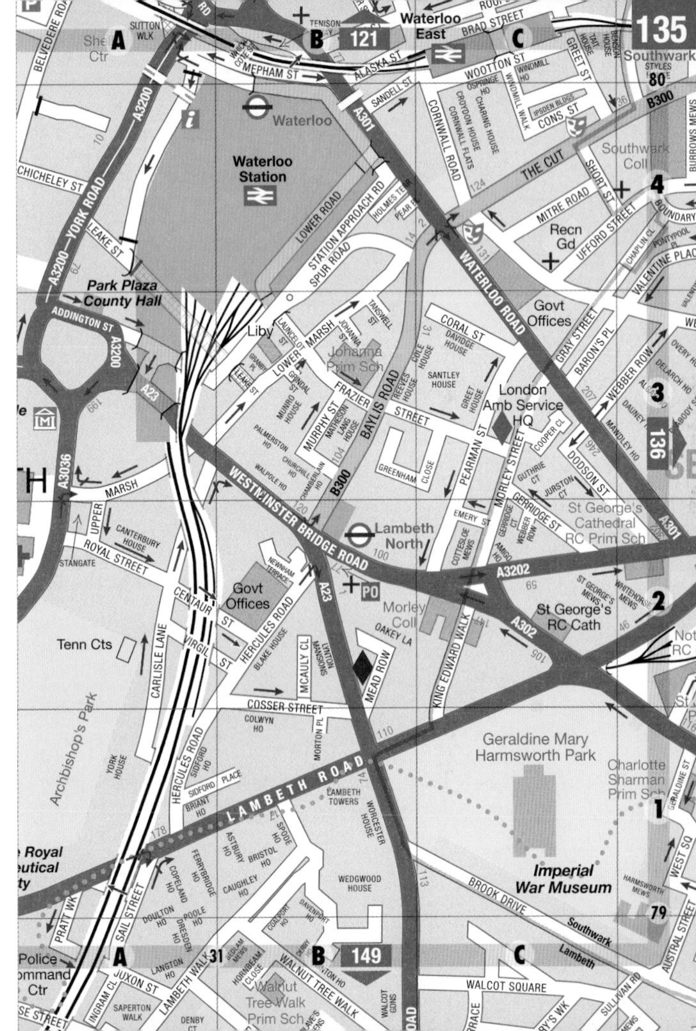

135
A
B
C
121
136
149
1
2
3
4
Waterloo East
BRAD STREET
TENISON WAY
SUTTON WLK
BELVEDERE ROAD
Shell Ctr
MEPHAM ST
ALASKA ST
SANDELL ST
WOOTTON ST
WINDMILL HO
WINDMILL WALK
OSPRINGE HO
CHARING HOUSE
CROYDON HOUSE
CORNWALL FLATS
CORNWALL ROAD
IPSDEN BLDGS
CONS ST
GREET ST
TAIT HOUSE
BENSON HOUSE
Southwark
B300
BURROWS MEWS
Southwark Coll
Waterloo
Waterloo Station
A3200
A301
YORK ROAD
CHICHELEY ST
LEAKE ST
LOWER ROAD
STATION APPROACH RD
HOLMES TERR
PEAR PL
SPUR ROAD
THE CUT
SHORT ST
MITRE ROAD
Recn Gd
UFFORD STREET
BOUNDARY RD
CHAPLIN CL
PONTYPOOL PL
VALENTINE PLACE
Park Plaza County Hall
ADDINGTON ST
A23
Liby
LAUNCELOT ST
GRANBY PL
LEAKE ST
LOWER MARSH
JOHANNA ST
TANSWELL ST
Johanna Prim Sch
WATERLOO ROAD
Govt Offices
CORAL ST
DAVIDGE HOUSE
COLE HOUSE
SANTLEY HOUSE
GRAY STREET
BARON'S PL
WEBBER ROW
OVERY HO
DELARCH HO
DAUNEY HO
MAWDLEY HO
PEABODY SQ
GRINDAL ST
MUNRO HOUSE
FRAZIER STREET
BAYLIS ROAD
REEVES HOUSE
GREET HOUSE
London Amb Service HQ
COOPER CL
DODSON ST
MURPHY ST
MATHESON LANG HOUSE
PALMERSTON HO
CHURCHILL HO
WALPOLE HO
CHAMBERLAIN HO
GREENHAM CLOSE
PEARMAN ST
MORLEY STREET
GUTHRIE CT
JURSTON CT
GERRIDGE ST
GERRIDGE CT
WEBBER ROW
St George's Cathedral RC Prim Sch
A3036
MARSH
UPPER
CANTERBURY HOUSE
ROYAL STREET
STANGATE
WESTMINSTER BRIDGE ROAD
Lambeth North
EMERY ST
COTTESLOE MEWS
AMIGO HO
A3202
ST GEORGE'S MEWS
WHITEHORSE MEWS
St George's RC Cath
A302
Notre RC G
CENTAUR ST
NEWNHAM TERRACE
Govt Offices
PO
Morley Coll
OAKEY LA
Tenn Cts
CARLISLE LANE
VIRGIL ST
HERCULES ROAD
BLAKE HOUSE
MCAULY CL
LYNTON MANSIONS
MEAD ROW
KING EDWARD WALK
COSSER STREET
COLWYN HO
MORTON PL
Archbishop's Park
YORK HOUSE
HERCULES ROAD
SIDFORD HO
SIDFORD PLACE
BRIANT HO
LAMBETH ROAD
LAMBETH TOWERS
WORCESTER HOUSE
Geraldine Mary Harmsworth Park
Charlotte Sharman Prim Sch
GERALDINE ST
WEST SQ
HARMSWORTH MEWS
Imperial War Museum
BROOK DRIVE
Southwark
Lambeth
AUSTRAL STREET
ASTBURY HO
SPODE HO
BRISTOL HO
CAUGHLEY HO
WEDGWOOD HOUSE
COPELAND HO
FERRYBRIDGE HO
DOULTON HO
POOLE HO
DRESDEN HO
COALPORT HO
DAVENPORT HO
DERBY HO
PRATT WK
SAIL STREET
Police Command Ctr
JUXON ST
LANGTON HO
LAMBETH WALK
BEDLAM MEWS
HORNBEAM CLOSE
Walnut Tree Walk Prim Sch
WALNUT TREE WALK
WALCOT GDNS
WALCOT SQUARE
SULLIVAN RD
INGRAM CL
SAPERTON WALK
DENBY CT

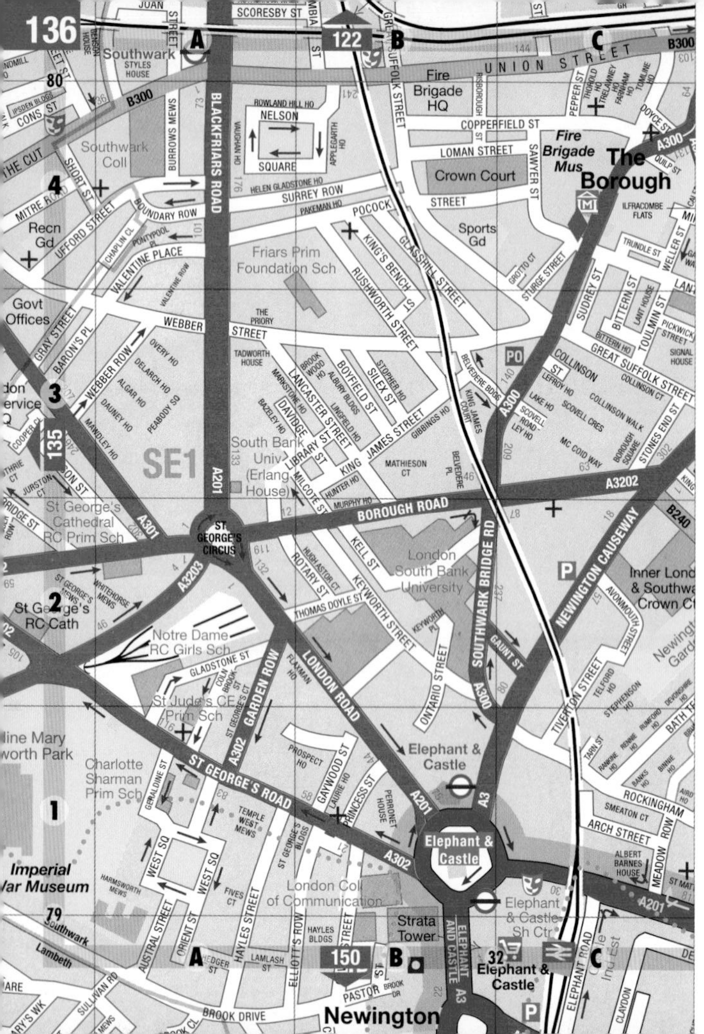

122
A
B
C
Southwark
Union Street
B300
Fire Brigade HQ
Blackfriars Road
Nelson Square
Copperfield St
Loman Street
Fire Brigade Mus
The Borough
Crown Court
Southwark Coll
The Cut
Surrey Row
Pocock Street
Sports Gd
Boundary Row
Ufford Street
Mitre Road
Recn Gd
Valentine Place
Friars Prim Foundation Sch
King's Bench St
Rushworth Street
Glasshill Street
Webber Street
Govt Offices
Gray Street
Webber Row
SE1
A201
A300
Great Suffolk Street
Collinson St
Borough Road
A3202
St George's Circus
A3203
South Bank Univ (Erlang House)
King James Street
London Road
London South Bank University
Southwark Bridge Rd
Newington Causeway
Inner London & Southwark Crown Ct
St George's Cathedral RC Prim Sch
St George's RC Cath
Notre Dame RC Girls Sch
St Jude's CE Prim Sch
Garden Row
St George's Road
A302
Elephant & Castle
A3
Tiverton Street
Rockingham Street
Arch Street
Charlotte Sharman Prim Sch
Imperial War Museum
West Sq
London Coll of Communication
Strata Tower
Elephant & Castle Sh Ctr
Brook Drive
Newington
150
32
Hayles Street
Elliott's Row
Austral Street
Orient St
1
2
3
4
79
80
135

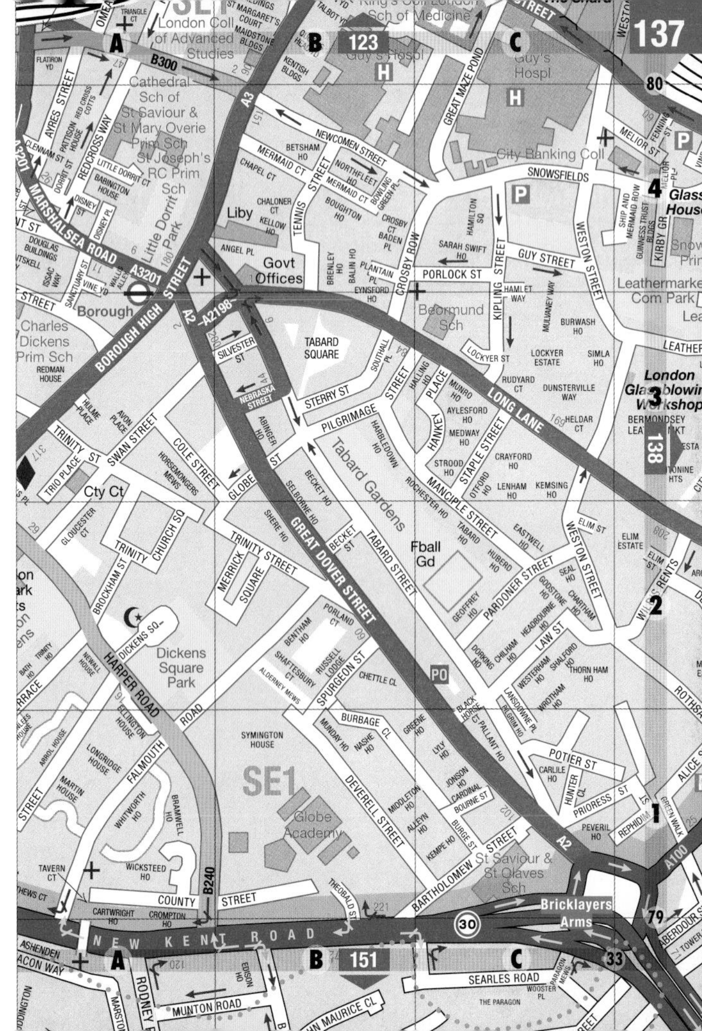

123
London Coll of Advanced Studies
King's Coll London Sch of Medicine
Guy's Hospl
B300
Cathedral Sch of St Saviour & St Mary Overie Prim Sch
St Joseph's RC Prim Sch
Little Dorrit Park
GREAT MAZE POND
City Banking Coll
NEWCOMEN STREET
SNOWSFIELDS
MELIOR ST
Glass House
A3201
MARSHALSEA ROAD
REDCROSS WAY
AYRES STREET
TENNIS STREET
Liby
Govt Offices
CROSBY ROW
PORLOCK ST
GUY STREET
KIPLING STREET
WESTON STREET
Leathermarket Com Park
Bermondsey Sch
Borough
BOROUGH HIGH STREET
A2
A2198
Charles Dickens Prim Sch
TABARD SQUARE
SILVESTER ST
NEBRASKA STREET
LONG LANE
LOCKYER ST
LOCKYER ESTATE
SIMLA HO
DUNSTERVILLE WAY
London Glassblowing Workshop
BERMONDSEY LEATHER MKT
138
STERRY ST
PILGRIMAGE STREET
Tabard Gardens
HANKEY PLACE
STAPLE STREET
MANCIPLE STREET
TRINITY ST
SWAN STREET
COLE STREET
GLOBE ST
GREAT DOVER STREET
City Ct
GLOUCESTER CT
TRINITY CHURCH SQ
MERRICK SQUARE
TRINITY STREET
BECKET ST
TABARD STREET
Fball Gd
PARDONER STREET
ELIM ESTATE
WILLOW RENTS
BROCKHAM ST
DICKENS SQ
Dickens Square Park
HARPER ROAD
SPURGEON ST
CHETTLE CL
PO
LAW ST
ROTHSAY
BURBAGE CL
SYMINGTON HOUSE
POTIER ST
PRIORESS ST
FALMOUTH ROAD
SE1
Globe Academy
DEVERELL STREET
BARTHOLOMEW STREET
St Saviour & St Olaves Sch
A100
ALICE ST
COUNTY STREET
B240
NEW KENT ROAD
30
Bricklayers Arms
79
33
ABERDOUR ST
151
SEARLES ROAD
THE PARAGON
MUNTON ROAD
RODNEY
MAURICE CL
A
B
C
1
2
3
4

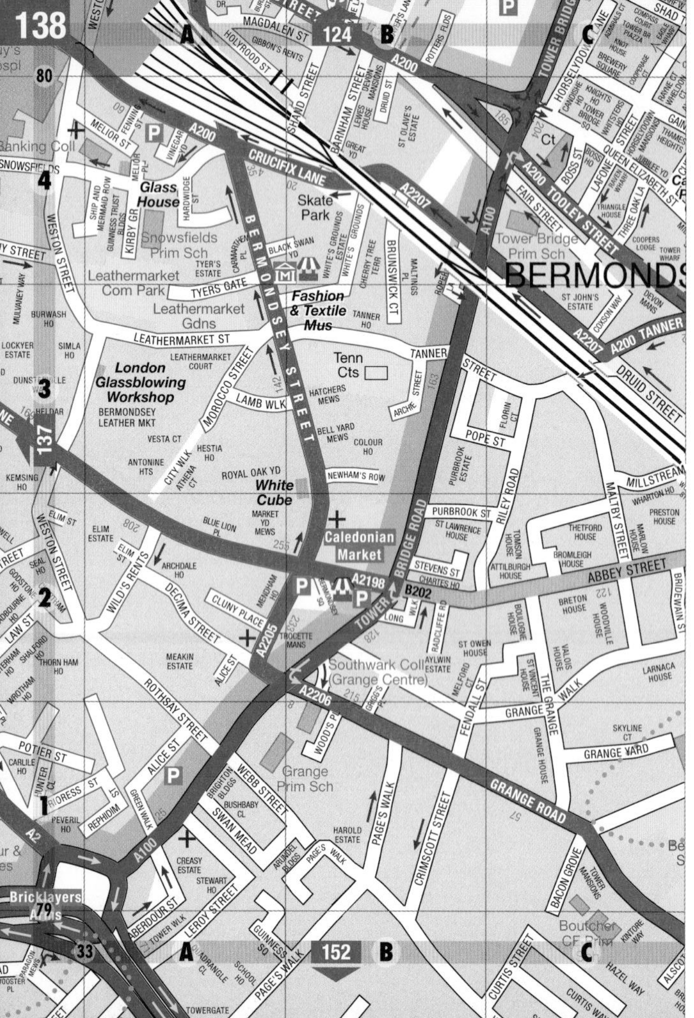

124
A
B
C
Glass House
Snowsfields Prim Sch
Leathermarket Com Park
Leathermarket Gdns
Fashion & Textile Mus
Skate Park
Tower Bridge Prim Sch
BERMONDSEY
London Glassblowing Workshop
BERMONDSEY LEATHER MKT
White Cube
Caledonian Market
Tenn Cts
Southwark Coll (Grange Centre)
Grange Prim Sch
Bricklayers Arms
Boutcher CF Prim
BERMONDSEY STREET
CRUCIFIX LANE
TOOLEY STREET
TOWER BRIDGE ROAD
LEATHERMARKET ST
WESTON STREET
TANNER STREET
ABBEY STREET
GRANGE ROAD
GRANGE WALK
ROTHSAY STREET
DECIMA STREET
DRUID STREET
MALTBY STREET
RILEY ROAD
CRIMSCOTT STREET
PAGE'S WALK
WEBB STREET
LEROY STREET
CURTIS STREET
A200
A2207
A100
A2198
A2205
A2206
B202
137
4
3
2
1
152

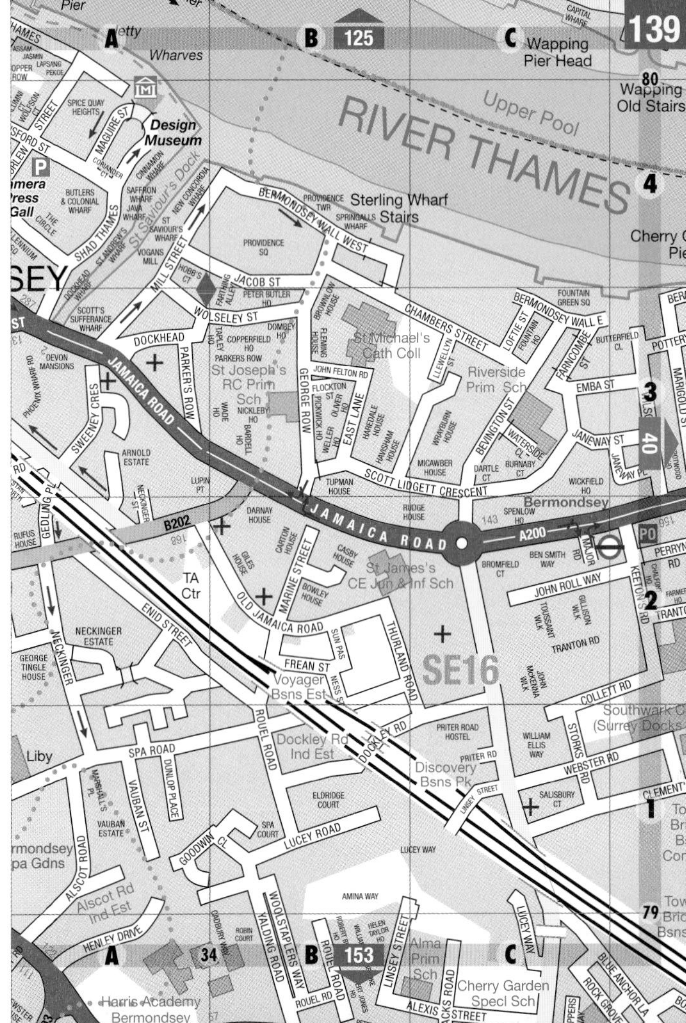
125
A
B
C
Pier
Wharves
Wapping
Pier Head
80
Wapping
Old Stairs
Upper Pool
RIVER THAMES
4
Cherry Ga
Pier
Design
Museum
SPICE QUAY
HEIGHTS
MAGUIRE ST
CORIANDER CT
CINNAMON WHARF
SAFFRON WHARF
JAVA WHARF
BUTLERS & COLONIAL WHARF
THE CIRCLE
SHAD THAMES
ST ANDREW'S WHARF
St Saviour's Dock
NEW CONCORDIA WHARF
ST SAVIOUR'S WHARF
VOGANS MILL
MILL STREET
HOBB'S CT
DOCKHEAD WHARF
SCOTT'S SUFFERANCE WHARF
SEY
BERMONDSEY WALL WEST
PROVIDENCE TWR
Sterling Wharf
Stairs
SPRINGALLS WHARF
PROVIDENCE SQ
JACOB ST
PETER BUTLER HO
FARTHING ALLEY
WOLSELEY ST
DOMBEY HO
BROWNLOW HOUSE
FLEMING HOUSE
CHAMBERS STREET
St Michael's
Cath Coll
FOUNTAIN GREEN SQ
BERMONDSEY WALL E
LOFTIE ST
FOUNTAIN HO
LLEWELLYN ST
Riverside
Prim Sch
FARNCOMBE ST
BUTTERFIELD CL
POTTERY ST
EMBA ST
MARIGOLD ST
3
40
JANEWAY ST
JANEWAY PL
BEVINGTON ST
WATERSIDE CL
BURNABY CT
DARTLE CT
MICAWBER HOUSE
WRAYBURN HOUSE
WICKFIELD HO
DOCKHEAD
PARKER'S ROW
TAPLEY HO
COPPERFIELD HO
PARKERS ROW
St Joseph's
RC Prim
Sch
WADE HO
NICKLEBY HO
BARDELL HO
GEORGE ROW
JOHN FELTON RD
FLOCKTON ST
PICKWICK HO
OLIVER HO
WELLER HO
EAST LANE
HAREDALE HOUSE
HAVISHAM HOUSE
DEVON MANSIONS
PHOENIX WHARF RD
SWEENEY CRES
JAMAICA ROAD
ARNOLD ESTATE
LUPIN PT
NECKINGER ST
TUPMAN HOUSE
SCOTT LIDGETT CRESCENT
RUDGE HOUSE
Bermondsey
SPENLOW HO
143
A200
B202
DARNAY HOUSE
CARTON HOUSE
CASBY HOUSE
GEDLING PL
RUFUS HOUSE
GILES HOUSE
TA
Ctr
MARINE STREET
BOWLEY HOUSE
St James's
CE Jun & Inf Sch
BROMFIELD CT
BEN SMITH WAY
MAJOR RD
PO
PERRYN RD
KEETON'S RD
JOHN ROLL WAY
GILLISON WLK
TOUSSAINT WLK
FARMER HO
TRANTON
2
TRANTON RD
OLD JAMAICA ROAD
ENID STREET
NECKINGER ESTATE
GEORGE TINGLE HOUSE
NECKINGER
SUN PAS
THURLAND ROAD
FREAN ST
Voyager
Bsns Est
NESS ST
SE16
JOHN McKENNA WLK
COLLETT RD
Southwark Coll
(Surrey Docks C
ROUEL ROAD
Dockley Rd
Ind Est
DOCKLEY RD
PRITER ROAD HOSTEL
PRITER RD
Discovery
Bsns Pk
WILLIAM ELLIS WAY
STORKS RD
WEBSTER RD
LINSEY STREET
SALISBURY CT
CLEMENT'S R
1
Liby
SPA ROAD
DUNLOP PLACE
MARSHALL'S PL
VAUBAN ST
VAUBAN ESTATE
ELDRIDGE COURT
SPA COURT
GOODWIN CL
LUCEY ROAD
LUCEY WAY
rmondsey
pa Gdns
ALSCOT ROAD
Alscot Rd
Ind Est
AMINA WAY
LUCEY WAY
Tower
Bridge
Bsns
Comp
79
Tower
Bridge
Bsns
HENLEY DRIVE
34
CADBURY WAY
ROBIN COURT
YALDING ROAD
WOOLSTAPLERS WAY
153
ROUEL ROAD
ROUEL RD
HELEN TAYLOR HO
LINSEY STREET
Alma
Prim
Sch
Cherry Garden
Specl Sch
ALEXIS STREET
BLUE ANCHOR LA
ROCK GROVE
Harris Academy
Bermondsey

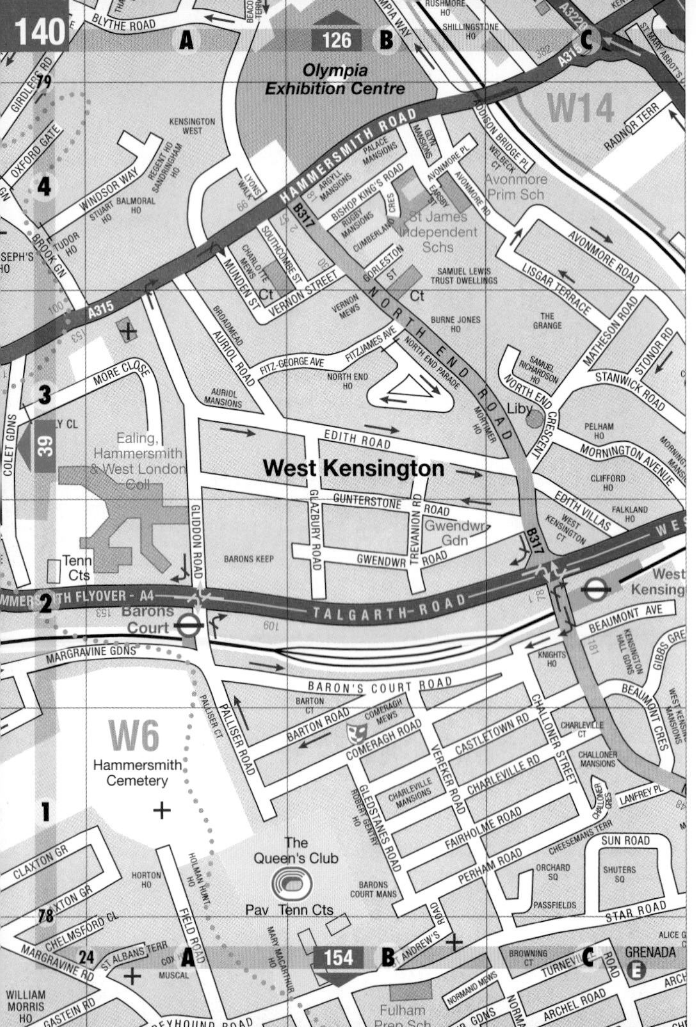

126
A
B
C
Olympia
Exhibition Centre
BLYTHE ROAD
RUSHMORE HO
SHILLINGSTONE HO
A3220
A315
ST MARY ABBOT'S
W14
RADNOR TERR
GIRDLERS RD
79
OXFORD GATE
KENSINGTON WEST
REGENT HO
SANDRINGHAM HO
WINDSOR WAY
STUART HO
BALMORAL HO
4
TUDOR HO
BROOK GN
HAMMERSMITH ROAD
LYONS WALK
ARGYLL MANSIONS
PALACE MANSIONS
GLYN MANSIONS
ADDISON BRIDGE PL
WELBECK CT
AVONMORE PL
Avonmore Prim Sch
BISHOP KING'S ROAD
RUGBY MANSIONS
CUMBERLAND CRES
EMBSY ST
AVONMORE RD
St James Independent Schs
B317
CHARLOTTE MEWS
SOUTHCOMBE ST
MUNDEN ST
VERNON STREET
GORLESTON ST
SAMUEL LEWIS TRUST DWELLINGS
AVONMORE ROAD
LISGAR TERRACE
Ct
A315
VERNON MEWS
NORTH END ROAD
BURNE JONES HO
THE GRANGE
MATHESON ROAD
STONOR RD
BROADMEAD
AURIOL ROAD
FITZ-GEORGE AVE
FITZJAMES AVE
NORTH END PARADE
SAMUEL RICHARDSON HO
STANWICK ROAD
MORE CLOSE
3
NORTH END HO
AURIOL MANSIONS
NORTH END CRESCENT
Liby
MORTIMER HO
COLET GDNS
39
PELHAM HO
Ealing, Hammersmith & West London Coll
EDITH ROAD
MORNINGTON AVENUE
West Kensington
CLIFFORD HO
GUNTERSTONE ROAD
GLAZBURY ROAD
TREVANION RD
Gwendwr Gdn
EDITH VILLAS
FALKLAND HO
WEST KENSINGTON CT
GLIDDON ROAD
BARONS KEEP
GWENDWR ROAD
Tenn Cts
West Kensington
2
TH FLYOVER - A4
TALGARTH ROAD
Barons Court
BEAUMONT AVE
KENSINGTON HALL GDNS
MARGRAVINE GDNS
KNIGHTS HO
BARON'S COURT ROAD
BEAUMONT CRES
BARTON CT
COMERAGH MEWS
CHALLONER STREET
PALLISER CT
PALLISER ROAD
BARTON ROAD
COMERAGH ROAD
CASTLETOWN RD
CHARLEVILLE CT
WEST KENSINGTON MANSIONS
W6
Hammersmith Cemetery
CHALLONER MANSIONS
CHARLEVILLE MANSIONS
VEREKER ROAD
CHARLEVILLE RD
GLEDSTANES ROAD
ROBERT GENTRY HO
LANFREY PL
CHALLONER CRES
1
FAIRHOLME ROAD
The Queen's Club
CHEESEMANS TERR
SUN ROAD
CLAXTON GR
HORTON HO
HOLMAN HUNT HO
PERHAM ROAD
ORCHARD SQ
SHUTERS SQ
BARONS COURT MANS
Pav
Tenn Cts
PASSFIELDS
STAR ROAD
78
CHELMSFORD CL
FIELD ROAD
MARY MACARTHUR HO
ST ANDREW'S ROAD
MARGRAVINE RD
24
ST ALBANS TERR
154
BROWNING CT
TURNEVILLE ROAD
GRENADA
MUSCAL
NORMAND MEWS
ARCHEL ROAD
WILLIAM MORRIS HO
GASTEIN RD
GREYHOUND ROAD
Fulham Prep Sch

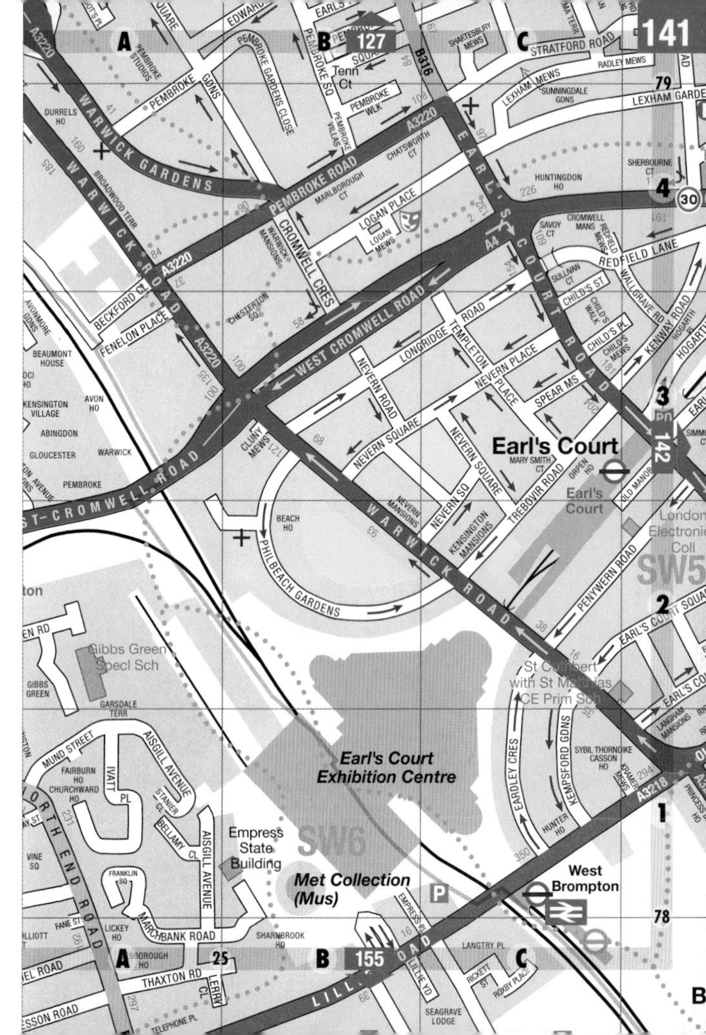

A
B
C
127
155
142
Earl's Court
Earl's Court Exhibition Centre
West Brompton
Met Collection (Mus)
Empress State Building
SW5
SW6
WARWICK GARDENS
WARWICK ROAD
WEST CROMWELL ROAD
PEMBROKE ROAD
EARL'S COURT ROAD
NORTH END ROAD
LILLIE ROAD
PHILBEACH GARDENS
NEVERN SQUARE
NEVERN PLACE
NEVERN ROAD
TREBOVIR ROAD
PENYWERN ROAD
LOGAN PLACE
CROMWELL CRES
LONGRIDGE ROAD
TEMPLETON PLACE
REDFIELD LANE
KENWAY ROAD
WALLGRAVE RD
STRATFORD ROAD
LEXHAM MEWS
LEXHAM GARDENS
EARDLEY CRES
KEMPSFORD GDNS
AISGILL AVENUE
MARCHBANK ROAD
THAXTON RD
MUND STREET
St Cuthbert with St Matthias CE Prim Sch
Gibbs Green Specl Sch
London Electronic Coll

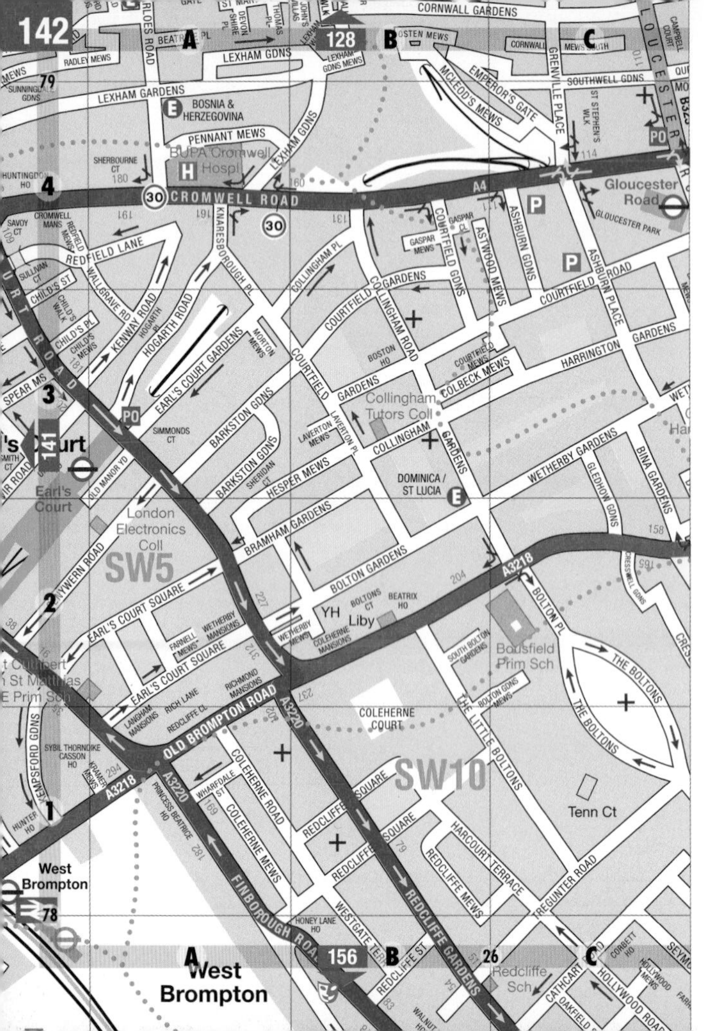

A
B
C
128
CORNWALL GARDENS
LEXHAM GDNS
LEXHAM GARDENS
BOSNIA & HERZEGOVINA
PENNANT MEWS
BUPA Cromwell Hospl
CROMWELL ROAD
A4
Gloucester Road
GLOUCESTER PARK
EMPEROR'S GATE
MCLEOD'S MEWS
GRENVILLE PLACE
SOUTHWELL GDNS
ST STEPHEN'S WLK
RADLEY MEWS
SUNNINGDALE GDNS
SHERBOURNE CT
HUNTINGDON HO
KNARESBOROUGH PL
REDFIELD LANE
WALLGRAVE RD
KENWAY ROAD
HOGARTH ROAD
EARL'S COURT GARDENS
COLLINGHAM PL
COURTFIELD GARDENS
COLLINGHAM ROAD
COURTFIELD GDNS
ASTWOOD MEWS
ASHBURN GDNS
ASHBURN PLACE
COURTFIELD ROAD
HARRINGTON GARDENS
COLBECK MEWS
Collingham Tutors Coll
COLLINGHAM GARDENS
WETHERBY GARDENS
GLEDHOW GDNS
BINA GARDENS
DOMINICA / ST LUCIA
BARKSTON GDNS
HESPER MEWS
BRAMHAM GARDENS
BOLTON GARDENS
SIMMONDS CT
Earl's Court
141
London Electronics Coll
SW5
EARL'S COURT SQUARE
WETHERBY MANSIONS
YH
Liby
A3218
BOLTON PL
Bousfield Prim Sch
THE BOLTONS
OLD BROMPTON ROAD
A3220
COLEHERNE COURT
THE LITTLE BOLTONS
SW10
COLEHERNE ROAD
COLEHERNE MEWS
REDCLIFFE SQUARE
HARCOURT TERRACE
REDCLIFFE MEWS
Tenn Ct
TREGUNTER ROAD
FINBOROUGH ROAD
REDCLIFFE GARDENS
WESTGATE TER
HONEY LANE HO
KEMPSFORD GDNS
SYBIL THORNDIKE CASSON HO
HUNTER HO
West Brompton
78
156
26
Redcliffe Sch
CATHCART ROAD
HOLLYWOOD ROAD
REDCLIFFE ST

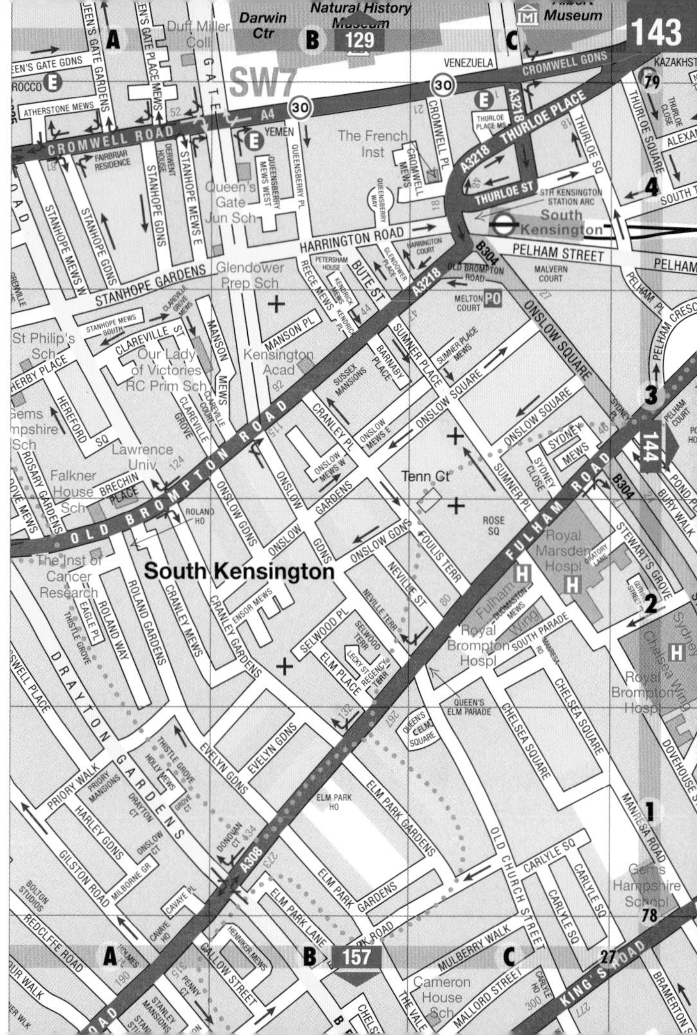
Natural History Museum
Darwin Ctr
Duff Miller Coll
Albert Museum
A
B
C
129
SW7
VENEZUELA
CROMWELL GDNS
KAZAKHSTAN
QUEEN'S GATE GDNS
ROCCO
ATHERSTONE MEWS
QUEEN'S GATE GARDENS
QUEEN'S GATE PLACE MEWS
GATE
A4
30
CROMWELL ROAD
YEMEN
FAIRBRIAR RESIDENCE
DERWENT HOUSE
STANHOPE MEWS E
STANHOPE GDNS
QUEENSBERRY MEWS WEST
QUEENSBERRY PL
QUEENSBERRY WAY
Queen's Gate Jun Sch
The French Inst
CROMWELL MEWS
CROMWELL PL
THURLOE PLACE MS
A3218
THURLOE PLACE
THURLOE SQ
THURLOE SQUARE
THURLOE CLOSE
ALEXANDER
THURLOE ST
STH KENSINGTON STATION ARC
South Kensington
SOUTH TER
4
STANHOPE MEWS W
STANHOPE GDNS
HARRINGTON ROAD
HARRINGTON COURT
PELHAM STREET
PELHAM
B304
OLD BROMPTON ROAD
MALVERN COURT
STANHOPE GARDENS
Glendower Prep Sch
PETERSHAM HOUSE
REECE MEWS
KENDRICK MEWS
KENDRICK PL
BUTE ST
GLENDOWER PLACE
MELTON COURT
PO
PELHAM PL
PELHAM CRESCENT
CREMVILLE
STANHOPE MEWS SOUTH
CLAREVILLE GROVE MEWS
CLAREVILLE ST
MANSON MEWS
MANSON PL
St Philip's Sch
HERBY PLACE
Our Lady of Victories RC Prim Sch
Kensington Acad
SUSSEX MANSIONS
BARNABY PLACE
SUMNER PLACE
SUMNER PLACE MEWS
ONSLOW SQUARE
3
HEREFORD SQ
Gems Hampshire Sch
CLAREVILLE GROVE
CLAREVILLE COURT
CRANLEY PL
ONSLOW MEWS E
SYDNEY PL
PELHAM COURT
ROSARY GARDENS
Lawrence Univ
OLD BROMPTON ROAD
ONSLOW MEWS W
ONSLOW GARDENS
SYDNEY MEWS
SYDNEY CLOSE
144
Falkner House Sch
BRECHIN PLACE
ROLAND HO
ONSLOW GDNS
Tenn Ct
SUMNER PL
FULHAM ROAD
B304
POND PLACE
BURY WALK
DOVE MEWS
ONSLOW GDNS
ROSE SQ
The Inst of Cancer Research
South Kensington
FOULIS TERR
NEVILLE ST
Royal Marsden Hospl
ORATORY LANE
STEWART'S GROVE
H
EAGLE PL
ROLAND WAY
ROLAND GARDENS
CRANLEY MEWS
CRANLEY GARDENS
ENSOR MEWS
NEVILLE TERR
SELWOOD PL
SELWOOD TERR
Fulham Wing
DUDMASTON MEWS
GUTHRIE STREET
2
THISTLE GROVE
DRAYTON GARDENS
LECKY ST
ELM PLACE
REGENCY TERR
Royal Brompton Hospl
SOUTH PARADE
MANRESA RD
Sydney Wing
Chelsea Wing
Royal Brompton Hospl
QUEEN'S ELM PARADE
CHELSEA SQUARE
QUEEN'S ELM SQUARE
THISTLE GROVE
HOLLY MEWS
EVELYN GDNS
DOVEHOUSE STREET
PRIORY WALK
PRIORY MANSIONS
DRAYTON CT
GROVE CT
ELM PARK HO
ELM PARK GARDENS
HARLEY GDNS
ONSLOW CT
DONOVAN CT
A308
OLD CHURCH STREET
1
MANRESA ROAD
GILSTON ROAD
MILBORNE GR
CARLYLE SQ
ELM PARK GARDENS
Gems Hampshire School
BOLTON STUDIOS
CAVAYE PL
ELM PARK LANE
78
REDCLIFFE ROAD
CAVAYE HO
HENNIKER MEWS
PARK ROAD
MULBERRY WALK
157
CARLYLE HO
KING'S ROAD
HOLMES PL
CALLOW STREET
PENNY CT
Cameron House Sch
MALLORD STREET
BRAMERTON ST
STANLEY MANSIONS
THE VALE
27

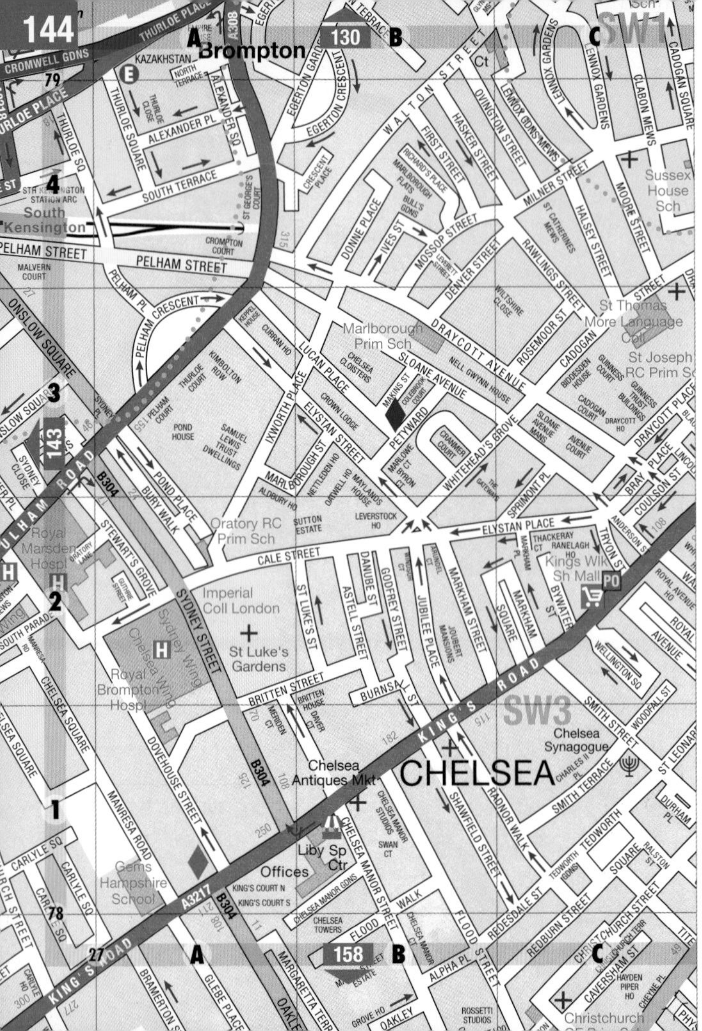
A
B
C
130
158
143
79
78
27
1
2
3
4
SW1
SW3
Brompton
CHELSEA
THURLOE PLACE
CROMWELL GDNS
KAZAKHSTAN
NORTH TERRACE
THURLOE SQUARE
THURLOE CLOSE
ALEXANDER PL
ALEXANDER SQ
SOUTH TERRACE
THURLOE SQ
STH KENSINGTON STATION ARC
South Kensington
PELHAM STREET
MALVERN COURT
CROMPTON COURT
ST GEORGE'S COURT
EGERTON GARDENS
EGERTON CRESCENT
EGERTON TERRACE
CRESCENT PLACE
WALTON STREET
FIRST STREET
HASKER STREET
OVINGTON STREET
LENNOX GARDENS
LENNOX GDNS MEWS
CLABON MEWS
CADOGAN SQUARE
MOORE STREET
Sussex House Sch
MILNER STREET
HALSEY STREET
ST CATHERINES MEWS
RAWLINGS STREET
DONNE PLACE
RICHARD'S PLACE
MARLBOROUGH FLATS
BULL'S GDNS
IVES ST
MOSSOP STREET
DENYER STREET
WILTSHIRE CLOSE
ROSEMOOR ST
CADOGAN STREET
St Thomas More Language Coll
St Joseph RC Prim Sch
DRAYCOTT AVENUE
NELL GWYNN HOUSE
Marlborough Prim Sch
PELHAM PL
PELHAM CRESCENT
ONSLOW SQUARE
KEPPEL HOUSE
CURRAN HO
LUCAN PLACE
CHELSEA CLOISTERS
SLOANE AVENUE
MAKINS ST
COLEBROOK COURT
PETYWARD
KIMBOLTON ROW
THURLOE COURT
PELHAM COURT
POND HOUSE
SAMUEL LEWIS TRUST DWELLINGS
IXWORTH PLACE
ELYSTAN STREET
CROWN LODGE
CRANMER COURT
WHITEHEAD'S GROVE
SLOANE AVENUE MANS
AVENUE COURT
CADOGAN COURT
BIDDESDEN HOUSE
GUINNESS COURT
GUINNESS TRUST BUILDINGS
DRAYCOTT HO
DRAYCOTT PLACE
BRAY PLACE
COULSON ST
SYDNEY CLOSE
FULHAM ROAD
B304
POND PLACE
BURY WALK
MARLBOROUGH ST
NETTLEDEN HO
OTTWELL HO
MAYLANDS HOUSE
ALDBURY HO
LEVERSTOCK HO
MARLOWE CT
BYRON CT
THE GATEWAYS
SPRIMONT PL
ELYSTAN PLACE
THACKERAY CT
RANELAGH HO
MARKHAM PL
ANDERSON ST
TRYON ST
Kings Wlk Sh Mall
PO
Royal Marsden Hospl
ORATORY LANE
STEWART'S GROVE
GUTHRIE STREET
Oratory RC Prim Sch
SUTTON ESTATE
CALE STREET
Imperial Coll London
St Luke's Gardens
ST LUKE'S ST
DANUBE ST
ASTELL STREET
GODFREY STREET
JUBILEE PLACE
JOUBERT MANSIONS
MARKHAM STREET
MARKHAM SQUARE
BYWATER ST
SYDNEY STREET
Sydney Wing
Chelsea Wing
Royal Brompton Hospl
SOUTH PARADE
CHELSEA SQUARE
BRITTEN STREET
BRITTEN HOUSE
MERIDEN CT
DAVER CT
BURNSALL ST
KING'S ROAD
WELLINGTON SQ
ROYAL AVENUE
ROYAL AVENUE HO
SMITH STREET
WOODFALL ST
Chelsea Synagogue
CHARLES II PL
SMITH TERRACE
ST LEONARD'S
DURHAM PL
DOVEHOUSE STREET
MANRESA ROAD
Chelsea Antiques Mkt
CHELSEA MANOR STUDIOS
SWAN CT
SHAWFIELD STREET
RADNOR WALK
TEDWORTH SQUARE
TEDWORTH GDNS
RALSTON ST
Liby Sp Ctr
Offices
KING'S COURT N
KING'S COURT S
CHELSEA MANOR GDNS
CHELSEA MANOR STREET
CHELSEA TOWERS
FLOOD WALK
FLOOD STREET
REDESDALE ST
REDBURN STREET
CHRISTCHURCH STREET
CHRISTCHURCH TERR
CAVERSHAM ST
HAYDEN PIPER HO
CHEYNE PL
CARLYLE SQ
Gems Hampshire School
A3217
CHURCH STREET
CARLYLE HO
BRAMERTON ST
GLEBE PLACE
MARGARETTA TERR
CHELSEA MANOR
ALPHA PL
GROVE HO
OAKLEY
ROSSETTI STUDIOS
Christchurch

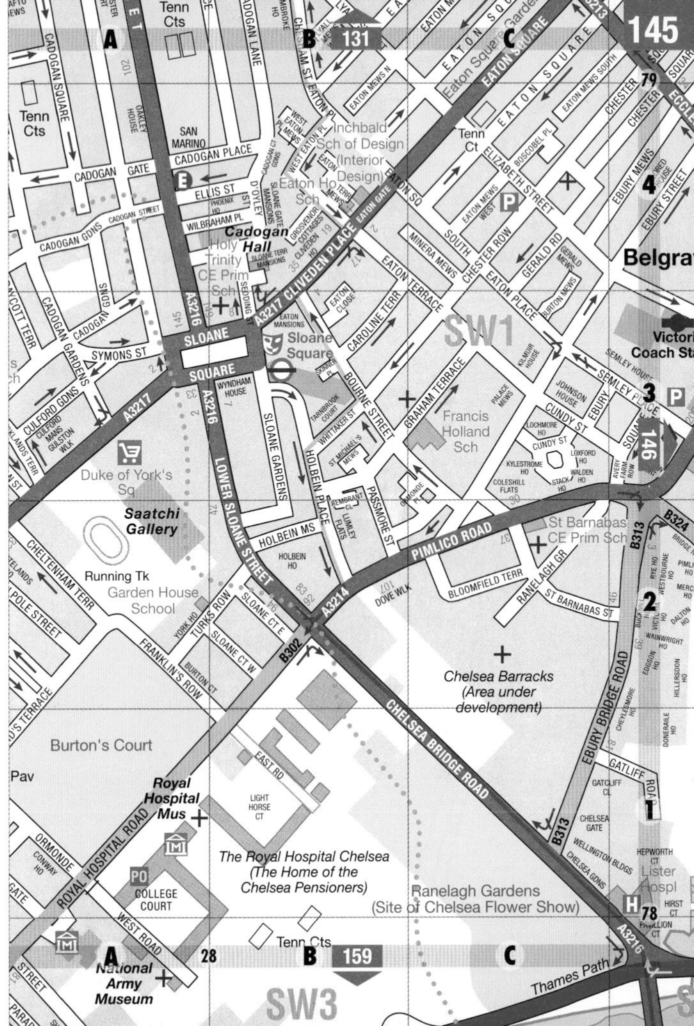
131
A
B
C
Eaton Square
Cadogan Square
Cadogan Place
Cadogan Gate
Sloane Square
Cadogan Hall
Holy Trinity CE Prim Sch
Inchbald Sch of Design (Interior Design)
Eaton Ho Sch
A3217 Cliveden Place
Eaton Terrace
Chester Row
Elizabeth Street
Eaton Place
Belgrav
Victoria Coach Stat
SW1
Bourne Street
Graham Terrace
Francis Holland Sch
Cundy St
Semley Place
146
Duke of York's Sq
Saatchi Gallery
Lower Sloane Street
Sloane Gardens
Holbein Place
Pimlico Road
St Barnabas CE Prim Sch
Cheltenham Terr
Running Tk
Garden House School
Franklin's Row
Turks Row
Chelsea Barracks (Area under development)
Ebury Bridge Road
Chelsea Bridge Road
Burton's Court
Royal Hospital Road
Royal Hospital Mus
The Royal Hospital Chelsea (The Home of the Chelsea Pensioners)
College Court
West Road
Ranelagh Gardens (Site of Chelsea Flower Show)
Lister Hospl
National Army Museum
Thames Path
159
SW3

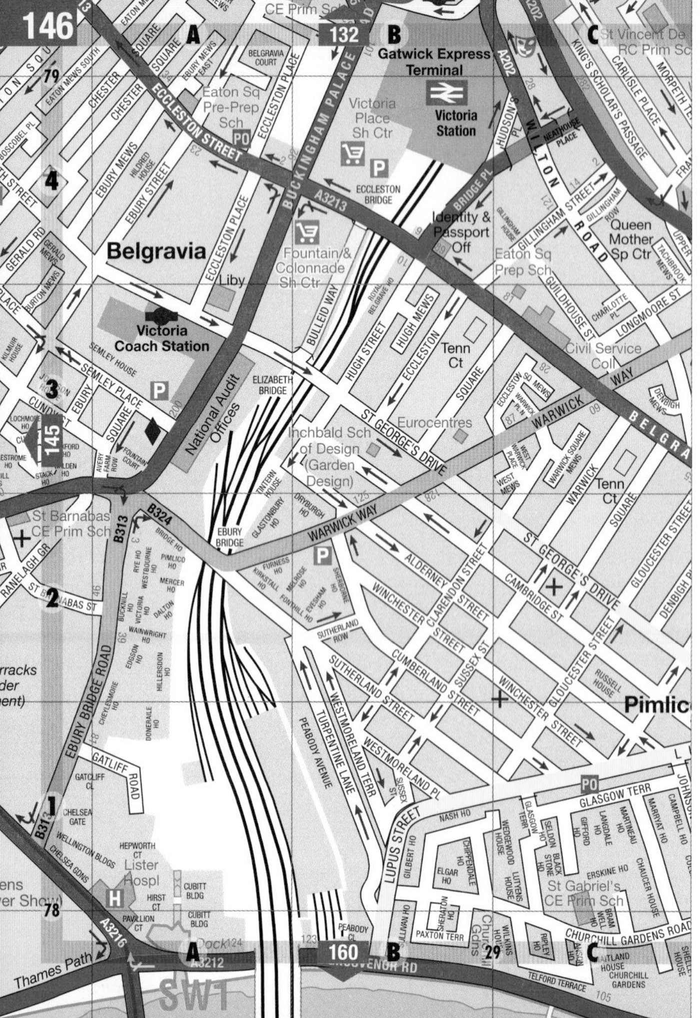
A
B
C
132
Gatwick Express Terminal
Victoria Station
St Vincent De RC Prim Sch
Belgravia Court
Eccleston Place
Buckingham Palace
Victoria Place Sh Ctr
Eaton Sq Pre-Prep Sch
Eccleston Street
Eccleston Bridge
A3213
Identity & Passport Off
Bridge Pl
Hudson's Pl
Wilton Road
Neathouse Place
Gillingham Street
Gillingham Row
Queen Mother Sp Ctr
King's Scholar's Passage
Carlisle Place
Morpeth Ter
Eaton Sq Prep Sch
Guildhouse St
Charlotte Pl
Longmoore St
Tachbrook Mews
Civil Service Coll
Belgravia
Chester Square
Eaton Square
Eaton Mews South
Ebury Mews
Ebury Mews East
Ebury Street
Hildred House
Boscobel Pl
Gerald Rd
Gerald Mews
Burton Mews
Kilmuir House
Victoria Coach Station
Fountain & Colonnade Sh Ctr
Liby
Bulleid Way
Royal Belgrave Ho
Hugh Street
Hugh Mews
Eccleston Square
Tenn Ct
Semley House
Semley Place
Ebury Square
Cundy St
Lochmore Ho
Avery Farm Row
Fountain Court
National Audit Offices
Elizabeth Bridge
St George's Drive
Eurocentres
Inchbald Sch of Design (Garden Design)
Eccleston Sq Mews
Warwick Way
Warwick Square
Warwick Square Mews
West Warwick Place
West Mews
Denbigh Mews
Belgrave Rd
145
St Barnabas CE Prim Sch
Ranelagh Gr
St Barnabas St
B313
B324
Ebury Bridge
Tintern House
Glastonbury Ho
Dryburgh Ho
Furness Ho
Kirkstall Ho
Melrose Ho
Fonthill Ho
Evesham Ho
Sherborne Ho
Bridge Ho
Pimlico Ho
Rye Ho
Westbourne Ho
Mercer Ho
Bucknill Ho
Victoria Ho
Dalton Ho
Wainwright Ho
Edgson Ho
Hillersdon Ho
Alderney Street
Clarendon Street
Winchester Street
Cambridge St
St George's Drive
Gloucester Street
Denbigh Street
Sutherland Row
Sutherland Street
Cumberland Street
Sussex St
Russell House
Pimlico
Ebury Bridge Road
Cheylesmore Ho
Doneraile Ho
Gatliff Road
Gatliff Cl
Westmoreland Terr
Westmoreland Pl
Turpentine Lane
Peabody Avenue
Lupus Street
Glasgow Terr
Nash Ho
Gilbert Ho
Chippendale Ho
Elgar Ho
Wedgewood House
Lutyens House
Seldon Ho
Black Stone Ho
Gifford Ho
Langdale Ho
Martineau Ho
Marryat Ho
Campbell Ho
Johnson
Erskine Ho
Chaucer House
St Gabriel's CE Prim Sch
Chelsea Gate
Wellington Bldgs
Chelsea Gdns
Hepworth Ct
Lister Hospl
Hirst Ct
Cubitt Bldg
Pavilion Ct
Sullivan Ho
Sheraton Ho
Paxton Terr
Churchill Gdns
Wilkins Ho
Ripley Ho
Churchill Gardens Road
Telford Terrace
Churchill Gardens
78
79
29
160
A3216
A3212
Grosvenor Rd
Thames Path
Dock
SW1
1
2
3
4

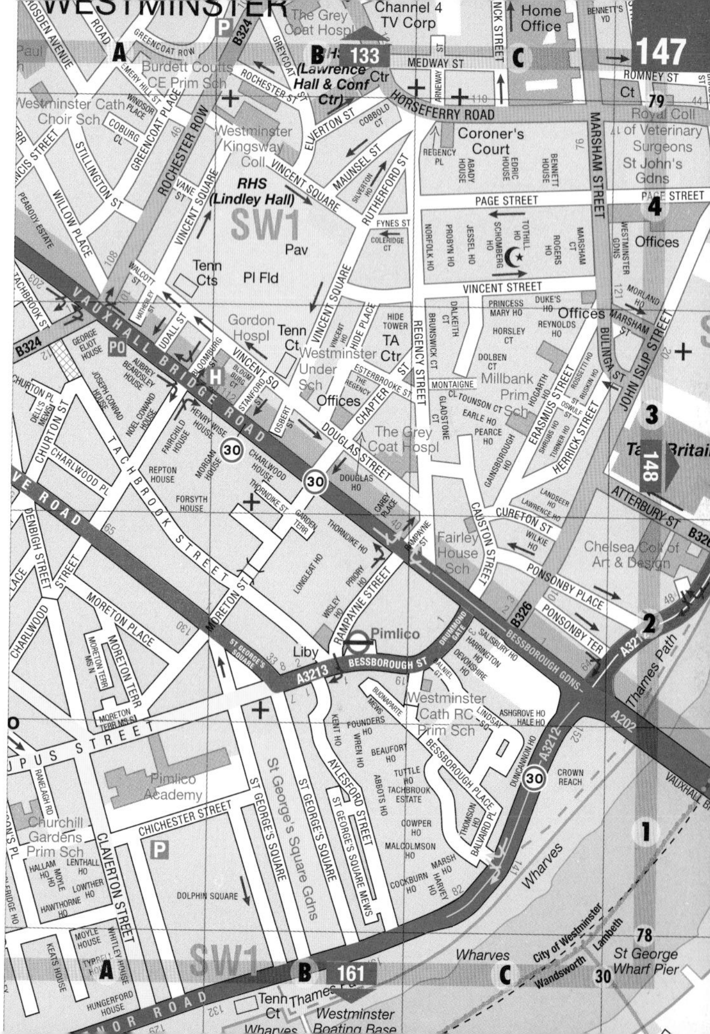

WESTMINSTER
Channel 4 TV Corp
The Grey Coat Hospl
Home Office
133
147
148
161
SW1
RHS (Lawrence Hall & Conf Ctr)
RHS (Lindley Hall)
Burdett Coutts CE Prim Sch
Westminster Cath Choir Sch
Westminster Kingsway Coll
Coroner's Court
Royal Coll of Veterinary Surgeons
St John's Gdns
HORSEFERRY ROAD
MARSHAM STREET
PAGE STREET
VINCENT STREET
VINCENT SQUARE
ROCHESTER ROW
VAUXHALL BRIDGE ROAD
TACHBROOK STREET
MORETON ST
BESSBOROUGH GDNS
BESSBOROUGH ST
BESSBOROUGH PLACE
PONSONBY PLACE
PONSONBY TER
JOHN ISLIP STREET
ATTERBURY ST
CAUSTON STREET
REGENCY STREET
DOUGLAS STREET
CHAPTER ST
RAMPAYNE STREET
ERASMUS STREET
HERRICK STREET
AYLESFORD STREET
ST GEORGE'S SQUARE
St George's Square Gdns
CHICHESTER STREET
DOLPHIN SQUARE
CLAVERTON STREET
LUPUS STREET
MORETON PLACE
MORETON TERR
CHURTON ST
CHARLWOOD PL
DENBIGH STREET
Gordon Hospl
Westminster Under Sch
Fairley House Sch
Millbank Prim Sch
Chelsea Coll of Art & Design
Tate Britain
Pimlico
Pimlico Academy
Churchill Gardens Prim Sch
Westminster Cath RC Prim Sch
Thames Path
Wharves
CROWN REACH
St George Wharf Pier
Westminster Boating Base
City of Westminster
Wandsworth
Lambeth
A3213
A3212
A202
B324
B326

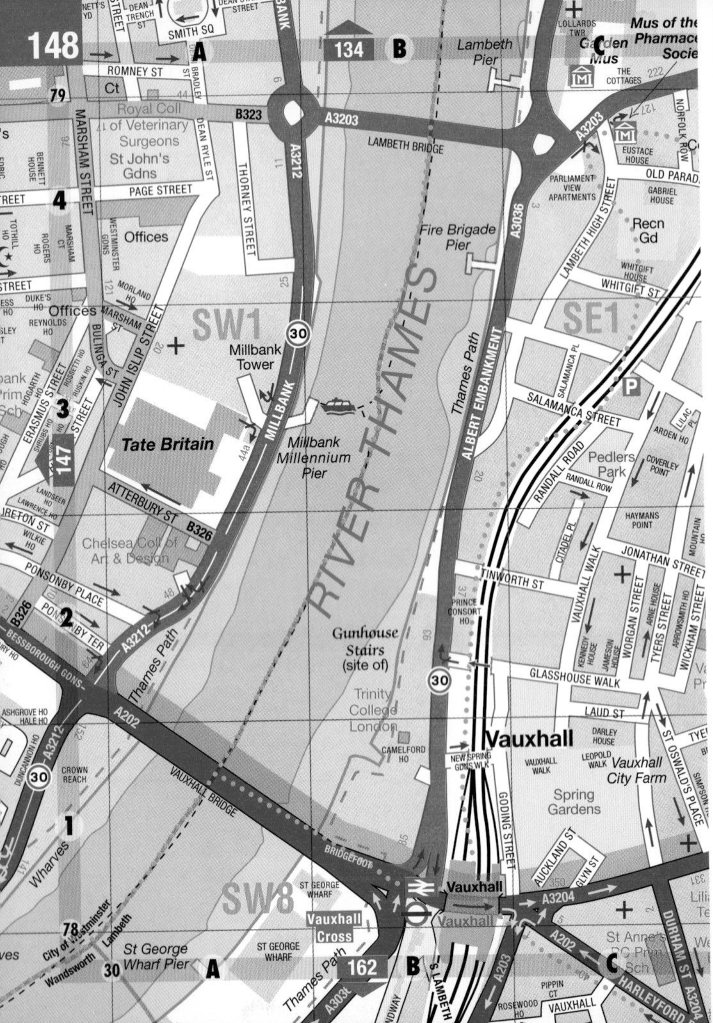

148
134
162
147
A
B
C
1
2
3
4
SMITH SQ
DEAN TRENCH ST
ROMNEY ST
BRADLEY ST
Royal Coll of Veterinary Surgeons
St John's Gdns
DEAN RYLE ST
MARSHAM STREET
PAGE STREET
THORNEY STREET
Offices
WESTMINSTER GDNS
MORLAND HO
DUKE'S HO
REYNOLDS HO
MARSHAM ST
BULINGA ST
JOHN ISLIP STREET
SW1
Millbank Tower
MILLBANK
Tate Britain
Millbank Millennium Pier
ATTERBURY ST
B326
B323
A3203
A3212
A3036
A202
A3204
A203
LAMBETH BRIDGE
Lambeth Pier
LOLLARDS TWR
Garden Mus
Mus of the Pharmaceutical Society
THE COTTAGES
EUSTACE HOUSE
OLD PARADE
NORFOLK ROW
PARLIAMENT VIEW APARTMENTS
LAMBETH HIGH STREET
GABRIEL HOUSE
Recn Gd
Fire Brigade Pier
WHITGIFT HOUSE
WHITGIFT ST
SE1
RIVER THAMES
Thames Path
ALBERT EMBANKMENT
SALAMANCA PL
SALAMANCA STREET
RANDALL ROAD
RANDALL ROW
Pedlers Park
COVERLEY POINT
ARDEN HO
LILAC PL
HAYMANS POINT
CITADEL PL
JONATHAN STREET
TINWORTH ST
VAUXHALL WALK
WORGAN STREET
TYERS STREET
ARNE HOUSE
ARROWSMITH HO
WICKHAM STREET
KENNEDY HOUSE
JAMESON HOUSE
GLASSHOUSE WALK
LAUD ST
PRINCE CONSORT HO
Gunhouse Stairs (site of)
Trinity College London
CAMELFORD HO
NEW SPRING GDNS WLK
Vauxhall
DARLEY HOUSE
LEOPOLD WALK
Vauxhall City Farm
ST OSWALD'S PLACE
Spring Gardens
GODING STREET
AUCKLAND ST
GLYN ST
DURHAM ST
St Anne's RC Prim Sch
HARLEYFORD
PIPPIN CT
ROSEWOOD HO
VAUXHALL
ERASMUS STREET
HOGARTH HO
ROSSETTI HO
RUSKIN HO
SHRUBS HO
LANDSEER HO
LAWRENCE HO
WILKIE HO
Chelsea Coll of Art & Design
PONSONBY PLACE
PONSONBY TER
BESSBOROUGH GDNS
ASHGROVE HO
HALE HO
DUNCANNON HO
CROWN REACH
VAUXHALL BRIDGE
BRIDGEFOOT
Wharves
SW8
ST GEORGE WHARF
Vauxhall Cross
St George Wharf Pier
City of Westminster
Lambeth
Wandsworth
BENNETT HOUSE
TOTHILL HO
ROGERS HO
MARSHAM CT

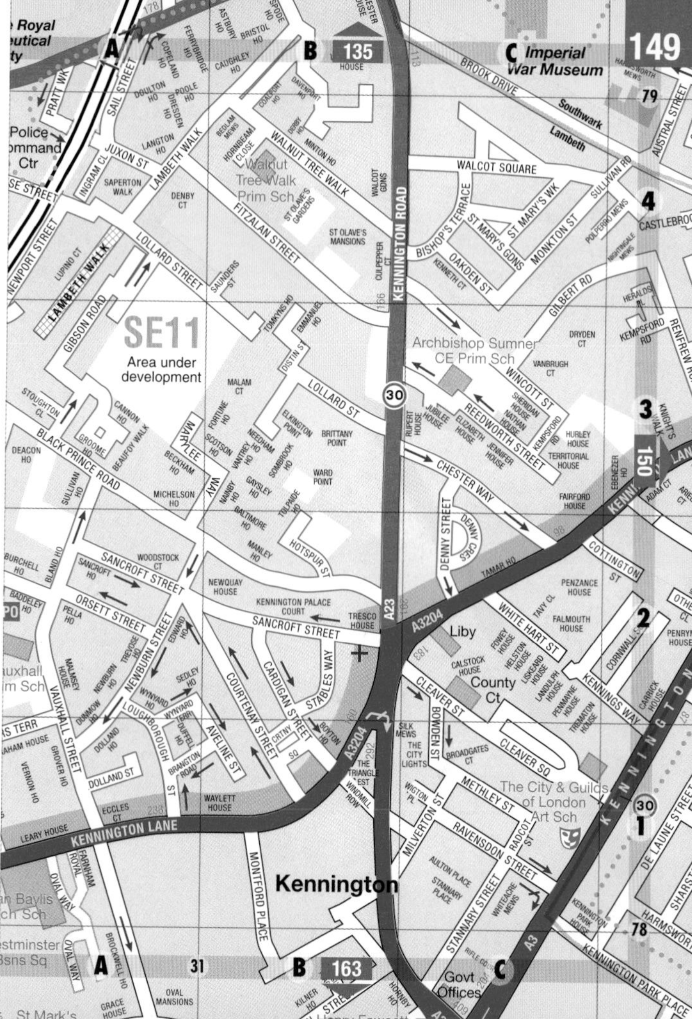
A
B
135
C
Imperial War Museum
Brook Drive
Southwark
Lambeth
79
Austral Street
Walcot Square
Sullivan Rd
4
Castlebrook Cl
Sail Street
Copeland Ho
Ferrybridge Ho
Astbury Ho
Bristol Ho
Spode Ho
Caughley Ho
Pratt Wk
Police Command Ctr
Doulton Ho
Poole Ho
Dresden Ho
Langton Ho
Juxon St
Ingram Cl
Saperton Walk
Lambeth Walk
Denby Ct
Bedlam Mews
Hornbeam Close
Walnut Tree Walk
Walnut Tree Walk Prim Sch
Minton Ho
Derby Ho
Coalport Ho
Davenport Ho
Walcot Gdns
Fitzalan Street
St Olave's Gardens
St Olave's Mansions
Kennington Road
Bishop's Terrace
St Mary's Gdns
St Mary's Wk
Monkton St
Polperro Mews
Nightingale Mews
Kenneth Ct
Oakden St
Gilbert Rd
Newport Street
Lupino Ct
Lambeth Walk
Lollard Street
Saunders St
Culpepper Ct
Heralds Pl
Kempsford Rd
Renfrew Road
Gibson Road
SE11
Area under development
Tomkyns Ho
Emmanuel Ho
Distin St
Archbishop Sumner CE Prim Sch
Dryden Ct
Vanbrugh Ct
Wincott St
Malam Ct
Lollard St
30
Stoughton Cl
Cannon Ho
Groome Ho
Beaufoy Walk
Marylee Way
Fortune Ho
Scotson Ho
Needham Ho
Elkington Point
Brittany Point
Rupert House
Jubilee House
Elizabeth House
Reedworth Street
Sheridan House
Nathan House
Jennifer House
Kempsford Rd
Hurley House
Territorial House
3
Knight's Walk
150
Lane
Deacon Ho
Black Prince Road
Beckham Ho
Vantrey Ho
Sombrook Ho
Ward Point
Chester Way
Ebenezer Ho
Adam Ct
Ariel Ct
Sullivan Ho
Michelson Ho
Nainby Ho
Gaysley Ho
Tolpaide Ho
Baltimore Ho
Denny Street
Denny Cres
Fairford House
Kennington Lane
Burchell Ho
Bland Ho
Woodstock Ct
Manley Ho
Hotspur St
Tamar Ho
Cottington St
Sancroft Ho
Sancroft Street
Newquay House
Penzance House
Isabella Ho
Othello Cl
Baddeley Ho
Orsett Street
Pella Ho
Kennington Palace Court
Tresco House
A23
A3204
Sancroft Street
Liby
White Hart St
Tavy Cl
Falmouth House
2
Penryn House
Vauxhall Prim Sch
Malmsey House
Newburn Street
Trevose Ho
Edward Ho
Courtenay Street
Cardigan Street
Stables Way
Calstock House
Fowey House
Helston House
Liskeard House
County Ct
Landulph House
Penmayne House
Trematon House
Cornwall Sq
Kennings Way
Carrick House
Kennington
Vauxhall Street
Newburn Ho
Donmow Ho
Sedley Ho
Wynyard Ho
Wynyard Terr
Loughborough St
Duffell Ho
Aveline St
Crtny Sq
Boyton Ho
A3204
Cleaver St
Bowden St
Silk Mews
The City Lights
Cleaver Sq
Broadgates Ct
The Triangle Est
Grover Ho
Vernon Ho
Dolland Ho
Dolland St
Brangton Road
Windmill Row
Methley St
The City & Guilds of London Art Sch
30
1
De Laune Street
Waylett House
Eccles Ct
Wigton Pl
Milverton St
Ravensdon Street
Radcot St
Leary House
Kennington Lane
Farnham Royal
Montford Place
Kennington
Aulton Place
Stannary Place
Stannary Street
Whiteacre Mews
A3
Kennington Park House
78
Harmsworth St
Oval Way
Lilian Baylis Tech Sch
Westminster Bsns Sq
Brockwell Ho
Kennington Park Place
A
31
B
163
C
Rifle Ct
Govt Offices
Oval Mansions
Grace House
Kilner Ho
Hornby Ho
St Mark's
Henry Fawcett

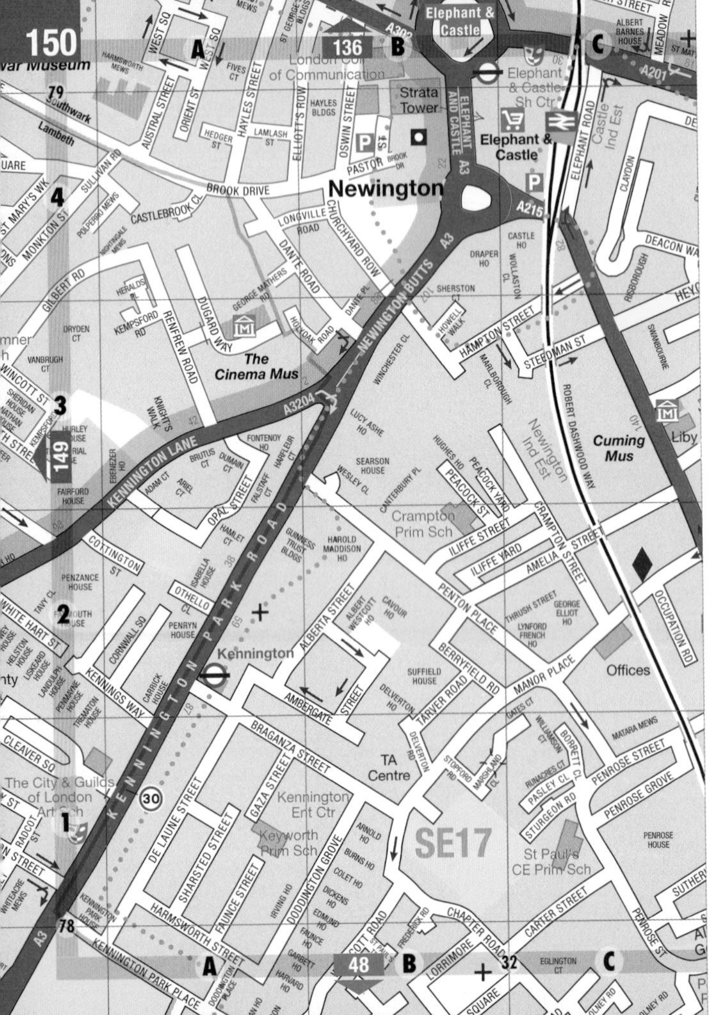
136
48
149
Elephant & Castle
Newington
SE17
Kennington
Strata Tower
London Coll of Communication
Elephant & Castle Sh Ctr
Castle Ind Est
The Cinema Mus
Cuming Mus
Liby
Newington Ind Est
Crampton Prim Sch
Kennington Ent Ctr
Keyworth Prim Sch
St Paul's CE Prim Sch
TA Centre
Offices
The City & Guilds of London Art Sch
Southwark
Lambeth
A3
A302
A201
A215
A3204
NEWINGTON BUTTS
KENNINGTON LANE
KENNINGTON PARK ROAD
KENNINGTON PARK PLACE
ELEPHANT AND CASTLE
ELEPHANT ROAD
BROOK DRIVE
WEST SQ
AUSTRAL STREET
ORIENT ST
HAYLES STREET
ELLIOTT'S ROW
OSWIN STREET
HEDGER ST
LAMLASH ST
HAYLES BLDGS
FIVES CT
PASTOR ST
CASTLEBROOK CL
LONGVILLE ROAD
DANTE ROAD
CHURCHYARD ROW
DANTE PL
HOLYOAK ROAD
DUGARD WAY
RENFREW ROAD
KEMPSFORD RD
HERALDS PL
GEORGE MATHERS RD
GILBERT RD
SULLIVAN RD
MONKTON ST
ST MARY'S WK
POLPERRO MEWS
KNIGHT'S WALK
OPAL STREET
BRUTUS CT
DUMAIN CT
ADAM CT
ARIEL CT
FALSTAFF CT
HAMLET CT
FONTENOY HO
HARFLEUR CT
COTTINGTON ST
OTHELLO CL
ISABELLA HOUSE
CORNWALL SQ
KENNINGS WAY
CARRICK HOUSE
PENRYN HOUSE
PENZANCE HOUSE
FAIRFORD HOUSE
DRYDEN CT
VANBRUGH CT
WINCOTT ST
WHITE HART ST
CLEAVER SQ
RADCOT ST
HARMSWORTH STREET
DE LAUNE STREET
SHARSTED STREET
FAUNCE STREET
GAZA STREET
BRAGANZA STREET
DODDINGTON GROVE
AMBERGATE STREET
ALBERTA STREET
ALBERT WESTCOTT HO
CAVOUR HO
GUINNESS TRUST BLDGS
HAROLD MADDISON HO
SEARSON HOUSE
LUCY ASHE HO
WESLEY CL
CANTERBURY PL
WINCHESTER CL
SHERSTON CT
HOWELL WALK
HAMPTON STREET
STEEDMAN ST
MARLBOROUGH CL
CASTLE HO
DRAPER HO
WOLLASTON CL
HUGHES HO
PEACOCK ST
PEACOCK YARD
ILIFFE STREET
ILIFFE YARD
AMELIA STREET
CRAMPTON STREET
PENTON PLACE
THRUSH STREET
GEORGE ELLIOT HO
LYNFORD FRENCH HO
BERRYFIELD RD
MANOR PLACE
TARVER ROAD
SUFFIELD HOUSE
DELVERTON HO
DELVERTON RD
STOPFORD RD
MARSHLAND CL
GATES CT
WILLIAMSON CT
BORRETT CL
RUNACRES CT
PASLEY CL
STURGEON RD
PENROSE STREET
PENROSE GROVE
PENROSE HOUSE
PENROSE ST
MATARA MEWS
ROBERT DASHWOOD WAY
OCCUPATION RD
SWANBOURNE
RISBOROUGH
CLAYDON
DEACON WAY
ALBERT BARNES HOUSE
MEADOW RO
CHAPTER ROAD
CARTER STREET
LORRIMORE SQUARE
FREDERICK RD
EGLINTON CT
ARNOLD HO
BURNS HO
COLET HO
DICKENS HO
EDMUND HO
FAUNCE HO
GARRETT HO
HARVARD HO
IRVING HO
DODDINGTON PLACE
KENNINGTON PARK HOUSE
WHITEACRE MEWS
HARMSWORTH MEWS
WEST MEWS
ST GEORGE'S BLDGS
TAVY CL
HELSTON HOUSE
LISKEARD HOUSE
LANDULPH HOUSE
PENMAYNE HOUSE
TREMATON HOUSE
EBENEZER HO
SHERIDAN HOUSE
A
B
C
1
2
3
4
30
78
79

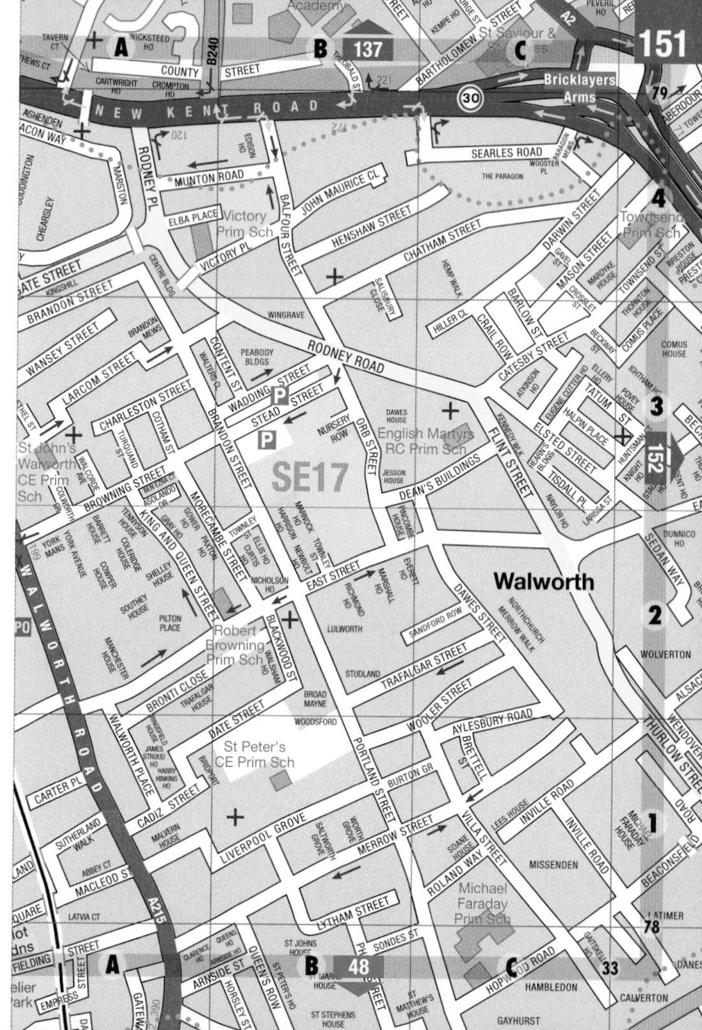

151
137
A
B
C
Academy
TAVERN CT
WICKSTEED HO
MEWS CT
COUNTY STREET
B240
CARTWRIGHT HO
CROMPTON HO
THEOBALD ST
BARTHOLOMEW STREET
KEMPE HO
St Saviour & St C... es
PEVERIL HO
A2
Bricklayers Arms
30
79
ABERDOUR ST
TOWER
NEW KENT ROAD
ASHENDEN
ACON WAY
RODNEY PL
MARSTON
CHEARSLEY
EDISON HO
MUNTON ROAD
ELBA PLACE
Victory Prim Sch
VICTORY PL
BALFOUR STREET
JOHN MAURICE CL
HENSHAW STREET
CHATHAM STREET
SEARLES ROAD
THE PARAGON
WOOSTER PL
PARAGON MEWS
DARWIN STREET
Townsend Prim Sch
4
GATE STREET
KINGSHILL
CENTRE BLDG
BRANDON STREET
WANSEY STREET
BRANDON MEWS
LARCOM STREET
WINGRAVE
SALISBURY CLOSE
HEMP WALK
HILLER CL
CRAIL ROW
BARLOW ST
GAVEL ST
MASON STREET
CROSSLET ST
MARDYKE HOUSE
TOWNSEND ST
THORNTON HOUSE
PRESTON HOUSE
PRESTON CL
COMUS PLACE
COMUS HOUSE
BECKWAY ST
CATESBY STREET
RODNEY ROAD
CONTENT ST
WALTERS CL
PEABODY BLDGS
WADDING STREET
STEAD STREET
NURSERY ROW
ORB STREET
DAWES HOUSE
English Martyrs RC Prim Sch
ATKINSON HO
EUGENE COTTER HO
ELLERY HO
TATUM ST
HALPIN PLACE
POVEY HOUSE
3
ETHEL ST
CHARLESTON STREET
COTHAM ST
TURQUAND ST
St John's Walworth CE Prim Sch
WALCORDE AVE
COLWORTH GR
BROWNING STREET
BEN EZRA CT
ASOLANDO DR
BRANDON STREET
MORECAMBE STREET
SE17
JESSON HOUSE
DEAN'S BUILDINGS
FLINT STREET
KENNEDY WLK
HEARN'S BLDGS
ELSTED STREET
TISDALL PL
NAYLOR HO
LARISSA ST
HUNTSMAN ST
KNIGHT HO
152
KING AND QUEEN STREET
GOWER HO
GRAY HO
PAXTON HO
TENNYSON HOUSE
BARRETT HOUSE
YORK MANS
YORK AVENUE
COLERIDGE HOUSE
COWPER HOUSE
SHELLEY HOUSE
TOWNLEY ST
ELLIS HO
CURTIS HO
HARRISON HO
MARMOCK HO
NEWBOLT HO
TOWNLEY ST
PINCOMBE HOUSE
SEDAN WAY
DUNNICO HO
NICHOLSON HO
EAST STREET
MARSHALL HO
RICHMOND HO
EVERETT HO
Walworth
199
WALWORTH ROAD
SOUTHEY HOUSE
PILTON PLACE
Robert Browning Prim Sch
BLACKWOOD ST
WALSHAM HO
LULWORTH
SANDFORD ROW
DAWES STREET
NORTHCHURCH
MERROW WALK
2
MANCHESTER HOUSE
BRONTI CLOSE
TRAFALGAR HOUSE
STUDLAND
TRAFALGAR STREET
WOLVERTON
ALSACE
BROAD MAYNE
WOODSFORD
WOOLER STREET
AYLESBURY ROAD
BRETTELL ST
WALWORTH PLACE
KINGSFIELD HOUSE
JAMES STROUD HO
HARRY HINKINS HO
BRIDPORT
DATE STREET
St Peter's CE Prim Sch
PORTLAND STREET
THURLOW STREET
WENDOVER
CARTER PL
CADIZ STREET
BURTON GR
INVILLE ROAD
LEES HOUSE
MICHAEL FARADAY HOUSE
1
BEACONSFIELD ROAD
SUTHERLAND WALK
MALVERN HOUSE
LIVERPOOL GROVE
SALTWOOD GROVE
WORTH GROVE
MERROW STREET
VILLA STREET
SOANE HOUSE
ROLAND WAY
MISSENDEN
ABBEY CT
MACLEOD ST
LATVIA CT
A215
LYTHAM STREET
Michael Faraday Prim Sch
LATIMER
78
SQUARE
FIELDING STREET
CLARENCE HO
QUEENS HO
ARNSIDE HO
ARNSIDE ST
QUEEN'S ROW
ST PETER'S HO
ST JOHNS HOUSE
SONDES ST
48
ST MARK'S HOUSE
ST MATTHEW'S HOUSE
HOPWOOD ROAD
GAITSKELL HO
33
DANESF
HAMBLEDON
CALVERTON
EMPRESS
Pelier Park
GATEWAY
390
HORSLEY ST
ST STEPHENS HOUSE
GAYHURST

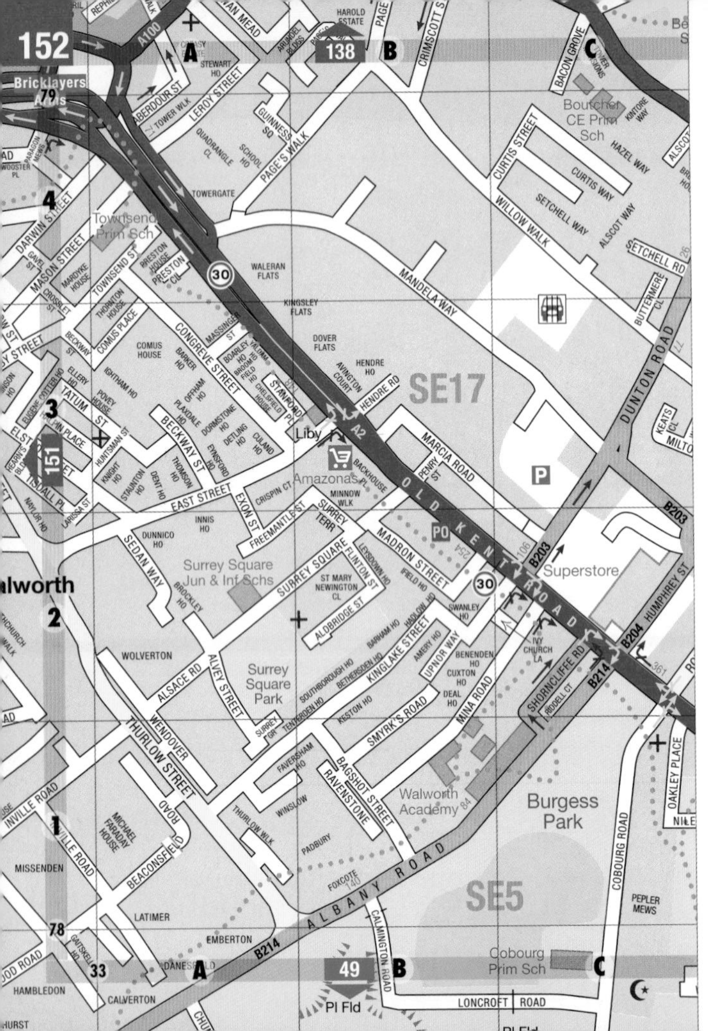

Bricklayers Arms
SE17
SE5
Walworth
Surrey Square Park
Surrey Square Jun & Inf Schs
Townsend Prim Sch
Boutcher CE Prim Sch
Walworth Academy
Burgess Park
Cobourg Prim Sch
OLD KENT ROAD
ALBANY ROAD
DUNTON ROAD
MANDELA WAY
EAST STREET
CONGREVE STREET
SURREY SQUARE
THURLOW STREET
KINGLAKE STREET
COBOURG ROAD
CALMINGTON ROAD
LONCROFT ROAD
Superstore
Amazonas
Liby
PO
138
151
49

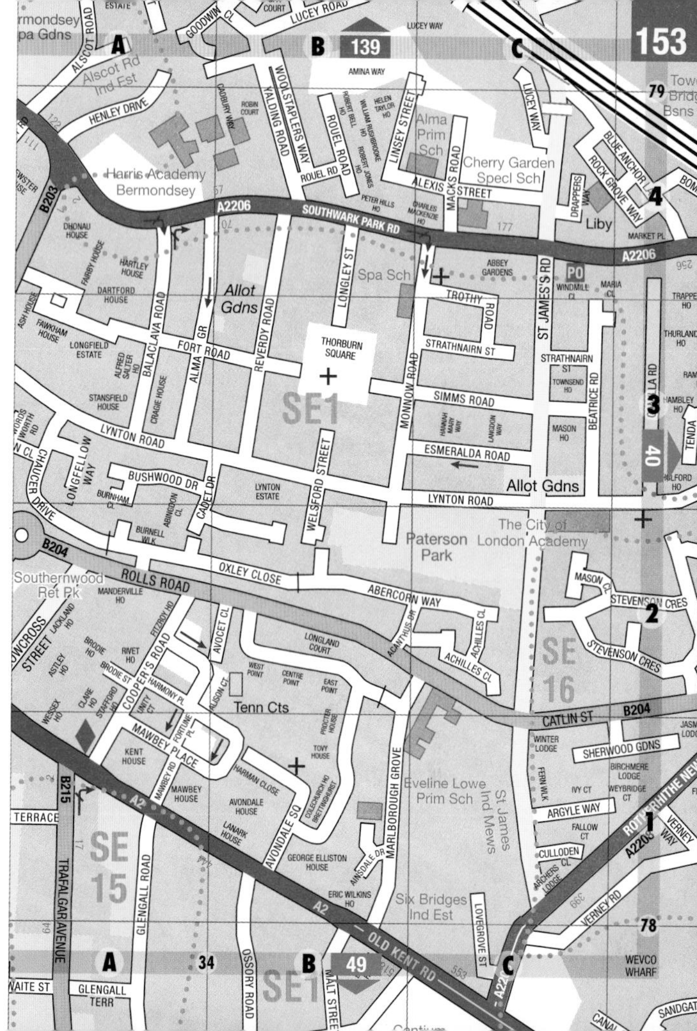

A
B
C
139
49
40
SE1
SE 16
SE 15
SOUTHWARK PARK RD
A2206
OLD KENT RD
A2
ROLLS ROAD
B204
CATLIN ST
LYNTON ROAD
FORT ROAD
SIMMS ROAD
ESMERALDA ROAD
THORBURN SQUARE
Harris Academy Bermondsey
Alma Prim Sch
Cherry Garden Specl Sch
Spa Sch
Allot Gdns
Paterson Park
The City of London Academy
Southernwood Ret Pk
Tenn Cts
Eveline Lowe Prim Sch
Six Bridges Ind Est
St James Ind Mews
ALEXIS STREET
LUCEY ROAD
LUCEY WAY
AMINA WAY
ROUEL ROAD
WOOLSTAPLERS WAY
YALDING ROAD
LINSEY STREET
MACKS ROAD
ST JAMES'S RD
TROTHY ROAD
STRATHNAIRN ST
MONNOW ROAD
BEATRICE RD
BALACLAVA ROAD
ALMA GR
REVERDY ROAD
LONGLEY ST
WELSFORD STREET
BUSHWOOD DR
CADET DR
CHAUCER DRIVE
LONGFELLOW WAY
OXLEY CLOSE
ABERCORN WAY
ACHILLES CL
STEVENSON CRES
MASON CL
COOPER'S ROAD
MAWBEY PLACE
HARMAN CLOSE
AVONDALE SQ
MARLBOROUGH GROVE
GLENGALL ROAD
TRAFALGAR AVENUE
OSSORY ROAD
LOVEGROVE ST
SHERWOOD GDNS
ARGYLE WAY
VERNEY RD
ROTHERHITHE NEW RD
HENLEY DRIVE
ALSCOT ROAD
GOODWIN CL
BLUE ANCHOR LA
ROCK GROVE WAY
MARKET PL
WEVCO WHARF
SANDGATE

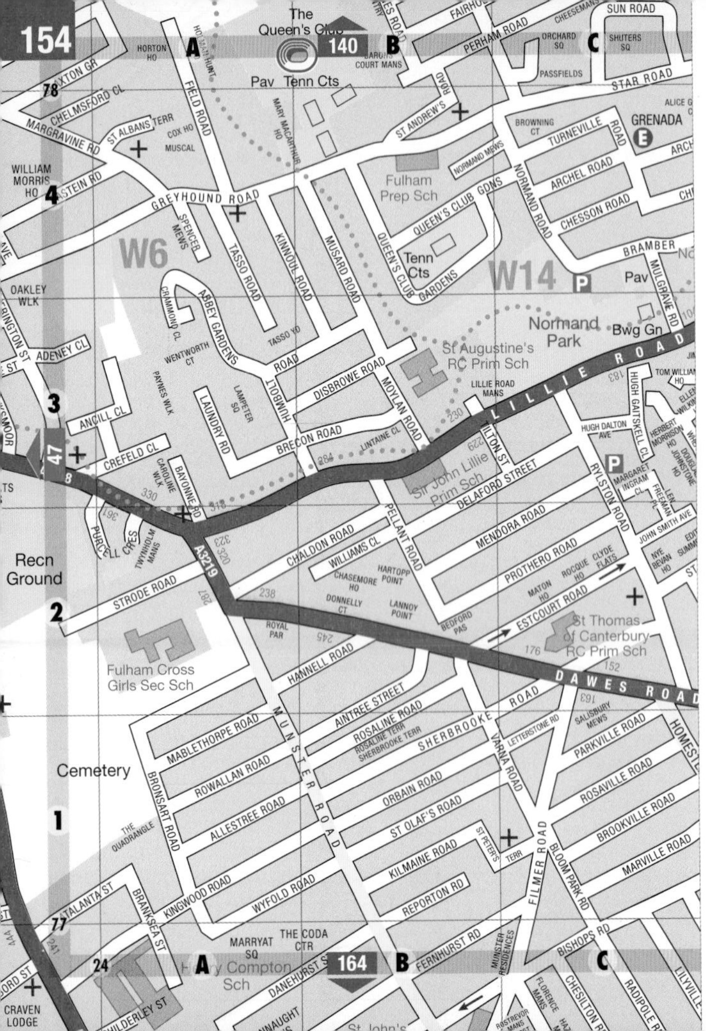
The Queen's Club
140
Pav Tenn Cts
W6
W14
GRENADA
Fulham Prep Sch
Tenn Cts
Normand Park
Bwg Gn
St Augustine's RC Prim Sch
Sir John Lillie Prim Sch
St Thomas of Canterbury RC Prim Sch
Fulham Cross Girls Sec Sch
Recn Ground
Cemetery
Henry Compton Sch
CRAVEN LODGE
47
164
A3219
LILLIE ROAD
DAWES ROAD
GREYHOUND ROAD
MARGRAVINE RD
FIELD ROAD
TASSO ROAD
KINNOUL ROAD
MUSARD ROAD
ABBEY GARDENS
QUEEN'S CLUB GARDENS
QUEEN'S CLUB GDNS
NORMAND ROAD
TURNEVILLE ROAD
ARCHEL ROAD
CHESSON ROAD
PERHAM ROAD
STAR ROAD
SUN ROAD
DISBROWE ROAD
MOYLAN ROAD
BRECON ROAD
CHALDON ROAD
STRODE ROAD
PELLANT ROAD
DELAFORD STREET
MENDORA ROAD
PROTHERO ROAD
ESTCOURT ROAD
RYLSTON ROAD
HANNELL ROAD
AINTREE STREET
ROSALINE ROAD
SHERBROOKE ROAD
MUNSTER ROAD
MABLETHORPE ROAD
ROWALLAN ROAD
ALLESTREE ROAD
BRONSART ROAD
ORBAIN ROAD
ST OLAF'S ROAD
KILMAINE ROAD
REPORTON RD
VARNA ROAD
FILMER ROAD
BLOOM PARK RD
PARKVILLE ROAD
ROSAVILLE ROAD
BROOKVILLE ROAD
MARVILLE ROAD
KINGWOOD ROAD
WYFOLD ROAD
FERNHURST RD
BISHOPS RD
DANEHURST ST
ATALANTA ST
BRANKSEA ST
CHILDERLEY ST
MARRYAT SQ
THE CODA CTR
MUGRAVE RD
HUGH GAITSKELL CL
JOHN SMITH AVE
PURCELL CRES
CREFELD CL
ANCILL CL
ADENEY CL
CHELMSFORD CL
ST ANDREW'S ROAD

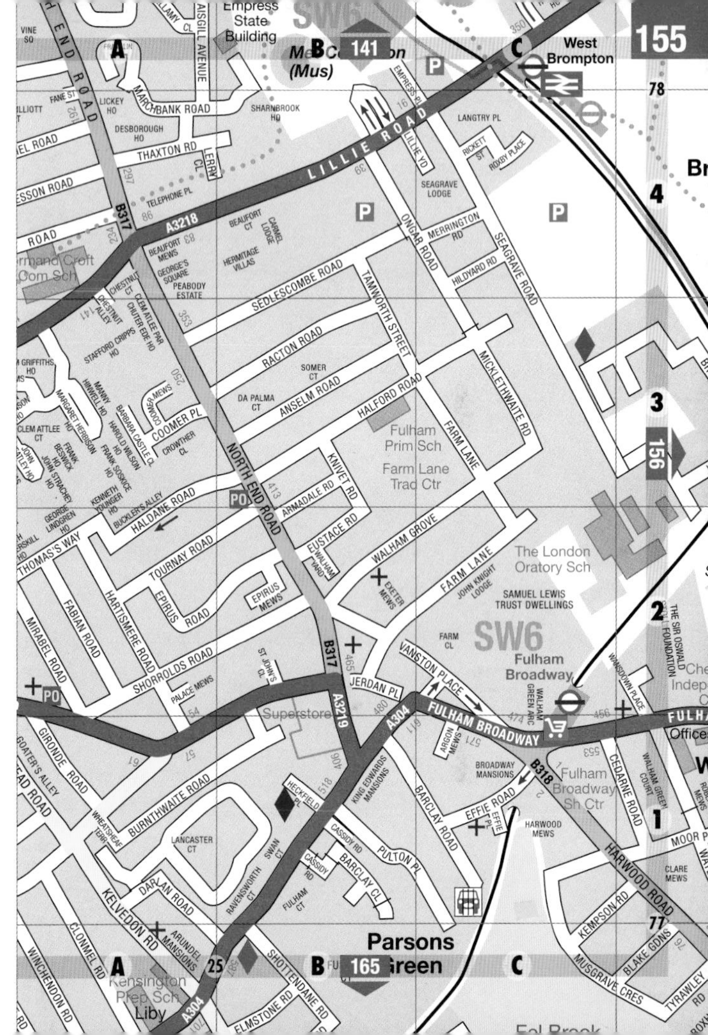
155
Empress State Building
141
(Mus)
West Brompton
LILLIE ROAD
A3218
B317
NORTH END ROAD
LANGTRY PL
RICKETT ST
ROXBY PLACE
SEAGRAVE LODGE
SEAGRAVE ROAD
ONGAR ROAD
MERRINGTON RD
HILDYARD RD
MICKLETHWAITE RD
FARM LANE
TAMWORTH STREET
SEDLESCOMBE ROAD
RACTON ROAD
ANSELM ROAD
HALFORD ROAD
SOMER CT
DA PALMA CT
Fulham Prim Sch
Farm Lane Trad Ctr
KNIVET RD
ARMADALE RD
EUSTACE RD
WALHAM GROVE
EXETER MEWS
JOHN KNIGHT LODGE
The London Oratory Sch
SAMUEL LEWIS TRUST DWELLINGS
SW6
FARM CL
VANSTON PLACE
Fulham Broadway
FULHAM BROADWAY
A304
A3219
B318
JERDAN PL
Superstore
ARGON MEWS
BROADWAY MANSIONS
EFFIE ROAD
EFFIE PL
HARWOOD MEWS
HARWOOD ROAD
Fulham Broadway Sh Ctr
CEDARNE ROAD
WALHAM GREEN COURT
WANSDOWN PLACE
THE SIR OSWALD STOLL FOUNDATION
156
BARCLAY ROAD
PULTON PL
BARCLAY CL
CASSIDY RD
KING EDWARDS MANSIONS
HECKFIELD PL
SWAN CT
RAVENSWORTH CT
FULHAM CT
LANCASTER CT
BURNTHWAITE ROAD
DARLAN ROAD
KELVEDON RD
ARUNDEL MANSIONS
CLONMEL RD
WINCHENDON RD
SHOTTENDANE RD
ELMSTONE RD
Kensington Prep Sch
Liby
Parsons Green
165
KEMPSON RD
BLAKE GDNS
MUSGRAVE CRES
TYRAWLEY RD
CLARE MEWS
MOOR P
SHORROLDS ROAD
PALACE MEWS
ST JOHN'S CL
EPIRUS ROAD
EPIRUS MEWS
TOURNAY ROAD
HARTISMERE ROAD
FABIAN ROAD
MIRABEL ROAD
GIRONDE ROAD
GOATER'S ALLEY
WHEATSHEAF TERR
THOMAS'S WAY
HALDANE ROAD
BUCKLER'S ALLEY
GEORGE LINDGREN HO
KENNETH YOUNGER HO
FRANK SOSKICE HO
HAROLD WILSON HO
BARBARA CASTLE CL
CROWTHER CL
COOMER PL
COOMER MEWS
MANNY SHINWELL HO
MARGARET HERBISON HO
CLEM ATTLEE CT
JOHN STRACHEY HO
FRANK BESWICK HO
STAFFORD CRIPPS HO
CLEMATTLEE PAR
CHUTER EDE HO
CHESTNUT CT
CHESTNUT ALLEY
PEABODY ESTATE
GEORGE'S SQUARE
BEAUFORT MEWS
BEAUFORT CT
CARMEL LODGE
HERMITAGE VILLAS
TELEPHONE PL
THAXTON RD
LERRY CL
DESBOROUGH HO
MARCHBANK ROAD
LICKEY HO
SHARNBROOK HO
FANE ST
AISGILL AVENUE
VINE SQ
EMPRESS PL
LILLIE YD
PO
A
B
C
1
2
3
4
77
78

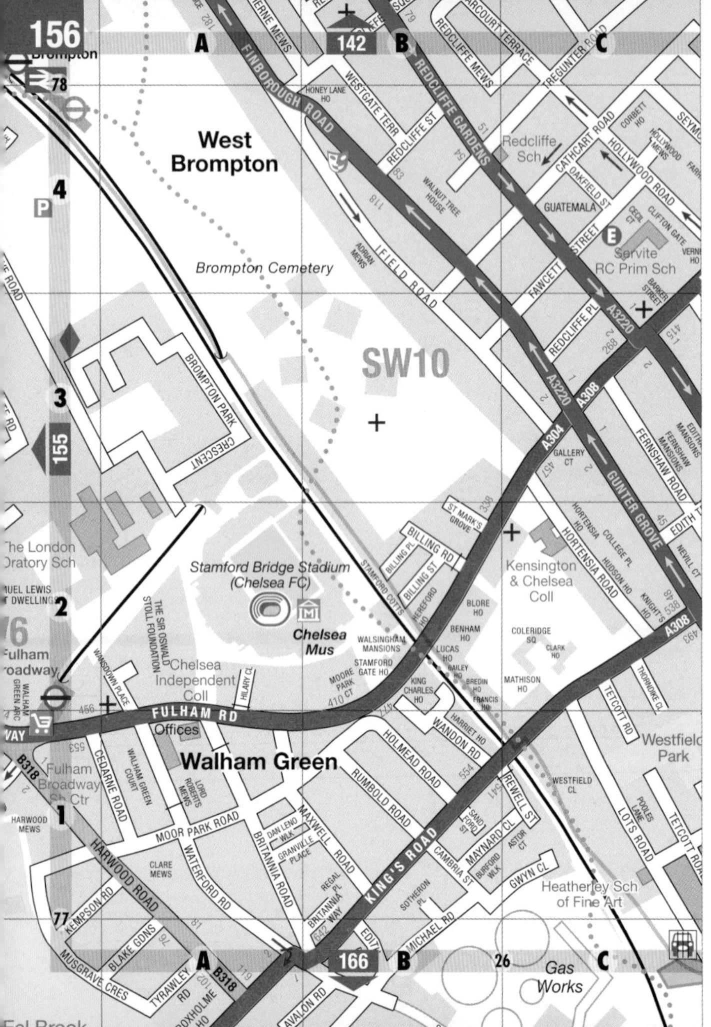

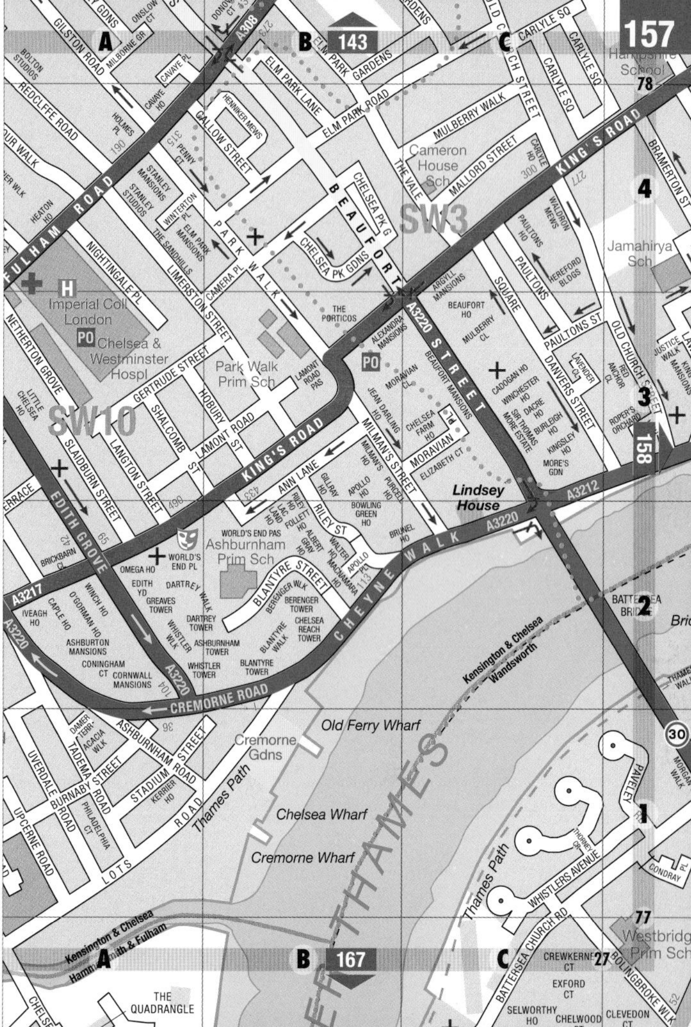
A
B
C
143
167
158
4
3
2
1
SW3
SW10
GILSTON ROAD
MILBORNE GR
ONSLOW CT
CAVAYE PL
CAVAYE HO
BOLTON STUDIOS
REDCLIFFE ROAD
HOLMES PL
FULHAM ROAD
A308
ELM PARK GARDENS
ELM PARK LANE
ELM PARK ROAD
HENNIKER MEWS
CALLOW STREET
PENNY CT
STANLEY MANSIONS
STANLEY STUDIOS
WINTERTON PL
ELM PARK MANSIONS
THE SANDHILLS
PARK WALK
BEAUFORT
CHELSEA PK G
CHELSEA PK GDNS
CARLYLE SQ
OLD CHURCH STREET
MULBERRY WALK
MALLORD STREET
CARLYLE HO
THE VALE
Cameron House Sch
KING'S ROAD
BRAMERTON ST
Hampshire School
78
WALDRON MEWS
PAULTONS HO
PAULTONS SQUARE
HEREFORD BLDGS
PAULTONS ST
Jamahirya Sch
HEATON HO
NIGHTINGALE PL
H
Imperial Coll London
PO
Chelsea & Westminster Hospl
LIMERSTON STREET
CAMERA PL
THE PORTICOS
ARGYLL MANSIONS
BEAUFORT HO
MULBERRY CL
A3220
STREET
ALEXANDRA MANSIONS
MORAVIAN CL
BEAUFORT MANSIONS
LAVENDER CL
RED ANCHOR CL
JUSTICE WALK
KING'S MANSIONS
LAWRENCE
NETHERTON GROVE
LITTLE CHELSEA HO
GERTRUDE STREET
Park Walk Prim Sch
LAMONT ROAD PAS
HOBURY ST
SHALCOMB ST
LAMONT ROAD
JEAN DARLING HO
CHELSEA FARM HO
MORAVIAN PL
CADOGAN HO
WINCHESTER HO
DACRE HO
SIR THOMAS MORE ESTATE
BURLEIGH HO
DANVERS STREET
KINGSLEY HO
MORE'S GDN
ROPER'S ORCHARD
SLAIDBURN STREET
LANGTON STREET
ANN LANE
MILMAN'S STREET
MILMAN'S HO
GILLRAY HO
APOLLO HO
PURCELL HO
ELIZABETH CT
Lindsey House
A3212
EDITH GROVE
RILEY HO
LACLAND HO
FOLLETT HO
RILEY ST
BOWLING GREEN HO
BRUNEL HO
WORLD'S END PAS
Ashburnham Prim Sch
ALBERT GRAY HO
WALTER HO
MACNAMARA HO
APOLLO PL
CHEYNE WALK
BRICKBARN CL
WORLD'S END PL
OMEGA HO
EDITH YD
DARTREY WALK
GREAVES TOWER
BLANTYRE STREET
BERENGER WLK
BERENGER TOWER
CHELSEA REACH TOWER
BATTERSEA BRIDGE
Bridge
A3217
IVEAGH HO
CAPLE HO
O'GORMAN HO
WINCH HO
ASHBURTON MANSIONS
CONINGHAM CT
CORNWALL MANSIONS
DARTREY TOWER
WHISTLER WLK
ASHBURNHAM TOWER
WHISTLER TOWER
BLANTYRE TOWER
BLANTYRE WALK
CREMORNE ROAD
Kensington & Chelsea
Wandsworth
THAMES WALK
Old Ferry Wharf
30
DAMER TERR
ACACIA WLK
TADEMA ROAD
ASHBURNHAM ROAD
STREET
Cremorne Gdns
MORGAN'S WALK
PAVELEY
UVERDALE ROAD
BURNABY STREET
STADIUM ST
KERRIER HO
PHILADELPHIA CT
Thames Path
THAMES
Chelsea Wharf
Cremorne Wharf
THORNEY CR
WHISTLERS AVENUE
CONDRAY PL
UPCERNE ROAD
LOTS ROAD
77
Westbridge Prim Sch
Hammersmith & Fulham
BATTERSEA CHURCH RD
CREWKERNE CT
27
BOLINGBROKE WLK
EXFORD CT
THE QUADRANGLE
SELWORTHY HO
CHELWOOD CT
CLEVEDON CT

144
157
168
A
B
C
1
2
3
4
SW3
KING'S ROAD
A3217
B304
A3212
A3031
B302
B305
Gems Hampshire School
Offices
KING'S COURT N
KING'S COURT S
CHELSEA MANOR GDNS
CHELSEA TOWERS
SWAN CT
FLOOD WALK
FLOOD STREET
REDESDALE ST
REDBURN STREET
CHRISTCHURCH STREET
CHRISTCHURCH TERR
CAVERSHAM ST
TEDWORTH SQUARE
TEDWORTH GDNS
RALSTON ST
HAYDEN PIPER HO
CHEYNE PL
Christchurch CE Prim Sch
ROBINSON ST
SWAN WALK
The English Gardening Sch
Chelsea Physic Garden
Thames Path
CHELSEA EMBANKMENT
MANOR STREET ESTATE
CHELSEA MANOR CT
ALPHA PL
GROVE HO
OAKLEY GARDENS
ROSSETTI STUDIOS
CHESIL CT
ST LOO CT
ST LOO AVE
ROSSETTI GDNS MANSIONS
CHEYNE CT
CHEYNE GDNS
CHEYNE MEWS
MARGARETTA TERR
OAKLEY STREET
PHENE ST
ADAIR HO
PIER HO
BRAMERTON ST
GLEBE PLACE
Jamahirya Sch
UPPER CHEYNE ROW
Carlyle's House
CHEYNE ROW
SHREWSBURY HO
CHELSEA ESTATE LAWRENCE MANS
LORDSHIP PLACE
CARLYLE MANS
CHEYNE WALK
LAWRENCE ST
KING'S MANSIONS
JUSTICE WALK
OLD CHURCH STREET
RED ANCHOR CL
ROPER'S ORCHARD
PETYT PLACE
CARLYLE SQ
CARLYLE HO
WALDRON MEWS
PAULTONS HO
PAULTONS SQUARE
PAULTONS ST
HEREFORD BLDGS
DANVERS STREET
LAVENDER CL
DACRE HO
SIR THOMAS MORE ESTATE
BURLEIGH HO
Cadogan Pier
RIVER THAMES
ALBERT BRIDGE (SUSPENSION)
Terrace Walk
Thames Path
BATTERSEA BRIDGE
Bridge Wharf
WATERSIDE POINT
RIVERSIDE
ALBION RIVERSIDE
THAMES WALK
RANSOMES MEWS
ANHALT ROAD
CRANBOURNE CT
GREAT EASTERN WHARF
Ransome's Dock
CARRIAGE DRIVE NORTH
Old English Garden
Pav
HESTER ROAD
RADSTOCK ST
ELCHO STREET
HOWIE ST
MORGAN'S WALK
Bsns Ctr
PARKGATE ROAD
ST MARY-LE-PARK CT
ALBANY MANSIONS
Govt Offices
ALBERT BRIDGE ROAD
Royal Coll of Art Sculpture Sch
BATTERSEA BRIDGE ROAD
PAVELEY RD
THORNEY CT
CONDRAY PL
WHISTLERS AVENUE
PO
SEARLES CL
JUER STREET
WORFIELD ST
STAFFORD MANSIONS
CARRIAGE DRIVE WEST
HENTY CL
HERON HO
MASKELYNE CL
JAGGER HO
MUSGRAVE CT
HYDE LA
Westbridge Prim Sch
CREWKERNE CT
EXFORD CT
BOLINGBROKE WLK
SELWORTHY HO
CHELWOOD CT
CLEVEDON CT
RANDALL CL
ETHELBURGA ST
ETHELBURGA TOWER
BATTERSEA CHURCH RD
30
P
Winter

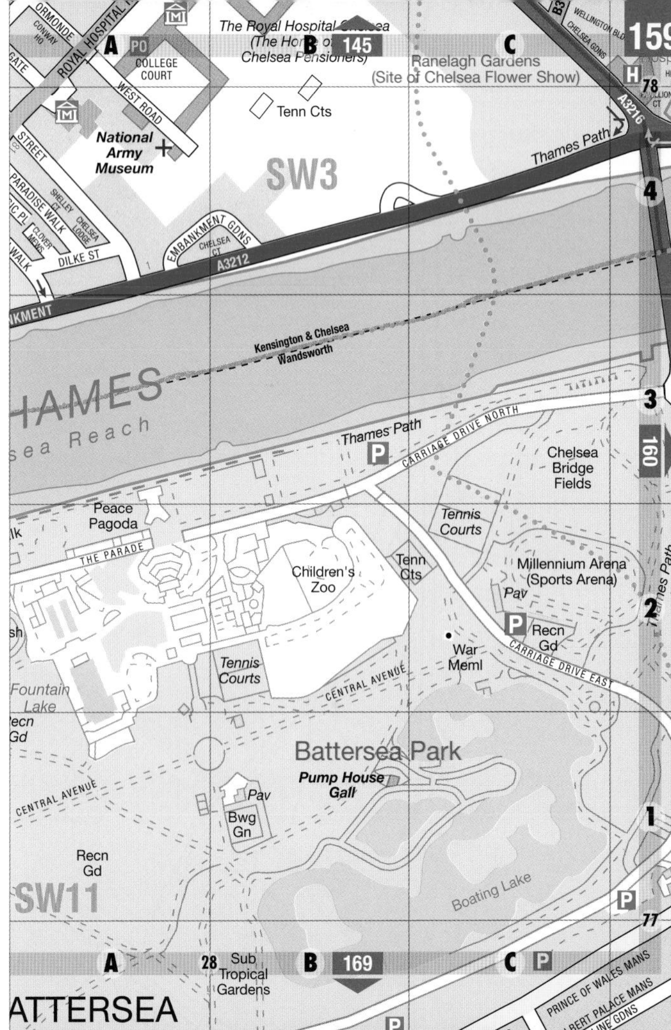

A
B
C
145
160
169
1
2
3
4
The Royal Hospital Chelsea
Chelsea Pensioners)
Ranelagh Gardens
(Site of Chelsea Flower Show)
ROYAL HOSPITAL
ORMONDE
CONWAY HO
PO
COLLEGE COURT
WEST ROAD
Tenn Cts
National Army Museum
STREET
PARADISE WALK
SHELLEY CT
CHELSEA LODGE
CLOVER MEWS
DILKE ST
EMBANKMENT GDNS
CHELSEA CT
A3212
SW3
Thames Path
A3216
WELLINGTON BLDGS
CHELSEA GDNS
HIRST CT
78
Kensington & Chelsea
Wandsworth
HAMES
sea Reach
Thames Path
CARRIAGE DRIVE NORTH
Chelsea Bridge Fields
Peace Pagoda
THE PARADE
Tennis Courts
Tenn Cts
Children's Zoo
Millennium Arena
(Sports Arena)
Pav
Recn Gd
War Meml
CARRIAGE DRIVE EAST
Tennis Courts
CENTRAL AVENUE
Fountain Lake
Recn Gd
Battersea Park
Pump House Gall
Pav
Bwg Gn
CENTRAL AVENUE
Recn Gd
SW11
Boating Lake
77
28
Sub Tropical Gardens
PRINCE OF WALES MANS
ALBERT PALACE MANS
ATTERSEA

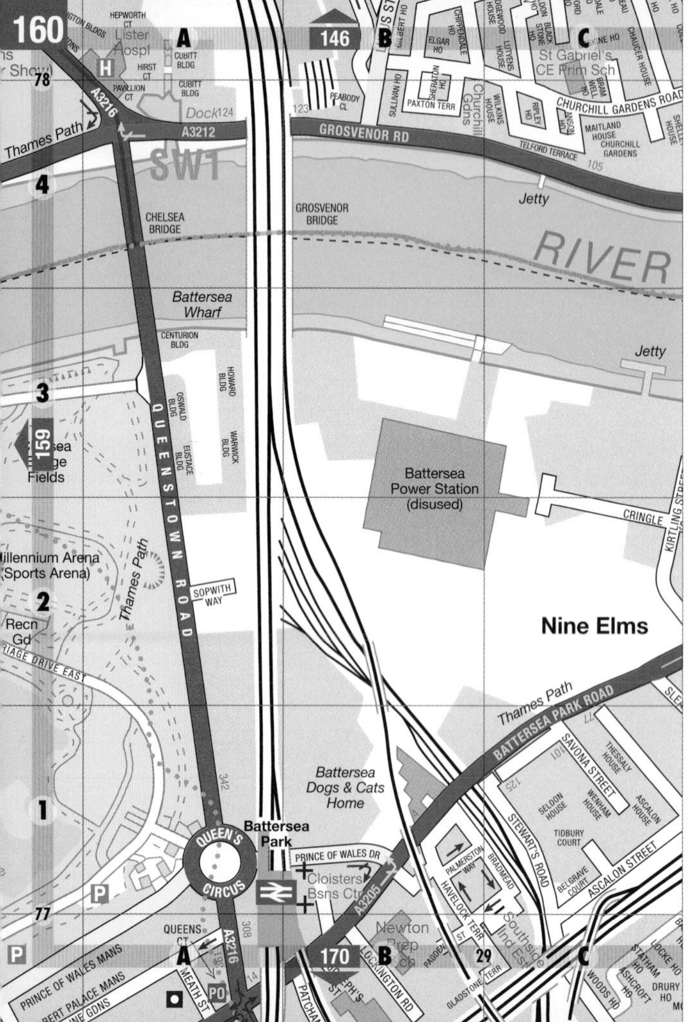
146
170
159
A
B
C
4
3
2
1
78
77
HEPWORTH CT
Lister Hospl
CUBITT BLDG
HIRST CT
PAVILLION CT
Dock
124
123
A3216
A3212
Thames Path
SW1
PEABODY CL
GILBERT HO
ELGAR HO
CHIPPENDALE HO
EDGEWOOD HOUSE
LUTYENS HOUSE
BLACK STONE HO
CHAUCER HOUSE
St Gabriel's CE Prim Sch
SULLIVAN HO
SHERATON HO
PAXTON TERR
Churchill Gdns
WILKINS HOUSE
RIPLEY HO
BRAMWELL HO
CHURCHILL GARDENS ROAD
MAITLAND HOUSE
CHURCHILL GARDENS
GROSVENOR RD
TELFORD TERRACE
105
Jetty
CHELSEA BRIDGE
GROSVENOR BRIDGE
RIVER
Battersea Wharf
CENTURION BLDG
HOWARD BLDG
OSWALD BLDG
EUSTACE BLDG
WARWICK BLDG
QUEENSTOWN ROAD
Battersea Power Station (disused)
CRINGLE
KIRTLING STREET
Fields
Millennium Arena (Sports Arena)
Thames Path
SOPWITH WAY
Recn Gd
CARRIAGE DRIVE EAST
Nine Elms
Thames Path
BATTERSEA PARK ROAD
SAVONA STREET
THESSALY HOUSE
101
125
Battersea Dogs & Cats Home
342
SELDON HOUSE
WENHAM HOUSE
ASCALON HOUSE
TIDBURY COURT
QUEEN'S CIRCUS
Battersea Park
PRINCE OF WALES DR
Cloisters Bsns Ctr
A3205
PALMERSTON WAY
BRADMEAD
STEWART'S ROAD
BELGRAVE COURT
ASCALON STREET
HAVELOCK TERR
Southside Ind Est
Newton Prep Sch
QUEENS CT
308
LOCKINGTON RD
PAGDEN ST
29
GLADSTONE TERR
STATHAM HO
LOCKE HO
ASHCROFT HO
DRURY HO
WOODS HO
PRINCE OF WALES MANS
ALBERT PALACE MANS
MEATH ST
PATCHAM
PO
P

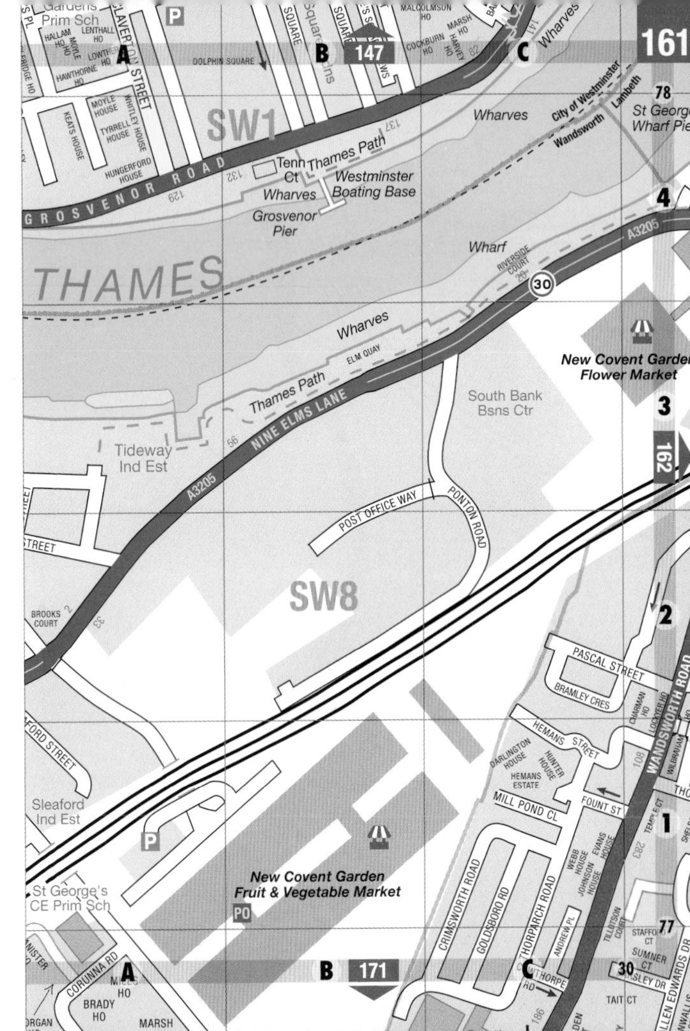
147
171
162
SW1
SW8
THAMES
GROSVENOR ROAD
Thames Path
Tenn Ct
Wharves
Westminster Boating Base
Grosvenor Pier
Wharf
St George Wharf Pier
City of Westminster
Lambeth
Wandsworth
RIVERSIDE COURT
A3205
NINE ELMS LANE
ELM QUAY
Tideway Ind Est
South Bank Bsns Ctr
New Covent Garden Flower Market
POST OFFICE WAY
PONTON ROAD
BROOKS COURT
PASCAL STREET
BRAMLEY CRES
HEMANS STREET
DARLINGTON HOUSE
HUNTER HOUSE
HEMANS ESTATE
MILL POND CL
FOUNT ST
WANDSWORTH ROAD
Sleaford Ind Est
New Covent Garden Fruit & Vegetable Market
PO
St George's CE Prim Sch
CORUNNA RD
CRIMSWORTH ROAD
GOLDSBORO RD
THORPARCH ROAD
ANDREW PL
WEBB HOUSE
JOHNSON HOUSE
EVANS HOUSE
TILLOTSON COURT
STAFFORD CT
SUMNER CT
ALLEN EDWARDS DR
TAIT CT
BRADY HO
MARSH HO
DOLPHIN SQUARE
MALCOLMSON HO
COCKBURN HO
MARSH HO
HARVEY HO
HALLAM HO
LENTHALL HO
MOYLE HO
LOWTHER HO
HAWTHORNE HO
MOYLE HOUSE
WHITLEY HOUSE
TYRRELL HOUSE
KEATS HOUSE
HUNGERFORD HOUSE
CLAVERTON STREET
Prim Sch
CHARMAN HO
LOCKYER HO
WILBRAHAM HO
TEMPLE CT
SHELDON CT

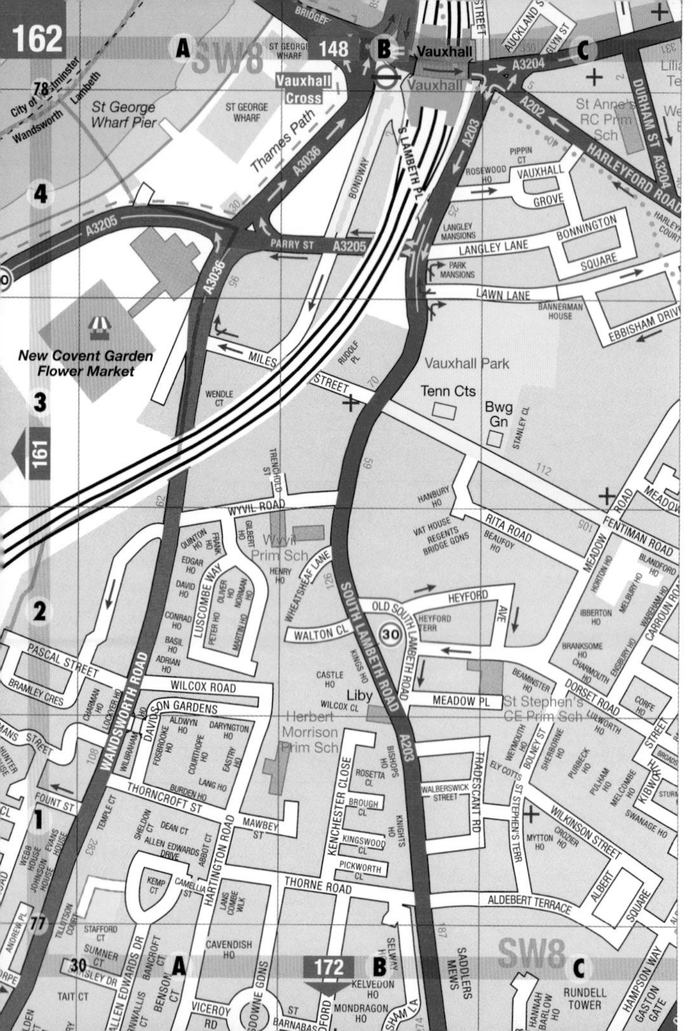
A
SW8
B
C
148
Vauxhall
Vauxhall Cross
ST GEORGE WHARF
St George Wharf Pier
City of Westminster
Lambeth
Wandsworth
78
Thames Path
A3036
A3204
A202
A203
HARLEYFORD ROAD
DURHAM ST
AUCKLAND ST
GLYN ST
St Anne's RC Prim Sch
S LAMBETH PL
BONDWAY
PIPPIN CT
ROSEWOOD HO
VAUXHALL GROVE
BONNINGTON SQUARE
LANGLEY MANSIONS
LANGLEY LANE
PARK MANSIONS
LAWN LANE
BANNERMAN HOUSE
EBBISHAM DRIVE
HARLEYFORD COURT
A3205
PARRY ST
4
New Covent Garden Flower Market
MILES STREET
RUDOLF PL
Vauxhall Park
Tenn Cts
Bwg Gn
STANLEY CL
WENDLE CT
3
161
TRENCHOLD ST
WYVIL ROAD
HANBURY HO
VAT HOUSE
REGENTS BRIDGE GDNS
RITA ROAD
BEAUFOY HO
FENTIMAN ROAD
MEADOW ROAD
QUINTON HO
FRANK HO
GILBERT HO
Wyvil Prim Sch
EDGAR HO
DAVID HO
LUSCOMBE WAY
OLIVER HO
NORMAN HO
HENRY HO
WHEATSHEAF LANE
SOUTH LAMBETH ROAD
OLD SOUTH LAMBETH ROAD
HEYFORD AVE
HEYFORD TERR
HORTON HO
BLANDFORD HO
MELBURY HO
WAREHAM HO
CARROUN ROAD
IBBERTON HO
2
CONRAD HO
PETER HO
MARTIN HO
BASIL HO
ADRIAN HO
WALTON CL
30
KINGS HO
CASTLE HO
BRANKSOME HO
CHARMOUTH HO
EISBURY HO
BEAMINSTER HO
DORSET ROAD
CORFE HO
PASCAL STREET
BRAMLEY CRES
WILCOX ROAD
WANDSWORTH ROAD
CHARMAN HO
LOCKYER HO
DAVIDSON GARDENS
Liby
WILCOX CL
MEADOW PL
St Stephen's CE Prim Sch
LULWORTH HO
ALDWYN HO
DARYNGTON HO
Herbert Morrison Prim Sch
WILBRAHAM HO
FOSBROOKE HO
COURTHOPE HO
EASTRY HO
BISHOPS HO
ROSETTA CL
WEYMOUTH HO
BOLNEY ST
SHERBORNE HO
PURBECK HO
KENCHESTER CLOSE
ELY COTTS
LANG HO
BURDEN HO
THORNCROFT ST
FOUNT ST
1
TEMPLE CT
SHELDON CT
DEAN CT
ALLEN EDWARDS DRIVE
ABBOT CT
HARTINGTON ROAD
MAWBEY ST
BROUGH CL
WALBERSWICK STREET
TRADESCANT RD
ST STEPHEN'S TERR
PULHAM HO
MELCOMBE HO
SWANAGE HO
KNIGHTS HO
KINGSWOOD CL
PICKWORTH CL
MYTTON HO
CROZIER HO
WILKINSON STREET
WEBB HOUSE
EVANS HOUSE
JOHNSON HOUSE
KEMP CT
CAMELLIA ST
LANSCOMBE WLK
THORNE ROAD
ALDEBERT TERRACE
ALBERT SQUARE
77
TILLOTSON COURT
ANDREW PL
STAFFORD CT
SUMNER CT
ALLEN EDWARDS DR
BANCROFT CT
CAVENDISH HO
SELWAY HO
SADDLERS MEWS
SW8
C
HAMPSON WAY
30
A
172
B
TAIT CT
BENSON CT
VICEROY RD
KELVEDON HO
MONDRAGON HO
ST BARNABAS
HANNAH BARLOW HO
RUNDELL TOWER
GASTON GATE

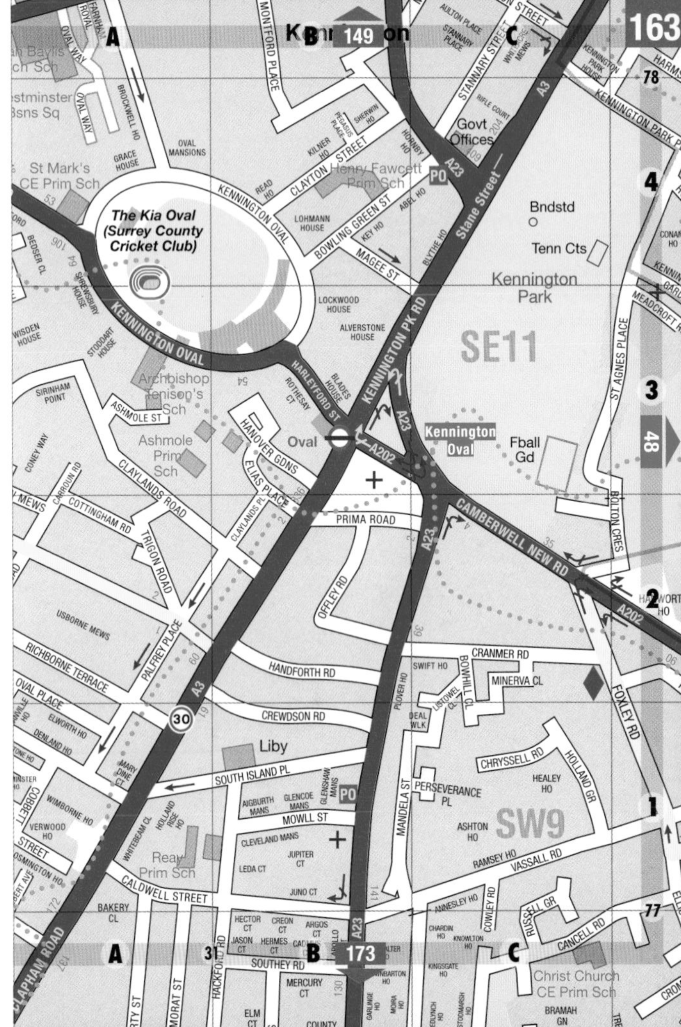

149
173
48
The Kia Oval
(Surrey County
Cricket Club)
KENNINGTON OVAL
Kennington
Park
SE11
SW9
Kennington
Oval
Oval
KENNINGTON PK RD
CAMBERWELL NEW RD
CLAPHAM ROAD
Stane Street
Govt
Offices
Bndstd
Tenn Cts
Fball
Gd
Henry Fawcett
Prim Sch
St Mark's
CE Prim Sch
Archbishop
Tenison's
Sch
Ashmole
Prim
Sch
Liby
Christ Church
CE Prim Sch
CLAYLANDS ROAD
COTTINGHAM RD
TRIGON ROAD
HANDFORTH RD
CREWDSON RD
SOUTH ISLAND PL
CALDWELL STREET
PRIMA ROAD
OFFLEY RD
CRANMER RD
FOXLEY RD
VASSALL RD
CHRYSSELL RD
HOLLAND GR
ST AGNES PLACE
BOLTON CRES
HARLEYFORD ST
BOWLING GREEN ST
CLAYTON STREET
MAGEE ST
STANNARY STREET
KENNINGTON PARK PLA
RICHBORNE TERRACE
OVAL PLACE
PALFREY PLACE
USBORNE MEWS
ASHMOLE ST
MOWLL ST
MANDELA ST
SOUTHEY RD
CANCELL RD

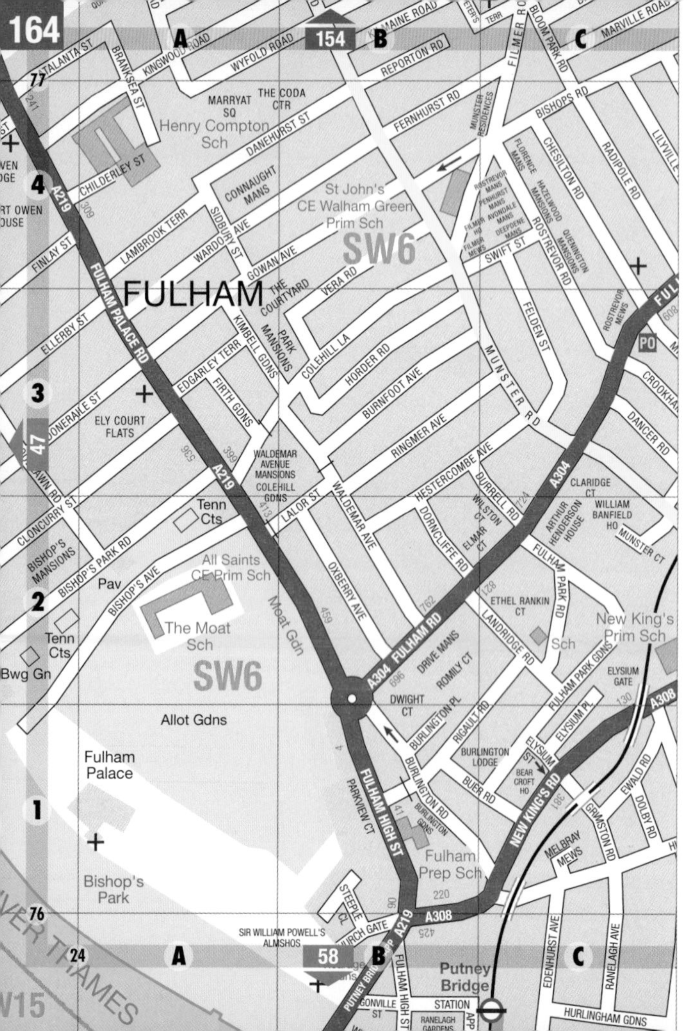

A
154
B
C
KINGWOOD ROAD
WYFOLD ROAD
KILMAINE ROAD
REPORTON RD
MARVILLE ROAD
BLOOM PARK RD
FILMER RD
ATALANTA ST
BRANKSEA ST
MARRYAT SQ
THE CODA CTR
Henry Compton Sch
DANEHURST ST
FERNHURST RD
MUNSTER RESIDENCES
BISHOPS RD
CHILDERLEY ST
CONNAUGHT MANS
St John's CE Walham Green Prim Sch
SW6
FLORENCE MANS
CHESILTON RD
RADIPOLE RD
LILYVILLE
ROSTREVOR MANS
PENHURST MANS
AVONDALE MANS
DEEPDENE MANS
HAZELWOOD MANSIONS
QUENINGTON MANSIONS
ROSTREVOR RD
FILMER HO
FILMER MEWS
SWIFT ST
LAMBROOK TERR
SIDBURY ST
WARDO AVE
GOWAN AVE
FINLAY ST
FULHAM
FULHAM PALACE RD
A219
THE COURTYARD
VERA RD
ELLERBY ST
KIMBELL GDNS
PARK MANSIONS
COLEHILL LA
HORDER RD
FELDEN ST
ROSTREVOR MEWS
PO
EDGARLEY TERR
FIRTH GDNS
BURNFOOT AVE
MUNSTER RD
CROOKHAM
DANCER RD
BONERALE ST
ELY COURT FLATS
47
RINGMER AVE
WALDEMAR AVENUE MANSIONS
COLEHILL GDNS
HESTERCOMBE AVE
DURRELL RD
A304
CLARIDGE CT
WILLIAM BANFIELD HO
ARTHUR HENDERSON HOUSE
CLONCURRY ST
Tenn Cts
LALOR ST
WALDEMAR AVE
DORNCLIFFE RD
WILSTON CT
ELMAR CT
MUNSTER CT
BISHOP'S MANSIONS
BISHOP'S PARK RD
All Saints CE Prim Sch
FULHAM PARK RD
Pav
BISHOP'S AVE
OXBERRY AVE
ETHEL RANKIN CT
Moat Gdn
The Moat Sch
LANDRIDGE RD
New King's Prim Sch
Sch
Bwg Gn
A304 FULHAM RD
DRIVE MANS
ROMILY CT
FULHAM PARK GDNS
ELYSIUM GATE
A308
DWIGHT CT
BURLINGTON PL
RIGAULT RD
ELYSIUM PL
Allot Gdns
BURLINGTON LODGE
ELYSIUM ST
Fulham Palace
BEAR CROFT HO
BUER RD
PARKVIEW CT
FULHAM HIGH ST
BURLINGTON RD
BURLINGTON GDNS
NEW KING'S RD
EWALD RD
GRIMSTON RD
DOLBY RD
Bishop's Park
MELBRAY MEWS
Fulham Prep Sch
STEEPLE CL
CHURCH GATE
RIVER THAMES
SIR WILLIAM POWELL'S ALMSHOS
58
EDENHURST AVE
RANELAGH AVE
Putney Bridge
PUTNEY BRIDGE APP
GONVILLE ST
STATION APP
RANELAGH GARDENS
HURLINGHAM GDNS
SW15

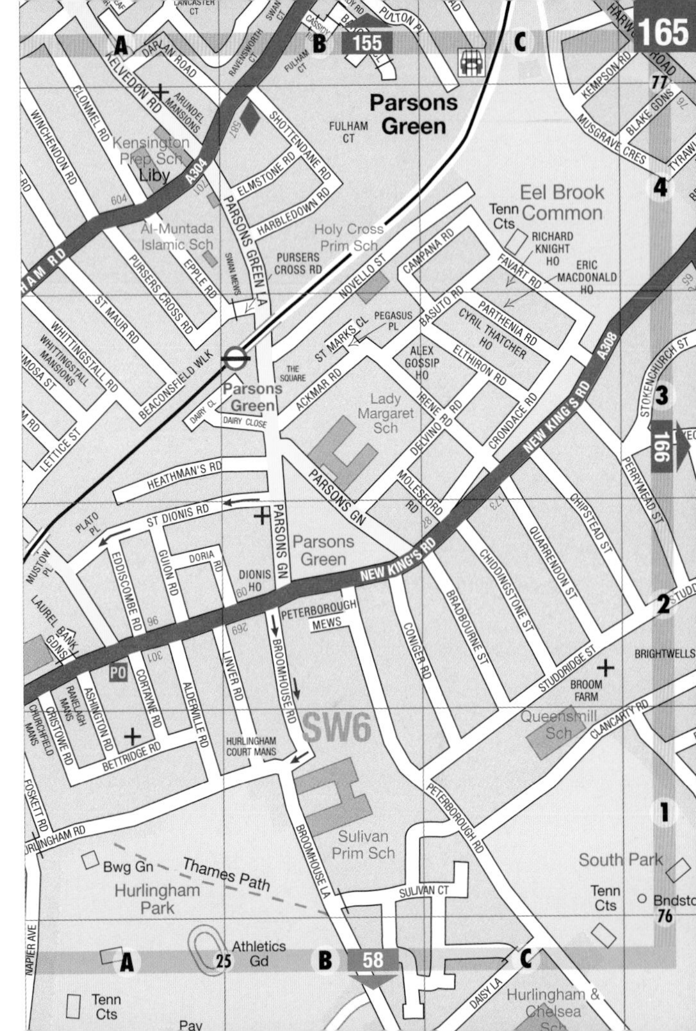

Parsons Green
FULHAM CT
Kensington Prep Sch
Liby
Al-Muntada Islamic Sch
Holy Cross Prim Sch
Eel Brook Common
Tenn Cts
RICHARD KNIGHT HO
ERIC MACDONALD HO
PURSERS CROSS RD
SHOTTENDANE RD
ELMSTONE RD
HARBLEDOWN RD
PARSONS GREEN LA
KELVEDON RD
DARLAN ROAD
ARUNDEL MANSIONS
CLONMEL RD
WINCHENDON RD
A304
EPPLE RD
SWAN MEWS
ST MAUR RD
WHITTINGSTALL RD
WHITTINGSTALL MANSIONS
BEACONSFIELD WLK
LETTICE ST
NOVELLO ST
CAMPANA RD
FAVART RD
PARTHENIA RD
BASUTO RD
CYRIL THATCHER HO
PEGASUS PL
ST MARKS CL
ALEX GOSSIP HO
ELTHIRON RD
THE SQUARE
ACKMAR RD
Parsons Green
DAIRY CL
DAIRY CLOSE
Lady Margaret Sch
IRENE RD
DELVINO RD
CRONDACE RD
A308
NEW KING'S RD
STOKENCHURCH ST
HEATHMAN'S RD
PARSONS GN
MOLESFORD RD
CHIPSTEAD ST
PERRYMEAD ST
ST DIONIS RD
PLATO PL
MUSTOW PL
EDDISCOMBE RD
GUION RD
DORIA RD
DIONIS HO
Parsons Green
QUARRENDON ST
CHIDDINGSTONE ST
BRADBOURNE ST
CONIGER RD
LAUREL BANK GDNS
PETERBOROUGH MEWS
BROOMHOUSE RD
LINVER RD
ALDERVILLE RD
CORTAYNE RD
PO
ASHINGTON RD
RANELAGH MANS
CRISTOWE RD
CHURCHFIELD MANS
BETTRIDGE RD
HURLINGHAM COURT MANS
SW6
STUDDRIDGE ST
BRIGHTWELLS
BROOM FARM
Queensmill Sch
CLANCARTY RD
FOSKETT RD
HURLINGHAM RD
PETERBOROUGH RD
Sulivan Prim Sch
BROOMHOUSE LA
Bwg Gn
Thames Path
Hurlingham Park
SULIVAN CT
South Park
Tenn Cts
Bndstd
NAPIER AVE
Athletics Gd
DAISY LA
Hurlingham & Chelsea Sch
Tenn Cts
Pav
KEMPSON RD
BLAKE GDNS
MUSGRAVE CRES
HARWOOD ROAD
TYRAWLEY
155
166
58
A
B
C
1
2
3
4

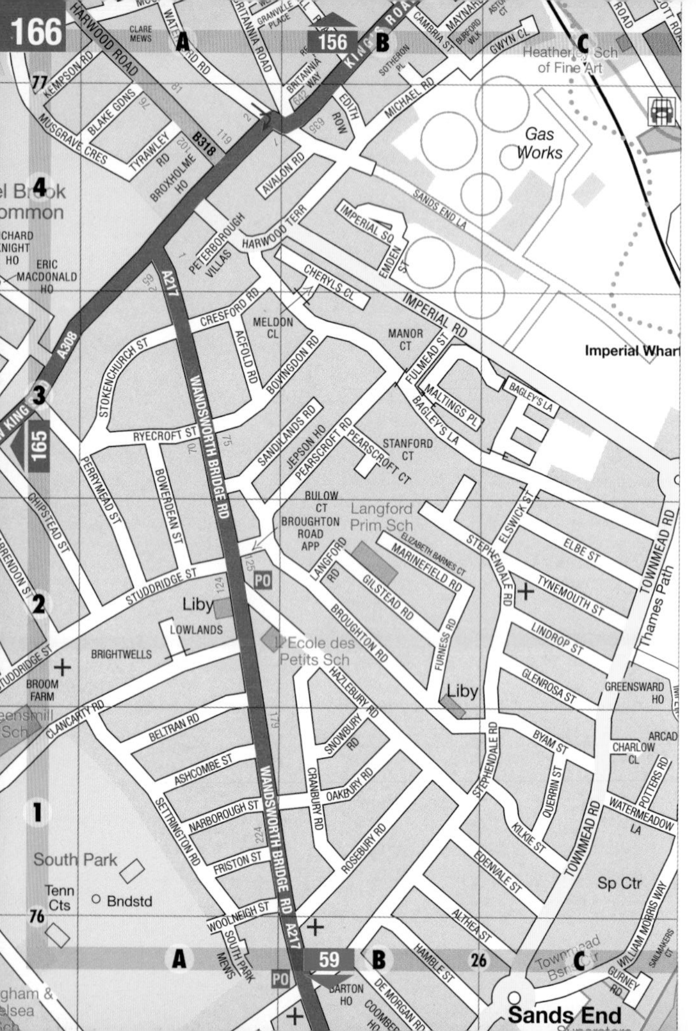

HARWOOD ROAD
CLARE MEWS
KEMPSON RD
BLAKE GDNS
MUSGRAVE CRES
TYRAWLEY RD
BROXHOLME HO
B318
BRITANNIA ROAD
GRANVILLE PLACE
BRITANNIA WAY
156
KINGS ROAD
EDITH ROW
AVALON RD
CAMBRIA ST
BURFORD WLK
GWYN CL
SOTHERON PL
MICHAEL RD
Heatherley Sch of Fine Art
Gas Works
SANDS END LA
IMPERIAL SQ
EMDEN ST
HARWOOD TERR
PETERBOROUGH VILLAS
CHERYLS CL
IMPERIAL RD
MANOR CT
Imperial Wharf
A217
A308
CRESFORD RD
MELDON CL
ACFOLD RD
BOVINGDON RD
STOKENCHURCH ST
RYECROFT ST
WANDSWORTH BRIDGE RD
FULMEAD ST
MALTINGS PL
BAGLEY'S LA
SANDILANDS RD
JEPSON HO
PEARSCROFT RD
PEARSCROFT CT
STANFORD CT
BULOW CT
BROUGHTON ROAD APP
Langford Prim Sch
ELIZABETH BARNES CT
MARINEFIELD RD
STEPHENDALE RD
ELSWICK ST
ELBE ST
TOWNMEAD RD
TYNEMOUTH ST
Thames Path
LINDROP ST
GLENROSA ST
GREENSWARD HO
165
CHIPSTEAD ST
PERRYMEAD ST
BOWERDEAN ST
STUDDRIDGE ST
Liby
LOWLANDS
BRIGHTWELLS
PO
L'Ecole des Petits Sch
LANGFORD RD
GILSTEAD RD
BROUGHTON RD
FURNESS RD
BROOM FARM
CLANCARTY RD
BELTRAN RD
ASHCOMBE ST
HAZLEBURY RD
SNOWBURY RD
OAKBURY RD
CRANBURY RD
BYAM ST
CHARLOW CL
POTTERS RD
QUERRIN ST
KILKIE ST
WATERMEADOW LA
SETTRINGTON RD
NARBOROUGH ST
FRISTON ST
ROSEBURY RD
EDENVALE ST
South Park
Tenn Cts
Bndstd
WOOLNEIGH ST
SOUTH PARK MEWS
ALTHEA ST
HAMBLE ST
Sp Ctr
WILLIAM MORRIS WAY
SAILMAKERS CT
Townmead Bsns Ctr
GURNEY RD
59
BARTON HO
DE MORGAN RD
Sands End

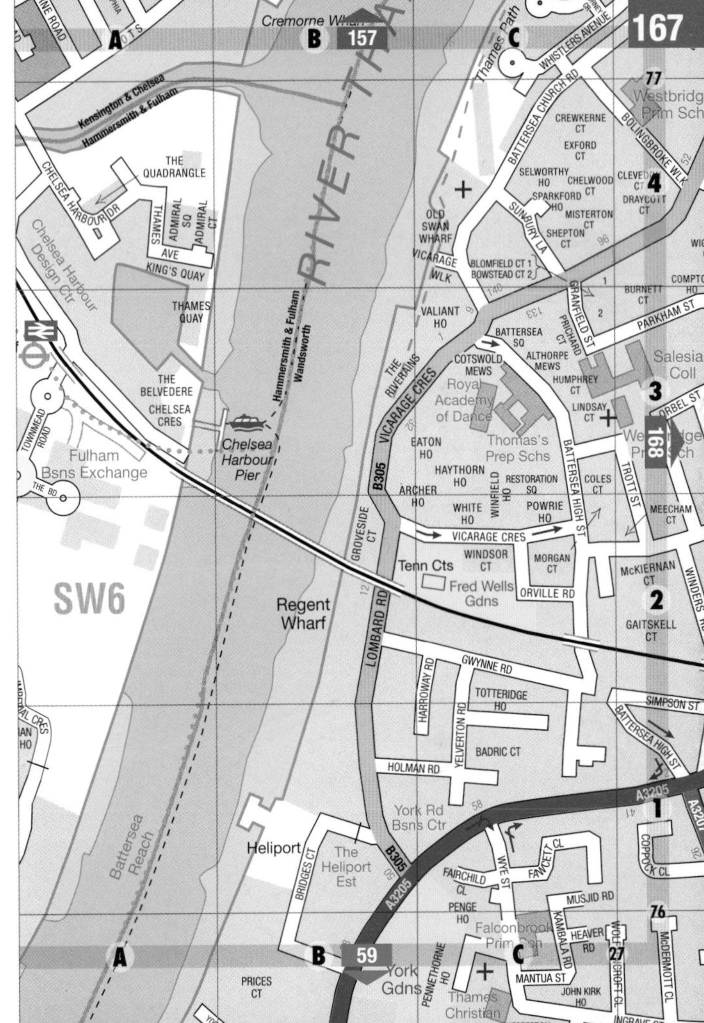
Cremorne Wharf
157
Thames Path
WHISTLERS AVENUE
77
Westbridge Prim Sch
Kensington & Chelsea
Hammersmith & Fulham
BATTERSEA CHURCH RD
CREWKERNE CT
EXFORD CT
BOLINGBROKE WLK
THE QUADRANGLE
RIVER THAMES
SELWORTHY HO
CHELWOOD CT
SPARKFORD HO
MISTERTON CT
SHEPTON CT
DRAYCOTT CT
SUNBURY LA
CHELSEA HARBOUR DR
THAMES AVE
ADMIRAL SQ
ADMIRAL CT
OLD SWAN WHARF
Chelsea Harbour Design Ctr
KING'S QUAY
VICARAGE WLK
BLOMFIELD CT 1
BOWSTEAD CT 2
THAMES QUAY
VALIANT HO
BURNETT CT
COMPTON HO
PARKHAM ST
GRANFIELD ST
PRICHARD CT
BATTERSEA SQ
Hammersmith & Fulham
Wandsworth
THE RIVERAINS
VICARAGE CRES
COTSWOLD MEWS
ALTHORPE MEWS
Salesian Coll
Royal Academy of Dance
HUMPHREY CT
THE BELVEDERE
CHELSEA CRES
LINDSAY CT
ORBEL ST
168
Chelsea Harbour Pier
Thomas's Prep Schs
TOWNMEAD ROAD
Fulham Bsns Exchange
EATON HO
HAYTHORN HO
BATTERSEA HIGH ST
COLES CT
TROTT ST
THE BD
B305
ARCHER HO
WINFIELD HO
RESTORATION SQ
WHITE HO
POWRIE HO
MEECHAM CT
GROVESIDE CT
VICARAGE CRES
WINDSOR CT
MORGAN CT
Tenn Cts
Fred Wells Gdns
McKIERNAN CT
WINDERS RD
SW6
Regent Wharf
ORVILLE RD
GAITSKELL CT
LOMBARD RD
GWYNNE RD
HARROWAY RD
TOTTERIDGE HO
SIMPSON ST
YELVERTON RD
BATTERSEA HIGH ST
BADRIC CT
HOLMAN RD
A3205
York Rd Bsns Ctr
Heliport
BRIDGES CT
The Heliport Est
B305
WYE ST
FAWCETT CL
COPPOCK CL
FAIRCHILD CL
Battersea Reach
A3205
PENGE HO
MUSJID RD
76
Falconbrook Prim Sch
KAMBALA RD
HEAVER RD
WOLFTENCROFT CL
McDERMOTT CL
59
PENNETHORNE HO
MANTUA ST
PRICES CT
York Gdns
Thames Christian Coll
JOHN KIRK HO
INGRAVE ST

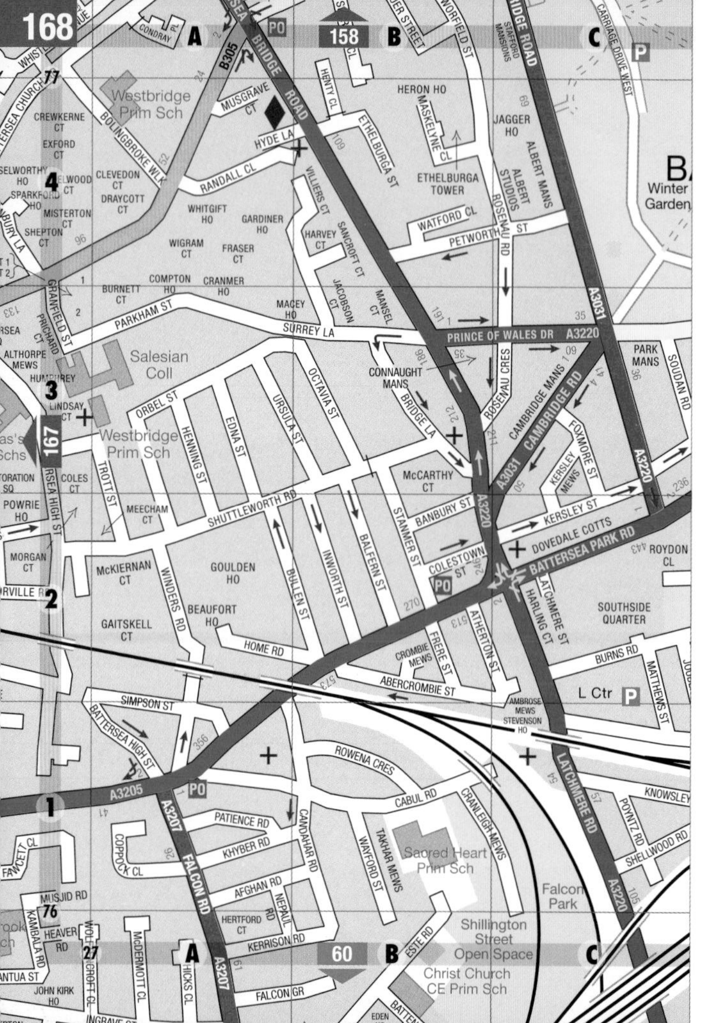

A
158
B
C
4
3
2
1
167
A
60
B
C
76
77
27
Westbridge Prim Sch
Salesian Coll
Westbridge Prim Sch
Sacred Heart Prim Sch
Winter Garden
Falcon Park
Shillington Street Open Space
Christ Church CE Prim Sch
L Ctr
SOUTHSIDE QUARTER
BATTERSEA BRIDGE ROAD
B305
MUSGRAVE CT
HYDE LA
RANDALL CL
BOLINGBROKE WLK
HENTY CL
ETHELBURGA ST
HERON HO
MASKELYNE CL
ETHELBURGA TOWER
JAGGER HO
ALBERT MANS
ALBERT STUDIOS
WORFIELD ST
STAFFORD MANSIONS
CARRIAGE DRIVE WEST
CONDRAY PL
CREWKERNE CT
EXFORD CT
SELWORTHY HO
SPARKFORD HO
CLEVEDON CT
DRAYCOTT CT
MISTERTON CT
SHEPTON CT
WHITGIFT HO
GARDINER HO
WIGRAM CT
FRASER CT
VILLIERS CT
HARVEY CT
SANCROFT CT
JACOBSON CT
MANSEL CT
WATFORD CL
PETWORTH ST
ROSENAU RD
BURNETT CT
COMPTON HO
CRANMER HO
MACEY HO
PARKHAM ST
SURREY LA
GRANFIELD ST
PRICHARD CT
ALTHORPE MEWS
HUMPHREY
LINDSAY CT
PRINCE OF WALES DR
A3220
A3031
PARK MANS
SOUDAN RD
CONNAUGHT MANS
BRIDGE LA
ROSENAU CRES
CAMBRIDGE MANS
CAMBRIDGE RD
FOXMORE ST
KERSLEY MEWS
KERSLEY ST
DOVEDALE COTTS
BATTERSEA PARK RD
ROYDON CL
ORBEL ST
HENNING ST
EDNA ST
URSULA ST
OCTAVIA ST
McCARTHY CT
BANBURY ST
STANMER ST
COLESTOWN ST
TROTT ST
COLES CT
POWRIE HO
MEECHAM CT
SHUTTLEWORTH RD
MORGAN CT
McKIERNAN CT
WINDERS RD
GOULDEN HO
BULLEN ST
INWORTH ST
BALFERN ST
BEAUFORT HO
GAITSKELL CT
HOME RD
CROMBIE MEWS
FRERE ST
ATHERTON ST
HARLING CT
LATCHMERE ST
BURNS RD
MATTHEWS ST
ABERCROMBIE ST
AMBROSE MEWS
STEVENSON HO
SIMPSON ST
BATTERSEA HIGH ST
ROWENA CRES
CABUL RD
CRANLEIGH MEWS
LATCHMERE RD
KNOWSLEY
POYNTZ RD
SHELLWOOD RD
A3205
A3207
FALCON RD
PATIENCE RD
KHYBER RD
COPPOCK CL
CANDAHAR RD
WAYFORD ST
TAKHAR MEWS
AFGHAN RD
NEPAUL RD
HERTFORD CT
KERRISON RD
FAWCETT CL
MUSJID RD
KAMBALA RD
HEAVER RD
WOLFTENCROFT CL
McDERMOTT CL
HICKS CL
ESTE RD
FALCON GR
JOHN KIRK HO
INGRAVE ST
EDEN HO
BATTEN
PO
P

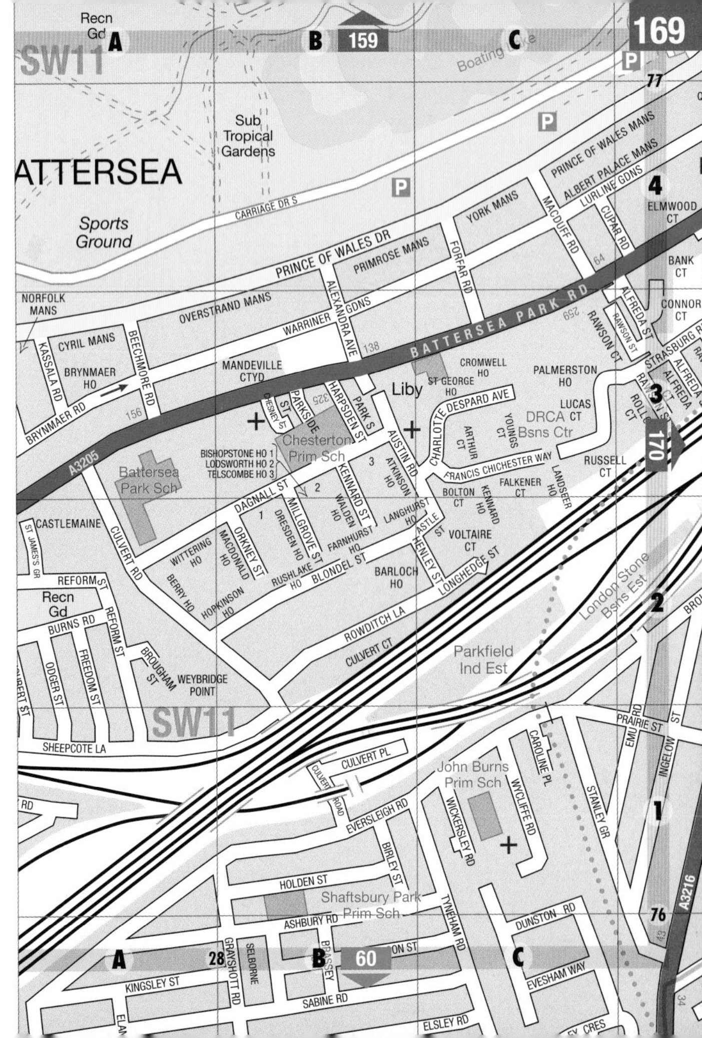

159
170
60
A
B
C
SW11
BATTERSEA
Recn Gd
Sub Tropical Gardens
Boating Lake
Sports Ground
CARRIAGE DR S
PRINCE OF WALES DR
PRINCE OF WALES MANS
ALBERT PALACE MANS
LURLINE GDNS
YORK MANS
MACDUFF RD
CUPAR RD
ELMWOOD CT
PRIMROSE MANS
FORFAR RD
BANK CT
CONNOR CT
ALEXANDRA AVE
OVERSTRAND MANS
WARRINER GDNS
BATTERSEA PARK RD
RAWSON CT
RAWSON ST
ALFREDA ST
STRASBURG RD
NORFOLK MANS
CYRIL MANS
KASSALA RD
BEECHMORE RD
BRYNMAER HO
BRYNMAER RD
MANDEVILLE CTYD
CROMWELL HO
PALMERSTON HO
ST GEORGE HO
Liby
CHESNEY ST
PARKSIDE ST
HARPSDEN ST
PARK S
CHARLOTTE DESPARD AVE
LUCAS CT
DRCA Bsns Ctr
ARTHUR CT
YOUNGS CT
ROLLO CT
A3205
Chesterton Prim Sch
AUSTIN RD
ATKINSON HO
FRANCIS CHICHESTER WAY
RUSSELL CT
BISHOPSTONE HO 1
LODSWORTH HO 2
TELSCOMBE HO 3
Battersea Park Sch
KENNARD ST
LANDSEER HO
FALKENER CT
BOLTON CT
KENNARD HO
DAGNALL ST
DRESDEN HO
MILLGROVE ST
WALDEN HO
LANGHURST HO
ASTLE ST
VOLTAIRE CT
CASTLEMAINE
ST JAMES'S GR
CULVERT RD
WITTERING HO
MACDONALD HO
ORKNEY ST
FARNHURST HO
HENLEY ST
LONGHEDGE ST
London Stone Bsns Est
REFORM ST
BERRY HO
HOPKINSON HO
RUSHLAKE HO
BLONDEL ST
BARLOCH HO
BURNS RD
ROWDITCH LA
CULVERT CT
Parkfield Ind Est
ODGER ST
FREEDOM ST
BROUGHAM ST
WEYBRIDGE POINT
PRAIRIE ST
EMU RD
INGELOW ST
SHEEPCOTE LA
CULVERT PL
CULVERT ROAD
CAROLINE PL
John Burns Prim Sch
WYCLIFFE RD
STANLEY GR
EVERSLEIGH RD
WICKERSLEY RD
BIRLEY ST
HOLDEN ST
Shaftsbury Park Prim Sch
TYNEHAM RD
ASHBURY RD
DUNSTON RD
A3216
GRAYSHOTT RD
SELBORNE
BRASSEY
EVESHAM WAY
KINGSLEY ST
SABINE RD
ELSLEY RD

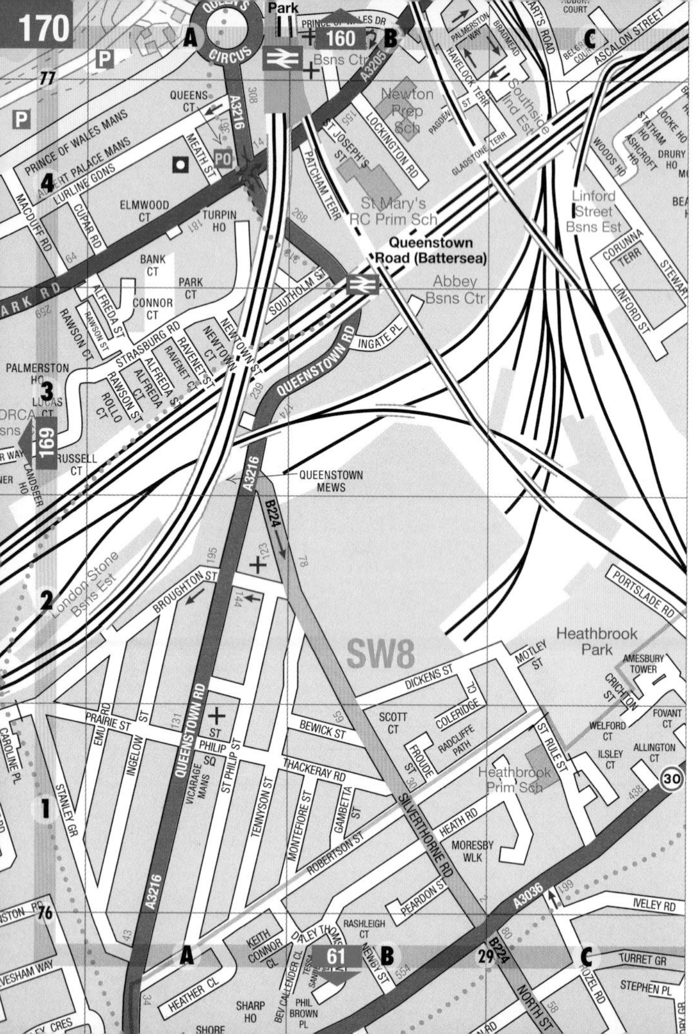

Queenstown Road (Battersea)
SW8
Heathbrook Park
Newton Prep Sch
St Mary's RC Prim Sch
Abbey Bsns Ctr
Linford Street Bsns Est
Southside Ind Est
London Stone Bsns Est
Heathbrook Prim Sch
QUEENSTOWN RD
SILVERTHORNE RD
QUEENS CIRCUS
PRINCE OF WALES DR
ASCALON STREET
PRINCE OF WALES MANS
ALBERT PALACE MANS
LURLINE GDNS
MACDUFF RD
CUPAR RD
ELMWOOD CT
TURPIN HO
BANK CT
PARK CT
CONNOR CT
ALFREDA ST
RAWSON ST
STRASBURG RD
RAVENET ST
NEWTOWN ST
SOUTHOLM ST
INGATE PL
PALMERSTON HO
LUCAS CT
RUSSELL CT
QUEENSTOWN MEWS
BROUGHTON ST
DICKENS ST
MOTLEY ST
COLERIDGE CT
SCOTT CT
BEWICK ST
PRAIRIE ST
EMU RD
INGELOW RD
ST PHILIP SQ
ST PHILIP ST
THACKERAY RD
TENNYSON ST
MONTEFIORE ST
GAMBETTA ST
ROBERTSON ST
HEATH RD
MORESBY WLK
PEARDON ST
FROUDE ST
RADCLIFFE PATH
ST RULE ST
CRICHTON ST
AMESBURY TOWER
WELFORD CT
ILSLEY CT
ALLINGTON CT
FOVANT CT
PORTSLADE RD
CORUNNA TERR
LINFORD ST
WOODS HO
STATHAM HO
ASHCROFT HO
LOCKE HO
DRURY HO
LOCKINGTON RD
ST JOSEPH'S ST
PATCHAM TERR
HAVELOCK TERR
GLADSTONE TERR
PAGDEN ST
PALMERSTON WAY
BRADMEAD
STANLEY GR
CAROLINE PL
VICARAGE MANS
IVELEY RD
TURRET GR
STEPHEN PL
ROZEL RD
NORTH ST
RASHLEIGH CT
NEWBY ST
KEITH CONNOR CL
BEV CALLENDER CL
PHIL BROWN PL
SHARP HO
HEATHER CL
EVESHAM WAY
A3216
A3205
A3036
B224
160
161
169
61

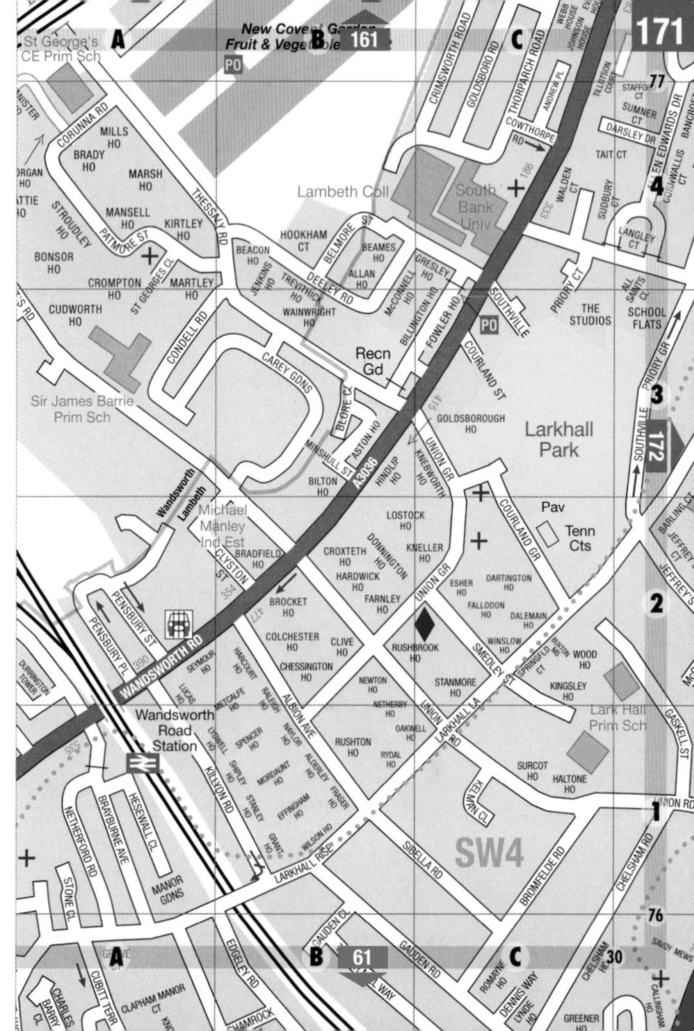

St George's CE Prim Sch
New Covent Garden Fruit & Vegetable
161
PO
CRIMSWORTH ROAD
GOLDSBORO RD
THORPARCH ROAD
ANDREW PL
WEBB HOUSE
JOHNSON HOUSE
TILLOTSON COURT
STAFFORD CT
77
SUMNER CT
DARSLEY DR
ALLEN EDWARDS DR
BANCROFT CT
CORUNNA RD
MILLS HO
BRADY HO
MARSH HO
COWTHORPE RD
TAIT CT
CORNWALLIS CT
186
Lambeth Coll
South Bank Univ
WALDEN CT
SUDBURY CT
333
MANSELL HO
KIRTLEY HO
THESSALY RD
STROUDLEY HO
PATMORE ST
HOOKHAM CT
BELMORE ST
BEAMES HO
BEACON HO
LANGLEY CT
BONSOR HO
JENKINS HO
TREVITHICK HO
DEELEY RD
ALLAN HO
GRESLEY HO
CROMPTON HO
MARTLEY HO
ST GEORGES CL
McCONNELL HO
BILLINGTON HO
FOWLER HO
SOUTHVILLE
PRIORY CT
ALL SAINTS CL
CUDWORTH HO
WAINWRIGHT HO
THE STUDIOS
SCHOOL FLATS
CONDELL RD
PO
CAREY GDNS
Recn Gd
COURLAND ST
PRIORY GR
Sir James Barrie Prim Sch
BLORE CL
415
GOLDSBOROUGH HO
3
Larkhall Park
MINSHULL ST
ASTON HO
UNION GR
KNEBWORTH HO
HINDLIP HO
SOUTHVILLE
172
BILTON HO
A3036
Wandsworth
Lambeth
Michael Manley Ind Est
LOSTOCK HO
COURLAND GR
Pav
Tenn Cts
BARLING CT
JEFFREY'S CT
JEFFREY'S RD
BRADFIELD HO
CROXTETH HO
DONNINGTON HO
KNELLER HO
CLYSTON ST
HARDWICK HO
UNION GR
ESHER HO
DARTINGTON HO
354
BROCKET HO
FARNLEY HO
FALLODON HO
DALEMAIN HO
2
PENSBURY PL
PENSBURY ST
477
COLCHESTER HO
CLIVE HO
RUSHBROOK HO
WINSLOW HO
BUXTON MS
SPRINGFLD CT
WOOD HO
SEYMOUR HO
HARCOURT HO
CHESSINGTON HO
SMEDLEY ST
KINGSLEY HO
390
WANDSWORTH RD
NEWTON HO
STANMORE HO
McCALL
DURRINGTON TOWER
LUCAS HO
METCALFE HO
RALEIGH HO
ALBION AVE
NETHERBY HO
UNION RD
LARKHALL LA
Lark Hall Prim Sch
GASKELL ST
Wandsworth Road Station
LYDWELL HO
SPENCER HO
NAYLOR HO
OAKWELL HO
335
RUSHTON HO
RYDAL HO
SHIPLEY HO
MORDAUNT HO
ALDERLEY HO
SURCOT HO
HALTONE HO
KILLYON RD
BRAYBURNE AVE
HESEWALL CL
STANLEY HO
EFFINGHAM HO
FRASER HO
KELMAN CL
1
UNION RD
NETHERFORD RD
GRANT HO
WILSON HO
SIBELLA RD
SW4
CHELSHAM RD
LARKHALL RISE
BROMFELDE RD
STONE CL
MANOR GDNS
76
GAUDEN CL
SAVOY MEWS
384
EDGELEY RD
GAUDEN RD
CHELSHAM HO
30
61
ROMAYNE HO
DENNIS WAY
CUBITT TERR
CHARLES BARRY CL
CLAPHAM MANOR CT
SHAMROCK
LYNDE HO
GREENER HO
CALLINGHAM HO
A
B
C
4

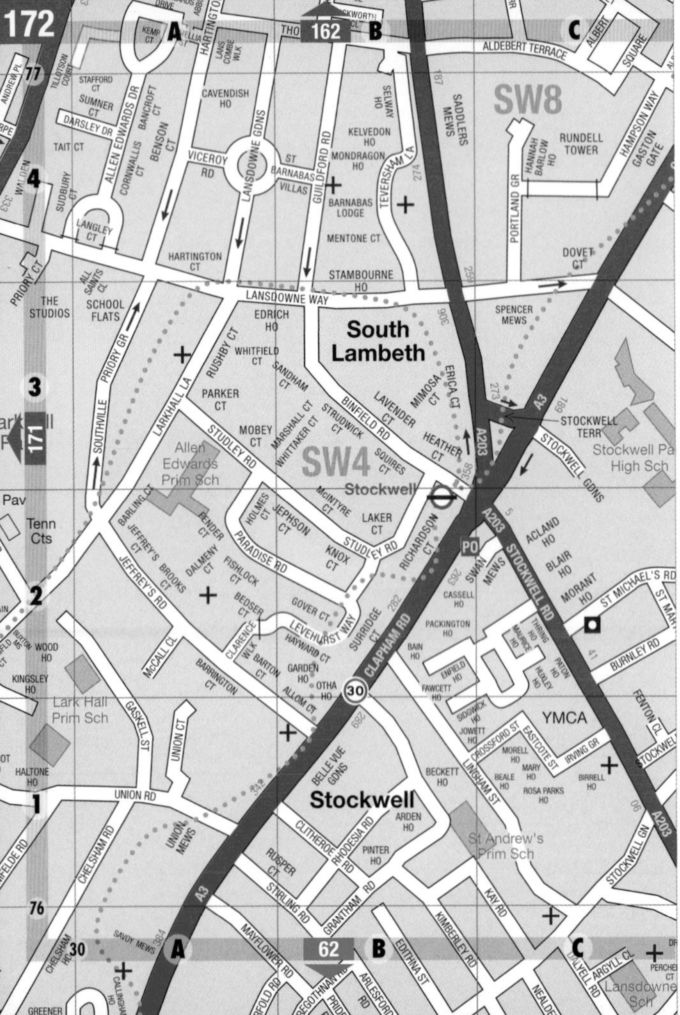

162
A
B
C
SW8
SW4
South Lambeth
Stockwell
ALDEBERT TERRACE
LANSDOWNE WAY
LANSDOWNE GDNS
GUILDFORD RD
VICEROY RD
ST BARNABAS VILLAS
BARNABAS LODGE
KELVEDON HO
MONDRAGON HO
MENTONE CT
STAMBOURNE HO
TEVERSHAM LA
SELWAY HO
SADDLERS MEWS
RUNDELL TOWER
HANNAH BARLOW HO
PORTLAND GR
HAMPSON WAY
GASTON GATE
DOVET CT
SPENCER MEWS
CAVENDISH HO
HARTINGTON CT
ALLEN EDWARDS DR
CORNWALLIS CT
BANCROFT CT
BENSON CT
STAFFORD CT
SUMNER CT
DARSLEY DR
TAIT CT
SUDBURY CT
LANGLEY CT
PRIORY CT
ALL SAINTS CL
THE STUDIOS
SCHOOL FLATS
PRIORY GR
SOUTHVILLE
LARKHALL LA
RUSHBY CT
EDRICH HO
WHITFIELD CT
SANDHAM CT
PARKER CT
MOBEY CT
MARSHALL CT
WHITTAKER CT
STRUDWICK CT
BINFIELD RD
LAVENDER CT
MIMOSA CT
ERICA CT
HEATHER CT
SQUIRES CT
STUDLEY RD
Allen Edwards Prim Sch
HOLMES CT
JEPHSON CT
McINTYRE CT
LAKER CT
KNOX CT
PARADISE RD
RICHARDSON CT
STOCKWELL TERR
STOCKWELL GDNS
Stockwell Park High Sch
A3
A203
ACLAND HO
BLAIR HO
MORANT HO
ST MICHAEL'S RD
STOCKWELL RD
SWAN MEWS
PO
CASSELL HO
PACKINGTON HO
BAIN HO
ENFIELD HO
FAWCETT HO
SIDGWICK HO
JOWETT HO
THRING HO
PATON HO
HUXLEY HO
BURNLEY RD
YMCA
FENTON CL
CROSSFORD ST
EASTCOTE ST
IRVING GR
MORELL HO
MARY HO
BEALE HO
ROSA PARKS HO
BIRRELL HO
BECKETT HO
LINGHAM ST
St Andrew's Prim Sch
STOCKWELL GN
BARLING CT
FENDER CT
JEFFREY'S CT
JEFFREY'S RD
BROOKS CT
DALMENY CT
FISHLOCK CT
BEDSER CT
GOVER CT
LEVEHURST WAY
CLARENCE WLK
HAYWARD CT
BARTON CT
GARDEN HO
OTHA HO
ALLOM CT
SURRIDGE CT
CLAPHAM RD
McCALL CL
BARRINGTON CT
GASKELL ST
UNION CT
Pav
Tenn Cts
WOOD HO
KINGSLEY HO
Lark Hall Prim Sch
HALTONE HO
UNION RD
CHELSHAM RD
UNION MEWS
BELLE VUE GDNS
ARDEN HO
PINTER HO
CLITHEROE RD
RHODESIA RD
RUSPER CT
STIRLING RD
GRANTHAM RD
KAY RD
KIMBERLEY RD
EDITHNA ST
MAYFLOWER RD
ARLESFORD RD
SAVOY MEWS
CHELSHAM HO
CALLINGHAM HO
GREENER HO
DALYELL RD
ARGYLL CL
PERCHER CT
Lansdowne Sch
NEALDEN
171
62
30

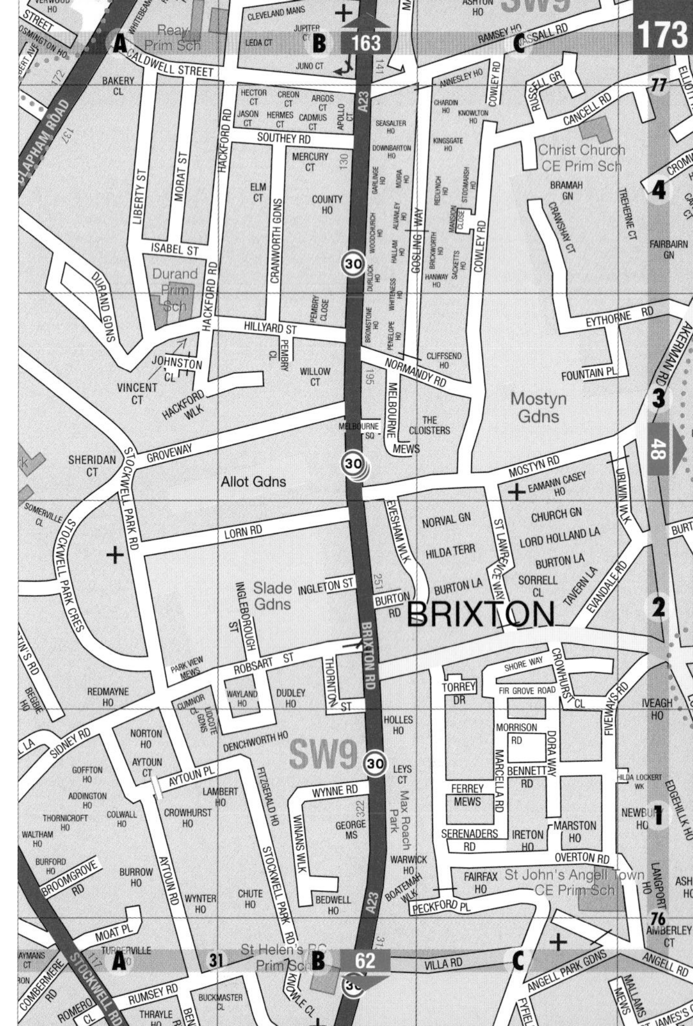

173
A
B
C
163
62
48
77
76
4
3
2
1
31
SW9
BRIXTON
CALDWELL STREET
CLEVELAND MANS
JUPITER CT
LEDA CT
JUNO CT
RAMSEY HO
ASHTON HO
VASSALL RD
Reay Prim Sch
BAKERY CL
CLAPHAM ROAD
HECTOR CT
CREON CT
ARGOS CT
JASON CT
HERMES CT
CADMUS CT
APOLLO CT
SOUTHEY RD
MERCURY CT
ELM CT
COUNTY HO
LIBERTY ST
MORAT ST
HACKFORD RD
CRANWORTH GDNS
ISABEL ST
Durand Prim Sch
DURAND GDNS
PEMBRY CLOSE
HILLYARD ST
PEMBRY CL
WILLOW CT
JOHNSTON CL
VINCENT CT
HACKFORD WLK
ANNESLEY HO
CHARDIN HO
KNOWLTON HO
SEASALTER HO
KINGSGATE HO
DOWNBARTON HO
GOSLING WAY
COWLEY RD
CLIFFSEND HO
HANWAY HO
SACKETTS HO
NORMANDY RD
MELBOURNE MEWS
MELBOURNE SQ
THE CLOISTERS
RUSSELL GR
CANCELL RD
Christ Church CE Prim Sch
BRAMAH GN
CRAWSHAY CT
TREHERNE CT
FAIRBAIRN GN
ELLIOTT RD
EYTHORNE RD
AKERMAN RD
FOUNTAIN PL
Mostyn Gdns
MOSTYN RD
EAMANN CASEY HO
CHURCH GN
URLWIN WLK
NORVAL GN
HILDA TERR
LORD HOLLAND LA
BURTON LA
SORRELL CL
TAVERN LA
EVANDALE RD
ST LAWRENCE WAY
EVESHAM WLK
BURTON RD
SHERIDAN CT
GROVEWAY
STOCKWELL PARK RD
Allot Gdns
SOMERVILLE CL
STOCKWELL PARK CRES
LORN RD
Slade Gdns
INGLETON ST
INGLEBOROUGH ST
BRIXTON RD
A23
PARK VIEW MEWS
ROBSART ST
THORNTON ST
REDMAYNE HO
BEGBIE HO
WAYLAND HO
DUDLEY HO
CUMNOR CL
UDCOTE GDNS
SHORE WAY
CROWHURST CL
TORREY DR
FIR GROVE ROAD
FIVEWAYS RD
IVEAGH HO
HOLLES HO
MORRISON RD
DORA WAY
SIDNEY RD
NORTON HO
DENCHWORTH HO
AYTOUN CT
AYTOUN PL
LEYS CT
BENNETT RD
MARCELLA RD
HILDA LOCKERT WK
EDGEHILL HO
GOFFTON HO
ADDINGTON HO
THORNICROFT HO
WALTHAM HO
COLWALL HO
CROWHURST HO
LAMBERT HO
FITZGERALD HO
WYNNE RD
WINANS WLK
GEORGE MS
Max Roach Park
FERREY MEWS
SERENADERS RD
IRETON HO
MARSTON HO
OVERTON RD
NEWBURY HO
BURFORD HO
BROOMGROVE RD
BURROW HO
AYTOUN RD
WYNTER HO
CHUTE HO
STOCKWELL PARK RD
BEDWELL HO
WARWICK HO
BOATEMAH WLK
FAIRFAX HO
St John's Angell Town CE Prim Sch
LANGPORT HO
ASHBY HO
PECKFORD PL
AMBERLEY CT
MOAT PL
TURBERVILLE HO
St Helen's RC Prim Sch
VILLA RD
ANGELL PARK GDNS
ANGELL RD
STOCKWELL RD
COMBERMERE RD
ROMERO CL
RUMSEY RD
THRAYLE HO
BUCKMASTER CL
KNOWLE CL
FYFIELD
MALLAMS MEWS
ST JAMES'S CR

Index

Church Rd **6** Beckenham BR2..........**53** C6 **228** C6

Place name	Location number	Locality, town or village	Postcode district	Standard scale reference	Enlarged scale reference
May be abbreviated on the map	Present when a number indicates the place's position in a crowded area of mapping	Shown when more than one place (outside London postal districts) has the same name	District for the indexed place	Page number and grid reference for the standard mapping	Page number and grid reference for the central London enlarged mapping, underlined in red

Public and commercial buildings are highlighted in magenta.
Places of interest are highlighted in blue
Cities, towns and villages are listed in CAPITAL LETTERS

Abbreviations used in the index

Acad	**Academy**
App	**Approach**
Arc	**Arcade**
Art Gall	**Art Gallery**
Ave	**Avenue**
Bglws	**Bungalows**
Bldgs	**Buildings**
Bsns Ctr	**Business Centre**
Bsns Pk	**Business Park**
Bvd	**Boulevard**
Cath	**Cathedral, Catholic**
CE	**Church of England**
Cemy	**Cemetery**
Cir	**Circus**
Circ	**Circle**
Cl	**Close**
Cnr	**Corner**
Coll	**College**
Com	**Community**
Comm	**Common**
Comp	**Comprehensive**
Con Ctr	**Conference Centre**
Cotts	**Cottages**
Cres	**Crescent**
Cswy	**Causeway**
Ct	**Court**
Ctr	**Centre**
Crkt	**Cricket**
Ctry Pk	**Country Park**
Cty	**County**
Ctyd	**Courtyard**
Dr	**Drive**
Ent Ctr	**Enterprise Centre**
Ent Pk	**Enterprise Park**
Est	**Estate**
Ex Ctr	**Exhibition Centre**
Ex Hall	**Exhibition Hall**
Fst	**First**
Gdn	**Garden**
Gdns	**Gardens**
Gn	**Green**
Gr	**Grove**
Gram	**Grammar**
Her Ctr	**Heritage Centre**
Ho	**House**
Hospl	**Hospital**
Hts	**Heights**
Ind Est	**Industrial Estate**
Inf	**Infant**
Inst	**Institute**
Int	**International**
Intc	**Interchange**
Jun	**Junior**
Junc	**Junction**
La	**Lane**
L Ctr	**Leisure Centre**
Liby	**Library**
Mans	**Mansions**
Mdw/s	**Meadow/s**
Meml	**Memorial**
Mid	**Middle**
Mix	**Mixed**
Mkt	**Market**
Mon	**Monument**
Mus	**Museum**
Obsy	**Observatory**
Orch	**Orchard**
Par	**Parade**
Pas	**Passage**
Pav	**Pavilion**
Pk	**Park**
Pl	**Place**
Prec	**Precinct**
Prep	**Preparatory**
Prim	**Primary**
Prom	**Promenade**
RC	**Roman Catholic**
Rd	**Road**
Rdbt	**Roundabout**
Ret Pk	**Retail Park**
Sch	**School**
Sec	**Secondary**
Sh Ctr	**Shopping Centre**
Sp	**Sports**
Specl	**Special**
Sports Ctr	**Sports Centre**
Sq	**Square**
St	**Street, Saint**
Sta	**Station**
Stad	**Stadium**
Tech	**Technical Technology**
Terr	**Terrace**
Trad Est	**Trading Estate**
Twr/s	**Tower/s**
Univ	**University**
Wlk	**Walk**
Yd	**Yard**

2 Willow Rd NW3 ... 12 A4
3 Mills Studios E14 ... 27 B2
30 St Mary Axe (The Gherkin) EC2 ... 110 B2
176 Gall NW5 ... 12 C2
201 Bishopgate EC2 ... 110 B4

A

Abady Ho SW1 ... 147 C4
Abberley Mews 9 SW8 ... 61 A4
Abbess Cl SW2 ... 75 A3
Abbeville Mews 3 SW4 ... 61 C3
Abbeville Rd SW4 ... 61 B2
Abbey Bsns Ctr SW8 ... 170 B4
Abbey Coll London SW1 ... 132 A1
Abbey Ct
 6 Bedford Pk W12 ... 38 A3
 Camberwell SE17 ... 151 A1
 St John's Wood NW8 ... 78 C2
Abbeyfield Rd SE16 ... 40 B2
Abbey Gdns
 10 Bermondsey SE16 ... 153 C4
 St John's Wood NW8 ... 79 A1
 West Kensington W6 ... 154 A3
Abbey Ho NW8 ... 89 A4
Abbey La E15 ... 27 C3
Abbey Lo NW8 ... 90 B3
Abbey Orchard St SW1 ... 133 C2
Abbey Orchard Street Est SW1 ... 133 C2
Abbey Rd
 St John's Wood NW8 ... 78 C2
 Wembley NW10 ... 20 A3
Abbey St SE1 ... 138 C2
Abbot Ct SW8 ... 162 A1
Abbot Ho 14 E14 ... 34 A2
Abbotsbury Cl
 Kensington W14 ... 126 C3
 Mill Meads E15 ... 27 B3
Abbotsbury Ho W14 ... 126 B4
Abbotsbury Mews SE15 ... 65 B4
Abbotsbury Rd W14 ... 126 C3
Abbotshade Rd 15 SE16 ... 32 C1
Abbots Ho
 Kensington W14 ... 126 C1
 Pimlico SW1 ... 147 B1
Abbots La SE1 ... 124 B1
Abbots Pk SW2 ... 74 C3
Abbot's Pl NW6 ... 78 A4
Abbot St E8 ... 16 B2
Abbotstone Ho 4 E5 ... 7 C2
Abbotstone Rd SW15 ... 57 B4
Abbotswell Rd SE4 ... 66 B2
Abbotswood Rd
 London SE22 ... 64 A3
 Streatham SW16 ... 73 C1
Abbott Ho SW12 ... 72 B4
Abbott Rd E14 ... 34 C3
Abbotts Cl N1 ... 15 B2
Abbotts Wharf 4 E14 ... 33 C3
Abchurch La EC2, EC4 ... 123 C4
Abchurch Yd EC4 ... 123 B4
Abdale Rd W12 ... 30 A1
Abel Ho 7 SE11 ... 163 B4
Aberavon Rd E3 ... 26 A2
Abercorn Cl NW8 ... 88 C4
Abercorn Mans NW8 ... 79 A1
Abercorn Mews 10 TW10 ... 54 B3
Abercorn Pl NW8 ... 78 C1
Abercorn Sch NW8 ... 79 A1
Abercorn Way SE1 ... 153 B2
Abercorn Wlk NW8 ... 88 C4
Abercrombie Ho 1 W12 ... 30 A2
Abercrombie St SW11 ... 168 B2
Aberdale Ct 22 SE16 ... 40 C4
Aberdare Gdns NW6 ... 11 A1
Aberdeen Ct
 Canonbury N5 ... 15 B3
 Paddington W2 ... 89 B1
Aberdeen Ctr N5 ... 15 B3
Aberdeen La N5 ... 15 B3
Aberdeen Mans WC1 ... 94 A2
Aberdeen Pk N5 ... 15 B3
Aberdeen Pl NW8 ... 89 B2
Aberdeen Rd
 Canonbury N5 ... 15 B4
 Dudden Hill NW10 ... 8 B3
Aberdeen Terr SE3 ... 52 C1
Aberdour St SE1 ... 152 A4
Aberfeldy Ho SE5 ... 48 A3
Aberfeldy St E14 ... 34 B3
Abersham Rd E8 ... 16 B3
Ability Plaza 8 E8 ... 16 B1
Ability Twrs EC1 ... 96 C4
Abingdon W14 ... 141 A3
Abingdon Cl
 Fulham SE1 ... 153 A2
 Kentish Town NW1 ... 13 C2
Abingdon Ct W8 ... 127 C1
Abingdon Gdns W8 ... 127 C1
Abingdon Ho E2 ... 24 B1 98 C2
Abingdon Mans W8 ... 127 B2
Abingdon Rd W8 ... 127 C1
Abingdon St SW1 ... 134 A2
Abingdon Villas W8 ... 127 C1
Abinger Gr SE8 ... 51 B4
Abinger Ho SE1 ... 137 B3
Abinger Mews W9 ... 23 C1
Abinger Rd W4 ... 38 A3
Ablett St SE16 ... 40 B1
Abney Gdns 5 N16 ... 7 B2
Abney Park Cemetery N16 ... 7 A2
Abney Park Ct N16 ... 7 B2
Aborfield 6 NW5 ... 13 B3
Aboyne Rd SW17 ... 71 C1
Abyssinia Cl SW11 ... 60 A3
Abyssinia Rd SW11 ... 60 A3
Acacia Cl SE8 ... 41 A2
Acacia Gdns NW8 ... 79 C2
Acacia Gr SE21 ... 75 C2
Acacia Ho
 Brockley SE4 ... 66 B3
 Stoke Newington N16 ... 6 C2
Acacia Pl NW8 ... 79 C2
Acacia Rd
 Acton W3 ... 28 B2
 St John's Wood NW8 ... 79 C2
Acacia Wlk SW10 ... 157 A1
Academy Ct 13 E2 ... 25 B2
Academy Gdns W8 ... 127 B4
Academy Sch The 9 NW3 ... 11 C4
Academy The 2 N19 ... 4 B3
Acad of Live & Recorded Arts SW18 ... 59 C1
Acanthus Dr SE1 ... 153 B2
Acanthus Rd SW11 ... 60 C4
Accommodation Rd NW11 ... 1 B3
Acer Ct 2 NW2 ... 9 C4
Acer Rd E8 ... 16 B1
Acfold Rd SW6 ... 166 A3
Achilles Cl SE1 ... 153 C2
Achilles Ho 16 E2 ... 25 A3
Achilles Rd NW6 ... 10 C3
Achilles St SE14 ... 51 A3
Achilles Way W1 ... 117 C1
Acklam Rd W10 ... 31 B4
Ackmar Rd SW6 ... 165 B3
Ackroyd Dr E3 ... 33 C4
Acland Burghley Sch NW5 ... 13 A4
Acland Cres SE5 ... 63 C4
Acland Ho SW9 ... 172 C2
Acland Rd NW2 ... 9 A2
Acol Ct 3 NW6 ... 10 C1
Acol Rd NW6 ... 11 A1
Acorn Ct 5 E3 ... 26 C3
Acorn Gdns W3 ... 28 C4
Acorn Par 7 SE15 ... 50 A3
Acorn Production Ctr N7 ... 14 A1
Acorns The 21 SW19 ... 69 C3
Acorn Wharf SE15 ... 49 C4
Acorn Wlk SE16 ... 33 A1
Acqua Ho TW9 ... 45 A3
Acre Dr SE22 ... 64 C3
Acre La SW2 ... 62 B3
Acris St SW18 ... 59 B2
ACTON ... 28 C1
Acton Bsns Ctr NW10 ... 20 C1
Acton Central Ind Est 4 W3 ... 28 A1
Acton Central Sta W3 ... 28 C1
ACTON GREEN ... 37 B2
Acton High Sch W3 ... 36 C4
Acton Hill Mews W3 ... 28 A1
Acton Ho
 5 Acton W3 ... 28 B3
 16 Haggerston E8 ... 24 B4
Acton La
 Acton Green W4 ... 37 B2
 Acton W3 ... 37 B4
 Harlesden NW10 ... 20 C3
Acton Main Line Sta W3 ... 28 B3
Acton Mews E8 ... 24 B4
Acton Park Ind Est W3 ... 37 C4
Acton St WC1 ... 94 C3
Acton Town Sta W3 ... 36 C4
Acton Vale Ind Pk W3 ... 29 B1
Acton & West London Coll 16 W3 ... 28 A1
Acuba Ho SW18 ... 71 A3
Acuba Rd SW18 ... 71 A2
Ada Ct
 Islington N1 ... 86 C3
 St John's Wood W9 ... 89 A3
Ada Gdns E14 ... 34 C3
Ada Ho 23 E2 ... 24 C4
Adair Ho SW3 ... 158 B4
Adair Rd W10 ... 23 A1
Adair Twr 7 W10 ... 23 A1
Ada Kennedy Ct 6 SE10 ... 52 B3
Adam Ct SE11 ... 150 A3
Adam & Eve Ct W1 ... 105 A2
Adam & Eve Mews W8 ... 127 C2
Adamfields NW3 ... 11 C1
Adams Gardens Est 5 SE16 ... 40 B4
Adams Ho 3 E14 ... 34 C3
Adams Mews SW17 ... 72 B2
Adamson Rd
 Hampstead NW3 ... 11 C1
 Newham E16 ... 35 C3
Adams Pl N7 ... 14 B3
Adam's Row W1 ... 117 C3
Adam St WC2 ... 120 B3
Adam Wlk SW6 ... 47 B3
Ada Pl E2 ... 24 C4
Ada Rd SE5 ... 49 A3
Adare Wlk SW16, SW2 ... 74 B2
Ada St E8 ... 25 A4
Adderley Gr SW11 ... 60 C2
Adderley St E14 ... 34 B3
Addey Ho SE8 ... 51 B3
Addey & Stanhope Sch 11 SE14 ... 51 C2
Addington Ct 7 SW14 ... 55 C4
Addington Ho 13 SW9 ... 173 A1
Addington Rd E3 ... 26 C2
Addington Sq SE5 ... 48 C3
Addington St SE1 ... 135 A3
Addis Ho 13 E1 ... 32 B4
Addison Ave W11 ... 31 A1 112 A1
Addison Bridge Pl W14 ... 140 C4
Addison Cres W14 ... 126 B2
Addison Gdns W14 ... 39 C3
Addison Gr W4 ... 38 A3
Addison Ho NW8 ... 89 B4
Addison Park Mans 12 W14 ... 39 C4
Addison Pl W11 ... 31 A1 112 A1
Addison Prim Sch W14 ... 39 C3
Addison Rd W14 ... 126 C2
Addle Hill EC4 ... 108 B1
Addlestone Ho 4 W10 ... 30 B4
Addy Ho SE16 ... 40 B2
Adela Ho 9 W6 ... 39 B1
Adelaide Ave SE4 ... 66 C3
Adelaide Cl SW9 ... 62 C3
Adelaide Ct
 Hackney E5 ... 18 A3
 St John's Wood NW8 ... 79 A1
Adelaide Gr W12 ... 29 C1
Adelaide Rd
 Primrose Hill NW3 ... 12 A1
 Richmond TW9 ... 54 B3
 2 Wandsworth SW18 ... 58 C2
Adelaide St WC2 ... 120 A3
Adela St W10 ... 23 A1
Adelina Gr E1 ... 32 B4
Adelina Mews SW12 ... 73 C3
Adeline Pl WC1 ... 105 C3
Adelphi Ct 20 SE16 ... 40 C4
Adelphi Terr WC2 ... 120 B3
Adeney Cl W6 ... 47 C4
Aden Gr N16 ... 15 C4
Aden Ho 15 E1 ... 32 C4
Aden Lo N16 ... 15 C4
Adeyfield Ho EC1 ... 97 C3
Adie Rd W6 ... 39 B3
Adisham Ho 4 E5 ... 17 A3
Adler St E1 ... 111 B2
Adley St E5 ... 18 A3
Admiral Ct
 Chelsea SW10 ... 167 A4
 Marylebone W1 ... 103 B3
Admiral Hyson Ind Est SE16 ... 40 A1
Admiral Mews W10 ... 22 C1
Admiral Pl SE16 ... 33 A1
Admirals Ct
 Bermondsey SE1 ... 124 C1
 32 Putney SW19 ... 69 C3
Admirals Gate SE10 ... 52 A2
Admiral Sq SW10 ... 167 A4
Admiral St SE8 ... 51 C2
Admirals Way E14 ... 41 C4
Admiral's Wlk NW3 ... 2 B1
Admiralty Arch SW1 ... 119 C2
Admiralty Cl 1 SE8 ... 51 C2
Admiral Wlk W9 ... 31 C4
Adolphus Rd N4 ... 6 A3
Adolphus St SE8 ... 51 B3
Adpar St W2 ... 101 B4
Adrian Bolt Ho 2 E2 ... 25 A2

Adrian Ho
Islington N1 85 A3
South Lambeth SW8 162 A2
Stratford E15 19 C1
Adrian Mews SW10 156 B4
Adriatic Bldg 18 E14 33 A2
Adriatic Ho 18 E1 25 C1
Adron Ho 13 SE16 40 B2
Adstock Ho 5 N1 15 A1
Adventurers Ct 17 E14 34 C2
Adys Lawn NW2 9 A2
Adys Rd SE15 64 B4
Aegean Apts 7 E16 35 C2
Aegon Ho 3 E14 42 A3
Affleck St N1 85 A1
Afghan Rd SW11 168 A1
Africa Ho WC2 106 C2
Afsil Ho EC1 107 C3
Aga Khan Univ WC1 105 C3
Agamemnon Rd NW6 10 B3
Agar Gr NW1 13 C1
Agar Pl NW1 13 B1
Agar St WC2 120 B3
Agate Rd W6 39 B3
Agatha Cl E1 32 B1
Agave Rd NW2 9 B4
Agdon St EC1 96 A2
Agincourt Rd NW3 12 B4
Agnes Ct 11 SW18 59 C3
Agnes Ho 13 W11 30 C2
Agnes Rd W3 38 B4
Agnes St E14 33 B3
Aicon Gall SW1 118 C4
Aigburth Mans 5 SW9 163 B1
Ailsa St E14 34 B4
Ainger Rd NW3 12 B1
Ainsdale NW1 92 C4
Ainsdale Dr SE1 153 B1
Ainsley St E2 25 A2
Ainslie Wlk 8 SW12 73 A4
Ainsty St 20 SE16 40 B4
Ainsworth Cl SE5 49 A1
Ainsworth Est NW8 78 C4
Ainsworth Ho NW8 78 B3
Ainsworth Rd E9 17 B1
Ainsworth Way NW8 78 C4
Aintree St SW6 154 B2
Aird Ho SE1 136 C1
Airdrie Cl N1 14 B1
Airedale Ave W4 38 B1
Airedale Ave S W4 38 B1
Airedale Rd SW12 72 B4
Airlie Gdns W8 31 C1 113 B1
Air St W1 119 A3
Aisgill Ave SW5 141 A1
Aiten Pl W6 38 C2
Aithan Ho 15 E14 33 B3
Aitken Cl E8 24 C4
Ajax Ho 15 E2 25 A3
Ajax Rd NW6 10 C3
Akbar Ho 7 E14 42 A2
Akehurst St SW15 68 C4
Akenside Ct 3 NW3 11 C3
Akenside Rd NW3 11 C3
Akerman Rd SW9 48 A2
Akintaro Ho 7 SE8 51 B4
Alamaro Lo 5 SE10 43 B3
Aland Ct SE16 41 A3
Alan Preece Ct NW6 9 C1
Alaska Bldg 12 SE13 52 A2
Alaska St SE1 121 B1
Alastor Ho 10 E14 42 B3
Albacore Cres SE13 67 A1
Alba Mews SW18, SW19 70 C2
Alban Ho
Hampstead NW3 11 B2
New Cross SE14 51 B2
Albans Cl SW16 74 A1
Albany W1 118 C3
Albany Cl SW14 55 A3
Albany Ct
College Pk NW10 22 A2
NW8 79 B1
Westminster SW1 133 B2
8 Whitechapel E1 111 B2
Albany Ctyd W1 119 A3
Albany Ho 6 TW8 44 A4
Albany Mans SW11 158 B1
Albany Mews
Camberwell SE5 48 B4
Islington N1 14 C1
Albany Par 4 TW8 44 A4
Albany Pas 12 TW10 54 A2
Albany Rd
Camberwell SE5 49 A4
Richmond TW10 54 A2
Albany St NW1 92 B4
Albany Terr 6 TW10 54 B2
Alba Pl W11 31 B3
Albemarle SW19 69 C2
Albemarle Coll W1 117 A4
Albemarle Ho
2 Brixton SW9 62 C4
Rotherhithe SE8 41 B2
Albemarle Mans NW3 11 A4
Albemarle Prim Sch SW19 70 A2
Albemarle St W1 118 C3
Albemarle Way EC1 96 A1
Alberta Ct 1 TW10 54 B2
Alberta Ho E14 34 B1
Alberta St SE17 150 B2
Albert Ave SW8 162 C1
Albert Barnes Ho SE1 136 C1
Albert Bigg Point E15 27 B4
Albert Bridge Rd SW11 158 C1
Albert Cl 11 E9 25 A4
Albert Cotts 2 E1 111 B4
Albert Ct
Knightsbridge SW7 129 B3
9 Putney SW19 70 A3
Albert Dr SW19 70 A3
Albert Emb SE1 148 B3
Albert Gate Ct SW1 130 C3
Albert Gdns E1 32 C3
Albert Gray Ho SW10 157 B2
Albert Hall Mans SW7 129 B3
Albert Mans
Battersea SW11 168 C4
Hornsey N8 5 A4
Albert Meml SW7 129 B3
Albert Mews W8 128 C2
Albert Palace Mans SW11 169 C4
Albert Pl W8 128 B3
Albert Rd
Finsbury Pk N4 5 B4
Kilburn NW6 23 B3
Richmond TW10 54 B2
Albert's Ct NW1 90 B2
Albert Sq SW8 162 C1
Albert St NW1 82 B3
Albert Starr Ho 7 SE8 40 C2
Albert Studios SW11 168 C4
Albert Terr
Camden Town NW1 81 B3
Stonebridge NW10 20 B4
Albert Terr Mews NW1 81 B3
Albert Way SE15 50 A3
Albert Westcott Ho SE17 150 B2
Albion Ave SW8 171 B1
Albion Cl W2 116 B4
Albion Coll WC1 106 B3
Albion Ct 7 W6 39 A2
Albion Dr E8 16 C1
Albion Est SE16 40 B4
Albion Gate W2 116 B4
Albion Gdns 1 W6 39 A2
Albion Gr N16 16 A4
Albion Ho
17 Deptford SE8 51 C3
EC1 108 A4
Albion Mews
Bayswater W2 116 B4
6 Hammersmith W6 39 A2
Islington N1 85 B4
Albion Pl
Broadgate EC2 109 C3
Clerkenwell EC1 108 A4
Hammersmith W6 39 A2
Albion Prim Sch 31 SE16 40 B4
Albion Rd N16 15 C4
Albion Riverside SW11 158 A2
Albion Sq E8 16 B1
Albion St
Bayswater W2 116 B4
Rotherhithe SE16 40 B4
Albion Terr E8 16 B1
Albion Way
Barbican EC1 108 C3
Lewisham SE13 67 B3
Albion Wlk N1 84 B1
Albion Works Studios 14 E8 16 C3
Albion Yd N1 84 B1
Albon Ho SW18 59 A1
Albrighton Rd SE5, SE22 64 A4
Albury Bldgs SE1 136 B3
Albury Ct SE8 51 C4
Albury Lo 7 SW2 74 B4
Albury St SE8 51 C4
Albyn Rd SE8 51 C2
Alchemea Coll of Audio Engineering N1 86 B4
Alconbury Rd E5 7 C2
Aldbourne Rd W12 29 C1
Aldbridge St SE17 152 B2
Aldburgh Mews W1 103 C2
Aldbury Ho SW3 144 A3
Aldebert Terr SW8 162 C1
Aldeburgh Pl SE10 43 C2
Aldeburgh St SE10 43 C1
Aldenham Ho NW1 83 A1
Aldenham St NW1 83 B1
Alden Ho E8 25 A4
Aldensley Rd W6 39 A3
Alderbrook Prim Sch 17 SW12 73 A4
Alderbrook Rd SW12 61 A1
Alderbury Rd SW13 46 C4
Aldergrove Ho 3 E5 7 C2
Alder Ho
Camberwell SE15 49 B4
1 Maitland Pk NW3 12 B2
St Johns SE4 66 C4
Alderley Ho 36 SW8 171 B1
Alder Lo SW6 47 C2
Aldermanbury EC2 109 A2
Aldermanbury Sq EC2 109 A3
Alderman's Wlk EC2 110 A3
Alder Mews 12 N19 4 B2
Alderney Ho 20 N1 15 B2
Alderney Mews SE1 137 B2
Alderney Rd E1 25 C1
Alderney St SW1 146 B2
Alder Rd SW14 55 C4
Aldersford Cl SE4 65 C3
Aldersgate Ct EC1 108 C3
Aldersgate St EC1 108 C3
Aldershot Rd NW6 23 B4
Alderson St W10 23 A1
Alderton Rd SE24 63 B4
Alderville Rd SW6 165 A2
Alderwick Ct N7 14 B2
Aldford St W1 117 C2
Aldgate EC3 110 B1
Aldgate East Sta E1 111 A2
Aldgate High St EC3 110 C1
Aldgate Sta EC3 110 C1
Aldham Ho SE4 51 B2
Aldine Ct W12 30 B1
Aldine St W12 39 B4
Aldington Ct 1 E8 16 C1
Aldred Rd NW6 10 C3
Aldren Rd SW17 71 B1
Aldrich Terr SW18 71 B2
Aldrick Ho N1 85 A2
Aldridge Ct W11 31 B4
Aldridge Rd Villas W11 31 B4
Aldsworth Cl W9 88 A1
Aldwich Ho WC2 107 A1
Aldworth Gr SE13 67 B1
Aldwych WC2 107 A1
Aldwych Bldgs WC2 106 B2
Aldwyn Ho SW8 162 A1
Alexander Ave NW10 9 A1
Alexander Ct SW18 59 B2
Alexander Fleming Laboratory Mus W2 101 C2
Alexander Ho 15 E14 41 C3
Alexander Mews 2 W2 100 A2
Alexander Pl SW7 144 A4
Alexander Rd N19 5 A2
Alexander Sq SW3 144 A4
Alexander St W2 31 C3
Alexandra Ave SW11 169 B3
Alexandra Cl SE8 51 B4
Alexandra Cotts SE14 51 B2
Alexandra Ct
Paddington W9 89 A2
4 Shacklewell N16 16 B4
5 Shepherd's Bush W12 38 C4
Alexandra Gdns W4 46 A3
Alexandra Gr N4 6 A3
Alexandra Ho 13 W6 39 B1
Alexandra Mans
Chelsea SW3 157 B3
Cricklewood NW2 9 C3
6 Hampstead NW6 10 C3
9 Shepherd's Bush W12 30 B1
Alexandra National Ho N4 6 A2
Alexandra Pl NW8 79 A4
Alexandra Rd
Acton W4 37 C4
Hampstead NW8 11 C1
Mortlake SW14 55 C4
Richmond TW9 44 B1
Alexandra St
5 Deptford SE14 51 A3
Newham E16 35 C4
Alex Gossip Ho SW6 165 B3
Alexis St SE16 153 C4
Alfearn Rd E5 17 B4
Alfie's Antique Mkt NW8 90 A1
Alford Ct N1 87 A1
Alford Pl N1 87 A1
Alfreda Ct SW11 170 A3

Alfreda St SW11 .. 170 A3
Alfred Butt Ho SW17 ... 72 B1
Alfred Cl W4 ... 37 C2
Alfred Ho E9 ... 18 A3
Alfred Mews W1, WC1 ... 105 B4
Alfred Nunn Ho NW10 ... 21 B4
Alfred Pl WC1 ... 105 B4
Alfred Rd
Acton W3 ... 28 B1
Paddington W2 ... 31 C4
Alfred Salter Ho SE1 ... 153 A3
Alfred Salter Prim Sch SE16 ... 40 C4
Alfred St E3 ... 26 B2
Alfreton Cl SW19 ... 69 C1
Alfriston Rd SW11 .. 60 B2
Algar Ho SE1 ... 136 A3
Algarve Rd SW18 ... 71 A3
Algernon Rd
Kilburn NW6 ... 23 C4
Lewisham SE13 ... 67 A3
Algiers Rd SE13 ... 66 C3
Alice Gilliott Ct W14 ... 155 A4
Alice La E3 ... 26 B4
Alice Owen Tech Ctr EC1 ... 96 A4
Alice Shepherd Ho [12] E14 ... 42 B4
Alice St SE1 ... 138 A1
Alice Walker Cl [8] SE24 ... 63 A3
Alie St E1 ... 111 A1
Aliwal Rd SW11 ... 60 A3
Alkerden Rd W4 ... 38 A1
Alkham Rd N16 ... 7 B2
Allam Ho W11 ... 31 A2 112 A4
Allanbridge N16 ... 7 A4
Allan Ho SW8 ... 171 B4
Allan Way W3 ... 28 B4
Allard Gdns SW4 ... 61 C2
Allardyce St SW4, SW9 ... 62 B3
Allbrook Ho [4] SW15 ... 68 C4
Allcroft Rd NW5 ... 12 C2
Allendale Cl SE5 ... 48 C2
Allen Edwards Dr SW8 ... 172 A4
Allen Edwards Prim Sch SW4 ... 172 A3
Allenford Ho SW15 ... 56 B1
All England Lawn Tennis & Croquet Club The SW19 ... 70 A1
Allen Ho W8 ... 127 C2
Allen Mans W8 ... 127 C2
Allen Rd
Old Ford E3 ... 26 B3
Stoke Newington N16 ... 16 A4
Allensbury Pl
[7] Camden Town NW1 ... 13 C1
Camden Town NW1 .. 14 A1
Allen St W8 ... 127 C1
Allenswood [12] SW19 ... 70 A3
Allerdale Ho [7] N4 .. 6 C4
Allerton Ho N1 ... 87 C1
Allerton Rd N16 ... 6 B2
Allerton St N1 ... 97 C4
Allerton Wlk [11] N7 .. 5 B2
Allestree Rd SW6 154 A1
Alleyn Cres SE21 ... 75 C2
Alleyn Ho
Bermondsey SE1 .. 137 B1
St Luke's EC1 ... 97 A1
Alleyn Pk SE21 ... 76 A1
Alleyn Rd SE21 ... 76 A1
Alleyn's Sch SE22 .. 64 A2
Allfarthing JMI Sch SW18 ... 59 B1
Allfarthing La SW18 ... 59 B1
Allgood St [10] E2 ... 24 B3
Allhallows La EC4 123 B3
Alliance Ct W3 ... 28 A4
Alliance Rd W3 ... 20 A1
Allied Ind Est W3 ... 29 A1
Allied Way W3 ... 38 A4
Allingham Ct NW3 .. 12 A3
Allingham Mews N1 ... 86 C2
Allingham St N1 ... 86 C2
Allington Ct [6] SW8 ... 170 C1
Allington Rd W10 .. 23 A3
Allington St SW1 . 132 B1
Allison Cl SE10 ... 52 B2
Allison Gr SE21 ... 76 A3
Allison Rd W3 ... 28 B2
Alliston Ho [27] E2 ... 24 B2 99 A3
Allitsen Rd NW8 ... 80 A2
All Nations Ho [10] E8 ... 17 A1
Allnutt Way SW4 ... 61 C2
Allom Ct [11] SW4 . 172 B1
Allonby Ho E14 ... 33 A4
Alloway Rd E3 ... 26 A2
Allport Ho SE5 ... 63 C4
Allport Mews [44] E1 ... 25 B1
All Saints CE Prim Sch
[8] Fulham SW6 ... 164 A2
Putney SW15 ... 57 B4
All Saints' CE Prim Sch
Blackheath Vale SE3 ... 53 A1
Child's Hill NW2 ... 1 B1
All Saints Church [9] N19 ... 4 C1
All Saints Ct
Lower Clapton E5 ... 17 B4
[10] Shadwell E1 ... 32 B2
All Saints Dr SE3 ... 53 B1
All Saints Ho [2] W11 ... 31 B4
All Saints Pas SW18 ... 58 C2
All Saints Rd W11 .. 31 B3
All Saints' Rd W3 ... 37 B3
All Saints St N1 ... 84 C2
All Saints Sta E14 .. 34 A2
Allsop Pl NW1 ... 91 A1
All Souls Ave NW10 ... 22 A4
All Souls CE Prim Sch W1 ... 104 C4
All Souls Pl W1 ... 104 B3
Alma Birk Ho [1] NW6 ... 10 B1
Almack Rd E5 ... 17 B4
Alma Gr SE1 ... 153 A3
Alma Ho [7] TW8 ... 44 A4
Alma Pl NW10 ... 22 A2
Alma Prim Sch [21] SE16 ... 153 C4
Alma Rd SW18 ... 59 B2
Alma Sq NW8 ... 89 A4
Alma St
Camden Town NW5 ... 13 A2
Stratford New Town E15 ... 19 C2
Alma Terr
Earl's Ct W8 ... 127 C1
Wandsworth SW18 .. 71 C4
Almeida St [10] N1 ... 15 A1
Almeric Rd SW11 ... 60 B3
Almington St N4 ... 5 B3
Almond Ave W5 ... 36 A3
Almond Cl SE15 ... 49 C1
Almond Ho SE4 ... 51 B1
Almond Rd SE16 ... 40 A2
Almorah Rd N1 ... 15 C1
Al-Muntada Islamic Sch SW6 ... 165 A4
Alperton St W10 ... 23 B1
Alphabet Sq E3 ... 33 C4
Alpha Cl NW8 ... 90 B3
Alpha Ct [6] NW5 ... 13 A2
Alpha Gr E14 ... 41 C4
Alpha Ho
[19] Brixton SW4 ... 62 B3
Kilburn NW6 ... 23 C3
Lisson Gr NW8 ... 90 B1
Alpha Pl
Chelsea SW3 ... 158 B4
Kilburn NW6 ... 23 C3
Alpha Rd SE14 ... 51 B2
Alpha St SE15 ... 49 C1
Alpine Gr [37] E9 ... 17 B1
Alpine Rd SE16 ... 40 C1
Alroy Rd N4 ... 5 C4
Alsace Rd SE17 ... 152 A2
Al Sadiq High Sch for Boys & Al Zahra Girls Sch NW6 ... 23 A4
Alscot Rd SE1 ... 139 A1
Alscot Road Ind Est SE1 ... 139 A1
Alscot Way SE1 ... 152 C4
Altair Ct N1 ... 15 C2
Altenburg Gdns SW11 ... 60 B3
Althea St SW6 ... 59 A4
Althorpe Mews SW11 ... 167 C3
Althorp Rd SW17 ... 72 B3
Altima Ct SE22 ... 64 C3
Alton Ho [3] E3 ... 27 A2
Alton Rd
Richmond TW10, TW9 ... 54 A3
Roehampton SW15 ... 68 C3
Alton St E14 ... 34 A4
Alumni Ct SE1 ... 139 A4
Alvanley Ct NW3 ... 11 A3
Alvanley Gdns NW6 ... 11 A3
Alvanley Ho [14] SW9 ... 173 B4
Alverstone Ave SW18, SW19 ... 70 C2
Alverstone Ho [11] SE11 ... 163 B3
Alverstone Rd NW2 .. 9 B1
Alverton St SE8 ... 51 B4
Alvey St SE17 ... 152 A2
Alvington Cres E8 .. 16 B3
Alwyn Ave W4 ... 37 C1
Alwyne La N1 ... 15 A1
Alwyne Pl N1 ... 15 B1
Alwyne Rd N1 ... 15 B1
Alwyne Sq N1 ... 15 B2
Alwyne Villas N1 ... 15 A1
Alwyn Gdns W3 ... 28 A3
Alzette Ho [11] E2 ... 25 C3
Aman Dalvi Ho [2] SW18 ... 70 A4
Amazonas SE1 ... 152 B3
Amazon St E1 ... 32 A3
Ambassador Ct [9] NW6 ... 10 C3
Ambassador Ho NW8 ... 79 A3
Ambassador Sq E14 ... 42 A2
Amber Ct N7 ... 14 C2
Ambergate St SE17 ... 150 B2
Amberley Ct [2] SW9 ... 63 A4
Amberley Rd W9 ... 31 C4
Amber Wharf [29] E2 ... 24 B4
Ambler Prim Sch [2] N4 ... 6 A2
Ambler Rd N4 ... 6 A1
Ambleside
[13] Putney SW19 ... 70 A3
Regent's Pk NW1 ... 82 B1
Ambleside Cl E9 ... 17 B3
Ambleside Point [1] SE15 ... 50 B3
Ambleside Rd NW10 ... 8 B1
Ambrosden Ave SW1 ... 133 A1
Ambrose Ho [9] E14 ... 33 C4
Ambrose Mews [2] SW11 ... 168 C2
Ambrose St SE16 ... 40 A2
Ambrose Wlk E3 ... 26 C3
AMC Bsns Ctr NW10 ... 20 A2
Amelia Cl W3 ... 37 A4
Amelia Ho [5] W6 ... 39 B1
Amelia St SE17 ... 150 C2
Amen Cnr EC4 ... 108 B1
Amen Ct EC4 ... 108 B1
American Intercontinental Univ W1 ... 103 C3
American Sch in London The NW8 . 79 B2
American Univ in London The [3] N7 .. 5 B1
America Sq EC3 .. 124 C4
America St SE1 ... 122 C1
Amerland Rd SW18 ... 58 B1
Amersham Gr SE14 ... 51 B3
Amersham Rd SE14 ... 51 B2
Amersham Vale SE14, SE8 ... 51 B3
Amery Gdns NW10 .. 22 A4
Amery Ho SE17 ... 152 B2
Amesbury Ave SW2 ... 74 B2
Amesbury Twr [4] SW8 ... 170 C2
Ames Cotts [12] E3 .. 33 A4
Ames Ho [10] E2 ... 25 C3
Amethyst Rd E15 ... 19 C4
Amhurst Ct N4 ... 6 C4
Amhurst Par N16 ... 7 B4
Amhurst Pk N4, N16 . 7 A4
Amhurst Rd E8, N16 ... 16 C4
Amhurst Terr E8 ... 16 C4
Amias Ho EC1 ... 96 C2
Amiel St [15] E1 ... 25 B1
Amies St SW11 ... 60 B4
Amigo Ho SE1 ... 135 C2
Amina Way SE16 .. 139 B1
Amner Rd SW11 ... 60 C1
Amor Rd W6 ... 39 B3
Amory Ho N1 ... 85 A2
Amott Rd SE15 ... 64 C4
Amoy Pl E14 ... 33 C2
Ampton Pl WC1 ... 94 C3
Ampton St WC1 ... 94 C3
Amstel Ct [12] SE15 .. 49 B3
Amsterdam Rd E14 ... 42 B3
Amundsen Ct [7] E14 ... 41 C1
Amwell St EC1 ... 95 B4
Amyruth Rd SE4 ... 66 C2
Anatola Rd N19 ... 4 B2
Anchorage Point [1] E14 ... 41 C4
Anchor Ho EC1 ... 96 C2
Anchor Mews SW12 ... 61 A1
Anchor Ret Pk E1 .. 25 B1
Anchor St SE16 ... 40 A2
Anchor Terr SE1 .. 123 A2
Anchor Yd EC1 ... 97 A2
Ancill Cl W6 ... 154 A3
Ancona Rd NW10 .. 21 C3
Andalus Rd SW9 ... 62 A4
Andaman Ho [3] E1 ... 33 A4
Andersens Wharf [9] E14 ... 33 B3
Anderson Cl W3 ... 28 C3
Anderson Ho [10] E14 ... 34 B2
Anderson Rd E9 ... 17 C2
Andersons Sq N1 .. 86 A3
Anderson St SW3 144 C2
Anderton Cl SE5 ... 63 C4
Andover Ho [5] N7 ... 5 B2
Andover Pl NW6 ... 78 A1
Andover Rd N7 ... 5 B2
Andoversford Ct [2] SE15 ... 49 A4
Andre St E8 ... 16 C3
Andrew Borde St WC2 ... 105 C2
Andrewes Ho EC2 109 A3
Andrew Ho
New Cross SE4 ... 51 B1
Putney SW15 ... 56 C2
Andrew Logan's Glasshouse SE1 . 138 A4
Andrew Marvell Ho [12] N16 ... 16 A4
Andrew Pl SW8 ... 171 C4
Andrew Reed Ho [3] SW18 ... 70 A4
Andrews Crosse WC2 ... 107 B1
Andrew's Rd E8 ... 25 A4

Andrew St E14 34 B3
Andrews Wharf 14 E8 25 A4
Andrews Wlk SE17 48 A4
Andrew Wilmot Ct SW18 71 B3
Anfield Cl SW12 73 B4
Angel EC1 86 B1
Angela Carter Cl SW9 62 C4
Angela Davis Ind Est 20 SW9 63 A3
Angel Ct
Broadgate EC2 109 C2
St James SW1 119 A1
5 Willesden NW2 8 C2
Angel Gate EC1 96 B4
Angel Ho N1 85 C1
Angelina Ho 2 SE15 49 C2
Angelis Appartments N1 86 B1
Angel La E15 19 C2
Angell Park Gdns 4 SW9 62 C4
Angell Rd SW9 63 A4
Angel Mews
Finsbury N1 85 C1
Putney SW15 68 C4
Stepney E1 32 A2
Angel Pas EC4 123 B3
Angel Pl SE1 137 B4
Angel Sq N1 85 C1
Angel St EC1 108 C2
Angel Sta EC1 85 C1
Angel Wlk W6 39 B2
Angerstein Bsns Pk SE10 43 C2
Angerstein La SE3 53 B2
Anglebury 5 W2 31 C3
Anglers La NW5 13 A2
Anglesey Ho 13 E14 33 C3
Anglia Ho 13 E14 33 A3
Anglo American Laundry SW17 71 B1
Anglo Rd 16 E3 26 B3
Angrave Ct 4 E8 24 B4
Angrave Pas 5 E8 24 B4
Angus Ho 12 SW12 73 C4
Angus St SE14 51 A3
Anhalt Rd SW11 158 B2
Animals in War Meml W1 117 A4
Anley Rd W14 39 C4
Annabel Cl E14 34 A3
Anna Cl E8 24 B4
Annandale Rd
Chiswick W4 38 A1
Greenwich SE10 43 B1
Anne Goodman Ho 3 E1 32 B3
Anne Kerr Ct 18 SW15 57 C1
Anne's Ct NW8 90 B2
Annesley Ho 15 SW9 173 B4
Annesley Wlk N19 4 B2
Annette Cres 16 N1 15 B1
Annette Ct N7 5 B1
Annette Rd N7 14 B4
Annie Besant Cl E3 26 B4
Anning St EC2 24 A1 98 B2
Annis Rd E9 18 A2
Ann La SW10 157 B3
Ann Moss Way SE16 40 B3
Ann's Cl SW1 131 B3
Ann's Pl E1 110 C3
Ansdell Rd SE15 50 B1
Ansdell St W8 128 B2
Ansdell Terr W8 128 B2
Ansell Ho E1 32 B4
Ansell Rd SW17 72 B1
Anselm Rd SW6 155 B3
Ansleigh Pl W11 30 C2
Anson Ho
Pimlico SW1 160 C4
6 Tower Hamlets E1 26 A1
Anson Prim Sch NW2 9 C3
Anson Rd
Cricklewood NW2 9 B3
Tufnell Pk N7 13 C4
Anstey Ct 6 W3 37 A4
Anstey Ho 7 E9 25 B4
Anstey Rd SE15 64 C4
Anstice Cl W4 46 A3
Antenor Ho 11 E2 25 A3
Anthony Cope Ct N1 97 C4
Anthony Ho NW8 90 A1
Anthony St E1 32 A3
Antilles Bay 19 E14 42 B4
Antilles Ho W3 28 C3
Antill Rd E3 26 A2
Antill Terr 5 E1 32 C3
Antonine Hts SE1 138 A3
Anton St E8 16 C3
Antony Ho
4 Deptford SE14 50 C3
2 Rotherhithe SE16 40 B2
Antrim Gr NW3 12 B2
Antrim Ho SW11 60 C4
Antrim Mans NW3 12 B2
Antrim Rd NW3 12 B2
Antrobus Rd W4 37 B3
AOP Gall EC2 98 A2
Apex Ind Est NW10 21 B1
Aphrodite Ct 11 E14 41 C2
Apollo Bldg 2 E14 41 C2
Apollo Ho
Chelsea SW10 157 B3
32 Hackney E2 25 A3
Highgate N6 3 B4
Apollo Ind Bsns Ctr 29 SE8 50 C4
Apollo Pl SW10 157 B2
Apollo Studios 18 NW5 13 C3
Apothecary St EC4 108 A1
Appach Rd SW2 62 C1
Appleby Ct W3 37 B4
Appleby Rd
Hackney E8 16 C1
Newham E16 35 C3
Appleby St E2 24 B3
Appledore Cl SW12, SW17 72 B2
Appleford 8 NW5 13 B3
Appleford Ho 6 W10 23 A1
Appleford Rd W10 23 A1
Applegarth Ho
Borough The SE1 136 B4
9 Camberwell SE15 49 C3
Applegarth Rd W14 39 C3
Apple Mkt WC2 120 B4
Appleshaw Ho 4 SE5 64 A4
Appleton Ct 30 E8 17 A3
Appletree Ct SE13 67 C3
Apple Tree Yd SW1 119 A2
Appold St EC2 110 A4
Appollo Ct 7 SW9 173 B4
Apprentice Way 5 E5 17 A4
Approach Cl N16 16 A4
Approach Rd E2 25 B3
Approach The W3 28 C3
April Ct 20 E2 24 C3
April St E8 16 B4
Apsley Ho
Stepney E1 32 B4
St John's Wood NW8 79 B2
Apsley Ho, The Wellington Mus SW1 131 C4
Apsley Way W1 131 C4
Aquila St NW8 79 C2
Aquinas St SE1 121 C1
Arabella Ct NW8 79 A2
Arabella Dr SW15 56 A3
Arabian Ho 3 E1 26 A1
Arabin Rd SE4 66 B3
Aragon Twr SE8 41 B2
Arakan Ho 4 N16 15 C4
Aral Ho 14 E1 25 C1
Arapiles Ho 6 E14 34 C3
Arbery Rd E3 26 A3
Arbon Ct N1 87 A3
Arbor Ct N16 6 C2
Arborfield Cl SW2 74 B3
Arborfield Ho 7 E14 33 C2
Arbour Ho 3 E1 32 C3
Arbour Sq E1 32 C3
Arbuthnot Rd SE14 50 C1
Arbutus St E8 24 B4
Arcade The
Broadgate EC2 110 A3
1 Tufnell Pk N7 14 A4
Arcadian Ho SW6 167 A1
Arcadian Pl SW18 70 B4
Arcadia St E14 33 C3
Arcadia Univ W2 114 A3
Archangel St SE16 40 C4
Archbishop Coggan Ho SE13 67 C3
Archbishop's Pl 1 SW2 74 B4
Archbishop Sumner CE Prim Sch SE11 149 C3
Archbishop Tenison's Sch SE11 163 A3
Archdale Ct W12 30 A1
Archdale Ho SE1 138 A2
Archdale Rd SE22 64 B3
Archel Rd W14 154 C4
Archer Ho
1 Battersea SW11 167 C2
24 Hoxton N1 24 A4
1 New Cross SE14 51 A2
Notting Hill W11 31 B2 113 A4
Archers Lo 22 SE16 153 C1
Archer Sq SE14 51 A4
Archer St W1 119 B4
Archery Cl W2 102 B1
Archery Fields Ho WC1 95 B4
Archery Stps W2 116 B4
Arches The WC2 120 B2
Archibald Mews W1 118 A3
Archibald Rd N7 13 C4
Archibald St E3 26 C2
Archie St SE1 138 B3
Arch St SE1 136 C1
Archway N19 4 B2
Archway Bsns Ctr 5 N19 4 C1
Archway Cl
North Kensington W10 30 C4
2 Upper Holloway N19 4 B2
Archway Hts 5 N19 4 B3
Archway L Ctr N19 4 B2
Archway Mews SW15 58 A3
Archway Rd N6 4 A4
Archway St SW13, SW14 56 A4
Archway Sta N19 4 B2
Arcola St E8 16 B3
Arctic St NW5 13 A3
Ardbeg Rd SE24 63 C2
Arden 17 SW19 69 C3
Arden Cres E14 41 C2
Arden Ho
21 Hoxton N1 24 A3
29 Stockwell SW9 172 B1
Vauxhall SE11 148 C3
Ardent Ho 30 E3 26 A3
Ardilaun Rd N5 15 B4
Ardleigh Rd N1 16 A2
Ardlui Rd SE27 75 B2
Ardmere Rd SE13 67 C1
Ardshiel Cl 6 SW15 57 C4
Ardwell Rd SW2 74 A2
Ardwick Rd NW2 10 C4
Ares Ct 16 E14 41 C2
Arethusa Ho 8 E14 42 A2
Argo Bsns Ctr 7 NW6 23 C2
Argon Mews SW6 155 C1
Argos Ct 5 SW9 173 B4
Argos Ho 8 E2 25 A3
Argosy Ho
Fitzrovia W1 92 B1
Rotherhithe SE8 41 A2
Argyle Ho E14 42 B3
Argyle Mans 4 NW2 9 C4
Argyle Pl W6 39 A2
Argyle Prim Sch WC1 94 A4
Argyle Rd E1 25 C1
Argyle Sq WC1 94 B4
Argyle St WC1 94 B4
Argyle Way SE16 153 C1
Argyle Wlk WC1 94 B3
Argyll Cl SW9 62 B4
Argyll Ct 15 SW2 74 A4
Argyll Mans
Chelsea SW3 157 C4
West Kensington W14 140 B4
Argyll Rd W8 127 C3
Argyll St W1 104 C1
Arica Ho SE16 40 A3
Arica Rd SE4 66 A4
Ariel Ct
5 Hammersmith W12 38 C3
Newington SE11 150 A3
Ariel Rd NW6 10 C2
Ariel Way W11, W12 30 C1
Aristotle Rd SW4 61 C4
Arizona Bldg 10 SE13 52 A2
Arkansas Ho 21 N19 4 C4
Ark Ct N16 7 B2
Arklow Ho SE17 48 C4
Arklow Rd SE14 51 B4
Arklow Road Trad Est SE14 51 B4
Arkwright Ho 23 SW2 74 A4
Arkwright Mans 1 NW3 11 B3
Arkwright Rd NW3 11 B3
Arlesey Cl SW15 58 A2
Arlesford Rd SW9 62 A4
Arlidge Ho EC1 107 C4
Arlingford Rd SW2 62 C1
Arlington Ave N1 87 A3
Arlington Cl SE13 67 C2
Arlington Ct 13 W3 28 A1
Arlington Gdns W4 37 B1
Arlington Ho
3 Deptford SE8 51 B4
Finsbury EC1 95 C4
1 Shepherd's Bush W12 30 A1
Arlington Lo SW2 62 B3
Arlington Park Mans 1 W4 37 B1
Arlington Pl 7 SE10 52 B3
Arlington Rd NW1 82 B3
Arlington Sq N1 87 A3
Arlington St SW1 118 C2
Arlington Way EC1 95 C4
Armada Ct 11 SE8 51 C4
Armadale Rd SW6 155 B3
Armada St 10 SE8 51 C4
Armagh Rd E3 26 B4
Arminger Rd W12 30 A1
Armitage Ho NW1 102 B4
Armitage Rd
Golders Green NW11 1 B3
Greenwich SE10 43 B1
Armour Cl N7 14 B2
Armoury Ho E3 26 A4
Armoury Rd SE8 52 A1

- Armoury Way SW18 ... 58 C2
- Armsby Ho 17 E1 ... 32 B4
- Armstrong Ho 8 SW15 ... 57 C1
- Armstrong Rd
  - East Acton W3 ... 29 B1
  - Knightsbridge SW7 ... 129 B1
  - 10 Willesden NW10 ... 8 A1
- Arnal Cres SW18 ... 70 A4
- Arncliffe NW6 ... 78 B3
- Arndale Wlk 6 SW18 ... 59 A2
- Arne Ho SE11 ... 148 C2
- Arne St WC2 ... 106 B1
- Arneway St SW1 ... 133 C1
- Arnewood Cl SW15 ... 68 C3
- Arnhem Pl E14 ... 41 C3
- Arnhem Way 3 SE22 ... 64 A2
- Arnhem Wharf E14 ... 41 C3
- Arnhem Wharf Prim Sch E14 ... 41 C3
- Arnold Cir E2 ... 24 B2 98 C3
- Arnold Est SE1 ... 139 A3
- Arnold Ho
  - Newington SE17 ... 150 B1
  - 9 Stoke Newington N16 ... 7 A1
- Arnold House Sch NW8 ... 79 B1
- Arnold Rd E3 ... 26 C2
- Arnot Ho 27 SE5 ... 48 B3
- Arnott Cl W4 ... 37 C2
- Arnould Ave SE5 ... 63 C3
- Arnside Ho 2 SE17 ... 48 C4
- Arnside St SE17 ... 48 B4
- Arodene Rd SW2 ... 62 B1
- Arragon Rd SW18 ... 70 C3
- Arran Ho
  - 5 Canary Wharf E14 ... 34 B1
  - Stoke Newington N16 ... 7 B3
- Arran Wlk N1 ... 15 B1
- Arrol Ho SE1 ... 137 A1
- Arrowe Ct 6 E5 ... 17 A4
- Arrow Ho 23 N1 ... 24 A4
- Arrow Rd E3 ... 27 A2
- Arrowsmith Ho SE11 ... 148 C2
- Arsenal Sta N5 ... 5 C1
- Arta Ho 26 E1 ... 32 B3
- Artcadia Lifestyle EC2 ... 110 C4
- Artemis Ct 14 E14 ... 41 C2
- Artemis Pl SW18 ... 70 B4
- Artesian Rd W2 ... 31 C3
- Arthur Ct
  - Battersea SW11 ... 169 C3
  - 10 North Kensington W10 ... 30 C3
  - Paddington W2 ... 100 A2
- Arthur Deakin Ho 1 E1 ... 111 B4
- Arthurdon Rd SE4 ... 66 C2
- Arthur Henderson Ho
  - 9 Crouch End N19 ... 4 C4
  - 9 Fulham SW6 ... 164 C2
- Arthur Newton Ho 19 SW11 ... 59 C4
- Arthur Rd N7 ... 14 B4
- Arthur St EC4 ... 123 C4
- Arthur Wade Ho 7 E2 ... 24 B2 99 A4
- Artichoke Hill 8 E1 ... 32 A2
- Artichoke Mews 5 SE5 ... 48 C2
- Artichoke Pl SE5 ... 48 C2
- Artillery Ho
  - Bow E3 ... 26 A4
  - Westminster SW1 ... 133 B1
- Artillery La
  - Broadgate E1 ... 110 B3
  - North Kensington W12 ... 29 C3
- Artillery Pas E1 ... 110 B3
- Artillery Pl SW1 ... 133 B1
- Artillery Row SW1 ... 133 B1
- Artisan Ct E8 ... 16 C2
- Artisan Mews 9 NW10 ... 22 C2
- Artisan Quarter 10 NW10 ... 22 C2
- Artizan St E1 ... 110 B2
- Arton Wilson Ho 12 SW15 ... 56 C2
- Arts Educational Sch The 14 W4 ... 38 A2
- Arundel Bldgs SE1 ... 138 B1
- Arundel Cl SW11 ... 60 A2
- Arundel Ct
  - Barnes SW13 ... 47 A4
  - Chelsea SW3 ... 144 B2
  - Putney SW15 ... 57 C2
- Arundel Gdns W11 ... 31 B2 112 C4
- Arundel Gr N16 ... 16 A3
- Arundel Ho
  - Islington N1 ... 86 B4
  - Richmond TW10 ... 54 C2
  - 3 South Acton W3 ... 37 A4
- Arundel Lo 9 N19 ... 5 A2
- Arundel Mans
  - Barnes SW13 ... 47 A4
  - Fulham SW6 ... 165 A4
- Arundel Pl N1, N7 ... 14 C2
- Arundel Sq N7 ... 14 C2
- Arundel St WC2 ... 121 A4
- Arundel Terr SW13 ... 47 A4
- Arungford Mews 12 SW2 ... 62 C2
- Arvon Rd N5 ... 14 C3
- Asaph Ho SE14 ... 51 B2
- Ascalon Ct 16 SW2 ... 74 B4
- Ascalon Ho SW8 ... 160 C1
- Ascalon St SW8 ... 160 C1
- Ascham St NW5 ... 13 B3
- Ascot Ct
  - 8 Brixton SW4 ... 62 A3
  - St John's Wood NW8 ... 89 B3
- Ascot Ho
  - 6 Acton Green W4 ... 37 B1
  - 1 Paddington W9 ... 31 C4
  - Regent's Pk NW1 ... 92 B4
- Ascot Lo NW6 ... 78 B2
- Ascot Par 9 SW4 ... 62 A3
- Ascott Ave W5 ... 36 A4
- Ashbourne Coll W8 ... 128 A3
- Ashbourne Ct E5 ... 18 A4
- Ashbourne Gr
  - Chiswick W4 ... 38 A1
  - East Dulwich SE22 ... 64 B3
- Ashbridge Ct 3 W6 ... 39 A3
- Ashbridge St NW8 ... 90 A1
- Ashbrook Rd N19 ... 4 C2
- Ashburn Gdns SW7 ... 142 C4
- Ashburnham Gr SE10 ... 52 A3
- Ashburnham Pl SE10 ... 52 A3
- Ashburnham Prim Sch SW10 ... 157 B2
- Ashburnham Rd
  - Chelsea SW10 ... 157 A1
  - Kensal Rise NW10 ... 22 B3
- Ashburnham Retreat 4 SE10 ... 52 A3
- Ashburnham Twr SW10 ... 157 B2
- Ashburn Pl SW7 ... 142 C3
- Ashburton Mans SW10 ... 157 A2
- Ashburton Rd E16 ... 35 C3
- Ashbury Rd SW11 ... 60 C4
- Ashby Ct NW8 ... 89 C2
- Ashby Gr N1 ... 15 B1
- Ashby Ho
  - 6 Brixton SW9 ... 48 A1
  - 17 Islington N1 ... 15 B1
- Ashby Mews
  - 10 Clapham Pk SW2 ... 62 A2
  - New Cross SE4 ... 51 B1
- Ashby Rd SE4 ... 51 B1
- Ashby St EC1 ... 96 B3
- Ashchurch Ct 2 W12 ... 38 C3
- Ashchurch Gr W12 ... 38 C3
- Ashchurch Park Villas W12 ... 38 C3
- Ashchurch Terr W12 ... 38 C3
- Ashcombe Ct 4 SW15 ... 58 A2
- Ashcombe Ho 39 E3 ... 27 A2
- Ashcombe St SW6 ... 166 A1
- Ashcroft Ho SW8 ... 170 C4
- Ashcroft Rd E3 ... 26 A2
- Ashcroft Sq 8 W6 ... 39 B2
- Ashcroft Tech Acad SW15 ... 58 B2
- Ash Ct
  - Clapham SW11 ... 60 C2
  - Marylebone W1 ... 102 C2
  - 6 Rotherhithe SE16 ... 33 A1
  - Upper Holloway N19 ... 4 B2
- Ashdale Ho N4 ... 6 C4
- Ashdene 6 SE15 ... 50 A3
- Ashdon Rd NW10 ... 21 B4
- Ashdown SW15 ... 57 C2
- Ashdown Cres NW5 ... 12 C3
- Ashdown Ct SE22 ... 76 C3
- Ashdown Ho 7 E5 ... 7 C2
- Ashdown Way SW17 ... 72 C2
- Ashdown Wlk 20 E14 ... 41 C2
- Ashenden SE17 ... 151 A4
- Ashenden Rd E5 ... 18 A3
- Ashen Gr SW19 ... 70 C2
- Ashentree Ct EC4 ... 107 C1
- Asher Way E1 ... 125 C3
- Ashfield Ho 5 N5 ... 15 B3
- Ashfield Rd W3 ... 29 B1
- Ashfield St
  - E1 ... 32 B4
  - 4 Whitechapel E1 ... 32 A4
- Ashfield Yd 21 E1 ... 32 B4
- Ashford Ct NW2 ... 9 C4
- Ashford Ho
  - 14 Brixton SW9 ... 63 A3
  - 11 Deptford SE8 ... 51 B4
- Ashford Rd NW2 ... 9 C4
- Ashford St N1 ... 24 A2 98 A4
- Ash Gr
  - Cricklewood NW2 ... 10 A4
  - Ealing W5 ... 36 A3
  - Hackney E8 ... 25 A4
- Ashgrove Ct 2 W9 ... 31 C4
- Ashgrove Ho SW1 ... 147 C2
- Ash Ho
  - 3 Canary Wharf E14 ... 42 B4
  - Fulham SE1 ... 153 A3
- Ashington 1 NW5 ... 13 A2
- Ashington Ho 16 E1 ... 25 A1
- Ashington Rd SW6 ... 165 A1
- Ashland Pl W1 ... 103 B4
- Ashleigh Ho SW14 ... 56 A4
- Ashleigh Rd SW14 ... 56 A4
- Ashley Cres SW11 ... 60 C4
- Ashley Ct
  - Hampstead NW3 ... 11 A3
  - 19 Kingsland N16 ... 16 A3
- Ashley Pl SW1 ... 132 C1
- Ashley Rd
  - Hornsey N19 ... 5 A4
  - Richmond TW9 ... 54 A4
- Ashlin Rd E15 ... 19 C4
- Ash Lo SW6 ... 47 C2
- Ashlone Rd SW15 ... 57 C4
- Ashmead Bsns Ctr 2 E16 ... 27 C1
- Ashmead Ho E9 ... 18 A3
- Ashmead Mews 1 SE8 ... 51 C1
- Ashmead Prim Sch SE8 ... 51 C1
- Ashmead Rd SE8 ... 51 C1
- Ashmere Gr 11 SW2, SW4 ... 62 A3
- Ashmere Ho 10 SW2 ... 62 A3
- Ashmill St NW8 ... 102 A4
- Ashmole Prim Sch SW8 ... 163 A3
- Ashmole St SW8 ... 163 A3
- Ashmore NW1 ... 13 C1
- Ashmore Cl SE15 ... 49 B3
- Ashmore Ho W14 ... 126 B1
- Ashmore Rd W9 ... 23 B2
- Ashmount Prim Sch N19 ... 4 B4
- Ashmount Rd N19 ... 4 C4
- Ashness Rd SW11 ... 60 B2
- Ashpark Ho 4 E14 ... 33 B3
- Ashtead Ct 15 SW19 ... 69 C3
- Ashtead Rd E5 ... 7 C4
- Ashton Ho
  - 13 Kennington SW9 ... 163 C1
  - Roehampton SW15 ... 69 A4
- Ashton Rd E15 ... 19 C3
- Ashton St E14 ... 34 B2
- Ashurst Lo 4 N5 ... 15 A3
- Ashwin St E8 ... 16 B2
- Ashworth Cl SE5 ... 48 C1
- Ashworth Mans W9 ... 88 B3
- Ashworth Rd W9 ... 88 B3
- Aske Ho 2 N1 ... 24 A2 98 A4
- Asker Ho N7 ... 14 A4
- Aske St N1 ... 24 A2 98 A4
- Askew Cres W12 ... 38 C4
- Askew Mans 14 W12 ... 38 C4
- Askew Rd W12 ... 38 C4
- Askham Ct W12 ... 29 C1
- Askham Rd W12 ... 29 C1
- Askill Dr SW15 ... 58 A2
- Asland Rd E15 ... 27 C4
- Aslett St SW18 ... 71 B4
- Asmara Rd NW2 ... 10 A3
- Asolando Dr SE17 ... 151 A3
- Aspect Ho 7 E14 ... 42 B4
- Aspen Cl
  - Ealing W5 ... 36 B4
  - 13 Upper Holloway N19 ... 4 B2
- Aspen Ct
  - 10 Acton W3 ... 28 B3
  - 12 Hackney E8 ... 16 C3
  - Richmond TW9 ... 44 C3
- Aspen Gdns 2 W6 ... 39 A1
- Aspen Ho
  - 8 Deptford SE15 ... 50 B4
  - 4 Maitland Pk NW3 ... 12 B2
  - Richmond TW9 ... 44 C3
- Aspenlea Rd W6 ... 47 C4
- Aspen Way E14 ... 34 B2
- Aspern Gr NW3 ... 12 A3
- Aspinall Ho SW12 ... 74 A3
- Aspinall Rd SE4 ... 65 C4
- Aspinden Rd SE16 ... 40 A2
- Aspire Bld 10 SW15 ... 58 B2
- Aspley Rd SW18 ... 59 A2
- Assam SE1 ... 125 A1
- Assam St E1 ... 111 B2
- Assata Mews N1 ... 15 A2
- Assembly Pas E1 ... 32 B4
- Assisi Ct SW12 ... 72 B3
- Astbury Bsns Pk 5 SE15 ... 50 B2
- Astbury Ho SE11 ... 135 B1
- Astbury Rd SE15 ... 50 B2
- Astell St SW3 ... 144 B2
- Aster Ho 3 SE13 ... 52 B1
- Aste St E14 ... 42 B4
- Astey's Row 1 N1 ... 15 B1
- Astle St SW11 ... 169 C2
- Astley Ave NW2 ... 9 B3
- Astley Ho
  - Fulham SE1 ... 153 A2
  - 39 Paddington W2 ... 31 C4
- Aston Ct N4 ... 6 B2
- Aston Ho
  - Notting Hill W11 ... 31 B2 113 A4

Aston Ho *continued*
South Lambeth SW8 171 B3
Aston St E14 33 A4
Astonville St SW18 70 C3
Astor Ct SW6 156 C1
Astoria Mans 18 SW16 74 A1
Astoria Par SW16 74 A1
Astoria Wlk SW9 62 C4
Astra Ho
4 Bow E3 26 B2
Hornsey N4 5 B4
Astrop Mews W6 39 B3
Astrop Terr W6 39 B4
Astwood Mews SW7 142 C4
Asylum Rd SE15 50 A3
Atalanta St SW6 47 C3 154 A1
Atheldene Rd SW18 71 B3
Athelstane Gr E3 26 B3
Athelstane Mews N4 5 C3
Athelstan Gdns 8 NW6 10 A1
Athelstan Ho
Hackney Wick E9 18 B3
Stoke Newington N16 16 A4
Athena Ct
Bermondsey SE1 138 A3
St John's Wood NW8 79 B2
Athenia Ho 7 E14 34 C3
Athenlay Rd SE15 65 C2
Athenoeum Ct N5 15 B4
Athens Gdns W9 23 C1
Atherden Rd E5 17 B4
Atherfield Ct SW18 59 A1
Atherfold Rd SW9 62 A4
Atherstone Ct W2 100 B4
Atherstone Mews SW7 143 A4
Atherton Rd SW13 46 C3
Atherton St SW11 168 B2
Athlone Cl 24 E5 17 A3
Athlone Ho
16 Camden Town NW5 12 C2
9 Stepney E1 32 B3
Athlone Rd SW2 74 C4
Athlone St NW5 12 C2
Athol Ct 15 N4 5 B2
Atholl Ho W9 88 C3
Athol Sq E14 34 B3
Atkins Ct 13 E3 26 B4
Atkins Lo W8 127 B4
Atkinson Ho
Battersea SW11 169 B3
15 Hackney E2 24 C3
Walworth SE17 151 C3
Atkins Rd SW4, SW12 73 C4
Atlanta Bldg 8 SE13 52 A2
Atlantic Ct 19 E14 34 C2
Atlantic Ho
5 Putney SW15 58 B2
4 Tower Hamlets E1 33 A4
Atlantic Rd SW2, SW9, SE24 62 C3
Atlas Mews
Dalston E8 16 B2
Islington N7 14 B2
Atlas Rd NW10 21 A2
Atney Rd SW15 58 A3
Atterbury St SW1 148 A3
Attilburgh Ho SE1 138 C2
Attlee Ho E1 111 A3
Attneave St WC1 95 B3
Atwater Cl SW2 74 C3
Atwell Rd 6 SE15 49 C1
Atwood Ave TW9 44 C1
Atwood Ho SE21 76 A1
Atwood Rd W6 39 A2
Aubert Ct N5 15 A4
Aubert Pk N5 15 A4
Aubert Rd N5 15 A4
Aubrey Beardsley Ho SW1 147 A3
Aubrey Mans NW1 102 A4
Aubrey Moore Point E15 27 B3
Aubrey Pl NW8 78 C1
Aubrey Rd W14 31 B1 113 A1
Aubrey Wlk W14 31 B1 113 A1
Auburn Cl SE14 51 A3
Aubyn Sq SW15 56 C2
Auckland Ho 11 W12 30 A2
Auckland Rd SW11 60 A3
Auckland St SE11 148 C1
Auden Pl NW1 81 B4
Audley Cl 8 SW11 60 C4
Audley Ct W1 118 A2
Audley Rd TW10 54 B2
Audley Sq W1 117 C2
Audley St W1 117 C2
Audrey Ho EC1 107 C3
Audrey St E2 24 C3
Augusta St E14 34 A3
Augustine Ho
Broadgate EC2 109 C2
New Cross SE4 51 B2
Augustine Rd W14 39 C3
Augustines Ct E9 17 B3
Augustus Cl W12 39 A3
Augustus Ct
8 Putney SW19 70 A3
Streatham SW16 73 C2
Augustus Ho NW1 92 C4
Augustus Rd
33 Putney SW19 69 C3
Putney SW19 70 A3
Augustus St NW1 92 B4
Aulton Pl SE11 149 C1
Aura Ho 3 TW9 45 A2
Auriga Mews N1 15 C3
Auriol Mans W14 140 A3
Auriol Rd W14 140 A3
Aurora Bldg 4 E14 34 B1
Aurora Ho E14 34 A3
Austen Ho 5 NW6 23 C2
Austin Friars EC2 109 C2
Austin Friars Ho EC2 109 C2
Austin Friars Sq EC2 109 C2
Austin Ho
6 Brixton SW2 62 B2
Austin Ho *continued*
1 New Cross SE14 51 B3
Austin Rd SW11 169 B3
Austins Ct SE15 64 C4
Austin St E2 24 B2 98 C3
Australia Rd W12 30 A2
Austral St SE11 150 A4
Autumn Rise 9 W4 37 C1
Autumn St E3 26 C4
Avalon Rd SW6 166 A4
Avebury Ct N1 87 B3
Avebury St N1 87 B3
Aveline St SE11 149 B1
Aveling Ho 12 N19 4 B1
Ave Maria La EC4 108 B1
Avenell Mans N5 15 A4
Avenell Rd N5 6 A1
Avenfield Ho W1 117 A4
Avening Rd SW18 70 C4
Avening Terr SW18 70 C4
Avenue Cl NW8 80 B3
Avenue Cres W3 37 A4
Avenue Ct
Chelsea SW3 144 C3
Cricklewood NW2 1 A1
Avenue Gdns
Mortlake SW14 56 A4
South Acton W3 37 A4
Avenue Ho
St John's Wood NW8 80 A1
Upper Clapton N16 7 C2
Willesden Green NW10 22 A3
Avenue Lo 12 NW8 11 C1
Avenue Mans
Clapham SW11 60 C3
Hampstead NW3 11 A3
Willesden NW2 9 A2
Avenue Park Rd SE21, SE27 75 A2
Avenue Rd
Crouch End N6 4 C4
Harlesden NW10 21 B3
Primrose Hill NW8 80 A4
South Acton W3 37 A4
Avenue The
Bedford Pk W4 38 A3
Brondesbury Pk NW6 23 A4
Clapham SW4 60 C2
Greenwich SE10 52 C3
Richmond TW9 44 B1
Wandsworth SW18, SW12 72 A4
Averill St W6 47 C4
Avery Farm Row SW1 146 A3
Avery Hill Coll (Mile End Annexe) E3 26 B1
Avery Row W1 118 B4
Aviary Cl E16 35 B4
Avignon Rd SE4 65 C4
Avingdor Ct 10 W3 28 B1
Avington Ct SE1 152 B3
Avis Sq E1 32 C3
Avocet Cl SE1 153 B2
Avon Ct
1 Acton W3 28 B3
10 Putney SW15 58 A2
Avondale Ct E16 35 A4
Avondale Ho
11 Bermondsey SE1 153 B1
6 Mortlake SW14 55 C4
Avondale Mans SW6 164 C4
Avondale Park Gdns W11 31 A2 112 A3
Avondale Park Prim Sch W11 31 A2 112 A3
Avondale Park Rd W11 31 A2 112 A4
Avondale Rd
Mortlake SW14 55 C4
Newham E16 35 A4
Avondale Rise SE15 64 B4
Avondale Sq SE1 153 B1
Avon Ho
2 Islington N1 14 C1
14 Stoke Newington N16 15 C4
West Kensington W14 141 A3
Avonhurst Ho NW6 10 A1
Avonley Rd SE14 50 B3
Avonmore Gdns W14 141 A3
Avonmore Pl W14 140 B4
Avonmore Prim Sch W14 140 B4
Avonmore Rd W14 140 C4
Avonmouth St SE1 136 C2
Avon Pl SE1 137 A3
Avon Rd SE4 66 C4
Avriol Ho W12 30 A1
Avro Ct E9 18 A3
Axford Ho SW2 75 A3
Axis Ct SE10 53 A4
Axminster Rd N7 5 B1
Aybrook St W1 103 B3
Aycliffe Rd W12 29 C1
Aylesbury Ho 13 SE15 49 C4
Aylesbury Rd SE17 151 C1
Aylesbury St EC1 96 A1
Aylesford Ho SE1 137 C3
Aylesford St SW1 147 B1
Aylesham Sh Ctr SE15 49 C2
Aylestone Ave NW6 22 C4
Aylmer Ho SE10 42 C1
Aylmer Rd W12 38 B4
Aylton Est 28 SE16 40 B4
Aylward St E1 32 C3
Aylwin Est SE1 138 B2
Aynhoe Mans W14 39 C2
Aynhoe Rd W14 39 C3
Ayres St SE1 137 A4
Ayrsome Rd N16 7 A1
Ayrton Gould Ho 9 E2 25 C2
Ayrton Rd SW7 129 B2
Aysgarth Rd SE21 76 A4
Ayshford Ho E1 25 A2
Ayston Ho 19 SE8 40 C2
Aytoun Ct 17 SW9 173 A1
Aytoun Pl SW9 173 A1
Aytoun Rd SW9 173 A1
Azalea Ho SE14 51 B3
Azania Mews NW5 13 A2
Azenby Rd SE15 49 B1
Azof St SE10 43 A2
Azov Ho 10 E1 26 A1
Aztec Ct 8 N16 16 A2
Azure Ho 28 E2 24 C2 99 B3

B

Baalbec Rd N5 15 A3
Babington Ct WC1 106 B4
Babington Ho SE1 137 A4
Babmaes St SW1 119 B3
Bacchus Wlk 12 N1 24 A3
Bache's St N1 97 C3
Back Church La E1 111 B1
Back Hill EC1 95 C1
Backhouse Pl SE1 152 B3
Back La NW3 11 B4
Bacon Gr SE1 138 C1
Bacon's Coll SE16 41 A4
Bacon's La N6 3 C3
Bacon St E2 24 B1 99 A2
Bacton NW5 12 C3
Bacton St E2 25 B2
Baddeley Ho SE11 149 A2
Baddow Wlk N1 86 C4
Baden Pl SE1 137 B4
Badminton Ct 9 N4 6 B4
Badminton Ho SE22 64 A3
Badminton Mews 9 E16 35 C1
Badminton Rd SW12 60 C1
Badric Ct SW11 167 C1
Badsworth Rd 3 SE5 48 B2
Bagley's La SW6 166 B3
Bagnigge Ho WC1 95 B3
Bagshot Ho NW1 92 B4
Bagshot St SE17 152 B1
Baildon 27 E2 25 B3
Baildon St SE8 51 B3
Bailey Ct 9 W12 38 C4
Bailey Ho SW10 156 B2
Bailey Mews
Brixton SW2 62 C2
Chiswick W4 45 A4
Bainbridge St WC1 105 C2
Bain Ho 23 SW9 172 B2
Baird Ho 29 W12 30 A2
Baird St EC1 97 A2
Baizdon Rd SE3 53 A1
Baker Ho 12 E3 27 A2
Baker Rd NW10 21 A4
Bakers Field N7 14 A4
Bakers Hall Ct EC3 124 B3
Baker's Mews W1 103 B2
Bakers Pas 22 NW3 11 B4
Bakers Rents 13 E2 24 B2 98 C3
Baker's Row EC1 95 B1
Baker St W1 103 A4
Baker Street W1 103 A4
Baker Street Sta NW1 91 A1

Baker's Yd EC1 ... 95 B1
Bakery Cl SW9 ... 163 A1
Balaclava Rd SE1 153 A3
Balchier Rd SE22 ... 65 A1
Balcombe Ho
Lisson Gr NW1 ... 90 C2
3 Streatham SW2 ... 74 B3
Balcombe St NW1 ... 90 C1
Balcorne St E9 ... 17 B1
Balderton Flats
W1 ... 103 C1
Balderton St W1 ... 103 C1
Baldock Ho 31 SE5 ... 48 B1
Baldock St E3 ... 27 A3
Baldrey Ho 1
SE10 ... 43 B1
Baldwin Cres SE5 ... 48 B2
Baldwin Ho 15
SW2 ... 74 C3
Baldwin Rd SW12 ... 60 C1
Baldwin's Gdns
EC1 ... 107 B4
Baldwin St EC1 ... 97 B3
Baldwin Terr N1 ... 86 C2
Baldwyn Gdns W3 ... 28 C2
Balearic Apts 3
E16 ... 35 C2
Bale Rd E1 ... 33 A4
Bales Coll W10 ... 22 C2
Balfern Gr W4 ... 38 A1
Balfern St SW11 ... 168 B2
Balfe St N1 ... 84 B1
Balfour Ho 4
W10 ... 30 C4
Balfour Mews W1 117 C2
Balfour Pl
Mayfair W1 ... 117 C3
Putney SW15 ... 57 A3
Balfour Rd
Highbury N5 ... 15 B4
North Acton W3 ... 28 B4
Balfour St SE17 ... 151 B4
Balfron Twr 4
E14 ... 34 B3
BALHAM ... 72 C3
Balham Gr SW12 ... 72 C4
Balham High Rd SW12,
SW17 ... 72 C3
Balham Hill SW12 ... 61 A1
Balham L Ctr
SW12 ... 73 A2
Balham New Rd
SW12 ... 73 A4
Balham Park Mans
SW12 ... 72 B3
Balham Park Rd SW12,
SW17 ... 72 C3
Balham Sta SW12 ... 73 A3
Balham Station Rd
SW12 ... 73 A3
Balin Ho SE1 ... 137 B4
Balkan Wlk E1 ... 32 A2
Balladier Wlk E14 ... 34 A4
Ballance Rd E9 ... 18 A2
Ballantine St
SW18 ... 59 B3
Ballantrae Ho
NW2 ... 10 B4
Ballard Ho SE10 ... 52 A4
Ballast Quay SE10 ... 42 C1
Ballater Rd SW2,
SW4 ... 62 A3
Ball Ct EC3 ... 109 C1
Ballin Ct 14 E14 ... 42 B4
Ballingdon Rd
SW11 ... 60 C1
Ballinger Point 18
E3 ... 27 A2
Balliol Ho 11
SW15 ... 57 C1
Balliol Rd W10 ... 30 C3
Ballogie Ave NW10 ... 8 A4
Ballow Cl 15 SE5 ... 49 A3
Ball's Pond Pl 3
N1 ... 15 C2
Ball's Pond Rd N1 ... 16 A2
Balman Ho 3
SE16 ... 40 C2
Balmer Rd E3 ... 26 B3
Balmes Rd N1 ... 87 C4
Balmoral Cl 1
SW15 ... 57 C1
Balmoral Ct
21 Rotherhithe
SE16 ... 32 C1
St John's Wood
NW8 ... 79 B2
Balmoral Gr N7 ... 14 B2
Balmoral Ho
2 Isle Of Dogs
E14 ... 42 A3
Stoke Newington N4 ... 6 B3
West Kensington
W14 ... 140 A4
Balmoral Mews
W12 ... 38 B3
Balmoral Rd NW2 ... 9 A2
Balmore Cl E14 ... 34 B3
Balmore St N19 ... 4 A2
Balmuir Gdns
SW15 ... 57 B3
Balnacraig Ave
NW10 ... 8 A4
Balniel Gate SW1 147 C2
Balsam Ho 9 E14 ... 34 A2
Baltic Apts 5 E16 ... 35 C2
Baltic Ho 7 SE5 ... 48 B1
Baltic St E EC1 ... 96 C1
Baltic St W EC1 ... 96 C1
Baltimore Ho
Clapham SW18 ... 59 B3
Kennington SE11 ... 149 B2
Balvaird Pl SW1 ... 147 C1
Balvernie Gr SW18 ... 70 C4
Bamber Rd 5
SE15 ... 49 B2
Bamborough Gdns 12
W12 ... 39 B4
Banbury Ct WC2 ... 120 A4
Banbury Ho 5 E9 ... 17 C1
Banbury Rd E9 ... 17 C1
Banbury St 3
SW11 ... 168 B2
Bancroft Ct SW8 ... 172 A4
Bancroft Ho 11 E1 ... 25 B1
Bancroft Rd E1 ... 25 C1
Banff Ho 1 NW3 ... 12 A2
Banfield Rd SE15 ... 65 A4
Bangabandhu Prim
Sch 38 E2 ... 25 B2
Bangalore St
SW15 ... 57 C4
Banim St W6 ... 39 A2
Banister Ho
Hackney E9 ... 17 C3
Nine Elms SW8 ... 171 A4
9 West Kilburn
W10 ... 23 A2
Banister Rd W10 ... 22 C2
Bank Ct SW11 ... 170 A4
Bank End SE1 ... 123 A2
Bank La SW15 ... 56 A2
Bank of England
EC2 ... 109 B1
Bank of England Mus
EC2 ... 109 B1
Banks Ho SE1 ... 136 C1
Bankside
Borough The SE1 ... 122 C3
Borough The SE1 ... 123 A2
Bankside Ave 1
SE13 ... 67 B4
Bankside Gall
SE1 ... 122 B3
Bankside Ho EC3 ... 110 B1
BankSide Mix SE1 122 C2
Bankside Pier
SE1 ... 122 C3
Bank St E14 ... 34 A1
Bank Sta EC3 ... 109 C1
Bank The N6 ... 4 A3
Bankton Rd SW2 ... 62 C3
Banner Ct 5 SE16 ... 40 B2
Banner Ho EC1 ... 97 A1
Bannerman Ho
SW8 ... 162 C3
Banner St EC1 ... 97 A2
Banning Ho 4
SW19 ... 69 C3
Banning St SE10 ... 43 A1
Bannister Cl SW2 ... 74 C3
Bannister Ho 28
SE14 ... 50 C4
Banqueting Ho
SW1 ... 120 A1
Banstead Ct
East Acton W12 ... 29 B2
Stoke Newington N4 ... 6 B3
Banstead St SE15 ... 65 B4
Bantock Ho 8
W10 ... 23 A2
Bantry Ho 13 E1 ... 25 C1
Bantry St SE5 ... 48 C3
Banville Ho SW8 ... 163 A1
Banyan Ho 8
NW3 ... 11 A2
Banyard Rd SE16 ... 40 A3
Baptist Gdns NW5 ... 12 C2
Barandon Wlk 6
W11 ... 30 C2
Barbanel Ho 26 E1 ... 25 B1
Barbara Brosnan Ct
NW8 ... 79 B1
Barbara Castle Cl
SW6 ... 155 A3
Barbara Rudolph Ct
5 N19 ... 5 A4
Barbauld Rd N16 ... 7 A1
Barber Beaumont Ho
21 E1 ... 25 C2
Barbers Rd E15 ... 27 A3
BARBICAN ... 109 A3
Barbican Ctr EC2 109 A4
Barb Mews W6 ... 39 B3
Barbon Alley EC3 ... 110 B2
Barbon Cl WC1 ... 106 C4
Barbrook Ho E9 ... 17 B2
Barchard St SW18 ... 59 A2
Barchester St E14 ... 34 A4
Barclay Cl SW6 ... 155 B1
Barclay Ho 21 E9 ... 17 B1
Barclay Rd SW6 ... 155 C1
Barcombe Ave
SW2 ... 74 B2
Bardell Ho 17 SE1 139 B3
Bardolph Rd
Richmond TW9 ... 54 B4
Tufnell Pk N7 ... 14 A4
Bard Rd W10 ... 30 C2
Bardsey Pl 41 E1 ... 25 B1
Bardsey Wlk 5
N1 ... 15 B2
Bardsley Ho 6
SE10 ... 52 B4
Bardsley La SE10 ... 52 B4
Barents Ho 10 E1 ... 25 C1
Barfett St W10 ... 23 B1
Barfleur La SE8 ... 41 B2
Barford Ho 23 E3 ... 26 B3
Barford St N1 ... 85 C3
Barforth Rd SE15 ... 65 A4
Barge House St
SE1 ... 121 C2
Barge La 10 E3 ... 26 B4
Barham Ho SE17 ... 152 B2
Baring Ct N1 ... 87 B3
Baring Ho 15 E14 ... 33 C3
Baring St N1 ... 87 B3
Barker Cl TW9 ... 45 A1
Barker Dr NW1 ... 13 C1
Barker Ho
Dulwich SE21 ... 76 A1
Walworth SE17 ... 152 A3
Barker Mews SW4 ... 61 A3
Barker St SW10 ... 156 C4
Barker Wlk SW16 ... 73 C1
Bark Pl W2 ... 114 A4
Barkston Gdns
SW5 ... 142 A3
Barkway Ct N4 ... 6 B2
Barkwith Ho 27
SE14 ... 50 C4
Barkworth Rd
SE16 ... 40 B1
Barlborough St
SE14 ... 50 C3
Barlby Gdns W10 ... 22 C1
Barlby Prim Sch
W10 ... 22 C1
Barlby Rd W10 ... 30 C4
Barleycorn Way
E14 ... 33 B2
Barley Mow Pas
Chiswick W4 ... 37 C1
Clerkenwell EC1 ... 108 B3
Barley Shotts Bsns Pk
W10 ... 31 B4
Barling 6 NW1 ... 13 A1
Barling Ct 1
SW4 ... 172 A2
Barlings Ho 2
SE4 ... 65 C3
Barloch Ho 14
SW11 ... 169 B2
Barlow Ho
14 Bermondsey
SE16 ... 40 A2
Notting Hill
W11 ... 31 A2 112 A4
Shoreditch N1 ... 97 B4
Barlow Pl W1 ... 118 B3
Barlow Rd
Acton W3 ... 28 A1
Brondesbury NW6 ... 10 B2
Barlow St SE17 ... 151 C3
Barmouth Ho 6 N7 ... 5 B2
Barmouth Rd
SW18 ... 59 B1
Barnabas Ho EC1 ... 96 C3
Barnabas Lo SW8 ... 172 B4
Barnabas Rd E9 ... 17 C3
Barnaby Pl SW7 ... 143 B3
Barnard Ct SW16 ... 74 B1
Barnard Ho 17 E2 ... 25 A2
Barnard Lo 10 W9 ... 31 C4
Barnard Mews
SW11 ... 60 A3
Barnardo Gdns 1
E1 ... 32 C2
Barnardo St E1 ... 32 C3
Barnard Rd SW11 ... 60 A3
Barnard's Inn EC4 107 C2
Barnbrough NW1 ... 82 C3
Barnby St NW1 ... 93 A4
Barn Cl 19 NW5 ... 13 C3
Barn Elms Sp Ctr
SW15 ... 47 B2
Barnersbury Ho
N7 ... 14 A4
BARNES ... 46 B2
Barnes Ave SW13 ... 46 C3
Barnes Bridge Sta
SW13 ... 46 A1
Barnes Common
SW13 ... 56 C4
Barnes Ct N1 ... 14 C1
Barnes High St
SW13 ... 46 B1
Barnes Ho
14 Bethnal Green
E2 ... 25 B3
Camden Town NW1 ... 82 B4
26 Deptford SE14 ... 50 C4
Hornsey N19 ... 5 A4
Barnes Hospl
SW14 ... 56 A4
Barnes Prim Sch
SW13 ... 56 B4
Barnes St E14 ... 33 A3
Barnes Sta SW13 ... 56 C4
Barnes Terr SE8 ... 41 B1
Barnet Gr
E2 ... 24 C2 99 B3
Barnet Ho 35 SE5 ... 48 B1
Barnett Ho E1 ... 110 C3
Barnett St 18 E1 ... 32 A3
Barn Field NW3 ... 12 B3
Barnfield Cl
London N4 ... 5 A4
Wandsworth SW17 ... 71 B1
Barnfield Pl E14 ... 41 C2
Barnham St SE1 ... 138 B4
BARNSBURY ... 14 A1
Barnsbury Gr N7 ... 14 B1
Barnsbury Ho 12
SW4 ... 61 C1
Barnsbury Pk N1 ... 14 C1
Barnsbury Rd N1 ... 85 B3
Barnsbury Sq N1 ... 14 C1
Barnsbury St N1 ... 14 C1
Barnsbury Terr N1 ... 14 B1
Barnsdale Ave E14 ... 41 C2
Barnsdale Rd W9 ... 23 B1
Barnsley St E1 ... 25 A1
Barn St N16 ... 7 A2
Barnstaple La
SE13 ... 67 B3
Barnston Wlk N1 ... 86 C4
Barnwell Ho 1
SE5 ... 49 A2
Barnwell Rd SW2 ... 62 C2
Barnwood Cl W9 ... 88 B1
Baron Cl N1 ... 85 B2
Baroness Rd 5
E2 ... 24 B2 99 A4
Barons Court Mans
W14 ... 140 B1

Baron's Court Rd W14 ... 140 B2
Barons Court Sta W14 ... 140 A2
Barons Gate 13 W4 ... 37 B3
Barons Keep W14 140 A2
Barons Lo 9 E14 ... 42 B2
Baronsmead Rd SW13 ... 46 C2
Baronsmede W5 ... 36 B4
Baron's Pl SE1 ... 135 C3
Baron St N1 ... 85 B2
Baron Wlk E16 ... 35 B4
Barque Mews SE8 ... 51 C4
Barradell Ho 15 W14 ... 39 C3
Barratt Ho 15 N1 ... 15 A1
Barratt Ind Pk E3 ... 27 B1
Barret Ho NW6 ... 23 C4
Barrett Ct 2 NW10 ... 21 A3
Barrett's Gr N16 ... 16 A3
Barretts Green Rd NW10 ... 20 C3
Barrett St W1 ... 103 C1
Barrhill Rd SW2 ... 74 A2
Barriedale SE14 ... 51 A1
Barrie Ho
Acton W3 ... 37 B4
Bayswater W2 ... 115 A3
Primrose Hill NW8 ... 80 B3
8 Stoke Newington N16 ... 7 A1
Barrington Cl NW5 ... 12 C3
Barrington Ct
9 Acton W3 ... 37 A4
Kentish Town NW5 ... 12 C3
31 South Lambeth SW9 ... 172 B1
Barrington Rd SW9 ... 63 A4
Barrowgate Ho W4 ... 37 C1
Barrowgate Rd W4 ... 37 C1
Barrow Hill Est NW8 ... 80 A1
Barrow Hill Jun Sch NW8 ... 80 A1
Barrow Hill Rd NW8 ... 80 A1
Barry Ct SW4 ... 61 B1
Barry Ho 4 SE16 ... 40 A1
Barry Lo N4 ... 5 B4
Barry Par SE22 ... 64 C3
Barry Rd SE22 ... 64 C2
Barset Rd SE15 ... 65 B4
Barston Rd SE27 ... 75 B1
Barstow Cres SW2 ... 74 B3
Bartell Ho SW2 ... 62 C1
Barter St WC1 ... 106 B3
Bartholomew Cl
Barbican EC1 ... 108 C3
Wandsworth SW18 ... 59 B3
Bartholomew Ct
16 Blackwall E14 ... 34 C2
St Luke's EC1 ... 97 A2
Bartholomew Ho 22 SE5 ... 48 B1
Bartholomew La EC2 ... 109 C1
Bartholomew Pas EC1 ... 108 B3
Bartholomew Pl EC1 ... 108 C3
Bartholomew Rd NW5 ... 13 B2
Bartholomew Sq
18 Bethnal Green E1 ... 25 A1
St Luke's EC1 ... 97 A2
Bartholomew St SE1 ... 137 C1
Bartholomew Villas NW5 ... 13 B2
Bartle Rd W11 ... 31 A3
Bartlett Cl E14 ... 33 C3
Bartlett Ct EC4 ... 107 C2
Bartok Ho W11 ... 31 B2 112 C3
Barton Cl
Hackney E9 ... 17 B3
Peckham SE15 ... 65 A4
Barton Ct
10 South Lambeth SW4 ... 172 A2
West Kensington W14 ... 140 B2
Barton Ho
8 Bromley E3 ... 27 A2
Islington N1 ... 15 A1
Sands End SW6 ... 59 A4
Barton Rd W14 ... 140 B1
Barton St SW1 ... 134 A2
Bartonway NW8 ... 79 B2
Bartram Rd SE4 ... 66 A1
Bartrip St E9 ... 18 B2
Barts & The London Sch of Medicine & Dentistry EC1 ... 96 B1
Barville Cl SE4 ... 66 A3
Barwell Ho 7 E2 ... 24 C1 99 C2
Barwick Ho 7 W3 ... 37 B4
Bascome St 13 SW2 ... 62 C1
Base Apartments 8 N1 ... 15 B1
Baseline Business Studios 18 W11 ... 30 C2
Basevi Way SE8 ... 52 A4
Bashley Rd NW10 ... 20 C1
Basildon Ct W1 ... 103 C4
Basil Ho
South Lambeth SW8 ... 162 A2
22 Whitechapel E1 ... 111 C2
Basil Mans SW1 ... 130 C3
Basil St
Knightsbridge SW1 ... 130 C3
Knightsbridge SW1, SW3 ... 130 C2
Basin App 20 E14 ... 33 A3
Basing Ct 13 SE15 ... 49 B2
Basingdon Way SE5 ... 63 C3
Basinghall Ave EC2 ... 109 B2
Basinghall St EC2 109 B2
Basing Hill NW11 ... 1 B3
Basing House Yd 22 E2 ... 24 A2 98 B4
Basing Pl E2 .24 A2 98 B4
Basing St W11 ... 31 B3
Basire St N1 ... 87 A4
Baskerville Ct SW18 ... 72 A4
Baskerville Gdns NW10 ... 8 A4
Baskerville Rd SW18 ... 72 A4
Baslow Wlk E5 ... 17 C4
Basnett Rd 9 SW11 ... 60 C4
Basque Ct 21 SE16 ... 40 C4
Bassano St SE22 ... 64 B2
Bassein Park Rd W12 ... 38 B4
Bassett House Sch 22 W10 ... 30 C3
Bassett Rd W10 ... 30 C3
Bassett St NW5 ... 12 C2
Bassingbourn Ho 3 N1 ... 15 A1
Bassingham Rd SW18 ... 71 B4
Bassishaw Highwalk EC2 ... 109 B3
Basswood Cl 5 SE15 ... 65 A4
Basterfield Ho EC1 96 C1
Bastion Highwalk EC2 ... 108 C3
Bastwick St EC1 ... 96 C2
Basuto Rd SW6 ... 165 C3
Batavia Ho 1 SE14 ... 51 A3
Batavia Mews 3 SE14 ... 51 A3
Batavia Rd SE14 ... 51 A3
Batchelor St N1 ... 85 C3
Bateman Ho 8 SE17 ... 48 A4
Bateman's Bldgs W1 ... 105 B1
Bateman's Row EC2 ... 24 A1 98 B2
Bateman St W1 ... 105 B1
Bate St 10 E14 ... 33 B2
Bath Cl SE15 ... 50 A3
Bath Ct
Finsbury EC1 ... 97 B3
3 Forest Hill SE26 ... 76 C1
Holborn EC1 ... 95 B1
Bathgate Ho 8 SW9 ... 48 A2
Bathgate Rd SW19 ... 69 C1
Bath Gr E2 ... 24 C3
Bath Ho
Bethnal Green E2 ... 24 C1 99 C2
Borough The SE1 ... 137 A2
Bath Pl
14 Hammersmith W6 ... 39 B1
11 Shoreditch EC2 ... 24 A2 98 A3
Bath Rd W4 ... 38 A2
Bath St EC1 ... 97 B3
Bath Terr SE1 ... 136 C2
Bathurst Gdns NW10 ... 22 A3
Bathurst Ho 2 W12 ... 30 A2
Bathurst Mews W2 ... 115 C4
Bathurst St W2 ... 115 C4
Batley Pl 3 N16 ... 7 B1
Batley Rd N16 ... 7 B1
Batman Cl W12 ... 30 A1
Batoum Gdns W6 ... 39 B3
Batson Ho 29 E1 ... 111 C1
Batson St W12 ... 38 C4
Batten Ho
7 London SW4 ... 61 B2
10 West Kilburn W10 ... 23 A2
Batten St SW11 ... 60 A4
BATTERSEA ... 169 A4
Battersea Bridge Rd SW11 ... 158 A1
Battersea Bsns Ctr SW11 ... 60 C4
Battersea Church Rd SW11 ... 167 C4
Battersea Dogs & Cats Home SW8 ... 160 B1
Battersea High St SW11 ... 167 B1
Battersea Hts SW11 ... 60 B4
Battersea Park SW11 ... 159 B1
Battersea Park Rd SW11, SW8 ... 169 A3
Battersea Park Sch SW11 ... 169 A3
Battersea Park Sta SW8 ... 160 A1
Battersea Power Station(dis) SW8 ... 160 B4
Battersea Rise SW11 ... 60 A3
Battersea Sq SW11 ... 167 C3
Battishill St 9 N1 ... 15 A1
Battlebridge Ct NW1 ... 84 B2
Battle Bridge La SE1 ... 124 A1
Battledean Rd N5 ... 15 A3
Battle Ho 8 SE15 ... 49 C4
Batty St E1 ... 111 C2
Baty Ho SW2 ... 74 B3
Baulk The SW18 ... 70 C4
Bavaria Rd N19 ... 5 A2
Bavent Rd SE5 ... 48 B1
Bawdale Rd SE22 ... 64 B2
Bawtree Rd SE14 ... 51 A3
Baxendale St E2 ... 24 C2 99 B4
Baxter Ho 11 E3 ... 27 A2
Baxter Rd N1 ... 15 C2
Baycliffe Ho 8 E9 ... 17 C2
Bay Ct
Ealing W5 ... 36 A3
7 Stepney E1 ... 25 C1
Bayer Ho EC1 ... 96 C1
Bayes Ct NW3 ... 12 B1
Bayfield Ho 3 SE4 ... 65 C3
Bayford Rd NW10 ... 22 C2
Bayford St Ind Ctr 4 E8 ... 17 A1
Bayford St 5 E8 ... 17 A1
Bayham Pl NW1 ... 83 A3
Bayham Rd W4 ... 37 C3
Bayham St NW1 ... 82 C3
Bayhurst Ho N4 ... 6 B4
Bayley St WC1 ... 105 B3
Baylis Rd SE1 ... 135 B3
Baynes Mews 2 NW3 ... 11 C2
Baynes St NW1 ... 13 B1
Bayon Ho 27 N19 ... 4 C4
Bayonne Rd W6 ... 154 A3
Bayston Rd N16 ... 7 B1
BAYSWATER ... 114 C4
Bayswater Rd W2 115 B3
Bayswater Rd Mkt W2 ... 115 A3
Bayswater Sta W2 ... 114 B4
Bayton Ct 2 E8 ... 16 C1
Baytree Rd SW2 ... 62 B3
Bazalgette Ho NW8 ... 89 C2
Bazeley Ho SE1 ... 136 A3
Bazely St E14 ... 34 B2
BBC Television Ctr W12 ... 30 B1
Beach Ho SW5 ... 141 B2
Beachy Rd E3 ... 18 C1
Beaconfield Terrace Rd W14 ... 126 A1
Beacon Gate SE14 ... 65 C4
Beacon Hill N7 ... 14 A3
Beacon Ho
11 Camberwell SE5 ... 49 A3
7 Isle Of Dogs E14 ... 42 A1
South Lambeth SW8 ... 171 B4
Beacon Rd SE13 ... 67 C1
Beaconsfield Cl
Acton Green W4 ... 37 B1
Greenwich SE3 ... 53 C4
Beaconsfield Rd
Acton W4 ... 37 C3
Greenwich SE3 ... 53 C3
Walworth SE17 ... 152 A1
Willesden NW10 ... 8 B2
Beaconsfield Wlk SW6 ... 165 A3
Beadon Rd W6 ... 39 B2
Beak St W1 ... 119 A4
Beale Ho 7 SW9 172 C1
Beale Pl E3 ... 26 B3
Beale Rd E3 ... 26 B4
Beames Ho SW8 ... 171 B4
Beames Rd NW10 ... 20 C4
Beaminster Ho SW8 ... 162 C2
Beamish Ho 7 SE16 ... 40 B2
Beanacre Cl E9 ... 18 B2
Bear Alley EC4 ... 108 A2
Bear Croft Ho 6 SW6 ... 164 C1
Beardsley Way W3 ... 37 C4
Bear Gdns SE1 ... 122 C2
Bear La SE1 ... 122 B1
Bear St WC2 ... 119 C4
Bearstead Rise SE4 ... 66 B2
Beaton Cl SE15 ... 49 B2
Beatrice Ho
1 Brixton SW2 ... 62 B2
4 Hammersmith W6 ... 39 B1
2 Stepney E1 ... 32 C4
Beatrice Pl W8 ... 128 A1
Beatrice Rd
Bermondsey SE1 ... 153 C3
Finsbury Pk N4 ... 5 C4
2 Richmond TW10 ... 54 B2
Beatrice Tate Sch 33 E2 ... 25 A2
Beatrice Webb Ho 4 E3 ... 26 A3

Beatrix Ho SW5 .. 142 B2
Beatrix Potter Prim Sch SW18 ... 71 B3
Beatson Wlk 23 SE16 ... 32 C1
Beattie Ho SW8 .. 171 A4
Beatty Ho 16 E14 ... 41 C4
Beatty Rd N16 ... 16 A4
Beauchamp Cl 17 W4 ... 37 B3
Beauchamp Pl SW3 ... 130 B1
Beauchamp Rd SW11 ... 60 B3
Beauchamp St EC1 ... 107 B3
Beauchamp Terr SW15 ... 57 A4
Beauclerc Rd W6 ... 39 A3
Beauclerk Ho 10 SW16 ... 74 A1
Beaufort Cl SW19 ... 69 A4
Beaufort Ct SW6 . 155 B4
Beaufort Gdns SW3 ... 130 B2
Beaufort Ho
Battersea SW11 ... 168 A2
Chelsea SW3 ... 157 C3
20 Millwall E14 ... 41 C4
Pimlico SW1 ... 147 B1
Beaufort Mans SW3 ... 157 C3
Beaufort Mews SW6 ... 155 A4
Beaufort St SW3 .. 157 B4
Beaufoy Ho
South Lambeth SW8 ... 162 C2
3 West Norwood SE27 ... 75 A1
Beaufoy Rd 11 SW8 ... 61 A4
Beaufoy Wlk SE11 149 A3
Beaulieu Cl SE5 ... 63 C4
Beaulieu Pl W4 ... 37 B3
Beaumanor Mans W2 ... 114 B4
Beaumaris Twr 2 W3 ... 37 A4
Beaumont SW15 ... 58 A2
Beaumont Ave
Richmond TW9 ... 54 B4
West Kensington W14 ... 140 C2
Beaumont Bldgs WC2 ... 106 B1
Beaumont Cres W14 ... 140 C1
Beaumont Ct
10 Acton Green W4 ... 37 B1
Marylebone W1 ... 103 C4
7 Mile End E1 ... 26 A2
Beaumont Gdns NW3 ... 1 C1
Beaumont Gr E1 ... 25 C1
Beaumont Ho
1 Streatham SW2 ... 74 A3
West Kensington W14 ... 141 A3
Wimbledon SW19 ... 70 C1
Beaumont Lo E8 ... 16 C2
Beaumont Pl NW1, WC1, W1 ... 93 A2
Beaumont Rd
Putney SW15, SW19 ... 70 A4
South Acton W4 ... 37 B3
Beaumont Rise N19 . 4 C3
Beaumont Sq E1 ... 32 C4
Beaumont St W1 . 103 C4
Beaumont Wlk NW3 ... 12 B1
Beauvale 6 NW1 ... 12 C1
Beauval Rd SE22 ... 64 B1
Beavis Ho N16 ... 7 A1
Beavor La W6 ... 38 C1
Beccles St E14 ... 33 B2
Beck Cl SE13 ... 52 A2
Beckers The N16 ... 16 C4
Becket Ho SE1 ... 137 B3
Becket St SE1 ... 137 B2
Beckett Cl
Streatham SW16 ... 73 C2
Willesden NW10 ... 8 A2
Beckett Ho
28 London SW9 ... 172 B1
15 Stepney E1 ... 32 B4
Beckfoot NW1 ... 83 A1
Beckford Cl W14 . 141 A3
Beckford Ho 18 N16 ... 16 A3
Beckford Prim Sch NW6 ... 10 B3
Beckham Ho SE11 ... 149 A3
Beck Ho N16 ... 7 A1
Beckington 18 NW5 ... 12 C2
Beckley Ho E3 ... 26 B1
Becklow Gdns
Chiswick W12 ... 38 B4
1 Shepherd's Bush W12 ... 38 C4
Becklow Mews 7 W12 ... 38 C4
Becklow Rd W12 ... 38 C4
Beck Rd E8 ... 25 A4
Beckton Rd E16 ... 35 B4
Beckway St SE17 . 152 A3
Beckwith Ho 22 E2 ... 25 A3
Beckwith Rd SE24 .. 63 C2
Bective Pl SW15 ... 58 B3
Bective Rd SW15 ... 58 B3
Bedale St SE1 ... 123 B1
Bedefield WC1 ... 94 B3
Bede Ho
London SE14 ... 51 B2
5 Putney SW15 ... 57 C1
Bedford Ave WC1 105 C3
Bedfordbury WC2 120 A3
Bedford Cl W4 ... 46 B4
Bedford Cnr 3 W4 ... 38 A2
Bedford Court Mans WC1 ... 105 C3
Bedford Ct
6 Richmond TW9 ... 54 B3
St James WC2 ... 120 A3
Bedford Gardens Ho W8 ... 31 C1 113 C1
Bedford Gdns W8 ... 31 C1 113 C1
Bedford Hill SW12 .. 73 A2
Bedford Ho
2 Acton W4 ... 38 A2
7 Stockwell SW4 ... 62 A3
BEDFORD PARK ... 38 A3
Bedford Park Cnr 5 W4 ... 38 A2
Bedford Park Mans 4 W4 ... 37 C2
Bedford Pas SW6. 154 B2
Bedford Pl WC1 .. 106 A4
Bedford Rd
Acton W4 ... 38 A3
Stockwell SW2, SW4 ... 62 A3
Bedford Row WC1 ... 107 A3
Bedford Sq WC1 .. 105 C3
Bedford St WC2 .. 120 B3
Bedford Way WC1 . 93 C1
Bedgebury Gdns SW19 ... 70 A2
Bedlam Mews SE11 ... 149 B4
Bedlow Cl NW8 ... 89 C1
Bedser Cl SE11 ... 163 A4
Bedser Ct 7 SW4 172 A2
Bedwell Ho 18 SW9 ... 173 B1
Beech Ave W3 ... 29 A1
Beech Cl
Deptford SE8 ... 51 B4
Putney SW15 ... 68 C4
Beechcroft Ave NW11 ... 1 B4
Beechcroft Ct
3 Golders Green NW11 ... 1 B4
Greenwich SE3 ... 53 C2
Beech Croft Ct N5 .. 15 A4
Beechcroft Rd
Mortlake SW14 ... 55 B4
Upper Tooting SW17 ... 72 A2
Beechcroft Way N19 ... 4 C3
Beech Ct
Child's Hill NW2 ... 1 B2
Marylebone W1 ... 102 C2
43 Notting Hill W2 ... 31 C4
7 Rotherhithe SE16 ... 33 A1
Beechdale Rd SW2 ... 62 B1
Beechdene 4 SE15 ... 50 A2
Beeches Rd SW17 .. 72 B1
Beeches The 1 N19 ... 5 A3
Beechey Ho 30 E1 .. 32 A1
Beech Gdns W5 ... 36 A3
Beech Ho
6 Maitland Pk NW3 ... 12 B2
22 Rotherhithe SE16 ... 40 B4
5 Stoke Newington N16 ... 6 C2
Beechmore Rd SW11 ... 169 A3
Beech St EC2 ... 109 A4
Beech Tree Cl N1 ... 14 C1
Beechwood Ave TW9 ... 44 C2
Beechwood Ct
Chiswick W4 ... 45 C4
Stamford Hill N16 ... 7 A4
Beechwood Gr W3 ... 29 A2
Beechwood Ho 23 E2 ... 24 C3
Beechwood Rd E8 .. 16 B2
Beechworth Cl NW3 ... 1 C2
Beecroft La SE4 ... 66 A2
Beecroft Mews SE4 ... 66 A2
Beecroft Rd SE4 ... 66 A2
Beehive Cl E8 ... 16 B1
Beehive Pl SW9 ... 62 C4
Beeston Cl 5 E8 ... 16 C3
Beeston Pl SW1 .. 132 B2
Beeston's Ho SE15 .. 65 A4
Beethoven St W10 .. 23 A2
Begbie Ho SW9 ... 173 A2
Begonia Wlk W12 .. 29 B3
Beira St SW12 ... 73 A4
Beis Chinuch Lebonos Girls Sch N4 ... 6 B4
Beis Hamedrash Elyon NW11 ... 1 A4
Beis Malka Girls Sch N16 ... 7 B3
Beis Rochel d'Satmar Girls Sch 1 N16 ... 7 A4
Bekesbourne St 17 E14 ... 33 A3
Beldanes Lo NW10 .. 8 C1
Belenoyd Ct SW16 .. 74 B1
Belfast Rd N16 ... 7 B2
Belfont Wlk N7 ... 14 A4
Belford Ho 7 E8 ... 24 B4
Belfort Rd SE15 ... 50 B1
Belfry Cl 33 SE16 ... 40 A1
Belgrade Ho N16 ... 16 A4
Belgrade Rd N16 ... 16 A4
Belgrave Cl 1 W3 .. 37 B4
Belgrave Ct
8 Acton Green W4 ... 37 B1
22 Limehouse E14 ... 33 B2
Nine Elms SW8 ... 160 C1
Belgrave Gdns
Kilburn NW8 ... 78 C3
St John's Wood NW8 ... 78 C3
Belgrave Mans NW8 ... 78 C3
Belgrave Mews N SW1 ... 131 B3
Belgrave Mews S SW1 ... 131 C2
Belgrave Mews W SW1 ... 131 B2
Belgrave Pl SW1 . 131 C1
Belgrave Rd
Barnes SW13 ... 46 B3
Westminster SW1 . 146 C3
Belgrave Sq SW1 . 131 B2
Belgrave St E1 ... 32 C3
Belgrave Yd SW1 . 132 A1
BELGRAVIA ... 146 A4
Belgravia Ct SW1 132 A1
Belgravia Ho 11 SW4 ... 61 C1
Belgrove St WC1 .. 94 B4
Belham Wlk 13 SE5 ... 48 C2
Belinda Rd 8 SW9 ... 63 A4
Belitha Villas N1 ... 14 C1
Bellamy Cl
13 Millwall E14 ... 41 C4
West Kensington SW5 ... 141 A1
Bellamy's Ct 16 SE16 ... 32 C1
Bellamy St SW12 ... 73 A4
Bellasis Ave SW2 ... 74 A2
Bell Ct SE13 ... 66 C2
Bell Dr SW18 ... 70 A4
Bellefields Rd SW9 ... 62 B4
Bellenden Prim Sch 5 SE15 ... 64 C4
Bellenden Rd SE15 . 49 B1
Bellenden Rd Ret Pk SE15 ... 49 C2
Bellendon Road Bsns Ctr SE15 ... 49 B1
Bellerbys Coll SE8 .. 51 C4
Belleville Prim Sch SW11 ... 60 B2
Belleville Rd SW11 . 60 B2
Belle Vue Gdns SW9 ... 172 B1
Bellevue Pl E1 ... 25 B1
Bellevue Rd
Barnes SW13 ... 46 C1
Upper Tooting SW17 ... 72 B3
Bellew St SW17 ... 71 B1
Bell Flats 4 NW2 ... 8 C2
Bellflower Ct SE13 .. 67 A3
Bellgate Mews NW5 ... 4 A1
Bellgrave Lo 9 W4 ... 37 A1
Bell Ho
Greenwich SE10 ... 52 B4
15 Streatham SW2 .. 74 C4
Bellina Mews NW5 . 13 B4
Bell Ind Est 2 W4 ... 37 B2
Bell Inn Yd EC3 ... 109 C1
Bell La
Newham E16 ... 35 C1
Spitalfields E1 ... 110 C3
Bell Language Sch W1 ... 92 C1
Bellmaker Ct 13 E3 ... 33 C4
Bell Moor NW3 ... 2 B1
Bello Cl SE24, SW2 .. 75 A3
Bellot Gdns 1 SE10 ... 43 A1
Bellot St SE10 ... 43 A1
Bell St NW1 ... 102 A4
Bell Wharf La EC4 ... 123 A4
Bellwood Rd SE15 .. 65 C3
Bell Yard Mews SE1 ... 138 B3
Bell Yd WC2 ... 107 B1
Belmont Cl SW4 ... 61 B4
Belmont Ct
Highbury N5 ... 15 B4
6 Stamford Hill N16 .. 7 A3
Belmont Gr
Chiswick W4 ... 37 C2
Lewisham SE13 ... 67 C4
Belmont Hall Ct SE13 ... 67 C4
Belmont Hill SE13 .. 67 C4
Belmont Mews SW19 ... 69 C2
Belmont Prim Sch 10 W4 ... 37 C2
Belmont Rd
Clapham SW4 ... 61 B4
London W4 ... 37 C2
Belmont St NW1 ... 12 C1

Belmont Terr W4 37 C2
Belmore Ho N7 13 C3
Belmore La N7 13 C3
Belmore St SW8 171 B4
Beloe Cl SW15 56 C3
Belper Ct 11 E5 17 C4
Belsham St E9 17 B2
Belsize Ave NW3 12 A3
Belsize Court Garages 1 NW3 11 C3
Belsize Cres NW3 11 C2
Belsize Ct NW3 11 C3
Belsize Gr NW3 12 A2
Belsize La NW3 11 C3
Belsize Mews NW3 11 C2
Belsize Park Gdns NW3 12 A2
Belsize Park Mews 1 NW3 11 C2
Belsize Park Sta NW3 12 A3
Belsize Pk NW3 11 C2
Belsize Pl NW3 11 C3
Belsize Rd NW6 78 B4
Belsize Sq NW3 11 C2
Belsize Terr NW3 11 C2
Beltane Dr SW19 69 C1
Belthorn Cres SW12 73 B4
Belton Rd NW2 8 C2
Belton Way E3 33 C4
Beltran Rd SW6 166 A1
Belvedere Bldgs SE1 136 B3
Belvedere Ct
Brondesbury NW2 9 C2
7 Clapham Pk SW4 61 C1
Putney SW15 57 B3
33 Shoreditch N1 24 A4
Belvedere Htss NW8 90 A2
Belvedere Mews SE15 65 B4
Belvedere Pl
Brixton SW2 62 B3
Lambeth SE1 136 B3
Belvedere Rd SE1 121 A1
Belvedere The SW10 167 A3
Belvoir Lo SE22 76 C4
Belvoir Rd SE22 76 C4
Bembridge Cl NW6 10 A1
Bembridge Ho
9 Deptford SE8 41 B2
Wandsworth SW18 59 A1
Bemerton St N1 84 C4
Bemish Rd SW15 57 C4
Benabo Ct 6 E8 16 C3
Benbow Ct W6 39 A3
Benbow Ho 12 SE8 51 C4
Benbow Rd W6 39 A3
Benbow St SE8 51 C4
Bence Ho 13 SE8 41 A2
Bendall Mews NW1 102 B4
Bendemeer Rd SW15 57 C4
Benden Ho SE13 67 B2
Bendon Valley SW18 71 A4
Benedict Rd SW9 62 B4
Benenden Ho SE17 152 B2
Ben Ezra Ct SE17 151 A3
Benfleet Ct 6 E8 24 B4
Bengal Ct EC3 109 C1
Bengal Ho E1 32 C4
Bengeworth Rd SE5 63 B4
Benham Ho SW10 156 B2
Benham's Pl 11 NW3 11 B4
Benhill Rd SE5 48 C2
Benington Ct N4 6 B2
Benjamin Cl E8 24 C4
Benjamin Franklin House SW1 120 A2
Benjamin Ho 12 W3 28 A1
Benjamin Mews SW12 73 B4
Benjamin St EC1 108 A4
Ben Jonson Ct 30 N1 24 A3
Ben Jonson Prim Sch E1 26 A1
Ben Jonson Rd E1 33 A4
Benledi Rd E14 34 C3
Bennelong Cl W12 30 A3
Bennerley Rd SW11 60 B2
Bennet's Hill EC4 122 B4
Bennett Ct
Hampstead NW6 11 A2
Lower Holloway N7 5 B1
7 South Acton W3 37 A4
Bennett Gr SE13 52 A2
Bennett Ho
2 Streatham SW4 73 C4
Westminster SW1 147 C4
Bennett St
Chiswick W4 38 A1
St James SW1 118 C2
Bennett's Yd SW1 133 C1
Benn Ho E2 24 C2 99 B3
Benn St E9 18 A2
Benns Wlk 8 TW9 54 A3
Bensbury Cl SW15 69 B4
Ben Smith Way 21 SE16 139 C2
Benson Ct
South Lambeth SW8 172 A4
1 Tufnell Pk N19 13 B4
Benson Ho
Lambeth SE1 121 C1
Shoreditch E2 24 B1 98 C2
Benson Quay E1 32 B2
Benthal Ct N16 7 C1
Benthal Prim Sch N16 7 C1
Benthal Rd N16 7 C1
Bentham Ct 11 N1 15 B1
Bentham Ho SE1 137 B2
Bentham Rd E9 17 C2
Bentinck Cl NW8 80 B1
Bentinck Ho 4 W12 30 A2
Bentinck Mans W1 103 C2
Bentinck Mews W1 103 C2
Bentinck St W1 103 C2
Bentley Cl SW19 70 C1
Bentley Ct SE13 67 B3
Bentley Dr NW2 10 B1
Bentley Ho
6 Bow E3 26 C1
4 Camberwell SE5 49 A2
Bentley Rd N1 16 A2
Bentworth Ct 1 E2 24 C1 99 B2
Bentworth Prim Sch W12 30 A3
Bentworth Rd W12 30 A3
Benwell Rd N7 14 C3
Benwick Cl SE16 40 A2
Benworth St E3 26 B2
Benyon Ho EC1 95 C4
Benyon Rd N1 87 C4
Benyon Wharf 31 E8 24 A4
Beormund Sch SE1 137 C3
Bequerel Ct SE10 43 B3
Berberis Ho 17 E3 33 C4
Berber Pl 2 E14 33 C2
Berber Rd SW11 60 B2
Berebinder Ho 21 E3 26 B3
Berenger Twr SW10 157 B2
Berenger Wlk SW10 157 B2
Berens Rd NW10 22 C2
Beresford Ct E9 18 A3
Beresford Ho
Dulwich SE21 76 A1
15 Stockwell SW4 62 A3
Beresford Lo N4 15 C3
Beresford Rd N5 15 C3
Beresford Terr 3 N5 15 B3
Bere St E1 32 C2
Berestede Rd 4 W6 38 B1
Bergen Ho 1 SE5 48 B1
Bergen Sq SE16 41 A3
Berger Prim Sch 30 E9 17 C2
Berger Rd E9 17 C2
Berghem Mews W14 39 C3
Bergholt Cres N16 7 A4
Bergholt Mews 4 NW1 13 C1
Berglen Ct E14 33 A2
Bering Sq E14 41 C1
Berisford Mews SW18 59 B1
Berkeley Ct
1 Golders Green NW11 1 B4
Marylebone NW1 91 A1
Willesden NW10 8 A4
Berkeley Gdns W8 31 C1 113 C1
Berkeley Ho
17 Bow E3 26 C2
8 Deptford SE8 41 B1
Berkeley Mews W1 103 A1
Berkeley Rd SW13 46 C2
Berkeley Sq W1 118 B3
Berkeley St W1 118 B2
Berkeley The NW11 2 A4
Berkeley Wlk 1 N7 5 B2
Berkley Gr NW1 12 C1
Berkley Rd NW1 12 B1
Berkshire Ho WC2 106 A2
Berkshire Rd E9 18 B2
Bermans Way NW10 8 B4
BERMONDSEY 40 A4
Bermondsey Leather Mkt SE1 138 A3
Bermondsey Sq SE1 138 B2
Bermondsey St SE1 138 A3
Bermondsey Sta SE16 40 A3
Bermondsey Trad Est SE16 40 B1
Bermondsey Wall E SE16 40 A4
Bermondsey Wall W SE1, SE16 139 B4
Bernard Angell Ho 4 SE10 52 C4
Bernard Cassidy St 2 E16 35 B4
Bernard Ho E1 110 C3
Bernard Shaw Ct 5 NW1 13 B1
Bernard Shaw Ho 2 NW10 20 C4
Bernard St WC1 94 B1
Bernay's Gr SW9 62 B3
Berners Ho N1 85 B2
Berners Mews W1 105 A3
Berners Pl W1 105 A2
Berners Rd N1 86 A3
Berners St W1 105 A2
Berner Terr 27 E1 111 C1
Bernhard Baron Ho 23 E1 111 C1
Bernhardt Cres NW8 90 A2
Bernie Grant Ho 40 E9 17 B1
Bernwood Ho 6 N4 6 C4
Berridge Mews NW6 10 C3
Berriman Rd N7 5 B1
Berry Cotts 2 E14 33 A3
Berryfield Rd SE17 150 B2
Berry Ho
10 Battersea SW11 169 A2
25 Bethnal Green E1 25 A1
Berrymead Gdns W3 37 B4
Berrymede Inf Sch W3 37 A4
Berrymede Jun Sch W3 37 A4
Berrymede Rd W4 37 C3
Berry Pl EC1 96 B3
Berry St EC1 96 B1
Berry Way W5 36 A3
Bertha Neubergh Ho 1 SE5 48 B2
Berthon St SE8 51 C4
Bertie Rd NW10 8 C2
Bertram St N19 4 A2
Bertrand Ho 11 SW16 74 A1
Bertrand St SE13 67 A4
Bertrum House Sch SW17 72 C2
Berwick St W1 105 A1
Berwick Street Mkt W1 105 A1
Berwyn Ho 3 N16 7 B3
Berwyn Rd
Mortlake SW14, TW10 55 A3
Streatham SE24 75 A3
Beryl Rd W6 39 C1
Besant Cl NW2 1 A1
Besant Ct N1 15 C3
Besant Ho NW8 78 C3
Besant Pl SE22 64 B3
Besant Rd NW2 10 A4
Besant Wlk N7 5 B2
Besford Ho 26 E2 24 C3
Bessant Dr TW9 45 A2
Bessborough Gdns SW1 147 C2
Bessborough Pl SW1 147 C2
Bessborough Rd SW15 68 C3
Bessborough St SW1 147 B2
Bessemer Ct 7 NW1 13 B1
Bessemer Grange Prim Sch SE5 64 A3
Bessemer Park Ind Est 3 SE24 63 A3
Bessemer Rd SE5 48 B1
Bessingham Wlk SE4 65 C2
Besson St SE14 50 C2
Bessy St E2 25 B2
Bestwood St SE8 40 C2
Beswick Mews 1 NW6 11 A2
Beta Pl 20 SW4 62 B3
Betchworth Ho 8 N7 13 C3
Bethersden Ho SE17 152 B2
Bethlehem Ho 13 E14 33 B2
BETHNAL GREEN 25 A2
Bethnal Green Rd
Bethnal Green E2 24 C2 99 B3
Shoreditch E1, E2 24 B1 99 A2
Bethnal Green Sta
Bethnal Green E1 25 A1
Bethnal Green E2 25 B2
Bethnal Green Tech Coll 49 E2 24 B2 99 A3
Bethune Rd
North Acton NW10 20 C1
Stamford Hill N16 7 A4
Bethwin Rd SE5 48 B3
Betsham Ho SE1 137 B4
Betterton Ho WC2 106 B1
Betterton St WC2 106 B1
Bettridge Rd SW6 165 A1
Betts Ho E1 32 A2
Betts St E1 32 A2
Betty Layward Prim Sch 1 N16 6 C1
Betty May Gray Ho 2 E14 42 B2
Bevan St N1 87 A3
Bev Callender Cl 4 SW8 61 A4

Bevenden St N1 ... 97 C4
Beveridge Rd 1 NW10 ... 8 A1
Beverley Cl
Barnes SW13 ... 46 C1
6 Wandsworth SW11 ... 59 C3
Beverley Cotts SW15 ... 68 A1
Beverley Ct
9 Acton Green W4 ... 37 B1
5 Acton W12 ... 38 A4
Brockley SE4 ... 66 B4
Islington N5 ... 15 A2
Beverley Gdns
Barnes SW13 ... 56 B4
Hendon NW11 ... 1 A4
Beverley Lo 6 TW10 ... 54 A2
Beverley Path 9 SW13 ... 46 B1
Beverley Rd
Barnes SW13 ... 56 B4
Chiswick W4 ... 38 B1
Beversbrook Rd N19 ... 4 C1
Beverstone Rd SW2 ... 62 B2
Beverston Mews NW1 ... 102 C3
Bevin Cl SE16 ... 33 A1
Bevin Ct WC1 ... 95 A4
Bevington Prim Sch 15 W10 ... 31 A4
Bevington Rd W10 ... 31 A4
Bevington St SE16 ... 139 C3
Bevin Ho
35 Bethnal Green E2 ... 25 B2
8 Bow E3 ... 26 C2
Bevin Sq SW17 ... 72 B1
Bevin Way WC1 ... 95 B4
Bevis Marks EC3 ... 110 B2
Bew Ct SE21 ... 76 C4
Bewdley Ho N4 ... 6 B4
Bewdley St N1 ... 14 C1
Bewick Mews SE15 ... 50 A3
Bewick St SW8 ... 170 B1
Bewley Ct SW2 ... 62 B1
Bewley Ho 7 E1 ... 32 A2
Bewley St E1 ... 32 A2
Bexhill Rd
Catford SE4 ... 66 B1
Mortlake SW14 ... 55 B4
Bexley Ho SE4 ... 66 A3
BFI Imax (Cinema) SE1 ... 121 B1
BFI Southbank SE1 ... 121 A2
Bianca Rd SE1, SE15 ... 49 C4
Bicester Rd TW9 ... 55 A4
Bickenhall Mans W1 ... 103 A4
Bickenhall St W1 ... 103 A4
Bickerton Rd N19 ... 4 B2
Bicknell Ho 33 E1 ... 111 C1
Bicknell Rd SE5 ... 63 B4
Bicknor Ho 2 E5 ... 17 A3
Bidborough St N1, WC1 ... 94 A3
Biddenham Ho 18 SE16 ... 40 C2
Bidder St E16 ... 35 A4
Biddesden Ho SW3 ... 144 C3
Biddestone Rd N7 ... 14 B4
Biddulph Mans W9 ... 88 B3
Biddulph Rd W9 ... 88 B3
Bidwell St SE15 ... 50 A2
Big Ben SW1 ... 134 B3
Biggerstaff Rd E15 ... 27 B4
Biggerstaff St N4 ... 5 C2
Bigg's Row SW15 ... 57 C4
Biggs Sq E9 ... 18 B2
Bigland Green Prim Sch 41 E1 ... 32 A3
Bigland St E1 ... 32 A3
Bilberry Ho 18 E3 ... 33 C4
Billie Holiday Ct NW10 ... 20 C3
Billingford Cl SE4 ... 65 C3
Billing Ho 7 E1 ... 32 C3
Billingley NW1 ... 82 C3
Billing Pl SW10 ... 156 B2
Billing Rd SW10 ... 156 B2
Billingsgate Mkt E14 ... 34 A1
Billing St SW10 ... 156 B2
Billington Ho SW8 ... 171 C3
Billington Rd SE14 ... 50 C3
Billiter Sq EC3 ... 110 B1
Billiter St EC3 ... 110 B1
Billson St E14 ... 42 B2
Bilton Ho SW8 ... 171 B3
Bilton Twrs W1 ... 103 A1
Bina Gdns SW5 ... 142 C3
Binbrook Ho 13 W10 ... 30 B4
Binden Rd W12 ... 38 B3
Binfield Ct SE5 ... 48 B1
Binfield Rd SW4 ... 172 B3
Bingfield St N1 ... 84 C4
Bingham Pl W1 ... 103 B4
Bingham St N1 ... 15 C2
Binley Ho SW15 ... 56 B1
Binney St W1 ... 103 C1
Binnie Ct SE10 ... 52 A3
Binnie Ho SE1 ... 136 C1
Binns Rd W4 ... 38 A1
Binns Terr 3 W4 ... 38 A1
Binstead Ho SW18 ... 59 A1
Binyon Ho 8 N16 ... 16 A4
Birbeck Ho 4 N19 ... 4 C3
Bircham Path SE4 ... 65 C3
Birch Cl
Newham E16 ... 35 A4
Peckham SE15 ... 49 C1
Upper Holloway N19 ... 4 B2
Birchdown Ho 32 E3 ... 27 A2
Birches The SE5 ... 49 A1
Birchfield Ho 3 E14 ... 33 C2
Birchfield St E14 ... 33 C2
Birchgrove Ho TW9 ... 45 A3
Birch Ho
New Cross Gate SE14 ... 51 B2
8 Tulse Hill SW2 ... 62 C1
Birchington Ct 2 NW6 ... 78 A4
Birchington Ho 1 E5 ... 17 A3
Birchington Rd NW6 ... 23 C4
Birchin La EC3 ... 109 C1
Birchlands Ave SW12 ... 72 B4
Birchmere Lo 18 SE16 ... 40 A1
Birchmere Row SE3 ... 53 B1
Birchmore Wlk N5 ... 6 B1
Birch Vale Ct NW8 ... 89 C2
Birchwood Dr NW3 ... 2 A1
Birdcage Wlk SW1 ... 133 B3
Birdhurst Rd SW18 ... 59 B2
Bird In Bush Rd SE15 ... 49 C3
Bird In Hand Yd 24 NW3 ... 11 B4
Birdsall Ho 5 SE5 ... 64 A4
Birdsfield La 12 E3 ... 26 B4
Bird St W1 ... 103 C1
Birdwood Ave 4 SE13 ... 67 C1
Birkbeck Ave W3 ... 28 B2
Birkbeck Coll W1 ... 105 B2
Birkbeck Ct W3 ... 28 C1
Birkbeck Gr W3 ... 37 C4
Birkbeck Hill SE21 ... 75 A3
Birkbeck Mews 5 E8 ... 16 B3
Birkbeck Pl SE21 ... 75 B2
Birkbeck Rd
Acton W3 ... 28 C1
Dalston E8 ... 16 B3
Birkbeck St E2 ... 25 A2
Birkbeck Univ of London WC1 ... 93 B2
Birkdale Cl 30 SE16 ... 40 A1
Birkenhead Ho 11 N7 ... 14 C3
Birkenhead St WC1 ... 94 B4
Birkwood Cl SW12 ... 73 C4
Birley Lo NW8 ... 79 C2
Birley St SW11 ... 169 B1
Birnam Rd N4 ... 5 B2
Birrell Ho 9 SW9 ... 172 C1
Birse Cres NW10 ... 8 A4
Birtwhistle Ho 5 E3 ... 26 B4
Biscay Ho 11 E1 ... 25 C1
Biscay Rd W6 ... 39 C1
Biscoe Way SE13 ... 67 C4
Biscott Ho 3 E3 ... 27 A1
Bisham Gdns N6 ... 3 C3
Bishop Challoner Collegiate Sch 28 E1 ... 32 B3
Bishop Ct 20 SW2 ... 62 C1
Bishop Duppa's Almshouses 7 TW10 ... 54 A2
Bishop King's Rd W14 ... 140 B4
Bishop's Ave SW6 ... 164 A2
Bishop's Bridge Rd W2 ... 100 C2
Bishops Cl W4 ... 37 B1
Bishop's Cl N19 ... 4 B1
Bishops Ct
13 Bayswater W2 ... 100 B2
Richmond TW9 ... 54 A4
Bishop's Ct
Holborn EC4 ... 108 A2
Holborn WC2 ... 107 B2
Bishopsdale Ho 8 NW6 ... 23 C4
Bishopsgate EC2 ... 110 A2
Bishopsgate Arc E1 ... 110 B3
Bishopsgate Churchyard EC2 ... 110 A2
Bishopsgate Inst EC2 ... 110 B3
Bishops Ho SW8 ... 162 B1
Bishop's Mans SW6 ... 47 C1
Bishops Mead SE5 ... 48 B3
Bishop's Park Rd SW6 ... 47 C1
Bishops Rd SW6 ... 164 C4
Bishops Sq E1 ... 110 B4
Bishop St N1 ... 86 C4
Bishop's Terr SE11 ... 149 C4
Bishopstone Ho 4 SW11 ... 169 B2
Bishop's Way E2 ... 25 B3
Bishopswood Rd N6 ... 3 B4
Bishop Wilfred Wood Cl SE15 ... 49 C1
Bisley Ho SW19 ... 69 C2
Bissextile Ho SE13 ... 52 A1
Bisson Rd E15 ... 27 B3
Bittern Ct 7 SE8 ... 51 C4
Bittern Ho SE1 ... 136 C3
Bittern St SE1 ... 136 C3
Blackall St EC2 ... 24 A1 98 A2
Blackburn Ct 21 SW2 ... 62 C1
Blackburne's Mews W1 ... 117 B3
Blackburn Rd NW6 ... 11 A2
Blackdown Ho E8 ... 16 C4
Blackett St SW15 ... 57 C4
Blackfriars Bridge EC4 ... 122 A3
Blackfriars Ct EC4 ... 122 A4
Black Friars La EC4 ... 108 A1
Blackfriars Pas EC4 ... 122 A4
Blackfriars Pier EC4 ... 122 A4
Blackfriars Rd SE1 ... 122 A1
Blackfriars Underpass EC4 ... 121 C4
Blackheath SE3 ... 53 A2
Blackheath Ave SE3 ... 53 A3
Blackheath Bsns Est SE10 ... 52 B2
Blackheath Gr SE3 ... 53 B1
Blackheath High Jun Sch SE3 ... 53 B1
Blackheath High Sch SE3 ... 53 C3
Blackheath Hill SE10 ... 52 B2
Blackheath Prep Sch SE3 ... 53 C2
Blackheath Rd SE10 ... 52 A2
Blackheath Rise SE13 ... 52 B1
BLACKHEATH VALE ... 53 B1
Blackheath Vale SE3 ... 53 A1
Blackheath Village SE3 ... 53 B1
Black Horse Ct SE1 ... 137 C2
Blackhorse Rd SE8 ... 51 A4
Blacklands Terr SW3 ... 145 A3
Black Lion La W6 ... 38 C2
Black Lion Mews 4 W6 ... 38 C2
Blackmore Ho
Islington N1 ... 85 A3
2 Wandsworth SW18 ... 59 A2
Blackmore Twr 1 W3 ... 37 B3
Blackpool Rd SE15 ... 50 A1
Black Prince Rd SE1, SE11 ... 149 A3
Black Roof Ho 9 SE5 ... 48 A2
Black's Rd W6 ... 39 B2
Blackstock Ho 2 N5 ... 6 A1
Blackstock Mews N4 ... 6 A1
Blackstock Rd N4, N5 ... 6 A2
Blackstone Ho
Dulwich SE21 ... 76 A1
Pimlico SW1 ... 146 C1
Blackstone Rd NW2 ... 9 B4
Black Swan Yd SE1 ... 138 A4
Blackthorn Ct
20 Camberwell SE15 ... 49 B3
4 Leyton E15 ... 19 C4
Blackthorn St E3 ... 26 C1
Blacktree Mews 11 SW9 ... 62 C4
BLACKWALL ... 34 C2
Blackwall Sta E14 ... 34 B2
Blackwall Trad Est E14 ... 34 C4
Blackwall Tunnel E14, SE10 ... 34 C1
Blackwall Tunnel App SE10 ... 43 A4
Blackwall Tunnel Northern Approach E14, E3 ... 27 B1
Blackwall Way E14 ... 34 B2
Blackwater Ho NW8 ... 101 C4
Blackwater St SE22 ... 64 B2
Blackwell Cl 10 E5 ... 17 C4
Blackwell Ho 3 SW4 ... 61 C1
Blackwood Ho 11 E1 ... 25 A1
Blackwood St SE17 ... 151 B2
Blade Mews SW15 ... 58 B3
Bladen Ho 4 E1 ... 32 C3

Blades Ct
4 Hammersmith W6 39 A1
Putney SW15 58 B3
Blades Ho 12 SE11 163 B3
Blades Lo 16 SW2 62 C1
Blagdon Rd SE13 67 A1
Blagrove Rd 1 W10 31 B4
Blair Cl N1 15 B2
Blair Ct NW8 79 B4
Blairderry Rd SW2 74 A2
Blairgowrie Ct 13 E14 34 C3
Blair Ho SW9 172 C2
Blair St E14 34 C3
Blake Coll W1 104 C4
Blake Ct
8 Bermondsey SE16 40 A1
Kilburn NW6 23 C2
Blake Gdns SW6 166 A4
Blake Ho
2 Deptford SE8 51 C4
Isle Of Dogs E14 42 A4
1 Kentish Town N19 13 C3
Lambeth SE1 135 B2
14 Stoke Newington N16 16 A4
Blake Mews 15 TW9 44 C2
Blakemore Rd SW16 74 A1
Blakeney Cl
5 Camden Town NW1 13 C1
4 Dalston E8 16 C3
Blakenham Ct W12 29 C1
Blaker Rd E15 27 B4
Blakes Cl W10 30 B4
Blake's Rd SE15 49 A3
Blanca Ho 16 N1 24 A3
Blanchard Way E8 16 C2
Blanch Cl SE15 50 B3
Blanchedowne SE5 63 C3
Blandfield Rd SW12 72 C4
Blandford Ct
Brondesbury Pk NW6 10 A1
6 De Beauvoir Town N1 16 A1
Blandford Ho SW8 162 C2
Blandford Rd W4 38 A3
Blandford Sq NW1 90 B1
Blandford St W1 103 B3
Bland Ho SE11 149 A2
Blantyre St SW10 157 B2
Blantyre Twr SW10 157 B2
Blantyre Wlk SW10 157 B2
Blashford NW3 12 B1
Blasker Wlk 8 E14 42 A1
Blaxland Ho 12 W12 30 A2
Blazer Ct NW8 89 C3
Blechynden Ho 17 W10 30 C3
Blechynden St W10 30 C2
Bleeding Heart Yd EC1 107 C3
Blemundsbury WC1 106 C4
Blendworth Point 4 SW15 69 A3
Blenheim 26 SW19 69 C3
Blenheim Cres
Notting Hill W11 31 A3
Notting Hill W11 31 A2 112 B4
Blenheim Ct
Barnsbury N7 14 A2
Richmond TW9 54 B4
17 Rotherhithe SE16 32 C1
Upper Holloway N19 5 A2
Blenheim Gdns
Clapham Pk SW2 62 B1
Dollis Hill NW2 9 B3
Blenheim Gr SE15 49 C1
Blenheim Pas NW8 78 C2
Blenheim Rd
Acton W4 38 A3
St John's Wood NW8 79 A2
Blenheim St W1 104 A1
Blenheim Terr NW8 78 C2
Blenkarne Rd SW11 60 B1
Blessed Sacrament RC Prim Sch N1 84 C3
Blessington Cl SE13 67 C4
Blessington Rd SE13 67 C3
Bletchley Ct N1 87 B1
Bletchley St N1 87 A1
Bletsoe Wlk N1 87 A2
Blick Ho 1 SE16 40 B3
Blincoe Cl SW19 69 C2
Blissett St SE10 52 B2
Bliss Mews 14 W10 23 A2
Blisworth Ho 12 E2 24 C4
Blithfield St W8 128 A1
Bloemfontein Ave W12 30 A1
Bloemfontein Rd W12 30 A2
Blomfield Ct
Battersea SW11 167 C4
Paddington W9 89 A2
Blomfield Ho 4 E14 34 A2
Blomfield Mans 3 W12 30 B1
Blomfield Rd W9 100 C4
Blomfield St EC2 109 C3
Blomfield Villas W9 100 C4
Blondel St SW11 169 B2
Blondin St E3 26 C3
Bloomberg Space EC1 109 C4
Bloomburg St SW1 147 A3
Bloomfield Ho 19 E1 111 B3
Bloomfield Pl W1 118 B4
Bloomfield Terr SW1 145 C2
Bloom Gr SE27 75 A1
Bloom Park Rd SW6 154 C1
BLOOMSBURY 106 A4
Bloomsbury Ct WC1 106 B3
Bloomsbury Ho 10 SW4 61 C1
Bloomsbury International Language Sch WC1 106 B3
Bloomsbury Pl
London SW18 59 B2
St Giles WC1 106 B3
Bloomsbury Sq WC1 106 B3
Bloomsbury St WC1 105 C3
Bloomsbury Way WC1 106 B3
Blore Cl SW8 171 B3
Blore Ct W1 119 B4
Blore Ho SW10 156 B2
Blossom Cl W5 36 A4
Blossom Pl E1 24 A1 98 B1
Blossom St E1 24 A1 98 B1
Blount St E14 33 A3
Blucher Rd SE5 48 B3
Blue Anchor Alley 4 TW9 54 A3
Blue Anchor La SE16 40 A2
Blue Anchor Yd E1 125 B4
Blue Ball Yd SW1 118 C1
Bluebell Cl 10 E9 25 B4
Blue Gate Fields Jun & Inf Schs 22 E1 32 B2
Bluegate Mews E1 32 A2
Blue Lion Pl SE1 138 A2
Blueprint Apartments 15 SW12 73 A4
Blundell Cl E8 16 C4
Blundell St N7 14 A2
Blurton Rd E5 17 C4
Blyth Cl 4 E14 42 C2
Blythe Ho 8 SE11 163 C4
Blythe Mews 2 W14 39 C3
Blythendale Ho 34 E2 24 C3
Blythe Rd W14 126 A1
Blythe St E2 25 A2
Blyth's Wharf E14 33 A2
Blythwood Rd N4 5 A4
BMI Fitzroy Square Hospl W1 92 C1
Bnois Jerusalem Girls Sch 2 N16 6 C4
Boades Mews 3 NW3 11 C4
Boadicea St N1 84 C3
Boardwalk Pl E14 34 B1
Boarley Ho SE17 152 A3
Boathouse Ctr The W10 22 C1
Boathouse Wlk 24 SE15 49 B3
Boat Lifter Way 19 SE16 41 A2
Bobbin Cl SW4 61 B4
Bob Marley Way 10 SE24 62 C3
Bobov Foundation Sch 4 N16 7 B4
Bocking St E8 25 A4
Boddicott Cl SW19 70 A2
Boddington Gdns W3 36 C4
Boddington Ho 2 SE14 50 B2
Bodeney Ho 10 SE5 49 A2
Boden Ho 4 E1 111 B4
Bodington Ct 2 W12 39 C4
Bodley Manor Way SE24 74 C4
Bodmin St SW18 70 C3
Bodney Rd E5, E8 17 A3
Bogart Ct 13 E14 33 C2
Bohemia Pl 1 E8 17 A2
Bohn Rd E1 33 A4
Boileau Rd SW13 47 A4
Boilerhouse SE1 124 C1
Boisseau Ho 31 E1 32 B4
Bolden St SE8 52 A1
Boldero Pl NW8 90 A1
Boleyn Rd N16 16 A3
Bolina Rd SE16 40 B1
Bolingbroke Gr SW11 60 B1
Bolingbroke Rd W14 39 C3
Bolingbroke Wlk SW11 168 A4
Bollo Bridge Rd W3 37 B4
Bollo Ct 2 W3 37 B3
Bollo La W3 37 A3
Bolney Gate SW7 130 A3
Bolney St SW8 162 C1
Bolsover St W1 92 B1
Bolt Ct EC4 107 C1
Bolton Cres SE5 48 A3
Bolton Ct SW11 169 C3
Bolton Gdns
Kensal Rise NW10 22 C3
South Kensington SW5 142 B2
Bolton Gdns Mews SW10 142 C2
Bolton Ho 4 SE10 43 A1
Bolton Pl SW5 142 C2
Bolton Rd
Chiswick W4 45 B3
Harlesden NW10 21 A4
Kilburn NW8 78 B3
Boltons Ct SW5 142 B2
Bolton St W1 118 B2
Boltons The SW10 142 C2
Bolton Studios SW10 143 A1
Bolton Wlk N7 5 B2
Bombay Ct 8 SE16 40 B4
Bombay St SE16 40 A2
Bomore Rd W11 31 A2 112 A4
Bonar Rd SE15 49 C3
Bonchurch Rd W10 31 A4
Bond Ct EC4 109 B1
Bond Ho 4 NW6 23 B3
Bonding Yard Wlk SE16 41 A3
Bond St W4 37 C2
Bond Street Sta W1 103 C1
Bondway SW8 162 B4
Bonfield Rd SE13 67 B3
Bonham Ho W11 31 B1 112 C2
Bonham Rd SW2 62 B2
Bonheur Rd W4 37 C4
Bonhill St EC2 97 C1
Bonington Ho N1 84 C1
Bonita Mews SE15 65 C4
Bonner Ho 3 SW15 56 C2
Bonner Prim Sch 39 E2 25 B2
Bonner Rd E2 25 B3
Bonner St E2 25 B3
Bonneville Gdns SW4 61 B1
Bonneville Prim Sch SW4 61 B1
Bonnington Sq SW8 162 C4
Bonny St NW1 13 B1
Bonsor Ho SW8 171 A4
Bonsor St SE5 49 A3
Bonthron Ho SW15 47 B1
Booker Cl 11 E3 33 B4
Boord St SE10 43 A3
Boothby Rd N19 4 C2
Booth Cl 10 E9 25 A4
Booth Ho 2 SW2 74 C4
Booth La EC4 122 C4
Booth's Pl W1 105 A3
Boot St N1 24 A2 98 A3
Bordon Wlk 5 SW15 68 C4
Boreas Wlk N1 86 B1
Boreham Ave E16 35 C3
Boreman Ho 11 SE10 52 B4
Borland Rd SE15 65 B3
Borneo St SW15 57 B4
Borough High St SE1 123 B2
Borough Mkt SE1 123 B1
Borough Rd SE1 136 B2
Borough Sq SE1 136 C3
Borough Sta SE1 137 A3
BOROUGH THE 136 C4
Borrett Cl SE17 150 C1
Borrodaile Rd SW18 59 A1
Borrowdale NW1 92 C3
Borthwick St SE8 41 C1
Boscastle Rd NW5 4 A1
Boscobel Ho 4 E8 17 A2
Boscobel Pl SW1 145 C4
Boscobel St NW8 89 C1
Boscombe Cl E5 18 A3
Boscombe Rd W12 38 C4
Boss Ho SE1 138 C4
Boss St SE1 138 C4
Boston Gdns W4 46 A4
Boston Ho
24 Camberwell SE5 48 B1
Earl's Ct SW5 142 B3
Lisson Gr NW1 90 C2
Boston Pl NW1 90 C1

Bosun Cl 22 E14 41 C4
Boswell Ct
- Bloomsbury WC1 106 B4
- 9 Hammersmith W14 39 C3
Boswell Ho WC1 106 B4
Boswell St WC1 106 B4
Bosworth Ho 4 W10 23 A1
Bosworth Rd W10 23 A1
Bothwell Cl E16 35 B4
Bothwell St 4 W6 47 C4
Botolph Alley EC3 124 A4
Botolph La EC3 124 A4
Bott's Mews W2 31 C3
Boughton Ho SE1 137 B4
Boulcott St E1 32 C3
Boulevard The
- Chelsea SW6 167 A3
- 4 Upper Tooting SW17 72 C2
Boulogne Ho SE1 138 C2
Boulter Ho 4 SE14 50 B2
Boulton Ho TW8 36 A1
Boundaries Mans 3 SW12 72 C3
Boundaries Rd SW12 72 C3
Boundary Ho
- Balham SW12 73 A3
- 1 Camberwell SE5 48 B3
- 15 Notting Hill W11 30 C1
Boundary La SE17 48 B4
Boundary Pas E2 24 B1 98 C2
Boundary Rd NW8 79 A4
Boundary Road Est NW8 78 C3
Boundary Row SE1 136 A4
Boundary St E2 24 B1 98 C2
Bourchier St W1 119 B4
Bourdon Pl W1 118 B4
Bourdon St W1 118 B3
Bourke Cl
- London SW4 62 A1
- Willesden NW10 8 A2
Bourlet Cl W1 104 C3
Bourne Ct W4 45 B4
Bourne Ho 5 SW4 61 B3
Bourne Mews W1 103 C1
Bournemouth Cl SE15 49 C1
Bournemouth Rd SE15 49 C1
Bourne Pl W4 37 C1
Bourne St SW1 145 B3
Bourne Terr W2 100 B4
Bousfield Prim Sch SW10 142 C2
Bousfield Rd SE14 50 C1
Boutcher CE Prim Sch SE1 152 C4
Boutflower Rd SW11 60 A3
Bouverie Mews N16 7 A2
Bouverie Pl W2 101 C2
Bouverie Rd N16 7 A2
Bouverie St EC4 107 C1
Bovingdon Cl 4 N19 4 B2
Bovingdon Rd SW6 166 B3
BOW 26 B3
Bowater Cl SW2 62 A1
Bowater Ho EC1 97 A1
Bow Brook The 20 E2 25 C3
Bow Church Sta E3 26 C2
BOW COMMON 34 A4
Bow Common La E3 26 B1
Bowden Ho 29 E3 27 A2
Bowden St SE11 149 C1
Bowditch SE8 41 B1
Bowen Ct 2 N5 15 A4
Bowen Dr SE21 76 A1
Bowen St E14 34 A3
Bower Ave SE3 53 A3
Bowerdean St SW6 166 A2
Bower Ho SE14 50 C2
Bowerman Ave SE14 51 A4
Bowerman Ct 1 N19 4 C2
Bower St E1 32 C3
Bowes-Lyon Hall 13 E16 35 C1
Bowes Rd W3 29 A2
Bowfell Rd W6 47 B4
Bowhill Cl SW9 163 C2
Bow Ho 1 E3 26 C2
Bowie Cl SW4 73 C4
Bow La EC2, EC4 109 A1
Bowland Ho N4 6 B4
Bowland Rd SW4 61 C3
Bowland Yd SW1 131 A3
Bowl Ct EC2 24 A1 98 B1
Bowles Rd 1 SE1 49 C4
Bowley Ho 6 SE16 139 B2
Bowling Green Cl SW19 69 A4
Bowling Green Ho SW10 157 B2
Bowling Green La EC1 95 C2
Bowling Green Pl SE1 137 B4
Bowling Green St SE11 163 B4
Bowling Green Wlk N1 24 A2 98 A4
Bowman Ave E16 35 B2
Bowman Mews
- St George in t East E1 125 B4
- Wandsworth SW18 70 B3
Bowman's Mews N7 5 A1
Bowman's Pl N7 5 A1
Bowmore Wlk NW1 13 C1
Bowness Cl 5 E8 16 B2
Bowness Ho SE15 50 B3
Bowood Rd SW11 60 C2
Bow Rd E3 26 C2
Bow Road Sta E3 26 C2
Bowry Ho 14 E14 33 B4
Bow Sec Sch 19 E3 26 C2
Bowsprit Point 1 E14 41 C3
Bow St WC2 106 B1
Bowstead Ct SW11 167 C3
Bow Triangle Bsns Ctr 17 E3 26 C1
Bowyer Ho
- 27 Shoreditch N1 24 A4
- Wandsworth SW18 59 A1
Bowyer Pl SE5 48 B3
Bowyer St 15 SE5 48 B3
Boxall Rd SE21 64 A1
Boxley Ho 3 E5 17 A3
Boxmoor Ho
- 16 Hackney E2 24 C4
- 9 Shepherd's Bush W11 30 C1
Box Tree Ho SE8 41 A1
Boxworth Gr N1 85 A4
Boyce Ho 1 W10 23 B2
Boyd Ct SW15 57 B1
Boydell Ct NW8 11 C1
Boyd St E1 111 C1
Boyfield St SE1 136 B3
Boyle St W1 118 C4
Boyne Ct NW10 8 C1
Boyne Rd SE13 67 C4
Boyne Terr Mews W11 31 B1 112 C2
Boyson Rd 10 SE17 48 C4
Boyton Cl E1 25 C1
Boyton Ho
- Kennington SE11 149 B1
- St John's Wood NW8 79 C2
Brabant Ct EC3 124 A4
Brabazon St E14 34 A4
Brabner Ho 3 E2 24 C2 99 B4
Brabourn Gr SE15 50 B1
Bracer Ho 1 N1 24 A3
Bracewell Rd W10 30 B4
Bracey Mews 1 N4 5 A2
Bracey St N4 5 A2
Bracken Ave SW12 72 C4
Brackenbury N4 5 B3
Brackenbury Gdns W6 39 A3
Brackenbury Prim Sch 4 W6 39 A3
Brackenbury Rd W6 39 A3
Bracken Gdns SW13 46 C1
Bracken Ho 15 E3 33 C4
Brackley Ave SE15 65 B4
Brackley Ct NW8 89 C2
Brackley Rd W4 38 A1
Brackley St EC1 109 A4
Brackley Terr 6 W4 38 A1
Bracklyn Ct N1 87 B2
Bracklyn St N1 87 B2
Bracknell Gate NW3 11 A3
Bracknell Gdns NW3 11 A4
Bracknell Way NW3 11 A4
Bradbeer Ho 24 E2 25 B2
Bradbourne St SW6 165 C2
Bradbury Ct 2 SE3 53 C3
Bradbury Ho E1 111 A2
Bradbury St 28 N16 16 A3
Bradby Ho NW8 78 B1
Braddon Rd TW9 54 B4
Braddyll St SE10 43 A1
Bradenham 11 SE17 48 C4
Bradenham Cl SE17 48 C4
Braden St W9 88 A1
Bradfield Ct 14 NW1 13 A1
Bradfield Ho 15 SW8 171 B2
Bradford Ho 4 W14 39 C3
Bradford Rd W3 38 A4
Bradgate Rd SE6 67 A1
Brading Rd SW2 74 B4
Brading Terr W12 38 C3
Bradiston Rd W9 23 B2
Bradley Cl N7 14 B2
Bradley Ho
- Bermondsey SE16 40 A2
- 1 Bromley E3 27 A2
Bradley Mews SW12 72 B3
Bradley's Cl N1 85 C2
Bradlord Ho SE21 76 A1
Bradmead SW8 160 C1
Bradmore Park Rd W6 39 A2
Brad St SE1 121 C1
Bradstock Ho E9 18 A1
Bradstock Rd E9 17 C2
Bradwell Ho 8 NW6 78 A3
Bradwell St 24 E1 25 C2
Brady Ho
- London SW4 61 C2
- South Lambeth SW8 171 A4
Brady St E1 25 A1
Braefoot Ct SW15 57 C2
Braemar SW15 57 C1
Braemar Ave SW18, SW19 70 C2
Braemar Ho W9 88 C3
Braemar Mans W8 128 B1
Braes St N1 15 A1
Braganza St SE17 150 A1
Braham Ho SE11 149 A1
Brahma Kumaris World Spiritual Univ NW10 8 C1
Braid Ave W3 29 A3
Braid Ho SE10 52 B2
Braidwood St SE1 124 A1
Brailsford Rd SW2 62 C1
Braintree Ho 6 E1 25 B1
Braintree St E2 25 B2
Braithwaite Ho EC1 97 B2
Braithwaite Twr W2 101 B4
Bramah Gn SW9 173 C4
Bramall Ct N7 14 B2
Bramber WC1 94 A3
Bramber Ct TW8 36 A2
Bramber Rd W14 154 C4
Brambledown 8 N4 5 A4
Bramble Gdns W12 29 B2
Bramble Ho 16 E3 33 C4
Brambling Ct 25 SE8 51 B4
Bramcote Gr SE16 40 B1
Bramcote Rd SW15 57 A3
Bramerton NW6 9 C1
Bramerton St SW3 158 A4
Bramfield Ct N4 6 B2
Bramfield Rd SW11 60 B2
Bramford Rd SW18 59 B3
Bramham Gdns SW5 142 B2
Bramham Ho SE22 64 A3
Bramlands Cl SW11 60 A4
Bramley Cres SW8 161 C2
Bramley Ct SE13 67 C2
Bramley Ho
- 19 North Kensington W10 30 C3
- Roehampton SW15 56 B1
Bramley Rd W10 30 C3
Brampton WC1 106 C3
Bramshaw Rd E9 17 C2
Bramshill Gdns NW5 4 A1
Bramshill Rd NW10 21 B3
Bramshurst NW8 78 B3
Bramston Rd
- Harlesden NW10 21 C3
- Wandsworth SW17 71 B1
Bramwell Ho
- Borough The SE1 137 A1
- Chelsea SW1 160 C4
Bramwell Mews N1 85 A4
Brancaster Ho
- 22 Globe Town E1 25 C2
- Islington N5 15 A3
Brancaster Rd SW16 74 A1
Branch Hill NW3 2 B1
Branch Pl N1 87 C4
Branch Rd E14 33 A2
Branch St SE15 49 A3
Brand Cl N4 6 A3
Branden Lo 13 W4 37 B1
Brandlehow Prim Sch SW15 58 B3
Brandlehow Rd SW15 58 B3
Brandon Mews
- Barbican EC2 109 B4
- Walworth SE17 151 A3
Brandon Rd N7 14 A1
Brandon St SE17 151 A3
Brandrams Wharf SE16 40 B4
Brandreth Rd SW17 73 A2
Brand St SE10 52 B3
Brangton Rd SE11 149 A1
Brangwyn Ct W14 126 A1
Branksea St SW6 154 A1
Branksome Ho SW8 162 C2
Branksome Rd SW2 62 A2
Bransby Ct 4 N16 16 A4
Branscombe NW1 83 A3

Branscombe St SE13 . . . 67 A4
Bransdale Cl NW6 . . 23 C4
Branstone Ct 9 TW9 . . . 44 B2
Branstone Rd TW9 . . 44 B2
Branston Ho N7 . . . . 14 C3
Brantwood Ho 9 SE5 . . . 48 B3
Brantwood Rd SE24 . . . 63 B2
Brasenose Dr SW13 . . . 47 B4
Brashley Road Cvn Site NW10 . . . 21 A2
Brassey Ho 1 E14 . . 42 A2
Brassey Rd NW6 . . . . 10 B2
Brassey Sq SW11 . . . 60 C4
Brassie Ave W3 . . . . 29 A3
Brass Talley Alley 31 SE16 . . . 40 C4
Brathay NW1 . . . . . . 83 A1
Brathway Rd SW18 . . . 70 C4
Bratley St 11 E1 . . . 24 C1 99 B1
Bravington Pl W9 . . 23 B1
Bravington Rd W9 . . 23 B2
Brawne Ho 12 SE17 . . . 48 A4
Braxfield Rd SE4 . . . 66 B3
Bray NW3 . . . . 12 A1
Brayard's Rd SE15 . . 50 A1
Braybrook St W12 . . 29 B3
Brayburne Ave SW4 . . . 171 A1
Bray Cres SE16 . . . . 40 C4
Braydon Rd N16 . . . . 7 C3
Bray Dr E16 . . . . 35 B2
Brayfield Terr N1 . . . 14 C1
Brayford Sq 12 E1 . . 32 B3
Bray Pl SW3 . . . . . 144 C3
Bread St EC2, EC4 . 109 A1
Breakspeare SE21 . . 76 B1
Breakspears Mews SE4 . . . 51 C1
Breakspears Rd SE4 . . . 66 C4
Breakwell Ct 16 W10 . . . 23 A1
Breamore Cl SW15 . . . 68 C3
Breamore Ho 21 SE15 . . . 49 C3
Bream's Bldgs EC4 . . . 107 B2
Bream St E3 . . . . . . 18 C1
Breasley Cl SW15 . . . 57 A3
Brechin Pl SW7 . . 143 A3
Brecknock Prim Sch 18 N7 . . . 13 C2
Brecknock Rd N19 . . 13 C3
Brecon Ho
Stamford Hill N16 . . . . 7 B3
Wandsworth SW18 . . 70 C4
Brecon Rd W6 . . . . 154 B3
Bredel Ho 1 E14 . . . 33 C4
Bredgar SE13 . . . . . . 67 A2
Bredgar Rd N19 . . . . . 4 B2
Bredinghurst SE22 . . 76 C4
Bredinghurst Sch SE15 . . . 65 C3
Bredin Ho SW10 . . 156 B2
Breer St SW6 . . . . . . 59 A4
Breezer's Ct 22 E1 . . . 125 C3
Breezer's Hill E1 . . 125 C3
Brehon Ho NW1 . . . 82 C3
Bremans Row 1 SW18 . . . 71 B2
Bremner Rd SW7 129 A2
Brenchley Gdns SE15, SE22, SE23 . . . 65 C1
Brenda Rd SW17 . . . 72 B2
Brendon Ave NW10 . . 8 A4
Brendon Ho W1 . . 103 B4
Brendon St W1 . . . 102 B2
Brenley Ho SE1 . . . 137 B4
Brennands Ct 14 N19 . . . 4 B1
Brent Adult Comm Education Service Coll 9 NW10 . . . 20 C4
Brent Ct 5 W12 . . . . 38 A3
Brentford Fountain L Ctr W4 . . . 36 C1
Brent Ho 16 E9 . . . . . 17 B2
Brenthouse Rd E9 . . 17 B2
Brenthurst Rd NW10 . . . 8 B2
Brent Mus NW10 . . . . 9 A2
Brent New Ent Ctr NW10 . . . 8 B2
Brenton Ct E9 . . . . . . 18 A3
Brenton St E14 . . . . . 33 A3
Brent Rd E16 . . . . 35 C4
Brent Trad Est NW10 . . . 8 A3
Brentwick Gdns TW8 . . . 36 A2
Brereton Ho 4 SW2 . . . 74 C4
Bressenden Pl SW1 . . . 132 C2
Breton Ho
Bermondsey SE1 . . 138 C2
St Luke's EC2 . . . . . . 97 A1
Brett Cl N16 . . . . 7 A2
Brett Cres NW10 . . . . 20 C4
Brettell St SE17 . . . 151 C1
Brett Ho 1 SW15 . . . 69 C4
Brett House Cl 2 SW15 . . . 69 C4
Brettinghurst 8 SE1 . . . 153 B1
Bretton Ho N19 . . . . . . 5 A3
Brett Pas 23 E8 . . . . . 17 A3
Brett Rd E8 . . . . 17 A3
Brewers Bldgs EC1 96 A4
Brewers Ct W2 . . . 100 C2
Brewer's Gn SW1 . 133 B2
Brewers Hall Gdns EC2 . . . 109 A3
Brewer St W1 . . . . 119 A4
Brewery Ind Est The N1 . . . 87 A1
Brewery Rd N7 . . . . . 14 A2
Brewery Sq
Bermondsey SE1 . . 124 C1
Clerkenwell EC1 . . . 96 B2
Brewhouse La
Putney SW15 . . . . 58 A4
Wapping E1 . . . . 32 A1
Brewhouse Wlk SE16 . . . 33 A1
Brewhouse Yd EC1 96 A2
Brewster Gdns W10 . . . 30 B4
Brewster Ho
Bermondsey SE1 . . 153 A4
Brewster Ho *continued*
Poplar E14 . . . . 33 B2
Briant Ho SE1 . . . . 135 A1
Briant St SE14 . . . . . . 50 C3
Briar Ct
7 Bow E3 . . . . 26 C3
9 Dalston E8 . . . . 16 B1
Briardale SW19 . . . . . 70 B3
Briardale Gdns NW3 . . . 1 C1
Briardale Ho 12 N16 . . . 7 A3
Briar Rd NW2 . . . . 9 B4
Briar Wlk
Putney SW15 . . . . 57 A3
West Kilburn W10 . . . 23 A1
Briarwood Rd SW4 . . . 61 C2
Briary Cl NW3 . . . . . . 12 A1
Briary Ct 10 E16 . . . . 35 B3
Brickbarn Cl SW10 . . . 157 A2
Brick Ct EC4 . . . . . . 107 B1
Brick Farm Cl TW9 . . . 45 A2
Brick La
Shoreditch E2 . . . 24 B2 99 A3
Spitalfields E1 . . . 24 B1 99 A1
Brick Lane Mkt E2. 99 A2
Bricklayers Arms SE1 . . . 137 C1
Brick St W1 . . . . . . 118 A1
Brickworth Ho 26 SW9 . . . 173 C4
Brideale Cl SE15 . . . . 49 B4
Bride Ct EC4 . . . . . 108 A1
Bride La EC4 . . . . . 108 A1
Bridel Mews N1 . . . 86 A3
Bride St N7 . . . . 14 B2
Bridewain St SE1 138 C2
Bridewell Pl
Holborn EC4 . . . . . . 108 A1
20 Wapping E1 . . . . . . 32 A1
Bridford Mews W1 . . . 104 B4
Bridge Acad The E2 . . . 24 B4
Bridge App NW3 . . . 12 C1
Bridge Ave W6 . . . . . 39 B1
Bridge Avenue Mans 1 W6 . . . 39 B1
Bridge Cl 13 W10 . . . 30 C3
Bridge Ct
9 Blackwall E14 . . . . 34 C2
7 Willesden NW10 . . . 8 A1
Bridge Field Ho 7 W2 . . . 100 A2
Bridgefoot SE1 . . . 148 B1
Bridge Gdns N16 . . . 15 C4
Bridge Ho
Brockley SE4 . . . . 66 B3
1 Camden Town NW1 . . . 12 C1
Homerton E9 . . . . 17 C3
Bridge House Quay E14 . . . 34 B1
Bridge La SW11 . . 168 B3
Bridgeland Rd E16 . 35 C2
Bridgeman Ho 19 E9 . . . 17 B1
Bridgeman Rd N1 . . 14 B1
Bridgeman St NW8 80 A1
Bridge Meadows SE14 . . . 50 C4
Bridgend Rd SW18 . 59 B3
Bridgen Ho 9 E1 . . 32 A3
Bridge Pk 7 SW18 . . . 58 C2
Bridge Pl SW1 . . . . 146 B4
Bridgeport Pl 4 E1 . . . 125 C2
Bridge Rd
Stratford Marsh E15 . . . 27 C4
Willesden NW10 . . . . . . 8 A2
Bridge Sch The
Clerkenwell EC1 . . . . 96 A2
Lower Holloway N7 . . 14 A3
Bridges Ct SW11 . 167 B1
Bridges Ho 15 SE5 . . 48 C3
Bridge St
Chiswick W4 . . . . 37 C2
Westminster SW1 . 134 B3
Bridge Terr E15 . . . . . 19 C1
Bridgeview 2 W6 . . 39 B1
Bridgewater Rd E15 . . . 27 B4
Bridgewater Sq EC2 . . . 108 C4
Bridgewater St EC2 . . . 108 C4
Bridgeway St NW1 83 A1
Bridge Wharf 18 E2 . . . 25 C3
Bridge Yd SE1 . . . . 123 C2
Bridgford St SW17, SW18 . . . 71 B1
Bridgman Rd W4 . . . 37 B3
Bridgnorth Ho 10 SE15 . . . 49 C4
Bridgwater Ho W2 . . . 100 C2
Bridle La W1 . . . . . 119 A4
Bridlington Ho SW18 . . . 59 B3
Bridport SE17 . . . . 151 A1
Bridport Ho N1 . . . . 87 C3
Bridport Pl N1 . . . . 87 C3
Bridstow Pl W2 . . . . . 31 C3
Brief St SE5 . . . . 48 A2
Brierfield NW1 . . . . 82 C3
Brierley Rd
Leyton E11 . . . . 19 C4
Upper Tooting SW12 . . . 73 B2
Brierly Gdns E2 . . . . 25 B3
Brigade St SE3 . . . . . 53 B1
Briggeford Cl 5 E5 . 7 C2
Briggs Ho 20 E2 . . . 24 B2 99 A4
Brightling Rd SE4 . . 66 B1
Brightlingsea Pl 5 E14 . . . 33 B2
Brightman Rd SW18 . . . 71 C3
Brighton Bldgs SE1 . . . 138 A1
Brighton Ct SW15 . . 58 B1
Brighton Gr SE14 . . . 51 A2
Brighton Ho 7 SE5 . . . 48 C2
Brighton Rd N16 . . . 16 A4
Brighton Terr SW9 . . 62 B3
Brightside Rd SE13 . . . 67 C1
Bright St E14 . . . . 34 A4
Brightwell Ct N7 . . . 14 B3
Brightwells 1 SW6 . . . 166 A2
Brig Mews SE8 . . . . . 51 C4
Brigstock Ho SE5 . . . 48 B1
Brill Pl NW1 . . . . 83 C1
Brimsdown Ho E3 . . 27 B1
Brindley Ho
37 Notting Hill W2 . . . 31 C4
22 Streatham SW12 . . . 74 A4
Brindley St SE14 . . . . 51 B2
Brine Ho 11 E3 . . . . . 26 A3
Brinklow Ho W2 . . 100 A3
Brinkworth Way E9 . . . 18 B2
Brinsley Ho 17 E1 . . 32 B3
Brinsley St 35 E1 . . . 32 A3
Brinton Wlk SE1 . . 122 A1
Brion Pl E14 . . . . 34 B4
Brisbane Ho 3 W12 . . . 30 A2
Brisbane St SE5 . . . . 48 C3
Briset St EC1 . . . . . . 96 A1
Briset Way N7 . . . . 5 B2
Bristol Gdns
Putney SW15 . . . . 69 B4
Westbourne Green W9 . . . 88 B1
Bristol Ho SE11 . . . 135 B1
Bristol Mews W9 . . 88 B1
Bristowe Cl 24 SW2 . . . 62 C1
Britannia Building N1 . . . 97 B4
Britannia Cl SW4 . . . 61 C3
Britannia Gate 11 E16 . . . 35 C1
Britannia Junc NW1 . . . 82 B4
Britannia L Ctr N1 . . 24 A4
Britannia Rd
23 Millwall E14 . . . . . 41 C2
Walham Green SW6 . . . 156 A1
Britannia Row N1 . 86 C4
Britannia St WC1 . . 94 C4
Britannia Way NW10 . . . 20 A1
Britannia Wlk N1 . . 97 B4
British Coll of Osteopathic Medicine NW3 . . . . 11 B2
British Dental Association Mus W1 . . . 104 A3
British Gr W4 . . . . . 38 B1
British Grove Pas 2 W4 . . . 38 B1
British Grove S 3 W4 . . . 38 B1
British Library The WC1 . . . 93 C4
British Mus WC1 . . 106 A3
British Optical Association Mus SW1 . . . 120 A2
British St E3 . . . . 26 B2
British Wharf Ind Est SE14 . . . 50 C4
Britley Ho 16 E14 . . . 33 B3
Brittage Rd 11 NW10 . . . 8 A1
Brittany Ho SW15 . . . 57 B3
Brittany Point SE11 . . . 149 B3
Britten Cl NW11 . . . . . 2 A3
Britten Ho SW3 . . . 144 B2
Britten St SW3 . . . 144 A2

Britton St EC1 96 A1
BRIXTON 62 C4
Brixton Day Coll 6 SW9 62 A4
Brixton Hill SW2 62 B1
Brixton Hill Ct 5 SW2 62 B2
Brixton Hill Pl SW2 74 A4
Brixton Mkt SW9 62 C3
Brixton Rd SW9 173 B2
Brixton Rec Ctr SW9 62 C4
Brixton Sta SW9 62 C3
Brixton Station Rd SW9 62 C4
Brixton Water La SW2 62 B2
Broadbent Cl N6 4 A3
Broadbent St W1 118 A4
Broadbridge Cl SE3 53 C3
Broad Common Est N16 7 C3
Broad Ct WC2 106 B1
Broadfield NW6 11 A2
Broadfield La NW1 14 A1
Broadfields Way NW10 8 B3
Broadford Ho 12 E1 26 A1
BROADGATE 110 A4
Broadgate EC2 110 A4
Broadgate Circ EC2 110 A3
Broadgates Ct SE11 149 C1
Broadgates Rd SW18 71 C3
Broadgate Twr The EC2 98 B1
Broadhinton Rd SW4 61 B4
Broadhurst Cl
Hampstead NW6 11 B2
9 Richmond TW10 54 B2
Broadhurst Gdns NW6 11 A2
Broadhurst Mans NW6 11 A2
Broad La EC2 110 A4
Broadlands N6 3 C4
Broadlands Ave SW16 74 A2
Broadlands Cl
Highgate N6 3 C4
Streatham SW16 74 A2
Broadlands Ct TW9 44 C3
Broadlands Lo N6 3 B4
Broadlands Mans 2 SW16 74 A2
Broadlands Rd N6 3 B4
Broadley St NW8 102 A4
Broadley Terr NW1 90 B1
Broadmayne SE17 151 B2
Broadmead W14 140 A3
Broadoak Ct 8 SW9 62 C4
Broadoak Ho 11 NW6 78 B3
Broad St Ave EC2 110 A3
Broad Sanctuary SW1 134 A3
Broadstone Ho SW8 162 C1
Broadstone Pl W1 103 B3
Broad Street Pl EC2 109 C3
Broadwalk Ho SW7 128 C3
Broadwalk La NW11 1 B4
Broadwall SE1 121 C2
Broadway
Stratford E15 19 C1
Westminster SW1 133 B2
Broadway Arc 3 W6 39 B2
Broadway Ho 2 E8 25 A4
Broadway Mans SW6 155 C1
Broadway Market E8 25 A4
Broadway Market Mews 21 E8 24 C4
Broadway Mews E5 7 B4
Broadway Mkt E8 25 A4
Broadway Ret Pk NW2 9 C4
Broadway Sh Ctr 5 W6 39 B2
Broadway The
Barnes SW13 46 A1
South Acton W3 36 C4
Broadway Wlk 4 E14 41 C3
Broadwick St W1 105 A1
Broad Wlk
Mayfair W1 117 B2
Regent's Pk NW1 81 C1
Richmond TW9 44 B3
Broad Wlk The W8 114 B1
Broadwood Terr W14 141 A4
Broad Yd EC1 96 A1
Brocas Cl NW3 12 A1
Brockbridge Ho SW15 56 B1
Brocket Ho 16 SW8 171 B2
Brockham Dr SW2 74 B4
Brockham Ho
Camden Town NW1 83 A3
11 Streatham SW2 74 B4
Brockham St SE1 137 A2
Brockhurst Ho N4 6 C4
Brockill Cres SE4 66 A3
Brocklebank Rd SW18 71 B4
Brocklebank Road Ind Est SE7 43 C2
Brocklehurst St SE14 50 C3
BROCKLEY 66 B3
Brockley Cross SE4 66 B4
Brockley Cross Bsns Ctr SE4 66 A4
Brockley Gdns SE4 51 B1
Brockley Gr SE4 66 B2
Brockley Hall Rd SE4 66 A2
Brockley Ho SE17 152 A2
Brockley Mews SE4 66 A2
Brockley Prim Sch SE4 66 B2
Brockley Rd SE4 66 B2
Brockley Sta SE4 66 A4
Brockley Way SE4 66 A2
Brockmer Ho 5 E1 32 A2
Brock Pl E3 27 A1
Brock St SE15 65 B4
Brockweir 28 E2 25 B3
Brockwell Ct 2 SW2 62 C2
Brockwell Ho SE11 163 A4
Brockwell Lido SE24 63 A1
Brockwell Park SE24 63 A1
Brockwell Park Gdns SE24 75 A4
Brockwell Park Row SW2 62 C1
Broderick Ho SE21 76 A1
Brodia Rd N16 7 A1
Brodick Ho 12 E3 26 B3
Brodie Ho SE1 153 A2
Brodie St SE1 153 A2
Brodlove La E1 32 C2
Brodrick Rd SW17 72 A2
Brody Ho E1 110 C3
Broken Wharf EC4 122 C4
Brokesley St E3 26 B2
Broke Wlk
Hackney E8 24 B4
1 Hackney E8 24 C4
Bromar Rd SE5 64 A4
Bromehead St 8 E1 32 B3
Bromell's Rd SW4 61 B3
Bromfelde Rd SW4 171 C1
Bromfield Ct 20 SE16 139 C2
Bromfield St N1 85 C2
Bromleigh Ho SE1 138 C2
BROMLEY E3 27 A2
Bromley-by-Bow Sta E3 98 A4
Bromley Hall Rd E14 34 B4
Bromley High St E3 27 A2
Bromley Lo 2 W3 28 B3
Bromley Pl W1 104 C4
Bromley St E1 32 C3
BROMPTON 130 A1
Brompton Arc SW1 131 A3
Brompton Oratory SW3 130 A1
Brompton Park Cres SW6 156 A3
Brompton Pl SW3 130 B2
Brompton Rd SW3 130 A1
Brompton Sq SW3 130 A2
Bromstone Ho 19 SW9 173 B3
Bromwich Ave N6 3 C2
Bromwich Ho 3 TW10 54 A1
Bromyard Ave W3 29 A2
Bromyard Ho
Acton W3 29 A1
3 Peckham SE15 50 A3
Bron Ct NW6 23 C4
BRONDESBURY 10 A2
Brondesbury Coll for Boys 10 NW6 10 A1
Brondesbury Ct NW2 9 C2
Brondesbury Mews 11 NW6 10 C1
BRONDESBURY PARK 22 C4
Brondesbury Park Sta NW6 23 A4
Brondesbury Pk NW6 9 C1
Brondesbury Rd NW6 23 C3
Brondesbury Sta NW6 10 B1
Brondesbury Villas NW6 23 C3
Bronsart Rd SW6 154 A1
Bronte Ct 8 W14 39 C3
Bronte Ho
Kilburn NW6 23 C2
6 Stoke Newington N16 16 A3
Bronti Cl SE17 151 A2
Bronwen Ct NW8 89 B3
Bronze St SE8 51 C3
Brookbank Rd SE13 67 A4
Brook Cl SW17 72 C2
Brook Com Prim Sch E8 16 C3
Brook Ct SW14 56 A4
Brookdale Rd SE6 67 A1
Brook Dr SE11 150 A4
Brooke Ct W10 23 A3
Brooke Ho 4 SE14 51 A2
Brooke Rd E5, N16 7 C1
Brookes Ct EC1 107 B4
Brooke's Mkt EC1 107 C4
Brooke St EC1 107 B3
Brookfield
Dartmouth Pk N6 3 C1
1 Finsbury Pk N4 5 C2
Brookfield Ho 23 E2 25 A3
Brookfield Pk NW5 4 A1
Brookfield Prim Sch N19 4 A2
Brookfield Rd
Acton W4 37 C4
Homerton E9 18 A2
Brookgate N16 6 C2
Brook Gate W1 117 A3
Brook Gdns SW13 56 B4
Brook Gn W6 39 C2
BROOK GREEN 39 C2
Brook Green Flats 11 W14 39 C3
Brook Ho
3 Clapham Pk SW4 61 B2
Ealing W3 36 C4
4 Hammersmith W6 39 B2
Marylebone WC1 105 B4
Brook Hos NW1 83 A1
Brooklands Ave SW18 71 A2
Brooklands Court Apartments 3 NW6 10 B1
Brooklands Ct 2 NW6 10 B1
Brooklyn Ct W12 30 B1
Brookmarsh Ind Est SE10 52 A3
Brook Mews N W2 115 A4
Brookmill Rd SE8 51 C2
Brooksbank Ho 7 E9 17 B2
Brooksbank St 9 E9 17 B2
Brooksby Ho 9 N1 14 C1
Brooksby Mews N1 14 C1
Brooksby St N1 14 C1
Brooksby's Wlk E9 17 C3
Brooks Ct
3 London SW4 172 A2
Nine Elms SW8 161 A2
Brooks Ho 6 SW2 74 C3
Brookside Rd N19 4 B2
Brooks La W4 44 C4
Brook's Mews W1 118 A4
Brooks Rd W4 36 C1
Brook St
Bayswater W2 115 C4
Mayfair W1 118 A4
Brookstone Ct SE15 65 A3
Brooksville Ave NW6 23 A4
Brookville Rd SW6 154 C1
Brookwood Ave SW13 46 B1
Brookwood Ho SE1 136 B3
Brookwood Rd SW18 70 C3
Broome Ct 3 TW9 44 C2
Broome Ho 7 E5 17 A3
Broome Way SE5 48 C3
Broom Farm SW6 165 C2
Broomfield 7 NW1 12 C1
Broomfield Ho SE17 152 A3
Broomfield House Sch TW9 44 B2
Broomfield Rd TW9 44 B2
Broomfield St E14 34 A4
Broomgrove Rd SW9 173 A1
Broomhill Rd SW18 58 C2
Broomhouse La SW6 58 C4
Broomhouse Rd SW6 165 B2
Broomsleigh St NW6 10 B3
Broomwood Hall (Lower Sch) 5 SW12 60 D1
Broomwood Hall Sch (Lower Sch) SW16 73 C1

Broomwood Hall Sch (Upper Sch) 3 SW12 ... 72 C4
Broomwood Rd SW11 ... 60 C2
Brougham Rd
Acton W3 ... 28 B3
Hackney E8 ... 24 C4
Brougham St SW11 ... 169 A2
Brough Cl SW8 ... 162 B1
Broughton Dr 19 SW9 ... 63 A3
Broughton Rd SW6 ... 166 B2
Broughton Road App 2 SW6 ... 166 A2
Broughton St SW8 ... 170 A2
Brouncker Rd W3 ... 37 B4
Browne Ho 13 SE8 ... 51 C3
Brownfield St E14 ... 34 B3
Brownflete Ho SE4 ... 66 A3
Brown Hart Gdns W1 ... 117 C4
Browning Cl W9 ... 89 A1
Browning Ct W14 154 C4
Browning Ho
2 London SE14 ... 51 A2
7 Shepherd's Bush W12 ... 30 B3
10 Stoke Newington N16 ... 16 A4
Browning Mews W1 ... 103 C3
Browning St SE17 151 A3
Brownlow Ho 10 SE16 ... 139 B3
Brownlow Mews WC1 ... 95 A1
Brownlow Rd
Hackney E8 ... 24 C4
Willesden NW10 ... 8 A1
Brownlow St WC1 107 A3
Brown's Bldgs EC3 ... 110 B1
Brown St W1 ... 102 C2
Brownswood Rd N4 . 6 B2
Broxash Rd SW11 ... 60 C1
Broxbourne Ho 1 E3 ... 27 A1
Broxholme Ho SW6 ... 166 A4
Broxholm Rd SE27, SW16 ... 74 C1
Broxwood Way NW8 ... 80 B3
Bruce Cl W10 ... 30 C4
Bruce Glasier Ho 13 N19 ... 4 C4
Bruce Ho
4 Clapham Pk SW4 ... 61 C1
3 North Kensington W10 ... 30 C4
Putney SW15 ... 57 A2
Bruce Rd E3 ... 27 A2
Bruckner St W10 ... 23 B2
Bruges Pl 16 NW1 ... 13 B1
Brune Ho E1 ... 110 C3
Brunei Gall WC1 .. 105 C4
Brunel Ct 8 SW13 ... 46 B1
Brunel Est W2 ... 31 C4
Brunel Ho
Chelsea SW10 ... 157 C2
4 Gospel Oak NW5 ... 13 A4
Millwall E14 ... 42 A1
New Cross SE8 ... 51 B3
25 Streatham SW2 ... 74 A4
Brunel Mews NW10 ... 22 C2
Brunel Mus SE16 ... 40 B4
Brunel Rd
Acton W3 ... 29 A4
Wapping SE16 ... 32 B1
Brunel St E16 ... 35 B3
Brune St E1 ... 110 C3
Brunlees Ho SE1 . 137 A1
Bruno Ct 5 E8 ... 16 C2
Brunswick Ct
Bermondsey SE1 .. 138 B4
Finsbury EC1 ... 96 A3
Westminster SW1 . 147 C3
Brunswick Gdns W8 ... 31 C1 113 C1
Brunswick Ho
4 Haggerston E2 ... 24 B3
Lisson Gr NW1 ... 90 C2
Brunswick Mews W1 ... 103 A2
Brunswick Park Prim Sch 22 SE5 ... 48 C3
Brunswick Pk SE5 ... 49 A2
Brunswick Pl N1 .. 97 C3
Brunswick Quay SE16 ... 40 C3
Brunswick Rd E14 ... 34 B3
Brunswick Sh Ctr WC1 ... 94 B2
Brunswick Sq WC1 94 B2
Brunswick Villas 2 SE5 ... 49 A2
Brunton Pl E14 ... 33 A3
Brushfield St E1 .. 110 C4
Brussels Rd SW11 ... 59 C3
Bruton La W1 ... 118 B3
Bruton Pl W1 ... 118 B3
Bruton St W1 ... 118 B3
Brutus Ct SE11 ... 150 A3
Bryan Ave NW10 ... 9 A1
Bryan Ct W1 ... 102 C2
Bryan Ho SE16 ... 41 B4
Bryan Rd SE16 ... 41 B4
Bryanston Ct W1 . 102 C2
Bryanston Ho 12 SE15 ... 49 B2
Bryanston Mans W1 ... 102 C4
Bryanston Mews E W1 ... 102 C3
Bryanston Mews W W1 ... 102 C2
Bryanston Pl W1 . 102 C3
Bryanston Sq W1 102 C2
Bryanston St W1 . 103 A1
Bryant Ct
Acton W3 ... 28 C1
Haggerston E2 ... 24 B3
Bryantwood Rd N5, N7 ... 14 C3
Bryce Ho 23 SE14 ... 50 C4
Brydale Ho 2 SE16 ... 40 C2
Brydges Pl WC2 .. 120 A3
Brydges Rd E15 ... 19 C3
Brydon Wlk N1 ... 84 B4
Bryer Ct EC2 ... 108 C4
Bryett Rd N7 ... 5 A1
Bryher Ho W4 ... 37 B1
Brymay Cl E3 ... 26 C3
Brymon Ct W1 ... 103 A3
Brynmaer Ho SW11 ... 169 A3
Brynmaer Rd SW11 ... 169 A3
Bryony Rd W12 ... 29 C2
BT Twr W1 ... 104 C4
Buccleuch Ho E5 ... 7 C4
Buchanan Ct 16 SE16 ... 40 C2
Buchanan Gdns NW10 ... 22 A3
Buchanan Ho
Dulwich SE21 ... 76 A1
Wandsworth SW18 ... 70 C4
Buchan Ho W3 ... 37 A4
Buchan Rd SE15 ... 65 B4
Bucharest Rd SW18 ... 71 B4
Buckfast St E2 ... 24 C2 99 C3
Buck Hill Wlk W2 115 C3
Buckhold Rd SW18 ... 58 C1
Buckhurst Ho 15 N7 ... 13 C3
Buckhurst St E1 ... 25 A1
Buckingham Ave SW1 ... 120 B3
Buckingham Gate SW1 ... 133 A2
Buckingham Ho
Finsbury Pk N4 ... 6 B3
Richmond TW10 ... 54 C2
Buckingham Mans NW6 ... 11 A3
Buckingham Mews
Harlesden NW10 ... 21 B3
7 Kingsland N1 ... 16 A2
Westminster SW1 . 132 C2
Buckingham Pal SW1 ... 132 C3
Buckingham Palace Rd SW1 ... 146 B4
Buckingham Pl SW1 ... 132 C2
Buckingham Rd
Harlesden NW10 ... 21 B3
Kingsland N1 ... 16 A2
Buckingham St WC2 ... 120 B3
Buckingham Yd NW10 ... 21 B3
Buckland Cres NW3 ... 11 C2
Buckland Ct 6 N1 . 24 A3
Buckland Ho 3 N1 ... 14 C1
Buckland St N1 ... 87 C1
Buckland Wlk 2 W3 ... 37 B4
Buckler's Alley SW6 ... 155 A2
Bucklersbury EC2, EC4 ... 109 B1
Buckle St
15 Whitechapel E1 ... 111 B2
Whitechapel E1 ... 111 A2
Buckley Ct 5 NW6 ... 10 B1
Buckley Rd NW6 ... 10 B1
Buckmaster Cl 1 SW9 ... 62 C4
Buckmaster Ho 1 N7 ... 14 B4
Buckmaster Rd SW11 ... 60 A3
Bucknall St WC1 .. 106 A2
Bucknell Cl SW2 ... 62 B3
Buckner Rd SW2 ... 62 B3
Buckridge Bldg EC1 ... 107 B4
Buckshead Ho 19 W2 ... 31 C4
Buck St NW1 ... 13 A1
Buckstone Cl SE23 .. 65 B1
Buckters Rents SE16 ... 33 A1
Buckthorne Rd SE4 ... 66 A2
Budge Row EC4 .. 109 B1
Budge's Wlk W2 .. 115 A2
Budleigh Ho 19 SE15 ... 49 C3
Buer Rd SW6 ... 164 B1
Bugsby's Way SE10 ... 43 B2
Buick Ho 4 E3 ... 26 C1
Building Crafts Coll The E15 ... 19 C1
Bulbarrow NW8 ... 78 B3
Bulinga St SW1 ... 147 C3
Bullace Row SE5 ... 48 C2
Bullards Pl 13 E2 ... 25 C2
Bulleid Way SW1 . 146 B3
Bullen Ho 13 E1 ... 25 A1
Bullen St SW11 ... 168 B2
Buller Cl SE15 ... 49 C3
Buller Rd NW10 ... 22 C2
Bullfinch Ct 4 SE21 ... 75 C2
Bullingham Mans W8 ... 127 C4
Bull Inn Ct WC2 .. 120 B3
Bullivant St 9 E14 . 34 B2
Bulls Alley SW14 ... 45 C1
Bull's Gdns SW3 .. 144 B4
Bulls Head Pas EC3 ... 110 A1
Bull Yd SE15 ... 49 C2
Bulmer Mews W11 ... 31 C1 113 B2
Bulow Ct 3 SW6 . 166 B2
Bulstrode Pl W1 .. 103 C3
Bulstrode St W1 .. 103 C2
Bulwer St W12 ... 30 B1
Bunbury Ho SE15 ... 49 C3
Bunhill Row EC1 ... 97 B1
Bunhouse Pl SW1 145 C2
Bunkers Hill NW11 ... 2 B4
Bunning Ho N7 ... 14 A4
Bunning Way N7 ... 14 B1
Bunsen Ho 2 E3 ... 26 A3
Bunsen St 3 E3 ... 26 A3
Bunyan Ct EC2 ... 108 C4
Buonaparte Mews SW1 ... 147 B2
Burbage Cl SE1 ... 137 B1
Burbage Ho
16 Deptford SE14 ... 50 C4
Shoreditch N1 ... 87 C3
Burbage Rd SE21, SE24 ... 75 C4
Burbage Sch 34 N1 ... 24 A3
Burcham St E14 ... 34 B3
Burchell Ho SE11 149 A2
Burchell Rd SE15 ... 50 A2
Burcher Gale Gr 5 SE15 ... 49 B3
Burcote Rd SW18 ... 71 C4
Burden Ho SW8 .. 162 A1
Burdenshott Ave TW10 ... 55 A3
Burder Cl N1 ... 16 A2
Burder Rd N1 ... 16 A2
Burdett Coutts & Townshend CE Prim Sch SW1 ... 147 C3
Burdett Mews 4 W2 ... 100 A2
Burdett Rd
Richmond TW9 ... 54 B4
Tower Hamlets E3 ... 33 B4
Burdon Ct 3 E8 ... 16 C2
Burford Ct SE8 ... 51 C4
Burford Ho
1 Brentford TW8 ... 36 A1
11 South Lambeth SW9 ... 173 A1
Burford Rd
Brentford TW8 ... 36 A1
5 Stratford Marsh E15 ... 27 C4
Burford Wlk SW6 . 156 B1
Burgate Ct 9 SW9 ... 62 C4
Burges Gr SW13 ... 47 A3
Burgess Bsns Pk SE5 ... 48 C3
Burgess Hill NW2 ... 10 C4
Burgess Ho 3 SE5 . 48 B3
Burgess Park Mans NW6 ... 10 C4
Burgess St E14 ... 33 C4
Burge St SE1 ... 137 C1
Burgh House & Hampstead Mus NW3 ... 11 C4
Burghley Hall Cl SW19 ... 70 A3
Burghley Ho SW19 .. 70 A1
Burghley Rd NW5 ... 13 A4
Burghley Twr W3 ... 29 B2
Burgh St N1 ... 86 B2
Burgon St EC4 ... 108 B1
Burgos Gr SE10 ... 52 A2
Burgoyne Rd SW9 ... 62 B4
Burhan Uddin Ho E1 ... 24 B1 98 C1
Buriton Ho 9 SW15 ... 69 A3
Burke Cl SW15 ... 56 A3
Burke Ho 1 SW11 ... 59 C3
Burke St E16 ... 35 B4
Burland Rd SW11 ... 60 B2
Burleigh Coll W6 ... 39 B2
Burleigh Ho
Chelsea SW3 ... 157 C3
5 North Kensington W10 ... 30 C4
Burleigh Pl SW15 ... 57 C2
Burleigh St WC2 .. 120 C4
Burley Ho E1 ... 32 C3
Burlington Arc W1 ... 118 C3
Burlington Ave TW9 ... 44 C2
Burlington Cl W9 ... 23 C1
Burlington Ct
Chiswick W4 ... 45 B3
Highgate N6 ... 3 C3

Burlington Danes Acad W12 30 A3
Burlington Gdns
Acton Green W4 37 B1
Acton W3 28 B1
4 Fulham SW6 164 B1
Marylebone W1 118 C3
Burlington Ho NW3 11 C3
Burlington La W4 45 C3
Burlington Lodge SW6 164 B1
Burlington Mews
Acton W3 28 B1
2 Putney SW15 58 B2
Burlington Pl SW6 164 B1
Burlington Rd
Acton Green W4 37 B1
Fulham SW6 164 B1
Burma Rd N16 15 C4
Burmarsh 6 NW5 12 C2
Burmester Ho SW17 71 B1
Burmester Rd SW17 71 B1
Burnaby Cres W4 45 B4
Burnaby Ct 31 SE16 139 C3
Burnaby Gdns W4 45 A4
Burnaby St SW10 157 A1
Burnand Ho 3 W14 39 C3
Burnbury Rd SW12 73 B3
Burne Jones Ho W14 140 B3
Burnell Ho 18 SW2 74 C3
Burnell Wlk SE1 153 A2
Burness Cl N7 14 B2
Burne St NW1 102 A4
Burnett Cl E9 17 B3
Burnett Ct SW11 168 A3
Burnett Ho 6 SE13 52 B1
Burney St SE10 52 B3
Burnfoot Ave SW6 164 B3
Burnham NW3 12 A1
Burnham Cl SE1 153 A3
Burnham Ct W2 114 B4
Burnham Est 8 E2 25 B2
Burnham St E2 25 B2
Burnhill Ho EC1 96 C3
Burnley Rd
London SW9 172 C2
Willesden NW10 8 C3
Burnsall St SW3 144 B2
Burns Ho
18 Bethnal Green E2 25 B2
1 Islington N7 14 B2
Kennington SE17 150 B1
11 Stoke Newington N16 16 A4
Burn's Ho NW10 21 A4
Burnside Cl SE16 32 C1
Burns Rd SW11 168 C2
Burn's Rd NW10 21 B4
Burnthwaite Rd SW6 155 A1
Burntwood Cl SW18 72 A3
Burntwood Ct SW17 71 B1
Burntwood Grange Rd SW18 72 A3
Burntwood La SW17 71 C2
Burntwood Sch SW17 71 C2
Buross St E1 32 A3
Burrage Ct 17 SE16 40 C2
Burrard Ho 11 E2 25 B3
Burrard Rd NW6 10 C4
Burr Cl E1 125 B2
Burrell St SE1 122 A2
Burrell's Wharf Sq E14 42 A1
Burrhill Ct SE16 40 C3
Burrow Ho 19 SW9 173 A1
Burrow Rd SE22 64 A3
Burrows Mews SE1 136 A4
Burrows Rd NW10 22 B2
Burrow Wlk SE21 75 B4
Burr Rd SW18 70 C4
Bursar St SE1 124 A1
Burslem St E1 111 C1
Burstock Rd SW15 58 A3
Burston Rd SW15 57 C2
Burtley Cl N4 6 B3
Burton Bank N1 15 C1
Burton Ct SW3 145 A2
Burton Gr SE17 151 B1
Burton Ho
8 Bermondsey SE16 40 A4
Brixton SE5 48 A2
Burton Lo 6 SW15 58 B2
Burton Mews SW1 145 C3
Burton Pl WC1 93 C3
Burton Rd
7 Brixton SW9 173 B2
Brixton SW9 48 A1
Brondesbury NW6 10 B1
Burtons Ct E15 19 C1
Burton St WC1 93 C2
Burtonwood Ho N4 6 C4
Burtt Ho 6 N1 24 A2 98 A4
Burwash Ho SE1 137 C3
Burwell Cl 27 E1 32 A3
Burwell Wlk 14 E3 26 C1
Burwood Ho 11 SW9 63 A3
Burwood Pl W2 102 B2
Bury Cl SE16 32 C1
Bury Ct EC3 110 B2
Buryfield Ct 23 SE8 40 C2
Bury Pl WC1 106 B3
Bury St
St James SW1 119 A2
Whitechapel EC3 110 B2
Bury Wlk SW3 144 A2
Busbridge Ho 24 E14 33 C4
Busby Mews 5 NW1 13 C2
Busby Pl NW5 13 C2
Bushbaby Cl SE1 138 A1
Bushberry Rd E9 18 A2
Bush Cotts 12 SW18 58 C2
Bush Ct 7 W12 39 C4
Bushell Cl SW2 74 B2
Bushell St 18 E1 125 C2
Bushey Down SW12 73 A2
Bushey Hall SE5 49 B2
Bushey Hill Rd SE5 49 B2
Bushfield Ho N5 15 B3
Bush Ind Est NW10 20 C1
Bush La EC4 123 B4
Bushnell Rd SW17 73 A1
Bush Rd
Bermondsey SE8 40 C2
Hackney E8 25 A4
Richmond TW9 44 B4
Bushwood Dr SE1 153 A3
Bushwood Rd TW9 44 C4
Business Design Ctr N1 85 C3
Buspace Studios 3 W10 23 A1
Butcher Row E1 32 C3
Butchers Rd E16 35 C3
Bute Gdns W6 39 C2
Bute House Prep Sch 2 W6 39 C2
Bute St SW7 143 B4
Bute Wlk 18 N1 15 C2
Butfield Ho 6 E9 17 B2
Butler Ho
32 Bethnal Green E2 25 B2
5 Brixton SW9 48 A2
11 Poplar E14 33 B3
Butler Pl SW1 133 B2
Butler Rd NW10 8 B1
Butlers & Colonial Wharf SE1 139 A4
Butler St 33 E2 25 B2
Butler's Wharf W SE1 124 C1
Butley Ct 8 E3 26 A3
Butterfield Cl 1 SE16 40 A4
Butterfly Wlk 2 SE5 48 C2
Buttermere NW1 92 B4
Buttermere Cl
Bermondsey SE1 152 C3
Leyton E11 19 C4
Buttermere Ct NW8 79 B4
Buttermere Dr SW15 58 A2
Buttermere Ho 13 E3 26 B2
Buttermere Wlk 9 E8 16 B2
Butterwick W6 39 B2
Butterworth Ct SW16 74 A1
Buttesland St N1 97 C4
Buxhall Cres E9 18 B2
Buxted Rd
Camberwell SE22 64 A3
Dalston E8 16 B1
Buxton Ct N1 97 A4
Buxton Gdns W3 28 A2
Buxton Ho 3 SW11 59 C3
Buxton Mews SW4 171 C2
Buxton Rd
Mortlake SW14 56 A4
Upper Holloway N19 4 C3
Buxton Rd *continued*
Willesden NW2 9 A2
Buxton St E1 24 B1 99 A1
Byam Shaw Sch of Art 8 N19 4 C2
Byam St SW6 166 C1
Byards Ct SE16 40 C3
Byas Ho 6 E3 26 B2
Byefield Cl SE16 41 A4
Byelands Cl 12 SE16 32 C1
Bye The W3 29 A3
Byeway The SW14 55 B4
Byfeld Gdns SW13 46 C2
Bygrove Prim Sch 21 E14 34 A3
Bygrove St E14 34 A3
Byng Pl WC1 93 B1
Byng St E14 41 C4
Byrne Ho 11 SW2 62 B2
Byrne Rd SW12 73 A2
Byron Cl E8 24 C4
Byron Ct
Chelsea SW3 144 B3
Dulwich SE21 76 C3
3 Hampstead NW6 11 B1
Paddington W9 23 C1
St Pancras WC1 94 C2
Byron Mews
Hampstead NW3 12 A4
2 Maida Vale W9 23 C1
Byron St E14 34 B3
Bythorn St SW9 62 B3
Byward St EC3 124 B3
Bywater Pl SE16 33 A1
Bywater St SW3 144 C2
Bywell Pl W1 104 C3
Byworth Wlk N19 5 A3

C

Cabbell St NW1 102 A3
Cabinet Off SW1 134 A4
Cabinet War Rooms & Churchill Mus SW1 133 C4
Cable Ho WC1 95 B4
Cable Pl SE10 52 B2
Cable St E1 32 A2
Cabot Ct SE16 40 C3
Cabot Sq E14 33 C1
Cabul Rd SW11 168 B1
Cactus Cl SE5 49 A1
Cactus Wlk W12 29 B3
Cadbury Way 1 SE16 153 B4
Caddington Rd NW2 1 A1
Cadell Cl E2 24 B3
Cadell Ho 12 E2 24 B3
Cade Rd SE10 52 C2
Cader Rd SW18 59 B1
Cadet Dr SE1 153 A2
Cade Tyler Ho 10 SE10 52 B2
Cadiz St SE17 151 A1
Cadman Cl SW9 48 A3
Cadmore Ho 4 N1 15 A1
Cadmus Cl 9 SW4 61 C4
Cadmus Ct 6 SW9 173 B4
Cadnam Lo E14 42 C3
Cadnam Point 15 SW15 69 A3
Cadogan Cl E9 18 B1
Cadogan Ct SW3 144 C3
Cadogan Ct Gdns SW1 145 B4
Cadogan Gate SW1 145 A4
Cadogan Gdns SW3 145 A3
Cadogan Hall SW1 145 B4
Cadogan Ho SW3 157 C3
Cadogan La SW1 131 B1
Cadogan Pier SW3 158 B3
Cadogan Pl SW1 131 A1
Cadogan Sq SW1 131 A1
Cadogan St SW3 144 C3
Cadogan Terr E9 18 B1
Caedmon Rd N7 14 B4
Caernarvon Ho W2 100 C2
Caesar Ct 25 E2 25 C3
Cahill St EC1 97 A1
Cahir St E14 42 A2
Caine Ho W3 37 A4
Caird St W10 23 B2
Cairns Ho 3 N7 14 B4
Cairns Rd SW11 60 A2
Caister Ho N7 14 B2
Caistor Ho 10 SW12 73 A4
Caistor Mews SW12 73 A4
Caistor Rd SW12 73 A4
Caithness Ho N1 84 C4
Caithness Rd W14 39 C3
Calabria Rd N5 15 A3
Calais Gate SE5 48 A2
Calais St SE5 48 A2
Calbourne Rd SW12 72 C4
Calcraft Ho 10 E2 25 B3
Caldecot Ct SE5 48 B1
Caldecot Rd SE5 48 B1
Calder Ct SE16 33 B1
Calderon Ho NW8 80 A2
Calderon Pl 20 W10 30 B4
Caldervale Rd SW4 61 C2
Caldew St SE5 48 C3
Caldwell St SW9 163 A1
Caldy Wlk 19 N1 15 B2
Caleb St SE1 137 A4
Caledonia Ho 15 E14 33 A3
Caledonian Market SE1 138 B2
Caledonian Rd
Islington N1 84 C3
Lower Holloway N7 14 B2
Caledonian Road & Barnsbury Sta N7 14 B1
Caledonian Road Sta N7 14 B2
Caledonian Sq 6 NW1 13 C2
Caledonian Wharf Rd E14 42 C2
Caledonia St N1 84 B1

Cale St SW3...... 144 A2
Caletock Way SE10..............43 B1
Calgarth NW1..... 83 A1
Calgary Ct 30 SE16 .40 B4
Caliban Twr 9 N1..24 A3
Calico Ho 4 SW11 .59 B4
Calico Row 5 SW11.............59 B4
Calidore Cl SW2....62 B1
California Bldg 2 SE13..............52 A2
Callaby Terr 11 N1................15 C2
Callahan Cotts 8 E1................32 B4
Callan Sch The W1............ 105 A2
Callcott Ct NW6....10 B1
Callcott Rd NW6....10 B1
Callcott St W8........31 C1 113 B2
Callendar Rd SW7............ 129 B2
Callingham Cl 13 E14..............33 B4
Callingham Ho 1 SW4...............62 A4
Callow St SW3 ... 157 B4
Calmington Rd SE5...............49 A4
Calshot Ho N1..... 84 C2
Calshot St N1..... 84 C1
Calstock NW1...... 83 B3
Calstock Ho SE11 149 C2
Calthorpe St WC1 . 95 A2
Calton Ave SE21....64 A1
Calver 13 NW5.....13 A4
Calverley Gr N19....4 C3
Calvert Ave E2..........24 B2 98 C3
Calvert Ct
1 London N19.......4 B3
5 Richmond TW9....54 B3
Calvert Ho 9 W12..30 A2
Calverton SE5......49 A4
Calvert Rd SE10....43 B1
Calvert's Bldgs SE1............. 123 B1
Calvert St NW1.... 81 B4
Calvin St E1..24 B1 98 C1
Calypso Cres 6 SE15..............49 B3
Calypso Way SE8, SE16..............41 B2
Cambalt Ho 3 SW15.............57 C2
Cambalt Rd SW15..57 C2
Cambay Ho 7 E1 ..26 A1
Camber Ho 4 SE15..............50 B4
Camberley Ho NW1............ 82 B1
CAMBERWELL.....48 B2
Camberwell Bsns Ctr SE5...............48 C3
Camberwell Church St SE5...............48 C2
Camberwell Coll of Arts
16 Camberwell SE5...............49 A2
25 Camberwell SE15............49 B3
Camberwell Glebe SE5...............49 A2
Camberwell Gn SE5...............48 C2
Camberwell Gr SE5...............49 A1
Camberwell Green SE5...............48 B2
Camberwell New Rd SW9..............48 A3
Camberwell Rd SE5...............48 B3
Camberwell Station Rd SE5............48 B2
Camberwell Trad Est SE5...............48 B2
Camborne Rd SW18..............70 C4
Cambourne Mews 6 W11..............31 A3
Cambray Rd SW12..73 B3
Cambria Ho 14 E14...............33 A3
Cambria Lo 3 SW15..............58 B2
Cambrian Cl SE27 ..75 A1
Cambrian Rd TW10..............54 B1
Cambria Rd SE5....63 B4
Cambria St SW6.. 156 B1
Cambridge Ave NW6..............23 C3
Cambridge Cir WC2............ 105 C1
Cambridge Cotts TW9..............44 C4
Cambridge Cres 20 E2...............25 A3
Cambridge Ct
26 Bethnal Green E2...............25 A3
7 Hammersmith W6..............39 B2
2 Kilburn NW6.....23 C3
Marylebone W2 ... 102 A3
Stamford Hill N16.....7 A4
Cambridge Gate NW1............. 92 A2
Cambridge Gate Mews NW1....... 92 B2
Cambridge Gdns
Kilburn NW6........23 C3
North Kensington W10..............31 A3
Cambridge Gr W6 ..39 A2
Cambridge Heath Rd E1, E2............25 A2
Cambridge Heath Sta E2...............25 A3
Cambridge Ho SW6..............58 A4
Cambridge Mans SW11........... 168 C3
Cambridge Pas 9 E9................17 B1
Cambridge Pl W8 128 B3
Cambridge Rd
Barnes SW13.......46 B1
Battersea SW11... 168 C3
Kilburn NW6........23 C2
Kilburn NW6........23 C3
Richmond TW9......44 C3
Cambridge Rd N W4...............37 A1
Cambridge Rd S 3 W4...............37 A1
Cambridge Sch 15 W6...............39 A2
Cambridge Sq W2............ 102 A2
Cambridge St SW1........... 146 C2
Cambridge Terr NW1............. 92 A3
Cambridge Terr Mews NW1............. 92 B3
Cambus Rd E16 ....35 C4
Cam Ct 2 SE15 ....49 B4
Camden Coll of English 8 NW1 ...12 C1
Camden Gdns NW1..............13 A1
Camden High St NW1.............. 82 C3
Camden Ho 6 SE8...............41 B1
Camdenhurst St E14..............33 A3
Camden Lock Mkt NW1..............13 A1
Camden Lock Pl NW1..............13 A1
Camden Mews NW1..............13 C2
Camden Mkt NW1 . 82 B4
Camden Park Rd NW1..............13 C2
Camden Pas N1... 86 A3
Camden Rd NW1.. 82 B4
Camden Road Sta NW1..............13 B1
Camden Row SE3...53 A1
Camden Sch for Girls The NW5..........13 B2
Camden Sq NW1 ...13 C2
Camden St NW1... 83 A3
Camden Studios NW1............. 83 A3
Camden Terr 17 NW1..............13 C2
CAMDEN TOWN....13 A1
Camden Town Sta NW1............. 82 B4
Camden Wlk N1.... 86 A3
Cameford Ct 20 SW12.............74 A4
Camelford NW1 ... 83 A3
Camelford Ct 15 W11..............31 A3
Camelford Ho SE1............. 148 B1
Camelford Wlk 13 W11..............31 A3
Camellia Ho SE8....51 B3
Camellia St SW8 . 162 A1
Camelot Ho 15 NW1..............13 C2
Camelot Prim Sch SE15..............50 A4
Camera Pl SW10.. 157 B4
Camera Press Gall SE1............. 138 C4
Cameret Ct 6 W11..............39 C4
Cameron Ct 3 SW19.............70 A3
Cameron Ho
Camberwell SE5.....48 B3
St John's Wood NW8............. 80 A2
Cameron House Sch SW10........... 157 C4
Cameron Pl SW16 ..74 C2
Camerton Cl 8 E8 .16 B2
Camilla Rd SE16....40 A2
Camlet St E2..........24 B1 98 C2
Camley St Natural Pk NW1............. 83 C3
Camley St NW1.... 83 C2
Camomile St EC3. 110 B2
Campaign Ct W9 ...23 B1
Campana Rd SW6 165 C4
Campbell Ct
Dulwich SE21.......76 C3
South Kensington SW7........... 128 C1
Campbell Gordon Way NW2................9 A4
Campbell Ho
Paddington W2..... 89 B1
Pimlico SW1...... 146 C1
30 Shepherd's Bush W12..............30 A2
Campbell Rd E3....26 C2
Campbell Wlk N1.. 84 B4
Campdale Rd N7....4 C1
Campden Gr W8.. 127 C4
Campden Hill W8. 127 B4
Campden Hill Ct W8............ 127 C4
Campden Hill Gate W8............ 127 B4
Campden Hill Gdns W8........31 C1 113 B2
Campden Hill Mans W8....... 31 C1 113 C2
Campden Hill Pl W14.......31 B1 113 A2
Campden Hill Rd W8............ 127 B4
Campden Hill Sq W14.......31 B1 113 A2
Campden Ho 4 NW6..............11 C1
Campden Hos W8........31 C1 113 B1
Campden House Cl W8............ 127 C4
Campden St W8........31 C1 113 B1
Campen Cl SW19...70 A2
Camperdown St E1.............. 111 A1
Campion Ho 15 N16...............16 A3
Campion Rd SW15..57 B2
Camplin St SE14....50 C3
Campshill Pl SE13 ..67 B2
Campshill Rd SE13 .67 B2
Campton Hill Twrs W8........31 C1 113 B2
Cam Rd E15........27 C4
Camsey Ho 8 SW2..............62 B2
Canada Cres W3....20 B1
Canada Gdns SE13..67 B2
Canada Rd W3 .....28 B4
Canada Sq E14.....34 A1
Canada St SE16.....40 C4
Canada Water Sta SE16..............40 C3
Canada Way W12...30 A2
Canal App SE8 .....51 A4
Canal Bldg N1..... 86 C2
Canal Bridge SE15..49 C4
Canal Bvd 7 NW1..13 C2
Canal Cl
Mile End E1.........26 A1
North Kensington W10..............22 C1
Canal Gr SE15......50 A4
Canal Head Public Sq
1 SE15 ....49 C2
Canal Path 22 E2...24 B4
Canalside Studios 29 N1................24 A4
Canal St SE5 ....48 C4
Canal Way W10.....22 C1
Canal Wlk N1 ..... 87 C4
CANARY WHARF...34 A1
Canary Wharf E14..34 A1
Canary Wharf Pier E14...............33 B1
Canary Wharf Sta E14...............34 A1
Canary Wharf Sta (DLR) E14.........33 C1
Canberra Prim Sch W12..............30 A2
Canbury Mews SE26..............76 C1
Cancell Rd SW9.. 173 C4
Candahar Rd SW11........... 168 B1
Candida Ct 9 NW1...............13 A1
Candishe Ho SE1 138 C4
Candle Gr SE15.....65 A4
Candlemakers 24 SW11.............59 C4
Candover St W1.. 104 C3
Candy St E3........26 B4
Canfield Gdns NW6..............11 A1
Canfield Pl NW6....11 B2
Canford Rd SW11...60 C2
Canham Rd W3.....38 A4
Cann Ho W14..... 126 B1
Canning Cross SE5...............49 A1
Canning Ho 23 W12..............30 A2
Canning Pas W8.. 128 C2
Canning Pl W8 ... 128 C2
Canning Pl Mews W8............. 128 C2
Canning Rd N5......6 A1
Cannington 14 NW5..............12 C2
CANNING TOWN ...35 B3
Canning Town E16..............35 A3
Canning Town Sta E16...............35 A3
Cannock Ho N4 .....6 C4
Cannon Dr 21 E14 ..33 C2
Cannon Hill NW6 ...10 C3
Cannon Ho SE11.. 149 A3
Cannon La NW3.....2 C1
Cannon Pl NW3 .....2 C1
Cannon St EC4 ... 123 A4
Cannon Street Rd E1................32 A3
Cannon Street Sta EC4............. 123 B4
Cannon Wharf Bsns Ctr 12 SE8.........41 A2
Canon Barnett Prim Sch E1.......... 111 A2
Canon Beck Rd SE16..............40 B4
CANONBURY 15 B2

Canonbury Bsns Ctr N1 87 A4
Canonbury Cres N1 15 B1
Canonbury Ct 21 N1 15 A1
Canonbury Gr N1 15 B1
Canonbury Hts 6 N1 15 C2
Canonbury La N1 15 A1
Canonbury Pk N N1 15 B2
Canonbury Pk S N1 15 B2
Canonbury Pl N1 15 A2
Canonbury Prim Sch 4 N1 15 A2
Canonbury Rd N1 15 A1
Canonbury Sq N1 15 A1
Canonbury St N1 15 B1
Canonbury Sta N1, N5 15 B3
Canonbury Villas N1 15 A1
Canonbury Yd E 26 N1 15 B2
Canon Murnane Rd SE1 138 C1
Canon Row SW1 134 A3
Canons Cl N2 2 C4
Canon St N1 86 C3
Canrobert St E2 25 A2
Cantelowes Rd NW1 13 C2
Canterbury SE13 67 B2
Canterbury Cl 16 SE5 48 B1
Canterbury Cres SW9 62 C4
Canterbury Ct
- Acton W3 29 A1
- Kilburn NW6 23 C3
Canterbury Gr SE27, SW16 74 C1
Canterbury Ho
- 6 Bromley E3 27 A2
- Lambeth SE1 135 A2
Canterbury Ind Pk 15 SE15 50 B4
Canterbury Mans NW6 11 A2
Canterbury Pl SE17 150 B3
Canterbury Rd NW6 23 C3
Canterbury Terr NW6 23 C3
Cantium Ret Pk SE1 49 C4
Canton St E14 33 C3
Cantrell Rd E3 26 C1
Canute Ct SW16 74 C1
Canute Gdns SE16 40 C2
Canvey St SE1 122 C2
Cape Henry Ct 15 E14 34 C2
Capel Ho 17 E9 17 B1
Capel Lo
- 5 Richmond TW9 44 B2
- 12 Streatham SW2 74 B4
Capener's Cl SW1 131 B3
Capern Rd SW18 71 B3
Capio Nightingale Hospl NW1 102 B4
Capital City Acad NW10 22 A4
Capital East Apts 8 E16 35 C2
Capital Interchange Way TW8 36 C1
Capital Sh Ctrs SW1 133 B3
Capital Wharf 14 E1 125 C1
Capland Ho NW8 89 C2
Capland St NW8 89 C2
Caple Ho SW10 157 A2
Caple Rd NW10 21 B3
Capper St WC1 93 A1
Capstan Ho 6 E14 42 B2
Capstan Rd SE8 41 B2
Capstan Sq E14 42 B4
Capstan Way SE16 33 A1
Capulet Mews 1 E16 35 C1
Caradoc Cl W2 31 C3
Caradoc St SE10 43 A1
Cara Ho 10 N1 14 C1
Caranday Villas 5 W11 30 C1
Caravel Cl E14 41 C3
Caravel Mews 14 SE8 51 C4
Caraway Hts E14 34 B2
Carbery Ave W3 36 B4
Carbis Rd E14 33 B3
Carbroke Ho 9 E9 25 B4
Carburton St W1 92 B1
Cardale St 1 E14 42 B3
Carden Rd SE15 65 A4
Cardiff Ho 9 SE15 49 C4
Cardigan Rd
- Barnes SW13 46 C1
- Bow E3 26 B3
- Richmond TW10 54 A1
Cardigan St SE11 149 B2
Cardigan Wlk 19 N1 15 B1
Cardinal Bourne St SE1 137 C1
Cardinal Cap Alley SE1 122 C3
Cardinal Hinsley Cl NW10 21 C3
Cardinal Hinsley Mathematics & Computing Coll NW10 21 C4
Cardinal Pl SW15 57 C3
Cardinal Pl SW1 132 C1
Cardinal Pole RC Sch
- London E9 17 C1
- London E9 18 A3
Cardinals Way N19 4 C3
Cardinal Vaughan Meml Sch The W14 126 A4
Cardinal Wlk SW1 132 C1
Cardine Mews SE15 50 A3
Cardington St NW1 93 A3
Cardozo Rd N7 14 A3
Cardross St W6 39 A3
Cardwell Rd 3 N7 14 A4
Career Ct 11 SE16 40 C4
Carew Cl N7 5 B2
Carew Ct 15 SE14 50 C4
Carew Ho SW16 74 C1
Carew St SE5 48 B1
Carey Ct 20 SE5 48 B3
Carey Gdns SW8 171 B3
Carey La EC2 108 C2
Carey Pl SW1 147 B3
Carey St WC2 107 A1
Carfax Pl SW4 61 C3
Carfree Cl 5 N1 14 C1
Cargill Rd SW18 71 B3
Carinthia Ct 5 SE8 41 A2
Carisbrooke Ct
- Acton W3 37 B4
- 1 Streatham SW16 74 B1
Carisbrooke Gdns SE15 49 B3
Carisbrooke Ho TW10 54 C2
Carker's La
- Crouch End N19 4 C4
- Gospel Oak NW5 13 A3
Carleton Gdns N19 13 B3
Carleton Rd N7 13 C4
Carlile Cl E3 26 B3
Carlile Ho SE1 137 C1
Carlingford Rd NW3 11 C4
Carlisle Ave
- Acton W3 29 A3
- Whitechapel EC3 110 C1
Carlisle Ho 6 NW5 4 B1
Carlisle La SE1 135 A2
Carlisle Pl SW1 132 C1
Carlisle Rd
- Finsbury Pk N4 5 C4
- Kilburn NW6 23 A4
Carlisle St W1 105 B1
Carlisle Wlk 6 E8 16 B2
Carlos Pl W1 118 A3
Carlow St NW1 82 C2
Carlson Ct SW15 58 B3
Carlton Cl NW3 1 C2
Carlton Ct
- Brixton SW9 48 A2
- Kilburn NW6 78 B2
- 8 Willesden NW2 9 B2
Carlton Dr SW15 58 A2
Carlton Gdns SW1 119 B1
Carlton Gr SE15 50 A2
Carlton Hill NW8 78 C2
Carlton Ho
- 8 Kilburn NW6 23 B3
- Kilburn NW6 23 C3
- Marylebone W1 103 A2
Carlton House Terr SW1 119 C2
Carlton Lo N4 5 C4
Carlton Mans
- Brixton SW9 62 C3
- Cricklewood NW2 9 C3
- Kensington W14 126 B4
- Maida Vale W9 88 B4
- 7 South Hampstead NW6 10 C1
- Stamford Hill N16 7 B3
Carlton Prim Sch NW5 12 C3
Carlton Rd
- Acton W4 37 C4
- Finsbury Pk N4 5 C4
- Mortlake SW14 55 B3
Carlton Sq E1 25 C1
Carlton St SW1 119 B3
Carltons The 5 SW15 58 A2
Carlton Tower Pl SW1 131 A2
Carlton Vale NW6 23 C3
Carlton Vale Inf Sch 12 NW6 23 B2
Carlyle Ho
- 4 Camberwell SE5 48 B3
- Chelsea SW3 157 C4
- 12 Stoke Newington N16 7 A1
Carlyle Mans SW3 158 A3
Carlyle Mews 24 E1 25 C1
Carlyle Pl SW15 57 C3
Carlyle Rd 1 NW10 20 C4
Carlyle's Ho SW3 158 A3
Carlyle Sq SW3 143 C1
Carmalt Gdns SW15 57 B3
Carmarthen Ho 8 SW15 69 B4
Carmarthen Pl SE1 138 A4
Carmel Ct W8 128 A4
Carmelite St EC4 121 C4
Carmel Lo SW6 155 B4
Carmen St E14 34 A3
Carmichael Cl 8 SW11 59 C4
Carmichael Ct 5 SW13 46 B1
Carmichael Ho 6 E14 34 B2
Carmichael Mews SW18 71 C4
Carminia Rd SW17 73 A2
Carnaby St W1 104 C1
Carnac St SE21, SE27 75 C1
Carna Ct TW9 54 A4
Carnegie Ho NW3 2 C1
Carnegie Pl SW19 69 C1
Carnegie St N1 85 A3
Carnicot Ho 9 SE15 50 A2
Carnoustie Dr N1 14 B1
Carnwath Ho SW6 59 A4
Carnwath Rd SW6 59 A4
Caroline Cl
- Bayswater W2 114 B3
- Streatham SW16 74 B1
Caroline Gdns E2 24 A2 98 B4
Caroline Ho
- Bayswater W2 114 B3
- 20 Hammersmith W6 39 B1
Caroline Martyn Ho 8 N19 4 C4
Caroline Pl
- Bayswater W2 114 B3
- Clapham SW11 169 C1
Caroline Pl Mews W2 114 B3
Caroline St E1 32 C3
Caroline Terr SW1 145 B3
Caroline Wlk W6 154 A3
Carol St NW1 82 C4
Caronia Ct 4 SE16 41 A2
Carpenter Ho
- 11 Tower Hamlets E14 33 C4
- 5 Tufnell Pk N19 13 C4
Carpenters Ct NW1 82 C4
Carpenter's Pl SW4 61 C3
Carpenters Prim Sch E15 27 B4
Carpenter St W1 118 A3
Carradale Ho 2 E14 34 B3
Carrara Cl 18 SW9 63 A3
Carrara Wharf SW6 58 A4
Carriage Dr E SW11 159 C2
Carriage Drive E SW11 159 C2
Carriage Drive N SW11, SW8 159 C3
Carriage Dr N
- Battersea SW8, SW11 158 C2
- Battersea SW8, SW11 159 C3
Carriage Dr S SW11 169 B4
Carriage Dr W SW11 158 C1
Carrick Ho
- Islington N7 14 B2
- Kennington SE11 150 A2
Carrick Mews SE8 51 C4
Carrington Ct SW11 60 A3
Carrington Ho W1 118 A1
Carrington Lo 3 TW10 54 A2
Carrington Rd TW10 54 C3
Carrington St W1 118 A1
Carrol Cl NW5 13 A4
Carroll Ct
- Acton W3 37 A3
- 4 Shacklewell E5 7 C1
Carroll Ho W2 115 B4
Carron Cl E14 34 A3
Carroun Rd SW8 162 C2
Carr St 5 E14 33 A3
Carslake Rd SW15 57 B1
Carson Rd
- Dulwich SE21 75 C2
- Newham E16 35 C4
Carter Ct EC4 108 B1
Carteret Ho 8 W12 30 A2
Carteret St SW1 133 B3
Carteret Way SE8 41 A2
Carter Ho
- 11 London SW2 62 C2
- Spitalfields E1 110 C3
Carter La EC4 108 B1
Carter Pl SE17 151 A1
Carters Cl 10 NW5 13 C2
Carter St SE17 150 C1
Carter's Yd SW18 58 C2
Carthew Rd W6 39 A3
Carthew Villas W6 39 A3
Carthusian St EC1 108 C4
Cartier Circ E14 34 B1
Carting La WC2 120 B3

Cartmel NW1 92 C4
Carton Ho
4 Bermondsey SE16 139 B2
12 Shepherd's Bush W11 30 C2
Cartoon Mus The WC1 106 A3
Cartwright Gdns WC1 94 A3
Cartwright Ho SE1 137 A1
Cartwright St E1 125 A3
Cartwright Way SW13 47 A3
Carvel Ho E14 42 B1
Carver Cl 15 W4 37 B3
Carver Rd SE24 63 B1
Carville Cres TW8 36 A2
Caryl Ho 6 SW19 69 C3
Carysfort Rd N16 15 C4
Casby Ho 7 SE16 139 B2
Casella Rd SE14 50 C3
Casey Cl NW8 90 B3
Casino Ave SE24 63 C2
Caspian Ho 10 E1 32 C4
Caspian St SE5 48 C3
Cassandra Ct 7 NW2 9 B2
Cass Bsns Sch EC1 97 B1
Cassell Ho 21 SW9 172 B2
Casserley Ho W4 37 C3
Cass Ho 23 E9 17 C2
Cassidy Rd SW6 155 B1
Cassilis Rd E14 41 C4
Cassinghurst SE24 63 C2
Cassland Rd E9 17 C2
Casson Ho 11 E1 111 B4
Casson St E1 111 B3
Castalia Sq 6 E14 42 B4
Castellain Mans W9 88 A2
Castellain Rd W9 88 B2
Castell Ho 11 SE8 51 C3
Castello Ave SW15 57 B2
Castelnau SW13 47 A3
Castelnau Gdns SW13 47 A4
Castelnau Mans SW13 47 A4
Castelnau Row SW13 47 A4
Casterbridge
Kilburn NW6 78 B4
3 Notting Hill W11 31 C3
Casterton St E8 17 A2
Castleacre W2 102 A1
Castle Baynard St EC4 122 C4
Castlebrook Cl SE11 150 A4
Castle Cl
12 Acton W3 37 B4
Homerton E9 18 A3
South Acton W3 37 A4
Wimbledon SW19 69 C1
Castlecombe Dr SW19 69 C4
Castle Ct EC3 109 C1
Castleden Ho NW6 11 C1
Castleford Ct NW8 89 C2
Castlefrank Ho 20 N1 24 A2 98 B4
Castlegate TW9 54 B4
Castlehaven Rd NW1 13 A1
Castle Ho
Newington SE1 150 C4
South Lambeth SW8 162 B2
Castle Ind Est SE17 150 C4
Castle La SW1 132 C2
Castlemaine 8 SW11 169 A2
Castlemaine St 2 E1 32 A4
Castle Mead SE5 48 B3
Castle Mews NW1 13 A2
Castle Pl
8 Acton W4 38 A2
Camden Town NW1 13 A2
Castle Rd NW1 13 A2
Castlereagh St W1 102 C2
Castleton Ho 3 E14 42 B2
Castletown Rd W14 140 B1
Castleview Cl N4 6 B2
Castle Way SW19 69 C1
Castlewood Ho WC1 105 C2
Castle Yd
Highgate N6 3 C4
Lambeth SE1 122 B2
Castor La E14 34 A2
Catalpa Ct SE13 67 C1
Caterham Rd SE13 67 C4
Catesby Ho 25 E9 17 B1
Catesby St SE17 151 C3
Cathay Ho SE16 40 A4
Cathay St 12 SE16 40 A4
Cathcart Hill N19 4 B1
Cathcart Rd SW10 156 C4
Cathcart St NW5 13 A2
Cathedral Ct EC4 108 B1
Cathedral Lo EC1 108 C4
Cathedral Sch of St Saviour & St Mary Overie Prim Sch SE1 137 A4
Cathedral St SE1 123 B2
Cathedral Wlk SW1 132 C2
Catherall Rd N5, N16 6 B1
Catherine Baird Ct 12 SW12 73 A4
Catherine Dr TW9 54 A3
Catherine Gr SE10 52 A2
Catherine Griffiths Ct EC1 95 C2
Catherine Ho 16 N1 24 A4
Catherine Pl SW1 132 C2
Catherine St WC2 120 C4
Catherine Wheel Alley E1 110 B3
Catherine Wheel Yd SW1 118 C1
Catherwood Ct N1 87 B1
Cathles Rd SW12 61 A1
Cathnor Rd W12 39 A4
Catlin St SE16 40 A1
Catman Ho N4 5 B3
Cato Rd SW4 61 C3
Cator St
Camberwell SE15 49 B3
Camberwell SE15 49 B4
Cato St W1 102 B2
Catton St WC1 106 C3
Caughley Ho SE11 135 B1
Caulfield Ct 15 NW1 13 B1
Caulfield Rd SE15 50 A1
Causeway The SW18 59 A2
Causton Cotts 3 E14 33 A3
Causton Ho SE5 48 B3
Causton Rd N6 4 A4
Causton St SW1 147 C2
Cautley Ave SW4 61 B2
Cavalry Gdns SW15 58 B2
Cavaye Ho SW10 157 A4
Cavaye Pl SW10 143 A1
Cavell Ct 5 N19 4 B2
Cavell Ho 8 N1 24 A4
Cavell St E1 32 A4
Cavendish Ave NW8 79 C1
Cavendish Cl
Brondesbury NW6 10 B2
3 Putney SW15 58 A2
St John's Wood NW8 89 C4
Cavendish Coll WC1 105 B4
Cavendish Ct EC2 110 B2
Cavendish Gdns SW4 61 B1
Cavendish Ho
South Lambeth SW8 172 A4
St John's Wood NW8 79 C1
Cavendish Jun & Inf Sch W4 46 A3
Cavendish Mans
2 Clapham Pk SW12 61 B1
Hackney E5 17 B3
Holborn EC1 95 B1
8 West Hampstead NW6 10 C3
Cavendish Mews N W1 104 B4
Cavendish Mews S W1 104 B3
Cavendish Par SW12 61 A1
Cavendish Pl
Balham SW4 61 A1
Brondesbury NW2 9 C2
Marylebone W1 104 B2
Cavendish Rd
Brondesbury NW6 10 B1
Chiswick W4 45 B2
Clapham Pk SW12 61 B1
Cavendish Sch 14 SE16 40 B2
Cavendish Sch The NW1 82 B4
Cavendish Sq W1 104 B2
Cavendish St N1 87 B1
Cavendish Terr 11 E3 26 B2
Cavendish The NW11 2 A4
Caversham Ho 7 SE15 49 C4
Caversham Rd NW5 13 B2
Caversham St SW3 158 C4
Caverswall St W12 30 B3
Cavour Ho SE17 150 B2
Caxton Gr E3 26 C2
Caxton Hall SW1 133 B2
Caxton Rd W12 39 C4
Caxton St N E16 35 B3
Caxton St SW1 133 B2
Caxton Wlk WC2 105 C1
Cayford Ho 1 NW3 12 B3
Cayley Prim Sch 22 E14 33 A3
Cayton Pl EC1 97 B3
Cayton St EC1 97 B3
Cazenove Mans 1 N16 7 C2
Cazenove Rd N16 7 C2
Cecil Ct
Chelsea SW10 156 C4
South Hampstead NW6 11 A1
St James WC2 120 A3
Cecilia Rd E8 16 C3
Cecil Mans 2 SW17 72 C2
Cecil Rd
Acton W3 28 B4
Harlesden NW10 21 A4
Cecil Rhodes Ho NW1 83 B2
Cedar Cl
Old Ford E3 26 B4
West Norwood SE21 75 B2
Cedar Ct
Islington N1 15 B1
Marylebone W1 102 B2
Mortlake SW14 55 B3
Wimbledon SW19 69 C1
Cedar Gr W5 36 A3
Cedar Ho
5 Cubitt Town E14 42 B4
Kensington W8 128 A2
New Cross Gate SE14 50 C2
5 Richmond TW9 45 A2
16 Rotherhithe SE16 40 C4
Cedar Lo
Brondesbury NW2 10 B2
Fulham SW6 47 C2
Cedarne Rd SW6 156 A1
Cedar Rd NW2 9 B4
Cedars Cl SE13 67 C4
Cedars Ct SW15 56 C1
Cedars Ho 21 SW2 62 B3
Cedars Mews SW4 61 A3
Cedars Rd
Barnes SW13 46 C1
Clapham SW4 61 A3
Cedars The E9 17 C1
Cedar Terr TW9 54 A3
Cedar Way NW1 83 B4
Cedra Ct N16 7 C3
Cedric Chambers NW8 89 B2
Celandine Cl E3, E14 33 C4
Celandine Dr E8 16 B1
Celbridge Mews W2 100 B2
Celestial Gdns SE13 67 C3
Celia Blairman Ho E1 110 C4
Celia Ct 7 TW9 44 B2
Celia Ho 10 N1 24 A3
Celia Rd N19 13 B4
Celtic St E14 34 A4
Cenacle Cl NW3 1 C1
Cenotaph SW1 134 A4
Centaur Ct 3 TW8 36 A1
Centaur St SE1 135 A2
Central Ave SW11 159 A1
Central Bsns Ctr NW10 8 A3
Central Foundation Boys' Sch EC2 97 C2
Central Foundation Lower Girls Sch The 10 E3 26 A2
Central Foundation Upper Girls Sch The 27 E3 26 B2
Central Ho E15 27 B3
Central Middlesex Hospl NW10 20 B2
Central Par W3 37 A4
Central St Martins Coll EC1 95 C1
Central St Martins College of Art & Design N1 84 A3
Central St Martins Coll of Art & Design W1 105 C1
Central St Martins Coll of Art & Design (The London Inst) WC1 106 C3
Central Sch of Ballet EC1 95 C1
Central Sch of Speech & Drama NW3 11 C1
Central St EC1 96 C3
Central Way NW10 20 B2
Centre Acad 2 SW11 59 C3
Centre Ave W3 28 C1
Centre Bldg SE17 151 A4
Centre Hts 5 NW3 11 C1
Centre Point 3 SE1 153 B2
Centre Point Ho WC2 105 C2
Centre St E2 25 A3
Centurion Bldg SW8 160 A3
Centurion Cl N7 14 B1
Centurion La E3 26 B3
Century Ho SE13 52 A1
Cephas Ave E1 25 B1
Cephas Ho 9 E1 25 B1
Cephas St E1 25 B1
Cerise Rd SE15 49 C2
Cerney Mews W2 115 B4
Cervantes Ct 12 W2 100 B1
Cester St E2 24 C4
Ceylon Rd
6 Hammersmith W14 39 C3
Kensington W14 126 A1

Chabot Dr SE15 65 A4
Chadacre Ho 10 SW9 63 A3
Chadbourn St E14 34 A4
Chadston Ho 17 N1 15 A1
Chadswell WC1 94 B3
Chadwell St EC1 95 C4
Chadwick Cl SW15 68 B4
Chadwick Rd
Harlesden NW10 21 B4
Peckham SE15 49 B1
Chadwick St SW1 133 B1
Chadworth Ho
Finsbury EC1 96 C3
Finsbury Pk N4 6 B3
Chagford Ho
38 Bromley E3 27 A2
Marylebone NW1 90 C1
Chagford St NW1 91 A1
Chalbury Ho 8 SW9 62 B3
Chalbury Wlk N1 85 B2
Chalcot Cres NW1 81 A4
Chalcot Gdns NW3 12 B2
Chalcot Mews SW16 74 A1
Chalcot Rd NW1 81 B4
Chalcot Sch 21 NW1 13 A1
Chalcot Sq NW1 12 C1
Chaldon Rd SW6 154 B2
Chale Rd SW2 62 A1
Chalfont Ct NW1 91 A1
Chalfont Ho 2 SE16 40 A3
Chalford 7 NW3 11 B2
Chalford Ct 15 SW15 57 C1
Chalkers Cnr TW9 55 A4
Chalk Farm Sta NW3 12 C1
Chalk Hill Rd W6 39 C2
Chalkwell Ho 10 E1 32 C3
Challenge Cl NW10 21 A4
Challenger Ho 7 E14 33 A2
Challice Way SW2 74 B3
Challoner Cres W14 140 C1
Challoner Mans W14 140 C1
Challoner St W14 140 C1
Chalmers Ho 13 SW11 59 B4
Chalmer's Wlk 14 SE17 48 A4
Chalner Ho SW2 74 C3
Chaloner Ct SE1 137 B4
Chalsey Lodge SE4 66 B3
Chalsey Rd SE4 66 B3
Chalton St NW1 83 B1
Chamberlain Cotts SE5 48 C2
Chamberlain Ho 6 E1 32 B2
Chamberlain St 7 NW1 12 B1
Chamberlayne Mans 3 NW10 22 C2
Chamberlayne Rd NW10 22 B4
Chambers La NW10 9 B1
Chambers Rd N7 14 A4
Chambers St SE16 139 C3
Chamber St E1 125 A4
Chambon Pl 7 W6 38 C2
Chambord Ho 24 E2 24 B2 99 A3
Chambord St E2 24 B2 99 A3
Champion Gr SE5 63 C4
Champion Hill SE5 63 C4
Champion Pk SE5 48 C1
Champlain Ho 26 W12 30 A2
Chancel Ct W1 119 B4
Chancellor Gr SE21 75 B1
Chancellor Ho
South Kensington SW7 129 A2
29 Wapping E1 32 A1
Chancellor Pas E14 33 C1
Chancellors' Ct WC1 106 C4
Chancellor's Rd W6 39 B1
Chancellors St W6 39 B1
Chancellors Wharf 21 W6 39 B1
Chancel St SE1 122 A1
Chancery Bldgs 14 E1 32 B2
Chancery Ho WC2 107 B3
Chancery La EC4 107 B2
Chancery Lane Sta WC1 107 B3
Chancery Mews SW17 72 A2
Chance St E2 24 B1 98 C2
Chandler Ave E16 35 C4
Chandlers Mews E14 41 C4
Chandler St E1 32 A1
Chandlers Way 11 SE24 74 C4
Chandler Way SE15 49 B3
Chandlery Ho 26 E1 111 B1
Chandos Pl WC2 120 A3
Chandos Rd
Cricklewood NW2 9 B3
Old Oak Comm NW10 21 A1
Stratford New Town E15 19 C3
Chandos St W1 104 B3
Chandos Way NW11 2 A3
Change Alley EC3 109 C1
Channel Gate Rd NW10 21 A2
Channel Ho E14 33 A4
Channel Sea Bsns Ctr E15 27 C3
Channelsea Rd E15 27 C4
Channing Jun Sch N6 3 C3
Channing Sch N6 4 A3
Chantrey Rd SW9 62 B4
Chantry Cl W9 23 B1
Chantry Cres NW10 8 B2
Chantry Ct SW6 58 A4
Chantry Sq W8 128 A1
Chantry St N1 86 B3
Chant Sq E15 19 C1
Chant St E15 19 C1
Chapel Cl NW10 8 B2
Chapel Ct SE1 137 B4
Chapel House St E14 42 A2
Chapel Mkt N1 85 B2
Chapel Pl
Islington N1 85 C2
Marylebone W1 104 A1
12 Shoreditch EC2 24 A2 98 A3
Chapel Side W2 114 A3
Chapel St
Paddington NW1 102 A3
Westminster SW1 131 C3
Chapleton Ho SW2 62 C2
Chaplin Cl SE1 136 A4
Chaplin Ho 6 SW9 62 C3
Chaplin Rd NW2 8 C2
Chaplow Cl SW6 166 C1
Chapman Ho
26 Stepney E1 32 A3
2 West Norwood SE27 75 A1
Chapman Rd E9 18 B2
Chapmans Park Ind Est NW10 8 B2
Chapman Sq SW19 69 C2
Chapman St E1 32 A2
Chapone Pl W1 105 B1
Chapter Cl 16 W4 37 B3
Chapter House & Jewel Twr SW1 134 A2
Chapter Rd
Kennington SE17 150 B1
Willesden NW2 8 C3
Chapter St SW1 147 B3
Chara Pl W4 45 C4
Charcot Ho SW15 56 B1
Charcroft Ct 11 W14 39 C4
Chard Ho 7 N7 5 B2
Chardin Ho 30 SW9 173 C4
Chardin Rd 11 W4 38 A2
Chardmore Rd N16 7 C3
Charecroft Way W12 39 C4
Charfield Ct W9 88 B1
Charford Rd E16 35 C4
Chargrove Cl 24 SE16 40 C4
Charing Cross SW1 120 A2
Charing Cross Hospl W6 39 C1
Charing Cross Rd WC2 105 C1
Charing Cross Sta WC2 120 B2
Charing Ho SE1 135 C4
Chariot Cl 3 E3 26 C4
Charlbert Ct NW8 80 A2
Charlbert St NW8 80 A2
Charles Allen Ho EC1 95 B4
Charles Auffray Ho 30 E1 32 B4
Charles Barry Cl SW4 61 B4
Charles Burton Ct E5 18 A4
Charles Coveney Rd 4 SE15 49 B2
Charles Darwin Ho 8 E2 25 A2
Charles Dickens Ho 1 E2 25 A2
Charles Dickens Mus The WC1 95 A1
Charles Dickens Prim Sch SE1 136 C3
Charles Edward Brooke Sch 11 SW9 48 A2
Charles Edward Brooke Sch (Dennen Site) 10 SE5 48 A2
Charles Flemwell Mews 7 E16 35 C1
Charles Haller St 25 SW2 74 C4
Charles Harrod Ct SW13 47 B4
Charles Hobson Ho 4 NW10 8 A1
Charles Hocking Ho 8 W3 37 B4
Charles II Pl SW3 144 C1
Charles II St SW1 119 B2
Charles La NW8 80 A2
Charles Lamb Ct N1 86 B2
Charles Mackenzie Ho 7 SE16 153 C4
Charles Pl NW1 93 A3
Charles Rowan Ho WC1 95 B3
Charles Sq N1 97 C3
Charles St
Barnes SW13 46 A1
Mayfair W1 118 A2
Charleston St SE17 151 A3
Charles Townsend Ho EC1 96 A2
Charles Utton Ct E8 16 C4
Charlesworth Ho 6 E14 33 C3
Charleville Ct SW5 140 C1
Charleville Mans W14 140 B1
Charleville Rd W14 140 C1
Charlotte Ct 10 W6 38 C2
Charlotte Despard Ave SW11 169 C3
Charlotte Ho 12 W6 39 B1
Charlotte Mews
Marylebone W1 105 A4
North Kensington W10 30 C3
West Kensington W14 140 A4
Charlotte Pl
Marylebone W1 105 A3
Westminster SW1 146 C3
Charlotte Rd
Barnes SW13 46 B2
Shoreditch EC2 24 A1 98 A2
Charlotte Row SW4 61 B4
Charlotte Sharman Prim Sch SE11 136 A1
Charlotte Sq 5 TW10 54 B1
Charlotte St W1 105 A4
Charlotte Terr N1 85 A3
Charlotte Turner Prim Sch SE8 51 C4
Charlton Ct
25 Hackney E2 24 B4
17 Kentish Town N7 13 C3
Charlton Ho
5 Brentford TW8 44 A4
Somers Town NW1 93 B4
Charlton King's Rd NW5 13 C3
Charlton Pl N1 86 A2
Charlton Rd NW10 21 A4
Charlton Way SE10, SE3 53 A2
Charlwood Ho
Richmond TW9 45 A3
1 Streatham SW2 74 B3
Westminster SW1 147 B3
Charlwood Pl SW1 147 A3
Charlwood Rd SW15 57 C3
Charlwood St SW1 147 A2
Charlwood Terr 5 SW15 57 C3
Charman Ho
18 London SW2 62 C1
South Lambeth SW8 162 A2
Charmian Ho 19 N1 24 A3
Charmouth Ct TW10 54 B2
Charmouth Ho SW8 162 C2
Charnock Ho 22 W12 30 A2
Charnwood Gdns E14 41 C2
Charrington Ho 42 E1 25 B1
Charrington St NW1 83 B2
Charter Bldgs 14 SE10 52 A2
Charter Ct
Finsbury Pk N4 5 C3
Marylebone W1 102 B3
Charter Ho WC2 106 B1
Charterhouse Bldgs EC1 96 C1
Charterhouse Mews EC1 108 B4
Charterhouse Rd E8 16 C3
Charterhouse Sq EC1 108 B4
Charterhouse Square Sch The EC1 108 B4
Charterhouse St EC1 108 A3
Charterhouse Works SW18 59 B3

Charteris Rd
Finsbury Pk N4 5 C3
Kilburn NW6 23 B4
Charteris Sp Ctr NW6 23 C4
Charter Sch SE24 63 C2
Chartes Ho SE1 138 B2
Chartfield Ave SW15 57 B2
Chartfield Sq SW15 57 C2
Chartham Ct 12 SW9 62 C4
Chartham Gr SE27 75 A1
Chartham Ho SE1 137 C2
Chart House The 5 E14 42 A1
Chartridge SE17 48 C4
Chart St N1 97 C4
Chartwell 25 SW19 69 C3
Chase Ct SW3 130 C1
Chase Ctr The NW10 20 C2
Chaseley Ct W4 37 A1
Chaseley St E14 33 A3
Chasemore Ho SW6 154 B2
Chase Rd NW10 20 C1
Chase Road Trad Est NW10 20 C1
Chase The SW4 61 A4
Chater Ho 6 E2 25 C2
Chatfield Rd SW11 59 B4
Chatham Ct SW11 60 B2
Chatham Ho 7 SE5 49 A1
Chatham Pl E9 17 B2
Chatham Rd SW11 60 B2
Chatham St SE17 151 C4
Chatsworth Ct
Brondesbury NW2 9 C2
Clapton Pk E5 17 C4
Earl's Ct W8 141 B4
Chatsworth Est E5 17 C4
Chatsworth Gdns W3 28 A1
Chatsworth Lo 1 W4 37 C1
Chatsworth Rd
Brondesbury NW2 9 C2
Chiswick W4 45 B4
Clapton Pk E5 17 C4
Chatsworth Way SE27 75 B1
Chattenden Ho 8 N4 6 C4
Chatterton Ct TW9 44 B1
Chatterton Rd N4 6 A1
Chatto Rd SW11 60 B2
Chaucer Ave TW9 44 C1
Chaucer Ct 17 N16 16 A4
Chaucer Dr SE1 153 A3
Chaucer Ho SW1 146 C1
Chaucer Rd
Acton W3 28 B1
Herne Hill SE24 63 A2
Chaulden Ho EC1 97 C3
Cheadle Ct NW8 89 C2
Cheadle Ho 17 E14 33 B3
Cheam St 6 SE15 65 A4
Cheapside EC2 109 A1
Chearsley SE17 151 A4
Cheddington Ho 9 E2 24 C4
Chedworth Cl E16 35 B3
Chedworth Ho 2 E5 7 C2
Cheesemans Terr W14 140 C1
Chelmer Rd E9 17 C3
Chelmsford Cl W6 47 C4
Chelmsford Ho 5 N7 14 B4
Chelmsford Sq NW10 22 B4
CHELSEA 144 B1
Chelsea Antiques Mkt SW3 144 B1
Chelsea Barracks SW1 145 C2
Chelsea Bridge SW1 160 A4
Chelsea Bridge Rd SW1 145 C1
Chelsea Cl NW10 20 C4
Chelsea Cloisters SW3 144 B3
Chelsea Coll of Art & Design SW1 148 A2
Chelsea Cres
Brondesbury NW2 10 B2
Chelsea SW10 167 A3
Chelsea Ct SW3 159 B4
Chelsea Emb SW3 158 C3
Chelsea Est SW3 158 A3
Chelsea Farm Ho SW10 157 C3
Chelsea Gate SW1 145 C1
Chelsea Gdns SW1 145 C1
Chelsea Harbour Design Ctr SW10 167 A4
Chelsea Harbour Dr SW10 167 A4
Chelsea Harbour Pier SW10 167 B3
Chelsea Ind Coll SW6 156 A1
Chelsea Lo SW3 159 A4
Chelsea Manor Ct SW3 158 B4
Chelsea Manor Gdns SW3 144 B1
Chelsea Manor St SW3 144 B1
Chelsea Manor Studios SW3 144 B1
Chelsea Mus SW6 156 B2
Chelsea Park Gdns SW3 157 B4
Chelsea Physic Gdn SW1 158 C4
Chelsea Reach Twr SW10 157 B2
Chelsea Sp Ctr SW3 144 B1
Chelsea Sq SW3 143 C1
Chelsea Twrs SW3 158 B4
Chelsea & Westminster Hospl SW10 157 A3
Chelsfield Ho SE17 152 A3
Chelsfield Point 3 E9 17 C1
Chelsham Ho 1 SW4 61 C4
Chelsham Rd SW4 61 C4
Cheltenham Pl
10 Acton W3 28 A1
Acton W3 37 B4
1 South Acton W3 37 A4
Cheltenham Rd SE15 65 B2
Cheltenham Terr SW3 145 A2
Chelverton Ct SW15 57 C3
Chelverton Rd SW15 57 C3
Chelwood NW5 12 C3
Chelwood Ct SW11 167 C4
Chelwood Gdns TW9 44 C1
Chelwood Ho W2 101 C1
Chenies Ho W2 114 A4
Chenies Mews WC1 93 B1
Chenies Pl NW1 83 C2
Chenies St WC1 105 B4
Chenies The NW1 83 C2
Cheniston Gdns W8 128 A2
Chepstow Cl SW15 58 A2
Chepstow Cres W11 31 C2 113 B4
Chepstow Ct W11 31 C2 113 B4
Chepstow Pl W2 31 C2 113 C4
Chepstow Rd W2 31 C3
Chepstow Villas W11 31 C2 113 B4
Chequers Ct EC1 97 B1
Chequers Ho NW8 90 A2
Chequer St EC1 97 A1
Cherbury Ct N1 87 C1
Cherbury St N1 87 C1
Cheriton Ho 9 E5 17 A3
Cheriton Sq SW17 72 C2
Cherry Cl 7 SW2 74 C4
Cherry Ct
Acton W3 29 A1
5 Rotherhithe SE16 33 A1
Cherry Garden Ho 7 SE16 40 A4
Cherry Garden Sch 20 SE16 153 C4
Cherry Garden St SE16 40 A4
Cherry Laurel Wlk SW2 62 B1
Cherry Tree Cl 11 E9 25 B4
Cherry Tree Ct
1 Camden Town NW1 13 B1
11 Peckham SE15 50 A2
Cherry Tree Dr SW16 74 A1
Cherrytree Ho 8 W10 22 C2
Cherry Tree Ho SE14 51 B1
Cherry Trees Sch The 22 E3 26 C2
Cherry Tree Terr SE1 138 B4
Cherry Tree Wlk EC1 97 A1
Cherrywood Cl E3 26 A2
Cherrywood Dr SW15 57 C2
Chertsey Ct SW14 55 A4
Chertsey Ho 37 E2 24 B2 98 C3
Cherwell Ho NW8 89 C1
Cheryls Cl SW6 166 B4
Chesham Cl SW1 131 B1
Chesham Ct SW18 71 C4
Chesham Flats W1 117 C4
Chesham Ho SW1 131 B1
Chesham Mews SW1 131 B2
Chesham Pl SW1 131 B1
Chesham St SW1 131 B1
Cheshire St E2 24 B1 99 A2
Chesholm Rd N16 7 A1
Cheshunt Ho 9 NW6 78 A3
Chesil Ct
17 Bethnal Green E2 25 B3
Chelsea SW3 158 B4
Chesilton Rd SW6 164 C4
Chesney Ct W9 23 C1
Chesney Ho SE13 67 C3
Chesney St SW11 169 B3
Chessington Ho 19 SW8 171 B2
Chesson Rd W14 155 A4
Chessum Ho E8 16 C2
Chester Ave TW10 54 B1
Chester Cl
Barnes SW13 57 A4
Knightsbridge SW1 132 A3
1 Richmond TW10 54 B1
Chester Close N NW1 92 B4
Chester Close S NW1 92 B3
Chester Cres E8 16 B3
Chester Ct
Bermondsey SE8 40 C1
4 Camberwell SE5 48 C3
Gospel Oak NW5 12 C4
Regent's Pk NW1 92 B3
Chesterfield Ct SE13 67 B4
Chesterfield Gdns
Greenwich SE10 52 C3
Mayfair W1 118 A2
Chesterfield Gr SE22 64 B2
Chesterfield Hill W1 118 A2
Chesterfield Ho
Highgate N6 3 C3
Mayfair W1 117 C2
Chesterfield Rd W4 45 B4
Chesterfield St W1 118 A2
Chesterfield Way SE15 50 B3
Chesterford Gdns NW3 11 A4
Chester Gate NW1 92 B3
Chester Ho
Dartmouth Pk N19 4 A2
1 Deptford SE8 51 B4
Chesterman Ct W4 46 A3
Chester Mews SW1 132 A2
Chester Pl NW1 92 A4
Chester Rd
Dartmouth Pk N19 4 A2
Regent's Pk NW1 92 A4
Chester Row SW1 145 C4
Chester Sq SW1 146 A4
Chester Sq Mews SW1 132 A1
Chester St
Bethnal Green E2 24 C1 99 C2
Westminster SW1 131 C2
Chester Terr NW1 92 A4
Chesterton Cl SW18 58 C2
Chesterton Ct W3 37 A3
Chesterton Ho
20 Battersea SW11 59 C4
3 Kensal Town W10 31 A4
Chesterton Prim Sch SW11 169 B3
Chesterton Rd W10 31 A4
Chesterton Sq W8 141 B3
Chester Way SE11 149 C3
Chestnut Alley SW6 155 A3
Chestnut Ave 11 SW14 55 C4
Chestnut Cl
New Cross Gate SE14 51 B2
1 Stoke Newington N16 6 C2
Chestnut Ct SW6 155 A4
Chestnut Gr SW12 72 C3
Chestnut Grove Sch 6 SW12 72 C3
Chestnut Ho
1 Acton W4 38 A2
Brockley SE4 66 B4
7 Maitland Pk NW3 12 B2
West Norwood SE27 75 B1
Chestnut Rd SE21, SE27 75 B1
Chestnuts The 1 N5 15 A4
Chettle Cl SE1 137 B2
Chetwode Ho NW8 90 A2
Chetwode Rd SW17 72 B1
Chetwynd Rd NW5 4 A1
Cheval Ct SW15 57 A3
Cheval Pl SW7 130 B2
Cheval St E14 41 C3
Chevening Rd
Cubitt Town SE10 43 B1
Kilburn NW6 23 A4
Cheverell Ho 25 E2 24 C3
Cheverton Rd N19 4 C3
Chevet St E9 18 A3
Chevington NW2 10 B2
Cheviot Ct 16 SE14 50 B3

Cheviot Gate NW2 1 A2
Cheviot Gdns NW2 1 A2
Cheviot Ho N16 7 B3
Chevron Cl E16 35 C3
Cheylesmore Ho SW1 146 A2
Cheyne Ct SW3 158 C4
Cheyne Gdns SW3 158 B3
Cheyne Mews SW3 158 B3
Cheyne Pl SW3 158 C4
Cheyne Row SW3 158 A3
Cheyne Wlk SW10 157 B2
Cheyney Ho 2 E9 17 C2
Chichele Mans NW2 9 C3
Chichele Rd NW2 9 C3
Chicheley St SE1 135 A4
Chichester Ct 2 NW1 13 B1
Chichester Ho NW6 23 C3
Chichester Rd
  Bayswater W2 100 B4
  Kilburn NW6 23 C3
Chichester Rents WC2 107 B2
Chichester St SW1 147 A1
Chichester Way E14 42 C2
Chicksand Ho 14 E1 111 B4
Chicksand St E1 111 A3
Chicksand Street E1 111 B3
Chiddingstone SE13 67 B2
Chiddingstone St SW6 165 C2
Chigwell Ct 1 E9 18 A2
Chigwell Hill E1 32 A2
Chiham Ho 5 SE15 50 B4
Chilcombe Ho 6 SW15 68 C4
Chilcot Cl 13 E14 34 A3
Childebert Rd SW17 73 A2
Childeric Prim Sch SE14 51 A3
Childeric Rd SE14 51 A3
Childerley St SW6 164 A4
Childers St SE8 51 B4
Child La SE10 43 B3
Childrens House Upper Sch 15 N1 16 A2
CHILD'S HILL 1 C2
Child's Hill Sch NW2 1 A1
Child's Mews SW5 141 C3
Child's Pl SW5 141 C3
Child's St SW5 141 C3
Child's Wlk SW5 141 C3
Chilham Ct 13 SW9 62 C4
Chilham Ho SE1 137 C2
Chillington Dr SW11 59 C3
Chillingworth Rd N7 14 C3
Chiltern Ct
  15 Deptford SE14 50 B3
Chiltern Ct *continued*
  Marylebone NW1 91 A1
Chiltern Ho
  Camberwell SE17 48 C4
  4 Kensal Town W10 31 A4
  5 Stamford Hill N16 7 B3
Chiltern Rd E3 26 C1
Chiltern St W1 103 B4
Chilton Gr SE8 41 A2
Chilton Rd TW9 54 C4
Chilton St E2 24 B1 99 A2
Chilver St SE10 43 B1
Chilworth Ct 8 SW19 69 C3
Chilworth Mews W2 101 B1
Chilworth St W2 101 A1
Chimney Ct 23 E1 32 A1
China Ct 1 E1 32 A1
China Hall Mews 16 SE16 40 B3
China Mews 17 SW2 74 B4
Chindit Ho 11 N16 15 C4
Ching Ct WC2 106 A1
Chinnocks Wharf E14 33 A2
Chipka St E14 42 B4
Chipley St SE14 51 A4
Chippendale Ho SW1 146 B1
Chippenham Gdns NW6 23 C2
Chippenham Mews W9 23 C1
Chippenham Rd W9 23 C1
Chip St SW4 61 C3
Chipstead Ho 4 SW2 74 A3
Chipstead St SW6 165 C2
Chirk Ct SE4 51 B1
Chisenhale Prim Sch 36 E3 26 A3
Chisenhale Rd E3 26 A3
Chisholm Ct 1 W6 38 C1
Chisholm Rd 13 TW10 54 B1
Chisledon Wlk E9 18 B2
Chislehurst Rd TW10 54 A2
Chislet 5 NW5 12 C2
Chiswell St
  Barbican EC1 109 B4
  Camberwell SE5 48 C3
CHISWICK 38 B1
Chiswick & Bedford Park Prep Sch 13 W4 38 A2
Chiswick Common Rd W4 37 C2
Chiswick Com Sch W4 45 C3
Chiswick Green Studios 1 W4 37 B2
Chiswick High Rd W4 38 A2
Chiswick High Road (North Circular Rd) W4 36 C1
Chiswick Ho W4 45 C4
Chiswick La W4 38 A1
Chiswick La S W4 46 B4
Chiswick Mall W4 38 B1
Chiswick Park Sta W4 37 B2
Chiswick Pier W4 46 B3
Chiswick Pk W4 37 A2
Chiswick Plaza W4 45 B4
Chiswick Quay W4 45 B2
Chiswick Rd W4 37 B2
Chiswick Rdbt W4 36 C1
Chiswick Sq W4 46 A4
Chiswick Sta W4 45 B3
Chiswick Staithe W4 45 B2
Chiswick Terr 6 W4 37 B2
Chiswick Village W4 45 A4
Chiswick Wharf W4 46 B4
Chitty St W1 105 A4
Chivalry Rd SW11 60 A2
Chivelston 27 SW19 69 C3
Chobham Gdns SW19 69 C2
Chobham Rd E15 19 C3
Cholmeley Cres N6 4 A4
Cholmeley Lo N6 4 A3
Cholmeley Pk N6 4 A4
Cholmley Gdns NW6 10 C3
Cholmondeley Ave NW10 21 C3
Chopin's Ct 13 E1 32 A1
Chopwell Cl E15 19 C1
Choumert Gr SE15 49 C1
Choumert Mews SE15 49 C1
Choumert Rd SE15 49 B1
Choumert Sq 4 SE15 49 C1
Chow Sq 2 E8 16 B3
Chrisp Ho SE10 53 A4
Chrisp St E14 34 A3
Christ Church TW9 54 A4
Christchurch Ave NW6 10 A1
Christ Church Bentinck CE Prim Sch NW1 102 B4
Christ Church Brondesbury CE Jun & Inf Sch NW6 10 B1
Christchurch CE Prim Sch SW3 158 C4
Christ Church CE Prim Sch
  Battersea SW11 60 A4
  Cubitt Town SE10 43 A1
Christ Church CE Prim Sch, Hampstead NW3 2 C1
Christchurch CE Sch E1 111 A3
Christ Church Ct
  1 Brondesbury Pk NW6 10 A1
  Harlesden NW10 21 A4
Christchurch Hill NW3 11 C4
Christchurch Ho 2 SW2 74 A3
Christchurch Pas NW3 2 B1
Christchurch Rd
  Mortlake SW14 55 B2
  Streatham SW2 74 C3
Christ Church Sch NW1 92 B4
Christchurch Sq 2 E9 25 B4
Christchurch St SW3 158 C4
Christ Church Streatham CE Prim Sch 18 SW2 74 B3
Christchurch Terr SW3 158 C4
Christchurch Way SE10 43 A1
Christian Ct SE16 33 B1
Christian St E1 111 C1
Christie Ct
  Maitland Pk NW3 12 A3
  2 Upper Holloway N19 5 A2
Christie Ho 2 SE10 43 B1
Christie Rd E9 18 A2
Christina Sq N4 6 A3
Christina St EC2 24 A1 98 A2
Christopher Boone's Almshouses SE13 67 C3
Christopher Cl SE16 40 C4
Christopher France Ho 6 E1 26 A2
Christopher Hatton Prim Sch EC1 95 B1
Christopher Lo 2 N6 4 C4
Christopher Pl NW1 93 C3
Christopher St EC2 97 C1
Christ's Sch TW10 54 C2
Christ the King RC Prim Sch 7 N4 5 B2
Christ the King Sixth Form Coll SE13 67 C4
Chryssell Rd SW9 163 C1
Chubworthy St 5 SE14 51 A4
Chudleigh Rd
  Hampstead NW6 9 C1
  London SE4 66 C2
Chudleigh St E1 32 C3
Chumleigh Gdns SE5 49 A4
Chumleigh St SE5 49 A4
Church App SE21 75 C1
Church Ave
  Camden Town NW1 13 A2
  Mortlake SW14 55 C4
Church Cl W8 128 A4
Church Cres E9 17 C1
Churchcroft Cl SW12 72 C4
Church Ct
  Holborn EC4 107 C1
  Rotherhithe SE16 41 B4
Churchdale Ct 1 W4 37 A1
CHURCH END NW10 8 B3
Church Entry EC4 108 B1
Church Estate Almshouses 8 TW9 54 B3
Churchfield Ho W2 89 B1
Churchfield Mans 5 SW6 165 A1
Churchfield Rd W3 28 B1
Churchfields SE10 52 B4
Church Garth 4 N19 4 C2
Church Gate SW6 58 A4
Church Gn 4 SW9 173 C2
Church Gr SE13 67 A2
Church Ho EC1 96 B2
Churchill Ct
  Finsbury Pk N4 5 C4
  Peckham SE15 49 C1
  Willesden NW2 9 A3
Churchill Gardens Prim Sch SW1 147 A1
Churchill Gdns SW1 160 C4
Churchill Gdns Rd SW1 160 C4
Churchill Pl E14 34 A1
Churchill Rd
  Gospel Oak NW5 13 A4
  Willesden NW2 9 A2
Churchill Wlk E9 17 B3
Church Mead SE5 48 B3
Churchmead Rd NW10 8 C2
Church Path W4 37 B3
Church Pl SW1 119 A3
Church Rd
  Acton W3 37 B4
  Barnes SW13 46 C2
  24 Canonbury N1 15 B2
  Richmond TW10, TW9 54 A2
  Willesden NW10 8 A1
Church Row NW3 11 B4
Church St
  Chiswick W4 46 B4
  Lisson Gr NW8 90 A1
Church Street Est NW8 89 C1
Church Studios 16 NW1 13 C2
Churchward Ho
  Camberwell SE17 48 A4
  West Kensington SW5 141 A1
Churchway NW1 93 C4
Church Wlk
  Barnes SW13 46 C2
  Canonbury N16 15 C4
  Child's Hill NW2 1 B1
  Dartmouth Pk N6 3 C1
Churchyard Row SE11 150 B4
Churnfield 2 N4 5 C2
Churston Cl 16 SW2 74 C3
Churston Mans WC1 95 A1
Churton Pl
  Brentford W4 45 A4
  Pimlico SW1 147 A3
Churton St SW1 147 A3
Chute Ho 17 SW9 173 B1
Chuter Ede Ho SW6 155 A3
Cicada Rd SW18 59 B2

Cicely Ho NW8 ... 79 C1
Cicely Rd SE15 ... 49 C2
Cinema Mus The SE11 ... 150 A3
Cinnabar Wharf Central 16 E1 ... 125 C2
Cinnabar Wharf East 15 E1 ... 125 C2
Cinnabar Wharf West 17 E1 ... 125 C2
Cinnamon Cl 8 SE15 ... 49 B3
Cinnamon Row 3 SW11 ... 59 B4
Cinnamon St E1 ... 32 A1
Cinnamon Wharf SE1 ... 139 A4
Circle Ho 14 E14 ... 34 C3
Circle The SE1 ... 139 A4
Circus Lo NW8 ... 89 B4
Circus Mews W1 ... 102 C4
Circus Pl EC2 ... 109 C3
Circus Rd NW8 ... 79 B1
Circus St SE10 ... 52 B3
Cirencester St W2 ... 100 A4
Cissbury Ho 6 SE26 ... 76 C1
Citadel Pl SE11 ... 148 C2
Citizen Ho N7 ... 14 C4
Citizen Rd N7 ... 14 C4
Citron Terr 4 SE15 ... 65 A4
Citrus Ho 14 SE8 ... 41 B1
City Banking Coll SE1 ... 137 C4
City Bsns Coll EC1 ... 96 B3
City Bsns Ctr 33 SE16 ... 40 B4
City Central Est EC1 ... 96 C3
City Coll N1 ... 97 B4
City Coll of London The WC1 ... 107 A3
City Forum EC1 ... 96 C4
City Garden Row N1 ... 86 B1
City Gate E1 ... 25 B1
City & Guilds of London Art Sch The SE11 ... 149 C1
City & Hackney Ctr for Mental Health (Hospl) E9 ... 18 A3
City Hall SE1 ... 124 B1
City Harbour E14 ... 42 A3
City & Islington 6th Form Coll EC1 ... 96 A4
City & Islington Coll (Ctr for Applied Sciences) EC1 ... 96 A4
City & Islington Coll (Ctr for Bsns, Arts & Technology) 8 N7 ... 14 A4
City & Islington Coll (Ctr for Health, Social & Child Care) 7 N7 ... 14 B4
City & Islington Coll (Ctr for Lifelong Learning) 3 N4 ... 6 A2
City Law Sch The EC1 ... 107 A3
City Lights The SE11 ... 149 C1
CITY OF LONDON ... 122 B4
City of London Acad-Islington N1 ... 86 C3
City of London Acad The SE1 ... 153 C2
City of London Information Ctr EC4 ... 108 B1
City of London Sch EC4 ... 122 C4
City of London Sch for Girls EC2 ... 109 A4
City of Westminster Coll W2 ... 101 B4
City of Westminster Coll, Cosway Street Ctr NW1 ... 102 B4
City of Westminster Coll, Maida Vale Ctr 1 W9 ... 88 A3
City of Westminster Coll, Queens Park Ctr 10 W9 ... 23 C2
City Rd EC1 ... 97 A4
City Thameslink Sta EC4 ... 108 A1
City University EC1 ... 96 A3
City Wlk SE1 ... 138 A3
Civil Service Coll SW1 ... 146 C3
Clabon Mews SW1 ... 144 C4
Clack St SE16 ... 40 B4
Claire Ct NW2 ... 10 A2
Claire Pl E14 ... 41 C3
Clancarty Rd SW6 ... 165 C1
Clandon Cl W3 ... 37 A4
Clandon St SE8 ... 51 C1
Clanfield Ho 12 SW15 ... 68 C3
Clanricarde Gdns W2 ... 31 C2 113 C3
CLAPHAM ... 61 A4
Clapham Common SW4 ... 61 A3
Clapham Common North Side SW4 ... 60 C3
Clapham Common South Side SW4 ... 61 B2
Clapham Common Sta SW4 ... 61 B3
Clapham Common West Side
Clapham SW4, SW11 ... 60 B3
Clapham SW11 ... 60 C2
Clapham Computer & Secretarial Coll 1 SW11 ... 60 B2
Clapham Court Terr 2 SW4 ... 62 A2
Clapham Cres SW4 ... 61 C3
Clapham Ct 3 SW4 ... 62 A2
Clapham High St SW4 ... 61 C3
Clapham High Street Sta SW4 ... 61 C4
Clapham Junction Est SW11 ... 60 A3
Clapham Junction Sta SW11 ... 60 A3
Clapham L Ctr SW4 ... 61 C4
Clapham Manor Ct 1 SW4 ... 61 B4
Clapham Manor Prim Sch 8 SW4 ... 61 B4
Clapham Manor St SW4 ... 61 C4
Clapham Mans SW4 ... 61 A1
Clapham North Bsns Ctr 10 SW4 ... 61 C4
Clapham North Sta SW4 ... 62 A4
CLAPHAM PARK ... 61 C2
Clapham Park Rd SW4 ... 61 C3
Clapham Park Terr 4 SW2 ... 62 A2
Clapham Rd SW9 ... 163 A2
Clapham South Sta SW4 ... 61 A1
Clapton Comm E5 ... 7 C4
Clapton Girls Tec Coll E5 ... 17 B4
CLAPTON PARK ... 17 C4
Clapton Pas E5 ... 17 B3
Clapton Sq E5 ... 17 B3
Clapton Terr E5 ... 7 C3
Clapton Way E5 ... 16 C4
Clara Grant Ho 10 E14 ... 41 C3
Clara Grant Prim Sch The 18 E3 ... 26 C1
Clare Ct WC1 ... 94 B3
Claredale Ho 3 E2 ... 25 A3
Claredale St E2 ... 24 C3
Clare Gdns W11 ... 31 A3
Clare Ho
Bermondsey SE1 ... 153 A2
6 Old Ford E3 ... 26 B4
Clare La N1 ... 15 B1
Clare Lawn Ave SW14 ... 55 C2
Clare Mews SW6 ... 156 A1
Clare Mkt WC2 ... 107 A1
Claremont 1 SW15 ... 58 A2
Claremont Cl
Finsbury N1 ... 85 C1
4 Streatham SW2 ... 74 B3
Claremont Ct 1 W9 ... 23 B3
Claremont Gr W4 ... 46 A3
Claremont Rd
Highgate N6 ... 4 B4
West Kilburn W9 ... 23 B3
Claremont Sq N1 ... 85 B1
Claremont St SE10 ... 52 A4
Clarence Ave SW4 ... 61 C1
Clarence Cres SW4 ... 61 C1
Clarence Ct 10 W6 ... 39 A2
Clarence Gate NW1 ... 91 A2
Clarence Gate Gdns NW1 ... 91 A1
Clarence Gdns NW1 ... 92 B3
Clarence Ho SE17 ... 48 B4
Clarence Ho SW1 ... 119 A1
Clarence La SW15 ... 56 B1
Clarence Mews
Balham SW12 ... 73 A4
Clarence Mews *continued*
Hackney E5 ... 17 A3
1 Rotherhithe SE16 ... 32 C1
Clarence Pl 25 E5 ... 17 A3
Clarence Rd
Brentford W4 ... 36 C1
Brondesbury NW6 ... 10 B1
Greenwich SE8 ... 52 A4
Lower Clapton E5 ... 17 A4
Richmond TW9 ... 44 C2
Clarence St 5 TW9 ... 54 A3
Clarence Terr NW1 ... 91 A2
Clarence Way NW1 ... 13 A1
Clarence Wlk 9 SW4 ... 172 A2
Clarendon Cl
Bayswater W2 ... 116 A4
38 Hackney E9 ... 17 B1
Clarendon Cross W11 ... 31 A2 112 B3
Clarendon Ct
Paddington W9 ... 89 A2
1 Richmond TW9 ... 44 C2
Willesden NW2 ... 9 B1
Clarendon Dr SW15 ... 57 B3
Clarendon Flats W1 ... 103 C1
Clarendon Gdns W9 ... 89 A1
Clarendon Gr NW1 ... 93 B4
Clarendon Ho NW1 ... 83 A1
Clarendon Mews W2 ... 116 A4
Clarendon Pl W2 ... 116 A4
Clarendon Rd W11 ... 31 A2 112 B3
Clarendon Rise SE13 ... 67 B3
Clarendon St SW1 ... 146 B2
Clarendon Terr W9 ... 89 A2
Clarendon Wlk 11 W11 ... 31 A3
Clare Pl SW15 ... 68 B4
Clare Rd
New Cross Gate SE14 ... 51 B2
Willesden NW10 ... 8 C1
Clare St E2 ... 25 A3
Clareville Ct SW7 ... 143 A3
Clareville Gr SW7 ... 143 A3
Clareville Grove Mews SW7 ... 143 A3
Clareville St SW7 ... 143 A3
Clarewood Ct W1 ... 102 C3
Clarewood Wlk SW9 ... 62 C3
Clarges Ho W1 ... 118 B2
Clarges Mews W1 ... 118 A2
Clarges St W1 ... 118 B2
Clariat Ct W3 ... 36 C4
Claribel Rd SW9 ... 48 A1
Claridge Ct SW6 ... 164 C3
Clarissa Ho 7 E14 ... 34 A3
Clarissa St E8 ... 24 B4
Clarke Ho 2 SW4 ... 61 B4
Clarke Path N16 ... 7 C3
Clarkes Mews W1 ... 103 C4
Clark Ho SW10 ... 156 C2
Clark Lawrence Ct 10 SW11 ... 59 C4
Clarkson Rd E16 ... 35 B3
Clarkson Row NW1 ... 82 C1
Clarkson St E2 ... 25 A2
Clark's Pl EC2 ... 110 A2
Clark St E1 ... 32 B4
Classic Mans 33 E9 ... 17 B1
Classinghall Ho 14 SW15 ... 57 C1
Claude Rd SE15 ... 50 A1
Claude St E14 ... 41 C2
Claudia Jones Way SW2 ... 62 A1
Claudia Pl SW19 ... 70 A3
Clavell St 8 SE10 ... 52 B4
Claverdale Rd SW2 ... 74 C4
Clavering Ave SW13 ... 47 A4
Clavering Ho SE13 ... 67 C3
Claverton St SW1 ... 147 A1
Clave St E1 ... 32 B1
Claxton Gr W6 ... 39 C1 140 A1
Claybank Gr SE13 ... 67 A4
Claybrook Rd W6 ... 47 C4
Claydon SE17 ... 150 C4
Clayhall Ct 20 E3 ... 26 B3
Claylands Pl SW8 ... 163 B2
Claylands Rd SW8 ... 163 A3
Claypole Rd E15 ... 27 B3
Clayponds Ave TW8 ... 36 A2
Clayponds Hospl W5 ... 36 A2
Clayponds La TW8 ... 36 A1
Clays Ct N16 ... 7 B3
Clay St W1 ... 103 A3
Clayton Cres N1 ... 84 C3
Clayton Ct N16 ... 7 C4
Clayton Ho 22 E9 ... 17 B1
Clayton Mews SE10 ... 52 C2
Clayton Rd SE15 ... 49 C2
Clayton St SE11 ... 163 B4
Clearbrook Way 13 E1 ... 32 B3
Clear Water Ho 9 TW10 ... 54 A2
Clearwater Terr 4 W11 ... 39 C4
Clearwell Dr W9 ... 88 B1
Cleaver Ho 6 NW3 ... 12 B1
Cleaver Sq SE11 ... 149 C1
Cleaver St SE11 ... 149 C2
Cleeve Ho 15 E2 ... 24 A2 98 B3
Cleeve Way SW15 ... 68 B4
Cleeve Workshops 14 E2 ... 24 A2 98 B3
Clegg St 16 E1 ... 32 A1
Cleland Ho 19 E2 ... 25 B3
Clematis St W12 ... 29 C2
Clem Atlee Par SW6 ... 155 A3
Clem Attlee Ct SW6 ... 155 A3
Clemence St E14 ... 33 B4

Clement Attlee Ho NW10 8 B1
Clement Ave SW4 61 C3
Clement Cl
Acton W4 37 C2
Hampstead NW6 9 B1
Clement Danes Ho 2 W12 30 A3
Clement Ho
14 Deptford SE8 41 A2
17 North Kensington W10 30 B4
Clements Ave 1 E16 35 C2
Clements Inn WC2 107 A1
Clements Inn Pas WC2 107 A1
Clement's La EC2, EC4 123 C4
Clement's Rd SE16 40 A3
Clemson Ho 9 E8 24 B4
Clennam St SE1 137 A4
Clenston Mews W1 102 C2
Clent Ho 4 N16 7 B3
Cleopatra's Needle WC2 120 C3
Clephane Rd 13 N1 15 B2
Clephane Rd N N1 15 B2
Clephane Rd S N1 15 C2
Clere Pl EC2 97 C2
Clere St EC2 97 C2
CLERKENWELL 96 A1
Clerkenwell Cl EC1 95 C1
Clerkenwell Gn EC1 96 A1
Clerkenwell Parochial CE Prim Sch EC1 95 B3
Clerkenwell Rd EC1 96 A1
Clermont Rd E9 25 B4
Clevedon Ct
Battersea SW11 168 A4
Dulwich SE21 75 C1
Clevedon Mans NW5 12 C4
Cleve Ho NW6 11 A1
Cleveland Ave W4 38 B2
Cleveland Ct W1 93 A1
Cleveland Gdns
Barnes SW13 46 B1
Paddington W2 100 C1
Cleveland Gr 39 E1 25 B1
Cleveland Mans
8 Brixton SW9 163 B1
4 Brondesbury NW6 10 B1
Paddington W9 23 C1
Cleveland Mews W1 104 C4
Cleveland Pl SW1 119 A2
Cleveland Rd
Barnes SW13 46 B1
Islington N1 15 C1
14 South Acton W4 37 B3
Cleveland Row SW1 119 A1
Cleveland Sq W2 100 C1
Cleveland St W1 92 C1
Cleveland Terr W2 101 A2
Cleveland Way E1 25 B1
Clevendon Cl N16 7 B1
Cleve Rd NW6 11 A1
Cleverly Cotts W12 29 B1
Cleverly Est W12 29 C2
Cley Ho SE4 65 C3
Clichy Ho 32 E1 32 B4
Clifden Mews E5 17 C3
Clifden Rd E5 17 C3
Cliff Ct 14 NW1 13 C2
Cliffe Ho 4 SE10 43 B1
Clifford Ave
Mortlake SW14 45 B1
Mortlake SW14, TW9 55 A4
Clifford Ct
Bayswater W2 100 A3
Wandsworth SW18 71 C4
Willesden NW10 8 A4
Clifford Dr SW9 63 A3
Clifford Gdns NW10 22 B3
Clifford Haigh Ho SW6 47 C3
Clifford Ho W14 140 C3
Clifford's Inn Pas EC4 107 B1
Clifford St W1 118 C3
Clifford Way NW10 8 B4
Cliff Rd NW1 13 C2
Cliff Road Studios 13 NW1 13 C2
Cliffsend Ho 23 SW9 173 C3
Cliff Terr SE8 51 C1
Cliffview Rd SE13 66 C4
Cliff Villas NW1 13 C2
Cliff Wlk E16 35 B4
Clifton Ave W12 29 B1
Clifton Cres SE15 50 A3
Clifton Ct
Finsbury Pk N4 5 C2
Paddington NW8 89 B2
Peckham SE15 50 A3
Putney SW15 57 C2
Clifton Gate SW10 156 C4
Clifton Gdns
Chiswick W4 37 C2
Paddington W9 88 C1
Clifton Gr E8 16 C2
Clifton Hill NW8 78 C3
Clifton Ho E2 24 B1 98 C2
Clifton Mans 4 SW9 62 C3
Clifton Pl
Paddington W2 101 C1
Rotherhithe SE16 40 B4
Clifton Rd
Harlesden NW10 21 C3
Newham E16 35 A4
Paddington W9 89 A2
Clifton Rise SE14 51 A3
Clifton St EC2 24 A1 98 A1
Clifton Terr N4 5 C2
Clifton Villas W9 100 C4
Clifton Way SE15 50 B3
Climsland Ho SE1 121 C2
Clinch Ct 11 E16 35 C4
Cline Ho SW15 56 C2
Clinger Ct N1 24 A4
Clink Prison Mus The SE1 123 B2
Clink St SE1 123 B2
Clinton Rd E3 26 A2
Clipper Appts 12 SE10 52 B4
Clipper Cl 3 SE16 40 C4
Clipper Ho E14 42 B1
Clipper Way SE13 67 B3
Clipstone Ho 10 SW15 56 C2
Clipstone Mews W1 104 C4
Clipstone St W1 104 C4
Clissold Cres N16 15 C4
Clissold Ct N4 6 B2
Clissold Ho 4 N16 6 C2
Clissold Rd N16 6 C1
Clitheroe Rd SW9 172 B1
Clive Ct W9 89 A2
Cliveden Ho SW1 145 B4
Cliveden Pl SW1 145 B4
Clive Ho
18 Clapham SW8 171 B2
Greenwich SE10 52 B4
Clive Rd SE21, SE27 75 C1
Cloak La EC4 123 B4
Clochar Ct NW10 21 B4
Clock Ho N16 7 B4
Clockhouse Cl SW19 69 B2
Clockhouse Pl SW15 58 A1
Clockhouse The SW19 69 B1
Clockmakers' Mus EC2 109 A2
Clock Tower Mews N1 87 A3
Clock Tower Pl 1 N7 14 A2
Clock View Cres 2 N7 14 A2
Cloister Rd
Acton W3 28 B4
Child's Hill NW2 1 B2
Cloisters Ct N6 4 A3
Cloisters The 22 SW9 173 C3
Clonbrock Rd N16 16 A4
Cloncurry St SW6 47 C1
Clone Ct 4 W12 38 A3
Clonmel Rd SW6 165 A4
Clonmore St SW18 70 B3
Clorane Gdns NW3 1 C1
Close The
Lewisham SE3 52 C1
Mortlake TW9 55 A4
Cloth Ct EC1 108 B3
Cloth Fair EC1 108 B3
Clothier St EC3 110 B2
Cloth St EC1 108 C4
Cloudesdale Rd SW17 73 A2
Cloudesley Mans N1 85 C3
Cloudesley Pl N1 85 C3
Cloudesley Rd N1 85 B3
Cloudesley Sq N1 85 C4
Cloudesley St N1 85 C3
Clove Cres E14 34 C2
Clovelly Ct NW2 9 B3
Clovelly Ho W2 100 C2
Clovelly Rd W4 37 C4
Clovelly Way E1 32 B3
Clover Mews SW3 159 A4
Clowes Ho 3 SW4 62 A3
Cloysters Gn E1 125 B2
Club Row E2 24 B1 98 C2
Clunbury St N1 87 C1
Clunie Ho SW1 131 A2
Cluny Mews SW5 141 B3
Cluny Pl SE1 138 A2
Cluse Ct N1 86 C2
Clutton St E14 34 A4
Clyde Ct NW1 83 C2
Clyde Flats SW6 154 C2
Clydesdale Gdns TW10 55 A3
Clydesdale Ho 4 W11 31 B3
Clydesdale Rd W11 31 B3
Clyde St SE8 51 B4
Clynes Ho 3 E2 25 C2
Clyro Ct N4 5 B3
Clyston St SW8 171 A2
Coach & Horses Yd W1 118 C4
Coach House La
Highbury N5 15 A4
Wimbledon SW19 69 C1
Coach House Mews SE23 65 C1
Coach House Yd 5 NW3 11 C4
Coachmaker Mews 5 SW9 62 A4
Coalbrook Mans 3 SW12 73 A3
Coaldale Wlk SE21 75 B4
Coalecroft Rd SW15 57 B2
Coalport Ho SE11 149 B4
Coatbridge Ho 8 N1 14 B1
Coates Ave SW18 60 A1
Coates Ct NW3 12 A3
Coate St E2 24 C3
Coates Wlk TW8 36 A1
Cobbett St SW8 163 A1
Cobble La N1 15 A1
Cobble Mews N4, N5 6 B1
Cobbold Ct SW1 147 B4
Cobbold Ind Est NW10 8 B2
Cobbold Mews W12 38 B4
Cobbold Rd
Bedford Pk W12 38 B4
Willesden NW10 8 B2
Cobb's Hall 1 SW6 47 C4
Cobb St E1 110 C3
Cobden Bldgs WC1 94 C4
Cobden Ho
11 Bethnal Green E2 24 C2 99 C4
Regent's Pk NW1 82 C2
Cobham Cl SW11 60 A1
Cobham Mews 3 NW1 13 C1
Coborn Mews 9 E3 26 B2
Coborn Rd E3 26 B2
Coborn St E3 26 B2
Cobourg Prim Sch SE5 49 B4
Cobourg Rd SE5 49 B4
Cobourg St NW1 93 A3
Coburg Cl SW1 147 A4
Coburg Cres SW2 74 C3
Coburg Dwellings 11 E1 32 B2
Cochrane Cl NW8 79 C1
Cochrane Ho 15 E14 41 C4
Cochrane Mews NW8 79 C1
Cochrane St NW8 79 C1
Coci Ho W14 141 A3
Cockburn Ho SW1 147 C1
Cock Hill E1 110 B3
Cock La EC1 108 B3
Cockpit Yd WC1 107 A4
Cockspur Ct SW1 119 C2
Cockspur St SW1 119 C2
Coda Ctr The SW6 164 B4
Code St E1 24 B1 99 A1
Codicote Ho 22 SE8 40 C2
Codicote Terr N4 6 B2
Codling Cl 12 E1 125 C2
Codrington Ct 3 SE16 33 A1
Codrington Ho 7 E1 25 A1
Codrington Mews W11 31 A3
Cody Rd E16 27 C1
Coffey St SE8 51 C3
Cohen Lo E5 18 A3
Coin St SE1 121 B2
Coity Rd NW5 12 C2
Cokers La SE21 75 C3
Coke St E1 111 C2
Colas Mews 7 NW6 23 C4
Colbeck Mews SW5 142 B3
Colberg Pl N16 7 B4
Colbert 1 SE5 49 B2
Colborne Ho 8 E14 33 C2
Colchester Ho 17 SW8 171 B2
Colchester St E1 111 A2
Coldbath Sq EC1 95 B2
Coldbath St SE13 52 A1
Cold Blow La SE14 50 C4
Coldharbour E14 34 B1
Coldharbour Ind Est SE5 48 B1
Coldharbour La SW9 63 A4
Coldharbour Pl SE5 48 C1
Coldstream Gdns SW18 58 B1
Colebeck Mews N1 15 A2
Colebert Ave E1 25 B1
Colebert Ho 21 E1 25 B1
Colebrook Cl SW19 69 C4
Colebrook Ct SW3 144 B3
Colebrooke Pl N1 86 B3
Colebrooke Row
Islington N1 84 B4
Islington N1 86 A2
Islington N1 86 B3
Colebrook Ho 1 E14 34 A3
Coleby Path 21 SE5 48 C3

Colechurch Ho 9 SE1 153 B1
Colefax Bldg 12 E1 111 C2
Coleford Rd SW18 59 B2
Colegrave Rd E15 19 C3
Colegrave Sch E15 19 C3
Colegrove Rd SE15 49 B4
Coleherne Ct SW10 142 B1
Coleherne Mans SW5 142 B2
Coleherne Mews SW10 142 A1
Coleherne Rd SW10 142 A1
Colehill Gdns SW6 164 A3
Colehill La SW6 164 B3
Cole Ho SE1 135 C3
Coleman Ct SW18 70 C4
Coleman Fields N1 87 A4
Coleman Mans N19 5 A4
Coleman Rd SE5 49 A3
Coleman St EC2 109 B2
Coleman Street Bldgs EC2 109 B2
Colenso Rd E5 17 B4
Coleraine Rd SE3 53 B4
Coleridge Cl SW8 170 B1
Coleridge Ct W14 39 C3
Coleridge Gdns NW6 11 B1
Coleridge Ho
Pimlico SW1 147 A1
Walworth SE17 151 A2
Coleridge Prim Sch N8 4 C4
Coleridge Rd N4, N7 5 C2
Coleridge Sq SW10 156 C2
Coles Ct SW11 167 C3
Coleshill Flats SW1 145 C3
Cole St SE1 137 A3
Colestown St 4 SW11 168 B2
Colet Gdns W14 39 C2
Colet Ho SE17 150 B1
Colette Ct 5 SE16 40 C4
Coley St WC1 95 A1
Colfe & Hatchcliffe's Glebe SE13 67 A2
Colgate Ho SE13 52 A1
Colin Blanchard Ho SE4 51 C1
Colin Ct SW16 73 C2
Colinette Rd SW15 57 B3
Colin Rd NW10 8 C2
Colinsdale N1 86 A3
Colin Winter Ho 45 E1 25 B1
Coliston Pas SW18 70 C4
Coliston Rd SW18 70 C4
Collamore Ave SW18 72 A3
Collard Pl NW1 13 A1
Collcutt Lo SW4 62 A3
College App SE10 52 B4
College Cl E5 17 B3
College Cres NW3 11 C2
College Cross N1 14 C1
College Ct
Chelsea SW3 145 A1
3 Hammersmith W6 39 B1
Hampstead NW3 11 C2
College Gdns
Dulwich SE21 76 A3
Upper Tooting SW17 72 A2
College Gr NW1 83 B4
College Green Ct SW9 63 A4
College Hill EC4 123 A4
College La NW5 13 A4
College Mews 5 SW18 59 A2
COLLEGE PARK 22 A2
College Park Cl SE13 67 C3
College Park Sch 20 W2 100 A1
College Pl
Camden Town NW1 83 A3
Chelsea SW10 156 C2
College Rd
Dulwich SE19, SE21 76 A2
Kensal Green NW10 22 B3
College St EC4 123 A4
College Terr E3 26 B2
Collent Ho 12 E9 17 B2
Collent St E9 17 B2
Collerston Ho SE10 43 B1
Collette Ho N16 7 B3
Collett Ho SE13 67 A4
Collett Rd SE16 139 C2
Colley Ho 12 N7 13 C3
Collier St N1 84 C1
Collingbourne Rd W12 30 A1
Collingham Gdns SW5 142 B3
Collingham Pl SW5 142 B4
Collingham Rd SW5 142 B3
Collingham Tutors Coll SW5 142 B3
Collington St SE10 42 C1
Collingwood Ho
27 Bethnal Green E1 25 A1
Marylebone W1 104 C4
Collingwood St E1 25 A1
Collins Ct E8 16 C2
Collins Ho
6 Cubitt Town SE10 43 B1
4 Poplar E14 34 B2
Collinson Ct SE1 136 C3
Collinson Ho 14 SE15 49 C3
Collinson St SE1 136 C3
Collinson Wlk SE1 136 C3
Collins Rd N5, N16 15 B4
Collins Sq SE3 53 B1
Collins St SE3 53 A1
Collins Yd N1 86 A3
Collison Pl N16 7 A3
Coll of Arms EC4 122 C4
Coll of Central London The EC2 24 A1 98 A2
Coll of Law The (Bloomsbury) EC1 105 B4
Coll of Law The (Moorgate) EC1 97 B1
Coll of NW London 15 NW6 23 C4
Coll of NW London (Willesden Centre) NW10 8 B3
Coll of Optometrists The SW1 120 A2
Coll Sharp Ct 42 E2 24 B2 98 C3
Coll's Rd SE15 50 B2
Collyer Pl SE15 49 C2
Colmans Wharf 5 E14 34 A4
Colmar Cl 3 E1 25 C1
Colmore Mews SE15 50 A2
Colnbrook St SE1 136 A2
Colne Ho NW8 89 C1
Colne Rd E5 18 A4
Cologne Rd SW11 59 C3
Colombo St SE1 122 A1
Colomb St SE10 43 A1
Colonades The 4 SE5 48 C2
Colonial Dr W4 37 B2
Colonnade WC1 94 B1
Colonnade Ho SE3 53 B1
Colonnades The 6 E8 17 A2
Colonnade The 12 SE8 41 B2
Colorado Bldg 9 SE13 52 A2
Colosseum Terr NW1 92 B2
Colour Ho SE1 138 B3
Colstead Ho 22 E1 32 A3
Colston Rd SW14 55 B3
Colthurst Cres N4 6 B2
Coltman Ho SE10 52 B4
Coltman St E14 33 A4
Columba Ho SE14 51 B2
Columbas Dr NW3 2 C3
Columbia Ho 18 E3 26 C2
Columbia Point 7 SE16 40 B3
Columbia Prim Sch 50 E2 24 B2 99 A4
Columbia Rd
9 Hackney E2 24 C3
Shoreditch E2 24 B2 98 C4
Columbia Road Flower Mkt E2 24 B2 99 A4
Colverson Ho 14 E1 32 B4
Colvestone Cres E8 16 B3
Colvestone Prim Sch E8 16 B3
Colville Gdns W11 31 B3
Colville Ho
32 Bethnal Green E2 25 B3
Notting Hill W11 31 B3
Colville Mews W11 31 B3
Colville Pl W1 105 A3
Colville Prim Sch 5 W11 31 B3
Colville Rd
Notting Hill W11 31 B3
South Acton W3 37 A3
Colville Sq W11 31 B3
Colville Terr W11 31 B3
Colwall Ho 18 SW9 173 A1
Colwell Rd SE22 64 B2
Colwick Cl N6 4 C4
Colwith Rd W6 47 B4
Colworth Gr SE17 151 A3
Colwyn Ho SE1 135 B1
Colyton Rd SE22 65 A2
Combe Ave SE3 53 B3
Combedale Rd SE10 43 C1
Combe Ho
Mortlake SW14 45 B1
20 Paddington W2 31 C4
Combemartin Rd SW18 70 A3
Combe Mews 4 SE3 53 B3
Comber Gr SE5 48 B3
Comber Grove Prim Sch 33 SE5 48 B3
Comber Ho SE5 48 B3
Combermere Rd SW9 62 B4
Combe The NW1 92 B3
Com Coll Hackney The 17 E8 25 A4
Comeragh Mews W14 140 B1
Comeragh Rd W14 140 B1
Comerford Rd SE4 66 B3
Comet Pl SE8 51 C3
Comet St SE8 51 C3
Comfort St 6 SE15 49 A4
Comins Ho SW4 61 B2
Commercial Rd
Stepney E1 32 B3
Whitechapel E1 111 C2
Commercial St E1 110 C4
Commercial Way
Peckham SE15 49 C3
Wembley NW10 20 A3
Commerell Pl SE10 43 B1
Commerell St SE10 43 A1
Commodity Quay E1 125 A3
Commodore Ct SE8 51 C2
Commodore Ho 7 E14 34 B2
Commodore St E1 26 A1
Commondale SW15 57 B4
Common Rd SW13 56 C4
Common View SW15 57 B4
Commonwealth Ave 25 W12 30 A2
Commonwealth Ho WC1 106 B2
Community La N7 13 C3
Community Rd E15 19 C3
Comodore Ho SW18 59 B3
Compania Bldg 12 E1 32 C2
Compass Ct SE1 124 C1
Compass Ho
Bayswater W2 100 A1
London SE8 52 A1
Compass Point 10 E14 33 C2
Compayne Gdns NW6 11 A1
Compton Ave
Islington N1 15 A2
London N6 3 A4
Compton Cl
Camberwell SE15 49 B3
Regent's Pk NW1 92 B3
Compton Cres W4 45 B4
Compton Ho SW11 168 A4
Compton Pas EC1 96 B2
Compton Pl WC1 94 A2
Compton Rd
Islington N1 15 A2
Kensal Green NW10 22 C2
Compton St EC1 96 B2
Compton Terr N1 15 A2
Comus Ho SE17 152 A3
Comus Pl SE17 152 A3
Comyn Rd SW11 60 A3
Comyns Cl E16 35 B4
Conant Ho SE11 48 A4
Conant Mews 1 E1 125 B4
Concanon Rd SW2, SW4 62 B3
Concert Hall App SE1 121 A1
Concord Bsns Ctr W3 28 A4
Concorde Way SE16 40 C2
Concordia Wharf 10 E14 34 B1
Concord Rd W3 20 A1
Condell Rd SW8 171 A3
Conder St E14 33 A3
Condray Pl SW11 158 A1
Conduit Ct WC2 120 A4
Conduit Ho SE10 52 C2
Conduit Mews W2 101 B1
Conduit Pas W2 101 B1
Conduit Pl W2 101 B1
Conduit St W1 118 C4
Conewood St N5 6 A1
Coney Acre SE21 75 B3
Coney Way SW8 163 A3
Congers Ho SE8 51 C3
Congress Ho WC1 105 C2
Congreve Ho 10 N16 16 A3
Congreve St SE17 152 A3
Conifer Ct 23 SW19 69 C3
Conifer Gdns SW16 74 B1
Conifer Ho SE4 66 B3
Coniger Rd SW6 165 B2
Coningham Ct SW10 157 A2

Coningham Mews W12 29 C1
Coningham Rd W12 39 A4
Coningsby Rd N4 6 A4
Conington Rd SE13 52 B1
Conisbrough NW1 82 C3
Coniston NW1 92 C4
Coniston Cl
Barnes SW13 46 B3
Chiswick W4 45 B3
Coniston Ct
Marylebone W2 102 B1
6 Rotherhithe SE16 40 C4
Conistone Way N7 14 A1
Coniston Ho
14 Bow E3 26 B2
18 Camberwell SE5 48 B3
Coniston Wlk E9 17 B3
Conlan St W10 23 A1
Conley Rd NW10 8 A2
Conley St SE10 43 A1
Connaught Ave SW14 55 B3
Connaught Cl W2 102 B1
Connaught Ho
College Pk NW10 22 A2
Mayfair W1 118 A3
Connaught House Sch W2 102 B1
Connaught Lo N4 5 C4
Connaught Mans
Battersea SW11 168 B3
3 Brixton SW9 62 C3
15 Canonbury N16 15 C4
Fulham SW6 164 A4
Connaught Pl W2 102 C1
Connaught Rd
Finsbury Pk N4 5 C4
Harlesden NW10 21 A3
5 Richmond TW10 54 B2
Connaught Sq W2 102 C1
Connaught St W2 102 B1
Connaught Works E3 26 A4
Connell Ct 6 SE14 50 C4
Connor Ct SW11 170 A3
Connor St E9 25 C4
Conrad Ho
8 Limehouse SE16 33 A2
South Lambeth SW8 162 A2
12 Stoke Newington N16 16 A3
Conrad Twr W3 37 A3
Consort Ho W2 114 B3
Consort Lo NW8 80 C3
Consort Rd SE15 50 A1
Cons St SE1 135 C4
Constable Ct 11 SE16 40 A1
Constable Ho
25 Millwall E14 41 C4
Primrose Hill NW3 12 B1
Constable Wlk SE21 76 A1
Constant Ho 26 E14 34 A2
Constantine Ho SW2 75 A3
Constantine Rd NW3 12 A4
Constitution Hill W1 132 B4
Consul Ho 5 E3 26 C1
Content St SE17 151 B3
Convent Gdns W11 31 B3
Convent of Jesus & Mary Language Coll NW10 21 B4
Convent of Jesus & Mary RC Inf Sch 9 NW2 9 B2
Conway Gr W3 28 C4
Conway Ho
Chelsea SW3 145 A1
5 Millwall E14 42 A2
6 Streatham SW2 74 A3
Conway Mews W1 92 C1
Conway St W1 92 C1
Conybeare NW3 12 A1
Conyer St 21 E3 26 A3
Cookham Cres SE16 40 C4
Cookham Ho E2 24 B1 98 C2
Cook's Rd
Camberwell SE17 48 A4
Stratford Marsh E15 27 A3
Coomassie Rd W9 23 B1
Coombe Ho 13 N7 13 C3
Coombe Rd W4 38 A1
Coomber Ho SW6 59 A4
Coombs St N1 86 B1
Coomer Mews SW6 155 A3
Coomer Pl SW6 155 A3
Cooperage The SE1 124 C1
Cooper Cl SE1 135 C3
Cooper Ho NW8 89 B1
Cooper Rd NW10 8 C3
Coopersale Rd E9 17 C3
Coopers Cl E1 25 B1
Coopers Ct
9 Acton W3 28 B1
Tower Hamlets E3 26 B1
Coopers La NW1 83 C1
Coopers Lo SE1 138 C4
Cooper's Rd SE1 153 A2
Cooper's Row EC3 124 C4
Cooper St 10 E16 35 B4
Coopers Yd N1 15 A1
Cope Ho EC1 97 A3
Copeland Dr E14 41 C2
Copeland Ho SE11 135 A1
Copeland Rd SE15 50 A1
Copenhagen Gdns W4 37 C4
Copenhagen Ho N1 85 B3
Copenhagen Pl E14 33 B3
Copenhagen Prim Sch N1 84 C3
Copenhagen St N1 84 C3
Cope Pl W8 127 B1
Cope St SE16 40 C2
Copford Wlk N1 86 C4
Copleston Rd SE15 64 B4
Copley Cl 15 SE17 48 A4
Copley St E1 32 C4
Coppedhall 2 SE21 75 C2
Copperas St SE8 52 A4
Copper Beech N6 3 C4
Copperbeech Cl NW3 11 C3
Copperfield Ho 12 SE1 139 B3
Copperfield Rd E3 33 A4
Copperfields Ct W3 36 C4
Copperfield St SE1 136 C4
Copper Mews 19 W4 37 B3
Copper Row SE1 124 C1
Coppice Dr SW15 57 A1
Coppin Ho SW2 75 A3
Coppock Cl SW11 168 A1
Copse Ct SW15 58 A2
Copthall Ave EC2 109 C2
Copthall Bldgs EC2 109 C2
Copthall Cl EC2 109 B2
Copthorne Ave SW12 73 C4
Coptic St WC1 106 A3
Copton Cl E3 33 C4
Coral Apts 6 E16 35 C2
Coral Ho 5 E1 26 A1
Coral Row 14 SW11 59 B4
Coral St SE1 135 C3
Coram Ho
Bloomsbury WC1 94 A2
9 Chiswick W4 38 A1
Coram Mans WC1 94 C1
Coram St WC1 94 A1
Corbden Cl SE15 49 B2
Corbet Ct EC3 109 C1
Corbet Ho N1 85 B3
Corbet Pl E1 110 C4
Corbett Ho SW10 156 C4
Corbett's La SE16 40 B2
Corbetts Pas 8 SE16 40 B2
Corbidge Ct SE8 52 A4
Corbiere Ho 5 N1 24 A4
Corbin Ho 7 E3 27 A2
Corbridge Cres E2 25 A3
Corbyn St N4, N19 5 A3
Corby Rd NW10 20 C3
Corby Way E3 26 C1
Cordelia Cl SE24 63 A3
Cordelia Ho 26 N1 24 A3
Cordelia St E14 34 A3
Cording St E14 34 A4
Cordwainers Ct 18 E9 17 B1
Corfe Ho SW8 162 C2
Corfe Lodge 15 SE21 75 C2
Corfe Twr 6 W3 37 B4
Corfield St E2 25 A2
Coriander Ave E14 34 C3
Coriander Ct SE1 139 A4
Corinne Rd N19 13 B4
Cork St Mews W1 118 C3
Cork Sq E1 32 A1
Cork St W1 118 C3
Corlett St NW1 102 A4
Cormont Rd SE5 48 A2
Cormorant Ct
36 Deptford SE8 51 B4
13 Dulwich SE21 75 C2
Cornbury Ho 5 SE8 51 B4
Cornelia St N7 14 B2
Cornell Bldg 9 E1 111 B2
Corner Fielde SW2 74 B3
Corner Gn SE3 53 C1
Corner House St WC2 120 A2
Cornerstone Ct 13 E1 24 C1 99 C1
Cornerways SW15 56 C3
Corney Rd W4 46 A4
Corney Reach Way W4 46 A3
Cornflower Terr SE22 65 A1
Cornford Gr SW12 73 A2
Cornhill EC3 109 C1
Cornick Ho 7 SE16 40 A3
Cornish Ho
Brentford TW8 36 B1
7 Camberwell SE17 48 A4
Cornmill La SE13 67 B4
Cornmow Dr NW10 8 C3
Cornwall Ave E2 25 B2
Cornwall Cres W11 31 A3
Cornwall Flats SE1 135 C4
Cornwall Gdns
Kensington SW7 128 B1
Willesden NW10 9 A2
Cornwall Gdns Wlk SW7 128 B1
Cornwall Gr W4 38 A1
Cornwall Ho
Marylebone NW1 91 A1
3 Putney SW15 69 B4
Cornwallis Ct SW8 172 A4
Cornwallis Ho 24 W12 30 A2
Cornwallis Rd N19 5 A2
Cornwallis Sq
3 Finsbury Park N4 5 C2
London N19 5 A2
Cornwall Mans
Chelsea SW10 157 A2
Marylebone NW1 91 A1
Cornwall Mews S SW7 128 C1
Cornwall Mews W SW7 128 B1
Cornwall Rd
Finsbury Pk N4 5 C4
Lambeth SE1 135 C4
Cornwall Sq SE11 150 A2
Cornwall St 4 E1 32 A2
Cornwall Terr NW1 91 A1
Cornwall Terrace Mews NW1 91 A1
Cornwood Dr E1 32 B3
Coronation Ave 1 N16 16 B4
Coronation Ct 19 W10 30 B4
Coronet St N1 24 A2 98 A3
Corporation Row EC1 95 C2
Corporation St N7 14 A3
Corpus Christi RC Prim Sch 19 SW2 62 B2
Corrance Rd SW2, SW4 62 A3
Corringham Ct NW11 1 C4
Corringham Ho 11 E1 32 C3
Corringham Rd NW11 1 C4
Corringway NW11 2 A4
Corry Dr SW9 63 A3
Corry Ho 2 E14 34 A2
Corsham St N1 97 C3
Corsica St N5 15 A2
Corsley Way E9 18 B2
Cortayne Rd SW6 165 A2
Cortis Rd SW15 57 A1
Cortis Terr SW15 57 A1
Corunna Rd SW8 171 A4
Corunna Terr SW8 170 C4
Corvette Sq 5 SE10 52 C4
Coryton Path W9 23 B1
Cosbycote Ave SE24 63 B2
Cosgrove Ho 11 E2 24 C4
Cosmo Pl WC1 106 B4
Cosmur Cl W12 38 B3
Cossall Wlk SE15 50 A2
Cossar Mews 10 SW2 62 C2
Cosser St SE1 135 B2
Costa St SE15 49 C1
Coston Wlk 4 SE4 65 C3
Cosway Mans NW1 102 B4
Cosway St NW1 102 B4
Cotall St E14 33 C4
Cotes Ho NW8 90 A1
Cotham St SE17 151 A3
Cotherstone Rd SW2 74 B3
Cotleigh Rd NW6 10 C1
Cotman Cl SW15 57 C2
Cotman Ho NW8 80 A2
Cotrill Gdns E8 17 A2
Cotswold Ct EC1 96 C2
Cotswold Gate NW2 1 A3
Cotswold Ho N16 7 B3
Cotswold Mews SW11 167 C3
Cottage Gn SE5 48 C3
Cottage Gr SW9 62 A4
Cottage Pl SW3 130 A1
Cottage St E14 34 A2
Cottages The SE1 134 C1
Cottage Wlk 2 N16 7 B1
Cottenham Ho 5 N19 5 A2
Cottesbrook St 9 SE14 51 A3
Cottesloe Ho NW8 90 A2
Cottesloe Mews SE1 135 C2
Cottesmore Ct W8 128 B2
Cottesmore Gdns W8 128 B2

Cottingham Rd SW8 ... 163 A2
Cottington St SE11 ... 150 A2
Cotton Ave W3 ... 28 C3
Cotton Ho
Bedford Pk W12 ... 38 B4
18 Streatham SW12 ... 74 A4
Cotton Row SW11 ... 59 C4
Cotton's Gdns E2 ... 24 A2 98 B4
Cottons La SE1 ... 123 C2
Cotton St E14 ... 34 B2
Cottrell Ct SE10 ... 43 B2
Couchman Ho 8 SW4 ... 61 B1
Coulgate St SE4 ... 66 A4
Coulsdon Ho 5 SW2 ... 74 A3
Coulson St SW3 ... 144 C2
Coulter Rd W6 ... 39 A3
Coults Cres NW5 ... 3 C1
Councillor St SE5 ... 48 B3
Counters Ct W14 ... 126 B2
Counter St SE1 ... 124 A1
Countess Rd NW5 ... 13 B3
Countisbury Ho SE26 ... 76 C1
County Gr SE5 ... 48 B2
County Ho
22 Herne Hill SE24 ... 63 A3
9 South Lambeth SW9 ... 173 B4
County St SE1 ... 137 A1
Courier Ho 17 SW2 ... 74 C4
Courland Gr SW8 ... 171 C3
Courland St SW8 ... 171 C3
Courtauld Ho 12 E2 ... 24 C3
Courtauld Inst of Art WC2 ... 120 C4
Courtauld Rd N19 ... 5 A3
Courtenay Ave N6 ... 3 A4
Courtenay Sq SE11 ... 149 B1
Courtenay St SE11 ... 149 B2
Courtfield Gdns SW5 ... 142 B3
Courtfield Ho EC1 ... 107 B4
Courtfield Mews SW7 ... 142 B3
Courtfield Rd SW7 ... 142 C3
Court Gdns N7 ... 14 C2
Courthill Rd SE13 ... 67 B3
Courthope Ho
14 Rotherhithe SE16 ... 40 B3
South Lambeth SW8 ... 162 A1
Courthope Rd NW3 ... 12 B4
Court La SE21 ... 76 B4
Courtlands TW10 ... 54 C2
Courtlands Ave TW9 ... 45 A1
Court Lane Gdns SE21 ... 76 A4
Court Mans 8 W6 ... 38 C2
Courtmead Cl SE24 ... 63 B1
Courtnell St W2 ... 31 C3
Courtney Ct N7 ... 14 C3
Courtney Ho W14 ... 126 B2
Courtney Rd N7 ... 14 C3
Courtrai Rd SE23 ... 66 A1
Court Royal SW15 ... 58 A2
Court St 3 E1 ... 32 A4
Courtville Ho 12 W10 ... 23 A2
Court Way W3 ... 28 B4
Courtyard The
Fulham SW6 ... 164 A3
Islington N1 ... 14 B1
13 Wandsworth SW18 ... 59 C3
Cousin La EC4 ... 123 B3
Couzens Ho 8 E3 ... 33 B4
Coval Gdns SW14 ... 55 A3
Coval La SW14 ... 55 A3
Coval Pas SW14 ... 55 B3
Coval Rd SW14 ... 55 B3
Covell Ct 16 SE8 ... 51 C3
Covent Garden Sta WC2 ... 106 B1
Coventry Cl NW6 ... 23 C4
Coventry Rd E1 ... 25 A1
Coventry St W1 ... 119 B3
Coverdale Rd
Brondesbury NW2 ... 10 A2
Hammersmith W12 ... 39 A4
Hampstead NW6 ... 9 C1
Coverham Ho 5 SE4 ... 65 C3
Coverley Cl E1 ... 111 C4
Coverley Point SE11 ... 148 C3
Cowcross St EC1 ... 108 A4
Cowdenbeath Path N1 ... 84 C4
Cowdray Hall Royal Coll of Nursing W1 ... 104 A2
Cowdray Ho 22 SE22 ... 64 A4
Cowdry Rd E9 ... 18 B2
Cowley Rd
Brixton SW9 ... 173 C4
East Acton W3 ... 29 B1
Mortlake SW14 ... 56 A4
Cowley St SW1 ... 134 A1
Cowling Cl W11 ... 31 A1 112 A2
Cowper Ho
Pimlico SW1 ... 147 C1
Walworth SE17 ... 151 A2
Cowper Rd
Acton W3 ... 28 C1
Stoke Newington N16 ... 16 A4
Cowper's Ct EC3 ... 109 C1
Cowper St EC1, EC2 ... 97 C2
Cowper Terr W10 ... 30 C4
Cowthorpe Rd SW8 ... 171 C4
Cox Ho W6 ... 154 A4
Coxson Way SE1 ... 138 C3
Coysh Ct 8 SW15 ... 58 A2
Crabtree Cl E2 ... 24 B3
Crabtree Hall SW6 ... 47 B3
Crabtree La SW6 ... 47 C3
Craddock St NW5 ... 12 C2
Cragie Ho SE1 ... 153 A3
Craigleith SW15 ... 57 C1
Craignair Rd SW2 ... 74 C4
Craig's Ct SW1 ... 120 A2
Craik Ct NW6 ... 23 B3
Crail Row SE17 ... 151 C3
Cramer St W1 ... 103 C3
Crammond Cl W6 ... 154 A3
Crampton Prim Sch SE17 ... 150 B2
Crampton St SE17 ... 150 C2
Cranbourn Alley WC2 ... 119 C4
Cranbourne Ct SW11 ... 158 B2
Cranbourne Rd E15 ... 19 B4
Cranbourn Ho 6 SE16 ... 40 A4
Cranbourn Pas 5 SE16 ... 40 A4
Cranbourn St WC2 ... 119 C4
Cranbrook NW1 ... 83 A3
Cranbrook Ho 5 E5 ... 17 A3
Cranbrook Rd
Chiswick W4 ... 38 A1
St Johns SE8 ... 51 C2
Cranbrook St E2 ... 25 C3
Cranbury Rd SW6 ... 166 B1
Crandale Ho 8 E5 ... 17 A3
Crandley Ct SE8 ... 41 A2
Crane Ave W3 ... 28 B2
Crane Ct
7 Acton W12 ... 38 A4
Holborn EC4 ... 107 C1
Crane Gr N7 ... 14 C2
Crane Ho
24 Bow E3 ... 26 A3
10 Peckham SE15 ... 49 B2
Crane Mead SE16 ... 40 C2
Crane St
Greenwich SE10 ... 42 C1
6 Peckham SE15 ... 49 B2
Cranfield Ct NW1 ... 102 B3
Cranfield Ho WC1 ... 106 B4
Cranfield Rd SE4 ... 66 B4
Cranford Cotts 8 E1 ... 32 C2
Cranford Lo SW19 ... 69 C2
Cranford St E1 ... 32 C2
Cranhurst Rd NW2 ... 9 B3
Cranleigh W11 ... 31 B1 112 C2
Cranleigh Ct
Richmond TW9 ... 54 C4
4 Stamford Hill N16 ... 7 A3
Cranleigh Hos NW1 ... 83 A1
Cranleigh Mews SW11 ... 168 C1
Cranleigh St NW1 ... 83 A1
Cranley Gdns SW7 ... 143 B2
Cranley Mews SW7 ... 143 A2
Cranley Pl SW7 ... 143 B3
Cranmer Ct SW3 ... 144 B3
Cranmer Ho SW11 ... 168 A4
Cranmer Rd SW9 ... 163 C2
Cranswick Rd SE16 ... 40 A1
Cranwell Cl E3 ... 27 A1
Cranwich Rd N16 ... 7 A4
Cranwood Ct EC1 ... 97 C3
Cranwood St EC1 ... 97 C3
Cranworth Gdns SW9 ... 173 B4
Cranworth Ho 6 N7 ... 14 B4
Craster Rd SW2 ... 74 B4
Craston Ho 2 SE5 ... 49 A1
Craven Cl N16 ... 7 C4
Craven Cottage (Fulham FC) SW6 ... 47 C2
Craven Ct NW10 ... 21 A4
Craven Hill W2 ... 115 A4
Craven Hill Gdns W2 ... 114 C4
Craven Hill Mews W2 ... 115 A4
Craven Ho 2 SW14 ... 55 C4
Craven Lo
Bayswater W2 ... 115 A4
Fulham SW6 ... 47 C2
Craven Mews 6 SW11 ... 60 C4
Craven Park Mews NW10 ... 21 A4
Craven Park Rd NW10 ... 21 A4
Craven Pas WC2 ... 120 A2
Craven Pk NW10 ... 21 A4
Craven Rd
Paddington W2 ... 101 A1
Stonebridge NW10 ... 20 C4
Craven St WC2 ... 120 A2
Craven Terr W2 ... 115 A4
Craven Wlk E5, N16 ... 7 C4
Crawford Bldgs NW1 ... 102 B3
Crawford Mews W1 ... 102 C3
Crawford Pas EC1 ... 95 C1
Crawford Pl W1 ... 102 B3
Crawford Place Dwellings NW1 ... 102 B3
Crawford Point 4 E16 ... 35 B3
Crawford Prim Sch SE5 ... 48 B2
Crawford Rd SE5 ... 48 B1
Crawford St W1 ... 102 C3
Crawshay Ct SW9 ... 173 C4
Crawshay Ho 13 N16 ... 15 C4
Crawthew Gr SE22 ... 64 B3
Crayford Ho
Bermondsey SE1 ... 137 C3
5 Lower Holloway N7 ... 14 A4
Crayford Rd N7 ... 14 A4
Crayle Ho EC1 ... 96 B2
Crealock St SW18 ... 59 A1
Creasy Est SE1 ... 138 A1
Crebor St SE22 ... 64 C1
Credenhill Ho 2 SE15 ... 50 A3
Crediton Hill NW6 ... 11 A3
Crediton Rd NW10 ... 22 C4
Credon Rd SE16 ... 40 A1
Creechurch La EC3 ... 110 B1
Creechurch Pl EC3 ... 110 B1
Creed Ct 5 E1 ... 26 A2
Creed Ho SE15 ... 65 A4
Creed La EC4 ... 108 B1
Creek Ho W14 ... 126 B2
Creek Rd SE10, SE8 ... 52 A4
Creek Road Ind Est SE8 ... 52 A4
Creekside SE8 ... 52 A3
Creekside Foyer SE8 ... 52 A4
Crefeld Cl W6 ... 154 A3
Creighton Cl W12 ... 30 A2
Creighton Rd NW6 ... 22 C3
Cremer Bsns Ctr 8 E2 ... 24 B3
Cremer Ho 9 SE8 ... 51 C3
Cremer St E2 ... 24 B3
Cremorne Rd SW10 ... 157 B2
Creon Ct 3 SW9 ... 173 B4
Crescent EC3 ... 124 C4
Crescent Arc 1 SE10 ... 52 B4
Crescent Court Bsns Ctr 1 E16 ... 27 C1
Crescent Ct SW4 ... 61 C2
Crescent Gdns SW19 ... 70 C1
Crescent Gr SW4 ... 61 B3
Crescent Ho SE13 ... 52 A1
Crescent La SW4 ... 61 C2
Crescent Mans
Islington N5 ... 15 A3
Notting Hill W11 ... 31 A2 112 B4
Crescent Pl SW3 ... 144 B4
Crescent Row EC1 ... 96 C1
Crescent St N1 ... 14 B1
Crescent Stables SW15 ... 58 A2
Crescent The
Acton W3 ... 29 A3
Barnes SW13 ... 46 C1
Wimbledon SW19 ... 70 C1
Crescent Way SE4 ... 66 C4
Crescent Wood Rd SE21, SE26 ... 76 C1
Cresford Rd SW6 ... 166 A3
Cressage Ho 9 TW8 ... 44 A4
Cressall Ho 14 E14 ... 41 C3
Cresset Ho 8 E9 ... 17 B2
Cresset Rd E9 ... 17 B2
Cresset St SW4 ... 61 C4
Cressfield Cl NW5 ... 12 C3
Cressida Rd N19 ... 4 C3
Cressingham Rd SE13 ... 67 B4
Cressington Cl 4 N16 ... 16 A3
Cresswell Gdns SW5 ... 142 C2
Cresswell Pl SW10 ... 143 A2
Cressy Ct
Hammersmith W6 ... 39 A3
6 Stepney E1 ... 32 B4
36 Stepney E1 ... 32 B4
Cressy Ho SW13 ... 57 A4
Cressy Hos 7 E1 ... 32 B4
Cressy Pl E1 ... 32 B4
Cressy Rd NW3 ... 12 B4
Cresta Ho
7 Bow E3 ... 26 C1
Hampstead NW6 ... 11 C1
Crestfield St N1, WC1 ... 94 B4
Crestview NW5 ... 4 A1
Crestway SW15 ... 57 A1
Creswick Ct W3 ... 28 A2
Creswick Rd W3 ... 28 A2

Creswick Wlk 7 E3 26 C2
Crewdson Rd SW9 163 B1
Crewe Pl NW10 21 B2
Crewkerne Ct SW11 167 C4
Crews St E14 41 C2
Crewys Rd
Child's Hill NW2 1 B2
London SE15 50 A1
Crichton St SW8 170 C2
Cricketers Mews 4 SW18 59 A2
Cricketfield Rd E5 17 A4
Cricklade Ave SW2 74 B2
CRICKLEWOOD 9 B4
Cricklewood Broadway NW2 9 C4
Cricklewood La NW2 1 B1
Cricklewood Sta NW2 9 C4
Crieff Rd SW18 59 B1
Criffel Ave SW2 73 C3
Crimscott St SE1 138 B1
Crimsworth Rd SW8 161 C1
Crinan St N1 84 B2
Cringle St SW8 160 C2
Cripplegate St EC1 109 A4
Crispe Ho N1 85 A3
Crispian Cl NW10 8 A4
Crispin Ct SE17 152 A3
Crispin Pl E1 110 C4
Crispin St E1 110 C3
Crisp Rd W6 39 B1
Cristowe Rd SW6 165 A1
Criterion Mews N19 4 C2
Crockerton Rd SW17 72 B2
Croft Ct SE13 67 B1
Croftdown Rd NW5 4 A1
Crofters Ct 9 SE8 41 A2
Crofters Way NW1 83 B4
Croft Ho
Putney SW15 58 A1
11 West Kilburn W10 23 A2
Crofton Ave W4 45 C3
Crofton Gate Way SE4 66 A2
Crofton Park Rd SE4 66 B1
Crofton Park Sta SE4 66 A2
Crofton Rd SE5 49 A1
Crofton Terr
Homerton E5 18 A3
Richmond TW9 54 B3
Crofts Ho 21 E2 24 C3
Crofts St E1 125 B3
Croft St SE8 41 A2
Croft The NW10 21 B3
Crogsland Rd NW1 12 C1
Cromartie Rd N19 4 C4
Cromarty Ho 8 E1 33 A4
Crombie Mews 5 SW11 168 B2
Cromdale Ct N16 7 B4
Cromer Ct
Streatham SW16 74 A1
Wandsworth SW18 58 B1
Crome Rd NW10 8 A2
Cromer St WC1 94 B3
Cromer Terr E8 16 C3
Cromer Villas Rd SW18 58 B1
Cromford Path 1 E5 17 C4
Cromford Rd SW18 58 C2
Crompton Ct SW3 144 A4
Crompton Ho
Borough The SE1 137 A1
Paddington W2 89 B1
South Lambeth SW8 171 A3
Crompton St W2 89 B1
Cromwell Ave
Hammersmith W6 39 A2
Highgate N6 4 A3
Cromwell Cl
Acton W3 28 B1
2 Gunnersbury W4 37 A1
Cromwell Cres SW5 141 B4
Cromwell Ctr NW10 20 C2
Cromwell Gdns SW7 129 C1
Cromwell Gr W6 39 B3
Cromwell Ho
Battersea SW11 169 C3
Putney SW15 56 C3
Cromwell Hospl (BUPA) SW5 142 A4
Cromwell Lo 40 E1 25 B1
Cromwell Mans SW5 141 C4
Cromwell Mews SW7 143 C4
Cromwell Pl
5 Acton W3 28 B1
Barbican EC1 109 A4
Highgate N6 4 A3
Mortlake SW14 55 B4
South Kensington SW7 143 C4
Cromwell Rd
Brixton SW9 48 A2
South Kensington SW7 143 A4
Cromwell Twr EC2 109 A4
Crondace Rd SW6 165 C3
Crondall Ct 7 N1 24 A3
Crondall Ho SW15 68 C3
Crondall Pl 15 N1 24 A3
Crondall St N1 24 A3
Crone Ct 5 NW6 23 B3
Cronin St SE15 49 B3
Crooked Billet Yd 18 E2 24 A2 98 B4
Crooke Rd SE8 41 A1
Crookham Rd SW6 164 C3
Croom's Hill SE10 52 C3
Croom's Hill Gr SE10 52 B3
Cropley Ct N1 87 B2
Cropley St N1 87 B2
Cropthorne Ct W9 89 A3
Crosby Ct SE1 137 B4
Crosby Ho 18 E14 42 B3
Crosby Row SE1 137 B4
Crosby Sq EC3 110 A2
Crosby Wlk
3 Dalston E8 16 B2
Streatham SE24 74 C4
Crosfield Ct 3 W10 30 C3
Crosfield Ho W11 31 A2 112 A3
Crosland Pl 5 SW11 60 C4
Crossbow Ho 15 N1 24 A4
Cross Cl SE15 50 A1
Cross Ct SE5 63 C4
Crossfield Rd NW3 11 C2
Crossfield St SE8 51 C3
Crossford St SW9 172 C1
Crossharbour Sta E14 42 A3
Cross Keys Cl W1 103 C3
Cross La EC3 124 A3
Crossleigh Ct 3 SE14 51 B3
Crosslet St SE17 151 C4
Crosslet Vale SE10 52 A2
Crossley St N7 14 C2
Crossman Hos 19 SW12 74 A4
Crossmount Ho 13 SE5 48 B3
Cross Rd SE5 49 A1
Cross St
Islington N1 86 B4
Mortlake SW13 56 A4
Crossthwaite Ave SE5, SE24 63 C3
Crosstrees Ho 7 E14 41 C3
Crosswall EC3 124 C4
Crossway E8, N16 16 A3
Crossway Ct SE4 51 A1
Crossways Acad SE4 51 A1
Croston St E8 24 C4
Crouch End Hill N8 4 C4
Crouch Hall Ct N19 5 A3
Crouch Hill N4, N8, N19 5 A4
Crouch Hill Sta N4 5 B4
Crouchmans Cl SE21, SE26 76 C1
Crowder St E1 32 A2
Crowfield Ho N5 15 B4
Crowfoot Cl E9 18 B3
Crowhurst Cl SW9 173 C2
Crowhurst Ho 21 SW9 173 A1
Crowland Ho NW8 78 C3
Crowland Terr N1 15 C1
Crowline Wlk 1 N1 15 B2
Crown Cl
Bow E3 26 C4
Hampstead NW6 11 A2
Crown Close Bsns Ctr 12 E3 26 C4
Crown Ct
City of London EC4 109 A1
4 Putney SW15 57 C3
St Giles WC2 106 B1
Crown Ct *continued*
St John's Wood NW8 90 B3
Crowndale Ct NW1 83 B2
Crowndale Rd NW1 83 A2
Crowne Ho SE1 123 A1
Crownfield Rd E15 19 C4
Crowngate Ho 33 E3 26 B3
Crownhill Rd NW10 21 B4
Crownleigh Ct SW2 62 C2
Crown Lo SW3 144 B3
Crown Mews 9 E1 32 C4
Crown Office Row EC4 121 B4
Crown Pas SW1 119 A1
Crown Pl
Broadgate EC2 110 A4
Kentish Town NW5 13 A2
Crown Reach SW1 147 C1
Crown St
Acton W3 28 A1
Camberwell SE5 48 B3
Crownstone Ct 1 SW2 62 C2
Crownstone Rd SW2 62 C2
Crown Terr TW9 54 B3
Crows Rd E3, E15 27 C2
Crowther Ave TW8 36 A2
Crowther Cl SW6 155 A3
Crowthorne Cl SW18 70 B3
Crowthorne Rd W10 30 C3
Croxley Rd W9 23 B2
Croxted Cl SE21 75 B4
Croxted Rd SE21, SE24 75 C3
Croxteth Ho 11 SW8 171 B2
Croydon Ho SE1 135 C4
Crozier Ho SW8 162 C1
Crozier Terr E9 17 C3
Crucifix La SE1 138 A4
Cruden Ho
15 Bow E3 26 B3
11 Camberwell SE17 48 A4
Cruden St N1 86 B3
Cruickshank St WC1 95 B4
Cruikshank Ho NW8 80 B2
Crusader Ho EC1 96 A1
Crusoe Mews N16 6 C2
Crutched Friars EC3 124 B4
Crystal Palace Rd SE22 64 C2
Crystal Wharf N1 86 B1
Cuba St E14 41 C4
Cubitt Bldg SW1 146 A1
Cubitt Ho 4 SW4 61 B1
Cubitt St WC1 95 A3
Cubitt Terr SW4 61 B4
CUBITT TOWN 42 B2
Cubitt Town Jun & Inf Sch E14 42 B3
Cuddington SE17 151 A4
Cudworth Ho SW8 171 A3
Cudworth St E1 25 A1
Cuffley Ho 3 W10 30 B4
Cuff Point 12 E2 24 B2 98 C4
Culand Ho SE17 152 A3
Culford Gdns SW3 145 A3
Culford Gr N1 16 A2
Culford Mans SW3 145 A3
Culford Mews N1 16 A2
Culford Rd
Kingsland N1 16 A2
Shoreditch N1 24 A4
Culham Ho
21 Paddington W2 31 C4
33 Shoreditch E2 24 B2 98 C3
Cullen Ho W9 23 B3
Cullen Way NW10 20 B1
Culling Rd SE16 40 B3
Cullingworth Rd NW10 9 A3
Culloden Cl 21 SE16 153 C1
Culloden Prim Sch 16 E14 34 B3
Cullum St EC3 124 A4
Culmore Rd SE15 50 B3
Culmstock Rd SW11 60 C2
Culpepper Ct SE11 149 B4
Culross Bldgs NW1 84 A2
Culross St W1 117 B3
Culver Ct SW18 59 A1
Culverden Rd SW12 73 B2
Culverhouse WC1 106 C3
Culverhouse Gdns SW16 74 B1
Culverin Ct 1 N7 14 B3
Culvert Ct SW11 169 B2
Culvert Pl SW11 169 B1
Culvert Rd SW11 169 A2
Culworth Ho NW8 80 A2
Culworth St NW8 80 A1
Cumber Ho SW18 70 C3
Cumberland Ave NW10 20 A2
Cumberland Bsns Pk NW10 20 A2
Cumberland Cl E8 16 B2
Cumberland Cres W14 140 B4
Cumberland Ct W1 103 A1
Cumberland Gate W1 117 A4
Cumberland Gdns WC1 95 B4
Cumberland Ho
Paddington W9 88 C1
1 Putney SW15 69 B4
Cumberland Mans
Marylebone W1 102 C2
7 West Hampstead NW6 10 C3
Cumberland Market NW1 92 B4

Cumberland Mills Sq E14 42 C1
Cumberland Park Ind Est NW10 21 C2
Cumberland Pk W3 28 B2
Cumberland Pl NW1 92 A4
Cumberland Rd
Acton W3 28 B2
Barnes SW13 46 C2
Richmond TW9 44 C3
Cumberland St SW1 146 B2
Cumberland Terr NW1 82 A1
Cumberland Terrace Mews NW1 82 A1
Cumberland Villas W3 28 B2
Cumberland Wharf 12 SE16 40 B4
Cumbrian Gdns NW2 1 A2
Cuming Mus SE17 150 C3
Cumming St N1 85 A1
Cumnor Cl 23 SW9 173 A2
Cunard Pl EC3 110 B1
Cunard Rd NW10 20 C2
Cunard Wlk 3 SE16 41 A2
Cundy St SW1 145 C3
Cunningham Ct W2 89 B1
Cunningham Ho 16 SE5 48 C3
Cunningham Pl NW8 89 B2
Cunnington St W4 37 B2
Cupar Rd SW11 169 C4
Cureton St SW1 147 C3
Curlew Ho
Brockley SE4 66 A3
7 Peckham SE15 49 B2
Curlew St SE1 139 A4
Curness St SE13 67 B3
Curran Ho SW3 144 A3
Curricle St W3 29 A1
Currie Ho 13 SW12 73 C4
Cursitor St EC4 107 B2
Curtain Pl EC2 24 A1 98 B2
Curtain Rd EC2 24 A1 98 B2
Curtis Dr W3 28 C3
Curtis Ho SE17 151 B2
Curtis St SE1 152 C4
Curtis Way SE1 152 C4
Curve Bldg The SE4 66 B2
Curve The W12 29 C2
Curwen Gall W1 105 B3
Curwen Rd W12 38 C4
Curzon Cres NW10 8 A1
Curzon Gate W1 117 C1
Curzon Sq W1 117 C1
Curzon St W1 118 A2
Custance Ho N1 87 B1
Custance St N1 97 B4
Custom House EC3 124 A3
Custom House Reach SE16 41 B3
Cutbush Ho N7 13 C3
Cutcombe Rd SE5 48 B1
Cuthbert Harrowing Ho EC1 96 C1
Cuthbert Ho W2 101 B4
Cuthbert St W2 89 B1
Cuthill Wlk 3 SE5 48 C2
Cutlers Gdns EC2 110 B2
Cutlers Gdns Arc EC2 110 B2
Cutlers Sq E14 41 C2
Cutler St EC2 110 B2
Cut The SE1 135 C4
Cutty Sark SE10 52 B4
Cutty Sark Ho 10 E14 42 A2
Cutty Sark Sta SE10 52 B4
Cuxton Ho SE17 152 B2
Cyclops Mews 12 E14 41 C2
Cygnet Ho NW8 78 C4
Cygnet House N 18 E14 34 A3
Cygnet House S 19 E14 34 A3
Cygnet St E1 24 B1 99 A2
Cygnus Bsns Ctr NW10 8 B2
Cynthia St N1 85 A1
Cyntra Pl 8 E8 17 A1
Cypress Cl 9 E5 7 C2
Cypress Ct 5 E11 19 C4
Cypress Gdns SE4 66 A2
Cypress Ho SE14 50 C2
Cypress Pl W1 93 A1
Cyprus Pl 23 E2 25 B3
Cyprus St E2 25 B3
Cyrena Rd SE22 64 B2
Cyril Jackson Prim Sch (North Bldg) 24 E14 33 B2
Cyril Jackson Prim Sch (South Bldg) 25 E14 33 B2
Cyril Mans SW11 169 A3
Cyril Thatcher Ho SW6 165 C3
Cyrus Ho EC1 96 B2
Cyrus St EC1 96 B2
Czar St SE8 51 C4

D

Dabb's La EC1 95 C1
Dabin Cres SE10 52 B2
Dacca St SE8 51 B4
Dace Rd E3 26 C4
Dacre Ho SW3 157 C3
Dacre St SW1 133 B2
Daffodil St W12 29 B2
Dafforne Rd SW17 72 C1
Dagmar Ct E14 42 B3
Dagmar Gdns NW10 22 C3
Dagmar Pas N1 86 B4
Dagmar Rd
Camberwell SE5 49 A2
Finsbury Pk N4 5 C4
Dagmar Terr N1 86 B4
Dagnall St SW11 169 B3
Dagnan Rd SW12 73 B4
Dagobert Ho 27 E1 32 B4
Daimler Ho 8 E3 26 C1
Dainton Ho 22 W2 31 C4
Daintry Way E9 18 B2
Dairy Cl NW10 21 C4
Dairyman Cl NW2 1 A1
Daisy Dormer Ct 11 SW9 62 B3
Daisy La SW6 58 C4
Dakin Pl 9 E1 33 A4
Dakota bldg 6 SE13 52 A2
Dalberg Rd SW2 62 C2
Dalbury Ho 6 SW9 62 B3
Dalby Rd SW18 59 B3
Dalby St NW5 13 A2
Dalebury Rd SW17 72 B2
Dale Croft N4 6 B1
Dalehaed NW1 82 C1
Daleham Gdns NW3 11 C2
Daleham Mews NW3 11 C2
Dale Ho
London SE4 66 A3
St John's Wood NW8 78 C4
Dalemain Ho 5 SW8 171 C2
Dalemain Mews 12 E16 35 C1
Dale Rd
Camberwell SE17 48 A4
Gospel Oak NW5 12 C3
Dale Row W11 31 A3
Dale St W4 38 A1
Daley Ho 6 W12 30 A3
Daley St E9 17 C2
Daley Thompson Way 7 SW8 61 A4
Dalgarno Gdns W10 30 B4
Dalgarno Way W10 22 B1
Daling Way E3 26 A3
Dalkeith Ct SW1 147 C3
Dalkeith Ho 6 SW9 48 A2
Dalkeith Rd SE21 75 B4
Dalling Rd W6 39 A2
Dallington Sch EC1 96 B2
Dallington St EC1 96 B2
Dalmeny Ave N7 13 C4
Dalmeny Avenue Est 3 N7 13 C4
Dalmeny Ct 4 SW4 172 A2
Dalmeny Rd N7 13 C4
Dalmeyer Rd NW10 8 B2
Dalmore Rd SE21 75 B2
Dalrymple Rd SE4 66 A3
DALSTON 16 C2
Dalston Jct E8 16 B2
Dalston Junction Sta E8 16 A2
Dalston Kingsland Sta E8 16 B3
Dalston La E8 16 C3
Dalton Ho
7 Balham SW12 73 A4
10 Bow E3 26 A3
19 Deptford SE14 50 C4
Dalton St SE27 75 A1
Dalwood St SE5 49 A2
Dalyell Rd SW9 62 B4
Damascene Wlk SE21 75 B3
Damer Ho 9 TW10 54 B1
Damer Terr SW10 157 A1
Dame St N1 86 C2
Damien Ct 12 E1 32 A3
Damien St E1 32 A3
Damory Ho 1 SE16 40 B2
Dan Bryant Ho 5 SW12 73 B4
Danbury St N1 86 B2
Danby Ho
23 Hackney E9 17 B1
3 West Kilburn W10 23 B2
Danby St SE15 64 B4
Dancer Rd
Fulham SW6 164 C3
Richmond TW9 54 C4
Dandridge Cl SE10 43 B1
Dandridge Ho E1 110 C4
Danebury 18 W10 30 B4
Danebury Ave SW15 56 B1
Danecroft Rd SE24 63 C2
Dane Ho 15 SE5 48 B1
Danehurst St SW6 164 A4
Danemere St SW15 57 B4
Dane Pl E3 26 B3
Danes Ct NW8 80 C3
Danesdale Rd E9 18 A2
Danesfield SE5 49 A4
Danes Ho 10 W10 30 B4
Dane St WC1 106 C3
Daneville Rd SE5 48 C2
Daniel Bolt Cl E14 34 A4
Daniel Ct W3 29 A2
Daniel Gdns SE15 49 B3
Daniell Ho N1 87 C2
Daniel's Rd SE15 65 B4
Dan Leno Wlk SW6 156 A1
Dansey Pl W1 119 B4
Dante Pl SE11 150 B3
Dante Rd SE11 150 A4
Danube Ct 13 SE15 49 B3
Danube St SW3 144 B2
Danvers Ho 35 E1 111 C1
Danvers St SW3 157 C3
Da Palma Ct SW6 155 B3
Daphne St SW18 59 B1
Daplyn St 6 E1 111 B4
D'arblay St W1 105 A1
Darcy Ho E8 25 A4
Darell Prim Sch TW9 54 C4
Darell Rd TW9 54 C4
Daren Ct N7 14 A4
Darent Ho NW8 101 C4
Darenth Rd N16 7 B3
Darfield NW1 82 C3
Darfield Rd SE4 66 B2
Darfield Way W10 30 C3
Darfur St 2 SW15 57 C4
Darien Ho
16 London SW11 59 C4
11 Stepney E1 32 C4
Darien Rd SW11 59 C4
Daring Ho 23 E3 26 A3
Darlan Rd SW6 155 A1
Darley Ho SE11 148 C1
Darley Rd SW11 60 B1
Darling Rd SE4 66 C4
Darling Row E1 25 A1
Darlington Ho SW8 161 C1
Darnall Ho 4 SE10 52 B2
Darnay Ho 3 SE16 139 B2
Darnell Ho 9 SE10 52 B3
Darnley Ho 7 E14 33 A3
Darnley Rd E9 17 B2
Darnley Terr 12 W11 30 C1
Darrell Rd SE22 64 C2
Darren Cl N4 5 B4
Darsley Dr SW8 172 A4
Dartford Ho SE1 153 A4
Dartford St SE17 48 B4
Dartington NW1 83 A3
Dartington Ho
Bayswater W2 100 A4
7 London SW8 171 C2
Dartle Ct 29 SE16 139 C3
Dartmoor Wlk 18 E14 41 C2
Dartmouth Cl W11 31 C3
Dartmouth Ct SE10 52 B2
Dartmouth Gr SE10 52 B2
Dartmouth Hill SE10 52 B2
Dartmouth Ho
Dartmouth Pk N19 4 A2
Lewisham SE10 52 B1
DARTMOUTH PARK 4 A1
Dartmouth Park Ave NW5 4 A1
Dartmouth Park Hill N19 4 A2
Dartmouth Park Rd NW5 4 A1
Dartmouth Pl W4 46 A4
Dartmouth Rd NW2 9 C2
Dartmouth Row SE10 52 B2
Dartmouth St SW1 133 C3
Dartmouth Terr SE10 52 C2
Darton Ct W3 28 B1
Dartrey Twr SW10 157 B2
Dartrey Wlk SW10 157 A2
Dart St W10 23 B2
Darville Rd N16 7 B1
Darwen Pl E2 25 A4
Darwin Ct NW1 81 C4
Darwin Ctr SW7 129 B1
Darwin Ho 8 SE13 52 B1
Darwin St SE17 151 C4
Daryngton Ho SW8 162 A1
Dashwood Ho SE21 76 B1
Data Point Bsns Ctr E16 27 C1
Datchelor Pl 14 SE5 48 C2
Datchet Ho NW1 92 B4

Datchett Ho [40] E2 ... 24 B2 98 C3
Datchwood Ct N4 ... 6 B1
Datchworth Ho [8] N1 ... 15 A1
Date St SE17 ... 151 B1
Daubeney Prim Sch E5 ... 18 A4
Daubeney Rd E5 ... 18 A4
Daubeney Twr [2] SE8 ... 41 B1
Dault Rd SW18 ... 59 B1
Dauney Ho SE1 ... 136 A3
Dave Adams Ho [8] E3 ... 26 B3
Davenant Ho [20] E1 ... 111 C4
Davenant Rd N19 ... 4 C2
Davenant St E1 ... 111 C3
Davenport Ho SE11 ... 135 B1
Davenport Mews [6] W12 ... 30 A1
Davenport Rd SE6 ... 67 B1
Daventry St NW1 ... 102 A4
Dave Porter Hts SW19 ... 70 A4
Daver Ct SW3 ... 144 B1
Davern Cl SE10 ... 43 B2
Davey Cl N7 ... 14 B2
Davey Rd E9 ... 18 C1
Davey's Ct WC2 ... 120 A4
Davey St SE15 ... 49 B4
David Devine Ho [7] E8 ... 16 C3
David Game Coll SW7 ... 143 B3
Davidge Ho SE1 ... 135 C3
Davidge St SE1 ... 136 B3
David Hewitt Ho [2] E3 ... 34 A4
David Ho
[8] Putney SW15 ... 56 C2
South Lambeth SW8 ... 162 A2
David Mews W1 ... 103 A4
Davidson Gdns SW8 ... 162 A2
Davidson Ho [7] N19 ... 13 B4
David St E15 ... 19 C3
Davies Laing & Dick Coll W1 ... 103 C2
Davies Mews W1 ... 118 A4
Davies St W1 ... 118 A4
Davina Ho
Brondesbury NW2 ... 10 B2
[14] Hackney E5 ... 17 A3
Da Vinci Ct [12] SE16 ... 40 A1
Davis Ho [35] W12 ... 30 A2
Davis Rd W3 ... 38 B4
Davisville Rd W12 ... 38 C4
Dawes Ho SE17 ... 151 B3
Dawes Rd SW6 ... 154 C2
Dawes St SE17 ... 151 C2
Dawlish Ave SW18 ... 71 A2
Dawlish Rd NW2 ... 9 C2
Dawnay Gdns SW18 ... 71 C2
Dawnay Rd SW17, SW18 ... 71 C2
Dawn Cres E15 ... 27 C4
Dawson Ho
[23] Bethnal Green E2 ... 25 B2
Dawson Ho *continued*
[5] Camberwell SE5 ... 49 A2
Dawson Pl W2 ... 31 C2 113 C4
Dawson Rd NW2 ... 9 B4
Dawson St E2 ... 24 B3
Day Ho [2] SE5 ... 48 B3
Daylesford Ave SW15 ... 56 C3
Daynor Ho [4] NW6 ... 23 C4
Daysbrook Rd SW2 ... 74 B3
Dayton Gr SE15 ... 50 B2
Deacon Ho SE11 ... 149 A3
Deacon Mews N1 ... 15 C1
Deacon Rd NW2 ... 8 C2
Deacon Way SE17 ... 151 A4
Deal Ho
Deptford SE15 ... 50 C4
Walworth SE17 ... 152 B2
Deal Porters Way SE16 ... 40 C3
Deal St E1 ... 111 B4
Dealtry Rd SW15 ... 57 B3
Deal Wlk [3] SW9 ... 163 C1
Dean Bradley St SW1 ... 134 A1
Dean Cl
Hackney E9 ... 17 B3
Rotherhithe SE16 ... 32 C1
Dean Coll of London [4] N7 ... 5 B1
Deancross St E1 ... 32 B3
Dean Ct
Acton W3 ... 28 C3
South Lambeth SW8 ... 162 A1
Deanery Mews W1 ... 117 C2
Deanery St W1 ... 117 C2
Dean Farrar St SW1 ... 133 C2
Deanhill Ct [2] SW14 ... 55 A3
Deanhill Rd SW14 ... 55 A3
Dean Ho
London N4 ... 6 B4
New Cross SE14 ... 51 B3
Stamford Hill N16 ... 7 B3
[18] Stepney E1 ... 32 B3
Dean Rd NW2 ... 9 B2
Dean Ryle St SW1 ... 148 A4
Dean's Bldgs SE17 ... 151 C3
Deans Cl W4 ... 45 A4
Dean's Ct EC4 ... 108 B1
Dean's Gateway [9] SE10 ... 51 C2
Deanshanger Ho [21] SE8 ... 40 C2
Dean's Mews W1 ... 104 B2
Dean St W1 ... 105 B1
Dean Stanley St SW1 ... 134 A1
Dean's Yd SW1 ... 133 C2
Dean Trench St SW1 ... 134 A1
Dearmer Ho [6] SW2 ... 74 C4
Deason St E15 ... 27 B4
Deauville Ct
[14] London SW4 ... 61 B1
[4] Rotherhithe SE16 ... 40 C4
Deauville Mans [13] SW4 ... 61 B1
De Barowe Mews
[4] Highbury N5 ... 15 A4
[1] London N5 ... 15 A3
Debdale Ho [20] E2 ... 24 C4
De Beauvoir Cres N1 ... 24 A4
De Beauvoir Ct N1 ... 15 C1
De Beauvoir Pl [5] N1 ... 16 A2
De Beauvoir Prim Sch [13] N1 ... 16 A2
De Beauvoir Rd N1 ... 16 A1
De Beauvoir Sq N1 ... 16 A1
DE BEAUVOIR TOWN ... 16 A1
Debenham Ct E8 ... 24 C4
Debnams Rd SE16 ... 40 B2
Decima St SE1 ... 138 A2
Deck Cl SE16 ... 32 C1
De Crespigny Pk SE5 ... 48 C1
Deeley Rd SW8 ... 171 B4
Deepdale N4 ... 6 A1
Deepdene Gdns SW2 ... 74 B4
Deepdene Ho N16 ... 6 C3
Deepdene Lo [5] SW2 ... 74 B4
Deepdene Mans SW6 ... 164 C4
Deepdene Rd SE5, SE24 ... 63 C3
Deerbrook Rd SE24, SW2 ... 75 A3
Dee Rd TW9 ... 54 B3
Deerdale Rd SE24 ... 63 B3
Deerhurst Ho [6] SE15 ... 49 C4
Deerhurst Rd NW2 ... 9 C2
Deer Lo SW6 ... 58 A4
Deeside Rd SW17 ... 71 C1
Dee St E14 ... 34 B3
Defoe Ave TW9 ... 44 C3
Defoe Ho
Barbican EC2 ... 108 C4
[5] Stoke Newington N16 ... 7 A1
Defoe Pl EC2 ... 108 C4
Defoe Rd
Rotherhithe SE16 ... 41 B4
Stoke Newington N16 ... 7 A1
De Gama Pl [3] E14 ... 41 C1
Dekker Ho [19] SE5 ... 48 C3
Dekker Rd SE21 ... 64 A1
Delafield Ho [25] E1 ... 111 C1
Delaford Rd SE16 ... 40 A1
Delaford St SW6 ... 154 B3
Delamere Ho [4] N4 ... 6 C4
Delamere Rd W5 ... 36 A4
Delamere St W2 ... 100 C3
Delamere Terr W2 ... 100 B4
Delancey Pas NW1 ... 82 B3
Delancey St NW1 ... 82 B3
Delancey Studios NW1 ... 82 B3
Delany Ho SE10 ... 52 B4
Delarch Ho SE1 ... 136 A3
De Laune St SE17 ... 150 A1
Delaware Rd W9 ... 88 A2
Delawyk Cres SE24 ... 63 C1
Delft Way [2] SE22 ... 64 A2
Delhi St N1 ... 84 B3
Delia St SW18 ... 71 A4
Delius Gr E15 ... 27 B3
Dellafield N4 ... 5 C2
Dell Cl E15 ... 27 C4
Dellow Ho [6] E1 ... 32 A2
Dellow St E1 ... 32 A2
Dell's Mews SW1 ... 147 A3
Deloraine Ho SE8 ... 51 C2
Deloraine St SE8 ... 51 C2
Delorme St W6 ... 47 C4
Delta Bldg [7] E14 ... 34 B3
Delta Ho N1 ... 97 B4
Delta Pk SW18 ... 59 A3
Delta Point [5] E2 ... 24 C2 99 B4
Delta St [4] E2 ... 24 C2 99 B4
Delverton Ho SE17 ... 150 B2
Delverton Rd SE17 ... 150 B1
Delvino Rd SW6 ... 165 C3
De Montfort Ct [1] SW16 ... 74 A1
De Montfort Rd SW16 ... 74 A2
De Morgan Rd SW6 ... 59 A4
Dempster Rd SW18 ... 59 B2
Denbigh Cl W11 ... 31 B2 113 A4
Denbigh Gdns TW10 ... 54 B2
Denbigh Ho
Knightsbridge SW1 ... 131 A2
[7] Notting Hill W11 ... 31 B3
Notting Hill W11 ... 31 B2 113 A4
Denbigh Mews SW1 ... 146 C3
Denbigh Pl SW1 ... 146 C2
Denbigh Rd W11 ... 31 B2 113 A4
Denbigh St SW1 ... 147 A2
Denbigh Terr W11 ... 31 B2 113 A4
Denbury Ho [43] E3 ... 27 A2
Denby Ct SE11 ... 149 A4
Dence Ho [15] E2 ... 24 C2 99 B3
Denchworth Ho [14] SW9 ... 173 B1
Dene Cl SE4 ... 66 A3
Denehurst Gdns
Acton W3 ... 28 A1
Richmond TW10 ... 54 C3
Dene Mans [1] NW6 ... 10 C2
Denesmead SE24 ... 63 B2
Denewood Rd N6 ... 3 B4
Dengie Wlk N1 ... 86 C4
Denham Ho [32] W12 ... 30 A2
Denham St SE10 ... 43 C1
Denholme Rd W9 ... 23 B2
Denland Ho SW8 ... 163 A1
Denman Ho [1] N16 ... 7 A2
Denman Rd SE15 ... 49 B1
Denman St W1 ... 119 B3
Denmark Gr N1 ... 85 B2
Denmark Hill SE5 ... 48 C1
Denmark Hill Sta SE5 ... 48 C1
Denmark Mans [14] SE5 ... 48 B1
Denmark Pl
[2] Bromley E3 ... 26 C2
Soho WC2 ... 105 C2
Denmark Rd
Camberwell SE5 ... 48 B1
Kilburn NW6 ... 23 B3
Denmark St WC2 ... 105 C2
Denmead Ho SW15 ... 56 B1
Denne Terr E8 ... 24 B4
Dennett's Gr SE14 ... 50 C1
Dennett's Rd SE14 ... 50 B2
Denning Cl NW8 ... 89 A3
Denning Mews SW12 ... 60 C1
Denning Point E1 ... 111 A2
Denning Rd NW3 ... 11 C4
Dennington Park Mansions [12] NW6 ... 10 C3
Dennington Park Rd NW6 ... 10 C2
Dennis Ct SE10 ... 52 B2
Dennis Ho [4] E3 ... 26 B3
Dennison Point E15 ... 19 B1
Dennis Severs' House E1 ... 110 B4
Dennis Way SW4 ... 61 C4
Denny Cres SE11 ... 149 C2
Denny St SE11 ... 149 C2
Densham Ho NW8 ... 79 C1
Denstone Ho [5] SE15 ... 49 C4
Dent Ho SE17 ... 152 A3
Denton NW1 ... 12 C2
Denton Ho N1 ... 15 A1
Denton St SW18 ... 59 A1
Dents Rd SW11 ... 60 B1
Denver Rd N16 ... 7 A4
Denyer Ho [1] NW5 ... 13 A4
Denyer St SW3 ... 144 B4
Denys Bldg EC1 ... 107 B4
Denzil Rd NW10 ... 8 B3
Deodar Rd SW15 ... 58 A3
Depot App NW2 ... 9 C4
Depot Rd W12 ... 30 B2
Depot St SE5 ... 48 C4
DEPTFORD ... 50 C3
Deptford Bridge SE8 ... 51 C2
Deptford Bridge Sta SE8 ... 51 C2
Deptford Broadway SE8, SE14 ... 51 C2
Deptford Church St SE8 ... 51 C3
Deptford Ferry Rd [24] E14 ... 41 C2
Deptford Gn SE8 ... 51 C4
Deptford Green Sch SE14 ... 51 B3
Deptford Green Sch (Annex) [12] SE14 ... 51 A3
Deptford High St SE8 ... 51 C3

Deptford Park Prim Sch 2 SE8 41 A1
Deptford Sta SE8 51 C3
Deptford Trad Est SE8 51 A4
Deptford Wharf SE8 41 B2
De Quincey Mews 3 E16 35 C1
Derby Ct 8 E5 17 C4
Derby Gate SW1 134 A4
Derby Ho SE11 149 B4
Derby Rd
- Mortlake SW14 55 A3
- South Hackney E9 25 C4

Derbyshire St E2 24 C2 99 C3
Derby St W1 117 C1
Dereham Ho 7 SE4 65 C3
Dereham Pl EC2 24 A1 98 B2
Derek Walcott Cl SE24 63 A2
Dericote St E8 25 A4
Dering St W1 104 B1
Dermody Gdns SE13 67 C2
Dermody Rd SE13 67 C2
Deronda Rd SE24, SW2 75 A3
Derrick Ho 13 SW2 74 C3
Derrycombe Ho 18 W2 31 C4
Derry St W8 128 A3
Dersingham Rd NW2 1 A1
Derwent NW1 92 C3
Derwent Ct
- 2 Hammersmith W6 38 C2
- 8 Rotherhithe SE16 40 C4

Derwent Gr SE22 64 B3
Derwent Ho
- South Kensington SW7 143 A4
- Tower Hamlets E3 26 B1

Derwent St SE10 43 A1
Derwentwater Mans 2 W3 28 B1
Derwentwater Prim Sch W3 28 B1
Derwentwater Rd W3 28 B1
Desborough Cl W2 100 B4
Desborough Ho W14 155 A4
Desenfans Rd SE21 64 A1
Design Mus SE1 139 A4
Desmond St SE14 51 A4
Despard Ho SW2 74 C2
Despard Rd N19 4 B3
Desvignes Dr SE13 67 C1
Dethick Ct E3 26 A4
Detling Ho SE17 152 A3
Devas St E3 27 A1
Deventer Cres 8 SE22 64 A2
De Vere Cotts W8 128 C2
De Vere Gdns W8 128 C3
Deverell St SE1 137 B1
De Vere Mews W8 128 C2
Devereux Ct WC2 107 B1
Devereux Ho 7 SW15 56 C2
Devereux La SW13 47 A3
Devereux Rd SW11 60 B1
Devitt Ho 5 E14 34 A2
Devizes St N1 87 C3
Devonhurst Pl 4 W4 37 C1
Devonia Rd N1 86 B2
Devon Mans SE1 138 B4
Devonport W2 102 A2
Devonport Ho
- Greenwich SE10 52 B4
- 23 Paddington W2 31 C4

Devonport Rd W12 39 A4
Devonport St E1 32 C3
Devonshire Cl W1 104 A4
Devonshire Ct
- 14 Balham SW12 73 A4
- 6 Richmond TW9 44 B2

Devonshire Dr SE10 52 A2
Devonshire Gdns W4 45 B3
Devonshire Gr SE15 50 A4
Devonshire Hall 15 E9 17 B2
Devonshire Ho
- Brondesbury NW6 10 B2
- Newington SE1 136 C2
- Paddington W2 101 C4
- 2 Putney SW15 69 B4
- Westminster SW1 147 C2

Devonshire House Prep Sch NW3 11 B3
Devonshire Mews 2 W4 38 A1
Devonshire Mews N W1 104 A4
Devonshire Mews S W1 104 A4
Devonshire Mews W W1 103 C4
Devonshire Pl
- Child's Hill NW2 1 C1
- Kensington W8 128 A1
- Marylebone W1 103 C4

Devonshire Place Mews W1 103 C4
Devonshire Rd W4 38 A1
Devonshire Row EC2 110 B3
Devonshire Row Mews W1 92 B1
Devonshire Sq EC2 110 B2
Devonshire St
- Chiswick W4 38 A1
- Marylebone W1 104 A4

Devonshire Terr W2 101 A1
Devons Rd E3 27 A1
Devons Road Sta E3 27 A1
Devon St SE15 50 A4
De Walden Ho NW8 80 A2
De Walden St W1 103 C3
Dewar St SE15 64 C4
Dewberry St E14 34 B4
Dewey Rd N1 85 B2
Dewhurst Rd W14 39 C3
Dewsbury Ct 5 W4 37 B2
Dewsbury Rd NW10 8 C3
Dewsbury Terr NW1 82 B4
D'eynsford Rd SE5 48 C2
Dhonau Ho SE16 153 A4
Diadem Ct W1 105 B2
Dial Wlk The W8 128 B4
Diamond Est SW17 72 A1
Diamond Ho 22 E3 26 A3
Diamond St SE15 49 A3
Diamond Terr SE10 52 B2
Diana Cl 27 SE8 51 B4
Diana Ho
- Barnes SW13 46 B2
- 4 Brixton SW2 62 B2

Diana, Princess of Wales Meml Fountain W2 129 C4
Diana, Princess of Wales Meml Wlk W2 114 C1
Dibden Ho 8 SE5 49 A3
Dibden St N1 86 C4
Dibdin Ho W9 78 A1
Dicey Ave NW2 9 B4
Dickens Ct EC1 96 A1
Dickens Ho
- Bloomsbury WC1 94 A2
- Kennington SE17 150 B1
- Kilburn NW6 23 C2
- Paddington NW8 89 C2

Dickenson Rd N8 5 A4
Dickens Sq SE1 137 A2
Dickens St SW8 170 B2
Dickinson Ho 18 E2 24 C2 99 B3
Dicksee Ho NW8 89 B1
Dick Shepherd Ct 17 SW2 62 C1
Dickson Ho 4 E1 32 A3
Didbin Ho N7 5 B2
Digby Bsns Ctr E9 17 C2
Digby Cres N4 6 B2
Digby Mans W6 39 B1
Digby Rd E9 17 C2
Digby St E2 25 B2
Diggon St E1 32 C4
Dighton Ct SE17 48 B4
Dighton Rd SW18 59 B3
Dignum St N1 85 B2
Digswell St N7 14 C2
Dilke St SW3 159 A4
Dilston Gr SE16 40 B2
Dilton Gdns SW15 69 A3
Dimes Pl 9 W6 39 A2
Dimson Cres E3 26 C2
Dinerman Ct NW8 79 A4
Dingle Gdns E14 33 C2
Dingley La SW16 73 C2
Dingley Pl EC1 97 A3
Dingley Rd EC1 96 C3
Dingwall Rd SW18 71 B4
Dinmont Ho 27 E2 24 C3
Dinmont St 1 E2 25 A3
Dinmore Ho 6 E9 25 B4
Dinnington Ho 17 E1 25 A1
Dinsdale Rd SE3 53 B4
Dinsmore Rd SW12 73 A4
Dinton Ho NW8 90 A2
Dinwiddy Ho N1 84 C1
Dionis Ho SW6 165 B2
Disbrowe Rd W6 154 B3
Discovery Bsns Pk 13 SE16 139 C1
Discovery Dock E E14 42 A4
Discovery Ho 1 E14 34 B2
Disney Pl SE1 137 A4
Disney St SE1 137 A4
Disraeli Cl 1 W4 37 C2
Disraeli Gdns SW15 58 B3
Disraeli Rd
- Acton NW10 20 C3
- Putney SW15 58 A3

Diss St E2 24 B2 98 C4
Distaff La EC4 122 C4
Distillery La W6 39 B1
Distillery Rd W6 39 B1
Distillery Wlk 14 TW8 44 A4
Distin St SE11 149 B3
Ditchburn St E14 34 B2
Ditton Ho 10 E5 17 A3
Divis Way SW15 57 A1
Dixon Clark Ct N1 15 A2
Dixon Ho 20 NW10 30 C3
Dixon Rd SE14 51 A2
Dixon's Alley 10 SE16 40 A4
Dixon Way 9 NW10 8 A1
Dobree Ave NW10 9 A1
Dobson Cl NW6 11 C1
Dobson Ho 18 SE14 50 C4
Doby Ct EC4 123 A4
Dockers Tanner Rd 26 E14 41 C2
Dockhead SE1 139 A3
Dockhead Wharf SE1 139 A4
Dock Hill Ave SE16 40 C4
Docklands Ct 20 E14 33 B3
Docklands Visitor Ctr E14 42 B4
Dockley Rd SE16 139 B1
Dockley Road Ind Est 11 SE16 139 B1
Dock Offices 12 SE16 40 B3
Dock Rd E16 35 B2
Dock St E1 125 B4
Doctor Spurstowe Almshouses 9 E8 17 A2
Docura Ho N7 5 B2
Docwras Bldgs N1 16 A2
Dodbrooke Rd SE27 75 A1
Dodd Ho 18 SE16 40 A2
Doddington Gr SE17 150 B1
Doddington Pl 4 SE17 48 A4
Dodson St SE1 135 C3
Dod St E14 33 C3
Dog & Duck Yd WC1 106 A4
Dog Kennel Hill SE22 64 A4
Dog Kennel Hill Sch 23 SE22 64 A4
Dog La NW10 8 A4
Dolben Ct SW1 147 C3
Dolben St SE1 122 B1
Dolby Rd SW6 164 C1
Doleman Ho 19 SE10 52 A2
Dolland Ho SE11 149 A1
Dolland St SE11 149 A1
Dollar Bay E14 42 B4
DOLLIS HILL 9 A4
Dollis Hill Sta NW2 8 C3
Dolman Rd W4 37 C2
Dolman St SW4 62 B3
Dolphin Cl 2 SE16 40 C4
Dolphin Ct N7 13 C4
Dolphin La E14 34 A2
Dolphin Sch SW11 60 B2
Dolphin Sq SW1 147 A1
Dolphin Twr 21 SE8 51 B4
Dombey Ho
- 13 Bermondsey SE1 139 B3
- 4 Shepherd's Bush W11 30 C1

Dombey St WC1 106 C4
Domelton Ho SW18 59 A1
Domett Cl SE5 63 C3
Domfe Pl E5 17 B4
Domingo St EC1 96 C1
Dominion St EC2 109 C4
Donaghue Cotts 11 E14 33 A4
Donaldson Rd NW6 23 B4
Donegal Ho 2 E1 25 B1
Donegal St N1 85 A1
Doneraile Ho SW1 146 A1
Doneraile St SW6 47 C2
Dongola Rd E1 33 A4
Don Gratton Ho 23 E1 111 B3
Donkey Alley SE22 64 C1
Donkin Ho 15 SE16 40 A2
Donne Ct SE24 63 B1
Donne Ho
- 18 Canonbury N16 15 C4
- 14 Deptford SE14 50 C4
- 11 Poplar E14 33 C3

Donnelly Ct SW6 154 B2
Donne Pl SW3 144 B4
Donnington Ct
- 11 Camden Town NW1 13 A1
- Willesden NW10 9 A1

Donnington Ho 12 SW8 171 B2
Donnington Prim Sch NW10 22 A4
Donnington Rd NW10 22 A4
Donovan Ct SW7 143 B1
Donovan Ho 4 E1 32 B2
Don Phelan Cl SE5 48 C2

Doon St SE1 121 B2
Doradus Ct 20 SW19 69 C3
Dora Ho
11 Shepherd's Bush W11 30 C2
1 Tower Hamlets E14 33 B3
Dorando Cl W12 30 A2
Doran Wlk
Stratford E15 19 B1
Stratford Marsh E15 27 B4
Dora St E14 33 B3
Dorcas Ct 9 SW18 59 C3
Dorchester Ct
1 De Beauvoir Town N1 16 A1
Herne Hill SE24 63 B2
Knightsbridge SW1 131 A1
5 Streatham SW16 74 A2
Dorchester Dr SE24 63 B2
Dorchester Gr W4 38 B1
Dorchester Ho TW9 45 A3
Dordrecht Rd W3 29 A1
Doria Rd SW6 165 A2
Doric Ho 7 E2 25 C3
Doric Way NW1 93 B4
Doris Emmerton Ct SW18 59 B3
Dorking Cl SE8 51 B4
Dorking Ho SE1 137 C2
Dorland Ct SW15 58 B1
Dorlcote Rd SW18 72 A4
Dorleston Ct N1 87 C4
Dorman Way NW8 79 B4
Dormay St SW18 59 A2
Dormstone Ho SE17 152 A3
Dornberg Cl SE3 53 C3
Dorncliffe Rd SW6 164 B2
Dorney NW3 12 A1
Dorney Ct SW6 58 A4
Dornfell St NW6 10 B3
Dornoch Ho 26 E3 26 B3
Dornton Rd SW12, SW17 73 B2
Dorothy Charrington Ho 1 SE22 64 C2
Dorothy Rd SW11 60 B4
Dorrell Pl 18 SW9 62 C4
Dorrien Wlk SW16 73 C2
Dorrington Point 20 E3 27 A2
Dorrington St EC1 107 B4
Dorrit Ho 2 W11 30 C1
Dorrit St SE1 137 A4
Dorset Bldgs EC4 108 A1
Dorset Cl NW1 102 C4
Dorset Ct 3 N1 16 A1
Dorset Mans 2 W6 47 C4
Dorset Mews SW1 132 A2
Dorset Pl E15 19 C2
Dorset Rd SW8 162 C2
Dorset Rise EC4 108 A1
Dorset Sq NW1 90 C1
Dorset St W1 103 A3
Dorton Cl 6 SE15 49 A3
Dorville Cres W6 39 A3
Doughty Ct 11 E1 32 A1
Doughty Mews WC1 94 C1
Doughty St WC1 94 C1
Douglas Bldgs SE1 137 A4
Douglas Ct 5 NW6 10 C1
Douglas Gracey Ho 1 SW18 70 A4
Douglas Ho
Putney SW15 56 C1
Westminster SW1 147 B3
Douglas Johnstone Ho SW6 154 C3
Douglas Mews NW2 1 A1
Douglas Path E14 42 B1
Douglas Rd
Islington N1 15 B1
Kilburn NW6 23 B4
5 Newham E16 35 C4
Douglas Rd N N1 15 B2
Douglas Rd S N1 15 B2
Douglas St SW1 147 B3
Douglas Waite Ho NW6 11 A1
Douglas Way SE8 51 B3
Doulton Ho SE11 149 A4
Doulton Mews 4 NW6 11 A2
Dounesforth Gdns SW18 71 A3
Douro Pl W8 128 B2
Douro St E3 26 C3
Douthwaite Sq 11 E1 125 C2
Dovecote Gdns 8 SW14 55 C4
Dove Ct EC2 109 B1
Dovedale Cotts 6 SW11 168 C2
Dovedale Ho N16 6 C4
Dovedale Rd SE22 65 A1
Dovehouse St SW3 144 A1
Dove Mews SW7 143 A2
Dovercourt Rd SE22 64 B1
Dover Ct
Clerkenwell EC1 96 A2
17 Greenwich SE10 52 A2
Dove Rd N1 15 C2
Doverfield Rd SW2 74 A4
Dover Flats SE1 152 B3
Dover Ho
Brixton SE5 48 A2
11 Deptford SE15 50 B4
Dover House Rd SW15 57 A2
Dover Mans 16 SW9 62 C4
Dove Row E2 24 C4
Dover Park Dr SW15 57 A1
Dover St W1 118 C2
Dover Terr TW9 44 C1
Dover Yd W1 118 C2
Doves Yd N1 85 B3
Dovet Ct SW8 172 C4
Doveton Ho 7 E1 25 B1
Doveton St 8 E1 25 B1
Dove Wlk SW1 145 B2
Dovey Lo 4 N1 14 C1
Dowdeny Cl 12 NW5 13 B3
Dowdeswell Cl SW15 56 A3
Dowding Ho N6 3 C4
Dowell Ho SE21 76 B1
Dowes Ho 13 SW16 74 A1
Dowgate Hill EC4 123 B4
Dowland St W10 23 A2
Dowlas St SE5 49 A3
Dowlen Ct 14 E14 41 C4
Dowler Ho 32 E1 111 C1
Downbarton Ho 11 SW9 173 B4
Downbury Mews 13 SW18 58 C2
Downend Ct 1 SE15 49 A4
Downer's Cotts SW4 61 B3
Downey Ho 6 E1 25 C1
Downfield Cl W9 88 A1
Downham Ct 1 N1 15 C1
Downham Rd N1 15 C1
Downing Ho
2 North Kensington W10 30 C3
4 Putney SW15 56 C2
Downing St SW1 134 A4
Down Pl W6 39 A1
Down St Mews W1 118 A1
Downs Ct 16 E8 17 A3
Downsell Prim Sch E15 19 C4
Downsell Rd E15 19 C4
Downshire Hill NW3 11 C4
Downside 2 SW15 58 A2
Downside Cres NW3 12 A3
Downs La 2 E5 17 A4
Downs Park Rd E5, E8 16 C3
Downs Rd E5, N16 16 C4
Down St W1 118 A1
Downsview Sch E5 17 A4
Downton Ave SW2 74 B2
Downtown Rd SE16 41 A4
Dowrey St N1 85 B4
Dowson Cl SE5 63 C3
Dowson Ct SE13 67 C4
Dowson Ho 8 E1 32 C3
Doyce St SE1 136 C4
Doyle Gdns NW10 22 A4
Doyle Ho W3 37 A4
D'Oyley St SW1 145 B4
Doynton St N19 4 A2
Draco St SE17 48 B4
Dragon Ct WC2 106 B2
Dragon Rd SE15 49 A4
Dragon Yd WC1 106 B2
Dragoon Rd SE8 41 B1
Dragor Rd NW10 20 B1
Drake Cl 30 SE16 40 C4
Drake Croft N16 6 C2
Drake Ct 5 W12 39 A4
Drakefell Rd SE4, SE14 65 C4
Drakefield Rd SW17 72 C1
Drake Ho
2 Limehouse E14 33 A2
20 Stepney E1 32 B4
Drakeley Ct N5 15 A4
Drake Rd SE4 66 C4
Drakes Ctyd NW6 10 B1
Drake St WC1 106 C3
Drama Ctr London EC1 95 C1
Draper Ho SE1 150 B4
Draper Pl N1 86 B4
Drapers Almhouses 5 E3 26 C2
Drapers Gdns EC2 109 C2
Drapers Rd E15 19 C4
Drappers Way 8 SE16 153 C4
Draycott Ave SW3 144 B3
Draycott Cl SE5 48 C3
Draycott Ct SW11 168 A4
Draycott Ho SW3 144 C3
Draycott Pl SW3 144 C3
Draycott Terr SW3 145 A3
Drayford Cl W9 23 B1
Dray Gdns SW2 62 B2
Draymans Ct 4 SW9 62 B4
Draymans Mews SE15 49 B1
Drayson Mews W8 127 C3
Drayton Ct SW10 143 A1
Drayton Gdns SW10 143 A1
Drayton Ho 14 SE5 48 C3
Drayton Park Mews 12 N5 14 C3
Drayton Park Prim Sch 13 N5 14 C3
Drayton Park Sta N5 14 C3
Drayton Pk N5, N7 14 C4
Drayton Rd NW10 21 B4
DRCA Business Ctr SW11 169 C3
Dreadnought St SE10 43 A3
Dresden Cl NW6 11 A2
Dresden Ho
5 Clapham SW11 169 B2
Lambeth SE11 149 A4
Dresden Rd N19 4 C3
Dressington Ave SE4 66 C1
Drewett Ho 31 E1 111 C1
Drew Ho 12 SW16 74 A1
Drewstead La SW16 73 C2
Drewstead Rd SW16 73 C2
Driffield Rd E3 26 A3
Driftway Ho 19 E3 26 B3
Drinkwater Ho 11 SE5 48 C3
Drive Mans 1 SW6 164 B2
Drive The
Acton W3 28 B3
Harlesden NW10 21 B4
Hendon NW11 1 A4
Islington N7 14 B2
Dr Johnson Ave SW17 73 A1
Dr Johnson's House EC4 107 C1
Droitwich Cl SE26 76 C1
Dromore Rd SW15 58 A1
Dron Ho E1 32 B4
Droop St W10 23 A1
Drovers Ct SE13 67 B4
Drovers Pl SE15 50 A3
Drovers Way N7 14 A2
Druce Rd SE21 64 A1
Druid St SE1 138 C3
Drummer Lo N7 5 B1
Drummond Cres NW1 93 B4
Drummond Gate SW1 147 C2
Drummond Ho 13 E2 24 C3
Drummond Rd SE16 40 A3
Drummonds Pl TW9 54 A3
Drummond St NW1 92 C2
Drury Ho SW8 170 C4
Drury La WC2 106 B1
Dryad St SW15 57 C4
Dryburgh Ho SW1 146 B2
Dryburgh Mans SW15 57 B4
Dryburgh Rd SW15 57 B4
Dryden Bldg 10 E1 111 B2
Dryden Cl SW4 61 C2
Dryden Ct SE11 149 C3
Dryden Ho
6 Camberwell SE5 49 A2
16 Stoke Newington N16 7 A1
Dryden St WC2 106 B1
Dryfield Wlk 1 SE8 51 C4
Drysdale Flats 3 E8 16 B3
Drysdale Ho 19 E2 24 A2 98 B4
Drysdale Pl N1 24 A2 98 B4
Drysdale St N1 24 A2 98 B4
Dublin Ave E8 24 C4
Ducal St 25 E2 24 B2 99 A3
Ducane Cl 6 W12 30 B3
Du Cane Ct SW12 72 C3
Du Cane Rd W12 29 C3
Ducavel Ho SW2 74 B3
Duchess Mews W1 104 B3
Duchess of Bedford Ho W8 127 B4
Duchess of Bedford's Wlk W8 127 B3
Duchess St W1 104 B3
Duchy St SE1 121 C2
Ducie Ho 2 SW15 57 B2
Ducie St SW4 62 B3
Duckett St E1 33 A4
Duck La W1 105 B1
Du Cros Rd W3 29 A1

DUDDEN HILL 8 C3
Dudden Hill La NW10 ...... 8 B3
Dudley Ct
Marylebone W1 ... 102 C1
St Giles WC2 ...... 106 A2
Dudley Ho
13 Brixton SW9 ... 173 B2
Paddington W2 .... 101 B3
Dudley Mews 14 SW2 ...... 62 C1
Dudley Rd
Kilburn NW6 .... 23 B3
Richmond TW9 ...... 44 B1
Dudley St W2 .... 101 B3
Dudmaston Mews SW3 ...... 143 C2
Duffell Ho SE11 .. 149 A1
Dufferin Ave EC1 .. 97 B1
Dufferin Ct EC1 .... 97 B1
Dufferin St EC1 .... 97 A1
Duffield Ho N4 ...... 6 B4
Duff Miller Coll SW7 ...... 129 A1
Duff St E14 .... 34 A3
Dufour's Pl W1 ... 105 A1
Dugard Way SE11 150 A3
Dugdale Ho 10 N7 .. 13 C3
Duke Humphrey Rd SE3 ...... 53 A1
Duke of Wellington Pl SW1, W1 ...... 131 C4
Duke of York's Sq SW3 ...... 145 A3
Duke of York St SW1 ...... 119 A2
Duke Rd W4 .... 37 C1
Duke St Hill SE1 .. 123 C2
Duke St St James's SW1 ...... 119 A2
Duke's Ave W4 ..... 37 C1
Dukes Ct
Dulwich SE22 .... 76 C3
East Dulwich SE22 ... 65 A2
Lewisham SE13 ..... 52 B1
Mortlake SW14 ..... 45 C1
Dukes Gate 4 W4 .. 37 B2
Dukes Head Yd N6 ... 4 A3
Duke's Ho SW1 .... 147 C4
Duke Shore Wharf E14 ...... 33 B2
Dukes La W8 ..... 128 A4
Duke's Mews W1 103 C2
Duke's Pl EC3 .... 110 B1
Dukes Point N6 ..... 4 A3
Duke's Rd WC1 .... 93 C3
Duke St W1 ...... 103 C1
Duke Street Mans W1 ...... 103 C1
Duke's Yd W1 .... 117 C4
Dulas St N4 .... 5 B3
Dulford St W11 ...... 31 A2 112 A4
Dulka Rd SW11 ..... 60 B2
Dulverton NW1 .... 83 A3
Dulverton Mans WC1 ...... 95 A1
DULWICH 76 A1
Dulwich Coll SE21 .. 76 A2
Dulwich Coll Prep Sch SE21 ...... 76 A1
Dulwich Com Hospl SE22 ...... 64 A3
Dulwich Comm SE21 ...... 76 A3
Dulwich Hamlet Jun Sch SE21 ...... 63 C1
Dulwich Lawn Cl SE22 ...... 64 B2
Dulwich L Ctr SE22 ...... 64 C3
Dulwich Mead SE24 ...... 63 B1
Dulwich Mews
1 East Dulwich SE22 ...... 64 B3
East Dulwich SE22 ... 64 B2
Dulwich Oaks The SE21 ...... 76 B1
Dulwich Picture Gall SE21 ...... 76 A4
Dulwich Rd SE24 ... 63 A1
DULWICH VILLAGE 76 A4
Dulwich Village SE21 ...... 64 A1
Dulwich Village CE Inf Sch SE21 ...... 64 A1
Dumain Ct SE11 .. 150 A3
Du Maurier Ho 2 NW3 ...... 12 B3
Dumbarton Ct 16 SW2 ...... 74 A4
Dumbarton Rd SW2 ...... 62 A1
Dumont Rd N16 ..... 7 A1
Dumphreys Ho 5 SW4 ...... 73 C4
Dumpton Pl NW1 ... 12 C1
Dunbar St SE27 ..... 75 B1
Dunbar Wharf 20 E14 ...... 33 B2
Dunboyne Rd NW3 . 12 B3
Dunbridge Ho SW15 ...... 56 B1
Dunbridge St
Bethnal Green E2 ...... 24 C1 99 C2
Bethnal Green E2 .... 25 A1
Duncan Ct 3 E14 ... 34 B4
Duncan Gr W3 ..... 29 A3
Duncan Ho 3 NW3 ...... 12 B1
Duncannon Ho SW1 ...... 147 C1
Duncannon St WC2 ...... 120 A3
Duncan Rd
Hackney E8 .... 25 A4
Richmond TW9 ...... 54 A3
Duncan St N1 ..... 86 A2
Duncan Terr N1 ... 86 A2
Dunch St 33 E1 .... 32 A3
Duncombe Ho 7 SW19 ...... 69 C3
Duncombe Prim Sch N19 ...... 5 A3
Duncombe Rd N19 .. 4 C3
Duncrievie Rd SE13 ...... 67 C1
Dundalk Ho 2 E1 .. 32 B3
Dundalk Rd SE4 .... 66 A4
Dundas Ho 12 E2 ... 25 B3
Dundas Rd SE15 .... 50 B1
Dundee Ct 36 E1 ... 32 A1
Dundee Ho W9 .... 88 C4
Dundee St E1 ...... 32 A1
Dundee Wharf E14 ...... 33 B2
Dundonald Rd NW10 ...... 22 C4
Dundry Ho 8 SE26 ...... 76 C1
Dunelm Gr SE27 .... 75 B1
Dunelm St E1 ...... 32 C3
Dunford Rd N7 ..... 14 B4
Dungarvan Ave SW15 ...... 56 C3
Dungeness Ho SW18 ...... 59 B3
Dunhill Point 12 SW15 ...... 69 A3
Dunkeld Ho 15 E14 ...... 34 C3
Dunlace Rd E5 ..... 17 C4
Dunlin Ct 12 SE21 .. 75 C2
Dunlin Ho 13 SE16 .. 40 C2
Dunloe Ct 7 E2 .... 24 B3
Dunloe St E2 .... 24 B3
Dunlop Pl SE16 ... 139 A1
Dunmore Point 15 E2 ...... 24 B2 98 C3
Dunmore Rd NW6 .. 23 A4
Dunmow Ho SE11 149 A2
Dunmow Rd E15 .... 19 C4
Dunmow Wlk N1 .. 86 C4
Dunnage Cres SE16 ...... 41 A2
Dunne Mews 11 NW5 ...... 13 B3
Dunnet Ho 27 E3 ... 26 B3
Dunnico Ho SE17 152 A2
Dunnock Ct 11 SE21 ...... 75 C2
Dunn's Pas WC1 .. 106 B2
Dunn St E8 .... 16 B3
Dunollie Pl NW5 .... 13 B3
Dunollie Rd NW5 ... 13 B3
Dunoon Ho N1 .... 84 C3
Dunraven Ho 12 TW9 ...... 44 B2
Dunraven Rd W12 .. 29 C1
Dunraven Sch SW16 ...... 74 B1
Dunraven St W1 .. 117 A4
Dunrobin Ct NW3 ... 11 A3
Dunsany Rd W14 ... 39 C3
Dunsfold Ho 4 SW2 ...... 74 B4
Dunsford Way SW15 ...... 57 A1
Dunsmure Rd N16 ... 7 A3
Dunstable Ct 3 SE3 ...... 53 C3
Dunstable Mews W1 ...... 103 C4
Dunstable Rd TW10, TW9 ...... 54 A3
Dunstall Ho 9 SE15 ...... 49 C2
Dunstan Ho SE4 .... 51 B1
Dunstan Hos 5 E1 ...... 32 B4
Dunstan Rd NW11 ... 1 C3
Dunstan's Gr SE22 .. 65 A1
Dunstan's Rd SE22 . 64 C1
Dunster Ct EC3 ... 124 B4
Dunster Gdns NW6 ...... 10 B1
Dunsterville Way SE1 ...... 137 C3
Dunston Rd
Clapham SW11 .... 169 C1
Hackney E8 .... 24 B4
Dunston St E8 ...... 24 B4
Dunton Ho 14 SW16 ...... 74 A1
Dunton Rd SE1 ... 152 C3
Duntshill Rd SW18 .. 71 A3
Dunworth Mews W11 ...... 31 B3
Duplex Ride SW1 131 A3
Durand Gdns SW9 ...... 173 A3
Durand Prim Sch SW9 ...... 173 A4
Durant St E2 . 24 C2 99 B4
Durban Ho 28 W12 ...... 30 A2
Durdans Ho 3 NW1 ...... 13 B1
Durfey Pl SE5 ...... 48 C3
Durford Cres SW15 ...... 69 A3
Durham Ct
Brockley SE4 .... 66 C4
4 Kilburn NW6 ..... 23 C3
Durham Ho
7 Dartmouth Pk NW5 ...... 4 B1
Lisson Gr NW8 ..... 90 B3
Durham House St WC2 ...... 120 B3
Durham Pl SW3 .. 144 C1
Durham Rd N4, N7 ... 5 B2
Durham Row E1 .... 33 A4
Durham St SE11 .. 162 C4
Durham Terr W2 .. 100 A2
Durley Rd N16 .... 7 A4
Durlock Ho 16 SW9 ...... 173 B4
Durlston Rd E5 ...... 7 C2
Durnford St 4 SE10 ...... 52 B4
Durnsford Ave SW18, SW19 ...... 70 C2
Durnsford Rd SW18, SW19 ...... 70 C1
Durrell Rd SW6 ... 164 C3
Durrels Ho W14 .. 141 A4
Durrington Rd E5 .. 18 A4
Durrington Twr 3 SW8 ...... 171 A2
Durrisdeer Ho NW2 ...... 10 B4
Durston NW5 .... 12 C3
Durward St E1 ..... 32 A4
Durweston Mews W1 ...... 103 A4
Durweston St W1 103 A3
Dutch Yd SW18 ..... 58 C2
Dutton Ho SW2 ..... 75 A3
Dutton St SE10 ..... 52 B2
Dwight Ct 3 SW6 164 B2
Dycer Ho 10 E9 ..... 17 C2
Dye House La E3 ... 26 C4
Dyer Ho SE4 .... 51 A1
Dyer's Bldgs EC1 . 107 B3
Dyer's La SW15 ..... 57 A3
Dykes Ct 11 SW2 ... 74 B3
Dylan Rd 2 SE24 ... 63 A3
Dylways SE5 .... 63 C3
Dymchurch Ho 12 E5 ...... 17 A3
Dymes Path SW19 .. 69 C2
Dymock St SW6 .... 59 A4
Dyne Rd NW6 ...... 10 B1
Dynevor Rd
Richmond TW10 ..... 54 A2
Shacklewell N16 ...... 7 B1
Dynham Rd NW6 ... 10 C1
Dyott St
Soho WC1 .... 105 C2
St Giles WC1, WC2 106 A2
Dysart St EC2 .... 24 A1 98 A1
Dyson Ho 3 SE10 .. 43 B1

E

Eade Rd N4 .... 6 B4
Eagle Cl SE16 ...... 40 B1
Eagle Ct
10 Dulwich SE21 .... 75 C2
Holborn EC1 ...... 108 A4
Eagle Dwellings EC1 ...... 97 A4
Eagle Ho
22 Bethnal Green E1 ...... 25 A1
Finsbury Pk N7 .... 5 B1
Eagle Hts 10 SW11 .. 60 A4
Eagle Lo NW11 ...... 1 B4
Eagle Mans N16 .... 16 B3
Eagle Mews N1 .... 16 A2
Eagle Pl
South Kensington SW7 ...... 143 A2
St James SW1 .... 119 A3
Eagle St WC1 ..... 106 C3
Eagle Wharf SE1 . 124 C1
Eagle Wharf Rd N1 ...... 87 A2
Eagle Works E1 .... 24 B1 99 A1
Eagling Cl E3 .... 26 C2
Ealing, Hammersmith & West London Coll W14 ...... 140 A2
Eamann Casey Ho 34 SW9 ...... 173 C3
Eamont Ct NW8 ... 80 B2
Eamont St NW8 ... 80 B2
Eardley Cres SW5 .. 141 C1
Earldom Rd SW15 .. 57 B3
Earle Ho SW1 .... 147 C3
Earlham St WC2 .. 106 A1
Earl Ho NW1 ...... 90 B1
Earlom Ho WC1 ... 95 B3
Earl Rd SW14 .... 55 B3
EARL'S COURT ... 141 C3
Earl's Court Ex Ctr SW5 ...... 141 B1
Earl's Court Gdns SW5 ...... 142 A3
Earl's Court Rd SW5, W8 ...... 141 C4
Earl's Court Sq SW5 ...... 142 A2
Earl's Court Sta SW5 ...... 141 C3
Earlsferry Way N1 .. 14 A1
EARLSFIELD 71 B3
Earlsfield Prim Sch SW18 ...... 71 B2
Earlsfield Rd SW18 ...... 71 B4
Earlsfield Sta SW18 ...... 71 B3
Earlsmead Rd NW10 ...... 22 B2
Earl St EC2 .... 110 A4
Earls Terr W8 ..... 127 A1
Earlsthorpe Mews 3 SW12 ...... 60 C1
Earlstoke St EC1 ... 96 A4

Earlston Gr E9 25 A4
Earls Wlk W8 127 B1
Earlswood Cl 10 SE10 43 A1
Earlswood Ho 2 SW2 74 B3
Earlswood St SE10 43 A1
Early Mews NW1 82 B4
Earnshaw Ho EC1 96 B3
Earnshaw St WC1, WC2 105 C2
Earsby St W14 140 B4
Earth Galleries SW7 129 C1
Eashing Point 5 SW15 69 A3
Easleys Mews W1 103 C2
EAST ACTON 29 A1
East Acton Arc W3 29 B3
East Acton Ct W3 29 A2
East Acton La W3 29 A2
East Acton Prim Sch W3 29 A2
East Acton Sta W12 29 B3
East Arbour St E1 32 C3
East Bank N16 7 A4
East Block 5 E1 32 C2
Eastbourne Ave W3 28 C3
Eastbourne Gdns SW14 55 B4
Eastbourne Mews W2 101 A2
Eastbourne Rd W4 45 B4
Eastbourne Terr W2 101 A2
Eastbury Gr W4 38 A1
Eastbury Terr E1 25 C1
Eastcastle St W1 105 A2
Eastcheap EC3 124 A4
East Churchfield Rd W3 28 C1
Eastcote St SW9 172 C1
East Cross Route
Bow E3 26 C4
Hackney Wick E9 18 B3
Eastdown Ho E8 16 C4
Eastdown Pk SE13 67 C3
EAST DULWICH 64 C2
East Dulwich Gr SE22 64 A2
East Dulwich Rd SE15, SE22 64 C3
East Dulwich Sta SE22 64 A3
East End Computing & Bsns Coll 37 E1 32 A3
Eastern Rd SE4 66 C3
East Ferry Rd E14 42 A2
Eastfields Ave SW18 58 C3
Eastfields Rd W3 28 B4
Eastfield St E14 33 A4
East Harding St EC4 107 C2
East Heath Rd NW3 2 C1
East Hill SW18 59 B2
East India Bldgs 9 E14 33 C2
East India Ct 7 SE16 40 B4
East India Dock Basin E14 35 A2
East India Dock Rd E14 34 A2
East India Dock Road Tunnel 18 E14 34 C3
East India Sta E14 34 C2
East La 5 SE16 139 B3
Eastlake Ho NW8 89 C1
Eastlake Rd SE5 48 B1
Eastlands Cres SE21 64 B1
Eastleigh Wlk 9 SW15 68 C4
Eastman Dental Hospl WC1 94 C2
Eastman Ho 7 SW4 61 B1
Eastman Rd W3 37 C4
Eastmearn Rd SE21, SE27 75 B2
East Mount St E1 32 A4
Eastney St SE10 42 C1
Easton Ho 4 SE27 75 A1
Easton St WC1 95 B2
East Parkside SE10 43 B4
East Pas EC1 108 C4
East Plaza E14 34 A1
East Point 4 SE1 153 B2
East Poultry Ave EC1 108 A3
East Putney Sta SW15 58 A2
East Rd
Chelsea SW1 145 B1
Shoreditch N1 97 C4
East Row W10 23 A1
Eastry Ho SW8 162 A1
EAST SHEEN 55 C3
East Sheen Ave SW14 55 C3
East Sheen Prim Sch SW14 56 A3
East Smithfield E1 125 A3
East St SE17 151 B2
East Surrey Gr SE15 49 B3
East Tenter St E1 111 A1
Eastvale W3 29 B1
East View NW3 2 C2
Eastway E3, E9 26 A4
Eastwell Ho SE1 137 C2
Eastwick Ct 2 SW19 69 C3
Eastwood Cl 2 N7 14 C3
Eaton Cl SW1 145 B3
Eaton Dr SW9 63 A3
Eaton Gate SW1 145 B4
Eaton Ho
Battersea SW11 167 C3
23 Limehouse E14 33 B2
Eaton House Sch SW1 145 B4
Eaton House The Manor Sch SW4 61 A3
Eaton La SW1 132 B1
Eaton Mans SW1 145 B3
Eaton Mews N SW1 131 C1
Eaton Mews S SW1 132 A1
Eaton Mews W SW1 145 C4
Eaton Pl SW1 131 C1
Eaton Row SW1 132 A1
Eaton Sq SW1 131 C1
Eaton Sq Pre-Prep Sch SW1 146 A4
Eaton Sq Prep Sch SW1 146 C3
Eaton Terr
Belgravia SW1 145 C4
Bow E3 26 A2
Eaton Terr Mews SW1 145 B4
Eatonville Rd SW17 72 B2
Eatonville Villas SW17 72 B2
Ebbisham Dr SW8 162 C3
Ebbsfleet Rd NW2 10 A4
Ebenezer Ho SE11 150 A3
Ebenezer Mussel Ho 5 E2 25 B3
Ebenezer St N1 97 B4
Ebley Cl SE15 49 B4
Ebner St SW18 59 A2
Ebony Ct NW10 8 B2
Ebony Ho
27 Bethnal Green E2 24 C2 99 B3
10 West Hampstead NW3 11 A2
Ebor Cotts SW15 68 A1
Ebor St E1, E2 24 B1 98 C2
Eburne Rd N7 5 A1
Ebury Bridge Rd SW1 145 C1
Ebury Mews
Belgravia SW1 146 A4
West Norwood SE27 75 A1
Ebury Mews E SW1 132 A1
Ebury Sq SW1 145 C3
Ebury St SW1 146 A4
Ecclesbourne Rd N1 15 B1
Eccles Ct SE11 149 A1
Eccles Rd SW11 60 B3
Eccleston Ho 1 SW2 62 C1
Eccleston Mews SW1 131 C1
Eccleston Pl SW1 146 A4
Eccleston Sq SW1 146 B3
Eccleston Sq Mews SW1 146 C3
Eccleston St SW1 146 A4
Eckford St N1 85 B2
Eckstein Rd SW11 60 A3
Edans Ct W12 38 B4
Edbrooke Rd W9 23 C1
Eddisbury Ho 7 SE26 76 C1
Eddiscombe Rd SW6 165 A2
Eddison Ct N19 5 A2
Eddystone Rd SE4 66 A2
Eddystone Twr SE8 41 A1
Edenbridge Cl 29 SE16 40 A1
Edenbridge Rd E9 17 C1
Eden Cl
Child's Hill NW3 1 C2
Kensington W8 127 C2
Edendale W3 28 A2
Eden Gr
Islington N7 14 B3
Willesden NW10 9 A2
Edenham Way W10 31 B4
Eden High Sch 9 W6 38 C1
Eden Ho
15 Battersea SW11 60 A4
Lisson Gr NW8 90 A1
Edenhurst Ave SW6 58 B4
Eden Lodge NW6 9 C1
Eden Mews SW17 71 B1
Edensmuir Ct SE3 53 C3
Edensor Gdns W4 46 A3
Edensor Rd W4 46 A3
Edenvale St SW6 166 C1
Eden Way E3 26 B4
Edgar Ho
Homerton E9 18 A3
South Lambeth SW8 162 A2
Edgar Kail Way SE22 64 A3
Edgarley Terr SW6 164 A3
Edgar Rd E3 27 A2
Edgar Wallace Cl 4 SE15 49 A3
Edgcott Ho 2 W10 30 B4
Edgecombe Ho
4 London SE5 49 A1
Putney SW19 70 A4
Edgecote Cl 7 W3 28 B1
Edgehill Ho 4 SW9 48 A1
Edgeley La SW4 61 C4
Edgeley Rd SW4 61 C4
Edgel St SW18 59 A3
Edge St W8 31 C1 113 C2
Edgeworth Ho NW8 78 C4
Edgson Ho SW1 146 A2
Edgware Acad WC2 106 B1
Edgware Rd W1, W2, NW1, NW8 102 A3
Edgware Road Sta (Bakerloo) NW1 102 A3
Edgware Road Sta (Met, Distr, Circle) NW1 102 B3
Edinburgh Cl 7 E2 25 B3
Edinburgh Ct 10 SE16 32 C1
Edinburgh Ho
3 Acton W3 28 C3
Maida Vale W9 88 B4
Edington 20 NW5 12 C2
Edison Bldg 7 E14 41 C4
Edison Ct SE10 43 B3
Edison Ho SE1 151 B4
Edis St NW1 81 C4
Editha Mans SW10 156 C3
Edith Cavell Cl 2 N19 5 A4
Edith Gr SW10 157 A2
Edith Ho 6 W6 39 B1
Edithna St SW9 62 A4
Edith Neville Cotts NW1 93 B4
Edith Neville Prim Sch NW1 83 B1
Edith Ramsay Ho 2 E1 33 A4
Edith Rd
Stratford New Town E15 19 C3
West Kensington W14 140 B3
Edith Row SW6 166 B4
Edith St E2 24 C3
Edith Summerskill Ho SW6 154 C2
Edith Terr SW10 156 C2
Edith Villas W14 140 C2
Edith Yd SW10 157 A2
Edmeston Cl E9 18 A2
Edmond Ct SE14 50 B2
Edmonton Ct 5 SE16 40 B3
Edmund Halley Way SE10 43 A4
Edmund Ho
Kennington SE17 150 B1
New Cross Gate SE14 51 B2
Edmundsbury Ct Est 16 SW9 62 B3
Edmund St SE5 48 C3
Edmund Waller Prim Sch SE14 50 C1
Ednam Ho SE15 49 C4
Edna St SW11 168 A3
Edred Ho E9 18 A4
Edrich Ho SW4 172 A3
Edric Ho SW1 147 C4
Edric Rd SE14 50 C3
Edridge Ho 9 SE27 75 A1
Edward Alleyn Ho SE21 76 A4
Edward Ct 2 E16 35 C4
Edward Dodd Ct N1 97 C4
Edward Edward's Ho SE1 122 A1
Edwardes Pl W8 127 A1
Edwardes Sq W8 127 A1
Edward Friend Ho 6 N16 7 A1
Edward Ho
Paddington W2 89 B1
Vauxhall SE11 149 A2
Edward Kennedy Ho 18 W10 23 A1
Edward Mann Cl 13 E1 32 C3
Edward Mews NW1 82 B1
Edward Pl SE8 51 B4
Edward Robinson Ho 3 SE14 50 C3
Edward's Cotts 11 N1 15 A1
Edward's La N16 7 A2
Edwards Mews
Islington N1 14 C1
Marylebone W1 103 B1
Edward Sq
Islington N1 84 C3

- **Edward Sq** *continued*
  - 1 Rotherhithe SE16 … 33 A1
- **Edward St** SE14 … 51 B3
- **Edward VII Mans** NW10 … 22 C2
- Edward Wilson Prim Sch 2 W2 … 100 A4
- **Edwin Ho** SE15 … 49 C3
- **Edwin's Mead** E9 … 18 A4
- **Edwin St**
  - Bethnal Green E1 … 25 B1
  - Newham E16 … 35 C4
- **Edwy Ho** E9 … 18 B4
- **Edwyn Ho** SW18 … 59 A1
- **Effie Pl** SW6 … 155 C1
- **Effie Rd** SW6 … 155 C1
- **Effingham Ho** 37 SW8 … 171 B1
- **Effra Ct** SW2 … 62 B2
- **Effra Mans** SW2 … 62 C2
- **Effra Par** SW2 … 62 C2
- **Effra Rd** SW2 … 62 C2
- Effra Road Ret Pk SW2 … 62 C2
- EF International Language Sch SE1 … 121 C1
- **Egbert Ho** E9 … 18 A3
- **Egbert St** NW1 … 81 B4
- **Egbury Ho** SW15 … 56 B1
- **Egerton Cres** SW3 … 144 B4
- **Egerton Ct** 5 TW10 … 54 A2
- **Egerton Dr** SE10 … 52 A2
- **Egerton Gdns**
  - Knightsbridge SW3 … 130 A1
  - Willesden NW10 … 22 B4
- **Egerton Gdns Mews** SW3 … 130 B1
- **Egerton Ho** W4 … 45 B4
- **Egerton Pl** SW3 … 130 B1
- **Egerton Rd** N16 … 7 B4
- **Egerton Terr** SW3 … 130 B1
- **Egham Cl** SW19 … 70 A2
- **Eglantine Rd** SW18 … 59 B2
- **Eglington Ct** SE17 … 48 B4
- **Egliston Mews** SW15 … 57 B4
- **Egliston Rd** SW15 … 57 B4
- **Egmont St** SE14 … 50 C3
- **Egremont Ho** SE13 … 52 A1
- **Egremont Rd** SE27 … 74 C1
- **Egret Ho** 11 SE16 … 40 C2
- **Eider Ct** 38 SE8 … 51 B4
- **Elaine Ct** 13 NW3 … 12 B2
- **Elaine Gr** NW5 … 12 C3
- **Elaine Ho** N4 … 5 A3
- **Elam Cl** SE5 … 48 A1
- **Elam St** SE5 … 48 A1
- **Elan Ct** E1 … 32 A4
- **Eland Rd** SW11 … 60 B4
- **Elba Pl** SE17 … 151 A4
- **Elbe St** SW6 … 166 C2
- **Elborough St** SW18 … 70 C3
- **Elbury Dr** E16 … 35 C3
- **Elcho St** SW11 … 158 B1
- **Elcot Ave** SE15 … 50 A3
- **Elderberry Rd** W5 … 36 A4
- **Elderfield Ho** 4 E14 … 33 C2
- **Elderfield Rd** E5 … 17 B4
- **Elder St** E1 … 24 B1 98 C1
- **Elder Wlk**
  - Islington N1 … 86 B4
  - 2 Lewisham SE13 … 67 B4
- **Eldon Ct** NW6 … 23 C4
- **Eldon Gr** NW3 … 11 C3
- **Eldon Ho** SW9 … 63 A4
- **Eldon Rd** W8 … 128 B1
- **Eldon St** EC2 … 109 C3
- **Eldon Way** NW10 … 20 A3
- **Eldridge Ct** SE16 … 139 B1
- **Eleanor Cl** SE16 … 40 C4
- **Eleanor Ct** 13 E2 … 24 C4
- **Eleanor Gr** SW13 … 56 A4
- **Eleanor Ho**
  - 18 Hammersmith W6 … 39 B1
  - 1 Kentish Town NW5 … 13 B3
- Eleanor Palmer Prim Sch 12 NW5 … 13 B4
- **Eleanor Rathbone Ho** 1 N6 … 4 C4
- **Eleanor Rd** E8 … 17 A1
- **Eleanor St** E3 … 26 C2
- **Electra Ct** 6 NW2 … 9 B2
- **Electric Ave** SW9 … 62 C3
- **Electric Ho** 13 E3 … 26 C2
- **Electric La** 2 SW9 … 62 C3
- **Electric Mans** 1 SW9 … 62 C3
- **Elephant & Castle**
  - Newington SE1 … 136 B1
  - Newington SE1 … 150 B4
- Elephant & Castle Sh Ctr SE1 … 150 C4
- Elephant & Castle Sta
  - Lambeth SE1 … 136 B1
  - Newington SE17 … 150 C4
- **Elephant La** SE16 … 40 B4
- **Elephant Rd** SE17 … 150 C4
- **Elfindale Rd** SE24 … 63 B2
- **Elfort Rd** N5 … 14 C4
- **Elf Row** E1 … 32 B2
- **Elgar Ave** W5 … 36 A4
- **Elgar Cl** SE8 … 51 C3
- **Elgar Ct** W14 … 126 A1
- **Elgar Ho**
  - Pimlico SW1 … 146 B1
  - South Hampstead NW6 … 11 B1
- **Elgar St** SE16 … 41 A3
- **Elgin Ave**
  - Hammersmith W12 … 39 A3
  - Westbourne Green W9 … 88 B4
- **Elgin Cl** W12 … 39 A4
- **Elgin Cres** W11 … 31 A2 112 B4
- **Elgin Ct** W9 … 88 A2
- **Elgin Ho** 8 E14 … 34 A3
- **Elgin Mans** W9 … 88 A3
- **Elgin Mews** W11 … 31 A3
- **Elgin Mews N** W9 … 88 B4
- **Elgin Mews S** W9 … 88 B4
- **Elgood Cl** W11 … 31 A1 112 A1
- **Elgood Ho** NW8 … 79 C1
- **Elham Ho** 13 E5 … 17 A3
- **Elia Mews** N1 … 86 A1
- **Elias Pl** SW8 … 163 B3
- **Elia St** N1 … 86 A1
- **Elim Est** SE1 … 138 A2
- **Elim St** SE1 … 138 A2
- **Eliot Cotts** SE3 … 53 A1
- **Eliot Ct** SW18 … 59 A1
- **Eliot Gdns** SW15 … 56 C3
- **Eliot Hill** SE13 … 52 B1
- **Eliot Ho** 10 TW10 … 54 B1
- **Eliot Mews** NW8 … 78 C1
- **Eliot Pk** SE13 … 52 B1
- **Eliot Pl** SE3 … 53 A1
- **Eliot Vale** SE3 … 52 C1
- **Elizabeth Ave**
  - Islington N1 … 15 C1
  - Shoreditch N1 … 87 A4
- **Elizabeth Barnes Ct** 5 SW6 … 166 B2
- **Elizabeth Blount Ct** 4 E14 … 33 A3
- **Elizabeth Cl**
  - Paddington W9 … 89 A1
  - 12 Poplar E14 … 34 A3
- **Elizabeth Cooper Lo** SW12 … 60 C1
- **Elizabeth Cotts** 5 TW9 … 44 C2
- **Elizabeth Ct**
  - Chelsea SW10 … 157 C3
  - East Dulwich SE22 … 64 C3
  - Marylebone NW8 … 90 B2
  - Westminster SW1 … 133 C1
- **Elizabeth Finn Ho** 1 W12 … 38 C3
- Elizabeth Garrett Anderson Hospl NW1 … 93 A1
- Elizabeth Garrett Anderson Language Coll N1 … 85 A1
- **Elizabeth Gdns** W3 … 29 B1
- **Elizabeth Ho**
  - 15 Hammersmith W6 … 39 B1
  - Lambeth SE11 … 149 C3
- Elizabeth Ind Est SE14 … 50 C4
- **Elizabeth Kenny Ho** N1 … 15 B2
- **Elizabeth Mews**
  - 28 Hackney E2 … 24 C3
  - Maitland Pk NW3 … 12 B2
- Elizabeth Selby Inf Sch 31 E2 … 24 C2 99 C4
- **Elizabeth Sq** 13 SE16 … 33 A2
- **Elizabeth St** SW1 … 145 C4
- **Elkington Point** SE11 … 149 B3
- **Elkstone Rd** W10 … 31 B4
- **Ellacombe Ho** 1 SW2 … 74 C4
- **Ellaline Rd** W6 … 47 C4
- **Ella Mews** NW3 … 12 B4
- **Elland Ho** 18 E14 … 33 B3
- **Elland Rd** SE15 … 65 B3
- **Ella Rd** N4, N8 … 5 A4
- **Ellenborough Ho** 5 W12 … 30 A2
- **Ellenborough Pl** SW15 … 56 C3
- **Ellen St** E1 … 111 C1
- **Ellen Wilkinson Ho**
  - 7 Globe Town E2 … 25 C2
- **Ellen Wilkinson Ho** *continued*
  - West Brompton SW6 … 155 A3
- **Ellerby St** SW6 … 47 C2
- **Ellerdale Cl** 15 NW3 … 11 B4
- **Ellerdale Rd** NW3 … 11 B3
- **Ellerdale St** SE13 … 67 A4
- **Ellerker Gdns** TW10 … 54 A1
- **Ellerslie Gdns** NW10 … 21 C4
- Ellerslie Ind Est SW2 … 62 A2
- **Ellerslie Rd** W12 … 30 A1
- **Ellerton Ct** W3 … 37 A4
- **Ellerton Rd**
  - Barnes SW13 … 46 C2
  - Wandsworth SW17, SW18 … 71 C3
- **Ellery Cl** 5 NW10 … 21 B3
- **Ellery Ho** SE17 … 151 C3
- **Ellery St** SE15 … 50 A1
- **Ellesmere Ct** W4 … 45 C4
- **Ellesmere Rd**
  - Bow E3 … 26 A3
  - Chiswick W4 … 45 C4
  - Willesden NW10 … 8 C3
- **Ellesmere St** E14 … 34 A3
- **Ellingfort Rd** E8 … 17 A1
- **Ellingham Rd**
  - Leyton E15 … 19 C4
  - Shepherd's Bush W12 … 38 C4
- **Ellington Ho** SE1 … 137 A1
- **Ellington St** N7 … 14 C2
- **Elliott Rd**
  - Acton W4 … 38 A2
  - Brixton SW9 … 48 A2
- Elliott Sch SW15 … 57 B1
- **Elliott's Pl** N1 … 86 B3
- **Elliott Sq** NW3 … 12 A1
- **Elliott's Row** SE11 … 150 B4
- **Ellis Cl** NW10 … 9 B2
- **Ellisfield Dr** SW15 … 68 C4
- **Ellis Franklin Ct** NW8 … 78 C2
- **Ellis Ho** SE17 … 151 B2
- **Ellison Ho** 1 SE13 … 52 B1
- **Ellison Rd** SW13 … 46 B1
- **Ellis St** SW1 … 145 B4
- **Ellsworth St** E2 … 25 A2
- **Ellwood Ct** 1 W9 … 88 B1
- **Elmar Ct** SW6 … 164 B2
- **Elm Bank Gdns** SW13 … 46 A1
- **Elm Bank Mans** SW13 … 46 A1
- **Elmbourne Rd** SW17 … 73 A1
- **Elmbridge Wlk** E8 … 16 C1
- **Elm Cl** N19 … 4 B2
- **Elmcourt Rd** SE21, SE27 … 75 A2
- **Elm Cres** W5 … 36 A4
- **Elmcroft** N6 … 4 B4
- **Elmcroft Ave** NW11 … 1 B4
- **Elmcroft Cres** NW11 … 1 A4
- **Elmcroft St** E5 … 17 B4
- **Elm Ct**
  - Brixton SW9 … 173 B4
  - Lewisham SE13 … 67 C4
  - 42 Notting Hill W2 … 31 C4
  - Strand EC4 … 121 B4
- Elm Ct Sch SE27 … 74 B4
- **Elmer Ho** NW1 … 102 A4
- **Elmfield Ho**
  - 6 Canonbury N5 … 15 B3
  - Paddington W9 … 23 C1
- **Elmfield Mans** 5 SW17 … 72 C2
- **Elmfield Rd** SW17 … 73 A2
- **Elmfield Way** W9 … 31 C4
- **Elm Friars Wlk** NW1 … 13 C1
- **Elm Gn** W3 … 29 A3
- **Elm Gr**
  - Cricklewood NW2 … 9 C4
  - Peckham SE15 … 49 C1
- Elmgreen Sch The SE27 … 75 A2
- **Elm Grove Rd**
  - Barnes SW13 … 46 C1
  - Ealing W5 … 36 A4
- **Elm Ho** 4 E14 … 42 B4
- **Elmhurst Mans** SW4 … 61 C4
- **Elmhurst St** SW4 … 61 C4
- **Elmhurst Villas** SE15 … 65 B3
- **Elmington Rd** SE5 … 48 C3
- **Elmira St** SE13 … 67 A4
- **Elm Lo** SW6 … 47 C2
- **Elmore Ho** SW9 … 48 A1
- **Elmore St** N1 … 15 C1
- **Elm Park Gdns** SW10 … 143 B1
- **Elm Park Ho** SW10 … 143 B1
- **Elm Park La** SW3 … 143 B1
- **Elm Park Mans** SW10 … 157 A4
- **Elm Park Rd** SW3 … 157 B4
- **Elm Pk** SW2 … 74 B4
- **Elm Pl** SW7 … 143 B2
- **Elm Quay** SW8 … 161 B3
- **Elm Rd** SW14 … 55 B3
- **Elm Row** NW3 … 2 B1
- **Elms Cres** SW4 … 61 C1
- **Elmshaw Rd** SW15 … 56 C2
- **Elmslie Point** 2 E3 … 33 B4
- **Elms Mews** W2 … 115 B4
- **Elms Rd** SW4 … 61 B2
- **Elm St** WC1 … 95 A1
- **Elms The**
  - Barnes SW13 … 56 B4
  - 3 Harlesden NW10 … 21 A3
- **Elmstone Rd** SW6 … 165 B4
- **Elm Terr** NW2 … 1 C1
- **Elmton Ct** NW8 … 89 B2
- **Elm Tree Cl** NW8 … 89 B4
- **Elm Tree Ct**
  - 5 Camberwell SE5 … 48 B2
  - St John's Wood NW8 … 89 B4
- **Elm Tree Rd** NW8 … 89 B4
- **Elm Way** NW10 … 8 A4
- **Elm Wlk** NW3 … 1 C2
- **Elmwood Ct** SW11 … 170 A4
- Elm Wood Prim Sch SE27 … 75 C1
- **Elmwood Rd**
  - Chiswick W4 … 45 B4
  - Herne Hill SE24 … 63 C2
- **Elmworth Gr** SE21 … 75 C2

Elnathan Mews W9 ... 88 B1
Elphinstone St N5 .. 15 A4
Elrington Rd E8 ... 16 C2
Elsa St E1 ... 33 A4
Elsdale Ho 14 E9 ... 17 B2
Elsdale St E9 ... 17 B1
Elsden Mews E2 ... 25 B3
Elsenham St SW18, SW19 ... 70 B2
Elsfield NW5 ... 13 A3
Elsham Rd W14 .. 126 A3
Elsham Terr W14 . 126 A3
Elsie Lane Ct W2 . 100 A3
Elsiemaud Rd SE4 .. 66 B2
Elsie Rd SE22 ... 64 B3
Elsinore Gdns NW2 .. 1 A1
Elsinore Ho
12 Camberwell SE5 ... 48 B1
Islington N1 ... 85 B3
Elsinore Way TW9 .. 55 A4
Elsley Rd SW11 ... 60 C4
Elsley Sch 8 SW17 ... 72 A2
Elspeth Rd SW11 ... 60 B3
Elstead Ho 9 SW2 . 74 B4
Elsted St SE17 ... 151 C3
Elstow Grange NW6 . 9 C1
Elswick Rd SE13 ... 52 A1
Elswick St SW6 ... 166 C2
Elsworthy Rd NW3. 80 A4
Elsworthy Rise NW3 ... 12 A1
Elsworthy Terr NW3 ... 12 A1
Elsynge Rd SW18 ... 59 C2
Elsynge Road Mans SW18 ... 59 C2
Elthiron Rd SW6 .. 165 C3
Elthorne Rd N19 ... 4 C2
Elthruda Rd SE13 ... 67 C1
Elton Ho 3 E3 ... 26 B4
Elton Pl N16 ... 16 A3
Elton St 11 N16 ... 16 A3
Eltringham St SW18 ... 59 B3
Elvaston Mews SW7 ... 129 A2
Elvaston Pl SW7 .. 129 A1
Elveden Ho 17 SW9 ... 63 A3
Elver Gdns 10 E2 ... 24 C2 99 C4
Elverson Rd SE8 ... 52 A1
Elverson Rd Sta SE8 ... 52 A1
Elverton St SW1 .. 147 B4
Elvin Ho 2 E9 ... 17 B2
Elvis Rd NW2 ... 9 B2
Elwin St E2 .. 24 C2 99 B4
Elwood Ho N5 ... 6 A1
Elwood St N4, N5 ... 6 A1
Elworth Ho SW8 .. 163 A1
Ely Cotts SW8 ... 162 C1
Ely Court Flats SW6 ... 164 A3
Ely Ct
Holborn EC1 ... 107 C3
3 Maida Vale NW6 ... 23 C3
Ely Ho 22 SE15 ... 49 C3
Ely Pl EC1 ... 107 C3
Elysium Gate 7 SW6 ... 164 C2
Elysium Pl SW6 .. 164 C1
Elysium St SW6 .. 164 C1
Elystan Ct SW15 ... 57 A2
Elystan Pl SW3 ... 144 C2
Elystan St SW3 ... 144 B3
Elystan Wlk N1 ... 85 B3
Emanuel Ave W3 ... 28 B3
Emanuel Ct W3 ... 28 C3
Emanuel Sch SW11 ... 60 A2
Embankment SW15 ... 47 C1
Embankment Gdns SW3 ... 159 A4
Embankment Pier WC2 ... 120 B2
Embankment Pl WC2 ... 120 B2
Embankment Sta WC2 ... 120 B2
Embassy Ct NW8 .. 79 C1
Embassy Ho 2 NW6 ... 10 C1
Emba St SE16 ... 139 C3
Ember Ct 2 W12 ... 38 A3
Emberton SE5 ... 49 A4
Emberton Ct EC1 .. 96 A3
Embleton Rd SE13 .. 67 A3
Emden St SW6 ... 166 B4
Emerald Rd NW10 .. 20 C4
Emerald St WC1 .. 106 C4
Emerson Ho N16 ... 16 A3
Emerson St SE1 .. 122 C2
Emery Hill St SW1 ... 133 A1
Emery St SE1 ... 135 C2
Emily St 7 E16 ... 35 B3
Emirates Airway SE10 ... 35 B1
Emirates Greenwich Peninsula SE10 ... 43 A4
Emirates Royal Dock E16 ... 35 C2
Emirates Stad (Arsenal FC) N7 ... 14 C4
Emlyn Gdns 3 W12 ... 38 A3
Emlyn Rd W12 ... 38 B3
Emmanuel CE Prim Sch NW6 ... 10 C3
Emmanuel Ho
Dulwich SE21 ... 75 C1
Lambeth SE11 ... 149 B3
Emmanuel Rd SW12 ... 73 C3
Emma St E2 ... 25 A3
Emminster NW6 ... 78 A4
Emmott Cl E1 ... 26 A1
Emperor's Gate SW7 ... 142 C4
Empingham Ho 20 SE8 ... 40 C2
Empire Ho SW3 .. 130 A1
Empire Sq N19 ... 5 A1
Empire Wharf E3 ... 26 A4
Empire Wharf Rd E14 ... 42 C2
Empress Mews 36 SE5 ... 48 B1
Empress Pl SW5 .. 141 B1
Empress St SE17 ... 48 B4
Empress State Building SW6 ... 141 B1
Empson St E3 ... 27 A1
Emsworth St SW2 .. 74 B2
Emu Rd SW8 ... 170 A1
Enard Ho 28 E3 ... 26 B3
Enbrook St W10 ... 23 A2
Enclave Ct EC1 ... 96 B2
Endell St WC2 ... 106 A1
Enderby St SE10 ... 43 A1
Endlesham Ct 2 SW12 ... 72 C4
Endlesham Rd SW12 ... 72 C4
Endsleigh Gdns WC1 ... 93 B2
Endsleigh Mans 4 SW16 ... 74 A1
Endsleigh Pl WC1 .. 93 C2
Endsleigh St WC1 . 93 C2
Endwell Rd SE4 ... 51 A1
Endymion Rd
Harringay N4 ... 6 A4
Tulse Hill SW2 ... 62 B1
Energen Cl NW10 ... 8 A2
Enfield Cloisters 7 N1 ... 24 A2 98 A4
Enfield Ho 24 SW9 ... 172 B2
Enfield Rd
De Beauvoir Town E8, N1 ... 16 A1
South Acton W3 ... 37 A4
Enford St W1 ... 102 C4
Engadine St SW18 .. 70 C3
Engate St SE13 ... 67 B3
England's La NW3 .. 12 B2
Englefield NW1 ... 92 C3
Englefield Rd N1 ... 16 A1
Englewood Rd SW12 ... 61 B1
English Gardening Sch The SW3 ... 158 C4
English Grounds SE1 ... 124 A1
English Martyrs RC Prim Sch
Walworth SE17 ... 151 C3
Whitechapel E1 ... 111 A1
English St E3 ... 26 B1
Enid St SE16 ... 139 A2
Enid Stacy Ho 11 N19 ... 4 C4
Enmore Ct SW14 ... 55 C2
Enmore Gdns SW14 ... 55 C2
Enmore Rd SW15 ... 57 B2
Ennerdale Ho 3 N4 ... 6 C4
Ennerdale Rd TW9 .. 44 B1
Ennersdale Rd SE13 ... 67 C2
Ennis Ho 16 E14 ... 34 A3
Ennismore Ave W4 ... 38 B2
Ennismore Gdns SW7 ... 130 A2
Ennismore Gdns Mews SW7 ... 130 A2
Ennismore Mews SW7 ... 130 A2
Ennismore St SW7 ... 130 A2
Ennis Rd N4 ... 5 C3
Ensbury Ho SW8 . 162 C2
Ensign Ct 12 E1 .. 125 C3
Ensign Ho 19 E14 .. 41 C4
Ensign St E1 ... 125 B4
Ensor Mews SW7 . 143 B2
Enterprise Ho 36 E9 ... 17 B1
Enterprise Way
College Pk NW10 ... 21 C2
Wandsworth SW18 .. 58 C3
Enterprize Way SE8 ... 41 B2
Epirus Mews SW6 155 B2
Epirus Rd SW6 ... 155 A2
Epping Cl E14 ... 41 C2
Epping Ho 8 E5 ... 7 C2
Epping Pl N1 ... 14 C2
Epple Rd SW6 ... 165 A4
Epstein Ct N1 ... 86 B3
Epworth St EC2 ... 97 C1
Equity Sq 29 E2 ... 24 B2 99 A3
Erasmus St SW1 .. 147 C3
Erconwald St W12 .. 29 B3
Eresby Ho SW7 ... 130 B3
Eresby Pl NW6 ... 10 C1
Erica Ct SW4 ... 172 B3
Erica Ho SE4 ... 66 B4
Erica St W12 ... 29 C2
Ericcson Cl SW18 ... 58 C2
Eric Fletcher Ct 15 N1 ... 15 B1
Eric Macdonald Ho SW6 ... 165 C3
Eric Rd NW10 ... 8 B2
Ericson Ho
London SE13 ... 67 C3
Stamford Hill N16 ... 7 B3
Eric St E3 ... 26 B1
Eric Wilkins Ho 14 SE1 ... 153 B1
Eridge Ho SE22 ... 64 B4
Eridge House Sch 13 SW6 ... 164 C2
Eridge Rd W4 ... 37 C3
Erin Ct NW2 ... 9 B2
Erlanger Rd SE14 ... 50 C1
Ermine Rd SE13 ... 67 A3
Ernest Bevin Coll SW17 ... 72 A2
Ernest Gdns W4 ... 45 A4
Ernest Simmonds Ho SE14 ... 50 B1
Ernest St E1 ... 25 C1
Ernshaw Pl SW15 ... 58 A2
Eros (Shaftesbury Meml Fountain) W1 ... 119 B3
Erpingham Rd SW15 ... 57 B4
Errington Rd W9 ... 23 B1
Errol St EC1 ... 97 A1
Erskine Ho SW1 .. 146 C1
Erskine Rd NW3 ... 12 B1
Escuan Lo N5 ... 15 B3
Esher Gdns SW19 ... 69 C2
Esher Ho 8 SW8 171 C2
Eskdale NW1 ... 82 C1
Esk Ho E3 ... 26 B1
Esme Ho SW15 ... 56 B3
Esmeralda Rd SE1 ... 153 C3
Esmond Ct W8 ... 128 B2
Esmond Gdns W4 .. 37 C2
Esmond Rd
Acton W4 ... 37 C3
Kilburn NW6 ... 23 B4
Esmond St SW15 ... 58 A3
Esparto St SW18 ... 71 A4
Espirit Ct E1 ... 110 C3
Espirit Ho 6 SW15 ... 58 A2
Essendine Mans W9 ... 23 C2
Essendine Prim Sch 1 W9 ... 23 C2
Essendine Rd W9 ... 23 C2
Essex Ct
Barnes SW13 ... 46 B1
Hammersmith W6 ... 39 B3
Holborn EC4 ... 107 B1
Essex Ho 2 E14 ... 34 A3
Essex Park Mews W3 ... 29 A1
Essex Pl W4 ... 37 B2
Essex Place Sq 5 W4 ... 37 C2
Essex Rd
Acton W3 ... 28 B2
Chiswick W4 ... 37 C2
Islington N1 ... 86 B4
Willesden NW10 ... 8 A1
Essex Road Sta N1 . 15 B1
Essex St WC2 ... 121 B4
Essex Villas W8 ... 127 B3
Essian St E1 ... 33 A4
Essington SW15 ... 58 A1
Estcourt Rd SW6 . 154 C2
Estella Ho 15 W11 .. 30 C2
Estelle Rd NW3 ... 12 B4
Esterbrooke St SW1 ... 147 B3
Este Rd SW11 ... 60 A4
Estoria Cl 22 SW2 .. 74 C4
Etal Ho N1 ... 15 A1
Etchingham Rd E15 ... 19 B4
Eternit Wlk SW6 ... 47 C2
Ethelbert Ho E9 ... 18 A4
Ethelbert St SW12 .. 73 A3
Ethelburga St SW11 ... 168 B4
Ethelburga Twr SW11 ... 168 B4
Ethelden Rd W12 ... 30 A1
Ethel Rankin Ct 8 SW6 ... 164 C2
Ethel St SE17 ... 151 A3
Ethelworth Ct 4 SW2 ... 74 C3
Etherow St SE22 ... 76 C4
Ethnard Rd SE15 ... 50 A4
Eton Ave NW3 ... 12 A1
Eton Cl SW18 ... 71 A4
Eton College Rd NW3 ... 12 B2
Eton Ct NW3 ... 11 C1
Eton Garages 11 NW3 ... 12 A2
Eton Hall NW3 ... 12 B2
Eton Ho
Hackney E9 ... 18 B2
Highbury N5 ... 15 A4
Eton Pl NW1 ... 12 C1
Eton Rd NW3 ... 12 B2
Eton Rise NW3 ... 12 B2
Eton St TW10 ... 54 A2
Eton Villas NW3 ... 12 B2
Etta St SE8 ... 51 A4
Ettrick St E14 ... 34 B3
Eugene Cotter Ho SE17 ... 151 C3
Eugenia Rd SE16 ... 40 B2
Eurocentres SW1 . 146 B3
Euro Cl NW10 ... 8 C2

Eurolink Bsns Ctr SW2 ... 62 C2
Europa Pl EC1 ... 96 C3
European Coll 45 E1 ... 111 B2
Eustace Bldg SW8 ... 160 A3
Eustace Ho SE11 . 148 C4
Eustace Rd SW6 .. 155 B2
Euston Rd NW1 ... 93 A2
Euston Sq NW1 ... 93 B3
Euston Square Sta WC1 ... 93 A2
Euston St NW1 ... 93 A3
Euston Sta NW1 ... 93 B3
Euston Underpass NW1 ... 92 C2
Evan Cook Cl SE15 .. 50 B2
Evandale Rd SW9 173 C2
Evangelist Rd NW5 ... 13 A4
Evans Cl E8 ... 16 B2
Evans Ho
34 Shepherd's Bush W12 ... 30 A2
South Lambeth SW8 ... 161 C1
Evelina Childrens' Hospl SE1 ... 134 C2
Evelina Mans 9 SE5 ... 48 C3
Evelina Rd SE15 ... 50 B1
Eveline Lowe Prim Sch 28 SE1 ... 153 C1
Evelyn Ct
Marylebone W1 ... 102 C1
Shacklewell E8 ... 16 C4
Shoreditch N1 ... 87 B1
Evelyn Denington Ct 2 N1 ... 15 A1
Evelyn Fox Ct W10 .. 30 B4
Evelyn Gdns
Richmond TW9 ... 54 A3
South Kensington SW7 ... 143 B1
Evelyn Grace Acad SE24 ... 63 A3
Evelyn Ho
Bedford Pk W12 ... 38 B4
3 Brixton SW2 ... 62 B2
18 Spitalfields E1 .. 111 B3
Evelyn Rd
Acton W4 ... 37 C3
Richmond TW9 ... 54 A4
Evelyn St
Greenwich SE10 ... 52 B4
SE8 ... 41 A1
Evelyn Terr TW9 ... 54 A4
Evelyn Wlk N1 ... 87 B1
Evelyn Yd W1 ... 105 B2
Evenwood Cl SW15 ... 58 A2
Everard Ho 33 E1 111 C1
Everatt Cl SW18 ... 58 B2
Everdon Rd SW13 .. 46 C4
Everest Pl E14 ... 34 B4
Everett Ho
Islington N7 ... 14 C4
Walworth SE17 ... 151 B2
Evergreen Sq 3 E8 ... 16 B1
Everilda St N1 ... 85 A3
Evering Rd E5, N16 ... 7 C1
Everington St W6 ... 47 C4
Everitt Rd NW10 ... 20 C2
Everleigh St N4 ... 5 B3
Eversfield Rd TW9 .. 44 B1
Evershed Ho E1 .. 111 A2
Evershed Wlk W4 .. 37 C2
Eversholt St NW1 .. 93 B4
Evershot Rd N4 ... 5 B3
Eversleigh Rd SW11 ... 169 B1
Eversley Ho 12 E2 ... 24 C2 99 B3
Everthorpe Rd SE15 ... 64 B4
Everton Bldgs NW1 ... 92 C3
Evesham Ct 2 TW10 ... 54 B1
Evesham Ho
1 Bethnal Green E2 ... 25 B3
Pimlico SW1 ... 146 B2
St John's Wood NW8 ... 78 C3
Evesham St W11 ... 30 C2
Evesham Way SW11 ... 60 C4
Evesham Wlk
Brixton SW9 ... 173 B2
Camberwell SE5 ... 48 C1
Ewald Rd SW6 ... 164 C1
Ewart Pl 13 E3 ... 26 B3
Ewe Cl N7 ... 14 A2
Ewen Cres SW2 ... 74 C4
Ewen Henderson Ct 10 SE14 ... 51 A3
Ewen Ho N1 ... 84 C3
Ewer St SE1 ... 122 C1
Ewhurst 19 SW15 ... 57 C1
Ewhurst Cl E1 ... 32 B4
Ewhurst Rd SE4 ... 66 B1
Exbury Ho
Hackney E9 ... 17 B2
4 London SW9 ... 62 B3
Excel Ct WC2 ... 119 C3
Excelsior Gdns SE13 ... 52 B1
Excelsior Ind Est SE16 ... 50 B4
Exchange Arc EC2 ... 110 B4
Exchange Ct WC2. 120 B3
Exchange Mans 2 NW11 ... 1 B4
Exchange Pl EC2 . 110 A4
Exeter Ct NW6 ... 23 C3
Exeter Ho
Paddington W2 ... 100 C2
11 Peckham SE15 ... 49 C4
Putney SW15 ... 57 B1
Exeter Mans NW2 .. 10 A2
Exeter Mews
Fulham SW6 ... 155 B2
12 Hampstead NW6 ... 11 A2
Exeter Rd
Brondesbury NW2 ... 10 A2
Newham E16 ... 35 C4
Exeter St WC2 ... 120 C4
Exeter Way 2 SE14 ... 51 B3
Exford Ct SW11 ... 167 C4
Exhibition Cl W12 .. 30 B2
Exhibition Rd SW7 ... 129 C2
Exmoor Ho 25 E3 ... 26 A3
Exmoor St W10 ... 30 C4
Exmouth Ho
Clerkenwell EC1 ... 95 C2
6 Millwall E14 ... 42 A2
Exmouth Market EC1 ... 95 C2
Exmouth Mews NW1 ... 93 A3
Exmouth Pl E8 ... 17 A1
Exmouth St E1 ... 32 B3
Exonbury NW8 ... 78 B3
Exon St SE17 ... 152 A3
Explorers Ct 6 E14 ... 34 C2
Express Wharf 10 E14 ... 41 C4
Exton St SE1 ... 121 B1
Eynella Rd SE21 ... 76 B4
Eynham Rd W12 ... 30 B3
Eynsford Coll W1 . 105 B2
Eynsford Ho
Borough The SE1 .. 137 B4
12 Deptford SE15 ... 50 B4
Walworth SE17 ... 152 A3
Eyot Gdns W6 ... 38 B1
Eyot Gn W4 ... 38 B1
Eyre Ct NW8 ... 79 B2
Eyre St Hill EC1 ... 95 B1
Eythorne Rd SW9 173 C3
Ezra St E2 ... 24 B2 99 A4

F

Fabian Rd SW6 ... 155 A2
Fabyc Ho TW9 ... 44 C3
Fairacres SW15 ... 56 C3
Fairbairn Gn 1 SW9 ... 48 A2
Fairbriar Residence SW7 ... 143 A4
Fairbridge Rd N19 ... 4 C2
Fairburn Ct SW15 ... 58 A2
Fairburn Ho
9 Stamford Hill N16 ... 7 A3
West Kensington SW5 ... 141 A1
Fairby Ho SE1 ... 153 A4
Faircharm Trad Est SE8 ... 52 A3
Fairchild Cl 6 SW11 ... 167 C1
Fairchild Ho
13 Hackney E9 ... 17 B1
Pimlico SW1 ... 147 A3
5 Shoreditch N1 ... 24 A2 98 A4
Fairchild Pl EC2 ... 24 A1 98 B1
Fairchild St EC2 ... 24 A1 98 B1
Fairclough St E1 . 111 C1
Faircourt 14 NW3 ... 12 B2
Faircroft N16 ... 6 C3
Fairdale Gdns SW15 ... 57 A3
Fairdene Ct N7 ... 14 A3
Fairfax Ho
11 Brixton SW9 ... 173 C1
6 Putney SW15 ... 56 C2
Fairfax Mews SW15 ... 57 B3
Fairfax Pl
Kensington W14 ... 126 B1
Fairfax Pl *continued*
South Hampstead NW6 ... 11 B1
Fairfax Rd
Acton W4 ... 38 A3
South Hampstead NW6 ... 11 B1
Fairfield
Camden Town NW1 ... 82 C3
4 Stepney E1 ... 32 B4
Fairfield Ct
Harlesden NW10 ... 21 C4
1 London SW18 ... 59 A2
Fairfield Dr SW18 .. 59 A2
Fairfield Rd E3 ... 26 C3
Fairfield St SW18 ... 59 A2
Fairfoot Rd E3 ... 26 C1
Fairford Ho SE11 . 149 C3
Fairhazel Gdns NW6 ... 11 B1
Fairheathe SW15 ... 57 C1
Fairholme Rd W14 ... 140 B1
Fairholt Cl N16 ... 7 A3
Fairholt Rd N16 ... 6 C3
Fairholt St SW7 .. 130 B2
Fairhurst 4 NW6 ... 11 B2
Fairlawn Ave W4 ... 37 B2
Fairlawn Ct 3 W4 .. 37 B2
Fairlawn Gr W4 ... 37 B2
Fairlawn Mans SE14 ... 50 C2
Fairlawns SW15 ... 57 C2
Fairlead Ho 6 E14 ... 41 C3
Fairley House Sch SW1 ... 147 C2
Fairlie Ct
22 Bromley E3 ... 27 A2
1 Tufnell Pk N7 ... 13 C4
Fairlight Ave NW10 ... 21 A3
Fairlight Ct 4 NW10 ... 21 A3
Fairlop Pl NW8 ... 89 C3
Fairmead Ho E9 ... 18 A4
Fairmead Rd N7, N19 ... 5 A1
Fairmont Ave E14 .. 34 C1
Fairmont Ho 1 E3 ... 26 C1
Fairmount Rd SW2 ... 62 B1
Fair St SE1 ... 138 C4
Fairstead Wlk N1 .. 86 C4
Fairthorn Rd SE7, SE10 ... 43 C1
Fairview Ho 14 SW2 ... 74 B4
Fairview Pl SW2 ... 74 B4
Fairwall Ho 9 SE5 ... 49 A2
Fairway Cl NW11 ... 2 B4
Fairway Ct 13 SE16 ... 40 C4
Fairway The W3 ... 29 A3
Fairweather Ho N7 ... 14 A4
Faith Ct NW2 ... 9 A2
Faithfull Ho N5 ... 15 B3
Fakruddin St E1 ... 24 C1 99 C1
Falconberg Ct W1 ... 105 C2
Falconberg Mews W1 ... 105 C2
Falconbrook Prim Sch 26 SW11 ... 59 C4
Falcon Cl
Chiswick W4 ... 45 B4
Lambeth SE1 ... 122 B2
Falcon Ct
9 Dulwich SE21 ... 75 C2
Holborn EC4 ... 107 B1
Islington N1 ... 86 B1
Falconer Wlk 12 N7 . 5 B2
Falcon Gr SW11 ... 60 A4
Falcon Ho 11 SE15 .. 49 B2
Falcon La SW11 ... 60 A4
Falcon Lo
11 Paddington W9 ... 31 C4
West Hampstead NW3 ... 11 A4
Falcon Pk Ind Est NW10 ... 8 A3
Falcon Point SE1 . 122 B3
Falcon Rd SW11 ... 60 A4
Falcons Pre Prep school The 1 W4 ... 45 A4
Falcons Prep Sch for Boys The TW9 ... 54 A3
Falcon Terr SW11 ... 60 A4
Falcon Way E14 ... 42 A2
Falconwood Ct SE3 ... 53 B1
Falkener Ct SW11 169 C3
Falkirk Ct 11 SE16 .. 32 C1
Falkirk Ho W9 ... 88 B4
Falkirk St N1 ... 24 A3
Falkland Ho
Kensington W8 ... 128 A1
West Kensington W14 ... 140 C2
Falkland Pl 2 NW5 ... 13 B3
Falkland Rd NW5 ... 13 B3
Falkner House Sch SW7 ... 143 A2
Fallodon Ho
6 London SW8 ... 171 C2
Paddington W11 ... 31 B4
Fallow Ct 20 SE16 153 C1
Fallowfield N4 ... 5 B2
Falmouth Ho
Bayswater W2 ... 116 A4
Kennington SE11 .. 149 C2
Falmouth Rd SE1 137 A1
Falmouth St E15 ... 19 C3
Falstaff Ct SE11 .. 150 A3
Falstaff Ho 18 N1 ... 24 A3
Fane St W14 ... 155 A4
Fan Mus The SE10 .. 52 B3
Fann St EC1 ... 97 A1
Fanshaw St N1 ... 24 A2 98 A4
Fanthorpe St SW15 ... 57 B4
Faraday Cl N7 ... 14 B2
Faraday Ho
2 Balham SW12 ... 73 A4
6 Gospel Oak NW5 ... 13 A4
Kensal Town W10 ... 31 A4
6 Poplar E14 ... 33 B2
Faraday Lo SE10 ... 43 B3
Faraday Rd
Acton W3 ... 28 B2
Kensal Town W10 ... 31 A4

Fareham Ho 13 SW15 ... 68 C3
Fareham St W1 ... 105 B2
Farjeon Ho NW6 ... 11 C1
Farleigh Pl N16 ... 16 B4
Farleigh Rd N16 ... 16 B4
Farley Ct
Kensington W14 ... 126 C2
Marylebone NW1 ... 91 B1
Farlington Pl SW15 ... 69 A4
Farlow Rd SW15 ... 57 C4
Farlton Rd SW18 ... 71 A4
Farm Ave NW2 ... 1 B1
Farm Cl SW6 ... 155 C2
Farmdale Rd SE10 ... 43 C1
Farmer Ho 4 SE16 ... 40 A3
Farmers Mkt W8 ... 113 C2
Farmers Rd SE5 ... 48 A3
Farmer St W8 ... 31 C1 113 B2
Farm La SW6 ... 155 C2
Farm Lane Trad Ctr SW6 ... 155 C3
Farmleigh Ho SW9 ... 63 A2
Farm Pl W8 ... 31 C1 113 B2
Farm Rd NW10 ... 20 C4
Farm St W1 ... 118 A3
Farnaby Ho 2 W10 ... 23 B2
Farnborough Ho 1 SW15 ... 68 C3
Farncombe St SE16 ... 139 C3
Farndale Ho 3 NW6 ... 78 A4
Farnell Mews SW5 ... 142 A2
Farnell Pl W3 ... 28 A2
Farnfield Ho 12 SW2 ... 62 B2
Farnham Ct 2 N16 ... 7 A3
Farnham Ho
Borough The SE1 ... 122 C1
Marylebone NW1 ... 90 B1
Farnham Pl SE1 ... 122 B1
Farnham Royal SE11 ... 149 A1
Farnhurst Ho 7 SW11 ... 169 B2
Farningham Ho 9 N4 ... 6 C4
Farnley Ho 13 SW8 ... 171 B2
Farnsworth Ct SE10 ... 43 B3
Farnworth Ho 5 E14 ... 42 C2
Faroe Rd W14 ... 39 C3
Farquhar Rd SW19 ... 70 C1
Farrance St E14 ... 33 C3
Farrant Ho 14 SW11 ... 59 C4
Farrell Ho E1 ... 32 B3
Farrer Ho SE8 ... 51 C3
Farriers Mews SE15 ... 65 B4
Farrier St NW1 ... 13 B1
Farrier Wlk SW10 ... 156 C4
Farringdon La EC1 ... 95 C1
Farringdon Rd EC1 ... 95 C1
Farringdon St EC4 ... 108 A2
Farringdon Sta EC1 ... 108 A4
Farrins Rents SE16 ... 33 A1
Farrow La SE14 ... 50 B3
Farrow Pl SE16 ... 41 A3
Farthingale Wlk E15 ... 19 C1
Farthing Alley 8 SE1 ... 139 B3
Farthing Fields 8 E1 ... 32 A1
Fashion Retail Acad The W1 ... 105 B2
Fashion St E1 ... 111 A3
Fashion & Textile Mus SE1 ... 138 A4
Fassett Rd E8 ... 16 C2
Fassett Sq E8 ... 16 C2
Fauconberg Ct W4 ... 45 B4
Fauconberg Rd W4 ... 45 B4
Faulkner Ho SW15 ... 47 B1
Faulkner's Alley EC1 ... 108 A4
Faulkner St SE14 ... 50 B2
Faunce Ho 1 SE17 ... 48 A4
Faunce St SE17 ... 150 A1
Favart Rd SW6 ... 165 C4
Faversham Ho
Camden Town NW1 ... 83 A3
Walworth SE17 ... 152 A1
Fawcett Cl SW11 ... 167 C1
Fawcett Est E5 ... 7 C3
Fawcett Ho 25 SW9 ... 172 B2
Fawcett Rd NW10 ... 8 B1
Fawcett St SW10 ... 156 C4
Fawe Park Rd SW15 ... 58 B3
Fawe St E14 ... 34 A4
Fawkham Ho SE1 ... 153 A3
Fawley Ct SE27 ... 75 A2
Fawley Lo 2 E14 ... 42 C2
Fawley Rd NW6 ... 11 A3
Fawnbrake Ave SE24 ... 63 B2
Fayetville Ho 26 N19 ... 4 C4
Faygate Rd SW2 ... 74 B2
Fazerley Ct 49 W2 ... 31 C4
Fearnley Ho SE5 ... 49 A1
Fearon St SE10 ... 43 C1
Feathers Pl SE10 ... 52 C4
Featherstone St EC1 ... 97 B2
Featley Rd SW9 ... 63 A4
Felbridge Ho 21 SE22 ... 64 A4
Felday Rd SE13 ... 67 A1
Felden St SW6 ... 164 C3
Feldman Cl N16 ... 7 C3
Felgate Mews 4 W6 ... 39 A2
Felix St 18 E2 ... 25 A3
Felixstowe Rd NW10 ... 22 A2
Fellbrigg Rd SE22 ... 64 B2
Fellbrigg St 21 E1 ... 25 A1
Fell Ho 11 N19 ... 4 B1
Fellows Ct E2 ... 24 B3
Fellows Rd NW3 ... 12 A1
Fells Haugh 6 W3 ... 28 B3
Felltram Way SE7 ... 43 C1
Felmersham Cl 2 SW4 ... 61 C3
Felsberg Rd SW2 ... 74 A4
Felsham Ho 5 SW15 ... 57 C4
Felsham Mews 14 SW15 ... 57 C4
Felsham Rd SW15 ... 57 C4
Felstead St E9 ... 18 B2
Felstead Wharf E14 ... 42 B1
Felton Ho N1 ... 87 C3
Felton St N1 ... 87 C3
Fenchurch Ave EC3 ... 110 A1
Fenchurch Bldgs EC3 ... 110 B1
Fenchurch Pl EC3 ... 124 B4
Fenchurch St EC3 ... 124 B4
Fenchurch Street Sta EC3 ... 124 B4
Fen Ct EC3 ... 124 A4
Fendall St SE1 ... 138 B1
Fender Ct 5 SW4 ... 172 A2
Fendt Cl 8 E16 ... 35 B3
Fenelon Pl W14 ... 141 A3
Fenham Rd SE15 ... 50 A3
Fenner Cl SE16 ... 40 A2
Fenner Ho 25 E1 ... 32 A1
Fenner Sq 9 SW11 ... 59 C4
Fenning St SE1 ... 138 A4
Fenn St E9 ... 17 B3
Fen St E16 ... 35 B2
Fenstanton 3 N4 ... 5 B3
Fenstanton Prim Sch 20 SW2 ... 74 C3
Fentiman Rd SW8 ... 162 C2
Fenton Cl
16 Dalston E8 ... 16 B2
South Lambeth SW9 ... 172 C1
Fenton Ho SE14 ... 51 A3
Fenton House NW3 ... 2 B1
Fentons SE3 ... 53 B3
Fenton St E1 ... 32 A3
Fenwick Gr SE15 ... 64 C4
Fenwick Pl SW9 ... 62 A4
Fenwick Rd SE15 ... 64 C4
Ferdinand Ho 1 NW1 ... 13 A1
Ferdinand Pl NW1 ... 12 C1
Ferdinand St NW1 ... 12 C1
Ferguson Dr W3 ... 28 C3
Ferguson Ho SE10 ... 52 B2
Ferguson's Cl E14 ... 41 C2
Fergus Rd N5 ... 15 A3
Fermain Ct E N1 ... 24 A4
Fermain Ct N N1 ... 24 A4
Fermain Ct W N1 ... 24 A4
Fermoy Rd W9 ... 23 B1
Fernbank Mews SW12 ... 61 B1
Fern Cl 3 N1 ... 24 A3
Ferncliff Rd E8 ... 16 C3
Ferncroft Ave NW3 ... 10 C4
Fern Ct SE14 ... 50 C1
Ferndale Com Sp Ctr SW9 ... 62 B3
Ferndale Ct 3 SE3 ... 53 B3
Ferndale Ho N16 ... 6 C3
Ferndale Rd SW4, SW9 ... 62 B3
Ferndene Rd SE24 ... 63 B3
Ferndown Lo 17 E14 ... 42 B3
Fernhead Rd W9 ... 23 B2
Fernhill Ho E5 ... 7 C2
Fernholme Rd SE15 ... 65 C2
Fernhurst Rd SW6 ... 164 B4
Fernie Ho SE22 ... 64 B4
Fernlea Rd SW12 ... 73 A3
Fernleigh Cl W9 ... 23 B2
Fernsbury St WC1 ... 95 B3
Fernshaw Mans SW10 ... 156 C3
Fernshaw Rd SW10 ... 156 C3
Fernside NW11 ... 1 C3
Fernside Rd SW12 ... 72 C4
Fern St E3 ... 26 C1
Ferntower Rd N5 ... 15 C3
Fern Wlk 18 SE16 ... 153 C1
Fernwood SW19 ... 70 B3
Ferrey Mews 19 SW9 ... 173 B1
Ferriby Cl N1 ... 14 C1
Ferrier Ind Est SW18 ... 59 A3
Ferrier Point 6 E16 ... 35 C4
Ferrier St SW18 ... 59 A3
Ferrings SE21 ... 76 A1
Ferris Rd SE22 ... 64 C3
Ferrybridge Ho SE11 ... 135 A1
Ferry La
Barnes SW13 ... 46 B4
Brentford TW8 ... 44 A4
Richmond TW9 ... 44 B4
Ferry Rd SW13 ... 46 C2
Ferry Sq 1 TW8 ... 44 A4
Ferry St E14 ... 42 B1
Festing Rd SW15 ... 57 C4
Festival Ct 5 E8 ... 16 B1
Festival Pier SE1 ... 120 C2
Fetter La EC4 ... 107 C2
Fettes Ho NW8 ... 79 C1
Ffinch St SE8 ... 51 C3
Field Ct
Hampstead NW3 ... 11 B3
Holborn WC1 ... 107 A3
Lower Holloway N7 ... 14 A3
Wimbledon SW19 ... 70 C1
Fieldgate Mans 25 E1 ... 111 C3
Fieldgate St E1 ... 111 C3
Field Ho NW10 ... 22 C2
Fieldhouse Rd SW12 ... 73 B3
Fielding Ho
Chiswick W4 ... 46 A4
6 Kilburn NW6 ... 23 C2
St John's Wood NW8 ... 78 C4
Fielding Mews SW13 ... 47 A4
Fielding Rd
Acton W4 ... 38 A3
Hammersmith W14 ... 39 C3
Fielding St SE17 ... 48 B4
Field Lo NW10 ... 8 B2
Field Rd W6 ... 154 A4
Fields Est E8 ... 16 C1
Field St WC1 ... 94 C4
Fieldsway Ho N5 ... 14 C3
Fieldview SW17, SW18 ... 71 C3
Fieldview Ct 2 N5 ... 15 A3
Fieldway Cres N5, N7 ... 14 C3
Fieldwick Ho 14 E9 ... 17 C2
Fife Rd
Mortlake SW14 ... 55 B2
Newham E16 ... 35 C4
Fife Terr N1 ... 85 A2
Fifth Ave W10 ... 23 A2
Fig Tree Cl NW10 ... 21 A4
Filey Ave N16 ... 7 C3
Filey Ho SW18 ... 59 B3
Filigree Ct SE16 ... 33 B1
Filmer Ho SW6 ... 164 B4
Filmer Mews SW6 ... 164 B4
Filmer Rd SW6 ... 154 C1
Filton Ct 14 SE14 ... 50 B3
Finborough Rd SW10 ... 156 B4
Finchdean Ho SW15 ... 68 B4
Finch Ho 1 SE8 ... 52 A3
Finch La EC2, EC3 ... 109 C1
Finchley Pl NW8 ... 79 B2
Finchley Rd
Hampstead NW3 ... 11 B2
St John's Wood NW8 ... 79 B2
Finchley Road & Frognal Sta NW3 ... 11 B3
Finchley Road Sta NW3 ... 11 B2
Finch Lo 15 W9 ... 31 C4
Finch Mews 3 SE15 ... 49 B2
Finch's Ct 10 E14 ... 34 A2
Findhorn St 8 E14 ... 34 B3
Findon Cl SW18 ... 58 C1
Findon Rd W12 ... 38 C4
Fineran Ct 16 SW11 ... 59 C3
Fingal St SE10 ... 43 B1
Fingest Ho NW8 ... 90 A2
Finland Rd SE4 ... 66 A4
Finland St SE16 ... 41 A3
Finlay St SW6 ... 47 C2
Finley Ct 21 SE5 ... 48 B3
Finmere Ho 1 N4 ... 6 B4
Finnemore Ho N1 ... 86 C4
Finn Ho N1 ... 97 C4
Finnis St E2 ... 25 A1
FINSBURY ... 95 C4
Finsbury Ave EC2 ... 109 C3
Finsbury Cir EC2 ... 109 C3
Finsbury Ct EC2 ... 109 B4
Finsbury L Ctr EC1 ... 96 C3
Finsbury Market EC2 ... 110 A4
Finsbury Mkt EC2 ... 24 A1 98 A1
FINSBURY PARK ... 5 C2
Finsbury Park Rd N4, N5 ... 6 A2
Finsbury Park Sta N4 ... 5 C2
Finsbury Pavement EC2 ... 109 C4

Finsbury Sq EC2 ... 109 C4
Finsbury St EC2 ... 109 B4
Finsen Rd SE5 ... 63 B4
Finstock Rd W10 ... 30 C3
Finton House Sch SW17 ... 72 B2
Finucane Ct TW9 ... 54 B4
Finwhale Ho E14 ... 42 A3
Fiona Ct 9 NW6 ... 23 B3
Firbank Rd SE15 ... 50 A1
Fircroft N1 ... 86 B4
Fircroft Prim Sch SW17 ... 72 B1
Fircroft Rd SW17 ... 72 B1
Fire Brigade Pier SE1 ... 148 B4
Firecrest Dr NW3 ... 2 A1
Firle Ho 7 W10 ... 30 B4
Fir Lo SW15 ... 57 A3
Firmston Ho 9 SW14 ... 55 C4
Firs Ave SW14 ... 55 B3
Firsby Rd N16 ... 7 C3
First Ave
  East Acton W3 ... 29 B1
  Mortlake SW14 ... 56 A4
  West Kilburn W10 ... 23 B1
First St SW3 ... 144 B4
Firth Gdns SW6 ... 164 A3
Fir Tree Ho 11 SE14 ... 50 B3
Fir Trees Cl SE16 ... 33 A1
Fisher Ho
  Islington N1 ... 85 B3
  9 Shadwell E1 ... 32 B2
  2 Tufnell Pk N19 ... 4 B1
Fishermans Dr SE16 ... 40 C4
Fisherman's Wlk E14 ... 33 C1
Fishers Cl SW16 ... 73 C1
Fishers Ct SE14 ... 50 C2
Fisher's La W4 ... 37 C2
Fisher St
  Holborn WC1 ... 106 C3
  Newham E16 ... 35 C4
Fisherton St NW8 ... 89 C2
Fisherton Street Est NW8 ... 89 C1
Fishlock Ct 6 SW4 ... 172 A2
Fish St Hill EC3 ... 123 C3
Fitch Ct SW2 ... 62 C2
Fitzalan St SE11 ... 149 B4
Fitzclarence Ho W11 ... 126 A4
Fitz-George Ave W14 ... 140 A3
Fitzgerald Ave SW14 ... 56 A4
Fitzgerald Ho
  15 Brixton SW9 ... 173 B1
  14 Poplar E14 ... 34 A3
Fitzgerald Rd SW14 ... 55 C4
Fitzhardinge Ho W1 ... 103 B2
Fitzhardinge St W1 ... 103 B2
Fitzherbert Ho 11 TW10 ... 54 B1
Fitzhugh Gr SW18 ... 59 C1
Fitzjames Ave W14 ... 140 B3
Fitzjohn's Ave NW3 ... 11 C3
Fitzjohns Mans NW3 ... 11 B2
Fitzjohns Prim Sch 4 NW3 ... 11 C3
Fitzmaurice Ho 17 SE16 ... 40 A2
Fitzmaurice Pl W1 ... 118 B2
Fitzneal St W12 ... 29 B3
FITZROVIA ... 104 A4
Fitzroy Cl N6 ... 3 B3
Fitzroy Cres W4 ... 45 C3
Fitzroy Ct W1 ... 93 A1
Fitzroy Ho
  Bermondsey SE1 ... 153 A2
  12 Tower Hamlets E14 ... 33 B3
Fitzroy Mews W1 ... 92 C1
Fitzroy Pk N6 ... 3 B3
Fitzroy Rd NW1 ... 81 B4
Fitzroy Sq W1 ... 92 C1
Fitzroy St W1 ... 92 C1
Fitzroy Yd NW1 ... 81 B4
Fitzwarren Gdns N19 ... 4 B3
Fitzwilliam Ave TW9 ... 44 B1
Fitzwilliam Mews E16 ... 35 C1
Fitzwilliam Rd SW4 ... 61 B4
Fives Ct SE11 ... 136 A1
Fiveways Rd SW9 ... 173 C1
Flamborough Ho 12 SE15 ... 49 C2
Flamborough St E14 ... 33 A3
Flamingo Ct 2 SE8 ... 51 C3
Flamsteed Ct 15 SE13 ... 52 A2
Flamsteed Ho SE10 ... 52 C3
Flanchford Rd W12 ... 38 B3
Flanders Ho N16 ... 7 A1
Flanders Mans 1 W4 ... 38 B2
Flanders Rd W4 ... 38 A2
Flanders Way E9 ... 17 C2
Flank St 9 E1 ... 125 B4
Flansham Ho 2 E14 ... 33 B3
Flask Cotts 4 NW3 ... 11 C4
Flask Wlk NW3 ... 11 C4
Flatiron Sq SE1 ... 123 A1
Flatiron Yd SE1 ... 123 A1
Flavell Mews SE10 ... 43 A1
Flaxman Ct W1 ... 105 B1
Flaxman Ho
  10 Chiswick W4 ... 38 A1
  Newington SE1 ... 136 B2
Flaxman Rd SE5 ... 48 A1
Flaxman Sp Ctr SE5 ... 48 B1
Flaxman Terr WC1 ... 93 C3
Flecker Ho 6 SE5 ... 48 C3
Fleece Wlk N7 ... 14 A2
Fleet Ct 1 W12 ... 38 A3
Fleetfield WC1 ... 94 B4
Fleet Ho
  6 Brixton SW2 ... 62 C2
  4 Limehouse E14 ... 33 A2
Fleet Pl EC4 ... 108 A2
Fleet Prim Sch 15 NW3 ... 12 B3
Fleet Rd NW3 ... 12 B3
Fleet Sq WC1 ... 95 A3
Fleet St EC4 ... 107 C1
Fleet Street Hill 10 E1 ... 24 C1 99 B1
Fleetway WC1 ... 94 B4
Fleet Wood 6 N16 ... 7 B2
Fleetwood Rd NW10 ... 8 C3
Fleetwood St N16 ... 7 A2
Fleming Cl 4 W9 ... 23 C1
Fleming Ct W2 ... 101 B4
Fleming Ho
  14 Bermondsey SE16 ... 139 B3
  Finsbury Pk N4 ... 6 B3
Fleming Rd SE17 ... 48 A4
Fletcher Bldgs WC2 ... 106 B1
Fletcher Ct 9 NW5 ... 13 A4
Fletcher Ho 16 N16 ... 16 A4
Fletcher Path 7 SE8 ... 51 C3
Fletcher Rd W4 ... 37 B3
Fletcher St 16 E1 ... 125 C4
Fleur De Lis St E1 ... 24 B1 98 C1
Fleur Gates 7 SW19 ... 69 C4
Flinders Ho 28 E1 ... 32 A1
Flinton St SE17 ... 152 B2
Flint St SE17 ... 151 C3
Flitcroft St WC2 ... 105 C1
Flitton Ho 7 N1 ... 15 A1
Flock Mill Pl SW18 ... 71 A3
Flodden Rd SE5 ... 48 B2
Flood St SW3 ... 158 B4
Flood Wlk SW3 ... 158 B4
Flora Cl E14 ... 34 A3
Flora Gardens Prim Sch 17 W6 ... 39 A2
Flora Gdns 2 W6 ... 39 A2
Floral St WC2 ... 120 A4
Florence Ct W9 ... 89 A3
Florence Gdns W4 ... 45 B4
Florence Ho
  20 Bermondsey SE16 ... 40 A1
  2 Brixton SW2 ... 62 B2
  10 Shepherd's Bush W11 ... 30 C2
  7 Wandsworth SW18 ... 59 C3
Florence Mans SW6 ... 164 C4
Florence Nightingale Ho 14 N1 ... 15 B2
Florence Nightingale Mus SE1 ... 135 A3
Florence Rd
  Acton W4 ... 37 C3
  Finsbury Pk N4 ... 5 C4
  New Cross Gate SE14 ... 51 B2
Florence St N1 ... 15 A1
Florence Terr
  Kingston u T SW15 ... 68 A1
  New Cross Gate SE14 ... 51 B2
Florence Way SW12 ... 72 B3
Flores Ho 13 E1 ... 32 C4
Florfield Rd E8 ... 17 A2
Florian SE5 ... 49 A2
Florian Rd SW15 ... 58 A3
Florida St E2 ... 24 C2 99 C3
Florida State Univ WC1 ... 105 C3
Florin Ct SE1 ... 138 C3
Floris Pl 7 SW4 ... 61 B4
Florys Ct 7 SW19 ... 70 A3
Floss St SW15 ... 47 B1
Flower & Dean Wlk E1 ... 111 A3
Flowersmead SW17 ... 72 C2
Flowers Mews 1 N19 ... 4 B2
Flower Wlk The SW7 ... 129 A4
Floyer Cl TW10 ... 54 B2
Flynn Ct 19 E14 ... 33 C2
Foley Ho 19 E1 ... 32 B3
Foley St W1 ... 104 C3
Folgate St E1 ... 110 C4
Foliot Ho N1 ... 84 C2
Foliot St W12 ... 29 B3
Follett Ho SW10 ... 157 B2
Follett St E14 ... 34 B3
Folly Wall E14 ... 42 B4
Fonda Ct 14 E14 ... 33 C2
Fontarabia Rd SW11 ... 60 C3
Fontenelle SE5 ... 49 A2
Fontenoy Ho SE11 ... 150 A3
Fontenoy Rd SW12, SW17 ... 73 B2
Fonthill Ho
  Kensington W14 ... 126 B2
  Pimlico SW1 ... 146 B2
Fonthill Mews N4 ... 5 B2
Fonthill Rd N4 ... 5 C2
Fontley Way SW15 ... 68 C4
Footpath The SW15 ... 56 C2
Forber Ho 25 E2 ... 25 B2
Forbes Ho 2 W4 ... 36 C1
Forbes St E1 ... 111 C1
Forburg Rd N16 ... 7 C3
Ford Cl 12 E3 ... 26 A3
Fordcombe 13 NW5 ... 12 C2
Fordham Ho 11 SE14 ... 51 A3
Fordham St 13 E1 ... 111 C2
Fordingley Rd W9 ... 23 B2
Ford Rd E3 ... 26 B3
Fords Park Rd E16 ... 35 C3
Ford Sq E1 ... 32 A4
Ford St
  Bow E3 ... 26 A3
  Canning Town E16 ... 35 B3
Fordwych Ct NW2 ... 10 A2
Fordwych Rd NW2 ... 10 A3
Fordyce Rd SE13 ... 67 B2
Forecastle Ct E14 ... 41 C4
Foreign & Commonwealth Office SW1 ... 134 A4
Foreland Ho W11 ... 31 A2 112 A4
Foreshore SE8 ... 41 B2
Fore St EC2 ... 109 A3
Forest Cl NW6 ... 10 A1
Forester Rd SE15 ... 65 A4
Forest Gr E8 ... 16 B2
Forest Hill Rd SE22 ... 65 A1
Forest Rd
  Dalston E8 ... 16 B2
  Richmond TW9 ... 44 C3
Fore Street Ave EC2 ... 109 B3
Forest Way 9 N19 ... 4 B2
Forfar Rd SW11 ... 169 C4
Forge Pl NW1 ... 12 C2
Forman Ho SE4 ... 65 C3
Formby Ct 9 N7 ... 14 C3
Formosa Ho 1 E1 ... 26 A1
Formosa St W9 ... 88 B1
Formunt Cl E16 ... 35 B4
Forrest Ct N7 ... 14 C2
Forrest Ho SW15 ... 47 B1
Forset Ct W1 ... 102 B2
Forset St W1 ... 102 B2
Forster Rd SW2 ... 74 A4
Forston St N1 ... 87 A2
Forsyth Gdns SE17 ... 48 A4
Forsyth Ho
  14 Hackney E9 ... 17 B1
  Pimlico SW1 ... 147 A3
Forsythia Ho SE4 ... 66 A4
Fortescue Ave 1 E8 ... 17 A1
Fortess Gr NW5 ... 13 B3
Fortess Rd NW5 ... 13 B4
Fortess Wlk NW5 ... 13 A3
Forthbridge Rd SW11 ... 60 C3
Forth Ho 30 E3 ... 26 B3
Forties The 9 NW5 ... 13 B3
Fortior Ct N6 ... 4 B4
Fortnam Rd N19 ... 4 C2
Fort Rd SE1 ... 153 A3
Fortrose Cl E14 ... 34 C3
Fortrose Gdns SW12, SW2 ... 74 A3
Fort St E1 ... 110 B3
Fortuna Cl N7 ... 14 B2
Fortune Ct 6 E8 ... 16 B1
Fortune Gate Rd NW10 ... 21 A4
Fortune Green Rd NW6 ... 10 C4
Fortune Ho
  Lambeth SE11 ... 149 B3
  St Luke's EC1 ... 97 A1
Fortune St EC1 ... 97 A1
Fortune Way NW10 ... 21 C2
Forty Acre La E16 ... 35 C4
Forum Cl 7 E3 ... 26 C4
Forward Bsns Ctr The 3 E16 ... 27 C1
Fosbrooke Ho SW8 ... 162 A1
Fosbury Ho 7 SW9 ... 62 B3
Fosbury Mews W2 ... 114 B3
Foscote Mews W9 ... 31 C4
Foskett Rd SW6 ... 165 A1
Fossil Rd SE13 ... 66 C4
Foster Ct
  6 Camden Town NW1 ... 13 B1
  Canning Town E16 ... 35 B2
Foster Ho SE14 ... 51 B2

Foster La EC2 .... 108 C2
Foster Rd
Acton W3 .... 29 A2
Chiswick W4 .... 37 C1
Foubert's Pl W1 .. 104 C1
Foulden Rd N16 .... 16 B4
Foulden Terr N16 ... 16 B4
Foulis Terr SW7 .. 143 C2
Foulser Rd SW17 ... 72 C1
Foundary Ho 6 E14 .... 34 A4
Founders Ct EC2 . 109 B2
Founders Ho SW1 147 B2
Foundling Ct WC1 . 94 A2
Foundling Mus The WC1 .... 94 B2
Foundry Cl SE16 .... 33 A1
Foundry Mews NW1 .... 93 A2
Foundry Pl
Stepney E1 .... 32 B4
Wandsworth SW18 .. 71 A4
Fountain & Colonnade Sh Ctr SW1 ...... 146 B4
Fountain Ct
Belgravia SW1 .... 146 A3
14 Shepherd's Bush W11 .... 39 C4
Strand EC4 .... 121 B4
Fountain Green Sq 34 SE16 .... 139 C3
Fountain Ho
33 Bermondsey SE16 .... 139 C3
3 Brondesbury Pk NW6 .... 10 A1
Mayfair W1 .... 117 B2
Fountain Mews
1 Highbury N5 ..... 15 B4
Maitland Pk NW3 .... 12 B2
Fountain Pl SW9 . 173 C3
Fountayne Rd N16 ... 7 C2
Fount St SW8 .... 161 C1
Fournier St E1 ... 111 A4
Fourscore Mans E8 .... 16 C1
Four Seasons Cl E3 .... 26 C3
Fourth Ave W10 .... 23 A2
Fovant Ct 5 SW8 170 C1
Fowey Cl E1 .... 32 A1
Fowey Ho SE11 ... 149 C2
Fowler Cl SW11 .... 59 C4
Fowler Ho
5 Camberwell SE5 .... 49 A1
Islington N1 .... 86 B4
South Lambeth SW8 .... 171 C3
Fowler Rd N1 ..... 86 B4
Fownes St SW11 .... 60 A4
Fox and Knot St EC1 .... 108 B4
Foxberry Ct SE4 .... 66 B3
Foxberry Rd SE4 .... 66 A4
Foxborough Gdns SE4 .... 66 C2
Foxbourne Rd SW17 .... 72 C2
Fox Cl
Bethnal Green E1 .... 25 B1
Newham E16 .... 35 C4
Foxcombe Rd 6 SW15 .... 68 C3
Foxcote SE5 ...... 152 B1
Foxcroft WC1 ...... 85 A1
Fox Ct EC1 .... 107 B3
Foxfield NW1 ...... 82 B3
Foxglove St W12 ... 29 B2
Foxham Rd N19 ..... 4 C1
Fox Ho 2 SW11 .... 59 C3
Foxley Cl E8 .... 16 C3
Foxley Ho 4 E3 .... 27 A2
Foxley Rd SW9 ..... 48 A3
Foxley Sq 3 SW9 .. 48 A2
Foxmore St SW11 168 C3
Fox Prim Sch W8 .... 31 C1 113 B1
Fox Rd E16 .... 35 B4
Fox's Yd E2 .. 24 B1 99 A2
Foxwell Mews SE4 . 66 A4
Foxwell St SE4 ..... 66 A4
Foyle Rd SE3 .... 53 B4
Fradel Lo N16 .... 6 C3
Framfield Rd N5 .... 15 A3
Frampton NW1 ..... 13 C1
Frampton Ct 3 W3 .... 37 B4
Frampton Ho NW8 . 89 C1
Frampton Park Rd E9 .... 17 B1
Frampton St NW8 . 89 C1
Francemary Rd SE4 .... 66 C2
Franche Court Rd SW17 .... 71 B1
Francis Chichester Way SW11 .... 169 C3
Francis Cl 6 E14 ... 42 C2
Francis Ct 12 SE14 . 50 C4
Francis Ho
Harlesden NW10 .... 21 B4
11 Shoreditch N1 .... 24 A4
Walham Green SW10 .... 156 B2
Francis Holland Sch
Belgravia SW1 .... 145 C3
Marylebone NW1 ... 90 C2
Francis Snary Lo 11 SW18 .... 58 C2
Francis St SW1 ... 147 A4
Francis Terr N19 ..... 4 B1
Francis Terrace Mews 16 N19 .... 4 B1
Francis Wlk N1 ..... 84 C4
Franconia Rd SW4 . 61 C2
Frank Barnes Sch 13 NW3 .... 11 C1
Frank Beswick Ho SW6 .... 155 A3
Frank Dixon Cl SE21 .... 76 A3
Frank Dixon Way SE21 .... 76 A3
Frankfurt Rd SE24 . 63 B2
Frankham Ho 8 SE8 .... 51 C3
Frankham St SE8 ... 51 C3
Frank Ho SW8 .... 162 A2
Frankland Cl SE16 . 40 A2
Frankland Ho 4 SW12 .... 73 A4
Frankland Rd SW7 .... 129 B1
Franklin Bldg 5 E14 .... 41 C4
Franklin Cl
Greenwich SE13 ..... 52 A2
West Norwood SE27 .... 75 A1
Franklin Ho
New Cross SE4 ...... 51 A1
Franklin Ho *continued*
26 Wapping E1 ...... 32 A1
Franklin Pl SE13 .... 52 A2
Franklin Sq SW5 . 141 A1
Franklin's Row SW3 .... 145 A2
Franklin St 43 E3 ... 27 A2
Franklyn Rd NW10 ... 8 B2
Frank Soskice Ho SW6 .... 155 A3
Frank Whymark Ho 4 SE16 .... 40 B4
Frans Hals Ct E14 .. 42 C3
Fraserburgh Ho 29 E3 .... 26 B3
Fraser Ct SW11 ... 168 A4
Fraser Ho
Brentford TW8 ...... 36 B1
40 Clapham SW8 .. 171 B1
Fraser Regnart Ct 12 NW5 .... 12 B3
Fraser St W4 .... 38 A1
Frazier St SE1 .... 135 B3
Frean St SE16 .... 139 B2
Frearson Ho WC1 .. 95 A4
Freda Corbett Cl 10 SE15 .... 49 C3
Frederica St 4 N7 .... 14 B1
Frederick Blg N1 ... 16 A2
Frederick Charrington Ho 4 E1 .... 25 B1
Frederick Cl W2 .. 116 C4
Frederick Cres SW9 .... 48 A3
Frederick Ct SW6 ... 58 A4
Frederick's Pl EC2 .... 109 B1
Frederick Sq 11 SE16 .... 33 A2
Frederick's Row EC1 .... 96 A4
Frederick St WC1 .. 94 C3
Frederick Terr E8 ... 16 B1
Frederic Mews SW1 .... 131 B3
Freedom St SW11 169 A2
Freegrove Rd N7 ... 14 A3
Freeling Ho NW8 .. 79 B4
Freeling St 7 N1 ... 14 B1
Freeman Ho 13 SW2 .... 74 A4
Freemantle St SE17 .... 152 A2
Freemens Hos 1 SW9 .... 62 B3
Freke Rd SW11 ..... 60 C4
Fremantle Ho 14 E1 .... 25 A1
Fremont St E9 ...... 25 B4
French Inst The SW7 .... 143 B4
French Pl E1 .... 24 A1 98 B2
Frendsbury Rd SE4 .... 66 A3
Frensham Ct N5 .... 15 B3
Frensham Dr SW15 .... 68 C2
Frensham St SE15 . 49 C4
Frere St 6 SW11 . 168 B2
Freshfield Ave E8 ... 16 B1
Freshfield Cl SE13 . 67 C3
Freshford St SW17, SW18 .... 71 B1
Freston Rd W10, W11 .... 30 C2
Freswick Ho 6 SE8 .... 41 A2
Freud Mus The NW3 .... 11 B2
Frewell Bldg EC1 . 107 B4
Frewin Rd SW18 .... 71 C3
Friar Mews SE27 ... 75 A1
Friars Ave
Putney SW15 .... 58 A2
Roehampton SW15 ... 68 B1
Friars Cl SE1 ..... 122 B1
Friars Gdns W3 ..... 28 C3
Friars Mead E14 .... 42 B3
Friars Place La W3 .... 28 C2
Friars Prim Foundation Sch SE1 .... 136 B3
Friars Stile Pl 9 TW10 .... 54 A1
Friars Stile Rd TW10 .... 54 A1
Friar St EC4 ...... 108 B1
Friars Way W3 ..... 28 C3
Friary Park Ct 12 W3 .... 28 B3
Friary Rd
Acton W3 .... 28 C3
Peckham SE15 ...... 49 C3
Friday Grove Mews 11 SW12 .... 73 B4
Friday St EC4 ..... 122 C4
Frideswide Pl NW5 .... 13 B3
Friendly Pl 16 SE13 .... 52 A2
Friendly St SE8 ..... 51 C2
Friendly Street Mews SE8 .... 51 C1
Friendship Way E15 .... 27 B4
Friend St EC1 ...... 96 A4
Friern Rd SE22 ..... 64 C1
Frigate Ho 7 E14 ... 42 B2
Frigate Mews SE8 . 51 C4
Frimley Cl SW19 .... 70 A2
Frimley Way E1 .... 25 C1
Frinstead Ho 1 W10 .... 30 C2
Friston St SW6 ... 166 A1
Frith Ho
Bethnal Green E2 .... 24 C2 99 B3
Paddington NW8 ... 89 C1
Frith Rd E11 .... 19 C4
Frith St W1 .... 105 B1
Frithville Ct 2 W12 .... 30 B1
Frithville Gdns W12 .... 30 B1
Frobisher Ct
1 Greenwich SE10 .... 52 C4
3 Shepherd's Bush W12 .... 39 B4
Frobisher Ho 27 E1 .... 32 A1
Frobisher Pas E14 .. 33 C1
Frobisher Pl SE14 .. 50 B2
Frobisher St SE10 .. 53 A4
Frogley Rd SE22 .... 64 B3
Frogmore SW18 .... 58 C2
Frogmore Est NW10 .... 20 B2
Frogmore Ind Est N5 .... 15 B4
Frognal NW3 .... 11 B3
Frognal Cl NW3 .... 11 B3
Frognal Ct NW3 .... 11 B2
Frognal Gdns NW3 . 11 B4
Frognal La NW3 .... 11 A3
Frognal Par NW3 ... 11 B2
Frognal Rise NW3 .. 11 B4
Frognal Way NW3 .. 11 B4
Frome Ho SE15 ..... 65 B3
Frome St N1 .... 86 C2
Fromow's Cnr 14 W4 .... 37 B1
Frontenac NW10 ..... 9 A1
Frostic Wlk E1 ... 111 A3
Froude St SW8 ... 170 B1
Frye Ct 5 E3 .... 26 B2
Frying Pan Alley E1 .... 110 C3
Fry Rd NW10 .... 21 B4
Fulbeck Ho N7 ..... 14 B2
Fulbourne St E1 .... 32 A4
Fulbrook Rd N19 ... 13 B4
Fulcher Ct 40 SE8 .. 51 B4
Fulcher Ho
13 Deptford SE8 .... 41 B1
10 Shoreditch N1 .... 24 A4
Fulford Mans 3 N19 .... 5 A1
Fulford St SE16 ..... 40 A4
FULHAM 47 C1
Fulham Broadway SW6 .... 155 C1
Fulham Broadway Sh Ctr SW6 .... 155 C1
Fulham Broadway Sta SW6 .... 155 C2
Fulham Bsns Exchange SW6 .. 167 A3
Fulham Cross Girls Sec Sch SW6 .... 154 A1
Fulham Ct SW6 ... 165 B4
Fulham High St SW6 .... 164 B1
Fulham Pal SW6 .. 164 A1
Fulham Palace Rd SW6, W6 .... 47 C4
Fulham Park Gdns SW6 .... 164 C2
Fulham Park Rd SW6 .... 164 C2
Fulham Prep Sch
6 Fulham SW6 ... 164 B1
Fulham W14 ...... 154 B4
Fulham Prim Sch SW6 .... 155 B3
Fulham Rd
Chelsea SW10 .... 157 A4
Fulham SW6 ...... 165 A4
Fuller Cl 4 E2 .... 24 C1 99 B2
Fullers Ho 6 SW18 .... 58 C2
Fullerton Rd SW18 . 59 B2
Fullwood's Mews N1 .... 97 C4
Fulmar Ct 6 SE21 .. 75 C2
Fulmar Ho
12 Bermondsey SE16 .... 40 C2
Marylebone NW8 ... 90 B1
Fulmead St SW6 .. 166 B3
Fulneck 1 E1 .... 32 B4

Fulthorp Rd SE3....53 C1
Fulton Mews W2 . 114 C4
Fulwood Pl WC1.. 107 A3
Fulwood Wlk SW19..............70 A3
Furber St W6.......39 A3
Furley Ho 7 SE15..49 C3
Furley Rd SE15.....49 C3
Furlong Rd N7.....14 C2
Furmage St SW18..71 A4
Furness Ho SW1.. 146 A2
Furness Lo 4 SW14.............55 A3
Furness Prim Sch NW10.............21 C3
Furness Rd
Harlesden NW10....21 C3
Sands End SW6 ... 166 B2
Furnival St EC4... 107 B2
Furrow La E9.......17 B3
Fursecroft W1..... 102 C2
Furze St E3........33 C4
Fusion Ct SW15....68 A1
Futters Ct 1 NW10.............21 A3
Fyfield N4...........5 C2
Fyfield Rd 5 SW9..62 C4
Fynes St SW1.... 147 B4

G

Gable Ho 12 W4....38 A2
Gables Cl SE5......49 A2
Gables The
3 Clapham SW4....61 B4
Hampstead NW3.....2 C2
Gabriel Ho SE11.. 148 C4
Gabrielle Ct NW3...11 C2
Gabriel Mews NW2..1 B2
Gabriel's Wharf SE1............ 121 B2
Gaddesden Ho EC1 97 C3
Gadsden Ho
6 Homerton E9.....17 C2
8 Kensal Town W10.............23 A1
Gagarin Ho SW11...59 C4
Gage Rd E16.......35 A4
Gage St WC1..... 106 B4
Gainford Ho 18 E2..25 A2
Gainford St N1.... 85 B4
Gainsborough Ct
6 Bermondsey SE16.............40 A1
Dulwich SE21.......76 A2
Shepherd's Bush W12.............39 B4
Gainsborough Gdns
Golders Green NW11.............1 B4
Hampstead NW3.....2 C1
Gainsborough Ho
Finsbury Pk N4.......5 B3
3 Hampstead NW3.............11 B4
5 Limehouse E14...33 A2
Westminster SW1 . 147 C3
Gainsborough Prim Sch E9.............18 C2
Gainsborough Rd
Bedford Pk W4......38 B2
Richmond TW9......54 B4
Gainsborough St 3 E9.................18 B2
Gainsborough Studios N1............... 87 B3
Gainsford St SE1 . 139 A4
Gairloch Ho 2 NW1..............13 C1
Gairloch Rd SE5....49 A1
Gaisford St NW5....13 B2
Gaitskell Ct SW11 168 A2
Gaitskell Ho SE17...48 C4
Gaitskell Way SE1 136 C4
Galata Rd SW13....46 C3
Galatea Sq SE15....65 A4
Galaxy Bldg 6 E14...............41 C2
Galaxy Ho EC2..... 97 C2
Galbraith St E14....42 B3
Gale Ho 10 SW2....62 B2
Galena Ho 5 W6....39 A2
Galena Rd W6......39 A2
Galen Pl WC1..... 106 B3
Galesbury Rd SW18.............59 B1
Gales Gdns E2......25 A2
Gale St E3.........33 C4
Galgate Cl 4 SW19.............70 A3
Galleon Cl SE16....40 C4
Galleon Ho 8 E14..42 B2
Galleries of Modern London EC1..... 108 C3
Gallery Ct SW10.. 156 C3
Gallery Rd SE21....75 C3
Galleywall Rd SE16.............40 A2
Galleywall Road Trad Est 12 SE16........40 A2
Galleywood Ho 1 W10..............30 B4
Gallia Rd N5.......15 A3
Galloway Rd W12...29 C1
Galsworthy Ave E14...............33 A4
Galsworthy Ct W3..37 A3
Galsworthy Ho 4 W11..............31 A3
Galsworthy Rd NW2..............10 A4
Galton St W10......23 A2
Galveston Ho 2 E1................26 A1
Galveston Rd SW15.............58 B2
Galway Cl 28 SE16..40 A1
Galway Ho
Finsbury EC1...... 97 A3
7 Stepney E1......32 C4
Galway St EC1..... 97 A3
Gambetta St 3 SW8............ 170 B1
Gambia St SE1... 122 B1
Gambler Ho EC1... 97 A3
Gamlen Rd SW15...57 C3
Gandolfi St 5 SE15.............49 A4
Ganley Ct 18 SW11 .59 C4
Gannet Ct 5 SE21..75 C2
Gannet Ho SE15....49 B2
Ganton St W1.... 105 A1
Garand Ct 2 N7....14 B3
Garbett Ho 2 SE17..............48 A4
Garbutt Pl W1.... 103 C3
Garden Cl SW15....69 A4
Garden Ct
4 Richmond TW9.............44 B2
12 South Acton W4..37 B3
St John's Wood NW8............ 89 B4
Strand EC4....... 121 B4
Garden Flats SW16.............74 A1
Garden Ho 12 SW9............ 172 B2
Garden House Sch SW3............ 145 A2
Garden La SW2.....74 B3
Garden Mews W2....... 31 C2 113 C3
Garden Mus SE1.. 134 C1
Garden Pl 28 E2....24 B4
Garden Rd
Richmond TW9......54 C4
St John's Wood NW8............ 89 A4
Garden Row SE1 . 136 A2
Garden Royal 16 SW15.............57 C1
Garden St E1.......32 C4
Gardens The
East Dulwich SE22.............64 C3
Stamford Hill N16.....7 B4
Garden Terr
Knightsbridge SW7........... 130 B3
Pimlico SW1...... 147 B2
Garden Wlk EC2.........24 A1 98 A2
Gardiner Ave NW2...9 B3
Gardiner Ct NW10..20 C4
Gardiner Ho SW11........... 168 A4
Gardner Ct N5......15 B4
Gardners La EC4.. 122 C4
Gardnor Mans 14 NW3..............11 B4
Gardnor Rd NW3...11 C4
Gard St EC1....... 96 B4
Gareth Ct SW16....73 C1
Garfield Ho W2... 102 C1
Garfield Mews 7 SW11.............60 C4
Garfield Rd SW11...60 C4
Garford St E14.....33 C2
Garland Ct 12 E14..33 C2
Garland Ho N16.....6 C1
Garlands Ho NW8 . 78 B2
Garlick Hill EC4.. 123 A4
Garlinge Ho 12 SW9............ 173 B4
Garlinge Rd NW2...10 B2
Garnault Mews EC1............. 95 C3
Garnault Pl EC1... 95 C3
Garner St E2.......24 C3
Garnet Rd NW10.....8 A2
Garnet St E1.......32 B2
Garnett Ho 5 NW3..............12 B3
Garnett Rd NW3....12 B3
Garnham Cl 2 N16..7 B2
Garnham St 1 N16..7 B2
Garnies Cl SE15....49 B3
Garrad's Rd SW16..73 C1
Garrard Wlk NW10...8 A2
Garratt Ho 8 N16...7 A3
Garratt La SW18....71 A3
Garratt Park Sec Specl Sch 6 SW18.............71 B2
Garraway Ct SW13..47 B3
Garraway Ho SE21..76 B1
Garrett Cl W3......28 C4
Garrett Ho 8 W12..30 A3
Garrett St EC1..... 97 A2
Garrick Cl SW18....59 B3
Garrick Ho
Chiswick W4........46 A4
Mayfair W1........ 118 A1
Garrick Rd TW9....44 C1
Garrick St WC2.... 120 A4
Garrick Yd WC2.... 120 A4
Garsdale Terr SW5........... 141 A2
Garsington Mews SE4...............66 B4
Garson Ho W2.... 115 B4
Garston Ho 6 N1..15 A1
Garter Way SE16...40 C4
Garth Ct W4........45 C4
Garth Ho NW2.......1 B2
Garth Rd
Child's Hill NW2......1 B2
8 Chiswick W4.....37 C1
Gartmoor Gdns SW19.............70 B3
Garton Ho 6 N6....4 C4
Garton Pl SW18....59 B1
Gartons Way SW11.............59 B4
Garway Rd W2... 100 A1
Gascoigne Pl 17 E2..........24 B2 98 C3
Gascony Ave NW6..10 C1
Gascoyne Ho 2 E9................17 C1
Gascoyne Rd E9....17 C1
Gaselee St E14.....34 B2
Gasholder Pl SE11............ 149 A1
Gaskarth Rd SW12..61 A1
Gaskell St SW4... 172 A2
Gaskin Ho N16......6 C1
Gaskin St N1...... 86 A4
Gaspar Cl SW7.... 142 B4
Gaspar Mews SW5............. 142 B4
Gasson Ho 24 SE14..............50 C4
Gastein Rd W6.....47 C4
Gastigny Ho EC1... 97 A3
Gaston Bell Cl TW9..............54 B4
Gaston Gate SW8 172 C4
Gataker Ho 5 SE16..............40 A3
Gataker St 6 SE16..............40 A3
Gatcliff Cl SW1... 145 C1
Gatcombe Ho 20 SE22..............64 A4
Gatcombe Rd
8 Newham E16.....35 C1
Tufnell Pk N19........4 C1
Gatefield Ct SE15...64 C4
Gateforth St NW8 . 90 A1
Gate Hill Ct W11.......31 B1 113 A2
Gatehouse Sch 26 E2................25 C3
Gatehouse Sq SE1............ 123 A2
Gateley Ho 6 SE4..65 C3
Gateley Rd SW9....62 B4
Gate Mews SW7.. 130 B3
Gatesborough St EC2.........24 A1 98 A2
Gates Ct SE17.... 150 C2
Gatesden WC1..... 94 B3
Gateside Rd SW17..72 B1
Gate St WC2...... 106 C2
Gateway SE17......48 B4
Gateway Arc N1... 86 A2
Gateway Ho SW12..61 A1
Gateway Ind Est NW10.............21 C1
Gateway Mews 4 E8................16 B3
Gateway Prim Sch NW8............. 89 C2
Gateways The SW3........... 144 B3
Gateway Trad Est NW10.............21 B2
Gathorne St 19 E2..25 C3
Gatliff Rd SW1... 146 A1
Gatonby St SE15....49 B2
Gatwick Ho 3 E14.33 B3
Gatwick Rd SW18...70 B4
Gauden Cl SW4.....61 C4
Gauden Rd SW4.....61 C4
Gaugin Ct 13 SE16..40 A1
Gaunt St SE1..... 136 C2
Gautrey Rd SE15....50 B1
Gavel St SE17.... 151 C4
Gaverick Mews 3 E14...............41 C2
Gaviller Pl 3 E5...17 A4
Gawber St E2......25 B2
Gawthorne Ct E3...26 C3
Gay Cl NW2.........9 A3
Gaydon Ho W2... 100 A4
Gayfere St SW1... 134 A1
Gayford Rd W12....38 B4
Gay Ho N16........16 A3
Gayhurst SE17......48 C4
Gayhurst Ho NW8 . 90 B2
Gayhurst Prim Sch 5 E8................16 C1
Gayhurst Rd E8....16 C1
Gaymead NW8.... 78 B3
Gay Rd E15.........27 C3
Gaysley Ho SE11.. 149 B3
Gay St SW15.......57 C4
Gayton Cres NW3...11 C4
Gayton Ho E3......26 C1
Gayton Rd NW3....11 C4
Gayville Rd SW11...60 B1
Gaywood Cl SW2...74 C3
Gaywood St SE1.. 136 B1
Gaza St SE17..... 150 A1
Gaze Ho 11 E14....34 C3
Gean Ct 3 E11.....19 C4
Geary Ho N7.......14 B3
Geary Rd NW10......8 C3
Geary St N7........14 B3
Gedling Ho SE22...64 B4
Gedling Pl SE1... 139 A2
Gees Ct W1...... 103 C1
Gee St EC1........ 96 C2
Geffrye Ct N1......24 A3
Geffrye Mus E2.....24 B3
Geffrye St E2.......24 B3
Geldart Rd SE15....50 A3
Geldeston Rd E5....7 C2
Gellatly Rd SE14....50 C1
Gemini Bsns Ctr E16...............27 C1
Gemini Ho 11 E3...26 C4

Gems Hampshire Sch (Main Sch) SW7 144 A1
Gems Hampshire Sch (The Early Years) SW7 143 A3
General Wolfe Rd SE10 52 C2
Genesis Bsns Pk NW10 20 A3
Geneva Ct
1 Putney SW15 57 C2
Stoke Newington N16 6 C3
Geneva Dr SW9 62 C3
Genoa Ave SW15 57 B2
Genoa Ho 19 E1 25 C1
Geoffrey Cl SE5 48 B1
Geoffrey Ct SE4 66 B4
Geoffrey Ho SE1 137 C2
Geoffrey Jones Ct NW10 21 C4
Geoffrey Rd SE4 66 B4
George Beard Rd 11 SE8 41 B2
George Beare Lo 9 SW4 61 B2
George Belt Ho 8 E2 25 C2
George Ct WC2 120 B3
George Downing Est N16 7 B2
George Eliot Ho SW1 147 A3
George Eliot Jun & Inf Schs NW8 79 B4
George Elliot Ho SE17 150 C2
George Elliston Ho 13 SE1 153 B1
George Eyre Ho NW8 79 C1
George Green's Sch E14 42 B1
George Inn Yd SE1 123 B1
George La SE13 67 B1
George Lansbury Ho
7 Bow E3 26 B2
3 Willesden NW10 8 A1
George Lashwood Ct 12 SW9 62 B3
George Leybourne Ho 15 E1 125 C4
George Lindgren Ho SW6 155 A2
George Loveless Ho 4 E2 24 B2 99 A4
George Mathers Rd SE11 150 A4
George Mews
27 Brixton SW9 173 B1
NW1 92 C3
George Peabody Ct NW1 102 A4
George Row SE16 139 B3
George's Rd N7 14 B3
George's Sq SW6 155 A4
George St
6 Canning Town E16 35 B3
Marylebone W1 103 A2
George Tingle Ho SE1 139 A2
Georgette Pl SE10 52 B3
George Vale Ho 35 E2 24 C3
George Walter Ho 11 SE16 40 B2
George Wyver Cl SW18 70 A4
George Yd
City of London EC3 109 C1
Mayfair W1 117 C4
Georgiana St NW1 83 A4
Georgian Ct 12 E9 25 B4
Georgina Gdns 10 E2 24 B2 99 A4
Geraldine Rd
Brentford W4 44 C4
Wandsworth SW18 59 B2
Geraldine St SE11 136 A1
Gerald Mews SW1 145 C4
Gerald Rd SW1 145 C4
Gerard Ct NW2 9 C3
Gerard Rd SW13 46 B2
Gerards Cl SE16 40 B1
Gernigan Ho SW18 59 C1
Gernon Rd E3 26 A3
Gerrard Ho 5 SE14 50 C3
Gerrard Pl W1 119 C4
Gerrard Rd N1 86 B2
Gerrard St W1 119 C4
Gerridge Ct SE1 135 C2
Gerridge St SE1 135 C2
Gerry Raffles Sq E15 19 C2
Gertrude St SW10 157 A3
Gervase St SE15 50 A3
Getters Talmud Torah 3 N16 6 C4
Ghent Way E8 16 B2
Gherkin The (30 St Mary Axe) EC2 110 B2
Giant Arches Rd SE24 63 B1
Gibbings Ho SE1 136 B3
Gibbins Rd E15 19 B1
Gibbon Ho NW8 89 C1
Gibbon Rd
Acton W3 29 A2
Nunhead SE15 50 B1
Gibbons Rd NW10 8 A2
Gibbon's Rents SE1 124 A1
Gibbon Wlk SW15 56 C3
Gibbs Gn W14 141 A2
Gibbs Green Rd W14 140 C2
Gibbs Green Specl Sch W14 141 A2
Gibbs Ho 6 SW12 73 A4
Gibraltar Ho NW10 21 A3
Gibraltar Wlk 23 E2 24 B2 99 A3
Gibson Cl E1 25 B1
Gibson Gdns N16 7 B2
Gibson Rd SE11 149 A3
Gibson Sq N1 85 C4
Gibson St SE10 43 A1
Gideon Rd SW11 60 C4
Giesbach Rd N19 4 C2
Giffen Square Mkt SE8 51 C3
Giffin St SE8 51 C3
Gifford Ho
5 Clapham SW4 61 C3
Greenwich SE10 42 C1
Gifford Ho *continued*
Pimlico SW1 146 C1
Gifford Rd NW10 8 A1
Gifford St N1 14 A1
Gilbert Ho
Barbican EC2 109 A3
Deptford SE8 51 C4
5 Globe Town E2 25 C2
Pimlico SW1 146 B1
South Lambeth SW8 162 A2
Gilbert Pl WC1 106 A3
Gilbert Rd SE11 149 C4
Gilbert Sheldon Ho W2 101 C4
Gilbertson Ho 11 E14 41 C3
Gilbert St W1 103 C1
Gilbeys Yd NW1 12 C1
Gilby Ho 5 E9 17 C2
Gilda Cres N16 7 C3
Gildea St W1 104 B3
Gilden Cres NW5 12 C3
Giles Ho
5 Bermondsey SE16 139 B2
Notting Hill W11 31 C3
Gilesmead SE5 48 C2
Gilkes Cres SE21 64 A1
Gilkes Pl SE21 64 A1
Gillam Ho 9 SE16 40 B2
Gill Ave E16 35 C3
Gillender St E3 27 B1
Gillespie Prim Sch N5 6 A1
Gillespie Rd N4, N5 6 A1
Gillett Pl 27 E8 16 A3
Gillett St E8, N16 16 A3
Gillfoot NW1 82 C1
Gillian St SE13 67 A2
Gillies St NW5 12 C3
Gilling Ct 5 NW3 12 A2
Gillingham Ho SW1 146 C4
Gillingham Mews SW1 146 C4
Gillingham Rd NW2 1 A1
Gillingham Row SW1 146 C4
Gillingham St SW1 146 C4
Gillison Wlk 19 SE16 139 C2
Gillman Ho 24 E2 24 C3
Gillray Ho SW10 157 B3
Gill St E14 33 B2
Gilmore Ho SW4 60 B3
Gilmore Rd SE13 67 C3
Gilpin Ave SW14 55 C3
Gilpin Cl W2 101 A4
Gilpin Rd E5 18 A4
Gilray Ho W2 115 B4
Gilstead Rd SW6 166 B2
Gilston Rd SW10 143 A1
Giltspur St EC1 108 B2
Gilwell Ct 7 E5 17 A4
Gipsy Cnr W3 28 C4
Gipsy La SW15 57 A4
Giraud St E14 34 A3
Girdlers Rd W14 39 C2
Girdlestone Wlk N19 4 B2
Girdwood Rd SW18, SW19 70 A4
Girling Ho 9 N1 24 A4
Gironde Rd SW6 155 A1
Girton Ho SW15 57 C1
Girton Villas 6 W10 30 C3
Gisburn Ho 23 SE15 49 C3
Gissing Wlk N1 14 C1
Glade The W12 39 A4
Glading Terr N16 7 B1
Gladsmuir Rd N19 4 B3
Gladstone Ct
Westminster SW1 147 C3
Willesden NW2 9 A3
Gladstone Ho 16 E14 33 C3
Gladstone Park Sch NW10 9 A3
Gladstone Rd W4 37 C3
Gladstone St SE1 136 A2
Gladstone Terr SW8 170 B4
Gladwin Ho NW1 83 A1
Gladwyn Rd SW15 57 C4
Gladys Rd NW6 10 C1
Glaisher St SE8 52 A4
Glamis Ct W3 37 A4
Glamis Est 3 E1 32 C2
Glamis Pl E1 32 B2
Glamis Rd E1 32 B2
Glanville Ho 4 SW12 73 B4
Glanville Rd SW2 62 A2
Glasbury Ho 5 SW9 62 B3
Glaserton Rd N16 7 A4
Glasgow Ho W9 78 B1
Glasgow Terr SW1 146 C1
Glasshill St SE1 136 B4
Glasshouse Fields E1 32 C2
Glasshouse St W1 119 A3
Glasshouse The SE13 67 B3
Glasshouse Wlk SE11 148 C2
Glasshouse Yd EC1 96 C1
Glass St 4 E2 25 A1
Glastonbury Ct 12 SE14 50 B3
Glastonbury Ho SW1 146 A2
Glastonbury Pl 22 E1 32 B3
Glastonbury St NW6 10 B3
Glaucus St E3 34 A4
Glazbury Rd W14 140 B2
Glazebrook Cl SE21 75 C2
Glebe Cl 1 W4 38 A1
Glebe Ho 8 SE16 40 A3
Glebelands Cl SE5 64 A4
Glebe Pl SW3 158 A4
Glebe Rd
Barnes SW13 46 C1
Dalston E8 16 B1
Willesden NW10 8 C2
Glebe St W4 38 A1
Gledhow Gdns SW5 142 C3
Gledstanes Rd W14 140 B1
Glegg Pl 3 SW15 57 C3
Glenaffric Ave E14 42 C2
Glen Albyn Rd SW19 69 C2
Glenalmond Ho 2 SW15 57 C1
Glenarm Rd E5 17 C4
Glenbrook Prim Sch SW4 61 C1
Glenbrook Rd NW6 10 C3
Glenburnie Rd SW17 72 B1
Glencoe Mans 6 SW9 163 B1
Glendall St SW9 62 B3
Glendarvon St SW15 57 C4
Glendower Gdns 10 SW14 55 C4
Glendower Pl SW7 143 B4
Glendower Prep Sch SW7 143 B4
Glendower Rd SW14 55 C4
Glendown Ho 2 E8 16 C3
Glendun Ct W3 29 A2
Glendun Rd W3 29 A2
Gleneagles Cl 21 SE16 40 A1
Glenelg Rd SW2 62 A2
Glenfield Rd SW12 73 B3
Glenfinlas Way SE5 48 A3
Glenforth St SE10 43 B1
Glengall Gr E14 42 B3
Glengall Pass 2 NW6 23 C4
Glengall Rd
Camberwell SE15 49 B4
Kilburn NW6 23 B4
Glengall Terr SE15 49 B4
Glengarnock Ave E14 42 B2
Glengarry Rd SE22 64 B2
Glenhurst Ave NW5 12 C4
Glenilla Rd NW3 12 A2
Glenister Rd SE10 43 B1
Glenkerry Ho 1 E14 34 B3
Glenloch Ct 2 NW3 12 A2
Glenloch Rd NW3 12 A3
Glenluce Rd SE3 53 C4
Glenmore SW15 57 C1
Glenmore Ho 6 TW10 54 A1
Glenmore Rd NW3 12 A2
Glennie Ct SE21 76 C3
Glennie Ho SE10 52 B2
Glennie Rd SE27, SW16 74 C1
Glenridding NW1 83 A1
Glenrosa St SW6 166 C2
Glenroy St W12 30 B3
Glensdale Rd SE4 66 B4
Glenshaw Mans 7 SW9 163 B1
Glentanner Way SW17 71 C1
Glentham Gdns SW13 47 A4

Glentham Rd SW13 47 A4
Glenthorne Mews W6 39 A2
Glenthorne Rd W6 39 A2
Glenthorpe SW15 56 C3
Glentworth St NW1 91 A1
Glenville Gr SE8 51 B3
Glenville Mews SW18 70 C4
Glenworth Ave E14 42 C2
Gliddon Rd W14 140 A2
Globe Acad SE1 137 C1
Globe Pond Rd SE16 33 A1
Globe Prim Sch 37 E2 25 B2
Globe Rd E1, E2 25 B1
Globe St SE1 137 B3
Globe Terr 9 E2 25 B2
Globe Theatre The SE1 122 C3
GLOBE TOWN 25 C2
Globe View EC4 122 C4
Globe Yd W1 104 A1
Gloucester W14 141 A3
Gloucester Ave NW1 81 C4
Gloucester Cir SE10 52 B3
Gloucester Cres NW1 82 A4
Gloucester Ct
- Borough The SE1 137 A2
- City of London EC3 124 B3
- Dulwich SE22 76 C3
- Golders Green NW11 1 B4
- Richmond TW9 44 C3
Gloucester Dr N4 6 A2
Gloucester Gate NW1 82 A2
Gloucester Gate Mews NW1 82 A2
Gloucester Gdns
- Golders Green NW11 1 B4
- Paddington W2 100 C2
Gloucester Ho
- Kilburn NW6 23 C3
- Richmond TW10 54 C2
Gloucester Mews W2 101 A1
Gloucester Mews W W2 101 A1
Gloucester Pk SW7 142 C4
Gloucester Pl W1 103 A4
Gloucester Pl Mews W1 103 A3
Gloucester Prim Sch SE15 49 A3
Gloucester Rd
- Acton W3 37 B4
- Richmond TW9 44 C3
- South Kensington SW7 142 C4
Gloucester Road Sta SW7 142 C4
Gloucester Sq
- 6 Hackney E2 24 C4
- Paddington W2 102 A1
Gloucester St SW1 146 C2
Gloucester Terr W2 101 A1
Gloucester Way EC1 95 C3
Gloucester Wlk W8 127 C4
Glover Ho
- London SE15 65 A3
- 2 South Hampstead NW6 11 B1
Glycena Rd SW11 60 B4
Glyn Ct SE27 74 C1
Glynde Mews SW3 130 B1
Glynde Reach WC1 94 B3
Glynde St SE4 66 B1
Glynfield Rd NW10 8 A1
Glyn Mans W14 140 B4
Glyn Rd E5 17 C4
Glyn St SE11 148 C1
Goater's Alley SW6 155 A1
Goat Wharf TW8 44 A4
Godalming Rd E14 34 A4
Goddard Ho SW19 69 C2
Goddard Pl N19 4 B1
Godfrey Ho EC1 97 B3
Godfrey St
- Chelsea SW3 144 B2
- Mill Meads E15 27 B3
Goding St SE11 148 B1
Godley Rd SW18 71 C3
Godliman St EC4 122 C4
Godman Rd SE15 50 A1
Godolphin Ho
- Primrose Hill NW3 12 A1
- 7 Streatham SW2 74 C3
Godolphin & Latymer Sch 16 W6 39 A2
Godolphin Pl W3 28 C2
Godolphin Rd W12 39 A4
Godson St N1 85 B2
Godstone Ct 1 N16 7 A3
Godstone Ho SE1 137 C2
Godwin Cl N1 87 A2
Godwin Ct NW1 83 A2
Godwin Ho
- 2 Haggerston E2 24 B3
- Kilburn NW6 78 A2
Goffers Ho SE3 53 A1
Goffers Rd SE3, SE13 53 A1
Goffton Ho 14 SW9 173 A1
Golborne Gdns
- 5 Kensal Town W10 23 A1
- West Kilburn W10 23 B1
Golborne Mews 9 W10 31 A4
Golborne Rd W10 31 A4
Golden Cross Mews 2 W11 31 B3
Golden Hinde The SE1 123 B2
Golden Hind Pl 5 SE8 41 B2
Golden La EC1 97 A1
Golden Lane Campus EC1 97 A1
Golden Lane L Ctr EC1 96 C1
Golden Plover Cl E16 35 C3
Golden Sq W1 119 A4
Golders Ct NW11 1 B4
Golders Gdns NW11 1 B4
GOLDERS GREEN 1 C4
Golders Green Coll NW11 1 C3
Golders Green Cres NW11 1 C4
Golders Green Rd NW11 1 A4
Golders Green Sta NW11 1 C3
Golders Hill Sch NW11 1 C4
Goldersleа NW11 1 C3
Golders Park Cl NW11 1 C3
Golders Way NW11 1 B4
Goldhawk Ind Est W6 39 A3
Goldhawk Mews 2 W12 39 A4
Goldhawk Rd W12 38 C3
Goldhawk Road Sta W12 39 B4
Goldhurst Terr NW6 11 B1
Goldie Ho N19 4 C4
Golding St E1 111 C1
Goldington Cres NW1 83 B2
Goldington Ct NW1 83 B3
Goldington St NW1 83 B2
Goldman Cl E2 24 C1 99 B2
Goldney Rd W9 23 C1
Goldsboro Rd SW8 161 C1
Goldsborough Ho SW8 171 C3
Goldsmith Ave W3 28 C2
Goldsmith Ct WC1 106 B2
Goldsmith Ho W3 28 C2
Goldsmith Rd
- Acton W3 28 C1
- Peckham SE15 49 C2
Goldsmiths Bldgs W3 28 C1
Goldsmiths Cl W3 28 C1
Goldsmiths Coll, Univ of London SE14 51 A2
Goldsmith's Pl 6 NW6 78 A3
Goldsmith's Row E2 24 C3
Goldsmith's Sq 17 E2 24 C3
Goldsmith St EC2 109 A2
Goldthorpe NW1 82 C3
Goldwell Ho SE22 64 A3
Goldwin Cl SE14 50 B2
Goldwing Cl E16 35 C3
Gomm Rd SE16 40 B3
Gondar Gdns NW6 10 B3
Gondar Mans NW6 10 B3
Gonson St SE8 52 A4
Gonston Cl SW19 70 A2
Gonville Ho 6 SW15 57 C1
Gonville St SW6 58 A4
Gooch Ho EC1 107 B4
Goodall Ho 10 SE4 65 C3
Goodenough Coll WC1 94 C2
Goodfaith Ho 18 E14 34 A2
Goodge Pl W1 105 A3
Goodge St W1 105 A3
Goodge Street Sta W1 105 B4
Goodhall St NW10 21 B2
Good Hart Pl E14 33 A2
Goodhope Ho 17 E14 34 A2
Goodinge Cl N7 14 A2
Goodinge Rd N7 14 A2
Goodman Cres SW2 73 C2
Goodman's Stile 17 E1 111 B2
Goodman's Yd E1, EC3 124 C4
Goodrich Com Prim Sch SE22 64 C1
Goodrich Ct 9 W10 30 C3
Goodrich Ho
- 20 Bethnal Green E2 25 B3
- Stamford Hill N16 7 A4
Goodrich Rd SE22 64 C1
Good Shepherd RC Prim Sch The W12 38 B4
Goodson Rd NW10 8 A1
Goodspeed Ho 20 E14 34 A2
Goodsway NW1 84 A2
Goodway Gdns E14 34 C3
Goodwill Ho 22 E14 34 A2
Goodwin Cl SE16 139 A1
Goodwin Ho 2 SE15 65 A4
Goodwin Rd W12 38 C4
Goodwins Ct WC2 120 A4
Goodwin St N4 5 C2
Goodwood Ct W1 104 B4
Goodwood Ho 3 W4 37 B1
Goodwood Mans 3 SW9 62 C4
Goodwood Rd SE14 51 A3
Goose Green Prim Sch SE22 64 B3
Goose Green Trad Est SE22 64 C3
Gophir La EC4 123 B4
Gopsall St N1 87 C3
Gordon Ave SW14 56 A3
Gordonbrock Prim Sch SE4 66 C2
Gordonbrock Rd SE4 66 C2
Gordon Ct 5 W12 30 B3
Gordondale Rd SW18, SW19 70 C2
Gordon Gr SE5 48 A1
Gordon Ho 17 E1 32 B2
Gordon Hospl SW1 147 B3
Gordon House Rd NW5 12 C4
Gordon Lo N16 6 C3
Gordon Mans WC1 93 B1
Gordon Pl W8 127 C4
Gordon Rd
- Chiswick W4 45 A4
- Leyton E15 19 B4
- Peckham SE15 50 A1
- Richmond TW9 44 B1
Gordon Sq WC1 93 C2
Gordon St WC1 93 B2
Gorefield Ho NW6 23 C3
Gorefield Pl NW6 23 C3
Gore Rd E9 25 B4
Gore St SW7 129 A2
Gorham Ho 12 SW4 61 B1
Gorham Pl W11 31 A2 112 A3
Goring St EC3 110 B2
Gorleston St W14 140 B4
Gorse Cl E16 35 C3
Gorsefield Ho 6 E14 33 C2
Gorst Rd
- London SW11 60 B1
- North Acton NW10 20 C1
Gorsuch Pl 1 E2 24 B2 98 C4
Gorsuch St E2 24 B2 98 C4
Gosberton Rd SW12 72 C3
Gosfield St W1 104 C3
Gosford Ho 25 E3 26 B3
Goslett Yd WC2 105 C2
Gosling Ho 2 E1 32 B2
Gosling Way SW9 173 B4
Gospatric Home Ho SW14 56 A4
GOSPEL OAK 12 C4
Gospel Oak Prim Sch NW5 12 C4
Gospel Oak Sta NW5 12 C4
Gosport Ho 9 SW15 68 C3
Gosset St E2 24 C2 99 B4
Gosterwood St SE8 51 A4
Goswell Pl EC1 96 B3
Goswell Rd EC1 96 B4
Gothic Ct 17 SE5 48 B3
Gottfried Mews NW5 13 B4
Gough Ho N1 86 B4
Gough Sq EC4 107 C2
Gough St WC1 95 A1
Gough Wlk 14 E14 33 C3
Goulden Ho SW11 168 A2
Gouldman Ho 33 E1 25 B1
Gould Terr 26 E8 17 A3
Goulston St E1 110 C2
Goulton Rd E5 17 A4
Govan St E2 24 C4
Gover Ct 8 SW4 172 B2
Gowan Ave SW6 164 A4
Gowan Ho 22 E2 24 B2 99 A3
Gowan Rd NW10 9 A2
Gower Cl SW4 61 B1
Gower Ct WC1 93 B2
Gower Ho SE17 151 A2
Gower Mews WC1 105 C4
Gower Pl NW1, WC1 93 B2

Gower Sch The 4 N7 14 A2
Gower St WC1 93 B1
Gower's Wlk E1 111 B1
Gowlett Rd SE15 64 C4
Gowrie Rd SW11 60 C4
Gracechurch St EC2, EC4 123 C4
Gracefield Gdns SW16 74 A1
Gracehill 2 E1 32 B4
Grace Ho SE11 163 A4
Grace Jones Cl E8 16 C2
Grace Pl E3 27 A2
Graces Mews NW8 79 A1
Grace's Mews SE5 49 A1
Grace's Rd SE5 49 A1
Grace St E3 27 A2
Graemesdyke Ave SW14 55 A3
Grafton Cres NW1 13 A2
Grafton Ct 10 E8 16 C3
Grafton Ho
16 Bow E3 26 C2
12 Deptford SE8 41 B1
Grafton Mans SW4 61 B3
Grafton Mews W1 92 C1
Grafton Pl NW1 93 C3
Grafton Prim Sch 5 N7 5 A1
Grafton Rd
Acton W3 28 B2
Gospel Oak NW5 12 C3
Grafton Sq SW4 61 B4
Grafton St W1 118 B3
Grafton Terr NW5 12 C3
Grafton Way W1 93 A1
Grafton Yd NW5 13 A2
Graham Ct 5 SE14 50 C4
Graham Ho
5 Balham SW12 73 A4
6 Tufnell Pk N19 13 C4
Graham Mans 2 E8 17 A2
Graham Rd
Acton W4 37 C3
Dalston E8 16 C2
Graham St N1 86 B1
Graham Terr SW1 145 C3
Graham Twr W3 37 A3
Grainger Ct 22 SE5 48 B3
Grampian Gdns NW2 1 A3
Grampians The 10 W14 39 C4
Granard Ave SW15 57 A2
Granard Ho 20 E9 17 C2
Granard Prim Sch SW15 57 A1
Granard Rd SW11, SW12 72 B4
Granary Rd E1 25 A1
Granary Sq
Islington N1 14 C2
N1 84 A3
Granary St NW1 83 B3
Granary The SE8 51 C3
Granby Pl SE1 135 B3
Granby St
Bethnal Green E2 24 C1 99 B2
Shoreditch E2 24 B1 99 A2
Granby Terr NW1 82 C1
Grand Ave EC1 108 B4
Grandfield Ct W4 45 C4
Grandison Rd SW11 60 B2
Grand Junction Wharf N1 86 C1
Grand Par SW14 55 B3
Grand Union Cl W9 31 B4
Grand Union Cres E8 24 C4
Grand Union Ind Est NW10 20 A3
Grand Vitesse Ind Est SE1 122 B1
Granfield St SW11 167 C3
Grangecourt Rd N16 7 A3
Grange Ct
Peckham SE15 49 B1
Strand WC2 107 A1
1 Willesden NW10 8 A4
Grangefield NW1 14 A1
Grange Gdns NW3 2 A1
Grange Gr N1 15 B2
Grange Ho
Bermondsey SE1 138 C1
Willesden NW10 9 A1
Grange La SE21 76 B2
Grangemill 11 NW5 13 A4
GRANGE MILLS 73 B3
Grange Mills SW12 73 B3
Grange Pl NW6 10 C1
Grange Prim Sch SE1 138 A1
Grange Rd
Barnes SW13 46 C2
Bermondsey SE1 138 C1
Gunnersbury W4 37 A1
Willesden NW10 9 A2
Grange St N1 87 C3
Grange The
Bermondsey SE1 138 C1
7 Gunnersbury W4 37 A1
Hammersmith W12 39 A3
19 Maitland Pk NW3 12 B2
South Acton W3 37 A4
West Kensington W14 140 C3
Grangeway NW6 10 C1
Grange Wlk SE1 138 C1
Grange Yd SE1 138 C1
Granite Apts E15 19 C2
Grannary The 10 SE16 40 B4
Gransden Ave E8 17 A1
Gransden Ho 1 SE8 41 B1
Gransden Rd W12 38 B4
Grantbridge St N1 86 B2
Grantham Ct 9 SE16 40 C4
Grantham Ho 12 SE15 49 C4
Grantham Pl W1 118 A1
Grantham Rd
Chiswick W4 46 A3
South Lambeth SW9 172 B1
Grant Ho
38 Clapham SW8 171 B1
Grant Ho *continued*
Clerkenwell EC1 108 B4
Grantley Ho
2 Deptford SE14 50 C4
5 Putney SW19 69 C3
Grantley St E1 25 C1
Grant Mus of Zoology WC1 93 B1
Grant Rd SW11 60 A4
Grant St N1 85 B2
Grantully Rd W9 88 A3
Granville Ct
8 Deptford SE14 51 A3
Shoreditch N1 87 C4
Granville Gr SE13 67 B4
Granville Ho 18 E14 33 C3
Granville Ind Est NW2 1 B2
Granville Mans 8 W12 39 B4
Granville Pk SE13 67 C4
Granville Pl
Marylebone W1 103 B1
Walham Green SW6 156 A1
Granville Point NW2 1 B2
Granville Rd
Child's Hill NW2 1 B2
Kilburn NW6 23 C3
Wandsworth SW18 70 B4
Granville Sq
3 Camberwell SE15 49 A3
Finsbury WC1 95 A3
Granville St WC1 95 A3
Grape St WC2 106 A2
Grasgarth Cl W3 28 B2
Grasmere NW1 92 B3
Grasmere Ave W3 28 C2
Grasmere Ct SW13 46 C4
Grasmere Ho 20 N16 15 C4
Grasmere Point 2 SE15 50 B3
Grasmere Prim Sch N16 15 C4
Grateley Ho 10 SW15 69 A3
Gratton Rd W14 126 A1
Graveley Ho 7 SE8 41 A2
Gravel La E1 110 C2
Gravesend Rd W12 29 C2
Grayfriars Pas EC1 108 B2
Gray Ho SE17 151 A2
Grayland Ct WC1 94 C3
Grayling Rd N16 6 C2
Grayling Sq E2 24 C2 99 C4
Grayshott Rd SW11 60 C4
Gray's Inn WC1 107 A4
Gray's Inn Pl WC1 107 A3
Gray's Inn Rd WC1 95 A2
Gray's Inn Sq WC1 107 B4
Grayson Ho EC1 97 A3
Gray St SE1 135 C3
Grayswood Point 14 SW15 68 C3
Gray's Yd W1 103 C2
Grazebrook Rd N16 6 C2
Great Arthur Ho EC1 96 C1
Great Bell Alley EC2 109 B2
Great Castle St W1 104 C2
Great Central St NW1 102 C4
Great Chapel St W1 105 B2
Great Chart St SW11 59 B3
Great Chertsey Rd SW14, W4 45 C2
Great Church La W6 39 C1
Great College St SW1 134 A2
Great Croft WC1 94 B3
Great Cross Ave SE3 53 A3
Great Cumberland Mews W1 102 C1
Great Cumberland Pl W1 103 A1
Great Dover St SE1 137 B2
Great Eastern Bldgs 10 E8 17 A2
Great Eastern Ent Ctr E14 42 A4
Great Eastern Pier E14 41 C1
Great Eastern Rd E15 19 C2
Great Eastern St EC2 24 A1 98 A2
Great Eastern Wharf SW11 158 B1
Great Field 7 NW5 13 B3
Greatfield Cl
London SE4 66 C3
4 Tufnell Pk N19 13 B4
Great George St SW1 134 A3
Great Guildford Bsns Sq SE1 122 C1
Great Guildford St SE1 122 C1
Greatham Wlk 8 SW15 68 C3
Great James St WC1 106 C4
Great Marlborough St W1 104 C1
Great Maze Pond SE1 137 C4
Great Newport St WC2 120 A4
Greatorex Ho 13 E1 111 B4
Greatorex St E1 111 B4
Great Ormond St Hospl for Children WC1 94 C1
Great Ormond St WC1 94 C1
Great Percy St WC1 95 B4
Great Peter St SW1 133 C1
Great Portland St W1 104 B4
Great Portland Street Sta W1 92 B1
Great Pulteney St W1 119 A4
Great Queen St WC2 106 B2
Great Russell Mans WC1 106 A3
Great Russell St WC1 106 A3
Great St Helen's EC3 110 A2
Great St Thomas Apostle EC4 123 A4
Great Scotland Yd SW1, WC2 120 A2
Great Smith St SW1 133 C2
Great Spilmans SE22 64 A2
Great Suffolk St SE1 122 B1
Great Sutton St EC1 96 B1
Great Swan Alley EC2 109 B2
Great Titchfield St W1 104 C3
Great Tower St EC3 124 A4
Great Trinity La EC4 123 A4
Great Turnstile WC2 107 A3
Great Western Rd W2, W9 31 B4
Great West Rd W4, W6 45 C4
Great West Road Cedars Rd W4 45 B4
Great West Road Hogarth La W4 46 A4
Great Winchester St EC2 109 C2
Great Windmill St W1 119 B4
Great Yd SE1 138 B4
Greaves Cotts 10 E14 33 A4
Greaves Twr SW10 157 A2
Grebe Ct 16 E14 42 B4
Greek Ct W1 105 C1
Greek Sch of London W3 28 A2
Greek St W1 105 C1
Greenacre Ct E8 16 C3
Greenacre Sq 26 SE16 40 C4
Green Arbour Ct EC1 108 A2
Greenaway Gdns NW3 11 A4
Greenaway Ho
Finsbury WC1 95 B3
St John's Wood NW8 78 C4
Green Bank E1 32 A1
Greenberry St NW8 80 A1
Green Cl NW11 2 B4
Greencoat Pl SW1 147 A4

Greencoat Row SW1 133 A1
Greencourt Ho 25 E1 25 C1
Greencroft Gdns NW6 11 B1
Green Ct 2 NW10 8 A4
Green Dale SE22 64 A2
Greendale Cl SE22 64 A2
Green Dragon Ct SE1 123 B1
Green Dragon Ho WC1 106 B2
Green Dragon La TW8 36 B1
Green Dragon Prim Sch TW8 44 A4
Green Dragon Yd 24 E1 111 B3
Greene Ct 20 SE14 50 C4
Greene Ho SE1 137 B1
Greenend Rd W4 38 A4
Greener Ho 3 SW4 61 C4
Greenfell Mans SE8 52 A4
Greenfield Gdns NW2 1 A1
Greenfield Ho 28 SW19 69 C3
Greenfield Rd E1 111 C2
Greenham Cl SE1 135 B3
Greenham Ho 5 E9 25 B4
Greenheath Bsns Ctr 3 E2 25 A1
Greenhill NW3 11 C4
Greenhill Pk NW10 21 A4
Greenhill Rd NW10 21 A4
Greenhill's Rents EC1 108 A4
Greenhills Terr 16 N1 15 C2
Green Ho The 5 SW19 70 A3
Green Hundred Rd SE15 49 C4
Greening Ho SE13 67 C3
Greenland Ho
Bermondsey SE8 40 C1
4 Mile End E1 26 A1
Greenland Mews SE8 40 C1
Greenland Pier SE8 41 B3
Greenland Pl NW1 82 B4
Greenland Quay SE16 40 C2
Greenland Rd NW1 82 C4
Greenland St NW1 82 B4
Green Lanes N4, N8, N15 6 A4
Greenleaf Cl 8 SW2 74 C4
Green Link Wlk TW9 45 A2
Greenman St N1 86 C4
Greenmead Prim Sch SW15 57 A2
Greenock Rd 11 W3 37 B3
Green Park SW1, W1 132 B4
Green Park Sta W1 118 C2
Greenroof Way SE10 43 B3
Greens Ct W1 119 B4
Green's Ct W11 31 B1 112 C1
Greenside Prim Sch W12 38 C4
Greenside Rd W12 38 C4
Green St W1 117 B4
Greenstead Gdns SW15 57 A2
Greenstreet Hill SE4 65 C4
Greensward Ho SW6 166 C2
Green Terr EC1 95 C3
Green The W3 29 A3
Greenview Cl W3 29 A1
Greenview Ct
East Dulwich SE22 64 C3
Wandsworth SW18 72 A4
Greenway Cl N4 6 B2
Greenwell St W1 92 B1
GREENWICH 43 C3
Greenwich Acad SE10 52 A2
Greenwich Bsns Ctr SE10 52 A3
Greenwich Bsns Pk SE10 52 A3
Greenwich Church St SE10 52 B4
Greenwich Coll 17 SE10 52 B3
Greenwich Ct 11 E1 32 A3
Greenwich High Rd SE10 52 A3
Greenwich Ho SE13 67 C1
Greenwich Ind Est SE10 52 A3
Greenwich Mkt 2 SE10 52 B4
Greenwich Park SE10 53 A3
Greenwich Park St SE10 52 C4
Greenwich Pier SE10 42 B1
Greenwich Quay SE8 52 A4
Greenwich South St SE10 52 B2
Greenwich Sta SE10 52 A3
Greenwich View Pl E14 42 A3
Green Wlk SE1 138 A1
Greenwood 8 SW19 69 C4
Green Wood NW5 13 B3
Greenwood Ho
Finsbury WC1 95 B3
8 Nunhead SE4 65 C3
Greenwood Pl NW5 13 A3
Greenwood Rd E8 16 C2
Greenwood Terr NW10 20 C3
Green Yd WC1 95 A2
Greet Ho SE1 135 C3
Greet St SE1 121 C1
Gregor Mews SE3 53 C3
Gregory Pl W8 128 A4
Greig Terr SE17 48 A4
Grenada Ho 18 E14 33 B2
Grenade St E14 33 B2
Grena Gdns TW9 54 B3
Grena Rd TW10, TW9 54 B3
Grenard Cl SE15 49 C3
Grendon Ho
29 Hackney E9 17 B1
Pentonville N1 84 C1
Grendon St NW8 90 A2
Grenfell Ho SE5 48 B3
Grenfell Rd W11 30 C2
Grenfell Twr 5 W11 30 C2
Grenfell Wlk 4 W11 30 C2
Grenier Apartments 11 SE15 50 A3
Grenville Ho
26 Bow E3 26 A3
4 Deptford SE8 51 C4
Grenville Lo N6 4 B4
Grenville Mans WC1 94 A2
Grenville Mews SW7 142 C3
Grenville Pl SW7 142 C4
Grenville Rd N19 5 A3
Grenville St WC1 94 B1
Gresham Almshouses 3 SW9 62 B3
Gresham Coll EC1 107 C3
Gresham Gdns NW11 1 A3
Gresham Pl 2 N19 4 C2
Gresham Rd SW9 62 C4
Gresham St EC2 109 A2
Gresham Way SW19 70 C1
Gresham Way Est SW19 71 A1
Gresley Ho SW8 171 C4
Gresley Rd N19 4 B4
Gressenhall Rd SW18 70 B4
Gresse St W1 105 B2
Greswell St SW6 47 C2
Greta Ho SE3 53 B4
Gretton Ho 2 E2 25 B2
Greville Hall NW6 78 B2
Greville Ho
Knightsbridge SW1 131 B2
Putney SW15 57 C4
Greville Lo 5 W2 100 A2
Greville Mews 5 NW6 78 A3
Greville Pl W9 78 B2
Greville Rd
Kilburn NW6 78 B2
Richmond TW10 54 B1
Greville St EC1 107 C4
Grey Coat Hospital The (Sch)
SW1 147 B3
SW1 133 B1
Greycoat Pl SW1 133 B1
Greycoat St SW1 133 B1
Grey Eagle St E1 24 B1 99 A1
Greyfriars 16 SE26 76 C1
Greyfriars Ho SE3 53 B4
Grey Ho 27 W12 30 A2
Greyhound Ct WC2 121 B4
Greyhound Rd
College Pk NW10 22 A2
Fulham W6 154 A4
Greyladies Gdns SE10 52 B1
Greystoke Ho SE15 49 C4
Greystoke Pl EC4 107 C2
Grey Turner Ho W12 29 C3
Grice Ct N1 15 B2
Grierson Rd SE23 66 A1
Griffin Cl NW10 9 A3
Griffin Ct
8 Brentford TW8 44 A4
Chiswick W4 38 B1
Shepherd's Bush W12 30 A1
Griffin Gate 1 SW15 57 C4
Griffon Ho 3 SW11 60 A4
Grigg's Pl SE1 138 B1
Grimaldi Ho N1 84 C2
Grimsby St
8 Bethnal Green E2 24 C1 99 A2
Shoreditch E2 24 B1 99 A2
Grimsel Path SE5 48 A3
Grimshaw Cl N6 3 C4
Grimston Rd SW6 164 C1
Grimthorpe Ho EC1 96 A2
Grimwade Cl SE15 65 B4
Grindall Ho 26 E1 25 A1
Grindal St SE1 135 B3
Grindley Ho 3 E3 33 B4
Grinling Gibbons Prim Sch 42 SE8 51 B4
Grinling Pl SE8 51 C4
Grinstead Rd SE8 41 A1
Grisedale NW1 92 C4
Grittleton Rd W9 23 C1
Groombridge Rd E9 17 C1
Groom Cres SW18 71 C4
Groome Ho SE11 149 A3
Groom Pl SW1 131 C2
Grosse Way SW15 57 A1
Grosvenor Ave
Canonbury N5 15 B3
Mortlake SW14 56 A4
Richmond TW10 54 A2
Grosvenor Bridge SW1 160 B4
Grosvenor Cotts SW1 145 B4
Grosvenor Court Mans W2 102 C1
Grosvenor Cres SW1 131 C3
Grosvenor Cres Mews SW1 131 B3
Grosvenor Ct
Brondesbury Pk NW6 22 C4
Gunnersbury W4 37 A1
22 Poplar E14 33 B3
Putney SW15 58 A2
Grosvenor Gdns
Cricklewood NW2 9 B3
Mortlake SW14 56 A4
Westminster SW1 132 B1
Grosvenor Gdns Mews E SW1 132 B2
Grosvenor Gdns Mews N SW1 132 A1
Grosvenor Gdns Mews S SW1 132 B1
Grosvenor Hill W1 118 A4
Grosvenor Hill Ct W1 118 A4
Grosvenor Ho E5 7 C3
Grosvenor Park SE5 48 B3
Grosvenor Pier SW1 161 B4
Grosvenor Pk SE5 48 B4
Grosvenor Pl SW1 132 A3
Grosvenor Rd
Acton Green W4 37 B1
Pimlico SW1 161 A4
Richmond TW10 54 A2
Grosvenor Residences 1 W14 39 C3
Grosvenor Sq W1 117 C4
Grosvenor St W1 118 A4
Grosvenor Terr SE5 48 B4
Grosvenor The NW11 2 A4
Grosvernor Wharf Rd E14 42 C2
Grote's Bldgs SE3 53 A1
Grote's Pl SE3 53 A1
Groton Rd SW18 71 A2
Grotto Ct SE1 136 C4
Grotto Pas W1 103 B4
Grove Crescent Rd E15 19 C2
Grove Ct
Camberwell SE5 49 A1
Clapham SW4 61 B4
South Kensington SW10 143 A1
St John's Wood NW8 89 B4
Grovedale Rd N19 4 C2
Grove Dwellings E1 32 B4
Grove End NW5 13 A4
Grove End Gdns NW8 79 A1
Grove End Ho NW8 89 B3
Grove End Rd NW8 89 B3
Grove Gdns NW8 90 B3
Grove Hall Ct
Bow E3 26 C3
St John's Wood NW8 89 A4
Grove Hill Rd SE5 64 A4
Grove Ho
Blackheath SE3 53 B1
Chelsea SW3 158 B4
Grove La SE5 64 A4
Groveland Ct EC4 109 A1
Grovelands Cl SE5 49 A1
Grove Lane Terr SE5 48 C1
Groveley Ho 7 N4 6 B4
Grove Lo SW4 61 B3

Grove Mans
London SW4 ....60 B3
2 Shepherd's Bush W6 ....39 B4
3 Stamford Hill N16..7 C3
Grove Mews W6....39 B3
GROVE PARK W4...45 B2
Grove Park Bridge W4 ....45 B3
Grove Park Gdns W4 ....45 B3
Grove Park Mews W4 ....45 B3
Grove Park Prim Sch W4 ....45 B4
Grove Park Rd W4..45 A3
Grove Park Terr W4 ....45 A4
Grove Pk SE5.......49 A1
Grove Pl
Acton W3 ....28 B1
Balham SW12.......61 A1
Hampstead NW3 .....2 C1
Grover Ct SE13 .....52 A1
Grove Rd
Acton W3 ....28 B1
Barnes SW13.......46 B1
Bow E3 ....26 A3
Richmond TW10.....54 B1
Willesden NW2.......9 B2
Grover Ho
4 London SW4.....61 B2
Vauxhall SE11..... 149 A1
Groveside Ct SW11 .... 167 B2
Grove St SE8 ....41 B1
Grove Terr NW5 ....13 A4
Grove Terrace Mews NW5 ....4 A1
Grove The
Dulwich SE21.......76 C3
Hendon NW11 ....1 A4
Highgate N6.........3 C3
Stroud Green N4 .....5 B4
Grove Vale SE22 ....64 B3
Groveway SW9 ... 173 A3
Grovewood 9 TW9 ....44 C2
Grovewood Ho NW2 ....1 B2
Grummant Rd SE15...............49 B2
Grundy St E14......34 A3
Guardian Angels RC Prim Sch 9 E3....26 A2
Guards Mus The SW1 .... 133 A3
Gubyon Ave SE24...63 A2
Gudden Dr E5.......17 A4
Guerin Sq E3.......26 B2
Guernsey Gr SE24 ..75 B4
Guernsey Ho 10 N1................15 B2
Guernsey Rd 11 N1................15 B2
Guildford Gr SE10 ..52 A2
Guildford Ho 23 SE5...............48 B1
Guildford Rd SW8 172 B4
Guildhall Art Gall EC2............. 109 B2
Guildhall Ho EC2 . 109 B2
Guildhall Sch Music & Drama EC2...... 109 A4
Guildhall Yd EC2.. 109 A2
Guildhouse St SW1 .... 146 C3
Guilford Pl WC1 ... 94 C1
Guilford St WC1 ... 94 B1
Guillemot Ct 28 SE8...............51 B4
Guinness Cl E9.....18 A1
Guinness Ct
Chelsea SW3 ..... 144 C3
Finsbury EC1 ...... 97 A3
Primrose Hill NW8.. 80 B3
Whitechapel E1 ... 111 A1
Guinness Sq SE1 . 152 A4
Guinness Trust Bldgs
Bermondsey SE1 .. 138 A4
7 Bethnal Green E2..............24 C3
Chelsea SW3 ..... 144 C3
Hammersmith W6 ...39 B1
Kennington SE11 .. 150 A2
Guion Rd SW6.... 165 A2
Gujarat Ho 1 N16...7 A1
Gulland Wlk 21 N1 .15 B2
Gullane Ho 24 E3...26 B3
Gulliver St SE16....41 B3
Gulston Wlk SW3 145 A3
Gunmakers La E3 ..26 A4
GUNNERSBURY....37 A2
Gunnersbury Avenue (North Circular Rd) W3 ....36 C3
Gunnersbury Cl 8 W4 ....37 A1
Gunnersbury Cres W3 ....36 C4
Gunnersbury Ct 8 W3 ....37 A4
Gunnersbury Dr W5 ....36 B4
Gunnersbury Gdns W3 ....36 C4
Gunnersbury La W3 ....36 C4
Gunnersbury Mews 6 W4 ....37 A1
Gunnersbury Park W3 ....36 C3
Gunnersbury Park Mus W3...........36 C3
Gunnersbury Sta W4 ....37 A1
Gunnersbury Triangle Nat Res W12 ......37 B2
Gunners Rd SW18 ..71 C2
Gunpowder Sq EC4............. 107 C2
Gun St E1........ 110 C3
Gunstor Rd N16 ....16 A4
Gunter Gr SW6... 156 C2
Gunterstone Rd W14 .... 140 B2
Gunthorpe St E1 . 111 A2
Gunwhale Cl SE16..32 C1
Gun Wharf
Old Ford E3.........26 A4
Wapping E1 ....32 B1
Gurdon Ho 7 E14..33 C3
Gurdon Rd SE7.....43 C1
Gurney Ho
3 Bayswater W2 .... 100 A2
14 Bethnal Green E2...............24 C3
Gurney Rd SW6 ....59 B4
Guthrie Ct SE1 ... 135 C3
Guthrie St SW3... 144 A2
Gutter La EC2 .... 108 C2
Guyscliff Rd SE13...67 B2
Guy's Hospl SE1.. 137 C4
Guy St SE1 .... 137 C4
Gwalior Rd SW15...57 C4
Gwendolen Ave SW15 ....57 C2
Gwendolen Cl SW15 ....57 C2
Gwendwr Rd W14 140 B2
Gwent Ct 13 SE16...32 C1
Gwilym Maries Ho 11 E2 ....25 A2
Gwyn Cl SW6..... 156 C1
Gwynne Cl W4 .....46 B4
Gwynne Ho
Finsbury WC1...... 95 B3
6 Streatham SW2 ..74 B3
Whitechapel E1 .....32 A4
Gwynne Pl WC1 ... 95 A3
Gwynne Rd SW11 167 C2
Gye Ho 2 SW4.....62 A3
Gylcote Cl SE5 .....63 C3

H

Haarlem Rd 12 W14 ....39 C3
Haberdasher Pl 4 N1..........24 A2 98 A4
Haberdashers' Aske's Hatcham Coll SE4...............51 A1
Haberdasher St N1.............. 97 C4
Hackford Rd SW9 173 A4
Hackford Wlk SW9 .... 173 B3
HACKNEY 17 A2
Hackney Central Sta E8 ....17 A2
Hackney Com Coll 33 N1..........24 A2 98 B4
Hackney Downs Sta E8 ....17 A3
Hackney Empire E8...............17 A2
Hackney Free & Parochial CE Sec Sch 18 E9..........17 B2
Hackney Gr E8 .....17 A2
Hackney Rd E2.....24 C3
HACKNEY WICK ...18 C2
Hackney Wick E9...18 B2
Hackney Wick Sta E9...............18 C2
Hackworth Point 24 E3...............27 A2
Hacon Sq 12 E8 ....17 A1
Haddo Ho
Gospel Oak NW5 ....13 A4
Greenwich SE10.....52 A4
Haddon Ct W3......29 B2
Haddo St SE10 .....52 B4
Haden Ct N4 ....5 C2
Hadfield Ho 37 E1.............. 111 C1
Hadleigh Cl 17 E1 ..25 B1
Hadleigh Ho 16 E1 .25 B1
Hadleigh St E2.....25 B2
Hadley Ct N16......7 C3
Hadley Gdns W4....37 C1
Hadley St NW1 .....13 A2
Hadlow Ho SE17.. 152 B2
Hadrian Cl 5 E3 ...26 C4
Hadrian Ct SE4....66 C4
Hadrian Est 33 E2 ..24 C3
Hadrian St SE10....43 A1
Hadstock Ho NW1. 93 C4
Hadyn Park Ct 13 W12 ....38 C4
Hadyn Park Rd W12 ....38 C4
Hafer Rd SW11.....60 B3
HAGGERSTON 24 B3
Haggerston Rd E8..24 B4
Haggerston Sch 15 E2...............24 B3
Haggerston Sta E2...............24 B4
Haggerston Studios 30 E8 ....24 B4
Hague Prim Sch 21 E2................25 A1
Hague St 30 E2..........24 C2 99 C3
Haig Ho 4 E2.....24 C3
Hailsham Ave SW2 .74 B2
Hainford Cl SE4 ....65 C3
Haining Cl 3 W4...36 C1
Hainton Cl E1 ......32 A3
Halcomb St N1.....24 A4
Halcrow St E1......32 A4
Haldane Pl SW18...71 A3
Haldane Rd SW6 . 155 A3
Haldon Rd SW18 ...58 B1
Hale Ho SW1..... 147 C2
Hales Ho 3 SW12..73 A4
Hales Prior N1 .... 84 C1
Hales St SE8 ....51 C3
Hale St E14 ....34 A2
Halesworth Rd SE13..............67 A4
Half Moon Cres N1.............. 85 A2
Half Moon Ct EC1 108 C3
Half Moon La SE24 .63 B1
Halfmoon Pas E1 111 A1
Half Moon St W1 . 118 B1
Halford Ho 9 SW15 ....57 C2
Halford Rd
Richmond TW10.....54 A2
West Brompton SW6 .... 155 B3
Haliday Ho N1......15 C2
Haliday Wlk 4 N1..15 C2
Halidon Cl E9 ......17 B3
Haliwell Ho 10 NW6............ 78 A3
Halkett Ho 1 E2 ...25 B4
Halkin Arc SW1 .. 131 A2
Halkin Mews SW1 131 B2
Halkin Pl SW1.... 131 B2
Halkin St SW1.... 131 C3
Hallam Ct W1 .... 104 B4
Hallam Ho
17 London SW9 ... 173 B4
Pimlico SW1...... 147 A1
Hallam Mews W1. 104 B4
Hallam Rd SW13....57 A4
Hallam St W1 .... 104 B4
Halley Gdns SE13...67 C3
Halley Ho
16 Bethnal Green E2...............24 C3
8 Cubitt Town SE10............43 B1
Halley Prim Sch E14...............33 A4
Halley St E14.......33 A4
Hallfield Jun & Inf Schs 21 W2 ..... 100 B1
Hall Gate NW8 .... 89 A4
Halliday Ho 40 E1 111 C1
Halliford St N1 .....15 C1
Halling Ho SE1 ... 137 C3
Hallings Wharf Studios 2 E15 ....27 C4
Halliwell Ct 4 SE22...............64 C2
Halliwell Rd SW2...62 B1
Hall Oak Wlk NW6..10 B2
Hall Pl W2 .... 89 B1
Hall Rd
Leyton E15 ....19 C4
St John's Wood NW8............ 89 A4
Hall Sch The NW3 ..11 C2
Hall Sch Wimbledon SW15 ....68 C1
Hall St EC1........ 96 B4
Hallsville Prim Sch E16...............35 C3
Hallsville Rd E16 ...35 B3
Hall Twr W2 ...... 101 C4
Halpin Pl SE17 ... 151 C3
Halsbury Ho 4 N7 .14 B4
Halsbury Rd W12...30 A1
Halsey St SW3.... 144 C4
Halsmere Rd SE5...48 A2
Halstead Ct N1 .... 87 C1
Halston Cl SW11....60 B1
Halstow 12 NW5....12 C2
Halstow Prim Sch 5 SE10..............43 C1
Halstow Rd
Greenwich SE3, SE10..............43 C1
Kensal Green NW10 ....22 C2
Halton Cross St N1.............. 86 B4
Haltone Ho 1 SW4 .... 171 C1
Halton Ho 22 N1 ...15 A1
Halton Mans N1....15 A1
Halton Pl N1 ...... 86 C4
Halton Rd N1...... 86 B4
Halyard Ho E14.....42 B3
Hambalt Rd SW4 ...61 B2
Hambledon SE17 ...48 C4
Hambledon Chase N4................5 A4
Hambledon Ho E5..17 A4
Hambledon Pl SE21..............76 B3
Hambledon Rd SW18 ....70 B4
Hamble St SW6.....59 A4
Hambley Ho 5 SE16...............40 A2
Hamblyn Ct N16.....7 B4
Hambridge Way SW2 ....74 C4
Hambrook Ct 12 NW5 ....13 A4
Hamers Ho 19 SW2 ....74 C4
Hamilton Cl
Rotherhithe SE16....41 A4
St John's Wood NW8............ 89 B3
Hamilton Ct W9 ... 88 C4

Hamilton Gdns NW8 . . . 89 A4
Hamilton Hall NW8 . . . 78 C1
Hamilton Ho
23 Bow E3 . . . 26 B2
Chiswick W4 . . . 46 A4
Kensington W8 . . . 128 A4
1 Poplar E14 . . . 33 B2
Putney SW15 . . . 56 C2
10 Richmond TW9 . . . 44 C2
St John's Wood NW8 . . . 89 B4
Hamilton La N5 . . . 15 A4
Hamilton Lo 37 E1 . . . 25 B1
Hamilton Mews W1 . . . 132 A4
Hamilton Pk N5 . . . 15 A4
Hamilton Pk W N5 . . . 15 A4
Hamilton Pl W1 . . . 117 C1
Hamilton Rd
Acton W4 . . . 38 A4
Hendon NW11 . . . 1 A4
Willesden NW10 . . . 8 C3
Hamilton Sq SE1 . . . 137 C4
Hamilton St SE8 . . . 51 C4
Hamilton Terr NW8 . . . 89 A4
Hamlet Ct
1 Hammersmith W6 . . . 38 C2
Kennington SE11 . . . 150 A2
Hamlet Gdns W6 . . . 38 C2
Hamlet Ind Ctr E9 . . . 18 C1
Hamlet Sq NW2 . . . 1 A1
Hamlets Way E3 . . . 26 B1
Hamlet The SE5 . . . 63 C4
Hamlet Way SE1 . . . 137 C4
Hammelton Gn 2 SW9 . . . 48 A2
Hammersley Ho 8 SE14 . . . 50 B3
HAMMERSMITH . . . 39 B2
Hammersmith Bridge Rd W6, SW13 . . . 39 B1
Hammersmith Broadway
Hammersmith W6 . . . 39 B1
5 Hammersmith W6 . . . 39 B2
Hammersmith Flyover W6 . . . 39 B1
Hammersmith Gr W6 . . . 39 B3
Hammersmith Hospl W12 . . . 30 A3
Hammersmith Rd
Hammersmith W6 . . . 39 C2
Kensington W14 . . . 140 B4
Hammersmith Sta W6 . . . 39 B2
Hammersmith Terr 6 W6 . . . 38 C1
Hammett St EC3 . . . 124 C4
Hammond Ho
10 Deptford SE14 . . . 50 B3
Millwall E14 . . . 42 A3
Hammond Lo 6 W9 . . . 31 C4
Hammond St NW5 . . . 13 B2
Hamond Sq N1 . . . 24 A3
Hampden Cl NW1 . . . 83 C2
Hampden Gurney CE Prim Sch W1 . . . 102 B2
Hampden Gurney St W1 . . . 102 C1
Hampden Rd N19 . . . 4 C2
Hampshire Ct 6 SW13 . . . 46 B1
Hampshire Hog La
3 Hammersmith W6 . . . 39 A1
11 Hammersmith W6 . . . 39 A2
Hampshire St NW5 . . . 13 C2
Hampson Way SW8 . . . 172 C4
HAMPSTEAD . . . 11 B2
Hampstead Coll of Fine Arts & Humanities 12 NW3 . . . 12 A2
Hampstead Com Mkt NW3 . . . 11 C4
Hampstead Gate NW3 . . . 11 B3
Hampstead Gn NW3 . . . 12 A3
Hampstead Gr NW3 . . . 2 B1
Hampstead Heath NW3 . . . 2 C2
Hampstead Heath Pre Prep Sch NW3 . . . 12 B4
Hampstead Heath Sta NW3 . . . 12 A4
Hampstead High Sch 3 NW3 . . . 11 B3
Hampstead High St NW3 . . . 11 C4
Hampstead Hill Gdns NW3 . . . 12 A4
Hampstead Hill Sch 1 NW3 . . . 12 A3
Hampstead La N6 . . . 3 A4
Hampstead Parochial CE Prim Sch 30 NW3 . . . 11 B4
Hampstead Rd NW1 . . . 92 C4
Hampstead Sch NW2 . . . 10 A4
Hampstead Sq 1 NW3 . . . 2 B1
Hampstead Sta NW3 . . . 11 B4
Hampstead Theatre NW3 . . . 11 C1
Hampstead West 4 NW6 . . . 10 C2
Hampstead Wlk 1 E3 . . . 26 B4
Hampton Cl NW6 . . . 23 C2
Hampton Ct
1 Islington N1 . . . 15 A2
19 Rotherhithe SE16 . . . 32 C1
Hampton St SE1 . . . 150 B3
Hamstead Gates 11 NW5 . . . 13 A2
Ham Yd W1 . . . 119 B4
Hana Mews E5 . . . 17 A4
Hanbury Ho
8 Bethnal Green E1 . . . 111 B4
South Lambeth SW8 . . . 162 B3
Hanbury Mews N1 . . . 87 A3
Hanbury Rd W3 . . . 37 A4
Hanbury St E1 . . . 111 A4
Hancock Nunn Ho 1 NW3 . . . 12 B1
Hancock Rd E3 . . . 27 B2
Handa Wlk 3 N1 . . . 15 B2
Hand Ct WC1 . . . 107 A3
Handel House Museum W1 . . . 118 B4
Handel Mans
Barnes SW13 . . . 47 B3
Bloomsbury WC1 . . . 94 B2
Handel St WC1 . . . 94 B2
Handforth Rd SW9 . . . 163 B2
Handley Rd E9 . . . 25 B4
Hands Wlk E16 . . . 35 C3
Hanford Cl SW18 . . . 70 C3
Hankey Pl SE1 . . . 137 C3
Hanley Ct N4 . . . 5 B3
Hanley Gdns N4 . . . 5 B3
Hanley Rd N4, N19 . . . 5 A3
Hanmer Wlk N7 . . . 5 B2
Hannah Mary Way 17 SE1 . . . 153 C3
Hannay La N8 . . . 4 C4
Hannay Wlk SW16 . . . 73 C2
Hannell Rd SW6 . . . 154 B2
Hannen Ho SE5 . . . 63 C4
Hannen Rd SE27 . . . 75 A1
Hannibal Rd E1 . . . 32 B4
Hannington Rd SW4 . . . 61 A4
Hanover Ave E16 . . . 35 C1
Hanover Cl TW9 . . . 44 C3
Hanover Ct
Shepherd's Bush W12 . . . 29 C1
Stamford Hill N16 . . . 7 B4
Hanover Gate Mans NW1 . . . 90 B2
Hanover Gdns SE11 . . . 163 B3
Hanover Ho NW8 . . . 80 A1
Hanover Mans 5 SW2 . . . 62 C2
Hanover Pk SE15 . . . 49 C2
Hanover Pl
16 Bow E3 . . . 26 B2
St Giles WC2 . . . 106 B1
Hanover Prim Sch N1 . . . 86 C2
Hanover Rd NW10 . . . 22 B4
Hanover Sq W1 . . . 104 B1
Hanover St W1 . . . 104 B1
Hanover Stps W2 . . . 102 B1
Hanover Terr NW1 . . . 90 C3
Hanover Terrace Mews NW1 . . . 90 B3
Hanover West Ind Est NW10 . . . 20 C2
Hanover Yd N1 . . . 86 C2
Hansard Mews W14 . . . 39 C4
Hanscomb Mews SW4 . . . 61 B3
Hans Cres SW1 . . . 130 C2
Hansler Ct 14 SW19 . . . 70 A3
Hansler Rd SE22 . . . 64 B2
Hanson Cl
Balham SW12 . . . 73 A4
Mortlake SW14 . . . 55 B4
Hanson Ho 2 E1 . . . 125 C4
Hanson St W1 . . . 104 C4
Hans Pl SW1 . . . 130 C2
Hans Rd SW3 . . . 130 C2
Hans St SW1 . . . 131 A1
Hanway Ho 25 SW9 . . . 173 C4
Hanway Pl W1 . . . 105 B2
Hanway St W1 . . . 105 B2
Hanworth Ho SE5 . . . 48 A3
Harben Rd NW6 . . . 11 B1
Harberson Rd SW12 . . . 73 A3
Harberton Rd N19 . . . 4 B3
Harbet Rd W2 . . . 101 C3
Harbinger Prim Sch 11 E14 . . . 42 A2
Harbinger Rd E14 . . . 42 A2
Harbin Ho 5 SW2 . . . 74 C3
Harbledown Ho SE1 . . . 137 B3
Harbledown Rd SW6 . . . 165 B4
Harbord Cl
Camberwell SE15 . . . 49 A3
London SE5 . . . 48 C1
Harbord Ho 5 SE16 . . . 40 C2
Harbord St SW6 . . . 47 C2
Harbour Ave SW10 . . . 167 A3
Harbour Exchange Sq E14 . . . 42 A4
Harbour Rd SE5 . . . 63 B4
Harbridge Ave SW15 . . . 68 C4
Harbut Rd SW11 . . . 59 C3
Harcombe Rd N16 . . . 7 A1
Harcourt Ho
27 Clapham SW8 . . . 171 B2
Marylebone W1 . . . 104 A2
4 Willesden NW10 . . . 9 B2
Harcourt Rd SE4 . . . 66 B4
Harcourt St W1 . . . 102 B3
Harcourt Terr SW10 . . . 142 B1
Hardcastle Ho
3 New Cross Gate SE14 . . . 51 A2
8 Peckham SE15 . . . 49 C2
Hardel Rise SW2 . . . 75 A3
Hardel Wlk SE24, SW2 . . . 74 C4
Harden Ho SE5 . . . 49 A1
Harders Rd SE15 . . . 50 A1
Hardess St SE24 . . . 63 B4
Hardham Ho 5 SW2 . . . 62 C1
Harding Cl SE17 . . . 48 B4
Hardinge Rd NW10 . . . 22 B4
Hardinge St E1 . . . 32 B3
Harding Ho SW13 . . . 47 A4
Hardington 2 NW1 . . . 12 C1
Hardwicke Ho 14 E3 . . . 27 A2
Hardwicke Mews WC1 . . . 95 A3
Hardwicke Rd W4 . . . 37 C2
Hardwick Ho
14 London SW8 . . . 171 B2
Marylebone NW8 . . . 90 B2
Hardwick St EC1 . . . 95 C3
Hardwick's Way SW18 . . . 58 C2
Hardwidge St SE1 . . . 138 A4
Hardy Ave 4 E16 . . . 35 C1
Hardy Cl SE16 . . . 40 C4
Hardy Cotts 2 SE10 . . . 52 C4
Hardy Ct SE3 . . . 53 B4
Hardy Rd SE3 . . . 53 B4
Hare and Billet Rd SE3 . . . 52 C1
Harecourt Rd N1 . . . 15 B2
Hare Ct EC4 . . . 107 B1
Haredale Ho 24 SE16 . . . 139 B3
Haredale Rd SE24 . . . 63 B3
Harefield Mews SE4 . . . 66 B4
Harefield Rd SE4 . . . 66 B4
Hare Marsh E2 . . . 24 C1 99 B2
Hare Pl EC4 . . . 107 C1
Hare Row E2 . . . 25 A3
Hare Wlk N1 . . . 24 A3
Harewood Ave NW1 . . . 90 B1
Harewood Pl W1 . . . 104 B1
Harewood Row NW1 . . . 102 B4
Harfield Gdns 1 SE5 . . . 64 A4
Harfleur Ct SE11 . . . 150 A3
Harford Ho
Camberwell SE5 . . . 48 B4
Notting Hill W11 . . . 31 B4
Harford Mews 6 N19 . . . 4 C1
Harford St E1 . . . 26 A1
Hargrave Mans 3 N19 . . . 4 C2
Hargrave Park Prim Sch 14 N19 . . . 4 B2
Hargrave Pk N19 . . . 4 B2
Hargrave Pl N7 . . . 13 C3
Hargrave Rd N19 . . . 4 B2
Hargraves Ho 14 W12 . . . 30 A2
Hargwyne St SW9 . . . 62 B4
Harkness Ho 30 E1 . . . 111 C1
Harlech Twr 5 W3 . . . 37 B4
Harlescott Rd SE15 . . . 65 C3
HARLESDEN . . . 21 B4
Harlesden Gdns NW10 . . . 21 B4
Harlesden Plaza 2 NW10 . . . 21 B3
Harlesden Prim Sch NW10 . . . 21 A3
Harlesden Rd NW10 . . . 21 C4
Harlesden Sta NW10 . . . 20 C3
Harleyford Ct SW8 . . . 162 C4
Harleyford Manor 8 W3 . . . 28 B1
Harleyford Rd SE11 . . . 162 C4
Harleyford St SE11 . . . 163 B3
Harley Gdns SW10 . . . 143 A1
Harley Gr E3 . . . 26 B2
Harley Ho NW1 . . . 91 C1
Harley Pl W1 . . . 104 A3
Harley Rd
Hampstead NW3 . . . 11 C1
Harlesden NW10 . . . 21 A3
Harley St W1 . . . 104 A3

Harley Villas NW10 ... 21 A3
Harling Ct 3 SW11 ... 168 C2
Harlowe Ho 13 E8 .. 24 B4
Harlynwood 19 SE5 ... 48 B3
Harman Cl
10 Bermondsey SE1 ... 153 B1
Cricklewood NW2 ... 1 A1
Harman Dr NW2 ... 10 A4
Harmon Ho 7 SE8 . 41 B2
Harmood Gr NW1 .. 13 A1
Harmood Ho 2 NW1 ... 13 A1
Harmood St NW1 ... 13 A1
Harmsworth St SE17 ... 150 A1
Harnage Ho TW8 ... 36 A1
Harney Ct SE14 ... 51 A2
Harold Ct 14 SE16 .. 40 C4
Harold Est SE1 ... 138 B1
Harold Ho 16 E2 ... 25 C3
Harold Laski Ho EC1 ... 96 B3
Harold Maddison Ho SE17 ... 150 B2
Harold Rd NW10 ... 20 C2
Harold Wilson Ho SW6 ... 155 A3
Harp Alley EC4 ... 108 A2
Harpenden Rd SE27, SW16 ... 75 A2
Harpenmead Point NW2 ... 1 B2
Harper Ho 3 SW9 .. 63 A4
Harper Mews SW17 ... 71 B1
Harper Rd SE1 ... 137 A2
Harp La EC3 ... 124 A3
Harpley Sq E1 ... 25 C1
Harpsden St SW11 ... 169 B3
Harpur Mews WC1 ... 106 C4
Harpur St WC1 ... 106 C4
Harrier Ho 9 SW11 ... 60 A4
Harriet Cl E8 ... 24 C4
Harriet Ho SW6 .. 156 B1
Harriet St SW1 ... 131 A3
Harriet Tubman Cl 21 SW2 ... 74 C4
Harriet Wlk SW1 . 131 A3
Harrington Ct
South Kensington SW7 ... 143 C4
9 West Kilburn W9 ... 23 B2
Harrington Gdns SW7 ... 142 C3
Harrington Ho
Regent's Pk NW1 ... 92 C4
Westminster SW1 . 147 C2
Harrington Rd SW7 ... 143 B4
Harrington Sq NW1 ... 82 C1
Harrington St NW1 92 C4
Harriott Cl SE10 ... 43 B2
Harriott Ho 11 E1 ... 32 B3
Harris Acad at Peckham SE15 ... 49 B2
Harris Acad Bermondsey SE1 ... 153 A4
Harris Girl's Acad SE15 ... 65 B2
Harris Ho
11 Bow E3 ... 26 C2
7 Brixton SW9 ... 62 C4
Harrison Ho SE17. 151 B2
Harrison Rd NW10 .. 20 C4
Harrisons Ct 1 SE14 ... 50 C4
Harrison St WC1 ... 94 B3
Harris St SE5 ... 48 C3
Harrodian Sch The SW13 ... 46 B3
Harrogate Ct 2 SE26 ... 76 C1
Harrold Ho 1 NW3 ... 11 B1
Harroway Rd SW11 ... 167 C2
Harrowby St W1 .. 102 B2
Harrowgate Ho 22 E9 ... 17 C2
Harrowgate Rd E9 .. 18 A1
Harrow La E14 ... 34 B2
Harrow Pl E1 ... 110 B2
Harrow Rd
Little Venice W2 ... 101 A3
Westbourne Green W2, W9 ... 23 C1
Harrow St NW1 ... 102 A4
Harry Gosling Prim Sch 41 E1 ... 111 C1
Harry Hinkins Ho SE17 ... 151 A1
Harry Lambourn Ho 10 SE15 ... 50 A3
Hartfield Terr E3 ... 26 C3
Hartham Cl N7 ... 14 A3
Hartham Rd N7 ... 14 A3
Hart Ho SW2 ... 74 C3
Hartington Ct
Chiswick W4 ... 45 A3
South Lambeth SW8 ... 172 A4
Hartington Rd
Chiswick W4 ... 45 B2
South Lambeth SW8 ... 162 A1
Hartismere Rd SW6 ... 155 A2
Hartlake Rd E9 ... 18 A2
Hartland NW1 ... 83 A3
Hartland Rd
Camden Town NW1 ... 13 A1
Kilburn NW6 ... 23 B4
Hartley Ho
Bermondsey SE1 .. 153 A4
Putney SW15 ... 56 C2
Hartley St E2 ... 25 B2
Hartnoll Ho 4 N7 .. 14 C3
Hartnoll St N7 ... 14 B3
Harton Lodge 2 SE8 ... 51 C2
Harton St SE8 ... 51 C2
Hartopp Ct 20 N16 ... 7 A1
Hartopp Point SW6 ... 154 B2
Hartshorn Alley EC3 ... 110 B1
Hart's La SE14 ... 51 A2
Hart St EC3 ... 124 B4
Hartswood Ho 10 SW2 ... 74 A3
Hartswood Rd W12 ... 38 B3
Hartwell Cl 12 SW2 ... 74 B3
Hartwell Ct SE22 ... 64 C3
Hartwell St E8 ... 16 B2
Harvard Ct NW6 ... 11 A3
Harvard Hill W4 ... 45 A4
Harvard Ho
3 Camberwell SE17 ... 48 A4
Putney SW15 ... 57 C1
Harvard Mans 18 SW11 ... 59 C3
Harvard Rd
11 Acton Green W4 ... 37 B1
Gunnersbury W4 ... 37 A1
Lewisham SE13 ... 67 B2
Harvey Ct SW11 .. 168 B4
Harvey Ho
10 Bethnal Green E1 ... 25 A1
Brentford TW8 ... 36 A1
Pimlico SW1 ... 147 C1
Shoreditch N1 ... 87 C3
Harvey Lo 8 W9 ... 31 C4
Harvey Point 7 E16 ... 35 C4
Harvey Rd 15 SE5 ... 48 C2
Harvey St N1 ... 87 C3
Harvington Wlk E8 ... 16 C1
Harvist Rd NW6 ... 23 A3
Harwood Ct
Putney SW15 ... 57 B3
Shoreditch N1 ... 87 C3
Harwood Point SE16 ... 41 B4
Harwood Rd SW6 156 A1
Harwood Terr SW6 ... 166 A4
Hascombe Ho 11 SW15 ... 69 A3
Hascombe Terr 2 SE5 ... 48 C1
Haselrigge Rd SW4 ... 61 C3
Hasker St SW3 ... 144 B4
Haslam Cl N1 ... 14 C1
Haslam Ho 12 N1 ... 15 B1
Haslam St SE15 ... 49 B2
Haslemere Ave SW18 ... 71 A2
Haslemere Ct 5 N16 ... 7 A3
Haslemere Ind Est SW18 ... 71 A2
Haslemere Rd N8 ... 5 A4
Hassard St E2 ... 24 B3
Hassett Rd E9 ... 18 A2
Hassop Rd NW2 ... 9 C4
Hastings Cl 17 SE15 ... 49 C3
Hastings Ho 18 W12 ... 30 A2
Hastings Hos WC1 . 94 A3
Hastings St WC1 ... 94 A3
Hatcham Mews Bsns Ctr SE14 ... 50 C2
Hatcham Park Mews SE14 ... 50 C2
Hatcham Park Rd SE14 ... 50 C2
Hatcham Rd SE15 ... 50 B4
Hatchard Rd N19 ... 5 A2
Hatchers Mews SE1 ... 138 B3
Hatcliffe Almshouses 8 SE10 ... 43 A1
Hatcliffe St SE10 ... 43 B1
Hatfield Cl SE14 ... 50 C3
Hatfield Ct SE3 ... 53 C3
Hatfield Ho EC1 ... 96 C1
Hatfield Rd W4 ... 37 C4
Hatfields SE1 ... 121 C2
Hathaway Ho 3 N1 ... 24 A2 98 A4
Hatherley Ct 6 W2 ... 100 A2
Hatherley Gr W2 . 100 A2
Hatherley Rd TW9 .. 44 B2
Hatherley St SW1 147 A3
Hathersage Ct N1 .. 15 C3
Hathersley Ho 3 SW2 ... 74 C4
Hathorne Cl 3 SE15 ... 50 A1
Hathway Ho 3 SE15 ... 50 B1
Hathway St 4 SE15 ... 50 B1
Hatley Rd N4, N7 ... 5 B2
Hat & Mitre Ct EC1 96 B1
Hatstone Ct 2 NW3 ... 11 B3
Hatteraick St 6 SE16 ... 40 B4
Hatton Gdn EC1 .. 107 C4
Hatton Ho 17 E1 .. 125 C4
Hatton Pl EC1 ... 107 C4
Hatton Row NW8 .. 89 C1
Hatton St NW8 ... 89 C1
Hatton Wall EC1 .. 107 C4
Haunch of Venison Yd W1 ... 104 A1
Hauteville Court Gdns 2 W6 ... 38 B3
Havana Rd SW18, SW19 ... 70 C2
Havannah St E14 ... 41 C4
Havelock Cl 13 W12 ... 30 A2
Havelock Ct 8 SE15 ... 50 A3
Havelock St N1 ... 84 B4
Havelock Terr SW8 ... 160 B1
Haven Cl SW19 ... 69 C1
Havenpool NW8 ... 78 B3
Haven St 18 NW1 ... 13 A1
Haven The TW9 ... 54 C4
Havercourt 3 NW3 ... 12 A2
Haverfield Gdns TW9 ... 44 C3
Haverfield Rd E3 ... 26 A2
Haverhill Rd SW12 .. 73 B3
Havering 8 NW1 ... 13 A1
Havering Ho N4 ... 6 B4
Havering St E1 ... 32 C3
Haversham Lo NW2 . 9 C3
Haversham Pl N6 ... 3 B2
Haverstock Hill NW3 ... 12 B2
Haverstock Rd NW5 ... 12 C3
Haverstock Sch 22 NW1 ... 12 C2
Haverstock St N1 .. 86 B1
Havil St SE5 ... 49 A2
Havisham Ho 25 SE16 ... 139 B3
Hawarden Gr SE24 .. 75 B4
Hawberry Lo N7 ... 14 A2
Hawes St N1 ... 15 A1
Hawgood St E3 ... 33 C4
Hawke Ho 20 E1 ... 25 C1
Hawke Pl 29 SE16 .. 40 C4
Hawkesbury Rd SW15 ... 57 A2
Hawkesdown House Sch W2 ... 31 C1 113 C1
Hawkesworth Ho 5 SW4 ... 61 B1
Hawke Twr 4 SE14 ... 51 A4
Hawk Ho 7 SW11 .. 60 A4
Hawkins Ho 3 SE8 ... 51 C4
Hawkins Rd NW10 ... 8 A1
Hawkley Gdns SE27 ... 75 A2
Hawkridge 19 NW5 ... 12 C2
Hawkshaw Cl 28 SW2 ... 74 A4
Hawkshead NW1 .. 92 C4
Hawkshead Rd
Acton W4 ... 38 A4
Willesden NW10 ... 8 B1
Hawkslade Rd SE15 ... 65 C2
Hawksley Rd N16 ... 7 A1
Hawks Mews 10 SE10 ... 52 B3
Hawksmoor Mews E1 ... 32 A2
Hawksmoor Pl 2 E2 ... 24 C1 99 B2
Hawksmoor St 5 W6 ... 47 C4
Hawkstone Rd SE16 ... 40 B2
Hawkwell Wlk N1 . 87 A4
Hawley Cres NW1 .. 13 A1
Hawley Inf Sch 23 NW1 ... 13 A1
Hawley Mews 4 NW1 ... 13 A1
Hawley Rd 3 NW1 ... 13 A1
Hawley St NW1 ... 13 A1
Haworth Ho 7 SW2 ... 62 C1
Hawstead Rd SE6 ... 67 A1
Hawthorn Ct
Putney SW15 ... 57 A4
Richmond TW9 ... 45 A2
Hawthorne Ave E3 .. 26 B4
Hawthorne Cl N1 ... 16 A2
Hawthorne Ho SW1 ... 147 A1
Hawthorn Ho SE14 . 51 B2
Hawthorn Rd NW10 .. 8 C1
Hawthorn Wlk W10 ... 23 A1
Hawtrey Rd NW3 ... 12 A1
Haycroft Gdns NW10 ... 22 A4
Haycroft Mans NW10 ... 21 C4
Haycroft Rd SW2 ... 62 A2
Hay Currie St E14 .. 34 A3

Hayday Rd E16 35 C4
Hayden Piper Ho SW3 158 C4
Hayden's Pl W11 31 B3
Haydon St E1, EC3 124 C4
Haydon Way SW11 59 C3
Haydon Wlk E1 111 A1
Hayes Ct
23 Camberwell SE5 48 B3
Streatham SW12 74 A3
Hayes Gr SE15, SE22 64 B3
Hayes Pl NW1 90 B1
Hayfield Pas E1 25 B1
Hayfield Yd 43 E1 25 B1
Hay Hill W1 118 B3
Hayhurst N1 86 B4
Hayles Bldgs SE11 150 B4
Hayles St SE11 150 A4
Hayling Cl 20 N16 16 A3
Haymans Point SE11 148 C2
Haymarket SW1 119 B3
Haymerle Ho 6 SE15 49 C3
Haymerle Rd SE15 49 C4
Haymerle Sch 15 SE15 49 C4
Hayne Ho W11 31 A1 112 A2
Haynes Ho 3 E9 17 C2
Hayne St EC1 108 B4
Hay's Galleria SE1 124 A2
Hay's La SE1 124 A2
Hay's Mews W1 118 A2
Hay St E2 24 C4
Hayter Ho W12 29 C2
Hayter Rd SW2 62 B2
Haythorn Ho SW11 167 C3
Hayton Cl 11 E8 16 B2
Hayward Ct 14 SW4 172 B2
Hayward Gallery SE1 121 A2
Hayward Gdns SW15 57 B1
Hayward Ho N1 85 B2
Haywards Pl EC1 96 A2
Hayward's Pl EC1 96 A2
Haywood Lo 23 N7 13 C3
Hazelbourne Rd SW12 61 A1
Hazel Cl
Peckham SE15 49 C1
Upper Holloway N19 4 B2
Hazel Ct 8 SE16 33 A1
Hazeldon Rd SE4 66 A2
Hazel Ho
London SE4 66 B4
12 Maitland Pk NW3 12 B2
Hazellville Rd N19 4 C3
Hazelmere Ct 10 SW2 74 B3
Hazelmere Rd NW6 23 B4
Hazel Rd NW10 22 B2
Hazel Way SE1 152 C4
Hazelwood Cl W5 36 A4
Hazelwood Ho 11 SE8 41 A2
Hazelwood Mans SW6 164 C4
Hazlebury Rd SW6 166 B2
Hazledene Rd W4 45 B4
Hazlewell Rd SW15 57 B2
Hazlewood Cres W10 23 A1
Hazlewood Twr W10 23 B1
Hazlitt Mews W14 126 A1
Hazlitt Rd W14 126 A1
Headbourne Ho SE1 137 C2
Headcorn 10 NW5 12 C2
Headfort Pl SW1 131 C3
Headington Rd SW18 71 B2
Headlam Rd SW4 73 C4
Headlam St E1 25 A1
Heads Mews W11 31 C3
Head St E1 32 C3
Heald St SE8, SE14 51 C2
Healey St NW1 13 A2
Healy Ho 2 E3 26 C1
Heanor Ct 4 E5 17 C4
Hearne Rd W4 44 C4
Hearn's Bldgs SE17 151 C3
Hearnshaw St 1 E14 33 A3
Hearn St EC2 24 A1 98 B1
Hearnville Rd SW12 72 C3
Heart Hospl The W1 103 C3
Heart Radio W11 30 C2
Heathbrook Prim Sch 11 SW4 170 C1
Heath Brow NW3 2 B1
Heath Cl NW11 2 A4
Heathcote Point 25 E9 17 C2
Heathcote St WC1 94 C3
Heathcroft NW11 2 A3
Heath Ct
2 Hampstead NW3 11 B2
Stoke Newington N16 6 C3
Heath Dr NW3 11 A4
Heather Cl SW8 61 A4
Heather Ct SW4 172 B3
Heather Ho 11 E14 34 B3
Heatherley Ct N16 7 C1
Heatherley Sch of Fine Art SW10 156 C1
Heather Lo N16 7 A3
Heather Wlk W10 23 A1
Heathfield Ave SW18 71 C4
Heathfield Ct
3 Bow E3 26 C3
5 Chiswick W4 37 C1
Wandsworth SW18 71 C4
Heathfield Gdns
Acton Green W4 37 B1
Blackheath SE3 53 A1
Wandsworth SW18 59 C1
Heathfield Ho SE3 53 A1
Heathfield House Sch 15 W4 37 B1
Heathfield Pk NW2 9 B2
Heathfield Rd
South Acton W3 37 A4
Wandsworth SW18 59 C1
Heathfield Sq SW18 71 C4
Heathfield Terr W4 37 C1
Heathgate Pl NW3 12 B4
Heath House Prep Sch 1 SE8 53 B1
Heath Hurst Rd NW3 12 A4
Heath La SE3 52 C1
Heathland Rd N16 7 A3
Heath Mans
5 Hampstead NW3 11 B4
Putney SW15 57 C1
Heathman's Rd SW6 165 A3
Heath Mead SW19 69 C1
Heathmere Prim Sch SW15 68 C3
Heath Park Gdns NW3 2 A1
Heathpool Ct 8 E1 25 A1
Heath Rd SW8 170 B1
Heath Rise SW15 57 C1
Heath Royal SW15 57 C1
Heathshott 8 TW10 54 A1
Heathside NW3 11 C4
Heathside Prep Sch 32 NW3 11 B4
Heath St NW3 2 B1
Heathstan Rd W12 29 C3
Heath View NW5 12 C4
Heathview Ct SW19 69 C2
Heathview Gdns SW15 69 B4
Heath Villas NW3 2 C1
Heathville Rd N4, N19 5 A4
Heathwall St SW11 60 B4
Heathway SE3 53 C3
Heathway Ct NW3 1 C2
Heathwood Ct SW12 73 B3
Heaton Ho
Chelsea SW10 157 A4
6 Peckham SE15 50 A1
Heaton Rd SE15 50 A1
Heaven Tree Cl N1 15 B3
Heaver Rd 23 SW11 59 C4
Hebden Ct 24 E2 24 B4
Hebdon Rd SW17 72 A1
Heber Prim Sch SE22 64 B1
Heber Rd
Cricklewood NW2 9 C4
East Dulwich SE22 64 B1
Hebron Rd W6 39 A3
Heckfield Pl SW6 155 B1
Heckford Ho E14 34 A3
Heckford St E1 32 C2
Hector Ct
1 London SW9 173 B4
Putney SW15 57 C2
Hector Ho 14 E2 25 A3
Heddington Gr N7 14 B3
Heddon St W1 118 C4
Hedger's Gr E9 18 A2
Hedger St SE11 150 A4
Hedingham Cl 6 N1 15 B1
Hedley Ct SW15 57 C1
Hedley Ho E14 42 B3
Hedley Row N5, N16 15 C3
Hedsor Ho E2 24 B1 98 C2
Heidegger Cres SW13 47 A3
Heights The NW3 11 B4
Heiron St SE17 48 A4
Helby Rd SW4 61 C1
Heldar Ct SE1 137 C3
Helena Pl 3 E9 25 B4
Helena Rd NW10 9 A3
Helena Sq 12 SE16 33 A2
Helen Gladstone Ho SE1 136 A4
Helen Ho 9 E2 25 A3
Helen Mackay Ho 10 E14 34 C3
Helen Peele Cotts 10 SE16 40 B3
Helenslea Ave NW11 1 C3
Helen's Pl E2 25 B2
Helen Taylor Ho 5 SE16 153 B4
Heliport Ind Est SW11 167 B1
Helix Ct 17 W11 30 C1
Helix Gdns SW2 62 B1
Helix Rd SW2 62 B1
Helix The SW19 69 C2
Hellings St E1 125 C1
Helmet Row EC1 97 A2
Helmsdale Ho NW6 78 A1
Helmsley Pl E8 17 A1
Helmsley St 7 E8 17 A1
Helperby Rd NW10 8 A1
Helsby Ct NW8 89 B2
Helsinki Sq SE16 41 A3
Helston NW1 83 A2
Helston Ho SE11 149 C2
Hemans Est SW8 161 C1
Hemans St SW8 161 C1
Hemberton Rd SW9 62 A4
Hemingford Rd N1 85 A4
Hemlock Rd W12 29 B2
Hemming St E1 24 C1 99 C1
Hemmingway Cl NW5 12 C4
Hemp Wlk SE17 151 C4
Hemstal Rd NW6 10 C1
Hemsworth Ct N1 24 A3
Hemsworth St N1 24 A3
Hemus Pl SW3 144 B1
Henchman St W12 29 B3
Henderson Ct
8 Deptford SE14 50 C4
Hampstead NW3 11 C3
Wandsworth SW18 72 A4
Henderson Dr NW8 89 B2
Henderson Rd SW18 72 A4
Hendham Rd SW17 72 B2
Hendre Ho SE1 152 B3
Hendre Rd SE1 152 B3
Hendrick Ave SW12 72 B4
Heneage La EC3 110 B1
Heneage Pl EC3 110 B1
Heneage St E1 111 A4
Henfield Cl N19 4 B3
Henley Cl SE16 40 B4
Henley Ct
Brondesbury NW2 9 C2
Peckham SE15 64 C4
Henley Dr SE1 153 A4
Henley Ho E2 24 B1 99 A2
Henley Prior N1 84 C1
Henley Rd NW10 22 B4
Henley St SW11 169 C2
Henniker Mews SW3 157 B4
Henniker Rd E15 19 C3
Henning St SW11 168 A3
Henrietta Cl SE8 51 C4
Henrietta Ho 11 W6 39 B1
Henrietta Mews WC1 94 B2
Henrietta Pl W1 104 A2
Henrietta St
Strand WC2 120 B4
Stratford New Town E15 19 B3
Henriques St E1 111 C1
Henry Cavendish Prim Sch 2 SW12 73 B3
Henry Compton Sch SW6 164 A4
Henry Dent Cl SE5 63 C4
Henry Dickens Ct W11 31 A1 112 A2
Henry Fawcett Prim Sch 15 SE11 163 B4
Henry Ho
Lambeth SE1 121 C1
South Lambeth SW8 162 A2
St John's Wood NW8 80 A2
Henry Jackson Ho 4 SW15 57 C4
Henry Jackson Rd SW15 57 C4
Henry Rd N4 6 B3
Henryson Rd SE4 66 C2
Henry Wise Ho SW1 147 A3
Henshall Point 19 E3 27 A2
Henshall St N1 15 C2
Henshaw St SE17 151 B4
Hensley Point 28 E9 17 C2
Henslowe Rd SE22 64 C2
Henslow Ho 12 SE15 49 C3
Henson Ave NW2 9 B3
Henson Ct 3 N5 15 B4
Henstridge Pl NW8 80 A3
Henty Cl SW11 168 B4
Henty Wlk SW15 57 A2
Hepburn Mews SW11 60 B2

Hepplestone Cl SW15 57 A1
Hepscott Rd E9 18 C1
Hepworth Ct
Chelsea SW1 146 A1
Islington N1 86 A4
Hera Ct 15 E14 41 C2
Heralds Pl SE11 150 A4
Herald St 5 E2 25 A1
Herbal Hill EC1 95 C1
Herbert Chapman Ct N5 15 A4
Herbert Cres SW1 131 A2
Herbert Gdns
Chiswick W4 45 A4
Willesden Green NW10 22 A3
Herbert Ho E1 110 C2
Herbert Mews 15 SW2 62 C1
Herbert Morrison Ho SW6 154 C3
Herbert Morrison Prim Sch SW8 162 A1
Herbert St NW5 12 C2
Herbrand Est WC1 94 A2
Herbrand St WC1 94 A2
Hercules Ct 7 SE14 51 A4
Hercules Pl N7 5 A1
Hercules Rd SE1 135 A1
Hercules St N7 5 A1
Hereford Bldgs SW3 157 C4
Hereford Ho
5 Brixton SW2 62 C3
25 Camberwell SE5 48 B1
Knightsbridge SW3 130 B2
Walham Green SW10 156 B2
Hereford Mans 10 W2 31 C3
Hereford Mews 11 W2 31 C3
Hereford Pl SE14 51 B3
Hereford Rd
Acton W3 28 B2
Bayswater W2 31 C2 113 C4
Hereford Retreat 5 SE15 49 C3
Hereford Sq SW7 143 A3
Hereford St E2 24 C1 99 B2
Hereward House Sch NW3 11 C2
Heritage Cl SW9 63 A4
Heritage Ct SE8 40 C1
Heritage Ho 22 SW19 69 C3
Hermes Cl 5 W9 23 C1
Hermes Ct 4 SW9 173 B4
Hermes St N1 85 B1
Hermitage Ct
2 Child's Hill NW2 1 C1
13 Wapping E1 125 C1
Hermitage Gdns NW2 1 C1
Hermitage La NW2 1 C1
Hermitage Prim Sch 19 E1 125 C2
Hermitage Row 9 E8 16 C3
Hermitage St W2 101 B3
Hermitage The
Barnes SW13 46 B2
Richmond TW10 54 A2
Hermitage Villas SW6 155 B4
Hermitage Wall E1 125 C1
Hermit Pl NW6 78 A3
Hermit St EC1 96 A4
Herndon Rd SW18 59 B2
HERNE HILL 63 B2
Herne Hill SE24 63 B3
Herne Hill Ho SE24 63 A1
Herne Hill Mans SE24 63 B1
Herne Hill Rd SE24 63 B3
Herne Hill Sch SE24 63 B2
Herne Hill Sta SE24 63 A1
Herne Hill Velodrome SE24 63 C1
Herne Pl SE24 63 A2
Heron Cl NW10 8 A2
Heron Ct
16 Cubitt Town E14 42 B3
7 Dulwich SE21 75 C2
Herondale Ave SW18 72 A3
Heron Dr N4 6 B2
Herongate N1 87 A4
Heron Ho
Battersea SW11 168 B4
Peckham SE15 49 B2
St John's Wood NW8 80 A1
Heron Pl
Marylebone W1 103 C2
Rotherhithe SE16 33 A1
Heron Quays E14 33 C1
Heron Quays Sta E14 33 C1
Heron Rd SE24 63 B3
Heron Trad Est W3 28 A4
Herrick Ho
18 Camberwell SE5 48 C3
17 Canonbury N16 15 C4
Herrick Rd N5 6 B1
Herrick St SW1 147 C3
Herries St W10 23 A3
Hersant Cl NW10 21 C4
Herschell's Mews SE5 63 B4
Hersham Cl SW15 68 C4
Hershell Ct 1 SW14 55 A3
Hertford Ave SW14 56 A3
Hertford Ct 16 SW11 60 A4
Hertford Lo 10 SW19 70 A3
Hertford Pl W1 93 A1
Hertford Rd N1 24 A4
Hertford St W1 118 A1
Hertmitage The 5 SE13 52 B1
Hertslet Rd N7 5 B1
Hertsmere Rd E14 33 C2
Hesewall Cl SW4 171 A1
Hesketh Pl W11 31 A2 112 A3
Heslop Ct 1 SW12 72 C3
Heslop Rd SW12 72 B3
Hesper Mews SW5 142 A3
Hesperus Cres E14 42 A2
Hessel St E1 32 A3
Hestercombe Ave SW6 164 B3
Hester Rd SW11 158 A1
Hester Terr TW9 54 C4
Hestia Ho SE1 138 A3
Heston Ho
Gunnersbury W4 37 A1
5 St Johns SE8 51 C2
Heston St SE14 51 C2
Hetherington Rd SW2, SW4 62 A3
Hethpool Ho W2 89 B1
Hetley Rd W12 39 A4
Hetty Rees Ct 6 N19 5 A4
Hevelius Cl SE10 43 B1
Hever Ho SE15 50 C4
Heversham Ho SE15 50 B4
Heward Ct SE13 52 B1
Hewer Ho 6 SW4 61 B2
Hewer St W10 30 C4
Hewett Ho SW15 47 B1
Hewett St EC2 24 A1 98 B1
Hewison St E3 26 B3
Hewlett Rd E3 26 A3
Hewling Ho 1 N16 16 A3
Hexagon The N6 3 B3
Hexham Rd SE27 75 B2
Hexton Ct N4 6 B2
Heybridge 9 NW1 13 A2
Heydon Ho 3 SE14 50 B2
Heyford Ave SW8 162 B2
Heyford Terr SW8 162 B2
Heygate St SE17 151 A4
Heylyn Sq E3 26 B2
Heysham La NW3 2 A1
Heythorp St SW18 70 B2
Heythrop Coll W8 128 A2
Heywood Ho
11 Deptford SE14 50 C4
6 Tulse Hill SW2 62 C1
Heyworth Rd E5 17 A4
Hibbert Ho 13 E14 41 C3
Hibbert St SW11 59 C4
Hichisson Rd SE15 65 B2
Hicken Rd SW2 62 B2
Hickes Ho 6 NW6 11 C1
Hickey's Almshouses 7 TW9 54 B3
Hickin St 2 E14 42 B3
Hickleton NW1 83 A3
Hickling Ho 10 SE16 40 A3
Hickmore Wlk SW4 61 B4
Hicks Cl SW11 60 A4
Hicks St SE8 41 A1
Hide Pl SW1 147 B3
Hide Twr SW1 147 B3
Hieover SE21 75 B2
Higgins Ho 7 N1 24 A4
Higginson Ho 2 NW3 12 B1
Higgs Ind Est 9 SE24 63 A4
Highbridge Ct 13 SE14 50 B3
High Bridge Wharf SE10 42 C1
Highburty Mans 24 N1 15 A1
HIGHBURY 15 A4
Highbury Cnr N5 15 A2
Highbury Corner N5 15 A2
Highbury Cres N5 14 C3
Highbury Fields Sch 4 N5 15 A3
Highbury Gr N5 15 A3
Highbury Grange N5 15 B4
Highbury Grove Ct N5 15 A2
Highbury Grove Sch 7 N5 15 B3
Highbury Hill N5 15 A4
Highbury & Islington Sta N1 15 A2
Highbury New Pk N5 15 B4
Highbury Pk N5 15 A4
Highbury Pl N5 15 A3
Highbury Pool N5 15 A2
Highbury Quadrant N5 6 B1
Highbury Quadrant Prim Sch N5 15 B4
Highbury Station Rd N1 14 C2
Highbury Terr N5 15 A3
Highbury Terrace Mews N5 15 A3
Highcliffe Dr SW15 56 B1
Highcroft Rd N19 5 A4
Highcross Way 4 SW15 68 C3
Highdown Rd SW15 57 A1
Highfield Ave NW11 1 A4
Highfield Cl SE13 67 C1
Highfield Mews NW6 11 A1
Highfield Rd W3 28 B4
Highfields Gr N6 3 B3
HIGHGATE 3 C4
Highgate Archway N6 4 B3
Highgate Ave N6 4 A4
Highgate Cemetery N19 4 A2
Highgate Cl N6 3 C4
Highgate High St N6 4 A3
Highgate Hill N19 4 B3
Highgate Ho 11 SE26 76 C1
Highgate Pre-Prep & Jun Sch N6 3 B4
Highgate Rd NW5 13 A4
Highgate Sch N6 3 C4
Highgate West Hill
Highgate N6 3 C3
London N6 3 C2
Highgrove Point 2 NW3 11 B4
High Holborn WC1 106 C3
High Holborn Ho WC1 107 A3
Highlands Ave W3 28 B2
Highlands Cl N4 5 A4
Highlands Heath SW15 69 B4
Highlever Rd W10 30 B4
High London 5 N6 4 C4
Highmore Rd SE3 53 A3
High Mount 11 N4 5 A4
High Park Ave TW9 44 C2
High Park Rd TW9 44 C2
High Par The SW16 74 A1
High Point N6 3 C4
High Rd NW10 8 C2
Highshore Rd SE15 49 B1
Highshore Sch 16 SE15 49 B2
High St
Acton W3 28 A1
Brentford TW8 44 A4
Stratford Marsh E15 27 B4
High Street Harlesden NW10 21 B3
High Street Kensington Sta W8 128 A3
High The SW16 74 A1
High Timber St EC4 122 C4
High Trees SW2 74 C3
Hightrees Ho SW12 60 C1
Highview N8 5 A4
Highview Ct 2 SW19 70 A3
High View Prim Sch 1 SW11 59 C3
Highway Bsns Pk The 7 E1 32 C2
Highway The E1 32 B2
Highway Trad Ctr The 6 E1 32 C2
Highwood Cl SE22 76 C3
Highwood Rd N19 5 A1
Highworth St NW1 102 B4
Hilary Cl SW6 156 A2
Hilary Rd W12 29 B2
Hilborough Ct 1 E8 24 B4
Hilborough Rd 1 E8 16 B1
Hilda Terr 2 SW9 173 C2
Hilditch Ho 7 TW10 54 B1
Hildred Ho SW1 146 A4
Hildreth St 6 SW12 73 A3
Hildreth Street Mews 2 SW12 73 A3
Hildyard Rd SW6 155 C4
Hiley Rd NW10 22 B2
Hilgrove Rd NW6 11 B1
Hillary Ct 13 W12 39 B4
Hillbeck Cl Deptford SE15 50 B3

Hillbeck Cl *continued*
Deptford SE15 ......50 B4
Hillbrow 7 TW10...54 A1
Hillbury Rd SW17...73 A1
Hillcourt Rd SE22...65 A1
Hillcrest
Camberwell SE24....63 C3
Highgate N6.........3 C4
Notting Hill W11......31 B2 112 C3
Hillcrest Ct NW2....10 A3
Hillcrest Rd W3 ....28 A1
Hill Ct
Hampstead NW3 ....12 A4
Putney SW15.......57 C2
Hilldrop Cres N7 ...13 C3
Hilldrop La N7 .....13 C3
Hilldrop Rd N7.....13 C3
Hillersdon Ave SW13 ....46 C1
Hillersdon Ho SW1 .... 146 A2
Hillery Cl SE17 ... 151 C3
Hill Farm Rd W10...30 C4
Hillfield Ct NW3....12 A3
Hillfield Ho N5.....15 B3
Hillfield Mans NW3..............12 A3
Hillfield Rd NW6....10 C3
Hillgate Pl
Balham SW12.......73 A4
Kensington W8.......31 C1 113 B2
Hillgate St W8........31 C1 113 B2
Hill House International Jun Sch SW1........ 131 A1
Hilliard Ho 15 E1...32 A1
Hilliard's Ct E1.....32 B1
Hillier Ho 1 NW1..13 C1
Hillier Rd SW11 ....60 B1
Hillingdon St SE17..48 A4
Hill Lo SW11 ....59 C3
Hillman Dr 12 NW10.............22 B1
Hillman St E8 ......17 A2
Hillmarton Rd N7 ..14 A3
Hillmead Dr SW9....63 A3
Hill Mead Prim Sch 28 SW9 ....63 A3
Hillmore Ct SE13 ...67 C4
Hill Rd NW8....... 79 A1
Hillrise Mans N19 ...5 A4
Hillrise Rd N19......5 A4
Hillsboro Rd SE22 ..64 A2
Hillsborough Ct 13 NW6............. 78 A3
Hillside
Greenwich SE10.....52 C3
Stonebridge NW10...20 C4
Hillside Cl NW8 ... 78 B2
Hillside Ct NW3 ....11 A3
Hillside Gdns SW2..74 C2
Hillside Rd SW2....74 C2
Hillsleigh Rd W14.......31 B1 113 A2
Hills Pl W1....... 104 C1
Hill St W1........ 118 A2
Hillstone Ct 5 E3 ..27 A1
Hilltop Ct
12 London SW18....59 C3
South Hampstead NW8.............11 B1
Hilltop Ho 7 N6 ....4 C4
Hilltop Rd NW6.....10 C1
Hill View NW1 ..... 81 A4
Hillway N6..........3 C2
Hill Wood Ho NW1 83 B1
Hillworth Rd SW2 ..74 C4
Hillyard St SW9 .. 173 B3
Hillyfield Cl E9.....18 A3
Hilly Fields Cres SE4...............66 C4
Hilsea Point 7 SW15 ....69 A3
Hilsea St E5........17 B4
Hilton Docklands Pier SE16..............33 B1
Hilton Ho
Lower Holloway N7..............14 A4
9 Nunhead SE4 ....65 C3
Hilversum Cres 10 SE22.............64 A2
Hinckley Rd SE15...64 C3
Hind Ct EC4...... 107 C1
Hinde Mews W1.. 103 C2
Hinde St W1 ..... 103 C2
Hind Gr E14........33 C3
Hindhead Point 6 SW15 ....69 A3
Hind Ho
13 Deptford SE14 ...50 C4
Islington N7........14 C4
Hindle Ho E8.......16 B3
Hindley Ho N7 ......5 B1
Hindlip Ho SW8 .. 171 B3
Hindmans Rd SE22.............64 C2
Hindmarsh Cl E1 . 125 C4
Hindrey Rd E5......17 A3
Hinstock NW6..... 78 A4
Hinton Rd SE24.....63 A4
Hippodrome Mews W11 ...... 31 A2 112 A3
Hippodrome Pl W11 ....31 A2 112 B3
Hirst Ct SW1 ..... 146 A1
Hitchin Sq E3 ......26 A3
Hithe Gr 15 SE16 ....40 B3
Hitherfield Prim Sch SW16 ....74 C2
Hitherfield Rd SW16, SW27 ....74 C1
Hither Green La SE13..............67 C1
Hither Green Prim Sch SE13.........67 C1
Hitherlands SW12 ..73 A2
HM Prison Wormwood Scrubs W12 ....29 C3
HMS Belfast SE1 . 124 B2
Hoadly Rd SW16....73 C2
Hobart Pl SW1 ... 132 A2
Hobbes Wlk SW15..57 A2
Hobb's Ct SE1.... 139 A4
Hobbs' Pl N1.......24 A3
Hobday St E14 .....34 A3
Hobhouse Ct SW1 119 C3
Hobsons Pl 7 E1. 111 B4
Hobury St SW10.. 157 B3
Hocker St 41 E2..........24 B2 98 C3
Hockett Cl SE8 .....41 B2
Hockley Ho 4 E9 ...17 B2
Hockliffe Ho 5 W10 ....30 B4
Hockney Ct 1 SE16..............40 A1
Hockworth Ho 7 N16................7 A3
Hocroft Ave NW2....1 B1
Hocroft Ct NW2 .....1 B1
Hocroft Rd NW2.....1 B1
Hocroft Wlk NW2....1 B1
Hodford Lo NW11 ...1 C2
Hodford Rd NW11 ...1 B3
Hodister Cl 26 SE5..48 B3
Hodnet Gr SE16 ....40 B2
Hoffman Sq N1.... 97 C4
Hofland Rd W14.. 126 A2
Hogan Mews W2 . 101 B4
Hogan Way E5 ......7 C2
Hogarth Bsns Pk W4...............46 A4
Hogarth Ct
8 Camden Town NW1.............13 B1
City of London EC3. 124 B4
24 Whitechapel E1 111 C1
Hogarth Ho SW1 . 147 C3
Hogarth Ind Est NW10.............21 C1
Hogarth La W4.....46 A4
Hogarth Pl SW5 .. 142 A3
Hogarth Rd SW5 . 142 A3
Hogarth Roundabout W4 ....46 A4
Hogarth's House W4 ....46 A4
Holbeach Mews 1 SW12 ....73 A3
Holbeck Row SE15..49 C3
Holbein Ho SW1.. 145 B2
Holbein Mews SW1 .... 145 B2
Holbein Pl SW1 .. 145 B3
Holberton Gdns NW10.............22 A2
HOLBORN 107 C3
Holborn EC1 ..... 107 C3
Holborn Cir EC1 .. 107 C3
Holborn Ho 1 W12 ....30 A3
Holborn Pl WC1 .. 106 C3
Holborn Sta WC1 106 C3
Holborn Viaduct EC1.............. 108 A3
Holbrook Cl N19.....4 A3
Holbrooke Ct N7 ...14 A4
Holbrook Ho
Acton W3 ....28 C4
5 Streatham SW2 ..74 B3
Holcombe Ho SW9...............62 A4
Holcombe Pl SE4...66 A4
Holcombe St W6 ...39 A2
Holcroft Ct W1 ... 104 C4
Holcroft Ho
Battersea SW11.....59 C4
Lewisham SE10 .....52 B2
Holcroft Rd E9 .....17 B1
Holdenby Rd SE4...66 A2
Holden Ho
12 Deptford SE8 ....51 C3
Islington N1....... 86 C3
Holden Point E15...19 C2
Holden St SW11 .. 169 B1
Holdernesse Rd 6 SW17 ....72 C2
Holderness Ho SE5...............64 A4
Holdsworth Ho 5 SW2..............74 C4
Holford Ho
6 Bermondsey SE16.............40 A2
Finsbury WC1...... 95 A4
Holford Pl WC1.... 95 A4
Holford Rd NW3.....2 B1
Holford St WC1.... 95 B4
Holford Yd WC1 ... 85 B1
Holgate Ave SW11..59 C4
Holland Gdns
Brentford TW8......44 A4
Kensington W14... 126 B2
Holland Gr SW9 .. 163 C1
Holland Park W11.......31 B1 112 C1
Holland Park Ave W11.......31 A1 112 B1
Holland Park Ct W14............ 126 B4
Holland Park Gdns W14............ 126 A4
Holland Park Mews W11.......31 B1 112 C1
Holland Park Pre Prep Sch W14 .... 126 C1
Holland Park Rd W14............ 127 A1
Holland Park Rdbt W12 ....39 C4
Holland Park Sch W8 .... 127 A4
Holland Park Sta W11.......31 B1 112 C1
Holland Pas N1 ... 86 C4
Holland Pl W8.... 128 A4
Holland Rd
West Kensington W14 .... 126 B2
Willesden Green NW10.............22 A3
Holland Rise Ho SW9 .... 163 A1
Holland St
Kensington W8.... 127 C4
Lambeth SE1 ..... 122 B2
Holland Villas Rd W14............ 126 A3
Holland Wlk
Kensington W14... 127 A3
Upper Holloway N19 ..4 C3
Hollar Rd N16.......7 B1
Hollen St W1...... 105 B2
Holles Ho 8 SW9 173 B2
Holles St W1...... 104 B2
Holley Rd W3 ......38 A4
Holliday Sq 6 SW11 ....59 C4
Hollies The SW12...73 B2
Hollies Way 1 SW12 ....72 C4
Hollingbourne Rd SE24..............63 B2
Hollins Ho N7 ......14 A4
Hollisfield WC1.... 94 B3
Holloway Rd
Lower Holloway N7..............14 B4
Upper Holloway N19 ..4 C2
Holloway Road Sta N7...............14 B3
Holloway Sch N7...13 C3
Holly Berry La 8 NW3.............11 B4
Hollybush Gdns E2...............25 A2
Holly Bush Hill 4 NW3..............11 B4
Hollybush Ho 23 E2...............25 A2
Hollybush Pl E2 ....25 A2
Holly Bush Steps 6 NW3..............11 B4
Holly Bush Vale 10 NW3..............11 B4
Holly Cl NW10.......8 A1
Hollycroft Ave NW3..1 C1
Hollydale Prim Sch 7 SE15..............50 B1
Hollydale Rd SE15..50 B1
Hollydene
Hither Green SE13............67 C1
5 Peckham SE15 ...50 A2
Holly Gr SE15.......49 C1
Hollyhedge Ho SE3...............52 C1
Holly Hedge Terr SE13..............67 C2
Holly Hill NW3......11 B4
Holly Lo W8...... 127 B4
Holly Lodge SE13...67 C3
Holly Lodge Gdns N6.................3 C3
Holly Lodge Mans N6.................3 C2
Holly Mews SW10 143 A1
Holly Mount NW3 ..11 B4
Hollymount Cl 9 SE10..............52 B2
Holly Park Est N4 ...5 B4
Holly Pk N4 ....5 B4
Holly Pl NW3.......11 B4
Holly Rd 6 W4.....37 C2
Holly St E8.........16 B1
Holly Terr N6........3 C3
Hollytree Cl SW19 ..69 C3
Holly Tree Ho SE4 ..66 B4
Holly Village N6 .....4 A2
Holly Wlk NW3 .....11 B4
Hollywood Lofts E1..........24 B1 98 C1
Hollywood Mews SW10 .... 156 C4
Hollywood Rd SW10 .... 156 C4
Holman Ho 2 E2...25 C2
Holman Hunt Ho W14 .... 140 A1
Holman Rd SW11. 167 B1
Holmbrook NW1... 83 A1
Holmbury Ct SW17 .72 B1
Holmbury Ho SW9..63 A2
Holmbush Rd SW15 ....58 A1
Holmcote Gdns N5.................15 B3
Holmdale Rd NW6..10 C3
Holmdene Ave SE24..............63 B2
Holmead Rd SW6. 156 B1
Holmefield Ct 4 NW3..............12 A2
Holmefield Ho W10 ....23 A1
Holmes Cl SE22 ....64 C3
Holmes Ct
18 South Acton W4 ....37 B3

Holmes Ct *continued*
18 South Lambeth SW4 172 A2
Holmesdale Ave SW14 55 A3
Holmesdale Ho 12 NW6 23 C4
Holmesdale Rd
Highgate N6 4 A4
Richmond TW9 44 B2
Holmesley Rd SE23 66 A1
Holmes Pl SW10 157 A4
Holmes Rd NW5 13 A3
Holmes Terr SE1 135 B4
Holmewood Gdns SW2 74 B4
Holmewood Rd SW2 74 B4
Holmhurst SE13 67 C1
Holmleigh Prim Sch N16 7 A3
Holmleigh Rd N16 7 A3
Holm Oak Cl SW15 58 B1
Holmsbury Ho 6 N7 13 C3
Holmsdale Ho 24 E14 34 A2
Holmside Ct SW12 60 C1
Holmside Rd SW12 60 C1
Holmsley Ho SW15 68 B4
Holm Wlk SE3 53 C1
Holmwood Ct 3 N16 7 B4
Holocaust Meml Gdn W2 131 A4
Holroyd Rd SW15 57 B2
Holsgrove Ct W3 29 A1
Holst Mans SW13 47 B3
Holsworthy Ho 49 E3 27 A2
Holsworthy Sq WC1 95 A1
Holt Ct SE10 52 B4
Holt Ho SW2 62 C1
Holton St E1 25 C1
Holwood Pl 7 SW4 61 C3
Holybourne Ave SW15 68 C4
Holy Cross Prim Sch SW6 165 B4
Holy Family RC Prim Sch 23 E14 33 C2
Holy Ghost RC Prim Sch 4 SW12 72 C4
Holyhead Cl E3 26 C2
Holyoake Ct SE16 41 B4
Holyoak Rd SE11 150 B3
Holyport Rd SW6 47 C3
Holyrood Ho N4 6 B3
Holyrood Mews
6 Greenwich SE7 43 C1
10 Newham E16 35 C1
Holyrood St SE1 124 A1
Holy Trinity CE Prim Sch
Belgravia SW1 145 B4
Dalston E8 16 B2
10 Hampstead NW3 11 B2
Richmond TW10 54 C3
Streatham SW2 74 B4
Holy Trinity & Saint Silas CE Prim Sch 22 NW1 13 A1
Holywell Cl
35 Bermondsey SE16 40 A1
2 Greenwich SE3 53 C4
Holywell La EC2 24 A1 98 B2
Holywell Row EC2 24 A1 98 A1
Homan Ho 6 SW4 73 C4
Homecross Ho 7 W4 37 C2
Homefield Rd W4 38 B1
Homefield St 14 N1 24 A3
Homeleigh Ct 8 SW16 74 A1
Homeleigh Rd SE15 65 C2
Homemead SW12 73 A2
Home Office SW1 133 C1
Home Park Rd SW19 70 B1
Home Rd SW11 168 A2
Homer Dr E14 41 C2
Homer Rd E9 18 A2
Homer Row W1 102 B3
Homer St W1 102 B3
HOMERTON 17 C1
Homerton Gr E9 17 C3
Homerton High St E9 17 C3
Homerton Rd E9 18 B3
Homerton Row E9 17 B3
Homerton Sta E9 17 C2
Homerton Terr E9 17 B2
Homerton University Hospl E9 17 C3
Homestall Rd SE22 65 B2
Homestead Rd SW6 155 A1
Homewoods 2 SW12 73 B4
Homildon Ho 10 SE26 76 C1
Honduras St EC1 96 C2
Honeybourne Rd NW6 11 A3
Honeybrook Rd SW12, SW4 73 B4
Honeyfield N4 5 C2
Honey La EC2 109 A1
Honey Lane Ho SW10 156 B4
Honeyman Cl NW6 9 C1
Honeywell Jun & Inf Schs 3 SW11 60 B1
Honeywell Rd SW11 60 B1
Honeywood Ho 5 SE15 49 C2
Honeywood Rd NW10 21 B3
Honiton Gdns 1 SE15 50 B1
Honiton Ho 29 SE5 48 B1
Honiton Rd NW6 23 B3
HONOR OAK 65 B2
Honor Oak Park Sta SE23 65 C1
Honor Oak Pk SE23 65 C1
Honor Oak Rise SE23 65 B1
Honwell Ho 24 W2 31 C4
Hood Ave SW14 55 B2
Hood Ct N7 5 B1
Hood Ho 17 SE5 48 C3
Hooke Ct SE10 52 B2
Hooke Ho 32 E3 26 A3
Hookham Ct SW8 171 B4
Hooks Cl SE15 50 A2
Hooper Ho 9 SW18 58 B2
Hooper Rd E16 35 C3
Hooper's Ct SW1 130 C3
Hooper's Mews 4 W3 28 B1
Hooper St E1 111 B1
Hoop La NW11 1 C4
Hope Cl
2 Brentford TW8 36 A1
Canonbury N1 15 B2
Hopefield Ave NW6 23 A3
Hope Gdns 10 W3 37 A4
Hope St SW11 59 C4
Hopetown St E1 111 A3
Hopewell St SE5 48 C3
Hop Gdns WC2 120 A3
Hopgood St 5 W12 30 B1
Hopkins Ho 17 E14 33 C3
Hopkinson Ho 1 SW11 169 B2
Hopkinson's Pl NW1 81 B4
Hopkins St W1 105 B1
Hopping La N1 15 A2
Hop St SE10 43 B2
Hopton Ho 5 SW9 48 A1
Hopton's Gdns SE1 122 B2
Hopton St SE1 122 B2
Hopwood Cl SW17 71 B1
Hopwood Rd SE17 48 C4
Hopwood Wlk E8 16 C1
Horatio Ho 13 E2 24 B3
Horatio Pl 9 E14 34 B1
Horatio St 11 E2 24 B3
Horbury Cres W11 31 C2 113 B3
Horbury Mews W11 31 B2 113 A3
Horder Rd SW6 164 B3
Hordle Prom E 15 SE15 49 B3
Hordle Prom N 4 SE15 49 B3
Hordle Prom S 7 SE15 49 B3
Horizon Bldg 22 E14 33 C2
Horizon Ind Est SE15 49 C3
Horizon Sch N16 16 A4
Horle Wlk SE5 48 A1
Hormead Rd W9 23 B1
Hornbeam Cl SE11 149 B4
Hornbeam Ho 2 NW3 12 B2
Hornbeam Sq 8 E3 26 B4
Hornblower Cl 2 SE16 41 A2
Hornby Cl NW3 11 C1
Hornby Ho 6 SE11 163 C4
Horndean Cl 3 SW15 68 C3
Horner Hos 18 N1 24 A4
Horne Way SW15 47 B1
Horn La
Acton W3 28 B3
Greenwich SE10 43 C2
Horn Link Way SE10 43 C2
Hornsby House Sch 7 SW12 72 C3
Hornsey La N6 4 B4
Hornsey Lane Gdns N6 4 B4
Hornsey Rd N7, N19 5 B2
Hornsey Rise Gdns N19 5 A4
Hornsey St N7 14 B3
Hornshay St SE15 50 B4
Hornton Ct W8 127 C3
Hornton Pl W8 127 C3
Hornton St W8 127 C4
Horrocks Ho SW15 57 A2
Horse & Dolphin Yd W1 119 C4
Horseferry Pl SE10 52 B4
Horseferry Rd
Limehouse E14 33 A2
Westminster SW1 147 C4
Horseferry Rd Est SW1 133 B1
Horse Guards Ave SW1 120 A1
Horse Guards Par SW1 119 C1
Horse Guards Rd SW1 133 C4
Horsell Rd N5 14 C3
Horselydown La SE1 124 C1
Horselydown Mans SE1 138 C4
Horsemongers Mews SE1 137 A3
Horsendon Ho 11 N7 13 C3
Horseshoe Cl E14 42 B1
Horse Yd N1 86 B4
Horsfield Ho 13 N1 15 B1
Horsford Rd SW2 62 B2
Horsley Ct SW1 147 C3
Horsley Ho 11 SE4 65 C3
Horsley St 3 SE17 48 C4
Horsman Ho SE5 48 B4
Horsman St SE5 48 B4
Horsmonden Rd SE4 66 B1
Horston Ho N4 6 B4
Hortensia Ho SW10 156 C2
Hortensia Rd SW10 156 C2
Horticultural Pl 6 W4 37 C1
Horton Ave NW2 10 A4
Horton Ho
13 Deptford SE15 50 B4
South Lambeth SW8 162 C2
West Kensington W14 140 A1
Horton Rd E8 17 A2
Horton St SE13 67 A4
Horwood Ho
24 Bethnal Green E2 25 A2
Marylebone NW8 90 B2
Hosack Rd SW12, SW17 72 C2
Hosier La EC1 108 B3
Hoskins St SE10 42 C1
Hospl for Tropical Diseases NW1 93 A1
Hospl of St John & St Elizabeth NW8 79 B1
Hotham Prim Sch SW15 57 C3
Hotham Rd SW15 57 B4
Hothfield Pl SE16 40 B3
Hotspur St SE11 149 B2
Houblon Rd TW10 54 A2
Houghton Cl 10 E8 16 B2
Houghton Sq SW9 62 A4
Houghton St WC2 107 A1
Houndsditch EC3 110 B2
Household Cavalry Mus SW1 120 A1
Houseman Way 20 SE5 48 C3
House Mill The E3 27 B2
Houses of Parliament SW1 134 B2
Hoveden Rd NW2 10 A3
Howard Bldg SW8 160 A3
Howard Cl
Acton W3 28 A3
Cricklewood NW2 10 A4
Howard Ct
Lewisham SE10 52 B2
Peckham SE15 64 C4
Howard Ho
6 Brixton SW9 62 C4
14 Deptford SE8 51 B4
Fitzrovia W1 92 B1
Howard Mews N5 15 A4
Howard Rd
Canonbury N16 15 C4
Cricklewood NW2 9 C4
Howard's La SW15 57 B3
Howbury Rd SE15 65 B4
Howcroft Ho 3 E3 26 B2
Howden St SE15 64 C4
Howell Ho 5 N7 13 C3
Howell Wlk SE1 150 B3
Howgate Rd SW14 55 C4
Howick Pl SW1 133 A1
Howie St SW11 158 A1
Howitt Cl
6 Maitland Pk NW3 12 A2
Stoke Newington N16 16 A4
Howitt Rd NW3 12 A2
Howland Ho 9 SW16 74 A1
Howland Mews E W1 105 A4
Howland St W1 105 A4
Howland Way SE16 41 A4
Howletts Rd SE24 63 B1
Howley Pl W2 101 A4

Howsman Rd SW13 46 C4
Howson Rd SE4 66 A3
Howson Terr TW10 54 A1
How's St E2 24 B3
HOXTON 24 A3
Hoxton Mkt 10 N1 24 A2 98 A3
Hoxton Point EC1 24 A2 98 A3
Hoxton Sq N1 24 A2 98 A3
Hoxton St N1 24 A3
Hoxton Sta E2 24 B3
Hoylake Rd W3 29 A3
Hoyland Cl 4 SE15 50 A3
Hoy St E16 35 B3
Hub Buildings The 4 SW12 73 A3
Hub E15 E15 27 A3
Huberd Ho SE1 137 C2
Hubert Gr SW9 62 A4
Hubert Ho NW8 90 A1
Hub The NW1 81 A1
Hucknall Ct NW8 89 B2
Huddart St 6 E3 33 B4
Huddleston Cl E2 25 B3
Huddlestone Rd NW2 9 A2
Huddleston Rd N7 13 B4
Hudson Cl 15 W12 30 A2
Hudson Ct 1 E14 41 C1
Hudson Ho
Chelsea SW10 156 C2
5 Notting Hill W11 31 A3
Hudsons Ho N1 97 C3
Hudson's Pl SW1 146 C4
Huggin Ct EC4 123 A4
Huggin Hill EC4 123 A4
Huggins Ho 9 E3 26 C2
Huggins Pl SW2 74 B3
Hughan Rd E15 19 C3
Hugh Astor Ct SE1 136 B2
Hugh Dalton Ave SW6 154 C3
Hughenden Ho NW8 90 A2
Hughendon Terr E15 19 B4
Hughes Ho
26 Bethnal Green E2 25 B2
Camberwell SE5 48 B2
15 Deptford SE8 51 C4
Newington SE17 150 B3
Hughes Mans E1 24 C1 99 C1
Hughes Terr 6 E16 35 B4
Hugh Gaitskell Cl SW6 154 C3
Hugh Gaitskell Ho
Stoke Newington N16 7 B2
Willesden NW10 8 B1
Hugh Mews SW1 146 B3
Hugh Morgan Ho 5 SW4 61 C4
Hugh Myddelton Prim Sch EC1 95 C3
Hugh Platt Ho 23 E2 25 A3
Hugh St SW1 146 B3
Hugo Ho SW1 131 A2
Hugon Rd SW6 59 A4
Hugo Rd N19 13 B4
Huguenot Ct 9 E1 111 B4
Huguenot Pl
London SW18 59 B2
Spitalfields E1 111 A4
Huguenot Sq SE15 65 A4
Hullbridge Mews N1 87 B4
Hull Cl SE16 32 C1
Hull Ct SE5 48 C1
Hull St EC1 96 C3
Hulme Pl SE1 137 A3
Humber Dr W10 22 C1
Humber Rd SE3 53 B4
Humberton Cl E9 18 A3
Humbolt Rd W6 154 A3
Hume Ct N1 15 A1
Hume Ho 14 W11 30 C1
Humphrey Ct SW11 167 C3
Humphrey St SE1 152 C2
Humphry Ho 10 SW15 57 C2
Hungerford Bridge WC2 120 C2
Hungerford Ho SW1 161 A4
Hungerford La WC2 120 B2
Hungerford Prim Sch 19 N7 13 C2
Hungerford Rd
12 Camden Town N7 13 C2
Lower Holloway N7 14 A3
Hungerford St 21 E1 32 A3
Hunsdon Rd SE14 50 C3
Hunslett St 26 E2 25 B3
Hunstanton Ho NW1 102 B4
Hunt Cl W11 30 C1
Hunter Cl
Borough The SE1 137 C1
Upper Tooting SW12 72 C3
Huntercombe-Roehampton Hospl The SW15 68 C4
Hunter Ct
8 London SE5 63 C3
27 Streatham SW2 74 C4
Hunter Ho
Bloomsbury WC1 94 B2
Lambeth SE1 136 B3
South Lambeth SW8 161 C1
1 Tufnell Pk N19 4 B1
West Brompton SW5 141 C1
Hunterian Mus WC2 107 A2
Hunter Lo 9 W9 31 C4
Hunter St WC1 94 B2
Huntingdon Ct SW14 55 B4
Huntingdon Gdns W4 45 B3
Huntingdon Ho SW5 141 C4
Huntingdon St
Canning Town E16 35 B3
Islington N1 14 B1
Huntingfield Rd SW15 56 C2
Huntingford Ho SW15 47 B1
Huntington Ho NW2 9 B2
Huntley St WC1 93 B1
Hunton St E1 111 B4
Hunts Cl SE3 53 C1
Hunt's Ct WC2 119 C3
Huntshaw Ho 37 E3 27 A2
Hunt's La E15 27 B3
Huntsman St SE17 152 A3
Huntspill St SW17 71 B1
Hunts Slip Rd SE21 76 A2
Huntsworth Mews NW1 90 C1
Hurdwick Ho NW1 82 C2
Hurdwick Pl NW1 82 C2
Hurleston Ho 11 SE8 41 B1
Hurley Cres SE16 40 C4
Hurley Ho
Lambeth SE11 149 C3
34 Shoreditch E2 24 B2 98 C3
Hurley Lo SE22 65 B1
Hurlingham Bsns Pk SW6 58 C4
Hurlingham & Chelsea Sec Sch SW6 58 C4
Hurlingham Court Mans SW6 165 B1
Hurlingham Ct SW6 58 B4
Hurlingham Gdns SW6 58 B4
Hurlingham Rd SW6 165 A1
Hurlingham Sch SW15 58 B3
Hurlingham Sq SW6 59 A4
Hurlock Ho 1 N5 6 A1
Hurlock St N5 6 A1
Huron Rd SW17 72 C1
Huron Univ WC1 106 A4
Hurstbourne Ho SW15 56 B1
Hurstdene Gdns N15 7 A4
Hurst Ho WC1 85 A1
Hurst St SE24 63 A1
Hurstway Wlk 2 W11 30 C2
Husbourne Ho 8 SE8 41 A2
Huson Cl NW3 12 A1
Hutching's St E14 41 C4
Hutching's Wharf 11 E14 41 C4
Hutchins Cl E15 19 B1
Hutchins Ho 8 SW4 73 C4
Hutchinson Ho 9 SE14 50 B3
Hutton Ct 4 N4 5 B3
Hutton Ho 19 E2 24 C2 99 B3
Hutton St EC4 107 C1
Huxbear St SE4 66 B2
Huxley Ho
4 London SW9 172 C2
Paddington NW8 89 C1
Huxley St W10 23 A2
Hyacinth Rd SW15 68 C3
Hyde Farm Mews SW12 73 C3
Hyde La SW11 168 A4
Hyde Park W2 116 C1
Hyde Park Cnr SW1 131 C4
Hyde Park Corner Sta SW1 131 C4
Hyde Park Cres W2 102 A1
Hyde Park Gate Mews SW7 129 A3
Hyde Park Gdns W2 115 C4
Hyde Park Gdns Mews W2 116 A4
Hyde Park Mans NW1 102 A3
Hyde Park Pl W2 116 B4
Hyde Park Sq W2 102 A1
Hyde Park Square Mews W2 102 A1
Hyde Park St W2 102 A1
Hyde Park Twrs W2 114 C3
Hyde Rd
Richmond TW10 54 B2
Shoreditch N1 24 A4
Hyde's Pl 12 N1 15 A1
Hyde St SE8 51 C4
Hydethorpe Rd SW12 73 B3
Hyde Vale SE10 52 B3
Hylda Ct NW5 3 C1
Hyndman Ho 4 N19 13 C4
Hyndman St SE15 50 A4
Hyperion Ho
27 Bow E3 26 A3
Streatham SW2 74 B4
Hyson Rd SE16 40 A1
Hythe Ho 14 SE16 40 B4
Hythe Rd NW10 21 C1
Hythe Road Ind Est NW10 21 C1

I

Ian Hamilton Ho NW1 93 B4
Ian Mikardo Sch 32 E3 27 A2
Ibberton Ho
Kensington W14 126 B1
South Lambeth SW8 162 C2
Ibbotson Ave E16 35 B3
Ibbott St 22 E1 25 B1
Iberia Ho 17 N19 4 C4
Ibis Ct 16 SE8 51 B4
Ibis La W4 45 B2
Ibsley Gdns SW15 68 C3
Ibstock Place Sch SW15 56 A1
Icarus Ho 21 E3 26 B2
Iceland Rd E3 26 C4
Iceland Wharf SE16 41 A2
Iceni Ct 23 E3 26 B4
Ice Wharf NW1 84 B2
Idaho Bldg 7 SE13 52 A2
Ida St E14 34 B3
Identity & Passport Office SW1 146 B4
Idmiston Rd SE21, SE27 75 B2
Idol La EC3 124 A3
Idonia St SE8 51 C3
Iffley Ho 47 E2 24 B2 98 C3
Iffley Rd W6 39 A3
Ifield Ho SE17 152 B2
Ifield Rd SW10 156 B4
Ifor Evans Pl E1 25 C1
Ightham Ho SE17 152 A3
Ikon Ho 21 E1 32 B2
Ilbert St W10 23 A2
Ilchester Gdns W2 114 A4
Ilchester Mans W8 127 B2
Ilchester Pl W14 127 A2
Ildersly Gr SE21 75 C2
Ilderton Prim Sch 16 SE16 40 B1
Ilderton Rd SE15, SE16 50 B4
Ilex Rd NW10 8 B2
Ilford Ho 14 N1 15 C2
Ilfracombe Flats SE1 137 A4
Iliffe St SE17 150 B2
Iliffe Yd SE17 150 B2
Ilkeston Ct 7 E5 17 C4
Ilminster Gdns SW11 60 A3
Ilsley Ct 8 SW8 170 C1
Imber St N1 87 B3
Imperial Ave 5 N16 16 A4
Imperial Cl NW2 9 A3
Imperial College London (Charing Cross) W6 39 C1
Imperial College London (Chelsea & Westminster) SW10 157 A3
Imperial College London (Hammersmith) W12 30 A3
Imperial College London (Royal Brompton) SW3 144 A2
Imperial College London (South Kensington) SW7 129 B2
Imperial College London (St Mary's) W2 101 C2
Imperial College Rd SW7 129 B2
Imperial Cres SW6 167 A1
Imperial Ct NW8 80 B2
Imperial Ho
1 Bow E3 26 A2
2 Poplar E14 33 B2
Strand WC2 106 C1
Imperial Rd SW6 166 B3
Imperial Sq SW6 166 B4
Imperial St E3 27 B2

Imperial Twrs 3 NW3 ... 11 B2
Imperial War Mus SE1, SE11 ... 135 C1
Imperial Wharf Sta SW10 ... 167 A3
Imre Cl W12 ... 30 A1
Inchbald Sch of Design (Garden Design) SW1 ... 146 B3
Inchbald Sch of Design (Interior Design) SW1 ... 145 B4
Independent Pl E8 ... 16 B3
Indescon Ct E14 ... 42 A4
Indiana Bldg 7 SE8 ... 51 C2
India St EC3 ... 110 C1
India Way W12 ... 30 A2
Indigo Mews N16 ... 6 C1
Indus Ct 16 SE15 ... 49 B3
Ingate Pl SW8 ... 170 B3
Ingelow Ho W8 ... 128 A4
Ingersoll Rd W12 ... 30 A1
Ingestre Pl W1 ... 105 A1
Ingestre Rd NW5 ... 13 A4
Ingham Rd NW6 ... 10 C4
Inglebert St EC1 ... 95 B4
Ingleborough St SW9 ... 173 B2
Ingleby Rd N7 ... 5 A1
Inglefield Sq 12 E1 ... 32 A1
Ingle Ho 3 SW12 ... 73 C3
Inglesham Wlk E9 ... 18 B2
Ingleside Gr SE3 ... 53 B4
Inglethorpe Ho 6 E5 ... 7 C2
Inglethorpe St SW6 ... 47 C2
Ingleton St SW9 ... 173 B2
Inglewood Cl E14 ... 41 C2
Inglewood Mans 11 NW6 ... 10 C3
Inglewood Rd NW6 ... 10 C3
Inglis Ho 1 SW15 ... 57 B2
Inglis St SE5 ... 48 A2
Ingram Ave NW11 ... 2 B4
Ingram Cl SE11 ... 149 A4
Ingram Ho E3 ... 26 A4
Ingram Lo 8 SW4 ... 61 C1
Ingrave St SW11 ... 60 A4
Ingrebourne Ho NW8 ... 101 C4
Ingress St 4 W4 ... 38 A1
Inigo Pl WC2 ... 120 A4
Inkerman Rd NW5 ... 13 A2
Inkerman Terr W8 ... 127 C1
Inkster Ho 8 SW11 ... 60 A4
Inman Rd
Harlesden NW10 ... 21 A4
Wandsworth SW18 ... 71 B4
Inner Circ NW1 ... 91 B4
Inner Park Rd SW19 ... 69 C2
Inner Temple EC4 ... 121 B4
Inner Temple La EC4 ... 107 B1
Innes Gdns SW15 ... 57 A1
Innisfree Ho NW2 ... 9 C2
Innis Ho SE17 ... 152 A2
Insley Ho 13 E3 ... 27 A2
Institute of Cancer Research The SW7 ... 143 A2
Institute Pl 31 E8 ... 17 A3
Inst of Child Health WC1 ... 94 C1
Inst of Neurology
Bloomsbury WC1 ... 106 B4
St Pancras WC1 ... 94 B1
Int Coll of Accountancy The SW17 ... 72 B1
Interchange The NW5 ... 13 A3
International Com Sch W1 ... 91 C1
International House Language Sch WC2 ... 106 B2
International Sch of London W3 ... 36 C2
Inver Ct
11 Bayswater W2 ... 100 B1
4 Hammersmith W6 ... 38 C3
Inverforth Cl NW3 ... 2 B2
Inverforth Ho NW3 ... 2 B2
Invergarry Ho NW6 ... 78 A1
Invermead Cl W6 ... 38 C2
Inverness Gdns W8 ... 114 A1
Inverness Mews W2 ... 114 B4
Inverness Pl W2 ... 114 B4
Inverness St NW1 ... 82 B4
Inverness Terr W2 ... 114 B4
Inverton Rd SE15 ... 65 C3
Invicta Cl 21 E3 ... 33 C4
Invicta Plaza SE1 ... 122 A2
Invicta Prim Sch SE3 ... 53 C3
Invicta Rd SE3, SE7 ... 53 C4
Inville Rd SE17 ... 151 C1
Inwen Ct SE8 ... 41 A1
Inwood Ct 12 NW1 ... 13 B1
Inwood Ho 19 SE22 ... 64 A4
Inworth St SW11 ... 168 B2
Inworth Wlk N1 ... 86 C4
Ion Ct 8 E2 ... 24 C3
Ionian Bldg 19 E14 ... 33 A2
Ionian Ho 22 E1 ... 25 C1
Ipsden Bldgs SE1 ... 135 C4
Ipswich Ho SE4 ... 65 C2
Iqra Ind Sch SW9 ... 62 C4
Irby Ho SW2 ... 62 C1
Ireland Yd EC4 ... 108 B1
Irene Rd SW6 ... 165 C3
Ireton Ho 22 SW9 ... 173 C1
Ireton St 12 E3 ... 26 C1
Iris Ct 8 SE15 ... 50 A1
Iroko Ho 7 NW3 ... 11 A2
Iron Bridge Cl NW10 ... 8 A3
Iron Bridge Ho NW3 ... 12 B1
Irongate Ho EC3 ... 110 B2
Iron Mill Pl SW18 ... 59 A1
Iron Mill Rd SW18 ... 59 A1
Ironmonger La EC2 ... 109 B1
Ironmonger Pas EC1 ... 97 A3
Ironmonger Row EC1 ... 97 A3
Ironmonger Row Baths EC1 ... 97 A3
Ironmongers Pl E14 ... 41 C2
Ironmonger's Pl 22 E14 ... 41 C2
Ironside Cl SE16 ... 40 C4
Ironside Ho E9 ... 18 A4
Ironworks 1 E3 ... 26 C4
Irvine Ct W1 ... 93 A1
Irvine Ho N7 ... 14 B2
Irving Gr SW9 ... 172 C1
Irving Ho SE17 ... 150 A1
Irving Mews N1 ... 15 B2
Irving Rd W14 ... 39 C3
Irving St WC2 ... 119 C3
Irwell Est 31 SE16 ... 40 B4
Irwin Gdns NW10 ... 22 A4
Isabella Ct 8 TW10 ... 54 B1
Isabella Ho
19 Hammersmith W6 ... 39 B1
Kennington SE11 ... 150 A2
Isabella Mews 11 E8 ... 16 A2
Isabella Rd E9 ... 17 B3
Isabel St SW9 ... 173 A4
Isambard Mews E14 ... 42 B3
Isambard Pl SE16 ... 32 B1
Iseldon Ct N7 ... 14 A4
Isel Way 4 SE22 ... 64 A2
Isis Cl SW15 ... 57 B3
Isis Ct W4 ... 45 A3
Isis Ho NW8 ... 89 C1
Isis St SW18 ... 71 B2
Islamia Girls' High Sch NW6 ... 23 A4
Islamia Prim Sch NW6 ... 23 A4
Islamic Coll for Advanced Studies 2 NW10 ... 9 A2
Island Gardens Sta E14 ... 42 B1
Island Ho E14 ... 27 B2
Island Rd SE16 ... 40 C2
Island Row E14 ... 33 B3
Islay Wlk 17 N1 ... 15 B2
Isleden Ho N1 ... 86 C4
Isledon Rd N4, N7 ... 5 C1
ISLE OF DOGS ... 42 B2
ISLINGTON ... 14 C2
Islington Arts & Media Sch 6 N4 ... 5 B3
Islington Bsns Ctr N1 ... 87 A4
Islington Est N1 ... 86 C4
Islington Gn N1 ... 86 A3
Islington High St N1 ... 86 A2
Islington Mus WC1 ... 96 A3
Islington Park Mews 1 N1 ... 15 A1
Islington Park St N1 ... 15 A1
Islington Tennis Ctr N7 ... 14 A2
Islip St NW5 ... 13 B3
Isokon Flats 3 NW3 ... 12 B3
Issac Way SE1 ... 137 A4
Italia Conti Acad of Theatre Arts EC1 ... 96 C1
Ivanhoe Ho
11 Balham SW12 ... 73 A4
34 Bow E3 ... 26 A3
Ivanhoe Rd SE5 ... 64 B4
Ivatt Pl W14 ... 141 A1
Iveagh Cl E9 ... 25 C4
Iveagh Ct EC3 ... 110 C1
Iveagh Ho
2 Brixton SW9 ... 48 A1
Chelsea SW10 ... 157 A2
Ivebury Ct 9 W10 ... 30 B3
Iveley Rd SW4 ... 170 C1
Iver Ct N1 ... 15 B2
Iverna Ct W8 ... 127 C2
Iverna Gdns W8 ... 127 C2
Iverson Rd NW6 ... 10 C2
Ives Rd E16 ... 35 A4
Ives St SW3 ... 144 B4
Ivimey St E2 ... 24 C2 99 C4
Ivinghoe Ho 14 N7 ... 13 C3
Ivor Ct NW1 ... 90 C2
Ivories The N1 ... 15 B1
Ivor Mayor Lo SW12 ... 60 C1
Ivor Pl NW1 ... 90 C1
Ivor St NW1 ... 13 B1
Ivory Ho
9 London SW11 ... 59 B4
St George in t East E1 ... 125 A2
Ivory Sq 15 SW18 ... 59 B4
Ivybridge Ho 18 SE22 ... 64 A4
Ivybridge La WC2 ... 120 B3
Ivy Church La SE1, SE17 ... 152 C2
Ivy Cres W4 ... 37 B2
Ivy Ct 19 SE16 ... 153 C1
Ivydale Prim Sch SE15 ... 65 C3
Ivydale Rd SE15 ... 65 C3
Ivyday Gr SW16 ... 74 B1
Ivy Lo W8 ... 31 C1 113 B2
Ivymount Rd SE27 ... 74 C1
Ivy Rd
Brockley SE4 ... 66 C3
Cricklewood NW2 ... 9 B4
Newham E16 ... 35 C3
Ivy St N1 ... 24 A3
Ixworth Pl SW3 ... 144 A3

J

Jacaranda Gr E8 ... 16 B1
Jackman Ho 24 E1 ... 32 A1
Jackman St E8 ... 25 A4
Jackson Cl E9 ... 17 C1
Jackson Ho 15 SW11 ... 59 C4
Jackson Rd N7 ... 14 B4
Jackson's La N6 ... 4 A4
Jack Taylor Sch NW8 ... 78 C4
Jack Tizard Sch W12 ... 30 A1
Jack Walker Ct N5 ... 15 A4
Jacobin Lo N7 ... 14 A3
Jacob Mans 15 E1 ... 32 A3
Jacobson Ct SW11 ... 168 B3
Jacobson Ho E1 ... 110 C2
Jacob St SE1 ... 139 B4
Jacob's Well Mews W1 ... 103 C2
Jacotts Ho W10 ... 22 B1
Jacqueline Ho 8 E1 ... 32 C4
Jacques Prevert Sch 3 W6 ... 39 C2
Jaggard Way SW12 ... 72 B4
Jagger Ho SW11 ... 168 C4
Jago Wlk SE5 ... 48 C3
Jamahirya Sch SW3 ... 158 A4
Jamaica Rd
Bermondsey SE1 ... 139 A3
Bermondsey SE16 ... 40 A3
Jamaica St E1 ... 32 B4
James Allen's Girls' Sch 12 SE22 ... 64 A2
James Allen's Pre-Prep Sch SE21 ... 63 C1
James Allen's Prep Sch 13 SE22 ... 64 A2
James Anderson Ct 29 E2 ... 24 A3
James Ave NW2 ... 9 B3
James Brine Ho 6 E2 ... 24 B2 99 A4
James Campbell Ho 2 E2 ... 25 B3
James Collins Cl W9 ... 23 B1
James Docherty Ho 4 E2 ... 25 B3
James Hammett Ho 9 E2 ... 24 B3
James Ho
Mile End E1 ... 26 A1
33 Rotherhithe SE16 ... 40 C4
James Joyce Wlk 7 SE24 ... 63 A3
James Leicester Hall of Residence N7 ... 14 A2
James Lind Ho 6 SE8 ... 41 B2
James Middleton Ho 20 E2 ... 25 A2
Jameson Ct 6 E2 ... 25 B3
Jameson Ho SE11 ... 148 C2
Jameson Pl 11 W3 ... 37 B4
Jameson St W8 ... 31 C1 113 C2
James's Cotts TW9 ... 44 C3
James St
Marylebone W1 ... 103 C1
Strand WC2 ... 120 B4
James Stewart Ho NW6 ... 10 B1
James Stroud Ho SE17 ... 151 A1
Jamestown Rd NW1 ... 82 A4
Jamestown Way E14 ... 34 C2
James Voller Way 30 E1 ... 32 B3
James Wolfe Prim Sch 16 SE10 ... 52 B3
Jamiatul Ummah Sch 40 E1 ... 32 A3
Jamuna Cl E14 ... 33 A4

Jane St E1 . . . . 32 A3
Janet St E14 . . . . 41 C3
Janeway Pl 2 SE16 . . . . 40 A4
Janeway St SE16 . 139 C3
Jansen Ho 5 SW15 . . . . 56 C2
Jansen Wlk SW11 . . 59 C3
Japan Cres N4 . . . . . . 5 B3
Jardine Rd E1 . . . . . . 32 C2
Jarman Ho
Bermondsey SE16 . . . 40 C2
16 Stepney E1 . . . . . . 32 B4
Jarrett Cl SW2 . . . . . 75 A3
Jarrow Rd SE16 . . . . 40 B1
Jarrow Way E9 . . . . . 18 A4
Jarvis Ho 3 SE15 . . 49 C2
Jarvis Rd SE22 . . . . . 64 A3
Jasmin SE1 . . . . . . 125 A1
Jasmine Sq 15 E3 . . 26 B4
Jasmin Ho SE4 . . . . . 66 B4
Jasmin Lo 17 SE16 . . 40 A1
Jason Ct
2 London SW9 . . . 173 B4
Marylebone W1 . . . 103 C2
Jasper Wlk N1 . . . . 97 B4
Java Wharf SE1 . . 139 A4
Jay Ho SW15 . . . . 47 B1
Jay Mews SW7 . . . 129 A3
Jean Darling Ho SW10 . . . . 157 B3
Jean Pardies Ho 23 E1 . . . . 32 B4
Jebb Ave SW2 . . . . . . 62 A1
Jebb St E3 . . . . 26 C3
Jedburgh St SW11 . . 60 C3
Jeddo Mews W12 . . 38 B4
Jeddo Rd W12 . . . . . . 38 B4
Jefferson Bldg 3 E14 . . . . 41 C4
Jeffrey's Ct 2 SW4 . . . . 172 A2
Jeffrey's Pl NW1 . . . 13 B1
Jeffrey's Rd SW4 172 A2
Jeffrey's St NW1 . . . 13 B1
Jeff Wooller Coll WC1 . . . . 106 B4
Jeger Ave E2 . . . . 24 B4
Jelf Rd SW2 . . . . 62 C2
Jellicoe Ho
5 Bethnal Green E2 . . . . 24 C3
Fitzrovia NW1 . . . . . . 92 B1
11 Putney SW15 . . . . 57 C2
Jemotts Ct 9 SE14 . . . . 50 C4
Jenkins Ho SW8 . . 171 B4
Jenkinson Ho 12 E2 . . . . 25 C2
Jenner Ave W3 . . . . . 28 C4
Jenner Ho SE3 . . . . . 53 A4
Jenner Pl SW13 . . . . 47 A4
Jenner Rd N16 . . . . . . 7 B1
Jennifer Ho SE11 149 C3
Jennings Ho SE10 . . 42 C1
Jennings Rd SE22 . . 64 B1
Jensen Ho 10 E3 . . . 26 C1
Jephson Ct 17 SW4 . . . . 172 B1
Jephson Ho 6 SE17 . . . . 48 A4
Jephson St SE5 . . . . . 48 C2
Jephtha Rd SW18 . . . 58 C1
Jerdan Pl SW6 . . . 155 B2
Jeremiah St 11 E14 . . . . 34 A3
Jeremy Bentham Ho 24 E2 . . . . 24 C2 99 C3
Jermyn St SW1 . . . 119 A2
Jerningham Ct SE14 . . . . 51 A2
Jerningham Rd SE14 . . . . 51 A2
Jerome Cres NW8 . 90 A2
Jerome Ho NW1 . . 102 B4
Jerome St E1 . . . . 24 B1 98 C1
Jerome Twr 5 W3 . . . . 37 A4
Jerrard St SE13 . . . . 67 A4
Jerrold Lo SW15 . . . . 57 B4
Jerrold St 24 N1 . . . . 24 A3
Jersey Ho 15 N1 . . . . 15 B2
Jersey Rd N1 . . . . 15 B2
Jersey St E2 . . . . 25 A2
Jerusalem Pas EC1 . . . . 96 A1
Jervis Bay Ho 9 E14 . . . . 34 C3
Jervis Ct
2 Greenwich SE10 . . . . 52 B2
Marylebone W1 . . . 104 B1
Jessel Ho
St Pancras WC1 . . . . 94 A3
Westminster SW1 . 147 C4
Jessica Rd SW18 . . . 59 B2
Jessie Blythe La 4 N19 . . . . 5 A4
Jessie Duffett Ho 11 SE5 . . . . 48 B3
Jesson Ho SE17 . . 151 B3
Jessop Ct N1 . . . . . . 86 B1
Jessop Ho 9 W4 . . . 37 C2
Jessop Sq E14 . . . . . . 33 C1
Jeston Ho 10 SE27 . . 75 A1
Jethou Ho 16 N1 . . . 15 B2
Jevons Ho 9 NW8 . 11 C1
Jewell Ho 3 SW12 . . . . 73 B4
Jewish Mus NW1 . . 82 B3
Jewry St EC3 . . . . . 110 C1
Jews Row SW18 . . . . 59 B3
Jeymer Ave NW2 . . . . 9 B3
Jeypore Rd SW18 . . . 59 B1
Jim Griffiths Ho SW6 . . . . 155 A3
Jim Veal Dr 3 N17 . . . . 14 A2
Joanna Ho 7 W6 . . 39 B1
Joan St SE1 . . . . . . 122 A1
Jocelin Ho N1 . . . . . 85 A3
Jocelyn Rd TW9 . . . . 54 A4
Jocelyn St SE15 . . . . 49 C2
Jockey's Fields WC1 . . . . 107 A4
Jodane Rd SE8 . . . . . 41 B2
Jodrell Rd E3 . . . . . . 18 B1
Johanna Prim Sch SE1 . . . . 135 B3
Johanna St SE1 . . 135 B3
John Adam St WC2 . . . . 120 B3
John Aird Ct W2 . . 101 A4
John Archer Way SW18 . . . . 59 C1
John Ashby Cl SW2 . . . . 62 A1
John Ball Prim Sch SE3 . . . . 53 A1
John Barker Ct NW6 . . . . 10 A1
John Betts' Ho W12 . . . . 38 C3
John Betts Prim Sch W6 . . . . 39 A3
John Bond Ho 2 E3 . . . . 26 B3
John Brent Ho 8 SE8 . . . . 40 C2
John Buck Ho NW10 . . . . 21 B4
John Burns Prim Sch 17 SW11 . . . . 169 C1
John Campbell Rd 26 N16 . . . . 16 A3
John Carpenter St EC4 . . . . 122 A4
John Cartwright Ho 7 E2 . . . . 25 A2
John Clynes Ct SW15 . . . . 57 A3
John Conwey Ho 23 SW2 . . . . 62 C1
John Dee Ho 3 SW14 . . . . 55 C4
John Donne Prim Sch 13 SE15 . . . . 50 A2
John Dwight Ho SW6 . . . . 59 A4
John Fearon Wlk 5 W10 . . . . 23 A2
John Felton Rd 19 SE16 . . . . 139 B3
John Fielden Ho 10 E2 . . . . 25 A2
John Fisher St E1 125 B4
John F Kennedy Specl Sch 6 E15 . . . . 27 C4
John Harris Ho SE15 . . . . 64 C4
John Harrison Way SE10 . . . . 43 B3
John Islip St SW1 148 A3
John Keall Ho 3 SW15 . . . . 57 C4
John Keble CE Prim Sch NW10 . . . . 21 B4
John Kennedy Ct 1 N1 . . . . 15 C2
John Kennedy Ho 1 SE16 . . . . 40 C2
John Kennedy Lo 2 N1 . . . . 15 C2
John King Ct 5 N19 . . . . 4 C2
John Kirk Ho
21 Battersea SW11 . . . . 59 C4
5 Streatham SW16 . . . . 74 A1
John Knight Lo SW6 . . . . 155 C2
John McDonald Ho 3 E14 . . . . 42 B3
John McKenna Wlk 17 SE16 . . . . 139 C2
John Maurice Cl SE17 . . . . 151 B4
John Nettleford Ho 14 E2 . . . . 25 A2
John Orwell Sports Ctr E1 . . . . 32 A1
John Parker Sq 7 SW11 . . . . 59 C4
John Parry Ct 28 N1 . . . . 24 A3
John Paul II Sch 9 SW19 . . . . 69 C4
John Penn Ho SE8 . . 51 B3
John Penn St SE13 . . . . 52 A2
John Perryn Prim Sch W3 . . . . 29 A3
John Prince's St W1 . . . . 104 B2
John Pritchard Ho 16 E1 . . . . 24 C1 99 C1
John Ratcliffe Ho 8 NW6 . . . . 23 C2
John Rennie Wlk 1 E1 . . . . 32 B1
John Roan Sch SE3 . . . . 53 A3
John Roll Way SE16 . . . . 139 C2
John Ruskin Prim Sch SE5 . . . . 48 B4
John Ruskin St SE5 . . . . 48 B4
John Scurr Ho 18 E14 . . . . 33 A3
John Scurr Prim Sch 46 E1 . . . . 25 B1
John Silkin La SE8 . 40 C1
John's Mews WC1 . 95 A1
John Smith Ave SW6 . . . . 154 C2
John Smith Mews E14 . . . . 34 C2
Johnson Cl E8 . . . . . . 24 C4
Johnson Ct 10 SW18 . . . . 59 C3
Johnson Ho
Belgravia SW1 . . . . 145 C3
23 Bethnal Green E2 . . . . 24 C2 99 C3
Somers Town NW1 . . 83 A1
South Lambeth SW8 . . . . 161 C1
Johnson Lo 12 W9 . . 31 C4
Johnson Rd NW10 . . 20 C4
Johnsons Ct EC4 . 107 C1
Johnson's Pl SW1 146 C1
Johnson St E1 . . . . . 32 B3
Johnsons Way NW10 . . . . 20 A1
John Spencer Sq N1 . . . . 15 A2
John's Pl E1 . . . . 32 A3
John St WC1 . . . . . . 95 A1
John Stainer Prim Sch SE4 . . . . 66 A4
Johnston Cl SW9 173 A3
Johnstone Ho SE13 . . . . 67 C4
John Strachey Ho SW6 . . . . 155 A3
John Trundle Ct EC4 . . . . 108 C4
John Tucker Ho 3 E14 . . . . 41 C3
John Wesley's House & Mus of Methodism EC1 . . . . 97 C2
John Wheatley Ho
14 London N19 . . . . 4 C4
West Brompton SW6 . . . . 155 A3
John Williams Cl SE14 . . . . 50 C4
Joiners Arms Yd 1 SE5 . . . . 48 C2
Joiner St SE1 . . . . . 123 C1
Joiners Yd N1 . . . . . 84 B1
Jolles Ho 9 E3 . . . . 27 A2
Jonathan Ct 9 W4 . . . . 38 A2
Jonathan St SE11 148 C2
Jones Ho
4 South Bromley E14 . . . . 34 C3
Stamford Hill N16 . . . . . 7 A3
Jones St W1 . . . . . 118 A3
Jones Wlk 6 TW10 . . . . 54 B1
Jonson Ho
Borough The SE1 . . 137 C1
16 Canonbury N16 . . . 15 C4
Jordan Ct SW15 . . . . 57 C3
Jordan Ho
12 London SE4 . . . . . 65 C3
Shoreditch N1 . . . . . . 87 C3
Jordans Ho NW8 . . 90 A1
Joscoyne Ho 5 E1 . . . . 32 A3
Joseph Ave W3 . . . . . 28 C3
Joseph Conrad Ho SW1 . . . . 147 A3
Joseph Ct N16 . . . . . . 7 A4
Joseph Hardcastle Cl SE14 . . . . 50 C3
Josephine Ave SW2 . . . . 62 B2
Joseph Irwin Ho 11 E14 . . . . 33 B2
Joseph Powell Cl 1 SW12 . . . . 61 B1
Joseph Priestley Ho 12 E2 . . . . 25 A2
Joseph St E3 . . . . 26 B1
Joseph Trotter Cl EC1 . . . . 95 C3
Joshua St E14 . . . . . . 34 B3
Joslings Cl W12 . . . . 29 C2
Josseline Ct 9 E3 . . 26 A3
Joubert Mans SW3 . . . . 144 B2
Joubert St SW11 . . 169 A2
Jowett Ho 27 SW9 . . . . 172 B1
Jowett St SE15 . . . . . 49 B3
Jubet Ho 9 N16 . . . 15 C4
Jubilee Bldgs NW8 79 B2
Jubilee Cl 4 NW10 . . . . 21 B3
Jubilee Cres E14 . . . 42 B3
Jubilee Ct N1 . . . . . 84 B4
Jubilee Hall Mkt WC2 . . . . 120 B4
Jubilee Ho SE11 . . 149 C3
Jubilee Hts NW2 . . . 10 B2
Jubilee JMI Sch N16 . . . . 7 C3
Jubilee Mans 10 E1 . . . . 32 B3
Jubilee Pl SW3 . . . 144 B2
Jubilee Prim Sch SW2 . . . . 62 C1
Jubilee St E1 . . . . 32 B4
Jubilee The 2 SE10 . . . . 52 A3
Jubilee Yd SE1 . . . 138 C4
Judd St WC1 . . . . . . 94 A3
Jude St E16 . . . . 35 B3
Judges' Wlk NW3 . . . 2 B1
Juer St SW11 . . . . . 158 B1

Julian Ave W3......28 A2
Julian Ct SW13......46 B2
Julian Pl E14......42 A1
Julia St NW5......12 C3
Juliet Ho 11 N1......24 A3
Julius Ct TW8......44 A3
Julius Ho 8 E14......34 C3
Julius Nyerere Cl N1......84 C3
Junction App
Battersea SW11......60 A4
Lewisham SE13......67 B4
Junction Mews W2......102 A2
Junction Pl W2......101 C2
Junction Rd N19......4 B1
Juniper Cres NW1......12 C1
Juniper Ct N16......6 C2
Juniper Dr SW18......59 B3
Juniper Ho
6 Peckham SE14, SE15......50 B3
9 Richmond TW9......45 A2
Juniper St 16 E1......32 B2
Juno Ct 11 SW9......163 B1
Juno Ho 2 E3......26 C4
Juno Way SE14......50 C4
Juno Way Ind Est SE14......50 C4
Jupiter Ct 10 SW9......163 B1
Jupiter Way N7......14 B2
Jupp Rd E15......19 C1
Jupp Rd W E15......27 C4
Jura Ho SE16......41 A2
Jurston Ct SE1......135 C3
Justice Wlk SW3......158 A3
Justines Pl E2......25 C2
Jutland Cl N19......5 A3
Jutland Ho 4 SE5......48 B1
Juxon St SE11......149 A4

K

Kambala Rd SW11......59 C4
Kara Way NW2......9 C4
Karen Ct
2 Camberwell SE5......64 A4
Forest Hill SE23......66 A1
Karen Ho 7 N16......15 C4
Kasmin Ct NW10......8 C1
Kassala Rd SW11......169 A3
Katherine Cl 3 SE16......32 C1
Katherine Ho 15 W10......23 A1
Katherine Sq W11......31 A1 112 A2
Kathleen Ave W3......28 B4
Kathleen Rd SW11......60 B4
Kay Rd SW9......172 C1
Kay St E2......24 C3
Kean Ho 5 SE17......48 A4
Kean St WC2......106 C1
Keates Est N16......7 B2
Keats Cl
Bermondsey SE1......152 C3
Hampstead NW3......12 A4
Keats Gr NW3......12 A4
Keats Ho
22 Bethnal Green E2......25 B2
30 Camberwell SE5......48 B3
Chelsea SW1......161 A4
Keats House (Mus) NW3......12 A4
Keats Pl EC2......109 B3
Keble Ho 4 SW15......57 C1
Keble Pl SW13......47 A4
Kedelston Ct E5......18 A4
Kedge Ho 16 E14......41 C3
Kedleston Wlk 21 E2......25 A2
Keel Cl SE16......32 C1
Keel Ct 8 E14......34 C2
Keeley St WC2......106 C1
Keeling Ho 4 E2......25 A3
Keelson Ho 9 E14......41 C3
Keen's Yd N1......15 A2
Keeper Wharf E1......32 C2
Keepier Wharf 15 E1......32 C2
Keep The SE3......53 C1
Keeton's Rd SE16......40 A3
Keevil Dr SW19......70 A4
Keighley Cl N7......14 A4
Keildon Rd SW11......60 B3
Keir Hardie Ho
Fulham W6......47 C4
15 Upper Holloway N19......4 C4
Willesden NW10......8 B1
Keir Hardy Prim Sch 13 E16......35 C4
Keith Connor Cl 5 SW8......61 A4
Keith Gr W12......29 C1
Keith Ho NW6......78 A1
Kelby Ho N7......14 B2
Kelfield Ct 1 W10......30 C3
Kelfield Gdns W10......30 C3
Kelfield Mews W10......30 C3
Kellett Ho N1......87 C3
Kellett Rd SW2......62 C3
Kellow Ho SE1......137 B4
Kell St SE1......136 B2
Kelly Ave SE15......49 B2
Kelly Ct 18 E14......33 C2
Kelly Mews 4 W9......23 B1
Kelly St NW1......13 A2
Kelman Cl SW4......171 C1
Kelmore Gr SE22......64 C3
Kelmscott Gdns W12......38 C3
Kelmscott House W6......39 A1
Kelmscott Rd SW11......60 B2
Kelross Rd N5......15 B4
Kelsall Mews TW9......45 A2
Kelsey St E2......24 C1 99 C2
Kelshall Ct N4......6 B2
Kelson Ho E14......42 B3
Kelso Pl W8......128 B2
Kelvedon Ho SW8......172 B4
Kelvedon Rd SW6......155 A1
Kelvin Ct
Chiswick W4......45 B3
Notting Hill W11......31 C2 113 B3
Kelvington Rd SE15......65 C2
Kelvin Rd N5......15 B4
Kelyway Ho 20 SW2......74 C4
Kember St N1......14 B1
Kemble Ho SW9......63 A4
Kemble St WC2......106 C1
Kemerton Rd SE5......63 B4
Kemey's St E9......18 A3
Kemp Ct SW8......162 A1
Kempe Ho SE1......137 C1
Kempe Rd NW6......22 C3
Kemp Ho
Finsbury EC1......97 B3
1 Globe Town E2......25 C3
Kempis Way 5 SE22......64 A2
Kemplay Rd NW3......11 C4
Kemp's Ct W1......105 B1
Kemps Dr E14......33 C2
Kempsford Gdns SW5......141 C1
Kempsford Rd
Lambeth SE11......149 C3
Newington SE11......150 A3
Kemps Gdns SE13......67 B2
Kempson Rd SW6......155 C1
Kempthorne Rd SE8......41 B2
Kempton Ct E1......32 A4
Kempton Ho 13 N1......24 A4
Kemsing Ho SE1......137 C3
Kemsing Rd SE10......43 C1
Kemsley SE13......67 A2
Kenbrook Ho
Kensington W14......127 A1
5 Kentish Town NW5......13 B3
Kenbury Gdns 10 SE5......48 B1
Kenbury Mans 18 SE5......48 B1
Kenbury St SE5......48 B1
Kenchester Cl SW8......162 B1
Kendal NW1......92 B4
Kendal Ave W3......28 A4
Kendal Cl SE5......48 A3
Kendal Ct NW2......10 A3
Kendal Ho
32 Hackney E9......17 B1
Islington N1......85 A2
Kendall Ct 3 SE22......64 C2
Kendall Pl W1......103 B3
Kendal Pl SW15......58 B2
Kendal Rd NW10......8 C4
Kendal St W2......102 B1
Kendal Stps W2......102 B1
Kender Prim Sch SE14......50 B2
Kender St SE14......50 B2
Kendoa Rd 1 SW4......61 C3
Kendon Ho E15......19 C1
Kendrick Ct 12 SE15......50 A2
Kendrick Mews SW7......143 B3
Kendrick Pl SW7......143 B3
Kenilford Rd SW12......73 A4
Kenilworth Ct SW6......58 A4
Kenilworth Rd
Bow E3......26 A3
Kilburn NW6......23 B4
Kenley Wlk W11......31 A2 112 A3
Kenmont Gdns NW10......22 A2
Kenmont Prim Sch NW10......22 A2
Kenmore Cl TW9......44 C3
Kenmore Ct NW6......10 C1
Kenmure Rd E8......17 A3
Kenmure Yd E8......17 A3
Kennacraig Cl 6 E16......35 C1
Kennard Ho 12 SW11......169 C3
Kennard Rd E15......19 C1
Kennard St 9 SW11......169 B3
Kennedy Cox Ho 9 E16......35 B4
Kennedy Ho SE11......148 C2
Kennedy Wlk SE17......151 C3
Kennet Cl SW11......59 C3
Kennet Ct 47 W2......31 C4
Kenneth Campbell Ho NW8......89 C2
Kenneth Cres NW2......9 A3
Kenneth Ct SE11......149 C4
Kennet Ho NW8......89 C1
Kenneth Younger Ho SW6......155 A3
Kennet Rd W9......23 B1
Kennet St E1......125 C2
Kennett Wharf La EC4......123 A4
Kenning Ho 6 N1......24 A4
Kenning St 18 SE16......40 B4
Kennings Way SE11......149 C2
KENNINGTON......149 B1
Kennington Ent Ctr SE17......150 A1
Kennington La SE11......149 A1
Kennington Oval SE11......163 A3
Kennington Palace Ct SE11......149 B2
Kennington Park Gdns SE17......48 A4
Kennington Park Ho SE11......149 C1
Kennington Park Pl SE11......48 A4
Kennington Park Rd SE11......150 A2
Kennington Rd SE11......149 B3
Kennington Sta SE17......150 A2
Kennoldes SE21......75 C2
Kenrick Pl W1......103 B3
KENSAL GREEN......22 B2
Kensal Green Cemy (All Souls) NW10......22 B2
Kensal Green Sta NW10......22 B2
Kensal Ho W10......22 C1
Kensal Rd W10......23 A1
KENSAL RISE......22 C3
Kensal Rise Prim Sch NW6......22 C3
Kensal Rise Sta NW10......22 C3
KENSAL TOWN......23 A1
KENSINGTON......127 C3
Kensington Acad SW6......156 A1
Kensington & Chelsea Coll
Chelsea SW10......156 C2
Kensington & Chelsea Coll *continued*
14 Kensal Town W10......31 A4
Kensington Church Ct W8......128 A3
Kensington Church St W8......31 C1 113 C1
Kensington Church Wlk W8......128 A3
Kensington Court Mans W8......128 B3
Kensington Court Mews W8......128 B2
Kensington Court Pl W8......128 B2
Kensington Ct W8......128 B3
Kensington Ct Gdns W8......128 B2
Kensington Gardens W2......115 A1
Kensington Gate W8......128 C2
Kensington Gdns Sq W2......100 A1
Kensington Gore SW7......129 B3
Kensington Hall Gdns W14......140 C2
Kensington High St W8......127 C2
Kensington Ho 3 NW5......13 B3
Kensington Hts W8......31 C1 113 B1
Kensington L Ctr W11......31 A2 112 A4
Kensington Mall W8......31 C1 113 C2
Kensington Mans SW5......141 C2
Kensington Olympia Sta W14......126 A2
Kensington Pal W8......114 B1
Kensington Palace Gdns W8......114 A2
Kensington Park Gdns W11......31 B2 113 A3
Kensington Park Mews W11......31 B3
Kensington Park Rd W11......31 B2 113 A4
Kensington Pl W8......31 C1 113 B2
Kensington Prep Sch SW6......165 A4
Kensington Rd SW7......129 A3
Kensington Sq W8......128 A3
Kensington Village W14......141 A3
Kensington W W14......140 A4
Kensworth Ho EC1......97 C3
Kent Ct 3 E2......24 B3
Kent Ho
Camberwell SE1......153 A1
13 Chiswick W4......38 A1
Marylebone W1......104 C2
Pimlico SW1......147 B1
Richmond TW10......54 C2

Kentish Bldgs SE1 ... 123 B1
KENTISH TOWN ... 13 B2
Kentish Town CE Prim Sch 13 NW5 ... 13 B3
Kentish Town City Farm NW5 ... 12 C3
Kentish Town Rd NW1 ... 13 A2
Kentish Town Sp Ctr NW5 ... 13 A2
Kentish Town Sta NW5 ... 13 B3
Kentish Town West Sta NW5 ... 13 A2
Kent Lo 9 SW19 ... 69 C3
Kentmere Ho SE15 ... 50 B4
Kenton Ct W14 ... 126 C1
Kenton Ho
20 Globe Town E1 ... 25 B1
Highbury N5 ... 5 C1
Kenton Rd E9 ... 17 C2
Kenton St WC1 ... 94 A2
Kent Pas NW1 ... 90 C2
Kent Pk Ind Est SE15 ... 50 A4
Kent Rd
Richmond TW9 ... 44 C3
South Acton W4 ... 37 B3
Kent St E2 ... 24 B3
Kent Terr NW1 ... 90 B3
Kentwell Cl SE4 ... 66 A3
Kentwode Gn SW13 ... 46 C3
Kent Yard SW7 ... 130 B3
Kenway Rd SW5 ... 142 A3
Ken Wilson Ho 19 E2 ... 24 C3
Kenwood Cl NW3 ... 2 C3
Kenwood Ho 15 SW9 ... 63 A3
Kenwood Ho NW3 ... 3 A3
Kenworthy Rd E9 ... 18 A2
Kenwrick Ho N1 ... 85 A3
Kenwyn Rd SW4 ... 61 C3
Kenyon Ho 31 SE5 ... 48 B3
Kenyon St SW6 ... 47 C2
Kepler Ho 9 SE10 ... 43 B1
Kepler Rd SW2, SW4 ... 62 A3
Keppel Ho
Brompton SW3 ... 144 A3
5 Deptford SE8 ... 41 B1
Keppel Row SE1 ... 122 C1
Keppel St WC1 ... 105 C4
Kerbela St 3 E2 ... 24 C1 99 B2
Kerbey St E14 ... 34 A3
Kerfield Cres SE5 ... 48 C2
Kerfield Pl SE5 ... 48 C2
Kerridge Ct 10 N1 ... 16 A2
Kerrier Ho SW10 ... 157 A1
Kerrington Ct 7 W12 ... 39 B4
Kerrison Rd
Battersea SW11 ... 60 A4
Mill Meads E15 ... 27 C4
Kerry N7 ... 14 A2
Kerry Ho 5 E1 ... 32 B3
Kerry Path SE8 ... 51 B4
Kerry Rd SE8 ... 51 B4
Kerscott Ho 30 E3 ... 27 A2
Kersfield Ho SW15 ... 57 C1
Kersfield Rd SW15 ... 57 C1
Kershaw Cl SW18 ... 59 C1
Kershaw Ho 7 SE27 ... 75 A1
Kersley Mews SW11 ... 168 C3
Kersley Rd N16 ... 7 A1
Kersley St SW11 ... 168 C2
Kerwick Cl 1 N7 ... 14 B1
Keslake Mans NW10 ... 22 C3
Keslake Rd NW6 ... 22 C3
Keston Ho SE17 ... 152 B2
Keston Rd SE15 ... 64 C4
Kestrel Ave SE24 ... 63 B2
Kestrel Ho
4 Battersea SW11 ... 60 A4
Finsbury EC1 ... 96 C4
Kestrel Pl SE14 ... 51 A4
Keswick Broadway 1 SW15 ... 58 B2
Keswick Ct 2 SE22 ... 64 C2
Keswick Ho 8 SE5 ... 48 B2
Keswick Hts 9 SW15 ... 58 A2
Keswick Lo E8 ... 16 B2
Keswick Rd SW15 ... 58 A2
Kett Gdns SW2 ... 62 B2
Kettleby Ho SW9 ... 63 A4
Ketton Ho 11 W10 ... 22 B1
Kevan Ho SE5 ... 48 B3
KEW ... 44 C4
Kew Bridge TW8 ... 36 B1
Kew Bridge Ct W4 ... 36 C1
Kew Bridge Distribution Ctr TW8 ... 36 B1
Kew Bridge Rd TW8 ... 36 B1
Kew Bridge Sta TW8 ... 36 B1
Kew Bridge Steam Mus TW8 ... 36 B1
Kew Coll TW9 ... 44 C3
Kew Foot Rd TW9 ... 54 A4
Kew Gardens Rd TW9 ... 44 C2
Kew Gardens (Royal Botanic) TW9 ... 44 A2
Kew Gardens Sta TW9 ... 44 C2
Kew Gn TW9 ... 44 B4
Kew Green TW9 ... 44 C4
Kew Green Prep Sch TW9 ... 44 B4
Kew Lo 11 TW9 ... 44 B2
Kew Pal TW9 ... 44 A3
Kew Pier TW9 ... 44 C4
Kew Rd TW9, W4 ... 44 B2
Kew Ret Pk TW9 ... 45 A2
Kew Riverside Prim Sch TW9 ... 45 A1
Key Cl E1 ... 25 A1
Keyes Ct SE22 ... 64 C2
Keyes Rd NW2 ... 9 C3
Keyham Ho 31 W2 ... 31 C4
Key Ho 9 SE11 ... 163 B4
Keymer Rd SW2 ... 74 B2
Keynsham Ho 2 N4 ... 6 B4
Keystone Cres N1 ... 84 B1
Keyworth Cl E5 ... 18 A4
Keyworth Pl SE1 ... 136 B2
Keyworth Prim Sch SE17 ... 150 A2
Keyworth St SE1 ... 136 B2
Kezia St SE8 ... 41 A1
Khyber Rd SW11 ... 168 A1
Kia Oval The (Surrey Cnty Crkt Club) SE11 ... 163 A4
Kibworth St SW8 ... 162 C1
Kidbrooke Gdns SE3 ... 53 C2
Kidderpore Ave NW3 ... 10 C4
Kidderpore Gdns NW3 ... 10 C4
Kiffen St EC2 ... 97 C2
Kilbrennan Ho 9 E14 ... 34 B3
KILBURN ... 23 C4
Kilburn Bridge 14 NW6 ... 23 C4
Kilburn Gate NW6 ... 78 A2
Kilburn High Rd NW6 ... 23 C4
Kilburn High Road Sta NW6 ... 78 A3
Kilburn Ho 11 W9 ... 23 B2
Kilburn La W10 ... 23 A3
Kilburn Park Rd NW6 ... 23 C2
Kilburn Park Sch 10 NW6 ... 23 B3
Kilburn Park Sta NW6 ... 23 C3
Kilburn Pl NW6 ... 23 C4
Kilburn Priory NW6 ... 78 A3
Kilburn Sq NW6 ... 23 C4
Kilburn Sta NW2 ... 10 B2
Kilburn Vale NW6 ... 78 A3
Kilburn Vale Est 13 NW6 ... 23 C4
Kilby Ct SE10 ... 43 B3
Kildare Ct W2 ... 31 C3
Kildare Gdns W2 ... 31 C3
Kildare Rd E16 ... 35 C4
Kildare Terr W2 ... 31 C3
Kildare Wlk E14 ... 33 C3
Kildoran Rd SW2 ... 62 A2
Kilgour Rd SE23 ... 66 A1
Kilkie St SW6 ... 166 C1
Killarney Rd SW18 ... 59 B1
Killick St N1 ... 84 C1
Killieser Ave SW2 ... 74 A2
Killip Cl E16 ... 35 B3
Killoran Ho 9 E14 ... 42 B3
Killowen Rd E9 ... 17 C2
Killyon Rd SW8 ... 171 B1
Kilmaine Rd SW6 ... 154 B1
Kilmarsh Rd W6 ... 39 B2
Kilmington Rd SW13 ... 46 C4
Kilmore Ho 17 E14 ... 34 A3
Kilmuir Ho SW1 ... 145 C3
Kiln Ct E14 ... 33 B2
Kilner Ho 3 SE11 ... 163 B4
Kilner St E14 ... 33 C4
Kiln Pl NW5 ... 12 C3
Kiloh Ct 1 SW11 ... 60 A4
Kilpatrick Ct N16 ... 7 B3
Kilpeck Ho 3 N4 ... 6 B4
Kilravock St W10 ... 23 A2
Kilronan 5 W3 ... 28 C3
Kimbell Gdns SW6 ... 164 A3
Kimber Ctr The SW18 ... 70 C4
Kimberley Ave SE15 ... 65 B4
Kimberley Ct NW6 ... 23 A4
Kimberley Ho 7 E14 ... 42 B3
Kimberley Rd
Kilburn NW6 ... 23 A4
Stockwell SW9 ... 62 A4
Kimber Rd SW18 ... 71 A4
Kimble Ho
Lisson Gr NW8 ... 90 B2
1 Lower Holloway N7 ... 14 A3
Kimbolton Row SW3 ... 144 A3
Kimpton Ct 12 SE5 ... 48 C2
Kimpton Ho SW15 ... 68 C4
Kimpton Rd SE5 ... 48 C2
Kinburn St SE16 ... 40 C4
Kincaid Rd SE15 ... 50 A3
Kincardine Gdns W9 ... 23 C1
Kindell Ho 4 SW14 ... 55 C4
Kinder Ho N1 ... 87 C2
Kindersley Ho 38 E1 ... 111 C1
Kinder St 19 E1 ... 32 A3
Kinefold Ho N7 ... 14 A2
Kinfauns Rd SW2 ... 74 C2
King Alfred Sch NW11 ... 2 A3
King Arthur Cl SE15 ... 50 B3
King Charles Ct 16 SE17 ... 48 A4
King Charles Ho SW6 ... 156 B2
King Charles St SW1 ... 134 A4
King Charles Terr 11 E1 ... 32 A2
King Charles Wlk 6 SW19 ... 70 A3
King David La E1 ... 32 B2
Kingdom St W2 ... 100 C3
Kingdon Ho 8 E14 ... 42 B3
Kingdon Rd NW6 ... 10 C2
Kingdown Cl W10 ... 30 C3
King Edward Mans 12 E8 ... 25 A4
King Edward Mews SW13 ... 46 C2
King Edwards Mans SW6 ... 155 B1
King Edward's Rd E9 ... 25 B4
King Edward St EC1 ... 108 C2
King Edward The Third Mews 11 SE16 ... 40 A4
King Edward VII Hospl for Officers W1 ... 103 C4
King Edward Wlk SE1 ... 135 C2
King Fahed Acad W3 ... 29 B2
Kingfield St E14 ... 42 B2
Kingfisher Ct
11 Battersea SW11 ... 60 A4
17 Cubitt Town E14 ... 42 B4
Kingfisher Ct *continued*
Putney SW19 ... 70 A2
Kingfisher Ho
16 Battersea SW18 ... 59 B4
Peckham SE15 ... 49 B2
West Kensington W14 ... 126 C2
Kingfisher Mews SE13 ... 67 A2
Kingfisher Sq 19 SE8 ... 51 B4
King Frederick IX Twr SE16 ... 41 B3
King George Sq TW10 ... 54 B1
King George St SE10 ... 52 B3
Kingham Cl
3 Shepherd's Bush W11 ... 39 C4
Wandsworth SW18 ... 71 B4
Kingham Ind Est NW10 ... 20 C2
King Henry's Rd NW3 ... 12 A1
King Henry's Reach W6 ... 47 B4
King Henry St N16 ... 16 A3
King Henry's Wlk N1 ... 16 A2
King Henry's Yd 5 N16 ... 16 A3
King Henry Terr 10 E1 ... 32 A2
King Ho 5 W12 ... 30 A3
Kinghorn St EC1 ... 108 C3
King James Ct SE1 ... 136 B3
King James St SE1 ... 136 B3
King John Ct EC2 ... 24 A1 98 B2
King John St E1 ... 32 C4
Kinglake St SE17 ... 152 B2
Kingly Ct W1 ... 119 A4
Kingly St W1 ... 118 C4
King & Queen St SE17 ... 151 A2
King's Arms Ct E1 ... 111 B3
King's Arms Yd EC2 ... 109 B2
Kings Ave SW4 ... 62 A1
Kings Avenue Sch SW4 ... 62 A2
King's Bench St SE1 ... 136 B4
King's Bench Wlk EC4 ... 107 C1
King's Boulevard NW1 ... 84 A1
Kingsbridge N16 ... 6 C3
Kingsbridge Ave W3 ... 36 B4
Kingsbridge Ct E14 ... 41 C2
Kingsbridge Rd W10 ... 30 B3
Kingsbury Rd N1 ... 16 A2
Kingsbury Terr N1 ... 16 A2
Kingsclere Cl SW15 ... 68 C4
Kingscliffe Gdns SW19 ... 70 B3
King's Coll SE24 ... 63 C1

Kings College Ct NW3 12 A1
King's College Hospl SE5 48 C1
Kings College Rd NW3 11 C1
King's Coll London (Denmark Hill Campus) SE5 48 B1
King's Coll London School of Medicine SE1 123 C1
King's Coll London (Strand Campus) WC2 121 A4
King's Coll London (St Thomas' Campus) SE1 134 C1
King's Coll London (Waterloo Campus) SE1 121 B1
Kingscote NW11 1 B3
Kingscote Rd W4 37 C3
Kingscote St EC4 122 A4
King's Court N SW3 144 A1
Kingscourt Rd SW16 74 A1
King's Court S SW3 144 A1
King's Cres N4, N5 6 B1
Kingscroft SW4 62 A1
Kingscroft Rd NW2 10 B2
KING'S CROSS 84 C2
King's Cross WC1 94 B4
King's Cross Bridge WC1 94 B4
King's Cross Rd WC1 95 A3
King's Cross, St Pancras N1 94 A4
King's Cross Sta N1 84 B1
Kings Ct
- 6 Barnsbury N7 14 B1
- Chiswick W6 38 C2
- East Dulwich SE22 64 C3
- Primrose Hill NW8 80 C3
- 10 Putney SW15 68 C4

Kingsdale Gdns W11 30 C1
Kingsdale Sch SE21 76 A1
Kingsdown Ave W3 29 A2
Kingsdown Cl
- 26 Deptford SE16 40 A1
- 8 Notting Hill W11 31 A3

Kingsdown Ct SW11 60 A1
Kingsdown Ho 1 E8 16 C3
Kingsdown Rd 4 N19 5 A2
Kings Farm Ave TW10 54 C3
Kingsfield Ho 18 N16 7 A1
Kingsford St NW5 12 B3
Kingsgate Est N1 16 A2
Kingsgate Ho 29 SW9 173 C4
Kingsgate Par SW1 133 A1
Kingsgate Pl NW6 10 C1
Kingsgate Prim Sch NW6 10 C1
Kingsgate Rd NW6 10 C1
King's Gdns 6 NW6 10 C1
King's Gr
- Peckham SE15 50 A2
- Peckham SE15 50 A3

Kingshall Mews SE13 67 B4
King's Head Yd SE1 123 B1
Kingshill SE17 151 A4
Kings Ho
- 10 Limehouse E14 33 B2
- South Lambeth SW8 162 B2

Kingshold Rd E9 17 B1
King's House Sch TW10 54 B2
King's House Sch (Jun) TW10 54 B2
King's Keep 6 SW15 57 C2
KINGSLAND 16 A2
Kingsland NW8 80 B3
Kingsland Gn 1 E8, N1 16 A2
Kingsland High St E8 16 B3
Kingsland Pas 2 E8 16 A2
Kingsland Rd E2 24 A3
Kingsland Sh Ctr 12 E8 16 B2
Kingslawn Cl SW15 57 A2
Kingsley Ct NW2 9 A2
Kingsley Flats SE1 152 B3
Kingsley Ho
- Chelsea SW3 157 C3
- 3 Clapham SW4 171 C2

Kingsley Mews
- Kensington W8 128 B1
- 15 St George in t East E1 32 A2

Kingsley Pl N6 3 C4
Kingsley Rd NW6 23 B4
Kingsley St SW11 60 B4
Kings Mall Sh Ctr W6 39 B2
King's Mans SW3 158 A3
Kingsmead TW10 54 B1
Kingsmead Ct N6 4 C4
Kingsmead Ho E9 18 A4
Kingsmead Prim Sch E9 18 A4
Kingsmead Rd SW2 74 C2
King's Mead Way E5, E9 18 A4
Kingsmere Cl 13 SW15 57 C4
Kingsmere Pl N16 6 C3
Kingsmere Rd SW19 69 C2
King's Mews
- 1 Clapham Pk SW4 62 A2
- Gray's Inn WC1 95 A1

Kingsmill NW8 79 C2
Kingsmill Terr NW8 79 C2
Kingsnorth Ho 12 W10 30 C3
King Solomon Acad NW1 102 A4
King's Par
- 3 Hammersmith W12 38 C3
- Willesden NW10 22 B4

Kings Pl W4 37 B2
Kings Pl N1 84 B2
King's Pl SE1 136 C3
King Sq EC1 96 C3
King's Quay SW10 167 A4
Kings Rd
- Richmond TW10, TW9 54 B2
- Willesden NW10 9 A1

King's Rd
- Chelsea SW3 144 B1
- Chelsea SW10 157 B3
- Mortlake SW14 55 C4

Kings Ride Gate TW10 54 C3
Kingsridge SW19 70 A2
King's Scholars' Pas SW1 146 C4
King St
- Acton W3 28 B1
- Hammersmith W6 38 C2
- St James SW1 119 A2
- Strand WC2 120 A4
- Whitechapel EC2 109 A1

King Stairs Cl SE16 40 A4
King's Terr NW1 82 C3
Kingston Ho 4 NW6 10 A1
Kingston Ho E SW7 130 A3
Kingston Ho N SW7 130 A3
Kingston Ho S SW7 130 A3
Kingston Rd SW15, SW19 69 A3
Kingston Univ (Roehampton Vale) SW15 68 B1
Kingston Vale SW15 68 A1
Kingstown St NW1 81 B4
King Street Cloisters 8 W6 39 A2
King Street Coll 10 W12 39 B2
Kingswater Pl SW11 158 A1
Kingsway
- Mortlake SW14, TW9 55 A4
- St Giles WC2 106 C2

Kingsway Coll 12 NW5 13 A2
Kingsway Mans WC1 106 C4
Kingsway Pl EC1 96 A2
Kingswear Rd NW5 4 A1
Kings Well 25 NW3 11 B4
Kings Wlk Sh Mall SW3 144 C2
Kingswood 31 E2 25 B3
Kingswood Ave NW6 23 A3
Kingswood Cl SW8 162 B1
Kingswood Ct
- Hither Green SE13 67 C1
- 7 Richmond TW10 54 B2

Kings Wood Ct 4 NW6 10 C1
Kingswood Rd
- South Acton W4 37 B3
- Streatham SW2 74 A4

Kingswood Terr W4 37 B3
Kings Yd E15 18 C2
Kington Ho 18 NW6 78 B3
Kingward Ho E1 111 B4
Kingweston Cl NW2 1 A1
King William La 3 SE10 43 A1
King William St EC4 123 C4
King William Wlk SE10 52 B4
Kingwood Rd SW6 154 A1
Kinloch St N7 5 B1
Kinnaird Ave W4 45 B3
Kinnear Rd W12 38 B4
Kinnerton Pl N SW1 131 A3
Kinnerton Pl S SW1 131 A3
Kinnerton St SW1 131 B3
Kinnerton Yd SW1 131 B3
Kinnoull Mans 10 E5 17 A4
Kinnoul Rd W6 154 A4
Kinross Ho N1 84 C4
Kinsale Rd SE15 64 C4
Kinsham Ho 5 E2 24 C1 99 C2
Kintore Way SE1 152 C4
Kintyre Ct 17 SW2 74 A4
Kintyre Ho 6 E14 34 B1
Kinver Ho N4 6 C4
Kipling Ho 20 SE5 48 B3
Kipling St SE1 137 C4
Kipling Twr 3 W3 37 B3
Kirby Est SE16 40 A3
Kirby Gr SE1 138 A4
Kirby St EC1 107 C4
Kirkeby Bldg EC1 107 B4
Kirkland Wlk 4 E8 16 B2
Kirkley Ho N16 7 A3
Kirkman Ho W1 105 B3
Kirkman Pl W1 105 B3
Kirkmichael Rd E14 34 B3
Kirkside Rd SE3 53 C4
Kirk St WC1 94 A1
Kirkstall Gdns SW2 74 A3
Kirkstall Ho SW1 146 A2
Kirkstall Rd SW2 74 A3
Kirkstead Ct E5 18 A4
Kirkstone NW1 92 C4
Kirkwall Pl E2 25 B2
Kirkwood Rd SE15 50 A1
Kirtley Ho SW8 171 A4
Kirtling St SW8 160 C2
Kirton Cl W4 37 C2
Kirton Gdns 23 E2 24 B2 99 A3
Kirwin Way SE5 48 A3
Kitcat Terr E3 26 C2
Kite Ho 5 SW11 60 A4
Kite Pl 9 E2 24 C2 99 C4
Kitson Rd
- Barnes SW13 46 C2
- Camberwell SE5 48 B3

Kittiwake Ct 26 SE8 51 B4
Kitto Rd SE14 50 C1
Kiver Rd N19 5 A2
Klea Ave SW4 61 B1
Kleffens Ct 2 SE3 53 B3
Kleine Wharf 30 N1 24 A4
Knapp Cl NW10 8 A2
Knapp Rd E3 26 C1
Knaresborough Dr SW18 71 A3
Knaresborough Ho 4 N4 6 B4
Knaresborough Pl SW5 142 A4
Knatchbull Rd
- Brixton SE5 48 A2
- Stonebridge NW10 20 C4

Knebworth Ho
- South Lambeth SW8 171 C3
- 2 Stoke Newington N16 16 A4

Knebworth Rd 3 N16 16 A4
Kneller Ho 9 SW8 171 C2
Kneller Rd SE4 66 A3
Knighten St E1 32 A1
Knighthead Point 26 E14 41 C4
Knight Ho SE17 152 A3
Knightleas Ct NW2 9 B2
Knightrider Ct EC4 122 C4
Knightrider St EC4 122 B4
Knights Arc SW1 130 C3
Knight's Ave W5 36 A4
KNIGHTSBRIDGE 130 A2
Knightsbridge SW1, SW7 130 C3
Knightsbridge Ct SW1 131 A3
Knightsbridge Gn SW1 130 C3
Knightsbridge Sch SW11 130 C1
Knightsbridge Sta SW1 131 A3
Knightsbridge Under Sch SW7 143 A3
Knights Cl E9 17 B3
Knights Ho
- Bermondsey SE1 138 C4
- South Lambeth SW8 162 B1
- West Kensington SW5 140 C2

Knight's Ho SW10 156 C2
Knights Rd E16 43 C4
Knight's Wlk SE11 150 A3
Knightswood Ct N6 4 C4
Knivet Rd SW6 155 B3
Knoll Ho NW8 78 C2
Knoll Rd SW18 59 B2

Knolly's Cl SE27, SW16 ... 74 C1
Knolly's Rd SE27, SW16 ... 74 C1
Knot Ho SE1 ... 124 C1
Knottisford St E2 ... 25 B2
Knowlden Ho 5 E1 ... 32 B2
Knowle Cl SW9 ... 62 C4
Knowledge Point Sch 6 N7 ... 14 B2
Knowles Hill Cres SE13 ... 67 C2
Knowles Ho
Wandsworth SW18 ... 59 A1
Willesden Green NW10 ... 21 C4
Knowles Wlk SW4 .. 61 B4
Knowlton Ho 32 SW9 ... 173 C4
Knowsley Rd SW11 ... 168 C1
Knox Ct 16 SW4 .. 172 B2
Knox Ho SW15 ... 47 B1
Knox St W1 ... 102 C4
Knoyle Ho W14 ... 126 B2
Knoyle St SE14 ... 51 A4
Kobi Nazrul Prim Sch 43 E1 ... 111 C2
Kossuth St SE10 ... 43 A1
Kotree Way 16 SE1 ... 153 C4
Kramer Mews SW5 ... 142 A1
Kreedman Wlk 8 E8 ... 16 C3
Kreisel Wlk TW9 ... 44 B4
Kylemore Ct 4 W12 ... 38 C4
Kylemore Rd NW6 .. 10 C1
Kylestrome Ho SW1 ... 145 C3
Kynance Mews SW7 ... 128 B1
Kynance Pl SW7 .. 128 C1
Kynaston Ho 7 SW2 ... 74 B3
Kynaston Rd N16 ... 7 A1
Kyrle Rd SW11 ... 60 C1
Kyverdale Rd N16 ... 7 B3

L

Laburnham Ct NW2 .. 1 B2
Laburnum Cl 5 SE15 ... 50 B3
Laburnum Ct 26 E2 ... 24 B4
Laburnum Ho
New Cross SE4 ... 51 B1
6 Stoke Newington N16 ... 6 C2
Laburnum St E2 ... 24 B4
Lacey Ho 7 SE13 ... 52 B1
Lacey Mews 9 E3 .. 26 C3
Lacine Ct 12 SE16 .. 40 C4
Lackington St EC2 ... 109 C4
Lackland Ho SE1 . 153 A2
Lacland Ho SW10 . 157 B2
Lacon Rd SE22 ... 64 C3
Lacy Rd SW15 ... 57 C3
Ladbroke Cres W11 ... 31 A3
Ladbroke Gdns W11 ... 31 B2 112 C4
Ladbroke Gr
Kensal Town W10 ... 31 A4
Notting Hill W11 ... 31 B2 112 C4
Ladbroke Grove Ho W11 ... 31 B2 112 C4
Ladbroke Grove Sta W10 ... 31 A3
Ladbroke Ho E1 .. 111 A3
Ladbroke Mews W11 ... 31 A1 112 B1
Ladbroke Rd W11 ... 31 B1 112 C2
Ladbroke Sq W11 ... 31 B2 113 A3
Ladbroke Terr W11 ... 31 B1 113 A2
Ladbroke Wlk W11 ... 31 B1 113 A2
Ladlands SE22 ... 76 C4
Ladybower Ct 6 E5 ... 17 C4
Ladycroft Rd SE13 .. 67 A4
Lady Elizabeth Ho SW14 ... 55 B4
Ladyfern Ho 19 E3 .. 33 C4
Lady Florence Ctyd 15 SE8 ... 51 C3
Lady Margaret Rd NW5 ... 13 B3
Lady Margaret Sch SW6 ... 165 B3
Lady Somerset Rd NW5 ... 13 A4
LADYWELL ... 66 C1
Ladywell Arena SE13 ... 67 A1
Ladywell Cl SE4 ... 66 C3
Ladywell Hts SE4 ... 66 B1
Ladywell Rd SE13 ... 67 A2
Ladywell Sta SE13 .. 67 A2
Ladywell Water Twr SE4 ... 66 C2
Lafitte Ho 22 N19 ... 4 C4
Lafone Ho 11 SW2 .. 74 A4
Lafone St SE1 ... 138 C4
Lagado Mews SE16 ... 32 C1
Lagonda Ho 11 E3 .. 26 C1
Lagonier Ho EC1 .. 97 A3
Laindon Ho 6 N16 .. 7 B3
Laing Ho SE5 ... 48 B3
Lainson St SW18 ... 70 C4
Lairdale Cl SE21 ... 75 B4
Laird Ho SE5 ... 48 B3
Lairs Cl N7 ... 14 A2
Laitwood Rd SW12 .73 A3
Lakanal 10 SE5 ... 49 A2
Lake Ho SE1 ... 136 C3
Laker Ct SW4 ... 172 B2
Laker Pl SW15 ... 58 A1
Lakeside Ct N4 ... 6 B3
Lakeside Rd W14 ... 39 C3
Lakeview 23 E3 ... 25 C3
Lake View Ct SW1 ... 132 B2
Lakis Cl NW3 ... 11 B4
Laleham Ho E2 ... 24 B1 98 C2
Lalor St SW6 ... 164 B2
Lambard Ho 4 SE10 ... 52 B3
Lamb Ct 16 E14 ... 33 A2
Lamberhurst Ho 14 SE15 ... 50 B4
Lambert Ave TW9 ... 55 A4
Lambert Ho
16 Brixton SW9 ... 173 B1
19 Crouch End N19 ... 4 C4
Lambert Rd SW2 ... 62 B2
Lambert St N1 ... 14 C1
LAMBETH ... 134 C3
Lambeth Acad SW4 ... 61 B2
Lambeth Coll (Brixton Ctr) SW2 ... 62 B2
Lambeth Coll (Clapham Ctr) SW4 ... 61 B2
Lambeth Coll (Vauxhall Ctr) SW8 ... 171 B4
Lambeth Ct 8 SW18 ... 58 C2
Lambeth High St SE1 ... 148 C4
Lambeth Hill EC4 ... 122 C4
Lambeth Hospl SW9 ... 62 B4
Lambeth North Sta SE1 ... 135 B2
Lambeth Pal SE1 . 134 C1
Lambeth Palace Rd SE1 ... 134 C2
Lambeth Pier SE1 ... 134 B1
Lambeth Rd SE1 .. 135 C1
Lambeth Twrs SE11 ... 135 B1
Lambeth Wlk SE11 ... 149 A4
Lambfold Ho N7 ... 14 A2
Lamb Ho
28 Camberwell SE5 ... 48 B3
11 Camberwell SE5 .. 48 C2
Greenwich SE10 ... 52 B4
Lamb La E8 ... 17 A1
Lamble St NW5 ... 12 C4
Lamb Office Ct WC1 ... 106 A4
Lambolle Pl NW3 ... 12 A2
Lambolle Rd NW3 .. 12 A2
Lambourn Cl 9 NW5 ... 13 B4
Lambourne Gr SE16 ... 40 C1
Lambourne Ho NW8 ... 101 C4
Lambourn Rd SW4 .61 A4
Lambrook Ho 13 SE15 ... 49 C2
Lambrook Terr SW6 ... 164 A4
Lamb's Bldgs EC1 . 97 B1
Lamb's Conduit Pas WC1 ... 106 C4
Lamb's Conduit St WC1 ... 94 C1
Lamb's Mews N1 .. 86 A3
Lamb's Pas EC1 ... 97 B1
Lamb St E1 ... 110 C4
Lambton Ct 2 N19 .. 5 A3
Lambton Mews 4 N19 ... 5 A3
Lambton Pl W11 ... 31 B2 113 A4
Lambton Rd N19 ... 5 A3
Lamb Wlk SE1 ... 138 A3
Lamerton Lo 10 TW9 ... 44 B2
Lamerton St 8 SE8 ... 51 C4
Lamington St 3 W6 ... 39 A2
Lamlash St SE11 .. 150 A4
Lamley Ho SE10 ... 52 A3
Lammas Rd E9 ... 17 C1
Lammermoor Rd SW12 ... 73 A4
Lamont Rd SW10 . 157 B3
Lamont Rd Pas SW10 ... 157 B3
Lampard Gr N16 ... 7 B3
Lampern Sq 8 E2 ... 24 C2 99 C4
Lampeter Sq W6 . 154 A3
Lamplighter Cl 34 E1 ... 25 B1
Lampson Ho 6 N19 ... 13 B4
Lanark Ho 12 SE1 . 153 B1
Lanark Mans
Paddington W9 ... 89 A2
15 Shepherd's Bush W12 ... 39 B4
Lanark Mews NW8 ... 89 A3
Lanark Pl W9 ... 89 A2
Lanark Rd W9 ... 88 C3
Lanark Sq E14 ... 42 A3
Lanbury Rd SE15 ... 65 C3
Lancashire Ct W1 ... 118 B4
Lancaster Ave SE21, SE27 ... 75 B2
Lancaster Cl
10 De Beauvoir Town N1 ... 16 A1
Kensington W2 ... 114 A3
Lancaster Cotts 1 TW10 ... 54 A1
Lancaster Ct
Bayswater W2 ... 115 A4
Parsons Green SW6 ... 155 A1
West Norwood SE27 ... 75 A2
Lancaster Dr
Canary Wharf E14 ... 34 B1
Maitland Pk NW3 ... 12 A2
Lancaster Gate W2 ... 115 A4
Lancaster Gate Sta W2 ... 115 B4
Lancaster Gr NW3 .. 12 A2
Lancaster hall 14 E16 ... 35 C1
Lancaster Ho SW15 ... 47 B1
Lancaster Ho SW1 ... 132 C4
Lancaster Ho SW18 ... 71 A4
Lancaster Lo 2 W11 ... 31 A3
Lancaster Mews
Bayswater W2 ... 115 A4
2 Richmond TW10 .. 54 A1
3 Wandsworth SW18 ... 59 A2
Lancaster Pk TW10 ... 54 A2
Lancaster Pl WC2 ... 120 C3
Lancaster Rd
Dudden Hill NW10 ... 8 C3
Finsbury Pk N4 ... 5 C4
Lancaster Rd *continued*
Notting Hill W11 ... 31 A3
Lancaster St SE1 . 136 B3
Lancaster Stables 10 NW3 ... 12 A2
Lancaster Terr W2 ... 115 B4
Lancaster Wlk W2 ... 115 A2
Lancefield Ho SE15 ... 65 A4
Lancefield St W10 .. 23 B2
Lancell St N16 ... 7 A2
Lancelot Pl SW7 .. 130 C3
Lancer Sq W8 ... 128 A4
Lanchester Ct W2 ... 102 C1
Lanchester Way SE14 ... 50 C2
Lancing St NW1 ... 93 B3
Lancresse Ct N1 ... 24 A4
Landale Ct SE10 ... 52 B2
Landale Ho 13 SE16 ... 40 B3
Landcroft Rd SE22 .. 64 B1
Landells Rd SE22 ... 64 C1
Landford Rd SW15 .. 57 B4
Landin Ho 1 E14 ... 33 C3
Landleys Field 21 N7 ... 13 C3
Landmann Ho 16 SE16 ... 40 A2
Landmann Way SE14 ... 40 C1
Landmark Hts E5 ... 18 A4
Landon Pl SW1 ... 130 C2
Landons Cl E14 ... 34 B1
Landon Wlk 16 E14 ... 34 A2
Landor Ct N16 ... 16 A3
Landor Ho 7 SE5 .. 48 C3
Landor Rd SW9 ... 62 A4
Landor Wlk 11 W12 ... 38 C4
Landrake NW1 ... 83 A3
Landridge Rd SW6 ... 164 C2
Landseer Ct 10 N19 .. 5 A2
Landseer Ho
Battersea SW11 ... 169 C3
Paddington NW8 ... 89 C2
Westminster SW1 . 147 C3
Landseer Rd N19 ... 5 A2
Landulph Ho SE11 ... 149 C2
Landward Ct W1 . 102 B2
Lane Ct SW11 ... 72 B4
Lanercost Cl SW2 .. 74 C2
Lanercost Rd SW2 .. 74 C2
Lane The NW8 ... 78 C1
Laneway SW15 ... 57 A2
Laney Bldg EC1 ... 107 B4
Lanfranc Rd E3 ... 26 A3
Lanfrey Pl W14 ... 140 C1
Langbourne Ave N6 . 3 C2
Langbourne Ho 7 SW2 ... 62 C2
Langbourne Mans N6 ... 3 C2
Langbourne Pl E14 ... 42 A1
Langbourne Prim Sch SE21 ... 76 A1
Langdale NW1 ... 92 C4
Langdale Cl
Camberwell SE17 ... 48 B4
Mortlake SW14 ... 55 A3

Langdale Ho SW1 146 C1
Langdale Rd SE10 . . 52 B3
Langdale St 25 E1 . . 32 A3
Langdon Ct
Finsbury EC1 . . . . . . 86 B1
Harlesden NW10 . . . . 21 A4
Langdon Ho 3 E14 . . . . 34 B3
Langdon Park Rd N6 . . . . 4 B4
Langdon Park Sch E14 . . . . 34 B3
Langdon Park Sta E14 . . . . 34 A4
Langdon Pk L Ctr E14 . . . . 34 B3
Langdon Pk Sta E3 . . . . 34 A4
Langdon Pl SW14 . . 55 B4
Langdon Way 18 SE1 . . . . 153 C3
Langford Cl
Shacklewell E8 . . . . . . 16 C3
St John's Wood NW8 . . . . 79 A2
Langford Ct NW8 . . 79 A1
Langford Gn SE5 . . . 64 A4
Langford Ho 5 SE8 . . . . 51 C4
Langford Pl NW8 . . 79 A2
Langford Prim Sch SW6 . . . . 166 B2
Langford Rd 4 SW6 . . . . 166 B2
Langham Ct 4 SW15 . . . . 57 C2
Langham Ho SW4 . . 61 B2
Langham Mans SW5 . . . . 142 A1
Langham Pl
Chiswick W4 . . . . 46 A4
Fitzrovia W1 . . . . . . 104 B3
Langham St W1 . . 104 B3
Lang Ho
South Lambeth SW8 . . . . 162 A1
3 Tufnell Pk N19 . . . . . 4 B1
Langholm Cl SW12 . . . . 73 C4
Langhorne Ct 10 NW8 . . . . 11 C1
Langhurst Ho 10 SW11 . . . . 169 B2
Langland Gdns NW3 . . . . 11 A3
Langland Ho 10 SE5 . . . . 48 C3
Langland Mans NW3 . . . . 11 A3
Langler Rd NW10 . . . 22 B3
Langley Ct
South Lambeth SW8 . . . . 172 A4
Strand WC2 . . . . . . 120 A4
Langley Dr W3 . . . . . 37 A4
Langley Ho
11 Lower Clapton E5 . . . . 17 A3
36 Paddington W2 . . . 31 C4
Langley La SW8 . . 162 B4
Langley Mans SW8 . . . . 162 B4
Langley St WC2 . . . 106 A1
Langmead Ho 24 E3 . . . . 27 A2
Langmore Ho 33 E1 . . . . 111 C1
Langport Ho 1 SW9 . . . . 48 A1
Langridge 15 NW5 . . 12 C2
Langroyd Rd SW17 . 72 B2
Langside Ave SW15 . . . . 56 C3
Lang St E1 . . . . 25 B1
Langston Hughes Cl 5 SE24 . . . . 63 A3
Langthorn Ct EC2 109 C2
Langthorne Lo 30 SW2 . . . . 74 C4
Langthorne St SW6 . . . . 47 C3
Langton Cl WC1 . . . 95 A2
Langton Ct SW15 . . . 58 B1
Langton Ho SE11 . 149 A4
Langton Pl SW18 . . . 70 C3
Langton Rd SW9 . . . 48 A3
Langton St SW10 . 157 A3
Langton Way SE3 . . . 53 C3
Langtry Pl SW6 . . . 155 C4
Langtry Rd NW8 . . . 78 A3
Langtry Wlk NW8 . . 78 C4
Lanhill Rd W9 . . . . . . 23 C1
Lanier Rd SE13 . . . . . 67 C1
Lanner Ho 2 SW11 . . . . 60 A4
Lannoy Point SW6 . . . . 154 B2
Lanrick Rd E14 . . . . . 35 A3
Lansbury Gdns 1 E14 . . . . 34 C3
Lansbury Lawrence Prim Sch 20 E14 . . . 34 A3
Lanscombe Wlk SW8 . . . . 162 A1
Lansdell Ho 9 SW2 . . . . 62 C1
Lansdowne Coll W2 . . . . 114 A3
Lansdowne Cres W11 . . . . 31 A2 112 B3
Lansdowne Dr E8 . . 16 C1
Lansdowne Gdns SW8 . . . . 172 A4
Lansdowne Gr NW10 . . . . 8 A4
Lansdowne Hill SE27 . . . . 75 A1
Lansdowne Ho W11 . . . . 31 B1 112 C2
Lansdowne Mews W11 . . . . 31 B1 112 C2
Lansdowne Pl SE1 . . . . 137 C2
Lansdowne Rd W11 . . . . 31 A2 112 B3
Lansdowne Rise W11 . . . . 31 A2 112 B3
Lansdowne Row W1 . . . . 118 B2
Lansdowne Sch 5 SW9 . . . . 62 B4
Lansdowne Terr WC1 . . . . 94 B1
Lansdowne Way SW4, SW8 . . . . 172 B3
Lansdowne Wlk W11 . . . . 31 B1 112 C2
Lansdowne Wood Cl 11 SE27 . . . . 75 A1
Lansdown Ho 28 SE5 . . . . 48 B1
Lantern Cl SW15 . . . . 56 C3
Lantern Ho E14 . . . . . 41 C4
Lanterns Ct E14 . . . . 41 C3
Lant Ho SE1 . . . . . . 136 C3
Lantry Ct 1 W3 . . . . 28 A1
Lant St SE1 . . . . 137 A3
Lanvanor Rd SE15 . . 50 B1
Lanyard Ho 4 SE8 . 41 B2
Lapford Cl W9 . . . . . . 23 B1
Lapsang SE1 . . . . . 125 A1
Lapwing Twr 31 SE8 . . . . 51 B4
Lapworth Ct W2 . . 100 B4
Lara Cl SE13 . . . . 67 B1
Larch Ave W3 . . . . . . 29 A1
Larch Cl
Balham SW12 . . . . 73 A2
15 Deptford SE8 . . . . . 51 B4
10 Upper Holloway N19 . . . . 4 B2
Larch Ct 41 W2 . . . . . 31 C4
Larches Ave SW14 . . 55 C3
Larchfield Ho 2 N5 . . . . 15 B3
Larch Ho 23 SE16 . . . 40 B4
Larchmore Ct N19 . . . 5 A2
Larch Rd NW2 . . . . 9 B4
Larcom St SE17 . . . 151 A3
Larden Rd W3 . . . . . 38 A4
La Retraite RC Girls Sch SW12 . . . . 73 B4
Larissa St SE17 . . . 151 C3
Larix Ct NW10 . . . . . . 21 C4
Larkfield Rd TW9 . . . 54 A3
Larkhall La SW4 . . 172 A3
Larkhall Rise SW4 . . . . 171 B1
Lark Row E2 . . . . 25 B4
Larmenier & Sacred Heart RC Prim Sch 4 W6 . . . . 39 C2
Larnaca Ho SE1 . . 138 C2
Larnach Rd W6 . . . . . 47 C4
Larpent Ave SW15 . . 57 B2
La Saint Union RC Sec Sch NW5 . . . . 3 C1
Lascelles Ho NW1 . 90 B1
Lassell St SE10 . . . . . 42 C1
Lasseter Pl SE3 . . . . . 53 B4
Latchmere Rd SW11 . . . . 168 C1
Latchmere St 5 SW11 . . . . 168 C2
Latham Ho E1 . . . . . . 32 C3
Latimer SE17 . . . . . 152 A1
Latimer Ho
11 Homerton E9 . . . . . 17 C2
Notting Hill W11 . . . . . . 31 B2 113 A3
Latimer Ind Est 1 NW10 . . . . 30 B3
Latimer Pl W10 . . . . . 30 B3
Latimer Rd W10 . . . . 30 B3
Latimer Road Sta W10 . . . . 30 C2
Latitude Ho NW1 . . 82 A3
Latona Rd SE15 . . . . . 49 C4
Lattimer Pl W4 . . . . . 46 A4
Latvia Ct SE17 . . . . 151 A1
Latymer Ct W6 . . . . . 39 C2
Latymer Upper Sch 14 W6 . . . . 38 C2
Lauderdale Mans W9 . . . . 88 B3
Lauderdale Rd W9. 88 B3
Lauderdale Twr EC2 . . . . 108 C4
Laud St SE11 . . . . . 148 C2
Laughton Ho 11 SW2 . . . . 62 C1
Launcelot St SE1 . 135 B3
Launceston Pl W8 . . . . 128 C1
Launch St E14 . . . . . . 42 B3
Laundress La N16 . . . 7 C1
Laundry La 7 N1 . . . 15 B1
Laundry Rd W6 . . . 154 A3
Laura Pl E5 . . . . 17 B4
Laurel Bank Gdns 3 SW6 . . . . 165 A2
Laurel Cl 8 N19 . . . . . 4 B2
Laurel Ct
Dalston E8 . . . . 16 B1
2 Putney SW15 . . . . 57 C2
9 Rotherhithe SE16 . . . . 33 A1
Laurel Ho
9 Deptford SE8 . . . . 51 B4
5 Hamstead NW3 . . 11 A2
Laurel Rd SW13 . . . . 46 C1
Laurel St E8 . . . . 16 B2
Laurence Mews 12 W12 . . . . 38 C4
Laurence Pountney Hill EC4 . . . . 123 B4
Laurence Pountney La EC4 . . . . 123 C4
Laurie Gr SE14 . . . . . 51 A2
Laurie Ho
Newington SE1 . . . . 136 B1
Notting Hill W8 . . . . 31 C1 113 B1
Laurier Rd NW5 . . . . . 4 A1
Lauriston Ho 6 E9 . . . . 17 C1
Lauriston Lo NW6 . . 10 B2
Lauriston Prim Sch 6 E9 . . . . 25 C4
Lauriston Rd E9 . . . . 17 C1
Lausanne Rd SE15 . . 50 B2
Lavell St N16 . . . . 15 C4
Lavender Cl SW3 . 157 C3
Lavender Ct SW4 . 172 B3
Lavender Gdns SW11 . . . . 60 B3
Lavender Gr E8 . . . . . 16 C1
Lavender Hill SW11 . . . . 60 C4
Lavender Ho
8 Richmond TW9 . . . . 45 A2
14 Rotherhithe SE16 . . . . 32 C1
Lavender Rd
Battersea SW11 . . . . . 59 C4
Rotherhithe SE16 . . . . 33 A1
Lavender Sweep SW11 . . . . 60 B3
Lavender Terr 12 SW11 . . . . 60 A4
Lavender Wlk SW11 . . . . 60 B3
Lavendon Ho NW8. 90 B2
Lavengro Rd SE27 . . 75 B2
Lavenham Rd SW18 . . . . 70 C3
Lavers Rd N16 . . . . 7 A1
Laverstoke Gdns SW15 . . . . 68 C4
Laverton Mews SW5 . . . . 142 B3
Laverton Pl SW5 . . 142 B3
Lavina Gr N1 . . . . . . 84 C2
Lavington Cl E9 . . . . 18 B2
Lavington St SE1 . 122 B1
Lawdale Jun Sch 32 E2 . . . . 24 C2 99 C4
Lawford Rd
Chiswick W4 . . . . 45 B3
De Beauvoir Town N1 . . . . 16 A1
Kentish Town NW5 . . . 13 B2
Lawfords Wharf 18 NW1 . . . . 13 B1
Lawless Ho 5 E14 . . 34 B2
Lawless St 12 E14 . . 34 A2
Lawley St E5 . . . . 17 B4
Lawman Ct 2 TW9 . . . . 44 B2
Lawn Cres TW9 . . . . . 44 C1
Lawnfield Ct NW6 . . . 9 C1
Lawn House Cl E14 . . . . 42 B4
Lawn La SW8 . . . . . 162 C4
Lawn Rd NW3 . . . . . . 12 B3
Lawns The N16 . . . . . 16 A3
Lawrence Ave NW10 . . . . 20 C4
Lawrence Bldgs 1 N16 . . . . 7 B1
Lawrence Cl
Bow E3 . . . . 26 C3
6 Shepherd's Bush W12 . . . . 30 A2
Lawrence Ct
4 South Acton W3 . . . . 37 B3
Stoke Newington N16 . 7 B1
Lawrence Ho
20 Camden Town NW1 . . . . 13 A1
Westminster SW1 . 147 C3
Lawrence La EC2 109 A2
Lawrence Mans SW3 . . . . 158 A3
Lawrence Pl N1 . . . 84 B4
Lawrence St
Canning Town E16 . . . . 35 B4
Chelsea SW3 . . . . . 158 A3
Lawrence Trad Est SE10 . . . . 43 A2
Lawrence Univ SW7 . . . . 143 A3
Lawson Cl SW19 . . . . 69 C1
Lawson Ct 1 N4 . . . . 5 B3
Lawson Ho 17 W12 . . . . 30 A2
Law St SE1 . . . . 137 C2
Lawton Rd E3 . . . . . . 26 A2
Laxfield Ct E8 . . . . . . 24 C4
Laxley Cl SE5 . . . . 48 A3
Laxton Path 1 SE4 . . . . 65 C3
Laxton Pl NW1 . . . . 92 B2
Layard Rd SE16 . . . . . 40 A2
Layard Sq SE16 . . . . . 40 A2
Laybourne Ho 18 E14 . . . . 41 C4
Laycock Prim Sch 5 N1 . . . . 15 A2
Laycock St N1 . . . . . . 14 C2
Layfield Ho 1 SE10 . . . . 43 C1
Laystall Ct EC1 . . . . 95 B1

Laystall St EC1 .... 95 B1
Layton Pl TW9 ...... 44 C2
Lazar Wlk 2 N7 ..... 5 B2
Leabank Sq E9 ..... 18 C2
Leabourne Rd N16 .. 7 C4
Leacroft Ave SW12 . 72 B4
Lea Ct 3 W12 ...... 38 A4
Leadenhall Building The EC3 ... 110 A1
Leadenhall Mkt EC3 ... 110 A1
Leadenhall Pl EC3 ... 110 A1
Leadenhall St EC3 ... 110 A1
Leadenham Ct 15 E3 ... 26 C1
Lea Ho NW8 ... 90 A1
Leahurst Rd SE13 ... 67 C2
Lea Int E9 ... 18 C3
Leake St
Lambeth SE1 ... 135 B3
South Bank SE1 ... 135 A4
Leamington Ct
4 Forest Hill SE26 ... 76 C1
North Acton W3 ... 28 C4
Leamington Ho 4 W11 ... 31 B4
Leamington Pk W3 ... 28 C4
Leamington Rd Villas W11 ... 31 B4
Leamore St W6 ... 39 B2
Leamouth Rd E14 .. 34 C3
Leander Ct
27 Hackney E9 ... 17 B1
St Johns SE8 ... 51 C2
Leander Rd SW2 ... 62 C1
Leary Ho SE11 ... 149 A1
Lea Sq 22 E3 ... 26 B4
Leatherdale St
32 Bethnal Green E1 ... 25 B1
19 Globe Town E1 ... 25 C2
Leatherhead Cl N16 . 7 B3
Leather La EC1 ... 107 C4
Leather La Mkt EC1 ... 107 C4
Leathermarket Ct SE1 ... 138 A3
Leathermarket St SE1 ... 138 A3
Leather Rd SE16 ... 40 C2
Leathwaite Rd SW11 ... 60 B2
Leathwell Rd SE8 ... 52 A1
Lebanon Gdns SW18 ... 58 C1
Lebanon Rd SW18 .. 58 C2
Lebus Ho NW8 ... 80 A1
Lechmere Rd NW2 ... 9 A2
Leckford Rd SW18 .. 71 B3
Leckhampton Pl 23 SW2 ... 74 C4
Lecky Ho NW2 ... 9 A4
Lecky St SW7 ... 143 B2
L'Ecole des Petits Sch SW6 ... 166 A2
Leconfield Ave SW13, SW15 ... 56 B4
Leconfield Ho SE5 .. 64 A4
Leconfield Rd N5 ... 15 C4
Lector Ct EC1 ... 95 C1
Leda Ct 9 SW9 .. 163 B1
Ledam Bldg EC1 .. 107 B4
Ledbury Ho 12 SE22 ... 64 A4
Ledbury Mews N W11 ... 31 C3
Ledbury Mews W W11 ... 31 C2 113 B4
Ledbury Rd W11 ... 31 C3
Ledbury St SE15 ... 49 C3
Ledo Ho 1 N16 ... 15 C4
Lee Conservancy Rd E9 ... 18 B3
Lee Ct SE13 ... 67 C3
Leeds Ct EC1 ... 96 A2
Lee Ho 3 N19 ... 13 C3
Leeke St WC1 ... 94 C4
Leeland Way NW10 .. 8 B4
Leerdam Dr E14 ... 42 B3
Lees Ct W1 ... 117 B4
Lees Ho SE17 ... 151 C1
Leeson Rd 11 SE24 ... 62 C3
Lees Pl W1 ... 117 B4
Lee St E8 ... 24 B4
Leet Ct N16 ... 15 C4
Leeve Ho 7 W9 ... 23 B2
Leeward Ct 3 E1 125 C2
Leeway SE8 ... 41 B1
Lefevre Wlk E3 ... 26 C4
Leffern Rd W12 ... 38 C4
Leff Ho 9 NW6 ... 10 A1
Lefroy Ho SE1 ... 136 C3
Lefroy Rd W12 ... 38 B4
Legard Rd N5 ... 6 A1
Leggatt Rd E15 ... 27 B3
Legge St SE13 ... 67 B2
Leghorn Rd NW10 .. 21 C3
Legion Cl N1 ... 14 C1
Legion Terr E3 ... 26 C4
Leicester Ct
46 Paddington W2 ... 31 C4
St James WC2 ... 119 C4
Leicester Ho
4 Brixton SW9 ... 63 A4
5 Putney SW15 ... 69 B4
Leicester Pl WC2 . 119 C4
Leicester Sq WC2 119 C3
Leicester Square Sta WC2 ... 119 C4
Leicester St WC2 . 119 C4
Leigham Ave SW16 ... 74 A1
Leigham Cl 5 SW16 ... 74 B1
Leigham Court Rd SW16 ... 74 B1
Leigham Hall 3 SW16 ... 74 A1
Leigham Hall Par 2 SW16 ... 74 A1
Leigham Vale SE27, SW16, SW2 ... 74 C2
Leigh Ct 22 SW2 ... 62 C1
Leighfield Ho 5 N4 . 6 B4
Leigh Gdns NW10 .. 22 B3
Leigh Ho 9 SW15 .. 56 C2
Leigh Orchard Cl SW16 ... 74 B1
Leigh Pl EC1 ... 107 B4
Leigh Rd N5 ... 15 A4
Leigh St WC1 ... 94 A3
Leighton Cres NW5 ... 13 B3
Leighton Gdns NW10 ... 22 B3
Leighton Gr NW5 ... 13 B3
Leighton House Mus W14 ... 127 A2
Leighton Pl NW5 ... 13 B3
Leighton Rd NW5 ... 13 B3
Leinster Ave SW14 .. 55 B3
Leinster Gdns W2 114 C4
Leinster Mews W2 ... 114 C4
Leinster Pl W2 ... 100 C1
Leinster Sq W2 ... 100 A1
Leinster Terr W2 .. 114 C4
Leitch Ho 8 NW8 .. 11 C1
Leithcote Path SW16 ... 74 B1
Leith Ho
7 Kentish Town N7 ... 13 C3
18 Streatham SW2 .. 74 B4
Leith Mans W9 ... 88 A3
Leith Yd 3 NW6 ... 23 C4
Lelitia Cl E8 ... 24 C4
Leman St E1 ... 111 B1
Lemmon Rd SE10 ... 53 A4
Le Moal Ho 28 E1 .. 32 B4
Lemsford Ct N4 ... 6 B2
Lena Gardens Prim Sch W6 ... 39 B3
Lena Gdns W6 ... 39 B3
Lendal Terr 7 SW4 ... 61 C4
Len Freeman Pl SW6 ... 154 C3
Lenham 11 NW5 ... 12 C2
Lenham Ho SE1 .. 137 C3
Lennon Rd NW2 ... 9 B2
Lennox Gdns
Knightsbridge SW1 ... 130 C1
Willesden NW10 ... 8 B4
Lennox Gdns Mews SW1 ... 144 C4
Lennox Ho 10 E9 ... 17 B2
Lennox Rd N4, N7 ... 5 C2
Lenthall Ho SW1 . 147 A1
Lenthall Rd E8 ... 16 C1
Lenthorp Rd SE10 .. 43 B2
Lenton Rise TW9 ... 54 A4
Len Williams Ct NW6 ... 23 C3
Leonard Ct
Bloomsbury WC1 ... 94 A2
Kensington W8 ... 127 B2
Leonard Day Ho 3 NW5 ... 13 A2
Leonard Pl 6 N16 .. 16 A4
Leonard St EC2 ... 97 C2
Leonora Ho W9 ... 88 C2
Leontine Cl SE15 ... 49 C3
Leopards Ct EC1 .. 107 B4
Leopold Bldgs 14 E2 ... 24 B2 98 C4
Leopold Mews E9 .. 25 B4
Leopold Prim Sch NW10 ... 8 B1
Leopold Rd NW10 ... 8 A1
Leopold St E3 ... 33 B4
Leopold Wlk SE11 148 C1
Leo St SE15 ... 50 A3
Leo Yd EC1 ... 96 B1
Leppoc Rd SW4 ... 61 C2
Leroy St SE1 ... 152 A4
Lerry Cl W14 ... 155 A4
Lerwick Ho SW18 ... 59 B3
Lesley Ct SW1 ... 133 B1
Leslie Prince Ct 8 SE5 ... 48 C3
Leslie Rd E11 ... 19 C4
Lessar Ave SW4 ... 61 B1
Lessar Ct SW4 ... 61 B1
Lester Ct 42 E3 ... 27 A2
Leswin Pl N16 ... 7 B1
Leswin Rd N16 ... 7 B1
Letchford Gdns NW10 ... 21 C2
Letchford Mews NW10 ... 21 C2
Letchmore Ho 7 W10 ... 22 B1
Lethaby Ho 15 SW4 ... 62 B3
Lethbridge Cl SE13 ... 52 B1
Letterstone Rd SW6 ... 154 C1
Lettice St SW6 ... 165 A3
Lett Rd E15 ... 19 C1
Lettsom St SE5 ... 49 A1
Levana Cl SW19 ... 70 A3
Levant Ho 17 E1 ... 25 C1
Levehurst Way SW4, SW9 ... 172 B2
Leven Rd E14 ... 34 C3
Lever Ct 15 E9 ... 17 C2
Leverett St SW3 .. 144 B4
Leverington Pl N1 . 97 C3
Lever St EC1 ... 96 C3
Leverstock Ho SW3 ... 144 B2
Leverton Pl NW5 ... 13 B3
Leverton St NW5 ... 13 B3
Levison Way 2 N19 ... 4 C3
Levita Ho NW1 ... 93 C4
Levyne Ct EC1 ... 95 B2
Lewesdon Cl 13 SW19 ... 69 C3
Lewes Ho
Bermondsey SE1 .. 138 B4
Peckham SE15 ... 49 C4
Leweston Pl N16 ... 7 B4
Lewey Ho E3 ... 26 B1
Lewin Rd SW14 ... 55 C4
Lewis Ct 5 SE16 ... 40 A1
Lewis Gr SE13 ... 67 B4
LEWISHAM ... 67 B3
Lewisham Bridge Prim Sch 3 SE13 ... 67 A4
Lewisham Bsns Ctr SE14 ... 50 C4
Lewisham Coll (Deptford Campus) 12 SE8 ... 51 C2
Lewisham Coll (Lewisham Way Campus) SE4 ... 51 C1
Lewisham High St SE13 ... 67 A2
Lewisham Hill SE13 ... 52 B1
Lewisham Hospl SE13 ... 67 A2
Lewisham Pk SE13 . 67 B1
Lewisham Rd SE13 . 52 B1
Lewisham Sh Ctr SE13 ... 67 B4
Lewisham St SW1 133 C3
Lewisham Sta SE13 ... 67 B4
Lewisham Way SE4, SE14 ... 51 B2
Lewis Pl E8 ... 16 C3
Lewis Silkin Ho 9 SE15 ... 50 B4
Lewis St NW1 ... 13 A2
Lexden Rd W3 ... 28 A1
Lexfield Ho N5 ... 15 B4
Lexham Gardens Mews W8 ... 128 B1
Lexham Gdns W8 142 A4
Lexham Mews W8 ... 141 C4
Lexham Wlk W8 .. 128 B1
Lexington St W1 .. 119 A4
Lexton Gdns SW12 .. 73 C3
Leyborne Pk TW9 ... 44 C2
Leybourne Ho 20 SE15 ... 50 B4
Leybourne Rd 17 NW1 ... 13 A1
Leybourne St 5 NW1 ... 13 A1
Leyden Mans 7 N19 ... 5 A4
Leyden St E1 ... 110 C3
Leydon Cl
Rotherhithe SE16 ... 32 C1
SE16 ... 32 C1
Ley Ho SE1 ... 136 C3
Leyland Ho 6 E14 .. 34 A2
Leylands SW18 ... 58 B1
Leylang Rd SE14 ... 50 C3
Leys Ct 9 SW9 ... 173 B1
Leysdown 9 NW5 .. 12 C2
Leysdown Ho SE17 ... 152 B2
Leysfield Rd W12 ... 38 C4
Leythe Rd W3 ... 37 B4
LEYTON ... 19 C4
Leyton Mill Ret Pk E10 ... 19 B4
Leyton Mills E10 ... 19 B4
Leyton Rd E15 ... 19 C2
Liardet St SE14 ... 51 A4
Liberia Rd N5 ... 15 A2
Liberty Mews SW12 ... 61 A1
Liberty St SW9 ... 173 A4
Libra Rd 7 E3 ... 26 B3
Library Mans 4 W12 ... 39 B4
Library Par NW10 .. 21 A4
Library Pl E1 ... 32 A2
Library St SE1 ... 136 B3
Lichfield Ct TW9 ... 54 A3
Lichfield Gdns TW10, TW9 ... 54 A2
Lichfield Ho 27 SE5 ... 48 B1
Lichfield Rd
Mile End E3 ... 26 A2
Richmond TW9 ... 44 B2
West Hampstead NW2 ... 10 A4
Lichfield Terr 1 TW9 ... 54 A2
Lickey Ho W14 ... 155 A4
Lidcote Gdns 22 SW9 ... 173 A1
Liddell Gdns NW10 ... 22 B3
Liddell Rd NW6 ... 10 C2
Lidfield Rd N16 ... 15 C4
Lidgate Rd 22 SE15 ... 49 B3

Lidiard Rd SW18 71 B2
Lidlington Pl NW1 83 A1
Lido The W2 116 A1
Lidyard Rd N19 4 B3
Liffey Ct NW10 8 C1
Liffords Pl SW13 46 B1
Lifford St SW15 57 C3
Lighter Cl 16 SE16 41 A2
Lighterman Mews 15 E1 32 C3
Lighterman's Rd E14 42 A4
Lighterman's Wlk SW18 58 C3
Light Horse Ct SW1 145 B1
Ligonier St E2 24 B1 98 C2
Lilac Ho SE4 66 B4
Lilac Pl SE11 148 C3
Lilac St W12 29 C2
Lilestone Est NW8 89 C1
Lilestone Ho NW8 89 C2
Lilestone St NW8 90 A2
Lilford Ho 21 SE5 48 B1
Lilford Rd SE5 48 A1
Lilian Baylis Ho N1 15 B2
Lilian Baylis Tech Sch SE11 149 A1
Lilley Cl E1 125 C1
Lillian Ave W3 36 C4
Lillian Cl 14 N16 7 A1
Lillian Rd SW13 47 A4
Lillie Ho N5 14 C3
Lillie Rd SW6 154 C3
Lillie Road Mans SW6 154 B3
Lillieshall Rd SW4 61 B4
Lillie Yd SW6 155 B4
Lillingston Ho N7 14 C4
Lily Cl W14 39 C2
Lily Pl EC1 107 C4
Lilyville Rd SW6 164 C4
Limborough Ho 5 E14 33 C4
Limburg Rd SW11 60 A3
Limeburner La EC4 108 A2
Lime Cl E1 125 C2
Lime Ct SW15 57 A4
Lime Gr W12 39 B4
Limeharbour E14 42 A4
Lime Ho 7 TW9 45 A2
LIMEHOUSE 33 A2
Limehouse Cswy E14 33 B2
Limehouse Ct 5 E14 33 C3
Lime House Ct 23 E14 33 B3
Limehouse Cut 4 E14 34 A4
Limehouse Fields Est 14 E14 33 A4
Limehouse Link (Tunnel) E14 33 B2
Limehouse Sta E14 33 A3
Limekiln Wharf 21 E14 33 B2
Limerick Cl SW12 73 B4
Limerick Ct 1 SW12 73 B4
Limerston St SW10 157 A3
Lime St Pas EC3 124 A4
Limes Ave
  Barnes SW13 46 B1
  Golders Green NW11 1 A4
Limes Ct NW6 9 C1
Limes Field Rd SW14 56 A4
Limesford Rd SE15 65 C3
Limes Gdns SW18 58 C1
Limes Gr SE13 67 B3
Lime St EC3 110 A1
Limes The
  Camberwell SE5 64 A4
  Kensington W2 31 C2 113 C3
Limes Wlk SE15 65 B3
Limetree Cl SW2 74 B3
Lime Tree Ct 14 E3 33 C4
Limpsfield Ave SW19 69 C2
Limscott Ho 35 E3 27 A2
Linacre Cl SE15 65 A4
Linacre Ct W6 39 C1
Linacre Rd NW2 9 A2
Linale Ho N1 87 B1
Linberry Wlk 3 SE8 41 B2
Lincoln Ave SW19 69 C1
Lincoln Ct N16 6 C4
Lincoln Ho
  Bloomsbury WC1 107 A3
  9 Dartmouth Pk NW5 4 B1
  2 Islington N1 15 B1
  Knightsbridge SW1 130 C3
Lincoln Mews NW6 23 B4
Lincoln's Inn WC2 107 A2
Lincoln's Inn Fields WC2 107 A2
Lincoln St SW3 144 C3
Lindale SW19 70 A2
Lindal Rd SE4 66 B2
Linden Ave NW10 22 C3
Linden Ct
  8 Battersea SW18 59 C3
  1 Shepherd's Bush W12 30 B1
Linden Gdns
  Chiswick W4 37 C1
  Notting Hill W2 31 C2 113 C3
Linden Gr SE15 65 B4
Linden Ho 10 SE8 51 B4
Linden Lodge Sch SW19 70 A3
Linden Mans N6 4 A3
Linden Mews
  Kensington W2 31 C2 113 C3
  Stoke Newington N1 15 C3
Lindens The W4 45 B2
Lindfield Gdns NW3 11 B3
Lindfield Hts NW3 11 B3
Lindfield St E14 33 C3
Lindisfarne Way E9 18 A4
Lindley Ho
  13 Peckham SE15 49 C3
  9 Stepney E1 32 B4
Lindley Pl TW9 44 C2
Lindley St E1 32 B4
Lindop Ho 8 E1 26 A1
Lindore Rd SW11 60 B3
Lindo St SE15 50 B1
Lindrop St SW6 166 C2
Lindsay Ct SW11 167 C3
Lindsay Sq SW1 147 C2
Lindsell St 6 SE10 52 B2
Lindsey Ho SW10 157 C2
Lindsey Mews 18 N1 15 B1
Lindsey St EC1 108 B4
Lind St SE8 52 A1
Linfield WC1 94 C3
Linford Christie Stadium The W12 30 A4
Linford Ho 17 E2 24 C4
Linford St SW8 170 C3
Linford Street Bsns Est SW8 170 C4
Lingard Ho 11 E14 42 B3
Lingards Rd SE13 67 B3
Lingfield Ho
  5 Acton Green W4 37 B1
  Lambeth SE1 136 B3
Lingham St SW9 172 C1
Ling Rd E16 35 C4
Ling's Coppice SE21 75 C2
Lingwell Rd SW17 72 A1
Lingwood Rd E5 7 C4
Linhope St NW1 90 C1
Linkenholt Mans 3 W6 38 B2
Link St E9 17 B3
Links Yd
  10 Spitalfields E1 111 B4
  Spitalfields E1 111 A4
Link The W3 28 A3
Linkway N4 6 B4
Linkwood Wlk NW1 13 C1
Linnell Ho
  Spitalfields E1 110 C4
  St John's Wood NW8 78 C4
Linnell Rd SE5 49 A1
Linnet Mews SW12 72 C4
Linom Rd SW4 62 A3
Linscott Rd E5 17 B4
Linsey St
  Bermondsey SE16 153 B4
  Bermondsey SE16 139 C1
Linslade Ho
  10 Hackney E2 24 C4
  Marylebone NW8 90 B2
Linstead St 1 NW6 10 C1
Linstead Way SW18, SW19 70 A4
Lintaine Cl W6 154 B3
Linthorpe Rd N16 7 A4
Linton Ho
  Lower Holloway N7 14 B4
  2 Tower Hamlets E3 33 C4
Linton St N1 87 A3
Linver Rd SW6 165 B2
Linwood Cl SE5 49 B1
Lion Cl SE4 66 C1
Lionel Ho 5 W10 31 A4
Lionel Mans 14 W14 39 C3
Lionel Mews 13 W10 31 A4
Lionel Road N TW8 36 A2
Lionel Road Prim Sch TW8 36 A2
Lionel Road S TW8 36 B1
Lion Gate Gdns TW9 54 B4
Lion Gate Mews SW18 70 C4
Lion House Sch SW15 57 C3
Lion Mills 36 E2 24 C3
Lion Yd SW4 61 C3
Lipton Rd 9 E1 32 C3
Lisburne Rd NW3 12 B4
Lisford St SE15 49 B2
Lisgar Terr W14 140 C4
Liskeard Gdns SE3 53 C2
Liskeard Ho SE11 149 C2
Lisle Ct NW2 1 A1
Lisle St WC2 119 C4
Lismore Cir NW5 12 C3
Lismore Wlk 4 N1 15 B2
Lissenden Gdns NW5 12 C4
Lissenden Mans NW5 12 C4
Lisson Cotts NW1 102 B4
Lisson Gr NW1, NW8 90 A2
LISSON GROVE 90 B1
Lisson Ho NW1 102 A4
Lisson St NW1 102 A4
Lister Cl W3 28 C4
Lister Ct N16 7 A2
Lister Ho
  Greenwich SE3 53 A4
  Marylebone W1 104 A2
  Spitalfields E1 111 C4
Lister Hospl SW1 146 A1
Lister Mews N7 14 B4
Liston Rd SW4 61 B4
Listowel Cl 2 SW9 163 C2
Listria Lo N16 7 B2
Listria Pk N16 7 B2
Litcham Ho 28 E1 25 C2
Litchfield Gdns NW10 8 C2
Litchfield St WC2 119 C4
Lithos Rd NW3 11 B2
Little Albany St NW1 92 B2
Little Argyll St W1 104 C1
Little Boltons The SW10 142 B1
Little Britain EC1 108 C3
Littlebury Rd SW4 61 C4
Little Chelsea Ho SW10 157 A3
Little Chester St SW1 132 A2
Little Cloisters SW1 134 A2
Little College St SW1 134 A2
Little Combe Cl 13 SW15 57 C1
Littlecote Cl SW19 70 A4
Little Cottage Pl SE10 52 A3
Little Deans Yd SW1 134 A2
Little Dimocks SW12 73 A2
Little Dorrit Ct SE1 137 A4
Little Edward St NW1 92 B4
Little Essex St WC2 121 B4
Littlefield Cl N19 13 B4
Little George St SW1 134 A3
Little Green St NW5 13 A4
Little Marlborough St W1 104 C1
Little Newport St WC2 119 C4
Little New St EC4 107 C2
Little Portland St W1 104 C2
Little Russell St WC1 106 A3
Little St James's St SW1 118 C1
Little St Leonards SW14 55 B4
Little Sanctuary SW1 134 A3
Little Smith St SW1 133 C2
Little Somerset St E1 110 C1
Little Titchfield St W1 104 C3
Littleton St SW18 71 B2
Little Trinity La EC4 123 A4
Little Turnstile WC1 106 C3
LITTLE VENICE 101 A4
Little Venice W9 100 C4
Littlewood SE13 67 B1
Livermere Ct 3 E8 24 B4
Livermere Rd E8 24 B4
Liverpool Gr SE17 151 B1
Liverpool Ho N7 14 C2
Liverpool Rd
  Islington N1 85 C3
  Islington N1, N7 14 C1
  Newham E16 35 A4
Liverpool St EC2 110 A3
Liverpool Street Sta EC2 110 A3
Livesey Pl SE15 49 C4
Livingstone Ho 16 SE5 48 B3
Livingstone Lo 13 W9 31 C4
Livingstone Pl E14 42 B1
Livingstone Rd
  13 Battersea SW11 59 C4
  Mill Meads E15 27 B4
Livity Sch The SW2 62 A2
Livonia St W1 105 A1

Lizard St EC1 97 A3
Llandovery Ho 1 E14 42 B4
Llanelly Rd NW2 1 B2
Llanvanor Rd NW2 1 B2
Llewellyn Ho 10 N19 4 B1
Llewellyn St SE16 139 C3
L'Ile aux Enfants NW5 12 C3
Lloyd Baker St WC1 95 B3
Lloyd Ct
  Ladywell SE13 67 A2
  6 West Norwood SE27 75 A1
Lloyd Ho N16 6 C1
Lloyd's Ave EC3 110 B1
Lloyd's Bldg EC3 110 A1
Lloyd's Pl SE3 53 A1
Lloyd Sq WC1 95 B4
Lloyd's Row EC1 96 A3
Lloyd St WC1 95 B4
Lloyd Villas SE4 51 C1
Lloyd Williamson Sch 17 W10 31 A4
Loampit Hill SE13 52 A1
Loampit Vale SE13 67 B4
Loanda Cl 17 E8 24 B4
Loats Rd SW2 62 A1
Locarno Rd 6 W3 28 B1
Lochaline St W6 47 B4
Lochbie 9 N4 5 A4
Lochinvar St SW12 73 A4
Lochmore Ho SW1 145 C3
Lochnagar St E14 34 B4
Lockbridge Ct 3 W9 31 C4
Locke Ho
  Nine Elms SW8 170 C4
  Stamford Hill N16 7 B3
Lockesfield Pl E14 42 A1
Lockgate Cl E9 18 B3
Lockhart Cl N7 14 B2
Lockhart St E3 26 B1
Lockhurst St E5 17 C4
Lockington Rd SW8 170 B4
Lockmead Rd SE13 67 B4
Lock Mews 9 NW1 13 C2
Lockside 17 E14 33 A2
Locksley St E14 33 B4
Lock View Ct 9 E14 33 A2
Lockwood Ho 10 SE11 163 B3
Lockwood Sq SE16 40 A3
Lockyer Est SE1 137 C3
Lockyer Ho
  7 Greenwich SE10 43 B1
  10 Putney SW15 57 C4
  South Lambeth SW8 162 A2
Lockyer St SE1 137 C3
Locton Gn 4 E3 26 B4
Loddiges Ho 5 E9 17 B1
Loddiges Rd E9 17 B1
Loddon Ho NW8 89 C1
Loder St SE15 50 B3
Lodge Ave SW14 56 A4
Lodge Rd NW8 90 A3
Lodge The 9 W4 38 A3
Lodore St E14 34 B3
Lodsworth Ho SW11 169 B3
Loftie St SE16 139 C3
Lofting Ho 8 N1 14 C1
Lofting Rd N1 14 C1
Lofts on the Park 24 E9 17 C2
Loftus Rd W12 30 A1
Loftus Rd (Queens Park Rangers FC) W12 30 A1
Logan Mews W8 141 B4
Logan Pl W8 141 B4
Loggetts SE21 76 A2
Lohmann Ho 5 SE11 163 B4
Lolesworth Cl E1 111 A3
Lollard St SE11 149 B3
Lollards Twr SE1 134 C1
Loman St SE1 136 B4
Lomas Dr 10 E8 16 B1
Lomas St E1 111 C4
Lombard Ct
  14 Acton W3 28 A1
  City of London EC3 123 C4
Lombard La EC4 107 C1
Lombard Rd SW11 167 B2
Lombard St EC3 109 C1
Lombardy Pl W2 114 B3
Lomley Ho 10 SW2 62 C1
Lomond Gr SE5 48 C3
Lomond Ho 10 SE5 48 C2
Loncroft Rd SE5 49 A4
Londesborough Ho 1 N16 16 A4
Londesborough Rd N16 16 A4
London Acad for Higher Education The E15 27 C4
London Acad of Computing & Electronics SW17 72 B1
London Bridge EC4, SE1 123 C3
London Bridge City Pier
  SE1 124 A2
  SE1 124 A2
London Bridge Experience The SE1 123 C2
London Bridge Hospl SE1 123 C2
London Bridge St SE1 123 C1
London Bridge Sta SE1 123 C1
London Bridge Wlk SE1 123 C2
London Britannia Coll N1 97 B4
London Business Sch NW1 90 C2
London Canal Mus N1 84 B2
London Central Mosque NW8 90 B3
London Chest Hospl E2 25 B3
London Christian Sch SE16 40 B3
London City Sh Ctr EC1 97 A1
London Clinic (Hospl) NW1 91 C1
London Coll of Advanced Studies SE1 123 B1
London Coll of Beauty Therapy W1 105 A1
London Coll of Bsns & Computer Studies 12 SW4 61 C3
London Coll of Communication (Sch of Printing & Publishing) SE11 136 B1
London Coll of Economics & Science NW10 20 B1
London Coll of Fashion (Curtain Rd) EC2 24 A1 98 B2
London Coll of Fashion (Golden La) EC1 96 C1
London Coll of Fashion (John Prince's St) W1 104 A1
London Coll of Fashion (Lime Grove) 18 W6 39 B4
London Coll of Fashion (Mare St) E8 17 B1
London Coll of International Business Studies WC1 106 B3
London Ct 3 SW18 58 C2
London Cty Hall SE1 134 C4
London Dungeon The SE1 123 C2
London Electronics Coll SW5 142 A2
London Eye (Millennium Wheel) SE1 134 C4
London Fields East Side E8 17 A1
London Fields Prim Sch 15 E8 25 A4
London Fields Sta E8 17 A1
London Fields West Side E8 16 C1
London Film Mus SE1 134 C4
London Fire Brigade Mus SE1 136 C4
London Glassblowing Workshop SE1 138 A3
London Ho 13 W6 38 C2
London Ho TW9 54 B4
London Ho NW8 80 B2
London Hospital Dental Inst 5 E1 32 A4
London Independent Hospl The E1 32 C4
London International Film Sch WC2 106 A1
London Irish Rifles Mus SW9 48 B2
London La E8 17 A1
London Meridian Coll 2 N7 5 B1
London Metrocity Coll 21 E3 26 C2
London Metropolitan Univ
  Islington N7 14 C3
  Whitechapel E1 110 C1
London Metropolitan Univ (Central Ho) 44 E1 111 B2
London Metropolitan Univ (Commercial Rd) 42 E1 111 C2
London Metropolitan Univ (Ladbrook Ho) 5 N5 15 A3
London Metropolitan Univ (Moorgate) EC2 109 C3
London Metropolitan Univ (Tower Hill) EC3 124 C4
London Metropolitian Univ (Spring Ho) 1 N7 14 C2
London Mews W2 101 C2
London Nautical Sch SE1 121 C2
London Oratory Sch The SW6 155 C2
London Oratory The SW7 130 A1
London Rd SE1 136 B2
London Sch of Economics & Political Science WC2 107 A1
London South Bank Univ SE1 136 B2
London St
  City of London EC3 124 B4
  Paddington W2 101 B1
London Stile 5 W4 36 C1
London Stock Exchange EC2 108 C2
London Terr 1 E2 24 C3
London Transport Mus WC2 120 B4
London Trocadero W1 119 B3
London Wall EC2 109 C3
London Wall Bldgs EC2 109 C3
London Wetland Ctr SW13 47 A3
London Wharf 4 E2 25 A4
London Zoo NW1 81 B2
Long Acre WC2 106 B1
Longbeach Rd SW11 60 B4
Longberrys NW2 1 B1
Longbridge Way SE13 67 B2
Longcliffe Ho SW18 59 A2
Long Dr W3 29 A3
Longfellow Way SE1 153 A3
Longfield Dr SW14 55 A2
Longfield Est SE1 153 A3
Longfield St SW18 70 C4
Longford Ct
  1 Bedford Pk W12 38 A4
  2 Clapton Pk E5 17 C4
Longford Ho 7 E1 32 B3
Longford St NW1 92 B2
Longford Wlk 9 SW2 74 C4
Longhope Cl SE15 49 B4
Longhurst Ho 8 W9 23 B2
Long La
  Bermondsey SE1 137 C3
  Holborn EC1 108 B4
Longland Ct
  Bermondsey SE1 153 B2
  Hackney E9 18 A3
Longlands Ct W11 31 B2 113 A4
Longleat Ho SW1 147 B2
Longleigh Ho 8 SE5 49 A2
Longlents Ho 3 NW10 20 C4
Longley Ho 5 N19 13 B4
Longley St SE1 153 B4
Longman Ho
  9 Globe Town E2 25 C3
  10 Shoreditch E8 24 B4
Long Meadow 20 N7 13 C3
Longmoor Point 14 SW15 69 A3
Longmore St SW1 146 C3
Longnor Rd E1 25 C2
Long Pond Rd SE3 53 A2
Long Rd SW4 61 B3
Longridge Ho SE1 137 A1
Longridge Rd SW5 141 C3
Longs Ct 2 TW9 54 B3
Long's Ct W1 119 C3
Longshore SE8 41 B2
Long St E2 24 B2 98 C4
Longstaff Cres SW18 70 C4
Longstaff Rd SW18 58 C1
Longstone Ave NW10 21 B4
Longthorne Ho 18 E3 26 B2
Longthorpe Ct 9 W6 38 C2
Longville Rd SE11 150 B4
Long Wlk SE1 138 B2
Longwood Dr SW15 56 C1
Long Yd WC1 94 C1
Lonsdale Ho
  Fulham SW6 58 C4
  6 Stoke Newington N4 6 B4
Lonsdale Mews
  Notting Hill W11 31 B3
  4 Richmond TW9 44 C2
Lonsdale Pl N1 14 C1
Lonsdale Rd
  Barnes SW13 46 B3
  Chiswick W4 38 B2
  Kilburn NW6 23 B4
  Notting Hill W11 31 B3

Lonsdale Sq
Islington N1 ... 14 C1
Islington N1 ... 85 C4
Lopez Ho 4 SW9 ... 62 A4
Loraine Rd
Chiswick W4 ... 45 A4
Islington N7 ... 14 B4
Lord David Pitt Ho 7 SE24 ... 62 C3
Lorden Wlk 13 E2 ... 24 C2 99 B3
Lord Hills Rd W2 . 100 B4
Lord Holland La 5 SW9 ... 173 C2
Lord Napier Pl W6 .. 38 C1
Lord North St SW1 ... 134 A1
Lord Roberts Mews SW6 ... 156 A1
Lords Cl SE21 ... 75 B2
Lord's Cricket Mus NW8 ... 89 C3
Lordship Gr N16 ... 6 C2
Lordship Ho 3 N16 . 6 C2
Lordship La SE22 ... 64 B1
Lordship Park Mews N16 ... 6 B2
Lordship Pk N16 ... 6 C2
Lordship Pl SW3 .. 158 A3
Lordship Rd N16 ... 6 C2
Lordship Terr N16 ... 6 C2
Lord's Indoor Cricket Sch NW8 ... 90 A4
Lord's (MCC & Middlesex Cty Cricket Ground) NW8 ... 89 C4
Lord's View NW8 .. 89 C3
Loreburn Ho 2 N7 ... 14 B4
Lorenzo St N1, WC1 ... 94 C4
Loris Rd W6 ... 39 B3
Lorn Ct SW9 ... 173 B2
Lorne Cl NW8 ... 90 B3
Lorne Ct SW15 ... 57 C1
Lorne Gdns 5 W11 ... 39 C4
Lorne Ho
Hornsey N4 ... 5 B4
7 Tower Hamlets E1 ... 33 A4
Lorne Rd
Finsbury Pk N4 ... 5 B3
3 Richmond TW10 .. 54 B2
Lorn Rd SW9 ... 173 B2
Lorraine Ct 10 NW1 ... 13 A1
Lorrimore Rd SE17 ... 48 A4
Lorrimore Sq SE17 . 48 A4
Lorton Ho 9 NW6 .. 23 C4
Lostock Ho 10 SW8 ... 171 B2
Lothair Rd S N4 ... 6 A4
Lothbury EC2 ... 109 B2
Lothian Rd SW9 ... 48 A2
Lothrop St W10 ... 23 A2
Lots Rd SW10 ... 157 A1
Loudoun Rd NW8 .. 79 A3
Loughborough Ct 7 SW9 ... 63 A4
Loughborough Junction Sta SW9 ... 63 A4
Loughborough Pk SW9 ... 63 A3
Loughborough Prim Sch SW9 ... 48 A1
Loughborough Rd SE5, SW9 ... 48 A1
Loughborough St SE11 ... 149 A1
Lough Rd N7 ... 14 B2
Louisa Cl E9 ... 25 C4
Louisa Gdns E1 ... 25 C1
Louisa Ho SW15 ... 56 B3
Louisa St E1 ... 25 C1
Louise Bennett Cl 9 SE24 ... 63 A3
Louise De Marillac Ho 26 E1 ... 32 B4
Louise White Ho 1 N19 ... 4 C3
Louisville Rd SW17 ... 72 C1
Louvaine Rd SW11 .. 59 C3
Lovat La EC3 ... 124 A3
Lovatt Ct SW12 ... 73 A3
Loveday Ho 2 SW2 ... 74 C3
Lovegrove St SE1 ... 49 C4
Lovegrove Wlk E14 ... 34 B1
Love La EC2 ... 109 A2
Lovelace Ho 12 E8 .. 24 B4
Lovelace Rd SE21 ... 75 B3
Lovelinch Cl SE15 ... 50 B4
Lovell Ho E8 ... 24 C4
Lovell Pl SE16 ... 41 A3
Loveridge Mews NW6 ... 10 B2
Loveridge Rd NW6 .. 10 B2
Lover's Wlk W1 .. 117 B1
Lovette Ho 4 E3 ... 26 C2
Lovetts Pl SW18 ... 59 A3
Love Wlk SE5 ... 48 C1
Low Cross Wood La SE21 ... 76 B1
Lowden Rd SE24 ... 63 B3
Lowder Ho 6 E1 ... 32 A1
Lowe Ave E16 ... 35 C4
Lowell Ho 10 SE5 ... 48 B3
Lowell St E14 ... 33 A3
Lower Addison Gdns W14 ... 126 A3
Lower Belgrave St SW1 ... 132 A1
LOWER CLAPTON .. 17 B4
Lower Clapton Rd E5 ... 17 B4
Lower Clarendon Wlk 9 W11 ... 31 A3
Lower Comm S SW15 ... 57 A4
Lower Grosvenor Pl SW1 ... 132 B2
Lower Grove Rd TW10 ... 54 B2
LOWER HOLLOWAY ... 14 A3
Lower James St W1 ... 119 A4
Lower John St W1 ... 119 A4
Lower Lea Crossing E14, E16 ... 35 A2
Lower Mall W6 ... 39 A1
Lower Marsh SE1 . 135 B3
Lower Merton Rise NW3 ... 12 A1
Lower Mortlake Rd TW9 ... 54 B4
Lower Pk
Acton W3 ... 20 B1
5 Putney SW15 ... 57 C2
LOWER PLACE ... 20 B3
Lower Place Bsns Ctr NW10 ... 20 B3
Lower Rd SE16 ... 40 B4
Lower Richmond Rd
Mortlake SW14, TW9 ... 55 A4
Putney SW15 ... 57 B4
Lower Robert St WC2 ... 120 B3
Lower Sloane St SW1 ... 145 B2
Lower Terr NW3 ... 2 B1
Lower Thames St EC3 ... 124 A3
Lowerwood Ct W11 ... 31 A3
Loweswater Ho E3 . 26 B1
Lowfield Rd
Dagenham W3 ... 28 B3
Hampstead NW6 ... 10 C1
Lowlands NW3 ... 12 A2
Lowman Rd N7 ... 14 B4
Lowndes Cl SW1 . 131 C1
Lowndes Ct
Knightsbridge SW1 ... 131 A2
Marylebone W1 ... 104 C1
Lowndes Lo SW1 . 131 A2
Lowndes Pl SW1 . 131 B1
Lowndes Sq SW1 . 131 A3
Lowndes St SW1 . 131 B2
Lowood Ho 12 E1 .. 32 B2
Lowood St E1 ... 32 A2
Lowry Ct 3 SE16 .. 40 A1
Lowther Ho
Pimlico SW1 ... 147 A1
11 Shoreditch E8 ... 24 B4
Lowther Prim Sch SW13 ... 46 C4
Lowther Rd
Barnes SW13 ... 46 B2
Islington N7 ... 14 C3
Lowth Rd SE5 ... 48 B1
Loxford Ho SW1 .. 145 C3
Loxham St WC1 ... 94 B3
Loxley Rd SW18 ... 71 C3
LTC Coll London W1 ... 104 C2
Lubavitch Boys Prim Sch 6 E5 ... 7 B4
Lubavitch Girls Prim Sch 8 N16 ... 7 B4
Lubavitch House Sch (Jun Boys) 9 E5 ... 7 B4
Lubbock Ho 21 E14 ... 34 A2
Lubbock St SE14 ... 50 B3
Lucan Ho N1 ... 87 C3
Lucan Pl SW3 ... 144 B3
Lucas Ct SW11 ... 169 C3
Lucas Ho
2 Clapham SW8 .. 171 A2
Walham Green SW10 ... 156 B2
Lucas St SE4, SE8 ... 51 C2
Lucas Vale Prim Sch 10 SE8 ... 51 C2
Lucerne Mews W8 ... 31 C1 113 C2
Lucerne Rd N5 ... 15 A4
Lucey Rd SE16 ... 139 B1
Lucey Way SE16 .. 153 C4
Lucien Rd SW18 ... 71 A2
Lucraft Ho 12 SW2 . 74 A4
Lucy Ashe Ho SE17 ... 150 B3
Lucy Brown Ho SE1 ... 123 A1
Lucy Cres W3 ... 20 B1
Ludgate Broadway EC4 ... 108 B1
Ludgate Cir EC4 .. 108 A1
Ludgate Hill EC4 . 108 B1
Ludgate Ho EC4 .. 108 A1
Ludgate Sq EC4 .. 108 B1
Ludham NW5 ... 12 B3
Ludlow Ct W3 ... 37 B4
Ludlow St EC1 ... 96 C2
Ludovick Wlk SW15 ... 56 A3
Ludwell Ho W14 .. 126 B2
Ludwick Mews SE14 ... 51 A3
Lugard Ho 2 W12 .. 30 A1
Lugard Rd SE15 ... 50 A2
Luke Ho 32 E1 ... 32 A3
Luke St EC2 .. 24 A1 98 A2
Lukin St E1 ... 32 B3
Lullingstone Ho 21 SE15 ... 50 B4
Lullingstone La SE13 ... 67 C1
Lulot Gdns N19 ... 4 A2
Lulworth
Camden Town NW1 ... 13 C1
Walworth SE17 ... 151 B2
Lulworth Ho SW8 162 C1
Lulworth Rd SE15 .. 50 A1
Lumiere Ct 7 SW17 ... 72 C2
Lumina Bldg 1 E14 ... 34 B1
Lumley Ct WC2 ... 120 B3
Lumley Flats SW1 145 B2
Lumley St W1 ... 103 C1
Lumsdon NW8 ... 78 B3
Lunan Ho 14 E3 ... 26 B3
Lund Point E15 ... 27 B4
Luntley Pl E1 ... 111 B3
Lupin Cl SW2 ... 75 A2
Lupino Ct SE11 ... 149 A4
Lupin Point SE1 .. 139 A3
Lupton St NW5 ... 13 B4
Lupus St SW1 ... 147 A1
Luralda Gdns E14 .. 42 C1
Lurgan Ave W6 ... 47 C4
Lurline Gdns SW11 ... 169 C4
Luscombe Ho SW18 ... 58 B2
Luscombe Way SW8 ... 162 A2
Lusher Ho SW15 ... 57 C1
Lushington Rd NW10 ... 22 A3
Lushington Terr 11 E8 ... 16 C3
Luton Pl SE10 ... 52 B3
Luton St NW8 ... 89 C1
Luttrell Ave SW15 .. 57 A2
Lutyens Ho SW1 .. 146 C1
Luxborough Ho W1 ... 103 B4
Luxborough St W1 ... 103 B4
Luxborough Twr W1 ... 103 B4
Luxemburg Gdns W6 ... 39 C2
Luxford St SE16 ... 40 C2
Luxmore St SE4 ... 51 B2
Luxor St SE5 ... 63 B4
Lyall Mews SW1 .. 131 B1
Lyall Mews W SW1 ... 131 B1
Lyall St SW1 ... 131 B1
Lyal Rd E3 ... 26 A3
Lycett Ho 10 SW2 .. 74 A4
Lycett Pl 3 W12 ... 38 C4
Lycott Gr SE22 ... 64 B2
Lydden Gr SW18 ... 71 A4
Lydden Rd SW18 ... 71 A4
Lydford NW1 ... 83 A3
Lydford Cl 22 N16 .. 16 A3
Lydford Rd
Brondesbury NW2 ... 9 C2
Paddington W9 ... 23 B1
Lydgate Ho 8 N16 ... 16 A3
Lydhurst Ave SW2 .. 74 B2
Lydney Cl
Camberwell SE15 ... 49 A3
Putney SW19 ... 70 A2
Lydon Rd SW4 ... 61 B4
Lydwell Ho 29 SW8 ... 171 B1
Lyford Rd SW18 ... 72 A3
Lygoe Ho 18 N6 ... 4 C4
Lygon Ho 2 E2 ... 24 C2 99 B4
Lygon Pl SW1 ... 132 A1
Lyham Cl SW2 ... 62 A1
Lyham Rd SW2 ... 62 A1
Lyle Pk SW15 ... 57 C1
Lyly Ho SE1 ... 137 C1
Lyme Gr E9 ... 17 B1
Lyme Grove Ho 2 E9 ... 17 B1
Lyme St NW1 ... 82 C4
Lyminge Gdns SW17, SW18 ... 72 A3
Lymington Mans NW6 ... 11 A2
Lymington Rd NW6 ... 11 A2
Lympstone Gdns SE15 ... 49 C3
Lynbrook Gr SE15 .. 49 A3
Lynch Wlk 2 SE8 .. 51 B4
Lyncott Cres SW4 .. 61 A3
Lyncourt SE3 ... 52 C1
Lyncroft Gdns NW6 ... 10 C3
Lyncroft Mans 4 NW6 ... 10 C3
Lyndale NW2 ... 1 B1
Lyndale Ave NW2 ... 1 B1
Lyndale Cl SE3 ... 53 B4
Lynde Ho 2 SW4 ... 61 C4
Lynden Gate SW15 . 69 A4
Lyndhurst Gdns NW3 ... 11 C3
Lyndhurst Gr SE5, SE15 ... 49 B1
Lyndhurst Ho 2 SW15 ... 68 C4
Lyndhurst House Prep Sch NW3 ... 11 C3

Lyndhurst Lo 3 E14 ... 42 C2
Lyndhurst Rd NW3 ... 11 C3
Lyndhurst Sch SE5 ... 48 C1
Lyndhurst Sq SE15 ... 49 B2
Lyndhurst Terr NW3 ... 11 C3
Lyndhurst Way SE15 ... 49 B1
Lyneham Wlk E5 ... 18 A3
Lynette Ave SW4 ... 61 B1
Lynford French Ho SE17 ... 150 C2
Lyngham Ct 10 N4 ... 5 A4
Lynhurst Ct NW8 ... 79 B3
Lyn Mews 12 E3 ... 26 B2
Lynmouth Rd N16 ... 7 B3
Lynne Ct NW6 ... 11 A1
Lynnett Ct E9 ... 18 A2
Lynn Ho SE15 ... 49 C4
Lynn Rd SW12 ... 73 A4
Lynton Cl NW10 ... 8 B3
Lynton Ct 9 W3 ... 28 B3
Lynton Est SE1 ... 153 B3
Lynton Ho 16 W2 ... 100 B1
Lynton Lo N5 ... 15 A3
Lynton Mans SE1 ... 135 B2
Lynton Rd
  Acton W3 ... 28 A2
  Bermondsey SE1 ... 153 A3
  Paddington NW6 ... 23 B3
Lynton Terr 4 W3 ... 28 B3
Lynx Terr SW19 ... 70 C1
Lyon Ho NW8 ... 90 A1
Lyons Pl NW8 ... 89 B1
Lyon St N1 ... 14 B1
Lyons Wlk W14 ... 140 A4
Lyric Rd SW13 ... 46 B2
Lysander Gr N19 ... 4 C3
Lysander Ho 10 E2 ... 25 A3
Lysander Mews N19 ... 4 B3
Lysia Ct SW6 ... 47 C3
Lysias Rd SW12 ... 61 A1
Lysia St SW6 ... 47 C3
Lysons Wlk SW15 ... 56 C2
Lytham St SE17 ... 151 B1
Lyttelton Cl NW3 ... 12 A1
Lytten Ct 6 W12 ... 38 C4
Lyttleton Ho 10 E9 ... 17 B1
Lytton Ct WC1 ... 106 B3
Lytton Gr SW15 ... 58 A1

M

Mabel Thornton Ho 12 N16 ... 15 C4
Mabledon Pl NW1, WC1 ... 93 C3
Mablethorpe Rd SW6 ... 154 A1
Mabley St E9 ... 18 A3
MacArthur Ho 4 SW2 ... 74 A4
Macartney Ho SE10 ... 52 C3
Macaulay CE Prim Sch SW4 ... 61 A3
Macaulay Ct SW4 ... 61 A4
Macaulay Ho
  2 Kensal Town W10 ... 31 A4
Macaulay Ho *continued*
  10 Stoke Newington N16 ... 7 A1
Macaulay Rd SW4 ... 61 A4
Macaulay Sq SW4 ... 61 A3
McAuley Cl SE1 ... 135 B2
Macauley Mews SE13 ... 52 B1
McAusland Ho 5 E3 ... 26 B3
Macbeth Ho 4 N1 ... 24 A3
Macbeth St W6 ... 39 A1
McBride Ho 6 E3 ... 26 B3
McCall Cl SW4 ... 172 A2
McCall Ho N7 ... 14 A4
Mccarthy Ct SW11 ... 168 B3
Macclesfield Rd EC1 ... 96 C4
Macclesfield St W1 ... 119 C4
McCoid Way SE1 ... 136 C3
Mcconnell Ho SW8 ... 171 B3
McCormick Ho 9 SW2 ... 74 C3
McCrone Mews 3 NW3 ... 11 C2
McCullum Rd E3 ... 26 B4
McDermott Cl SW11 ... 60 A4
McDermott Rd SE15 ... 64 C4
Macdonald Ho 2 SW11 ... 169 B2
Macdonald Rd N19 ... 4 B2
McDougall Ct TW9 ... 44 C1
Mcdougall Ho E2 ... 24 C2 99 B3
McDowall Cl E16 ... 35 B4
McDowall Rd SE5 ... 48 B2
Macduff Rd SW11 ... 169 C4
Mace Cl E1 ... 32 A1
Mace St E2 ... 25 C3
McEwan Way E15 ... 27 C4
Macey Ho
  Battersea SW11 ... 168 A3
  10 Greenwich SE10 ... 52 B4
Macfarlane Rd W12 ... 30 B1
Macfarren Ho 7 W10 ... 23 A2
MacFarren Pl NW1 ... 91 C1
McGlashon Ho 15 E1 ... 24 C1 99 B1
McGregor Ct 8 N1 ... 24 A2 98 B4
MacGregor Ho 2 SW12 ... 73 C3
McGregor Rd W11 ... 31 B4
Machell Rd SE15 ... 65 B4
McIndoe Ct N1 ... 87 B4
McIntosh Ho 14 SE16 ... 40 B2
McIntyre Ct 19 SW4 ... 172 B2
Mackay Ho 33 W12 ... 30 A2
Mackay Rd SW4 ... 61 A4
McKenna Ho 3 E3 ... 26 B3
Mackennal St NW8 ... 80 B2
Mackenzie Cl 7 W12 ... 30 A2
Mackenzie Rd N7 ... 14 B2
Mackenzie Wlk E14 ... 33 C1
McKerrell Rd SE15 ... 49 C2
Mackeson Rd NW3 ... 12 B4
Mackie Ho 18 SW2 ... 74 C4
Mackie Rd SW2 ... 74 C4
McKiernan Ct 2 SW11 ... 168 A2
McKinnon Wood Ho 16 E2 ... 24 C2 99 B3
Mackintosh La E9 ... 17 C3
Macklin St WC2 ... 106 B2
Mackonochie Ho EC1 ... 107 B4
Mackrow Wlk 11 E14 ... 34 B2
Macks Rd SE16 ... 153 C4
Mackworth Ho NW1 ... 92 C4
Mackworth St NW1 ... 92 C4
Mac Laren Mews SW15 ... 57 B3
Maclean Rd SE23 ... 66 A1
Mcleod Ct SE21 ... 76 C3
McLeod's Mews SW7 ... 142 B4
Macleod St SE17 ... 151 A1
Maclise Rd W14 ... 126 A1
McManus Ho 2 SW11 ... 59 C4
Mcmillan Ho SE4 ... 66 A4
Macmillan Ho
  Cricklewood NW4 ... 9 A4
  Lisson Gr NW8 ... 90 B3
McMillan St SE8 ... 51 C4
Mcmorran Ho 4 N7 ... 14 A4
Macnamara Ho SW10 ... 157 B2
Mcneil Rd SE5 ... 49 A1
McNicol Dr NW10 ... 20 B3
Maconochies Rd 9 E14 ... 42 A1
Macquarie Way E14 ... 42 A2
Macready Ho W1 ... 102 B3
Macready Pl 2 N7 ... 14 A4
Macroom Ho W9 ... 23 B2
Macroom Rd W9 ... 23 B2
Mac's Pl EC4 ... 107 C2
Madame Tussaud's NW1 ... 91 B1
Madani Girls Sch 36 E1 ... 32 A3
Maddams St E3 ... 27 A1
Maddocks Ho 3 E1 ... 32 A2
Maddock Way SE17 ... 48 A4
Maddox St W1 ... 118 B4
Madinah Rd
  7 Dalston E8 ... 16 C2
  London E8 ... 16 C3
Madison Ho E3 ... 27 B2
Madras Pl N7 ... 14 C2
Madrid Rd SW13 ... 46 C3
Madron St SE17 ... 152 B2
Mafeking Ave TW8 ... 44 A4
Magdala Ave N19 ... 4 B2
Magdalene Cl 7 SE15 ... 50 A1
Magdalene Ho 7 SW15 ... 57 C1
Magdalen Pas E1 ... 125 A4
Magdalen Rd SW18 ... 71 C3
Magdalen St SE1 ... 124 A1
Magee St SE11 ... 163 B4
Magellan Ho 16 E1 ... 25 C1
Magellan Pl 25 E14 ... 41 C2
Magnin Cl 5 E8 ... 24 C4
Magnolia Ct
  Richmond TW9 ... 45 A2
  Wandsworth SW11 ... 60 B1
Magnolia Ho 13 SE8 ... 51 B4
Magnolia Pl SW4 ... 62 A2
Magnolia Rd W4 ... 45 A4
Magnolia Wharf W4 ... 45 A4
Magpie Ho 7 E3 ... 26 B4
Magpie Pl SE14 ... 51 A4
Magri Wlk 22 E1 ... 32 B4
Maguire St SE1 ... 139 A4
Mahatma Gandhi Ind Est 1 SE24 ... 63 A3
Mahogany Cl SE16 ... 33 A1
Mahoney Ho SE14 ... 51 B2
Maida Ave W2 ... 89 A1
MAIDA VALE ... 88 A4
Maida Vale W9 ... 88 C3
Maida Vale Sta W9 ... 88 B4
Maiden La
  Borough The SE1 ... 123 A2
  Camden Town NW1 ... 13 C1
  Strand WC2 ... 120 B4
Maidenstone Hill SE10 ... 52 B2
Maidstone Bldgs SE1 ... 123 B1
Maidstone Ho 4 E14 ... 34 A3
Mail Coach Yd 23 E2 ... 24 A2 98 B4
Main Yd E9 ... 18 C2
Maismore St SE15 ... 49 C4
Maitland Cl 3 SE10 ... 52 A3
Maitland Ct W2 ... 115 B4
Maitland Ho
  Chelsea SW1 ... 160 C4
  16 South Hackney E2 ... 25 B3
MAITLAND PARK ... 12 B2
Maitland Park Rd NW3 ... 12 B2
Maitland Park Villas NW3 ... 12 B2
Maitland Pl E5 ... 17 B4
Majestic Ct N4 ... 6 A3
Major Cl SW9 ... 63 A4
Majorie Mews 6 E1 ... 32 C3
Major Rd E15 ... 19 C3
Makepeace Ave N6 ... 3 C2
Makepeace Mans N6 ... 3 C2
Makins St SW3 ... 144 B3
Malabar Ct 20 W12 ... 30 A2
Malabar St E14 ... 41 C4
Malam Ct SE11 ... 149 B3
Malam Gdns 3 E14 ... 34 A2
Malay Ho 2 E1 ... 32 B1
Malbrook Rd SW15 ... 57 A3
Malcolm Ho 13 N1 ... 24 A3
Malcolm Pl E2 ... 25 B1
Malcolm Rd E1 ... 25 B1
Malcolmson Ho SW1 ... 147 C1
Malden Cres NW1 ... 12 C2
Malden Pl NW5 ... 12 C3
Malden Rd NW5 ... 12 C2
Maldon Cl
  Camberwell SE5 ... 64 A4
  Shoreditch N1 ... 87 A4
  Stratford New Town E15 ... 19 C3
Maldon Rd W3 ... 28 B2
Malet Pl WC1 ... 93 B1
Malet St WC1 ... 105 C4
Maley Ave SE27 ... 75 A2
Malfort Rd SE5 ... 64 A4
Malins Ct SW12 ... 60 C1
Mallams Mews 1 SW9 ... 63 A4
Mallard Cl
  1 Hackney E9 ... 18 B2
  Kilburn NW6 ... 23 C4
Mallard Ho
  8 Camberwell SE15 ... 49 B2
  St John's Wood NW8 ... 80 A1
Mallard Point 6 E3 ... 26 C2
Mallet Ho 11 SW15 ... 56 C2
Mallet Rd SE13 ... 67 C1
Mall Galleries SW1 ... 119 C2
Malling SE13 ... 67 A2
Mallinson Rd SW11 ... 60 B2
Mallinson Sp Ctr N6 ... 3 B4
Mallon Gdns E1 ... 111 A3
Mallord St SW3 ... 157 C4
Mallory Bldgs EC1 ... 96 A1
Mallory Cl SE4 ... 66 A3
Mallory St NW8 ... 90 B2
Mallow Ct SE13 ... 52 B1
Mallow St EC1 ... 97 B2
Mall Rd W6 ... 39 A1
Mall Studios 9 NW3 ... 12 B3
Mall The
  Mortlake SW14 ... 55 B2
  St James SW1 ... 119 B1
Malmesbury 30 E2 ... 25 B3
Malmesbury Prim Sch 25 E3 ... 26 B2
Malmesbury Rd
  Bow E3 ... 26 B3
  Newham E16 ... 35 A4
Malmesbury Terr E16 ... 35 B4
Malmsey Ho SE11 ... 149 A2
Malmsmead Ho E9 ... 18 A3
Malorees Jun & Inf Schs NW6 ... 9 C1
Malpas Rd
  Hackney E8 ... 17 A2
  New Cross SE4 ... 51 B1
Malta St EC1 ... 96 B2
Maltby St SE1 ... 138 C2
Malthouse Dr W4 ... 46 B4

Malthouse Pas SW13 ... 46 A1
Malting Ho E14 ... 33 B2
Maltings W4 ... 36 C1
Maltings Cl SW13 ... 46 A1
Maltings Lo W4 ... 46 A3
Maltings Pl
Bermondsey SE1 ... 138 B4
Parsons Green SW6 ... 166 B3
Malt Mill SE1 ... 124 C1
Malton Mews 1 W10 ... 31 A3
Malton Rd W10 ... 31 A3
Maltravers St WC2 ... 121 B4
Malt St SE1 ... 49 C4
Malva Cl SW18 ... 59 A2
Malvern Cl W10 ... 31 B4
Malvern Ct
15 Shepherd's Bush W12 ... 38 C4
South Kensington SW7 ... 143 C4
Malvern Gdns NW2 ... 1 A2
Malvern Ho
London N16 ... 7 B3
SE17 ... 151 A1
Malvern Mews NW6 ... 23 C2
Malvern Pl NW6 ... 23 B2
Malvern Rd
Dalston E8 ... 16 C1
Maida Vale NW6 ... 23 C2
Upper Holloway N19 ... 4 C3
Malvern Terr N1 ... 85 B4
Malwood Rd SW12 ... 61 A1
Malyons Rd SE13 ... 67 A2
Malyons Terr SE13 ... 67 A2
Managers St 8 E14 ... 34 B1
Manaton Cl SE15 ... 65 A4
Manbre Rd W6 ... 47 B4
Manchester Dr W10 ... 23 A1
Manchester Gr E14 ... 42 B1
Manchester Ho SE17 ... 151 A2
Manchester Mans N19 ... 4 C4
Manchester Mews W1 ... 103 B3
Manchester Rd E14 ... 42 B3
Manchester Sq W1 ... 103 C2
Manchester St W1 ... 103 B3
Manchuria Rd SW11 ... 60 C1
Manciple St SE1 ... 137 C2
Mandalay Ho 6 N16 ... 15 C4
Mandalay Rd SW4 ... 61 B2
Mandarin Ct 6 SE8 ... 51 C4
Mandela Cl 36 W12 ... 30 A2
Mandela Ho 18 E2 ... 24 B2 98 C4
Mandela Rd E16 ... 35 C3
Mandela St
Camden Town NW1 ... 83 A4
Kennington SW9 ... 163 B1
Mandela Way SE1 ... 152 B4
Manderville Ho SE1 ... 153 A2
Mandeville Cl 5 SE3 ... 53 B3
Mandeville Ct NW3 ... 11 A3
Mandeville Ctyd SW11 ... 169 B3
Mandeville Ho 8 SW4 ... 61 B2
Mandeville Pl W1 ... 103 C2
Mandrake Rd SW17 ... 72 B1
Mandrell Rd SW2 ... 62 A2
Manette St W1 ... 105 C1
Manfred Ct 7 SW15 ... 58 B2
Manfred Rd SW15 ... 58 B2
Manger Rd N7 ... 14 A2
Manilla St E14 ... 41 C4
Manitoba Ct 29 SE16 ... 40 B4
Manley Ct N16 ... 7 B1
Manley Ho SE11 ... 149 B2
Manley St NW1 ... 81 B4
Manneby Prior N1 ... 85 A1
Mannering Ho 16 SW2 ... 62 B2
Manningford Cl EC1 ... 96 A4
Manning Ho 3 W11 ... 31 A3
Manning Pl TW10 ... 54 B1
Manningtree Cl SW19 ... 70 A3
Manningtree St 2 E1 ... 111 B2
Manny Shinwell Ho SW6 ... 155 A3
Manor Ave SE4 ... 51 B1
Manor Circus TW9 ... 54 C4
Manor Ct
7 Brixton SW2 ... 62 B2
Camberwell SE15 ... 49 B2
Gunnersbury W3 ... 36 C2
Parsons Green SW6 ... 166 B3
Streatham SW16 ... 74 A1
Manorfield Cl 3 N19 ... 13 B4
Manorfield Prim Sch 8 E14 ... 34 A4
Manor Gdns
8 Chiswick W4 ... 38 A1
Clapham SW4 ... 171 A1
Gunnersbury W3 ... 36 C2
Richmond TW10, TW9 ... 54 B3
Upper Holloway N7 ... 5 A1
Manor Gr
Deptford SE15 ... 50 B4
Richmond TW9 ... 54 C4
Manor Gt SW15 ... 58 A2
Manor Ho NW1 ... 102 B4
Manor House Ct W9 ... 88 C1
Manor House Dr NW6 ... 9 C1
Manor House Sta N4 ... 6 A3
Manor Lo NW2 ... 9 C2
Manor Mans
7 Hampstead NW3 ... 12 A2
Tufnell Pk N7 ... 5 A1
Manor Mews
New Cross SE4 ... 51 B1
Paddington NW6 ... 23 C3
Manor Oak Mans SE22 ... 65 A1
Manor Par N16 ... 7 B2
Manor Park Par SE13 ... 67 C3
Manor Park Rd NW10 ... 21 B4
Manor Pk TW9 ... 54 B3
Manor Pl SE17 ... 150 C2
Manor Rd
Richmond TW10, TW9 ... 54 B3
Stamford Hill N16 ... 7 A3
Manor Specl Sch NW10 ... 22 B4
Manor Street Est SW3 ... 158 B4
Manor The W1 ... 118 A3
Manor Way W3 ... 36 C2
Manresa Rd SW3 ... 144 A1
Mansel Ct SW11 ... 168 B3
Mansell Ho SW8 ... 171 A4
Mansell Rd W3 ... 37 C4
Mansell St E1 ... 111 A1
Manse Rd N16 ... 7 B1
Mansfield Ct 27 E2 ... 24 B4
Mansfield Ho SW15 ... 57 C1
Mansfield Mews W1 ... 104 A3
Mansfield Pl 28 NW3 ... 11 B4
Mansfield Rd
Acton W3 ... 20 A1
Maitland Pk NW3 ... 12 B4
Mansfield St W1 ... 104 A3
Mansford St E2 ... 24 C3
Mansion Cl SW9 ... 173 C4
Mansion Gdns NW3 ... 2 A1
Mansion Ho EC4 ... 109 B1
Mansion House Pl EC3, EC4 ... 109 B1
Mansion House St EC2 ... 109 B1
Mansion House Sta EC4 ... 123 A4
Mansions The NW6 ... 10 B3
Manson Mews SW7 ... 143 B3
Manson Pl SW7 ... 143 B3
Manston NW1 ... 13 B1
Manstone Rd NW2 ... 10 A3
Manston Ho W14 ... 126 B1
Mantell Ho SW4 ... 61 B2
Mantle Rd SE4 ... 66 A4
Manton Ho N16 ... 6 C1
Mantua St 22 SW11 ... 59 C4
Mantus Cl E1 ... 25 B1
Mantus Rd E1 ... 25 B1
Manville Gdns SW17 ... 73 A1
Manville Rd SW17 ... 73 A1
Manwood Rd SE4 ... 66 B1
Many Gates SW12 ... 73 A2
Mapesbury Ct NW2 ... 10 A3
Mapesbury Rd NW2 ... 10 A2
Mapeshill Pl NW2 ... 9 B2
Mapes Ho 7 NW6 ... 10 A1
Mape St E2 ... 25 A1
Maple Ave W3 ... 29 A1
Maple Cl SW4 ... 61 C1
Maple Ct 3 NW2 ... 9 C4
Mapledene Est E8 ... 16 C1
Mapledene Rd E8 ... 16 C1
Maple Ho
11 Maitland Pk NW3 ... 12 B2
5 New Cross SE8 ... 51 B3
4 Richmond TW9 ... 45 A2
Maple Leaf Sq 27 SE16 ... 40 C4
Maple Lo SW15 ... 58 A1
Maple Mews NW6 ... 78 A2
Maple Pl W1 ... 93 A1
Maples Pl E1 ... 32 A4
Maple St
5 Bethnal Green E2 ... 25 A3
Fitzrovia W1 ... 93 A1
Maplestead Rd SW2 ... 74 B4
Mapleton Cres SW18 ... 59 A1
Mapleton Rd SW18 ... 59 A1
Maple Wlk W10 ... 22 C1
Maplin St E3 ... 26 B2
Marada Ho NW6 ... 10 A1
Marais W4 ... 45 B3
Marban Rd W9 ... 23 B2
Marble Arch W1 ... 117 A4
Marble Arch Sta W1 ... 103 A1
Marble Cl W3 ... 28 A1
Marbleford Ct 4 N6 ... 4 C4
Marble Ho W9 ... 23 B1
Marcella Rd SW9 ... 173 B1
Marchant Ho 13 SW2 ... 62 B2
Marchant St SE14 ... 51 A4
Marchbank Rd W14 ... 155 A4
March Ct SW15 ... 57 A3
Marchmont Rd TW10 ... 54 B2
Marchmont St WC1 ... 94 A2
Marchwood Cl 9 SE5 ... 49 A3
Marcia Rd SE1 ... 152 B3
Marcilly Rd SW18 ... 59 C2
Marcol Ho W1 ... 104 B2
Marcon Ct 23 E8 ... 17 A3
Marcon Pl E8 ... 17 A3
Marco Rd W6 ... 39 B3
Marcus Ct TW8 ... 44 A3
Marcus Garvey Mews SE22 ... 65 A2
Marcus Garvey Way 8 SE24 ... 62 C3
Marcus Ho 14 SE15 ... 49 B2
Marcus St SW18 ... 59 A1
Marcus Terr SW18 ... 59 A1
Marden Ho 6 E8 ... 17 A3
Marden Sq SE16 ... 40 A3
Mardyke Ho SE17 ... 151 C4
Maresfield Gdns NW3 ... 11 B2
Mare St E8 ... 17 A1
Margaret Bondfield Ho
5 Bow E3 ... 26 A3
Margaret Bondfield Ho *continued*
22 Kentish Town N7 ... 13 C3
Margaret Ct W1 ... 104 C2
Margaret Herbison Ho SW6 ... 155 A3
Margaret Ho 16 W6 ... 39 B1
Margaret Ingram Cl SW6 ... 154 C3
Margaret Mcmillan Ho 10 N19 ... 4 C4
Margaret Rd N16 ... 7 B3
Margaret Rutherford Pl 3 SW12 ... 73 B3
Margaret St W1 ... 104 C2
Margaretta Terr SW3 ... 158 B4
Margaret White Ho NW1 ... 93 B4
Margate Rd SW2 ... 62 A2
Margery Fry Ct N7 ... 5 A1
Margery St WC1 ... 95 B3
Margravine Gdns
Hammersmith W6 ... 39 C1
West Kensington W14 ... 140 A2
Margravine Rd W6 ... 154 A4
Marham Gdns SW17, SW18 ... 72 A3
Maria Cl 13 SE1 ... 153 C4
Maria Fidelis Convent Sch (Lower) NW1 ... 93 A3
Maria Fidelis Convent Sch (Upper) NW1 ... 93 B4
Marian Ct E9 ... 17 B3
Marian Pl E2 ... 25 A3
Marian Sq E2 ... 25 A3
Marian St 2 E2 ... 25 A3
Marian Way NW10 ... 8 B1
Maria Terr E1 ... 25 C1
Maribor 13 SE10 ... 52 B3
Marie Curie SE5 ... 49 A2
Marie Lloyd Ct 13 SW9 ... 62 B3
Marie Lloyd Gdns 1 N19 ... 5 A4
Marie Lloyd Ho N1 ... 87 B1
Marie Stopes Ct 3 N19 ... 5 A4
Marigold St SE16 ... 40 A4
Marina Ct 12 E3 ... 26 C2
Marina Point 4 E14 ... 42 A3
Marinefield Rd SW6 ... 166 B2
Marinel Ho 23 SE5 ... 48 B3
Mariners Mews E14 ... 42 C2
Marine St SE16 ... 139 B2
Marine Twr 29 SE8 ... 51 B4
Marion Richardson Prim Sch 17 E1 ... 32 C3
Marischal Rd SE13 ... 67 C4
Maritime Greenwich Coll 18 SE8 ... 51 C3
Maritime Ho 5 SW4 ... 61 B4
Maritime Quay 5 E14 ... 41 C1
Maritime St E3 ... 26 B1

Marius Mans [3] SW17 72 C2
Marius Rd SW17 72 C2
Marjorie Gr SW11 60 B3
Market Ct W1 104 C2
Market La W12 39 B4
Market Mews W1 118 A1
Market Pl
[3] Acton W3 28 B1
[1] Bermondsey SE16 40 A2
Marylebone W1 104 C2
Market Rd
Barnsbury N7 14 A2
Richmond TW9 54 C4
Market Sq E14 34 A3
Market St E1 110 C4
Market Studios [14] W12 39 B4
Market Way E14 34 A3
Market Yd Mews SE1 138 A2
Markham Pl SW3 144 C2
Markham Sq SW3 144 C2
Markham St SW3 144 B2
Mark Ho [3] E2 25 C3
Mark La EC3 124 B4
Markland Ho W10 30 C2
Mark Mans W12 38 C4
Marksbury Ave TW9 54 C4
Mark Sq EC2 24 A1 98 A2
Mark St EC2 24 A1 98 A2
Markstone Ho SE1 136 A3
Markyate Ho [6] W10 22 B1
Marland Ho SW1 131 A2
Marlborough
[11] Putney SW19 69 C3
St John's Wood W9 88 C4
Marlborough Ave [3] E8 24 C4
Marlborough Cl SE17 150 B3
Marlborough Cres W4 38 A3
Marlborough Ct
Kensington W8 141 B4
Marylebone W1 104 C1
Marlborough Flats SW3 144 B4
Marlborough Gr SE1 153 B1
Marlborough Hill NW8 79 A3
Marlborough Ho
Marylebone NW1 92 B2
Richmond TW10 54 C2
Stoke Newington N4 6 B3
Marlborough Ho SW1 119 A1
Marlborough Ho SW19 69 C1
Marlborough Lo
[36] Stepney E1 25 B1
St John's Wood NW8 78 C1
Marlborough Mans [5] NW6 10 C3
Marlborough Mews [18] SW2 62 B3
Marlborough Pl NW8 79 A2
Marlborough Prim Sch SW3 144 B3
Marlborough Rd
Acton Green W4 37 B1
Richmond TW10 54 B1
St James SW1 119 A1
Upper Holloway N19 5 A2
Marlborough St SW3 144 B3
Marlborough Trad Est TW9 45 A2
Marlborough Yd N19 4 C2
Marlbury NW8 78 B3
Marley Ho [14] W11 30 C2
Marley Wlk NW2 9 B3
Marlin Ho SW15 58 A2
Marloes Rd W8 128 A1
Marlow Ct NW6 9 C1
Marlowe Bsns Ctr [2] SE14 51 A3
Marlowe Ct SW3 144 B3
Marlowe Ho [15] N16 16 A4
Marlowes The NW8 79 B4
Marlow Ho
Bermondsey SE1 138 C2
[15] Kensington W2 100 B1
[44] Spitalfields E2 24 B2 98 C3
Marlow Studio Workshops [43] E2 24 B2 98 C3
Marlow Way SE16 40 C4
Marl Rd SW18 59 B3
Marlston NW1 92 B3
Marlton St SE10 43 B1
Marmara Apts [4] E16 35 C2
Marmion Ho [13] SW12 73 A4
Marmion Mews [4] SW11 60 C4
Marmion Rd SW11 60 C3
Marmont Rd SE15 49 C3
Marmora Ho E1 33 A4
Marmora Rd SE22 65 B1
Marner Prim Sch [6] E3 27 A1
Marne St W10 23 A2
Marney Rd SW11 60 C3
Marnfield Cres SW2 74 B3
Marnham Ave NW2 10 A4
Marnock Ho SE17 151 B2
Marnock Rd SE4 66 B2
Maroon St E14 33 A4
Marquess Rd N1 15 C2
Marquis Ct N4 5 B3
Marquis Rd
Finsbury Pk N4 5 C3
Kentish Town NW1 13 C2
Marrick Cl SW15 56 C3
Marrick Ho [19] NW6 78 B3
Marriott Rd N4 5 B3
Marryat Ct [12] W6 39 A2
Marryat Ho SW1 146 C1
Marryat Sq SW6 164 A4
Marsala Rd SE13 67 A3
Marsalis Ho [3] E3 26 C2
Marsden Rd SE15 64 B4
Marsden St NW5 12 C2
Marshall Cl SW18 59 B1
Marshall Ct SW4 172 B3
Marshall Ho
Paddington NW6 23 B3
Shoreditch N1 87 C2
Walworth SE17 151 B2
Marshall Rd E10 19 A4
Marshall St L Ctr W1 105 A1
Marshall's Pl SE16 139 A1
Marshall St W1 105 A1
Marshalsea Rd SE1 137 A4
Marsham Ct
[19] Putney SW19 69 C3
Westminster SW1 147 C4
Marsham St SW1 147 C4
Marsh Ct E8 16 C2
Marshfield St E14 42 B3
Marsh Gate Bsns Ctr E15 27 B3
Marshgate Sch TW10 54 B2
Marsh Hill E9 18 A3
Marsh Ho
Nine Elms SW8 171 A4
Pimlico SW1 147 C1
Marsh St E14 42 A2
Marsh Wall E14 42 A4
Marshwood Ho [10] NW6 23 C4
Marsland Cl SE17 150 B1
Marsom Ho N1 87 B1
Marston SE17 151 A4
Marston Cl NW6 11 B1
Marston Ho [23] SW9 173 C1
Marsworth Ho [8] E2 24 C4
Martaban Rd N16 7 B2
Martello St E8 17 A1
Martello Terr E8 17 A1
Martell Rd SE21 75 C1
Martel Pl E8 16 B2
Martha's Bldgs EC1 97 B2
Martha St E1 32 B3
Martin Ct [15] E14 42 B4
Martindale SW14 55 B2
Martindale Ave [2] E16 35 C2
Martindale Ho [23] E14 34 A2
Martindale Rd SW12 73 A4
Martineau Ho SW1 146 C1
Martineau Mews N5 15 A4
Martineau Rd N5 15 A4
Martin Ho
Newington SE1 137 A1
South Lambeth SW8 162 A2
Martin La EC4 123 C4
Martlett Ct WC2 106 B1
Martlett Lo NW3 11 A4
Martley Ho SW8 171 A4
Martock Ct [10] SE15 50 A2
Marton Rd [2] N16 7 A1
Marvel Ho [5] SE5 48 C3
Marville Rd SW6 154 C1
Marvin St [3] E8 17 A2
Marwell Ct SE3 52 C1
Mary Adelaide Cl SW15 68 A1
Mary Adelaide Ho W2 101 C4
Mary Ann Bldgs SE8 51 C4
Mary Datchelor Cl SE5 48 C2
Mary Dine Ct SW8 163 A1
Mary Gn NW8 78 B4
Mary Ho
[8] Hammersmith W6 39 B1
[6] Stockwell SW9 172 C1
Mary James Ho [32] E2 24 C3
Mary Jones Ho [20] E14 33 C2
Maryland Rd
Paddington W9 23 C1
Stratford New Town E15 19 C3
Marylands Rd W9 88 A1
Maryland Wlk N1 86 C4
Mary Lawrenson Pl [1] SE3 53 C3
MARYLEBONE 104 B2
Marylebone Flyover NW1 102 A3
Marylebone High St W1 103 C4
Marylebone La W1 103 C2
Marylebone Mews W1 104 A3
Marylebone Pas W1 105 A2
Marylebone Rd NW1 103 A4
Marylebone St W1 103 C3
Marylebone Sta NW1 90 C1
Marylee Way SE11 149 A3
Mary McArthur Ho [12] N19 4 C4
Mary Macarthur Ho
[15] Globe Town E2 25 C2
W14 154 A4
Maryon Mews NW3 12 A4
Mary Pl W11 31 A2 112 A3
Mary's Ct NW8 90 B2
Mary Secole Cl [21] E8 24 B4
Mary Smith Ct SW5 141 C3
Mary St
[5] Canning Town E16 35 B4
Shoreditch N1 87 A3
Mary Terr NW1 82 C3
Mary Wharrie Ho [4] NW3 12 B1
Masbro' Rd W14 39 C3
Mascotte Rd [2] SW15 57 C3
Masefield Ct N5 15 C3
Masefield Ho [4] NW6 23 C2
Mashie Rd W3 29 A3
Maskall Cl SW2 74 C3
Maskell Rd SW17 71 B1
Maskelyne Cl SW11 168 B4
Mason Cl
Bermondsey SE16 153 C2
Newham E16 35 C2
Mason Ho
[15] Bermondsey SE1 153 C3
[16] Hackney E9 17 B1
Mason's Arms Mews W1 118 B4
Mason's Ave EC2 109 B2
Mason's Pl EC1 96 C4
Mason St SE17 151 C4
Mason's Yd
Finsbury EC1 96 B4
St James SW1 119 A2
Massie Rd E8 16 C2
Massinger St SE1, SE17 152 A3
Massingham St E1 25 C1
Mast Ct [17] SE16 41 A2
Masterman Ho [1] SE5 48 C3
Masters Dr SE16 40 A1
Masters Lo [24] E1 32 B3
Master's St [16] E1 32 C4
Mast House Terr E14 41 C2
Masthouse Terrace Pier SE8 41 C1
Mastin Ho SW18 70 C3
Mast L Ctr The SE16 40 C3
Mastmaker Rd E14 41 C4
Matara Mews SE17 150 C1
Matching Ct [14] E3 26 C2
Matham Gr SE22 64 B3
Matheson Lang Ho SE1 135 B3
Matheson Rd W14 140 C3
Mathews Yd WC2 106 A1
Mathieson Ct SE1 136 B3
Mathison Ho SW10 156 C2
Matilda Gdns [10] E3 26 C3
Matilda Ho E1 125 B2
Matilda St N1 85 A4
Matlock Cl SE24 63 B3
Matlock Ct
[7] Herne Hill SE5 63 C3
St John's Wood NW8 78 C2
Matlock St E14 33 A3
Maton Ho SW6 154 C2
Matson Ho
[9] Bermondsey SE16 40 A3
[16] Homerton E9 17 C2
Matthew Cl W10 22 C1
Matthew Parker St SW1 133 C3
Matthews Ct N5 15 B4
Matthews Ho [3] E14 33 C4
Matthews St SW11 168 C2
Matthias Ct [12] TW10 54 A1

Matthias Ho 2 N16 ... 16 A3
Matthias Rd N16 ... 16 A3
Mattingly Way 3 SE15 ... 49 B3
Maude Ho 3 E2 ... 24 C3
Maude Rd SE5 ... 49 A2
Maudlins Gn E1 ... 125 B2
Maudsley Ho TW8 ... 36 A1
Maudsley Hospl SE5 ... 48 C1
Maud St E16 ... 35 B4
Maud Wilkes Cl 10 NW5 ... 13 B3
Maugham Ct 5 W3 ... 37 B3
Mauleverer Rd SW2 ... 62 A2
Maundeby Wlk NW10 ... 8 A2
Maunsel St SW1 ... 147 B4
Maurer Ct 2 SE10 ... 43 B3
Mauretania Bldg 11 E1 ... 32 C2
Maurice Ct 4 E1 ... 26 A2
Maurice Ho 1 SW9 ... 172 C2
Maurice St W12 ... 30 A3
Mauritius Rd SE10 ... 43 A2
Maury Rd N16 ... 7 C1
Maverton Rd E3 ... 26 C4
Mavor Ho N1 ... 85 A3
Mawbey Ho SE1 ... 153 A1
Mawbey Pl SE1 ... 153 A1
Mawbey Rd SE1 ... 153 A1
Mawbey St SW8 ... 162 A1
Mawdley Ho SE1 ... 135 C3
Mawson Ct N1 ... 87 C3
Mawson Ho EC1 ... 107 B4
Mawson La W4 ... 46 B4
Maxden Ct SE15 ... 64 C4
Maxted Rd SE15 ... 64 B4
Maxwell Ct SE21 ... 76 C3
Maxwell Rd SW6 ... 156 B1
Maya Cl SE15 ... 50 A1
Mayall Rd SE24 ... 63 A2
Maybury Ct W1 ... 103 C3
Maybury Gdns NW10 ... 9 A2
Maybury Mews N6 ... 4 B4
Maydew Ho SE16 ... 40 B2
Maydwell Ho 6 E14 ... 33 C4
MAYFAIR ... 118 A3
Mayfair Pl W1 ... 118 B2
Mayfield Ave W4 ... 38 A2
Mayfield Cl
Clapham Pk SW4 ... 61 C2
Dalston E8 ... 16 B2
Mayfield Ho
31 Bethnal Green E2 ... 25 A3
Stamford Hill N16 ... 7 A4
Mayfield Mans SW15 ... 58 B2
Mayfield Rd
Acton W3 ... 28 A2
Bedford Pk W12 ... 38 A4
Dalston E8 ... 16 B1
Mayflower Cl SE16 ... 40 C2
Mayflower Prim Sch 22 E14 ... 34 A3
Mayflower Rd SW9 ... 62 A4
Mayflower St 1 SE16 ... 40 B4
Mayford NW1 ... 83 A2
Mayford Cl SW12 ... 72 B4
Mayford Rd SW12 ... 72 C4
Maygood Ho N1 ... 85 B2
Maygood St N1 ... 85 B2
Maygrove Rd NW6 ... 10 B2
Mayhew Ct 2 SE5 ... 63 C3
Maylands Ho SW3 ... 144 B3
Maylie Ho 4 SE16 ... 40 A4
Maynard Cl SW6 ... 156 B1
Maynard Ho E1 ... 26 A2
Maynards Quay E1 ... 32 B2
Mayne Ct E8 ... 16 C4
Mayo Ho 10 E1 ... 32 B4
Mayola Rd E5 ... 17 B4
Mayo Rd NW10 ... 8 A2
May's Buildings Mews SE10 ... 52 C3
Mays Ct WC2 ... 120 A3
May's Ct SE10 ... 52 C3
Maysoule Rd SW11 ... 59 C3
May St W14 ... 141 A1
Mayston Mews 3 SE10 ... 43 C1
Maythorne Cotts SE13 ... 67 C1
Mayton St N7 ... 5 B1
May Tree Ho SE4 ... 66 B4
Maytree Wlk SW2 ... 74 C2
Mayward Ho 7 SE5 ... 49 A2
Maze Hill SE10, SE3 ... 53 A4
Maze Hill Lodge 7 SE10 ... 52 C4
Maze Hill Sta SE10 ... 53 A4
Mazenod Ave NW6 ... 10 C1
Maze Rd TW9 ... 44 C3
Mead Cl 3 NW1 ... 12 C1
Meadcroft Rd SE17 ... 48 A4
Meade Cl W4 ... 44 C4
Meader Ct SE14 ... 50 C3
Mead Ho W11 ... 31 B1 112 C2
Mead Lo W4 ... 37 C4
Meadowbank NW3 ... 12 B1
Meadow Bank 8 SW15 ... 58 B2
Meadowbank Cl SW6 ... 47 B3
Meadow Cl E9 ... 18 B3
Meadowcroft 8 W4 ... 36 C1
Meadowgate Sch SE4 ... 66 A4
Meadow Mews SW8 ... 162 C3
Meadow Pl
Chiswick W4 ... 46 A3
South Lambeth SW8 ... 162 B2
Meadow Rd SW8 ... 162 C2
Meadow Row SE1 ... 136 C1
Mead Pl E9 ... 17 B2
Mead Row SE1 ... 135 B2
Meadway The SE3 ... 52 C1
Meakin Est SE1 ... 138 A2
Meakin Ho N7 ... 14 B3
Meard St W1 ... 105 B1
Meath Cres E1, E2 ... 25 C2
Meath Ho SE24 ... 63 A1
Meath St SW11 ... 170 A4
Mecklenburgh Pl WC1 ... 94 C2
Mecklenburgh Sq WC1 ... 94 C2
Mecklenburgh St WC1 ... 94 C2
Medburn St NW1 ... 83 B2
Medcroft Gdns SW14 ... 55 B3
Medfield St SW15 ... 69 A4
Medhurst Cl 19 E3 ... 26 A3
Median Rd E5 ... 17 B3
Medina Ct N7 ... 5 C1
Medina Gr N7 ... 5 C1
Medina Ho SE15 ... 65 B3
Medina Rd N7 ... 5 C1
Medlar St SE5 ... 48 B2
Medley Rd NW6 ... 10 C2
Medora Rd SW2 ... 74 B4
Medresco Ho NW3 ... 11 C3
Medusa Rd SE6, SE13 ... 67 A1
Medway Bldgs E3 ... 26 A3
Medway Ct WC1 ... 94 A3
Medway Ho
Bermondsey SE1 ... 137 C3
Paddington NW8 ... 102 A4
Stoke Newington N16 ... 15 C4
Medway Mews 35 E3 ... 26 A3
Medway Rd E3 ... 26 A3
Medway St SW1 ... 133 C1
Medwin St SW4 ... 62 B3
Meecham Ct 1 SW11 ... 168 A2
Meeson St E5 ... 18 A4
Meeting House Alley 7 E1 ... 32 A1
Meeting House La SE15 ... 50 A3
Mehetabel Rd E9 ... 17 B3
Melba Way SE13 ... 52 A2
Melbourne Ct
Hackney E5 ... 18 A4
Paddington W9 ... 89 A2
Melbourne Gr SE22 ... 64 B3
Melbourne Ho W8 ... 31 C1 113 B1
Melbourne Mews SW9 ... 173 B3
Melbourne Pl WC2 ... 107 A1
Melbourne Sq 21 SW9 ... 173 B3
Melbray Mews 11 SW6 ... 164 C1
Melbreak Ho 11 SE22 ... 64 A4
Melbury Ct W8 ... 127 A2
Melbury Dr SE5 ... 49 A3
Melbury Ho SW8 ... 162 C2
Melbury Rd W14 ... 127 A2
Melchester 5 W11 ... 31 B3
Melchester Ho 1 N19 ... 4 C1
Melcombe Ct NW1 ... 102 C4
Melcombe Ho SW8 ... 162 C1
Melcombe Pl NW1 ... 102 C4
Melcombe Prim Sch 6 W6 ... 47 C4
Melcombe St NW1 ... 91 A1
Meldon Cl SW6 ... 166 B4
Melford Ct
Bermondsey SE1 ... 138 B2
Dulwich SE22 ... 76 C4
Melford Rd SE21, SE22 ... 76 C3
Melgund Rd N5 ... 14 C3
Melina Ct
Putney SW15 ... 56 C4
St John's Wood NW8 ... 89 B3
Melina Pl NW8 ... 89 B3
Melina Rd W12 ... 39 A4
Melior Pl SE1 ... 138 A4
Melior St SE1 ... 138 A4
Melisa Ct N6 ... 4 C4
Mellington Ct 2 N16 ... 7 C1
Mellis Ave TW9 ... 45 A2
Mellish Ho 2 E1 ... 32 A3
Mellish St E14 ... 41 C3
Mellitus St W12 ... 29 B3
Mell St 6 SE10 ... 43 A1
Melody La N5 ... 15 B3
Melody Rd SW18 ... 59 B2
Melon Pl W8 ... 127 C4
Melon Rd SE15 ... 49 C2
Melrose Ave
Cricklewood NW2 ... 9 B3
Wimbledon SW19 ... 70 C1
Melrose Ct SW18 ... 58 B1
Melrose Gdns W6 ... 39 B3
Melrose Ho
Maida Vale NW6 ... 23 C2
Pimlico SW1 ... 146 B2
Melrose Rd
1 Barnes SW13 ... 46 B1
Wandsworth SW18 ... 58 B1
Melrose Terr W6 ... 39 B3
Melton Ct SW7 ... 143 C3
Melton Ho E5 ... 7 C2
Melton St NW1 ... 93 B3
Melville Court Flats 8 W12 ... 39 A4
Melville Ct
4 Brentford W4 ... 36 C1
Rotherhithe SE8 ... 41 A2
Melville Ho SE10 ... 52 B2
Melville Pl 4 N1 ... 15 B1
Melville Rd SW13 ... 46 C2
Melville Villas Rd W3 ... 28 C1
Melvin Ct 11 TW9 ... 44 C2
Melwood Ho 23 E1 ... 32 A3
Melyn Cl N7 ... 13 B4
Memel Ct EC1 ... 96 C1
Memel St EC1 ... 96 C1
Menai Pl 2 E3 ... 26 C3
Menard Ct EC1 ... 97 A3
Mendham Ho SE1 ... 138 A2
Mendip Ct
12 Battersea SW11 ... 59 B4
Deptford SE14 ... 50 B4
Mendip Dr NW2, NW11 ... 1 A2
Mendip Ho 2 N4 ... 6 C4
Mendip Hos 12 E2 ... 25 B2
Mendip Rd SW11 ... 59 B4
Mendora Rd SW6 ... 154 C2
Menelik Rd NW2 ... 10 B4
Menorah Prim Sch NW11 ... 1 A4
Menotti St 6 E2 ... 24 C1 99 C2
Menteath Ho 9 E14 ... 33 C3
Mentmore Terr E8 ... 17 A1
Mentone Ct SW8 ... 172 B4
Meon Rd W3 ... 37 B4
Mephan St SE1 ... 121 B1
Merbury Cl SE13 ... 67 C2
Mercator Pl 4 E14 ... 41 C1
Mercator Rd SE13 ... 67 C3
Merceron Ho 3 E2 ... 25 B2
Merceron St E1 ... 25 A1
Mercers Cl SE10 ... 43 B2
Mercer's Cotts 8 E3 ... 33 A3
Mercers Mews N7 ... 13 C4
Mercers Pl W6 ... 39 C2
Mercers Rd N19 ... 4 C1
Mercer St WC2 ... 106 A1
Merchant Ct E1 ... 32 B1
Merchants Ho SE10 ... 42 C1
Merchant Sq W2 ... 101 B3
Merchant St E3 ... 26 B2
Merchant Taylors' Hall EC3 ... 109 C1
Merchon Ho N7 ... 13 B4
Mercia Gr SE13 ... 67 B3
Mercia Ho 9 SE5 ... 48 B1
Mercie Ct SE22 ... 76 C3
Mercier Rd SW15 ... 58 A2
Mercury Ct
8 Brixton SW9 ... 173 B4
10 Millwall E14 ... 41 C2
Mercury Ho 6 E3 ... 26 C4
Mercury Way SE14 ... 50 C4
Mercy Terr SE13 ... 67 A2
Mere Cl SW15, SW19 ... 69 C4
Meredith Ave NW2 ... 9 B3
Meredith Ho 17 N16 ... 16 A3
Meredith Mews SE4 ... 66 B3
Meredith St EC1 ... 96 A3
Meredith Twr W3 ... 37 A3
Meredyth Rd SW13 ... 46 C1
Meretone Cl SE4 ... 66 A3
Mereton Mans 6 SE8 ... 51 C2
Mereworth Ho 3 SE15 ... 50 B4
Merganser Ct 17 SE8 ... 51 B4
Meridan Ct SE13 ... 67 C3
Meriden Ct SW3 ... 144 A1
Meriden Ho 25 N1 ... 24 A4
Meridian Courtyard SE10 ... 52 C3
Meridian Ho SE10 ... 43 A2
Meridian Pl E14 ... 42 B4
Meridian Prim Sch 9 SE10 ... 52 C4
Meridian Sq E15 ... 19 C1
Merivale Rd SW15 ... 58 A3
Merlin Ho
7 Chiswick W4 ... 37 C1
West Hampstead NW3 ... 11 A4

Merlin Sch The 11 SW15 ... 58 A2
Merlins Ct WC1 ... 95 B3
Merlin St EC1 ... 95 B3
Mermaid Ct
 Bermondsey SE1 .. 137 B4
 Rotherhithe SE16 ... 33 B1
Mermaid Ho 8 E14 ... 34 B2
Mermaid Twr 22 SE8 ... 51 B4
Meroe Ct N16 ... 7 A2
Merredene St SW2 ... 62 B1
Merriam Ave 2 E9 ... 18 B2
Merricks Ct 5 SW14 ... 55 A3
Merrick Sq SE1 ... 137 B2
Merrington Rd SW6 ... 155 C4
Merritt Rd SE4 ... 66 B2
Merrivale NW1 ... 83 A3
Merrow St SE17 .. 151 B1
Merrow Wlk SE17 151 C2
Merryfield SE3 ... 53 B1
Merryweather Ct 13 N19 ... 4 B1
Mersey Ho 10 N7 ... 14 C3
Merstone Ho SW18 ... 59 A1
Merthyr Terr SW13 ... 47 A4
Merton Ave W4 ... 38 B2
Merton Ho SW18 ... 70 C3
Merton La N6 ... 3 B2
Merton Rd SW18 ... 70 C4
Merton Rise NW3 ... 12 A1
Merton Road Ind Est SW18 ... 70 C4
Merttins Rd SE15 ... 65 C2
Meru Cl NW5 ... 12 C3
Mervan Rd SW2 ... 62 C3
Messaline Ave W3 .. 28 B3
Messina Ave NW6 .. 10 C1
Messiter Ho N1 ... 85 A3
Metcalfe Ho 28 SW8 ... 171 B2
Met Collection (Mus) SW6 ... 141 B1
Meteor St SW11 ... 60 C3
Methley Ho 8 N7 ... 5 B2
Methley St SE11 .. 149 C1
Methodist Central Hall SW1 ... 133 C3
Methwold Rd W10 .. 30 C4
Metropolis Apartments 5 SW12 ... 73 A3
Metropolitan Benefit Societies Almshouses 3 N1 ... 16 A2
Metropolitan Bsns Ctr 9 N1 ... 16 A1
Metropolitan Cl 23 E14 ... 33 C4
Mews St E1 ... 125 B2
Mews The
 Shoreditch N1 ... 87 A4
 5 Upper Holloway N19 ... 5 A3
Mexborough NW1 . 82 C3
Mexfield Rd SW15 .. 58 B2
Meyer Ho 1 SW12 ... 73 A4
Meymott St SE1 .. 122 A1
Meynell Cres E9 ... 17 C1
Meynell Gdns E9 ... 17 C1
Meynell Rd E9 ... 17 C1
Meyrick Ho 8 E14 . 33 C4
Meyrick Rd
 Battersea SW11 ... 60 A4
 Willesden NW10 ... 8 C2
Miah Terr 9 E1 .. 125 C1
Micawber Ct N1 ... 97 A4
Micawber Ho 27 SE16 ... 139 C3
Micawber St N1 ... 97 A4
Michael Cliffe Ho EC1 ... 95 C3
Michael Faraday Ho SE17 ... 151 C1
Michael Faraday Prim Sch SE17 ... 151 C1
Michael Manley Ind Est 12 SW8 ... 171 A2
Michael Rd SW6 .. 166 B4
Michael Tippett Sch The SE24 ... 63 B3
Michelangelo Ct 14 SE16 ... 40 A1
Michelle Ct W3 ... 28 C2
Michels Almshouses 11 TW10 ... 54 A2
Michelsdale Dr 3 TW9 ... 54 A3
Michelson Ho SE11 ... 149 A3
Michel's Row 2 TW9 ... 54 A3
Michigan Ho E14 ... 41 C3
Mickledore NW1 .. 83 A1
Micklethwaite Rd SW6 ... 155 C3
Mickleton Ho 30 W2 ... 31 C4
Middlefield NW8 .. 79 B4
Middle Row W10 ... 23 A1
Middle Row Prim Sch 21 W10 ... 23 A1
Middlesex Ct 5 W4 ... 38 B2
Middlesex Ho W1 105 A4
Middlesex Pas EC1 ... 108 B3
Middlesex Pl 13 E9 ... 17 B2
Middlesex St E1 .. 110 C2
Middlesex Univ (Archway Campus) 15 N19 ... 4 B2
Middle St EC1 ... 108 C4
Middle Temple EC4 ... 121 B4
Middle Temple La EC4 ... 121 B4
Middleton Dr SE16 . 40 C4
Middleton Gr N7 ... 14 A3
Middleton Ho
 Dalston E8 ... 16 B1
 Newington SE1 ... 137 B1
Middleton Mews N7 ... 14 A3
Middleton Pl W1 . 104 C3
Middleton Rd
 Dalston E8 ... 16 B1
 Golders Green NW11 .. 1 C4
Middleton St E2 ... 25 A2
Middleton Way SE13 ... 67 C3
Middle Yd SE1 ... 124 A2
Midford Pl W1 ... 93 A1
Midhope Ho WC1 .. 94 B3
Midhope St WC1 .. 94 B3
Midhurst Ct N8 ... 5 A4
Midhurst Ho 6 E14 ... 33 B3
Midhurst Way E5 ... 16 C4
Midland Pl E14 ... 42 B1
Midland Rd NW1 .. 94 A4
Midland Terr NW10 ... 21 A1
Midlothian Ho NW2 . 9 A4
Midlothian Rd E3 .. 26 B1
Midmoor Rd SW12 .. 73 B3
Midship Cl SE16 ... 32 C1
Midship Point E14 .. 41 C4
Midstrath Rd NW10 .. 8 A4
Midway Ho EC1 ... 96 B4
Milborne Gr SW10 ... 143 A1
Milborne Ho 11 E9 . 17 B2
Milborne St E9 ... 17 B2
Milbrook Ct NW3 ... 2 B3
Milcote St SE1 ... 136 B3
Mildmay Ave N1 ... 15 C2
Mildmay Ct N1 ... 15 C3
Mildmay Gr N N1 ... 15 C3
Mildmay Gr S N1 ... 15 C3
Mildmay Ho 6 SW15 ... 57 B2
Mildmay Mission Hospl E2 ... 24 B2 98 C3
Mildmay Pk N1 ... 15 C3
Mildmay Rd N1 ... 16 A3
Mildmay St N1 ... 15 C2
MILE END ... 26 A1
Mile End Hospl E2 .. 25 C2
Mile End Park L Ctr & Stad E3 ... 33 B4
Mile End Pl E1 ... 25 C1
Mile End Rd E1, E3 .. 25 C1
Mile End Sta E3 ... 26 B2
Miles Bldgs NW1 . 102 A4
Miles Coverdale Prim Sch 16 W12 ... 39 B4
Miles Ct E1 ... 32 A3
Miles Ho 5 SE10 ... 43 A1
Miles Lo E15 ... 19 C3
Miles Pl NW8 ... 101 C4
Miles St SW8 ... 162 B3
Milestone Green SW14 ... 55 C3
Milfoil St W12 ... 29 C2
Milford Ct 3 N16 ... 7 A3
Milford La WC2 ... 121 B4
Milford Mews SW16 ... 74 B1
Milk St EC2 ... 109 A2
Milkwell Yd 7 SE5 ... 48 B2
Milkwood Rd SE24 . 63 A3
Milk Yd E1 ... 32 B2
Millais Rd E11 ... 19 C4
Milland Ho 11 SW15 ... 68 C3
Millard Cl 21 N16 ... 16 A3
Millard Rd SE8 ... 41 B1
Millbank SW1 ... 148 A3
Millbank Millennium Pier SW1 ... 148 B3
Millbank Prim Sch SW1 ... 147 C3
Millbrooke Ct 7 SW15 ... 58 A2
Millbrook Ho 4 SE15 ... 49 C4
Millbrook Pl NW1 . 82 C2
Millbrook Rd SW9 .. 63 A4
Millender Wlk SE16 ... 40 B2
Millennium Bridge SE1, EC4 ... 122 C3
Millennium City Acad W1 ... 104 B3
Millennium Dr E14 ... 42 C2
Millennium Harbour E14 ... 41 C4
Millennium Pl 27 E2 ... 25 A3
Millennium Prim Sch The SE10 ... 43 B3
Millennium Sq SE1 ... 139 A4
Millennium Way SE10 ... 43 A3
Miller Ho 9 SW2 ... 74 A4
Miller's Ave E8, N16 ... 16 B3
Miller's Ct 1 W4 ... 38 B1
Miller St NW1 ... 82 C2
Miller's Terr 1 E8 .. 16 B3
Miller's Way W6 ... 39 B4
Millers Wharf Ho E1 ... 125 B1
Miller Wlk SE1 ... 121 C1
Millfield N4 ... 5 C2
Millfield La N6 ... 3 B2
Millfield Pl N6 ... 3 C2
Millfields Com Sch E5 ... 17 B4
Millgrove St 6 SW11 ... 169 B2
Millharbour E14 ... 42 A4
Mill Hill SW13 ... 56 C4
Mill Hill Gr 11 W3 .. 28 A1
Mill Hill Rd
 Barnes SW13 ... 46 C1
 South Acton W3 ... 37 A4
Mill Hill Terr 9 W3 ... 28 A1
Mill Ho 4 SE13 ... 67 B4
Milligan St E14 ... 33 B2
Milliners Ho SW18 .. 58 C3
Millington Ho N16 ... 6 C1
Mill La NW6 ... 10 B3
Millman Ct WC1 ... 94 C1
Millman Mews WC1 ... 94 C1
Millman Pl WC1 ... 95 A1
Millman St WC1 ... 94 C1
Millmark Gr SE14 ... 51 A1
MILL MEADS ... 27 C3
Millner Ct SE4 ... 51 B1
Mill Pl E14 ... 33 A3
Mill Pond Cl SW8 161 C1
Millpond Est SE16 .. 40 A4
Mill Row N1 ... 24 A4
Mills Ct EC2 .. 24 A2 98 A3
Mills Gr 1 E14 ... 34 B4
Mills Ho SW8 ... 171 A4
Millshott Cl SW6 ... 47 B2
Mills Row W4 ... 37 C2
Mill St
 Bermondsey SE1 .. 139 A4
 Mayfair W1 ... 118 C4
Millstone Cl E15 ... 19 C2
Millstream Ho 14 SE16 ... 40 A4
Millstream Rd SE1 ... 138 C3
Mill Trad Est The NW10 ... 20 B2
MILLWALL ... 41 C3
Millwall Dock Rd E14 ... 41 C3
Millwood St 10 W10 ... 31 A4
Mill Yd E1 ... 125 B4
Milman Rd NW6 ... 23 A3
Milman's Ho SW10 ... 157 B3
Milman's St SW10 157 B3
Milner Bldg N16 ... 6 C1
Milner Ho 1 SW11 ... 59 C4
Milner Pl N1 ... 85 C4
Milner Sq N1 ... 15 A1
Milner St SW3 ... 144 C4
Milnthorpe Rd W4 .. 45 C4
Milo Rd SE22 ... 64 B1
Milrood Ho 5 E1 ... 32 C4
Milroy Wlk SE1 ... 122 A2
Milson Rd W14 ... 126 A2
Milsted Ho 23 E5 ... 17 A3
Milton Ave
 Becontree NW10 ... 20 C4
 Crouch End N6 ... 4 B4
 Stonebridge NW10 ... 20 B4
Milton Cl SE1 ... 152 C3
Milton Court Rd SE14 ... 51 A4
Milton Ct
 Fulham SW6 ... 58 A4
 St Luke's EC2 ... 109 B4
 9 Wandsworth SW18 ... 58 C2
Milton Gr N16 ... 16 A4
Milton Ho
 19 Bethnal Green E2 ... 25 B2
 2 Camberwell SE5 .. 48 C3
Milton House Mans E8 ... 16 B4
Milton Pk N6 ... 4 B4
Milton Pl 3 N7 ... 14 C3
Milton Rd
 Acton W3 ... 28 C1
 Crouch End N6 ... 4 B4
 Mortlake SW14 ... 55 C4
 Tulse Hill SE24 ... 63 A2
Milton St EC1, EC2 109 B4
Milverton NW5 ... 12 C3
Milverton Rd NW6 ... 9 B1
Milverton St SE11 149 C1
Milward St E1 ... 32 A4
Mimosa Ct SW4 .. 172 B3
Mimosa St SW6 .. 165 A3
Mina Rd SE17 ... 152 B2
Minchin Ho 10 E14 ... 33 C3
Mincing La EC3 ... 124 A4
Minera Mews SW1 ... 145 C4
Minerva Cl SW9 .. 163 C2
Minerva Rd NW10 .. 20 C2
Minerva St E2 ... 25 A3
Minerva Wlk EC1 . 108 B2
Minet Ave NW10 ... 21 A3
Minet Gdns NW10 .. 21 A3
Minet Ho 20 E1 ... 111 B1
Minet Rd SE5, SW9 .. 48 A1

Minford Gdns W14 39 C4
Mingard Wlk N7 5 B1
Ming St E14 33 C2
Minnow Wlk SE17 152 B3
Minories EC3 124 C4
Minshull St SW8 171 B3
Minson Rd E9 25 C4
Minstead Gdns SW15 68 B4
Minster Ct EC3 124 B4
Minster Rd NW2 10 A3
Mint Bsns Pk 12 E16 35 C4
Mintern St N1 87 C2
Minton Ho SE11 149 B4
Minton Mews 3 NW6 11 A2
Mint St SE1 137 A4
Mirabel Rd SW6 155 A2
Miranda Cl 19 E1 32 B4
Miranda Ho 17 N1 24 A3
Miranda Rd N19 4 B3
Missenden SE17 151 C1
Missenden Ho NW8 90 A2
Mission Pl SE15 49 C2
Mission Sq 13 TW8 44 A4
Mission The
13 Bermondsey SE16 40 A4
14 Poplar E14 33 B3
Misterton Ct SW11 167 C4
Mistral SE5 49 A2
Mitali Pas 21 E1 111 B1
Mitcham Ho 9 SE5 48 B2
Mitchell Brook Prim Sch NW10 8 A2
Mitchell Ct SW14 56 A3
Mitchell Ho
Gunnersbury W4 37 A1
6 Islington N1 14 C1
31 Shepherd's Bush W12 30 A2
Mitchell's Pl SE21 76 A4
Mitchell St EC1 97 A2
Mitchison Rd N1 15 C2
Mitford Rd N19 5 A2
Mitre Bridge Ind Pk W10 22 A1
Mitre Rd SE1 135 C4
Mitre Sq EC3 110 B1
Mitre St EC3 110 B1
Mitre The 9 E14 33 B2
Mitre Way W10 30 A4
Mizzen Ct E14 41 C4
Moatfield NW6 10 A1
Moat Pl
Acton W3 28 A3
Stockwell SW9 62 B4
Moat Sch The 7 SW6 164 A2
Moberly Rd SW4 73 C4
Mobey Ct SW4 172 A3
Mocatta Ho 9 E1 25 A1
Modbury Gdns NW5 12 C2
Modder Pl SW15 57 C3
Model Cotts SW14 55 B4
Modling Ho 8 E2 25 C3
Moelwyn Hughes Ct N7 13 C3
Moffat Ho 24 SE5 48 B3
Mohawk Ho 33 E3 26 A3
Moira Ct SW17 72 C2
Moira Ho 13 SW9 173 B4
Molasses Ho 1 SW11 59 B4
Molasses Row 2 SW11 59 B4
Mole Ct 2 W12 38 A4
Mole Ho NW8 89 C1
Molesey Ho E2 24 B1 98 C2
Molesford Rd SW6 165 B3
Molesworth Ho 9 SE17 48 A4
Molesworth St SE13 67 B4
Molly Huggins Cl SW12 73 B4
Molton Ho N1 85 A3
Molyneux Ho W1 102 B2
Molyneux St W1 102 B3
Mona Rd SE15 50 B1
Mona St E16 35 B4
Monck's Row SW18 58 B1
Monck St SW1 133 C1
Monckton Ct W14 126 C2
Monclar Rd SE5 63 C3
Moncorvo Cl SW7 130 A3
Moncrieff St SE15 49 C1
Mondragon Ho SW8 172 B4
Monet Ct 15 SE16 40 A1
Moneyer Ho N1 97 B4
Monica Shaw Ct NW1 83 C1
Monier Rd E3 18 C1
Monkbretton Ho E2 24 C2 99 B3
Monk Ct W12 29 C1
Monk Dr E16 35 C2
Monkridge 3 N8 4 C4
Monksfield N4 5 C2
Monkswell Ho E2 24 C2 99 B3
Monkton Ho
32 Bermondsey SE16 40 C4
22 Hackney E5 17 A3
Monkton St SE11 149 C4
Monkwell Sq EC2 109 A3
Monmouth Cl W4 37 C3
Monmouth Gr TW8 36 A2
Monmouth Ho
5 Camden Town NW5 13 A2
Wandsworth SW18 58 C1
Monmouth Pl W2 100 A1
Monmouth Rd W2 31 C3
Monmouth St WC2 106 A1
Monnery Rd N19 4 B1
Monnow Rd SE1 153 B3
Monroe Dr SW14 55 A2
Monroe Ho
16 Crouch End N19 4 C4
Lisson Gr NW8 90 B3
Monro Ho
16 Hampstead NW3 11 B4
Putney SW15 57 A2
Monro Way E5 16 C4
Monsal Ct E5 18 A4
Monsell Ct 4 N4 6 A1
Monsell Rd N4, N5 6 A1
Monson Rd
Deptford SE14 50 C3
Willesden Green NW10 22 A3
Montagu Ct W1 103 A3
Montague Ave SE4 66 C3
Montague Cl SE1 123 B2
Montague Pl WC1 105 C4
Montague Rd
Richmond TW10 54 A1
Shacklewell E8 16 C3
Montague Sq SE15 50 B3
Montague St
Bloomsbury WC1 106 A4
City of London EC1 108 C3
Montagu Mans W1 103 A3
Montagu Mews N W1 103 A3
Montagu Mews S W1 103 A2
Montagu Mews W W1 103 A2
Montagu Pl W1 103 A3
Montagu Row W1 103 A3
Montagu Sq W1 103 A2
Montagu St W1 103 A2
Montaigne Cl SW1 147 C3
Montana Bldg 4 SE13 52 A2
Montana Rd SW17 72 C1
Montcalm Ho E14 41 C3
Montclare St E2 24 B1 98 C2
Monteagle Ct 27 N1 24 A3
Monteagle Way
Nunhead SE15 65 A4
Shacklewell E5 7 C1
Montefiore Ct 2 N16 7 B3
Montefiore St 2 SW8 170 B1
Montego Cl 9 SW2 62 C3
Montem Prim Sch 5 N7 5 B1
Montem St N4 5 B3
Monteray Studios W10 23 A3
Montesquieu Terr 3 E16 35 B3
Montford Pl SE11 149 B1
Montfort Ho
4 Bethnal Green E2 25 B2
Cubitt Town E14 42 B3
Montfort Pl SW19 69 C3
Montgomery Ct W4 45 B4
Montgomery Ho 5 SW14 55 C4
Montgomery Lo 38 E1 25 B1
Montgomery Rd W4 37 B2
Montgomery St E14 34 A1
Montholme Rd SW11 60 B1
Monthope Rd 17 E1 111 B3
Montolieu Gdns SW15 57 A2
Montpelier Gr NW5 13 B3
Montpelier Mews SW7 130 B2
Montpelier Pl
Knightsbridge SW7 130 B2
21 Stepney E1 32 B3
Montpelier Rd SE15 50 A2
Montpelier Rise NW11 1 A4
Montpelier Row SE3 53 B1
Montpelier Sq SW7 130 B3
Montpelier St SW7 130 B2
Montpelier Terr SW7 130 B3
Montpelier Vale SE3 53 B1
Montpelier Way NW11 1 A4
Montpelier Wlk SW7 130 B2
Montreal Pl WC2 120 C4
Montrell Rd SW2 74 A3
Montrose Ave NW6 23 A3
Montrose Ct SW7 129 C3
Montrose Ho
Belgravia SW1 131 C3
Millwall E14 41 C3
Montrose Pl SW1 131 C3
Montrose Villas 5 W6 38 C1
Montserrat Rd SW15 58 A3
Monument EC3 123 C4
Monument Gdns SE13 67 B2
Monument St EC3 123 C4
Monument Sta EC3 123 C4
Monza Bldg The E1 32 B2
Monza St E1 32 B2
Moodkee St SE16 40 B3
Moody Rd SE15 49 B2
Moody St E1 25 C2
Moon St N1 86 A4
Moorcroft Rd SW16 74 A1
Moore Cl SW14 55 B4
Moore Ct N1 86 A3
Moore Ho
16 Bethnal Green E2 25 B2
5 Greenwich SE10 43 B1
7 Shadwell E1 32 B2
Wandsworth SW17 71 C1
Moore Park Ct SW6 156 B2
Moore Park Rd SW6 156 A1
Moore St SW3 144 C4
Moorfields EC2 109 B3
Moorfields Eye Hospl EC1 97 B3
Moorfields Highwalk EC2 109 B3
Moorgate EC2 109 B3
Moorgate Pl EC2 109 B2
Moorgate Sta EC2 109 B3
Moorgreen Ho EC1 96 A4
Moorhouse EC2 109 B3
Moorhouse Rd W2 31 C3
Moor La EC2 109 B3
Moorland Rd SW9 63 A3
Moor Pl EC2 109 B3
Moor St W1 105 C1
Morant Ho SW9 172 C2
Morant St E14 33 C2
Mora Prim Sch NW2 9 B4
Mora Rd NW2 9 B4
Mora St EC1 97 A3
Morat St SW9 173 A4
Moravian Cl SW3 157 C3
Moravian Pl SW10 157 C3
Moravian St 10 E2 25 B2
Moray Ho 9 E1 26 A1
Moray Mews N4, N7 5 B2
Moray Rd N4, N7 5 B2
Mordaunt Ho
4 Becontree NW10 20 C4
34 Clapham SW8 171 B1
Mordaunt Rd NW10 20 C4
Mordaunt St SW9 62 B4
Morden Hill SE13 52 B1
Morden Ho 19 SW2 62 C1
Morden La SE13 52 B2
Morden Mount Prim Sch 1 SE13 52 A1
Morden Rd SE3 53 C1
Morden Road Mews SE3 53 C1
Morden St SE13 52 A2
Morden Wharf Rd SE10 43 A3
Mordern Ho NW1 90 B1
Morecambe Cl 3 E1 32 C4
Morecambe St SE17 151 A2
More Cl
Canning Town E16 35 B3
West Kensington W14 140 A3
Moredown Ho 3 E8 16 C3
More House Sch SW1 131 A1
Moreland Ct 3 NW2 1 C1
Moreland Prim Sch EC1 96 B3
Moreland St EC1 96 B4
Morella Rd SW11, SW12 72 B4
Morell Ho 5 SW9 172 C1
More London Pl SE1 124 A1
Moresby Wlk 6 SW8 170 B1
More's Gdn SW3 157 C3
Moreton Ho SE16 40 A3
Moreton Pl SW1 147 A2
Moreton St SW1 147 B2

Moreton Terr SW1 147 A2
Moreton Terr Mews N SW1 147 A2
Moreton Terr Mews S SW1 147 A2
Moreton Twr 3 W3 28 A1
Morgan Ct 5 SW11 167 C2
Morgan Ho
Nine Elms SW8 171 A4
Pimlico SW1 147 A3
Morgan Rd
Islington N7 14 C3
Notting Hill W10 31 B4
Morgans La SE1 124 A1
Morgan St
Canning Town E16 35 B4
Globe Town E3 25 C2
Morgan's Wlk SW11 158 A1
Moriatry Cl N7 14 A4
Morie St SW18 59 A2
Morkyns Wlk SE21 76 A1
Morland Cl NW11 2 A3
Morland Ct W12 39 A4
Morland Est E8 16 C1
Morland Ho
Kilburn NW6 23 C4
Notting Hill W11 31 A3
Somers Town NW1 83 A1
Westminster SW1 148 A4
Morland Mews N1 14 C1
Morley Coll SE1 135 C2
Morley Ct SE13 67 B3
Morley Ho
Stoke Newington N16 7 C2
Streatham SW2 74 A4
W1 104 B2
Morley Rd SE13 67 B3
Morley St SE1 135 C3
Morna Rd SE5 48 B1
Morning La E9 17 B2
Morningside Prim Sch 17 E9 17 B2
Mornington Ave W14 140 C3
Mornington Avenue Mans W14 140 C3
Mornington Cres
Camden Town NW1 82 C2
NW1 82 C2
Mornington Crescent Sta NW1 82 C2
Mornington Ct NW1 82 C2
Mornington Gr E3 26 C2
Mornington Mews 2 SE5 48 B2
Mornington Pl
4 New Cross SE8 51 B3
Regent's Pk NW1 82 C2
Mornington Rd SE14, SE8 51 B3
Mornington St NW1 82 B2
Mornington Terr NW1 82 B2
Morocco St SE1 138 A3
Morpeth Gr E9 25 C4
Morpeth Rd E9 25 C4
Morpeth Sch E2 25 B2
Morpeth St E2 25 C2
Morpeth Terr SW1 146 C4
Morrel Ct 11 E2 24 C3
Morris Blitz Ct 2 N16 16 B4
Morris Ct 3 SE5 63 C3
Morris Gdns SW18 70 C4
Morris Ho
17 Bethnal Green E2 25 B2
Lisson Gr NW8 90 A1
1 Stockwell SW4 62 A3
10 Tufnell Pk N19 13 B4
Morrish Rd SW2 74 A4
Morrison Bldgs 5 E1 111 B2
Morrison Ho SW2 74 C3
Morrison St SW11 60 C4
Morris Pl N4 5 C2
Morris Rd E14 34 A4
Morriss Ho 9 SE16 40 A4
Morris St E1 32 A3
Morshead Mans W9 23 C2
Morshead Rd W9 23 C2
Mortain Ho 9 SE16 40 A2
Morten Cl SW4 61 C1
Mortimer Cl
1 Child's Hill NW2 1 B1
Streatham SW16 73 C2
Mortimer Cres NW6 78 B3
Mortimer Ct NW8 79 A1
Mortimer Est NW6 78 A3
Mortimer Ho
6 Shepherd's Bush W11 30 C1
West Kensington W14 140 B3
Mortimer Lo 11 SW19 70 A3
Mortimer Market WC1 93 A1
Mortimer Pl NW6 78 A3
Mortimer Rd
De Beauvoir Town N1 16 A1
Kensal Green NW10 22 B2
Mortimer Sq W11 30 C2
Mortimer St W1 105 A3
Mortimer Terr NW5 13 A4
MORTLAKE 55 B4
Mortlake High St SW14 55 C4
Mortlake Ho 7 W4 37 B2
Mortlake Rd SW14, TW9 44 C2
Mortlake Sta SW14 55 B4
Mortlake Terr TW9 44 C3
Mortlock Cl SE15 50 A2
Morton Cl 29 E1 32 B3
Morton Ho SE17 48 A4
Morton Mews SW5 142 A3
Morton Pl SE1 135 B1
Morton Rd N1 15 B1
Morval Rd SW2 62 C2
Morven Rd SW17 72 B1
Morville Ho SW18 59 C1
Morville St E3 26 C3
Morwell St WC1 105 C3
Moscow Pl W2 114 A4
Moscow Rd W2 114 A4
Mosedale NW1 92 B3
Moseley Row SE10 43 B2
Mosque Tower 26 E1 111 C3
Mossbourne Com Acad E8 16 C3
Mossbury Rd SW11 60 A4
Moss Cl E1 111 C4
Mossford St E3 26 B1
Mossington Gdns SE16 40 B2
Mossop St SW3 144 B4
Mostyn Gdns NW10 22 C3
Mostyn Gr E3 26 C3
Mostyn Lo N5 15 B4
Mostyn Rd SW9 173 C3
Motcomb St SW1 131 B2
Mothers Sq The 13 E5 17 A4
Motley Ave EC2 24 A1 98 A2
Motley St SW8 170 C2
Moules Ct SE5 48 B3
Moulins Rd E9 17 B1
Moulsford Ho
5 Lower Holloway N7 14 A3
32 Paddington W2 31 C4
Mounsey Ho 13 W10 23 A2
Mount Adon Pk SE21, SE22 76 C4
Mountague Pl 2 E14 34 B2
Mountain Ho SE11 148 C2
Mount Angelus Rd SW15 68 B4
Mount Ararat Rd TW10 54 A2
Mountbatten Ho N6 3 C4
Mountbatten Mews SW18 71 B3
Mount Carmel 3 N7 14 B3
Mount Carmel RC Tech Coll for Girls 6 N19 4 C3
Mountearl Gdns SW16, SW2 74 B1
Mount Ephraim La SW16 73 C1
Mount Ephraim Rd SW16 73 C1
Mountfield NW2 1 B2
Mountfield Ct SE13 67 C1
Mount Ford St E1 111 B2
Mountfort Cres N1 14 C1
Mountfort Terr 1 N1 14 C1
Mountgrove Rd N5 6 B1
Mountjoy Ho EC2 108 C3
Mount Lodge SW4 61 C3
Mount Mills EC1 96 B3
Mount Nod Rd SW16, SW2 74 B1
Mount Pl 7 W3 28 A1
Mount Pleasant WC1 95 B1
Mount Pleasant Cres N4 5 B4
Mount Pleasant Rd
Lewisham SE13 67 B1
Willesden NW10 22 B4
Mount Pleasant Villas N4 5 B4
Mount Rd SW18, SW19 71 A2
Mount Row W1 118 A3
Mounts Pond Rd SE3, SE13 52 C1
Mount Sq The 3 NW3 2 B1
Mount St W1 117 C3
Mount Terr E1 32 A4
Mount The
Hampstead NW3 2 B1
Kensington W8 31 C1 113 B1
Mount Tyndal NW3 2 C3
Mount Vernon NW3 11 B4
Mountview 5 SW16 74 B1
Mountview Cl NW11 2 B3
Mount Villas SE27 75 A1
Mourne Ho NW3 11 B2
Mowatt Cl N19 4 C3
Mowbray Rd NW6 10 A1
Mowlem Prim Sch 36 E2 25 B3
Mowlem St E2 25 A3
Mowll St SW9 163 B1
Moxon St W1 103 B3
Moye Cl 10 E2 24 C3
Moylan Rd W6 154 B3
Moyle Ho SW1 161 A4
Moyne Ho 16 SW9 63 A3
Mozart St W10 23 B2
Mudchute Pk & Farm E14 42 B2
Mudchute Sta E14 42 A2
Mudie Ho 8 SW2 74 A4
Mudlarks Blvd 3 SE10 43 B3
Muirdown Ave SW14 55 C3
Muir Dr SW18 60 A1
Muirfield W3 29 A3
Muirfield Cl 23 SE16 40 A1
Muirfield Cres E14 42 A3
Muir Rd E5 7 C1
Mulberry Bsns Ctr SE16 40 C4
Mulberry Cl
Chelsea SW3 157 C3
East Dulwich SE22 64 C1
Hampstead NW3 11 C4
Mulberry Ct
Finsbury EC1 96 B3
Islington N5 15 A3
1 Leyton E11 19 C4
10 Paddington W9 23 B2
Mulberry Ho
1 Bethnal Green E2 25 B2
8 Deptford SE8 51 B4
Mulberry House Sch NW2 10 A3
Mulberry Mews SE14 51 B2
Mulberry Pl W6 38 C1
Mulberry Rd E8 16 B1
Mulberry Sch for Girls
39 Stepney E1 32 A3
16 St George in t East E1 32 A2
Mulberry St 7 E1 111 B2
Mulberry Wlk SW3 157 C4
Mulgrave Rd
West Kensington W14 154 C4
Willesden NW10 8 B4
Mulkern Rd N19 4 C3
Mullard Ho WC1 105 B4
Mullens Ho 7 SW15 57 B2
Mullen Twr EC1 95 B1
Muller Rd SW4 61 C1
Mullet Gdns 7 E2 24 C2 99 C4
Mulletsfield WC1 94 B3
Mull Ho 17 E3 26 B3
Mullins Path SW14 55 C4
Mulready St NW8 90 A1
Multi Way W3 38 A4
Multon Ho E9 17 B1
Multon Rd SW18 71 C4
Mulvaney Way SE1 137 C3
Mumford Rd SE24 63 A2
Muncaster Rd SW11 60 C2
Mundania Ct SE22 65 A1
Mundania Rd SE22 65 B1
Munday Ho SE1 137 B1
Munday Rd E16 35 C2
Munden Ho 5 E3 27 A2
Munden St W14 140 A4
Mund St W14 141 A1
Mundy Ho 6 W10 23 A2
Mundy St N1 24 A2 98 B4
Munro Ho
Bermondsey SE1 137 C3
Lambeth SE1 135 B3
Munro Mews W10 31 A4
Munster Ct SW6 164 C2
Munster Rd SW6 154 B2
Munster Residences SW6 164 B4
Munster Sq NW1 92 B2
Munton Rd SE1, SE17 151 A4
Murchison Ho 1 W10 31 A4
Murdoch Ho 4 SE16 40 B3
Murdock Cl E16 35 B3
Murdock St SE15 50 A4
Murfett Cl SW19 70 A2
Muriel St N1 85 A4
Murphy Ho SE1 136 B2
Murphy St SE1 135 B3
Murray Gr N1 87 B1
Murray Mews NW1 13 C1
Murray St NW1 13 C1
Murray Terr NW3 11 C4
Musard Rd W6 154 B4

Musbury St E1 ... 32 B3
Muscal W6 ... 154 A4
Muscatel Pl SE5 ... 49 A2
Muschamp Rd SE15 ... 64 B4
Muscott Ho 15 E2 ... 24 C4
Muscovy St EC3 ... 124 B4
Museum & Galleries of Modern London EC2 ... 108 C3
Museum Ho 7 E2 ... 25 B2
Museum La SW7 ... 129 B1
Museum Mans WC1 ... 106 A3
Museum of Brands, Packaging & Advertising W11 ... 31 B3
Museum of Childhood (V&A) E2 ... 25 B2
Museum of Instruments SW7 ... 129 B2
Museum of London EC2 ... 108 C3
Museum of London Docklands E14 ... 33 C2
Museum of the Order of St John EC1 ... 96 A1
Museum of the Royal Pharmaceutical Society SE1 ... 148 C4
Museum St WC1 ... 106 A2
Museum Way W3 ... 36 C4
Musgrave Cres SW6 ... 165 C4
Musgrave Ct SW11 ... 168 A4
Musgrove Ho 1 E9 ... 17 C2
Musgrove Rd SE14 ... 51 A2
Musical Mus The TW8 ... 44 B4
Musjid Rd 7 SW11 ... 167 C1
Mustow Pl 2 SW6 ... 165 A2
Mutrix Rd NW6 ... 23 C4
Mutton Pl NW1 ... 12 C2
Myatt Garden Prim Sch SE4 ... 51 B1
Myatt Ho SE5 ... 48 A1
Myatt Rd SW9 ... 48 A2
Myatts Field Ct SE5 ... 48 B2
Mycenae Rd SE3 ... 53 C4
Myddelton Pas EC1 ... 95 C4
Myddelton Sq EC1 ... 95 C4
Myddelton St EC1 ... 95 C3
Myddleton Ave N4 ... 6 B2
Myers Ho 5 SE5 ... 48 B3
Myers La SE14 ... 50 C4
Mylius Cl SE14 ... 50 B2
Mylne Cl W6 ... 38 C1
Mylne St EC1 ... 85 B1
Mynterne Ct 16 SW19 ... 69 C3
Myrdle Ct 14 E1 ... 111 C2
Myrdle St E1 ... 111 C2
Myron Pl SE13 ... 67 B4
Myrtle Ho SE14 ... 50 C2
Myrtle Rd W3 ... 28 B1
Myrtle Wlk 20 N1 ... 24 A3
Mysore Rd SW11 ... 60 B3
Myton Rd SE21 ... 75 C1
Mytton Ho SW8 ... 162 C1

N

N1 Sh Ctr N1 ... 85 C2
Nags Head N7 ... 14 B4
Nags Head Ct EC1 ... 97 A1
Nags Head Sh Ctr The N7 ... 14 B4
Naima Jewish Prep Sch 4 NW6 ... 78 A2
Nainby Ho SE11 ... 149 B3
Nairne Gr SE5, SE24 ... 63 C3
Nairn St E14 ... 34 B4
Naldera Gdns SE3 ... 53 C4
Nalton Ho 4 NW6 ... 11 B1
Namco Sta SE1 ... 134 C4
Nankin St E14 ... 33 C3
Nansen Rd SW11 ... 60 C4
Nant Ct NW2 ... 1 B2
Nantes Cl SW18 ... 59 B3
Nant Rd NW2 ... 1 B2
Nant St E2 ... 25 A2
Naoroji St WC1 ... 95 B3
Napier Ave
Deptford E14 ... 41 C1
Fulham SW6 ... 58 B4
Napier Cl
New Cross SE14, SE8 ... 51 B3
West Kensington W14 ... 126 C2
Napier Ct
Fulham SW6 ... 58 B4
Shoreditch N1 ... 87 B2
Napier Gr N1 ... 87 A2
Napier Ho SE17 ... 48 A4
Napier Pl W14 ... 126 C1
Napier Rd
College Pk NW10 ... 22 A2
Kensington W14 ... 126 C1
Napier Terr N1 ... 15 A1
Narbonne Ave SW4 ... 61 B2
Narborough St SW6 ... 166 A1
Narcissus Rd NW6 ... 10 C3
Narford Rd E5 ... 7 C2
Narrow St
6 Acton W3 ... 28 A1
Limehouse E14 ... 33 A2
Nascot St W12 ... 30 B3
Naseby Cl NW6 ... 11 B1
Nashe Ho SE1 ... 137 B1
Nash Ho
5 Millwall E14 ... 41 C3
Pimlico SW1 ... 146 B1
Nash Rd SE4 ... 66 A2
Nash St NW1 ... 92 B4
Nasmyth St W6 ... 39 A3
Nassau Rd SW13 ... 46 B2
Nassau St W1 ... 104 C3
Nassington Rd NW3 ... 12 B4
Nathan Ho SE11 ... 149 C3
Nathaniel Cl E1 ... 111 A3
National Archives The TW9 ... 45 A3
National Army Mus SW3 ... 159 A4
National Gallery W1 ... 119 C3
National Hospl for Neurology & Neurosurgery WC1 ... 94 B1
National Maritime Mus SE10 ... 52 C4
National Portrait Gallery W1 ... 119 C3
National Tennis Ctr SW15 ... 56 A2
National Theatre SE1 ... 121 A2
Natural History Mus SW7 ... 129 B1
Nautilus Bldg The EC1 ... 95 C4
Naval Row E14 ... 34 B2
Navarino Gr E8 ... 16 C2
Navarino Mans E8 ... 16 C2
Navarino Rd E8 ... 16 C2
Navarre St E2 ... 24 B1 98 C2
Navenby Wlk 13 E3 ... 26 C1
Navy St SW4 ... 61 C4
Naxos Bldg 9 E14 ... 41 C4
Naylor Bldg W 4 E1 ... 111 B2
Naylor Ho
33 Clapham SW8 ... 171 B1
Walworth SE17 ... 151 C2
5 West Kilburn W10 ... 23 B2
Naylor Rd SE15 ... 50 A3
Nayor Bldg E 6 E1 ... 111 B2
Nazareth Cl SE15 ... 50 A1
Nazrul St E2 ... 24 B2 98 C4
Nealden St SW9 ... 62 B4
Neal St WC2 ... 106 A1
Neal's Yd WC2 ... 106 A1
Neasden Cl NW10 ... 8 A3
Neasden Junc NW10 ... 8 A4
Neasden La NW10 ... 8 A3
Neasden Sta NW10 ... 8 A3
Neathouse Pl SW1 ... 146 C4
Nebraska Bldg 11 SE13 ... 52 A2
Nebraska St SE1 ... 137 B3
Neckinger SE16 ... 139 A2
Neckinger Est SE16 ... 139 A2
Neckinger St SE1 ... 139 A2
Nectarine Way SE13 ... 52 A1
Nedahall Ct 4 NW11 ... 1 B4
Needham Ho SE11 ... 149 B3
Needham Rd W11 ... 31 C3
Needleman St SE16 ... 40 C4
Needwood Ho N4 ... 6 B3
Neilson-Terry Ct 9 SW9 ... 62 B3
Neil Wates Cres 17 SW2 ... 74 C3
Nella Rd W6 ... 47 C4
Nelldale Rd SE16 ... 40 B2
Nell Gwynn Ho SW3 ... 144 B3
Nelson Cl 2 NW6 ... 23 C2
Nelson Ct SE16 ... 33 B1
Nelson Docks SE16 ... 33 B1
Nelson Gdns E2 ... 24 C2 99 C4
Nelson Pas EC1 ... 97 A4
Nelson Pl N1 ... 86 B1
Nelson Rd SE10 ... 52 B4
Nelson's Monument WC2 ... 120 A2
Nelson Sq SE1 ... 136 A4
Nelsons Row SW4 ... 61 C3
Nelson St
Canning Town E16 ... 35 B2
Stepney E1 ... 32 A3
Nelsons Yd NW1 ... 82 C2
Nelson Terr N1 ... 86 B1
Nemoure Rd W3 ... 28 B2
Nepaul Rd 17 SW11 ... 60 A4
Nepean St SW15 ... 68 C4
Neptune Ct 13 E14 ... 41 C2
Neptune Ho
2 Rotherhithe SE16 ... 40 B3
14 Stoke Newington N16 ... 16 A3
Neptune St SE16 ... 40 B3
Nesham Ho 14 N1 ... 24 A4
Nesham St E1 ... 125 B2
Ness St 9 SE16 ... 139 B2
Nestor Ho 13 E2 ... 25 A3
Netheravon Rd W4 ... 38 B1
Netheravon Rd S W4 ... 38 B1
Netherby Ho 23 SW8 ... 171 B1
Nethercombe Ho 1 SE3 ... 53 C4
Nethercott Ho 27 E3 ... 27 A2
Netherfield Rd SW17 ... 72 C1
Netherford Rd SW4 ... 171 A1
Netherhall Gdns NW3 ... 11 B3
Netherhall Int Coll NW3 ... 11 B2
Netherhall Way NW3 ... 11 B3
Netherleigh Cl N6 ... 4 A3
Netherton Gr SW10 ... 157 A3
Netherwood Rd W14 ... 39 C4
Netherwood St NW6 ... 10 C2
Netley 13 SE5 ... 49 A2
Netley Prim Sch NW1 ... 92 C3
Netley Rd TW8 ... 44 A4
Netley St NW1 ... 92 C3
Nettlecombe NW1 ... 13 C1
Nettleden Ho SW3 ... 144 B3
Nettlefold Pl SE27 ... 75 A1
Nettleton Rd SE14 ... 50 C2
Nevada St SE10 ... 52 B4
Nevena Ct 3 SW2 ... 62 C2
Nevern Mans SW5 ... 141 B2
Nevern Pl SW5 ... 141 C3
Nevern Rd SW5 ... 141 B3
Nevern Sq SW5 ... 141 C3
Nevil Ho 7 SW9 ... 48 A1
Nevill Ct SW10 ... 156 C2
Neville Cl
Acton W3 ... 37 B4
Paddington NW6 ... 23 B3
Neville Cl *continued*
Peckham SE15 ... 49 C2
Somers Town NW1 ... 83 C1
Neville Ct 10 SW12 ... 73 B4
Neville Gill Cl SW18 ... 59 A1
Neville Rd NW6 ... 23 B3
Neville St SW7 ... 143 B2
Neville Terr SW7 ... 143 B2
Nevill Rd N16 ... 7 A1
Nevinson Cl SW18 ... 59 C1
Nevis Rd SW17 ... 72 C2
Nevitt Ho N1 ... 87 C1
Newall Ho SE1 ... 137 A2
Newark Cres NW10 ... 20 C2
Newark Ho 3 SW9 ... 48 A1
Newark St E1 ... 32 A4
New Atlas Wharf E14 ... 41 C3
New Bentham Ct 10 N1 ... 15 B1
Newbery Ho N1 ... 15 B1
Newbold Cotts 4 E1 ... 32 B3
Newbolt Ho SE17 ... 151 B2
New Bond St W1 ... 118 B4
New Bridge St EC4 ... 108 A1
New Broad St EC2 ... 110 A3
New Bsns Ctr The NW10 ... 21 B2
Newburgh Rd W3 ... 28 B1
Newburgh St W1 ... 105 A1
New Burlington Mews W1 ... 118 C4
New Burlington Pl W1 ... 118 C4
New Burlington St W1 ... 118 C4
Newburn Ho SE11 ... 149 A2
Newburn St SE11 ... 149 A2
Newbury Ct E5 ... 18 A3
Newbury Ho
Brixton SW9 ... 48 A1
14 Kensington W2 ... 100 B1
Newbury Mews NW5 ... 12 C2
Newbury St EC1 ... 108 C4
New Butt La SE8 ... 51 C3
Newby NW1 ... 92 C4
Newby Pl E14 ... 34 B2
Newby St SW8 ... 61 A4
New Caledonian Mkt SE1 ... 138 B2
New Caledonian Wharf SE16 ... 41 B3
New Campden Ct 9 NW3 ... 11 B4
Newcastle Cl EC4 ... 108 A2
Newcastle Ct EC4 ... 123 A4
Newcastle Ho W1 ... 103 B4
Newcastle Pl W2 ... 101 C4
Newcastle Row EC1 ... 95 C1
New Cavendish St W1 ... 104 A3
New Change EC4 ... 108 C1
New Charles St EC1 ... 96 B4

New Church Rd
[32] Camberwell SE5 . . . . 48 B3
Camberwell SE5 . . . . 48 C4
New College Ct [6] NW3 . . . . 11 B2
New College Mews [7] N1 . . . . 14 C1
New College Par [1] NW3 . . . . 11 C1
Newcombe Ho N5 . . 15 B3
Newcombe St W8 . . . . 31 C1 113 C2
Newcomen Ho [5] NW5 . . . . 13 A4
Newcomen Rd SW11 . . . . 59 C4
Newcomen St SE1 . . . . 137 B4
New Compton St WC2 . . . . 106 A1
New Concordia Wharf SE1 . . . . 139 A4
Newcourt Ho [26] E2 . . . . 25 A2
Newcourt St NW8 . 80 A1
New Covent Garden Flower Market SW8 . . . . 162 A3
New Covent Garden Fruit & Vegetable Mkt SW8 . . . . 161 B1
New Crane Pl E1 . . . 32 B1
New Crescent Yd [1] NW10 . . . . 21 B3
NEW CROSS 51 B2
New Cross SE14 . . . . 51 B3
NEW CROSS GATE 50 C2
New Cross Gate SE14 . . . . 50 C2
New Cross Gate Sta SE14 . . . . 51 A3
New Cross Rd SE14 . . . . 51 A2
New Cross Sta SE14 . . . . 51 B3
New Ct
City of London EC4 . . . . 107 B1
[26] Hampstead NW3 . . . . 11 B4
Stoke Newington N16 . . . . 6 C3
New Den (Millwall FC) The SE16 . . . . 40 B1
Newdigate Ho [5] E14 . . . . 33 B3
Newell St E14 . . . . 33 B3
New End NW3 . . . . 2 B1
New End Prim Sch [33] NW3 . . . . 11 B4
New End Sq NW3 . . . 11 C4
Newent Cl SE15 . . . . 49 A3
New Fetter La EC4 . . . . 107 C2
Newfield Prim Sch NW10 . . . . 8 B1
Newgate St EC1 . . 108 B2
New Globe Wlk SE1 . . . . 122 C2
New Goulston St E1 . . . . 110 C2
Newham Sixth Form Coll (Stratford Ctr) [7] E15 . . . . 19 C1
Newham's Row SE1 . . . . 138 B3
Newhaven La [3] E16 . . . . 35 C4
New Hope Christian Sch [1] SE22 . . . . 64 B3
NEWINGTON 150 B4
Newington Barrow Way N7 . . . . 5 B1
Newington Butts SE1, SE11 . . . . 150 B3
Newington Cswy SE1 . . . . 136 C2
Newington Gn N16 . . . . 15 C3
Newington Green Mans N16 . . . . 15 C3
Newington Green Prim Sch [1] N16 . . 15 C3
Newington Green Rd N1 . . . . 15 C3
Newington Ind Est SE17 . . . . 150 C3
New Inn Broadway EC2 . . . . 24 A1 98 B2
New Inn Sq EC2 . . . . 24 A1 98 B2
New Inn St EC2 . . . . 24 A1 98 B2
New Inn Yd EC2 . . . . 24 A1 98 B2
New James Ct SE15 . . . . 65 A4
New Kent Rd SE1 151 A4
New King's Prim Sch [12] SW6 . . . . 165 A2
New King's Rd SW6 . . . . 165 C3
New King St SE8 . . . 51 C4
Newland Ct EC1 . . . 97 B2
Newland Ho [17] SE14 . . . . 50 C4
Newlands NW1 . . . . 92 C4
Newlands Quay E1 . 32 B2
New London St EC3 . . . . 124 B4
Newlyn NW1 . . . . 83 A3
Newman Pas W1 . 105 A3
Newman's Ct EC3 109 C1
Newman's Row WC2 . . . . 107 A3
Newman St W1 . . . 105 A3
Newmill Ho E3 . . . . 27 B1
Newmount NW3 . . . . 11 C3
New Mount St E15 . . 19 C1
Newnes Path SW15 . . . . 57 A3
Newnham Ho [9] SW15 . . . . 57 C1
Newnham Terr SE1 . . . . 135 B2
New North Com Sch N1 . . . . 86 C4
New North Pl EC2 . . . . 24 A1 98 A2
New North Rd N1 . 87 B3
New North Road Bridge N1 . . . . 87 B3
New North St WC1 . . . . 106 C4
Newnton Cl N4 . . . . 6 C4
New Oxford St WC1 . . . . 106 A2
New Palace Yd SW1 . . . . 134 A3
New Park Ct [26] SW2 . . . . 74 A4
New Park Par [14] SW2 . . . . 74 A4
New Park Rd SW2 . . 74 A4
New Place Sq SE16 . . . . 40 A3
Newport Ave E14 . . 34 C2
Newport Ct WC2 . . 119 C4
Newport Ho [2] E3 . . 26 A2
Newport Pl WC2 . . 119 C4
Newport Rd SW13 . . 46 C2
Newport St SE11 . 149 A4
New Priory Ct [9] NW6 . . . . 10 C1
New Providence Wharf E14 . . . . 34 C1
Newquay Ho SE11 149 B2
New Quebec St W1 . . . . 103 A1
New Rd E1 . . . . 32 A4
New River Ct N5 . . . 15 C4
New River Way N4 . . 6 C4
New Row WC2 . . . . 120 A4
New St Sq EC4 . . . 107 C2
New Scotland Yard SW1 . . . . 133 B2
New Shepherd's Bush Mkt [6] W12 . . . . 39 B4
New Spring Gdns Wlk SE11 . . . . 148 B1
New Sq WC2 . . . . 107 A2
New Square Pas WC2 . . . . 107 B2
New St EC2 . . . . 110 B3
Newstead Ho N1 . . 85 C2
Newton Ave W3 . . . . 37 B4
Newton Gr W4 . . . . 38 A2
Newton Ho
[22] Clapham SW8 . . 171 B2
Paddington NW8 . . . 78 B4
[1] Stepney E1 . . . . 32 A2
Newton Pl E14 . . . . 41 C2
Newton Point [1] E16 . . . . 35 B3
Newton Prep Sch SW8 . . . . 170 B4
Newton Rd
Acton W3 . . . . 37 B4
Kensington W2 . . . . 100 A1
Stratford New Town E15 . . . . 19 C3
Newton St WC2 . . . 106 B2
Newton's Yd [14] SW18 . . . . 58 C2
New Tower Bldgs [21] E1 . . . . 32 A1
Newtown Ct
Battersea SW11 . . . 170 A3
Clapham SW4 . . . . 61 A2
New Union Cl E14 . . 42 B3
New Union St EC2 . . . . 109 B3
New Wharf Rd N1 . 84 B2
Niagara Cl N1 . . . . 87 A2
Niagara Ct [6] SE16 . . . . 40 B3
Nicholas Ct
Chiswick W4 . . . . 46 A3
Golders Green NW11 . . 1 C4
Nicholas Ho [2] SW15 . . . . 56 C2
Nicholas La EC2, EC4 . . . . 123 C4
Nicholas Pas EC3 123 C4
Nicholas Rd
Bethnal Green E1 . . . . 25 B1
[20] Shepherd's Bush W11 . . . . 30 C2
Nicholay Rd N19 . . . . 4 C3
Nicholl Ho N4 . . . . 6 B3
Nicholl St E2 . . . . 24 C4
Nichols Cl N4 . . . . 5 C3
Nichols Ct E2 . . . . 24 B3
Nicholson Ho SE17 . . . . 151 B2
Nicholson St SE1 122 A1
Nickleby Ho
[18] Bermondsey SE1 . . . . 139 B3
[7] Shepherd's Bush W11 . . . . 30 C1
Nickols Wlk SW18 . . 59 A3
Nicoll Ct NW10 . . . . 21 A4
Nicoll Rd NW10 . . . . 21 A4
Nicosia Rd SW18 . . . 72 A4
Nigel Bldg EC1 . . . 107 B4
Nigel Playfair Ave W6 . . . . 39 A1
Nigel Rd SE15 . . . . 64 C4
Nightingale Cl W4 . . 45 B4
Nightingale Ct
[14] Cubitt Town E14 . . . . 42 B3
Finsbury Pk N4 . . . . 5 B2
Nightingale Gr SE13 . . . . 67 C2
Nightingale Ho
[21] Hoxton E1 . . . . 24 A4
[4] North Kensington W12 . . . . 30 B3
[7] St George in t East E1 . . . . 125 B2
Nightingale La SW11, SW12 . . . . 60 C1
Nightingale Lo [5] W9 . . . . 31 C4
Nightingale Mans [4] SW12 . . . . 60 C1
Nightingale Mews
[1] Bow E3 . . . . 26 A3
Newington SE11 . . . 150 A4
Nightingale Pl SW10 . . . . 157 A4
Nightingale Prim Sch E5 . . . . 16 C4
Nightingale Rd
[22] Canonbury N1 . . . . 15 B2
Dagenham NW10 . . . . 21 B3
Nightingale Sch SW17 . . . . 72 A2
Nightingale Sq SW12 . . . . 72 C4
Nightingale Wlk SW18, SW4 . . . . 61 A1
Nile Cl N16 . . . . 7 B1
Nile Ho N1 . . . . 97 B4
Nile St N1 . . . . 97 B4
Nile Terr SE1, SE15 . . . . 153 A1
Nimegen Way [9] SE22 . . . . 64 A2
Nimrod Pas [4] N1 . . 16 A2
NINE ELMS 160 C2
Nine Elms La SW8 . . . . 161 B3
Nisbet Ho E9 . . . . 17 C3
Niton Rd TW9 . . . . 54 C4
Niton St SW6 . . . . 47 C3
Nobel Ho [8] SE5 . . . 48 B1
Noble Ct E1 . . . . 32 A2
Noble St EC2 . . . . 108 C2
Noel Coward Ho SW1 . . . . 147 A3
Noel Ho [3] NW3 . . . . 11 C1
Noel Rd
Acton W3 . . . . 28 A3
Islington N1 . . . . 86 B2
Noel St W1 . . . . 105 A1
Noko NW10 . . . . 22 C2
Nolan Way E5 . . . . 16 C4
Noll Ho N7 . . . . 5 B2
Norbiton Rd E14 . . . . 33 B3
Norbroke St W12 . . . 29 B2
Norburn St W10 . . . . 31 A4
Norcombe Ho [2] N19 . . . . 4 C1
Norcott Rd N16 . . . . 7 C1
Norcroft Gdns SE22 . . . . 76 C4
Norden Ho [25] E2 . . . 25 A2
Nore Ct NW10 . . . . 8 C1
Norfolk Cres W2 . . 102 B2
Norfolk Ho
City of London EC4 . . . . 122 C4
Greenwich SE3 . . . . 53 A4
[4] Putney SW15 . . . . 69 B4
Richmond TW10 . . . . 54 C2
Shacklewell E8 . . . . 16 B4
St Johns SE8 . . . . 51 C2
Westminster SW1 . 147 C4
Norfolk House Rd SW16 . . . . 74 A1
Norfolk Mans
Battersea SW11 . . . 169 A3
[10] Wandsworth SW18 . . . . 58 C2
Norfolk Mews [12] W10 . . . . 31 A4
Norfolk Pl W2 . . . . 101 C2
Norfolk Rd
St John's Wood NW8 . . . . 79 C3
Willesden NW10 . . . . 8 A1
Norfolk Row SE1, SE11 . . . . 148 C4
Norfolk Sq W2 . . . 101 C2
Norfolk Sq Mews W2 . . . . 101 C1
Norgrove St SW12 . . 72 C4
Norland Ho [13] W11 . . . . 30 C1
Norland Pl W11 . . . . 31 A1 112 B1
Norland Place Sch W11 . . . . 31 A1 112 A1
Norland Rd [16] W11 . . . . 30 C1
Norland Sq W11 . . . . 31 A1 112 B1
Norley Vale SW15 . . . 68 C3
Norman Butler Ho [10] W10 . . . . 23 A1
Normanby Cl SW15 . . . . 58 B2
Normanby Rd NW10 . 8 B4
Norman Ct
Dulwich SE22 . . . . 76 C4
Finsbury Pk N4 . . . . 5 C4
Willesden NW10 . . . . 8 C1
Normand Croft Com Sch W14 . . . . 155 A4
Normand Mews W14 . . . . 154 B4
Normand Rd W14 154 C4

Normandy Ho 8 E14 42 B4
Normandy Rd SW9 173 B3
Norman Gr E3 26 A3
Norman Ho SW8 162 A2
Normanhurst Rd SW2 74 B2
Norman Rd SE10 52 A3
Norman St EC1 97 A3
Normanton Ave SW18, SW19 70 C2
Normanton Ho 6 SW4 61 B1
Norman Way W3 28 A3
Norris Ho
12 Hoxton N1 24 A4
15 South Hackney E9 25 B4
Norris St SW1 119 B3
Norroy Rd SW15 57 C3
Norse Ho 13 SE5 48 B1
Norstead Pl SW15 68 C2
NORTH ACTON 20 C2
North Acton Rd NW10 20 C2
North Acton Sta W3 28 C4
Northampton Gr N1 15 C3
Northampton Pk N1 15 C2
Northampton Rd EC1 95 C2
Northampton Sq EC1 96 A3
Northampton St N1 15 B1
North Audley St W1 117 B4
North Ave 8 TW9 44 C2
Northaw Ho 4 W10 22 B1
North Bank NW8 90 A3
North Block 19 E1 32 B2
Northbourne Ho 21 E5 17 A3
Northbourne Rd SW4 61 C2
North Bridge House Sch 18 NW3 11 B2
North Bridge House Senior Sch NW1 82 A3
Northbrook CE Sch SE12 67 C2
Northburgh St EC1 96 B2
North Carriage Dr W2 116 B4
Northchurch SE17 151 C2
Northchurch Ho 19 E2 24 C4
Northchurch Rd N1 15 C1
Northchurch Terr N1 16 A1
North Circular Rd NW2, NW10 8 A3
North Colonnade The E14 34 A1
Northcote Lodge Sch SW11 60 B1
Northcote Rd
Wandsworth SW11 60 B2
Willesden NW10 8 A1
Northcourt W1 105 A4
North Cres
Marylebone WC1 105 B4
Newham E16 27 C1
Northcroft Ct 8 W12 38 C4
North Cross Rd SE22 64 C2
North Ct SW1 134 A1
Northdown St N1 84 C1
North Dulwich Sta SE21 63 C2
NORTH END 2 B2
North End NW3 2 B2
North End Ave NW3 2 B2
North End Cres W14 140 C3
North End Ho W14 140 B3
North End Par W14 140 B3
North End Rd
Golders Green NW11 2 A3
West Kensington W14 141 A1
North End Way NW3 2 B2
Northern Hts N8 4 C4
Northesk Ho 6 E1 25 A1
North Eyot Gdns 5 W6 38 B1
Northey St E14 33 A2
Northfield Hall N6 3 C4
Northfield Ho 3 SE15 49 C4
Northfield Rd N16 7 A4
Northfields SW18 58 C3
Northfields Prospect SW18 58 C3
Northfields Rd W3 28 B4
Northfleet Ho SE1 137 B4
North Flower Wlk W2 115 B3
North Gate NW8 80 A1
Northgate Ct 14 SW9 62 C4
North Gower St NW1 93 A3
North Gr N6 3 C4
North Greenwich Pier SE10 35 B1
North Greenwich Sta SE10 43 A4
North Hill Ct N6 3 C4
North Ho 3 SE8 41 B1
Northiam WC1 94 B3
Northiam St E9 25 A4
Northington St WC1 95 A1
NORTH KENSINGTON 30 C4
Northlands St SE5 48 B1
Northleigh Ho 36 E3 27 A2
North Lo SW4 61 A3
North Lodge Cl SW15 57 C2
North London Science Ctr 12 N1 14 C1
North Mews WC1 95 A1
Northolme Rd N5 15 B4
North Pas SW18 58 C2
Northpoint Sq 8 NW1 13 C2
North Pole Rd W10 30 B4
Northport St N1 87 C3
North Rd
Barnsbury N7 14 A2
Brentford TW8 44 A4
Highgate N6 3 C4
Richmond TW9 44 C1
North Ride W2 116 A3
North Rise W2 102 B1
North Row W1 117 B4
NORTH SHEEN 44 C1
North Sheen Sta TW10 54 C3
North Side Wandsworth Comm SW18 59 C2
North St SW4 61 B4
Northstead Rd SW2 74 C2
North Tenter St E1 111 A1
North Terr SW3 130 A1
Northumberland Alley EC3 110 B1
Northumberland Ave WC2 120 A2
Northumberland Ho NW5 13 B2
Northumberland Mans E5 17 B4
Northumberland Pl W2 31 C3
Northumberland St WC2 120 A2
Northumbria Ct 10 TW9 54 A3
Northumbria St E14 33 C3
North Verbena Gdns 2 W6 38 C1
Northview 1 N7 5 A1
Northview Cres NW10 8 B4
Northview Prim Sch NW10 8 B4
North Villas NW1 13 C2
Northway Rd SE5 63 B4
Northways Par 2 NW3 11 C1
North West London Jewish Day Sch NW6 10 A1
Northwest Pl N1 85 C2
North Wharf Rd W2 101 B3
Northwick Cl NW8 89 B2
Northwick Ho NW8 89 A2
Northwick Terr NW8 89 B2
North Wlk W2 114 C3
Northwold Prim Sch E5 7 C2
Northwold Rd E5, N16 7 C2
North Wood Lo NW3 11 A4
Northwood Rd N6 4 A4
North Worple Way SW14 55 C4
Norton Folgate E1 110 B4
Norton Ho
14 Globe Town E2 25 C3
30 Stepney E1 32 A3
18 Stockwell SW9 173 A1
Norval Gn 1 SW9 173 C2
Norvic Ho 5 SE5 48 B1
Norway Gate SE16 41 A3
Norway Pl E14 33 B3
Norway St SE10 52 A4
Norwich Ho 6 E14 34 A3
Norwich St EC4 107 B2
Norwood Cl NW2 1 A1
Norwood Ho 25 E14 34 A2
Norwood NHS Ctr SE27 75 A1
Norwood Rd SE24, SE27 75 A3
Notley St SE5 48 C3
Notre Dame RC Girls Sch SE1 136 B1
Notting Barn Rd W10 22 C1
Nottingdale Sq W11 31 A1 112 A2
Nottingham Ct WC2 106 A1
Nottingham Ho
33 Camberwell SE5 48 B1
Stoke Newington N4 6 B3
Nottingham Pl W1 103 B4
Nottingham Rd SW17 72 B3
Nottingham St W1 103 B4
Nottingham Terr NW1 91 B1
NOTTING HILL 112 C3
Notting Hill Gate W11 31 C1 113 B2
Notting Hill Gate Sta W11 31 C1 113 B2
Notting Hill Prep Sch 17 W11 31 A3
Nottingwood Ho W11 31 A2 112 A4
Nova Bldg 1 E14 41 C2
Nova Ct E 3 E14 34 B1
Nova Ct W 2 E14 34 B1
Novello St SW6 165 B4
Nowell Rd SW13 46 C4
Noyna Rd SW17 72 B1
Nucleus NW10 20 B2
Nuding Cl SE13 66 C4
Nuffield Lo 14 W9 31 C4
Nugent Ct 3 N19 5 A3
Nugent Rd N19 5 A3
Nugent Terr NW8 79 A1
Nun Ct EC2 109 B2
NUNHEAD 65 B3
Nunhead Cres SE15 65 A4
Nunhead Gn SE15 65 A4
Nunhead Gr SE15 65 B4
Nunhead La SE15 65 A4
Nunhead Sta SE15 50 B1
Nursery Cl
New Cross SE4 51 B1
Putney SW15 57 C3
Nursery La
North Kensington W10 30 B4
Nursery La *continued*
Shoreditch E2 24 B4
Nursery Rd
Hackney E9 17 B2
Stockwell SW9 62 B3
Nursery Row SE17 151 B3
Nutbourne St W10 23 A2
Nutbrook St SE15 64 C4
Nutcroft Rd SE15 50 A3
Nutfield Rd
East Dulwich SE22 64 B3
Leyton E15 19 B4
Nutford Pl W1 102 C2
Nuthurst Ave SW2 74 B2
Nutley Terr NW3 11 C2
Nutmeg La E14 34 C3
Nuttall St N1 24 A3
Nutt St SE15 49 B3
Nye Bevan Ho SW6 154 C2
Nye's Wharf SE1, SE15 49 C4
Nylands Ave TW9 44 C1
Nynehead St SE14 51 A3
Nyton Cl N19 5 A3

O

O2 Ctr NW6 11 B2
O2 Millennium Dome The SE10 35 A1
Oakbank Gr SE24 63 B3
Oakbury Rd SW6 166 B1
Oakcourt 17 SE15 49 B3
Oak Cres E16 35 A4
Oakcroft Ct SE3 53 C2
Oakcroft Rd SE13 52 C1
Oakdale Ct N19 5 A2
Oakdale Rd SE15 65 B4
Oakdene 3 SE15 50 A2
Oakdene Ho 11 N16 7 A3
Oakden St SE11 149 C4
Oakeford Ho W14 126 B1
Oakend Ho 10 N4 6 C4
Oakeshott Ave N6 3 C2
Oakey La SE1 135 B2
Oakfield Ct
Clapham Pk SW4 62 A1
Finsbury Pk N8 5 A4
Oakfield Prep Sch SE21 75 C3
Oakfield Rd
Finsbury Pk N4 5 C4
Wimbledon SW19 69 C1
Oakfield St SW10 156 C4
Oakford Rd NW5 13 B4
Oak Gr NW2 10 A4
Oakham Ho 5 W10 22 B1
Oakhill Ave NW3 11 A4
Oakhill Ct
Honor Oak SE23 65 B1
Putney SW15 58 B2
Oak Hill Lo NW3 11 A4
Oak Hill Park Mews NW3 11 B4
Oak Hill Pk NW3 11 A4
Oakhill Pl SW15 58 C2
Oakhill Rd SW15 58 B2
Oak Hill Way NW3 11 B4

Oak Ho
13 Cubitt Town E14 42 B4
8 Maitland Pk NW3 12 B2
2 Richmond TW9 45 A2
9 Stoke Newington N16 6 C2
Oakhurst Gr SE22 64 C3
Oakington Rd W9 23 C1
Oakington Way N8 5 A4
Oak La E14 33 B2
Oaklands Ct
Dagenham NW10 21 A4
5 Shepherd's Bush W12 30 A1
Oaklands Gr W12 29 C1
Oaklands Ho SE4 66 B4
Oaklands Mews 1 NW2 9 C4
Oaklands Pas NW2 9 C4
Oaklands Pl 8 SW4 61 C3
Oaklands Rd
Cricklewood NW2 9 C4
Mortlake SW14 55 C4
Oaklands Sec Sch 31 E2 25 A2
Oakley Cres EC1 86 B1
Oakley Dr SE13 67 C1
Oakley Gdns SW3 158 B4
Oakley Ho SW1 145 A4
Oakley Pl SE1 152 C1
Oakley Rd N1 15 C1
Oakley Sq NW1 83 A2
Oakley St SW3 158 A4
Oakley Wlk W6 47 C4
Oak Lodge 14 SE21 75 C2
Oak Lodge Sch SW12 72 C4
Oakman Ho 29 SW19 69 C3
Oakmead Rd SW12 73 A3
Oak Park Gdns SW19 69 C3
Oak Park Mews N16 7 B1
Oakshaw Rd SW18 71 A4
Oakshott Ct NW1 83 B1
Oaks Sh Ctr The W3 28 B1
Oaks The
Brondesbury Pk NW6 9 C1
Willesden NW10 9 A1
Oak Tree Ct
Acton W3 28 A2
8 Clapham Pk SW4 62 A2
Oak Tree Ho W9 88 A2
Oak Tree Rd NW8 90 A3
Oakview Lo NW11 1 B4
Oak Village NW5 12 C4
Oak Way W3 29 A1
Oakwell Ho 24 SW8 171 B1
Oakwood Cl SE13 67 C1
Oakwood Ct W14 126 C2
Oakwood La W14 126 C2
Oakworth Rd W10 30 C4
Oast Ct 8 E14 33 B2
Oast Lo W4 46 A3
Oat La EC2 109 A2
Oatlands Ct 3 SW19 69 C3
Oatwell Ho SW3 144 B3
Oban Ho E14 34 C3
Oban St E14 34 C3
Oberon Ho 5 N1 24 A3
Oberstein Rd 15 SW11 59 C3
Oborne Cl SE24 63 A2
O'Brian Ho 10 E1 25 C2
Observatory Gdns W8 127 C4
Observatory Mews E14 42 C2
Observatory Rd
Kensington SW7 129 B1
Mortlake SW14 55 B3
Occupation Rd SE17 150 C2
Ocean St E1 32 C4
Ocean Wharf E14 41 C4
Ockbrook 3 E1 32 B4
Ockendon Rd N1 15 C2
Ockley Rd SW16 74 A1
Octagon Arc EC2 110 A3
Octagon The NW3 10 C4
Octavia Ho W10 23 A1
Octavia Mews 1 W9 23 B1
Octavia St SW11 168 B3
Octavius St SE8 51 C3
Odell Wlk SE13 67 B4
Odeon Ct
Dagenham NW10 21 A4
1 Newham E16 35 C4
Odessa Rd NW10 21 C3
Odessa St SE16 41 B3
Odette Duval Ho 29 E1 32 B4
Odger St SW11 169 A2
Odhams Wlk WC2 106 B1
Odin Ho 6 SE5 48 B1
O'Donnell Ct WC1 94 B2
O'Driscoll Ho 4 W12 30 A3
Offa's Mead E9 18 A4
Offenbach Ho 12 E2 25 C3
Offerton Rd SW4 61 B4
Offham Ho SE17 152 A3
Offley Ho 10 E9 17 C2
Offley Rd SW9 163 B2
Offord Rd N1 14 B1
Offord St N1 14 B1
Ogilvie Ho 12 E1 32 C3
Oglander Rd SE15 64 B4
Ogle St W1 104 C4
O'Gorman Ho SW10 157 A2
Ohio Bldg 13 SE13 52 A2
Oil Mill La W6 38 C1
Okehampton Rd NW10 22 C4
Okeover Manor SW4 61 A3
Olaf St W11 30 C2
Old Bailey EC4 108 B1
Old Bailey (Central Criminal Court) EC4 108 B2
Old Barrack Yd SW1 131 B3
Old Bellgate Wharf E14 41 C3
Old Bethnal Green Rd E2 25 A2
Old Billingsgate Wlk EC3 124 A3
Old Bldgs WC2 107 B2
Old Bond St W1 118 C3
Old Brewery Mews NW3 11 C4
Old Broad St EC2 109 C2
Old Brompton Rd SW5, SW7 143 A3
Old Burlington St W1 118 C3
Oldbury Ct E9 18 A3
Oldbury Pl W1 103 C4
Old Castle St E1 111 A2
Old Cavendish St W1 104 A1
Old Change Ct EC4 108 C1
Old Chiswick Yd W4 46 A4
Old Church Rd E1 32 C3
Old Church St SW3 143 C1
Old Compton St W1 105 B1
Old Court Ho W8 128 A3
Old Court Pl W8 128 A3
Old Covent Gdn WC2 120 B4
Old Dairy Mews
5 Balham SW12 72 C3
4 Camden Town NW5 13 A2
Old Deer Park Gdns TW9 54 A4
Old Devonshire Rd SW12 73 A4
Old Dock Cl TW9 44 C4
Oldfield Gr SE16 40 C2
Oldfield Ho 14 W4 38 A1
Oldfield Mews N6 4 B4
Oldfield Rd
Bedford Pk W3, W12 38 B4
Stoke Newington N16 7 A1
Willesden NW10 8 B1
Old Fish St Hill EC4 122 C4
Old Fleet La EC4 108 A2
OLD FORD 26 B4
Old Ford Prim Sch 33 E3 26 B3
Old Ford Rd E2, E3 25 C3
Old Ford Trad Est E3 26 C4
Old Forge Mews W12 39 A4
Old Forge Rd N19 4 C2
Old Gloucester St WC1 106 B4
Oldham Terr W3 28 B1
Oldhill St N16 7 C3
Old Hospital Cl SW12, SW17 72 B3
Olding Ho 6 SW12 73 B4
Old Jamaica Bsns Est 23 SE16 139 B1
Old Jamaica Rd SE16 139 B2
Old James St SE15 65 A4
Old Jewry EC2 109 B1
Old Kent Rd
Deptford SE1, SE15 50 A4
Walworth SE1 152 B2
Old Laundry The 14 SW18 59 C3
Old Manor Ct NW8 79 A2
Old Manor Yd SW5 142 A3
Old Market Sq 11 E2 24 B2 99 A4
Old Marylebone Rd NW1 102 B3
Old Mitre Ct EC4 107 C1
Old Montague St E1 111 B3
Old Nichol St E2 24 B1 98 C2
Old North St WC1 106 C4
OLD OAK COMMON 21 B1
Old Oak Common La NW10 21 A1
Old Oak La NW10 21 B2
Old Oak Prim Sch W12 29 B3
Old Oak Rd W3 29 B2
Old Orch The NW3 12 B4
Old Palace Prim Sch 51 E3 27 A2
Old Paradise St SE11 148 C4
Old Park Ave SW12 60 C1
Old Park La W1 118 A1
Old Pearson St SE10 52 A3
Old Pye St SW1 133 B2
Old Pye Street Est SW1 133 B1
Old Quebec St W1 103 A1
Old Queen St SW1 133 C3
Oldridge Rd SW12 73 A4
Old Royal Free Pl N1 85 C3
Old Royal Free Sq N1 85 C3
Old School Sq 12 E14 33 C3
Old School The WC1 107 A4
Old Seacoal La EC4 108 A1
Old South Lambeth Rd SW8 162 B2
Old Spitalfields Mkt E1 110 C4
Old Sq WC2 107 B2
Old St EC1 97 C2
Old Stable Mews N5 6 B1
Old Street Sta EC1 97 C2
Old Sun Wharf E14 33 A2
Old Swan Wharf SW11 167 C4
Old Theatre Ct SE1 123 A2
Old Town SW4 61 B4
Old Vicarage Sch 13 TW10 54 A1
Old Woolwich Rd SE10 42 C1
Old York Rd SW18 59 A2
O'Leary Sq E1 32 B4
Olga Prim Sch 37 E3 26 A3
Olga St 20 E3 26 A3
Oliphant St W10 23 A2
Olive Blythe Ho 14 W10 23 A1
Oliver Bsns Pk NW10 20 B3
Oliver Cl W4 45 A4
Olive Rd NW2 9 B4
Oliver Goldsmith Prim Sch 18 SE5 49 B2
Oliver Ho
22 Bermondsey SE16 139 B3
Notting Hill W11 31 A2 112 A3
South Lambeth SW8 162 A2
Oliver House Prep Sch 1 SW4 61 A1
Oliver Mews SE15 49 C1
Oliver's Yd EC1 97 C2
Olive Tree Ho 7 SE15 50 B4
Olive Tree Sch The SE13 67 A1
Olivette St 1 SW15 57 C3
Olive Waite Ho NW6 11 A1
Ollerton Gn E3 26 B4
Ollgar Cl W12 29 B1
Olliffe St E14 42 B3
Olmar St SE1 49 C4
Olney Ho NW8 90 B2
Olney Rd SE17 48 B4
Olympia Ex Ctr W14 126 B1
Olympian Ct 8 E14 41 C2
Olympia Way W14 126 B1
Olympia Yd W2 114 B3
Olympic Ho 10 W10 30 B3
Olympic Park E15 19 A2
Olympic Stadium E15 19 A1
Olympus Sq E5 7 C1
Oman Ave NW2 9 B4
Oman Ct NW4 9 A4
Ombersley Ho N4 6 B4
Omeara St SE1 123 A1
Omega Cl E14 42 A3
Omega Ho SW10 157 A2
Omega Pl N1 84 B1
Omega St SE14 51 C2
Omega Works E3 18 C1
Ommaney Rd SE14 51 A2
Omnibus Bsns Ctr N7 14 A3
Ondine Rd SE15 64 B3
Onedin Point 10 E1 125 C3
Onega Gate SE16 41 A3
O'Neill Ho NW8 79 C1
One New Change Sh Ctr EC4 108 C1
One Tree Cl SE23 65 B1
Ongar Ho 15 N1 15 C2
Ongar Rd SW6 155 C4
Onslow Ave TW10 54 A2
Onslow Avenue Mans 10 TW10 54 A2

- Onslow Cl W9 23 B2
- Onslow Ct SW10 143 A1
- Onslow Gdns SW7 143 B2
- Onslow Lo 28 SW2 74 C4
- Onslow Mews E SW7 143 B3
- Onslow Mews W SW7 143 B3
- Onslow Rd TW10 54 A1
- Onslow Sq SW7 143 C3
- Onslow St EC1 95 C1
- Ontario St SE1 136 B2
- Ontario Way E14 33 C2
- Opal St SE11 150 A2
- Open Air Theatre, Regent's Pk NW1 91 B3
- Openview SW17, SW18 71 C2
- Opera Ct 7 N19 4 C1
- Operating Theatre Mus & Herb Garret The SE1 123 C1
- Ophelia Gdns NW2 1 A1
- Ophir Terr SE15 49 C2
- Opie Ho NW8 80 B2
- Oppenheim Rd SE13 52 B1
- Oppidan Apartments NW6 10 C2
- Oppidans Rd NW3 12 B1
- Orange Pl SE16 40 B3
- Orangery Gallery The W8 126 C3
- Orange St WC2 119 C3
- Orange Yd WC2 105 C1
- Oransay Rd 25 N1 15 B2
- Oratory La SW3 143 C2
- Oratory RC Prim Sch SW3 144 A2
- Orbain Rd SW6 154 B1
- Orbel St SW11 168 A3
- Orb St SE17 151 B3
- Orchard Cl
  - Honor Oak SE23 65 B1
  - 21 Islington N1 15 B1
  - Kensal Town W10 31 A4
- Orchard Ct
  - Barnes SW13 56 B4
  - Marylebone W1 103 B2
- Orchard Dr SE3 53 A1
- Orchard Hill SE13 52 A2
- Orchard Ho
  - Camberwell SE5 48 B2
  - 11 Rotherhithe SE16 40 B3
  - Shepherd's Bush W12 29 C1
- Orchard House Sch 15 W4 37 A2
- Orchard Mead Ho NW11 1 C2
- Orchard Mews N1 15 C1
- Orchard Pl E14 35 A2
- Orchard Prim Sch 41 E9 17 B1
- Orchard Rd
  - Highgate N6 4 A4
  - Richmond TW9 54 C4
- Orchard Rise TW10 55 A3
- Orchardson Ho NW8 89 C1
- Orchardson St NW8 89 C1
- Orchard Sq W14 140 C1
- Orchard St W1 103 C2
- Orchard The
  - Acton Green W4 37 C2
  - Lewisham SE3 52 C1
- Orchid Cl SE13 67 C2
- Orchid St W12 29 C2
- Orde Hall St WC1 106 C4
- Orde Ho 10 N16 15 C4
- Ordell Ct 36 E3 26 B3
- Ordell Rd E3 26 B3
- Ordnance Cres SE10 43 A4
- Ordnance Hill NW8 79 C3
- Ordnance Mews NW8 79 C2
- Ordnance Rd E16 35 B4
- Oregano Dr E14 34 C3
- Oregon Bldg 5 SE13 52 A2
- Orestes Mews 1 NW6 10 C3
- Orford Ct SE27 75 A2
- Oriana Ho 3 E14 33 B2
- Oriel Ct NW3 11 B4
- Oriel Dr SW13 47 B4
- Oriel Rd
  - Hackney E9 18 A2
  - Homerton E9 17 C2
- Orient St SE11 150 A4
- Orion Bsns Ctr SE14 40 C1
- Orion Ho 20 E1 25 A1
- Orion Point 5 E14 41 C2
- Orkney Ho N1 84 C4
- Orkney St SW11 169 B2
- Orlando Rd SW4 61 B4
- Orleston Mews N7 14 C2
- Orleston Rd N7 14 C2
- Orlop St SE10 43 A1
- Orme Ct W2 114 A3
- Orme Ct Mews W2 114 B3
- Orme Ho 8 E8 24 B4
- Orme La W2 114 A3
- Ormeley Rd SW12 73 A3
- Ormerod Ho 3 SW9 62 A4
- Orme Sq W2 114 A3
- Ormiston Gr W12 30 A1
- Ormiston Rd SE10 43 C1
- Ormond Cl WC1 106 B4
- Ormonde Ct SW15 57 B3
- Ormonde Gate SW3 145 A1
- Ormonde Mans WC1 106 B4
- Ormonde Pl SW1 145 C3
- Ormonde Rd SW14 55 B4
- Ormonde Terr NW8 80 C3
- Ormond Ho 7 N16 6 C2
- Ormond Mans WC1 94 C1
- Ormond Mews WC1 94 B1
- Ormond Rd N4, N19 5 A3
- Ormond Yd SW1 119 A2
- Ormrod Ct W11 31 B3
- Ormsby Lo 7 W4 38 A3
- Ormsby Pl N16 7 B1
- Ormsby St E2 24 B3
- Ormside St SE15 50 B4
- Ornan Rd NW3 12 A3
- Orpen Ho SW5 141 C3
- Orpen Wlk N16 7 A1
- Orpheus Ho 25 N19 4 C4
- Orpheus St SE5 48 C2
- Orsett Mews W2 100 C2
- Orsett St SE11 149 A2
- Orsett Terr W2 100 C2
- Orsman Rd N1 24 A4
- Orton St E1 125 B1
- Orville Rd SW11 167 C2
- Orwell Ct
  - Hackney E8 24 C4
  - Highbury N5 15 B4
- Orwell Ho W12 29 C2
- Osbaldeston Rd N16 7 C3
- Osbert St SW1 147 B3
- Osborn Cl E8 24 C4
- Osborne Rd
  - Finsbury Pk N4 5 C3
  - Hackney E9 18 B2
  - South Acton W3 37 A4
  - Willesden NW2 9 A2
- Osborn St E1 111 A4
- Osbourne Ho TW10 54 C2
- Oscar Faber Pl 8 N1 16 A1
- Oscar St SE8 51 C1
- Oseney Cres NW5 13 C2
- Osier Ct E1 25 C1
- Osier La SE10 43 B3
- Osier Mews W4 46 B4
- Osiers Rd SW18 58 C3
- Osier St E1 25 B1
- Oslo Ct NW8 80 A1
- Oslo Ho 2 SE5 48 B1
- Oslo Sq SE16 41 A3
- Oslow Cl W10 23 B2
- Osmani Prim Sch E1 111 C4
- Osman Rd W6 39 B3
- Osmington Ho SW8 163 A1
- Osmund St W12 29 B4
- Osnaburgh St NW1 92 B2
- Osnaburgh Terr NW1 92 B2
- Osprey Ct NW3 11 A3
- Osprey Ho
  - Camberwell SE15 49 B2
  - 3 Limehouse E14 33 A2
- Ospringe Ho SE1 121 C1
- Ospringe Rd NW5 13 B4
- Osram Ct W6 39 B3
- Osric Path 8 N1 24 A3
- Ossian Mews N4 5 B4
- Ossian Rd N4 5 B4
- Ossington Bldgs W1 103 B3
- Ossington Cl W2 31 C2 113 C3
- Ossington St W2 114 A3
- Ossory Rd SE1 49 C4
- Ossulston St NW1 83 C2
- Ostade Rd SW2 74 B4
- Osten Mews SW7 128 B1
- Osterley Ho 5 E14 34 A3
- Osterley Rd N16 16 A4
- Oswald Bldg SW8 160 A3
- Oswald's Mead E9 18 A4
- Osward Rd SW12, SW17 72 B2
- Oswell Ho 9 E1 32 A1
- Oswin St SE11 150 B4
- Oswyth Rd SE5 49 A1
- Otford Cres SE4 66 B1
- Otford Ho
  - Bermondsey SE1 137 C3
  - 6 Deptford SE15 50 B4
- Otha Ho 13 SW9 172 B2
- Othello Cl SE11 150 A2
- Otis St E3 27 B2
- Otley Ho N5 6 A1
- Ottaway Ct E5 7 C1
- Ottaway St E5 7 C1
- Otterburn Ho 12 SE5 48 B3
- Otter Cl E15 27 B4
- Otto St SE17 48 A4
- Our Lady of Dolours RC Prim Sch 1 W2 100 A4
- Our Lady of Lourdes RC Prim Sch
  - 1 Lewisham SE13 67 C4
  - London NW10 20 B4
- Our Lady of Victories RC Prim Sch
  - 7 Putney SW15 57 C3
  - South Kensington SW7 143 A3
- Our Lady Queen of Heaven RC Prim Sch 10 SW19 69 C4
- Our Lady RC Prim Sch
  - Camden Town NW1 83 A4
  - 28 Poplar E14 33 B3
- Our Lady & St Joseph RC Prim Sch 14 N1 16 A2
- Our Lady's Convent RC High Sch 3 N15 7 A4
- Ouseley Rd SW12 72 B3
- Outer Circ NW8 81 A1
- Outgate Rd NW10 8 B1
- Outram Pl N1 84 B4
- Outwich St EC3 110 B2
- Outwood Ho 3 SW2 74 B4
- Oval Mans SE11 163 A4
- Oval Pl SW8 163 A2
- Oval Rd NW1 82 A4
- Oval Sta SE11 163 B3
- Oval The E2 25 A3
- Oval Way SE11 149 A1
- Overbury Ho 3 E5 17 C4
- Overbury St E5 17 C4
- Overcliff Rd SE13 66 C4
- Overhill Rd SE21, SE22 76 C4
- Overlea Rd E5 7 C4
- Oversley Ho 17 W2 31 C4
- Overstone Ho 19 E14 33 C3
- Overstone Rd W6 39 B2
- Overstrand Mans SW11 169 B3
- Overton Ho SW15 68 B4
- Overton Rd SW9 173 C1
- Overy Ho SE1 136 A3
- Ovex Cl E14 42 B4
- Ovington Ct SW3 130 B1
- Ovington Gdns SW3 130 B1
- Ovington Mews SW3 130 B1
- Ovington Sq SW3 130 B1
- Ovington St SW3 144 B4
- Owen Ho 11 N19 13 B4
- Owen's Ct EC1 96 A4
- Owen's Row EC1 96 A4
- Owen St EC1 86 A1
- Owgan Cl SE5 48 C3
- Oxberry Ave SW6 164 B2
- Oxbridge Ct 4 W4 37 A1
- Oxendon St SW1, W1 119 B3
- Oxenford St SE15 64 B4
- Oxenham Ho 13 SE8 51 C4
- Oxenholme NW1 83 A1
- Oxestalls Rd SE8 41 A1
- Oxford & Cambridge Mans NW1 102 B3
- Oxford Cir W1 104 C1
- Oxford Circus Ave W1 104 C1
- Oxford Circus Sta W1 104 C1
- Oxford Ct
  - City of London EC4 123 B4
  - Gunnersbury W4 37 A1
  - 48 Paddington W2 31 C4
- Oxford Dr SE1 124 A1
- Oxford Gardens Prim Sch 21 W10 30 C3
- Oxford Gate W6 39 C2
- Oxford Gdns
  - Brentford W4 44 C4
  - North Kensington W10 30 C3
- Oxford Ho N4 5 C3
- Oxford Rd
  - Finsbury Pk N4 5 C3
  - Paddington NW6 23 C3
  - Putney SW15 58 A3
  - Stratford E15 19 C2
- Oxford Rd N W4 37 A1
- Oxford Rd S W4 37 A1
- Oxford Sq W2 102 B1
- Oxford St W1 104 B1
- Oxley Cl SE1 153 A2
- Oxonian St SE22 64 B3
- OXO Tower SE1 121 C3
- Oxo Tower Wharf SE1 121 C3
- Oxted Ct N16 7 A3
- Oyster Row E1 32 B3
- Ozolins Way E16 35 C3

P

- Pablo Neruda Cl 4 SE24 63 A3
- Pace Pl E1 32 A3
- Pacific Ho 15 E1 25 C1
- Pacific Rd E16 35 C3
- Pacific Wharf SE16 32 C1
- Packenham Ho
  - 24 Crouch End N19 4 C4
  - 21 Spitalfields E2 24 B2 99 A4
- Packington Sq N1 86 C4
- Packington St N1 86 B3
- Padbury SE17 152 B1

Padbury Ct E2 24 B2 99 A3
Padbury Ho NW8 90 B2
Paddenswick Ct [2] W6 39 A3
Paddenswick Rd W6 38 C3
PADDINGTON 100 C3
Paddington Acad [7] W9 23 C1
Paddington Gn W2 101 B4
Paddington Green Prim Sch NW8 89 B1
Paddington St W1 103 B4
Paddington Sta W2 101 B2
Paddock Cl SE3 53 C1
Paddock Prim Sch SW11 60 C3
Paddock Sch SW15 56 B3
Paddock Way [11] SW15 69 B4
Padfield Rd SE5 63 B4
Padstone Ho [50] E3 27 A2
Padstow Ho [12] E14 33 B2
Pagden St SW8 170 B4
Pageant Cres SE16 33 B1
Pageantmaster Ct EC4 108 A1
Page Ho SE10 52 B4
Page St SW1 147 C4
Page's Wlk SE1 138 B1
Page's Yd W4 46 A4
Paget Ho [15] E2 25 B3
Paget Rd N16 6 C3
Paget St EC1 96 A4
Pagham Ho [8] W10 22 B1
Pagnell St SE14 51 B3
Pagoda Ave TW9 54 B4
Pagoda Gdns SE3 52 C1
Pagoda Gr SE27 75 B2
Paine Ct SE3 53 B4
Painsthorpe Rd [3] N16 7 A1
Painswick Ct [1] SE15 49 B3
Painters Mews SE16 153 C4
Pakeman Ho SE1 136 B4
Pakeman Prim Sch [1] N7 5 B1
Pakeman St N7 5 B1
Pakenham Cl SW12 72 C3
Pakenham St WC1 95 A2
Palace Ave W8 128 B4
Palace Cl [4] E9 18 B2
Palace Ct
Hampstead NW3 11 A3
Kensington W2 114 A3
Streatham SW2 74 C2
Palace Garden Mews W8 31 C1 113 C2
Palace Gate W8 128 C3
Palace Gdns Mews W8 114 B1
Palace Gn W8 114 A1
Palace Mans W14 140 B4
Palace Mews
Belgravia SW1 145 C3
Fulham SW6 155 A2
Palace Pl SW1 132 C2
Palace Rd SE27, SW16, SW2 74 C2
Palace St SW1 132 C2
Palatine Ave N16 16 A4
Palatine Rd N16 16 A4
Palazzo Apartments [11] N1 16 A1
Palemead Cl SW6 47 C2
Palermo Rd NW10 21 C3
Palewell Common Dr SW14 55 C2
Palewell Pk SW14 55 C3
Palfrey Pl SW8 163 A2
Palgrave Gdns NW1 90 B2
Palgrave Ho
[7] Camberwell SE5 48 B3
[4] Maitland Pk NW3 12 B3
Palgrave Rd W12 38 B3
Palissy St [35] E2 24 B2 98 C3
Pallant Ho SE1 137 C1
Pallester Ct NW11 1 A3
Palliser Ct W14 140 A1
Palliser Ho
[3] Greenwich SE10 52 C4
[21] Stepney E1 25 C1
Palliser Rd W14 140 A1
Pallister Terr SW15 68 B2
Pall Mall SW1 119 B1
Pall Mall E SW1 119 C2
Pall Mall Pl SW1 119 A1
Palm Ct
[18] Camberwell SE15 49 B3
Stoke Newington N16 6 C2
Palmer Ho
[6] Deptford SE14 50 C3
[8] Kentish Town NW5 13 B4
[5] Tufnell Pk N19 4 B1
Palmer Pl N7 14 C3
Palmers Rd
Globe Town E2 25 C3
Mortlake SW14 55 B4
Palmer St SW1 133 B2
Palmerston Ct [22] E3 25 C3
Palmerston Ho
Battersea SW11 169 C3
Kensington W8 31 C1 113 B1
Palmerston Rd
Acton Green W3 37 B3
Brondesbury NW6 10 B1
Hampstead NW6 10 C1
Mortlake SW14 55 B3
Palmerston Way SW8 160 B1
Palm Gr W5 36 A3
Palm Tree Ho [2] SE14 50 C3
Pamela Ct NW10 8 C1
Pamela Ho [14] E8 24 B4
Pamlion Ct N4 5 A4
Panama Ho [6] E1 32 C4
Pancras La EC2 109 B1
Pancras Rd NW1 83 C2
Pancras Way E3 26 C3
Pandian Way [4] NW5 13 C2
Pandora Rd NW6 10 C2
Pangbourne NW1 92 C3
Pangbourne Ave W10 30 B4
Pangbourne Ho [4] N7 14 A3
Pankhurst Cl [7] SE14 50 C3
Pankhurst Ho [2] NW10 30 B3
Panmure Cl N5 15 A4
Pan Penisula Sq E14 42 A4
Pansy Gdns W12 29 C2
Panton St SW1 119 B3
Panyer Alley EC2 108 C2
Paper Mill Wharf E14 33 A2
Papworth Gdns N7 14 B3
Papworth Way SW2 74 C4
Parade Mans [19] SE5 48 B1
Parade Mews SE27, SW2 75 A2
Parade The SW11 159 A2
Paradise Pas N7 14 C3
Paradise Rd
Richmond TW10 54 A2
South Lambeth SW4 172 A2
Paradise Row E2 25 A2
Paradise St SE16 40 A4
Paradise Wlk SW3 159 A4
Paragon Christian Acad E5 17 C4
Paragon Cl E16 35 C3
Paragon Ho SE3 53 B1
Paragon Mews SE1 151 C4
Paragon Pl SE3 53 B1
Paragon Rd E9 17 B2
Paragon The
Kidbrooke SE3 53 C1
Walworth SE17 151 C4
Paramount Bldg EC1 96 A2
Paramount Ct WC1 93 A1
Parbury Rd SE23 66 A1
Pardoner St SE1 137 C2
Pardon St EC1 96 B2
Parfett St E1 111 C2
Parfitt Cl NW11 2 B3
Parfrey St W6 47 B4
Paris Gdn SE1 122 A2
Paris Ho [12] E2 25 A3
Park Ave
Golders Green NW11 2 A3
Mortlake SW14 55 C3
Willesden NW2 9 B2
Park Ave N NW10 9 A3
Park Cl
Kensington W14 127 A2
Knightsbridge SW1 130 C3
[13] South Hackney E9 25 B4
Park Cres W1 92 A1
Park Crescent Mews E W1 92 B1
Park Crescent Mews W W1 92 A1
Park Ct
Battersea SW11 170 A4
Clapham Pk SW4 61 C2
Dulwich SE21 75 C1
[12] Hammersmith W6 38 C2
Upper Tooting SW12 72 C3
Park Dr
Acton W3 36 C3
Golders Green NW11 2 A3
Mortlake SW14 55 C3
Park Dwellings [7] NW3 12 B3
Park End NW3 12 A4
Parker Ct
Shoreditch N1 87 A4
South Lambeth SW4 172 A3
Parke Rd SW13 46 C2
Parker Mews WC2 106 B2
Parkers Row [15] SE16 139 B3
Parker's Row SE1 139 A3
Parker St WC2 106 B2
Parkfield Ave SW14 56 A3
Parkfield Ct SE14 51 B2
Parkfield Ind Est SW11 169 C2
Parkfield Rd
New Cross SE14 51 B2
Willesden NW10 9 A1
Parkfields SW15 57 B3
Parkfield St N1 85 C2
Park Flats N6 3 A4
Parkgate Gdns SW14 55 C2
Parkgate House Sch SW11 60 C3
Parkgate Mews N6 4 B4
Parkgate Rd SW11 158 B1
Park Hall SE10 52 C3
Park Hall Rd SE21 75 C1
Park Hall Road Trad Est SE21 75 C1
Parkham St SW11 168 A3
Park Heights Ct [21] E14 33 B3
Park Hill
Clapham Pk SW4 61 C2
Richmond TW10 54 B1
Park Hill Ct SW17 72 B1
Parkhill Rd NW3 12 B3
Park Hill Wlk [10] NW3 12 B3
Park Ho
[8] Camberwell SE5 48 C2
Finsbury Pk N4 6 A2
[35] Hackney E9 17 B1
Richmond TW10 54 A1
Parkholme Rd E8 16 C2
Parkhouse St SE5 48 C3
Parkhurst Ct N7 14 A4
Parkhurst Rd N7 14 A4
Parkinson Ct
Finsbury N1 97 B3
Shoreditch EC1 97 C4
Parkinson Ho [6] E9 17 B1
Park La
Mayfair W1 117 B3
Mill Meads E15 27 C4
Parkland Ct W14 126 A4
Parkland Gdns [12] SW19 69 C3
Parklands
East Dulwich SE22 65 A2
Highgate N6 4 A4
Parklands Cl SW14 55 B2
Park Lea Ct N16 7 A4
Parklife Oxford St W1 103 B1
Park Lo
[11] South Hampstead NW8 11 C1
[10] Wapping E1 32 A1
Willesden NW2 9 B4
Park Lofts [9] SW4 62 A2
Park Lorne NW8 90 B3
Park Mans
Battersea SW11 168 C3
Bedford Pk W6 38 B3
Fulham SW6 164 B3
Knightsbridge SW1 130 C3
St John's Wood NW8 80 A1
Vauxhall SW8 162 B4
Parkmead SW15 57 A1
Park Mews
Greenwich SE10 43 B1
Kensal Rise W10 23 A3
Park Par
Acton W3 36 C3
Dagenham NW10 21 B3
Park Piazza [3] SE13 67 C1
Park Pl
Canary Wharf E14 33 C1
Gunnersbury W3 36 C2
Shoreditch N1 87 C4
St James SW1 118 C2
Park Place Dr W3 36 C3
Park Place Ho [8] SE10 52 C4
Park Place Villas W2 101 A4
Park Rd
Chiswick W4 45 C4
Dagenham NW10 21 A4
Lisson Gr NW1, NW8 90 B2
Richmond TW10 54 B1
Park Rd E W3 37 B4
Park Rd N
Chiswick W4 37 C1
South Acton W3 37 A4
Park Road E [11] W3 37 A4
Park Row SE10 52 C4
PARK ROYAL 20 A2
Park Royal NW10 20 A4
Park Royal Bsns Ctr NW10 20 B1
Park Royal Metro Ctr NW10 20 A1
Park Royal Rd NW10, W3 20 B1
Park S SW11 169 B3
Park St James NW8 80 C3

Park Sheen 3 SW14 ... 55 A3
Parkshot TW9 ... 54 A3
Parkside
East Acton W3 ... 29 A1
Greenwich SE3 ... 53 B3
Park Side NW2 ... 9 A4
Parkside Bsns Est SE8 ... 51 A4
Parkside Cres N7 ... 5 C1
Parkside Est E9 ... 25 C4
Parkside (Private) Hospl SW19 ... 69 C1
Parkside St SW11 169 B3
Park Sq E NW1 ... 92 B2
Park Square Mews NW1 ... 92 A1
Park Sq W NW1 ... 92 A1
Park St
Borough The SE1 ... 123 A2
Mayfair W1 ... 117 B3
Parkstead Rd SW15 ... 57 A2
Parkstone Rd 5 SE15 ... 49 C1
Park Stps W2 ... 116 B4
Park The NW11 ... 2 A3
Parkthorne Rd SW12 ... 73 C4
Park Twrs W1 ... 118 A1
Park View
Dagenham W3 ... 28 B4
Highbury N5 ... 15 B4
Willesden NW2 ... 9 B4
Parkview Ct SW6 . 164 B1
Park View Ct SW18 ... 58 C1
Park View Ho SE24 ... 63 A1
Park View Mans N4 .. 6 A4
Park View Mews 24 SW9 ... 172 C2
Park View Rd NW10 .. 8 B4
Park Village E NW1 ... 82 B1
Park Village W NW1 ... 82 A2
Parkville Rd SW6 154 C1
Park Vista SE10 ... 52 C4
Park Walk Prim Sch SW10 ... 157 B3
Parkwat Cres E15 .. 19 B3
Parkway NW1 ... 82 A3
Park Way W3 ... 36 C2
Parkway Ho SW14 .. 55 C3
Park West W2 ... 102 B1
Park West Pl W1, W2 ... 102 B2
Park Wlk
Chelsea SW10 ... 157 B4
Highgate N6 ... 3 C4
Parkwood NW8 ... 80 C3
Parkwood Prim Sch 1 N4 ... 6 A2
Parliament Ct NW3 ... 12 A4
Parliament Hill NW3 ... 12 A4
Parliament Hill Mans NW5 ... 12 C4
Parliament Hill Sch NW5 ... 12 C4
Parliament Mews SW14 ... 45 B1
Parliament Sq SW1 ... 134 A3
Parliament St SW1 ... 134 A4
Parliament View Apartments SE11 ... 148 C4
Parma Cres SW11 .. 60 B3
Parminter Ind Est 20 E2 ... 25 A3
Parmiter St E2 ... 25 A3
Parmoor Ct EC1 ... 96 C2
Parnell Cl W12 ... 39 A3
Parnell Ho WC1 .. 105 C2
Parnell Rd E3 ... 26 B4
Parnham St E14 ... 33 A3
Parolles Rd N19 ... 4 B3
Parr Ct N1 ... 87 B2
Parrington Ho 1 SW4 ... 61 C1
Parr Pl W4 ... 38 B2
Parr St N1 ... 87 B2
Parry Ho 32 E1 ... 32 A1
Parry Rd W10 ... 23 A2
Parry St SW8 ... 162 B4
Parsifal Coll 1 NW3 ... 10 C4
Parsifal Ho NW3 ... 10 C4
Parsifal Rd NW6 ... 10 C3
Parsonage St E14 .. 42 B2
Parsons Gn SW6 . 165 B3
PARSONS GREEN ... 165 B4
Parsons Green La SW6 ... 165 B4
Parsons Green Sta SW6 ... 165 B3
Parsons Ho
Paddington W2 ... 89 B1
21 Streatham SW12 ... 74 A4
Parsons Lo NW6 ... 11 A1
Parthenia Rd SW6 ... 165 C3
Partington Cl N19 ... 4 C3
Parton Lo 14 E8 ... 16 B2
Partridge Ct EC1 .. 96 A2
Partridge Ho 22 E3 ... 26 B3
Pascall Ho SE17 ... 48 B4
Pascal St SW8 ... 161 C2
Pascoe Rd SE13 ... 67 C2
Pasley Cl SE17 ... 150 C1
Passfield Dr E14 ... 34 A4
Passfields W14 ... 140 C1
Passing Alley EC1 .. 96 B1
Passmore St SW1 145 B2
Pastor St SE1, SE11 ... 150 B4
Patcham Terr SW8 ... 170 B4
Patent Ho E14 ... 34 A4
Paternoster La EC4 ... 108 B2
Paternoster Sq EC4 ... 108 B2
Pater St W8 ... 127 B1
Patience Rd SW11 ... 168 A1
Patience Villas SE13 ... 67 C4
Patio Cl SW4 ... 61 C1
Patmore Ho 9 N16 ... 16 A3
Patmore St SW8 .. 171 A4
Patmos Rd SW9 ... 48 A2
Paton Cl E3 ... 26 C2
Paton Ho 3 SW9 172 C2
Paton St EC1 ... 96 C3
Patrick Coman Ho EC1 ... 96 A3
Patrick Connolly Gdns 41 E3 ... 27 A2
Patriot Sq E2 ... 25 A3
Patrol Pl SE6 ... 67 A1
Pat Shaw Ho 2 E1 ... 25 C1
Patshull Pl NW5 ... 13 B2
Patshull Rd NW5 ... 13 B2
Patten Ho N4 ... 6 B3
Patten Rd SW18 ... 72 A4
Patterdale NW1 ... 92 B3
Patterdale Rd SE15 ... 50 B3
Pattina Wlk SE16 ... 33 A1
Pattinson Point 10 E16 ... 35 C4
Pattison Ho
Borough The SE1 .. 137 A4
1 Stepney E1 ... 32 C3
Pattison Rd NW2 ... 1 C1
Pat Williams Ho SE27 ... 75 B1
Paul Daisley Ct 2 NW6 ... 10 A1
Paulet Rd SE5 ... 48 A2
Paul Ho 13 W10 ... 23 A1
Pauline Ho 21 E1 111 C4
Paul Julius Cl E14 .. 34 C2
Paul St EC2 .. 24 A1 98 A2
Paultons Ho SW3 157 C4
Paultons Sq SW3 157 C4
Paultons St SW3 . 157 C3
Pauntley Ho 6 N19 . 4 B3
Pauntley St 4 N19 .. 4 B3
Pavan Ct 29 E2 ... 25 B2
Paveley Dr SW11 . 158 A1
Paveley Ho N1 ... 84 C1
Paveley St NW8 ... 90 B2
Pavement The
Brentford W5 ... 36 A3
Clapham SW4 ... 61 B3
Pavilion Ct
7 Hampstead NW3 ... 11 B4
Hampstead NW3 ... 11 C3
3 Paddington NW6 ... 23 C2
Pavilion Mans 10 SW9 ... 62 B3
Pavilion Rd SW1 .. 131 A1
Pavilion Sq SW17 ... 72 B1
Pavilion St SW1 .. 131 A1
Pavilion Terr 8 W12 ... 30 B3
Pavillion Ct SW1 . 160 A4
Pavitt Ct NW10 ... 8 C1
Paxton Cl TW9 ... 44 B1
Paxton Ho SE17 .. 151 A2
Paxton Rd W4 ... 46 A4
Paxton Terr SW1 .. 160 B4
Paymal Ho 33 E1 ... 32 B4
Payne Ho N1 ... 85 A3
Payne Rd E3 ... 27 A3
Paynesfield Ave SW14 ... 55 C4
Payne St SE8 ... 51 B4
Paynes Wlk W6 ... 154 A3
Peabody Ave SW1 146 B1
Peabody Bldgs
6 Camberwell SE5 ... 48 C2
Walworth SE17 ... 151 B3
Peabody Cl SW1 .. 160 B4
Peabody Ct
9 Camberwell SE5 ... 48 C2
St Luke's EC1 ... 97 A1
Peabody Est
18 Bethnal Green E2 ... 25 A3
Borough The SE1 .. 122 C1
Fulham SW6 ... 155 A4
17 Hammersmith W6 ... 39 B1
Holborn EC1 ... 95 C1
Lambeth SE1 ... 121 C1
North Kensington W10 ... 30 B4
4 Ratcliff E1 ... 32 C2
7 St George in t East E1 ... 125 B4
St Luke's EC1 ... 97 A1
Strand WC2 ... 106 C1
Streatham SE24 ... 75 B4
Westminster SW1 . 147 A4
Peabody Hill SE21 .. 75 B3
Peabody Sq SE1 .. 136 A3
Peabody Twr EC1 .. 97 A1
Peabody Yd N1 ... 86 C4
Peace Pagoda SW3 ... 159 A2
Peach Rd W10 ... 23 A2
Peachum Rd SE3 ... 53 B4
Peach Walk Mews 24 E3 ... 25 C3
Peacock St SE17 . 150 B3
Peacock Yd SE17 . 150 B3
Peak Ho N4 ... 6 B3
Pearce Ho
Camden Town N19 ... 4 B1
7 Streatham SW2 .. 74 A4
Westminster SW1 . 147 C3
Pear Cl SE14 ... 51 A3
Pear Ct 31 SE15 ... 49 B3
Peardon St SW8 .. 170 B1
Pearfield Ho 1 N5 ... 15 B3
Pearl St E1 ... 32 A1
Pearmain Ho 9 SE13 ... 52 B1
Pearman St SE1 .. 135 C3
Pear Pl SE1 ... 135 B4
Pearscroft Ct SW6 ... 166 B3
Pearscroft Rd SW6 ... 166 B3
Pearse St 3 SE15 .. 49 A4
Pearson Cl 4 SE5 .. 48 B2
Pearson Ho SW15 .. 47 B1
Pearson's Ave SE8, SE14 ... 51 C2
Pearson St E2 ... 24 B3
Peartree Ave SW17 ... 71 B1
Pear Tree Cl 23 E2 .. 24 B4
Pear Tree Ct
Holborn EC1 ... 95 C1
Putney SW15 ... 57 A3
Pear Tree Ho SE4 ... 66 B3
Peartree La E1 ... 32 B2
Peartree St EC1 ... 96 C2
Peartree Way SE10 ... 43 C2
Peary Pl E2 ... 25 B2
Peckarmans Wood SE21, SE26 ... 76 C1
Peckett Sq 3 N5 ... 15 A4
Peckford Pl SW9 . 173 C1
PECKHAM ... 49 C2
Peckham Gr SE15 .. 49 A3
Peckham High St SE15 ... 49 C2
Peckham Hill St SE15 ... 49 C3
Peckham Park Prim Sch 25 SE15 ... 49 C3
Peckham Park Rd SE15 ... 49 C3
Peckham Rd SE5 ... 49 A2
Peckham Rye
East Dulwich SE22 ... 64 C3
Peckham SE15, SE22 ... 65 A3
Peckham Rye Sta SE15 ... 49 C1
Peckwater Ho 2 NW5 ... 13 C2
Peckwater St NW5 . 13 B3
Pedlars Wlk N7 ... 14 A3
Pedley St E1 . 24 B1 99 A1
Pedro St E5 ... 17 C4
Pedworth Gdns 4 SE16 ... 40 B2
Peel Gr E2 ... 25 B3
Peel Pass W8 ... 31 C1 113 B1
Peel Prec NW6 ... 23 C3
Peel St W8 .. 31 C1 113 B1
Peerless St EC1 ... 97 B3
Pegasus Cl N16 ... 15 C4
Pegasus Ct
11 Acton W3 ... 28 B3
Brentford TW8 ... 36 B1
College Pk NW10 ... 22 A2
Pegasus Ho 9 E1 .. 25 C1
Pegwell Ho 19 E5 .. 17 A3
Pekin St E14 ... 33 C3
Pekoe SE1 ... 125 A1
Peldon Ct TW10 ... 54 B2
Pelham Cl SE5 ... 64 A4
Pelham Cres SW7 144 A3
Pelham Ct SW3 ... 144 A3
Pelham Ho W14 .. 140 C3
Pelham Pl SW7 ... 144 A3
Pelham St SW7 ... 143 C4
Pelican Ho 8 SE8 .. 41 B2
Pelican Pas 3 E1 .. 25 B1
Pelier St SE17 ... 48 B4
Pella Ho SE11 ... 149 A2
Pellant Rd SW6 ... 154 B2
Pellatt Rd SE22 ... 64 B2
Pellerin Rd N16 ... 16 A3
Pellew Ho 15 E1 ... 25 A1
Pelling St E14 ... 33 C3
Pelter St E2 .. 24 B2 98 C4
Pelton Rd SE10 ... 43 A1
Pember Rd NW10 ... 22 C2
Pemberton Ct 18 E1 ... 25 C2
Pemberton Gdns N19 ... 4 B1
Pemberton Pl 2 E8 ... 17 A1
Pemberton Row EC4 ... 107 C2
Pemberton Terr N19 ... 4 B1
Pembridge Cres W11 ... 31 C2 113 B4
Pembridge Gdns W2 ... 31 C2 113 B3

Pembridge Hall Prep Sch for Girls W2 ... 31 C2 113 C3
Pembridge Mews W11 ... 31 C2 113 B4
Pembridge Pl
Notting Hill W2 ... 31 C2 113 C4
1 Wandsworth SW15 ... 58 C2
Pembridge Rd W11 ... 31 C2 113 B3
Pembridge Sq W2 ... 31 C2 113 C3
Pembridge Villas W11 ... 31 C2 113 B4
Pembroke W14 ... 141 A3
Pembroke Ave N1 ... 84 B4
Pembroke Bldgs NW10 ... 21 C2
Pembroke Cl SW1 ... 131 C3
Pembroke Gdns W8 ... 141 A4
Pembroke Gdns Cl W8 ... 127 B1
Pembroke Ho
Acton W3 ... 37 B4
Chelsea SW1 ... 131 B1
5 Clapham Pk SW2 ... 62 A2
17 Kensington W2 ... 100 B1
Putney SW15 ... 56 C2
Pembroke Lo 2 SW16 ... 74 B1
Pembroke Mews
8 Bow E3 ... 26 A2
Kensington W8 ... 127 B1
Pembroke Pl W8 ... 127 B1
Pembroke Rd W8 ... 141 B4
Pembroke Sq W8 ... 127 B1
Pembroke St N1 ... 84 B4
Pembroke Studios W8 ... 127 A1
Pembroke Terr NW8 ... 79 B3
Pembroke Villas W8 ... 141 B4
Pembroke Wlk W8 ... 141 B4
Pembury Cl E5 ... 17 A3
Pembury Ho SE5 ... 49 A1
Pembury Pl 15 E5, E8 ... 17 A3
Pembury Rd E5 ... 17 A3
Pemell Cl 30 E1 ... 25 B1
Pemell Ho 31 E1 ... 25 B1
Penally Pl N1 ... 87 C4
Penang St E1 ... 32 A1
Penarth Ctr The SE15 ... 50 B4
Penarth St SE15 ... 50 B4
Pencombe Mews W11 ... 31 B2 113 A4
Pencraig Way SE15 ... 50 A4
Penda's Mead E9 ... 18 A4
Pendennis Ho 15 SE8 ... 41 A2
Penderyn Way N7 ... 13 C4
Pendle Ho 13 SE26 ... 76 C1
Pendley Ho 18 E2 ... 24 C4
Pendrell Ho WC2 ... 105 C1
Pendrell Rd SE4 ... 51 A1
Penelope Ho 20 SW9 ... 173 B3
Penfield Lo 7 W9 ... 31 C4
Penfields Ho N7 ... 14 A2
Penfold Pl NW1 ... 102 A4
Penfold St NW8 ... 89 C1
Penford St SE5 ... 48 A1
Penhurst Mans SW6 ... 164 C4
Peninsula Ct E14 ... 42 A3
Peninsula Ret Pk TW9 ... 43 C2
Peninsular Park Rd SE7 ... 43 C2
Penmayne Ho SE11 ... 149 C2
Pennack Rd SE15 ... 49 B4
Penn Almshouses 1 SE10 ... 52 B2
Pennant Mews W8 ... 142 A4
Pennard Mans 5 W12 ... 39 B4
Pennard Rd W12 ... 39 B4
Pennefather Ho N1 ... 15 C2
Penner Cl SW19 ... 70 A2
Pennethorne Cl E9 ... 25 B4
Pennethorne Ho SW11 ... 59 C4
Pennethorne Rd SE15 ... 50 A3
Penn Ho NW8 ... 90 A1
Pennine La NW2 ... 1 A2
Pennine Mans NW2 ... 1 A2
Pennine Par NW2 ... 1 A2
Pennington Ct
4 Rotherhithe SE16 ... 33 A1
23 St George in t East E1 ... 125 C3
Pennington St E1 ... 32 A2
Penn Rd N7 ... 14 A4
Penn St N1 ... 87 C3
Penny Ct SW10 ... 157 A4
Pennyfields E14 ... 33 C2
Pennyford Ct NW8 ... 89 B2
Penny Mews SW12 ... 73 A4
Pennymore Wlk W9 ... 23 B1
Penny Rd NW10 ... 20 A2
Penpoll Rd E8 ... 17 A2
Penrhyn Cres SW14 ... 55 B3
Penrith Cl SW15 ... 58 A2
Penrith Pl SE27 ... 75 A2
Penrose Gr SE17 ... 150 C1
Penrose Ho SE17 ... 150 C1
Penrose St SE17 ... 150 C1
Penryn Ho SE11 ... 150 A2
Penryn St NW1 ... 83 B2
Penry St SE1 ... 152 B3
Pensbury Pl SW8 ... 171 A2
Pensbury St SW8 ... 171 A2
Pensford Ave TW9 ... 44 C1
Penshurst 2 NW5 ... 12 C2
Penshurst Ho 1 SE15 ... 50 B4
Penshurst Rd E9 ... 17 C1
Pentland Cl NW11 ... 1 A2
Pentland Gdns SW18 ... 59 B1
Pentland Ho
17 Camden Town NW5 ... 12 C2
7 Stamford Hill N16 ... 7 B3
Pentland Rd 1 NW6 ... 23 C2
Pentland St SW18 ... 59 B1
Pentlow St SW15 ... 57 B4
Pentney Rd SW12 ... 73 B3
Penton Gr N1 ... 85 B1
Penton Ho N1 ... 85 B1
Penton Pl SE17 ... 150 B2
Penton Rise WC1 ... 95 A4
Penton St N1 ... 85 B1
PENTONVILLE ... 85 A1
Pentonville Rd WC1 ... 84 C1
Pentridge St SE15 ... 49 B3
Penwith Rd SW18 ... 71 A2
Penwood Ho SW15 ... 56 B1
Penywern Rd SW5 ... 141 C2
Penzance Ho SE11 ... 149 C2
Penzance Pl W11 ... 31 A1 112 B2
Penzance St W11 ... 31 A1 112 A2
Peony Gdns W12 ... 29 C2
Peperfield WC1 ... 94 C3
Pepler Ho 17 W10 ... 23 A1
Pepler Mews SE1 ... 152 C1
Peploe Rd NW6 ... 22 C3
Peppermead Sq SE13 ... 66 C2
Pepper St
Borough The SE1 ... 136 C4
Millwall E14 ... 42 A3
Peppie Cl N16 ... 7 A2
Pepys Cres 2 E16 ... 35 C1
Pepys Ent Ctr 13 SE8 ... 41 B2
Pepys Ho
14 Bethnal Green E2 ... 25 B2
Clapham Pk SW4 ... 61 C2
Pepys Rd SE14 ... 50 C1
Pepys St EC3 ... 124 B4
Perceval Ave NW3 ... 12 A3
Percheron Ct 3 SW9 ... 62 B4
Perch St E8 ... 16 B4
Percival Rd SW14 ... 55 B3
Percival St EC1 ... 96 B3
Percy Cir WC1 ... 95 A4
Percy Laurie Ho 6 SW15 ... 57 C3
Percy Mews W1 ... 105 B3
Percy Pas W1 ... 105 B3
Percy Rd
Newham E16 ... 35 A4
Shepherd's Bush W12 ... 38 C4
Percy St W1 ... 105 B3
Peregrine Ho
6 Battersea SW11 ... 60 A4
Finsbury EC1 ... 96 B4
Perham Rd W14 ... 140 B1
Perifield SE21 ... 75 B3
Perkins Ho 15 E14 ... 33 B4
Perkins Rents SW1 ... 133 B1
Perkins Sq SE1 ... 123 A2
Perley Ho 9 E3 ... 33 B4
Perotti Ho SW6 ... 59 A4
Perran Rd SE24, SW2 ... 75 A2
Perren St NW5 ... 13 A2
Perrers Rd W6 ... 39 A2
Perring Est E3 ... 33 C4
Perrin's Ct 20 NW3 ... 11 B4
Perrin's La NW3 ... 11 B4
Perrin's Wlk NW3 ... 11 B4
Perronet Ho SE1 ... 136 B1
Perry Ave W3 ... 28 C3
Perry Ct 6 E14 ... 41 C1
Perry Ho 24 SW2 ... 74 A4
Perrymead St SW6 ... 166 A3
Perryn Ho W3 ... 29 A2
Perryn Rd
Acton W3 ... 28 C2
1 Bermondsey SE16 ... 40 A3
Perry's Pl W1 ... 105 B2
Perrywood Ho 17 E5 ... 17 A3
Perseverance Works 17 E2 ... 24 A2 98 B4
Perth Ct 5 SE5 ... 63 C3
Perth Ho N1 ... 14 B1
Perth Rd N4 ... 5 C3
Petchey Acad The E8 ... 16 B3
Peter Ave NW10 ... 9 A1
Peter Best Ho 1 E1 ... 32 A3
Peterboat Cl SE10 ... 43 A2
Peterborough Ct EC4 ... 107 C1
Peterborough Mews SW6 ... 165 B2
Peterborough Rd SW6 ... 58 C4
Peterborough Villas SW6 ... 166 A4
Peter Butler Ho 9 SE1 ... 139 B3
Peterchurch Ho SE15 ... 50 A4
Petergate SW11 ... 59 B3
Peter Harrison Planetarium SE10 ... 52 C3
Peter Heathfield Ho 4 E15 ... 27 C4
Peter Hills Ho 6 SE16 ... 153 B4
Peter Hills Sch 29 SE16 ... 32 C1
Peter Ho SW8 ... 162 A2
Peter James Ent Ctr NW10 ... 20 B2
Peterley Bsns Ctr 21 E2 ... 25 A3
Peter Scott Visitor Centre SW13 ... 47 A2
Peters Ct 9 W2 ... 100 B2
Peter's Ct SW4 ... 62 A1
Petersfield Rd W3 ... 37 B4
Petersfield Rise SW15 ... 69 A3
Petersham Ho SW7 ... 143 B4
Petersham La SW7 ... 128 C2
Petersham Mews SW7 ... 129 A1
Petersham Pl SW7 ... 129 A2
Peter's La EC1 ... 108 B4
Peter St W1 ... 119 B4
Peterstow Cl SW19 ... 70 A2
Petherton Ct NW10 ... 22 C4
Petherton Ho N4 ... 6 B3
Petherton Rd N5 ... 15 B3
Petiver Cl 26 E9 ... 17 B1
Petley Rd W6 ... 47 C3
Peto Pl NW1 ... 92 B2
Peto St N E16 ... 35 B3
Petrel Ct 8 SE21 ... 75 C2
Petrie Cl NW2 ... 10 A2
Petrie Mus of Egyptian Archaeology WC1 ... 93 B1
Petros Gdns 1 NW3 ... 11 B2
Petticoat Lane Mkt EC2 ... 110 C3
Petticoat Sq E1 ... 110 C2
Petticoat Twr E1 ... 110 C2
Pettiward Cl SW15 ... 57 B3
Petty France SW1 ... 133 B2
Petty Wales EC3 ... 124 B3
Petworth Ho 16 SE22 ... 64 A4
Petworth St SW11 ... 168 B4
Petyt Pl SW3 ... 158 A3
Petyward SW3 ... 144 B3
Pevensey Ct
4 South Acton W3 ... 37 A4
West Norwood SW16 ... 74 C1
Pevensey Ho 5 E1 ... 33 A4
Peveril Ho SE1 ... 137 C1
Pewsham Ho N4 ... 6 B3
Peyton Pl SE10 ... 52 B3
Pharamond NW2 ... 9 C2
Phelps Ho 11 SW15 ... 57 C4
Phelp St SE17 ... 48 C4
Phene St SW3 ... 158 B4
Philadelphia Ct SW10 ... 157 A1
Philbeach Gdns SW5 ... 141 B2
Phil Brown Pl 3 SW8 ... 61 A4
Philchurch Pl 36 E1 ... 111 C1
Philia Ho 4 NW1 ... 13 B1
Philip Blairman Ho E1 ... 24 B1 98 C1
Philip Ct W2 ... 101 B4
Philip Ho 12 NW6 ... 78 A3
Philip Turner Est 28 E9 ... 17 B1
Philip Wlk SE15 ... 64 C4
Phillimore Ct W8 ... 127 C3
Phillimore Gardens Cl W8 ... 127 B2
Phillimore Gdns
Kensington W8 ... 127 B3
Willesden NW10 ... 22 B4
Phillimore Pl W8 ... 127 B3
Phillimore Terr W8 ... 127 C2
Phillimore Wlk W8 ... 127 C2
Phillip Ho E1 ... 111 A3

Phillipp St N1 ... 24 A4
Philpot La EC3 ... 124 A4
Philpot Sq SW6 ... 59 A4
Philpot St E1 ... 32 A3
Philson Mans 13 E1 ... 32 A3
Phipps Ho 16 W12 ... 30 A2
Phipp St EC2 ... 24 A1 98 A2
Phoebeth Rd SE4 ... 66 C2
Phoenix Bsns Ctr 22 E3 ... 33 C4
Phoenix Cl 18 E8 ... 24 B4
Phoenix Ct
4 Brentford TW8 ... 36 A1
2 Deptford SE14 ... 51 A4
Millwall E14 ... 41 C2
Phoenix High Sch W12 ... 29 C2
Phoenix Ho SW1 ... 145 B4
Phoenix Lodge Mans 1 W6 ... 39 B2
Phoenix Pl WC1 ... 95 A2
Phoenix Rd NW1 ... 93 B4
Phoenix Sch The 12 NW3 ... 11 B2
Phoenix Sec & Prim Sch 26 E3 ... 26 B2
Phoenix St WC2 ... 105 C1
Phoenix Wharf Rd SE1 ... 139 A3
Phyllis Hodges Ho NW1 ... 83 B1
Physic Pl SW3 ... 158 C4
Piccadilly W1 ... 118 C2
Piccadilly Arc SW1 ... 118 C2
Piccadilly Cir W1 ... 119 B3
Piccadilly Circus Sta SW1 ... 119 B3
Piccadilly Ct 5 N7 ... 14 B2
Piccadilly Pl W1 ... 119 A3
Pickard St EC1 ... 96 B4
Pickering Cl E9 ... 17 C1
Pickering Ho
18 Kensington W2 ... 100 B1
Stoke Newington N4 ... 6 C4
Pickering Mews 9 W2 ... 100 B2
Pickering Pl SW1 ... 119 A1
Pickering St N1 ... 86 B4
Pickets St SW12 ... 73 A4
Pickfords Wharf N1 ... 86 C1
Pickwick Ho
21 Bermondsey SE16 ... 139 B3
3 Shepherd's Bush W11 ... 30 C1
Pickwick Rd SE21 ... 76 A4
Pickwick St SE1 ... 136 C3
Pickworth Cl SW8 ... 162 B1
Picton Ho 1 SW4 ... 74 A4
Picton Pl W1 ... 103 C1
Picton St SE5 ... 48 C3
Picture Ho 6 SW16 ... 74 A2
Pied Bull Ct WC1 ... 106 B3
Pied Bull Yd WC1 ... 106 B3
Pier Head E1 ... 32 A1
Pierhead Wharf 37 E1 ... 32 A1
Pier Ho SW3 ... 158 B3
Piermont Rd SE22 ... 65 A2
Pierpoint Bldg 4 E14 ... 41 C4
Pierrepoint Rd W3 ... 28 A2
Pierrepoint Row N1 ... 86 A2
Pier St E14 ... 42 B2
Pier Terr SW18 ... 59 B3
Piggott Ho 2 E2 ... 25 C3
Pigott St E14 ... 33 C3
Pilgrimage St SE1 ... 137 B3
Pilgrim Ho SE1 ... 137 C1
Pilgrims Cloisters 10 SE5 ... 49 A3
Pilgrims Ct SE3 ... 53 C2
Pilgrim's La NW3 ... 11 C4
Pilgrims Mews 12 E14 ... 34 C2
Pilgrim's Pl 6 NW3 ... 11 C4
Pilgrim St EC4 ... 108 A1
Pilgrims Way N19 ... 4 C3
Pilgrims Way Prim Sch 22 SE15 ... 50 B4
Pilkington Rd 4 SE15 ... 50 A1
Pilot Ind Ctr NW10 ... 21 A1
Pilsden Cl SW19 ... 69 C3
Pilton Pl SE17 ... 151 A2
Pimilico Sta SW1 ... 147 B2
PIMLICO ... 146 C1
Pimlico Acad SW1 ... 147 A1
Pimlico Rd SW1 ... 145 C2
Pimlico Wlk 1 N1 ... 24 A2 98 A4
Pinchin St E1 ... 125 C4
Pincombe Ho SE17 ... 151 B2
Pincott Pl SE4 ... 65 C4
Pindar St EC2 ... 110 A4
Pindock Mews W9 ... 88 B1
Pine Apple Ct SW1 ... 132 C2
Pine Ave E15 ... 19 C3
Pine Cl 11 N19 ... 4 B2
Pinedene 2 SE15 ... 50 A2
Pinefield Cl E14 ... 33 C2
Pine Gr N4, N19 ... 5 B2
Pine Ho
Bow E3 ... 26 A4
21 Rotherhithe SE16 ... 40 B4
Pinehurst Ct 6 W11 ... 31 B3
Pinelands Cl 7 SE3 ... 53 B3
Pine Lo SW15 ... 58 A1
Pine Rd NW2 ... 9 C4
Pines Ct 14 SW19 ... 69 C3
Pine St EC1 ... 95 B2
Pine Tree Ho SE14 ... 50 C3
Pine Tree Way 1 SE13 ... 67 A4
Pinewood Ct SW4 ... 61 C1
Pinkham Mans W4 ... 36 C1
Pinnace Ho E14 ... 42 B3
Pinnacle Ho EC3 ... 124 A3
Pinnacle The EC2 ... 110 A1
Pinnacle The 7 N1 ... 15 C2
Pinner Ct NW8 ... 89 B2
Pinner Ho 30 SE5 ... 48 B1
Pintail Ct 39 SE8 ... 51 B4
Pinter Ho 30 SW9 ... 172 B1
Pioneer Cl
10 Bow Comm E14 ... 34 A4
London W12 ... 30 A3
Pioneer St SE15 ... 49 C2
Pioneer Way W12 ... 30 B3
Piper Cl N7 ... 14 B3
Pipers Ho SE10 ... 42 C1
Pippin Ho 17 W10 ... 30 C2
Pirate Castle The NW1 ... 82 A4
Pirbright Rd SW18 ... 70 C3
Pitcairn Ho 1 E9 ... 17 B1
Pitfield Ho N5 ... 15 B3
Pitfield St N1 ... 24 A3
Pitman Ho 4 SE8 ... 51 C2
Pitman St SE5 ... 48 B3
Pitmaston Ho 2 SE13 ... 52 B1
Pitsea Pl E1 ... 32 C3
Pitsea St E1 ... 32 C3
Pitt Ho 4 SW11 ... 59 C3
Pitt's Head Mews W1 ... 117 C1
Pitt St W8 ... 127 C4
Pixley St E14 ... 33 B3
Planetree Ct W6 ... 39 C2
Plane Tree Ho SE8 ... 51 A4
Plantain Pl SE1 ... 137 B4
Plantation La EC3 ... 124 A4
Plantation The SE3 ... 53 C1
Platehouse The 3 E14 ... 42 A1
Platina St EC2 ... 97 C2
Plato Pl 1 SW6 ... 165 A2
Plato Rd SW2 ... 62 A3
Platt's La NW3 ... 1 C1
Platt St NW1 ... 83 B2
Plaxdale Ho SE17 ... 152 A3
Playfair St W6 ... 39 B1
Playfield Cres SE22 ... 64 B2
Playford Rd
Finsbury Pk N4 ... 5 B2
Finsbury Pk N4 ... 5 C2
Playhouse Yd EC4 ... 108 A1
Playon (Canary Wharf Indoor Sports) E14 ... 34 B1
Plaza Sh Ctr W1 ... 105 A2
Pleasance Rd SW15 ... 57 A2
Pleasance The SW15 ... 57 A3
Pleasant Pl N1 ... 15 A1
Pleasant Row NW1 ... 82 B3
Plender Ct NW1 ... 83 A3
Plender St NW1 ... 83 A3
Pleshey Rd N7 ... 13 C4
Plevna St E14 ... 42 B3
Pleydell Ave W6 ... 38 B2
Pleydell Ct EC4 ... 107 C1
Pleydell St EC4 ... 107 C1
Plimsoll Cl E14 ... 34 A3
Plimsoll Rd N4 ... 6 A1
Plough Ct EC3 ... 123 C4
Plough La SE22 ... 64 B1
Ploughmans Cl NW1 ... 83 B4
Plough Mews 19 SW11 ... 59 C3
Plough Pl EC4 ... 107 C2
Plough Rd SW11 ... 59 C3
Plough St 16 E1 ... 111 B2
Plough Terr SW11 ... 59 C3
Plough Way SE16 ... 41 A2
Plough Yd EC2 ... 24 A1 98 B1
Plover Ho 4 SW9 ... 163 B2
Plover Way SE16 ... 41 A3
Plowman Ho SW19 ... 69 C2
Plumbers Row E1 ... 111 C2
Plumbridge St 7 SE10 ... 52 B2
Plume Ho SE10 ... 52 A4
Plummer Ct SE13 ... 67 A1
Plummer Rd SW4 ... 73 C4
Plumtree Ct EC4 ... 108 A2
Plymouth Ho 20 SE10 ... 52 A2
Plymouth Rd E16 ... 35 C4
Plymouth Wharf E14 ... 42 C2
Plympton Ave NW6 ... 10 B1
Plympton Pl NW1 ... 90 A1
Plympton Rd NW6 ... 10 B1
Plympton St NW8 ... 90 A1
Pocklington Ct SW15 ... 68 C3
Pocklington Lo 6 W12 ... 38 C3
Pocock St SE1 ... 136 B4
Podmore Rd SW18 ... 59 B3
Poets Cnr SW1 ... 134 A2
Poets Mews 3 SE24 ... 63 A2
Poet's Rd N5 ... 15 C3
Point Cl SE10 ... 52 B2
Pointer Sch The SE3 ... 53 C3
Pointers Cl E14 ... 42 A1
Point Hill SE10 ... 52 B2
Point Ho SE10 ... 52 B2
Point Pleasant SW18 ... 58 C3
Point Wharf La TW8 ... 44 A3
Poland Ho 3 E15 ... 27 C4
Poland St W1 ... 105 A1
Polesworth Ho 16 W2 ... 31 C4
Polish Inst & Sikorski Mus SW7 ... 129 C3
Polish Univ Abroad 16 W6 ... 38 C2
Pollard Cl
Islington N7 ... 14 B4
Newham E16 ... 35 C2
Pollard Ho N1 ... 84 C1
Pollard Row E2 ... 24 C2 99 C4
Pollard St E2 ... 24 C2 99 C4
Pollen St W1 ... 104 B1
Pollitt Dr NW8 ... 89 C2
Pollock Ho W10 ... 23 A1
Pollock's Toy Mus W1 ... 105 A4
Polperro Mans 3 NW6 ... 10 C3
Polperro Mews SE11 ... 150 A4
Polygon Rd NW1 ... 83 B1
Polygon The
1 Clapham SW4 ... 61 B3
Polygon The *continued*
St John's Wood NW8 ... 79 C4
Pomell Way E1 ... 111 A2
Pomeroy Ct W11 ... 31 A3
Pomeroy Ho 5 E2 ... 25 C3
Pomeroy St SE14 ... 50 B2
Pomfret Rd SE5 ... 63 A4
Pomoja La N19 ... 5 A2
Pomona Ho 10 SE8 ... 41 A2
Pond Cl SE3 ... 53 C1
Pond Cotts SE21 ... 76 A3
Ponder St 5 N7 ... 14 B1
Pondfield Ho 4 N5 ... 15 B3
Pond Ho SW3 ... 144 A3
Pond Mead SE21 ... 63 C1
Pond Pl SW3 ... 144 A3
Pond Rd SE3 ... 53 B1
Pond Sq N6 ... 3 C3
Pond St NW3 ... 12 A3
Ponler St E1 ... 32 A3
Ponsard Rd NW10 ... 22 A2
Ponsford St E9 ... 17 B2
Ponsonby Ho 13 E2 ... 25 B3
Ponsonby Pl SW1 ... 147 C2
Ponsonby Rd SW15 ... 69 A4
Ponsonby Terr SW1 ... 147 C2
Ponton Ho SW2 ... 74 C3
Ponton Rd SW8 ... 161 C3
Pont St Mews SW1 ... 130 C1
Pont St SW1 ... 131 A1
Pontypool Pl SE1 ... 136 A4
Poole Ct N1 ... 16 A1
Poole Ho SE11 ... 135 A1
Poole Rd E9 ... 17 C2
Pooles Bldgs EC1 ... 95 B1
Pooles La SW10 ... 156 C1
Pooles Park Prim Sch 16 N4 ... 5 B2
Pooles Pk N4 ... 5 C2
Poole St N1 ... 87 B3
Pooley Ho E1 ... 25 C2
Pool Ho NW8 ... 101 C4
Poolmans St SE16 ... 40 C4
Poonah St E1 ... 32 B3
Pope Ho
7 Bermondsey SE16 ... 40 A2
3 Camberwell SE5 ... 48 C3
Pope John Prim Sch W12 ... 30 A2
Pope's Head Alley EC3 ... 109 C1
Pope's La W5 ... 36 A3
Pope's Rd SW9 ... 62 C4
Pope St SE1 ... 138 B3
Popham Ct N16 ... 7 A1
Popham Gdns TW9 ... 55 A4
Popham Rd N1 ... 86 C4
Popham St
Islington N1 ... 86 B4
Shoreditch N1 ... 86 C4
POPLAR ... 33 C3
Poplar Bath St 11 E14 ... 34 A2
Poplar Bsns Pk E14 ... 34 B2

Poplar Cl E9 ... 18 B3
Poplar Ct 4 SW16 ... 74 B1
Poplar Gr W6 ... 39 B4
Poplar High St E14 ... 34 A2
Poplar Ho
- Brockley SE4 ... 66 B3
- 19 Rotherhithe SE16 ... 40 C4

Poplar Mews 4 W12 ... 30 B1
Poplar Pl W2 ... 114 B4
Poplar Rd SE24 ... 63 B3
Poplar Sta E14 ... 34 A2
Poplars The NW5 ... 13 B3
Poplar Wlk SE24 ... 63 B3
Poppins Ct EC4 ... 108 A1
Porchester Ct W2 100 B1
Porchester Gate W2 ... 114 C3
Porchester Gdn Mews W2 ... 100 B1
Porchester Gdns W2 ... 114 B4
Porchester Ho 8 E1 ... 32 A3
Porchester Mews W2 ... 100 B2
Porchester Pl W2 102 B1
Porchester Rd W2 ... 100 B2
Porchester Sq W2 ... 100 B2
Porchester Terr W2 ... 114 C4
Porchester Terr N W2 ... 100 B2
Porden Rd SW2 ... 62 B3
Porland Ct SE1 ... 137 B2
Porlock Ho 5 SE26 ... 76 C1
Porlock St SE1 ... 137 C4
Porson Ct SE13 ... 67 A4
Portal Cl SE27 ... 74 C1
Portal Way W3 ... 28 C4
Portbury Cl 17 SE15 ... 49 C2
Portchester Cl SE24 ... 63 C3
Portelet Ct 1 N1 ... 24 A4
Portelet Rd E1 ... 25 C2
Porten Hos W14 ... 126 A1
Porten Rd W14 ... 126 A1
Porter Sq N19 ... 5 A3
Porter St
- Borough The SE1 ... 123 A2
- Marylebone W1 ... 103 A4

Porteus Rd W2 ... 101 A4
Portfleet Pl 34 N1 ... 24 A4
Portgate Cl W9 ... 23 B1
Port Ho 6 SW11 ... 59 B4
Port House The 6 E14 ... 42 A1
Portia Way E3 ... 26 B1
Porticos The SW3 157 B3
Portinscale Rd SW15 ... 58 B2
Portishead Ho 29 W2 ... 31 C4
Portland Ave N16 ... 7 B4
Portland Ct
- 7 De Beauvoir Town N1 ... 16 A1
- 1 Deptford SE14 ... 51 A4

Portland Gr SW8 ... 172 C4
Portland Ho 19 SW2 ... 74 C3
Portland Hospl for Women & Children The W1 ... 92 B1
Portland Mews W1 ... 105 A1
Portland Pl W1 ... 104 B3
Portland Place Sch W1 ... 104 B4
Portland Rd
- Notting Hill W11 ... 31 A1 112 B2
- Notting Hill W11 ... 31 A2 112 A3

Portland Rise N4 ... 6 B3
Portland Sq 4 E1 ... 32 A1
Portland St SE17 ... 151 B1
Portland Village W6 ... 39 B3
Portman Ave SW14 ... 55 C4
Portman Cl W1 ... 103 B2
Portman Gate NW1 ... 90 B1
Portman Hts 1 NW3 ... 1 C1
Portman Mews S W1 ... 103 B1
Portman Pl E2 ... 25 B2
Portman Sq W1 ... 103 B2
Portman St W1 ... 103 B1
Portman The NW11 ... 1 C4
Portman Twrs W1 ... 103 A2
Portnall Rd W9 ... 23 B2
Portobello Ct Est W11 ... 31 B3
Portobello Mews W11 ... 31 C2 113 B3
Portobello Rd W11 ... 31 B2 113 A4
Portobello Road Mkt W10 ... 31 A4
Portpool La EC1 ... 107 B4
Portree St E14 ... 34 C3
Port Royal Pl 8 N16 ... 16 A3
Portsea Hall W2 ... 102 B1
Portsea Ho 8 SW15 ... 69 A3
Portsea Mews W2 ... 102 B1
Portsea Pl W2 ... 102 B1
Portslade Rd SW8 170 C2
Portsmouth Rd SW15 ... 69 B4
Portsmouth St WC2 ... 107 A1
Portsoken St E1, EC3 ... 124 C4
Portswood Pl SW15 ... 56 B1
Portugal St WC2 ... 107 A1
Poseidon Ct 9 E14 ... 41 C2
Postern The EC2 ... 109 A3
Post Office Way SW8 ... 161 B2
Potier St SE1 ... 137 C1
Potterne Cl 5 SW19 ... 69 C4
Potters Cl 5 SE15 ... 49 A3
Potters Fields SE1 ... 124 B1

Potters Lo E14 ... 42 B1
Potters Rd SW6 ... 166 C1
Pottery La W11 ... 31 A1 112 B2
Pottery Rd TW8 ... 44 A4
Pottery St SE16 ... 40 A4
Pott St E2 ... 25 A2
Poullett Ho SW2 ... 75 A3
Poulton Cl E8 ... 17 A2
Poultry EC2 ... 109 B1
Pound La NW10 ... 8 C2
Pountney Rd SW11 ... 60 C4
Povey Ho
- Tulse Hill SW2 ... 62 C1
- Walworth SE17 ... 152 A3

Powell's Wlk W4 ... 46 B4
Powergate Bsns Pk NW10 ... 20 C2
Power Ho 18 TW9 ... 44 C2
Power Ho The W4 ... 38 B2
Power Rd W4 ... 36 C2
Powerscroft Rd E5 ... 17 B4
Powis Gdns
- Golders Green NW11 ... 1 B4
- Notting Hill W11 ... 31 B3

Powis Ho WC2 ... 106 B2
Powis Mews W11 ... 31 B3
Powis Pl WC1 ... 94 B1
Powis Rd E3 ... 27 A2
Powis Sq W11 ... 31 B3
Powis Terr W11 ... 31 B3
Powlesland Ct 21 E14 ... 33 A3
Powlett Ho NW1 ... 13 A2
Powlett Pl NW1 ... 13 A1
Pownall Rd E8 ... 24 C4
Powrie Ho 4 SW11 ... 167 C2
Poynder Ct 3 N7 ... 14 A3
Poynders Ct 9 SW4 ... 61 B1
Poynders Gdns SW12 ... 73 B4
Poynders Rd SW12, SW4 ... 73 C4
Poynings Rd N19 ... 4 B1
Poynter Ho
- Paddington NW8 ... 89 B2
- 10 Shepherd's Bush W11 ... 30 C1

Poyntz Rd SW11 ... 168 C1
Poyser St E2 ... 25 A3
Praed Mews W2 ... 101 C2
Praed St W2 ... 101 C2
Prague Pl SW2 ... 62 A2
Prah Rd N4 ... 5 C2
Prairie St SW8 ... 170 A1
Pratt Mews NW1 ... 82 C3
Pratt St NW1 ... 82 C4
Pratt Wlk SE1, SE11 ... 149 A4
Preachers Ct EC1 ... 96 B1
Prebend Gdns W4, W6 ... 38 B2
Prebend Mans 4 W4 ... 38 B2
Prebend St N1 ... 86 C4
Precinct The
- Islington N1 ... 86 C3
- Islington N5 ... 15 A3

Premier Corner NW6 ... 23 B3
Premier Ho 25 N1 ... 15 A1

Premier Park Rd NW10 ... 20 A3
Premier Pk NW10 ... 20 A3
Premier Pl 17 E14 ... 33 C2
Prendergast Ho 7 SW4 ... 73 C4
Prendergast Ladywell Fields Coll SE4 ... 66 C1
Prendergast Sch SE4 ... 66 C3
Prescot St E1 ... 125 A4
Prescott Ho 13 SE17 ... 48 A4
Prescott Pl SW4 ... 61 C3
Presentation Mews SW2 ... 74 B3
President Dr E1 ... 32 A1
President Ho EC1 ... 96 B3
President St EC1 ... 96 C4
Prestage Way 13 E14 ... 34 B2
Prested Rd SW11 ... 60 A3
Preston Cl SE1 ... 152 A4
Preston Gdns NW10 ... 8 A2
Preston Ho
- Bermondsey SE1 ... 138 C2
- Walworth SE1 ... 152 A4

Preston Pl
- Richmond TW10 ... 54 A2
- Willesden NW2 ... 8 C2

Preston's Rd E14 ... 34 B1
Prestwich Terr SW4 ... 61 C2
Prestwood Ho 8 SE16 ... 40 A3
Prestwood St N1 ... 87 A1
Priam Ho 17 E2 ... 25 A3
Price Cl SW17 ... 72 B1
Price Ho N1 ... 86 C3
Prices Ct SW11 ... 59 C4
Price's St SE1 ... 122 B2
Price's Yd N1 ... 85 A3
Prichard Ct
- Battersea SW11 ... 167 C3
- Islington N7 ... 14 B3

Prideaux Ho WC1 ... 95 A4
Prideaux Pl
- Acton W3 ... 28 C2
- St Pancras WC1 ... 95 A4

Prideaux Rd SW9 ... 62 A4
Pride Ct N1 ... 85 C2
Priestley Cl N16 ... 7 B4
Priestley Ho
- 2 Camden Town NW5 ... 13 A2
- St Luke's EC1 ... 97 A2

Priestman Point 25 E3 ... 27 A2
Priests Bridge SW14 ... 56 A4
Priest's Ct EC2 ... 108 C2
Prima Rd SW9 ... 163 B2
Primrose Cl 6 E3 ... 26 C3
Primrose Ct
- 2 Child's Hill NW2 ... 1 B1
- Primrose Hill NW8 ... 80 C3
- 11 Streatham SW12 ... 73 C4

Primrose Gdns NW3 ... 12 A2
PRIMROSE HILL ... 12 B1
Primrose Hill EC4 107 C1
Primrose Hill Ct NW3 ... 12 B1
Primrose Hill Rd NW1, NW3 ... 12 B1

Primrose Hill Sch NW1 ... 81 C4
Primrose Hill Studios NW1 ... 81 B4
Primrose Ho
- 7 Peckham SE15 ... 49 C2
- 1 Richmond TW9 ... 44 B2

Primrose Mans SW11 ... 169 B4
Primrose Mews 9 NW1 ... 12 B1
Primrose Sq E9 ... 25 B4
Primrose St EC2 ... 110 B4
Primrose Wlk 6 SE14 ... 51 A3
Primula St W12 ... 29 C3
Prince Albert Ct NW8 ... 80 C3
Prince Albert Rd NW8 ... 80 C3
Prince Arthur Ct 18 NW3 ... 11 B4
Prince Arthur Mews 17 NW3 ... 11 B4
Prince Arthur Rd NW3 ... 11 B3
Prince Charles Rd SE3 ... 53 B2
Prince Consort Ho SE1 ... 148 B2
Prince Consort Rd SW7 ... 129 B2
Princedale Rd W11 ... 31 A1 112 B2
Prince Edward Mans W2 ... 31 C2 113 C4
Prince Edward Rd E9 ... 18 B2
Prince George Rd N16 ... 16 A4
Princelet St E1 ... 111 A4
Prince of Orange La 3 SE10 ... 52 B3
Prince of Wales Dr SW11 ... 169 B4
Prince of Wales Mans
- Battersea SW11 ... 169 C4
- Clapham SW4 ... 61 A2

Prince of Wales Pas NW1 ... 92 C3
Prince of Wales Rd
- Blackheath Vale SE3 ... 53 B2
- Camden Town NW5 ... 12 C2

Prince Of Wales Terr
- Chiswick W4 ... 38 A1
- Kensington W8 ... 128 B3

Prince Regent Ct 2 SE16 ... 33 A1
Prince Regent Mews NW1 ... 92 C3
Princes Arc SW1 ... 119 A2
Princes Ave W3 ... 36 C3
Princes Cir WC2 ... 106 A2
Princes Cl N4 ... 6 A3
Princes Coll WC1 106 A2
Princes Court Bsns Ctr 14 E1 ... 32 A2
Princes Ct
- Brondesbury NW2 ... 10 A3
- Hampstead NW3 ... 11 C4
- Stepney E1 ... 32 A2

Prince's Ct SE16 ... 41 B3
Princes Gate SW7 129 C3

Prince's Gate SW7 ... 130 A3
Princes Gate Ct SW7 ... 129 C3
Princes Gate Mews SW7 ... 129 C2
Princes Gdns SW7 ... 129 C2
Princes Ho W11 ... 31 C2 113 B3
Prince's Mews
1 Hammersmith W6 ... 39 A1
Kensington W2 ... 114 A4
Princes Pl
Notting Hill W11 ... 31 A1 112 A2
St James SW1 ... 119 A2
Princes Rd
Kew TW9 ... 44 B2
Richmond TW10 ... 54 B2
Prince's Rd SW14 ... 55 C4
Princes Rise SE13 ... 52 B1
Princes Riverside Rd 7 SE16 ... 32 C1
Princess Alexandra School of Nursing The 6 E1 ... 32 A4
Princess Alice Ho 1 W10 ... 22 B1
Princess Beatrice Ho SW10 ... 142 A1
Princess Cres N4 ... 6 A2
Princess Ct
Hampstead NW6 ... 11 A1
Kensington W2 ... 114 B4
Marylebone W1 ... 102 C3
Princess Frederica CE Jun & Inf Sch NW10 ... 22 B3
Princess Grace Hospl The W1 ... 91 B1
Princess Louise Cl W2 ... 101 C4
Princess Mary Ho SW1 ... 147 C3
Princess May Prim Sch 6 N16 ... 16 B4
Princess May Rd N16 ... 16 A4
Princess Mews NW3 ... 11 C2
Prince's Sq W2 ... 114 A4
Princess Rd
Camden Town NW1 ... 81 C4
Paddington NW6 ... 23 C3
Princess St SE1 ... 136 B1
Princes St W1 ... 104 B1
Prince's St
City of London EC2 ... 109 B1
Richmond TW10, TW9 ... 54 A2
Prince St SE8 ... 51 B4
Princes Way
Acton W3 ... 36 C3
Putney SW15, SW19 ... 70 A3
Princes Yd W11 ... 31 A1 112 B1
Princethorpe Ho W2 ... 100 A4
Princeton Ct 12 SW15 ... 57 C4
Princeton Mans WC1 ... 106 C3
Princeton St WC1 106 C4
Principal Sq E9 ... 17 C3
Printers Mews E3 ... 26 A4
Printer St EC4 ... 107 C2
Printing House Yd 16 E2 ... 24 A2 98 B3
Printon Ho 16 E3 ... 33 B4
Print Village Ind Est SE15 ... 49 B1
Prior Bolton St N1 ... 15 A2
Prioress Ho 2 E3 ... 27 A2
Prioress Rd SE27 ... 75 A1
Prioress St SE1 ... 137 C1
Priors Lo 4 TW10 ... 54 A1
Prior St SE10 ... 52 B3
Prior Weston Prim Sch EC1 ... 97 B2
Priory Ave W4 ... 38 A3
Priory Ct
City of London EC4 ... 108 B1
Homerton E9 ... 17 C3
Nunhead SE15 ... 65 B3
Roehampton SW15 ... 56 B3
South Lambeth SW8 ... 171 C4
Priory Gdns
Barnes SW13 ... 56 B4
6 Chiswick W4 ... 38 A2
Priory Gn N1 ... 84 C2
Priory Gr SW8 ... 172 A3
Priory Ho
Clerkenwell EC1 ... 96 A2
Pimlico SW1 ... 147 B2
Spitalfields E1 ... 110 C4
Priory Hospl Grange Roehampton SW15 ... 56 B3
Priory Hts N1 ... 85 A2
Priory La SW15 ... 56 B2
Priory Lo 7 W4 ... 36 C1
Priory Mans
17 Maitland Pk NW3 ... 12 B2
South Kensington SW10 ... 143 A1
Priory Park Rd NW6 ... 23 B4
Priory Rd
Bedford Pk W4 ... 37 C3
Hampstead NW6 ... 11 A1
Richmond TW9 ... 44 C3
Priory St 16 E3 ... 27 A2
Priory Terr NW6 ... 78 A4
Priory The SE1 ... 136 A3
Priory Wlk SW10 ... 143 A1
Pritchard Ho 38 E2 ... 24 C3
Pritchard's Rd E2 ... 24 C3
Priter Rd SE16 ... 139 C1
Priter Road Hostel 14 SE16 ... 139 C1
Probert Rd SW2 ... 62 C2
Probyn Ho SW1 ... 147 C4
Probyn Rd SW2 ... 75 A2
Procter Ho 12 SE5 ... 48 C3
Procter St WC1 ... 106 C3
Proctor Ho 5 SE1 ... 153 B1
Prome Ho 3 N16 ... 15 C4
Promenade Approach Rd W4 ... 46 A3
Promenade The W4 ... 46 A2
Prospect Cotts SW18 ... 58 C3
Prospect Ho
1 Dalston E8 ... 16 B2
Islington N1 ... 85 B1
Newington SE1 ... 136 B1
14 North Kensington W10 ... 30 C3
Prospect House Sch 11 SW15 ... 69 C4
Prospect Pl
5 Child's Hill NW2 ... 1 B1
2 Chiswick W4 ... 37 C1
6 Deptford SE8 ... 51 B4
12 Hampstead NW3 ... 11 B4
7 Lower Holloway N7 ... 14 A4
Wapping E1 ... 32 B1
Prospect Quay SW18 ... 58 C3
Prospect Rd NW2 ... 1 C1
Prospect St SE16 ... 40 A4
Prospect Wharf E1 ... 32 B2
Prospero Rd N19 ... 4 C3
Prothero Rd SW6 154 C2
Proud Ho 16 E1 ... 32 A3
Prout Gr NW10 ... 8 B4
Provence St N1 ... 86 C2
Providence Cl E9 ... 25 C4
Providence Ct
Islington N1 ... 86 A3
Mayfair W1 ... 117 C4
Providence Pl N1 ... 86 A3
Providence Row N1 ... 84 C1
Providence Row Cl 30 E1 ... 25 A2
Providence Sq 36 SE1 ... 139 B4
Providence Yd 1 E2 ... 24 C2 99 B4
Provost Ct NW3 ... 12 B2
Provost Rd NW3 ... 12 B1
Provost St N1 ... 97 B4
Prowse Pl NW1 ... 13 B1
Prudent Pas EC2 ... 109 A1
Prusom's Island 8 E1 ... 32 B1
Prusom St E1 ... 32 A1
Pryors The NW3 ... 2 C1
Pudding La EC3 ... 123 C4
Pudding Mill La E15 ... 27 A4
Pudding Mill Lane Sta E15 ... 27 A4
Puddle Dock EC4 ... 122 B4
Pugin Ct N1 ... 14 C1
Pulborough Rd SW18 ... 70 B4
Pulham Ho SW8 ... 162 C1
Pullman Ct SW2 ... 74 B3
Pullman Gdns SW15 ... 57 B1
Pulross Rd SW9 ... 62 B4
Pulteney Cl 20 E3 ... 26 B4
Pulteney Terr N1 ... 85 A4
Pulton Ho SE4 ... 66 A3
Pulton Pl SW6 ... 155 B1
Puma Ct E1 ... 110 C4
Pump Ct EC4 ... 107 B1
Pump House Cl SE16 ... 40 B4
Pumphouse Educational Mus The SE16 ... 33 A1
Pump House Gall SW11 ... 159 B1
Pumping Ho 8 E14 ... 34 C2
Pumping Station Rd W4 ... 46 A4
Pump La SE14 ... 50 B3
Punderson's Gdns E2 ... 25 A2
Purbeck Ho SW8 ... 162 C1
Purbrook Est SE1 ... 138 B3
Purbrook Ho 2 SW15 ... 69 A3
Purbrook St SE1 ... 138 B2
Purcell Cres SW6 154 A2
Purcell Ho SW10 ... 157 B3
Purcell Mews 2 NW10 ... 8 A1
Purcell St N1 ... 24 A3
Purchese St NW1 ... 83 C1
Purday Ho 4 W10 ... 23 B2
Purdon Ho 11 SE15 ... 49 C2
Purdy St E3 ... 27 A1
Purley Ave NW2 ... 1 A2
Purley Pl N1 ... 15 A1
Purser Ho 3 SW2 ... 62 C1
Pursers Cross Rd SW6 ... 165 A4
Purves Rd NW10 ... 22 B3
Pusey Ho 20 E14 ... 33 C3
Puteaux Ho 6 E2 ... 25 C3
PUTNEY ... 57 B2
Putney Bridge App SW6 ... 58 A4
Putney Bridge Rd SW15 ... 58 B3
Putney Bridge Sta SW6 ... 58 B4
Putney Comm SW15 ... 57 B4
Putney Exchange Shopping Ctr SW15 ... 57 C3
PUTNEY HEATH ... 57 B1
Putney Heath SW15 ... 57 B1
Putney Heath La SW15 ... 57 C1
Putney High Sch SW15 ... 57 C2
Putney High St SW15 ... 58 A3
Putney Hill
12 Putney SW15 ... 69 B4
Putney SW15 ... 57 C2
Putney L Ctr SW15 ... 57 B3
Putney Park Ave SW15 ... 56 C3
Putney Park La SW15 ... 57 A2
Putney Park Sch SW15 ... 57 A3
Putney Pier SW15 ... 58 A4
Putney School of Art & Design SW15 ... 58 A3
Putney Sta SW15 ... 58 A3
PUTNEY VALE ... 68 C1
Putney Wharf Twr SW15 ... 58 A4
Pykewell Lo 13 E8 ... 16 C3
Pylon Trad Est E16 ... 34 C4
Pymers Mead SE21 ... 75 B3
Pynfolds SE16 ... 40 A4
Pynnersmead SE24 ... 63 B2
Pyrford Ho 12 SW9 ... 63 A3
Pyrland Rd
Richmond TW10 ... 54 B1
Stoke Newington N5 ... 15 C3
Pyrmont Gr SE27 ... 75 A1
Pyrmont Rd W4 ... 44 C4
Pytchley Rd SE22 ... 64 A4

Q

Quadrangle Cl SE1 ... 152 A4
Quadrangle The
Chelsea SW10 ... 167 A4
Fulham SW6 ... 154 A1
Herne Hill SE24 ... 63 B2
3 North Kensington W12 ... 30 B3
Paddington W2 ... 102 A2
Quadrant Arc W1 119 A3
Quadrant Bsns Ctr NW6 ... 23 A4
Quadrant Gr NW5 ... 12 B3
Quadrant The
4 Kensal Green W10 ... 22 C2
Richmond TW9 ... 54 A3
Quaker Ct EC1 ... 97 A2
Quaker St E1 ... 24 B1 98 C1
Quality Ct WC2 ... 107 B2
Quantock Ho N16 ... 7 B3
Quantock Mews 3 SE15 ... 49 C1
Quarrendon St SW6 ... 165 C2
Quarry Rd SW18 ... 59 B1
Quarterdeck The E14 ... 41 C4
Quayside Ct 6 SE16 ... 32 C1
Quebec & Crown Wharves E14 ... 33 B3
Quebec Ind Est SE16 ... 41 A3
Quebec Mews W1 ... 103 A1
Quebec Way SE16 ... 41 A4
Quebec Wharf 32 E8 ... 24 A4
Quedgeley Ct 3 SE15 ... 49 B4
Queen Alexandra Mans WC1 ... 94 A3
Queen Anne Mews W1 ... 104 B3
Queen Anne Rd E9 ... 17 C2
Queen Anne's Gate SW1 ... 133 B3
Queen Anne's Gdns
Bedford Pk W4 ... 38 A3
Ealing W5 ... 36 A4
Queen Anne's Gr
Bedford Pk W4 ... 38 A3
Ealing W5 ... 36 A4

Queen Anne St W1 104 A3
Queen Anne Terr 9 E1 32 A2
Queen Caroline St W6 39 B1
Queen Charlotte's & Chelsea Hospl W12 29 C3
Queen Ct WC1 94 B1
Queen Elizabeth Ct 5 N1 15 C2
Queen Elizabeth Hall & Purcell Room SE1 121 A2
Queen Elizabeth Ho SW12 72 C4
Queen Elizabeth II Con Ctr SW1 133 C3
Queen Elizabeth II Jubilee Sch 5 W9 23 B1
Queen Elizabeth's Cl N16 6 C2
Queen Elizabeth's Coll 15 SE10 52 B3
Queen Elizabeth St SE1 138 C4
Queen Elizabeth's Wlk N16 6 C2
Queen Elizabeth Wlk SW13 47 A2
Queenhithe EC4 123 A4
Queen Margaret Flats 22 E2 25 A2
Queen Margarets Ct N1 16 A3
Queen Margaret's Gr N1 16 A3
Queen Mary's Gdns NW1 91 B3
Queen Mary's Univ Hospl SW15 56 C1
Queen Mary, Univ of London E1 26 A1
Queen Mother Sp Ctr SW1 146 C4
Queen of Denmark Ct SE16 41 B3
Queen St Pl EC4 123 A4
Queensberry Mews W SW7 143 B4
Queensberry Pl SW7 143 B4
Queensberry Way SW7 143 B4
Queensborough Mews W2 114 C4
Queensborough Pas W2 114 C4
Queensborough Terr W2 114 B4
Queensbridge Ct 1 E2 24 B3
Queensbridge Inf Sch 11 E8 16 B1
Queensbridge Rd
Dalston E8 16 B1
Shoreditch E2, E8 24 B4
Queensbury St 22 N1 15 B1
Queen's CE Prim Sch The TW9 44 C3
Queen's Cir SW11 160 A1
Queen's Club Gdns W14 154 B4
Queen's Club The W14 140 B1
Queen's Coll W1 104 A3
Queen's Coll Prep Sch W1 104 A4
Queens Cres TW10 54 B2
Queen's Cres NW5 12 C2
Queens Ct
Battersea SW11 170 A4
Camberwell SE5 49 A1
4 Limehouse E14 33 B2
Queen's Ct
Barnes SW13 56 C4
Kensington W2 114 B3
3 Richmond TW10 54 B1
St John's Wood NW8 79 B2
Queensdale W11 30 C1
Queensdale Cres W11 30 C1
Queensdale Pl W11 31 A1 112 A1
Queensdale Rd
Notting Hill W11 30 C1
Notting Hill W11 31 A1 112 A1
Queensdale Wlk W11 31 A1 112 A1
Queensdown Rd E5 17 A4
Queen's Dr N4 6 A2
Queen's Elm Par SW3 143 C2
Queen's Elm Sq SW3 143 C1
Queen's Gallery SW1 132 B3
Queen's Gate SW7 129 A1
Queensgate Gdns SW15 57 A3
Queen's Gate Gdns SW7 129 A1
Queensgate Ho 32 E3 26 B3
Queen's Gate Jun Sch SW7 143 B4
Queen's Gate Mews SW7 129 A2
Queensgate Pl 10 NW6 10 C1
Queen's Gate Pl SW7 129 A1
Queen's Gate Pl Mews SW7 129 A1
Queen's Gate Terr SW7 129 A2
Queens Gate Villas E9 18 A1
Queen's Gdns W2 114 C4
Queen's Gr NW8 79 C3
Queen's Head Pas EC2 108 C2
Queen's Head St N1 86 B3
Queen's Head Yd SE1 123 B1
Queens Ho 1 SE17 48 C4
Queen's House The SE10 52 C4
Queensland Rd N7 14 C4
Queens Manor Sch SW6 47 C3
Queens Mans NW6 11 A3
Queen's Mans W6 39 C2
Queensmead NW8 79 C4
Queensmere Cl SW19 69 C2
Queensmere Ct SW13 46 C4
Queensmere Rd SW19 69 C2
Queen's Mews W2 114 A4
Queensmill Rd SW6 47 C3
Queensmill Sch SW6 165 C1
Queens Par 3 NW2 9 B2
Queens Park Com Sch NW6 22 C4
Queens Park Ct 5 W10 22 C2
Queen's Park Prim Sch 20 W10 23 A1
Queen's Park Sta NW6 23 B3
Queen Sq WC1 106 B4
Queen's Quay EC4 123 A4
Queen's Rd
Mortlake SW14 55 C4
New Cross Gate SE14, SE15 50 B2
Richmond TW10 54 B1
Queen's Ride SW13 57 A4
Queen's Rise TW10 54 B1
Queen's Road Sta SE15 50 B2
Queen's Row SE17 48 C4
Queen St
City of London EC4 123 A4
Mayfair W1 118 A2
Queens Terr NW8 79 B2
Queenstown Mews SW8 170 A3
Queenstown Rd SW8 160 A2
Queenstown Road (Battersea) Sta SW8 170 B4
Queensville Rd SW12, SW4 73 C4
Queensway W2 114 B4
Queensway Sta W2 114 B3
Queen's Wlk SW1 118 C1
Queenswood Ct 7 SW4 62 A2
Queens Yd E9 18 C2
Queen's Yd W1 93 A1
Queen Victoria Meml SW1 132 C4
Queen Victoria St EC4 122 C4
Queen Victoria Terr 12 E1 32 A2
Quelch Ho 2 N19 13 C3
Quemerford Rd N7 14 B3
Quendon Ho 9 W10 22 B1
Quenington Ct 5 SE15 49 B4
Quenington Mans SW6 164 C4
Quennel Ho 7 SW12 73 B4
Querrin St SW6 166 C1
Quested Ct 27 E8 17 A3
Quex Mews NW6 23 C4
Quex Rd NW6 23 C4
Quick Rd W4 38 A1
Quick St N1 86 B1
Quick Street Mews N1 86 A1
Quickswood NW3 12 A1
Quill La SW15 57 C3
Quill St N4 5 C1
Quilp St SE1 136 C4
Quilter St E2 24 C2 99 B4
Quilting Ct 23 SE16 40 C4
Quince Rd SE13 52 A1
Quintin Ct W4 45 B3
Quintin Kynaston Sch NW8 79 B3
Quintock Ho 2 TW9 44 C2
Quinton Ho SW8 162 A2
Quinton St SW18 71 B2
Quixley St 1 E14 34 C2
Quorn Rd SE22 64 A4

R

Rabbit Row W8 31 C1 113 C2
Raby St E14 33 A3
Racine 15 SE5 49 A2
Racton Rd SW6 155 B3
Radbourne Cl E5 17 C4
Radbourne Rd SW12 73 C3
Radcliff Bldg EC1 107 B4
Radcliffe Ave NW10 21 C3
Radcliffe Coll
Marylebone W1 104 C1
Soho W1 105 B2
Radcliffe Ho 10 SE16 40 A2
Radcliffe Path 5 SW8 170 B1
Radcliffe Rd SE1 138 B2
Radcliffe Sq SW15 57 C1
Radcot St SE11 149 C1
Raddington Rd W10 31 A4
Radford Ho
7 Bow Comm E14 34 A4
Islington N7 14 B3
Radford Rd SE13 67 B1
Radipole Rd SW6 164 C4
Radland Rd E16 35 C3
Radlett Pl NW8 80 A4
Radley Ct 25 SE16 40 C4
Radley Ho NW1 90 C2
Radley Lo 30 SW19 69 C3
Radley Mews W8 127 C1
Radley Terr 1 E16 35 B4
Radnor Lo W2 101 C1
Radnor Mews W2 101 C1
Radnor Pl W2 102 A1
Radnor Rd
Kensal Rise NW6 23 A4
Peckham SE15 49 C3
Radnor St EC1 97 A3
Radnor Terr W14 140 C4
Radnor Way NW10 20 A1
Radnor Wlk
Chelsea SW3 144 C1
21 Millwall E14 41 C2
Radstock St SW11 158 A1
Radway Ho 38 W2 31 C4
Radwell Ho SW2 62 C2
Raebarn Ct 6 SW16 74 A1
Raeburn St SW2 62 A3
Ragged School Mus E3 33 A4
Raglan Ct SW9 62 C4
Raglan St NW5 13 A2
Ragley Cl W3 37 B4
Rahere Ho EC1 96 C4
Railey Mews NW5 13 B3
Railton Rd SE24 63 A2
Railway App SE1 123 C2
Railway Ave SE16 40 B4
Railway Cotts W6 39 B4
Railway Gr SE14 51 B3
Railway Rise SE22 64 A3
Railway Side SW13 56 A4
Railway St N1 84 B1
Railway Terr SE13 67 A2
Rainbow Ave E14 42 A1
Rainbow Ct 3 SE14 51 A4
Rainbow Montessori Sch NW6 11 A1
Rainbow Quay SE16 41 A3
Rainbow Sch 5 SW17 71 B2
Rainbow St SE5 49 A3
Raines Ct N16 7 B2
Raine's Foundation Lower Sch 32 E2 25 A2
Raine's Foundation Sch 34 E2 25 B3
Raine St E1 32 A1
Rainford Ho 9 N7 5 B2
Rainham Cl SW11 60 A1
Rainham Ho NW1 83 A3
Rainham Rd NW10 22 B2
Rainhill Way E3 26 C2
Rainsborough Ave SE8 41 A2
Rainsford Ct NW10 20 A3
Rainsford Ho 14 SW2 62 B2
Rainsford Rd NW10 20 A3
Rainsford St W2 102 A2
Rainton Rd SE7 43 C1
Rainville Rd W6 47 B4
Raleigh Ct
7 Hammersmith W12 39 A4
2 Rotherhithe SE16 32 C1
Raleigh Gdns SW2 62 B1
Raleigh Ho
30 Clapham SW8 171 B2
Isle of Dogs E14 42 A4
Raleigh Mews N1 86 B3
Raleigh Rd TW9 54 B4

Raleigh St N1 86 B3
Ralph Ct 8 W2 100 B2
Ralston St SW3 144 C1
Ramar Ho 12 E1 111 B4
Ramilles Cl SW2 62 A1
Ramilles Ho W1 105 A1
Ramillies Pl W1 104 C1
Ramillies Rd W4 37 C3
Ramillies St W1 104 C1
Rampart St E1 32 A3
Rampayne St SW1 147 B2
Ramsay Ho NW8 80 A2
Ramsay Rd W3 37 B4
Ramsdean Ho 1 SW15 69 A3
Ramsden Rd SW12 72 C4
Ramsey Ct
Putney SW15 57 B1
6 Upper Holloway N19 4 C2
Ramsey Ho
5 Battersea SW11 59 C3
14 Kennington SW9 163 C1
Ramsey St E2 24 C1 99 C2
Ramsey Wlk N1 15 C2
Ramsfort Ho 4 SE16 40 A2
Ramsgate St E8 16 B2
Ram St SW18 59 A2
Randal Cremer JMI Sch 16 E2 24 B3
Randall Cl SW11 168 A4
Randall Pl SE10 52 B3
Randall Rd SE11 148 C3
Randall Row SE11 148 C3
Randell's Rd N1 84 B4
Randolf Ct
Paddington NW6 78 A1
St John's Wood NW8 78 C3
Randolph Ave W9 88 C3
Randolph Cres W9 88 C2
Randolph Gdns NW6 78 A1
Randolph Mews W9 89 A1
Randolph Rd W9 89 A1
Randolph St NW1 13 B1
Ranelagh Ave
Barnes SW13 46 C1
Fulham SW6 58 B4
Ranelagh Gardens Mans SW6 58 A4
Ranelagh Gardens (site of Chelsea Flower Show) SW1 145 C1
Ranelagh Gdns
3 Bedford Pk W6 38 B3
Chiswick W4 45 B3
Fulham SW6 58 B4
Ranelagh Gr SW1 145 C2
Ranelagh Ho SW3 144 C2
Ranelagh Mans 4 SW6 165 A2
Ranelagh Rd
Dagenham NW10 21 B3
Pimlico SW1 147 A1
Rangdon St EC3 110 C1
Ranger's House (The Wernher Collection) SE10 52 C2
Rangers Sq SE10 52 C2
Rangoon Ho 5 N16 15 C4
Rankine Ho SE1 136 C1
Ranmere St SW12 73 A3
Rann Ho 1 SW14 55 C4
Rannoch Rd W6 47 C4
Ransomes Dock Bsns Ctr SW11 158 B1
Ransomes Mews SW11 158 B2
Ranston St NW1 102 A4
Ranulf Rd NW2 10 B4
Ranwell Cl 18 E3 26 B4
Ranwell Ho 17 E3 26 B4
Raphael Ct 9 SE16 40 A1
Raphael St SW7 130 C3
Rapley Ho 14 E2 24 C2 99 B3
Rashleigh Ct 8 SW8 61 A4
Rashleigh Ho WC1 94 A3
Rastell Ave SW12 73 C3
RATCLIFF 32 C2
Ratcliffe Cross St E1 32 C3
Ratcliffe Ho 10 E14 33 A3
Ratcliffe La 16 E14 33 A3
Ratcliffe Orch 9 E1 32 C2
Rathbone Ho
5 Canning Town E16 35 B3
Kilburn NW6 23 C4
Rathbone Mkt 3 E16 35 B4
Rathbone Pl W1 105 B2
Rathbone St
Canning Town E16 35 B3
Fitzrovia W1 105 A3
Rathgar Rd SW9 63 A4
Rathmell Dr SW4 61 C1
Rattray Rd SW2 62 C2
Raul Rd SE15 49 C2
Raveley St NW5 13 B4
Ravenet Ct
Battersea SW11 170 A3
Clapham SW4 61 A2
Ravenet St SW11 170 A3
Ravenfield Rd SW17 72 B1
Raven Ho 10 SE16 40 C2
Ravenna Rd SW15 57 C2
Raven Row E1 32 A4
Ravensbourne Ho NW8 102 A4
Ravensbourne Mans 9 SE8 51 C4
Ravensbourne Pl SE13 52 A1
Ravensbury Rd SW18 71 A2
Ravensbury Terr SW18 71 A2
Ravenscar NW1 82 C3
Ravenscourt 1 N16 7 C1
Ravenscourt Ave W6 38 C2
Ravenscourt Gdns W6 38 C2
Ravenscourt Ho 13 W6 39 A2
Ravenscourt Park Mans 1 W6 39 A3
Ravenscourt Park Prep Sch W6 38 C2
Ravenscourt Park Sta W6 39 A2
Ravenscourt Pk W6 38 C2
Ravenscourt Pl W6 39 A2
Ravenscourt Rd W6 39 A2
Ravenscourt Sq W6 38 C3
Ravenscourt Theatre Sch 14 W6 39 A2
Ravenscroft Ave NW11 1 B4
Ravenscroft Cl 4 E16 35 C4
Ravenscroft Ct NW11 1 B4
Ravenscroft Point 26 E9 17 C2
Ravenscroft Rd
Acton W4 37 B2
Newham E16 35 C4
Ravenscroft St E2 24 B2 99 A4
Ravensdon St SE11 149 C1
Ravenshaw St NW6 10 B3
Ravenslea Rd SW11, SW12 72 B4
Ravensmede Way W4 38 B2
Ravenstone SE17 152 B1
Ravenstone Prim Sch SW12 72 C2
Ravenstone St SW12 72 C3
Ravenswood Rd SW12 73 A4
Ravensworth Ct SW6 155 B1
Ravensworth Rd NW10 22 A2
Raven Wharf SE1 138 C4
Ravey St EC2 24 A1 98 A2
Rav Pinter Cl N16 7 A4
Rawlings St SW3 144 C4
Rawlinson Ho SE13 67 C3
Rawlinson Point 8 E16 35 B4
Rawreth Wlk N1 87 A4
Rawson Ct SW11 169 C3
Rawson St SW11 170 A3
Rawstorne Pl EC1 96 A4
Rawstorne St EC1 96 A4
Rayburne Ct W14 126 A2
Raydon St N19 4 A2
Ray Ho
7 North Kensington W10 30 C3
Shoreditch N1 87 C3
Raymede Twr 2 W10 30 C4
Raymond Bldgs WC1 107 A4
Raymouth Rd SE16 40 A2
Raynald Ho 15 SW16 74 A1
Rayne Ct SE1 138 C4
Rayne Ho
1 Balham SW12 60 C1
Paddington W9 88 A2
Rayner Ct 10 W12 39 B4
Rayner's Rd SW15 58 A2
Raynes Ct NW2 10 A4
Raynham W2 102 A2
Raynham Ho 1 E1 25 C1
Raynham Rd W6 39 A2
Raynor Pl
23 Canonbury N1 15 B1
N1 87 A4
Ray St EC1 95 C1
Ray Wlk N7 5 B2
Reachview Cl 17 NW1 13 B1
Reade Ct 6 W3 37 B3
Reade Wlk 5 NW10 8 A1
Read Ho 4 SE11 163 B4
Reading Ho
Paddington W2 100 C1
Peckham SE15 49 C4
Reading La E8 17 A2
Reapers Cl NW1 83 B4
Reardon Ho 5 E1 32 A1
Reardon Path 31 E1 32 A1
Reardon St E1 32 A1
Reaston St SE14 50 C3
Reay Prim Sch SW9 163 A1
Reckitt Rd W4 38 A1
Record St SE16 50 B4
Rector St N1 86 C3
Rectory Gdns 6 SW4 61 B4
Rectory Gr SW4 61 B4
Rectory Rd
Barnes SW13 46 C1
1 London W3 28 B1
Shacklewell N16 7 B1
Rectory Road Sta N16 7 B1
Rectory Sq E1 32 C4
Reculver Ho 2 SE15 50 B4
Reculver Rd SE16 40 C1
Red Anchor Cl SW3 158 A3
Redan Pl W2 100 A1
Redan St W14 39 C3
Redan Terr SE5 48 A1
Redbourne Ho 7 E14 33 B3
Redbourn Ho 10 W10 22 B1
Redbridge Gdns SE5 49 A3
Redburn St SW3 158 C4
Redcar St SE5 48 B3
Redcastle Cl E1 32 B2
Redchurch St E2 24 B1 98 C2
Redcliffe Cl SW5 142 A1
Redcliffe Gdns
Chiswick W4 45 A3
Fulham SW10 156 B4
Redcliffe Mews SW10 142 B1
Redcliffe Pl SW10 156 C3
Redcliffe Rd SW10 157 A4
Redcliffe Sch SW10 156 C4
Redcliffe Sq SW10 142 B1
Redcliffe St SW10 156 B4
Redclyf Ho 13 E1 25 B1
Redcroft 5 NW6 10 C2
Red Cross Cotts SE1 137 A4
Redcross Way SE1 123 A1
Reddins Rd SE15 49 C4
Rede Pl W2 31 C2 113 C4
Redesdale St SW3 158 C4
Redfern Rd NW10 8 A1
Redfield La SW5 142 A4
Redfield Mews SW5 141 C4
Redfiff Est SE16 41 B3
Redford Wlk N1 86 C4
Redgate Terr SW15 57 C1
Redgrave Rd SW15 57 C4
Redhill Ct SW2 74 C2
Redhill St NW1 92 B4
Red House Sq 20 N1 15 B1
Redington Gdns NW3 11 A4
Redington Ho N1 85 A2
Redington Rd NW3 11 A4
Redlands Prim Sch 35 E1 32 B4
Redlands Way SW2 74 B4
Red Lion Cl 9 SE17 48 C4
Red Lion Ct EC4 107 C1
Red Lion Row SE17 48 B4
Red Lion Sq WC1 106 C3
Red Lion St WC1 106 C3
Red Lion Yd W1 117 C2
Redlynch Ct W14 126 B3
Redlynch Ho 27 SW9 173 C4
Redman Bldg EC1 107 B4
Redman Ho SE1 137 A3
Redman's Rd E1 32 B4
Redmayne Ho 15 SW9 173 A2
Redmead La E1 125 B1
Redmill Ho 24 E1 25 A1
Redmond Ho N1 85 A3
Redmore Rd W6 39 A2
Red Pl W1 117 B4
Red Post Hill SE21, SE24 63 C2
Redriff Prim Sch SE16 41 A4
Redriff Rd SE16 41 A3
Red Rover SW13 56 C4
Redrup Ho 21 SE14 50 C4
Redruth Rd E9 25 B4
Red Sq The N16 6 C1
Redstart Cl SE14 51 A3

Redvers St E2 . . . 24 A2 98 B4
Redwald Rd E5 . . . 17 C4
Redwood Cl
4 Bow E3 . . . 26 C3
Rotherhithe SE16 . . . 33 A1
Redwood Ct
Brondesbury NW6 . . . 10 A1
Crouch End N19 . . . 4 C4
Redwood Mews 2 SW4 . . . 61 A4
Redwoods SW15 . . . 68 C3
Reece Mews SW7 143 B4
Reed Cl E16 . . . 35 C4
Reedham St SE15 . . . 64 C4
Reed Ho SW15 . . . 56 C1
Reedholm Villas N16 . . . 15 C4
Reed Pl
Battersea SW11 . . . 60 A3
Clapham SW4 . . . 61 C3
Reed's Pl NW1 . . . 13 B1
Reedworth St SE11 . . . 149 C3
Reef Ho E14 . . . 42 B3
Rees St N1 . . . 87 A3
Reeves Ho
Lambeth SE1 . . . 135 B3
Mayfair W1 . . . 117 B3
Reeves Mews W1 117 C3
Reeves Rd E3 . . . 27 A1
Reflection Ho 9 E2 . . . 24 C1 99 B2
Reform St SW11 . . 169 A2
Regal Cl E1 . . . 111 C4
Regal La NW1 . . . 81 C3
Regal Pl
8 Tower Hamlets E3 . . . 26 B2
Walham Green SW6 . . . 156 B1
Regan Way N1 . . . 24 A3
Regatta Point TW8 . 44 B4
Regency Ct
9 Bow E3 . . . 26 B3
14 South Hackney E9 . . . 25 B4
Regency Ho NW1 . . 92 B2
Regency Lo NW3 . . . 11 C1
Regency Mews
Camberwell SW9 . . . 48 A3
1 Willesden NW10 . . . 8 C2
Regency Pl SW1 . . 147 C4
Regency St SW1 . . 147 C3
Regency Terr SW7 . . . 143 B2
Regency Wlk 8 TW10 . . . 54 A2
Regeneration Rd SE16 . . . 40 C1
Regent Ct
Lisson Gr NW8 . . . 90 A3
1 Stamford Hill N16 . . 7 B4
Regent Ho W14 . . 140 A4
Regent Pl W1 . . . 119 A4
Regent Rd SE24 . . . 63 A2
Regents Bridge Gdns SW8 . . . 162 B2
Regents Canal Ho 19 E14 . . . 33 A3
Regent's Coll NW1 91 B2
Regents Ct E8 . . . 24 C4
Regents Gate Ho 20 E14 . . . 33 A2
Regents Lo 9 SW2 . . . 74 B3
Regents Mews NW8 . . . 79 A2
REGENT'S PARK . . . 92 A4
Regent's Park NW1 . . . 81 B1
Regent's Park Barracks NW1 . . . 82 B1
Regent's Park Rd
Camden Town NW1 . . . 81 B4
Primrose Hill NW3 . . . 12 C1
Regent's Park Sta NW1 . . . 92 A1
Regent's Park Terr NW1 . . . 82 A4
Regent's Pl SE3 . . . 53 C1
Regents Plaza 2 NW6 . . . 78 A2
Regent Sq
23 Bromley E3 . . . 27 A2
St Pancras WC1 . . . 94 B3
Regent's Row E8 . . . 24 C4
Regent St
Brentford W4 . . . 36 C1
7 Kensal Green NW10 . . . 22 C2
Mayfair W1 . . . 118 C4
Regents Wharf
3 Hackney E2 . . . 25 A4
Islington N1 . . . 84 C2
Reginald Pl 6 SE8 . . . 51 C3
Reginald Rd SE8 . . . 51 C3
Reginald Sq SE8 . . . 51 C3
Regina Point SE16 . . 40 B3
Regina Rd N4 . . . 5 B3
Regis Ct NW1 . . . 102 C4
Regis Pl 17 SW2 . . . 62 B3
Regis Rd NW5 . . . 13 A3
Regnart Bldgs NW1 . . . 93 A3
Reid Ct SW14 . . . 45 B1
Reighton Rd E5 . . . 7 C2
Reizel Cl N16 . . . 7 B3
Relay Rd W12 . . . 30 B1
Relf Rd SE15 . . . 64 C4
Reliance Sq E2 . . . 24 A1 98 B2
Relton Ct W3 . . . 36 C4
Relton Mews SW7 . . . 130 B2
Rembrandt Cl E14 . . 42 C3
Rembrandt Ct 10 SE16 . . . 40 A1
Rembrant Cl SW1 145 B3
Remington St N1 . . 86 B1
Remnant St WC2 . 106 C2
Remsted Ho 7 NW6 . . . 78 A3
Remus Rd E3 . . . 18 C1
Renaissance Wlk 4 SE10 . . . 43 B3
Renbold Ho 5 SE10 . . . 52 B2
Rendlesham Ho 3 E5, N16 . . . 7 C1
Rendlesham Rd E5 . . 7 C1
Renforth St SE16 . . . 40 B4
Renfrew Ho NW6 . . 78 A1
Renfrew Rd SE11 150 A3
Rennell Ho 18 E9 . . . 17 C2
Rennell St SE13 . . . 67 B4
Rennie Cotts 29 E1 . . . 25 B1
Rennie Ct SE1 . . . 122 A2
Rennie Ho SE1 . . . 136 C1
Rennie St SE1 . . . 122 A2
Renoir Ct 7 SE16 . . 40 A1
Renton Cl SW2 . . . 62 B1
Rephidim St SE1 . 138 A1
Replingham Rd SW18 . . . 70 C3
Reporton Rd SW6 154 B1
Repton Ho SW1 . . 147 A3
Repton St E14 . . . 33 A3
Reservoir Rd SE4 . . . 51 A1
Reservoir Studios 14 E1 . . . 32 C3
Resolution Way 14 SE8 . . . 51 C3
Restell Cl SE3 . . . 53 A4
Reston Pl SW7 . . . 128 C3
Restoration Sq SW11 . . . 167 C3
Retcar Pl N19 . . . 4 A2
Retford St E2 . . . 24 A3
Retreat Ho 5 E9 . . . 17 B2
Retreat Pl E9 . . . 17 B2
Retreat The SW14 . . 56 A4
Reunion Row E1 . . . 32 A2
Reveley Sq SE16 . . . 41 A4
Revelon Rd SE4 . . . 66 A4
Revelstoke Rd SW18, SW19 . . . 70 C2
Reverdy Rd SE1 . . 153 B3
Rewell St SW6 . . . 156 C1
Rex Pl W1 . . . 117 C2
Reynard Cl SE4 . . . 66 A4
Reynard Pl SE14 . . . 51 A4
Reynolds Cl NW11 . . . 2 A4
Reynolds Ho
Finsbury Pk N4 . . . 5 A3
18 South Hackney E2 . . . 25 B3
St John's Wood NW8 . . . 79 C1
Westminster SW1 . 147 C3
Reynolds Pl 12 TW10 . . . 54 B1
Reynolds Rd
Acton Green W4 . . . 37 B3
Nunhead SE15 . . . 65 B3
Reynolds Sp Ctr W3 . . . 36 C4
Rffra Rd Ret Pk SW2 . . . 62 C2
Rheidol Mews N1 . 86 C2
Rheidol Terr N1 . . . 86 C3
Rhizotron & Xstrata Treetop Walkway TW9 . . . 44 A2
Rhoda St E2 . . 24 B1 99 A2
Rhodes Ho
Shepherd's Bush W12 . . . 30 A1
Shoreditch N1 . . . 97 B4
Rhodesia Rd SW9 172 B1
Rhodes St N7 . . . 14 B3
Rhodeswell Rd E14 . . . 33 B3
Rhondda Gr E3 . . . 26 B2
Rhyl Prim Sch 21 NW5 . . . 12 C2
Rhyl St NW5 . . . 12 C2
Ribblesdale Ho 11 NW6 . . . 23 C4
Ribbon Dance Mews SE5 . . . 48 C2
Ribstone Ho 12 E9 . . 17 C2
Ricardo St E14 . . . 34 A3
Riceyman Ho WC1 . 95 B3
Richard Anderson Ct 1 SE14 . . . 50 C3
Richard Atkins Prim Sch 28 SW2 . . . 74 A4
Richard Burbidge Mans SW13 . . . 47 B4
Richard Cloudesley Sch (Prim Dept) EC1 . . . 97 A1
Richard Cloudesley Sch (Secondary Dept) EC1 . . . 96 C1
Richard Cobden Prim Sch NW1 . . . 83 A3
Richard Fox Ho N4 . . 6 B1
Richard Ho 10 SE16 . . . 40 B2
Richard Knight Ho SW6 . . . 165 C4
Richard Neale Ho 2 E1 . . . 32 A2
Richardson Cl 19 E8 . . . 24 B4
Richardson Ct 20 SW4 . . . 172 B2
Richardson Ho 10 E14 . . . 33 C4
Richardson's Mews W1 . . . 92 C1
Richard's Pl SW3 . 144 B4
Richard St 20 E1 . . . 32 A3
Richbell WC1 . . . 106 B4
Richbell Pl WC1 . . 106 C4
Richborne Terr SW8 . . . 163 A2
Richborough Ho
10 Deptford SE15 . . . 50 B4
14 Hackney E5 . . . 17 A4
Richborough Rd NW2 . . . 10 A4
Richbourne Ct W1 . . . 102 B2
Richford Gate W6 . . 39 B3
Richford St W6 . . . 39 B3
Rich Ind Est SE15 . . 50 A4
Rich La SW5 . . . 142 A2
Richland Ho 4 SE15 . . . 49 C2
Richman Ho 10 SE8 . . . 41 B1
Rich Mix E1 . . . 99 A2
RICHMOND . . . 54 B3
Richmond Ave
Islington N1 . . . 85 A4
Willesden NW10 . . . 9 B2
Richmond Bldgs W1 . . . 105 B1
Richmond Circus TW9 . . . 54 A3
Richmond Coll W8 . . . 128 B2
Richmond Cres N1 85 B4
Richmond Ct SW1 . . . 131 A3
Richmond Gr N1 . . 15 A1
Richmond Healthcare Hamlet Hospl TW9 . . . 54 A4
RICHMOND HILL . . . 54 A1
Richmond Hill TW10 . . . 54 A1
Richmond Hill Ct 5 TW10 . . . 54 A1
Richmond Ho
12 Forest Hill SE26 . . . 76 C1
Regent's Pk NW1 . . . 82 B1
Walworth SE17 . . . 151 B2
Richmond International Bsns Ctr 5 TW9 . . . 54 B3
Richmond Mans
Earl's Ct SW5 . . . 142 A2
Putney SW15 . . . 58 A4
Richmond Mews W1 . . . 105 B1
Richmond Park Rd SW14 . . . 55 C3
Richmond Rd
Dalston E8 . . . 16 C1
Ealing W5 . . . 36 A4
Richmond Sta TW9 . . . 54 A3
Richmond Terr SW1 . . . 134 A4
Richmond Way W12, W14 . . . 39 C4
Rich St E14 . . . 33 B2
Rickard Cl SW2 . . . 74 C3
Rickett St SW6 . . . 155 C4
Rickman Ho 23 E2 . . 25 B1
Rickman St 24 E1 . . 25 B1
Rick Roberts Way E15 . . . 27 C3
Rickthorne Rd 7 N19 . . . 5 A2
Riddell Ct SE1 . . . 152 C2
Ridgdale St E3 . . . 27 A3
Ridge Hill NW11 . . . 1 A3
Ridge Rd NW2 . . . 1 B1
Ridgeway 11 TW10 . . . 54 A1
Ridgeway Dr W3 . . 36 C3
Ridgeway Gdns N6 . . 4 B4
Ridgeway The
Acton W3 . . . 36 C3
Golders Green NW11 . . 1 B3
Ridgewell Cl N1 . . . 87 A4
Ridgmount Gdns WC1 . . . 105 B4
Ridgmount Pl WC1 . . . 105 B4
Ridgmount Rd SW18 . . . 59 A2
Ridgmount St WC1 . . . 105 B4
Ridgway Rd SW9 . . . 63 A4
Riding House St W1 . . . 104 C3
Ridings Cl N6 . . . 4 B4
Riding The NW11 . . . 1 B4
Ridley Ho 14 SW11 . . . 60 A4
Ridley Rd
Dalston E8 . . . 16 B3
Willesden Green NW10 . . . 21 C3
Ridley Road Mkt E8 . . . 16 B3
Riffel Rd NW2 . . . 9 B3
Rifle Ct SE11 . . . 163 C4
Rifle Pl W11 . . . 30 C1
Rifle St E14 . . . 34 A4
Riga Ho 12 E1 . . . 32 C4
Rigault Rd SW6 . . 164 B1
Rigden St E14 . . . 34 A3
Rigeley Rd NW10 . . . 21 C2
Rigge Pl SW4 . . . 61 C3
Rigg Ho 2 SW4 . . . 74 A4

Rignold Ho 6 SE5 49 A1
Riley Ho
9 Bow E3 26 C1
Chelsea SW10 157 B3
1 Streatham SW4 73 C4
Riley Rd SE1 138 C2
Riley St SW10 157 B2
Rill Ho 16 SE5 49 A3
Rimini Ct SW12 72 B3
Rinaldo Rd SW12 73 A4
Ringcroft St N7 14 C3
Ringford Ho SW18 58 B2
Ringford Rd SW18 58 C1
Ring Ho 15 E1 32 B2
Ringmer Ave SW6 164 B3
Ringmer Gdns 3 N19 5 A2
Ringmer Ho 15 SE22 64 A4
Ring Rd W12 30 B1
Ringsfield Ho SE17 151 A1
Ringwood Gdns
17 Millwall E14 41 C2
Roehampton SW15 68 C3
Ripley Gdns SW14 55 C4
Ripley Ho
Mortlake SW14 56 A4
Nine Elms SW1 160 C4
Ripley's Believe It or Not! SW1 119 B3
Riplington Ct SW15 69 A4
Ripplevale Gr N1 14 B1
Risborough SE17 150 C4
Risborough Ho NW8 90 B2
Risborough St SE1 136 B4
Risdon Ho 26 SE16 40 B4
Risdon St 27 SE16 40 B4
Riseholme Ct E9 18 B2
Riseholme Ho 14 SE22 64 A4
Riseldine Rd SE23 66 A1
Risinghill St N1 85 B2
Rising Sun Ct EC1 108 B3
Risley Ho 7 E9 17 C2
Rita Rd SW8 162 C2
Ritchie Ho
Crouch End N19 4 C4
8 Rotherhithe SE16 40 B3
12 South Bromley E14 34 C3
Ritchie St N1 85 C2
Ritherdon Rd SW17 73 A2
Ritson Ho N1 84 C3
Ritson Rd E8 16 C2
Rivaz Pl E9 17 B2
Riven Ct 10 W2 100 B1
Riverains The SW11 167 B3
River Barge Cl E14 42 B4
Rivercourt Rd W6 39 A1
River Ct SE1 122 A3
Riverdale Dr SW18 71 A3
Riverfleet WC1 94 B4
Riverford Ho 28 W2 31 C4
River Ho SW13 46 A1
River House Montessori Sch E14 42 A4
Rivermead Ct SW6 58 B4
Rivermead Ho E9 18 A3
River Pl N1 15 B1
River Plate Ho EC2 109 C3
Riversdale Prim Sch SW18 70 C3
Riversdale Rd N5 6 B1
Riversdene N5 6 B1
Rivers Ho 10 TW8 36 C1
Riverside
Battersea SW11 158 B2
11 Rotherhithe SE16 40 B4
St Pancras WC1 94 B4
Riverside Bsns Ctr SW18 71 A3
Riverside Ct SW8 161 C4
Riverside Dr W4 46 A2
Riverside Gdns W6 39 A1
Riverside Health & Racquets Club Chiswick The W4 46 A2
Riverside Ho 14 N1 15 B1
Riverside Mans 4 E1 32 B1
Riverside Prim Sch 37 SE16 139 C3
Riverside Rd
Mill Meads E15 27 B3
Wandsworth SW17, SW19 71 B1
Riverside Wlk Mkt WC2 121 A2
Riverside Workshops SE1 123 A2
River St EC1 95 B4
River Terr
London W6 39 B1
St James SW1 120 C3
Riverton Cl W9 23 B2
Riverview Gdns SW13 47 A4
Riverview Gr W4 45 A4
Riverview Rd W4 45 A4
River Way SE10 43 B3
Rivet Ho SE1 153 A2
Rivington Ct NW10 21 C4
Rivington Pl EC2 24 A2 98 B3
Rivington St EC2 24 A2 98 A3
Rivington Wlk 4 E8 24 C4
Rixon St N7 5 C1
Roach Rd E3 18 C1
Roads Pl N19 5 A2
Roan St SE10 52 B4
Robert Adam St W1 103 B2
Roberta St E2 24 C2 99 C3
Robert Bell Ho 2 SE16 153 B4
Robert Blair Prim Sch N7 14 A2
Robert Browning Prim Sch SE17 151 B2
Robert Cl W9 89 A1
Robert Dashwood Way SE17 150 C3
Robert Gentry Ho W14 140 B1
Robert Jones Ho 3 SE16 153 B4
Robert Keen Cl 18 SE15 49 C2
Robert Lowe Cl SE14 50 C3
Robert Owen Ho
Fulham SW6 47 C2
8 Spitalfields E2 24 B2 99 A4
Robert Owen Lo 4 E5 17 A4
Roberts Ct
Islington N1 86 B3
Willesden NW10 8 A2
Roberts Ho 5 SE27 75 A1
Roberts Mews SW1 131 B1
Robertson Ho 11 SE10 52 B2
Robertson St SW8 170 B1
Robert's Pl EC1 95 C2
Robert St
Regent's Pk NW1 92 B3
Strand WC2 120 B3
Robert Sutton Ho 20 E1 32 B3
Robeson St 7 E3 33 B4
Robin Ct 15 E14 42 B3
Robin Gr
Dartmouth Pk N6 3 C2
Highgate N6 3 C2
Robin Ho NW8 80 A1
Robin Hood SW15 68 A1
Robin Hood Gdns 12 E14 34 B2
Robin Hood La E14 34 B2
Robinscroft Mews 18 SE10 52 A2
Robins Ct TW10 54 A1
Robin's Ct SW4 62 A1
Robinsfield Inf Sch NW8 80 A2
Robinson Ct
Islington N1 86 B4
4 Richmond TW9 54 B3
Robinson Ho
4 North Kensington W10 30 C3
12 Tower Hamlets E14 33 C4
Robinson Rd E2 25 B3
Robinson St SW3 158 C4
Robinswood Mews 6 N5 15 A3
Robsart St SW9 173 B2
Robson Ave NW10 8 C1
Robson Rd SE21, SE27 75 B1
Roby Ho EC1 96 C2
Rochdale Way 4 SE8 51 C3
Roche Ho 15 E14 33 B2
Rochelle Cl SW11 59 C3
Rochelle Ct 14 E1 32 B3
Rochelle St 31 E2 24 B2 98 C3
Rochemont Wlk 2 E8 24 C4
Roche Sch The 15 SW18 58 C2
Rochester Ct
1 Bethnal Green E2 25 A1
9 Camden Town NW1 13 B1
Rochester Ho
Bermondsey SE1 137 C3
18 Deptford SE15 50 B4
Rochester Mews NW1 13 B1
Rochester Pl NW1 13 B1
Rochester Rd NW1 13 B2
Rochester Row SW1 147 A4
Rochester Sq NW1 13 B1
Rochester St SW1 133 B1
Rochester Terr NW1 13 B2
Rochester Wlk SE1 123 B2
Rochford Wlk 3 E8 16 C1
Rochfort Ho 4 SE8 41 B1
Rock Ave 13 SW14 55 C4
Rockell's Pl SE22 65 A1
Rockfield Ho SE10 52 B4
Rock Grove Way SE16 153 C4
Rockhall Rd NW2 9 C4
Rockingham Cl SW15 56 B3
Rockingham St SE1 136 C1
Rockland Rd SW15 58 A3
Rockley Ct 9 W14 39 C4
Rockley Rd W14 39 C4
Rocks La SW13 56 C4
Rock St N4 5 C2
Rockstraw Ho 5 NW3 12 B1
Rockwood Ct N16 7 C4
Rocliffe St N1 86 B1
Rocque Ho SW6 154 C2
Rodborough Rd NW11 1 C3
Rodenhurst Ct SW4 61 C2
Rodenhurst Rd SW4 61 C1
Roden St N7 5 B1
Roderick Ho 3 SE16 40 B2
Roderick Rd NW3 12 B4
Rodgers Ho 4 SW4 73 C4
Rodin Ct N1 86 A3
Roding Ct 6 W12 38 A4
Roding Ho N1 85 B3
Roding Mews E1 125 C2
Roding Rd E5 18 A3
Rodmarton St W1 103 A3
Rodmell WC1 94 B3
Rodmere St SE10 43 A1
Rodney Ct NW8 89 A2
Rodney Ho
4 Cubitt Town E14 42 A2
Islington N1 85 A1
Notting Hill W11 31 C2 113 B4
Rodney Pl SE17 151 A4
Rodney Rd SE17 151 B3
Rodney St N1 85 A1
Rodway Rd SW15 68 C4
Rodwell Rd SE22 64 B1
Roedean Cres SW15 56 A2
ROEHAMPTON 68 A4
Roehampton Church Sch SW15 69 A4
Roehampton Cl SW15 56 C3
Roehampton Ct SW13 56 C4
Roehampton Gate SW15 56 A1
Roehampton High St SW15 68 C4
Roehampton La
Putney SW15 56 C1
Roehampton SW15 69 A3
Roehampton Vale SW15 68 B2
Roffey St E14 42 B4
Rogate Ho E5 7 C1
Roger Dowley Ct 8 E2 25 B3
Roger's Almshouses 2 SW9 62 B3
Rogers Ct 16 E14 33 C2
Rogers Est 28 E2 25 B2
Rogers Ho SW1 147 C4
Rogers Rd E16 35 B3
Roger St WC1 95 A1
Rokeby Ho
9 Balham SW12 73 A4
Bloomsbury WC1 94 C1
Rokeby Rd SE4 51 B1
Rokeby Sch E15 19 C1
Rokeland Ho SE4 66 A3
Roland Gdns SW7 143 A2
Roland Ho SW7 143 A2
Roland Mews 1 E1 32 C4
Roland Way
South Kensington SW7 143 A2
Walworth SE17 151 C1
Rollins St SE15 50 B4
Rollit Ho N7 14 C3
Rollit St N7 14 C3
Rollo Ct SW11 170 A3
Rolls Bldgs EC4 107 C2
Rollscourt Ave SE24 63 B2
Rolls Pas EC4 107 B2
Rolls Rd SE1 153 A2
Rolt St SE8 51 A4
Roman Cl W3 37 A4
Roman Ct 4 N7 14 B2
Romanfield Rd SW2 74 B4
Roman Rd
Chiswick W4 38 B2
Globe Town E2, E3 25 C3
25 Old Ford E3 26 B4
Roman Road Mkt 1 E3 26 B3
Roman Way
Barnsbury N7 14 B2
4 Deptford SE15 50 B3
Roma Read Cl SW15 69 A4
Romayne Ho SW4 61 C4
Romberg Rd SW17 72 C1
Romborough Gdns SE13 67 B2

- Romborough Way SE13 ... 67 B2
- Romer Ho 9 SW2 ... 62 B2
- Romero Cl SW9 ... 62 B4
- Romeyn Rd SW16 ... 74 B1
- Romford Ho 17 N1 ... 15 C2
- Romford St E1 ... 32 A4
- Romilly Rd N4 ... 6 A2
- Romilly St W1 ... 119 C4
- Romily Ct 2 SW6 ... 164 B2
- Romney Cl
  - 7 Deptford SE14 ... 50 B3
  - North End NW11 ... 2 B3
- Romney Ct
  - 9 Hammersmith W12 ... 39 B4
  - 9 Hampstead NW3 ... 12 A2
- Romney Ho 2 E14 ... 34 C2
- Romney Mews W1 ... 103 B4
- Romney Rd SE10 ... 52 C4
- Romney St SW1 ... 134 A1
- Romola Rd SE24, SW2 ... 75 A3
- Ronald Ross Prim Sch 6 SW19 ... 70 A4
- Ronaldshay N4 ... 5 C3
- Ronalds Rd N5 ... 14 C3
- Ronald St E1 ... 32 B3
- Rona Rd NW3 ... 12 C4
- Rona Wlk 20 N1 ... 15 C2
- Rondu Rd NW2 ... 10 A3
- Rood La EC3 ... 124 A4
- Rookery Rd SW4 ... 61 B3
- Rooke Way SE10 ... 43 B1
- Rookwood Rd N16 ... 7 C4
- Roosevelt Ct 15 SW19 ... 70 A3
- Rootes Dr W10 ... 30 C4
- Ropemaker Rd SE16 ... 41 A3
- Ropemaker's Fields 7 E14 ... 33 B2
- Ropemaker St EC2 ... 109 B4
- Roper La SE1 ... 138 B3
- Roper's Orch SW3 ... 158 A3
- Ropers Wlk 13 SE24 ... 74 C4
- Ropery St E3 ... 26 B1
- Rope St SE16 ... 41 A3
- Ropewalk Gdns 18 E1 ... 111 C2
- Ropley St 6 E2 ... 24 C3
- Rosa Alba Mews N5 ... 15 B4
- Rosalind Ho 25 N1 ... 24 A3
- Rosaline Rd SW6 ... 154 B1
- Rosaline Terr SW6 ... 154 B1
- Rosa Parks Ho 8 SW9 ... 172 C1
- Rosary Ct 17 E1 ... 32 C4
- Rosary Gdns SW7 ... 143 A3
- Rosary RC Prim Sch NW3 ... 12 A3
- Rosaville Rd SW6 ... 154 C1
- Rosbury SW15 ... 58 A1
- Roscastle Rd SE4 ... 66 A2
- Roscoe St EC1 ... 97 A1
- Roscommon Ho 2 NW3 ... 11 C3
- Rose Alley
  - Borough The SE1 ... 123 A2
  - Broadgate EC2 ... 110 B3
- Rosebank
  - 2 Dagenham W3 ... 28 C3
  - Fulham SW6 ... 47 B3
- Rosebank Gdns
  - Bow E3 ... 26 B3
  - 1 Dagenham W3 ... 28 C3
- Rosebank Way W3 ... 28 C3
- Rosebank Wlk NW1 ... 13 C1
- Rosebay Ho 20 E3 ... 33 C4
- Roseberry Pl E8 ... 16 B2
- Roseberry St SE16 ... 40 A2
- Rosebery Ave EC1 ... 95 C3
- Rosebery Ct
  - Holborn EC1 ... 95 B2
  - Mayfair W1 ... 118 A2
- Rosebery Ho 21 E2 ... 25 B3
- Rosebery Rd SW2 ... 62 A1
- Rosebery Sq EC1 ... 95 B1
- Rosebury Rd SW6 ... 166 B1
- Rose Bush Ct NW3 ... 12 B3
- Rosecroft Ave NW3 ... 1 C1
- Rose & Crown Ct EC2 ... 108 C2
- Rose & Crown Yd SW1 ... 119 A1
- Rose Ct
  - 7 Dalston E8 ... 16 B1
  - Islington N1 ... 86 A3
  - Spitalfields E1 ... 111 A3
- Rosedale Ct N5 ... 15 A4
- Rosedale Ho N16 ... 6 C3
- Rosedale Rd TW9 ... 54 A3
- Rosedale Terr W6 ... 39 A3
- Rosedene NW6 ... 22 C4
- Rosedene Ave SW16 ... 74 B1
- Rosedew Rd W6 ... 47 C4
- Rosefield Gdns E14 ... 33 C2
- Roseford Ct 16 W12 ... 39 C4
- Rosegate Ho 32 E3 ... 26 B3
- Rosehart Mews 8 W11 ... 31 C3
- Rosehill Rd SW18 ... 59 B2
- Rose Joan Mews NW6 ... 10 C4
- Roseland Ho SW6 ... 58 A4
- Roseleigh Ave N5 ... 15 A4
- Rosemary Branch Bridge N1 ... 87 C4
- Rosemary Ct 35 SE8 ... 51 B4
- Rosemary Dr 16 E14 ... 34 C3
- Rosemary Gdns SW14 ... 55 B4
- Rosemary Ho
  - Shoreditch N1 ... 87 C3
  - Willesden NW10 ... 22 A4
- Rosemary La SW14 ... 55 B4
- Rosemary Rd
  - Camberwell SE15 ... 49 B3
  - Wandsworth SW17 ... 71 B1
- Rosemary St N1 ... 87 C4
- Rosemary Works Sch N1 ... 87 C3
- Rosemead Prep Sch SE27 ... 75 B2
- Rosemont Mans 11 NW3 ... 11 A2
- Rosemont Rd
  - Acton W3 ... 28 A2
  - Richmond TW10 ... 54 A1
  - South Hampstead NW3 ... 11 B2
- Rosemoor St SW3 ... 144 C3
- Rosemount Ct 2 W3 ... 28 A1
- Rosemount Lo W3 ... 28 A2
- Rosenau Cres SW11 ... 168 C3
- Rosenau Rd SW11 ... 168 C4
- Rosendale Prim Sch SE21 ... 75 B4
- Rosendale Rd SE21, SE24 ... 75 B3
- Roseneath Rd SW11 ... 60 C1
- Rosenthal Ho SE6 ... 67 A1
- Rosenthal Rd SE6 ... 67 B1
- Rosenthorpe Rd SE15 ... 65 C2
- Roserton St E14 ... 42 B4
- Rose Sq SW7 ... 143 C2
- Rose St
  - Holborn EC4 ... 108 B2
  - Strand WC2 ... 120 A4
- Rose Theatre SE1 ... 122 C2
- Rosethorn Cl SW12 ... 73 C4
- Rosetta Cl SW8 ... 162 B1
- Roseway SE21 ... 63 C1
- Rosewood Ct 2 E11 ... 19 C4
- Rosewood Gdns SE13 ... 52 B1
- Rosewood Ho 9 NW3 ... 11 A2
- Rosewood Sq W12 ... 29 C3
- Rosher Cl E15 ... 19 C1
- Rosina St E9 ... 17 C2
- Roskell Rd SW15 ... 57 C4
- Roslin Ho 2 E1 ... 32 C2
- Roslin Rd W3 ... 37 A3
- Rosmead Rd W11 ... 31 A2 112 B4
- Rosoman Pl EC1 ... 95 C2
- Rosoman St EC1 ... 95 C3
- Ross Ct
  - 1 Hackney E5 ... 17 A4
  - 4 Putney SW15 ... 69 C4
- Rossdale Rd SW15 ... 57 B3
- Rosse Gdns SE13 ... 67 C1
- Rossendale Way NW1 ... 83 A4
- Rossetti Ct WC1 ... 105 B4
- Rossetti Gdns Mans SW3 ... 158 C4
- Rossetti Ho SW1 ... 147 C3
- Rossetti Mews NW8 ... 79 C3
- Rossetti Rd SE16 ... 40 A1
- Rossetti Studios SW3 ... 158 B4
- Ross Ho 18 E1 ... 32 A1
- Rossington St E5 ... 7 C2
- Rossiter Rd SW12 ... 73 A3
- Rosslyn Ave SW13 ... 56 B4
- Rosslyn Ct NW3 ... 12 A3
- Rosslyn Hill NW3 ... 11 C3
- Rosslyn Ho 8 TW9 ... 44 B2
- Rosslyn Mans
  - 8 Hampstead NW3 ... 11 B2
  - South Hampstead NW6 ... 11 B2
- Rosslyn Mews 7 NW3 ... 11 C4
- Rosslyn Park Mews NW3 ... 11 C3
- Rossmore Ct NW1 ... 90 C2
- Rossmore Rd NW1 ... 90 B2
- Rostrevor Mans SW6 ... 164 C4
- Rostrevor Mews SW6 ... 164 C3
- Rostrevor Rd SW6 ... 164 C4
- Rotary Lo 12 SE27 ... 75 A1
- Rotary St SE1 ... 136 B2
- Rothay NW1 ... 92 B4
- Rothbury Rd E9 ... 18 C1
- Rotheley Ho 39 E9 ... 17 B1
- Rotherfield Ct
  - De Beauvoir Town N1 ... 15 C1
  - Shoreditch N1 ... 87 B4
- Rotherfield Prim Sch N1 ... 87 A4
- Rotherfield St
  - Islington N1 ... 15 B1
  - Shoreditch N1 ... 87 A4
- Rotherham Wlk SE1 ... 122 A1
- ROTHERHITHE ... 40 C3
- Rotherhithe Bsns Est 6 SE16 ... 40 B2
- Rotherhithe New Rd SE16 ... 40 A1
- Rotherhithe Old Rd SE16 ... 40 C2
- Rotherhithe Prim Sch 24 SE16 ... 40 C2
- Rotherhithe St SE16 ... 40 B4
- Rotherhithe Sta SE16 ... 40 B4
- Rotherhithe Tunnel SE16 ... 32 C1
- Rother Ho SE15 ... 65 A3
- Rotherwick Rd NW11 ... 1 C4
- Rotherwood Rd SW15 ... 57 C4
- Rothery St N1 ... 86 B4
- Rothesay Ave SW14, TW10 ... 55 A3
- Rothesay Ct 13 SE11 ... 163 B3
- Rothley Ct NW8 ... 89 B2
- Rothsay St SE1 ... 138 A1
- Rothsay Wlk 19 E14 ... 41 C2
- Rothschild Rd W4 ... 37 B3
- Rothwell St
  - 10 Hampstead NW1 ... 12 B1
  - Primrose Hill NW1 ... 81 A4
- Roth Wlk N7 ... 5 B2
- Rotten Row SW1 ... 130 C4
- Rotterdam Dr E14 ... 42 B3
- Rouel Rd
  - Bermondsey SE16 ... 153 B4
  - Bermondsey SE16 ... 139 B1
- Roundacre SW19 ... 69 C2
- Roundel Cl SE4 ... 66 B3
- Roundhouse Theatre NW1 ... 12 C1
- Roundwood Rd NW10 ... 8 B1
- Rounton Rd E3 ... 26 C1
- Roupell Rd SW2 ... 74 B3
- Roupell St SE1 ... 121 C1
- Rousden St NW1 ... 13 B1
- Routh Rd SW18 ... 72 A4
- Rover Ho 28 N1 ... 24 A4
- Rowallan Rd SW6 ... 154 A1
- Rowan Cl W5 ... 36 A4
- Rowan Ct
  - 19 Camberwell SE15 ... 49 B3
  - Wandsworth SW11 ... 60 B1
- Rowan Ho
  - 9 Bow E3 ... 26 B4
  - Dagenham NW10 ... 21 A1
  - 5 Maitland Pk NW3 ... 12 B2
- Rowan Rd W6 ... 39 C2
- Rowan Terr W6 ... 39 C2
- Rowan Wlk
  - 7 Dartmouth Pk N19 ... 4 B2
  - Kensal Town W10 ... 23 A1
- Rowberry Cl SW6 ... 47 B3
- Rowcross St SE1 ... 153 A2
- Rowditch La SW11 ... 169 B2
- Rowdon Ave NW10 ... 9 A1
- Rowe Ho E9 ... 17 B2
- Rowe La E9 ... 17 B3
- Rowena Cres SW11 ... 168 B1
- Rowfant Rd SW12, SW17 ... 72 C2
- Rowhill Mans 11 E5 ... 17 A4
- Rowhill Rd E5 ... 17 A4
- Rowington Cl W2 ... 100 A4
- Rowland Hill Ho SE1 ... 136 A4
- Rowland Hill St NW3 ... 12 A3
- Rowley Gdns N4 ... 6 B4
- Rowley Ho SE8 ... 51 C4
- Rowley Ind Pk W3 ... 37 A3
- Rowley Way NW8 ... 78 C4
- Rowntree Cl NW6 ... 10 C2
- Rowse Cl E15 ... 27 B4
- Rowstock 1 NW5 ... 13 C2
- Rowstock Gdns N7 ... 13 C3
- Roxby Pl SW6 ... 155 C4
- Roxford Ho 2 E3 ... 27 A1
- Roxley Rd SE13 ... 67 A1
- Roxwell 10 NW1 ... 13 A2
- Roxwell Rd W12 ... 38 C4
- Royal Academy of Dramatic Art WC1 ... 105 B4
- Royal Acad of Arts W1 ... 118 C3
- Royal Acad of Dance SW11 ... 167 C3
- Royal Acad of Music NW1 ... 91 C1
- Royal Albert Hall SW7 ... 129 B3
- Royal Arc W1 ... 118 C3
- Royal Armouries The E1 ... 124 C3
- Royal Ave SW3 ... 144 C2

Royal Avenue Ho SW3 ... 144 C2
Royal Ballet Upper Sch The WC2 ... 106 B1
Royal Brompton Hospl
Chelsea SW3 ... 143 B2
Chelsea SW3 ... 144 A2
Royal Cir SE27 ... 75 A1
Royal Cl
Deptford SE8 ... 51 B4
Putney SW19 ... 69 C2
Stamford Hill N16 ... 7 A3
Royal College of Physicians Liby NW1 ... 92 B2
Royal College St NW1 ... 83 A4
Royal Coll of Anaesthetists WC1 ... 106 C3
Royal Coll of Art SW7 ... 129 B3
Royal Coll of Art Sculpture Sch SW11 ... 158 A1
Royal Coll of Midwives W1 ... 104 A3
Royal Coll of Music SW7 ... 129 B2
Royal Coll of Obstetricians & Gynaecologists NW1 ... 90 C3
Royal Coll of Ophthalmologists NW1 ... 91 B1
Royal Coll of Paediatrics & Child Health W1 ... 107 A4
Royal Coll of Pathologists SW1 ... 119 B1
Royal Coll of Physicians NW1 ... 92 B2
Royal Coll of Radiologists W1 ... 104 B4
Royal Coll of Science SW7 ... 129 B2
Royal Coll of Speech Language Therapists SE1 ... 123 B1
Royal Coll of Surgeons WC2 ... 107 A2
Royal Coll of Veterinary Surgeons SW1 ... 134 A1
Royal Courts of Justice WC2 ... 107 B1
Royal Cres W11 ... 31 A1 112 A1
Royal Crescent Mews W11 ... 30 C1
Royal Ct
City of London EC3 ... 109 C1
Rotherhithe SE16 ... 41 B3
Royal Duchess Mews 16 SW12 ... 73 A4
Royal Exchange EC3 ... 109 C1
Royal Exchange Bldgs EC3 ... 109 C1
Royal Festival Hall SE1 ... 121 A1
Royal Free Hospl NW3 ... 12 A3
Royal Fusiliers Mus E1 ... 124 C3
Royal Geographical Society SW7 ... 129 C3
Royal Hill SE10 ... 52 B3
Royal Hill Ct 2 SE10 ... 52 B3
Royal Horticultural Society (Lawrence Hall & Conf Ctr) SW1 ... 133 B1
Royal Horticultural Society (Lindley Hall) SW1 ... 147 B4
Royal Hospital Chelsea The SW1 ... 145 B1
Royal Hospital Rd SW3 ... 145 A1
Royal Hospl for Neuro-Disability The SW15 ... 58 A1
Royal Hospl Mus SW3 ... 145 A1
Royal Institute of British Architects W1 ... 104 B4
Royal Institution Mus The SW1 ... 118 C3
Royal Langford Apartments 3 NW6 ... 78 A2
Royal London Est The NW10 ... 20 C3
Royal London Hospl for Integrated Medicine WC1 ... 106 B4
Royal London Hospl Mus E1 ... 32 A4
Royal London Hospl (Whitechapel) The E1 ... 32 A4
Royal Marsden Hospl SW3 ... 143 C2
Royal Mews The SW1 ... 132 B2
Royal Mint Pl 6 E1 ... 125 B4
Royal Mint St E1 ... 125 A4
Royal National Orthopaedic Hospl W1 ... 92 B1
Royal National TNE Hospl The WC1 ... 94 C4
Royal Naval Pl SE14 ... 51 B3
Royal Oak Ct 9 N1 ... 24 A2 98 A4
Royal Oak Pl SE22 ... 65 A1
Royal Oak Rd 5 E8 ... 17 A2
Royal Oak Sta W2 ... 100 B3
Royal Oak Yd SE1 ... 138 A3
Royal Observatory The SE10 ... 52 C3
Royal Opera Arc SW1 ... 119 B2
Royal Orchard Cl SW18 ... 70 A4
Royal Par
Blackheath Vale SE3 ... 53 B1
Fulham SW6 ... 154 A2
12 Richmond TW9 ... 44 C2
Royal Pl 11 SE10 ... 52 B3
Royal Rd SE17 ... 48 A4
Royal Sch Hampstead The 8 NW3 ... 11 C4
Royal St SE1 ... 135 A2
Royalty Ho W1 ... 105 B1
Royalty Mews W1 ... 105 B1
Royalty Studios W11 ... 31 A3
Royal United Services Mus SW1 ... 120 A1
Royal Veterinary Coll NW1 ... 83 B3
Royal Victoria Sta E16 ... 35 C2
Royal Victor Pl E3 ... 25 C3
Roycroft Cl SW2 ... 74 C3
Roydon Cl 7 SW11 ... 168 C2
Roy Ridley Ho 6 SW4 ... 61 C4
Roy Sq E14 ... 33 A2
Royston Ct
New Cross SE4 ... 51 B1
3 Richmond TW9 ... 44 B2
Royston Ho 14 SE15 ... 49 C4
Royston Rd TW10 ... 54 A2
Royston St 24 E2 ... 25 B3
Rozel Ct 3 N1 ... 24 A4
Rozel Rd SW4 ... 61 B4
Ruby St SE15 ... 50 A4
Ruby Triangle SE15 ... 50 A4
Ruckholt Rd E9, E10 ... 18 C4
Rucklidge Ave NW10 ... 21 C3
Rudall Cres NW3 ... 11 C4
Rudbeck Ho 11 SE15 ... 49 C3
Ruddington Cl E5 ... 18 A4
Rudge Ho 1 SE16 ... 139 C2
Rudgwick Terr NW8 ... 80 B3
Rudhall Ho 4 SW2 ... 62 C1
Rudloe Rd SW12 ... 73 B4
Rudolf Pl SW8 ... 162 B3
Rudolph Rd NW6 ... 23 C3
Rudstone Ho 10 E3 ... 27 A2
Rudyard Ct SE1 ... 137 C3
Rufford St N1 ... 84 B4
Rufford Street Mews N1 ... 14 A1
Rufford Twr 5 W3 ... 28 A1
Rufus Bsns Ctr SW18 ... 71 A2
Rufus Ho SE1 ... 139 A2
Rufus St N1 ... 24 A2 98 A3
Rugby Mans W14 ... 140 B4
Rugby Rd W4 ... 38 A4
Rugby St WC1 ... 94 C1
Rugg St E14 ... 33 C2
Rugless Ho 2 E14 ... 42 B4
Rugmere 4 NW1 ... 12 C1
Rumball Ho 14 SE5 ... 49 A3
Rumbold Rd SW6 ... 156 B1
Rum Cl E1 ... 32 B2
Rumford Ho SE1 ... 136 C1
Rumsey Rd SW9 ... 62 B4
Runacres Ct SE17 ... 150 C1
Runcorn Pl W11 ... 31 A2 112 A4
Rundell Twr SW8 ... 172 C4
Running Horse Yd 12 TW8 ... 44 A4
Runnymede Ct SW15 ... 68 C3
Runnymede Ho
Hackney E9 ... 18 A4
Richmond TW10 ... 54 C2
Rupack St 3 SE16 ... 40 B4
Rupert Ct W1 ... 119 B4
Rupert Gdns SW9 ... 48 A1
Rupert Ho
SE11 ... 149 C3
8 Upper Holloway N19 ... 4 C1
Rupert Rd
Bedford Pk W4 ... 38 A3
Paddington NW6 ... 23 B3
Upper Holloway N19 ... 4 C2
Rupert St W1 ... 119 B4
Rusbridge Cl E8 ... 16 C3
Ruscoe Rd E16 ... 35 B3
Rusham Rd SW12 ... 72 B4
Rushbrook Ho 20 SW8 ... 171 B2
Rushby Ct SW4 ... 172 A3
Rush Common Mews 18 SW2 ... 74 B4
Rushcroft Rd SW2, SW9 ... 62 C3
Rushcutters Ct 18 SE16 ... 41 A2
Rushey Mead SE4 ... 66 C2
Rushford Rd SE4 ... 66 B1
Rush Hill Mews 3 SW11 ... 60 C4
Rush Hill Rd SW11 ... 60 C4
Rushlake Ho 3 SW11 ... 169 B2
Rushmead 5 E2 ... 25 A2
Rushmere Ho 2 SW15 ... 68 C3
Rushmore Cres 9 E5 ... 17 C4
Rushmore Ho
9 Kentish Town N7 ... 13 C3
W14 ... 126 B1
Rushmore Prim Sch 12 E5 ... 17 C4
Rushmore Rd
Clapton Pk E5 ... 17 C4
Hackney E5 ... 18 A4
Rusholme Rd SW15 ... 58 A1
Rushton Ho 26 SW8 ... 171 B1
Rushton St N1 ... 87 C2
Rushworth St SE1 ... 136 B3
Ruskin Ave TW9 ... 44 C3
Ruskin Ct SE5 ... 63 C4
Ruskin Ho SW1 ... 147 C3
Ruskin Park Ho SE5 ... 63 C4
Ruskin Wlk SE24 ... 63 B2
Rusper Ct SW9 ... 172 B1
Russell Cl W4 ... 46 B4
Russell Ct
Battersea SW11 ... 169 C3
Bloomsbury WC1 ... 94 A1
5 Peckham SE15 ... 50 A1
St James SW1 ... 119 A1
Russell Gdns W14 ... 126 A2
Russell Gdns Mews W14 ... 126 A2
Russell Gr 33 SW9 ... 173 C4
Russell Ho
21 Poplar E14 ... 33 C3
SW1 ... 146 C2
Russell Kerr Cl W4 ... 45 B3
Russell Lo SE1 ... 137 B2
Russell Mans WC1 ... 106 B4
Russell Pickering Ho 2 SW4 ... 62 A4
Russell Pl
Hampstead NW3 ... 12 A3
Rotherhithe SE16 ... 41 A3
Russell Rd W14 ... 126 B1
Russell Sq WC1 ... 94 A1
Russell Square Ho WC1 ... 94 A1
Russell Square Mans WC1 ... 106 B4
Russell Square Sta WC1 ... 94 A1
Russell St WC2 ... 120 B4
Russell's Wharf 2 W9 ... 23 B1
Russell Wlk 4 TW10 ... 54 B1
Russell Yd SW15 ... 58 A3
Russet Cres N7 ... 14 B3
Russett Way SE13 ... 52 A1
Russia Dock Rd SE16 ... 33 A1
Russia La E2 ... 25 B3
Russia Row EC2 ... 109 A1
Rusthall Ave W4 ... 37 C3
Rusthall Mans 3 W4 ... 37 C2
Ruston Mews W11 ... 31 A3
Ruston St E3 ... 26 B4
Rust Sq SE5 ... 48 C3
Ruth Ct 16 E3 ... 26 A3
Rutherford Ho 12 E1 ... 25 A1
Rutherford St SW1 ... 147 B4
Ruth Ho W10 ... 23 A1
Ruthin Rd SE3 ... 53 C4
Ruthven St E9 ... 25 C4
Rutland Cl SW14 ... 55 B4
Rutland Ct
Herne Hill SE5 ... 63 C3
SW7 ... 130 B3
Rutland Gate SW7 ... 130 B3
Rutland Gate Mews SW7 ... 130 A3
Rutland Gdns SW7 ... 130 B3
Rutland Gdns Mews SW7 ... 130 B3
Rutland Gr W6 ... 39 A1
Rutland Ho
10 Putney SW15 ... 69 B4
W8 ... 128 A1
Rutland Mews 21 NW8 ... 78 B3
Rutland Mews E SW7 ... 130 B2
Rutland Mews S SW7 ... 130 A2
Rutland Mews W SW7 ... 130 A2

Rutland Park Gdns 1 NW2 . . . 9 B2
Rutland Park Mans 2 NW2 . . . 9 B2
Rutland Pk NW2 . . . 9 B2
Rutland Pl EC1 . . . 108 B4
Rutland Rd E9 . . . 25 C4
Rutland St SW7 . . 130 B2
Rutland Studios NW10 . . . 21 C2
Rutley Cl SE11 . . . 48 A4
Rutt's Terr SE14 . . . 50 C2
Ruvigny Gdns SW15 . . . 57 C4
Ruvigny Mans 7 SW15 . . . 57 C4
Rycott Path SE22 . . . 76 C4
Ryculff Sq SE3 . . . 53 B1
Rydal Ho 25 SW8 . 171 B1
Rydal Water NW1 . . 92 C3
Ryde Ho 1 NW6 . . . 23 C4
Ryder Ct SW1 . . . 119 A2
Ryder Dr SE16 . . . 40 A1
Ryder Ho 18 E1 . . . 25 B1
Ryder St SW1 . . . 119 A2
Ryder's Terr NW8 . . 78 C2
Ryder Yd SW1 . . . 119 A2
Ryde Vale Rd SW12 . . . 73 B2
Rydon St N1 . . . 87 A4
Rydston Cl 2 N7 . . . 14 B1
Ryecotes Mead SE21 . . . 76 A3
Ryecroft Rd SE13 . . . 67 B2
Ryecroft St SW6 . . 166 A3
Ryedale SE22 . . . 65 A1
Ryefield Path 7 SW15 . . . 68 C3
Ryegates 2 SE15 . . . 50 A1
Rye Hill Pk SE15 . . . 65 B3
Rye Ho 17 SE16 . . . 40 B4
Rye La SE15 . . . 49 C1
Rye Lane Mkt SE15 . . . 49 C1
Rye Oak Sch 7 SE15 . . . 65 A4
Rye Rd SE15 . . . 65 C3
Rye Wlk SW15 . . . 57 C2
Ryfold Rd SW19 . . . 70 C1
Ryland Rd NW5 . . . 13 A2
Rylett Cres W12 . . . 38 B3
Rylett Rd W12 . . . 38 B3
Rylston Rd SW6 . . 154 C3
Rymer St SE24 . . . 63 A1
Rysbrack St SW1 . 130 C2

S

Saatchi Gallery SW3 . . . 145 A2
Sabbarton St 9 E16 . . . 35 B3
Sabella Ct E3 . . . 26 B3
Sabine Rd SW11 . . . 60 C4
Sable St N1 . . . 15 A1
Sacketts Ho 24 SW9 . . . 173 C4
Sackville Ho 16 SW16 . . . 74 A1
Sackville St W1 . . 119 A3
Sacred Heart High Sch 9 W6 . . . 39 B2
Sacred Heart Prim Sch, Battersea SW11 . . . 168 B1
Sacred Heart RC Prim Sch SW15 . . . 56 C2
Sacred Heart RC Sec Sch 10 SE5 . . . 48 B2
Sacred Heart Sch N7 . . . 14 B3
Saddlers Mews SW8 . . . 172 B4
Sadler Ho 17 Bromley E3 . . . 27 A2
EC1 . . . 96 A4
Saffron Ave E14 . . . 34 C2
Saffron Ct 10 N1 . . . 15 C2
Saffron Hill EC1 . . 107 C4
Saffron Ho 6 TW9 . . . 45 A2
Saffron St EC1 . . . 107 C4
Saffron Wharf SE1 . . . 139 A4
Sage Mews SE22 . . . 64 B2
Sage St E1 . . . 32 B2
Sage Way WC1 . . . 94 C3
Sailacre Ho 10 SE10 . . . 43 B1
Sail Ct 10 E14 . . . 34 C2
Sailmakers Ct SW6 . . . 59 B4
Sail St SE11 . . . 149 A4
Sainfoin Rd SW17 . . 72 C2
St Agnes Cl E9 . . . 25 B4
St Agnes Pl SE11 . . . 48 A4
St Agnes RC Prim Sch 15 E3 . . . 27 A2
London NW2 . . . 1 A1
St Aidan's Prim Sch N4 . . . 5 C4
St Aidan's Rd SE22 . 65 A2
St Albans Ave W4 . . 37 C3
St Alban's CE Prim Sch EC1 . . . 107 B4
St Alban's Cl NW11 . . 1 C3
St Alban's Gr W8 . 128 B2
St Albans La NW11 . . 1 C3
St Albans Mans W8 . . . 128 B2
St Alban's Pl N1 . . . 86 A3
St Alban's Rd Dagenham NW10 . . . 21 A4
Dartmouth Pk NW5 . . . 4 A1
St Alban's St SW1 119 B3
St Albans Studios W8 . . . 128 B2
St Albans Terr W6 . . . 154 A4
St Alban's Villas NW5 . . . 3 C1
St Alfege Pas SE10 . 52 B4
St Alfege with St Peter's CE Prim Sch SE10 . . . 52 B4
St Aloysius Convent NW1 . . . 93 B4
St Aloysius RC Coll 9 N19 . . . 4 B3
St Aloysius RC Inf Sch NW1 . . . 93 B4
St Aloysius RC Jun Sch NW1 . . . 83 B1
St Alphage Gdn EC2 . . . 109 A3
St Alphage Highwalk EC2 . . . 109 A3
St Alphonsus Rd SW4 . . . 61 C3
St Andrew & St Francis CE Prim Sch 6 NW2 . . . 8 C2
St Andrew's (Barnsbury) Prim Sch N1 . . . 85 A4
St Andrews Chambers W1 . . . 105 A2
St Andrews Cl 25 SE16 . . . 40 A1
St Andrews Ct W4 . . 45 B2
St Andrew's Ct 2 SW18 . . . 71 B2
St Andrew's Gr N16 . 6 C3
St Andrew's Greek Sch NW1 . . . 13 B2
St Andrew's Hill EC4 . . . 108 B1
St Andrews Ho 11 SE16 . . . 40 A3
St Andrews Mans 9 E5 . . . 17 A4
St Andrew's Mans W1 . . . 103 B3
St Andrews Mews Greenwich SE3 . . . 53 C3
4 Streatham SW12 . . . 73 C3
St Andrew's Mews N16 . . . 7 A3
St Andrew's Pl NW1 . . . 92 B2
St Andrew's Prim Sch 33 SW9 . . . 172 B1
St Andrews Rd W3 . . . 29 A3
St Andrew's Rd W14 . . . 154 B4
Willesden NW2 . . . 9 A2
St Andrew's Sq W11 . . . 31 A3
St Andrew St EC4 107 C3
St Andrews Way E3 . . . 27 A1
St Andrew's Wharf SE1 . . . 139 A4
St Anne RC Prim Sch 18 E1 . . . 24 C1 99 B1
St Anne's CE Prim Sch 6 SW18 . . . 59 A2
St Anne's Cl N6 . . . 3 C1
St Anne's Ct Kensal Rise NW6 . . . 23 A4
W1 . . . 105 B1
St Anne's Flats NW1 . . . 93 B4
St Anne's Pas E14 . . 33 B3
St Anne's RC Prim Sch SE11 . . . 162 C4
St Anne's Row E14 . 33 B3
St Anne St E14 . . . 33 B3
St Anne's Trad Est 25 E14 . . . 33 B3
St Ann's Cres SW18 . . . 59 B1
St Ann's Gdns NW5 . . . 12 C2
St Ann's Hill SW18 . . 59 B1
St Ann's Ho WC1 . . 95 B3
St Ann's La SW1 . . 133 C1
St Ann's Park Rd SW18 . . . 59 B1
St Anns Rd Barnes SW13 . . . 46 B2
St Anns Rd *continued* Shepherd's Bush W11 . . . 30 C2
St Ann's St SW1 . . 133 C2
St Ann's Terr NW8 . 79 C2
St Ann's Villas W11 . . . 31 A1 112 A1
St Anselm's Pl W1 . . . 118 A4
St Anselm's RC Prim Sch SW17 . . . 72 C1
St Anthonys Cl 5 SW17 . . . 72 A2
St Anthony's Cl 8 E1 . . . 125 B2
5 Hackney Wick E9 . . . 18 B2
St Anthony's Ct 2 Balham SW12 . . . 60 C1
Upper Tooting SW17 . . . 72 C2
St Anthony's Flats NW1 . . . 83 B1
St Anthony's RC Prim Sch SE22 . . . 64 C1
St Anthony's Sch 8 NW3 . . . 11 C3
St Asaph Ct SE4 . . . 65 C4
St Asaph Rd SE4 . . . 65 C4
St Aubins Ct N1 . . . 87 C4
St Augustine's CE High Sch 5 NW6 . . . 23 C3
St Augustine's Ho NW1 . . . 93 B4
St Augustine's Prim Sch 5 NW6 . . . 78 A2
St Augustine's RC Prim Sch W6 . . . 154 B3
St Augustine's Rd NW1 . . . 13 C1
St Austell Rd SE13 . . 52 C1
St Barnabas CE Prim Sch SW1 . . . 145 C2
St Barnabas Cl 11 SE22 . . . 64 A2
St Barnabas & St Philip CE Prim Sch W8 . . . 127 B1
St Barnabas St SW1 . . . 145 C2
St Barnabas Terr E9 . . . 17 C3
St Barnabas Villas SW8 . . . 172 B4
St Bartholomew's Hospl EC1 . . . 108 B3
St Bartholomew's Mus EC1 . . . 108 B3
St Bede's RC Inf Sch SW12 . . . 73 C3
St Benets Cl 6 SW17 . . . 72 A2
St Benet's Pl EC3 . 123 C4
St Bernadette RC Jun Sch 12 SW12 . . . 73 B4
St Bernard Ho 6 E14 . . . 42 B3
St Botolph St E1, EC3 . . . 110 C2
St Brelades Ct N1 . . 87 C4
St Bride's EC4 . . . 108 A1
St Bride's Ave EC4 . . . 108 A1
St Bride's Pas EC4 . . . 108 A1
St Bride St EC4 . . . 108 A2
St Catherines Cl 7 SW17 . . . 72 A2
St Catherine's Ct 8 W4 . . . 38 A3
St Catherine's Dr SE14 . . . 50 C1
St Catherines Mews SW3 . . . 144 C4
St Cecilia's CE Sch SW18 . . . 70 B3
St Chad's Pl WC1 . . 94 C4
St Chad's St WC1 . . 94 B4
St Charles' Hospl W10 . . . 30 C4
St Charles Pl W10 . . 31 A4
St Charles RC Prim Sch 7 W10 . . . 30 C4
St Charles RC Sixth Form Coll 8 W10 . . . 30 C4
St Charles Sq W10 . . 30 C4
St Christina's RC Prep Sch NW8 . . . 80 B2
St Christophers Ct 15 N19 . . . 4 B1
St Christopher's Ho NW1 . . . 83 B1
St Christopher's Pl W1 . . . 103 C2
St Christopher's Sch 5 NW3 . . . 11 C3
St Clair Ho 17 E3 . . . 26 B2
St Clare St EC3 . . . 110 C1
St Clement Danes CE Prim Sch WC2 . . . 106 C1
St Clement & St James CE Prim Sch W11 . . . 31 A1 112 A2
St Clements Ct Barnsbury N7 . . . 14 B2
7 SE14 . . . 50 C4
8 Shepherd's Bush W11 . . . 30 C2
St Clement's Ct EC3 . . . 123 C4
St Clements Ho E1 . . . 110 C3
St Clement's La WC2 . . . 107 A1
St Clements Mans 3 SW6 . . . 47 C4
St Clements St N7 . . 14 C1
St Columb's Ho 11 W10 . . . 31 A4
St Crispins Cl NW3 . . . 12 A4
St Cross St EC1 . . . 107 C4
St Cuthbert's Rd NW2 . . . 10 B2
St Cuthbert with St Matthias CE Prim Sch SW5 . . . 142 A2
St Davids Cl 27 SE16 . . . 40 A1
St David's Sq E14 . . 42 A1
St Dionis Rd SW6 165 A2
St Dominic RC Prim Sch 14 NW5 . . . 12 B3
St Dominics RC Prim Sch 6 E9 . . . 18 A2
St Donatt's Rd London SE14 . . . 51 B2
New Cross Gate SE4 . . . 51 B1

St Dunstan Ave W3 28 C2
St Dunstan Gdns W3 28 C2
St Dunstan's Alley EC3 124 A3
St Dunstan's Ct EC4 107 C1
St Dunstan's Hill EC3 124 A3
St Dunstan's La EC3 124 A3
St Dunstan's Rd W6 39 C1
St Edmunds Cl 3 SW17 72 A2
St Edmund's Cl NW8 80 C3
St Edmund's Ct NW8 80 C3
St Edmunds RC Prim Sch E14 41 C2
St Edmund's Sq SW13 47 B4
St Edmund's Terr NW8 80 C3
St Edward's RC Prim Sch NW1 90 B1
St Elizabeth RC Prim Sch 33 E2 25 B3
St Elizabeth's RC Prim Sch TW10 54 B1
St Elmo Rd W12 38 B4
St Elmos Rd SE16 41 A4
St Ermin's Hill SW1 133 B2
St Ervan's Rd W10 31 B4
St Eugene de Mazenod RC Prim Sch 12 NW6 10 C1
St Faith's CE Prim Sch 1 SW18 59 B2
St Faith's Rd SE24 75 A3
St Francesca Cabrini RC Prim Sch SE23 65 B1
St Francis' Ho NW1 83 B1
St Francis of Assisi Prim Sch 19 W11 30 C2
St Francis Pl SW12 61 A1
St Francis RC Prim Sch 26 SE15 49 C3
St Francis Rd SE22 64 A3
St Francis Xavier Coll SW12 61 A1
St Frideswides Mews 5 E14 34 B3
St Gabriel's CE Prim Sch SW1 146 C1
St Gabriels Cl 3 E14 34 A4
St Gabriel's Rd NW2 9 C3
St George Ho SW11 169 C3
ST GEORGE IN THE EAST 32 A2
St George's Ave N7 13 C4
St George's Bldgs SE11 136 B1
St George's Cath NW1 92 B4
St George's Cath RC Prim Sch SE1 136 A2
St George's CE Prim Sch 18 SE5 49 A3
SW8 161 A1
St George's Circ SE1 136 A2
St Georges Cl SW8 171 A4
St Georges Coll N7 5 C1
St Georges Ct SW15 58 B3
St George's Ct
Brompton SW3 144 A4
Kensington SW7 128 C1
Newington SE1 136 A1
St George's Dr SW1 146 C2
St George's Field W2 102 B1
St George's Gr SW17 71 C1
St Georges Hanover Sq Sch W1 117 C3
St George's Ho NW1 83 A1
St George's La EC3 124 A4
St Georges Mews 11 NW1 12 B1
St George's Mews
2 Rotherhithe SE8 41 B2
SE1 135 C2
St Georges Pl N7 13 C4
St George's Pools E1 32 A2
St George's RC Cath SE1 135 C2
St George's RC Sec Sch W9 78 B1
St Georges Rd W4 37 C4
St George's Rd
Newington SE1 136 A1
Richmond TW9 54 B4
St George's Residences 4 SW2 62 C2
St Georges's Ct EC4 108 A2
St Georges Sq 1 E14 33 A2
St George's Sq
Rotherhithe SE8 41 B2
SW1 147 B1
St George's Square Mews SW1 147 B1
St George St W1 118 B4
St Georges Terr
Hampstead NW1 12 B1
NW1 81 A4
St George's Way SE15 49 A4
St George the Martyr CE Prim Sch WC1 95 A1
St George Wharf SW8 162 A4
St George Wharf Pier SW8 162 A4
St Gerards Cl SW4 61 B2
St German's Pl SE3 53 C2
St Gildas' RC Jun Sch 13 N8 5 A4
ST GILES 106 A2
St Giles Cir WC1 105 C2
St Giles Coll WC1 106 B4
St Giles Ct WC2 106 A2
St Giles High St WC2 105 C2
St Giles Ho SW16 74 A1
St Giles Pas WC2 105 C1
St Giles Rd SE5 49 A2
St Giles Terr EC1 109 A3
St Giles Twr 3 SE5 49 A2
St Gilles Ho 15 E2 25 C3
St Helena Ho WC1 95 B3
St Helena Rd SE16 40 C2
St Helena St WC1 95 B3
St Helens Gdns W10 30 C3
St Helen's Pl EC3 110 A2
St Helen's RC Sch 17 SW9 62 C4
St Helier Ct 4 N1 24 A4
St Hildas Cl 2 SW17 72 A2
St Hilda's Cl NW6 9 C1
St Hilda's Rd SW13 47 A4
St Hildas Wharf E1 32 B1
St Hubert's Ho 2 E14 41 C3
St Hughes Cl 4 SW17 72 A2
St Ives Ct NW2 10 A2
ST JAMES 119 B2
St James Ct
26 Bethnal Green E2 24 C2 99 C3
9 Brentford W4 36 C1
St James' Ct
Bedford Pk W4 37 C3
SW1 133 A2
St James Ho N5 14 C3
St James Independent Schs W14 140 B4
St James Ind Mews 16 SE1 153 C1
St James' Mans NW6 10 C1
St James Mews E14 42 B3
St James's SE14 51 A2
St James & St Michael's CE Prim Sch W2 115 A4
St James's App EC2 24 A1 98 A1
St James's Ave E2 25 B3
St James's CE Prim Sch SE14 51 A2
St James School Flats 5 N7 14 C3
St James's Cl
NW8 80 C3
Upper Tooting SW17 72 B2
St James's Cloisters 2 SE22 64 B3
St James's Cres SW9 62 C4
St James's Dr
Balham SW12, SW17 72 B4
Upper Tooting SW17 72 B3
St James's Gdns W11 31 A1 112 A2
St James's Gr SW11 169 A2
St James's Market SW1 119 B3
St James's Pal SW1 119 A1
St James's Park Sta SW1 133 B2
St James's Pas EC3 110 B1
St James's Pk SW1 133 B4
St James's Pl SW1 118 C1
St James's Rd
Bermondsey SE1, SE16 153 C4
Peckham SE1 49 C4
St James's Sq SW1 119 A2
St James's St SW1 118 C2
St James St W6 39 B1
St James's Terr
NW8 80 C4
2 Upper Tooting SW12 72 C3
St James's Terrace Mews NW8 80 C3
St James The Great RC Prim Sch 17 SE15 49 B2
St James Wlk EC1 96 A2
St Joan of Arc RC Prim Sch N5 15 B4
St John of Jerusalem CE Prim Sch 42 E9 17 B1
ST JOHN'S 51 C1
St John & St James CE Prim Sch 1 E9 17 B3
St John's Angell Town CE Prim Sch 28 SW9 173 B1
St John's Ave
Dagenham NW10 21 B4
Putney SW15 57 C2
St John's CE Prim Sch 35 E2 25 B3
St John's CE Walham Green Prim Sch SW6 164 B4
St John's Church Rd E9 17 B3
St John's Cl SW6 155 B2
St John's Concert Hall SW1 134 A1
St John's Cres SW9 62 C4
St Johns Ct 39 E1 32 A1
St John's Ct
Finsbury Pk N4 6 A2
Hammersmith W6 39 A2
Lewisham SE13 52 B1
5 South Hampstead NW3 11 B2
Saint John's Ct N5 15 A4
St John's Dr SW18 71 A3
St John's Est SE1 138 C3
St John's Gdns W11 31 B2 112 C3
St John's Gr
3 Barnes SW13 46 B1
St John's Gr *continued*
1 Richmond TW9 54 A3
Upper Holloway N19 4 B2
St John's Highbury Vale CE Prim Sch N5 6 A1
St John's Hill SW11 59 C3
St John's Hill Gr SW11 59 C3
St Johns Ho 5 SE17 48 C4
St John's Ho 1 E14 42 B2
St John's La EC1 108 B4
St John's Lodge 8 SE8 51 C2
St John's Mans E5 17 B3
St John's Park Mans N19 4 B1
St John's Path EC1 96 A1
St John's Pk SE3 53 C3
St John's Pl EC1 96 A1
St John's RC Prim Sch SE16 41 A4
St John's Rd
Battersea SW11 60 A3
Canning Town E16 35 C3
Richmond TW9 54 A3
St John's & St Clements CE Jun & Inf Sch 4 SE15 64 C4
St John's Sq EC1 96 A1
St Johns Sta SE8 51 C1
St John St EC1 96 A2
St John's Terr W10 22 C1
St John's Therapy Ctr SW11 59 C3
St John's Upper Holloway CE Prim Sch 7 N19 4 C2
St John's Vale SE8 51 C1
St John's Villas
Upper Holloway N19 4 C2
W8 128 B1
St John's Walworth CE Prim Sch SE17 151 A3
St John's Way N19 4 C3
ST JOHN'S WOOD 79 B1
St John's Wood Ct NW8 89 C3
St John's Wood High St NW8 80 A1
St John's Wood Park NW8 79 B4
St John's Wood Pre-Prep Sch NW8 90 A4
St John's Wood Rd NW8 89 C3
St John's Wood Sta NW8 79 B2
St John's Wood Terr NW8 80 A2
St John the Baptist VA CE Prim Sch N1 87 C1
St John the Divine CE Jun & Inf Sch SE5 48 A3
St John the Evangelist RC Prim Sch N1 86 A2

St Joseph's Cl W10 31 A4
St Josephs Ct [3] NW10 21 B3
St Joseph's Flats NW1 93 B4
St Joseph's Ho W6 39 C2
St Joseph's Hospice E9, E8 25 A4
St Joseph's RC Inf & Jun Schs [36] SE5 48 B3
St Joseph's RC Prim Sch
- Chelsea SW3 144 C3
- [19] Deptford SE8 51 C3
- [11] Greenwich SE10 43 A1
- Paddington W9 88 C3
- Rotherhithe SE16 40 B3
- St Giles WC2 106 B2
- Upper Holloway N19 4 A3
- [16] Wandsworth SW18 58 C2
- [8] Willesden NW10 8 A1

St Joseph's St SW8 170 B4
St Joseph's Vale SE3 67 C4
St Jude & St Paul's CE Prim Sch [12] N1 16 A2
St Jude's CE Prim Sch
- [4] London SE24 63 A2
- SE1 136 A1

St Judes Ho [6] W10 23 B2
St Jude's Rd E2 25 A3
St Jude St N16 16 A3
St Julian's Rd NW6 23 C4
St Katharine's Ho N1 85 B2
St Katharine's Prec NW1 82 A2
St Katharine's Way E1 125 A2
St Katherine's Pier E1 125 A2
St Katherine's Row EC3 110 B1
St Katherine's Wlk [1] W11 30 C1
St Kilda's Rd N16 7 A3
St Laurence's Cl NW6 22 C4
St Lawrence Ct N1 87 C4
St Lawrence Ho SE1 138 B2
St Lawrence St E14 34 B1
St Lawrence Terr W10 31 A4
St Lawrence Way SW9 173 C2
St Leonards Ct SW14 55 B4
St Leonard's Ct N1 97 C4
St Leonard's Hospl N1 24 A3
St Leonards Rd SW14 55 B4
St Leonard's Rd
- Becontree NW10 20 C1
- South Bromley E14 34 B4

St Leonard's Sq NW5 12 C2
St Leonard's St E3 27 A2
St Leonard's Terr SW3 145 A1
St Loo Ave SW3 158 B4
St Loo Ct SW3 158 C4
St Luke Prim CE Sch [9] E16 35 B3
ST LUKE'S 97 A2
St Luke's Ave SW4 61 C3
St Luke's CE Prim Sch
- [7] Cubitt Town E14 42 C2
- Paddington W9 23 B2
- Shoreditch EC1 97 A3

St Luke's Cl EC1 97 A2
St Luke's Ct W11 31 B3
St Luke's Mews W11 31 B3
St Luke's Rd W11 31 B4
St Luke's Sq E16 35 B3
St Luke's St SW3 144 B2
St Margaret's Cres SW15 57 A2
St Margaret's Ct
- Putney SW15 57 A3
- SE1 123 B1

St Margaret's La W8 128 A1
St Margarets Lo W3 37 A4
St Margaret's Rd
- Brockley SE4 66 B3
- Kensal Green NW10 22 B2

St Margaret's Sch NW3 11 A4
St Margaret St SW1 134 A3
St Mark's CE Prim Sch SE11 163 A4
St Marks Cl [5] SE10 52 B3
St Mark's Cres NW1 81 C4
St Marks Gate E9 18 B1
St Mark's Gr SW10 156 B2
St Marks Ho [6] SE17 48 C4
St Mark's Mans [14] N4 5 B2
St Mark's Pl W11 31 A3
St Mark's Prim Sch [11] N19 5 A2
St Marks Rd
- [15] North Kensington NW10 30 C3
- North Kensington W10 30 C4

St Mark's Rd W11 31 A3
St Mark's Rise E8 16 B3
St Mark's Sq NW1 81 B3
St Mark St E1 111 A1
St Martin-in-the-Fields High Sch [21] SW2 74 C3
St Martin's Almshouses NW1 82 C4
St Martin's Cl NW1 82 C4
St Martins Ct N1 24 A4
St Martin's Ct
- WC2 120 A4
- West Norwood SE27 75 A2

St Martin's La WC2 120 A3
St Martin's Le Grand EC1 108 C2
St Martin's Pl WC2 120 A3
St Martin's Rd SW9 172 C2
St Martin's St WC2 119 C3
St Martin's Way SW17 71 B1
St Mary Abbots CE Prim Sch W8 128 A3
St Mary Abbot's Ct W14 126 C1
St Mary Abbot's Pl W8 127 A1
St Mary Abbots Terr W14 127 A1
St Mary at Hill EC3 124 A3
St Mary Axe EC3 110 B2
St Marychurch St SE16 40 B4
St Mary Graces Ct E1 125 A3
St Marylebone CE Sch The W1 103 C4
St Mary le Bow Church EC2 109 A1
St Mary- le-Park Ct SW11 158 B1
St Mary Magdalene Acad N7 14 C2
St Mary Magdalene CE Prim Sch
- [3] Paddington W2 100 A4
- [10] Peckham SE15 50 A1

St Mary Magdalen's RC Prim Sch
- Brockley SE4 66 A3
- [14] Mortlake SW14 55 C4

St Mary Magdelen's RC Jun Sch [1] NW2 9 A2
St Mary Newington Cl SE17 152 B2
St Mary of the Angels RC Prim Sch [12] W2 31 C3
St Mary RC Prim Sch [22] W10 23 A1
St Mary & St Michael Prim Sch [27] E1 32 B3
St Mary & St Pancras CE Prim Sch NW1 83 B1
St Mary's Bryanston Square CE Sch W1 102 C4
St Mary's CE Prim Sch
- Islington N1 86 B4
- London SE13 67 A2
- [15] Putney SW15 57 C4
- Willesden NW10 8 A2

St Mary's Ct W6 38 B3
St Mary's Est [2] SE16 40 B4
St Mary's Flats NW1 93 B4
St Mary's Gate W8 128 A1
St Mary's Gdns SE11 149 C4
St Mary's Gr
- Barnes SW13 57 A4
- Chiswick W4 45 A4
- Islington N1 15 A2
- Richmond TW10, TW9 54 B3

St Mary's Ho N1 86 B4
St Mary's Hospl W2 101 C2
St Mary's Hospl Medical Sch W2 101 C2
St Mary's Kilburn CE Prim Sch [16] NW6 23 C4
St Mary's Mans
- Dagenham NW10 21 A4
- Paddington W2 101 B4

St Mary's Mews NW6 11 A1
St Mary's Path N1 86 B4
St Mary's Pl W8 128 A1
St Mary's RC Prim Sch
- Chiswick W4 46 A4
- [10] Clapham Pk SW4 61 B2
- Clapham SW8 170 B4
- Hammersmith W14 39 C3
- Paddington NW6 23 C3

St Mary's Rd
- Golders Green NW11 1 A4
- Harlesdon NW10 21 A4
- Nunhead SE15 50 B1

St Mary's Sch Hampstead NW3 11 C3
St Mary's Sq W2 101 B4
St Mary's Stoke Newington CE Prim Sch [2] N16 7 A2
St Mary's Terr W2 101 B4
St Mary's Twr EC1 97 A1
St Mary's Wlk SE11 149 C4
St Matthews CE Sch SW1 133 C2
St Matthews Ct SE1 136 C1
St Matthew's Ho [8] SE17 48 C4
St Matthew's Lo NW1 83 A2
St Matthew's Rd SW2 62 B2
St Matthew's Row E2 24 C1 99 B2
St Matthew St SW1 133 B1
St Matthias CE Prim Sch E2 24 B1 99 A2
St Matthias's CE Prim Sch [32] N16 16 A4
St Mauritius Ho SE13 67 B2
St Maur Rd SW6 165 A3
St Michael & All Angels CE Acad [35] SE5 48 A3
St Michael's Alley EC3 109 C1
St Michael's Cath Coll [38] SE16 139 B3
St Michael's CE Prim Sch
- Camden Town NW1 82 C4

St Michael's CE Prim Sch *continued*
- Highgate N6 3 C4
- Wandsworth SW18 70 B4

St Michaels Ct [2] E14 34 B4
St Michael's Ct NW11 1 B4
St Michael's Flats NW1 83 B1
St Michael's Gdns W10 31 A4
St Michael's Rd
- Cricklewood NW2 9 B4
- Stockwell SW9 172 C2

St Michael's St W2 102 A2
St Michael Steiner Sch The [18] SW18 58 C2
St Mildred's Ct EC2 109 B1
St Monica's RC Prim Sch [24] N1 24 A2 98 A4
St Nicholas' Flats NW1 83 B1
St Nicholas Ho SE8 51 C4
St Nicholas Mans SW17 72 B2
St Nicholas St SE8 51 C2
St Norbert Gn SE4 66 A3
St Norbert Rd SE4 66 A3
St Olaf's Rd SW6 154 B1
St Olaves Ct W2 114 A3
St Olave's Ct EC2 109 B1
St Olave's Est SE1 138 B4
St Olave's Gdns SE11 149 B4
St Olave's Mans SE11 149 B4
St Olav's Sq [32] SE16 40 B4
St Osmund's RC Prim Sch SW13 46 B2
St Oswald's Pl SE11 148 C1
St Oswulf St SW1 147 C3
St Owen Ho SE1 138 B2
ST PANCRAS 94 B4
St Pancras Almshouses [13] NW5 12 B3
St Pancras Commercial Ctr NW1 83 A4
St Pancras Hospl NW1 83 B3
St Pancras International Sta WC1 94 A4
St Pancras Way NW1 83 B4
St Patrick's Coll W1 105 B2
St Patrick's RC Prim Sch NW5 13 A3
St Paul's Ave
- Rotherhithe SE16 32 C1
- Willesden NW2 9 B2

St Paul's Cath EC4 108 C1
St Paul's Cath Sch EC4 108 C1
St Paul's CE Prim Sch
- [23] Hammersmith W6 39 B1

St Paul's CE Prim Sch *continued*
Hampstead NW3 .... 12 B1
SE17 .... 150 C2
St Paul's Church Yd EC4 .... 108 C1
St Pauls Cl W5 .... 36 B4
St Pauls Cres NW1 .... 13 C1
St Paul's Ct
Clapham SW4 .... 61 C3
[6] Upper Holloway N19 .... 5 A2
St Paul's Dr E15 .... 19 C3
St Paul's Girls' Sch [1] W6 .... 39 C2
St Pauls Mews NW1 .... 13 C1
St Paul's Pl N1 .... 15 C2
St Pauls Rd TW9 .... 54 B4
St Paul's Rd N1 .... 15 B2
St Paul's Sch SW13 .... 38 C1
St Paul's Sta EC2 .... 108 C2
St Pauls Steiner Sch [22] N1 .... 15 C2
St Paul St N1 .... 87 A3
St Paul's Terr SE17 .... 48 A4
St Pauls View WC1 .... 95 B3
St Paul's Way E3 .... 33 C4
St Paul's Way Com Sch [25] E3 .... 33 C4
St Paul's with St Michael's Prim Sch [24] E8 .... 24 C4
St Paul with St Luke CE Prim Sch [18] E3 .... 33 B4
St Peter & St Paul RC Prim Sch EC1 .... 96 B2
St Peter's Alley EC3 .... 109 C1
St Peter's Ave [37] E2 .... 24 C3
St Petersburgh Mews W2 .... 114 A4
St Petersburgh Pl W2 .... 114 A3
St Peter's CE Prim Sch
[15] Chiswick W6 .... 38 C1
[9] E1 .... 32 B1
[6] Paddington W9 .... 23 C1
SE17 .... 151 B1
SW1 .... 132 B1
St Peter's Church Ct N1 .... 86 B3
St Peters Cl [1] SW17 .... 72 A2
St Peter's Cl E2 .... 24 C3
St Peters Ct
New Cross SE4 .... 51 B1
[28] Stepney E1 .... 25 B1
St Peter's Gdns SE27 .... 74 C1
St Peter's Gr W6 .... 38 C2
St Peters Ho WC1 .... 94 B3
St Peter's Ho
[4] SE17 .... 48 C4
Stamford Hill N16 .... 7 A4
St Peter's Pl W9 .... 88 A1
St Peter's Rd W6 .... 38 C1
St Peter's Sq
Chiswick W6 .... 38 B1
Hackney E2 .... 24 C3
St Peter's St N1 .... 86 B3
St Peter's Street Mews N1 .... 86 B2
St Peter's Terr SW6 .... 154 B1
St Peter's Villas [5] W6 .... 38 C2
St Peter's Way N1 .... 16 A1
St Peter's Wharf [8] W6 .... 38 C1
St Philip Ho WC1 .... 95 B3
St Philip Sq [1] SW8 .... 170 A1
St Philip's Rd E8 .... 16 C2
St Philip's Sch SW7 .... 143 A3
St Philip St SW8 .... 170 A1
St Philip's Way N1 .... 87 A3
St Quentin Ho SW18 .... 59 C1
St Quintin Ave W10 .... 30 C4
St Quintin Gdns [21] W10 .... 30 B4
St Regis Hts NW3 .... 2 A1
St Richard's Ho NW1 .... 93 B4
St Rule St SW8 .... 170 C1
St Saviours SW4 .... 61 A3
St Saviour & St Olaves CE Sch SE1 .... 137 C1
St Saviour's CE Prim Sch
[9] Bow Comm E14 .... 34 A4
Camberwell SE24 .... 63 B4
[26] Paddington W9 .... 88 B1
St Saviours Ho [35] SE1 .... 139 B3
St Saviour's RC Prim Sch SE13 .... 67 B3
St Saviour's Rd SW2 .... 62 B2
St Saviour's Wharf SE1 .... 139 A4
St Scholastica's RC Prim Sch [6] E5 .... 7 C1
St Silas Pl NW5 .... 12 C2
St Simon's Ave SW15 .... 57 B2
St Stephen's Ave W12 .... 39 A4
St Stephen's CE Prim Sch
Paddington W2 .... 31 C4
[17] Shepherd's Bush W12 .... 39 B4
[2] St Johns SE8 .... 51 C1
SW8 .... 162 C2
St Stephen's Cl
Maitland Pk NW5 .... 12 B3
NW8 .... 80 B3
St Stephen's Cres W2 .... 31 C3
St Stephen's Gdns
Notting Hill W2 .... 31 C3
[4] Putney SW15 .... 58 B2
St Stephen's Gr SE13 .... 67 B4
St Stephens Ho [7] SE17 .... 48 C4
St Stephen's Mews [34] W2 .... 31 C4
St Stephen's Rd E3 .... 26 B3
St Stephen's Row EC4 .... 109 B1
St Stephen's Terr SW8 .... 162 C1
St Stephen's Wlk SW7 .... 142 C4
St Swithin's La EC4 .... 123 B4
St Swithun's Rd SE13 .... 67 C2
St Theresas Cl E9 .... 18 C4
St Thomas' CE Prim Sch [23] W10 .... 23 A1
St Thomas Ct [14] NW1 .... 13 B1
St Thomas Ho [2] E1 .... 32 C3
St Thomas More Language Coll SW3 .... 144 C3
St Thomas of Canterbury RC Prim Sch SW6 .... 154 C2
St Thomas Rd E16 .... 35 C3
St Thomas' Rd W4 .... 45 B4
St Thomas's Gdns NW5 .... 12 C2
St Thomas's Hospl SE1 .... 134 C2
St Thomas's Pl [20] E9 .... 17 B1
St Thomas's Rd
Dagenham NW10 .... 21 A4
Highbury N4, N5 .... 5 C1
St Thomas's Sq E9 .... 17 B1
St Thomas St SE1 .... 123 C1
St Thomas's Way SW6 .... 155 A2
St Thomas the Apostle Coll SE15 .... 50 B2
St Ursula's Convent Sch SE10 .... 52 C3
St Vincent De Paul Ho [24] E1 .... 32 B4
St Vincent De Paul RC Prim Sch SW1 .... 133 A2
St Vincent Ho SE1 .... 138 C2
St Vincent's RC Prim Sch
Acton W3 .... 28 A2
Marylebone W1 .... 103 C3
St Vincent St W1 .... 103 C3
Salamanca Pl SE1 .... 148 C3
Salamanca St SE1, SE11 .... 148 C3
Salcombe Gdns SW4 .... 61 A3
Salcombe Lo NW5 .... 12 C4
Salcombe Rd [23] N16 .... 16 A3
Salcombe Villas [13] TW10 .... 54 A2
Salcot N4 .... 5 B2
Salcott Rd SW11 .... 60 B2
Salehurst Rd SE4 .... 66 B1
Salem Ho [13] E9 .... 17 C2
Salem Rd W2 .... 114 B4
Sale Pl W2 .... 102 A2
Salesian Coll SW11 .... 168 A3
Sale St E2 .... 24 C1 99 C2
Salford Ho [5] E14 .... 42 B2
Salford Rd SW12, SW2 .... 73 C3
Salisbury Cl SE17 .... 151 B4
Salisbury Ct
[15] Bermondsey SE16 .... 139 C1
Chiswick W4 .... 38 A2
EC4 .... 108 A1
Hackney E9 .... 18 A3
Salisbury Ho
[2] Islington N1 .... 15 A2
Islington N1 .... 86 A4
[3] Poplar E14 .... 34 A3
Westminster SW1 .... 147 C2
Wimbledon SW19 .... 69 C1
Salisbury Mews SW6 .... 154 C1
Salisbury Pl
Camberwell SW9 .... 48 A3
Marylebone W1 .... 102 C4
Salisbury Rd TW9 .... 54 A3
Salisbury Sq EC4 .... 107 C1
Salisbury St
[10] Acton W3 .... 37 B4
NW8 .... 90 A1
Salisbury Terr SE15 .... 65 B4
Salisbury Wlk N19 .... 4 B2
Salmon La E14 .... 33 A3
Salmon St [13] E14 .... 33 B3
Saltcoats Rd W4 .... 38 A4
Saltdene N4 .... 5 B3
Salter Rd
Rotherhithe SE16 .... 32 C1
SE16 .... 33 A1
Salters' Hall Ct EC4 .... 123 B4
Salters Rd W10 .... 22 C1
Salter St
College Pk NW10 .... 21 C2
[11] Poplar E14 .... 33 C2
Salterton Rd N7 .... 5 B1
Saltoun Rd SW2, SW9 .... 62 C3
Saltram Cres W9 .... 23 C2
Saltwell St E14 .... 33 C2
Saltwood Gr SE17 .... 151 B1
Saltwood Ho [19] SE15 .... 50 B4
Salusbury Prim Sch NW6 .... 23 B4
Salusbury Rd NW6 .... 23 A4
Salutation Rd SE10 .... 43 A2
Salvin Rd SW15 .... 57 C4
Salway Rd E15 .... 19 C2
Salween Ho [2] N16 .... 15 C4
Sambrook Ho [25] E1 .... 32 B4
Samels Ct W6 .... 38 C1
Samford Ho N1 .... 85 B3
Samford St NW8 .... 90 A1
Sam Manners Ho [7] SE10 .... 43 A1
Sam March Ho [5] E14 .... 34 C3
Sampson St E1 .... 125 C1
Samuel Cl
SE14 .... 50 C4
Shoreditch E8 .... 24 B4
Samuel Ct N1 .... 24 A2 98 A3
Samuel Ho [15] E8 .... 24 B4
Samuel Jones Ind Est [7] SE15 .... 49 A3
Samuel Lewis Bldgs N1 .... 14 C2
Samuel Lewis Trust Dwellings
[6] Camberwell SE5 .... 48 B2
Chelsea SW3 .... 144 A3
Walham Green SW6 .... 155 C2
West Kensington W14 .... 140 B4
Samuel Rhodes Sch N1 .... 85 B4
Samuel Richardson Ho W14 .... 140 C3
Samuel's Cl [2] W6 .... 39 B2
Samuel St SE15 .... 49 B3
Sancroft Ct SW11 .... 168 B4
Sancroft Ho SE11 .... 149 A2
Sancroft St SE11 .... 149 A2
Sanctuary Mews [15] E8 .... 16 B2
Sanctuary St SE1 .... 137 A4
Sanctuary The
[35] Wapping E1 .... 32 A1
Westminster SW1 .... 133 C2
Sandale Cl N16 .... 6 C1
Sandall Ho [7] E3 .... 26 A3
Sandall Rd NW5 .... 13 B2
Sandalwood Cl [11] E1 .... 26 A1
Sandalwood Ho [6] NW3 .... 11 A2
Sandbourne
[4] Kensington W11 .... 31 C3
[14] Paddington NW8 .... 78 B4
Sandbourne Rd SE4 .... 51 A1
Sandbrook Rd N16 .... 7 A1
Sandby Ho
[11] Camberwell SE5 .... 49 A2
[6] Kilburn NW6 .... 23 C4
Sandell St SE1 .... 135 B4
Sanderling Ct [20] SE8 .... 51 B4
Sanders Ho WC1 .... 95 B4
Sanderson Cl NW5 .... 13 A4
Sanderson Ho [7] SE8 .... 41 B1
Sanderstead Ave NW2 .... 1 A2
Sanderstead Cl SW12 .... 73 B4
Sanders Way [3] N19 .... 4 C3
Sandfield WC1 .... 94 B3
Sandford Ct N16 .... 7 A3
Sandford Row SE17 .... 151 C2
Sandford St SW6 .... 156 B1
Sandgate Ho [15] E5 .... 17 A4
Sandgate La SW17, SW18 .... 72 A3
Sandgate St SE15 .... 50 A4
Sandgate Trad Est SE15 .... 50 A4
Sandham Ct SW4 .... 172 B3
Sandhills The SW10 .... 157 A4
Sandhurst Ct SW2 .... 62 A3
Sandhurst Ho [12] E1 .... 32 B4

Sandilands Rd SW6 166 A3
Sandison St SE15 64 C4
Sandland St WC1 107 A3
Sandlings Cl SE15 50 A1
Sandmere Rd SW4 62 A3
Sandon Ho 5 SW2 74 A4
Sandown Ho 2 W4 37 B1
Sandpiper Cl SE16 41 B4
Sandpiper Ct
13 Cubitt Town E14 42 B3
1 SE8 51 C3
Sandridge St 3 N19 4 B2
Sandringham Cl 1 SW19 69 C3
Sandringham Ct
Marylebone W1 105 A1
Putney SW15 57 C1
18 Rotherhithe SE16 32 C1
St John's Wood W9 89 A3
Sandringham Flats WC2 119 C4
Sandringham Ho
Richmond TW10 54 C2
W14 140 A4
Sandringham Rd
Dalston E8 16 B3
Golders Green NW11 1 A4
Willesden NW2 9 A2
Sandrock Rd SE13 66 C4
SANDS END 59 B4
Sands End La SW6 166 B4
Sandstone TW9 44 C3
Sandstone Pl N19 4 A2
Sandways 6 TW9 44 C2
Sandwell Cres 2 NW6 10 C2
Sandwell Mans 3 NW6 10 C2
Sandwich Ho
15 Rotherhithe SE16 40 B4
WC1 94 A3
Sandwich St WC1 94 A3
Sandycombe Ctr TW9 54 C4
Sandycombe Rd TW9 44 C1
Sandy Lo N6 4 B4
Sandy Rd NW3 2 A2
Sandy's Row E1 110 B3
Sanford La 3 N16 7 B2
Sanford St SE14, SE8 51 A4
Sanford Terr N16 7 B1
Sanford Wlk
SE14 51 A4
4 Stoke Newington N16 7 B2
Sangora Rd 17 SW11 59 C3
San Ho 29 E9 17 C2
Sankey Ho 22 E2 25 B3
Sansom St
Camberwell SE5 48 C2
SE5 48 C3
Sans Wlk EC1 96 A2
Santley Ho SE1 135 C3
Santley St SW4 62 B3
Santos Rd SW18 58 C2
Sapcote Trad Ctr NW10 8 B2
Saperton Wlk SE11 149 A4
Sapperton Ct EC1 96 C2
Sapphire Ct 13 E1 125 B4
Sapphire Rd SE8 41 A2
Saracen's Head Yd EC2 110 B1
Saracen St E14 33 C3
Sarah Ho
Roehampton SW15 56 B3
8 Stepney E1 32 A3
Sarah Swift Ho SE1 137 C4
Sara Lane Ct 31 N1 24 A3
Saratoga Rd E5 17 B4
Sardinia Ho WC2 106 C1
Sardinia St WC2 106 C2
Sarjant Path SW19 69 C2
Sark Ho 9 N1 15 B2
Sarnersfield Ho SE15 50 A4
Sarratt Ho 6 W10 30 B4
Sarre Rd NW2 10 B3
Sarsden Bldgs W1 103 C1
Sarsfeld Rd SW12, SW17 72 B3
Sartor Rd SE15 65 C3
Sarum Hall Sch NW3 12 A1
Sarum Ho W11 31 B2 113 A3
Sassoon Ho SE15 50 B1
Satchwell Rd 17 E2 24 C2 99 B3
Saturn Ho 4 E3 26 C4
Saul Ct 4 SE15 49 B4
Saunders Cl 14 E14 33 B2
Saunders Ho 11 SW2 74 C3
Saunders Ness Rd E14 42 C2
Saunders St SE11 149 B4
Savage Gdns EC3 124 B4
Savana N16 7 A2
Savannah Cl 9 SE15 49 B3
Savernake Ho N4 6 C4
Savernake Rd NW3 12 B4
Saville Rd W4 37 C3
Saville Row W1 118 C4
Savill Ho 2 SW4 61 C1
Savona St SW8 160 C1
Savoy Circus W3 29 B2
Savoy Ct
Earl's Ct SW5 141 C4
Strand WC2 120 B3
Savoy Hill WC2 120 C3
Savoy Mews SW9 62 A4
Savoy Pier WC2 120 C3
Savoy Pl WC2 120 C3
Savoy Row WC2 120 C4
Savoy St WC2 120 C3
Savoy Stps WC2 120 C3
Savoy Way WC2 120 C3
Sawkins Cl SW19 70 A2
Sawley Rd W12 29 C1
Sawmill Yd E3 26 A4
Sawyer St SE1 136 C4
Saxby Rd SW2 74 A4
Saxonbury Ct
16 Kentish Town N7 13 C3
2 Lower Holloway N7 14 A3
Saxoncroft Ho SW16 73 C1
Saxon Dr W3 28 A4
Saxonfield Cl SW2 74 B4
Saxon Hall W2 114 A3
Saxon Ho 4 SW4 61 C3
Saxon Rd E3 26 B3
Saxton Cl SE13 67 C4
Sayer Ho SE4 66 A3
Sayes Court St SE8 51 B4
Sayes Ct SE8 51 B4
Scafell NW1 92 C4
Scala St W1 105 A4
Scampston Mews 5 W10 30 C3
Scandrett St 38 E1 32 A1
Scarba Wlk N1 15 C2
Scarborough Rd N4 5 C3
Scarborough St E1 111 A1
Scarlette Manor Wlk 10 SE24 74 C4
Scarsbrook Ho 2 SW2 62 C1
Scarsdale Pl W8 128 A2
Scarsdale Villas W8 127 C1
Scarth Rd SW13 56 B4
Scawen Rd SE8 41 A1
Scawfell St E2 24 B3
Sceptre Ho 10 E1 25 B1
Sceptre Rd E2 25 B2
Schiller International Univ SE1 121 B1
Schofield Wlk SE3 53 C3
Sch of Pharmacy WC1 94 B2
Sch of the Islamic Republic of Iran The 6 NW6 23 C3
Scholars Ct 5 N19 4 C3
Scholars Rd SW12 73 B3
Scholefield Rd N19 4 C2
Scholey Ho SW11 60 A4
Schomberg Ho SW1 147 C4
Schonfeld Sq N16 6 C3
School App 21 E2 24 A2 98 B4
Schoolbank Rd SE10 43 B2
School Bell Cloisters 17 E3 26 A3
Schoolbell Mews 18 E3 26 A3
School Flats SW8 172 A3
School Ho SE1 152 A4
Schoolhouse La E1 32 C2
School Rd NW10 20 C1
School Sq SE10 43 B3
Schooner Cl
Cubitt Town E14 42 C3
1 Rotherhithe SE16 40 C4
Schubert Rd SW15 58 B2
Science Mus SW7 129 B1
Sclater St E1 24 B1 99 A2
Scoles Cres SW2 74 C3
Scoresby St SE1 122 A1
Scorton Ho 2 N1 24 A3
Scotch Ho SW1 130 C3
Scoter Ct 23 SE8 51 B4
Scotia Bldg 10 E1 32 C2
Scotia Ct 3 SE16 40 B3
Scotia Rd 24 SW2 74 C4
Scotland Pl SW1 120 A1
Scotney Ho E9 17 B2
Scotson Ho SE11 149 B3
Scotswood St EC1 95 C2
Scott Ave SW15, SW18 58 A1
Scott Ct
Acton W4 37 C4
4 Clapham SW11 170 B1
17 Stoke Newington N16 7 A1
Scott Ellis Gdns NW8 89 B3
Scott Ho
2 Barnsbury N7 14 B2
Islington N1 87 B4
Lisson Gr NW8 90 A1
17 Millwall E14 41 C4
Scott Lidgett Cres SE16 139 C3
Scotts Ct 6 W12 39 A4
Scott's Rd W12 39 A4
Scott's Sufferance Wharf SE1 139 A3
Scott St E1 25 A1
Scott's Yd EC4 123 B4
Scoulding Ho 12 E14 41 C3
Scoulding Rd E16 35 C3
Scouler St E14 34 C2
Scout App NW10 8 A4
Scout La SW4 61 B4
Scovell Cres SE1 136 C3
Scovell Rd SE1 136 C3
Scriven Ct 2 E8 24 B4
Scriven St E8 24 B4
Scrooby St SE6 67 A1
Scrope Bldg EC1 107 B4
Scrubs La NW10, W10, W12 22 A1
Scrutton Cl SW12 73 C4
Scrutton St EC2 24 A1 98 A1
Scutari Rd SE22 65 B2
Scylla Rd SE15 65 A4
Seabright St 27 E2 25 A2
Seacole Cl W3 28 C4
Seacon Twr 8 E14 41 C4
Seaford Ho 13 SE16 40 B4
Seaford St WC1 94 B3
Seaforth Cres N5 15 B3
Seaforth Lo 2 SW13 46 B1
Seaforth Pl SW1 133 A2
Seagrave Lo SW6 155 C4
Seagrave Rd SW6 155 C4
Seagrove Cl E1 32 C4
Seagull La E16 35 C2
Seal Ho SE1 137 C2
SEA LIFE London Aquarium SE1 134 C3
Seal St E8 16 B4
Searle Pl N4 5 B3
Searles Cl SW11 158 B1
Searles Rd SE1 151 C4
Searson Ho SE17 150 B3
Sears St SE5 48 C3
Seasalter Ho 10 SW9 173 B4
Seaton Cl SW15 69 A4
Seaton Point E5 16 C4
Seavington Ho 3 SE5 64 A4
Sebastian Ho 22 N1 24 A3
Sebastian St EC1 96 B3
Sebbon St N1 15 A1
Sebright Ho 22 E2 24 C3
Sebright Pas 29 E2 24 C3
Sebright Sch 39 E2 24 C3
Secker Ho SW9 48 A1
Secker St SE1 121 B1
Second Ave
East Acton W3 29 B1
Kensal Town W10 23 A1
Mortlake SW14 56 A4
Sedan Way SE17 152 A2
Sedding St SW1 145 B4
Seddon Ho EC2 108 C4
Seddon St WC1 95 A3
Sedgeford Rd W12 29 B1
Sedgewick Ho SW19 69 C2
Sedgley Ho N4 5 B2
Sedgmoor Pl SE5 49 A3
Sedgwick St E9 17 C3
Sedleigh Rd SW18 58 B1
Sedlescombe Rd SW6 155 B4
Sedley Ho SE11 149 A2
Sedley Pl W1 104 A1
Seething La EC3 124 B4
Sefton St SW15 57 B4
Sekforde St EC1 96 A2
Selbie Ave NW10 8 B3
Selborne 2 SW11 60 C4
Selborne Ho SE1 137 B3
Selborne Rd 1 SE5 48 C1
Selby Ho 10 SW4 61 B1
Selby Sq 1 W10 23 A2
Selby St E1 24 C1 99 C1
Selden Ho 2 SE15 50 B1
Selden Rd SE15 50 B1
Selden Wlk N7 5 B2
Seldon Ho
Nine Elms SW8 160 C1
Pimlico SW1 146 C1
Selhurst Cl SW19 69 C3
Selina Ho NW8 89 C2
Selkirk Ho
N1 84 C4
4 Stoke Newington N16 7 A1
Sellons Ave NW10 21 B4
Selma Ho 7 W12 30 A3
Selman Ho 3 E9 18 A2
Selsdon Way E14 42 A3
Selsea Pl N16 16 A3
Selsey St E14 33 C4
Selway Ho SW8 172 B4
Selwood Ho 1 N4 6 C4
Selwood Pl SW7 143 B2
Selwood Terr SW7 143 B2

Selworthy Ho SW11 167 C4
Selwyn Ave TW9 54 B4
Selwyn Ct 8 TW10 54 B2
Selwyn Ho 3 SW15 57 C1
Selwyn Rd
Bow E3 26 B3
Willesden NW10 8 A1
Semley Gate E9 18 B2
Semley Ho SW1 146 A3
Semley Pl SW1 146 A3
Senate St SE15 50 B1
Senators Lo 31 E3 26 A3
Sendall Ct 12 SW11 59 C4
Senior St W2 100 A4
Senrab St E1 32 C3
Seraph Ct EC1 96 C4
Serenaders Rd 20 SW9 173 B1
Sergeant Ind Est The SW18 59 A1
Serica Ct 14 SE10 52 B3
Serjeants' Inn EC4 107 C1
Serlby Ct W14 126 C2
Serle St WC2 107 A2
Sermon La EC4 108 C1
Serpentine Ct 10 SE16 40 C4
Serpentine Gallery W2 129 C4
Serpentine Rd W2 116 C1
Serpentine The W2 116 B1
Service Route No 1 E15 19 C1
Service Route No 2 1 E15 19 C1
Service Route No 3 2 E15 19 C1
Servite Ho SE13 52 A2
Servite RC Prim Sch SW10 156 C4
Setchell Rd SE1 152 C4
Setchell Way SE1 152 C4
Seth St 25 SE16 40 B4
Settlers Ct 11 E14 34 C2
Settles St E1 111 C2
Settrington Rd SW6 166 A1
Seven Dials WC2 106 A1
Seven Islands L Ctr SE16 40 B3
Seven Mills Prim Sch 27 E14 41 C4
Sevenoaks Rd SE4 66 B1
Seven Sisters Rd
Finsbury Pk N4 6 A2
Stoke Newington N4, N7, N15 6 B4
Seven Stars Cnr W12 38 C3
Seven Stars Yd E1 111 A4
Severnake Cl E14 41 C2
Severn Ave 2 W10 23 A2
Severn Way NW10 8 B3
Severus Rd SW11 60 A3
Seville Ho 10 E1 125 C1
Seville Mews N1 16 A1
Seville St SW1 131 A3
Sevington St W9 88 A1
Seward St EC1 96 C3
Sewardstone Rd E2 25 B3
Sewell Ho 7 N16 16 A3
Sextant Ave E14 42 C2
Sexton Ct 7 E14 34 C2
Sexton's Ho 5 SE13 52 B4
Seymour Ct
Putney SW15 57 A3
Upper Clapton N16 7 C3
Seymour Gdns SE4 66 A4
Seymour Ho
Bloomsbury WC1 94 A2
1 Clapham SW8 171 A2
Somers Town NW1 93 C3
Seymour Mews W1 103 B2
Seymour Pl W1 102 C2
Seymour Rd
Acton W4 37 B2
Wandsworth SW18 58 B1
Wimbledon SW19 69 C1
Seymour St W1 103 A1
Seymour Wlk SW10 156 C4
Seyssel St E14 42 B2
Shaa Rd W3 28 C2
Shabana Ct 3 W12 30 A1
Shackleton Ct
3 Dulwich SE21 75 C2
2 Isle of Dogs E14 41 C1
4 Shepherd's Bush W12 39 A4
Shackleton Ho 5 E1 32 B1
SHACKLEWELL 16 B4
Shacklewell Ho 3 E8 16 B4
Shacklewell La E8 16 B3
Shacklewell Prim Sch 5 E8 16 B4
Shacklewell Rd N16 16 B4
Shacklewell Row E8 16 B4
Shacklewell St 30 E2 24 B2 99 A3
Shad Thames SE1 139 A4
SHADWELL 32 B2
Shadwell Gdns E1 32 B2
Shadwell Pierhead E1 32 B2
Shadwell Pl 1 E1 32 B2
Shadwell Sta E1 32 A2
Shaftesbury Ave W1 119 C4
Shaftesbury Ct
Borough The SE1 137 B2
1 Herne Hill SE5 63 C3
Shoreditch N1 87 B1
Streatham SW16 73 C1
Shaftesbury Ctr NW10 22 C1
Shaftesbury Gdns NW10 21 A1
Shaftesbury Ho
11 Canning Town E16 35 B3
13 Stoke Newington N16 7 A1
W2 114 B4
Shaftesbury Lo 9 E14 34 A3
Shaftesbury Mews
2 Clapham Pk SW4 61 B2
W8 127 C1
Shaftesbury Park Chambers 1 SW11 60 C4
Shaftesbury Rd
Finsbury Pk N4, N19 5 A3
Richmond TW9 54 A4
Shaftesbury St N1 87 B1
Shafteswood Ct SW17 72 B1
Shafto Mews SW1 131 A1
Shafton Rd E9 25 C4
Shaftsbury Park Prim Sch 16 SW11 169 B1
Shafts Ct EC3 110 A1
Shahjalal Ho 18 E2 24 C3
Shakespeare Ave 7 NW10 20 C4
Shakespeare Ho 3 E9 17 B1
Shakespeare Rd
Acton W3 28 B1
Brixton SE24 63 A3
Stonebridge NW10 20 C4
Shakespeare's Globe Theatre (site of) SE1 123 A2
Shakespeare Twr EC2 109 A4
Shakspeare Mews 7 N16 16 A4
Shakspeare Wlk N16 16 A4
Shalbourne Sq E9 18 B2
Shalcomb St SW10 157 A3
Shalden Ho SW15 56 B1
Shalfleet Dr W10 30 C2
Shalford NW10 21 C4
Shalford Ct N1 86 A2
Shalford Ho SE1 137 C2
Shalimar Gdns W3 28 B2
Shalimar Lo W3 28 B2
Shalimar Rd W3 28 B2
Shalstone Rd SW14, TW9 55 A4
Shamrock St SW4 61 C4
Shandon Ct SE4 51 A1
Shandon Rd SW4 61 B1
Shand St SE1 138 B4
Shandy St E1 25 C1
Shan Ho WC1 94 C1
Shannon Ct
11 Peckham SE15 49 B3
Stoke Newington N16 7 A1
Willesden NW10 8 C2
Shannon Gr SW9 62 B3
Shannon Pl NW8 80 B2
Shanti Ct SW18 70 C3
Shapla Prim Sch 25 E1 125 C3
Shardcroft Ave SE24 63 A2
Shardeloes Rd SE14 51 B1
Shard's Sq SE15 49 C4
Shard The SE1 123 C1
Sharebourne Ho SW2 62 C2
Sharman Ho 13 E14 34 B3
Sharnbrook Ho W6 155 B4
Sharon Gdns E9 25 B4
Sharon Rd W4 37 C1
Sharp Ho SW8 61 A4
Sharples Hall St 8 NW1 12 B1
Sharpness Ct 2 SE15 49 B3
Sharratt St SE15 50 B4
Sharsted St SE17 150 A1
Sharwood WC1 85 A1
Shaver's Pl SW1 119 B3
Shawbury Ct SE22 64 B2
Shawbury Rd SE22 64 B2
Shaw Cres 6 E14 33 A3
Shaw Ct
8 Acton Green W3 37 B3
11 Battersea SW11 59 C4
Upper Holloway N19 5 A2
Shawfield St SW3 144 B1
Shawford Ct 8 SW15 68 C4
Shaw Rd SE22 64 A3
Shearling Way N7 14 A2
Shearsmith Ho 19 E1 125 C4
Shearwater Ct 24 SE8 51 B4
Sheba Pl E1 24 B1 99 A1
Sheen Common Dr SW14, TW10 54 C2
Sheen Court Rd TW10 54 C3
Sheen Ct TW10 54 C3
Sheendale Rd TW9 54 B3
Sheen Gate Gdns SW14 55 B3
Sheengate Mans SW14 55 C3
Sheen Gr N1 85 B4
Sheen La SW14 55 B3
Sheen Mount Prim Sch SW14 55 A2
Sheen Pk TW10, TW9 54 A3
Sheen Rd TW10, TW9 54 B3
Sheen Wood SW14 55 B2
Sheepcote La SW11 169 A1
Sheep La E8 25 A4
Sheffield Ho 15 SE15 49 B2
Sheffield Sq 2 E3 26 B2
Sheffield St WC2 106 C1
Sheffield Terr W8 31 C1 113 C1
Shelbourne Ho 20 N19 4 C4
Shelburne Ct SW15 57 C2
Shelburne Rd N7 14 B4
Shelbury Rd SE22 65 A2
Sheldon Ct SW8 162 A1
Sheldon Ho 9 E9 17 C2
Sheldon Pl E2 25 A3
Sheldon Rd NW2 9 C4
Sheldon Sq W2 101 A3
Sheldrake Ho 15 SE16 40 C2
Sheldrake Pl W8 127 B4
Shelduck Ct 37 SE8 51 B4
Shelford Pl N16 6 C1
Shelgate Rd SW11 60 B2
Shell Ctr SE1 121 A1
Shelley Cl SE15 50 A1
Shelley Ct
Finsbury Pk N4 5 B3
SW3 159 A4
Shelley Ho
21 Bethnal Green E2 25 B2
Chelsea SW1 160 C4
9 Stoke Newington N16 16 A4
Walworth SE17 151 A2
Shelley Rd NW10 20 C4
Shellgrove Rd 31 N16 16 A3
Shellness Rd E5 17 A3
Shell Rd SE13 67 A4
Shellwood Rd SW11 168 C1
Shelmerdine Cl E3 33 C4
Shelton St WC2 106 A1
Shene Bldg EC1 107 B4
Shene Sch SW14 56 A3
Shenfield St N1 24 A3
Shenley Rd SE5 49 A2
Shepard Ho 17 SW11 59 C4
Sheperdess Pl N1 97 A4
Shepherd Cl W1 117 B4
Shepherdess Wlk N1 87 A1
Shepherd Ho
Barnsbury N7 14 A2
10 Poplar E14 34 A3
Shepherd Mkt W1 118 A1
SHEPHERD'S BUSH 30 A1
Shepherd's Bush Gn W12 39 B4
Shepherd's Bush Market W12 39 B4
Shepherd's Bush Mkt Sta W12 30 B1
Shepherd's Bush Overground Sta W12 39 C4
Shepherd's Bush Pl W12 39 C4
Shepherd's Bush Rd W6 39 B3
Shepherd's Bush Sta W12 39 C4
Shepherds Ct 8 W12 39 C4
Shepherd's La E9 17 C2
Shepherds Pl W1 117 B4
Shepherd St W1 118 A1
Shepherd's Wlk NW3 11 C4
Sheppard Dr SE16 40 A1
Sheppard Ho
31 Hackney E2 24 C3
8 Streatham SW2 74 C3
Shepperton Rd N1 87 B4
Sheppey Ho 16 E5 17 A4

Shepton Ct SW11 167 C4
Shepton Hos 11 E2 25 B2
Sherard Ct N19 5 A1
Sherard Ho 24 E9 17 B1
Sheraton Ho SW1 160 B4
Sheraton St W1 105 B1
Sherborne Ho
Pimlico SW1 146 B2
South Lambeth SW8 162 C1
Sherborne La EC4 123 C4
Sherborne St N1 87 B4
Sherbourne Ct SW5 142 A4
Sherbrooke Ho 9 E2 25 B3
Sherbrooke Rd SW6 154 B1
Sherbrooke Terr SW6 154 B1
Shere Ho SE1 137 B2
Sherfield Gdns SW15 56 B1
Sheridan Bldgs WC2 106 B1
Sheridan Ct
Earl's Ct SW5 142 A3
South Hampstead NW6 11 B1
South Lambeth SW9 173 A3
Sheridan Ho SE11 149 C3
7 Stoke Newington N16 7 A1
Sheridan Pl SW13 56 B4
Sheridan St 34 E1 32 A3
Sheringdale Prim Sch SW18 70 B3
Sheringham NW8 79 C4
Sheringham Ho NW1 102 B4
Sheringham Mews 4 SW18 71 B2
Sheringham Rd N7 14 C2
Sherlock Ct NW8 79 B4
Sherlock Holmes Mus NW1 91 A1
Sherlock Mews W1 103 B4
Sherren Ho 35 E1 25 B1
Sherrick Green Rd NW10 9 A3
Sherriff Ct NW6 10 C2
Sherriff Rd NW6 10 C2
Sherrin Rd E10 19 A4
Sherston Ct
Finsbury WC1 95 B3
Newington SE1 150 B4
Sherwin Ho 1 SE11 163 B4
Sherwin Rd SE14 50 C2
Sherwood NW6 10 A1
Sherwood Cl SW13 57 A4
Sherwood Ct
11 Battersea SW11 59 B4
St Johns SE13 52 A1
W1 102 C3
Sherwood Gdns
Bermondsey SE16 40 A1
Sherwood Gdns *continued*
Millwall E14 41 C2
Sherwood Ho N4 6 B4
Sherwood St W1 119 A4
Shetland Rd E3 26 B3
Shillaker Ct W3 29 B1
Shillibeer Pl W1 102 B3
Shillingford Ho 40 E3 27 A2
Shillingford St 23 N1 15 A1
Shillingstone Ho W14 126 B1
Shinfield St W12 30 B3
Shipka Rd SW12 73 A3
Ship La SW14 45 B1
Shiplake Ho 45 E2 24 B2 98 C3
Shipley Ho 32 SW8 171 B1
Ship & Mermaid Row SE1 138 A4
Ship St SE8 51 C2
Ship Tavern Pas EC3 124 A4
Shipton Ho
7 Camden Town NW5 12 C2
14 Haggerston E2 24 B3
Shipton St E2 24 B2 99 A4
Shipwright Rd SE16 41 A4
Shipwright Yd SE1 124 A1
Shirbutt St E14 34 A2
Shire Pl SW18 71 B4
Shirland Mews W9 23 B2
Shirland Rd W9 23 C1
Shirley Gr SW11 60 C4
Shirley Ho 13 SE5 48 C3
Shirley Rd W4 37 C4
Shirley St E16 35 B3
Shirlock Rd NW3 12 B4
Shoe La EC4 107 C2
Shooters Hill Rd SE3, SE10 53 A2
Shoot-Up Hill NW2 10 A2
Shopstop SW11 60 A3
Shore Bsns Ctr 31 E9 17 B1
SHOREDITCH 87 C1
Shoreditch Ct 2 E8 16 B1
Shoreditch High St Sta E2 24 B1
Shoreditch High St E2 24 A1 98 B2
Shoreditch Ho N1 97 C3
Shoreham Cl SW18 59 A2
Shore Ho SW8 61 A4
Shore Mews 30 E9 17 B1
Shore Pl E9 17 B1
Shore Rd E9 17 B1
Shorncliffe Rd SE1 152 C2
Shorrolds Rd SW6 155 A2
Shortcroft Mead Ct NW10 8 C3
Shorter St EC3 125 A4
Shortlands W6 39 C2
Short Rd W4 46 A4
Shorts Gdns WC2 106 A1
Short St SE1 135 C4
Shottendane Rd SW6 165 B4
Shottfield Ave SW14 56 A3
Shottsford 1 W11 31 C3
Shoulder of Mutton Alley 10 E14 33 A2
Shouldham St W1 102 B3
Shreveport Ho 23 N19 4 C4
Shrewsbury Ave SW14 55 C3
Shrewsbury Cres NW10 20 C4
Shrewsbury Ho
Chelsea SW3 158 A3
Kennington SE11 163 A3
Shrewsbury Mews 33 W2 31 C4
Shrewsbury Rd W2 31 C3
Shrewsbury St W10 22 B1
Shropshire Ho WC1 93 A1
Shroton St NW1 102 B4
Shrubbery Cl N1 87 A3
Shrubland Rd E8 24 C4
Shrubs Ho SW1 147 C3
Shurland Gdns SE15 49 B3
Shuters Sq W14 140 C1
Shuttle St E1 24 C1 99 B1
Shuttleworth Rd SW11 168 A2
Sibella Rd SW4 171 C1
Sicilian Ave WC1 106 B3
Sidbury St SW6 164 A4
Siddons Ct WC2 106 C1
Siddons Ho 8 NW3 12 B3
Siddons La NW1 91 A1
Sidford Ho SE1 135 A1
Sidford Pl SE1 135 A1
Sidgwick Ho 26 SW9 172 B1
Sidings Mews N7 14 C4
Sidlaw Ho N16 7 B3
Sidmouth Ho
18 Camberwell SE15 49 C3
Marylebone W1 102 B2
26 Streatham SW2 74 C4
Sidmouth Mews WC1 94 C3
Sidmouth Par NW2 9 B1
Sidmouth Rd NW2 9 B1
Sidmouth St WC1 94 C3
Sidney Boyd Ct NW6 10 C1
Sidney Godley (VC) Ho 31 E2 25 B2
Sidney Gr EC1 86 A1
Sidney Ho 4 E2 25 C3
Sidney Miller Ct 8 W3 28 A1
Sidney Rd SW9 173 A1
Sidney Sq E1 32 B4
Sidney St E1 32 B4
Sidworth St 6 E8 17 A1
Siebert Rd SE3 53 C4
Siege Ho 10 E1 32 A3
Sigdon Rd E8 16 C3
Signal Ho
9 London E8 17 A1
SE1 136 C3
Signmakers Yd NW1 82 B3
Silbury Ho 9 SE26 76 C1
Silbury St N1 97 B4
Silchester Rd W10 30 C3
Silesia Bldgs E8 17 A1
Silex St SE1 136 B3
Silkin Mews 24 SE15 49 C3
Silk Mews SE11 149 C1
Silk Mills Path SE13 67 B4
Silk Mills Sq E9 18 B2
Silk St EC2 109 A4
Sillitoe Ho N1 87 C3
Silsoe Ho NW1 82 B1
Silverbirch Wlk 1 NW3 12 C2
Silverburn Ho 4 SW9 48 A2
Silver Cl SE14 51 A3
Silver Cres W4 37 A2
Silver Ct N19 4 B1
Silverdale NW1 92 C4
Silverdale Ct EC1 96 B2
Silvermere Rd SE6 67 A1
Silver Pl W1 119 A4
Silver Rd
Shepherd's Bush W12 30 C2
St Johns SE13 67 A4
Silverthorn 17 NW6 78 B3
Silverthorne Rd SW8 170 B1
Silverton Rd W6 47 C4
Silvertown Way E16 35 C1
Silver Wlk SE16 33 B1
Silvester Ho
27 Bethnal Green E2 25 B2
1 Notting Hill W11 31 B3
6 Stepney E1 32 A3
Silvester Rd SE22 64 B2
Silvester St SE1 137 B3
Silwex Ho E1 24 B1 98 C1
Silwood St SE16 40 B1
Simla Ho SE1 137 C3
Simmonds Ct SW5 142 A3
Simmons Ho
20 Bethnal Green E2 24 C2 99 B3
Finsbury Pk N7 5 B2
Simms Ct SW6 58 A4
Simms Rd SE1 153 C3
Simon Cl W11 31 B2 113 A4
Simon Ct W9 23 C2
Simon Lo 31 SW19 69 C3
Simon Marks Jewish Prim Sch 8 N16 7 B2
Simons Wlk E15 19 C3
Simpson Dr W3 28 C3
Simpson Ho
Lisson Gr NW8 90 A3
Vauxhall SE11 148 C1
Simpson's Rd E14 34 A2
Simpson St SW11 168 A1
Sinclair Ct N5 15 B2
Sinclair Gdns W14 39 C4
Sinclair Ho 1 SW12 73 C3
Sinclair Mans 13 W12 39 C4
Sinclair Pl SE4 66 C1
Sinclair Rd W14 126 A2
Sinclairs Ho 18 E3 26 B3
Singer St EC2 97 C3
Sion Ho SE13 67 B3
Sion-Manning RC Sch for Girls
16 Kensal Town W10 31 A4
6 North Kensington W10 30 C4
Sir Abraham Dawes Cotts SW15 58 A3
Sir Alexander Cl W3 29 B1
Sir Alexander Rd W3 29 B1
Sirdar Rd W11 31 A2 112 A3
Sir Francis Drake Prim Sch 1 SE8 41 A1
Sirinham Point SW8 163 A3
Sirius Bldg 13 E1 32 C2
Sir James Barrie Prim Sch SW8 171 A3
Sir John Cass Foundation & Redcoat CE Sec Sch 19 E1 32 C4
Sir John Cass's Foundation Prim Sch EC3 110 B1
Sir John Kirk Cl 33 SE5 48 B3
Sir John Lillie Prim Sch SW6 154 B3
Sir John Soane's Mus WC2 106 C2
Sir Oswald Stoll Foundation The SW6 156 A2
Sir Thomas Abney Prim Sch N16 6 C3
Sir Thomas More Est SW3 157 C3
Sir William Burrough Prim Sch 27 E14 33 B3
Sir William Powell's Almshos SW6 58 A4
Sise La EC4 109 B1
Siskin Ho 14 SE16 40 C2
Sispara Gdns SW18 58 B1
Sissinghurst Ho 17 SE15 50 B4
Sister Mabel's Way 15 SE15 49 C3
Sisters Ave SW11 60 B3
Sisters of St Marcellina Sch 34 NW3 11 B4
Sistova Rd SW12 73 A3
Sisulu Pl SW9 62 C4
Sitarey Ct 4 W12 30 A1
Site of Changing of the Guard SW1 132 C3
Sivill Ho 9 E2 24 B2 99 A4

Siward Rd SW17 71 B1
Six Bridges Ind Est 15 SE1 153 C1
Sixth Ave W10 23 A2
Skardu Rd NW2 10 A3
Skeena Hill SW18, SW19 70 A4
Skeggs Ho 5 E14 42 B3
Skegness Ho 3 N7 14 B1
Skelbrook St SW18 71 B2
Skelgill Rd SW15 58 B3
Skelton Cl 7 E8 16 B2
Skelton Ho N16 16 A3
Skelwith Rd W6 47 B4
Skenfrith Ho SE15 50 A4
Sketchley Gdns SE16 40 C1
Skiffington Cl SW2 74 C3
Skinner Pl SW1 145 B3
Skinners Company Sch (Upper) 10 N16 7 B4
Skinners La EC4 123 A4
Skinner St EC1 95 C2
Skipsea Ho SW18 59 C1
Skipton Ho SE4 66 A3
Skipwith Bldg EC1 107 B4
Skipworth Rd E9 25 B4
Skua Ct 33 SE8 51 B4
Skyline Ct SE1 138 C1
Skyline Plaza Bldg 19 E1 111 C2
Skylines E14 42 B4
Slade Ct NW2 10 A3
Sladen Pl 12 E5 17 A4
Slagrove Pl SE13 67 A2
Slaidburn St SW10 157 A3
Slaithwaite Rd SE13 67 B3
Slaney Ct NW10 9 B1
Slaney Pl 1 N7 14 C3
Sleaford Ho 16 E3 26 C1
Sleaford Ind Est SW8 161 A1
Sleaford St SW8 161 A1
Sleat Ho 11 E3 26 B3
Slievemore Cl 8 SW4 61 C4
Sligo Ho 8 E1 25 C1
Slingsby Pl WC2 120 A4
Slippers Pl SE16 40 A3
Slipway Ho 1 E14 42 A1
Sloane Ave SW3 144 B3
Sloane Avenue Mans SW3 144 C3
Sloane Ct E SW3 145 B2
Sloane Ct W SW3 145 B2
Sloane Gate Mans SW1 145 B4
Sloane Gdns SW1 145 B3
Sloane Ho 7 E9 17 B1
Sloane Sq SW1 145 A3
Sloane Square Sta SW1 145 B3
Sloane St SW1 131 A1
Sloane Terr SW1 145 B4
Sloane Terr Mans SW1 145 B4
Sly St 17 E1 32 A3
Smallbrook Mews W2 101 B1
Smalley Cl N16 7 B1
Smart's Pl WC1, WC2 106 B2
Smart St E2 25 C2
Smeaton Ct SE1 136 C1
Smeaton Rd SW18 70 C4
Smeaton St E1 32 A1
Smedley St SW4 171 C2
Smeed Rd E3 18 C1
Smiles Pl SE13 52 B1
Smith Cl SE16 32 C1
Smithfield Mkt EC1 108 B3
Smithfield St EC1 108 A3
Smith's Ct W1 119 B4
Smith Sq SW1 134 A1
Smith St SW3 144 C1
Smith's Yd SW18 71 B2
Smith Terr SW3 144 C1
Smithwood Cl SW19 70 A2
Smithy St E1 32 B4
Smithy Street Sch 34 E1 32 B4
Smugglers Way SW18 59 A3
Smyrk's Rd SE17 152 B1
Smyrna Mans 8 NW6 10 C1
Smyrna Rd NW6 10 C1
Smythe St E14 34 A2
Snarsgate St W10 30 B4
Sneath Ave NW11 1 B4
Sneyd Rd NW2 9 B4
Snowberry Cl E11 19 C4
Snowbury Rd 6 SW6 166 B1
Snowden St EC2 24 A1 98 A1
Snowe Ho SE27 75 A1
Snow Hill EC1 108 A3
Snowman Ho NW6 78 B4
Snowsfields SE1 137 C4
Snowsfields Prim Sch SE1 138 A4
Soames St SE15 64 B4
Soane Ct 10 NW1 13 B1
Soane Ho SE17 151 C1
Soaphouse La TW8 44 A3
Sobell L Ctr N7 5 B1
SOHO 105 B1
Soho W1 105 B2
Soho Parish CE Prim Sch W1 119 B4
Soho Sq W1 105 B2
Soho St W1 105 B2
Sojourner-Truth Cl 11 E8 17 A2
Solander Gdns
13 Shadwell E1 32 B2
Stepney E1 32 A2
Soldene Ct N7 14 B2
Solebay St E1 26 A1
Solent Ho 6 E1 33 A4
Solent Rd NW6 10 C3
Soley Mews WC1 95 B4
Solidarity Ho 5 NW10 9 B2
Solna Ave SW15 57 B2
Solomon's Pas SE15 65 A3
Solon New Rd SW4 62 A3
Solon Rd SW2 62 A3
Solway Ho 12 E1 25 C1
Solway Rd SE22 64 C3
Somali Rd NW2 10 B3
Somborne Ho 11 SW15 68 C4
Sombrook Ho SE11 149 B3
Somer Ct SW6 155 B3
Somerfield Rd N4 6 A2
Somerfield St SE16 40 C1
Somerford Gr N16 16 B4
Somerford Grove Est N16 16 B4
Somerford St E1 25 A1
Somerford Way SE16 41 A4
Somerleyton Rd SW9 62 C3
Somers Cl NW1 83 B2
Somers Cres W2 102 A1
Somerset Gdns
Highgate N6 3 C4
St Johns SE13 52 A1
Somerset Ho WC2 121 A4
Somerset Ho SW19 70 A1
Somerset Lo SW15 57 A3
Somerset Rd
Bedford Pk W4 37 C3
Wimbledon SW19 70 A1
Somerset Sq W14 126 C3
Somers Pl SW2 74 B4
Somers Rd SW2 62 B1
SOMERS TOWN 93 C4
Somers Town Est NW1 83 A1
Somerton Ave TW9 55 A4
Somerton Rd
Cricklewood NW2 1 A1
Nunhead SE15 65 A3
Somerville Ave SW13 47 B4
Somerville Cl SW9 173 A2
Somerville Ho 10 SW15 57 C1
Somerville Point SE16 41 B4
Sonderburg Rd 13 N7 5 B2
Sondes St SE17 48 C4
Sonia Gdns NW10 8 B4
Sonning Ho 32 E2 24 B2 98 C3
Sophia Cl N7 14 B2
Sophia Ho 10 W6 39 B1
Sophia Sq 14 SE16 33 A2
Sopwith Way SW8 160 A2
Sorrel La 17 E14 34 C3
Sorrell Cl
6 Brixton SW9 173 C2
SE14 51 A3
Soseki Mus SW4 61 A4
Sotheby Rd N5 15 B4
Sotheran Cl E8 24 C4
Sotheron Pl SW6 156 B1
Soudan Rd SW11 168 C3
Souldern Rd 10 W14 39 C3
SOUTH ACTON 37 A3
South Acton Sta W3, W4 37 B3
South Africa Rd W12 30 A2
Southall Pl SE1 137 B3
Southam Ho 9 W10 23 A1
Southampton Bldgs WC2 107 B3
Southampton Pl WC1 106 B3
Southampton Rd NW5 12 B3
Southampton Row WC1 106 B4
Southampton St WC2 120 B4
Southampton Way SE5 49 A3
Southam St W10 23 A1
South Audley St W1 117 C2
South Ave TW9 44 C1
SOUTH BANK 120 C1
South Bank Bsns Ctr SW8 161 C3
Southbank International Sch 14 NW3 11 B2
Southbank International Sch (Westminster Campus) W1 104 A4
Southbank Int Sch W11 31 C2 113 B3
South Bank Univ SW8 171 C4
South Bank University (Erlang House) SE1 136 A3
South Bermondsey Sta SE16 40 B1
South Black Lion La 7 W6 38 C1
South Bldg SW1 133 A2
South Block 20 E1 32 B2
South Bolton Gdns SW10 142 B2
Southborough Ho SE17 152 B2
Southborough Rd E9 25 C4
SOUTH BROMLEY 34 C4
South Building SE10 52 C3
Southbury NW8 79 A4
South Camden Com Sch NW1 83 B2
South Carriage Dr SW1, SW7 130 C4
South Chelsea Coll 22 SW9 62 B3
South Colonnade The E14 34 A1
Southcombe St W14 140 A4
Southcote Rd N19 13 B4
Southcott Ho
31 Bromley E3 27 A2
W9 89 A1
South Cres
Newham E16 27 C1
WC1 105 B3
Southcroft 8 NW10 20 C4
South Ct 17 SW15 57 C1
Southdean Gdns SW19 70 B2
Southdown N7 14 A2
South Eastern Univ 3 N7 5 B1
South Eaton Pl SW1 145 C4
South Edwardes Sq W8 127 B1
South End W8 128 B2
South End Cl NW3 12 A4
South End Gn NW3 12 A4
South End Rd NW3 12 A4
South End Row W8 128 B2
Southerngate Way SE14 51 A3
Southern Gr E3 26 B1
Southern Row W10 23 A1
Southern St N1 84 C2
Southern Way SE10 43 B3
Southernwood Ret Pk SE1 153 A2
Southerton Rd W6 39 B2
Southey Ho SE17 151 A2
Southey Mews E16 35 C1
Southey Rd SW9 173 B4
Southfield Lo W4 37 C4
Southfield Prim Sch W4 38 A4
Southfield Rd W4 37 C4
SOUTHFIELDS 71 A3
Southfields Com Coll SW18 70 C3
Southfields Rd SW18 58 C1
Southfields Sta SW18 70 B3
Southgate Ct N1 15 C1
Southgate Gr N1 15 C1
Southgate Rd N1 87 C4
South Gr N6 3 C3
South Grove Ho N6 3 C3
SOUTH HACKNEY 25 B4
SOUTH HAMPSTEAD 11 B1
South Hampstead High Sch 11 NW3 11 C2
South Hampstead Sta NW8 11 B1
South Hill Pk NW3 12 A4
South Hill Pk Gdns NW3 12 A4
Southill St E14 34 A3
South Island Pl SW9 163 B1
SOUTH KENSINGTON 143 A3
South Kensington Sta SW7 143 C4
South Kensington Station Arc SW7 143 C4
SOUTH LAMBETH 172 B3
South Lambeth Pl SW8 162 B4
South Lambeth Rd SW8 162 B2
Southlands Dr SW19 69 C2

South Lo NW8 89 B4
South London Gall SE5 49 A2
South London Montessori Sch SW11 168 A3
Southmead Prim Sch 16 SW19 70 A3
Southmead Rd SW19 70 A3
South Molton La W1 104 A1
South Molton Rd E16 35 C3
South Molton St W1 104 A1
Southmoor Way E9 18 B3
Southolm St SW11 170 B3
South Par W4 37 C2
South Parade SW3 143 C2
South Park Mews SW6 59 A4
South Pl EC2 109 C3
South Pl Mews EC2 109 C3
South Quay Plaza E14 42 A4
South Quay Sta E14 42 A4
South Rise W2 116 B4
South Row SE3 53 B1
South Sea St SE16 41 B3
Southside N7 13 C4
South Side W6 38 B3
Southside Ind Est SW8 170 C4
Southside Quarter 4 SW11 168 C2
Southside Sh Ctr SW18 59 A1
South Sq WC1 107 B3
South St W1 117 C2
South Tenter St E1 111 A1
South Terr SW7 144 A4
South Thames Coll (Putney Ctr) 12 SW15 57 C2
South Thames Coll (Roehampton Ctr) SW15 56 C1
South Thames Coll (Wandsworth Ctr) 7 SW18 59 A2
Southvale Rd SE3 53 A1
Southview Ave NW10 8 B3
South Villas NW1 13 C2
Southville
- London SW8 171 C3
- South Lambeth SW8 172 A3

SOUTHWARK 40 B2
Southwark Bridge SE1, EC4 123 A3
Southwark Bridge Rd SE1 123 A1
Southwark Cath SE1 123 B2
Southwark Coll SE1 136 A4
Southwark Coll (Blackfriars Ctr) SE1 122 A1
Southwark Coll (Camberwell Ctr) 17 SE5 49 A3
Southwark Coll (Grange Ctr) SE1 138 B1
Southwark Coll (Surrey Docks Ctr) 12 SE16 40 A3
Southwark Park Est 11 SE16 40 A2
Southwark Park Prim Sch 19 SE16 40 A3
Southwark Park Rd SE16 153 B4
Southwark Pk Sports Complex SE16 40 B2
Southwark St SE1 122 C1
Southwark Sta SE1 122 A1
Southwater Cl 8 E14 33 B3
Southway Cl 9 W12 39 A4
Southwell Gdns SW7 142 C3
Southwell Ho
- 8 Bermondsey SE16 40 A2
- 13 Stoke Newington N16 16 A3

Southwell Rd SE5 63 B4
South Wharf Rd W2 101 C2
Southwick Mews W2 101 C2
Southwick Pl W2 102 A1
Southwick St W2 102 A2
Southwick Yd W2 102 A1
Southwold Mans W9 23 C2
Southwood Ave N6 4 A4
Southwood Ct EC1 96 A3
Southwood Ho W11 31 A2 112 A4
Southwood Hts N6 4 A4
Southwood La N6 3 C4
Southwood Lawn Rd N6 4 A4
Southwood Park N6 3 C4
Southwood Smith Ho 4 E2 25 A2
Southwood Smith St N1 86 A3
South Worple Ave SW14 56 A4
Southwyck Ho SW9 62 C3
South Yd EC1 109 B4
Sovereign Cl E1 32 A2
Sovereign Cres SE16 33 A2
Sovereign Ct
- 3 Richmond TW9 54 B3
- 13 Stepney E1 32 A2

Sovereign Ho 23 E1 25 A1
Sovereign Mews 6 E2 24 B3
Sovereign Pk NW10 20 A1
Space Bsns Pk NW10 20 A2
Spa Ct 12 SE16 139 B1
Spafield St EC1 95 B2
Spalding Ho SE4 66 A2
Spanby Rd E3 26 C1
Spaniards Cl NW11 2 C3
Spaniards End NW3 2 C3
Spaniards Rd NW3 2 B2
Spanish Billingual Sch W10 31 A4
Spanish Pl W1 103 C2
Spanish Rd SW18 59 B2
Spa Rd SE16 139 A1
Sparke Terr 2 E16 35 B3
Sparkford Ho SW11 167 C4
Sparks Cl W3 28 C3
Sparsholt Rd N19 5 B3
Sparta St SE10 52 B2
Spa Sch SE1 153 B4
Spa View 6 SW16 74 B1
Speakers' Corner W1 117 A4
Speakman Ho SE4 66 A4
Spear Mews SW5 141 C3
Spears Rd N19 5 A3
Spectrum Ho NW5 12 C4
Spedan Cl NW3 2 B1
Speechly Mews E8 16 B3
Speed Ho EC2 109 B4
Speedwell St 5 SE8 51 C3
Speedy Pl WC1 94 A3
Speldhurst Rd
- Bedford Pk W4 37 C3
- Homerton E9 17 C1

Spellbrook Wlk N1 87 A4
Spelman Ho 15 E1 111 B3
Spelman St E1 111 B4
Spence Cl SE16 41 B4
Spencer Gdns SW14 55 B2
Spencer Ho
- 31 Clapham SW8 171 B1
- 24 Putney SW19 69 C3
- Vale of Health NW3 2 C1
- Wimbledon SW19 69 C1

Spencer House Mus SW1 118 C1
Spencer Mews
- Fulham W6 154 A4
- South Lambeth SW9 172 C3

Spencer Park Ct SW18 59 C2
Spencer Pk SW18 59 C2
Spencer Pl
- 16 Islington N1 15 A1
- SW1 133 A1

Spencer Rd
- Acton W3 28 B1
- Chiswick W4 45 B3
- Wandsworth SW18 59 C2

Spencer Rise NW5 4 A1
Spencer St EC1 96 A3
Spencer Way 35 E1 32 A3
Spencer Wlk
- 23 Hampstead NW3 11 B4
- Putney SW15 57 C3

Spencer Yd SE3 53 B1
Spenlow Ho 2 SE16 139 C2
Spenser Gr N16 16 A4
Spenser Mews SE21 75 C3
Spenser Rd SE24 63 A2
Spenser St SW1 133 A2
Spens Ho WC1 94 C1
Spensley Wlk N16 6 C1
Spert St E14 33 A2
Spey St E14 34 B4
Spezia Rd NW10 21 C3
Spice Ct
- 10 Battersea SW11 59 B4
- 2 St George in t East E1 125 C2

Spice Quay Htss SE1 125 A1
Spicer Cl SE5, SW9 48 A1
Spicer Ho E2 24 C2 99 B3
Spindrift Ave E14 42 A2
Spinnaker Ho 21 E14 41 C4
Spinney The
- Barnes SW13 47 A4
- Streatham SW16 73 C1

Spire Ct 10 TW10 54 A1
Spire Ho W2 115 A4
Spirit Quay E1 32 A1
SPITALFIELDS 111 A4
Spital Sq E1 110 B4
Spital St E1 111 B4
Spital Yd E1 110 B4
Splendour Wlk SE16 40 B1
Spode Ho SE11 135 B1
Spode Wlk NW3 11 A3
Sporle Ct 5 SW11 59 C4
Sprewell SW15 58 A1
Spriggs Ho 14 N1 15 A1
Sprimont Pl SW3 144 C2
Springall St 9 SE15 50 A3
Springalls Wharf 2 SE16 139 B4
Springbank Wlk NW1 13 C1
Spring Cott 10 W12 38 C4
Spring Ct NW2 10 B2
Springdale Rd N16 15 C4
Springett Ho 18 SW2 62 B2
Springfield Ct
- 7 Dagenham W3 28 B3
- Hampstead NW3 12 A1

Springfield Ho
- Acton W3 28 B1
- 1 Camberwell SE5 49 A1
- 13 Dalston E8 16 B2

Springfield La NW6 78 A3
Springfield Rd NW8 79 A3
Springfield University Hospl SW17 72 A1
Springfield Wlk NW6 78 A3
Spring Gdns
- Islington N5 15 B3
- SW1 120 A2

Spring Gr W4 44 C4
Spring Grove Rd TW10 54 B2
Spring Hill E5 7 C4
Springhill Cl SE5 63 C4
Spring Ho WC1 95 B3
Spring Mews W1 103 A4
Springpark Dr N4 6 B3
Spring Pl NW5 13 A3
Springrice Rd SE13 67 C1
Spring St W2 101 B1
Spring Terr TW10 54 A2
Springtide Cl 10 SE15 49 C2
Springvale Ave TW8 36 A1
Springvale Terr 5 W14 39 C3
Springwater WC1 106 C4
Springwell Ave NW10 21 B4
Spring Wlk E1 111 C4
Springwood Cl 8 E3 26 C3
Spruce Ct W5 36 A3
Spruce Ho 15 SE16 40 C4
Sprules Rd SE4 51 A1
Spurgeon St SE1 137 B2
Spurling Rd SE22 64 B3
Spur Rd SE1 135 B4
Spurstowe Rd E8 17 A2
Spurstowe Terr E8 17 A3
Square Rigger Row 7 SW11 59 B4
Square The
- Hammersmith W6 39 B1
- SW6 165 B3

Squarey St SW17 71 B1
Squire Gdns NW8 89 B3
Squires Ct SW4 172 B3
Squire's Mount NW3 2 C1
Squirrels The SE13 67 C4
Squirries St E2 24 C2 99 C3
Stable Ho 9 SE16 40 B4
Stables Way SE11 149 B2
Stable Way W10 30 B3
Stable Yd Rd SW1 133 A4
Stacey St
- Highbury N7 5 C1
- Soho WC2 105 C1

Stack Ho SW1 145 C3
Stackhouse St SW1 130 C2
Stacy Path 13 SE5 49 A3
Stadium St SW10 157 A1
Stafford Cl NW6 23 C2
Stafford Cripps Ho
- 30 Bethnal Green E2 25 B2
- SW6 155 A3

Stafford Ct
- Kensington W8 127 C2
- South Lambeth SW8 172 A4

Stafford Ho SE1 153 A2
Stafford Mans
- 13 Hammersmith W14 39 C3
- 14 Stockwell SW4 62 A3
- SW11 158 C1

Stafford Pl SW1 .. 132 C2
Stafford Rd
Bow E3 ... 26 B3
Maida Vale NW6 ... 23 C2
Staffordshire St
Peckham SE15 ... 49 C2
Peckham SE15 ... 50 A2
Stafford St W1 ... 118 C2
Stafford Terr W8 .. 127 B2
Stag La SW15 ... 68 B2
Stagshaw Ho 17 SE22 ... 64 A4
Stainer St SE1 ... 123 C1
Staining La EC2 .. 109 A2
Stainsbury St 25 E2 ... 25 B3
Stainsby Rd E14 ... 33 C3
Stalbridge Flats W1 ... 103 C1
Stalbridge Ho NW1 ... 82 C1
Stalbridge St NW1 ... 102 B4
Stalham St SE16 ... 40 A3
Stambourne Ho SW8 ... 172 B4
Stamford Bridge Stadium (Chelsea FC) SW6 ... 156 A2
Stamford Brook Ave W6 ... 38 B3
Stamford Brook Gdns 1 W6 ... 38 B3
Stamford Brook Mans 2 W6 ... 38 B2
Stamford Brook Rd W6 ... 38 B3
Stamford Brook Sta W6 ... 38 B2
Stamford Cl 2 NW3 ... 2 B1
Stamford Cotts SW10 ... 156 B2
Stamford Ct W6 ... 38 C2
Stamford Gr E 1 N16 ... 7 C3
Stamford Gr W 4 N16 ... 7 C3
STAMFORD HILL ... 7 A3
Stamford Hill N16 ... 7 B3
Stamford Hill Mans 1 N16 ... 7 B3
Stamford Hill Sta N16 ... 7 A4
Stamford Lo 2 N16 . 7 B4
Stamford Mans 2 N16 ... 7 C3
Stamford Rd N1 ... 16 A2
Stamford St SE1 .. 121 C2
Stamp Pl E2 .. 24 B2 99 A4
Stanard Cl N16 ... 7 A4
Stanborough Ho 4 E3 ... 27 A1
Stanborough Pas E8 ... 16 B2
Stanbridge Mans SW15 ... 57 B4
Stanbridge Rd SW15 ... 57 B4
Stanbrook Ct W1 118 C2
Stanbury Ct 16 NW3 ... 12 B2
Stanbury Rd
Nunhead SE15 ... 50 B1
Peckham SE15 ... 50 A1
Standard Pl 13 EC2 ... 24 A2 98 B3
Standard Rd NW10 ... 20 C1
Standen Rd SW18 .. 70 C4
Standish Ho 6 W6 ... 38 C2
Standish Rd W6 ... 38 C2
Stanesgate Ho 20 SE15 ... 49 C3
Stanfield Ho NW8 . 89 C2
Stanfield Rd 14 E3 .. 26 A3
Stanford Ct
Kensington W8 ... 128 B1
Walham Green SW6 ... 166 B3
Stanford Pl SE1 .. 152 A3
Stanford Rd W8 .. 128 B2
Stanford St SW1 .. 147 B3
Stangate SE1 ... 135 A2
Stanhope Cl 28 SE16 ... 40 C4
Stanhope Gate W1 ... 117 C2
Stanhope Gdns SW7 ... 143 A4
Stanhope Ho
4 Putney SW15 ... 57 B2
SE8 ... 51 B3
Stanhope Mews E SW7 ... 143 A4
Stanhope Mews S SW7 ... 143 A3
Stanhope Mews W SW7 ... 143 A4
Stanhope Par NW1 92 C4
Stanhope Pl W2 .. 102 C1
Stanhope Rd N6 ... 4 B4
Stanhope Row W1 ... 118 A1
Stanhope St NW1 .. 92 C3
Stanhope Terr W2 ... 115 C4
Stanier Cl SW5 ... 141 A1
Stanlake Mews 7 W12 ... 30 B1
Stanlake Rd W12 ... 30 B1
Stanlake Villas 8 W12 ... 30 B1
Stanley Cl SW8 ... 162 C3
Stanley Cohen Ho EC1 ... 96 C1
Stanley Cres W11 ... 31 B2 112 C4
Stanley Gdns
Bedford Pk W3 ... 38 A4
Cricklewood NW2 ... 9 B3
W11 ... 31 B2 112 C4
Stanley Gr SW11 .. 169 C1
Stanley Ho
35 Clapham SW8 .. 171 B1
22 Poplar E14 ... 33 C3
Stanley Holloway Ct E16 ... 35 C3
Stanley Mans SW10 ... 157 A4
Upper Tooting SW17 ... 72 B2
Stanley Rd
Acton Green W3 ... 37 B3
Mill Meads E15 ... 27 C4
Mortlake SW14 ... 55 A3
Stanley St SE14, SE8 ... 51 B3
Stanley Studios SW10 ... 157 A4
Stanley Terr 8 N19 .. 5 A2
Stanliff Ho 8 E14 .. 41 C3
Stanmer St SW11 . 168 B2
Stanmore Gdns TW9 ... 54 B4
Stanmore Ho 21 SW8 ... 171 C2
Stanmore Pl NW1 . 82 B4
Stanmore Rd TW9 .. 54 B4
Stanmore St N1 ... 84 C4
Stannard Cotts 27 E1 ... 25 B1
Stannard Mews E8 ... 16 C2
Stannard Rd E8 ... 16 C2
Stannary Pl SE11 . 149 C1
Stannary St SE11 . 149 C1
Stansbury Sq 3 W10 ... 23 A2
Stansfeld Ho SE1 153 A3
Stansfield Rd SW9 .. 62 B4
Stanstead Ho E3 .. 27 B1
Stansted Express Terminal EC2 ... 110 A4
Stanswood Gdns SE5 ... 49 A3
Stanton Ct N16 ... 6 C4
Stanton Ho 9 SE10 ... 52 B4
Stanton Rd SW13 ... 46 B1
Stanway Ct 23 N1 .. 24 A3
Stanway St N1 ... 24 A3
Stanwick Rd W14 140 C3
Stanworth St SE1 139 A3
Staplefield Cl 3 SW2 ... 74 A3
Stapleford Cl SW19 ... 70 A4
Staplehurst Ct 1 SW11 ... 60 B1
Staplehurst Ho 18 E5 ... 17 A3
Staple Inn WC2 ... 107 B3
Staple Inn Bldgs WC2 ... 107 B3
Staples Cl SE16 ... 33 A1
Staple St SE1 ... 137 C3
Stapleton Hall N4 ... 5 B4
Stapleton Hall Rd N4 ... 5 B4
Stapleton Ho 19 E2 ... 25 A2
Stapleton Rd SW17 ... 72 C1
Star Alley EC3 ... 124 B4
Starboard Way E14 ... 41 C3
Starcross St NW1 .. 93 A3
StarDome NW1 ... 91 B1
Starfield Rd W12 ... 38 C4
Star & Garter Mans 8 SW15 ... 57 C4
Star Lane Sta E16 .. 35 A4
Starliner Ct N7 ... 14 C2
Starling Ho NW8 .. 80 A2
Star Pl E1 ... 125 A3
Star Rd W14 ... 140 C1
Star St W2 ... 102 A2
Star Works NW10 .. 21 C2
Star Yd WC2 ... 107 B2
Statham Ct N7 ... 5 A1
Statham Gr N16 ... 6 C1
Statham Ho SW8 . 170 C4
Station App
Dagenham NW10 ... 21 B2
Fulham SW6 ... 58 A4
Station App *continued*
Richmond TW9 ... 44 C2
Station Approach Rd W4 ... 45 B3
Station Approach Road SE1 ... 135 B4
Station Ave
5 Brixton SW9 ... 63 A4
14 Richmond TW9 ... 44 C2
Station Cres SE3 ... 43 C1
Station Ct 5 SE15 .. 50 B1
Stationers Hall Ct EC4 ... 108 B1
Station Gdns W4 ... 45 B3
Station Mews Terr 4 SE3 ... 43 C1
Station Par
Cricklewood NW2 ... 9 B2
Richmond TW9 ... 44 C2
4 Upper Tooting SW12 ... 72 C3
Station Pas SE15 ... 50 B2
Station Pl N4 ... 5 C2
Station Rd
Barnes SW13 ... 46 B1
Camden Town N19 ... 4 B1
Harlesden NW10 ... 21 B3
Lewisham SE13 ... 67 B4
Station Rise SE27 ... 75 A2
Station St E15 ... 19 C1
Station Terr
Camberwell SE5 ... 48 B2
Kensal Rise NW10 ... 22 C3
Staunton Ho SE17 152 A3
Staunton St SE8 ... 51 B4
Staveley NW1 ... 92 C4
Staveley Cl
Hackney E9 ... 17 B3
Lower Holloway N7 .. 14 A4
New Cross Gate SE15 ... 50 B2
8 Peckham SE15 ... 50 A2
Staveley Gdns W4 .. 45 C2
Staveley Ho SE4 ... 66 A2
Staveley Rd W4 ... 45 C3
Stavers Ho 31 E3 ... 26 B3
Staverton Rd NW2 ... 9 B1
Stave Yard Rd SE16 ... 33 A1
Stavordale Lo W14 ... 127 A2
Stavordale Rd N5 .. 15 A4
Stayner's Rd E1 ... 25 C1
Steadman Ct EC1 .. 97 A2
Stead St SE17 ... 151 B3
Stean St E8 ... 24 B4
Stebbing Ho 8 W11 ... 30 C1
Stebondale St E14 .. 42 B2
Stebon Prim Sch 26 E14 ... 33 C4
Stedham Pl WC1 . 106 A2
Steedman St SE17 ... 150 C3
Steele Rd
Acton Green W4 ... 37 B3
Becontree NW10 ... 20 B3
Steele's Mews N NW3 ... 12 B2
Steele's Mews S NW3 ... 12 B2
Steele's Rd NW3 ... 12 B2
Steel's La 23 E1 ... 32 B3
Steen Way 7 SE22 ... 64 A2
Steep Hill SW16 ... 73 C1
Steeple Cl SW6 ... 164 B1
Steeple Ct 19 E1 ... 25 A1
Steeple Wlk N1 ... 87 A4
Steerforth St SW18 ... 71 B2
Steers Way SE16 ... 41 A4
Stelfax Ho WC1 ... 95 A4
Stellman Cl E5 ... 7 C1
Stephan Cl E8 ... 24 C4
Stephen Ct 18 SW19 ... 69 C3
Stephendale Rd SW6 ... 166 C2
Stephen Fox Ho 7 W4 ... 38 A1
Stephen Hawking Sch 23 E14 ... 33 A3
Stephen Mews W1 ... 105 B3
Stephen Pl SW4 ... 61 B4
Stephen Saunders Ct SW11 ... 60 A2
Stephens Ct SE4 ... 66 A4
Stephenson Ho
2 Gospel Oak NW5 ... 13 A4
6 Maitland Pk NW3 ... 12 B3
Newington SE1 ... 136 C2
Stephenson St
Dagenham NW10 ... 21 B2
Newham E16 ... 35 A4
Stephenson Way NW1 ... 93 A2
Stephen St W1 ... 105 B3
STEPNEY ... 32 C4
Stepney City E1 ... 32 B4
Stepney City Farm E1 ... 32 C4
Stepney E1 ... 32 C4
Stepney Cswy E1 ... 32 C3
Stepney Gn E1 ... 32 C4
Stepney Greencoat CE Prim Sch The 26 E14 ... 33 B3
Stepney Green Ct 4 E1 ... 32 C4
Stepney Green Maths & Computing Coll 18 E1 ... 32 C4
Stepney Green Sta E1 ... 25 C1
Stepney High St E1 ... 32 C4
Stepney Way E1 ... 32 B4
Sterling Cl NW10 ... 8 C1
Sterling Gdns SE14 ... 51 A4
Sterling Pl W5 ... 36 A2
Sterling St SW7 .. 130 B2
Sterndale Rd W14 .. 39 C3
Sterne St W12 ... 39 C4
Sternhall La SE15 ... 64 C4
Sternhold Ave SW12, SW2 ... 73 C2
Sterry St SE1 ... 137 B3
Steve Biko Ct W10 .. 22 C1
Steve Biko Rd N7 ... 5 C1
Stevedore St 3 E1 ... 32 A1
Stevenage Rd SW6 ... 47 C2
Stevens Ave E9 ... 17 B2

Stevenson Cres SE16 ... 40 A1
Stevenson Ho
1 Battersea SW11 ... 168 C1
6 Clapham Pk SW2 ... 62 A2
NW8 ... 78 C4
Stevens St SE1 ... 138 B2
Steventon Rd W12 .. 29 B2
Stewart Headlam Prim Sch 28 E1 ... 25 A1
Stewart Ho SE1 .. 138 A1
Stewart Rd E15 ... 19 C4
Stewart's Gr SW3 144 A2
Stewart's Rd SW8 170 C4
Stewart St E14 ... 42 B4
Stew La EC4 ... 122 C4
Steyne Ho
15 Acton W3 ... 28 A1
11 Acton W3 ... 28 B1
Steyne Rd W3 ... 28 A1
Stifford Ho E1 ... 32 B4
Stile Hall Gdns W4 ... 36 C1
Stile Hall Par 6 W4 ... 36 C1
Stileman Ho 4 E3 .. 33 B4
Stillingfleet Rd SW13 ... 46 C4
Stillington St SW1 ... 147 A4
Stillness Jun & Inf Schs SE23 ... 66 A1
Stillness Rd SE23 ... 66 B1
Stirling Ct
Clerkenwell EC1 ... 96 A2
Strand WC2 ... 106 C1
Stirling Mans NW6 . 11 B2
Stirling Rd
South Acton W3 ... 37 A3
Stockwell SW9 ... 172 B1
Stoatley Ho 10 SW15 ... 68 C3
Stockbeck NW1 ... 83 A1
Stockfield Rd SW16 ... 74 B1
Stockholm Ho E1 125 C4
Stockholm Rd SE16 ... 40 B1
Stockholm Way E1 ... 125 B2
Stockhurst Cl SW15 ... 47 C1
Stockleigh Hall NW8 ... 80 B2
Stock Orchard Cres N7 ... 14 B3
Stock Orchard St N7 ... 14 B3
Stocks Ct 5 E1 ... 25 C1
Stocks Pl 16 E14 ... 33 B2
Stockton Ho 16 E2 . 25 A2
STOCKWELL ... 62 A4
Stockwell Ave SW9 ... 62 B4
Stockwell Gdns SW9 ... 172 C3
Stockwell Gn SW9 ... 172 C1
Stockwell La SW9 172 C1
Stockwell Park Cres SW9 ... 173 A2
Stockwell Park High Sch SW9 ... 172 C3
Stockwell Park Rd SW9 ... 173 A3
Stockwell Park Wlk SW9 ... 62 C4
Stockwell Prim Sch 6 SW9 ... 62 B4
Stockwell St SE10 .. 52 B4
Stockwell Sta SW4 ... 172 B2
Stockwell Terr SW9 ... 172 C3
Stoddart Ho SW8 163 A3
Stodmarsh Ho 28 SW9 ... 173 C4
Stoford Cl 4 SW19 ... 70 A4
Stokenchurch St SW6 ... 166 A3
STOKE NEWINGTON ... 7 A2
Stoke Newington Church St N16 ... 7 A2
Stoke Newington Comm N16 ... 7 B2
Stoke Newington High St N16 ... 7 B1
Stoke Newington Rd N16 ... 16 B4
Stoke Newington Sch N16 ... 6 C1
Stoke Newington Sta N16 ... 7 B2
Stoke Pl NW10 ... 21 B2
Stokesley St W12 ... 29 B3
Stondon Pk SE23 ... 66 A1
Stone Bldgs WC2 107 A3
STONEBRIDGE ... 20 B4
Stonebridge Ctr 6 NW10 ... 20 C4
Stonebridge Prim Sch NW10 ... 20 C4
Stone Cl SW4 ... 171 A1
Stonecutter St EC4 ... 108 A2
Stonefield N4 ... 5 B2
Stonefield Mans N1 ... 85 B3
Stonefield St N1 ... 85 C4
Stonegate 8 NW5 .. 12 C2
Stonehill Cl SW14 .. 55 C2
Stonehill Rd
Brentford W4 ... 36 C1
Mortlake SW14 ... 55 C2
Stonehills Ct SE21 .. 76 A1
Stonehill's Mans 3 SW16 ... 74 A2
Stonehouse NW1 .. 83 A3
Stonehouse Ct EC2 ... 110 B2
Stonehouse Ho 27 W2 ... 31 C4
Stoneleigh Lo 13 TW9 ... 44 B2
Stoneleigh Mews 15 E3 ... 26 A3
Stoneleigh Pl W11 .. 30 C2
Stoneleigh St W11 .. 30 C2
Stoneleigh Terr N19 ... 4 A2
Stonell's Rd SW11 .. 60 B2
Stonenest St N4 ... 5 B3
Stones End St SE1 ... 136 C3
Stoneyard La E14 ... 34 A2
Stoney La EC3 ... 110 B2
Stoney St SE1 ... 123 B2
Stonhouse St SW4 .. 61 C3
Stonor Rd W14 ... 140 C3
Stopes St SE15 ... 49 B3
Stopford Rd SE17 . 150 B1
Stopher Ho SE1 .. 136 B3
Storace Ho 6 SW4 ... 62 A3
Storers Quay E14 ... 42 C2
Store St
Bloomsbury WC1 ... 105 B4
Stratford New Town E15 ... 19 C3
Storey Ct NW8 ... 89 B3
Storey Ho 13 E14 ... 34 A2
Storey's Gate SW1 ... 133 C3
Stories Rd SE5 ... 64 A4
Storks Rd SE16 ... 139 C1
Stormont House Sch E5 ... 17 A4
Stormont Rd
Clapham SW11 ... 60 C3
Highgate N6 ... 3 B4
Storrington WC1 .. 94 B3
Story St N1 ... 14 B1
Stothard Ho 25 E1 .. 25 B1
Stothard Pl E2 ... 110 B4
Stothard St 12 E1 .. 25 B1
Stott Cl SW18 ... 59 C1
Stoughton Cl
Roehampton SW15 ... 68 C3
SE11 ... 149 A3
Stourcliffe Cl W1 102 C2
Stourcliffe St W1 102 C1
Stourhead Cl 6 SW19 ... 69 C4
Stour Rd E3 ... 18 C1
Stowage SE8 ... 52 A4
Stowe Ho 11 N16 ... 7 A1
Stowe Rd W12 ... 39 A4
Stracey Rd NW10 ... 20 C4
Stradbroke Rd N5 .. 15 B4
Stradella Rd SE24 .. 63 B1
Straffan Lo 8 NW3 ... 12 A2
Strafford Ho 9 SE8 ... 41 B1
Strafford Rd W3 ... 37 B4
Strafford St E14 ... 41 C4
Strahan Rd E3 ... 26 A2
Straightsmouth SE10 ... 52 B3
Straker's Rd SE15 .. 65 A3
Strale Ho 17 N1 ... 24 A4
STRAND ... 120 C4
Strand
Strand WC2 ... 120 C4
Strand WC2 ... 107 A1
Strand Dr TW9 ... 45 A3
Strand La WC2 ... 121 A4
STRAND ON THE GREEN ... 44 C4
Strand-on-the-Green W4 ... 44 C4
Strand-on-the-Green Schs 5 W4 ... 44 C4
Strang Ho N1 ... 86 C3
Strangways Terr W14 ... 126 C1
Stranraer Way N1 .. 14 A1
Strasburg Rd SW11 ... 170 A3
STRATFORD ... 19 B2
Stratford Bus Sta E15 ... 19 C1
Stratford Coll (Newham 6th Form Coll) E15 ... 19 C2
Stratford Gr SW15 .. 57 C3
Stratford High St Sta E15 ... 27 C4
Stratford International Sta E15 ... 19 B2
STRATFORD MARSH ... 27 A4
STRATFORD NEW TOWN ... 19 B3
Stratford Pl W1 .. 104 A1
Stratford Rd W8 .. 127 C1
Stratford Sh Ctr E15 ... 19 C1
Stratford Sta E15 ... 19 C1
Stratford Studios W8 ... 128 A1
Stratford Villas NW1 ... 13 C1
Stratford Workshops E15 ... 27 C4
Strathan Cl SW18 ... 58 A1
Strathblaine Rd SW11 ... 59 C3
Strathdon Dr SW17 ... 71 C1
Strathearn Ho W2 ... 116 A4
Strathearn Pl W2 116 A4
Stratheden Par SE3 ... 53 C3
Stratheden Rd SE3 ... 53 C3
Strathleven Rd SW2 ... 62 A2
Strathmore Ct NW8 ... 90 A4
Strathmore Gdns W8 ... 31 C1 113 C2
Strathmore Rd SW19 ... 70 C1
Strathnairn St SE1 ... 153 C3
Strathray Gdns NW3 ... 12 A2
Strath Terr SW11 ... 60 A3
Strathville Rd SW18 ... 71 A2
Stratton Ct 4 N1 ... 16 A1
Strattondale St E14 ... 42 B3
Stratton St W1 ... 118 B2
Strauss Rd W4 ... 37 C4
Streamline Mews SE22 ... 76 C3
Streatham Cl SW16 ... 74 A2
Streatham & Clapham High Sch SW16 ... 73 C1
Streatham Ct SW16 ... 74 A1
STREATHAM HILL .. 74 A3
Streatham Hill SW2 ... 74 A3
Streatham Hill & Clapham High Sch 14 SW2 ... 74 B3
Streatham Hill Sta SW2 ... 74 A2
Streatham Pl SW2 .. 74 A4
Streatham St WC1 ... 106 A2
Streathbourne Rd SW17 ... 72 C1
Streathem Wells Prim Sch SW2 ... 74 C2
Streatleigh Par 4 SW16 ... 74 A2
Streatley Pl
27 Hampstead NW3 ... 11 B4
Hampstead NW3 ... 11 C4
Streatley Rd NW6 ... 10 B1
Streimer Rd E15 ... 27 B3
Strelley Way W3 ... 29 A2
Stretton Mans 16 SE8 ... 51 C4
Strickland Ct SE15 .. 64 C4
Strickland Ho 26 E2 ... 24 B2 99 A3
Strickland Row SW18 ... 71 C4
Strickland St SE8 ... 51 C2
Stringer Hos 19 N1 ... 24 A4
Strode Ho 3 SW2 .. 74 C3
Strode Rd
SW6 ... 154 A2
Willesden NW10 ... 8 C2
Strome Ho NW6 ... 78 A1
Stronsa Rd W12 ... 38 B4
Strood Ho SE1 ... 137 C3
Stroud Cres SW15 .. 68 C1
Stroud Green Prim Sch N4 ... 5 C3
Stroud Green Rd N4 ... 5 C3
Stroudley Ho SW8 ... 171 A4
Stroudley Wlk E3 ... 27 A2
Stroud Rd SW19 ... 70 C1
Strout's Pl 2 E2 ... 24 B2 98 C4
Strudwick Ct SW4 ... 172 B3
Strutton Ground SW1 ... 133 B1
Strype St E1 ... 110 C3
Stuart Ave W5 ... 36 B4
Stuart Ho
Hammersmith W6 ... 39 B3
1 Homerton E9 ... 17 C1
5 Stockwell SW4 ... 62 A3
W14 ... 140 A4
Stuart Mill Ho N1 . 84 C1
Stuart Rd
Acton W3 ... 28 B1
Maida Vale NW6 ... 23 C2
Nunhead SE15 ... 65 B3
Wimbledon SW19 ... 70 C1
Stubbs Dr SE16 ... 40 A1
Stubbs Ho
Finsbury Pk N4 ... 5 B3
1 Globe Town E2 ... 25 C2
Stucley Pl 19 NW1 .. 13 A1
Studdridge St SW6 ... 165 C2
Studd St N1 ... 86 A4
Studholme Ct NW3 ... 10 C4
Studholme St SE15 ... 50 A3
Studio Pl SW1 ... 131 A3
Studios NW8 ... 78 C2
Studios The
4 Clapham SW4 ... 61 B3

Studios The *continued* SW8 171 C3
Studland SE17 151 B2
Studland Ho E14 33 A3
Studland St W6 39 A2
Studley Cl E5 18 A3
Studley Ct [13] E14 34 C2
Studley Rd SW4 172 B2
Stukeley St WC2 106 B2
Stunell Ho [23] SE14 50 C4
Sturdee Ho [2] E2 24 C3
Sturdy Ho [28] E3 26 A3
Sturdy Rd SE15 50 A1
Sturgeon Rd SE17 150 C1
Sturge St SE1 136 C4
Sturmer Way N7 14 B3
Sturminster Ho SW8 163 A1
Sturry St E14 34 A3
Sturt St N1 87 A1
Stutfield St E1 111 C1
Stuttle Ho [14] E1 24 C1 99 B1
Styles Gdns SW9 63 A4
Styles Ho SE1 122 A1
Stylus Apartments [25] E1 32 B3
Sudbourne Prim Sch [18] SW2 62 B2
Sudbourne Rd SW2 62 B2
Sudbrooke Rd SW12 60 C1
Sudbury Ct SW8 171 C4
Sudbury Ho SW18 59 A2
Sudeley St N1 86 B1
Sudlow Rd SW18 58 C2
Sudrey St SE1 136 C3
Suffield Ho SE17 150 B2
Suffolk Ho [8] NW5 4 B1
Suffolk La EC4 123 B4
Suffolk Pl SW1 119 C2
Suffolk Rd
Barnes SW13 46 C3
Willesden NW10 8 A1
Suffolk St SW1 119 C2
Sugar House La E15 27 B3
Sugar Loaf Wlk [6] E2 25 B2
Sugden Rd SW11 60 C3
Sulby Ho SE4 66 A3
Sulgrave Gdns [11] W6 39 B4
Sulgrave Rd W6 39 B3
Sulina Rd SW2 74 A4
Sulivan Ct SW6 165 B1
Sulivan Ent Ctr SW6 58 C4
Sulivan Prim Sch SW6 165 B1
Sulivan Rd SW6 58 C4
Sulkin Ho [11] E2 25 C2
Sullivan Cl SW11 60 A4
Sullivan Ct
Stamford Hill N16 7 B3
SW5 141 C4
Sullivan Ho
Chelsea SW1 160 B4
Vauxhall SE11 149 A3
Sullivan Rd SE11 149 C4
Sultan St SE5 48 B3
Sumatra Rd NW6 10 C2
Sumburgh Rd SW12 60 C1

Summercourt Rd E1 32 B3
Summerfield Ave NW6 23 A3
Summer Ho SE13 67 C3
Summerhouse Rd N16 7 A2
Summerlands Ave W3 28 B2
Summerley St SW18 71 A2
Summers St EC1 95 B1
SUMMERSTOWN 71 B1
Summit Ct NW2 10 A3
Summit Est N16 7 C4
Sumner Ave SE15 49 B2
Sumner Bldgs SE1 122 C2
Sumner Ct SW8 172 A4
Sumner Ho [1] E3 34 A4
Sumner Pl SW7 143 C3
Sumner Place Mews SW7 143 C3
Sumner Rd SE15 49 B3
Sumner St SE1 122 C2
Sumpter Cl NW3 11 B2
Sun Alley [6] TW9 54 A3
Sun Alliance Ho WC2 107 B2
Sunbeam Cres W10 22 B1
Sunbeam Rd NW10 20 C1
Sunbury Ave SW14 55 C3
Sunbury Ct [3] SE14 50 C4
Sunbury Ho [33] E2 24 B2 98 C3
Sunbury La SW11 167 C4
Sunbury Workshops [39] E2 24 B2 98 C3
Sun Ct EC3 109 C1
Sunderland Ct SE22 76 C4
Sunderland Ho [26] W2 31 C4
Sunderland Terr W2 100 A2
Sundew Ave W12 29 C2
Sundra Wlk [28] E1 25 C1
Sundridge Ho [4] E9 17 C1
Sunley Ho E1 111 A3
Sunlight Sq [29] E2 25 A2
Sunningdale Ave W3 29 A2
Sunningdale Cl [22] SE16 40 A1
Sunningdale Gdns W8 127 C1
Sunninghill Ct [9] W3 37 B4
Sunninghill Rd SE13 52 A1
Sunnyhill Cl E5 18 A4
Sunnymead Rd SW15 57 A2
Sunnyside [4] NW2 1 B1
Sunnyside Ho [3] NW2 1 B1
Sunnyside Rd N19 4 C4
Sun Pas [8] SE16 139 B2
Sunray Ave SE5, SE24 63 C3
Sun Rd W14 140 C1

Sun St Pas EC2 110 A3
Sunset Rd SE5 63 C3
Sun St EC2 109 C4
Sunwell Cl SE15 50 A2
Surcot Ho [2] SW4 171 C1
Surma Cl E1 24 C1 99 C1
Surrendale Pl W9 23 C1
Surrey Canal Rd SE14, SE8 50 C4
Surrey Cres [1] W4 36 C1
Surrey Docks Farm SE16 41 B4
Surrey Docks Watersports Ctr SE8 41 B2
Surrey Gr SE17 152 A1
Surrey Ho [8] SE16 32 C1
Surrey La SW11 168 B3
Surrey Quays Rd SE16 40 C4
Surrey Quays Sh Ctr SE16 40 C3
Surrey Quays Sta SE16 40 C2
Surrey Rd SE15 65 C2
Surrey Row SE1 136 B4
Surrey Sq SE17 152 B2
Surrey Square Inf Sch SE17 152 A2
Surrey Square Jun Sch SE17 152 A2
Surrey St WC2 121 A4
Surrey Terr SE17 152 B2
Surrey Water Rd SE16 32 C1
Surrey Wharf SE1 49 C4
Surridge Ct [15] SW9 172 B2
Surr St N7 14 A3
Susan Constant Ct [18] E14 34 C2
Susannah St E14 34 B3
Sussex Cl N19 5 A2
Sussex Ct
[4] Barnes SW13 46 B1
Greenwich SE10 52 B4
Paddington W2 101 B1
Sussex Gdns W2 101 C1
Sussex Ho
Hampstead NW3 12 A2
Richmond TW9 44 B1
Sussex House Sch SW3 144 C4
Sussex Lo W2 101 C1
Sussex Mans
South Kensington SW7 143 B3
Strand WC2 120 B4
Sussex Mews E W2 101 C1
Sussex Mews W W2 115 C4
Sussex Pl
[22] Hammersmith W6 39 B1
Lisson Gr NW1 90 C2
Paddington W2 101 C1
Sussex Sq W2 115 C4
Sussex St SW1 146 B2
Sussex Way
Upper Holloway N7 5 B1
Upper Holloway N7, N19 5 A2
Upper Holloway N19 4 C3

Sutherland Ave W9 88 C2
Sutherland Ct
[3] Paddington W9 23 C1
Stoke Newington N16 6 C1
Sutherland Gdns SW14 56 A4
Sutherland Gr SW18, SW19 70 B4
Sutherland Ho
Kensington W8 128 A1
[7] Putney SW15 69 B4
[9] South Hampstead NW6 11 B2
Sutherland Pl W2 31 C3
Sutherland Rd W4 46 A4
Sutherland Row SW1 146 B2
Sutherland Sq SE17 150 C1
Sutherland St SW1 146 B2
Sutherland Wlk SE17 151 A1
Sutterton St N7 14 B2
Sutton Court Mans W4 45 B4
Sutton Court Rd W4 45 B4
Sutton Ct
Chiswick W4 45 B4
[8] Hackney E5 17 A4
Sutton Est SW3 144 B2
Sutton Est The [8] W10 30 B4
Sutton House E9 17 B3
Sutton La EC1 96 B1
Sutton La N W4 37 B1
Sutton La S W4 45 B4
Sutton Pl E9 17 B3
Sutton Row W1 105 C2
Sutton Sq E9 17 B3
Sutton St E1 32 B3
Suttons Way EC1 97 A1
Sutton Way W10 30 B4
Sutton Wlk SE1 121 A1
Swaby Rd SW17, SW18 71 B2
Swaffield Prim Sch SW18 71 B4
Swaffield Rd SW18 71 B4
Swain's La N6 4 A2
Swainson Ho N7 14 C4
Swainson Rd W3 38 B4
Swain St NW8 90 A2
Swallow Cl SE14 50 C2
Swallow Ct [4] W9 31 C4
Swallowfield NW1 92 B3
Swallow Ho NW8 80 A2
Swallow Pl
[24] Poplar E14 33 B3
W1 104 B1
Swallow St W1 119 A3
Swanage Ct [5] N1 16 A1
Swanage Ho SW8 162 C1
Swanage Rd SW18 59 B1
Swanbourne SE17 150 C3
Swanbourne Ho NW8 90 A2
Swan Bsns Ctr [8] W4 37 C2
Swan Ct
Chelsea SW3 144 B1

Swan Ct *continued*
Parsons Green SW6 155 B1
Poplar E14 33 B3
Swan Ctr SW17 71 B1
Swandon Way SW18 59 A3
Swanfield St E2 24 B2 99 A3
Swan Ho N1 15 C1
Swan La EC4 123 C3
Swan Lane Pier EC4 123 B3
Swanlea Sch E1 25 A1
Swanley Ho SE17 152 B2
Swan Mead SE1 138 A1
Swan Mews
Stockwell SW9 172 C2
SW6 165 B4
Swanmore Ct SW18 59 B1
Swanne Ho [12] SE10 52 B3
Swan Pas [5] E1 125 B3
Swan Pl SW13 46 B1
Swan Rd SE16 40 B4
Swanscombe Ho [11] W11 30 C1
Swanscombe Point [7] E16 35 B4
Swanscombe Rd
[5] Chiswick W4 38 A1
Shepherd's Bush W11 30 C1
Swan St SE1 137 A3
Swanton Gdns SW19 69 C3
Swanwick Cl SW15 68 B4
Swan Wlk SW3 158 C4
Swan Yd N1 15 A2
Swaton Rd E3 26 C1
Swaythling Ho SW15 56 B1
Swedenborg Gdns E1 32 A2
Sweden Gate SE16 41 A2
Swedish Quays SE16 41 A3
Swedish Sch The SW13 46 C4
Sweeney Cres SE1 139 A3
Sweyn Pl SE3 53 C1
Swift Ho
[16] Stepney E1 32 B3
[15] Stoke Newington N16 7 A1
[1] SW9 163 C2
Swift St SW6 164 C4
Swinbrook Rd W10 31 A4
Swinburne Ct [4] SE5 63 C3
Swinburne Ho [15] E2 25 B2
Swinburne Rd SW15 56 C3
Swindon St W12 30 B1
Swinford Gdns SW9 63 A4
Swingfield Ho [4] E9 25 B4
Swinley Ho NW1 92 B4

Swinnerton St E9 ... 18 A3
Swinton Ho 21 E2 ... 24 C2 99 B3
Swinton Pl WC1 ... 94 C4
Swinton St WC1 ... 94 C4
Swiss Cottage NW3 ... 11 C1
Swiss Cottage L Ctr NW3 ... 11 C1
Swiss Cottage Sch
14 South Hampstead NW3 ... 11 C1
St John's Wood NW8 ... 79 C4
Swiss Cottage Sta NW3 ... 11 C1
Swiss Ct SW1 ... 119 C3
Swiss Terr 7 NW3 ... 11 C1
Switch Ho 4 E14 ... 34 C2
Sybil Phoenix Cl SE8 ... 40 C1
Sybil Thorndike Casson Ho SW5 . 141 C1
Sybil Thorndike Ho 12 N1 ... 15 B2
Sycamore Ave E3 ... 26 B4
Sycamore Cl W3 ... 29 A1
Sycamore Ct
Kilburn NW6 ... 23 C4
Tufnell Pk N19 ... 4 C1
Sycamore Gdns W6, W12 ... 39 A3
Sycamore Gr SE6 ... 67 B1
Sycamore Ho
10 Maitland Pk NW3 ... 12 B2
17 Rotherhithe SE16 ... 40 C4
3 Shepherd's Bush W6 ... 39 A4
2 Stoke Newington N16 ... 6 C2
Sycamore Lo SW15 ... 57 A4
Sycamore Mews 4 SW4 ... 61 B4
Sycamore St EC1 .. 96 C1
Sycamore Wlk 1 W10 ... 23 A1
Sydcote SE21 ... 75 B3
Sydenham Hill SE21, SE22, SE23, SE26, SE19 ... 76 C1
Sydenham Hill Sta SE21 ... 76 B1
Sydenham Hill Wood Nature Reserve SE26 ... 76 C1
Sydner Mews N16 .. 16 B4
Sydner Rd N16 ... 16 B4
Sydney Cl SW3 ... 143 C3
Sydney Ho 4 W4 ... 38 A2
Sydney Mews SW3 ... 143 C3
Sydney Pl SW7 ... 144 A3
Sydney Rd TW10, TW9 ... 54 A3
Sydney St SW3 ... 144 A2
Sylva Cotts 3 SE8 .. 51 C2
Sylva Ct 3 SW15 ... 69 C4
Sylvan Ct 1 NW6 .. 78 A4
Sylvan Gr
Hampstead NW2 ... 9 C4
Sylvan Gr *continued*
SE15 ... 50 A4
Sylvester Ho 7 E8 ... 17 A2
Sylvester Path 8 E8 ... 17 A2
Sylvester Rd E8 ... 17 A2
Sylvia Ct N1 ... 87 B1
Sylvia Pankhurst Ho 14 E2 ... 25 C2
Sylvia Young Theatre Sch NW1 ... 90 B1
Symes Mews NW1 . 82 C2
Symington Ho SE1 ... 137 B1
Symington Mews E9 ... 17 C3
Symister Mews N1 ... 24 A2 98 A3
25 Shoreditch N1 ... 24 A2 98 A3
Symons Cl 6 SE15 . 50 B1
Symons St SW3 .. 145 A3
Symphony Mews 15 W10 ... 23 A2
Syracuse Univ W11 ... 31 B2 112 C5
Syringa Ho SE4 ... 66 B4

T

Tabard Ct 6 E14 ... 34 B3
Tabard Ho SE1 ... 137 C2
Tabard Sq SE1 ... 137 B3
Tabard St SE1 ... 137 B2
Tabernacle St EC2 . 97 C2
Tableer Ave SW4 ... 61 C2
Tabley Rd N7 ... 14 A4
Tabor Rd W6 ... 39 A3
Tachbrook Est SW1 ... 147 C1
Tachbrook Mews SW1 ... 146 C4
Tachbrook St SW1 ... 147 A3
Tack Mews SE4 ... 66 C4
Tadema Ho NW8 .. 89 C1
Tadema Rd SW10 157 A1
Tadmor St W12 ... 30 C1
Tadworth Ho SE1 136 A3
Taeping St E14 ... 42 A2
Taffrail Ho 2 E14 .. 42 A1
Taft Way 44 E3 ... 27 A2
Tailworth St 16 E1 ... 111 B3
Tait Ct
16 Old Ford E3 ... 26 B4
SW8 ... 171 C4
Tait Ho
SE1 ... 121 C1
2 Tufnell Pk N19 ... 13 B4
Takhar Mews SW11 ... 168 B1
Talacre Com Sp Ctr NW5 ... 13 A2
Talacre Rd NW5 ... 12 C2
Talbot Ct EC3 ... 123 C4
Talbot Grove Ho 10 W11 ... 31 A3
Talbot Ho
Highbury N7 ... 5 C1
Poplar E14 ... 34 A3
Talbot Pl SE3 ... 53 A1
Talbot Rd
Camberwell SE22 ... 64 A3
Talbot Rd *continued*
Notting Hill W2 ... 31 C3
Notting Hill W11 ... 31 B3
Talbot Sq W2 ... 101 B1
Talbot Wlk
Notting Hill W11 ... 31 A3
Willesden NW10 ... 8 A2
Talbot Yd SE1 ... 123 B1
Talcott Path 12 SW2 ... 74 C3
Talfourd Pl SE15 ... 49 B2
Talfourd Rd SE15 ... 49 B2
Talgarth Rd
Hammersmith W6 ... 39 B1
W14 ... 140 B2
Talia Ho E14 ... 42 B3
Talleyrand Ho SE5 .. 48 B1
Tallis St EC4 ... 121 C4
Talma Rd SW2 ... 62 C3
Talmud Torah Machzikei Hadass Sch E5 ... 7 C4
Talmud Torah Tiferes Shlomo 1 NW11 ... 1 A2
Talmud-Torah Yetev-Lev 6 N16 ... 7 C3
Talwin St E3 ... 27 A2
Tamar Cl 24 E3 ... 26 B4
Tamar Ho
10 Cubitt Town E14 ... 42 B4
SE11 ... 149 C2
Tamarind Ct 8 W3 ... 28 B3
Tamarind Ho 4 SE15 ... 49 C3
Tamarind Yd 5 E1 ... 125 C2
Tamarisk Sq W12 ... 29 B2
Tamworth N7 ... 14 A2
Tamworth St SW6 155 B3
Tangier Rd TW10 ... 55 A4
Tangley Gr SW15 ... 68 B4
Tangmere WC1 ... 94 C3
Tanhurst Ho 27 SW2 ... 74 A4
Tankerton St WC1 . 94 B3
Tanner Ho SE1 ... 138 B3
Tanner's Hill SE8 ... 51 C2
Tanners Mews SE8 ... 51 B2
Tanner St SE1 ... 138 B3
Tanners Yd 33 E2 ... 25 A3
Tannery Ho 22 E1 111 B4
Tannington Terr N5 .. 5 C1
Tansley Cl N7 ... 13 C3
Tanswell St SE1 .. 135 B3
Tantallon Rd SW12 ... 72 C3
Tant Ave E16 ... 35 B3
Tanza Rd NW3 ... 12 B4
Tapley Ho 11 SE1 . 139 B3
Taplow NW3 ... 11 C1
Taplow Ho 36 E2 ... 24 B2 98 C3
Taplow St N1 ... 87 A1
Tappesfield Rd SE15 ... 65 B4
Tapp St E1 ... 25 A1
Taranto Ho 14 E1 ... 32 C4
Tarbert Rd SE22 ... 64 A2
Tarbert Wlk E1 ... 32 B2
Tarling Rd E16 ... 35 B3
Tarling St E1 ... 32 B3
Tarnbrook Ct SW1 ... 145 B3
Tarn St SE1 ... 136 C1
Tarns The NW1 ... 92 C4
Tarplett Ho 22 SE14 ... 50 C4
Tarragon Cl SE14 ... 51 A3
Tarranbrae NW6 ... 10 A1
Tarrant Ho E2 ... 25 B2
Tarrant Pl W1 ... 102 C3
Tarrantt Ho W14 .. 126 A2
Tarriff Cres SE8 ... 41 B2
Tarrington Cl SW16 ... 73 C1
Tartan Ho 12 E14 ... 34 B3
Tarver Rd SE17 ... 150 B2
Tarves Way SE10 ... 52 A3
Tasker Ho 17 E14 ... 33 B4
Tasker Lo W8 ... 127 B4
Tasker Rd NW3 ... 12 B3
Tasman Ct 9 E14 .. 42 A2
Tasman Ho 17 E1 ... 32 A1
Tasman Rd SW9 ... 62 A4
Tasso Rd W6 ... 154 A4
Tasso Yd W6 ... 154 A3
Tatchbury Ho SW15 ... 56 B1
Tate Britain SW1 . 148 A3
Tate Ho 13 E2 ... 25 C3
Tate Modern EC4 . 122 B2
Tatham Pl NW8 ... 79 C2
Tatnell Rd SE23 ... 66 A1
Tatton Cres E5, N16 .. 7 B4
Tatum St SE17 ... 151 C3
Tauheed Cl N4 ... 6 B2
Taunton Ho W2 ... 100 C1
Taunton Mews NW1 ... 90 C1
Taunton Pl NW1 ... 90 C2
Tavern Ct SE1 ... 137 A1
Taverner Ho N16 ... 6 C1
Taverners Cl W11 ... 31 A1 112 A1
Taverner Sq 4 N5 .. 15 B4
Tavern La SW9 ... 173 C2
Tavistock Cl N16 ... 16 A3
Tavistock Cres W11 ... 31 B4
Tavistock Ct WC1 .. 93 C2
Tavistock Ho 3 W11 ... 31 B4
Tavistock Mews 3 W11 ... 31 B3
Tavistock Pl WC1 .. 94 A2
Tavistock Rd
Dagenham NW10 ... 21 B3
Notting Hill W11 ... 31 B4
Tavistock Sq WC1 .. 93 C2
Tavistock St WC2 . 120 B4
Tavistock Terr N19 ... 4 C1
Tavistock Twr SE16 ... 41 A3
Taviton St WC1 ... 93 B2
Tavy Cl SE11 ... 149 C2
Tawhid Boys Sch N16 ... 7 B2
Tawny Way SE16 ... 40 C2
Taybridge Rd SW11 ... 60 C3
Tayburn Cl E14 ... 34 B3
Tay Ho 10 E3 ... 26 B3
Tayler Ct NW8 ... 79 B4
Taylor Ave TW9 ... 45 A1
Taylor Cl SE8 ... 51 B4
Taylor Ho 10 SW2 ... 74 C3
Taylor's Gn W3 ... 29 A3
Taylor's La NW10 ... 8 A1
Tayport Cl N1 ... 14 A1
Tayside Ct 6 SE5 ... 63 C3
Teak Cl SE16 ... 33 A1
Tealby Ct N7 ... 14 B2
Teal Ct 30 SE8 ... 51 B4
Teale St E2 ... 24 C3
Teal St 1 SE10 ... 43 B3
Teather St 12 SE5 .. 49 A3
Tebbs Ho 14 SW2 ... 74 C4
Tedman Ct SE13 ... 67 B3
Ted Roberts Ho 25 E2 ... 25 A3
Tedworth Gdns SW3 ... 144 C1
Tedworth Sq SW3 144 C1
Teesdale Cl E2 ... 25 A3
Teesdale St E2 ... 25 A3
Teesdale Yd 34 E2 .. 25 A3
Tee The W3 ... 29 A3
Teignmouth Cl 6 SW4 ... 61 C3
Teignmouth Rd NW2 ... 9 C2
Telegraph Hill NW3 .. 2 A1
Telegraph Pl E14 ... 42 A2
Telegraph Rd SW15 ... 69 B4
Telegraph St EC2 . 109 B2
Telephone Pl SW6 ... 155 A4
Telfer Cl 4 W3 ... 37 B4
Telfer Ho EC1 ... 96 B3
Telferscot Prim Sch 5 SW12 ... 73 C3
Telferscot Rd SW12 ... 73 C3
Telford Ave SW12, SW2 ... 74 A3
Telford Avenue Mans 7 SW2 ... 74 A3
Telford Ho
8 Kensal Town W10 ... 31 A4
SE1 ... 136 C2
Telford Parade Mans 8 SW2 ... 74 A3
Telford Rd W10 ... 31 A4
Telford Terr SW1 . 160 C4
Telford Way W3 ... 29 A4
Tell Gr SE22 ... 64 B3
Telscombe Ho SW11 ... 169 B3
Temair Ho 1 SE10 . 52 B3
Temeraire Pl TW8 .. 36 B1
Temeraire St SE16 .. 40 B4
Temperley Rd SW12 ... 72 C4
Templar Ho NW2 ... 10 B2
Templar St SE5 ... 48 A1
Temple Ave EC4 .. 121 C4
Temple Bar EC4 .. 108 B1
Temple Bar EC4 .. 108 B1
Templecombe Rd E9 ... 25 B4
Temple Ct
Stepney E1 ... 32 C4
SW8 ... 162 A1
Temple Dwellings 7 E2 ... 25 A3
Temple Gr Hatcham Sch SE14 ... 50 C1
Temple Ho
13 Battersea SW11 ... 60 A4
4 Tufnell Pk N7 ... 4 B1
Temple La EC4 ... 107 C1

Templemead Cl W3 .... 29 A3
Templemead Ho E9 .... 18 A4
TEMPLE MILLS 19 A3
Temple Mills La
London E10, E15 .... 19 B4
Stratford E15 .... 19 A4
Temple Mills Rd E9 .... 18 C4
Temple Pl WC2 .... 121 A4
Temple Rd
Acton Green W4 .... 37 B3
Richmond TW9 .... 54 B4
Temple Sheen SW14 .... 55 B2
Temple Sheen Rd SW14 .... 55 B3
Temple St E2 .... 25 A3
Temple Sta WC2 .... 121 B4
Templeton Cl 25 N16 .... 16 A3
Templeton Pl SW5 .... 141 C3
Temple West Mews SE11 .... 136 A1
Templewood Ave NW3 .... 2 A1
Templewood Gdns NW3 .... 2 A1
Templewood Point NW2 .... 1 B2
Tenbury Ct SW12 .... 73 C3
Tenby Ho
Islington N7 .... 14 C4
W2 .... 100 C1
Tench St E1 .... 32 A1
Tenda Rd SE16 .... 40 A2
Tendring Ho SW2 .... 62 C1
Tenham Ave SW2 .... 73 C2
Tenison Ct W1 .... 118 C4
Tenison Way SE1 .... 121 B1
Tenniel Cl W2 .... 114 B4
Tennis St SE1 .... 137 B4
Tennyson Ho SE17 .... 151 A2
Tennyson Rd NW6 .... 23 B4
Tennyson St SW8 .... 170 A1
Tensing Ho N1 .... 15 A2
Tenterden Ho SE17 .... 152 B2
Tenterden St W1 .... 104 B1
Tenter Ground E1 .... 110 C3
Tent St E1 .... 25 A1
Tequila Wharf E14 .... 33 A3
Terborch Way 6 SE22 .... 64 A2
Tercelet Terr NW3 .... 11 B4
Teredo St SE16 .... 40 C3
Terling Ho 9 W10 .... 30 B4
Terling Wlk N1 .... 86 C4
Terminus Pl SW1 .... 132 B1
Tern Ho 9 SE15 .... 49 B2
Terrace Gdns SW13 .... 46 B1
Terrace La TW10 .... 54 A1
Terrace Rd E9 .... 17 B1
Terrace The
Barnes SW13, SW14 .... 46 A1
EC4 .... 107 C1
Kilburn NW6 .... 23 C4
10 Rotherhithe SE8 .... 41 B2
Terrano Ho 1 TW9 .... 45 A2
Terrapin Ct SW17 .... 73 A1
Terrapin Rd SW17 .... 73 A1
Terrick St W12 .... 30 A3
Territorial Ho SE11 .... 149 C3
Terry Ho SW2 .... 74 C3
Tersha St TW9 .... 54 B3
Tessa Sanderson Pl 6 SW8 .... 61 A4
Testerton Wlk 3 W11 .... 30 C2
Tetcott Rd SW10 .... 156 C1
Teversham La SW8 .... 172 B4
Teviot St E14 .... 34 B4
Teyham Ct 2 SW11 .... 60 B1
Thackeray Ct
Chelsea SW3 .... 144 C2
West Kensington W14 .... 126 A1
Thackeray Ho
College Pk NW10 .... 21 C2
WC1 .... 94 A2
Thackeray Mews 6 E8 .... 16 C2
Thackeray Rd SW8 .... 170 B1
Thackeray's Almshouses SE6 .... 67 A1
Thackeray St W8 .... 128 B2
Thalia Cl SE10 .... 52 C4
Tham Cl 10 SE24 .... 63 A4
Thame Rd SE16 .... 40 C4
Thames Ave SW10 .... 167 A4
Thames Bank SW14 .... 45 B1
Thames Christian Coll 25 SW11 .... 59 C4
Thames Circ E14 .... 41 C2
Thames Cres W4 .... 46 A3
Thames Ct 10 SE15 .... 49 B3
Thames Hts SE1 .... 138 C4
Thameside Ctr TW8 .... 44 B4
Thames Link Ho 7 TW9 .... 54 A3
Thames Pl SW15 .... 57 C4
Thames Quay
Millwall E14 .... 42 A4
SW10 .... 167 A3
Thames Rd W4 .... 45 A4
Thames Reach W6 .... 47 B4
Thames Row TW9 .... 44 B4
Thames St SE10 .... 52 A4
Thames Village W4 .... 45 B2
Thames Wlk SW11 .... 158 A2
Thane Mans N7 .... 5 B1
Thanet Ho
WC1 .... 94 A3
1 West Norwood SE27 .... 75 A1
Thanet Lo NW2 .... 10 A2
Thanet St WC1 .... 94 A3
Thane Villas N7 .... 5 B1
Thane Works N7 .... 5 B1
Thavies Inn EC4 .... 107 C2
Thaxted Ct N1 .... 87 C1
Thaxted Ho SE16 .... 40 B2
Thaxton Rd W14 .... 155 A4
Thayer St W1 .... 103 C2
Theatre Royal E10 .... 19 C2
Theatre Sq E15 .... 19 C2
Theatre St SW11 .... 60 B4
Theberton St N1 .... 86 A4
Theed St SE1 .... 121 C1
Thelbridge Ho 28 E3 .... 27 A2
Theobalds Ct N4 .... 6 B2
Theobald's Rd WC1 .... 106 C4
Theobald St SE1 .... 137 B1
Theodore Ct SE13 .... 67 C1
Theodore Ho 1 SW15 .... 56 C2
Theodore Rd SE13 .... 67 C1
Therapia Rd SE22 .... 65 B1
Theresa Rd W6 .... 38 C2
Therfield Ct N4 .... 6 B2
Thermopylae Gate E14 .... 42 A2
Theseus Ho 2 E14 .... 34 C3
Theseus Wlk N1 .... 86 B1
Thessaly Ho SW8 .... 160 C1
Thessaly Rd SW8 .... 171 A4
Thetford Ho SE1 .... 138 C2
Thetis Terr TW9 .... 44 C4
Third Ave
East Acton W3 .... 29 B1
West Kilburn W10 .... 23 A2
Thirleby Rd SW1 .... 133 A1
Thirlmere NW1 .... 92 B4
Thirlmere Ho 19 N16 .... 15 C4
Thirsk Rd SW11 .... 60 C3
Thistle Gr SW7 .... 143 A1
Thistle Ho 10 E14 .... 34 B3
Thistlewood Cl 3 N7 .... 5 B2
Thistly Ct SE8 .... 52 A4
Thomas Baines Rd SW11 .... 59 C4
Thomas Burt Ho 9 E2 .... 25 A2
Thomas Buxton Jun & Inf Sch 17 E1 .... 24 C1 99 C1
Thomas Crowell Ct 29 N1 .... 16 A3
Thomas Doyle St SE1 .... 136 B2
Thomas Fairchild Com Sch N1 .... 87 A2
Thomas Ho
3 Hackney E9 .... 17 B2
4 Stockwell SW4 .... 62 A3
Thomas Hollywood Ho 3 E2 .... 25 B3
Thomas Jones Prim Sch 16 W11 .... 31 A3
Thomas London Ind Day Sch W8 .... 128 B2
Thomas Milner Ho 8 SE15 .... 49 C3
Thomas More Ho EC2 .... 108 C3
Thomas More Sq E1 .... 125 B3
Thomas More St E1 .... 125 B2
Thomas Neal's Ctr WC1 .... 106 A1
Thomas North Terr 4 E16 .... 35 B4
Thomas Pl W8 .... 128 A1
Thomas Rd E14 .... 33 C4
Thomas Road Ind Est 2 E14 .... 33 C3
Thomas's Prep Sch Clapham SW11 .... 60 B2
Thomas's Prep Schs SW11 .... 167 C3
Thompson Ave
Richmond TW9 .... 54 C4
6 SE5 .... 48 B3
Thompson Ho
11 Kensal Town W10 .... 23 A1
SE14 .... 50 C4
Thompson Rd SE22 .... 64 B1
Thomson Ct 4 E8 .... 16 C2
Thomson Ho
Pimlico SW1 .... 147 C1
Walworth SE17 .... 152 A3
Thorburn Ho SW1 .... 131 B3
Thorburn Sq SE1 .... 153 B3
Thoresby Ho N16 .... 6 C1
Thoresby St N1 .... 97 A4
Thornaby Ho 15 E2 .... 25 A2
Thornbill Ho 1 SE15 .... 49 C3
Thornbury Cl N16 .... 16 A3
Thornbury Ct W11 .... 31 C2 113 B4
Thornbury Ho N6 .... 4 B3
Thornbury Rd SW2 .... 62 A1
Thornbury Sq N6 .... 4 B3
Thorncliffe Ct SW2 .... 62 A1
Thorncliffe Rd SW2 .... 62 A1
Thorncombe Rd SE22 .... 64 A2
Thorncroft St SW8 .... 162 A1
Thorndale Ho 10 N16 .... 7 A3
Thorndean St SW18 .... 71 B2
Thorndike Cl SW10 .... 156 C2
Thorndike Ho SW1 .... 147 B2
Thorndike Rd 21 N1 .... 15 C2
Thorndike St SW1 .... 147 B3
Thorne Cl E16 .... 35 C3
Thorne Ho
34 Bethnal Green E2 .... 25 B2
4 Cubitt Town E14 .... 42 B3
Thorne Pas 7 SW13 .... 46 B1
Thorne Rd SW8 .... 162 B1
Thorness Ct SW18 .... 59 B1
Thorne St SW13, SW14 .... 56 A4
Thornewill Ho 8 E1 .... 32 B2
Thorney Cres SW11 .... 157 C1
Thorneycroft Ho 11 W4 .... 38 A1
Thorney Ct W8 .... 128 C3
Thorney Hedge Rd W4 .... 37 A2
Thorney St SW1 .... 148 A4
Thornfield Ho 5 E14 .... 33 C2
Thornfield Rd W12 .... 39 A4
Thornford Rd SE13 .... 67 B2
Thorngate Rd W9 .... 23 C1
Thornham Gr E15 .... 19 C3
Thorn Ham Ho SE1 .... 137 C2
Thornham St SE10 .... 52 A4
Thornhaugh St WC1 .... 93 C1
Thornhill Bridge Wharf N1 .... 84 C3
Thornhill Cres N1 .... 14 B1
Thornhill Gr N1 .... 14 C1
Thornhill Ho
12 Chiswick W4 .... 38 A1
Islington N1 .... 14 C1
Thornhill Mews SW15 .... 58 B3
Thornhill Prim Sch 11 N1 .... 14 C1
Thornhill Rd N1 .... 85 B4
Thornhill Sq N1 .... 14 B1
Thornicroft Ho 12 SW9 .... 173 A1
Thornley Pl 2 SE10 .... 43 A1
Thornsett Rd SW18 .... 71 A3
Thornton Ave
Chiswick W4 .... 38 A2
Streatham SW2 .... 73 C3
Thornton Ct N7 .... 14 A3
Thornton Gdns SW12 .... 73 C3
Thornton Ho SE17 .... 152 A3
Thornton Pl W1 .... 103 A4
Thornton Rd
Mortlake SW14 .... 55 C4
Streatham SW12, SW2 .... 73 C3
Thornton St SW9 .... 173 B2
Thornville St SE8 .... 51 C2
Thornwood Gdns W8 .... 127 B4
Thornwood Lo W8 .... 127 B4
Thornycroft Ct TW9 .... 44 B1
Thorold Ho
SE1 .... 136 C4
6 Streatham SW2 .... 74 A4
Thorparch Rd SW8 .... 161 C1
Thorpebank Rd W12 .... 29 C1
Thorpe Cl W10 .... 31 A3
Thorpedale Rd N4 .... 5 B3
Thorpe Ho N1 .... 85 A3
Thorverton Rd NW2 .... 1 A1
Thoydon Rd E3 .... 26 A3
Thrale St SE1 .... 123 A1
Thrasher Cl 20 E8 .... 24 B4
Thrawl St E1 .... 111 A3
Thrayle Ho 2 SW9 .... 62 B4
Threadgold Ho 8 N1 .... 15 C2
Threadneedle St EC2, EC3 .... 109 C1
Three Colts La E2 .... 25 A1
Three Colt St E14 .... 33 B2

Three Cups Yd WC1 107 A3
Three Kings Yd W1 118 A4
Three Mill La E3 27 B2
Three Nun Ct EC2 109 A2
Three Oak La SE1 138 C4
Threshers Pl W11 31 A2 112 A4
Thring Ho 2 SW9 172 C2
Throgmorton Ave EC2 109 C2
Throgmorton St EC2 109 C2
Thrush St SE17 150 C2
Thurland Ho 3 SE16 40 A2
Thurland Rd SE16 139 B2
Thurleigh Ave SW12 60 C1
Thurleigh Ct SW12 60 C1
Thurleigh Rd SW12 60 C1
Thurloe Cl SW7 144 A4
Thurloe Ct SW3 144 A3
Thurloe Pl SW7 143 C4
Thurloe Place Mews SW7 143 C4
Thurloe Sq SW7 144 A4
Thurloe St SW7 143 C4
Thurlow Hill SE21 75 B2
Thurlow Ho 17 SW16 74 A1
Thurlow Park Rd SE21, SE24 75 B2
Thurlow Rd NW3 11 C3
Thurlow St SE17 152 A1
Thurlow Terr NW5 12 C3
Thurlow Twrs SE27 74 C1
Thurlow Wlk SE17 152 A1
Thurnscoe NW1 82 C3
Thursley Gdns SW19 69 C2
Thursley Ho 10 SW2 74 B4
Thurso Ho NW6 78 A1
Thurston Ind Est SE13 67 A4
Thurston Rd SE8, SE13 52 A1
Thurtle Rd E2 24 B3
Tibbatt's Rd E3 27 A1
Tibberton Sq N1 86 C4
Tibbets Cl SW19 69 C3
Tibbet's Corner SW19 69 C4
Tibbet's Ride SW19 69 C4
Tiber Cl 10 E3 26 C4
Tiber Gdns N1 84 B3
Tickford Ho NW8 90 A3
Tidal Basin Rd E16 35 B2
Tidbury Ct SW8 160 C1
Tidemill Prim Sch 20 SE8 51 C3
Tideswell 10 NW5 13 A4
Tideswell Rd SW15 57 B3
Tideway Ct 9 SE16 32 C1
Tideway Ho E14 41 C4
Tideway Ind Est SW8 161 A3
Tideway Wharf SW13 46 A1
Tideway Yd SW13 46 A1
Tidey St E3 33 C4
Tidworth Ho 13 SE22 64 A4
Tidworth Rd E3 26 C1
Tierney Rd SW2 74 A3
Tierney Terr SW2 74 A3
Tiger Ho WC1 93 C3
Tiger Way E5 17 A4
Tignel Ct W3 36 C4
Tilbury Cl 14 SE15 49 B3
Tilbury Ho 4 SE14 50 C4
Tildesley Rd SW15 57 B1
Tilehurst NW1 92 B3
Tilehurst Rd SW17, SW18 71 C3
Tile Kiln La N6 4 B3
Tileyard Rd N7 14 A1
Tilford Gdns SW19 69 C3
Tilford Ho 8 SW2 74 B4
Tilia Rd E5 17 A4
Tilia Wlk 21 SW9 63 A3
Tiller Ho 28 N1 24 A4
Tiller L Ctr E14 41 C3
Tiller Rd E14 41 C3
Tillet Sq SE16 41 A4
Tillet Way 6 E2 24 C2 99 B4
Tilling Ho 1 SE15 65 A4
Tillman Ho 8 SW2 74 B3
Tillman St E1 32 A3
Tilloch St 9 N1 14 B1
Tillotson Ct SW8 161 C1
Tilney Ct EC1 97 A2
Tilney Gdns 12 N1 15 C2
Tilney St W1 117 C2
Tilson Cl 2 SE15 49 A3
Tilson Gdns SW2, SW4 74 A4
Tilson Ho SW2 74 A4
Tilton St SW6 154 B3
Tiltwood The W3 28 B2
Timberland Cl 16 SE15 49 C3
Timberland Rd E1 32 A3
Timber Mill Way SW4 61 C4
Timber Pond Rd SE16 40 C4
Timber St EC1 96 C2
Time Sq E8 16 B3
Timothy Cl 1 SW4 61 B2
Timsbury Wlk 5 SW15 68 C3
Tina Ct SW16 74 C1
Tindal St SW9 48 A2
Tinniswood Cl N5 14 C3
Tinsley Rd E1 32 B4
Tintagel Cres SE22 64 B3
Tintagel Ct EC1 96 A2
Tintern Cl SW15 58 A2
Tintern Ho
Belgravia SW1 146 A3
Regent's Pk NW1 82 B1
Tintern St SW4 62 A3
Tinworth St SE11 148 B2
Tipthorpe Rd SW11 60 C4
Tiptree 7 NW1 13 A1
Tisbury Ct W1 119 B4
Tisdall Pl SE17 151 C3
Tissington Ct 4 SE16 40 C2
Titan Bsns Est 3 SE8 51 C3
Titan Ct TW8 36 B1
Titchborne Row W2 102 B1
Titchfield Rd NW8 80 C4
Titchwell Rd SW18 71 C3
Tite St SW3 158 C4
Titmuss St W12 39 B4
Tiverton Rd NW6, NW10 22 C4
Tiverton St SE1 136 C2
Tivoli Ct SE16 33 B1
Tobago St 12 E14 41 C4
Tobin Cl NW3 12 A1
Toby La E1 26 A1
Todber Ho W14 126 A2
Todds Wlk N7 5 B2
Tokenhouse Yd EC2 109 B2
Token Yd SW15 58 A3
Toland Sq SW15 56 C2
Tolchurch 2 W11 31 C3
Toldos Sch N16 7 A3
Tolhurst Dr 4 W10 23 A2
Tollbridge Cl W10 23 A1
Tollet St E1 25 C1
Tollgate Dr SE21 76 A2
Tollgate Ho 1 NW6 78 A2
Tollhouse Way N19 4 B2
Tollington Ct N4 5 B2
Tollington Ho 4 N19 5 A1
Tollington Pk N4 5 B2
Tollington Pl N4 5 B2
Tollington Rd N7 14 B4
Tollington Way N7 5 A1
Tolmers Sq NW1 93 A2
Tolpaide Ho SE11 149 B3
Tolpuddle St N1 85 B2
Tolsford Rd E5 17 A3
Tom Groves Cl E15 19 C3
Tom Hood Cl E15 19 C3
Tom Jenkinson Rd 5 E16 35 C1
Tomkyns Ho SE11 149 B3
Tomline Ho SE1 122 C1
Tomlin's Gr E3 26 C2
Tomlinson Cl
5 Gunnersbury W4 37 A1
Spitalfields E2 24 B2 99 A3
Tomlin's Terr E14 33 A3
Tomlins Wlk 4 N7 5 B2
Tompion Ho EC1 96 B2
Tompion St EC1 96 B3
Tom Smith Cl SE10 53 A4
Tomson Ho SE1 138 C2
Tom Williams Ho SW6 154 C3
Tonbridge Hos WC1 94 A3
Tonbridge St WC1 94 A3
Toneborough 16 NW8 78 B3
Tonsley Hill SW18 59 A2
Tonsley Pl SW18 59 A2
Tonsley Rd SW18 59 A2
Tonsley St SW18 59 A2
Took's Ct EC4 107 B2
Tooley St SE1 124 A1
Tooting Bec Sta SW17 72 C1
Topham Ho 8 SE10 52 B3
Topham St EC1 95 B2
Topiary Sq TW9 54 B4
Topmast Point 23 E14 41 C4
Torah Vodaas NW11 1 B3
Tora Temimah Prim Sch NW2 9 A4
Torbay Ct 13 NW1 13 A1
Torbay Mans NW6 23 B4
Torbay Rd NW6 10 B1
Torbay St 15 NW1 13 A1
Tor Ct W8 127 C4
Tor Gdns W8 127 B4
Tornay Ho
Hackney E9 17 B1
N1 84 C2
Torquay St W2 100 A3
Torrence Ho 6 N19 4 B2
Torrens Ct SE5 63 C4
Torrens Rd SW2 62 B2
Torrens St EC1 86 A1
Torres Sq E14 41 C1
Torriano Ave NW5 13 C3
Torriano Cotts NW5 13 B3
Torriano Jun & Inf Schs 24 NW5 13 C3
Torriano Mews NW5 13 B3
Torridge Gdns SE15 65 B3
Torridon Ho NW6 78 A1
Torrington Pl
Bloomsbury WC1 105 B4
St George in t East E1 125 C2
Torrington Sq WC1 93 C1
Tortington Ho 1 SE15 50 A3
Torwood Rd SW15 56 C2
Tothill Ho SW1 147 C4
Tothill St SW1 133 C3
Totland Ho SW18 59 A1
Tottan Terr E1 32 C3
Tottenhall 5 NW1 12 C1
Tottenham Court Rd W1 105 A4
Tottenham Court Road Sta W1 105 C2
Tottenham Mews W1 105 A4
Tottenham Rd N1 16 A2
Tottenham St W1 105 A4
Totteridge Ho SW11 167 C2
Touchard Ho N1 97 C3
Toulmin St SE1 136 C3
Toulon St SE5 48 B3
Toulouse Ct 2 SE16 40 A1
Tounson Ct SW1 147 C3
Tournay Rd SW6 155 A2
Toussaint Wlk 18 SE16 139 C2
Tovy Ho 6 SE1 153 B1
Towcester Rd E3 27 B1
Tower 42 EC2 110 A2
Tower Bldgs 22 E1 32 A1
Tower Br App E1, EC3 124 C3
Tower Bridge E1, EC3, SE1 124 C2
Tower Bridge Bsns Complex SE16 40 A3
Tower Bridge Bsns Sq SE16 40 A2
Tower Bridge Ex E1 124 C2
Tower Bridge Piazza SE1 124 C1
Tower Bridge Prim Sch SE1 138 C4
Tower Bridge Rd SE1 138 A3
Tower Bridge Sq SE1 138 C4
Tower Cl NW3 11 C3
Tower Ct
Brockley SE4 66 A3
Stamford Hill E5 7 B4
St Giles WC2 106 A1
St John's Wood NW8 80 B2
Towergate SE1 152 A4
Towergate Ho 35 E3 26 B3
Tower Gateway Sta EC3 124 C4
TOWER HAMLETS 33 B4
Tower Hamlets Coll
25 Poplar E14 34 A3
27 Poplar E14 34 A2
16 Stepney E1 32 C3
Tower Hill EC3 125 A3
Tower Hill Sta EC3 124 C4
Tower House Sch SW14 55 B3
Tower Mans SE1 138 C1
Tower Mews E5 18 A3
Tower Millennium Pier EC3 124 B2
Tower Mill Rd
7 Camberwell SE15 49 A4
1 SE15 49 A3
Tower of London The EC3 124 C3
Tower Pl E EC3 124 B3
Tower Pl W EC3 124 B3
Tower Rd NW10 8 C1
Tower Rise TW9 54 A4
Tower Royal EC4 123 B4
Towers Pl TW10 54 A2
Tower St WC2 106 A1
Towers The
Dartmouth Pk NW5 4 A1
1 Richmond TW9 54 B3
Tower Terr SE4 66 A3
Towerview SE13 66 C2
Tower Wharf SE1 138 C4
Tower Wlk SE1 152 A4
Towncourt Path N4 6 B3
Townhall Ave 3 W4 37 C1
Town Hall Rd SW11 60 B4
Town Hos EC1 96 B1
Townley Rd SE22 64 A2
Townley St SE17 151 B2

Townmead Bsns Ctr SW6 ... 59 B4
Townmead Rd
Richmond TW9 ... 45 A1
Sands End SW6 ... 166 C1
Townsend Ho 14 SE1 ... 153 C3
Townsend Ind Est NW10 ... 20 B3
Townsend Mews 3 SW18 ... 71 B2
Townsend Prim Sch SE17 ... 152 A4
Townsend Rd NW8 ... 80 B2
Townsend St SE1, SE17 ... 152 A4
Townsend Yd N6 ... 4 A3
Townshend Ct NW8 ... 80 B2
Townshend Est NW8 ... 80 A2
Townshend Rd
Primrose Hill NW8 ... 80 A3
Richmond TW9 ... 54 B3
Townshend Terr TW9 ... 54 B3
Towns Ho 4 SW4 ... 61 C4
Towpath Wlk E9 ... 18 B3
Towton Rd SE27 ... 75 B2
Toxteth Ho N4 ... 6 B4
Toynbee St E1 ... 110 C3
Toynbee Studios E1 ... 111 A3
Tracey Ave NW2 ... 9 B3
Tracy Ho 15 E3 ... 26 B2
Tradescant Ho 15 E9 ... 17 B1
Tradescant Rd SW8 ... 162 B1
Trade Twr 8 SW11 ... 59 B4
Trade Winds Ct 1 E1 ... 125 C2
Trading Estate Rd NW10 ... 20 B1
Traemore Ct SW16 ... 74 C1
Trafalgar Ave SE15 ... 49 B4
Trafalgar Cl 1 SE16 ... 41 A2
Trafalgar Gdns
Stepney E1 ... 32 C4
W8 ... 128 B2
Trafalgar Gr SE10 ... 52 C4
Trafalgar Ho SE17 ... 151 A2
Trafalgar Mews E9 ... 18 B2
Trafalgar Point 2 N1 ... 15 C1
Trafalgar Rd SE10 ... 43 A1
Trafalgar Sq SW1 ... 119 C2
Trafalgar St SE17 ... 151 C2
Trafalgar Way E14 ... 34 B1
Trafford Ho N1 ... 87 C2
Tragail SW15 ... 58 A2
Trahorn Cl E1 ... 25 A1
Traitors Gate EC3 ... 124 C2
Tralee Ct 31 SE16 ... 40 A1
Tramway Ave E15 ... 19 C1
Trance Way W3 ... 36 C3
Tranmere Ho 7 N7 ... 14 C3
Tranmere Rd SW17, SW18 ... 71 B2
Tranquil Pas SE3 ... 53 B1
Tranquil Vale SE3 ... 53 A1
Transept St NW1 ... 102 B3
Transom Cl SE16 ... 41 A2
Transom Sq E14 ... 42 A1
Tranton Rd SE16 ... 40 A3
Trappes Ho 2 SE16 ... 40 A2
Travers Ho 6 SE10 ... 52 C4
Travers Rd N7 ... 5 C1
Travis Ho SE10 ... 52 B2
Treadgold Ho 7 W11 ... 30 C2
Treadgold St W11 ... 30 C2
Treadway St E2 ... 25 A3
Treasury Bldgs SW1 ... 134 A4
Treaty St N1 ... 84 C3
Trebeck St W1 ... 118 A1
Treborough Ho W1 ... 103 B4
Trebovir Rd SW5 ... 141 C3
Treby St E3 ... 26 B1
Trecastle Way 2 N7 ... 13 C4
Tredegar Mews 10 E3 ... 26 B2
Tredegar Rd E3 ... 26 B3
Tredegar Sq E3 ... 26 B2
Tredegar Terr E3 ... 26 B2
Trederwen Rd E8 ... 24 C4
Treen Ave SW13 ... 56 B4
Trees The N16 ... 6 C4
Trefil Wlk N7 ... 14 A4
Trefoil Rd SW18 ... 59 B2
Tregarvon Rd SW11 ... 60 C3
Trego Rd E9 ... 18 C1
Tregothnan Rd SW9 ... 62 A4
Tregunter Rd SW10 ... 142 C1
Treherne Ct SW9 ... 48 A2
Trehern Rd 12 SW14 ... 55 C4
Trehurst St E5 ... 18 A3
Trelawney Est E9 ... 17 B2
Trelawney Ho SE1 ... 136 C4
Trelawn Rd SW2 ... 62 C2
Trellis Sq 1 E3 ... 26 B2
Tremadoc Rd SW4 ... 61 C3
Tremaine Cl SE4 ... 51 C1
Trematon Ho SE11 ... 149 C2
Tremlett Gr N19 ... 4 B1
Tremlett Mews 17 N19 ... 4 B1
Trenchard St SE10 ... 42 C1
Trenchold St SW8 ... 162 A3
Trendell Ho 8 E14 ... 33 C3
Trenmar Gdns NW10 ... 22 A2
Trentham Ct W3 ... 28 C4
Trentham St SW18 ... 70 C3
Trent Ho SE15 ... 65 B3
Trent Rd SW2 ... 62 B2
Treport St SW18 ... 71 A4
Tresco Ho SE11 ... 149 B2
Tresco Rd SE15 ... 65 A3
Tresham Cres NW8 ... 90 A2
Tresham Wlk E9 ... 17 B3
Tresidder Ho 10 SW4 ... 73 C4
Tressel Cl 20 N1 ... 15 A1
Tressillian Cres SE4 ... 66 C4
Tressillian Rd SE4 ... 66 C4
Trevanion Rd W14 ... 140 B2
Trevelyan Gdns NW10 ... 22 B4
Trevelyan Ho
16 Globe Town E2 ... 25 C2
SE5 ... 48 A3
Treveris St SE1 ... 122 B1
Treverton St W10 ... 22 C1
Treverton Twr 1 W10 ... 30 C4
Treves Ho E1 ... 24 C1 99 C1
Treville St SW15 ... 69 A4
Trevithick Ho
13 Bermondsey SE16 ... 40 A2
3 Gospel Oak NW5 ... 13 A4
SW8 ... 171 B4
Trevithick St SE8 ... 51 C4
Trevor Pl SW7 ... 130 B3
Trevor Roberts Sch NW8 ... 11 C1
Trevor Sq SW7 ... 130 B3
Trevor St SW7 ... 130 B3
Trevose Ho SE11 ... 149 A2
Trewint St SW18 ... 71 B2
Triangle Ct SE1 ... 123 A1
Triangle Est The SE11 ... 149 B1
Triangle Ho SE1 ... 138 C4
Triangle Pl SW4 ... 61 C3
Triangle Rd 7 E8 ... 25 A4
Triangle The
Crouch End N19 ... 4 C4
EC1 ... 96 B2
16 Hackney E8 ... 25 A4
Trident Ho 14 E14 ... 34 B3
Trident St SE16 ... 40 C2
Trieste Ct SW12 ... 72 B3
Trig La EC4 ... 122 C4
Trigon Rd SW8 ... 163 A2
Trillington Ho W12 ... 29 C1
Trimdon NW1 ... 83 A3
Trimmer Wlk 11 TW8 ... 44 A4
Trim St SE8 ... 51 B4
Trinder Gdns N19 ... 5 A3
Trinder Rd N4, N19 ... 5 A3
Trinidad Ho 17 E14 ... 33 B2
Trinidad St E14 ... 33 B2
Trinity Church Rd SW13 ... 47 A4
Trinity Church Sq SE1 ... 137 A2
Trinity Cl
3 Clapham SW4 ... 61 B3
Lewisham SE13 ... 67 C3
Trinity Coll London SE1 ... 148 B1
Trinity Coll of Music SE10 ... 52 B4
Trinity Cotts TW9 ... 54 B4
Trinity Cres SW17 ... 72 C2
Trinity Ct
Finsbury WC1 ... 94 C2
Trinity Ct *continued*
2 Hoxton N1 ... 24 A4
Rotherhithe SE16 ... 41 A4
Willesden NW2 ... 9 B3
Trinity Gdns
E16 ... 35 B4
Stockwell SW2, SW9 ... 62 B3
Trinity Gn E1 ... 32 B4
Trinity Gr 8 SE10 ... 52 B2
Trinity Ho SE1 ... 137 A2
Trinity Homes 14 SW2 ... 62 B3
Trinity Mews SW18 ... 70 C3
Trinity Pl EC3 ... 124 C3
Trinity Rd
Richmond TW9 ... 54 B4
Wandsworth SW17, SW18 ... 72 A4
Trinity Rise SE24, SW2 ... 75 A4
Trinity St Mary's Prim Sch 8 SW12 ... 72 C3
Trinity Sq EC3 ... 124 B4
Trinity St
9 Newham E16 ... 35 C4
SE1 ... 137 B2
Trinity Way W3 ... 29 B2
Trio Pl SE1 ... 137 A3
Tristan Ct 34 SE8 ... 51 B4
Triton Ct EC2 ... 97 C1
Triton Ho 2 E14 ... 42 A2
Tritton Rd SE21, SE27 ... 75 C1
Trocette Mans SE1 ... 138 B2
Trojan Ct NW6 ... 10 A1
Trojan Ind Est NW10 ... 8 B2
Troon Cl 34 SE16 ... 40 A1
Troon Ho 9 E14 ... 33 A3
Troon St E1 ... 33 A3
Tropical Ct 2 W10 ... 22 C2
Trossachs Rd SE22 ... 64 A2
Trothy Rd SE1 ... 153 C3
Trotman Ho 1 SE14 ... 50 B2
Trott St SW11 ... 168 A3
Trotwood Ho 3 SE16 ... 40 A4
Troubridge Ct 12 W4 ... 37 B1
Troutbeck NW1 ... 92 B3
Troutbeck Rd SE14 ... 51 A2
Trouville Rd SW4 ... 61 B1
Trowbridge Est 6 E15 ... 18 B2
Trowbridge Rd E9 ... 18 B2
Trower Ho 5 E9 ... 18 A2
Troy Ct W8 ... 127 B2
Troyes Ho NW3 ... 12 B3
Troy Town SE15 ... 64 C4
Troy Town Flats SE15 ... 64 C4
Truman's Rd 24 N16 ... 16 A3
Trump St EC2 ... 109 A1
Trundle St SE1 ... 136 C4
Trundleys Rd SE8 ... 51 A4
Trundley's Rd SE8 ... 40 C1
Trundley's Terr SE8 ... 40 C2
Truro Ho 25 W2 ... 31 C4
Truro St NW5 ... 12 C2
Trussley Rd W6 ... 39 B3
Trust Wlk SE21 ... 75 A3
Tryon Cres E9 ... 25 B4
Tryon St SW3 ... 144 C2
Tubbs Rd NW10 ... 21 B3
Tudor Cl
Crouch End N6 ... 4 B4
Hampstead NW3 ... 12 A2
Tulse Hill SW2 ... 62 B1
Tudor Coll WC1 ... 94 A3
Tudor Ct
Kingsland N1 ... 16 A2
5 Rotherhithe SE16 ... 32 C1
South Acton W5 ... 36 C4
Tudor Est NW10 ... 20 A3
Tudor Gdns SW14 ... 56 A4
Tudor Gr E9 ... 17 B1
Tudor Ho
Brook Green W14 ... 39 C2
34 Hackney E9 ... 17 B1
Tudor Mews 2 NW10 ... 8 C2
Tudor Rd E9 ... 25 A4
Tudor St EC4 ... 121 C4
Tudor Way W3 ... 36 C4
Tufnell Ct 19 E3 ... 26 B4
Tufnell Mans 7 N7 ... 13 C4
TUFNELL PARK ... 13 C4
Tufnell Park Mans 2 N7 ... 5 A1
Tufnell Park Prim Sch N7 ... 13 C4
Tufnell Park Rd N19, N7 ... 13 C4
Tufnell Park Sta N19 ... 13 B4
Tufton Ct SW1 ... 134 A1
Tufton St SW1 ... 134 A1
Tuke Sch SE15 ... 50 A2
Tullis Ho 12 E9 ... 17 B1
TULSE HILL ... 75 A4
Tulse Hill
Tulse Hill SW2 ... 74 C4
Tulse Hill SW27 ... 75 A2
Tulse Hill Sta SE27 ... 75 A2
Tulse Ho SW2 ... 62 C1
Tulsemere Rd SE21, SE27 ... 75 B2
Tunbridge Ct 1 SE26 ... 76 C1
Tunbridge Ho EC1 ... 96 A4
Tunis Rd W12 ... 30 A1
Tunley Gn 12 E14 ... 33 B4
Tunley Rd
Dagenham NW10 ... 21 A4
Upper Tooting SW12, SW17 ... 72 C2
Tunnel Avenue Trad Est SE10 ... 42 C4
Tunnel Rd SE16 ... 40 B4
Tunstall Ct 14 TW9 ... 44 B2
Tunstall Rd SW9 ... 62 B3
Tunstall Wlk 10 TW8 ... 44 A4
Tunworth Cres SW15 ... 56 B1
Tun Yd SW8 ... 61 A4

Tupman Ho 26 SE16 . . . 139 B3
Turberville Ho 1 SW9 . . . 62 B4
Turenne Cl SW18 . . . 59 B3
Turin St E2 . . . 24 C2 99 B3
Turk's Head Yd EC1 . . . 108 A4
Turks Row SW3 . . 145 A2
Turle Rd N4 . . . 5 B2
Turlewray Cl N4 . . . 5 B3
Turnagain La EC4 108 A2
Turnberry Cl 24 SE16 . . . 40 A1
Turnberry Quay 1 E14 . . . 42 A3
Turnbull Ho N1 . . . 86 B4
Turnchapel Mews 1 SW4 . . . 61 A4
Turner Cl 7 SW9 . . . 48 A2
Turner Ct
9 Herne Hill SE5 . . . 63 C3
24 Rotherhithe SE16 . . . 40 B4
Turner Ho
Finsbury Pk N4 . . . 5 B3
24 Millwall E14 . . . 41 C4
St John's Wood NW8 . . . 80 A2
Strand WC2 . . . 120 B3
Westminster SW1 . 147 C3
Turner Lo 10 SW19 . . . 69 C3
Turner Pl SW11 . . . 60 A2
Turners Ct E15 . . . 19 B4
Turner's Rd E3 . . . 33 B4
Turner St
Canning Town E16 . . . 35 B3
Stepney E1 . . . 32 A4
Turneville Rd W14 . . . 154 C4
Turney Rd SE21 . . . 75 C4
Turney Sch SE21 . . . 75 B4
Turnham Green Sta W4 . . . 38 A2
Turnham Green Terr W4 . . . 38 A2
Turnham Ho SE4 . . . 66 A3
Turnham Prim Sch 1 SE4 . . . 66 A3
Turnham Rd SE4 . . . 66 A3
Turnmill Ho 8 SW2 . . . 62 C2
Turnmill St EC1 . . . 108 A4
Turnour Ho 31 E1 . . 32 A3
Turnpike Cl SE8 . . . 51 B3
Turnpike Ho EC1 . . 96 B3
Turnpin La 3 SE10 . . . 52 B4
Turpentine La SW1 . . . 146 B1
Turpin Ho SW11 . . 170 A4
Turpin Way N19 . . . 4 C3
Turquand St SE17 151 A3
Turret Gr SW4 . . . 61 B4
Turville Ho NW8 . . . 90 A2
Turville St E2 . . . 24 B1 98 C2
Tuscan Ho 36 E2 . . . 25 B2
Tuskar St SE10 . . . 43 A1
Tuttle Ho SW1 . . . 147 C1
Tweed Ho E14 . . . 27 B1
Tweezer's Alley WC2 . . . 121 B4
Twelvetrees Bsns Pk E16 . . . 27 C1
Twelvetrees Cres E3 . . . 27 B1
Twig Folly Cl 21 E2 . . . 25 C3
Twilley St SW18 . . . 71 A4
Twine Ct E1 . . . 32 B2
Twinings Mus WC2 . . . 107 B1
Twisden Rd NW5 . . . 13 A4
Twycross Mews SE10 . . . 43 A2
Twyford CE High Sch W3 . . . 28 A1
Twyford Ho N5 . . . 6 A1
Twyford Sp Ctr W3 . . . 28 A1
Twyford St N1 . . . 84 C4
Twynholm Mans SW6 . . . 154 A2
Tyburn Tree (site of) W2 . . . 116 C4
Tyburn Way W1 . . 117 A4
Tyer's Est SE1 . . . 138 A4
Tyers Gate SE1 . . . 138 A3
Tyers St SE11 . . . 148 C2
Tyers Terr SE11 . . . 149 A1
Tyler Cl E2 . . . 24 B3
Tyler Ho SE3 . . . 52 C1
Tyler St
Greenwich SE10 . . . 43 A1
SE10 . . . 53 A4
Tylney Ho 10 E1 . . . 32 A3
Tymperley Ct SW19 . . . 70 A3
Tyndale La N1 . . . 15 A1
Tyndale Mans N1 . . . 15 A1
Tyndale Terr 13 N1 . . . 15 A1
Tyneham Cl 10 SW11 . . . 60 C4
Tyneham Rd SW11 . . 60 C4
Tynemouth St SW6 . . . 166 C2
Tyne St E1 . . . 111 A2
Tynsdale Rd NW10 . . . 8 A2
Tynte Ct E9 . . . 18 A3
Tynwald Ho 14 SE26 . . . 76 C1
Type St E2 . . . 25 C3
Tyrawley Rd SW6 166 A4
Tyrells Ct 3 SE15 . . . 65 A4
Tyrrell Ho SW1 . . . 161 A4
Tyrrell Rd SE22 . . . 64 C3
Tyrwhitt Rd SE4 . . . 66 C4
Tysoe St EC1 . . . 95 C3
Tyssen Com Prim Sch N16 . . . 7 C3
Tyssen Rd N16 . . . 7 B1
Tyssen St
Dalston E8 . . . 16 B2
Hoxton N1 . . . 24 A3
Tysson Ho E9 . . . 18 A1
Tytherton 29 E2 . . . 25 B3
Tytherton Rd N19 . . . 4 C1

U

Uamvar St E14 . . . 34 A4
Udall St SW1 . . . 147 A3
Udimore Ho 11 W10 . . . 30 B4
Uffington Rd NW10 . . . 22 A4
Ufford St SE1 . . . 135 C4
Ufton Gr N1 . . . 15 C1
Ufton Rd N1 . . . 16 A1
Uhura Sq 19 N16 . . . 7 A1
Ujima Ct N19 . . . 5 A3
Ullin St E14 . . . 34 B4
Ullswater SW15 . . . 57 C1
Ullswater Ho SE15 . . 50 B4
Ullswater Rd
Barnes SW13 . . . 46 C3
West Norwood SE27, SW16 . . . 75 A2
Ulster Pl NW1 . . . 92 A1
Ulster Terr NW1 . . . 92 A2
Ulundi Rd SE3 . . . 53 A4
Ulva Rd SW15 . . . 57 C3
Ulverscroft Rd SE22 . . . 64 C2
Ulverstone Rd SE27 . . . 75 A2
Ulysses Rd NW6 . . . 10 B3
Umberston St E1 . . . 32 A3
Umbria St SW15 . . . 56 C1
Una Ho 7 NW5 . . . 13 A2
Undercliff SE10 . . . 52 B2
Undercliff Rd SE13 . . . 67 A4
Underhill Ho 7 E14 . . . 33 C4
Underhill Pas NW1 82 B4
Underhill St NW1 . . 82 B3
Undershaft EC3 . . 110 A1
Underwood Ho W6 . . . 39 A3
Underwood Rd E1 . . . 24 C1 99 C1
Underwood Row N1 . . . 97 A4
Underwood St N1 . 97 A4
Undine Rd E14 . . . 42 A2
Unicorn Bldg 14 E1 . . . 32 C2
Unicorn Sch TW9 . . . 44 B2
Union Cl E11 . . . 19 C4
Union Ct
45 Paddington W2 . . . 31 C4
2 Richmond TW10 . . 54 A2
South Lambeth SW4 . . . 172 A1
Whitechapel EC2 . . 110 A2
Union Dr E1 . . . 26 A1
Union Gr SW8 . . . 171 C2
Union Mews 32 SW9 . . . 172 A1
Union Pk 11 SE10 . . . 43 B1
Union Rd SW8 . . . 171 C1
Union Sq N1 . . . 87 A3
Union St
Mill Meads E15 . . . 27 C4
SE1 . . . 122 C1
Union Wharf N1 . . . 87 A2
Union Wlk E2 . . . 24 A2 98 B4
Union Yd W1 . . . 104 B1
United International Coll W1 . . . 104 B3
Unity Cl NW10 . . . 8 C2
Unity Mews NW1 . . 83 B2
Univ Coll Jun Sch 31 NW3 . . . 11 B4
Univ Coll London
Bloomsbury WC1 . . . 93 B2
Bloomsbury WC1 . . . 94 B2
Univ Coll London (Windeyer Inst) W1 . . . 105 A4
Univ Coll London (Wolfson Ho) NW1 . . . 93 A3
University Coll Hospl WC1 . . . 93 A2
University Coll Sch NW3 . . . 11 B3
University Mans 9 SW15 . . . 57 C4
University St WC1 . 93 A1
Univ of California WC1 . . . 105 C3
Univ of East London (Duncan Ho) 7 E15 . . . 27 C4
Univ of Greenwich SE10 . . . 52 C4
Univ of London WC1 . . . 93 C1
Univ of London (King's Coll Hall) SE5 . . . 63 C4
Univ of London (Queen Mary & Westfield Coll) E1 . . . 26 A1
Univ of Notre Dame SW1 . . . 119 C3
Univ of Notre Dame SW1 . . . 119 C2
Univ of Roehampton (Digby Stuart Coll) SW15 . . . 56 C2
Univ of Roehampton (Froebel Coll) SW15 . . . 56 B1
Univ of Roehampton (Southlands Coll) SW15 . . . 56 C2
Univ of Roehampton (Whitelands Coll) SW15 . . . 68 C4
Univ of Westminster (Cavendish Campus) W1 . . . 104 C4
Univ of Westminster (Marylebone Campus) W1 . . . 103 B4
Univ of Westminster (Regent Campus) W1 . . . 104 C3
Univ of Westminster (Regent Campus, Univ HQ) W1 . . . 104 B2
Univ of Westminster (Wigram House Halls of Residence) SW1 . . . 133 A1
Unwin Cl SE15 . . . 49 C4
Unwin Rd SW7 . . . 129 C2
Upbrook Mews W2 . . . 101 A1
Upcerne Rd SW10 157 A1
Upcott Ho
33 Bromley E3 . . . 27 A2
4 Hackney E9 . . . 17 B1
Upgrove Manor Way 12 SE24 . . . 74 C4
Upham Park Rd W4 . . . 38 A2
Upland Rd SE22 . . . 64 C1
Uplands Cl SW14 . . . 55 A2
Upnall Ho 16 SE15 . . 50 B4
Upnor Way SE17 . . 152 B2
Upper Addison Gdns W14 . . . 126 A4
Upper Bank St E14 . . . 34 A1
Upper Bardsey Wlk 7 N1 . . . 15 B2
Upper Belgrave St SW1 . . . 131 C2
Upper Berkeley St W1 . . . 103 A1
Upper Brockley Rd SE4 . . . 51 B1
Upper Brook St W1 . . . 117 B4
Upper Caldy Wlk 18 N1 . . . 15 B2
Upper Camelford Wlk 14 W10 . . . 31 A3
Upper Cheyne Row SW3 . . . 158 A4
Upper Clarendon Wlk 12 W11 . . . 31 A3
Upper Dengie Wlk N1 . . . 86 C4
Upper Grosvenor St W1 . . . 117 B3
Upper Ground SE1 . . . 121 B2
Upper Gulland Wlk 23 N1 . . . 15 B2
Upper Hampstead Wlk 29 NW3 . . . 11 B4
Upper Handa Wlk 2 N1 . . . 15 B2
Upper Harley St NW1 . . . 91 C1
Upper Hawkwell Wlk N1 . . . 87 A4
UPPER HOLLOWAY . 4 C2
Upper Holloway Sta N19 . . . 4 C2
Upper James St W1 . . . 119 A4
Upper John St W1 . . . 119 A4
Upper Lismore Wlk 8 N1 . . . 15 B2
Upper Mall W6 . . . 39 A1
Upper Marsh SE1 135 A2
Upper Montague St W1 . . . 102 C3
Upper North St E3, E14 . . . 33 C4
Upper Park Rd NW3 . . . 12 B3
Upper Phillimore Gdns W8 . . . 127 B3
Upper Ramsey Wlk 19 N1 . . . 15 C2
Upper Rawreth Wlk N1 . . . 87 A4
Upper Richmond Rd SW15 . . . 57 B3
Upper Richmond Rd W TW10, SW14, SW15 . . . 55 B3
Upper St Martin's La WC2 . . . 120 A4
Upper St N1 . . . 86 A3
Upper Tachbrook St SW1 . . . 147 A4
Upper Talbot Wlk 7 W10 . . . 31 A3
Upper Terr NW3 . . . 2 B1

Upper Thames St EC4 123 A4
Upper Tollington Pk N4 5 C3
UPPER TOOTING 72 B1
Upper Tooting Park Mans 1 SW17 72 C2
Upper Tooting Pk SW17 72 B2
Upper Tooting Rd SW17 72 B1
Upper Tulse Hill SW2 74 B3
Upper Wimpole St W1 103 C4
Upper Woburn Pl NW1, WC1 93 C3
Upstall St SE5 48 A2
Upton Cl NW2 1 A1
Urban Mews N4 6 A4
Urlwin St SE5 48 B4
Urlwin Wlk SW9 48 A2
Urmston Dr SW19 70 A3
Urmston Ho 4 E14 42 B2
Ursula Mews N4 6 B3
Ursula St SW11 168 A3
Urswick Rd E5, E9 17 B3
Usborne Mews SW8 163 A2
Usher Rd E3 26 B3
Usk Rd SW11 59 B3
Usk St E2 25 C2
Utah Bldg 3 SE13 52 A2
Utopia Ho 3 NW2 8 C2
Utopia Village NW1 81 B4
Uverdale Rd SW10 157 A1
Uxbridge Rd W12 30 A1
Uxbridge St W8 31 C1 113 B2

V

Vadnie Bish Ho NW5 13 B2
Vaine Ho 4 E9 18 A2
Vale Cl W9 88 C3
Vale Ct
East Acton W3 29 B1
St John's Wood W9 88 C3
Vale End SE22 64 B3
Vale Est The W3 29 A1
Vale Gr
Acton W3 28 C1
Stoke Newington N4 6 B4
Valens Ho 1 SW2 74 C3
Valentia Pl SW9 62 C3
Valentine Ho
11 Clapham Pk SW4 61 B1
26 Old Ford E3 26 B4
Valentine Pl SE1 136 A4
Valentine Rd E9 17 C2
Valentine Row SE1 136 A3
VALE OF HEALTH 2 C1
Vale of Health NW3 2 C1
Vale Rd N4 6 B4
Vale Rise NW11 1 B3
Vale Row N5 6 A1
Vale Royal N7 14 A1
Vale Sch The SW7 128 C1
Vale The
Cricklewood NW11 1 A2
East Acton W3 29 A1
SW3 157 C4
Valetta Rd W3 38 B4
Valette Ho E9 17 B2
Valette St E8 17 A2
Valiant Ho
9 Cubitt Town E14 42 B4
SW11 167 C3
Vallance Rd E1 24 C1 99 C1
Valliere Rd NW10 21 C2
Val McKenzie Ave N7 5 C1
Valmar Rd SE5 48 B2
Valmar Trad Est SE5 48 B2
Valois Ho SE1 138 C2
Valonia Gdns SW18 58 B1
Vanbern Ho NW5 12 C2
Vanbrugh Ct SE11 149 C3
Vanbrugh Fields SE3 53 B3
Vanbrugh Hill SE10, SE3 53 B4
Vanbrugh Ho 8 E9 17 B1
Vanbrugh Park Rd SE3 53 B3
Vanbrugh Park Rd W SE3 53 B3
Vanbrugh Pk SE3 53 B3
Vanbrugh Rd W4 37 C3
Vanbrugh Terr SE3 53 B2
Vanburgh Ho E1 110 C4
Vancover Ho 33 E1 32 A1
Vanderbilt Rd SW18 71 B3
Vanderbilt Villas 1 W12 39 C4
Vandon Ct SW1 133 A2
Vandon Pas SW1 133 A2
Vandon St SW1 133 A2
Vandyke Cl SW15 57 C1
Vandy St EC2 24 A1 98 A1
Vane Cl NW3 11 C4
Vane St SW1 147 A4
Vange Ho 12 W10 30 B4
Van Gogh Ct E14 42 C3
Vanguard Bldg 6 E14 41 C4
Vanguard Ho 11 E8 17 A1
Vanguard St SE8 51 C2
Vanneck Sq SW15 56 C2
Vanner Point 27 E9 17 C2
Vansittart St 7 SE14 51 A3
Vanston Pl SW6 155 C2
Vantage Mews 7 E14 34 B1
Vantage Pl W8 127 C1
Vantrey Ho SE11 149 B3
Varcoe Rd SE16 40 B1
Vardens Rd SW11 59 C3
Varden St E1 32 A3
Vardon Cl W3 28 C3
Vardon Ho SE10 52 B2
Varey Ho E1 26 A2
Varley Ho 5 NW6 23 C4
Varma Ct SE3 53 C2
Varna Rd SW6 154 C1
Varndell St NW1 92 C4
Varnishers Yard N1 84 B1
Varsity Row SW14 45 B1
Vascroft Est NW10 20 A1
Vassall Ho 3 E3 26 A2
Vassall Rd SW9 163 C1
Vat Ho SW8 162 B2
Vauban Est SE16 139 A1
Vauban St SE16 139 A1
Vaudeville Ct N4 5 C2
Vaughan Ave W6 38 B2
Vaughan Est 3 E2 24 B2 98 C4
Vaughan Ho SE1 136 A4
Vaughan Rd SE5 63 B4
Vaughan St SE16 41 B4
Vaughan Way E1 125 C2
Vaughan Williams Cl SE8 51 C3
VAUXHALL 148 B1
Vauxhall Bridge Rd SW1 147 A3
Vauxhall City Farm SE1 148 C1
Vauxhall Cross SE1, SW8 148 B1
Vauxhall Gr SW8 162 C4
Vauxhall Prim Sch SE11 149 A2
Vauxhall St SE11 149 A2
Vauxhall Sta SE11 148 B1
Vauxhall Wlk SE11 148 C2
Vawdrey Cl E1 25 B1
Vaynor Ho N7 14 A4
Vectis Ct SW18 59 A1
Veda Rd SE13 66 C3
Velde Way 1 SE22 64 A2
Vellacott Ho 3 W12 30 A3
Velletri Ho 17 E2 25 C3
Venables St NW8 101 C4
Vencourt Pl W6 38 C2
Venetian Rd SE5 48 B1
Venice Ct 14 SE5 48 B3
Venn Ho N1 85 A3
Venn St SW4 61 B3
Ventnor Rd SE14 50 C3
Ventura Ho 12 SW2 62 A3
Venue St E14 34 B4
Venus Ho
7 Millwall E14 41 C2
8 Old Ford E3 26 C4
Vera Ct 1 W2 100 A2
Vera Rd SW6 164 B4
Verbena Gdns 4 W6 38 C1
Verdun Rd SW13 46 C3
Vere Bank SW19 70 B3
Vereker Rd W14 140 B1
Vere St W1 104 A1
Verity Cl W11 31 A3
Verity Ho 20 E3 26 B2
Vermeer Ct E14 42 C3
Vermont Rd SW18 59 A1
Verne Ct 9 W3 37 B3
Verneer Gdns SE15 65 B3
Verney Ho
Lisson Gr NW8 90 A2
Verney Ho *continued*
South Kensington SW10 156 C4
Verney Rd SE16 40 A1
Verney Way SE16 40 A1
Vernon Ct NW2 1 B1
Vernon Ho SE11 149 A1
Vernon Mews W14 140 B3
Vernon Pl WC1 106 B3
Vernon Rd
Bow E3 26 B3
Mortlake SW14 55 C4
Vernon Rise WC1 95 A4
Vernon Sq WC1 95 A4
Vernon St W14 140 B3
Vernon Yd W11 31 B2 112 C4
Verona Ct
Chiswick W4 38 A1
10 SE14 50 C4
Veronica Ho
Brockley SE4 66 B4
46 Bromley E3 27 A2
Veronica Rd SW17 73 A2
Verran Rd SW12 73 A4
Verulam Bldgs WC1 107 A4
Verulam Ho 1 W6 39 B4
Verulam St EC1 107 B4
Vervain Ho 2 SE15 49 C3
Verwood Ho SW8 163 A1
Verwood Lo 1 E14 42 C2
Vesage Ct EC1 107 C3
Vesey Path 15 E14 34 A3
Vespan Rd W12 38 C4
Vesta Ct SE1 138 A3
Vesta Ho 9 E3 26 C4
Vesta Rd SE4, SE14 51 A1
Vestry Mews 12 SE5 49 A2
Vestry Rd SE5 49 A2
Vestry St N1 97 B4
Viaduct Pl 28 E2 25 A2
Viaduct St E2 25 A2
Vian St SE13 67 A4
Vibart Gdns SW2 74 B4
Vibart Wlk N1 84 B4
Vicarage Ave SE3 53 C3
Vicarage Cres SW11 167 B3
Vicarage Ct
7 Putney SW15 68 C4
W8 128 A4
Vicarage Dr SW14 55 C2
Vicarage Gate W8 114 A1
Vicarage Gdns
Mortlake SW14 55 C2
W8 31 C1 113 C1
Vicarage Gr SE5 48 C2
Vicarage Rd SW14 55 C2
Vicarage Wlk SW11 167 C4
Vicar's Cl E9 25 B4
Vicars Hill SE13 67 A3
Vicar's Rd NW5 12 C3
Viceroy Ct NW8 80 B2
Viceroy Rd SW8 172 A4
Vic Johnson Ho 21 E3 26 B4
Vickery Ct EC1 97 A2
Vickery Ho 13 SW4 62 A3
Vickery's Wharf 3 E14 33 C3
Victor Cazalet Ho N1 86 A4
Victoria & Albert Mus SW7 129 C1
Victoria Arc SW1 132 B1
Victoria Ave EC2 110 B3
Victoria Bldgs 13 E8 25 A4
Victoria Chambers EC2 24 A1 98 A2
Victoria Coach Sta SW1 146 A3
Victoria Coll WC2 107 B2
Victoria Cotts
7 Richmond TW9 44 C2
3 Spitalfields E1 111 B4
Victoria Ct
5 Clapham Pk SW4 61 C1
South Acton W3 36 C4
4 St George in t East E1 125 B3
Victoria Dr SW19 69 C3
Victoria Emb WC2 121 B3
Victoria Gdns W11 31 C1 113 B2
Victoria Gr W8 128 C2
Victoria Gr Mews W2 114 A3
Victoria Hall 15 E16 35 C1
Victoria Ho
6 Clapham Pk SW4 61 C1
2 Shepherd's Bush W12 38 C4
SW1 146 A2
Victoria Ind Est W3 29 A4
Victoria Mans
8 Islington N7 14 C3
Willesden NW10 9 A1
Victoria Mews
Kilburn NW6 23 C4
Wandsworth SW18 71 B3
Victoria Mills 1 E15 27 C4
Victorian Gr N16 7 A1
Victorian Rd N16 7 B1
Victoria Park Ct 11 E9 17 B1
Victoria Park Ind Ctr E9 18 B1
Victoria Park Lofts E9 25 C4
Victoria Park Rd E9 17 C1
Victoria Park Sq E2 25 B2
Victoria Pas NW8 89 B2
Victoria Place Sh Ctr SW1 146 B4
Victoria Rd
Finsbury Pk N4 5 B3
Kensington W8 128 C2
Kilburn NW6 23 B4
Mortlake SW14 55 C4
North Acton NW10 21 A1

Victoria Rise SW4 ... 61 A4
Victoria Sq SW1 ... 132 B2
Victoria St SW1 ... 133 A1
Victoria Sta SW1 ... 146 B4
Victoria Terr
Dagenham NW10 ... 21 A1
Finsbury Pk N4 ... 5 C3
Victoria (Underground) SW1 ... 132 B1
Victoria Villas TW9 ... 54 B3
Victoria Wharf E14 ... 33 A2
Victoria Yd 28 E1 ... 111 C1
Victor Rd NW10 ... 22 A2
Victory Pl
6 Limehouse E14 ... 33 A2
SE17 ... 151 B4
Victory Prim Sch SE17 ... 151 A4
Victory Way SE16 ... 41 A4
Victory Wlk SE8 ... 51 C2
Video Ct N4 ... 5 A4
View Cl N6 ... 3 B4
Viewfield Rd SW18 ... 58 B1
Viewpoint 3 N5 ... 15 A3
Vigo St W1 ... 118 C3
Viking Cl 13 E3 ... 26 A3
Viking Ho 3 SE5 ... 48 B1
Village Cl NW3 ... 11 C3
Village Mount 19 NW3 ... 11 B4
Village Sch The NW3 ... 12 B2
Village The SW11 ... 60 B4
Village Way SE21 ... 63 C1
Villa Rd SW9 ... 62 C4
Villas On The Heath NW3 ... 2 B1
Villa St SE17 ... 151 C1
Villiers Ct SW11 ... 168 B4
Villiers Rd NW2 ... 8 C2
Villiers St WC2 ... 120 B2
Vince Ct N1 ... 97 C3
Vincent Ct
Finsbury Pk N4 ... 5 A3
Marylebone W1 ... 102 C2
South Lambeth SW9 ... 173 A3
Vincent Mews 1 E3 ... 26 C3
Vincent Rd W3 ... 37 B3
Vincents Cl SE16 ... 41 A4
Vincent Sq SW1 ... 147 B4
Vincent St
Canning Town E16 ... 35 B4
Westminster SW1 ... 147 C4
Vincent Terr N1 ... 86 B2
Vince St EC1 ... 97 C3
Vine Cl E5 ... 16 C4
Vine Ct E1 ... 111 C3
Vinegar St E1 ... 32 A1
Vinegar Yd SE1 ... 138 A4
Vine Hill EC1 ... 95 B1
Vine La SE1 ... 124 B1
Vine Rd SW13 ... 56 B4
Vine St Bridge EC1 ... 95 C1
Vine Sq W14 ... 141 A1
Vine St
W1 ... 119 A3
Vine St *continued*
Whitechapel EC3 ... 110 C1
Vineyard Path SW14 ... 55 C4
Vineyard Prim Sch The TW10 ... 54 A1
Vineyard The TW10 ... 54 A2
Vineyard Wlk EC1 ... 95 B2
Viney Ct 9 SW4 ... 61 C1
Vine Yd SE1 ... 137 A4
Viney Rd SE13 ... 67 A4
Vining St SW2, SW9 ... 62 C3
Vinson Ho N1 ... 87 C1
Vintners Ct EC4 ... 123 A4
Viola Sq W12 ... 29 B2
Violet Cl 32 SE8 ... 51 B4
Violet Hill NW8 ... 78 C1
Violet Hill Ho NW8 ... 78 C1
Violet Rd E3 ... 27 A1
Violet St E2 ... 25 A1
Virgil Pl W1 ... 102 C3
Virgil St SE1 ... 135 A2
Virginia Ct 7 SE16 ... 40 C4
Virginia Ho 3 E14 ... 34 B2
Virginia Prim Sch 48 E2 ... 24 B2 98 C3
Virginia Rd 19 E2 ... 24 B2 98 C3
Virginia St E1 ... 125 C3
Virginia Wlk SW2 ... 62 B1
Viscount Ct 9 W11 ... 31 C3
Viscount St EC1 ... 108 C4
Vision Coll of Theology E9 ... 18 B2
Vista Bldgs 19 E3 ... 26 B2
Vitae Apartments 7 W6 ... 38 C3
Vittoria Ho N1 ... 85 A3
Vittoria Prim Sch N1 ... 85 B2
Vivian Comma Cl 3 N4 ... 6 A1
Vivian Ct NW6 ... 78 A2
Vivian Ho N4 ... 6 C4
Vivian Rd E3 ... 26 A3
Vivian Sq SE15 ... 65 A4
Vogans Mill SE1 ... 139 A4
Vogler Ho 3 E1 ... 32 B2
Vollasky Ho 5 E1 ... 111 B4
Voltaire
2 Camberwell SE5 ... 49 B2
15 Richmond TW9 ... 44 B2
Voltaire Ct 13 SW11 ... 169 C2
Voltaire Rd SW4 ... 61 C4
Volt Ave NW10 ... 21 A2
Vorley Rd N19 ... 4 B2
Voss St E2 ... 24 C2 99 C3
Voyager Bsns Est 10 SE16 ... 139 B2
Vulcan Rd SE4 ... 51 B1
Vulcan Sq E14 ... 41 C2
Vulcan Terr SE4 ... 51 B1
Vulcan Way N7 ... 14 B2
Vyner Ct E5 ... 7 C2
Vyner Rd W3 ... 28 C2
Vyner St E2 ... 25 A4

W

Wadcroft Ct SE4 ... 66 B4
Wadding St SE17 ... 151 B3
Waddington Rd E15 ... 19 C2
Waddington St E15 ... 19 C2
Wade Ho 16 SE1 ... 139 B3
Wadeson St E2 ... 25 A3
Wade's Pl E14 ... 34 A2
Wadham Gdns NW3 ... 80 A4
Wadham Rd SW15 ... 58 A3
Wadhurst Rd W4 ... 37 C3
Wager St E3 ... 26 B1
Waghorn St SE15 ... 64 C4
Wagner St SE15 ... 50 B3
Wainford Cl SW19 ... 69 C3
Wainwright Ho 3 E1 ... 32 B1
Waite St SE15 ... 49 B4
Waithman St EC4 ... 108 A1
Wakefield Ho 6 SE15 ... 49 C2
Wakefield Mews WC1 ... 94 B3
Wakefield St WC1 ... 94 B3
Wakeford Cl SW4 ... 61 B2
Wakeham St 9 N1 ... 15 C2
Wakehurst Rd SW11 ... 60 B2
Wakeling Ho 8 SE27 ... 75 A1
Wakeling St 11 E14 ... 33 A3
Wakelin Ho 19 N1 ... 15 A1
Wakeman Rd NW10 ... 22 C2
Wakley St EC1 ... 96 A4
Walberswick St SW8 ... 162 B1
Walbrook EC4 ... 123 B4
Walbrook Ct 32 N1 ... 24 A3
Walbrook Wharf EC4 ... 123 B4
Walburgh St E1 ... 32 A3
Walcorde Ave SE17 ... 151 A3
Walcot Gdns SE11 ... 149 B4
Walcot Ho 9 SE22 ... 64 A4
Walcot Sq SE11 ... 149 C4
Walcott St SW1 ... 147 A4
Waldeck Gr SE27 ... 75 A1
Waldeck Rd
Brentford W4 ... 44 C4
Mortlake SW14 ... 55 B4
Waldeck Terr SW14 ... 55 B4
Waldegrave Ho 5 SW15 ... 57 B2
Waldemar Ave SW6 ... 164 B2
Waldemar Avenue Mans SW6 ... 164 A3
Walden Ct SW8 ... 171 C4
Walden Ho
8 Clapham SW11 ... 169 B2
SW1 ... 145 C3
Walden St E1 ... 32 A3
Waldo Cl SW4 ... 61 B2
Waldo Rd NW10 ... 22 A2
Waldorf Sch of S W London SW16 ... 73 C2
Waldron Ho 17 SW2 ... 62 B2
Waldron Mews SW3 ... 157 C4
Waldron Rd SW18 ... 71 B1
Walerand Rd SE13 ... 52 B1
Waleran Flats SE1 ... 152 A4
Wales Cl SE15 ... 50 A4
Wales Farm Rd W3 ... 28 C4
Waley St 1 E1 ... 33 A4
Walford Ho 28 E1 ... 32 A3
Walford Rd N16 ... 16 A4
Walham Ct 15 NW3 ... 12 B2
Walham Gr SW6 ... 155 B2
WALHAM GREEN ... 156 A1
Walham Green Arc SW6 ... 155 C2
Walham Yd SW6 ... 155 B2
Walker Ho NW1 ... 83 B1
Walker Mews 9 SW2 ... 62 C2
Walkerscroft Mead SE21 ... 75 B3
Walker's Ct W1 ... 119 B4
Walkers Lo 18 E14 ... 42 B4
Walker's Pl SW15 ... 58 A3
Walkinshaw Ct 9 N1 ... 15 B1
Walkynscroft 1 SE15 ... 50 A1
Wallace Collection W1 ... 103 B2
Wallace Ct NW1 ... 102 B3
Wallace Ho N7 ... 14 B2
Wallace Lo N4 ... 5 C3
Wallace Rd N1, N5 ... 15 B2
Wallbutton Rd SE4 ... 51 A1
Wall Ct N4 ... 5 B3
Waller Rd SE14 ... 50 C1
Wallett Ct 11 NW1 ... 13 B1
Wallflower St W12 ... 29 B2
Wallgrave Rd SW5 ... 142 A3
Wallingford Ave W10 ... 30 C3
Wallis Alley SE1 ... 137 A4
Wallis Cl SW11 ... 59 C4
Wallis Ho 5 SE14 ... 51 A2
Wallis Rd E9 ... 18 C2
Wallorton Gdns SW14 ... 55 C3
Wallside EC2 ... 109 A3
Wall St N1 ... 15 C2
Wallwood St E14 ... 33 B4
Walmer Ho 8 W10 ... 30 C3
Walmer Pl W1 ... 102 C4
Walmer Rd
North Kensington W10 ... 30 B3
W11 ... 31 A2 112 A3
Walm La NW2 ... 9 B2
Walney Wlk 6 N1 ... 15 B2
Walnut Cl SE8 ... 51 B4
Walnut Ho 11 E3 ... 26 B4
Walnut Tree Cl SW13 ... 46 B2
Walnut Tree Ho SW10 ... 156 B4
Walnut Tree Rd
Brentford TW8 ... 44 A4
Greenwich SE10 ... 43 A1
Walnut Tree Walk Prim Sch SE11 ... 149 B4
Walnut Tree Wlk SE11 ... 149 B4
Walpole Ave TW9 ... 44 B1
Walpole Ct
7 Hammersmith W14 ... 39 C3
South Hampstead NW6 ... 11 B1
Walpole Gdns W4 ... 37 B1
Walpole Mews NW8 ... 79 B3
Walpole St SW3 ... 145 A2
Walsham Cl N16 ... 7 C3
Walsham Ho
New Cross Gate SE14 ... 50 C1
SE17 ... 151 B2
Walsham Rd SE14 ... 50 C1
Walsingham NW8 ... 79 C4
Walsingham Lo SW13 ... 46 C2
Walsingham Mans SW6 ... 156 B2
Walsingham Pl SW4, SW11 ... 60 C1
Walsingham Rd E5 ... 7 C1
Walter Besant Ho 20 E1 ... 25 C2
Walter Ct 3 W3 ... 28 B3
Walter Green Ho SE15 ... 50 B2
Walter Ho SW10 ... 157 B2
Walter Northcott Ho 2 NW6 ... 10 C3
Walters Cl SE17 ... 151 A3
Walters Ho
3 Camberwell SE5 ... 49 A1
Islington N1 ... 86 B4
10 Kennington SE17 ... 48 A4
Walter Sickert Hall N1 ... 86 C1
Walter St E2 ... 25 C2
Walters Way SE23 ... 65 C1
Walter Taylor Ct SE4 ... 66 B3
Walter Terr E1 ... 32 C3
Walterton Rd W9 ... 23 C1
Waltham Green Ct SW6 ... 156 A1
Waltham Ho
NW8 ... 78 C4
10 Stockwell SW9 ... 173 A1
Walton Cl SW8 ... 162 B2
Walton Gdns W3 ... 28 A4
Walton Ho
E2 ... 24 B1 99 A2
Upper Holloway N7 ... 5 B1
Wandsworth SW18 ... 58 C1
Walton Pl SW3 ... 130 C2
Walton St SW3 ... 130 B1
Walton Way W3 ... 28 A4
Walt Whitman Cl 6 SE24 ... 63 A3
WALWORTH ... 151 C2
Walworth Acad SE17 ... 152 B1
Walworth Pl SE17 ... 151 A1

Walworth Rd SE17 151 A2
Wanborough Dr SW15 69 A3
Wandle Ct 4 W12 38 A4
Wandle Ho NW8 102 A4
Wandsworth SW18 71 A4
Wandle Rd SW17 72 A2
Wandle Way SW18 71 A3
Wandon Rd SW6 156 B1
WANDSWORTH 58 C1
Wandsworth Bridge Rd SW6 166 A3
Wandsworth Common Sta SW12 72 B4
Wandsworth Common West Side SW18 59 B2
Wandsworth Gyratory SW18 59 A2
Wandsworth High St SW18 59 A2
Wandsworth Plain SW18 59 A2
Wandsworth Rd SW8 162 A1
Wandsworth Road Sta SW4 171 A1
Wandsworth Town Sta SW18 59 A3
Wangford Ho 13 SW9 63 A3
Wanless Rd SE24 63 B4
Wanley Rd SE5 63 C3
Wansbeck Rd E3, E9 18 B1
Wansdown Pl SW6 156 A2
Wansdworth Riverside Quarter Pier SW6 58 C4
Wansey St SE17 151 A3
WAPPING 32 A1
Wapping Dock St 19 E1 32 A1
Wapping High St E1 32 A1
Wapping La E1 32 A1
Wapping Sta E1 32 B1
Wapping Wall E1 32 B1
Warbeck Rd W12 39 A4
Warburg Ho E2 24 C2 99 B3
Warburton Cl 6 N1 16 A2
Warburton Ct SE15 64 C4
Warburton Ho 5 E8 25 A4
Warburton Rd 8 E8 25 A4
Warburton St 6 E8 25 A4
Wardalls Ho 12 SE8 51 B4
Wardell Ho 7 SE10 52 B4
Warden Rd NW5 12 C2
Wardens Gr SE1 122 C1
Wardle St E9 17 C3
Wardley St SW18 71 A4
Wardlow 8 NW5 13 A4
Wardo Ave SW6 164 A4
Wardour Mews W1 105 A1
Wardour St W1 105 B1
Ward Point SE11 149 B3
Ward Rd
Camden Town N19 4 B1
Mill Meads E15 27 C4
Wardrobe Pl EC4 108 B1
Wardrobe Terr EC4 122 B4
Wareham Ct 2 N1 16 A1
Wareham Ho SW8 162 C2
Warfield Rd NW10 22 C2
Warfield Yd 6 NW10 22 C2
Wargrave Ho 46 E2 24 B2 98 C3
Warham St SE5 48 A3
Waring Ho 25 E2 24 C2 99 C3
Warley Ho N1 15 C2
Warley St E2 25 C2
Warlock Rd W9 23 C1
Warlters Cl N7 14 A4
Warlters Rd N7 14 A4
Warltersville Mans N19 5 A4
Warltersville Rd N4, N8, N19 5 A4
War Meml Homes W4 45 C3
Warmington Rd SE24 63 B1
Warmsworth NW1 82 C4
Warndon St SE16 40 B2
Warneford St E9 25 A4
Warner Ho
4 Homerton E9 17 C2
Lewisham SE13 52 A1
NW8 88 C4
Warner Pl E2 24 C2 99 C4
Warner Rd SE5 48 B2
Warner St EC1 95 B1
Warner Yd EC1 95 B1
Warnford Ho SW15 56 A1
Warnham WC1 94 C3
Warnham Ho 6 SW2 74 B4
Warple Mews W3 38 A4
Warple Way W3, W12 38 A4
Warren Ave SW14, TW10 55 A3
Warren Cl SE21 75 B4
Warren Ct N1 85 B2
Warrender Rd N19 13 B4
Warren Gdns E15 19 C3
Warren Ho 21 E3 27 A2
Warren Mews W1 92 C1
Warren St W1 92 C1
Warren Street Sta NW1 93 A2
Warriner Gdns SW11 169 B3
Warrington Cres W9 88 C2
Warrington Gdns W9 88 C1
Warspite Ho 3 E14 42 A2
Warton Rd E15 27 B4
Warwick W14 141 A3
Warwick Ave W9 88 C1
Warwick Avenue Sta W9 88 C1
Warwick Bldg SW8 160 A3
Warwick Chambers W8 127 B2
Warwick Cres W2 100 C4
Warwick Ct WC1 107 A3
Warwick Dr SW15 57 A4
Warwick Gdns W14 141 A4
Warwick Ho
10 Brixton SW9 173 B1
6 Putney SW15 69 B4
Stoke Newington N4 6 B3
Warwick House St SW1 119 C2
Warwick La EC4 108 B1
Warwick Lo NW2 10 A3
Warwick Mans SW5 141 B4
Warwick Pas EC4 108 B2
Warwick Pl W9 100 C4
Warwick Pl N SW1 146 C3
Warwick Rd W14, SW5 141 A4
Warwick Row SW1 132 B2
Warwickshire Path SE8 51 B3
Warwick Sq
Holborn EC4 108 B2
Pimlico SW1 146 C2
Warwick Sq Mews SW1 146 C3
Warwick St W1 119 A4
Warwick Way SW1 146 B4
Warwick Yd EC1 97 A1
Wasdale NW1 92 B3
Washbrook Ho SW2 62 C1
Washington Bldg 1 SE13 52 A2
Washington Cl 45 E3 27 A2
Washington Ho SW1 130 C3
Washington Rd SW13 46 C3
Watchfield Ct 7 W4 37 B1
Watcombe Cotts TW9 44 C4
Watercress Pl 12 N1 16 A1
Waterford Rd SW6 156 A1
Waterford Way NW10 8 C3
Water Gardens The W2 102 B2
Watergate EC4 122 A4
Watergate St SE8 51 C4
Watergate Wlk WC2 120 B2
Waterhead NW1 92 C4
Waterhouse Cl
Hammersmith W6 39 C1
Hampstead NW3 11 C3
Waterhouse Sq EC1 107 B3
Wateridge Cl E14 41 C3
Water La
16 Camden Town NW1 13 A1
SE14 50 B3
Waterloo Bridge SE1, WC2 121 A3
Waterloo Cl E9 17 B3
Waterloo East Sta SE1 121 C1
Waterloo Gdns
26 Islington N1 15 A1
South Hackney E2 25 B3
Waterloo Millennium Pier SE1 134 C4
Waterloo Pl
Kew TW9 44 C4
9 Richmond TW9 54 A3
SW1 119 B2
Waterloo Rd SE1 135 C4
Waterloo Sta SE1 135 B4
Waterloo Terr N1 15 A1
Waterlow Ct NW11 2 A4
Waterlow Rd N19 4 B3
Waterman Bldg 2 E14 41 C4
Watermans Arts Ctr TW8 44 A4
Watermans Ct 2 TW8 44 A4
Waterman St SW15 57 C4
Waterman Way E1 32 A1
Watermark Pl EC4 123 B3
Watermead Ho E9 18 B3
Watermeadow La SW6 166 C1
Water Mews SE15 65 B3
Watermill Ct SE13 67 A4
Watermint Quay N16 7 C4
Water's Edge SW6 47 B2
Waterside N1 86 C1
Waterside Cl
30 Bermondsey SE16 139 C3
Old Ford E3 26 B4
Waterside Ct SE13 67 C3
Waterside Pl NW1 81 C4
Waterside Point SW11 158 B2
Waterson St E2 24 B2 98 C4
Waters Pl SW15 47 B1
Water St WC2 121 B4
Water Tower Pl N1 86 A3
Waterview Ho 13 E14 33 A4
Waterway Ave 2 SE13 67 A4
Waterworks Rd SW2 62 B1
Watford Cl SW11 168 B4
Watford Rd E16 35 C4
Watkins Ho 11 E14 42 B4
Watkinson Rd N7 14 B2
Watling Ct EC4 109 A1
Watling Gdns NW2 10 A2
Watling St
4 Camberwell SE15 49 A4
City of London EC4 109 A1
Watney Cotts SW14 55 B4
Watney Mkt E1 32 A3
Watney Rd SW14 55 B4
Watney St E1 32 A3
Watson Cl N16 15 C3
Watson Ho 3 SW2 74 A4
Watsons Mews W1 102 B3
Watson's St SE8 51 C3
Watts Gr E3 34 A4
Watts Ho 6 W10 31 A4
Watts St
SE15 49 B2
Wapping E1 32 A1
Wat Tyler Rd SE10 52 C2
Wavel Ct
7 Streatham SW16 74 A1
7 Wapping E1 32 B1
Wavel Mews NW6 11 A1
Wavendon Ave W4 37 C1
Waveney Ave SE15 65 A3
Waveney Cl 20 E1 125 C2
Waveney Ho SE15 65 A3
Waverley Ct
5 Brondesbury NW6 10 A1
W1 103 C4
Waverley Pl
Finsbury Pk N4 6 A3
St John's Wood NW8 79 B2
Waverley Rd N8 5 A4
Waverly Ct NW3 12 B2
Waverton Ho 2 E3 26 B4
Waverton Rd SW18 71 B4
Waverton St W1 118 A2
Wavertree Ct 9 SW2 74 A3
Wavertree Rd SW2 74 B3
Waxham NW5 12 B3
Waxlow Rd NW10 20 C3
Wayford St SW11 168 B1
Wayland Ave E8 16 C3
Wayland Ho 12 SW9 173 B2
Waylett Ho SE11 149 B1
Waylett Pl SE27 75 A1
Wayman Ct E8 17 A2
Waynflete Sq
18 North Kensington W10 30 C3
16 Shepherd's Bush W10 30 C2
Waynflete St SW18 71 B2
Wayside
Golders Green NW11 1 A3
Mortlake SW14 55 B2
Weald Cl 16 SE16 40 A1
Weardale Ho N4 6 B4
Weardale Rd SE13 67 C3
Wearmouth Ho 1 E3 33 B4
Wear Pl 13 E2 25 A2
Wearside Rd SE13 67 A3
Weatherbury 6 W2 31 C3
Weatherbury Ho 3 N19 4 C1
Weatherley Cl E3 33 B4
Weaver Ct 2 E2 25 A1

Weaver Ho 12
E1 ....24 C1 99 B1
Weaver's La SE1 .. 124 B1
Weaver St
E1 ....24 C1 99 B1
Weavers Way
6 Camden Town
NW1 ....13 C1
NW1 .... 83 B4
Webb Cl NW10 ....22 B1
Webb Ct W3 ....37 A4
Webber Row SE1 136 A3
Webber St SE1 ... 136 A3
Webb Est E5 ....7 C4
Webb Ho SW8 .... 161 C1
Webb Pl NW10 ....21 B2
Webb Rd SE3 ....53 B4
Webb's Rd SW11 ...60 B2
Webb St SE1 .... 138 A1
Webheath 6 NW6 ..10 B1
Webster Ho 16
N16 ....16 A3
Webster Rd SE16 . 139 C1
Weddell Ho 23 E1 ..25 C1
Wedderburn Rd
NW3 ....11 C3
Wedgewood Ho
SW1 .... 146 C1
Wedgewood Mews
W1 .... 105 C1
Wedgewood Wlk
NW3 ....11 A3
Wedgwood Ho
17 Globe Town
E2 ....25 C2
SE11 .... 135 B1
Wedlake St W10 ....23 A1
Wedmore Gdns
N19 ....4 C2
Wedmore Mews
N19 ....4 C1
Wedmore St N19 ....4 C1
Weech Rd NW6 ....10 C4
Weedington Rd
NW5 ....12 C3
Weedon Ho W12 ....29 C3
Weekley Sq SW11 ..59 C4
Weighhouse St
W1 .... 103 C1
Weimar St SW15 ....58 A4
Weir Ho 8 SW12 ...73 B4
Weir Rd
Streatham SW12 ....73 B4
Wimbledon SW18,
SW19 ....71 A1
Weiss Rd SW15 ....57 C4
Welbeck Ct W14 .. 140 C4
Welbeck Mans 10
NW6 ....10 C3
Welbeck St W1 ... 104 A2
Welbeck Way W1 104 A2
Welbury Ct E8 ....16 A1
Welby Ho N19 ....4 C4
Welby St SE5 ....48 A2
Weldon Ct SE8 ....51 C1
Welford Ct
12 Camden Town
NW1 ....13 A1
7 Clapham SW8 .. 170 C1
Welland Ho SE15 ...65 B3
Welland Mews 21
E1 .... 125 C2
Welland St SE10 ....52 B4
Wellclose Sq E1 .. 125 C4
Wellclose St 20
E1 .... 125 C3
Well Ct EC4 .... 109 A1
Wellday Ho 2 E9 ..18 A2
Welldon Ct 1
SE21 ....75 C2
Weller Ho 23
SE16 .... 139 B3
Weller St SE1 .... 136 C4
Welles Ct 15 E14 ...33 C2
Wellesley Ave W6 ..39 A3
Wellesley Ct W9 ... 88 C4
Wellesley Ho NW1 . 93 B3
Wellesley Pl
Camden Town
NW5 ....12 C3
NW1 .... 93 B3
Wellesley Rd
Gospel Oak NW5 ....12 C3
Gunnersbury W4 ....37 A1
Wellesley St E1 ....32 C4
Wellesley Terr N1 .. 97 A4
Wellfit St 6 SE24 ...63 A4
Wellgarth Rd NW11 ..2 A3
Wellington Arch
SW1 .... 131 C4
Wellington Bldgs
15 Bow E3 ....26 C2
SW1 .... 145 C1
Wellington Cl
Kensington W11 ....31 C3
New Cross Gate
SE14 ....50 C2
Wellington Ct
Knightsbridge
SW1 .... 130 C3
St John's Wood
NW8 .... 79 C1
Strand WC2 .... 120 A4
Wandsworth SW18 ..60 A2
Wellington Gr
SE10 ....52 C3
Wellington Ho 18
NW3 ....12 B2
Wellington Hospl The
NW8 .... 79 C1
Wellington Mans
N16 ....16 B4
Wellington Mews
East Dulwich
SE22 ....64 C3
3 Islington N7 ....14 B2
Streatham SW16 ....73 C1
Wellington Pl NW8 89 C4
Wellington Prim Sch
20 E3 ....26 C2
Wellington Rd
Kensal Green
NW10 ....22 C2
St John's Wood
NW8 .... 79 C1
Wimbledon SW19 ....70 C2
Wellington Row
E2 ....24 C2 99 B4
Wellington Sq
Islington N1 .... 84 B4
SW3 .... 144 C2
Wellington St
WC2 .... 120 C4
Wellington Terr 2
E1 ....32 A1
Wellington Way
E3 ....26 C2
Well La SW14 ....55 B2
Well Rd NW3 ....2 C1
Wells Ct
21 Hampstead
NW3 ....11 B4
1 Paddington
NW6 ....23 C3
Stoke Newington
N1 ....16 A3
Wells Ho
Finsbury EC1 .... 96 A4
12 Kensal Town
W10 ....23 A1
New Cross Gate
SE4 ....51 A1
9 Rotherhithe
SE16 ....40 B3
Wells Ho The 2
NW3 ....11 C4
Wells House Rd
NW10 ....29 A4
Wellside Gdns
SW14 ....55 B2
Wells Mews W1 .. 105 A2
Wells Pl SW18 ....71 B4
Wells Rd W12 ....39 B4
Wells Rise NW8 .... 80 C3
Wells Sq WC1 .... 95 A3
Wells St W1 .... 105 A2
Well St E9 ....17 B1
Wells Terr N4 ....5 C2
Wells Way
Brompton SW7 .... 129 B2
Camberwell SE5 ....49 A4
Well Wlk NW3 ....2 C1
Wellwood Ct
SW15 ....57 B3
Welmar Works
SW4 ....61 C3
Welsford St SE1 .. 153 B3
Welsh Ho 14 E1 ....32 A1
Welshpool Ho 22
E8 ....24 C4
Welshpool St 1
E8 ....25 A4
Welstead Ho 29
E1 ....32 A3
Welstead Way W4 ..38 B2
Weltje Rd W6 ....38 C1
Welton Ct SE5 ....49 A2
Welton Ho E1 ....32 C4
Welwyn St E2 ....25 B2
Wembury Mews N6 ..4 B4
Wembury Rd N6 ....4 A4
Wemyss Rd SE3 ....53 B1
Wendell Park Prim
Sch W12 ....38 B4
Wendell Rd W12 ....38 B4
Wendle Ct SW8 ... 162 A3
Wendling NW5 ....12 B3
Wendon St E3 ....26 B4
Wendover SE17 ... 152 A1
Wendover Ct
Acton W3 ....20 A1
Becontree W3 ....20 B1
4 Child's Hill NW2 ...1 C1
W1 .... 103 B3
Wendover Ho W1 . 103 B3
Wendover Rd
NW10 ....21 B3
Wengham Ho W12 ..29 C2
Wenham Ho SW8 160 C1
Wenlake Ho EC1 ... 96 C2
Wenlock Ct N1 .... 87 C1
Wenlock Rd N1 .... 87 A1
Wenlock St N1 .... 87 B1
Wennington Rd
E3 ....25 C3
Wensdale Ho E5 ....7 C2
Wensleydale Ho 8
N4 ....6 B4
Wentworth Cres
SE15 ....49 C3
Wentworth Ct
W6 .... 154 A3
Wandsworth SW18 ..59 A1
Wentworth Dwellings
E1 .... 110 C2
Wentworth Ho 4
SE3 ....53 C3
Wentworth Mews
E3 ....26 B2
Wentworth St E1 . 111 A3
Werrington St
NW1 .... 83 A1
Werter Rd SW15 ....58 A3
Wesleyan Pl NW5 ..13 A4
Wesley Ave NW10 ..20 C2
Wesley Cl
Finsbury Pk N7 ....5 B2
SE17 .... 150 B3
Wesley Ct W1 .... 103 C3
Wesley Ho SE24 ....63 C1
Wesley Rd NW10 ...20 B4
Wesley Sq W11 ....31 A3
Wesley St W1 .... 103 C3
Wessex Ct SW15 ....57 C2
Wessex Gardens Prim
Sch NW11 ....1 A3
Wessex Gdns NW11 ..1 A3
Wessex Ho
SE1 .... 153 A1
4 Tufnell Pk N19 ....4 C1
Wessex St E2 ....25 B2
Wessex Way NW11 ..1 A3
West 12 Sh Ctr
W12 ....39 C4
Westacott Cl N19 ....4 C3
West Acton Prim Sch
W3 ....28 A3
West Arbour St E1 ..32 C3
West Bank N16 ....7 A4
Westbere Rd NW2 ..10 A3
West Block 18 E1 ...32 B2
Westbourne Ave
W3 ....28 C3
Westbourne Cres
W2 .... 115 B4
Westbourne Ct
W2 .... 100 C2
Westbourne Gdns
W2 .... 100 A2
Westbourne Gr
Notting Hill W2,
W11 ....31 C3
W11 ....31 B2 113 A4
WESTBOURNE
GREEN 88 A2
Westbourne Gr Mews
7 W11 ....31 C3
Westbourne Gr Terr
W2 .... 100 A1
Westbourne Ho
SW1 .... 146 A2
Westbourne Park Rd
Notting Hill W2 ....31 C3
Notting Hill W11 ....31 B3
Westbourne Park Sta
W11 ....31 B4
Westbourne Park
Villas W2 .... 100 A3
Westbourne Rd
N7 ....14 B2
Westbourne St
W2 .... 115 B4
Westbourne Terr
W2 .... 101 A2
Westbourne Terrace
Mews W2 .... 100 C2
Westbourne Terrace
Rd W2 .... 100 C3
Westbridge Cl
W12 ....29 C1
Westbridge Prim Sch
SW11 .... 168 A4
Westbridge Rd
SW11 .... 168 A4
WEST
BROMPTON 156 A4
West Brompton Sta
SW5 .... 141 C1
Westbrook Ho
5 Bethnal Green
E2 ....25 B2
5 Clapham Pk
SW4 ....61 B2
Westbury Ct SW4 ...61 A1
Westbury Ho 6
NW10 ....8 A1
Westbush Ct 1
W12 ....39 A4
West Carriage Dr
W2 .... 116 A2
West Central St
WC1 .... 106 A2
Westchester Ho
W2 .... 102 C1
Westcliff Ho 13
N1 ....15 C2
Westcombe Ct 1
SE3 ....53 B3
Westcombe Hill SE3,
SE10 ....53 C4
Westcombe Park Rd
SE3 ....53 B3
Westcombe Park Sta
SE3 ....43 C1
Westcott Ho 1
E14 ....34 A2
Westcott Rd SE17 ...48 A4
West Cotts NW6 ....10 C3
Westcroft Cl NW2 ..10 A4
Westcroft Ct 3
W6 ....38 C2
Westcroft Sq W6 ...38 C2
Westcroft Way
NW2 ....10 A4
West Cromwell Rd
W14 .... 141 A2
West Cross Route W10,
W11 ....30 C2
Westdean Cl
SW18 ....59 A1
Westdown Rd E15 ..19 B4
WEST DULWICH ...75 B2
West Dulwich Sta
SE21 ....75 C3
West Eaton Pl
SW1 .... 145 B4
West Eaton Pl Mews
SW1 .... 145 B4
West Ella Rd NW10 ..8 A1
West End Ct NW6 ...11 A1
West End La NW6 ..11 A2
Westerdale Ct N5 ..15 A4
Westerdale Rd 2
SE10 ....43 C1
Westerham NW1 .. 82 C3

Westerham Ho SE1 137 C2
Western Ave W3 28 C3
Western Avenue Bsns Pk W3 20 A1
Western Beach Apts E16 35 C1
Western Ct
4 Dagenham W3 28 C3
3 Kilburn W9 23 B3
Western Eye Hospl The NW1 102 C4
Western Gateway E16 35 C2
Western Ho 3 W9 23 B1
Western La SW12 72 C4
Western Mews W9 23 B1
Western Pl 19 SE16 40 B4
Western Rd
Becontree NW10 20 B1
Brixton SW9 62 C4
Western Terr 3 W6 38 C1
Western Wharf 2 SE15 49 C4
Westferry Cir E14 33 C1
Westferry Rd E14 41 C3
Westferry Sta E14 33 C2
Westfield NW3 10 C4
Westfield Cl SW10 156 C1
Westfield Ct 1 W10 22 C2
Westfield Ho 6 SE16 40 C2
Westfield London Sh Ctr W12 30 C1
Westfields SW13 56 B4
Westfields Ave SW13 56 A4
Westfields Rd W3 28 A4
Westfield Stratford Sh Ctr EH15 19 B2
Westfield Way E1 26 A1
West Garden Pl W2 102 B1
Westgate Bsns Ctr
2 Kensal Town W10 23 A1
North Kensington W10 22 C1
Westgate Ct 15 SW9 62 C4
Westgate St E8 25 A4
Westgate Terr SW10 156 B4
West Gdns E1 32 A2
West Gr SE10 52 C2
Westgrove La SE10 52 B2
West Halkin St SW1 131 B2
West Hall Rd TW9 45 A2
WEST HAMPSTEAD 10 C4
West Hampstead Mews NW6 11 A2
West Hampstead Sta NW6 10 C2
West Hampstead Thameslink Sta NW6 10 C2
West Harding St EC4 107 C2
Westhay Gdns SW14 55 A2
West Heath Ave NW11 1 C3
West Heath Cl NW3 1 C1
West Heath Ct NW11 1 C3
West Heath Dr NW11 1 C3
West Heath Gdns NW3 1 C1
West Heath Rd NW3 2 A1
WEST HILL 58 B1
West Hill SW15 58 A1
Westhill Ct W11 31 B2 113 A4
West Hill Ct N6 3 C1
Westhill Pk
Dartmouth Pk N6 3 C2
Highgate N6 3 B2
West Hill Prim Sch 17 SW18 58 C2
West Hill Rd SW18 58 B1
West Ho 9 SW12 73 B4
Westhope Ho 29 E2 24 C2 99 C3
Westhorpe Rd SW15 57 B4
West House Cl SW19 70 A3
West India Ave E14 33 C1
West India Dock Rd E14 33 C2
West India Ho 1 E14 33 C2
West India Quay Sta E14 33 C2
WEST KENSINGTON 140 B3
West Kensington Ct W14 140 C2
West Kensington Mans W14 140 C1
West Kensington Sta W14 140 C2
WEST KILBURN 23 A2
West La SE16 40 A4
Westlake 12 SE16 40 B2
Westland Pl N1 97 B4
Westlands Terr 3 SW12 61 B1
Westleigh Ave SW15 57 B2
Westly Ct NW2 9 C2
Westmacott Ho NW8 89 C1
West Mall W11 31 C1 113 C2
Westmark Point 13 SW15 69 A3
Westmead SW15 57 A1
West Mews SW1 146 C3
Westmill Ct N4 6 B2
WESTMINSTER 133 A1
Westminster Abbey SW1 134 A2
Westminster Abbey Choir Sch SW1 133 C2
Westminster Acad W2 31 C4
Westminster Acad (Sch of English) W1 105 A2
Westminster Boating Base SW1 161 B4
Westminster Bridge SE1, SW1 134 B3
Westminster Bridge Rd SE1 134 C3
Westminster Cath SW1 132 C1
Westminster Cath Choir Sch SW1 147 A4
Westminster Cath RC Prim Sch SW1 147 C2
Westminster City Hall SW1 133 A2
Westminster City Sch SW1 133 A2
Westminster Coll W1 119 B4
Westminster Ct
22 Rotherhithe SE16 32 C1
5 Wandsworth SW18 58 C2
Westminster Dragoons Mus SW6 58 A4
Westminster Gdns SW1 148 A4
Westminster Kingsway Coll (King's Cross Centre) WC1 94 C3
Westminster Kingsway Coll (Regent's Park Ctr) NW1 92 C2
Westminster Kingsway Coll (Victoria Centre) SW1 147 B4
Westminster Millennium Pier SW1 134 B3
Westminster Pier SW1 134 B3
Westminster Sch SW1 134 A2
Westminster Sta SW1 134 B3
Westminster Under Sch SW1 147 B3
Westmore Ct SW15 58 A2
Westmoreland Ho NW10 21 C2
Westmoreland Pl SW1 146 B1
Westmoreland Rd
Barnes SW13 46 C2
Camberwell SE17 48 C4
Westmoreland St W1 103 C3
Westmoreland Terr SW1 146 B1
WEST NORWOOD 75 B1
West Norwood Sta SE27 75 A1
Westonbirt Ct 6 SE15 49 B4
Weston Ct N4 6 B1
West One Ho W1 104 C3
West One Sh Ctr W1 104 A1
Weston Ho
6 Brondesbury NW6 10 A1
Weston Ho *continued*
8 South Hackney E9 25 B4
Weston Rd W4 37 B3
Weston Rise N1, WC1 95 A4
Weston St SE1 137 C4
Weston Wlk 3 E8, E9 17 A1
Westover Hill NW3 1 C2
Westover Rd SW18 59 B1
West Park Ave TW9 45 A2
West Park Rd TW9 44 C2
West Parkside
Greenwich SE10 43 B3
Greenwich SE10 43 C2
West Plaza E14 34 A1
Westpoint SW15 57 C1
West Point 2 SE1 153 B2
Westpoint Trad Est W3 28 A4
Westport St E1 32 C3
West Poultry Ave EC1 108 A3
West Quarters W12 29 C3
West Rd
Chelsea SW3 159 A4
Clapham Pk SW4 61 C2
Westrow SW15 57 B1
West Row W10 23 A1
West Sheen Vale TW9 54 B3
Westside 11 W6 38 C2
Westside Ct 1 W9 23 C1
West Silvertown Sta E16 35 C1
West Smithfield EC1 108 B3
West Sq SE11 136 A1
West St
30 Bethnal Green E2 25 A3
Soho WC2 105 C1
West Temple Sheen SW14 55 A2
West Tenter St E1 111 A1
Westvale Mews W3 38 A4
Westview Cl
North Kensington W10 30 B3
Willesden NW10 8 B3
Westville Rd W12 38 C4
West Warwick Pl SW1 146 C3
Westway W10, W12 29 C2
Westway (Elevated Rd) W10 31 B4
Westway Lo 35 W2 31 C4
Westwell 4 NW5 12 C2
Westwick Gdns W14 39 C4
Westwood Bsns Ctr NW10 21 A1
Westwood Gdns SW13 56 B4
Westwood Ho
6 Shepherd's Bush W12 30 B1
5 Stoke Newington N4 6 C4
Westwood Park Trad Est W3 20 A1
Westwood Rd SW13 56 B4
Wetherby Gdns SW5 142 C3
Wetherby Mans SW5 142 A2
Wetherby Mews SW5 142 B2
Wetherby Pl SW7 143 A3
Wetherby Prep Sch W11 31 C2 113 B4
Wetherell Rd E9 25 C4
Wevco Wharf SE15 50 A4
Wexford Ho 11 E1 32 B4
Wexford Rd SW12 72 B4
Weybourne St SW18 71 B2
Weybridge Ct 18 SE16 40 A1
Weybridge Ho N4 6 B4
Weybridge Point 11 SW11 169 A2
Weydown Cl SW19 70 A3
Weyhill Ho 26 SE5 48 B1
Weyhill Rd 11 E1 111 C2
Wey Ho NW8 89 C1
Weymouth Ct
5 Haggerston E2 24 B3
15 Streatham SW2 74 B4
Weymouth Ho
Fitzrovia W1 104 B4
South Lambeth SW8 162 C1
Weymouth Mews W1 104 A4
Weymouth St W1 104 A4
Weymouth Terr E2 24 B3
Whadcoat St N4 5 C2
Whaddon Ho
10 Camberwell SE5 64 A4
SW1 131 A3
Wharfdale Rd N1 84 B2
Wharfedale Ct 5 E5 17 C4
Wharfedale St SW10 142 A1
Wharf La 19 E14 33 B3
Wharf Pl E2 25 A4
Wharf Rd N1 86 C1
Wharfside Rd E16 35 A4
Wharf St E16 35 A4
Wharf View Ct 15 E14 34 B3
Wharncliffe Ho 3 SW15 57 B2
Wharton Cl NW10 8 A2
Wharton Ho SE1 138 C2
Wharton St WC1 95 A3
Whateley Rd SE22 64 B2
Whatman Ho 10 E14 33 B3
Wheatland Ho 7 SE22 64 A4

Wheatlands Rd SW17 .... 72 C1
Wheatley Ho
Gospel Oak NW5 .... 13 A4
3 Putney SW15 .... 68 C4
Wheatley St W1 .. 103 C3
Wheat Sheaf Cl E14 .... 42 A2
Wheatsheaf La
Fulham SW6 .... 47 B3
SW8 .... 162 B2
Wheatsheaf Terr SW6 .... 155 A1
Wheatstone Ho 7 W10 .... 31 A4
Wheatstone Rd W10 .... 31 A4
Wheeler Ct 4 SW11 .... 59 C4
Wheeler Gdns N1 . 84 B4
Wheeler La E1 ... 110 C4
Wheelhouse The 4 E14 .... 42 A1
Wheelwright St N7 .... 14 B1
Wheldon Ct SE1 .. 138 C4
Wheler Ho E1 .... 24 B1 98 C1
Wheler St E1 .... 24 B1 98 C1
Whellock Rd W4 ... 38 A3
Whetstone Park WC2 .... 106 C2
Whewell Rd N19 ..... 5 A2
Whichcote St SE1 121 B1
Whidborne Bldgs WC1 .... 94 A3
Whidborne Cl SE8 .. 51 C1
Whidborne St WC1 94 B3
Whippingham Ho 22 E3 .... 26 B2
Whiskin St EC1 .... 96 A3
Whistler Mews 23 SE15 .... 49 B3
Whistlers Ave SW11 .... 157 C1
Whistler St N5 ..... 15 A3
Whistler Twr SW10 .... 156 C1
Whistler Wlk SW10 .... 157 A2
Whiston Ho 18 N1 .. 15 A1
Whiston Rd E2 ..... 24 C4
Whitbread Ctr EC1. 97 B1
Whitbread Rd SE4 .. 66 B3
Whitburn Rd SE13 .. 67 B3
Whitby Ave NW10 .. 20 A2
Whitby Ct 6 N7 .... 14 A4
Whitby Ho NW8 ... 78 C3
Whitby St E1 .... 24 B1 98 C2
Whitcher Cl SE14 ... 51 A4
Whitcher Pl NW1 ... 13 B2
Whitchurch Ho 16 W10 .... 30 C3
Whitchurch Rd W11 .... 30 C2
Whitcomb Ct W1 119 C3
Whitcomb St WC2 .... 119 C3
Whitcome Mews TW9 .... 45 A2
Whiteacre Mews SE11 .... 149 C1
Whiteadder Way E14 .... 42 A2
Whitear Wlk E15 ... 19 C2
Whitebeam Cl SW9 .... 163 A1
Whitebeam Ho 3 NW3 .... 12 B2
White Bear Pl 1 NW3 .... 11 C4
White Bear Yd EC1 95 B1
WHITECHAPEL .. 110 C1
Whitechapel Gall E1 .... 111 A2
Whitechapel High St E1 .... 111 A2
Whitechapel Mkt E1 .... 111 C3
Whitechapel Rd E1 .... 32 A4
Whitechapel Sta E1 .... 32 A4
Whitechurch La 3 E1 .... 111 B2
Whitechurch Pas 1 E1 .... 111 B2
White City W10 ..... 30 B3
White City Cl W12 .. 30 B2
White City Est W12 .... 30 A2
White City Rd W12 . 30 B2
White City Sta W12 .... 30 B2
Whitecliff Ho SW18 .... 59 A1
White Conduit St N1 .... 85 C2
Whitecross Pl EC2 .... 109 C4
Whitecross St EC1. 97 A1
White Cube (Gall) N1 .... 24 A2 98 A3
SE1 .... 138 B2
SW1 .... 111 A2
Whitefield Cl SW15 .... 58 A1
Whitefriars St EC4 .... 107 C1
Whitehall SW1 ... 134 A4
Whitehall Ct SW1. 120 B1
Whitehall Gdns
Chiswick W4 .... 45 A4
SW1 .... 120 A1
Whitehall Mans 3 N19 .... 4 B3
Whitehall Park Rd W4 .... 45 A4
Whitehall Pk N19 .... 4 B3
Whitehall Pl WC2, SW1 .... 120 A1
White Hart Ct EC2 .... 110 A3
White Hart La
Mortlake SW13 ..... 56 A4
Willesden NW10 ...... 8 B2
White Hart St
Holborn EC4 ...... 108 B2
Kennington SE11 .. 149 C2
White Hart Yd SE1 .... 123 B1
Whitehaven St NW8 .... 90 A1
Whitehead Cl SW18 .... 71 B4
Whitehead Ho 8 SW15 .... 57 C2
Whitehead's Gr SW3 .... 144 B3
White Ho
2 Battersea SW11 .... 167 C2
3 Streatham SW4 .. 73 C4
Whitehorn Ho 6 E1 .... 32 B1
White Horse La E1 .... 32 C4
Whitehorse Mews SE1 .... 136 A2
Whitehorse Rd E1 .. 33 A4
White Horse Rd E1 .... 33 A3
White Horse St W1 .... 118 B1
White Horse Yd EC2 .... 109 B2
White Ho The NW1 92 B2
White House Prep Sch SW12 .... 73 C3
White Kennett St E1 .... 110 B2
Whitelands Cres SW18 .... 70 A4
Whitelands Ho SW3 .... 145 A2
Whiteley Ho 9 SW4 .... 73 C4
Whiteleys Ctr 19 W2 .... 100 B1
White Lion Ct EC3 .... 110 A1
White Lion Hill EC4 .... 122 B4
White Lion St N1 .. 85 C1
White Lo NW11 ...... 1 B3
Whitelock Ho 21 E9 .... 17 C2
White Lyon Ct EC2 .... 108 C4
Whiteness Ho 18 SW9 .... 173 B4
White Post La E9 ... 18 C2
White Post St SE14, SE15 .... 50 B3
White Rd EC2 .... 110 A3
White's Grounds SE1 .... 138 B4
White's Grounds Est SE1 .... 138 B4
White's Row E1 .. 110 C3
White's Sq SW4 ... 61 C3
Whitestone La NW3 . 2 B1
Whitestone Wlk NW3 .... 2 B1
Whitethorn St E3 ... 33 C4
White Twr Way E1 .. 33 A4
Whitfield Ct SW4 172 A3
Whitfield Gdns W1 .... 105 A4
Whitfield Ho NW8 . 90 A1
Whitfield Pl W1 .. 93 A1
Whitfield St W1 .. 105 A4
Whitgift Ho
Battersea SW11 ... 168 A4
Lambeth SE11 .... 148 C4
Whitgift St SE11 .. 148 C4
Whitington Ave EC3 .... 110 A1
Whitley Ho SW1 .. 161 A4
Whitlock Dr SW19 .. 70 A3
Whitman Ho 20 E2 . 25 B2
Whitman Rd E3 .... 26 A1
Whitmore Gdns NW10 .... 22 B3
Whitmore Ho 20 E1 .... 24 A4
Whitmore Prim Sch N1 .... 87 C3
Whitmore Rd N1 ... 24 A4
Whitnell Ct 7 SW15 .... 57 C2
Whitnell Way SW15 .... 57 C2
Whitney Ho 6 SE22 .... 64 A4
Whitstable Ho 11 W10 .... 30 C3
Whitsters Ho SE1 138 C4
Whittaker Ct SW4 172 B3
Whittaker St SW1 145 B3
Whittaker Way 19 SE1 .... 153 C4
Whittingham Ct W4 .... 46 A3
Whittingstall Mans SW6 .... 165 A3
Whittingstall Rd SW6 .... 165 A3
Whittington Hospl The N19 .... 4 B2
Whittlebury Ho N4 .. 6 B4
Whittlesey St SE1 121 C1
Whitton NW3 .... 12 B1
Whitton Wlk E3 .... 26 C2
Whitworth Ho SE1 .... 137 A1
Whitworth St SE10 . 43 A1
Whorlton Rd SE15 .. 65 A4
Whytlaw Ho 10 E3 .. 33 B4
Wicker St 24 E1 .... 32 A3
Wickfield Ho 32 SE16 .... 139 C3
Wickford Ho 5 E1 .... 25 B1
Wickford St E1 ..... 25 B1
Wickham Cl E1 ..... 32 B4
Wickham Gdns SE4 .... 66 B4
Wickham Ho SW15 .... 57 C1
Wickham Mews SE4 .... 51 B1
Wickham Rd SE4 ... 66 B4
Wickham St SE11 148 C2
Wick La
Hackney E3 .... 18 B1
Stratford Marsh E3 .. 26 C4
Wicklow Ho N16 ..... 7 B3
Wicklow St WC1 ... 94 C4
Wick Rd
Hackney E9 .... 17 C2
Hackney E9 .... 18 A2
Wickstead Ho TW8 .... 36 B1
Wicksteed Ho SE1 .... 137 A1
Wick Village 7 E15 .... 18 B3
Wickway Ct 7 SE15 .... 49 B4
Wickwood St SE5 ... 48 A1
Widdenham Rd N7 .... 14 B4
Widecombe Ho 32 SE5 .... 48 B1
Widegate St E1 ... 110 B3
Widford 8 NW1 .... 13 A2
Widford Ho N1 .... 86 A1
Widley Rd W9 ...... 23 C1
Widnes Ho 6 N7 ... 14 C3
Wigmore Hall W1 104 A2
Wigmore Pl W1 .. 104 A2
Wigmore St W1 .. 103 C2
Wigram Ct SW11 . 168 A4
Wigram Ho 7 E14 .. 34 A2
Wigton Pl SE11 ... 149 C1
Wilberforce Ho 3 SW11 .... 59 C4
Wilberforce Mews 9 SW4 .... 61 C3
Wilberforce Prim Sch W10 .... 23 A2
Wilberforce Rd
Finsbury Pk N4 .... 6 A2
Highbury N4, N5 ...... 6 B1
Wilbraham Ho SW8 .... 162 A1
Wilbraham Pl SW1 .... 145 B4
Wilby Mews W11 .... 31 B1 113 A2
Wilcox Cl SW8 .... 162 B2
Wilcox Ho 5 E3 .... 33 B4
Wilcox Pl SW1 .... 133 A1
Wilcox Rd SW8 ... 162 A2
Wildcroft Manor SW15 .... 69 B4
Wildcroft Rd SW15 .... 69 B4
Wild Ct WC2 ..... 106 C2
Wilde Cl E8 .... 24 C4
Wilde Pl SW18 ..... 71 C4
Wilderness Mews SW4 .... 61 A3
Wilderton Rd N16 ... 7 A4
Wild Goose Dr SE14 .... 50 B2
Wilding Ho 17 E9 ... 17 C2
Wild's Rents SE1 . 138 A2
Wild St WC2 ...... 106 C1
Wildwood Gr NW3 ... 2 B3
Wildwood Rd NW11 . 2 B4
Wildwood Rise NW11 .... 2 B3
Wildwood Terr NW3, NW11 .... 2 B3
Wilfred Fienburgh Ho N7 .... 13 C4
Wilfred St SW1 ... 132 C2
Wilfrid Gdns W3 ... 28 B4
Wilkes Rd 3 TW8 .. 44 A4
Wilkes St E1 ..... 111 A4
Wilkie Ho SW1 ... 147 C2
Wilkin St Mews NW1 .... 13 A2
Wilkins Ho SW1 .. 160 C4
Wilkinson Ho N1 .. 87 C1
Wilkinson St SW8 162 C1
Wilkinson Way W4 .... 37 C4
Wilkin St NW5 ...... 13 A2
Wilks Pl N1 .... 24 A3
Willan Wall E16 .... 35 B2
Willard St SW8 ..... 61 A4
Willbury Ho 4 N7 ... 13 C3
Willcott Rd W3 ..... 28 A1
Willenfield Rd NW10 .... 20 B3
WILLESDEN 8 B1
Willesden Community Hospl The NW10 .... 8 C1
WILLESDEN GREEN 22 A4

Willesden Green Sta NW2 . . . 9 B2
Willesden Junction Sta NW10 . . . 21 B2
Willesden La NW2, NW6 . . . 9 C2
Willesden Sports Ctr W10 . . . 22 A4
Willes Rd NW5 . . . 13 A2
Willett Ho SW9 . . . 62 A4
William Banfield Ho 10 SW6 . . . 164 C2
William Blake Ho 2 SE15 . . . 49 C1
William Bonney Est 10 SW4 . . . 61 C3
William Booth Meml Training Coll SE5 . . . 48 C1
William Brown Ct SE27 . . . 75 A2
William Caslon Ho 28 E2 . . . 25 A3
William Channing Ho 6 E2 . . . 25 A2
William Cl SE13 . . . 67 B4
William Davis Prim Sch 19 E2 . . . 24 C1 99 B2
William Dromey Ct NW6 . . . 10 B1
William Dunbar Ho NW6 . . . 23 B3
William Ellis Sch NW5 . . . 3 C1
William Ellis Way 16 SE16 . . . 139 C1
William Evans Ho 9 SE8 . . . 40 C2
William Gdns SW15 . . . 57 A2
William Guy Gdns 47 E3 . . . 27 A2
William Harvey Ho 1 SW19 . . . 70 A3
William Hogarth Sch The 15 W4 . . . 38 A1
William Hunt Mans SW13 . . . 47 B4
William IV St WC2 . . . 120 A3
William Margrie Cl 1 SE15 . . . 49 C1
William Mews SW1 . . . 131 A3
William Morris Acad W6 . . . 39 C1
William Morris Ho W6 . . . 47 C4
William Morris Way SW6 . . . 166 C1
William Patten Prim Sch 9 N16 . . . 7 B2
William Pl 37 E3 . . . 26 B3
William Rathbone Ho 3 E2 . . . 25 A2
William Rd NW1 . . . 92 C3
William Rushbrooke Ho 4 SE16 . . . 153 B4
William Saville Ho 2 NW6 . . . 23 B3
William's Bldgs 1 E2 . . . 25 B1
Williams Cl SW6 . . . 154 B2
Williams Coll EC1 . . . 107 C3
Williams Ho
10 Bow E3 . . . 26 C2
Williams Ho *continued*
9 Hackney E9 . . . 25 A4
14 Streatham SW2 . . . 74 C3
Williams La SW14 . . . 45 B1
Williamson Cl SE10 . . . 43 B1
Williamson Ct SE17 . . . 150 C1
Williamson St N7 . . . 14 A4
William Sq 15 SE16 . . . 33 A2
William St SW1 . . . 131 A3
William Tyndale Prim Sch 27 N1 . . . 15 A1
William Winter Ct 29 SW2 . . . 74 C4
Willingham Cl 4 NW5 . . . 13 B3
Willingham Terr NW5 . . . 13 B3
Willington Rd SW9 . . . 62 A4
Willis Ho 8 E14 . . . 34 A2
Willis St E14 . . . 34 A3
Willoughby Ho
EC2 . . . 109 B3
34 Wapping E1 . . . 32 A1
Willoughby Rd NW3 . . . 11 C4
Willoughby St WC1 . . . 106 A3
Willoughbys The SW14 . . . 56 A3
Willow Ave SW13 . . . 46 B1
Willowbank SW6 . . . 58 A4
Willowbank Rd SE15 . . . 49 B4
Willow Bridge Rd N1 . . . 15 B2
Willow Cotts TW9 . . . 44 C4
Willow Ct
Brixton SW9 . . . 173 B3
Chiswick W4 . . . 46 A3
EC2 . . . 24 A1 98 A2
Islington N7 . . . 14 B3
40 Paddington W2 . . . 31 C4
3 Streatham SW16 . . . 74 B1
Willowdene
Highgate N6 . . . 3 B4
1 Peckham SE15 . . . 50 A2
5 SE15 . . . 50 A3
Willow Farm La SW15 . . . 57 A4
Willow Hall NW3 . . . 11 C4
Willow Ho
9 Maitland Pk NW3 . . . 12 B2
North Kensington W10 . . . 22 C1
Willow Lo
Fulham SW6 . . . 47 C2
Putney SW15 . . . 57 A4
Willow Lodge 10 SW8 . . . 61 A4
Willowmere SE13 . . . 67 A2
Willow Pl SW1 . . . 147 A4
Willow Rd
Ealing W5 . . . 36 A4
Hampstead NW3 . . . 11 C4
Willow St EC2 . . . 24 A1 98 A2
Willows Terr NW10 . . . 21 B3
Willow Tree Cl
14 Old Ford E3 . . . 26 B4
Willow Tree Cl *continued*
Wandsworth SW18 . . . 71 A3
Willow Vale W12 . . . 29 C1
Willow Way 9 W11 . . . 30 C2
Willow Wlk SE1 . . . 152 C4
Willsbridge Ct 1 SE15 . . . 49 B4
Wilman Gr E8 . . . 16 C1
Wilmcote Ho W2 . . . 100 A4
Wilmer Gdns 22 N1 . . . 24 A4
Wilmer Ho 6 E3 . . . 26 A3
Wilmer Lea Cl E15 . . . 19 C1
Wilmer Pl N16 . . . 7 B2
Wilmers Ct 5 NW10 . . . 20 C4
Wilmington Ave W4 . . . 45 C3
Wilmington Sq WC1 . . . 95 B3
Wilmington St WC1 . . . 95 B3
Wilmot Cl SE15 . . . 49 C3
Wilmot Pl NW1 . . . 13 B1
Wilmot St E2 . . . 25 A1
Wilna Rd SW18 . . . 71 B4
Wilsham St W11 . . . 31 A1 112 A2
Wilshaw Ho 10 SE8 . . . 51 C3
Wilshaw St SE14 . . . 51 C2
Wilson Gr SE16 . . . 40 A4
Wilson Ho
39 Clapham SW8 . . . 171 B1
South Hampstead NW6 . . . 11 B1
Wilson Rd SE5 . . . 49 A2
Wilson's Pl E14 . . . 33 B3
Wilson's Rd W6 . . . 39 C1
Wilson St EC2 . . . 109 C4
Wiltern Ct NW2 . . . 10 A2
Wilton Ave W4 . . . 38 A1
Wilton Cres SW1 . . . 131 B3
Wilton Ct
4 Richmond TW10 . . . 54 A2
7 Stepney E1 . . . 32 A3
Wilton Est E8 . . . 16 C2
Wilton Ho 8 SE22 . . . 64 A4
Wilton Mews SW1 . . . 131 C2
Wilton Pl SW1 . . . 131 B3
Wilton Rd SW1 . . . 146 C4
Wilton Row SW1 . . . 131 B3
Wilton Sq N1 . . . 87 B4
Wilton St SW1 . . . 132 A2
Wilton Terr SW1 . . . 131 B2
Wilton Villas N1 . . . 87 B3
Wilton Way E8 . . . 16 C2
Wiltshire Cl SW3 . . . 144 C3
Wiltshire Ct 2 N4 . . . 5 B3
Wiltshire Rd SW9 . . . 62 C4
Wiltshire Row N1 . . . 87 C3
Wimbart Rd SW2 . . . 74 B4
Wimbledon Lawn Tennis Mus SW19 . . . 70 A1
Wimbledon Park Ct SW19 . . . 70 B3
Wimbledon Park Montessori Sch SW18 . . . 70 C2
Wimbledon Park Prim Sch SW19 . . . 71 A2
Wimbledon Park Rd SW18, SW19 . . . 70 B3
Wimbledon Park Side SW19 . . . 69 C3
Wimbledon Park Sta SW19 . . . 70 C1
Wimbledon Stadium Bsns Ctr SW17 . . . 71 A1
Wimbledon Windmill Mus SW19 . . . 69 B1
Wimbolt St E2 . . . 24 C2 99 B4
Wimborne Ho
Canning Town E16 . . . 35 B2
Marylebone NW1 . . . 90 B1
South Lambeth SW8 . . . 163 A1
Upper Tooting SW12 . . . 73 B1
Wimbourne Ct N1 . . . 87 B2
Wimbourne St N1 . . . 87 B2
Wimpole Mews W1 . . . 104 A3
Wimpole St W1 . . . 104 A2
Winans Wlk SW9 . . . 173 B1
Winant Ho 19 E14 . . . 34 A2
Wincanton Rd SW18 . . . 70 B4
Winchelsea Cl SW15 . . . 57 C2
Winchelsea Ho 16 SE16 . . . 40 B4
Winchelsea Rd NW10 . . . 20 C4
Winchendon Rd SW6 . . . 165 A4
Winchester Ave NW6 . . . 10 A1
Winchester Cl SE17 . . . 150 B3
Winchester Ct
Richmond TW9 . . . 54 B4
W8 . . . 128 A4
Winchester Ho
Bayswater W2 . . . 100 C1
Chelsea SW3 . . . 157 C3
24 Tower Hamlets E3 . . . 26 B2
Winchester Pal SE1 . . . 123 B2
Winchester Pl
6 Dalston E8 . . . 16 B3
Highgate N6 . . . 4 A3
Winchester Rd
Highgate N6 . . . 4 A3
South Hampstead NW3 . . . 11 C1
Winchester Sq SE1 . . . 123 B2
Winchester St
Acton W3 . . . 37 B4
SW1 . . . 146 B2
Winchester Wlk SE1 . . . 123 B2
Winchfield Ho SW15 . . . 56 B1
Winch Ho
Isle of Dogs E14 . . . 42 A3
SW10 . . . 157 A2
Winchilsea Ho NW8 . . . 89 C3
Wincott St SE11 . . . 149 C3
Windermere
NW1 . . . 92 B4
12 Putney SW15 . . . 57 C1
Windermere Ave NW6 . . . 23 A4
Windermere Ct SW13 . . . 46 B4
Windermere Ho E3 . . . 26 B1
Windermere Point 3 SE15 . . . 50 B3
Windermere Rd N19 . . . 4 B2
Winders Rd SW11 . . . 168 A2
Windham Rd TW9 . . . 54 B4
Windlass Pl SE8 . . . 41 A2
Windlesham Gr SW19 . . . 69 C3
Windmill WC1 . . . 106 C4
Windmill Alley 7 W4 . . . 38 A2
Windmill Cl
12 Bermondsey SE1 . . . 153 C4
4 Lewisham SE13 . . . 52 B1
Windmill Ct NW2 . . . 10 A2
Windmill Dr
Clapham SW4 . . . 61 A2
Cricklewood NW2 . . . 1 A1
Windmill Gdns SW2 . . . 62 B1
Windmill Hill
1 Hampstead NW3 . . . 11 B4
Hampstead NW3 . . . 2 B1
Windmill Ho
4 Millwall E14 . . . 41 C2
SE1 . . . 121 C1
Windmill La E15 . . . 19 C2
Windmill Pas 10 W4 . . . 38 A2
Windmill Rd
Chiswick W4 . . . 38 A2
Roehampton SW19 . . . 69 A1
Wandsworth SW18 . . . 59 C1
Windmill Row SE11 . . . 149 B1
Windmill St W1 . . . 105 B3
Windmill Wlk SE1 . . . 135 C4
Windrose Cl SE16 . . . 40 C4
Windrush Cl
Battersea SW11 . . . 59 C3
Chiswick W4 . . . 45 B3
4 Hackney E8 . . . 16 C1
Windrush Ho NW8 . . . 101 C4
Windrush Rd NW10 . . . 20 C4
Windrush Sq
Brixton SW9 . . . 62 C3
SW2 . . . 62 C3
Windsock Cl 1 SE16 . . . 41 B2
Windsor Ct
Battersea SW11 . . . 167 C2
Bayswater W2 . . . 114 A4
Chelsea SW3 . . . 144 B2
2 Clapham SW4 . . . 61 B3
Fulham SW6 . . . 58 A4
20 Rotherhithe SE16 . . . 32 C1
4 Wandsworth SW18 . . . 58 C2
West Hampstead NW3 . . . 10 C4
Windsor Gdns W9 . . . 23 C1

Windsor Ho
4 Acton Green W4 37 B1
Brondesbury NW2 10 A2
4 Globe Town E2 25 C2
Regent's Pk NW1 92 B4
Shoreditch N1 87 A2
Stoke Newington N4 6 B3
Windsor Pl SW1 147 A4
Windsor Rd
Richmond TW9 44 B1
Upper Holloway N7 5 A1
Willesden NW2 9 A2
Windsor St N1 86 B4
Windsor Terr N1 97 A4
Windsor Way W14 140 A4
Windsor Wharf E9 18 B3
Windsor Wlk SE5 48 C1
Windspoint Dr SE15 50 A4
Windus Rd N16 7 B3
Windus Wlk N16 7 B3
Wine Cl E1 32 B2
Wine Office Ct EC4 107 C2
Winfield Ho 3 SW11 167 C2
Winford Ct 16 SE15 49 C2
Winford Ho E3 18 B1
Winforton St SE10 52 B2
Winfrith Rd SW18 71 B3
Wingate Ho
26 Bromley E3 27 A2
8 Stoke Newington N16 15 C4
Wingate Rd W6 39 A3
Wingfield Ct 5 E14 34 C2
Wingfield Ho
Paddington NW6 78 A2
16 Spitalfields E2 24 B2 98 C3
Wingfield Mews SE15 64 C4
Wingfield St SE15 64 C4
Wingford Rd SW2 62 A1
Wingham 3 NW5 12 C2
Wingmore Rd SE24 63 B4
Wingrad Ho 18 E1 32 B4
Wingrave SE17 151 B3
Wingrave Rd W6 47 B4
Wingreen 15 NW8 78 B4
Winicotte Ho W2 101 C4
Winifrede Paul Ho 7 NW5 13 A4
Winkley St 6 E2 25 A3
Winkworth Cotts 14 E1 25 B1
Winnett St W1 119 B4
Winnington Ho
19 Kensal Town W10 23 A1
8 SE5 48 B3
Winscombe St N19 4 A2
Winsham Gr SW11 60 C2
Winsham Ho NW1 93 C4
Winslade Rd SW2 62 A2
Winsland Mews W2 101 B2
Winsland St W2 101 B2
Winsley St W1 105 A2
Winslow SE17 152 A1
Winslow Rd W6 47 B4
Winstanley Rd SW11 59 C4
Winston Churchill's Britain at War Experience SE1 124 A1
Winston Ho WC1 93 C2
Winston Rd N16 15 C4
Winston Wlk 2 W4 37 C2
Winterbourne Ho W11 31 A2 112 A3
Winter Box Wlk TW10 54 B2
Winterbrook Rd SE24 63 B1
Winterfold Cl SW19 70 A2
Winterleys 7 NW6 23 B3
Winter Lo 17 SE16 153 C1
Winterslow Ho 20 SE5 48 B1
Winterton Ho 15 E1 32 B3
Winterton Pl SW10 157 A4
Winterwell Rd SW2 62 A2
Winthorpe Rd SW15 58 A3
Winthrop Ho 10 W12 30 A2
Winthrop St E1 32 A4
Winton Prim Sch N1 84 C1
Wirrall Ho 15 SE26 76 C1
Wisbech 5 N4 5 B3
Wisden Ho SW8 163 A3
Wise Rd E15 27 C4
Wiseton Rd SW17 72 B3
Wisley Ho SW1 147 B2
Wisley Rd SW11 60 C2
Wisteria Ho SE4 66 A4
Wisteria Rd SE13 67 C3
Wistow Ho 14 E2 24 C4
Witanhurst La N6 3 C3
Witan St E2 25 A2
Witchwood Ho 10 SW9 62 C4
Witcombe Point 14 SE15 49 C2
Witechapel Sp Ctr E1 32 B4
Witham Ct SW17 72 B1
Witham Ho 31 SE5 48 B1
Witherington Rd N5 14 C3
Withers Pl EC1 97 A2
Withycombe Rd SW19 69 C4
Withy Ho 4 E1 25 C1
Witley Ct WC1 94 A1
Witley Ho 2 SW2 74 B4
Witley Point 8 SW15 69 A3
Witley Rd N19 4 B2
Wittering Ho 9 SW11 169 A2
Wivenhoe Cl SE15 65 A4
Wix Prim Sch SW4 61 A3
Wix's La SW4 61 A3
Woburn Ct
32 Bermondsey SE16 40 A1
Richmond TW9 54 B4
Woburn Pl WC1 94 A1
Woburn Sq WC1 93 C1
Woburn Wlk WC1 93 C3
Wodeham Gdns 1 E1 32 A4
Wodehouse Ave SE15 49 B2
Wodehouse Ct 10 W3 37 B3
Woking Cl SW15 56 B3
Wolcot Ho NW1 83 A1
Wolfe Cres 34 SE16 40 C4
Wolfe Ho 19 W12 30 A2
Wolfson Ct
Golders Green NW11 1 A4
SE1 139 A4
Wolftencroft Cl SW11 59 C4
Wollaston Cl SE1 150 C4
Wollotan Ho N1 85 C2
Wolseley Ave SW18, SW19 70 C2
Wolseley Gdns W4 45 A4
Wolseley Rd W4 37 B2
Wolseley St SE1 139 A3
Wolsey Ct NW6 11 B1
Wolsey Ho 3 NW5 13 C2
Wolsey Mews NW5 13 B2
Wolsey Rd N1 15 C3
Wolsey St E1 32 B4
Wolverley St E2 25 A2
Wolverton SE17 152 A2
Wolverton Gdns W6 39 C2
Women's Liby The EC2 110 C2
Wontner Cl 5 N1 15 B1
Wontner Rd SW12, SW17 72 B2
Woodall Cl 15 E14 34 A2
Woodberry Down N4 6 B4
Woodberry Down Com Prim Sch N4 6 B4
Woodberry Gr N4 6 B4
Woodbine Terr E9 17 B2
Woodborough Rd SW15 57 A3
Woodbourne Ave SW16 73 C1
Woodbourne Cl SW16 74 A1
Woodbridge Cl 10 N7 5 B2
Woodbridge Ct N16 6 C1
Woodbridge St EC1 96 A2
Woodchester Sq W2 100 A4
Woodchurch Ho 15 SW9 173 B4
Woodchurch Rd NW6 11 A1
Wood Cl E2 24 C1 99 B2
Woodcock Ho 4 E14 33 C4
Woodcote Ho 4 SE8 51 B4
Woodcott Ho 1 SW15 68 C4
Woodcroft Mews SE8 41 A2
Wood Dene 6 SE15 50 A2
Woodfall Rd N4 5 C2
Woodfall St SW3 144 C1
Woodfarrs SE5 63 C3
Wood Field NW3 12 B3
Woodfield Ave SW16 73 C1
Woodfield Ct SW16 73 C1
Woodfield Gr SW16 73 C1
Woodfield La SW16 73 C1
Woodfield Pl W9 23 B1
Woodfield Rd W9 31 B4
Woodford Ct 15 W12 39 C4
Woodger Rd W12 39 B4
Woodhall NW1 92 C3
Woodhall Ave SE21 76 B1
Woodhall Dr SE21 76 B1
Woodhall Ho SW18 59 C1
Woodheyes Rd NW10 8 A3
Wood Ho
4 Clapham SW4 171 C2
6 Paddington NW6 23 B3
Woodhurst Rd W3 28 B2
Woodison St E3 26 A1
Wood La W12 30 B2
Woodland Cres
18 Rotherhithe SE16 40 C4
SE10 53 A4
Woodland Gr SE10 43 A1
Woodland Hts SE3 53 A4
Woodland Mews SW16 74 A1
Woodlands SW4 61 A3
Woodlands Ave W3 28 A1
Woodlands Ct NW10 22 C4
Woodlands Gt SW15 58 B2
Woodlands Park Rd SE10 53 A4
Woodlands Rd SW13 56 B4
Woodland St 2 E8 16 B2
Woodlands The
Highbury N5 15 B4
12 Hornsey N8 5 A4
Woodlands Way SW15 58 B2
Woodland Wlk
9 Greenwich SE10 43 A1
Hampstead NW3 12 A3
Wood Lane High Sch W12 30 A3
Wood Lane Sta W12 30 B2
Woodlawn Cl SW15 58 B2
Woodlawn Rd SW6 47 C2
Woodlea Rd N16 7 A1
Woodleigh Gdns SW16 74 A1
Woodman Mews TW9 45 A2
Woodmans Gr NW10 8 B3
Woodmans Mews W12 30 A4
Woodmere Cl 11 SW11 60 C4
Woodpecker Mews SE13 67 C3
Woodpecker Rd 6 SE14 51 A4
Wood Point 8 E16 35 C4
Woodquest Ave SE24 63 B2
Woodruff Ho 12 SW2 62 C1
Woodrush Cl 4 SE14 51 A3
Woodseer St E1 111 B4
Woodsford SE17 151 B1
Woodsford Sq W14 126 B4
Woods Ho SW8 170 C4
Wood's Mews W1 117 B4
Woodsome Rd NW5 4 A1
Wood's Pl SE1 138 B1
Woodspring Rd SW19 70 A2
Wood's Rd SE15 50 A2
Wood St
Chiswick W4 38 A1
City of London EC2 109 A2
Woodstar Ho 3 SE15 49 C3
Woodstock Ave NW11 1 A4
Woodstock Ct SE11 149 A2
Woodstock Gr W12 39 C4
Woodstock Ho 2 N5 15 B4
Woodstock Mews W1 103 C3
Woodstock Rd
Bedford Pk W4 38 A3
Finsbury Pk N4 5 C3
Golders Green NW11 1 B3
Woodstock St W1 104 A1
Woodstock Studios 17 W12 39 C4
Woodstock Terr E14 34 A2
Woodthorpe Rd SW15 57 A3
Woodview Cl N4 6 A4
Woodville Ct 3 SE10 52 B2
Woodville Ho SE1 138 C2
Woodville Rd
Golders Green NW11 1 A4
Paddington NW6 23 B3
Stoke Newington N16 16 A3
Woodwarde Rd SE22 64 A1
Woodwell St SW18 59 B2

Wood Wharf SE10 . . 52 B4
Woodyard Cl NW5 . . 12 C3
Woodyard La SE21 . . 76 A4
Woolcombes Ct 4 SE16 . . 32 C1
Wooler St SE17 . . 151 C2
Woolf Ct 7 W3 . . 37 B3
Woolf Mews WC1 . . 94 A2
Woolley Ho SW9 . . 63 A4
Woollon Ho 1 E1 . . 32 B3
Woolmore Prim Sch 14 E14 . . 34 B2
Woolmore St E14 . . 34 B2
Woolneigh St SW6 . . 166 A1
Woolpack Ho 1 E9 . . 17 B2
Woolridge Way E9 . . 17 B1
Woolstaplers Way SE16 . . 153 B4
Woolstone Ho 7 E2 . . 24 C4
Woolven Ho SE3 . . 53 B4
Wooster Gdns E14 . . 34 C3
Wooster Pl SE1 . . 151 C4
Wootton St SE1 . . 121 C1
Worcester Ct 44 W2 . . 31 C4
Worcester Dr W4 . . 38 A4
Worcester Gdns SW11 . . 60 B2
Worcester Ho
Bayswater W2 . . 100 C1
3 Islington N1 . . 15 B1
Lambeth SE11 . . 135 B1
9 Putney SW15 . . 69 B4
Worcester Mews 2 NW6 . . 11 A2
Wordsworth Ho NW6 . . 23 C2
Wordsworth Pl 11 NW5 . . 12 B3
Wordsworth Rd
Bermondsey SE1 . . 153 A3
Stoke Newington N16 . . 16 A4
Worfield St SW11 . . 158 B1
Worgan St
Rotherhithe SE16 . . 40 C2
SE11 . . 148 C2
Working Men's Coll The NW1 . . 83 A2
World's End Pas SW10 . . 157 B2
World's End Pl SW10 . . 157 A2
World Trade Ctr London E14 . . 42 A4
Worlidge St W6 . . 39 B1
Worlingham Rd SE22 . . 64 B3
Wormholt Park Prim Sch W12 . . 29 C2
Wormholt Rd W12 . . 29 C1
Wormwood St EC2 . . 110 A2
Wornington Rd W10 . . 31 A4
Woronzow Rd NW8 . . 80 A3
Worple St SW14 . . 55 C4
Worple Way TW10 . . 54 A3
Worship St EC2 . . 24 A1 98 A1
Worsley Gr E5 . . 16 C4
Worsopp Dr SW4 . . 61 B2
Worth Gr SE17 . . 151 B1
Worthington Ho
EC1 . . 95 C4
16 Streatham SW2 . . 74 C4
Wotton Ct 14 E14 . . 34 C2
Wotton Rd 18 SE8 . . 51 B4
Wouldham Rd E16 . . 35 B3
Wrayburn Ho 28 SE16 . . 139 C3
Wray Cres N4 . . 5 B2
Wray Ct N4 . . 5 B2
Wray Ho 11 SW2 . . 74 A3
Wren Ave NW2 . . 9 B4
Wren Cl E16 . . 35 B3
Wren Ho
29 Bow E3 . . 26 A3
SW1 . . 147 B1
Wren Landing E14 . . 33 C1
Wrenn Ho SW13 . . 47 B4
Wren Rd SE5 . . 48 C2
Wren St WC1 . . 95 A2
Wrentham Ave NW10 . . 22 C3
Wren View N6 . . 4 B3
Wrestlers Ct EC3 . . 110 A2
Wrexham Rd E3 . . 26 C3
Wrigglesworth St SE14 . . 50 C3
Wright Cl SE13 . . 67 C3
Wright Ho SW15 . . 57 A2
Wright's Gn SW4 . . 61 C3
Wright's La W8 . . 128 A2
Wright's Rd E3 . . 26 B3
Wrights Wlk SW14 . . 55 C4
Wrotham Ho SE1 . . 137 C2
Wrotham Rd 13 NW1 . . 13 B1
Wrottesley Rd NW10 . . 21 C3
Wroughton Rd SW11 . . 60 B1
Wroxton Rd SE15 . . 50 B1
Wulfstan St W12 . . 29 B3
Wyatt Cl SE16 . . 41 B4
Wyatt Dr SW13 . . 47 A3
Wyatt Ho
Blackheath Vale SE3 . . 53 B1
NW8 . . 89 C1
Wyatt Park Mans 1 SW2 . . 74 A2
Wyatt Park Rd SW2 . . 74 B2
Wyatt Rd N5 . . 6 B1
Wybert St NW1 . . 92 C2
Wycherley Cl SE3 . . 53 B3
Wychwood End N6 . . 4 B4
Wychwood Ho N4 . . 6 B4
Wyclif Ct EC1 . . 96 A3
Wycliffe Ho 13 N16 . . 16 A4
Wyclif St EC1 . . 96 A3
Wycombe Ct SE3 . . 53 C3
Wycombe Gdns NW11 . . 1 C2
Wycombe Ho NW8 . . 90 A2
Wycombe Pl SW18 . . 59 B1
Wycombe Sq W8 . . 31 C1 113 B1
Wyersdale Ho N4 . . 6 B4
Wye St SW11 . . 167 C1
Wyfold Rd SW6 . . 154 A1
Wyke Rd E3 . . 18 C1
Wyldes Cl NW11 . . 2 B3
Wyllen Cl E1 . . 25 B1
Wymering Mans 9 W9 . . 23 C2
Wymering Rd W9 . . 23 C2
Wymondham Ct NW8 . . 79 C4
Wymond St SW15 . . 57 B4
Wynan Rd E14 . . 42 A1
Wyndham Cres N19 . . 4 B1
Wyndham Deedes Ho 30 E2 . . 24 C3
Wyndham Ho SW1 . . 145 B3
Wyndham Mews W1 . . 102 C3
Wyndham Pl W1 . . 102 C3
Wyndham Rd SE5 . . 48 B3
Wyndhams Ct 4 E8 . . 16 B1
Wyndham St W1 . . 102 C4
Wyndham Yd W1 . . 102 C3
Wyneham Rd SE24 . . 63 C2
Wynford Rd N1 . . 85 A2
Wynne Ho SE14 . . 50 C2
Wynne Rd SW9 . . 173 B1
Wynnstay Gdns W8 . . 127 C2
Wynter Ho 20 SW9 . . 173 A1
Wynter St SW11 . . 59 B3
Wynton Pl W3 . . 28 A3
Wynyard Ho SE11 . . 149 A2
Wynyard Terr SE11 . . 149 A2
Wynyatt Ho EC1 . . 96 A4
Wynyatt St EC1 . . 96 A4
Wytham Ho NW8 . . 89 C1
Wythburn Ct W1 . . 102 C2
Wythburn Pl W1 . . 102 C2
Wyvil Prim Sch SW8 . . 162 B2
Wyvil Rd SW8 . . 162 A2
Wyvis St E14 . . 34 A4

Y

Yabsley St E14 . . 34 B1
Yaldam Ho SE1 . . 152 A3
Yalding Ho 20 E5 . . 17 A3
Yalding Rd SE16 . . 153 B4
Yale Ct NW6 . . 11 A3
Yardley St WC1 . . 95 B3
Yard The N1 . . 84 B1
Yarmouth Pl W1 . . 118 A1
Yarnfield Sq 15 SE15 . . 49 C2
Yarrow Ho
12 Cubitt Town E14 . . 42 B3
16 North Kensington W10 . . 30 B4
Yatesbury Ct E5 . . 18 A3
Yates Ct NW2 . . 9 C2
Yates Ho 22 E2 . . 24 C2 99 C4
Yatton Ho 15 W10 . . 30 B4
Yeadon Ho 14 W10 . . 30 B4
Yearby Ho W10 . . 22 B1
Yeate St N1 . . 15 C1
Yeats Cl NW10 . . 8 A2
Yeldham Ho W6 . . 39 C1
Yeldham Rd W6 . . 39 C1
Yelverton Rd SW11 . . 167 C1
Yeoman Cl SE27 . . 75 A1
Yeoman's Row SW3 . . 130 B1
Yeoman St SE8 . . 41 A2
Yeoman's Yd E1 . . 125 A4
Yeo St E3 . . 34 A4
Yeovil Ho
Finsbury Pk N7 . . 5 B2
North Kensington W10 . . 22 B1
Yerbury Prim Sch N19 . . 4 C1
Yerbury Rd N19 . . 4 C1
Yeshivo Horomo Talmudical Coll N16 . . 6 C3
Yesodey Hatorah Jun Sch for Girls 7 N16 . . 7 B4
Yesodey Hatorah Sec Sch for Girls 5 N16 . . 7 B4
Yet Lev Ct E5 . . 7 C3
Yewfield Rd NW10 . . 8 B2
Yew Gr NW2 . . 9 C4
Yew Ho SE14 . . 51 B1
Yew Tree Cl 3 SE13 . . 67 B4
Yew Tree Ct 8 N16 . . 6 C2
Yew Tree Rd W12 . . 29 B2
Yoakley Rd N16 . . 7 A2
Yoke Cl N7 . . 14 A2
Yonge Pk N4, N7 . . 5 C1
York Ave
Mortlake SW14 . . 55 B2
Walworth SE17 . . 151 A2
York Bldgs WC2 . . 120 B3
York Bridge NW1 . . 91 B2
York Cl 17 SE5 . . 48 B1
York Gate NW1 . . 91 C1
York Gr SE15 . . 50 B2
York Hall L Ctr E2 . . 25 B3
York Hill SE27, SW16 . . 75 A1
York Ho
Acton W3 . . 28 B2
Chelsea SW3 . . 145 A2
Islington N5 . . 14 C3
Kensington W8 . . 128 A4
11 Kentish Town N7 . . 13 C2
Kew TW9 . . 44 C2
Lambeth SE1 . . 135 A1
Marylebone W1 . . 102 C4
Pentonville N1 . . 84 C1
Richmond TW10 . . 54 C2
York House Pl W8 . . 128 A4
Yorkley Ho 3 W10 . . 22 B1
York Mans
Battersea SW11 . . 169 C4
Marylebone W1 . . 103 B4
Walworth SE17 . . 151 A2
York Mews NW5 . . 13 A3
York Pl
Battersea SW11 . . 59 C4
WC2 . . 120 B3
York Place Mans NW1 . . 103 A4
York Rd
Battersea SW11, SW18 . . 59 C4
Dagenham W3 . . 28 C3
4 Richmond TW10 . . 54 B2
SE1 . . 135 A4
York Rise NW5 . . 4 A1
York Road Bsns Ctr SW11 . . 167 B1
York St Chambers W1 . . 102 C4
Yorkshire Cl N16 . . 7 A1
Yorkshire Grey Pl 13 NW3 . . 11 B4
Yorkshire Grey Yd WC1 . . 106 C3
Yorkshire Rd E14 . . 33 A3
York Sq 12 E14 . . 33 A3
York St W1 . . 103 A4
York Terr E NW1 . . 91 C1
York Terr W NW1 . . 91 B1
Yorkton St E2 . . 24 C3
York Water Gate The SW1 . . 120 B2
York Way
Barnsbury N1, N7, NW1 . . 14 A1
N1 . . 84 B3
York Way Ct
Islington N1 . . 84 C3
Islington N1 . . 84 B3
Young's Bldgs EC1 . . 97 A2
Youngs Ct SW11 . . 169 C3
Young St W8 . . 128 A3
Yoxall Ho 2 W10 . . 22 B1
Yukon Rd SW12 . . 73 A4

Z

Zabludowicz Collection NW5 . . 12 C2
Zampa Rd SE16 . . 40 B1
Zander Ct E2 . . 24 C2 99 C4
Zangwill Ho NW6 . . 23 B3
Zealand Ho 11 SE5 . . 48 B1
Zealand Rd E3 . . 26 A3
Zennor Rd SW12 . . 73 B3
Zenoria St SE22 . . 64 B3
Zetland Ho W8 . . 128 A2
Zetland St E14 . . 34 B4
Zeus Ho N1 . . 97 B3
Zion Ho 6 E1 . . 32 B3
Zoar St SE1 . . 122 C2
Zodiac Ho 3 E3 . . 26 C1
Zoffany St N19 . . 4 C2

List of numbered locations

This atlas shows thousands more place names than any other London street atlas. In some busy areas it is impossible to fit the name of every place.

Where not all names will fit, some smaller places are shown by a number. If you wish to find out the name associated with a number, use this listing.

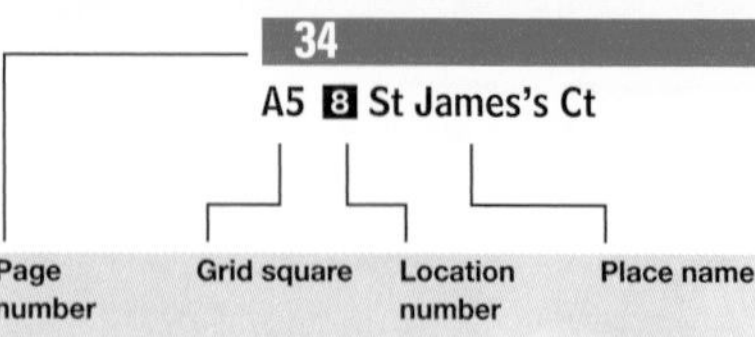

1

A2 1 Talmud Torah Tiferes Shlomo
B1 1 Mortimer Cl
2 Primrose Ct
3 Sunnyside Ho
4 Sunnyside
5 Prospect Pl
B4 1 Berkeley Ct
2 Exchange Mans
3 Beechcroft Ct
4 Nedahall Ct
C1 1 Portman Hts
2 Hermitage Ct
3 Moreland Ct
4 Wendover Ct

2

B1 1 Hampstead Sq
2 Stamford Cl
3 Mount Sq The

4

B1 1 Hunter Ho
2 Fisher Ho
3 Lang Ho
4 Temple Ho
5 Palmer Ho
6 Carlisle Ho
7 Durham Ho
8 Suffolk Ho
9 Lincoln Ho
10 Llewellyn Ho
11 Fell Ho
12 Aveling Ho
13 Merryweather Ct
14 Brennands Ct
15 St Christophers Ct
16 Francis Terrace Mews
17 Tremlett Mews
B2 1 Flowers Mews
2 Archway Cl
3 Sandridge St
4 Bovingdon Cl
5 Cavell Ct
6 Torrence Ho
7 Rowan Wlk
8 Laurel Cl
9 Forest Way
10 Larch Cl
11 Pine Cl
12 Alder Mews
13 Aspen Cl
14 Hargrave Park Prim Sch
15 Middlesex Univ (Archway Campus)
B3 1 Calvert Ct
2 Academy The
3 Whitehall Mans
4 Pauntley St
5 Archway Hts
6 Pauntley Ho
9 St Aloysius RC Coll
C1 1 Melchester Ho
2 Norcombe Ho
3 Weatherbury Ho
4 Wessex Ho
5 Archway Bsns Ctr
6 Harford Mews
7 Opera Ct
8 Rupert Ho
9 All Saints Church
C2 1 Bowerman Ct
2 Gresham Pl
3 Hargrave Mans
4 Church Garth
5 John King Ct
6 Ramsey Ct
7 St John's Upper Holloway CE Prim Sch
8 Byam Shaw Sch of Art
C3 1 Louise White Ho
2 Levison Way
3 Sanders Way
4 Birbeck Ho
5 Scholars Ct
6 Mount Carmel RC Tech Coll for Girls
C4 1 Eleanor Rathbone Ho
2 Christopher Lo
3 Monkridge
4 Marbleford Ct
5 High London
6 Garton Ho
7 Hilltop Ho
8 Caroline Martyn Ho
9 Arthur Henderson Ho
10 Margaret Mcmillan Ho
11 Enid Stacy Ho
12 Mary McArthur Ho
13 Bruce Glasier Ho
14 John Wheatley Ho
15 Keir Hardie Ho
16 Monroe Ho
17 Iberia Ho
18 Lygoe Ho
19 Lambert Ho
20 Shelbourne Ho
21 Arkansas Ho
22 Lafitte Ho
23 Shreveport Ho
24 Packenham Ho
25 Orpheus Ho
26 Fayetville Ho
27 Bayon Ho

5

A1 1 Northview
2 Tufnell Park Mans
3 Fulford Mans
4 Tollington Ho
5 Grafton Prim Sch
A2 1 Bracey Mews
2 Christie Ct
3 Ringmer Gdns
4 Kingsdown Rd
5 Cottenham Ho
6 St Paul's Ct
7 Rickthorne Rd
8 Stanley Terr
9 Arundel Lo
10 Landseer Ct
11 St Mark's Prim Sch
A3 1 Beeches The
2 Lambton Ct
3 Nugent Ct
4 Lambton Mews
5 Mews The
A4 1 Marie Lloyd Gdns
2 Edith Cavell Cl
3 Marie Stopes Ct
4 Jessie Blythe La
5 Barbara Rudolph Ct
6 Hetty Rees Ct
7 Leyden Mans
8 Brambledown
9 Lochbie
10 Lyngham Ct
11 High Mount
12 Woodlands The
13 St Gildas' RC Jun Sch
B1 1 Pakeman Prim Sch
2 London Meridian Coll
3 American Univ in London The
3 South Eastern Univ
4 Dean Coll of London
5 Montem Prim Sch
B2 1 Berkeley Wlk
2 Lazar Wlk
3 Thistlewood Cl
4 Tomlins Wlk
5 Andover Ho
6 Barmouth Ho
7 Chard Ho
7 Christ the King RC Prim Sch
8 Methley Ho
9 Rainford Ho
10 Woodbridge Cl
11 Allerton Wlk
12 Falconer Wlk
13 Sonderburg Rd
14 St Mark's Mans
15 Athol Ct
16 Pooles Park Prim Sch
B3 1 Lawson Ct
2 Wiltshire Ct
3 Fenstanton
4 Hutton Ct
5 Wisbech
6 Islington Arts & Media Sch
C2 1 Brookfield
2 Churnfield
3 Cornwallis Sq

6

A1 1 Hurlock Ho
2 Blackstock Ho
3 Vivian Comma Cl
4 Monsell Ct
A2 1 Parkwood Prim Sch
2 Ambler Prim Sch
3 City & Islington Coll (Ctr for Life-long Learning)
B4 1 Finmere Ho
2 Keynsham Ho
3 Kilpeck Ho
4 Knaresborough Ho
5 Leighfield Ho
6 Lonsdale Ho
7 Groveley Ho
8 Wensleydale Ho
9 Badminton Ct
C1 1 Betty Layward Prim Sch
C2 1 Chestnut Cl
2 Sycamore Ho
3 Lordship Ho
4 Clissold Ho
5 Beech Ho
6 Laburnum Ho
7 Ormond Ho
8 Yew Tree Ct
9 Oak Ho
C4 1 Selwood Ho
2 Bnois Jerusalem Girls Sch
2 Mendip Ho
3 Ennerdale Ho
3 Getters Talmud Torah
4 Delamere Ho
5 Westwood Ho
6 Bernwood Ho
7 Allerdale Ho
8 Chattenden Ho
9 Farningham Ho
10 Oakend Ho

7

A1 1 Gujarat Ho
2 Marton Rd
3 Painsthorpe Rd
4 Selkirk Ho
5 Defoe Ho
6 Edward Friend Ho
7 Sheridan Ho
8 Barrie Ho
9 Arnold Ho
10 Macaulay Ho
11 Stowe Ho
12 Carlyle Ho
13 Shaftesbury Ho
14 Lillian Cl
15 Swift Ho
16 Dryden Ho
17 Scott Ct
18 Kingsfield Ho
19 Uhura Sq
20 Hartopp Ct
A2 1 Denman Ho

2 St Mary's Stoke Newington CE Prim Sch
A3 1 Godstone Ct
2 Farnham Ct
3 Milford Ct
4 Cranleigh Ct
5 Haslemere Ct
6 Belmont Ct
7 Hockworth Ho
8 Garratt Ho
9 Fairburn Ho
10 Thorndale Ho
11 Oakdene Ho
12 Briardale Ho
A4 1 Beis Rochel d'Satmar Girls Sch
3 Our Lady's Convent RC High Sch
B1 1 Lawrence Bldgs
2 Cottage Wlk
3 Batley Pl
B2 1 Garnham St
2 Garnham Cl
3 Sanford La
4 Sanford Wlk
5 Abney Gdns
6 Fleet Wood
8 Simon Marks Jewish Prim Sch
9 William Patten Prim Sch
B3 1 Stamford Hill Mans
2 Montefiore Ct
3 Berwyn Ho
4 Clent Ho
5 Chiltern Ho
6 Laindon Ho
7 Pentland Ho
B4 1 Regent Ct
2 Stamford Lo
3 Holmwood Ct
4 Bobov Foundation Sch
5 Yesodey Hatorah Sec Sch for Girls
6 Lubavitch Boys Prim Sch
7 Yesodey Hatorah Jun Sch for Girls
8 Lubavitch Girls Prim Sch
9 Lubavitch House Sch (Jun Boys)
10 Skinners Company Sch (Upper)
C1 1 Ravenscourt
2 Mellington Ct
3 Rendlesham Ho
4 Carroll Ct
6 St Scholastica's RC Prim Sch
C2 1 Cazenove Mans
2 Chedworth Ho
3 Aldergrove Ho
4 Abbotstone Ho
5 Briggeford Cl
6 Inglethorpe Ho
7 Ashdown Ho
8 Epping Ho
9 Cypress Cl
C3 1 Stamford Gr E
2 Stamford Mans
3 Grove Mans
4 Stamford Gr W
6 Talmud-Torah Yetev-Lev

8

A1 1 Beveridge Rd
2 Purcell Mews
3 George Lansbury Ho
4 Charles Hobson Ho
5 Reade Wlk
6 Westbury Ho
7 Bridge Ct
8 St Joseph's RC Prim Sch
9 Dixon Way
10 Armstrong Rd
11 Brittage Rd
A4 1 Grange Ct
2 Green Ct
C2 1 Regency Mews
2 Tudor Mews
3 Utopia Ho
4 Bell Flats
5 Angel Ct
6 St Andrew & St Francis CE Prim Sch

9

A2 1 St Mary Magdelen's RC Jun Sch
2 Islamic Coll for Advanced Studies
B2 1 Rutland Park Gdns
2 Rutland Park Mans
3 Queens Par
4 Harcourt Ho
5 Solidarity Ho
6 Electra Ct
7 Cassandra Ct
8 Carlton Ct
9 Convent of Jesus & Mary RC Inf Sch
C4 1 Oaklands Mews
2 Acer Ct
3 Maple Ct
4 Argyle Mans

10

A1 1 Christ Church Ct
2 Paul Daisley Ct
3 Fountain Ho
4 Kingston Ho
5 Waverley Ct
6 Weston Ho
7 Mapes Ho
8 Athelstan Gdns
9 Leff Ho
10 Brondesbury Coll for Boys
B1 1 Alma Birk Ho
2 Brooklands Ct
3 Brooklands Court Apartments
4 Cleveland Mans
5 Buckley Ct
6 Webheath
C1 1 Linstead St
2 Embassy Ho
3 Acol Ct
4 Kings Wood Ct
5 Douglas Ct
6 King's Gdns
7 Carlton Mans
8 Smyrna Mans
9 New Priory Ct
10 Queensgate Pl
11 Brondesbury Mews
12 St Eugene de Mazenod RC Prim Sch
C2 1 Dene Mans
2 Sandwell Cres
3 Sandwell Mans
4 Hampstead West
5 Redcroft
C3 1 Orestes Mews
2 Walter Northcott Ho
3 Polperro Mans
4 Lyncroft Mans
5 Marlborough Mans
6 Alexandra Mans
7 Cumberland Mans
8 Cavendish Mans
9 Ambassador Ct
10 Welbeck Mans
11 Inglewood Mans
12 Dennington Park Mansions
C4 1 Parsifal Coll

11

A2 1 Beswick Mews
2 Worcester Mews
3 Minton Mews
4 Doulton Mews
5 Laurel Ho
6 Sandalwood Ho
7 Iroko Ho
8 Banyan Ho
9 Rosewood Ho
10 Ebony Ho
11 Rosemont Mans
12 Exeter Mews
B1 1 Harrold Ho
2 Glover Ho
3 Byron Ct
4 Nalton Ho
B2 1 Petros Gdns
2 Heath Ct
3 Imperial Twrs
4 Fairhurst
5 St John's Ct
6 New College Ct
7 Chalford
8 Rosslyn Mans
9 Sutherland Ho
10 Holy Trinity CE Prim Sch
12 Phoenix Sch The
13 North Bridge House Sch
14 Southbank International Sch
B3 1 Arkwright Mans
2 Hatstone Ct
3 Hampstead High Sch
B4 1 Windmill Hill
2 Highgrove Point
3 Gainsborough Ho
4 Holly Bush Hill
5 Heath Mans
6 Holly Bush Steps
7 Pavilion Ct
8 Holly Berry La
9 New Campden Ct
10 Holly Bush Vale
11 Benham's Pl
12 Prospect Pl
13 Yorkshire Grey Pl
14 Gardnor Mans
15 Ellerdale Cl
16 Monro Ho
17 Prince Arthur Mews
18 Prince Arthur Ct
19 Village Mount
20 Perrin's Ct
21 Wells Ct
22 Bakers Pas
23 Spencer Wlk
24 Bird In Hand Yd
25 Kings Well
26 New Ct
27 Streatley Pl
28 Mansfield Pl
29 Upper Hampstead Wlk
30 Hampstead Parochial CE Prim Sch
31 Univ Coll Jun Sch
32 Heathside Prep Sch
33 New End Prim Sch
34 Sisters of St Marcellina Sch
C1 1 New College Par
2 Northways Par
3 Noel Ho
4 Campden Ho
5 Centre Hts
6 Hickes Ho
7 Swiss Terr
8 Leitch Ho
9 Jevons Ho
10 Langhorne Ct
11 Park Lo
12 Avenue Lo
13 Frank Barnes Sch
14 Swiss Cottage Sch
C2 1 Belsize Park Mews
2 Baynes Mews
3 McCrone Mews
11 South Hampstead High Sch
C3 1 Belsize Court Garages
2 Roscommon Ho
3 Akenside Ct
4 Fitzjohns Prim Sch
5 St Christopher's Sch
8 St Anthony's Sch
C4 1 White Bear Pl
2 Wells Ho The
3 Boades Mews
4 Flask Cotts
5 Coach House Yd
6 Pilgrim's Pl
7 Rosslyn Mews
8 Royal Sch Hampstead The
9 Academy Sch The

12

A2 1 Banff Ho
2 Glenloch Ct
3 Havercourt
4 Holmefield Ct
5 Gilling Ct
6 Howitt Cl
7 Manor Mans
8 Straffan Lo
9 Romney Ct
10 Lancaster Stables
11 Eton Garages
12 Hampstead Coll of Fine Arts & Humanities
A3 1 Hampstead Hill Sch
B1 1 Hancock Nunn Ho
2 Higginson Ho
3 Duncan Ho
4 Mary Wharrie Ho
5 Rockstraw Ho
6 Cleaver Ho
7 Chamberlain St
8 Sharples Hall St
9 Primrose Mews
10 Rothwell St
11 St Georges Mews
B2 1 Alder Ho
2 Hornbeam Ho
3 Whitebeam Ho
4 Aspen Ho
5 Rowan Ho
6 Beech Ho
7 Chestnut Ho
8 Oak Ho
9 Willow Ho
10 Sycamore Ho
11 Maple Ho
12 Hazel Ho
13 Elaine Ct
14 Faircourt
15 Walham Ct
16 Stanbury Ct
17 Priory Mans
18 Wellington Ho
19 Grange The
B3 1 Cayford Ho
2 Du Maurier Ho
3 Isokon Flats
4 Palgrave Ho
5 Garnett Ho
6 Stephenson Ho
7 Park Dwellings
8 Siddons Ho
9 Mall Studios
10 Park Hill Wlk
11 Wordsworth Pl
12 Fraser Regnart Ct
13 St Pancras Almshouses
14 St Dominic RC Prim Sch
15 Fleet Prim Sch
C1 1 Bridge Ho
2 Hardington
3 Mead Cl
4 Rugmere
5 Tottenhall
6 Beauvale
7 Broomfield
8 Camden Coll of English
C2 1 Silverbirch Wlk
2 Penshurst
3 Wingham
4 Westwell
5 Chislet
6 Burmarsh
7 Shipton Ho
8 Stonegate
9 Leysdown
10 Headcorn
11 Lenham
12 Halstow
13 Fordcombe
14 Cannington
15 Langridge
16 Athlone Ho
17 Pentland Ho
18 Beckington
19 Hawkridge
20 Edington
21 Rhyl Prim Sch
22 Haverstock Sch

13

A1 1 Ferdinand Ho
2 Harmood Ho
3 Hawley Rd
4 Hawley Mews
5 Leybourne St
6 Barling
7 Tiptree
8 Havering
9 Candida Ct
10 Lorraine Ct
11 Donnington Ct
12 Welford Ct
13 Torbay Ct
14 Bradfield Ct
15 Torbay St
16 Water La
17 Leybourne Rd
18 Haven St
19 Stucley Pl
20 Lawrence Ho
21 Chalcot Sch
22 Holy Trinity & Saint Silas CE Prim Sch
23 Hawley Inf Sch
A2 1 Ashington
2 Priestley Ho
3 Leonard Day Ho
4 Old Dairy Mews
5 Monmouth Ho
6 Alpha Ct
7 Una Ho
8 Widford
9 Heybridge
10 Roxwell
11 Hamstead Gates
12 Kingsway Coll
A4 1 Denyer Ho
2 Stephenson Ho
3 Trevithick Ho
4 Brunel Ho
5 Newcomen Ho
6 Faraday Ho
7 Winifrede Paul Ho
8 Wardlow
9 Fletcher Ct
10 Tideswell
11 Grangemill
12 Hambrook Ct
13 Calver
B1 1 Cherry Tree Ct
2 Chichester Ct
3 Durdans Ho
4 Philia Ho
5 Bernard Shaw Ct
6 Foster Ct
7 Bessemer Ct
8 Hogarth Ct
9 Rochester Ct
10 Soane Ct
11 Wallett Ct
12 Inwood Ct
13 Wrotham Rd
14 St Thomas Ct
15 Caulfield Ct
16 Bruges Pl
17 Reachview Cl
18 Lawfords Wharf
B3 1 Eleanor Ho
2 Falkland Pl
3 Kensington Ho
4 Willingham Cl
5 Kenbrook Ho
6 Aborfield
7 Great Field
8 Appleford
9 Forties The
10 Maud Wilkes Cl
11 Dunne Mews
12 Dowdeny Cl
13 Kentish Town CE Prim Sch
B4 1 Benson Ct
2 Tait Ho
3 Manorfield Cl
4 Greatfield Cl
5 Longley Ho
6 Lampson Ho
7 Davidson Ho
8 Palmer Ho
9 Lambourn Cl
10 Morris Ho
11 Owen Ho
12 Eleanor Palmer Prim Sch
C1 1 Hillier Ho
2 Gairloch Ho
3 Cobham Mews
4 Bergholt Mews
5 Blakeney Cl
6 Weavers Way
7 Allensbury Pl
C2 1 Rowstock
2 Peckwater Ho
3 Wolsey Ho
4 Pandian Way
5 Busby Mews
6 Caledonian Sq
7 Canal Bvd
8 Northpoint Sq
9 Lock Mews
10 Carters Cl
11 York Ho
12 Hungerford Rd
13 Cliff Road Studios
14 Cliff Ct
15 Camelot Ho
16 Church Studios
17 Camden Terr
18 Brecknock Prim Sch
19 Hungerford Prim Sch
C3 1 Blake Ho
2 Quelch Ho
3 Lee Ho
4 Willbury Ho
5 Howell Ho
6 Holmsbury Ho
7 Leith Ho
8 Betchworth Ho
9 Rushmore Ho
10 Dugdale Ho
11 Horsendon Ho
12 Colley Ho
13 Coombe Ho
14 Ivinghoe Ho
15 Buckhurst Ho
16 Saxonbury Ct
17 Charlton Ct
18 Apollo Studios
19 Barn Cl
20 Long Meadow
21 Landleys Field
22 Margaret Bondfield Ho
23 Haywood Lo
24 Torriano Jun & Inf Schs
C4 1 Fairlie Ct
2 Trecastle Way
3 Dalmeny Avenue Est
4 Hyndman Ho
5 Carpenter Ho
6 Graham Ho
7 Tufnell Mans

14

A2 1 Clock Tower Pl
2 Clock View Cres
3 Jim Veal Dr
4 Gower Sch The
A3 1 Kimble Ho
2 Saxonbury Ct
3 Poynder Ct
4 Pangbourne Ho
5 Moulsford Ho
A4 1 Arcade The
2 Macready Pl
3 Cardwell Rd
4 Mcmorran Ho
5 Crayford Ho
6 Whitby Ct
7 Prospect Pl
8 City & Islington Coll (Ctr for Bsns, Arts & Technology)
B1 1 Kerwick Cl
2 Rydston Cl
3 Skegness Ho
4 Frederica St
5 Ponder St
6 Kings Ct
7 Freeling St
8 Coatbridge Ho
9 Tilloch St
B2 1 Burns Ho
2 Scott Ho
3 Wellington Mews
4 Roman Ct
5 Piccadilly Ct
6 Knowledge Point Sch
B3 1 Culverin Ct
2 Garand Ct
3 Mount Carmel
B4 1 Buckmaster Ho
2 Loreburn Ho
3 Cairns Ho
4 Halsbury Ho
5 Chelmsford Ho
6 Cranworth Ho
7 City & Islington Coll (Ctr for Health, Social & Child Care)
C1 1 Mountfort Terr
2 Avon Ho
3 Buckland Ho
4 Dovey Lo
5 Carfree Cl
6 Mitchell Ho
7 New College Mews
8 Lofting Ho
9 Brooksby Ho
10 Cara Ho
11 Thornhill Prim Sch
12 North London Science Ctr
C2 1 London Metropolitian Univ (Spring Ho)
C3 1 Slaney Pl
2 Eastwood Cl
3 Milton Pl
4 Hartnoll Ho
5 St James School Flats
6 Widnes Ho
7 Tranmere Ho
8 Victoria Mans
9 Formby Ct
10 Mersey Ho
11 Birkenhead Ho
12 Drayton Park Mews
13 Drayton Park Prim Sch

15

A1 1 Islington Park Mews
2 Evelyn Denington Ct
3 Bassingbourn Ho
4 Cadmore Ho
5 Adstock Ho
6 Garston Ho
7 Flitton Ho
8 Datchworth Ho
9 Battishill St
10 Almeida St
11 Edward's Cotts
12 Hyde's Pl
13 Tyndale Terr
14 Spriggs Ho
15 Barratt Ho
16 Spencer Pl
17 Chadston Ho
18 Whiston Ho
19 Wakelin Ho
20 Tressel Cl
21 Canonbury Ct
22 Halton Ho
23 Shillingford St
24 Highbury Mans
25 Premier Ho
26 Waterloo Gdns
27 William Tyndale Prim Sch
A2 1 Hampton Ct
2 Salisbury Ho
4 Canonbury Prim Sch
5 Laycock Prim Sch
A3 1 De Barowe Mews
2 Fieldview Ct
3 Viewpoint
4 Ashurst Lo
4 Highbury Fields Sch
5 London Metropolitan Univ (Ladbrook Ho)
6 Robinswood Mews
A4 1 Chestnuts The
2 Bowen Ct
3 Peckett Sq
4 De Barowe Mews
B1 1 Astey's Row
2 Lincoln Ho
3 Worcester Ho
4 Melville Pl
5 Wontner Cl
6 Hedingham Cl
7 Laundry La
8 Base Apartments
9 Walkinshaw Ct
10 New Bentham Ct
11 Bentham Ct
12 Haslam Ho
13 Horsfield Ho
14 Riverside Ho
15 Eric Fletcher Ct
16 Annette Cres
17 Ashby Ho
18 Lindsey Mews
19 Cardigan Wlk
20 Red House Sq
21 Orchard Cl
22 Queensbury St
23 Raynor Pl
B2 1 Crowline Wlk
2 Upper Handa Wlk
3 Handa Wlk
4 Lismore Wlk
5 Bardsey Wlk
6 Walney Wlk
7 Upper Bardsey Wlk
8 Upper Lismore Wlk
9 Sark Ho
10 Guernsey Ho
11 Guernsey Rd
12 Sybil Thorndike Ho
13 Clephane Rd
14 Florence Nightingale Ho
15 Jersey Ho
16 Jethou Ho
17 Islay Wlk
18 Upper Caldy Wlk
19 Caldy Wlk
20 Alderney Ho
21 Gulland Wlk
22 Nightingale Rd
23 Upper Gulland Wlk
24 Church Rd
25 Oransay Rd
26 Canonbury Yd E
B3 1 Pearfield Ho
2 Larchfield Ho
3 Beresford Terr
4 Pondfield Ho
5 Ashfield Ho
6 Elmfield Ho
7 Highbury Grove Sch
B4 1 Fountain Mews
2 Woodstock Ho
3 Henson Ct
4 Taverner Sq
C1 1 Downham Ct
2 Trafalgar Point
C2 1 John Kennedy Ct
2 John Kennedy Lo
3 Ball's Pond Pl
4 Haliday Wlk
5 Queen Elizabeth Ct
6 Canonbury Hts
7 Pinnacle The
8 Threadgold Ho
9 Wakeham St
10 Saffron Ct
11 Callaby Terr
12 Tilney Gdns
13 Westcliff Ho
14 Ilford Ho
15 Ongar Ho
16 Greenhills Terr
17 Romford Ho
18 Bute Wlk
19 Upper Ramsey Wlk
20 Rona Wlk
21 Thorndike Rd
22 St Pauls Steiner Sch
C3 1 Newington Green Prim Sch
C4 1 Ledo Ho
2 Salween Ho
3 Prome Ho

4 Arakan Ho
5 Rangoon Ho
6 Mandalay Ho
7 Karen Ho
8 Wingate Ho
9 Jubet Ho
10 Orde Ho
11 Chindit Ho
12 Mabel Thornton Ho
13 Crawshay Ho
14 Avon Ho
15 Connaught Mans
16 Jonson Ho
17 Herrick Ho
18 Donne Ho
19 Thirlmere Ho
20 Grasmere Ho

16

A1 1 Dorchester Ct
2 Wareham Ct
3 Dorset Ct
4 Stratton Ct
5 Swanage Ct
6 Blandford Ct
7 Portland Ct
8 Oscar Faber Pl
9 Metropolitan Bsns Ctr
10 Lancaster Cl
11 Palazzo Apartments
12 Watercress Pl
A2 1 Kingsland Gn
2 Kingsland Pas
3 Metropolitan Benefit Societies Almshouses
4 Nimrod Pas
5 De Beauvoir Pl
6 Warburton Cl
7 Buckingham Mews
8 Aztec Ct
10 Kerridge Ct
11 Isabella Mews
12 St Jude & St Paul's CE Prim Sch
13 De Beauvoir Prim Sch
14 Our Lady & St Joseph RC Prim Sch
15 Childrens House Upper Sch
A3 1 Hewling Ho
2 Matthias Ho
3 Port Royal Pl
4 Cressington Cl
5 King Henry's Yd
6 Bronte Ho
7 Sewell Ho
8 Lydgate Ho
9 Patmore Ho
10 Congreve Ho
11 Elton St
12 Conrad Ho
13 Southwell Ho
14 Neptune Ho
15 Campion Ho
16 Webster Ho
17 Meredith Ho
18 Beckford Ho
19 Ashley Ct
20 Hayling Cl
21 Millard Cl
22 Lydford Cl
23 Salcombe Rd
24 Truman's Rd
25 Templeton Cl
26 John Campbell Rd
27 Gillett Pl
28 Bradbury St
29 Thomas Crowell Ct
31 Shellgrove Rd
A4 1 Londesborough Ho
2 Knebworth Ho
3 Knebworth Rd
4 Bransby Ct
5 Imperial Ave
6 Leonard Pl
7 Shakspeare Mews
8 Binyon Ho
9 Shelley Ho
10 Browning Ho
11 Burns Ho
12 Andrew Marvell Ho
13 Wycliffe Ho
14 Blake Ho
15 Marlowe Ho
16 Fletcher Ho
17 Chaucer Ct
32 St Matthias's CE Prim Sch
B1 1 Hilborough Rd
2 Shoreditch Ct
3 Evergreen Sq
4 Wyndhams Ct
5 Festival Ct
6 Fortune Ct
7 Rose Ct
8 Ability Plaza
9 Briar Ct
10 Lomas Dr
11 Queensbridge Inf Sch
B2 1 Prospect Ho
2 Woodland St
3 Crosby Wlk
4 Kirkland Wlk
5 Bowness Cl
6 Carlisle Wlk
7 Skelton Cl
8 Camerton Cl
9 Buttermere Wlk
10 Houghton Cl
11 Hayton Cl
12 Kingsland Sh Ctr
13 Springfield Ho
14 Parton Lo
15 Sanctuary Mews
16 Fenton Cl
B3 1 Miller's Terr
2 Chow Sq
3 Drysdale Flats
4 Gateway Mews
5 Birkbeck Mews
6 Winchester Pl
B4 1 Coronation Ave
2 Morris Blitz Ct
3 Shacklewell Ho
4 Alexandra Ct
5 Shacklewell Prim Sch
6 Princess May Prim Sch
C1 1 Aldington Ct
2 Bayton Ct
3 Rochford Wlk
4 Windrush Cl
5 Gayhurst Prim Sch
C2 3 Burdon Ct
4 Thomson Ct
5 Bruno Ct
6 Thackeray Mews
7 Madinah Rd
C3 1 Kingsdown Ho
2 Glendown Ho
3 Moredown Ho
4 Blakeney Cl
5 Beeston Cl
6 Benabo Ct
7 David Devine Ho
8 Kreedman Wlk
9 Hermitage Row
10 Grafton Ct
11 Lushington Terr
12 Aspen Ct
13 Pykewell Lo
14 Albion Works Studios

17

A1 1 Fortescue Ave
2 Pemberton Pl
3 Weston Wlk
4 Bayford St Ind Ctr
5 Bayford St
6 Sidworth St
7 Helmsley St
8 Cyntra Pl
9 Signal Ho
10 All Nations Ho
11 Vanguard Ho
12 Hacon Sq
A2 1 Bohemia Pl
2 Graham Mans
3 Marvin St
4 Boscobel Ho
5 Royal Oak Rd
6 Colonnades The
7 Sylvester Ho
8 Sylvester Path
9 Doctor Spurstowe Almshouses
10 Great Eastern Bldgs
11 Sojourner-Truth Cl
A3 1 Birchington Ho
2 Bicknor Ho
3 Boxley Ho
4 Adisham Ho
5 Cranbrook Ho
6 Marden Ho
7 Broome Ho
8 Crandale Ho
9 Cheriton Ho
10 Ditton Ho
11 Langley Ho
12 Dymchurch Ho
13 Elham Ho
14 Davina Ho
15 Pembury Pl
16 Downs Ct
17 Perrywood Ho
18 Staplehurst Ho
19 Pegwell Ho
20 Yalding Ho
21 Northbourne Ho
22 Monkton Ho
23 Milsted Ho
24 Athlone Cl
25 Clarence Pl
26 Gould Terr
27 Quested Ct
28 Brett Pas
29 Marcon Ct
30 Appleton Ct
31 Institute Pl
A4 1 Ross Ct
2 Downs La
3 Gaviller Pl
4 Robert Owen Lo
5 Apprentice Way
6 Arrowe Ct
7 Gilwell Ct
8 Sutton Ct
9 St Andrews Mans
10 Kinnoull Mans
11 Rowhill Mans
12 Sladen Pl
13 Mothers Sq The
14 Richborough Ho
15 Sandgate Ho
16 Sheppey Ho
B1 1 Pitcairn Ho
2 Lyme Grove Ho
3 Shakespeare Ho
4 Upcott Ho
5 Loddiges Ho
6 Parkinson Ho
7 Sloane Ho
8 Vanbrugh Ho
9 Cambridge Pas
10 Lyttleton Ho
11 Victoria Park Ct
12 Tullis Ho
13 Fairchild Ho
14 Forsyth Ho
15 Tradescant Ho
16 Mason Ho
17 Capel Ho
18 Cordwainers Ct
19 Bridgeman Ho
20 St Thomas's Pl
21 Barclay Ho
22 Clayton Ho
23 Danby Ho
24 Sherard Ho
25 Catesby Ho
26 Petiver Cl
27 Leander Ct
28 Philip Turner Est
29 Grendon Ho
30 Shore Mews
31 Shore Bsns Ctr
32 Kendal Ho
33 Classic Mans
34 Tudor Ho
35 Park Ho
36 Enterprise Ho
37 Alpine Gr
38 Clarendon Cl
39 Rotheley Ho
40 Bernie Grant Ho
41 Orchard Prim Sch
42 St John of Jerusalem CE Prim Sch
B2 1 Woolpack Ho
2 Elvin Ho
3 Thomas Ho
4 Hockley Ho
5 Retreat Ho
6 Butfield Ho
7 Brooksbank Ho
8 Cresset Ho
9 Brooksbank St
10 Lennox Ho
11 Milborne Ho
12 Collent Ho
13 Middlesex Pl
14 Elsdale Ho
15 Devonshire Hall
16 Brent Ho
17 Morningside Prim Sch
18 Hackney Free & Parochial CE Sec Sch
B3 1 St John & St James CE Prim Sch
C1 1 Stuart Ho
2 Gascoyne Ho
3 Chelsfield Point
4 Sundridge Ho
5 Banbury Ho
6 Lauriston Ho
C2 1 Musgrove Ho
2 Cheyney Ho
3 Haynes Ho
4 Warner Ho
5 Gilby Ho
6 Gadsden Ho
7 Risley Ho
8 Baycliffe Ho
9 Sheldon Ho
10 Offley Ho
11 Latimer Ho
12 Ribstone Ho
13 Salem Ho
14 Fieldwick Ho
15 Lever Ct
16 Matson Ho
17 Wilding Ho
18 Rennell Ho
19 Dycer Ho
20 Granard Ho
21 Whitelock Ho
22 Harrowgate Ho
23 Cass Ho
24 Lofts on the Park
25 Heathcote Point
26 Ravenscroft Point
27 Vanner Point
28 Hensley Point
29 San Ho
30 Berger Prim Sch
C4 1 Cromford Path
2 Longford Ct
3 Overbury Ho
4 Heanor Ct
5 Wharfedale Ct
6 Ladybower Ct
7 Ilkeston Ct
8 Derby Ct
9 Rushmore Cres
10 Blackwell Cl
11 Belper Ct
12 Rushmore Prim Sch

18

A2 1 Chigwell Ct
2 Wellday Ho
3 Selman Ho
4 Vaine Ho
5 Trower Ho
6 St Dominics RC Prim Sch
B2 1 Mallard Cl
2 Merriam Ave
3 Gainsborough St
4 Palace Cl
5 St Anthony's Cl
6 Trowbridge Est
B3 7 Wick Village

19

C1 1 Service Route No 2
2 Service Route No 3
7 Newham Sixth Form Coll (Stratford Ctr)

C4 1 Mulberry Ct
2 Rosewood Ct
3 Gean Ct
4 Blackthorn Ct
5 Cypress Ct

20

C4 1 Carlyle Rd
2 Bernard Shaw Ho
3 Longlents Ho
4 Mordaunt Ho
5 Wilmers Ct
6 Stonebridge Ctr
7 Shakespeare Ave
8 Southcroft
9 Brent Adult Comm Education Service Coll

21

A3 1 Futters Ct
2 Barrett Ct
3 Elms The
4 Fairlight Ct
B3 1 New Crescent Yd
2 Harlesden Plaza
3 St Josephs Ct
4 Jubilee Cl
5 Ellery Cl

22

B1 1 Princess Alice Ho
2 Yoxall Ho
3 Yorkley Ho
4 Northaw Ho
5 Oakham Ho
6 Markyate Ho
7 Letchmore Ho
8 Pagham Ho
9 Quendon Ho
10 Redbourn Ho
11 Ketton Ho
12 Hillman Dr
C2 1 Westfield Ct
2 Tropical Ct
3 Chamberlayne Mans
4 Quadrant The
5 Queens Park Ct
6 Warfield Yd
7 Regent St
8 Cherrytree Ho
9 Artisan Mews
10 Artisan Quarter

23

A1 1 Sycamore Wlk
2 Westgate Bsns Ctr
3 Buspace Studios
4 Bosworth Ho
5 Golborne Gdns
6 Appleford Ho
7 Adair Twr
8 Gadsden Ho
9 Southam Ho
10 Norman Butler Ho
11 Thompson Ho
12 Wells Ho
13 Paul Ho
14 Olive Blythe Ho
15 Katherine Ho
16 Breakwell Ct
17 Pepler Ho
18 Edward Kennedy Ho
19 Winnington Ho
20 Queen's Park Prim Sch
21 Middle Row Prim Sch
22 St Mary RC Prim Sch
23 St Thomas' CE Prim Sch
A2 1 Selby Sq
2 Severn Ave
3 Stansbury Sq
4 Tolhurst Dr
5 John Fearon Wlk
6 Mundy Ho
7 Macfarren Ho
8 Bantock Ho
9 Banister Ho
10 Batten Ho
11 Croft Ho
12 Courtville Ho
13 Mounsey Ho
14 Bliss Mews
15 Symphony Mews
B1 1 Octavia Mews
2 Russell's Wharf
3 Western Ho
4 Kelly Mews
5 Queen Elizabeth II Jubilee Sch
B2 1 Boyce Ho
2 Farnaby Ho
3 Danby Ho
4 Purday Ho
5 Naylor Ho
6 St Judes Ho
7 Leeve Ho
8 Longhurst Ho
9 Harrington Ct
10 Mulberry Ct
11 Kilburn Ho
12 Carlton Vale Inf Sch
B3 1 Claremont Ct
2 William Saville Ho
3 Western Ct
4 Bond Ho
5 Crone Ct
6 Wood Ho
7 Winterleys
8 Carlton Ho
9 Fiona Ct
10 Kilburn Park Sch
C1 1 Westside Ct
2 Byron Mews
3 Sutherland Ct
4 Fleming Cl
5 Hermes Cl
6 St Peter's CE Prim Sch
7 Paddington Acad
C2 1 Pentland Rd
2 Nelson Cl
3 Pavilion Ct
4 Masefield Ho
5 Austen Ho
6 Fielding Ho
7 Argo Bsns Ctr
8 John Ratcliffe Ho
9 Wymering Mans
10 City of Westminster Coll, Queens Park Ctr
11 Essendine Prim Sch
C3 1 Wells Ct
2 Cambridge Ct
3 Ely Ct
4 Durham Ct
5 St Augustine's CE High Sch
6 Sch of the Islamic Republic of Iran The
C4 1 Ryde Ho
2 Glengall Pass
3 Leith Yd
4 Daynor Ho
5 Varley Ho
6 Sandby Ho
7 Colas Mews
8 Bishopsdale Ho
9 Lorton Ho
10 Marshwood Ho
11 Ribblesdale Ho
12 Holmesdale Ho
13 Kilburn Vale Est
14 Kilburn Bridge
15 Coll of NW London
16 St Mary's Kilburn CE Prim Sch

24

A2 1 Pimlico Wlk
2 Aske Ho
3 Hathaway Ho
4 Haberdasher Pl
5 Fairchild Ho
6 Burtt Ho
7 Enfield Cloisters
8 McGregor Ct
9 Royal Oak Ct
10 Hoxton Mkt
11 Bath Pl
12 Chapel Pl
13 Standard Pl
14 Cleeve Workshops
15 Cleeve Ho
16 Printing House Yd
17 Perseverance Works
18 Crooked Billet Yd
19 Drysdale Ho
20 Castlefrank Ho
21 School App
22 Basing House Yd
23 Mail Coach Yd
24 St Monica's RC Prim Sch
25 Symister Mews
33 Hackney Com Coll
A3 1 Bracer Ho
2 Scorton Ho
3 Fern Cl
4 Macbeth Ho
5 Oberon Ho
6 Buckland Ct
7 Crondall Ct
8 Osric Path
9 Caliban Twr
10 Celia Ho
11 Juliet Ho
12 Bacchus Wlk
13 Malcolm Ho
14 Homefield St
15 Crondall Pl
16 Blanca Ho
17 Miranda Ho
18 Falstaff Ho
19 Charmian Ho
20 Myrtle Wlk
21 Arden Ho
22 Sebastian Ho
23 Stanway Ct
24 Jerrold St
25 Rosalind Ho
26 Cordelia Ho
27 Monteagle Ct
28 John Parry Ct
29 James Anderson Ct
30 Ben Jonson Ct
31 Sara Lane Ct
32 Walbrook Ct
33 Burbage Sch
A4 1 Portelet Ct
2 Trinity Ct
3 Rozel Ct
4 St Helier Ct
5 Corbiere Ho
6 Kenning Ho
7 Higgins Ho
8 Cavell Ho
9 Girling Ho
10 Fulcher Ho
11 Francis Ho
12 Norris Ho
13 Kempton Ho
14 Nesham Ho
15 Crossbow Ho
16 Catherine Ho
17 Strale Ho
18 Horner Hos
19 Stringer Hos
20 Whitmore Ho
21 Nightingale Ho
22 Wilmer Gdns
23 Arrow Ho
24 Archer Ho
25 Meriden Ho
26 Rover Ho
27 Bowyer Ho
28 Tiller Ho
29 Canalside Studios
30 Kleine Wharf
31 Benyon Wharf
32 Quebec Wharf
33 Belvedere Ct
34 Portfleet Pl
B2 1 Gorsuch Pl
2 Strout's Pl
3 Vaughan Est
4 George Loveless Ho
5 Baroness Rd
6 James Brine Ho
7 Arthur Wade Ho
8 Robert Owen Ho
9 Sivill Ho
10 Georgina Gdns
11 Old Market Sq
12 Cuff Point
13 Bakers Rents
14 Leopold Bldgs
15 Dunmore Point
16 Wingfield Ho
17 Gascoigne Pl
18 Mandela Ho
19 Virginia Rd
20 Briggs Ho
21 Packenham Ho
22 Gowan Ho
23 Kirton Gdns
24 Chambord Ho
25 Ducal St
26 Strickland Ho
27 Alliston Ho
28 Gibraltar Wlk
29 Equity Sq
30 Shacklewell St
31 Rochelle St
32 Sonning Ho
33 Culham Ho
34 Hurley Ho
35 Palissy St
36 Taplow Ho
37 Chertsey Ho
38 Sunbury Ho
39 Sunbury Workshops
40 Datchett Ho
41 Hocker St
42 Coll Sharp Ct
43 Marlow Studio Workshops
44 Marlow Ho
45 Shiplake Ho
46 Wargrave Ho
47 Iffley Ho
48 Virginia Prim Sch
49 Bethnal Green Tech Coll
50 Columbia Prim Sch
B3 1 Queensbridge Ct
2 Godwin Ho
3 Kent Ct
4 Brunswick Ho
5 Weymouth Ct
6 Sovereign Mews
7 Dunloe Ct
8 Cremer Bsns Ctr
9 James Hammett Ho
10 Allgood St
11 Horatio St
12 Cadell Ho
13 Horatio Ho
14 Shipton Ho
15 Haggerston Sch
16 Randal Cremer JMI Sch
B4 1 Hilborough Ct
2 Scriven Ct
3 Livermere Ct
4 Angrave Ct
5 Angrave Pas
6 Benfleet Ct
7 Belford Ho
8 Orme Ho
9 Clemson Ho
10 Longman Ho
11 Lowther Ho
12 Lovelace Ho
13 Harlowe Ho
14 Pamela Ho
15 Samuel Ho
16 Acton Ho
17 Loanda Cl
18 Phoenix Cl
19 Richardson Cl
20 Thrasher Cl
21 Mary Secole Cl
22 Canal Path
23 Pear Tree Cl
24 Hebden Ct
25 Charlton Ct
26 Laburnum Ct
27 Mansfield Ct
28 Garden Pl
29 Amber Wharf
30 Haggerston Studios
C1 1 Bentworth Ct
2 Hawksmoor Pl
3 Kerbela St
4 Fuller Cl
5 Kinsham Ho
6 Menotti St
7 Barwell Ho
8 Grimsby St
9 Reflection Ho

10 Fleet Street Hill
11 Bratley St
12 Weaver Ho
13 Cornerstone Ct
14 Stuttle Ho
15 McGlashon Ho
16 John Pritchard Ho
17 Thomas Buxton Jun & Inf Sch
18 St Anne RC Prim Sch
19 William Davis Prim Sch
C2 1 Providence Yd
2 Lygon Ho
3 Brabner Ho
4 Delta St
5 Delta Point
6 Tillet Way
7 Mullet Gdns
8 Lampern Sq
9 Kite Pl
10 Elver Gdns
11 Cobden Ho
12 Eversley Ho
13 Lorden Wlk
14 Rapley Ho
15 Dence Ho
16 McKinnon Wood Ho
17 Satchwell Rd
18 Dickinson Ho
19 Hutton Ho
20 Simmons Ho
21 Swinton Ho
22 Yates Ho
23 Johnson Ho
24 Jeremy Bentham Ho
25 Waring Ho
26 St James Ct
27 Ebony Ho
28 Azure Ho
29 Westhope Ho
30 Hague St
31 Elizabeth Selby Inf Sch
32 Lawdale Jun Sch
C3 1 London Terr
2 Sturdee Ho
3 Maude Ho
4 Haig Ho
5 Jellicoe Ho
6 Ropley St
7 Guinness Trust Bldgs
8 Ion Ct
9 Columbia Rd
10 Moye Cl
11 Morrel Ct
12 Courtauld Ho
13 Drummond Ho
14 Gurney Ho
15 Atkinson Ho
16 Halley Ho
17 Goldsmith's Sq
18 Shahjalal Ho
19 Ken Wilson Ho
20 April Ct
21 Crofts Ho
22 Sebright Ho
23 Beechwood Ho
24 Gillman Ho
25 Cheverell Ho
26 Besford Ho
27 Dinmont Ho
28 Elizabeth Mews
29 Sebright Pas
30 Wyndham Deedes Ho
31 Sheppard Ho
32 Mary James Ho
33 Hadrian Est
34 Blythendale Ho
35 George Vale Ho
36 Lion Mills
37 St Peter's Ave
38 Pritchard Ho
39 Sebright Sch
C4 1 Broke Wlk
2 Rochemont Wlk
3 Marlborough Ave
4 Rivington Wlk
5 Magnin Cl
6 Gloucester Sq
7 Woolstone Ho
8 Marsworth Ho
9 Cheddington Ho
10 Linslade Ho
11 Cosgrove Ho
12 Blisworth Ho
13 Eleanor Ct
14 Wistow Ho
15 Muscott Ho
16 Boxmoor Ho
17 Linford Ho
18 Pendley Ho
19 Northchurch Ho
20 Debdale Ho
21 Broadway Market Mews
22 Welshpool Ho
23 Ada Ho
24 St Paul's with St Michael's Prim Sch

25

A1 1 Rochester Ct
2 Weaver Ct
3 Greenheath Bsns Ctr
4 Glass St
5 Herald St
6 Northesk Ho
7 Codrington Ho
8 Heathpool Ct
9 Mocatta Ho
10 Harvey Ho
11 Blackwood Ho
12 Rutherford Ho
13 Bullen Ho
14 Fremantle Ho
15 Pellew Ho
16 Ashington Ho
17 Dinnington Ho
18 Bartholomew Sq
19 Steeple Ct
20 Orion Ho
21 Fellbrigg St
21 Hague Prim Sch
22 Eagle Ho
23 Sovereign Ho
24 Redmill Ho
25 Berry Ho
26 Grindall Ho
27 Collingwood Ho
28 Stewart Headlam Prim Sch
A2 1 Charles Dickens Ho
2 Adrian Bolt Ho
3 William Rathbone Ho
4 Southwood Smith Ho
5 Rushmead
6 William Channing Ho
7 John Cartwright Ho
8 Charles Darwin Ho
9 Thomas Burt Ho
10 John Fielden Ho
11 Gwilym Maries Ho
12 Joseph Priestley Ho
13 Wear Pl
14 John Nettleford Ho
15 Thornaby Ho
16 Stockton Ho
17 Barnard Ho
18 Gainford Ho
19 Stapleton Ho
20 James Middleton Ho
21 Kedleston Wlk
22 Queen Margaret Flats
23 Hollybush Ho
24 Horwood Ho
25 Norden Ho
26 Newcourt Ho
27 Seabright St
28 Viaduct Pl
29 Sunlight Sq
30 Providence Row Cl
31 Oaklands Sec Sch
32 Raine's Foundation Lower Sch
33 Beatrice Tate Sch
A3 1 Dinmont St
2 Marian St
3 Claredale Ho
4 Keeling Ho
5 Maple St
6 Winkley St
7 Temple Dwellings
8 Argos Ho
9 Helen Ho
10 Lysander Ho
11 Antenor Ho
12 Paris Ho
13 Nestor Ho
14 Hector Ho
15 Ajax Ho
16 Achilles Ho
17 Priam Ho
18 Peabody Est
19 Felix St
20 Cambridge Cres
21 Peterley Bsns Ctr
22 Beckwith Ho
23 Brookfield Ho
24 Parminter Ind Est
25 Ted Roberts Ho
26 Cambridge Ct
27 Millennium Pl
28 William Caslon Ho
29 Hugh Platt Ho
30 West St
31 Mayfield Ho
32 Apollo Ho
33 Tanners Yd
34 Teesdale Yd
A4 1 Welshpool St
2 Broadway Ho
3 Regents Wharf
4 London Wharf
5 Warburton Ho
6 Warburton St
7 Triangle Rd
8 Warburton Rd
9 Williams Ho
10 Booth Cl
11 Albert Cl
12 King Edward Mans
13 Victoria Bldgs
14 Andrews Wharf
15 London Fields Prim Sch
16 Triangle The
17 Com Coll Hackney The
B1 1 William's Bldgs
2 Donegal Ho
3 Pelican Pas
4 Frederick Charrington Ho
5 Wickford Ho
6 Braintree Ho
7 Doveton Ho
8 Doveton St
9 Cephas Ho
10 Sceptre Ho
11 Bancroft Ho
12 Stothard St
13 Redclyf Ho
14 Winkworth Cotts
15 Amiel St
16 Hadleigh Ho
17 Hadleigh Cl
18 Ryder Ho
20 Kenton Ho
21 Colebert Ho
22 Ibbott St
23 Rickman Ho
24 Rickman St
25 Stothard Ho
26 Barbanel Ho
27 Stannard Cotts
28 St Peters Ct
29 Rennie Cotts
30 Pemell Cl
31 Pemell Ho
32 Leatherdale St
33 Gouldman Ho
34 Lamplighter Cl
35 Sherren Ho
36 Marlborough Lo
37 Hamilton Lo
38 Montgomery Lo
39 Cleveland Gr
40 Cromwell Lo
41 Bardsey Pl
42 Charrington Ho
43 Hayfield Yd
44 Allport Mews
45 Colin Winter Ho
46 John Scurr Prim Sch
B2 1 Mulberry Ho
2 Gretton Ho
3 Merceron Ho
4 Montfort Ho
5 Westbrook Ho
6 Sugar Loaf Wlk
7 Museum Ho
8 Burnham Est
9 Globe Terr
10 Moravian St
11 Shepton Hos
12 Mendip Hos
13 Academy Ct
14 Pepys Ho
15 Swinburne Ho
16 Moore Ho
17 Morris Ho
18 Burns Ho
19 Milton Ho
20 Whitman Ho
21 Shelley Ho
22 Keats Ho
23 Dawson Ho
24 Bradbeer Ho
25 Forber Ho
26 Hughes Ho
27 Silvester Ho
28 Rogers Est
29 Pavan Ct
30 Stafford Cripps Ho
31 Sidney Godley (VC) Ho
32 Butler Ho
33 Butler St
34 Thorne Ho
35 Bevin Ho
36 Tuscan Ho
37 Globe Prim Sch
38 Bangabandhu Prim Sch
39 Bonner Prim Sch
B3 1 Evesham Ho
2 James Campbell Ho
3 Thomas Hollywood Ho
4 James Docherty Ho
5 Ebenezer Mussel Ho
6 Jameson Ct
7 Edinburgh Cl
8 Roger Dowley Ct
9 Sherbrooke Ho
10 Calcraft Ho
11 Burrard Ho
12 Dundas Ho
13 Ponsonby Ho
14 Barnes Ho
15 Paget Ho
16 Maitland Ho
17 Chesil Ct
18 Reynolds Ho
19 Cleland Ho
20 Goodrich Ho
21 Rosebery Ho
22 Sankey Ho
23 Cyprus Pl
24 Royston St
25 Stainsbury St
26 Hunslett St
27 Baildon
28 Brockweir
29 Tytherton
30 Malmesbury
31 Kingswood
32 Colville Ho
33 St Elizabeth RC Prim Sch
34 Raine's Foundation Sch
35 St John's CE Prim Sch
36 Mowlem Prim Sch
B4 1 Halkett Ho
2 Christchurch Sq
3 Helena Pl
4 Swingfield Ho
5 Greenham Ho
6 Dinmore Ho
7 Anstey Ho
8 Weston Ho
9 Carbroke Ho
10 Bluebell Cl
11 Cherry Tree Cl

12 Georgian Ct
13 Park Cl
14 Regency Ct
15 Norris Ho
C1 1 Raynham Ho
2 Pat Shaw Ho
3 Colmar Cl
4 Withy Ho
5 Stocks Ct
6 Downey Ho
7 Bay Ct
8 Sligo Ho
9 Pegasus Ho
10 Barents Ho
11 Biscay Ho
12 Solway Ho
13 Bantry Ho
14 Aral Ho
15 Pacific Ho
16 Magellan Ho
17 Levant Ho
18 Adriatic Ho
19 Genoa Ho
20 Hawke Ho
21 Palliser Ho
22 Ionian Ho
23 Weddell Ho
24 Carlyle Mews
25 Greencourt Ho
26 Sundra Wlk
C2 1 Stubbs Ho
2 Holman Ho
3 Clynes Ho
4 Windsor Ho
5 Gilbert Ho
6 Chater Ho
7 Ellen Wilkinson Ho
8 George Belt Ho
9 Ayrton Gould Ho
10 O'Brian Ho
11 Sulkin Ho
12 Jenkinson Ho
13 Bullards Pl
14 Sylvia Pankhurst Ho
15 Mary Macarthur Ho
16 Trevelyan Ho
17 Wedgwood Ho
18 Pemberton Ct
19 Leatherdale St
20 Walter Besant Ho
21 Barber Beaumont Ho
22 Brancaster Ho
23 Litcham Ho
24 Bradwell St
C3 1 Kemp Ho
2 Piggott Ho
3 Mark Ho
4 Sidney Ho
5 Pomeroy Ho
6 Puteaux Ho
7 Doric Ho
8 Modling Ho
9 Longman Ho
10 Ames Ho
11 Alzette Ho
12 Offenbach Ho
13 Tate Ho
14 Norton Ho
15 St Gilles Ho
16 Harold Ho
17 Velletri Ho
18 Bridge Wharf
19 Gathorne St
20 Bow Brook The
21 Twig Folly Cl
22 Palmerston Ct
23 Lakeview
24 Peach Walk Mews
25 Caesar Ct
26 Gatehouse Sch
C4 6 Lauriston Prim Sch

26

A1 1 Formosa Ho
2 Galveston Ho
3 Arabian Ho
4 Greenland Ho
5 Coral Ho
6 Anson Ho
7 Cambay Ho
8 Lindop Ho
9 Moray Ho
10 Azov Ho
11 Sandalwood Cl
12 Broadford Ho
A2 1 Imperial Ho
2 Newport Ho
3 Vassall Ho
4 Maurice Ct
5 Creed Ct
6 Christopher France Ho
7 Beaumont Ct
8 Pembroke Mews
9 Guardian Angels RC Prim Sch
10 Central Foundation Lower Girls Sch The
A3 1 Nightingale Mews
2 Bunsen Ho
3 Bunsen St
4 Beatrice Webb Ho
5 Margaret Bondfield Ho
6 Wilmer Ho
7 Sandall Ho
8 Butley Ct
9 Josseline Ct
10 Dalton Ho
11 Brine Ho
12 Ford Cl
13 Viking Cl
14 Stanfield Rd
15 Stoneleigh Mews
16 Ruth Ct
17 School Bell Cloisters
18 Schoolbell Mews
19 Medhurst Cl
20 Olga St
21 Conyer St
22 Diamond Ho
23 Daring Ho
24 Crane Ho
25 Exmoor Ho
26 Grenville Ho
27 Hyperion Ho
28 Sturdy Ho
29 Wren Ho
30 Ardent Ho
31 Senators Lo
32 Hooke Ho
33 Mohawk Ho
34 Ivanhoe Ho
35 Medway Mews
36 Chisenhale Prim Sch
37 Olga Prim Sch
B2 1 Trellis Sq
2 Sheffield Sq
3 Howcroft Ho
4 Astra Ho
5 Frye Ct
6 Byas Ho
7 George Lansbury Ho
8 Regal Pl
9 Coborn Mews
10 Tredegar Mews
11 Cavendish Terr
12 Lyn Mews
13 Buttermere Ho
14 Coniston Ho
15 Tracy Ho
16 Hanover Pl
17 St Clair Ho
18 Longthorne Ho
19 Vista Bldgs
20 Verity Ho
21 Icarus Ho
22 Whippingham Ho
23 Hamilton Ho
24 Winchester Ho
25 Malmesbury Prim Sch
26 Phoenix Sec & Prim Sch
27 Central Foundation Upper Girls Sch The
B3 1 Roman Road Mkt
2 John Bond Ho
3 McKenna Ho
4 Dennis Ho
5 McAusland Ho
6 McBride Ho
7 Libra Rd
8 Dave Adams Ho
9 Regency Ct
10 Tay Ho
11 Sleat Ho
12 Brodick Ho
13 Ewart Pl
14 Lunan Ho
15 Cruden Ho
16 Anglo Rd
17 Mull Ho
18 Sinclairs Ho
19 Driftway Ho
20 Clayhall Ct
21 Berebinder Ho
22 Partridge Ho
23 Barford Ho
24 Gullane Ho
25 Gosford Ho
26 Dornoch Ho
27 Dunnet Ho
28 Enard Ho
29 Fraserburgh Ho
30 Forth Ho
31 Stavers Ho
32 Rosegate Ho
33 Crowngate Ho
34 Queensgate Ho
35 Towergate Ho
36 Ordell Ct
37 William Pl
38 Old Ford Prim Sch
B4 1 Hampstead Wlk
2 Waverton Ho
3 Elton Ho
4 Locton Gn
5 Birtwhistle Ho
6 Clare Ho
7 Magpie Ho
8 Hornbeam Sq
9 Rowan Ho
10 Barge La
11 Walnut Ho
12 Birdsfield La
13 Atkins Ct
14 Willow Tree Cl
15 Jasmine Sq
16 Tait Ct
17 Ranwell Ho
18 Ranwell Cl
19 Tufnell Ct
20 Pulteney Cl
21 Vic Johnson Ho
22 Lea Sq
23 Iceni Ct
24 Tamar Cl
25 Roman Rd
26 Valentine Ho
C1 1 Fairmont Ho
2 Healy Ho
3 Zodiac Ho
4 Buick Ho
5 Consul Ho
6 Bentley Ho
7 Cresta Ho
8 Daimler Ho
9 Riley Ho
10 Jensen Ho
11 Lagonda Ho
12 Ireton St
13 Navenby Wlk
14 Burwell Wlk
15 Leadenham Ct
16 Sleaford Ho
17 Bow Triangle Bsns Ctr
18 Clara Grant Prim Sch The
C2 1 Bow Ho
2 Denmark Pl
3 Marsalis Ho
4 Lovette Ho
5 Drapers Almhouses
6 Mallard Point
7 Creswick Wlk
8 Bevin Ho
9 Huggins Ho
10 Williams Ho
11 Harris Ho
12 Marina Ct
13 Electric Ho
14 Matching Ct
15 Wellington Bldgs
16 Grafton Ho
17 Berkeley Ho
18 Columbia Ho
19 Bow Sec Sch
20 Wellington Prim Sch
21 London Metrocity Coll
22 Cherry Trees Sch The
C3 1 Vincent Mews
2 Menai Pl
3 Heathfield Ct
4 Redwood Cl
5 Acorn Ct
6 Primrose Cl
7 Briar Ct
8 Springwood Cl
9 Lacey Mews
10 Matilda Gdns
C4 1 Ironworks
2 Juno Ho
3 Chariot Cl
4 Saturn Ho
5 Hadrian Cl
6 Mercury Ho
7 Forum Cl
8 Venus Ho
9 Vesta Ho
10 Tiber Cl
11 Gemini Ho
12 Crown Close Bsns Ctr

27

A1 1 Broxbourne Ho
2 Roxford Ho
3 Biscott Ho
4 Stanborough Ho
5 Hillstone Ct
6 Marner Prim Sch
A2 1 Bradley Ho
2 Prioress Ho
3 Alton Ho
4 Foxley Ho
5 Munden Ho
6 Canterbury Ho
7 Corbin Ho
8 Barton Ho
9 Jolles Ho
10 Rudstone Ho
11 Baxter Ho
12 Baker Ho
13 Insley Ho
14 Hardwicke Ho
15 St Agnes RC Prim Sch
16 Priory St
17 Sadler Ho
18 Ballinger Point
19 Henshall Point
20 Dorrington Point
21 Warren Ho
22 Fairlie Ct
23 Regent Sq
24 Hackworth Point
25 Priestman Point
26 Wingate Ho
27 Nethercott Ho
28 Thelbridge Ho
29 Bowden Ho
30 Kerscott Ho
31 Southcott Ho
32 Birchdown Ho
33 Upcott Ho
34 Langmead Ho
35 Limscott Ho
36 Northleigh Ho
37 Huntshaw Ho
38 Chagford Ho
39 Ashcombe Ho
40 Shillingford Ho
41 Patrick Connolly Gdns
42 Lester Ct
43 Franklin St
44 Taft Way
45 Washington Cl
46 Veronica Ho
47 William Guy Gdns
48 Denbury Ho
49 Holsworthy Ho
50 Padstone Ho
51 Old Palace Prim Sch
52 Ian Mikardo Sch
C1 1 Crescent Court Bsns Ctr
2 Ashmead Bsns Ctr
3 Forward Bsns Ctr The
C4 1 Victoria Mills

2 Hallings Wharf Studios
3 Poland Ho
4 Peter Heathfield Ho
5 Burford Rd
6 John F Kennedy Specl Sch
7 Univ of East London (Duncan Ho)

28

A1 1 Lantry Ct
2 Rosemount Ct
3 Moreton Twr
4 Acton Central Ind Est
5 Rufford Twr
6 Narrow St
7 Mount Pl
8 Sidney Miller Ct
9 Mill Hill Terr
10 Cheltenham Pl
11 Mill Hill Gr
12 Benjamin Ho
13 Arlington Ct
14 Lombard Ct
15 Steyne Ho
16 Acton & West London Coll
B1 1 Rectory Rd
2 Derwentwater Mans
3 Market Pl
4 Hooper's Mews
5 Cromwell Pl
6 Locarno Rd
7 Edgecote Cl
8 Harleyford Manor
9 Coopers Ct
10 Avingdor Ct
11 Steyne Ho
B3 1 Avon Ct
2 Bromley Lo
3 Walter Ct
4 Lynton Terr
5 Acton Ho
6 Fells Haugh
7 Springfield Ct
8 Tamarind Ct
9 Lynton Ct
10 Aspen Ct
11 Pegasus Ct
12 Friary Park Ct
C3 1 Rosebank Gdns
2 Rosebank
3 Edinburgh Ho
4 Western Ct
5 Kilronan

30

A1 1 Arlington Ho
2 Lugard Ho
3 Shabana Ct
4 Sitarey Ct
5 Oaklands Ct
6 Davenport Mews
A2 1 Abercrombie Ho
2 Bathurst Ho
3 Brisbane Ho
4 Bentinck Ho
5 Ellenborough Ho
6 Lawrence Cl
7 Mackenzie Cl
8 Carteret Ho
9 Calvert Ho
10 Winthrop Ho
11 Auckland Ho
12 Blaxland Ho
13 Havelock Cl
14 Hargraves Ho
15 Hudson Cl
16 Phipps Ho
17 Lawson Ho
18 Hastings Ho
19 Wolfe Ho
20 Malabar Ct
21 Charnock Ho
22 Canning Ho
23 Cornwallis Ho
24 Commonwealth Ave
25 Champlain Ho
26 Grey Ho
27 Durban Ho
28 Baird Ho
29 Campbell Ho
30 Mitchell Ho
31 Denham Ho
32 Mackay Ho
33 Evans Ho
34 Davis Ho
35 Mandela Cl
A3 1 Holborn Ho
2 Clement Danes Ho
3 Vellacott Ho
4 O'Driscoll Ho
5 King Ho
6 Daley Ho
7 Selma Ho
8 Garrett Ho
B1 1 Linden Ct
2 Frithville Ct
3 Blomfield Mans
4 Poplar Mews
5 Hopgood St
6 Westwood Ho
7 Stanlake Mews
8 Stanlake Villas
9 Alexandra Mans
B3 1 Latimer Ind Est
2 Pankhurst Ho
3 Quadrangle The
4 Nightingale Ho
5 Gordon Ct
6 Ducane Cl
7 Browning Ho
8 Pavilion Terr
9 Ivebury Ct
10 Olympic Ho
B4 1 Galleywood Ho
2 Edgcott Ho
3 Cuffley Ho
4 Addlestone Ho
5 Hockliffe Ho
6 Sarratt Ho
7 Firle Ho
8 Sutton Est The
9 Terling Ho
10 Danes Ho
11 Udimore Ho
12 Vange Ho
13 Binbrook Ho
14 Yeadon Ho
15 Yatton Ho
16 Yarrow Ho
17 Clement Ho
18 Danebury
19 Coronation Ct
20 Calderon Pl
21 St Quintin Gdns
C1 1 St Katherine's Wlk
2 Dorrit Ho
3 Pickwick Ho
4 Dombey Ho
5 Caranday Villas
6 Mortimer Ho
7 Nickleby Ho
8 Stebbing Ho
9 Boxmoor Ho
10 Poynter Ho
11 Swanscombe Ho
12 Darnley Terr
13 Norland Ho
14 Hume Ho
15 Boundary Ho
16 Norland Rd
17 Helix Ct
C2 1 Frinstead Ho
2 Hurstway Wlk
3 Testerton Wlk
4 Grenfell Wlk
5 Grenfell Twr
6 Barandon Wlk
7 Treadgold Ho
8 St Clements Ct
9 Willow Way
10 Florence Ho
11 Dora Ho
12 Carton Ho
13 Agnes Ho
14 Marley Ho
15 Estella Ho
16 Waynflete Sq
17 Pippin Ho
18 Baseline Business Studios
19 St Francis of Assisi Prim Sch
20 Nicholas Rd
C3 1 Kelfield Ct
2 Downing Ho
3 Crosfield Ct
4 Robinson Ho
5 Scampston Mews
6 Girton Villas
7 Ray Ho
8 Walmer Ho
9 Goodrich Ct
10 Arthur Ct
11 Whitstable Ho
12 Kingsnorth Ho
13 Bridge Cl
14 Prospect Ho
15 St Marks Rd
16 Whitchurch Ho
17 Blechynden Ho
18 Waynflete Sq
19 Bramley Ho
20 Dixon Ho
21 Oxford Gardens Prim Sch
22 Bassett House Sch
C4 1 Treverton Twr
2 Raymede Twr
3 Bruce Ho
4 Balfour Ho
5 Burleigh Ho
6 Sion-Manning RC Sch for Girls
7 St Charles RC Prim Sch
8 St Charles RC Sixth Form Coll

31

A3 1 Malton Mews
2 Lancaster Lo
3 Manning Ho
4 Galsworthy Ho
5 Hudson Ho
6 Cambourne Mews
7 Upper Talbot Wlk
8 Kingsdown Cl
9 Lower Clarendon Wlk
10 Talbot Grove Ho
11 Clarendon Wlk
12 Upper Clarendon Wlk
13 Camelford Wlk
14 Upper Camelford Wlk
15 Camelford Ct
16 Thomas Jones Prim Sch
17 Notting Hill Prep Sch
A4 1 Murchison Ho
2 Macaulay Ho
3 Chesterton Ho
4 Chiltern Ho
5 Lionel Ho
6 Watts Ho
7 Wheatstone Ho
8 Telford Ho
9 Golborne Mews
10 Millwood St
11 St Columb's Ho
12 Norfolk Mews
13 Lionel Mews
14 Kensington & Chelsea Coll
15 Bevington Prim Sch
16 Sion-Manning RC Sch for Girls
17 Lloyd Williamson Sch
B3 1 Silvester Ho
2 Golden Cross Mews
3 Tavistock Mews
4 Clydesdale Ho
5 Colville Prim Sch
5 Melchester
6 Pinehurst Ct
7 Denbigh Ho
B4 1 Blagrove Rd
2 All Saints Ho
3 Tavistock Ho
4 Leamington Ho
C3 1 Shottsford
2 Tolchurch
3 Casterbridge
4 Sandbourne
5 Anglebury
6 Weatherbury
7 Westbourne Gr Mews
8 Rosehart Mews
9 Viscount Ct
10 Hereford Mans
11 Hereford Mews
12 St Mary of the Angels RC Prim Sch
C4 1 Ascot Ho
2 Ashgrove Ct
3 Lockbridge Ct
4 Swallow Ct
5 Nightingale Lo
6 Hammond Lo
7 Penfield Lo
8 Harvey Lo
9 Hunter Lo
10 Barnard Lo
11 Falcon Lo
12 Johnson Lo
13 Livingstone Lo
14 Nuffield Lo
15 Finch Lo
16 Polesworth Ho
17 Oversley Ho
18 Derrycombe Ho
19 Buckshead Ho
20 Combe Ho
21 Culham Ho
22 Dainton Ho
23 Devonport Ho
24 Honwell Ho
25 Truro Ho
26 Sunderland Ho
27 Stonehouse Ho
28 Riverford Ho
29 Portishead Ho
30 Mickleton Ho
31 Keyham Ho
32 Moulsford Ho
33 Shrewsbury Mews
34 St Stephen's Mews
35 Westway Lo
36 Langley Ho
37 Brindley Ho
38 Radway Ho
39 Astley Ho
40 Willow Ct
41 Larch Ct
42 Elm Ct
43 Beech Ct
44 Worcester Ct
45 Union Ct
46 Leicester Ct
47 Kennet Ct
48 Oxford Ct
49 Fazerley Ct

32

A1 1 China Ct
2 Wellington Terr
3 Stevedore St
4 Portland Sq
5 Reardon Ho
6 Lowder Ho
7 Meeting House Alley
8 Farthing Fields
9 Oswell Ho
10 Park Lo
11 Doughty Ct
12 Inglefield Sq
13 Chopin's Ct
14 Welsh Ho
15 Hilliard Ho
16 Clegg St
17 Tasman Ho
18 Ross Ho
19 Wapping Dock St
20 Bridewell Pl
21 New Tower Bldgs
22 Tower Bldgs
23 Chimney Ct
24 Jackman Ho
25 Fenner Ho
26 Franklin Ho
27 Frobisher Ho
28 Flinders Ho
29 Chancellor Ho
30 Beechey Ho
31 Reardon Path
32 Parry Ho
33 Vancover Ho
34 Willoughby Ho
35 Sanctuary The
36 Dundee Ct

32 A1

37 Pierhead Wharf
38 Scandrett St
39 St Johns Ct

A2
1 Newton Ho
2 Richard Neale Ho
3 Maddocks Ho
4 Cornwall St
5 Brockmer Ho
6 Dellow Ho
7 Bewley Ho
8 Artichoke Hill
9 Queen Anne Terr
10 King Henry Terr
11 King Charles Terr
12 Queen Victoria Terr
13 Sovereign Ct
14 Princes Court Bsns Ctr
15 Kingsley Mews
16 Mulberry Sch for Girls

A3
1 Peter Best Ho
2 Mellish Ho
3 Porchester Ho
4 Dickson Ho
5 Joscoyne Ho
6 Silvester Ho
7 Wilton Ct
8 Sarah Ho
9 Bridgen Ho
10 Tylney Ho
11 Greenwich Ct
12 Damien Ct
13 Philson Mans
14 Siege Ho
15 Jacob Mans
16 Proud Ho
17 Sly St
18 Barnett St
19 Kinder St
20 Richard St
21 Hungerford St
22 Colstead Ho
23 Melwood Ho
24 Wicker St
25 Langdale St
26 Chapman Ho
27 Burwell Cl
28 Walford Ho
29 Welstead Ho
30 Norton Ho
31 Turnour Ho
32 Luke Ho
33 Dunch St
34 Sheridan St
35 Brinsley St
36 Spencer Way
38 Madani Girls Sch
37 East End Computing & Bsns Coll
39 Mulberry Sch for Girls
40 Jamiatul Ummah Sch
41 Bigland Green Prim Sch

A4
1 Wodeham Gdns
2 Castlemaine St
3 Court St
4 Ashfield St
5 London Hospital Dental Inst
6 Princess Alexandra School of Nursing The

B1
1 John Rennie Wlk
2 Malay Ho
3 Wainwright Ho
4 Riverside Mans
5 Shackleton Ho
6 Whitehorn Ho
7 Wavel Ct
8 Prusom's Island
9 St Peter's CE Prim Sch

B2
1 Shadwell Pl
2 Gosling Ho
3 Vogler Ho
4 Donovan Ho
5 Knowlden Ho
6 Chamberlain Ho
7 Moore Ho
8 Thornewill Ho
9 Fisher Ho
10 All Saints Ct
11 Coburg Dwellings
12 Lowood Ho
13 Solander Gdns
14 Chancery Bldgs
15 Ring Ho
16 Juniper St
17 Gordon Ho
18 West Block
19 North Block
20 South Block
21 Ikon Ho
22 Blue Gate Fields Jun & Inf Schs

B3
1 Woollon Ho
2 Dundalk Ho
3 Anne Goodman Ho
4 Newbold Cotts
5 Kerry Ho
6 Zion Ho
7 Longford Ho
8 Bromehead St
9 Athlone Ho
10 Jubilee Mans
11 Harriott Ho
12 Brayford Sq
13 Clearbrook Way
14 Rochelle Ct
15 Winterton Ho
16 Swift Ho
17 Brinsley Ho
18 Dean Ho
19 Foley Ho
20 Robert Sutton Ho
21 Montpelier Pl
22 Glastonbury Pl
23 Steel's La
24 Masters Lo
25 Stylus Apartments
26 Arta Ho
27 St Mary & St Michael Prim Sch
28 Bishop Challoner Collegiate Sch
29 Morton Cl
30 James Voller Way

B4
1 Fulneck
2 Gracehill
3 Ockbrook
4 Fairfield
5 Dunstan Hos
6 Cressy Ct
7 Cressy Hos
8 Callahan Cotts
9 Lindley Ho
10 Mayo Ho
11 Wexford Ho
12 Sandhurst Ho
13 Addis Ho
14 Colverson Ho
15 Beckett Ho
16 Jarman Ho
17 Armsby Ho
18 Wingrad Ho
19 Miranda Cl
20 Drake Ho
21 Ashfield Yd
22 Magri Wlk
23 Jean Pardies Ho
24 St Vincent De Paul Ho
25 Sambrook Ho
26 Louise De Marillac Ho
27 Dagobert Ho
28 Le Moal Ho
29 Odette Duval Ho
30 Charles Auffray Ho
31 Boisseau Ho
32 Clichy Ho
33 Paymal Ho
34 Smithy Street Sch
35 Redlands Prim Sch
36 Cressy Ct

C1
1 Clarence Mews
2 Raleigh Ct
3 Katherine Cl
4 Woolcombes Ct
5 Tudor Ct
6 Quayside Ct
7 Princes Riverside Rd
8 Surrey Ho
9 Tideway Ct
10 Edinburgh Ct
11 Falkirk Ct
12 Byelands Cl
13 Gwent Ct
14 Lavender Ho
15 Abbotshade Rd
16 Bellamy's Ct
17 Blenheim Ct
18 Sandringham Ct
19 Hampton Ct
20 Windsor Ct
21 Balmoral Ct
22 Westminster Ct
23 Beatson Wlk
24 Peter Hills Sch

C2
1 Barnardo Gdns
2 Roslin Ho
3 Glamis Est
4 Peabody Est
5 East Block
6 Highway Trad Ctr The
7 Highway Bsns Pk The
8 Cranford Cotts
9 Ratcliffe Orch
10 Scotia Bldg
11 Mauretania Bldg
12 Compania Bldg
13 Sirius Bldg
14 Unicorn Bldg
15 Keepier Wharf

C3
1 Pattison Ho
2 St Thomas Ho
3 Arbour Ho
4 Bladen Ho
5 Antill Terr
6 Majorie Mews
7 Billing Ho
8 Dowson Ho
9 Lipton Rd
10 Chalkwell Ho
11 Corringham Ho
12 Ogilvie Ho
13 Edward Mann Cl
14 Reservoir Studios
15 Lighterman Mews
16 Tower Hamlets Coll
17 Marion Richardson Prim Sch

C4
1 Roland Mews
2 Beatrice Ho
3 Morecambe Cl
4 Stepney Green Ct
5 Milrood Ho
6 Panama Ho
7 Galway Ho
8 Jacqueline Ho
9 Crown Mews
10 Caspian Ho
11 Darien Ho
12 Riga Ho
13 Flores Ho
14 Taranto Ho
15 Aden Ho
16 Master's St
17 Rosary Ct
18 Stepney Green Maths & Computing Coll
19 Sir John Cass Foundation & Redcoat CE Sec Sch

33

A1
1 Edward Sq
2 Prince Regent Ct
3 Codrington Ct
4 Pennington Ct
5 Cherry Ct
6 Ash Ct
7 Beech Ct
8 Hazel Ct
9 Laurel Ct

A2
1 St Georges Sq
2 Drake Ho
3 Osprey Ho
4 Fleet Ho
5 Gainsborough Ho
6 Victory Pl
7 Challenger Ho
8 Conrad Ho
9 Lock View Ct
10 Shoulder of Mutton Alley
11 Frederick Sq
12 Helena Sq
13 Elizabeth Sq
14 Sophia Sq
15 William Sq
16 Lamb Ct
17 Lockside
18 Adriatic Bldg
19 Ionian Bldg
20 Regents Gate Ho

A3
1 Hearnshaw St
2 Berry Cotts
3 Causton Cotts
4 Elizabeth Blount Ct
5 Carr St
6 Shaw Cres
7 Darnley Ho
8 Mercer's Cotts
9 Troon Ho
10 Ratcliffe Ho
11 Wakeling St
12 York Sq
13 Anglia Ho
14 Cambria Ho
15 Caledonia Ho
16 Ratcliffe La
17 Bekesbourne St
18 John Scurr Ho
19 Regents Canal Ho
20 Basin App
21 Powlesland Ct
22 Cayley Prim Sch
23 Stephen Hawking Sch

A4
1 Waley St
2 Edith Ramsay Ho
3 Andaman Ho
4 Atlantic Ho
5 Pevensey Ho
6 Solent Ho
7 Lorne Ho
8 Cromarty Ho
9 Dakin Pl
10 Greaves Cotts
11 Donaghue Cotts
12 Ames Cotts
13 Waterview Ho
14 Limehouse Fields Est

B2
1 Hamilton Ho
2 Imperial Ho
3 Oriana Ho
4 Queens Ct
5 Brightlingsea Pl
6 Faraday Ho
7 Ropemaker's Fields
8 Oast Ct
9 Mitre The
10 Bate St
11 Joseph Irwin Ho
12 Padstow Ho
13 Bethlehem Ho
14 Saunders Cl
15 Roche Ho
16 Stocks Pl
17 Trinidad Ho
18 Grenada Ho
19 Kings Ho
20 Dunbar Wharf
21 Limekiln Wharf
22 Belgrave Ct
23 Eaton Ho
24 Cyril Jackson Prim Sch (North Bldg)
25 Cyril Jackson Prim Sch (South Bldg)

B3
1 Dora Ho
2 Flansham Ho
3 Gatwick Ho
4 Ashpark Ho
5 Newdigate Ho
6 Midhurst Ho
7 Redbourne Ho
8 Southwater Cl
9 Andersens Wharf
10 Whatman Ho
11 Butler Ho
12 Fitzroy Ho
13 Salmon St
14 Mission The
15 Aithan Ho
16 Britley Ho
17 Cheadle Ho
18 Elland Ho
19 Wharf La
20 Docklands Ct
21 Park Heights Ct

22 Grosvenor Ct
23 Lime House Ct
24 Swallow Pl
25 St Anne's Trad Est
26 Stepney Greencoat CE Prim Sch The
27 Sir William Burrough Prim Sch
28 Our Lady RC Prim Sch
B4 1 Wearmouth Ho
2 Elmslie Point
3 Grindley Ho
4 Stileman Ho
5 Wilcox Ho
6 Huddart St
7 Robeson St
8 Couzens Ho
9 Perley Ho
10 Whytlaw Ho
11 Booker Cl
12 Tunley Gn
13 Callingham Cl
14 Bowry Ho
15 Perkins Ho
16 Printon Ho
17 Tasker Ho
18 St Paul with St Luke CE Prim Sch
C2 1 West India Ho
2 Berber Pl
3 Birchfield Ho
4 Elderfield Ho
5 Thornfield Ho
6 Gorsefield Ho
7 Arborfield Ho
8 Colborne Ho
9 East India Bldgs
10 Compass Point
11 Salter St
12 Garland Ct
13 Bogart Ct
14 Fonda Ct
15 Welles Ct
16 Rogers Ct
17 Premier Pl
18 Kelly Ct
19 Flynn Ct
20 Mary Jones Ho
21 Cannon Dr
22 Horizon Bldg
23 Holy Family RC Prim Sch
C3 1 Landin Ho
2 Thomas Road Ind Est
3 Vickery's Wharf
4 Abbotts Wharf
5 Limehouse Ct
6 Charlesworth Ho
7 Gurdon Ho
8 Trendell Ho
9 Menteath Ho
10 Minchin Ho
11 Donne Ho
12 Old School Sq
13 Anglesey Ho
14 Gough Wlk
15 Baring Ho
16 Gladstone Ho
17 Hopkins Ho
18 Granville Ho
19 Overstone Ho
20 Pusey Ho
21 Russell Ho
22 Stanley Ho
C4 1 Bredel Ho
2 Linton Ho
3 Matthews Ho
4 Woodcock Ho
5 Limborough Ho
6 Maydwell Ho
7 Underhill Ho
8 Meyrick Ho
9 Ambrose Ho
10 Richardson Ho
11 Carpenter Ho
12 Robinson Ho
13 Bellmaker Ct
14 Lime Tree Ct
15 Bracken Ho
16 Bramble Ho
17 Berberis Ho
18 Bilberry Ho
19 Ladyfern Ho
20 Rosebay Ho
21 Invicta Cl
22 Phoenix Bsns Ctr
23 Metropolitan Cl
24 Busbridge Ho
25 St Paul's Way Com Sch
26 Stebon Prim Sch

34

A2 1 Westcott Ho
2 Corry Ho
3 Malam Gdns
4 Blomfield Ho
5 Devitt Ho
6 Leyland Ho
7 Wigram Ho
8 Willis Ho
9 Balsam Ho
10 Finch's Ct
11 Poplar Bath St
12 Lawless St
13 Storey Ho
14 Abbot Ho
15 Woodall Cl
16 Landon Wlk
17 Goodhope Ho
18 Goodfaith Ho
19 Winant Ho
20 Goodspeed Ho
21 Lubbock Ho
22 Goodwill Ho
23 Martindale Ho
24 Holmsdale Ho
25 Norwood Ho
26 Constant Ho
27 Tower Hamlets Coll
A3 1 Colebrook Ho
2 Essex Ho
3 Salisbury Ho
4 Maidstone Ho
5 Osterley Ho
6 Norwich Ho
7 Clarissa Ho
8 Elgin Ho
9 Shaftesbury Lo
10 Shepherd Ho
11 Jeremiah St
12 Elizabeth Cl
13 Chilcot Cl
14 Fitzgerald Ho
15 Vesey Path
16 Ennis Ho
17 Kilmore Ho
18 Cygnet House N
19 Cygnet House S
20 Lansbury Lawrence Prim Sch
21 Bygrove Prim Sch
22 Mayflower Prim Sch
23 Tower Hamlets Coll
A4 1 Sumner Ho
2 David Hewitt Ho
3 St Gabriels Cl
4 Limehouse Cut
5 Colmans Wharf
6 Foundary Ho
7 Radford Ho
8 Manorfield Prim Sch
9 St Saviour's CE Prim Sch
10 Pioneer Cl
B1 1 Lumina Bldg
2 Nova Ct W
3 Nova Ct E
4 Aurora Bldg
5 Arran Ho
6 Kintyre Ho
7 Vantage Mews
8 Managers St
9 Horatio Pl
10 Concordia Wharf
B2 1 Discovery Ho
2 Mountague Pl
3 Virginia Ho
4 Collins Ho
5 Lawless Ho
6 Carmichael Ho
7 Commodore Ho
8 Mermaid Ho
9 Bullivant St
10 Anderson Ho
11 Mackrow Wlk
12 Robin Hood Gdns
13 Prestage Way
14 Woolmore Prim Sch
B3 1 Glenkerry Ho
2 Carradale Ho
3 Langdon Ho
4 Balfron Twr
5 St Frideswides Mews
6 Tabard Ct
7 Delta Bldg
8 Findhorn St
9 Kilbrennan Ho
10 Thistle Ho
11 Heather Ho
12 Tartan Ho
13 Sharman Ho
14 Trident Ho
15 Wharf View Ct
16 Culloden Prim Sch
B4 1 Mills Gr
2 St Michaels Ct
3 Duncan Ct
C2 1 Quixley St
2 Romney Ho
3 Pumping Ho
4 Switch Ho
5 Wingfield Ct
6 Explorers Ct
7 Sexton Ct
8 Keel Ct
9 Bridge Ct
10 Sail Ct
11 Settlers Ct
12 Pilgrims Mews
13 Studley Ct
14 Wotton Ct
15 Cape Henry Ct
16 Bartholomew Ct
17 Adventurers Ct
18 Susan Constant Ct
19 Atlantic Ct
C3 1 Lansbury Gdns
2 Theseus Ho
3 Adams Ho
4 Jones Ho
5 Sam March Ho
6 Arapiles Ho
7 Athenia Ho
8 Julius Ho
9 Jervis Bay Ho
10 Helen Mackay Ho
11 Gaze Ho
12 Ritchie Ho
13 Blairgowrie Ct
14 Circle Ho
15 Dunkeld Ho
16 Rosemary Dr
17 Sorrel La
18 East India Dock Road Tunnel

35

B3 1 Newton Point
2 Sparke Terr
3 Montesquieu Terr
4 Crawford Point
5 Rathbone Ho
6 George St
7 Emily St
8 Fendt Cl
9 Sabbarton St
9 St Luke Prim CE Sch
10 Briary Ct
11 Shaftesbury Ho
B4 1 Radley Terr
2 Bernard Cassidy St
3 Rathbone Mkt
4 Thomas North Terr
5 Mary St
6 Hughes Terr
7 Swanscombe Point
8 Rawlinson Point
9 Kennedy Cox Ho
10 Cooper St
C1 1 Capulet Mews
2 Pepys Cres
3 De Quincey Mews
4 Hardy Ave
5 Tom Jenkinson Rd
6 Kennacraig Cl
7 Charles Flemwell Mews
8 Gatcombe Rd
9 Badminton Mews
10 Holyrood Mews
11 Britannia Gate
12 Dalemain Mews
13 Bowes-Lyon Hall
14 Lancaster hall
15 Victoria Hall
C2 1 Clements Ave
2 Martindale Ave
3 Balearic Apts
4 Marmara Apts
5 Baltic Apts
6 Coral Apts
7 Aegean Apts
8 Capital East Apts
C4 1 Odeon Ct
2 Edward Ct
3 Newhaven La
4 Ravenscroft Cl
5 Douglas Rd
6 Ferrier Point
7 Harvey Point
8 Wood Point
9 Trinity St
10 Pattinson Point
11 Clinch Ct
12 Mint Bsns Pk
13 Keir Hardy Prim Sch

36

A1 1 Burford Ho
2 Hope Cl
3 Centaur Ct
4 Phoenix Ct
C1 1 Surrey Cres
2 Forbes Ho
3 Haining Cl
4 Melville Ct
5 London Stile
6 Stile Hall Par
7 Priory Lo
8 Meadowcroft
9 St James Ct
10 Rivers Ho

37

A1 1 Churchdale Ct
2 Cromwell Cl
3 Cambridge Rd S
4 Oxbridge Ct
5 Tomlinson Cl
6 Gunnersbury Mews
7 Grange The
8 Gunnersbury Cl
9 Bellgrave Lo
A2 15 Orchard House Sch
A4 1 Cheltenham Pl
2 Beaumaris Twr
3 Arundel Ho
4 Pevensey Ct
5 Jerome Twr
6 Anstey Ct
7 Bennett Ct
8 Gunnersbury Ct
9 Barrington Ct
10 Hope Gdns
11 Park Road E
B1 1 Arlington Park Mans
2 Sandown Ho
3 Goodwood Ho
4 Windsor Ho
5 Lingfield Ho
6 Ascot Ho
7 Watchfield Ct
8 Belgrave Ct
9 Beverley Ct
10 Beaumont Ct
11 Harvard Rd
12 Troubridge Ct
13 Branden Lo
14 Fromow's Cnr
15 Heathfield House Sch
B2 1 Chiswick Green Studios
2 Bell Ind Est
3 Fairlawn Ct
4 Dukes Gate
5 Dewsbury Ct
6 Chiswick Terr
7 Mortlake Ho
B3 1 Blackmore Twr
2 Bollo Ct
3 Kipling Twr

4 Lawrence Ct
5 Maugham Ct
6 Reade Ct
7 Woolf Ct
8 Shaw Ct
9 Verne Ct
10 Wodehouse Ct
11 Greenock Rd
12 Garden Ct
13 Barons Gate
14 Cleveland Rd
15 Carver Cl
16 Chapter Cl
17 Beauchamp Cl
18 Holmes Ct
19 Copper Mews
B4 1 Belgrave Cl
2 Buckland Wlk
3 Frampton Ct
4 Telfer Cl
5 Harlech Twr
6 Corfe Twr
7 Barwick Ho
8 Charles Hocking Ho
9 Sunninghill Ct
10 Salisbury St
11 Jameson Pl
12 Castle Cl
C1 1 Chatsworth Lo
2 Prospect Pl
3 Townhall Ave
4 Devonhurst Pl
5 Heathfield Ct
6 Horticultural Pl
7 Merlin Ho
8 Garth Rd
9 Autumn Rise
C2 1 Disraeli Cl
2 Winston Wlk
3 Rusthall Mans
4 Bedford Park Mans
5 Essex Place Sq
6 Holly Rd
7 Homecross Ho
8 Swan Bsns Ctr
9 Jessop Ho
10 Belmont Prim Sch

38

A1 1 Glebe Cl
2 Devonshire Mews
3 Binns Terr
4 Ingress St
5 Swanscombe Rd
6 Brackley Terr
7 Stephen Fox Ho
8 Manor Gdns
9 Coram Ho
10 Flaxman Ho
11 Thorneycroft Ho
12 Thornhill Ho
13 Kent Ho
14 Oldfield Ho
15 William Hogarth Sch The
A2 1 Chestnut Ho
2 Bedford Ho
3 Bedford Cnr
4 Sydney Ho
5 Bedford Park Cnr
6 Priory Gdns
7 Windmill Alley
8 Castle Pl
9 Jonathan Ct
10 Windmill Pas
11 Chardin Rd
12 Gable Ho
13 Chiswick & Bedford Park Prep Sch
14 Arts Educational Sch The
A3 1 Fleet Ct
2 Ember Ct
3 Emlyn Gdns
4 Clone Ct
5 Brent Ct
6 Abbey Ct
7 Ormsby Lo
8 St Catherine's Ct
9 Lodge The
A4 1 Longford Ct
2 Mole Ct
3 Lea Ct
4 Wandle Ct
5 Beverley Ct
6 Roding Ct
7 Crane Ct
B1 1 Miller's Ct
2 British Grove Pas
3 British Grove S
4 Berestede Rd
5 North Eyot Gdns
B2 1 Flanders Mans
2 Stamford Brook Mans
3 Linkenholt Mans
4 Prebend Mans
5 Middlesex Ct
B3 1 Stamford Brook Gdns
2 Hauteville Court Gdns
3 Ranelagh Gdns
C1 1 Chisholm Ct
2 North Verbena Gdns
3 Western Terr
4 Verbena Gdns
5 Montrose Villas
6 Hammersmith Terr
7 South Black Lion La
8 St Peter's Wharf
9 Eden High Sch
15 St Peter's CE Prim Sch
C2 1 Hamlet Ct
2 Derwent Ct
3 Westcroft Ct
4 Black Lion Mews
5 St Peter's Villas
6 Standish Ho
7 Chambon Pl
8 Court Mans
9 Longthorpe Ct
10 Charlotte Ct
11 Westside
12 Park Ct
13 London Ho
14 Latymer Upper Sch
16 Polish Univ Abroad
C3 1 Elizabeth Finn Ho
2 Ashchurch Ct
3 King's Par
4 Inver Ct
5 Ariel Ct
6 Pocklington Lo
7 Vitae Apartments
C4 1 Becklow Gdns
2 Victoria Ho
3 Lycett Pl
4 Kylemore Ct
5 Alexandra Ct
6 Lytten Ct
7 Becklow Mews
8 Northcroft Ct
9 Bailey Ct
10 Spring Cott
11 Landor Wlk
12 Laurence Mews
13 Hadyn Park Ct
14 Askew Mans
15 Malvern Ct

39

A1 1 Prince's Mews
2 Aspen Gdns
3 Hampshire Hog La
4 Blades Ct
A2 1 Albion Gdns
2 Flora Gdns
3 Lamington St
4 Felgate Mews
5 Galena Ho
6 Albion Mews
7 Albion Ct
8 King Street Clois-ters
9 Dimes Pl
10 Clarence Ct
11 Hampshire Hog La
12 Marryat Ct
13 Ravenscourt Ho
14 Ravenscourt Thea-tre Sch
15 Cambridge Sch
16 Godolphin & Latymer Sch
17 Flora Gardens Prim Sch
A3 1 Ravenscourt Park Mans
2 Paddenswick Ct
3 Ashbridge Ct
4 Brackenbury Prim Sch
A4 1 Westbush Ct
2 Goldhawk Mews
3 Sycamore Ho
4 Shackleton Ct
5 Drake Ct
6 Scotts Ct
7 Raleigh Ct
8 Melville Court Flats
9 Southway Cl
B1 1 Bridge Avenue Mans
2 Bridgeview
3 College Ct
4 Beatrice Ho
5 Amelia Ho
6 Edith Ho
7 Joanna Ho
8 Mary Ho
9 Adela Ho
10 Sophia Ho
11 Henrietta Ho
12 Charlotte Ho
13 Alexandra Ho
14 Bath Pl
15 Elizabeth Ho
16 Margaret Ho
17 Peabody Est
18 Eleanor Ho
19 Isabella Ho
20 Caroline Ho
21 Chancellors Wharf
22 Sussex Pl
23 St Paul's CE Prim Sch
B2 1 Phoenix Lodge Mans
2 Samuel's Cl
3 Broadway Arc
4 Brook Ho
5 Hammersmith Broadway
6 Broadway Sh Ctr
7 Cambridge Ct
8 Ashcroft Sq
9 Sacred Heart High Sch
10 King Street Coll
B4 1 Verulam Ho
2 Grove Mans
3 Frobisher Ct
4 Library Mans
5 Pennard Mans
6 New Shepherd's Bush Mkt
7 Kerrington Ct
8 Granville Mans
9 Romney Ct
10 Rayner Ct
11 Sulgrave Gdns
12 Bamborough Gdns
13 Hillary Ct
14 Market Studios
15 Lanark Mans
16 Miles Coverdale Prim Sch
17 St Stephen's CE Prim Sch
18 London Coll of Fashion (Lime Grove)
C2 1 St Paul's Girls' Sch
2 Bute House Prep Sch
3 Jacques Prevert Sch
4 Larmenier & Sacred Heart RC Prim Sch
C3 1 Grosvenor Resi-dences
2 Blythe Mews
3 Burnand Ho
4 Bradford Ho
5 Springvale Terr
6 Ceylon Rd
7 Walpole Ct
8 Bronte Ct
9 Boswell Ct
10 Souldern Rd
11 Brook Green Flats
12 Haarlem Rd
13 Stafford Mans
14 Lionel Mans
15 Barradell Ho
C4 1 Vanderbilt Villas
2 Bodington Ct
3 Kingham Cl
4 Clearwater Terr
5 Lorne Gdns
6 Cameret Ct
7 Bush Ct
8 Shepherds Ct
9 Rockley Ct
10 Grampians The
11 Charcroft Ct
12 Addison Park Mans
13 Sinclair Mans
14 Fountain Ct
15 Woodford Ct
16 Roseford Ct
17 Woodstock Studios

40

A1 1 Hockney Ct
2 Toulouse Ct
3 Lowry Ct
4 Barry Ho
5 Lewis Ct
6 Gainsborough Ct
7 Renoir Ct
8 Blake Ct
9 Raphael Ct
10 Rembrandt Ct
11 Constable Ct
12 Da Vinci Ct
13 Gaugin Ct
14 Michelangelo Ct
15 Monet Ct
16 Weald Cl
17 Jasmin Lo
18 Birchmere Lo
19 Weybridge Ct
20 Florence Ho
21 Gleneagles Cl
22 Sunningdale Cl
23 Muirfield Cl
24 Turnberry Cl
25 St Andrews Cl
26 Kingsdown Cl
27 St Davids Cl
28 Galway Cl
29 Edenbridge Cl
30 Birkdale Cl
31 Tralee Ct
32 Woburn Ct
33 Belfry Cl
34 Troon Cl
35 Holywell Cl
A2 1 Market Pl
2 Trappes Ho
3 Thurland Ho
4 Ramsfort Ho
5 Hambley Ho
6 Holford Ho
7 Pope Ho
8 Southwell Ho
9 Mortain Ho
10 Radcliffe Ho
11 Southwark Park Est
12 Galleywall Road Trad Est
13 Trevithick Ho
14 Barlow Ho
15 Donkin Ho
16 Landmann Ho
17 Fitzmaurice Ho
18 Dodd Ho
A3 1 Perryn Rd
2 Chalfont Ho
3 Prestwood Ho
4 Farmer Ho
5 Gataker Ho
6 Gataker St
7 Cornick Ho
8 Glebe Ho
9 Matson Ho
10 Hickling Ho
11 St Andrews Ho
12 Southwark Coll (Surrey Docks Ctr)
13 Southwark Park Prim Sch
A4 1 Butterfield Cl
2 Janeway Pl
3 Trotwood Ho

4 Maylie Ho
5 Cranbourn Pas
6 Cranbourn Ho
7 Cherry Garden Ho
8 Burton Ho
9 Morriss Ho
10 Dixon's Alley
11 King Edward The Third Mews
12 Cathay St
13 Mission The
14 Millstream Ho
B1 15 Ilderton Prim Sch
B2 1 Damory Ho
2 Antony Ho
3 Roderick Ho
4 Pedworth Gdns
5 Banner Ct
6 Rotherhithe Bsns Est
7 Beamish Ho
8 Corbetts Pas
9 Gillam Ho
10 Richard Ho
11 George Walter Ho
12 Westlake
13 Adron Ho
14 Cavendish Sch
15 McIntosh Ho
B3 1 Blick Ho
2 Neptune Ho
3 Scotia Ct
4 Murdoch Ho
5 Edmonton Ct
6 Niagara Ct
7 Columbia Point
8 Ritchie Ho
9 Wells Ho
10 Helen Peele Cotts
11 Orchard Ho
12 Dock Offices
13 Landale Ho
14 Courthope Ho
15 Hithe Gr
16 China Hall Mews
B4 1 Mayflower St
2 St Mary's Est
3 Rupack St
4 Frank Whymark Ho
5 Adams Gardens Est
6 Hatteraick St
7 East India Ct
8 Bombay Ct
9 Stable Ho
10 Grannary The
11 Riverside
12 Cumberland Wharf
13 Seaford Ho
14 Hythe Ho
15 Sandwich Ho
16 Winchelsea Ho
17 Rye Ho
18 Kenning St
19 Western Pl
20 Ainsty St
21 Pine Ho
22 Beech Ho
23 Larch Ho
24 Turner Ct
25 Seth St
26 Risdon Ho
27 Risdon St
28 Aylton Est
29 Manitoba Ct
30 Calgary Ct
31 Irwell Est
32 St Olav's Sq
33 City Bsns Ctr
34 Albion Prim Sch
C2 1 John Kennedy Ho
2 Brydale Ho
3 Balman Ho
4 Tissington Ct
5 Harbord Ho
6 Westfield Ho
7 Albert Starr Ho
8 John Brent Ho
9 William Evans Ho
10 Raven Ho
11 Egret Ho
12 Fulmar Ho
13 Dunlin Ho
14 Siskin Ho
15 Sheldrake Ho
16 Buchanan Ct
17 Burrage Ct
18 Biddenham Ho
19 Ayston Ho
20 Empingham Ho
21 Deanshanger Ho
22 Codicote Ho
23 Buryfield Ct
24 Rotherhithe Prim Sch
C4 1 Schooner Cl
2 Dolphin Cl
3 Clipper Cl
4 Deauville Ct
5 Colette Ct
6 Coniston Ct
7 Virginia Ct
8 Derwent Ct
9 Grantham Ct
10 Serpentine Ct
11 Career Ct
12 Lacine Ct
13 Fairway Ct
14 Harold Ct
15 Spruce Ho
16 Cedar Ho
17 Sycamore Ho
18 Woodland Cres
19 Poplar Ho
20 Adelphi Ct
21 Basque Ct
22 Aberdale Ct
23 Quilting Ct
24 Chargrove Cl
25 Radley Ct
26 Greenacre Sq
27 Maple Leaf Sq
28 Stanhope Cl
29 Hawke Pl
30 Drake Cl
31 Brass Talley Alley
32 Monkton Ho
33 James Ho
34 Wolfe Cres

41

A1 1 Sir Francis Drake Prim Sch
2 Deptford Park Prim Sch
A2 1 Trafalgar Cl
2 Hornblower Cl
3 Cunard Wlk
4 Caronia Ct
5 Carinthia Ct
6 Freswick Ho
7 Graveley Ho
8 Husbourne Ho
9 Crofters Ct
10 Pomona Ho
11 Hazelwood Ho
12 Cannon Wharf Bsns Ctr
13 Bence Ho
14 Clement Ho
15 Pendennis Ho
16 Lighter Cl
17 Mast Ct
18 Rushcutters Ct
19 Boat Lifter Way
B1 1 Gransden Ho
2 Daubeney Twr
3 North Ho
4 Rochfort Ho
5 Keppel Ho
6 Camden Ho
7 Sanderson Ho
8 Berkeley Ho
9 Strafford Ho
10 Richman Ho
11 Hurleston Ho
12 Grafton Ho
13 Fulcher Ho
14 Citrus Ho
B2 1 Windsock Cl
2 St George's Mews
3 Linberry Wlk
4 Lanyard Ho
5 Golden Hind Pl
6 James Lind Ho
7 Harmon Ho
8 Pelican Ho
9 Bembridge Ho
10 Terrace The
11 George Beard Rd
12 Colonnade The
13 Pepys Ent Ctr
C1 1 Hudson Ct
2 Shackleton Ct
3 De Gama Pl
4 Mercator Pl
5 Maritime Quay
6 Perry Ct
7 Amundsen Ct
C2 1 Nova Bldg
2 Apollo Bldg
3 Gaverick Mews
4 Windmill Ho
5 Orion Point
6 Galaxy Bldg
7 Venus Ho
8 Olympian Ct
9 Poseidon Ct
10 Mercury Ct
11 Aphrodite Ct
12 Cyclops Mews
13 Neptune Ct
14 Artemis Ct
15 Hera Ct
16 Ares Ct
17 Ringwood Gdns
18 Dartmoor Wlk
19 Rothsay Wlk
20 Ashdown Wlk
21 Radnor Wlk
22 Ironmonger's Pl
23 Britannia Rd
24 Deptford Ferry Rd
25 Magellan Pl
26 Dockers Tanner Rd
C3 1 Bowsprit Point
2 St Hubert's Ho
3 John Tucker Ho
4 Broadway Wlk
5 Nash Ho
6 Fairlead Ho
7 Crosstrees Ho
8 Stanliff Ho
9 Keelson Ho
10 Clara Grant Ho
11 Gilbertson Ho
12 Scoulding Ho
13 Hibbert Ho
14 Cressall Ho
15 Alexander Ho
16 Kedge Ho
C4 1 Anchorage Point
2 Waterman Bldg
3 Jefferson Bldg
4 Pierpoint Bldg
5 Franklin Bldg
6 Vanguard Bldg
7 Edison Bldg
8 Seacon Twr
9 Naxos Bldg
10 Express Wharf
11 Hutching's Wharf
12 Tobago St
13 Bellamy Cl
14 Dowlen Ct
15 Cochrane Ho
16 Beatty Ho
17 Scott Ho
18 Laybourne Ho
19 Ensign Ho
20 Beaufort Ho
21 Spinnaker Ho
22 Bosun Cl
23 Topmast Point
24 Turner Ho
25 Constable Ho
26 Knighthead Point
27 Seven Mills Prim Sch

42

A1 1 Slipway Ho
2 Taffrail Ho
3 Platehouse The
4 Wheelhouse The
5 Chart House The
6 Port House The
7 Beacon Ho
8 Blasker Wlk
9 Maconochies Rd
A2 1 Brassey Ho
2 Triton Ho
3 Warspite Ho
4 Rodney Ho
5 Conway Ho
6 Exmouth Ho
7 Akbar Ho
8 Arethusa Ho
9 Tasman Ct
10 Cutty Sark Ho
11 Harbinger Prim Sch
A3 1 Turnberry Quay
2 Balmoral Ho
3 Aegon Ho
4 Marina Point
B2 1 St John's Ho
2 Betty May Gray Ho
3 Castleton Ho
4 Urmston Ho
5 Salford Ho
6 Capstan Ho
7 Frigate Ho
8 Galleon Ho
9 Barons Lo
B3 1 Cardale St
2 Hickin St
3 John McDonald Ho
4 Thorne Ho
5 Skeggs Ho
6 St Bernard Ho
7 Kimberley Ho
8 Kingdon Ho
9 Killoran Ho
10 Alastor Ho
11 Lingard Ho
12 Yarrow Ho
13 Sandpiper Ct
14 Nightingale Ct
15 Robin Ct
16 Heron Ct
17 Ferndown Lo
18 Crosby Ho
B4 1 Llandovery Ho
2 Rugless Ho
3 Ash Ho
4 Elm Ho
5 Cedar Ho
6 Castalia Sq
7 Aspect Ho
8 Normandy Ho
9 Valiant Ho
10 Tamar Ho
11 Watkins Ho
12 Alice Shepherd Ho
13 Oak Ho
14 Ballin Ct
15 Martin Ct
16 Grebe Ct
17 Kingfisher Ct
18 Walkers Lo
19 Antilles Bay
C2 1 Verwood Lo
2 Fawley Lo
3 Lyndhurst Lo
4 Blyth Cl
5 Farnworth Ho
6 Francis Cl
7 St Luke's CE Prim Sch

43

A1 1 Bellot Gdns
2 Thornley Pl
3 King William La
4 Bolton Ho
5 Miles Ho
6 Mell St
7 Sam Manners Ho
8 Hatcliffe Almshouses
9 Woodland Wlk
10 Earlswood Cl
11 St Joseph's RC Prim Sch
B1 1 Baldrey Ho
2 Christie Ho
3 Dyson Ho
4 Cliffe Ho
5 Moore Ho
6 Collins Ho
7 Lockyer Ho
8 Halley Ho
9 Kepler Ho
10 Sailacre Ho
11 Union Pk
B3 1 Teal St
2 Maurer Ct
3 Mudlarks Blvd
4 Renaissance Wlk
5 Alamaro Lo
C1 1 Layfield Ho
2 Westerdale Rd
3 Mayston Mews

4 Station Mews Terr
5 Halstow Prim Sch
6 Holyrood Mews

44

A4 1 Ferry Sq
2 Watermans Ct
3 Wilkes Rd
4 Albany Par
5 Charlton Ho
6 Albany Ho
7 Alma Ho
8 Griffin Ct
9 Cressage Ho
10 Tunstall Wlk
11 Trimmer Wlk
12 Running Horse Yd
13 Mission Sq
14 Distillery Wlk
B2 1 Primrose Ho
2 Lawman Ct
3 Royston Ct
4 Garden Ct
5 Capel Lo
6 Devonshire Ct
7 Celia Ct
8 Rosslyn Ho
9 Branstone Ct
10 Lamerton Lo
11 Kew Lo
12 Dunraven Ho
13 Stoneleigh Lo
14 Tunstall Ct
15 Voltaire
C2 1 Clarendon Ct
2 Quintock Ho
3 Broome Ct
4 Lonsdale Mews
5 Elizabeth Cotts
6 Sandways
7 Victoria Cotts
8 North Ave
9 Grovewood
10 Hamilton Ho
11 Melvin Ct
12 Royal Par
13 Power Ho
14 Station Ave
15 Blake Mews
C4 5 Strand-on-the-Green Schs

45

A2 1 Terrano Ho
2 Oak Ho
3 Aura Ho
4 Maple Ho
5 Cedar Ho
6 Saffron Ho
7 Lime Ho
8 Lavender Ho
9 Juniper Ho
A4 1 Falcons Pre Prep school The

46

B1 1 Melrose Rd
2 Seaforth Lo
3 St John's Gr
4 Sussex Ct
5 Carmichael Ct
6 Hampshire Ct
7 Thorne Pas
8 Brunel Ct
9 Beverley Path

47

C4 1 Cobb's Hall
2 Dorset Mans
3 St Clements Mans
4 Bothwell St
5 Hawksmoor St
6 Melcombe Prim Sch

48

A1 1 Langport Ho
2 Iveagh Ho
3 Newark Ho
4 Edgehill Ho
5 Hopton Ho
6 Ashby Ho
7 Nevil Ho
A2 1 Fairbairn Gn
2 Hammelton Gn
3 Foxley Sq
4 Silverburn Ho
5 Butler Ho
6 Dalkeith Ho
7 Turner Cl
8 Bathgate Ho
9 Black Roof Ho
10 Charles Edward Brooke Sch (Dennen Site)
11 Charles Edward Brooke Sch
A3 35 St Michael & All Angels CE Acad
A4 1 Faunce Ho
2 Garbett Ho
3 Harvard Ho
4 Doddington Pl
5 Kean Ho
6 Jephson Ho
7 Cornish Ho
8 Bateman Ho
9 Molesworth Ho
10 Walters Ho
11 Cruden Ho
12 Brawne Ho
13 Prescott Ho
14 Chalmer's Wlk
15 Copley Cl
16 King Charles Ct
B1 1 Bergen Ho
2 Oslo Ho
3 Viking Ho
4 Jutland Ho
5 Norvic Ho
6 Odin Ho
7 Baltic Ho
8 Nobel Ho
9 Mercia Ho
10 Kenbury Gdns
11 Zealand Ho
12 Elsinore Ho
13 Norse Ho
14 Denmark Mans
15 Dane Ho
16 Canterbury Cl
17 York Cl
18 Kenbury Mans
19 Parade Mans
20 Winterslow Ho
21 Lilford Ho
22 Bartholomew Ho
23 Guildford Ho
24 Boston Ho
25 Hereford Ho
26 Weyhill Ho
27 Lichfield Ho
28 Lansdown Ho
29 Honiton Ho
30 Pinner Ho
31 Baldock Ho
32 Widecombe Ho
33 Nottingham Ho
34 Witham Ho
35 Barnet Ho
36 Empress Mews
B2 1 Bertha Neubergh Ho
2 Mornington Mews
3 Badsworth Rd
4 Pearson Cl
5 Elm Tree Ct
6 Samuel Lewis Trust Dwellings
7 Milkwell Yd
8 Keswick Ho
9 Mitcham Ho
10 Sacred Heart RC Sec Sch
B3 1 Boundary Ho
2 Day Ho
3 Burgess Ho
4 Carlyle Ho
5 Myers Ho
6 Thompson Ave
7 Palgrave Ho
8 Winnington Ho
9 Brantwood Ho
10 Lowell Ho
11 Jessie Duffett Ho
12 Otterburn Ho
13 Crossmount Ho
14 Venice Ct
15 Bowyer St
16 Livingstone Ho
17 Gothic Ct
18 Coniston Ho
19 Harlynwood
20 Carey Ct
21 Finley Ct
22 Grainger Ct
23 Hayes Ct
24 Moffat Ho
25 Marinel Ho
26 Hodister Cl
27 Arnot Ho
28 Lamb Ho
29 Kipling Ho
30 Keats Ho
31 Kenyon Ho
32 New Church Rd
33 Sir John Kirk Cl
34 Comber Grove Prim Sch
35 St Joseph's RC Inf & Jun Schs
C1 1 Selborne Rd
2 Hascombe Terr
C2 1 Joiners Arms Yd
2 Butterfly Wlk
3 Cuthill Wlk
4 Colonades The
5 Artichoke Mews
6 Peabody Bldgs
7 Brighton Ho
8 Park Ho
9 Peabody Ct
10 Lomond Ho
11 Lamb Ho
12 Kimpton Ct
13 Belham Wlk
14 Datchelor Pl
15 Harvey Rd
C3 1 Masterman Ho
2 Milton Ho
3 Pope Ho
4 Chester Ct
5 Marvel Ho
6 Flecker Ho
7 Landor Ho
8 Leslie Prince Ct
9 Evelina Mans
10 Langland Ho
11 Drinkwater Ho
12 Procter Ho
13 Shirley Ho
14 Drayton Ho
15 Bridges Ho
16 Cunningham Ho
17 Hood Ho
18 Herrick Ho
19 Dekker Ho
20 Houseman Way
21 Coleby Path
22 Brunswick Park Prim Sch
C4 1 Queens Ho
2 Arnside Ho
3 Horsley St
4 St Peter's Ho
5 St Johns Ho
6 St Marks Ho
7 St Stephens Ho
8 St Matthew's Ho
9 Red Lion Cl
10 Boyson Rd
11 Bradenham

49

A1 1 Springfield Ho
2 Craston Ho
3 Walters Ho
4 Edgecombe Ho
5 Fowler Ho
6 Rignold Ho
7 Chatham Ho
A2 1 Barnwell Ho
2 Brunswick Villas
3 St Giles Twr
4 Bentley Ho
5 Dawson Ho
6 Dryden Ho
7 Mayward Ho
8 Longleigh Ho
9 Fairwall Ho
10 Bodeney Ho
11 Sandby Ho
12 Vestry Mews
13 Netley
14 Lakanal
15 Racine
16 Camberwell Coll of Arts
A3 1 Tower Mill Rd
2 Tilson Cl
3 Granville Sq
4 Edgar Wallace Cl
5 Potters Cl
6 Dorton Cl
7 Samuel Jones Ind Est
8 Dibden Ho
9 Marchwood Cl
10 Pilgrims Cloisters
11 Beacon Ho
12 Teather St
13 Stacy Path
14 Rumball Ho
15 Ballow Cl
16 Rill Ho
17 Southwark Coll (Camberwell Ctr)
18 St George's CE Prim Sch
A4 1 Downend Ct
2 Andoversford Ct
3 Pearse St
4 Watling St
5 Gandolfi St
6 Comfort St
7 Tower Mill Rd
B2 1 Colbert
2 Voltaire
3 Finch Mews
4 Charles Coveney Rd
5 Bamber Rd
6 Crane St
7 Curlew Ho
8 Mallard Ho
9 Tern Ho
10 Crane Ho
11 Falcon Ho
12 Bryanston Ho
13 Basing Ct
14 Marcus Ho
15 Sheffield Ho
16 Highshore Sch
17 St James The Great RC Prim Sch
18 Oliver Goldsmith Prim Sch
B3 1 Painswick Ct
2 Sharpness Ct
3 Mattingly Way
4 Hordle Prom N
5 Burcher Gale Gr
6 Calypso Cres
7 Hordle Prom S
8 Cinnamon Cl
9 Savannah Cl
10 Thames Ct
11 Shannon Ct
12 Amstel Ct
13 Danube Ct
14 Tilbury Cl
15 Hordle Prom E
16 Indus Ct
17 Oakcourt
18 Palm Ct
19 Rowan Ct
20 Blackthorn Ct
21 Pear Ct
22 Lidgate Rd
23 Whistler Mews
24 Boathouse Wlk
25 Camberwell Coll of Arts
B4 1 Willsbridge Ct
2 Cam Ct
3 Quedgeley Ct
4 Saul Ct
5 Quenington Ct
6 Westonbirt Ct
7 Wickway Ct
C1 1 William Margrie Cl
2 William Blake Ho
3 Quantock Mews
4 Choumert Sq
5 Parkstone Rd
6 Atwell Rd
C2 1 Canal Head Public Sq
2 Angelina Ho
3 Jarvis Ho
4 Richland Ho
5 Honeywood Ho
6 Wakefield Ho

7 Primrose Ho
8 Hardcastle Ho
9 Dunstall Ho
10 Springtide Cl
11 Purdon Ho
12 Flamborough Ho
13 Lambrook Ho
14 Witcombe Point
15 Yarnfield Sq
16 Winford Ct
17 Portbury Cl
18 Robert Keen Cl
C3 1 Thornbill Ho
2 Vervain Ho
3 Woodstar Ho
4 Tamarind Ho
5 Hereford Retreat
6 Haymerle Ho
7 Furley Ho
8 Thomas Milner Ho
9 Applegarth Ho
10 Freda Corbett Cl
11 Rudbeck Ho
12 Henslow Ho
13 Lindley Ho
14 Collinson Ho
15 Sister Mabel's Way
16 Timberland Cl
17 Hastings Cl
18 Sidmouth Ho
19 Budleigh Ho
20 Stanesgate Ho
21 Breamore Ho
22 Ely Ho
23 Gisburn Ho
24 Silkin Mews
25 Peckham Park Prim Sch
26 St Francis RC Prim Sch
C4 1 Bowles Rd
2 Western Wharf
3 Northfield Ho
4 Millbrook Ho
5 Denstone Ho
6 Deerhurst Ho
7 Caversham Ho
8 Battle Ho
9 Cardiff Ho
10 Bridgnorth Ho
11 Exeter Ho
12 Grantham Ho
13 Aylesbury Ho
14 Royston Ho
15 Haymerle Sch

50

A1 1 Walkynscroft
2 Ryegates
3 Hathorne Cl
4 Pilkington Rd
5 Russell Ct
6 Heaton Ho
7 Magdalene Cl
8 Iris Ct
10 St Mary Magdalene CE Prim Sch
A2 1 Willowdene
2 Pinedene
3 Oakdene
4 Beechdene
5 Hollydene
6 Wood Dene
8 Staveley Cl
9 Carnicot Ho
10 Martock Ct
11 Cherry Tree Ct
12 Kendrick Ct
13 John Donne Prim Sch
A3 1 Tortington Ho
2 Credenhill Ho
3 Bromyard Ho
4 Hoyland Cl
5 Willowdene
6 Ashdene
7 Acorn Par
8 Havelock Ct
9 Springall St
10 Harry Lambourn Ho
11 Grenier Apartments
B1 1 Honiton Gdns
2 Selden Ho
3 Hathway Ho
4 Hathway St
5 Station Ct
6 Symons Cl
7 Hollydale Prim Sch
B2 1 Trotman Ho
2 Boddington Ho
3 Heydon Ho
4 Boulter Ho
5 Astbury Bsns Pk
B3 1 Ambleside Point
2 Grasmere Point
3 Windermere Point
4 Roman Way
5 Laburnum Cl
6 Juniper Ho
7 Romney Cl
8 Hammersley Ho
9 Hutchinson Ho
10 Hammond Ho
11 Fir Tree Ho
12 Glastonbury Ct
13 Highbridge Ct
14 Filton Ct
15 Chiltern Ct
16 Cheviot Ct
B4 1 Penshurst Ho
2 Reculver Ho
3 Mereworth Ho
4 Camber Ho
5 Chiham Ho
6 Otford Ho
7 Olive Tree Ho
8 Aspen Ho
9 Lewis Silkin Ho
10 Richborough Ho
11 Dover Ho
12 Eynsford Ho
13 Horton Ho
14 Lamberhurst Ho
15 Canterbury Ind Pk
16 Upnall Ho
17 Sissinghurst Ho
18 Rochester Ho
19 Saltwood Ho
20 Leybourne Ho
21 Lullingstone Ho
22 Pilgrims Way Prim Sch
C3 1 Richard Anderson Ct
2 Palm Tree Ho
3 Edward Robinson Ho
4 Antony Ho
5 Gerrard Ho
6 Palmer Ho
7 Pankhurst Cl
C4 1 Harrisons Ct
2 Grantley Ho
3 Sunbury Ct
4 Tilbury Ho
5 Graham Ct
6 Connell Ct
7 St Clements Ct
8 Henderson Ct
9 Jemotts Ct
10 Verona Ct
11 Heywood Ho
12 Francis Ct
13 Hind Ho
14 Donne Ho
15 Carew Ct
16 Burbage Ho
17 Newland Ho
18 Dobson Ho
19 Dalton Ho
20 Greene Ct
21 Redrup Ho
22 Tarplett Ho
23 Stunell Ho
24 Gasson Ho
25 Bryce Ho
26 Barnes Ho
27 Barkwith Ho
28 Bannister Ho
29 Apollo Ind Bsns Ctr

51

A2 1 Archer Ho
2 Browning Ho
3 Hardcastle Ho
4 Brooke Ho
5 Wallis Ho
A3 1 Batavia Ho
2 Marlowe Bsns Ctr
3 Batavia Mews
4 Woodrush Cl
5 Alexandra St
6 Primrose Wlk
7 Vansittart St
8 Granville Ct
9 Cottesbrook St
10 Ewen Henderson Ct
11 Fordham Ho
12 Deptford Green Sch (Annex)
A4 1 Portland Ct
2 Phoenix Ct
3 Rainbow Ct
4 Hawke Twr
5 Chubworthy St
6 Woodpecker Rd
7 Hercules Ct
B3 1 Austin Ho
2 Exeter Way
3 Crossleigh Ct
4 Mornington Pl
5 Maple Ho
B4 1 Chester Ho
2 Lynch Wlk
3 Arlington Ho
4 Woodcote Ho
5 Cornbury Ho
6 Prospect Pl
7 Akintaro Ho
8 Mulberry Ho
9 Laurel Ho
10 Linden Ho
11 Ashford Ho
12 Wardalls Ho
13 Magnolia Ho
14 Howard Ho
15 Larch Cl
16 Ibis Ct
17 Merganser Ct
18 Wotton Rd
19 Kingfisher Sq
20 Sanderling Ct
21 Dolphin Twr
22 Mermaid Twr
23 Scoter Ct
24 Shearwater Ct
25 Brambling Ct
26 Kittiwake Ct
27 Diana Cl
28 Guillemot Ct
29 Marine Twr
30 Teal Ct
31 Lapwing Twr
32 Violet Cl
33 Skua Ct
34 Tristan Ct
35 Rosemary Ct
36 Cormorant Ct
37 Shelduck Ct
38 Eider Ct
39 Pintail Ct
40 Fulcher Ct
42 Grinling Gibbons Prim Sch
C1 1 Ashmead Mews
2 St Stephen's CE Prim Sch
C2 1 Admiralty Cl
2 Harton Lodge
3 Sylva Cotts
4 Pitman Ho
5 Heston Ho
6 Mereton Mans
7 Indiana Bldg
8 St John's Lodge
9 Dean's Gateway
10 Lucas Vale Prim Sch
11 Addey & Stanhope Sch
12 Lewisham Coll (Deptford Campus)
C3 1 Sandpiper Ct
2 Flamingo Ct
3 Titan Bsns Est
4 Rochdale Way
5 Speedwell St
6 Reginald Pl
7 Fletcher Path
8 Frankham Ho
9 Cremer Ho
10 Wilshaw Ho
11 Castell Ho
12 Holden Ho
13 Browne Ho
14 Resolution Way
15 Lady Florence Ctyd
16 Covell Ct
17 Albion Ho
18 Maritime Greenwich Coll
19 St Joseph's RC Prim Sch
20 Tidemill Prim Sch
C4 1 Dryfield Wlk
2 Blake Ho
3 Hawkins Ho
4 Grenville Ho
5 Langford Ho
6 Mandarin Ct
7 Bittern Ct
8 Lamerton St
9 Ravensbourne Mans
10 Armada St
11 Armada Ct
12 Benbow Ho
13 Oxenham Ho
14 Caravel Mews
15 Hughes Ho
16 Stretton Mans

52

A1 1 Morden Mount Prim Sch
A2 1 Washington Bldg
2 California Bldg
3 Utah Bldg
4 Montana Bldg
5 Oregon Bldg
6 Dakota bldg
7 Idaho Bldg
8 Atlanta Bldg
9 Colorado Bldg
10 Arizona Bldg
11 Nebraska Bldg
12 Alaska Bldg
13 Ohio Bldg
14 Charter Bldgs
15 Flamsteed Ct
16 Friendly Pl
17 Dover Ct
18 Robinscroft Mews
19 Doleman Ho
20 Plymouth Ho
A3 1 Finch Ho
2 Jubilee The
3 Maitland Cl
4 Ashburnham Retreat
B1 1 Ellison Ho
2 Pitmaston Ho
3 Aster Ho
4 Windmill Cl
5 Hertmitage The
6 Burnett Ho
7 Lacey Ho
8 Darwin Ho
9 Pearmain Ho
B2 1 Penn Almshouses
2 Jervis Ct
3 Woodville Ct
4 Darnall Ho
5 Renbold Ho
6 Lindsell St
7 Plumbridge St
8 Trinity Gr
9 Hollymount Cl
10 Cade Tyler Ho
11 Robertson Ho
B3 1 Temair Ho
2 Royal Hill Ct
3 Prince of Orange La
4 Lambard Ho
5 St Marks Cl
6 Ada Kennedy Ct
7 Arlington Pl
8 Topham Ho
9 Darnell Ho
10 Hawks Mews
11 Royal Pl
12 Swanne Ho
13 Maribor
14 Serica Ct
15 Queen Elizabeth's Coll
16 James Wolfe Prim Sch
17 Greenwich Coll
B4 1 Crescent Arc
2 Greenwich Mkt

52 B4

3 Turnpin La
4 Durnford St
5 Sexton's Ho
6 Bardsley Ho
7 Wardell Ho
8 Clavell St
9 Stanton Ho
10 Macey Ho
11 Boreman Ho
12 Clipper Appts
C4 1 Frobisher Ct
2 Hardy Cotts
3 Palliser Ho
4 Bernard Angell Ho
5 Corvette Sq
6 Travers Ho
7 Maze Hill Lodge
8 Park Place Ho
9 Meridian Prim Sch

53

B1 1 Heath House Prep Sch
B3 1 Westcombe Ct
2 Kleffens Ct
3 Ferndale Ct
4 Combe Mews
5 Mandeville Cl
7 Pinelands Cl
C3 1 Mary Lawrenson Pl
2 Bradbury Ct
3 Dunstable Ct
4 Wentworth Ho
C4 1 Nethercombe Ho
2 Holywell Cl

54

A1 1 Lancaster Cotts
2 Lancaster Mews
3 Bromwich Ho
4 Priors Lo
5 Richmond Hill Ct
6 Glenmore Ho
7 Hillbrow
8 Heathshott
9 Friars Stile Pl
10 Spire Ct
11 Ridgeway
12 Matthias Ct
13 Old Vicarage Sch
A2 1 Lichfield Terr
2 Union Ct
3 Carrington Lo
4 Wilton Ct
5 Egerton Ct
6 Beverley Lo
7 Bishop Duppa's Almshouses
8 Regency Wlk
9 Clear Water Ho
10 Onslow Avenue Mans
11 Michels Almshouses
12 Albany Pas
13 Salcombe Villas
A3 1 St John's Gr
2 Michel's Row
3 Michelsdale Dr
4 Blue Anchor Alley
5 Clarence St
6 Sun Alley
7 Thames Link Ho
8 Benns Wlk
9 Waterloo Pl
10 Northumbria Ct
B1 1 Chester Cl
2 Evesham Ct
3 Queen's Ct
4 Russell Wlk
5 Charlotte Sq
6 Jones Wlk
7 Hilditch Ho
8 Isabella Ct
9 Damer Ho
10 Eliot Ho
11 Fitzherbert Ho
12 Reynolds Pl
13 Chisholm Rd
B2 1 Alberta Ct
2 Beatrice Rd
3 Lorne Rd
4 York Rd
5 Connaught Rd
6 Albany Terr
7 Kingswood Ct
8 Selwyn Ct
9 Broadhurst Cl
B3 1 Towers The
2 Longs Ct
3 Sovereign Ct
4 Robinson Ct
5 Calvert Ct
6 Bedford Ct
7 Hickey's Almshouses
8 Church Estate Almshouses
9 Richmond International Bsns Ctr
10 Abercorn Mews

55

A3 1 Hershell Ct
2 Deanhill Ct
3 Park Sheen
4 Furness Lo
5 Merricks Ct
C4 1 Rann Ho
2 Craven Ho
3 John Dee Ho
4 Kindell Ho
5 Montgomery Ho
6 Avondale Ho
7 Addington Ct
8 Dovecote Gdns
9 Firmston Ho
10 Glendower Gdns
11 Chestnut Ave
12 Trehern Rd
13 Rock Ave
14 St Mary Magdalen's RC Prim Sch

56

C2 1 Theodore Ho
2 Nicholas Ho
3 Bonner Ho
4 Downing Ho
5 Jansen Ho
6 Fairfax Ho
7 Devereux Ho
8 David Ho
9 Leigh Ho
10 Clipstone Ho
11 Mallet Ho
12 Arton Wilson Ho

57

B2 1 Inglis Ho
2 Ducie Ho
3 Wharncliffe Ho
4 Stanhope Ho
5 Waldegrave Ho
6 Mildmay Ho
7 Mullens Ho
C1 1 Balmoral Cl
2 Glenalmond Ho
3 Selwyn Ho
4 Keble Ho
5 Bede Ho
6 Gonville Ho
7 Magdalene Ho
8 Armstrong Ho
9 Newnham Ho
10 Somerville Ho
11 Balliol Ho
12 Windermere
13 Little Combe Cl
14 Classinghall Ho
15 Chalford Ct
16 Garden Royal
17 South Ct
18 Anne Kerr Ct
19 Ewhurst
C2 1 Geneva Ct
2 Laurel Ct
3 Cambalt Ho
4 Langham Ct
5 Lower Pk
6 King's Keep
7 Whitnell Ct
8 Whitehead Ho
9 Halford Ho
10 Humphry Ho
11 Jellicoe Ho
12 South Thames Coll (Putney Ctr)
C3 1 Olivette St
2 Mascotte Rd
3 Glegg Pl
4 Crown Ct
5 Charlwood Terr
6 Percy Laurie Ho
7 Our Lady of Victories RC Prim Sch
C4 1 Griffin Gate
2 Darfur St
3 John Keall Ho
4 Henry Jackson Ho
5 Felsham Ho
6 Ardshiel Cl
7 Ruvigny Mans
8 Star & Garter Mans
9 University Mans
10 Lockyer Ho
11 Phelps Ho
12 Princeton Ct
13 Kingsmere Cl
14 Felsham Mews
15 St Mary's CE Prim Sch

58

A2 1 Claremont
2 Downside
3 Cavendish Cl
4 Ashcombe Ct
5 Carltons The
6 Espirit Ho
7 Millbrooke Ct
8 Coysh Ct
9 Keswick Hts
10 Avon Ct
11 Merlin Sch The
B2 1 Keswick Broadway
2 Burlington Mews
3 Cambria Lo
4 St Stephen's Gdns
5 Atlantic Ho
6 Burton Lo
7 Manfred Ct
8 Meadow Bank
9 Hooper Ho
10 Aspire Bld
C2 1 Pembridge Pl
2 Adelaide Rd
3 London Ct
4 Windsor Ct
5 Westminster Ct
6 Fullers Ho
7 Bridge Pk
8 Lambeth Ct
9 Milton Ct
10 Norfolk Mans
11 Francis Snary Lo
12 Bush Cotts
13 Downbury Mews
14 Newton's Yd
15 Roche Sch The
16 St Joseph's RC Prim Sch
17 West Hill Prim Sch
18 St Michael Steiner Sch The

59

A2 1 Fairfield Ct
2 Blackmore Ho
3 Lancaster Mews
4 Cricketers Mews
5 College Mews
6 Arndale Wlk
6 St Anne's CE Prim Sch
7 South Thames Coll (Wandsworth Ctr)
B2 1 St Faith's CE Prim Sch
B4 1 Molasses Ho
2 Molasses Row
3 Cinnamon Row
4 Calico Ho
5 Calico Row
6 Port Ho
7 Square Rigger Row
8 Trade Twr
9 Ivory Ho
10 Spice Ct
11 Sherwood Ct
12 Mendip Ct
13 Chalmers Ho
14 Coral Row
15 Ivory Sq
16 Kingfisher Ho
C3 1 Burke Ho
1 High View Prim Sch
2 Centre Acad
2 Fox Ho
3 Buxton Ho
4 Pitt Ho
5 Ramsey Ho
6 Beverley Cl
7 Florence Ho
8 Linden Ct
9 Dorcas Ct
10 Johnson Ct
11 Agnes Ct
12 Hilltop Ct
13 Courtyard The
14 Old Laundry The
15 Oberstein Rd
16 Fineran Ct
17 Sangora Rd
18 Harvard Mans
19 Plough Mews
C4 1 Milner Ho
2 McManus Ho
3 Wilberforce Ho
4 Wheeler Ct
5 Sporle Ct
6 Holliday Sq
7 John Parker Sq
8 Carmichael Cl
9 Fenner Sq
10 Clark Lawrence Ct
11 Shaw Ct
12 Sendall Ct
13 Livingstone Rd
14 Farrant Ho
15 Jackson Ho
16 Darien Ho
17 Shepard Ho
18 Ganley Ct
19 Arthur Newton Ho
20 Chesterton Ho
21 John Kirk Ho
22 Mantua St
23 Heaver Rd
24 Candlemakers
25 Thames Christian Coll
26 Falconbrook Prim Sch

60

A4 1 Kiloh Ct
2 Lanner Ho
3 Griffon Ho
4 Kestrel Ho
5 Kite Ho
6 Peregrine Ho
7 Hawk Ho
8 Inkster Ho
9 Harrier Ho
10 Eagle Hts
11 Kingfisher Ct
12 Lavender Terr
13 Temple Ho
14 Ridley Ho
15 Eden Ho
16 Hertford Ct
17 Nepaul Rd
B1 1 Staplehurst Ct
2 Teyham Ct
3 Honeywell Jun & Inf Schs
B2 1 Clapham Computer & Secretarial Coll
C1 1 Rayne Ho
2 St Anthony's Ct
3 Earlsthorpe Mews
4 Nightingale Mans
C4 1 Shaftesbury Park Chambers
2 Selborne
3 Rush Hill Mews
4 Marmion Mews
5 Crosland Pl
6 Craven Mews
7 Garfield Mews
8 Audley Cl
9 Basnett Rd
10 Tyneham Cl
11 Woodmere Cl
D1 5 Broomwood Hall (Lower Sch)

61

A1 1 Oliver House Prep Sch
A4 1 Turnchapel Mews

2 Redwood Mews
3 Phil Brown Pl
4 Bev Callender Cl
5 Keith Connor Cl
6 Tessa Sanderson Pl
7 Daley Thompson Way
8 Rashleigh Ct
9 Abberley Mews
10 Willow Lodge
11 Beaufoy Rd
B1 1 Joseph Powell Cl
2 Cavendish Mans
3 Westlands Terr
4 Cubitt Ho
5 Hawkesworth Ho
6 Normanton Ho
7 Eastman Ho
8 Couchman Ho
9 Poynders Ct
10 Selby Ho
11 Valentine Ho
12 Gorham Ho
13 Deauville Mans
14 Deauville Ct
B2 1 Timothy Cl
2 Shaftesbury Mews
3 Brook Ho
4 Grover Ho
5 Westbrook Ho
6 Hewer Ho
7 Batten Ho
8 Mandeville Ho
9 George Beare Lo
10 St Mary's RC Prim Sch
B3 1 Polygon The
2 Windsor Ct
3 Trinity Cl
4 Studios The
5 Bourne Ho
B4 1 Clapham Manor Ct
2 Clarke Ho
3 Gables The
4 Sycamore Mews
5 Maritime Ho
6 Rectory Gdns
7 Floris Pl
8 Clapham Manor Prim Sch
C1 1 Parrington Ho
2 Savill Ho
3 Blackwell Ho
4 Bruce Ho
5 Victoria Ct
6 Victoria Ho
7 Belvedere Ct
8 Ingram Lo
9 Viney Ct
10 Bloomsbury Ho
11 Belgravia Ho
12 Barnsbury Ho
C3 1 Kendoa Rd
2 Felmersham Cl
3 Abbeville Mews
4 Saxon Ho
5 Gifford Ho
6 Teignmouth Cl
7 Holwood Pl
8 Oaklands Pl
9 Wilberforce Mews
10 William Bonney Est
12 London Coll of Bsns & Computer Studies
C4 1 Chelsham Ho
2 Lynde Ho

3 Greener Ho
4 Towns Ho
5 Hugh Morgan Ho
6 Roy Ridley Ho
7 Lendal Terr
8 Slievemore Cl
9 Cadmus Cl
10 Clapham North Bsns Ctr

62

A2 1 King's Mews
2 Clapham Court Terr
3 Clapham Ct
4 Clapham Park Terr
5 Pembroke Ho
6 Stevenson Ho
7 Queenswood Ct
8 Oak Tree Ct
9 Park Lofts
10 Ashby Mews
A3 1 Morris Ho
2 Gye Ho
3 Clowes Ho
4 Thomas Ho
5 Stuart Ho
6 Storace Ho
7 Bedford Ho
8 Ascot Ct
9 Ascot Par
10 Ashmere Ho
11 Ashmere Gr
12 Ventura Ho
13 Vickery Ho
14 Stafford Mans
15 Beresford Ho
A4 1 Callingham Ho
2 Russell Pickering Ho
3 Ormerod Ho
4 Lopez Ho
5 Coachmaker Mews
6 Brixton Day Coll
B2 1 Beatrice Ho
2 Florence Ho
3 Evelyn Ho
4 Diana Ho
5 Brixton Hill Ct
6 Austin Ho
7 Manor Ct
8 Camsey Ho
9 Romer Ho
10 Gale Ho
11 Byrne Ho
12 Farnfield Ho
13 Marchant Ho
14 Rainsford Ho
15 Springett Ho
16 Mannering Ho
17 Waldron Ho
18 Sudbourne Prim Sch
19 Corpus Christi RC Prim Sch
B3 1 Freemens Hos
2 Roger's Almshouses
3 Gresham Almshouses
4 Exbury Ho
5 Glasbury Ho
6 Dalbury Ho
7 Fosbury Ho
8 Chalbury Ho
9 Neilson-Terry Ct
10 Pavilion Mans
11 Daisy Dormer Ct

12 George Lashwood Ct
13 Marie Lloyd Ct
14 Trinity Homes
15 Lethaby Ho
16 Edmundsbury Ct Est
17 Regis Pl
18 Marlborough Mews
19 Alpha Ho
20 Beta Pl
21 Cedars Ho
22 South Chelsea Coll
B4 1 Turberville Ho
2 Thrayle Ho
3 Percheron Ct
4 Draymans Ct
5 Lansdowne Sch
6 Stockwell Prim Sch
C1 1 Eccleston Ho
2 Scarsbrook Ho
3 Purser Ho
4 Rudhall Ho
5 Hardham Ho
6 Heywood Ho
7 Haworth Ho
8 Birch Ho
9 Lansdell Ho
10 Lomley Ho
11 Laughton Ho
12 Woodruff Ho
13 Bascome St
14 Dudley Mews
15 Herbert Mews
16 Blades Lo
17 Dick Shepherd Ct
18 Charman Ho
19 Morden Ho
20 Bishop Ct
21 Blackburn Ct
22 Leigh Ct
23 John Conwey Ho
24 Bristowe Cl
C2 1 Crownstone Ct
2 Brockwell Ct
3 Nevena Ct
4 St George's Residences
5 Hanover Mans
6 Fleet Ho
7 Langbourne Ho
8 Turnmill Ho
9 Walker Mews
10 Cossar Mews
11 Carter Ho
12 Arungford Mews
C3 1 Electric Mans
2 Electric La
3 Connaught Mans
4 Clifton Mans
5 Hereford Ho
6 Chaplin Ho
7 Lord David Pitt Ho
8 Marcus Garvey Way
9 Montego Cl
10 Bob Marley Way
11 Leeson Rd
C4 1 Buckmaster Cl
2 Albemarle Ho
3 Goodwood Mans
4 Angell Park Gdns
5 Fyfield Rd
6 Howard Ho
7 Harris Ho
8 Broadoak Ct
9 Burgate Ct
10 Witchwood Ho

11 Blacktree Mews
12 Chartham Ct
13 Chilham Ct
14 Northgate Ct
15 Westgate Ct
16 Dover Mans
17 St Helen's RC Sch
18 Dorrell Pl

63

A2 3 Poets Mews
4 St Jude's CE Prim Sch
A3 1 Mahatma Gandhi Ind Est
2 Dylan Rd
3 Bessemer Park Ind Est
4 Pablo Neruda Cl
5 Langston Hughes Cl
6 Walt Whitman Cl
7 James Joyce Wlk
8 Alice Walker Cl
9 Louise Bennett Cl
10 Chadacre Ho
11 Burwood Ho
12 Pyrford Ho
13 Wangford Ho
14 Ashford Ho
15 Kenwood Ho
16 Moyne Ho
17 Elveden Ho
18 Carrara Cl
19 Broughton Dr
20 Angela Davis Ind Est
21 Tilia Wlk
22 County Ho
23 Hill Mead Prim Sch
A4 1 Mallams Mews
2 Amberley Ct
3 Harper Ho
4 Leicester Ho
5 Station Ave
6 Wellfit St
7 Loughborough Ct
8 Belinda Rd
9 Higgs Ind Est
10 Tham Cl
C3 1 Shaftesbury Ct
2 Mayhew Ct
3 Morris Ct
4 Swinburne Ct
5 Perth Ct
6 Tayside Ct
7 Matlock Ct
8 Hunter Ct
9 Turner Ct

64

A2 1 Velde Way
2 Delft Way
3 Arnhem Way
4 Isel Way
5 Kempis Way
6 Terborch Way
7 Steen Way
8 Deventer Cres
9 Nimegen Way
10 Hilversum Cres
11 St Barnabas Cl
12 James Allen's Girls' Sch
13 James Allen's Prep Sch
A4 1 Harfield Gdns

2 Karen Ct
3 Seavington Ho
4 Appleshaw Ho
5 Birdsall Ho
6 Whitney Ho
7 Wheatland Ho
8 Wilton Ho
9 Walcot Ho
10 Whaddon Ho
11 Melbreak Ho
12 Ledbury Ho
13 Tidworth Ho
14 Riseholme Ho
15 Ringmer Ho
16 Petworth Ho
17 Stagshaw Ho
18 Ivybridge Ho
19 Inwood Ho
20 Gatcombe Ho
21 Felbridge Ho
22 Cowdray Ho
23 Dog Kennel Hill Sch
B3 1 Dulwich Mews
1 New Hope Christian Sch
2 St James's Cloisters
C2 1 Dorothy Charrington Ho
2 Keswick Ct
3 Kendall Ct
4 Halliwell Ct
C4 4 St John's & St Clements CE Jun & Inf Sch
5 Bellenden Prim Sch

65

A4 1 Tilling Ho
2 Goodwin Ho
3 Tyrells Ct
4 Citron Terr
5 Basswood Cl
6 Cheam St
7 Rye Oak Sch
C3 1 Laxton Path
2 Barlings Ho
3 Bayfield Ho
4 Coston Wlk
5 Coverham Ho
6 Gateley Ho
7 Dereham Ho
8 Greenwood Ho
9 Hilton Ho
10 Goodall Ho
11 Horsley Ho
12 Jordan Ho

66

A3 1 Turnham Prim Sch

67

A4 1 Pine Tree Way
2 Waterway Ave
3 Lewisham Bridge Prim Sch
B4 1 Bankside Ave
2 Elder Wlk
3 Yew Tree Cl
4 Mill Ho
C1 3 Park Piazza
4 Birdwood Ave

C4 1 Our Lady of Lourdes RC Prim Sch

68

C3 1 Farnborough Ho
2 Rushmere Ho
3 Horndean Cl
4 Highcross Way
5 Timsbury Wlk
6 Foxcombe Rd
7 Ryefield Path
8 Greatham Wlk
9 Gosport Ho
10 Stoatley Ho
11 Milland Ho
12 Clanfield Ho
13 Fareham Ho
14 Grayswood Point
C4 1 Woodcott Ho
2 Lyndhurst Ho
3 Wheatley Ho
4 Allbrook Ho
5 Bordon Wlk
6 Chilcombe Ho
7 Vicarage Ct
8 Shawford Ct
9 Eastleigh Wlk
10 Kings Ct
11 Somborne Ho

69

A3 1 Ramsdean Ho
2 Purbrook Ho
3 Portsea Ho
4 Blendworth Point
5 Eashing Point
6 Hindhead Point
7 Hilsea Point
8 Witley Point
9 Buriton Ho
10 Grateley Ho
11 Hascombe Ho
12 Dunhill Point
13 Westmark Point
14 Longmoor Point
15 Cadnam Point
B4 1 Cumberland Ho
2 Devonshire Ho
3 Cornwall Ho
4 Norfolk Ho
5 Leicester Ho
6 Warwick Ho
7 Sutherland Ho
8 Carmarthen Ho
9 Worcester Ho
10 Rutland Ho
11 Paddock Way
12 Putney Hill
C3 1 Sandringham Cl
2 Eastwick Ct
3 Oatlands Ct
4 Banning Ho
5 Grantley Ho
6 Caryl Ho
7 Duncombe Ho
8 Chilworth Ct
9 Kent Lo
10 Turner Lo
11 Marlborough
12 Parkland Gdns
13 Lewesdon Cl
14 Pines Ct
15 Ashtead Ct
16 Mynterne Ct
17 Arden
18 Stephen Ct
19 Marsham Ct
20 Doradus Ct
21 Acorns The
22 Heritage Ho
23 Conifer Ct
24 Spencer Ho
25 Chartwell
26 Blenheim
27 Chivelston
28 Greenfield Ho
29 Oakman Ho
30 Radley Lo
31 Simon Lo
32 Admirals Ct
33 Augustus Rd
C4 1 Brett Ho
2 Brett House Cl
3 Sylva Ct
4 Ross Ct
5 Potterne Cl
6 Stourhead Cl
7 Fleur Gates
8 Greenwood
9 John Paul II Sch
10 Our Lady Queen of Heaven RC Prim Sch
11 Prospect House Sch

70

A3 1 William Harvey Ho
2 Highview Ct
3 Cameron Ct
4 Galgate Cl
5 Green Ho The
6 King Charles Wlk
7 Florys Ct
8 Augustus Ct
9 Albert Ct
10 Hertford Lo
11 Mortimer Lo
12 Allenswood
13 Ambleside
14 Hansler Ct
15 Roosevelt Ct
16 Southmead Prim Sch
A4 1 Douglas Gracey Ho
2 Aman Dalvi Ho
3 Andrew Reed Ho
4 Stoford Cl
6 Ronald Ross Prim Sch

71

B2 1 Bremans Row
2 St Andrew's Ct
3 Townsend Mews
4 Sheringham Mews
5 Rainbow Sch
6 Garratt Park Sec Specl Sch

72

A2 1 St Peters Cl
2 St Hildas Cl
3 St Edmunds Cl
4 St Hughes Cl
5 St Anthonys Cl
6 St Benets Cl
7 St Catherines Cl
8 Elsley Sch
C2 1 Upper Tooting Park Mans
2 Cecil Mans
3 Marius Mans
4 Boulevard The
5 Elmfield Mans
6 Holdernesse Rd
7 Lumiere Ct
C3 1 Heslop Ct
2 St James's Terr
3 Boundaries Mans
4 Station Par
5 Old Dairy Mews
6 Chestnut Grove Sch
7 Hornsby House Sch
8 Trinity St Mary's Prim Sch
C4 1 Hollies Way
2 Endlesham Ct
3 Broomwood Hall Sch (Upper Sch)
4 Holy Ghost RC Prim Sch

73

A3 1 Holbeach Mews
2 Hildreth Street Mews
3 Coalbrook Mans
4 Hub Buildings The
5 Metropolis Apartments
6 Hildreth St
A4 1 Meyer Ho
2 Faraday Ho
3 Hales Ho
4 Frankland Ho
5 Graham Ho
6 Gibbs Ho
7 Dalton Ho
8 Ainslie Wlk
9 Rokeby Ho
10 Caistor Ho
11 Ivanhoe Ho
12 Catherine Baird Ct
13 Marmion Ho
14 Devonshire Ct
15 Blueprint Apartments
16 Royal Duchess Mews
17 Alderbrook Prim Sch
B3 2 Henry Cavendish Prim Sch
3 Margaret Rutherford Pl
B4 1 Limerick Ct
2 Homewoods
3 Jewell Ho
4 Glanville Ho
5 Dan Bryant Ho
6 Olding Ho
7 Quennel Ho
8 Weir Ho
9 West Ho
10 Neville Ct
11 Friday Grove Mews
12 St Bernadette RC Jun Sch
C3 1 Sinclair Ho
2 MacGregor Ho
3 Ingle Ho
4 St Andrews Mews
5 Telferscot Prim Sch
C4 1 Riley Ho
2 Bennett Ho
3 White Ho
4 Rodgers Ho
5 Dumphreys Ho
6 Homan Ho
7 Prendergast Ho
8 Hutchins Ho
9 Whiteley Ho
10 Tresidder Ho
11 Primrose Ct
12 Angus Ho
13 Currie Ho

74

A1 1 De Montfort Ct
2 Leigham Hall Par
3 Leigham Hall
4 Endsleigh Mans
5 John Kirk Ho
6 Raebarn Ct
7 Wavel Ct
8 Homeleigh Ct
9 Howland Ho
10 Beauclerk Ho
11 Bertrand Ho
12 Drew Ho
13 Dowes Ho
14 Dunton Ho
15 Raynald Ho
16 Sackville Ho
17 Thurlow Ho
18 Astoria Mans
A2 1 Wyatt Park Mans
2 Broadlands Mans
3 Stonehill's Mans
4 Streatleigh Par
5 Dorchester Ct
6 Picture Ho
A3 1 Beaumont Ho
2 Christchurch Ho
3 Staplefield Cl
4 Chipstead Ho
5 Coulsdon Ho
6 Conway Ho
7 Telford Avenue Mans
8 Telford Parade Mans
9 Wavertree Ct
10 Hartswood Ho
11 Wray Ho
A4 1 Picton Ho
2 Rigg Ho
3 Watson Ho
4 MacArthur Ho
5 Sandon Ho
6 Thorold Ho
7 Pearce Ho
8 Mudie Ho
9 Miller Ho
10 Lycett Ho
11 Lafone Ho
12 Lucraft Ho
13 Freeman Ho
14 New Park Par
15 Argyll Ct
16 Dumbarton Ct
17 Kintyre Ct
18 Cotton Ho
19 Crossman Hos
20 Cameford Ct
21 Parsons Ho
22 Brindley Ho
23 Arkwright Ho
24 Perry Ho
25 Brunel Ho
26 New Park Ct
27 Tanhurst Ho
28 Hawkshaw Cl
29 Richard Atkins Prim Sch
B1 1 Carisbrooke Ct
2 Pembroke Lo
3 Willow Ct
4 Poplar Ct
5 Leigham Cl
5 Mountview
6 Spa View
B3 1 Charlwood Ho
2 Earlswood Ho
3 Balcombe Ho
4 Claremont Cl
5 Holbrook Ho
6 Gwynne Ho
7 Kynaston Ho
8 Tillman Ho
9 Regents Lo
10 Hazelmere Ct
11 Dykes Ct
12 Hartwell Cl
13 Christ Church Streatham CE Prim Sch
14 Streatham Hill & Clapham High Sch
B4 1 Archbishop's Pl
2 Witley Ho
3 Outwood Ho
4 Dunsfold Ho
5 Deepdene Lo
6 Warnham Ho
7 Albury Lo
8 Tilford Ho
9 Elstead Ho
10 Thursley Ho
11 Brockham Ho
12 Capel Lo
13 Leith Ho
14 Fairview Ho
15 Weymouth Ct
16 Ascalon Ct
17 China Mews
18 Rush Common Mews
C3 1 Valens Ho
2 Loveday Ho
3 Strode Ho
4 Ethelworth Ct
5 Harbin Ho
6 Brooks Ho
7 Godolphin Ho
8 Sheppard Ho
9 McCormick Ho
10 Taylor Ho
11 Saunders Ho
12 Talcott Path
13 Derrick Ho
14 Williams Ho
15 Baldwin Ho
16 Churston Cl
17 Neil Wates Cres
18 Burnell Ho
19 Portland Ho
20 Fenstanton Prim Sch
21 St Martin-in-the-Fields High Sch
C4 1 Ellacombe Ho
2 Booth Ho
3 Hathersley Ho
4 Brereton Ho
5 Holdsworth Ho
6 Dearmer Ho
7 Cherry Cl
8 Greenleaf Cl
9 Longford Wlk

10 Scarlette Manor Wlk
11 Chandlers Way
12 Upgrove Manor Way
13 Ropers Wlk
14 Tebbs Ho
15 Bell Ho
16 Worthington Ho
17 Courier Ho
18 Mackie Ho
19 Hamers Ho
20 Kelyway Ho
21 Harriet Tubman Cl
22 Estoria Cl
23 Leckhampton Pl
24 Scotia Rd
25 Charles Haller St
26 Sidmouth Ho
27 Hunter Ct
28 Onslow Lo
29 William Winter Ct
30 Langthorne Lo

75

A1 1 Thanet Ho
2 Chapman Ho
3 Beaufoy Ho
4 Easton Ho
5 Roberts Ho
6 Lloyd Ct
7 Kershaw Ho
8 Wakeling Ho
9 Edridge Ho
10 Jeston Ho
11 Lansdowne Wood Cl
12 Rotary Lo
C2 1 Welldon Ct
2 Coppedhall
3 Shackleton Ct
4 Bullfinch Ct
5 Gannet Ct
6 Fulmar Ct
7 Heron Ct
8 Petrel Ct
9 Falcon Ct
10 Eagle Ct
11 Dunnock Ct
12 Dunlin Ct
13 Cormorant Ct
14 Oak Lodge
15 Corfe Lodge

76

C1 1 Tunbridge Ct
2 Harrogate Ct
3 Bath Ct
4 Leamington Ct
5 Porlock Ho
6 Cissbury Ho
7 Eddisbury Ho
8 Dundry Ho
9 Silbury Ho
10 Homildon Ho
11 Highgate Ho
12 Richmond Ho
13 Pendle Ho
14 Tynwald Ho
15 Wirrall Ho
16 Greyfriars

www.philips-maps.co.uk

First published in 2001 by
Philip's, a division of
Octopus Publishing Group Ltd
www.octopusbooks.co.uk
Endeavour House,
189 Shaftesbury Avenue
London WC2H 8JY
An Hachette UK Company
www.hachette.co.uk

Fifth edition 2012
First impression 2012
LONEA

Spiral-bound
ISBN 978-1-84907-208-3

Perfect-bound
ISBN 978-1-84907-209-0

Hardback (red)
ISBN 978-1-84907-210-6

Hardback (navy)
ISBN 978-1-84907-211-3

Hardback (Union Jack)
ISBN 978-1-84907-228-1

Data for the speed cameras supplied by **PocketGPSWorld.com Ltd**

Printed and bound in China

NOTES

NOTES

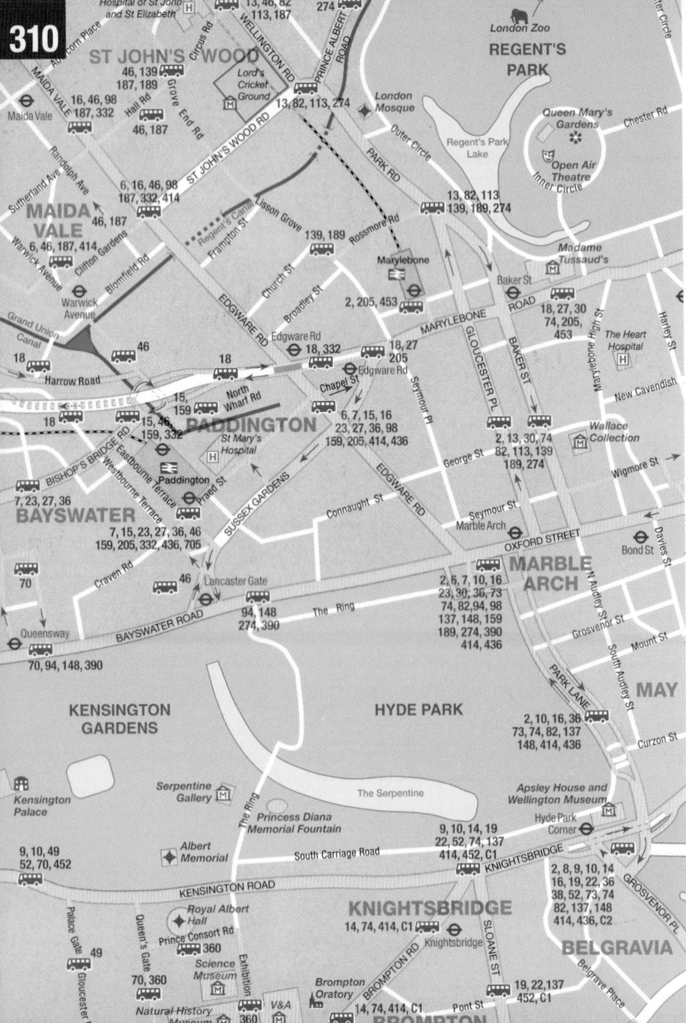

Hospital of St John and St Elizabeth
13, 46, 82
113, 187
274
London Zoo
REGENT'S PARK
Abercorn Place
ST JOHN'S WOOD
Circus Rd
WELLINGTON RD
PRINCE ALBERT ROAD
46, 139
187, 189
Lord's Cricket Ground
MAIDA VALE
Grove End Rd
Hall Rd
16, 46, 98
187, 332
Maida Vale
46, 187
13, 82, 113, 274
London Mosque
Queen Mary's Gardens
Chester Rd
Regent's Park Lake
Outer Circle
Open Air Theatre
Inner Circle
ST JOHN'S WOOD RD
PARK RD
Randolph Ave
Sutherland Ave
6, 16, 46, 98
187, 332, 414
13, 82, 113
139, 189, 274
MAIDA VALE
46, 187
Regent's Canal
Lisson Grove
Frampton St
Rossmore Rd
139, 189
Warwick Avenue
6, 46, 187, 414
Clifton Gardens
Blomfield Rd
Madame Tussaud's
Marylebone
Church St
Baker St
Warwick Avenue
Broadley St
2, 205, 453
ROAD
18, 27, 30
74, 205,
453
EDGWARE RD
MARYLEBONE
Harley St
Grand Union Canal
Marylebone High St
The Heart Hospital
Edgware Rd
18, 332
GLOUCESTER PL
BAKER ST
46
18, 27
205
18
18
Edgware Rd
Seymour Pl
Harrow Road
Chapel St
New Cavendish
North Wharf Rd
15,
159
6, 7, 15, 16
23, 27, 36, 98
159, 205, 414, 436
18
15, 46,
159, 332
PADDINGTON
Wallace Collection
2, 13, 30, 74
82, 113, 139
189, 274
St Mary's Hospital
BISHOP'S BRIDGE RD
Eastbourne Terrace
Westbourne Terrace
Paddington
Praed St
SUSSEX GARDENS
EDGWARE RD
George St
Wigmore St
7, 23, 27, 36
BAYSWATER
Connaught St
Seymour St
Marble Arch
7, 15, 23, 27, 36, 46
159, 205, 332, 436, 705
OXFORD STREET
Bond St
Davies St
MARBLE ARCH
70
Craven Rd
46
Lancaster Gate
2, 6, 7, 10, 16
23, 30, 36, 73
74, 82, 94, 98
137, 148, 159
189, 274, 390
414, 436
N Audley St
94, 148
274, 390
The Ring
BAYSWATER ROAD
Queensway
Grosvenor St
Mount St
70, 94, 148, 390
South Audley St
PARK LANE
MAY
KENSINGTON GARDENS
HYDE PARK
2, 10, 16, 36
73, 74, 82, 137
148, 414, 436
Curzon St
Kensington Palace
Serpentine Gallery
The Serpentine
Apsley House and Wellington Museum
The Ring
Princess Diana Memorial Fountain
Hyde Park Corner
9, 10, 14, 19
22, 52, 74, 137
414, 452, C1
9, 10, 49
52, 70, 452
Albert Memorial
South Carriage Road
KNIGHTSBRIDGE
2, 8, 9, 10, 14
16, 19, 22, 36
38, 52, 73, 74
82, 137, 148
414, 436, C2
KENSINGTON ROAD
GROSVENOR PL
Palace Gate
Queen's Gate
Royal Albert Hall
KNIGHTSBRIDGE
14, 74, 414, C1
Knightsbridge
SLOANE ST
Prince Consort Rd
360
BELGRAVIA
49
Science Museum
Exhibition
BROMPTON RD
Belgrave Place
70, 360
Brompton Oratory
19, 22, 137
452, C1
Natural History Museum
V&A
360
14, 74, 414, C1
Pont St
BROMPTON

Central London bus routes

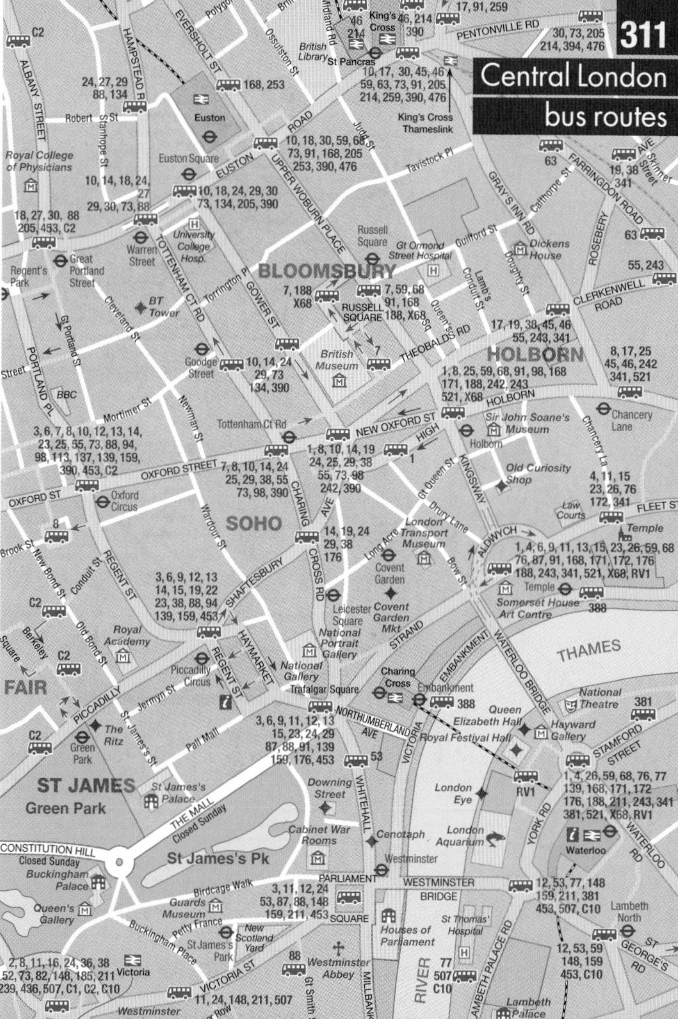

MAYOR OF LONDON

Website tfl.gov.uk

24 hour travel information 0843 222 1234*

Reg. user No. 11/2125/P

High Barnet
Totteridge & Whetstone
Woodside Park
West Finchley
Mill Hill East
Finchley Central
East Finchley
Highgate
Archway
Tufnell Park
Crouch Hill
Gospel Oak
stead
ath
Kentish Town West
Kentish Town
Camden Road
arm
Town
gton
cent
King's Cross St. Pancras
Euston Square
Farringdon
Russell Square
Barbican
Moorgate
Angel
Old Street
Holborn
Chancery Lane
St. Paul's
Covent Garden
Bank
Leicester Square
Mansion House
Cannon Street
Monument
Tower Hill
Fenchurch Street
Charing Cross
Blackfriars
Temple
Embankment
London Bridge
Southwark
Borough
Lambeth North
Elephant & Castle
Oval
well
Brixton

Cockfosters
Oakwood
Southgate
Arnos Grove
Bounds Green
Wood Green
Turnpike Lane
Manor House
Harringay Green Lanes
South Tottenham
Upper Holloway
Seven Sisters
Tottenham Hale
Blackhorse Road
Walthamstow Central
Arsenal
Finsbury Park
Holloway Road
Caledonian Road
Highbury & Islington
Caledonian Road & Barnsbury
Canonbury
Dalston Kingsland
Dalston Junction
Haggerston
Hoxton
Hackney Central
Homerton
Hackney Wick
Walthamstow Queen's Road
Leyton Midland Road
Stratford International
Liverpool Street
Shoreditch High Street
Bethnal Green
Mile End
Bow Road
Bow Church
Aldgate East
Aldgate
Whitechapel
Stepney Green
Shadwell
Tower Gateway
Wapping
Rotherhithe
Bermondsey
Canada Water
Surrey Quays
New Cross Gate
New Cross
Brockley
Honor Oak Park
Forest Hill
Sydenham
Penge West
Anerley
Crystal Palace
Norwood Junction
West Croydon

Epping
Theydon Bois
Debden
Loughton
Buckhurst Hill
Roding Valley
Chigwell
Grange Hill
Hainault
Fairlop
Barkingside
Newbury Park
Woodford
South Woodford
Snaresbrook
Redbridge
Wanstead
Gants Hill
Leytonstone
Leytonstone High Road
Leyton
Wanstead Park
Stratford
Woodgrange Park
Stratford High Street
Pudding Mill Lane
Abbey Road
Bromley-by-Bow
West Ham
Star Lane
Upminster
Upminster Bridge
Hornchurch
Elm Park
Dagenham East
Dagenham Heathway
Becontree
Upney
Barking
East Ham
Upton Park
Plaistow
Devons Road
Langdon Park
All Saints
Limehouse
Westferry
Poplar
East India
Blackwall
Canning Town
Royal Victoria
Custom House for ExCeL
Prince Regent
Royal Albert
Beckton Park
Cyprus
Gallions Reach
Beckton
Emirates Royal Docks
West Silvertown
Pontoon Dock
London City Airport
King George V
Woolwich Arsenal
West India Quay
Canary Wharf
Heron Quays
South Quay
Crossharbour
Mudchute
Island Gardens
Cutty Sark for Maritime Greenwich
Greenwich
Deptford Bridge
Elverson Road
Lewisham
North Greenwich for The O2
Emirates Greenwich Peninsula
Under construction
River Thames

Transport for London

*You pay no more than 5p per minute if calling from a BT landline. There may be a connection charge. Charges from mobiles or other landline providers may vary.

Improvement works may affect your journey, please check before you travel

Version A TfL 12.2011

West End theatres and cinemas

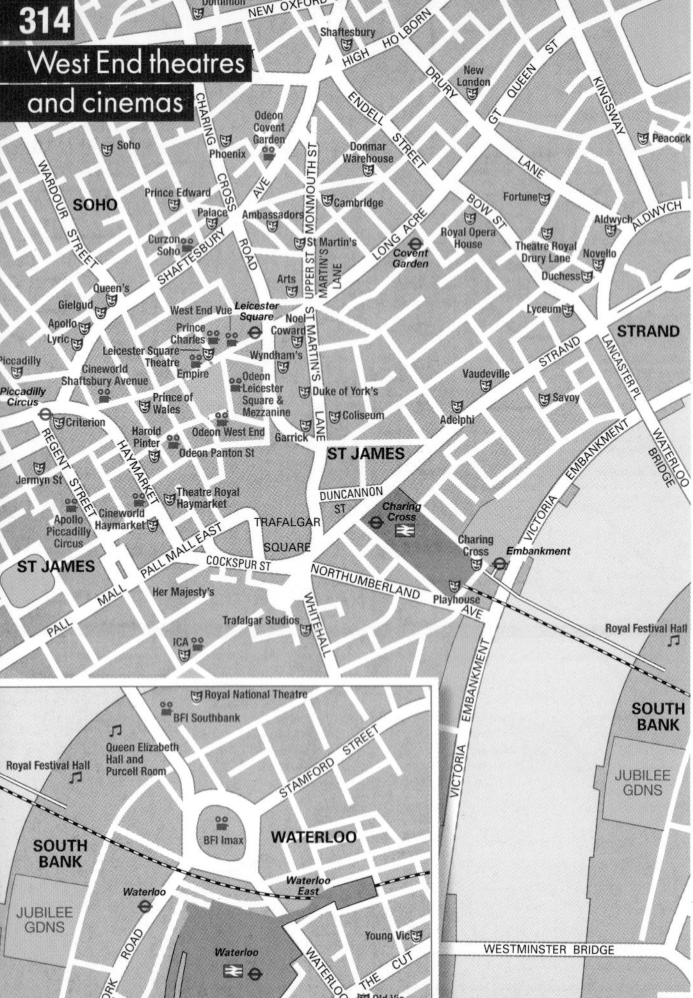